Handbook of the
Sociology of Emotions

Handbooks of Sociology and Social Research

Series Editor:
Howard B. Kaplan, *Texas A&M University, College Station, Texas*

HANDBOOK OF DISASTER RESEARCH
Edited by Havidán Rodríguez, E. L. Quarantelli, and Russell Dynes

HANDBOOK OF DRUG ABUSE PREVENTION
Theory, Science and Prevention
Edited by Zili Sloboda and William J. Bukowski

HANDBOOK OF THE LIFE COURSE
Edited by Jeyaln T. Mortimer and Michael J. Shanahan

HANDBOOK OF POPULATION
Edited by Dudley L. Poston and Michael Micklin

HANDBOOK OF RELIGION AND SOCIAL INSTITUTIONS
Edited by Helen Rose Ebaugh

HANDBOOK OF SOCIAL MOVEMENTS
Edited by Conny Roggeband and Bert Klandermans

HANDBOOK OF SOCIAL PSYCHOLOGY
Edited by John Delamater

HANDBOOK OF SOCIOLOGICAL THEORY
Edited by Jonathan H. Turner

HANDBOOK OF THE SOCIOLOGY OF EDUCATION
Edited by Maureen T. Hallinan

HANDBOOK OF THE SOCIOLOGY OF EMOTION
Edited by Jan E. Stets and Jonathan H. Turner

HANDBOOK OF THE SOCIOLOGY OF GENDER
Edited by Janet Saltzman Chafetz

HANDBOOK OF THE SOCIOLOGY OF MENTAL HEALTH
Edited by Carol S. Aneshensel and Jo C. Phelan

HANDBOOK OF THE SOCIOLOGY OF THE MILITARY
Edited by Giuseppe Caforio

HANDBOOK OF THE SOCIOLOGY OF RACIAL AND ETHNIC RELATIONS
Edited by Hernán Vera and Joseph R. Feagin

Handbook of the
Sociology of Emotions

Edited by

Jan E. Stets
University of California
Riverside, California

and

Jonathan H. Turner
University of California
Riverside, California

 Springer

Jan E. Stets
Department of Sociology
University of California
Riverside, CA 92521
USA
jan.stets@ucr.edu

Jonathan H. Turner
Department of Sociology
University of California
Riverside, CA 92521
USA
jonathan.turner@ucr.edu

ISBN-13: 978-0-387-73991-5   e-ISBN-13: 978-0-387-30715-2

Library of Congress Control Number: 2005936762

springer.com

Contributors

David Boyns. Department of Sociology, California State University, Northridge, CA 91330

Kathy Charmaz. Department of Sociology, Sonoma State University, Rohnert Park, CA 94928

Gordon Clanton. Department of Sociology, San Diego State University, San Diego, CA 92182

Candace Clark. Kure Beach, NC 28449

Martha Copp. Department of Sociology and Anthropology, East Tennessee State University, Johnson City, TN 37614

Mark H. Davis. Department of Psychology, Eckerd College, St. Petersburg, FL 33711

Brooke Di Leone. Department of Psychology, Pennsylvania State University, University Park, PA 16802

Diane H. Felmlee. Department of Sociology, University of California, Davis, CA 95616

Jessica Fields. Department of Sociology, San Francisco State University, San Francisco, CA 94132

Linda E. Francis. School of Social Welfare, SUNY at Stony Brook, Stony Brook, NY 11794

David D. Franks. Department of Sociology, Virginia Commonwealth University, Richmond, VA 23284

Dallas N. Garner. Department of Psychology, Pennsylvania State University, University Park, PA 16802

Jeff Goodwin. Department of Sociology, New York University, New York, NY 10012

Alena M. Hadley. Department of Psychology, Pennsylvania State University, University Park, PA 16802

Michael Hammond. Department of Sociology, University of Toronto, Toronto, Ontario, Canada M5S 2J4

James M. Jasper. New York, NY 10011

Guillermina Jasso. Department of Sociology, New York University, New York, NY 10012

Howard B. Kaplan. Department of Sociology, Texas A&M University, College Station, TX 77843

Theodore D. Kemper. Department of Sociology, St. John's University, Jamaica, NY 11439

Sherryl Kleinman. Department of Sociology, University of North Carolina, Chapel Hill, NC 27599

Edward J. Lawler. Department of Organizational Behavior, School of Industrial and Labor Relations and Department of Sociology, Cornell University, Ithaca, NY 14853

Kathryn J. Lively. Department of Sociology, Dartmouth College, Hanover, NH 03755

Melinda J. Milligan. Department of Sociology, Sonoma State University, Rohnert Park, CA 94928

Gretchen Peterson. Department of Sociology, California State University, Los Angeles, CA 90032

Cecilia L. Ridgeway. Department of Sociology, Stanford University, Stanford, CA 94305

Dawn T. Robinson. Department of Sociology, University of Georgia, Athens, GA 30602

Scott Schieman. Department of Sociology, University of Toronto, Toronto, Ontario, Canada M5S 2J4

Christopher S. Schmitt. Department of Sociology, University of California, Riverside, CA 92521

Stephanie A. Shields. Department of Psychology, Pennsylvania State University, University Park, PA 16802

Lynn Smith-Lovin. Department of Sociology, Duke University, Durham, NC 27708

Susan Sprecher. Department of Sociology and Anthropology, Illinois State University, Normal, IL 61790

Jan E. Stets. Department of Sociology, University of California, Riverside, CA 92521

Erika Summers-Effler. Department of Sociology, University of Notre Dame, Notre Dame, IN 46556

Robert A. Thamm. Department of Sociology, San Jose State University, San Jose, CA 95192

Shane R. Thye. Department of Sociology, University of South Carolina, Columbia, SC 29208

Jonathan H. Turner. Department of Sociology, University of California, Riverside, CA 92521

Allison K. Wisecup. Department of Sociology, Duke University, Durham, NC 27708

Contents

Introduction... 1
Jan E. Stets and Jonathan H. Turner
References... 6

I. BASIC PROCESSES

1. The Classification of Emotions................................... 11
Robert A. Thamm
Traditional Classification Approaches.................................. 11
Contemporary Classification Systems.................................. 14
Relevant Factors in Classifying Emotions.............................. 16
Culture, Structure, and Appraisal..................................... 16
The Classification Scheme... 17
"Classic" Construction of Emotion Categories.......................... 18
Levels of Emotion Differentiation..................................... 20
Conclusions.. 34
References... 35

2. The Neuroscience of Emotions.................................. 38
David D. Franks
Why the Emotional Brain?.. 39
Sociology and the Neuroscience Divide................................. 40
Some Generalizations about the Emotional Brain........................ 41
The Functional Anatomy of Emotion in the Brain........................ 42
Top to Down Brain Structures.. 45
The Debate About the Limbic System.................................... 49
Neuroscience and Unconscious Emotion.................................. 51
On the Relationship of Cognition and Emotion: The Interaction of Cognitive
    and Emotional Processes in the Brain.............................. 55
Conclusion... 59
Notes.. 60
References... 60

3. **Gender and Emotion** 63
   Stephanie A. Shields, Dallas N. Garner, Brooke Di Leone, and Alena M. Hadley
   A Framework for Studying Gender and Emotion   65
   Beliefs About the Gender-Emotion Connection   68
   Power and Status   71
   Sexuality   74
   Conclusion   78
   References   79

II. THEORIES

4. **Power and Status and the Power-Status Theory of Emotions** 87
   Theodore D. Kemper
   Power and Status Theory   87
   Relational Metaprocesses   93
   The Power-Status Theory of Emotions   96
   Tests of the Theory   108
   Research Agenda   109
   Conclusion   110
   Notes   111
   References   111

5. **Cultural Theory and Emotions** 114
   Gretchen Peterson
   Defining Emotions   115
   The Self and Emotions   115
   Cultural Content   116
   Empirical Work on Emotion Culture   118
   Variations in Emotion Culture   121
   Learning the Emotion Culture: Emotional Socialization   122
   Research on Emotional Socialization   123
   Managing Emotions   124
   Research on Emotion Management   126
   Commercialization of Emotion Management   127
   Research on Emotional Labor   129
   Conclusion   131
   Notes   133
   References   133

6. **Ritual Theory** 135
   Erika Summers-Effler
   The Interaction Order   136
   Interaction Order Dynamics   137
   Second-Order System Dynamics   140
   Thinking and the Self   141
   Network Processes   146
   Small Groups   147
   Constraints on the Interaction Order   149

Conclusion 152

References 153

7. **Symbolic Interactionism, Inequality, and Emotions** 155
Jessica Fields, Martha Copp, and Sherryl Kleinman
Theoretical Framings and Foundations 156
Linking the Emotional and the Social 158
Everyday Emotional Practices and Contexts 159
Who We Are, How We Feel: Emotions, Identity, and Beliefs 164
Emotion, Ideology, and Sustained Social Inequalities 168
Methodological Perspectives for Interactionist Studies of Emotion 173
Conclusion 174
References 175

8. **Affect Control Theory** 179
Dawn T. Robinson, Lynn Smith-Lovin, and Allison K. Wisecup
Symbolic Interactionist Roots of Affect Control Theory 180
Definitions 181
The Formal Structure of the Theory 184
Empirical Studies of Emotion Using Affect Control Theory 191
Emotions in Understanding Social Movements and Politics 193
A Brief Comparison with a Close Theoretical Cousin 196
Directions for Future Research 198
Notes 199
References 199

9. **Identity Theory and Emotions** 203
Jan E. Stets
Identity Theory and Research 204
Future Research 220
Conclusion 221
Notes 222
References 222

10. **Self Theory and Emotions** 224
Howard B. Kaplan
Self Theory as an Integrative Framework for the Sociology of Emotions 224
Emotions as Self-Referent Responses 229
Emotional Experiences/Expressions as Self-Cognitive Stimuli for
    Self-Evaluation 230
Emotional (Self-Feeling) Responses to Self-Cognition-Stimulated
    Self-Evaluations 232
Emotions and Self-Enhancing/Self-Protective Responses 241
Emotional Responses as Self-Enhancing/Self-Protective Mechanisms 244
Self-Enhancing/Self-Protective Mechanisms and Self-Feelings (Emotion) 245
Retrospect and Prospect 247
References 249

11. Emotion-Based Self Theory 254
David Boyns
Sociological Approaches to the Self 255
Locating the Emotion-Based Self in the Sociology of Emotions 258
Conclusion and Future Directions 271
References 272

12. Psychoanalytic Sociological Theories and Emotion 276
Jonathan H. Turner
Freud's Theory in a More Sociological Guise 276
Redirection of Psychoanalytic Theory and Research 279
Sociological Theories of Pride and Shame 280
Expanding the Theory of Emotions: A New Kind of Synthesis Between
    Sociology and Psychoanalytic Ideas 281
Conclusion 292
References 293

13. Social Exchange Theory of Emotions 295
Edward J. Lawler and Shane R. Thye
The Problem 296
Social Exchange Theories: Background 298
Emotion and Emotional Processes 301
Relational Cohesion Theory 305
Extensions of Relational Cohesion Theory 308
Affect Theory of Social Exchange 311
Conclusion and Future Directions 316
References 318

14. Emotion in Justice Processes 321
Guillermina Jasso
Justice Analysis: Understanding the Operation of the Sense of Justice 322
A Closer Look at the Justice Evaluation Function 327
The Long Reach of Justice: Theoretical Justice Analysis 331
Emotion in Justice Processes: Basic Framework and New Extensions 332
A New Extension: Impartiality in the Justice Process 334
Empirical Assessment of Impartiality 339
Emotion in a New Unified Theory of Sociobehavioral Processes 341
Appendix 343
Notes 344
References 344

15. Expectation States Theory and Emotions 347
Cecilia L. Ridgeway
Early Studies of Status and Affect 348
Expectation States Theory 349
Is Affect Inherent in Status Processes? 351
Cultural Schemas of Status and Emotion 353
Legitimacy Dynamics, Emotions, and the Containment of Conflict 355

How Do Emotions and Sentiments Shape Status?.. 358
Feeling with the Group and Solidarity... 364
Conclusion.. 364
References.. 365

16. Evolutionary Theory and Emotions 368
Michael Hammond
Evolutionary Existentialism... 369
The Evolutionary Biology of Emotions 370
Emotions and Social Evolution 375
Conclusion.. 384
References.. 384

III. SELECT EMOTIONS

17. Love 389
Diane H. Felmlee and Susan Sprecher
Is Love an Emotion? 390
Classic Psychological Approaches to Love... 393
Sociological Perspectives on Love 397
The Future of Scholarship on Love.. 401
Conclusion.. 405
References.. 406

18. Jealousy and Envy 410
Gordon Clanton
Recognizing Jealousy and Envy 411
Jealousy.. 412
Envy... 424
Conclusion.. 439
References.. 440

19. Empathy.. 443
Mark H. Davis
Empathy: An Organizational Framework 444
Research Evidence Relevant to the Model... 447
Future Directions 460
Conclusion.. 462
References.. 462

20. Sympathy... 467
Christopher S. Schmitt and Candace Clark
Sympathy Conceptualized 469
Dimes of Sympathy: Emotional Gifts, Exchange, and Micropolitics................... 474
Courtroom Trials... 481
Communities of Sympathy.. 484
Conclusion.. 485

Notes 487
References 487

21. **Anger** 493
     Scott Schieman
     Conceptualization of Anger 494
     Social Causes of Anger Processes 495
     The Social Distribution of Anger 503
     Power, the Sense of Control, and the Utility of Anger 507
     Conclusion 509
     References 510

22. **Grief** 516
     Kathy Charmaz and Melinda J. Milligan
     Positioning the Literature on Grief 517
     What Is Grief? 518
     Psychological Theorizing: Attachment and Identification 520
     Historical and Cross-Cultural Studies: Evidence for the Social and
         Cultural Construction of Grief 521
     Emotions and Social Movements: The Place of Grief 523
     Situating Grief in Social Structure 525
     Reconceptualizing Grief 529
     Loss of Self 532
     Research on Variations in the Experience of Grief 534
     Conclusion 537
     Notes 538
     References 538

23. **Moral Emotions** 544
     Jonathan H. Turner and Jan E. Stets
     What Is Morality? 544
     A Biology of Morality? 546
     The Moral Self 548
     Social Structure and Moral Emotions 549
     Toward A Sociology of Moral Emotions 556
     The Psychodynamics of Moral Emotions 560
     Conclusion: Moral Emotions and the Moral Order 564
     References 565

IV. EMOTIONS IN SOCIAL LIFE

24. **Emotions in the Workplace** 569
     Kathryn J. Lively
     The Managed Heart 570
     Conclusion 583
     Notes 585
     References 586

25. Emotions and Health 591
Linda E. Francis
The Sociology of Emotions and Health 592
The Division: Biomedical Positivism and Social Constructionism in
    Research on Emotions and Health 595
Bridging the Gap: Stress and Interactionism 600
Discussion 604
Conclusion 605
References 606

26. Emotions and Social Movements 611
Jeff Goodwin and James M. Jasper
Fearing Emotions: A Brief History 612
Rediscovering Emotions: Recent Research 617
Theorizing Emotions: Engaging Broader Theories 624
Conclusion 630
References 631

Index 637

Introduction

Jan E. Stets
Jonathan H. Turner

We began assembling the chapters for this handbook at about the same time that we completed *The Sociology of Emotions*, in which we reviewed the theory and research on emotions over the past 30 years (Turner and Stets 2005). It became very clear to us in writing this book that the sociology of emotions has made remarkable progress since its emergence in the late 1970s. Clear theoretical and research traditions are evident, and the field now stands at the forefront of microsociology and, increasingly, macrosociology. *The Sociology of Emotions* will be, we hope, a useful reference work, but it is also important to hear directly from the authors who are at the forefront of this field. Hence, for this handbook we have assembled a strong cast of authors to review the range of topics that presently define the sociology of emotions.

As Massey argued in his 2001 Presidential Address to the American Sociological Association, sociology must develop models of how humans think *and* feel (Massey 2002). Moreover, sociology can no longer ignore the neurology of emotions by simply declaring biology to be a "black box" into which sociologists should not tread, nor can sociologists shy away from evolutionary analyses of how humans' emotional capacities have emerged. It is essential, therefore, to understand emotions in their most complete and robust form—a charge that we took seriously in assembling the chapters for this handbook.

In any book of this nature, it is necessary to divide the chapters into topic areas. Although there is always a certain degree of arbitrariness in such an exercise, our division of materials into four areas best reflects the state of the field in sociology. The first section of the book deals with basic processes that undergird the sociology of emotions. In Chapter 1, Robert Thamm explores the classification of emotions. How many emotions are there? Along what dimensions do they fall? Can a succinct classificatory scheme be developed for the sociology of emotions? These are the kinds of questions that have guided Thamm in his effort to develop a scheme that captures the

JAN E. STETS AND JONATHAN H. TURNER • Department of Sociology, University of California, Riverside, CA 92521 full range of emotions in a parsimonious conceptual scheme. To define and classify the range of human emotions is, we feel, a good place to begin the study of human emotions.

Chapter 2 by David Franks heeds Massey's call for sociological analysis on the neurological basis of human emotions. Franks, who has called for a "neurosociololgy," is the perfect scholar to review the neurology of emotions. He has the credentials of a symbolic interactionist and is, therefore, sympathetic to a social constructionist perspective on emotions while recognizing the need for sociologists to understand the neurological substrate generating all human emotions. (See Franks and Smith, 1999, for the first effort to assemble work by sociologists on the brain and emotions.)

In Chapter 3, Stephanie Shields, a leading researcher on gender and emotions (Shields 2002), and several collaborators (Dallas Garner, Brooke DiLeone, and Alena Hadley) review the literature on how gender hierarchies are sustained by prescriptions for emotions that define gender boundaries. Thus, cultural prescriptions for the feeling and expression of emotions in microencounters also operate to sustain macrolevel social structures, such as gendered inequalities.

The second section of the book is devoted to a review of the various sociological theories of emotional dynamics that have informed empirical work. The authors in this section are all leading figures within a particular theoretical tradition, and each provides a review of the key emotional dynamics emphasized by theory and research within their respective theoretical programs. Chapter 4 by Theodore D. Kemper, one of the early founders of the sociology of emotions in the 1970s, opens this review of sociological theories. Kemper's theory has always emphasized power and status as the principal structural conditions affecting emotional arousal. For Kemper, individuals' relative power and status, as well as their expectations for power and status and their gain or loss of relative power and status in interaction, determine their emotional experiences in all social settings.

Chapter 5 by Gretchen Peterson examines another of the early approaches to the sociology of emotions—the effects of culture on emotions. Feeling and display rules as well as emotion ideologies in a society's culture always define what emotions can and should be felt and expressed in situations. The power of culture to constrain emotional experiences often places individuals under stress when cultural expectations and actual feelings come into conflict. Under these conditions, individuals must often adopt a variety of cognitive and behavioral strategies to cope with the disjuncture between the demands of feeling rules and other cultural prescriptions and proscriptions, on the one side, and the feelings and emotional displays of persons, on the other side.

In Chapter 6, Erika Summers-Effler reviews yet another early tradition in the sociology of emotions—ritual theorizing. Randall Collins (2004) has been the foremost proponent of an interaction ritual theory of emotions. By drawing from Emile Durkheim ([1912] 1965) and Erving Goffman (1967), he has enumerated the conditions under which emotions are aroused during the course of interaction. When individuals are co-present, reveal a common focus of attention and mood, and represent focused encounters with symbols, positive emotional energy is built up. Conversely, when these conditions fail to be sustained, emotional energy will decline or even turn negative. Summers-Effler, a former student of Collins, extends this theoretical legacy by introducing new dimensions to interaction ritual theory, namely human biology, a view of self, and a more explicit set of connections among biology, culture, self, and ritual.

Chapters 7–12, which draw from symbolic interactionism, one of sociology's earliest and most enduring theoretical traditions, underscore the continued viability of the insights of George Herbert Mead as these insights are recast to study human emotions. Chapter 7 by Jessica Fields, Martha Copp, and Sherryl Kleinman draws inspiration not only from the pioneering work of George Herbert Mead (1934) but also Herbert Blumer (1969) and Erving Goffman (1959). Of particular interest for Fields and her colleagues is how emotions sustain inequitable arrangements in society.

All symbolic interactionist theories emphasize the central place of self and identity. When self and identity are confirmed in situations, individuals experience positive emotions, whereas when self and identity are not confirmed, individuals feel negative emotions and are motivated to seek confirmation. In Chapter 8, one variant of symbolic interactionism—affect control theory—is reviewed by several of its leading proponents: Dawn Robinson, Lynn Smith-Lovin, and Allison Wisecup. In this theory, emphasis is on the level of congruence among individuals' more fixed sentiments or beliefs and more transient impressions about self, others, behaviors, and situations. Individuals are motivated to perceive congruence between transient impressions and more fundamental sentiments about self, other, behavior, and situations. When deflection (or the perception of incongruence) occurs, the emotions aroused work as a motive force to restore congruence.

Chapter 9 by Jan Stets reviews and extends yet another symbolic interaction theory of emotions—identity theory—which argues that individuals seek to maintain congruence between their identity standard meanings and perceptions of themselves in situations. When congruence occurs, one's identity is verified. Specific emotional states, such as shame, guilt, anger, depression, and distress, emerge when there is incongruence between identity standard meanings and self-in-situation meanings, activating control processes to restore incongruence and achieve identity verification.

Chapter 10 by Howard Kaplan, a long-standing researcher on self processes (Kaplan 1986), integrates a number of approaches into a view of emotions as ultimately self-referential. Emotions are not only the basis for self-evaluation; they are also a stimulus to self-enhancing and to self-protecting strategies for sustaining the integrity of self. Chapter 11 by David Boyns reviews self-theories by arraying them along two dimensions: intrapersonal/interpersonal and positivistic/social constructionist. By classifying theories in this way, Boyns is able to explicate the fundamental differences among theories emphasizing the central place of self in emotional arousal while providing guidelines for how to build a more robust theory of self and emotions.

In Chapter 12, Jonathan Turner reviews how psychoanalytic ideas can be grafted onto symbolic interactionist theories. For Turner and others who work in the more psychoanalytic tradition (e.g., Scheff 1988), defense mechanisms are often activated when individuals experience shame, guilt, and other negative emotions about self. As emotions move below the level of consciousness, they are typically transmuted into new, more intense emotions that distort efforts to bring self and the responses of others back into line and that disrupt rather than repair social bonds.

Chapter 13 by Edward Lawler and Shane Thye review theoretical work on emotions in exchange theory. When individuals mutually exchange and reveal relational cohesion (i.e., have equal dependence on each other's resources), positive emotions are aroused that increase commitment to the exchange relation, thereby reinforcing relational cohesion. Indeed, the positive affect becomes yet another resource in the exchange. Lawler and they have extended these basic ideas to a more general theory in which the nature of the exchange (reciprocal, negotiation, productive, and generalized) influences the emotions aroused as well as the attributions given by individuals to self, others, and social structures. In making this extension, the affect theory of exchange presents a more general theory of the conditions generating social solidarity.

In Chapter 14, Guillermina Jasso explores a topic that has been central to exchange theories in sociology from their very beginnings: distributive justice and fairness. Individuals always make justice evaluations in which they compare their shares of resources against a standard of justice. If these shares are at a standard of justice, individuals will experience positive emotions, whereas if they fall below or above the standard, persons will experience negative emotions. Thus, individuals are always comparing their exchange payoffs to what they perceive as just shares; and these evaluations have effects not only on microlevel exchanges but also on macrolevel social processes. With these simple but elegantly expressed ideas (through formal propositions), Jasso is able to make many derivations that predict emotions and behaviors in a wide variety of social situations.

Chapter 15 by Cecilia Ridgeway brings another long-standing theoretical research program—expectation states theorizing—to the study of emotions. Status hierarchies generate expectation states for the respective performances of higher- and lower-ranking individuals, but it is also possible that positive or negative emotions about individuals may also influence expectations for performances and the allocation of status. Ridgeway finds more support for the effects of the status hierarchy on the emotions that individuals feel and express than on the effects of preexisting feelings about actors on the development of status hierarchies. In general, higher-status individuals experience more positive emotions and direct more negative emotions to lower-status persons, while these lower-status actors experience more negative emotions but direct more positive emotions to higher-status persons.

Chapter 16 by Michael Hammond is the final theoretical chapter and heeds Massey's call for an evolutionary analysis on the origins of human emotions. Hammond reviews several theories that differ in their arguments on the relative effects of culture and biology on humans' emotional capacities. For William Wentworth and D. Yardly (1994), culture and the social construction of emotions have more impact than biology on humans' emotional responses, whereas for Hammond (2004) and Jonathan Turner (2000), the biological substrate of emotions as it was used to build social structures is given more significance. On either side of these arguments, the important point is that these theories signal the importance of looking at human emotions from an evolutionary perspective.

The third section of this volume reviews the sociological work on specific sets of emotions. Early theorizing and research on emotions often conceptualized emotions in rather global terms, such as continuum of emotions varying along a "positive" and "negative" scale. Over the past decades, however, a considerable amount of insight into the dynamics of specific emotions has accumulated (Stets 2003). Not all potential emotions are examined in this section, but some of the most important emotions are explored. In Chapter 17, Diane Felmlee and Susan Sprecher review love as an emotion that emerges in social relationships. In particular, they discuss the differences between sociological and psychological analyses of love, with the former stressing the structural, cultural, and historical influences on how love is experienced and expressed and the latter emphasizing the diverse types of love that exist.

Chapter 18 by Gordon Clanton examines the emotions of jealousy and envy, which are often conflated when in fact they involve very different affective states. Jealousy involves actual or potential loss of valued objects or relationships, whereas envy is an emotion activated when a person does not possess valued objects or relationships held by others. Although these emotions are painful and often repressed, Clanton emphasizes that they serve important social functions, such as preserving social bonds and maintaining social order (see also Clanton and Smith 1998 [1977]).

Chapters 19 and 20 address topics that are often seen as related: empathy and sympathy. Empathy involves a person actually feeling the emotions of another, whereas sympathy involves feeling sorrow and compassion for the fate of another. Chapter 19 by Mark Davis expands upon his earlier work on empathy (Davis 1994), presenting a model that outlines the antecedents, processes, intrapersonal outcomes, and interpersonal outcomes of empathy. Chapter 20 by Christopher Schmitt and Candace Clark builds upon earlier work by Clark (1997) on the sociology of sympathy. In their analysis, the giving and receiving of sympathy is not only regulated by cultural rules, but like any valued resource, sympathy is subject to exchange dynamics revolving around games of microeconomics and micropolitics.

In Chapter 21, Scott Schieman focuses on anger. For Scheiman, anger is a social emotion that is likely to arise under specific social situations and among specific social categories (gender, age, and class), while being mediated by the dynamics of power. Thus, rather than emphasizing the biological basis of anger or the intrapersonal/psychological processes involved in anger, the sociology of anger examines the social conditions under which anger is aroused, expressed, and controlled in interpersonal relations.

Chapter 22 by Kathy Charmaz and Melinda Milligan examines grief as an emotion that, unlike anger, is generally considered to be directed inward. Charmaz and Milligan demonstrate, however, that the sociology of grief can correct for this perception by documenting the conditions under which grief is aroused. For instance, there are conditions increasing the likelihood that grief will be socially constructed, that grief will be employed in social movements, and that grief will be played out in a culturally prescribed manner. Thus, like all emotions, sociocultural conditions influence not only when grief is experienced but also the forms of expression that it takes.

Chapter 23 represents our attempt to look at what are often termed the "moral emotions." Moral emotions are always regulated by cultural codes specifying what is good and bad or appropriate and inappropriate. There are, in our view, four types of moral emotions: self-directed emotions of shame and guilt; other-directed emotions like contempt, anger, and disgust for violations of moral codes; sympathizing and empathizing responses to the distress of others; and emotions revolving around praise and elevation of others for their moral behaviors. As we also emphasize, however, a rather large palate of negative and positive emotions can become moral emotions under specific conditions. Moreover, because evaluations of self and others in moral terms often generate negative emotions about selves, defense mechanisms can intervene and distort the connection between self and the moral order. Yet, despite these distorting effects of repression, the social order cannot be sustained without moral emotional arousal.

The last section of this volume explores how emotions are implicated in life processes, specifically the workplace, health, and social movements. These chapters illustrate how the sociology of emotions can add additional layers of insight to these and other key domains of social life. In Chapter 24, Kathryn Lively critically assesses Arlie Hochschild's (1983) analysis of emotions in the workplace. In light of more recent data on emotional labor and the psychological costs for displaying normatively prescribed emotions that are not felt, many of Hochschild's and others' earlier conclusions can be questioned, or at least qualified. What emerges from the data is a more nuanced assessment on the dynamics of emotional labor than is evident in either Hochschild's or others' earlier analyses. Chapter 25 by Linda Francis compares psychological and sociological approaches to health issues. Sociologists tend to use a social constructionist argument to study health care, whereas psychologists employ a biomedial model emphasizing physiological processes. Both approaches have their limitations, and Francis argues that the personality and social structure approach of stress research and the symbolic interactionist approach have greater potential for studying emotions and health from both biological and sociocultural perspectives.

Finally, in Chapter 26, Jeff Goodwin and James Jasper build upon their earlier work on the importance of emotions to social movement participation (Goodwin and Jasper 2004). For too long, they argue, the literature on social movements has been dominated by rational choice and resource mobilization models, which, despite their virtues, do not adequately explore the range of emotions that initially attract or sustain individuals' involvement in social movements. Because social movements are ultimately about mobilizing individuals to a cause, it is rather surprising that the motive force behind such mobilization—a range of emotions—has not been fully conceptualized in the social movement literature.

In conclusion, the fine essays in this volume offer a sense for how far the sociology of emotions has come over the past three decades. These chapters do not examine every area of sociological analysis on emotions, but they represent a broad representative overview of what the sociology of emotions has accomplished. As the sociology of emotions continues to infiltrate virtually every subfield within sociology and beyond, a handbook published 10 years from now should be twice as large and even more comprehensive.

If there are deficiencies exposed in these representative chapters, they revolve around the lack of theoretical integration and the lack of sociological work on the full palate of human emotions. In the future, then, sociological work on emotions needs to, first, begin the process of theoretical integration so that a more unified sociological theory of emotions emerges and, second, continue theorizing and research on specific emotions or sets of emotions so that the complete set of human emotions can be understood sociologically. As long as theories remain confined within relatively narrow conceptual traditions, the sociology of emotions will sustain rather than break down the boundaries that now partition sociological theory and research. Also, to the extent that only a few select emotions are studied or are examined along crude continua such as positive and negative emotions, the potential contribution of sociology to the analysis of emotions will be correspondingly limited. Moreover, if sociology is to produce more general theories of emotions, it is essential that these theories include a more robust conception of human emotional experiences.

Thus, a great deal has been accomplished in just three decades since the modern reemergence of sociologists' interests in emotions—as is so ably illustrated by the authors in this volume. Yet, a great deal more needs to been done in the next decade to ensure that the sociology of emotions will realize its full potential in explaining what is central to the human experience: the arousal and expression of emotions that direct and drive human behavior, interaction, and social organization.

REFERENCES

Blumer, Herbert. 1969. *Symbolic Interactionism*. Englewood Cliffs, NJ: Prentice-Hall.

Clanton, Gordon, and Lynn G. Smith. 1998 [1977]. *Jealousy*. Lanham, MD: University Press of America.

Clark, Candace. 1997. *Misery and Company: Sympathy in Everyday Life*. Chicago: University of Chicago Press.

Collins, Randall. 2004. *Interaction Rituals*. Princeton, NJ: Princeton University Press.

Davis, Mark H. 1994. *Empathy: A Social Psychological Approach*. Boulder, CO: Westview Press.

Durkheim, Emile. [1912] 1965. *The Elementary Forms of the Religious Life*. New York: Free Press.

Franks, David D., and Thomas S. Smith. 1999. *Mind, Brain, and Society: Toward a Neurosociology of Emotion*. Stamford, CT: JAI Press.

Goffman, Erving. 1959. *The Presentation of Self in Everyday Life*. Garden City, NY: Doubleday.

———. 1967. "On Face-Work." Pp. 5–45 in *Interaction Ritual*, edited by E. Goffman. New York: Doubleday.

Goodwin, Jeff, and James M. Jasper. 2004. *Rethinking Social Movements: Structure, Meaning, and Emotion*. Lanham, MD: Rowman and Littlefield.

Hammond, Michael. 2004. "The Enhancement Imperative and Group Dynamics in the Emergence of Religion and Ascriptive Inequality." *Advances in Group Processes* 21: 167–188.

Hochschild, Arlie R. 1983. *The Managed Heart: Commercialization of Human Feeling*. Berkeley: University of California Press.

Kaplan, Howard B. 1986. *Social Psychology of Self-Referent Behavior*. New York: Plenum.

Massey, Douglas S. 2002. "2001 Presidential Address: A Brief History of Human Society: The Origin and Role of Emotion in Social Life." *American Sociological Review* 67: 1–29.

Mead, George H. 1934. *Mind, Self, and Society*. Chicago: University of Chicago Press.

Scheff, Thomas J. 1988. "Shame and Conformity: The Deference-Emotion System." *American Sociological Review* 53: 395–406.

Shields, Stephanie A. 2002. *Speaking from the Heart: Gender and the Social Meaning of Emotion*. New York: Cambridge University Press.

Stets, Jan E. 2003. "Emotions and Sentiments." Pp. 309–335 in *Handbook of Social Psychology*, edited by J. DeLamater. New York: Kluwer-Plenum.

Turner, Jonathan H. 2000. *On the Origins of Human Emotions: A Sociological Inquiry into the Evolution of Human Affect.* Stanford, CA: Stanford University Press.

Turner, Jonathan H., and Jan E. Stets. 2005. *The Sociology of Emotions*. New York: Cambridge University Press.

Wentworth, William M., and D. Yardly. 1994. "Deep Sociality: A Bioevolutionary Perspective on the Sociology of Human Emotions." Pp. 21–55 in *Social Perspectives on Emotion*, edited by D. D. Franks, W. M. Wentworth, and J. Ryan. Greenwich, CT: JAI Press.

SECTION I

BASIC PROCESSES

CHAPTER 1

The Classification of Emotions

Robert A. Thamm

There comes a time in the progression of any scientific endeavor when the elemental dimensions of a discipline need to be more fully defined, elaborated, and differentiated. This was achieved in chemistry by the Russian chemist Dimitry Mendeleyev (1834–1907) in his construction of the periodic table of elements and in biology by the Swedish botanist Carolus Linnaeus (1707–1778) in his classification of plants and animals.

However, nothing this universal and comprehensive has been attempted in the study of human relations and emotions. As Kemper (1978:24) has pointed out "we have no general statements concerning either a full range of emotions or a full range of interaction conditions that might produce emotions." Optimistically, de Rivera (1977:98) postulated that "it should be possible to specify relations between various emotions and to create a language for emotional life much the same way chemistry reveals necessary relations between atoms and elements" and Ortony et al. (1988) commented that such a system could well be parsimonious.

So, is it too presumptuous to suggest that all human emotions are related members of a single system, a system in which the properties of each emotion category can be differentiated from the properties of each of the others? This chapter addresses that possibility. The objectives include (1) an examination of traditional classification approaches, (2) a review of contemporary theorists' contributions, (3) an investigation of relevant factors in classifying emotions, and (4) a proposed Linnaean-like classification scheme.

TRADITIONAL CLASSIFICATION APPROACHES

From various traditions, philosophers have postulated a set number of salient human emotions. Aristotle maintained that there were 15 basic emotions, Descartes listed 6, Hume listed only 2, Spinoza mentioned 3, Hobbes mentioned 7, Aquinas had 11, and Nietzsche, Darwin, and others

ROBERT A. THAMM • Department of Sociology, San Jose State University, San Jose, CA 95192 proposed various numbers for basic emotions. These schemes typically involved a rather arbitrary selection of emotion labels based on religious or philosophical assumptions. (See Gardiner et al. ([1937] 1970) for an extensive review of many of these traditional conceptualizations.)

Until the present, scholars have not been able to specify the differences among a wide range of emotion categories in any systematic way. For example, they have not been able to successfully differentiate specific meanings for common emotion labels such as guilt, regret, embarrassment, and shame. It is also probable that for this reason, they have failed to reach agreement on which emotions are elemental and which are not. In most cases, labels are equated with the emotion (e.g., shame *is* the emotion).

Many of these scholars have some agreement on which emotions are elemental and which are not. However, elemental structures of any natural phenomenon (emotion in this case) cannot be decided simply by taking a survey of those doing theoretical manipulations, no matter how well the investigators are thought of.

Labeling Approaches

During the past few decades, a controversy has emerged between the "prototypical" labeling approach and the "structural dimension" approach to the classification of emotions. The prototypical approach concentrates on the "resemblance" among emotion concepts, stressing internal structure with no sharp boundaries, whereas the dimensional approach takes the classical view that there are necessary and sufficient, mutually exclusive, conditions by virtue of which emotion categories are differentiated (see Russell 1991). Shaver et al. (1987) argued that the prototypical approach is more sensitive to the finer details of the emotion, and Morgan and Heise (1988) countered that the dimensional approach is a more efficient way to represent the emotion domain.

In a conciliatory response, MacKinnon and Keating (1989:83) concluded that "the two schools of thought may be more complementary than irreconcilable." The immediate concern, however, is not which is the best approach to the classification of emotions, but which of the two is more effective in generating mutually exclusive emotion categories and which approach should be primary in the overall classification process.

Initiating the classification of human emotions by attempting to demonstrate interconnections among a list of emotion "concepts" or "labels" is rather futile. It is analogous to labeling the various species of "flowers" prior to examining the necessary and sufficient conditions that define and differentiate their foliages and other inherent structural attributes. Viable classifications systems of any natural phenomenon cannot evolve with attempts to assign labels to categories prior to the elaboration of each category's underlying structural dimensions, conditions, and states. In classifying emotions, best-fit labels can only be researched and assigned after the variations of structural conditions that define emotion categories have been differentiated.

The primary concern in understanding emotion is not how labels are interconnected, but in the attempt to find the causal preconditions that best differentiate them. Or, as Clore and Ortony (1988:391) have argued, the goal must not be to define emotion words but to discover the structure of the conditions to which such words apply. In this regard, Solomon (2002:134) argued that "the quest for basic emotions should be understood and pursued in such a way as to capture the richness and variety of human existence, not by way of reducing our emotional lives to the pre-set workings of a limited number of *affect programs*" (emphasis added).

Overall, the widespread speculation in labeling primary emotions has been unproductive in providing seminal models for an extensive differentiation of emotion categories. In discussing this futility, Weiner (1982) maintained that the search for taxonomy of emotions has not been successful, and there is little agreement concerning how many emotions there are, or what these emotions are to be called.

The failure of prototypical approaches to successfully differentiate a large number of emotion categories is in their faulty assumptions about what causes emotion in the first place. It is less fruitful to begin a classification scheme of emotions with a list of emotion terms or concepts than with an elaboration of the social conditions that predict them. For this reason, a "dimensional approach" will be applied in the proposed classification scheme as a more effective tool in differentiating a larger number and wider range of emotion categories.

Psychoevolutionary Approaches

The psychoevolutionary approach to emotions originated with the assumption that emotions evolve out of the human need to survive (Darwin 1872). It is unclear, however, just how such basic survival functions can be meaningfully applied in a scheme to classify emotions. Such attempts have not been entirely successful. For example, Plutchik (1980) suggested in his psychoevolutionary approach that there are four basic dimensions ("existential problems of life") essential in his emotion theory. They included (1) hierarchy, (2) territory, (3) identity, and (4) temporality, as if to suggest that other dimensions are unnecessary or incidental for a comprehensive classification system.

Tenhouten (1996:194) offered a critique of Plutchik's proposition that two emotions combine as "adjacent primary emotions" to equal "secondary emotions." Although some of his combinations have face validity, at least one of his pairs of primaries equaling a secondary emotion, as well as other definitions, is problematic. Combinations are defined rather arbitrarily, and combining two primary labels to equal a secondary avoids the possibility of a third or fourth component. Tenhouten (1995) also noted that Plutchik's theory posits that a cognitive evaluation of a "stimulus" precedes an emotional reaction. What is missing is an elaboration of the concept of "stimulus." Tenhouten argued that from a sociological perspective, environmental forces, processes, and structures should be the focus in explaining emotions rather than "existential problems."

In summary, Plutchik's classification of emotion labels is limited in that it (1) is arbitrary, (2) based on the selection of only four dimensions, and (3) is a prototypical labeling approach to emotion classification. However, the major limitation in his theory is the inability to account for the social preconditions (stimuli) to emotions (i.e., a detailed mechanism by which emotions are appraised and socially differentiated).

Socioevolutionary Approaches

In the following year, Tenhouten (1996) proposed his own evolutionary scheme as an extension of Plutchik's theory. He offered a reformulation of Plutchik's model for the prediction of primary and secondary emotions in listing 10 additional emotions as adaptive reactions to the 4 elementary forms of social relations. He referred to this new model as "socioevolutionary" because it held that the emotional experience is a result of social relationships and that emotions have a long evolutionary history. For a *socioevolutionary* approach, such as Tenhouten's, to be viable in the classification of emotions, it would have to demonstrate how social forms in relationships somehow evolved over time and culture from a single origin, in terms of kind and sequence, and then show how the evolution of these social relational forms are relevant to the differentiation of emotion categories.

In this pursuit, the evolution of social structures needs more attention and might very well be of taxonomic interest. However, how such a socioevolutionary model would be directly translated into emotion categories is still a mystery. It is not as simple as listing emotion labels for categories in temporal ordering of their appearances in an evolutionary chain of concurrent social structures. This approach might some day aid in understanding the origin and development of structural emotions, but at this stage of development, it seems of limited value in systematically differentiating emotion categories.

In contrast to these approaches, it is proposed that emotions can only be defined, differentiated, and categorized in terms of *social structural dimensions* and *variations* that predict them, just as biological or chemical labels of "trees" or "hydrogen" are defined in terms of their unique structural characteristics. The elaboration of these structural dimensions and conditions is a primary focus in the construction of the proposed classification scheme.

CONTEMPORARY CLASSIFICATION SYSTEMS

Over the past 30 years, several scholars have proposed methods of classifying emotions. Among the most prominent, representing various approaches, include Kemper (1978), Plutchik (1980), Hochschild (1983), Ortony et al. (1988), and Turner (2002). They will be directly reviewed in terms of how they evolved emotion categories to differentiate the meanings of emotions and how they came to assign labels to the various categories they generated.

Kemper first published his theory of emotions in the late 1970s and his theory is perhaps still the state of the art. His primary assumption in classifying structural emotions is that they flow from the outcomes of relations of power and status in interpersonal interaction. His approach is from a social structural perspective, assuming that as structural variations change, so do emotion experiences. He saw actors in given social relations being attributed with different amounts of power or status, ranging from *deficient* to *adequate* to *excessive*. How much power or status a person was attributed with predicts the subsequent emotion. As a result of his research, he assigned emotion labels for these structural variations. In the classification of emotions, Kemper's most salient contribution is that the dimensions of power and status are essential in differentiating emotion categories and labels.

A few years after Kemper's theory came out, Plutchik, a psychologist, introduced his psychoevolutionary synthesis of emotions. His theory proposed that there are eight basic adaptive patterns that provide a basis for all emotions. He then elaborated a formal structural model describing the relations among primary emotions, and from these, he identified "derivative" emotions. In these derivations, as was outlined above, he considered the various ways the primary emotions are mixed in order to synthesize more complex emotions. In his "wheel," any adjacent pair of primary emotions could be combined to form an intermediate mixed emotion, just as any two adjacent colors on the color circle form an intermediate hue. His classification approach included having subjects judge the similarity of emotion terms and place them in a circle according to their similarity in order to provide a conceptual basis for a dictionary of emotions. Also, he saw the organization of his emotion categories as being analogous to the periodic table in chemistry.

Bordering a sociological perspective, he considered evaluations of stimulus situations as good or bad and argued the importance of valences and polarity (opposites) in emotion categories. His methodology included a subjective or introspective language approach including terms used to describe inner-feeling states such as angry, happy, and sad. In addition, he introduced an intensity dimension suggesting that emotion terms can be graded. In summary, his major contributions to emotion classification included the dimensions of polarity, valences, mixed emotion categories, compounded emotions, intensity, analogy, and the possibility of a dictionary of emotions.

In 1983, Hochschild elaborated a classification system from a constructionist and affect-control theory perspective. She saw emotions as managing "temporary roles" involving "expecting and wanting." Her notions on classification involved charting emotions as a result of the individual's "momentary focus." She listed emotion labels and categories in terms of what individuals liked or wanted, in terms of what they had or did not have, or had lost, and in terms of what individuals approve or disapprove. One of her contributions to the classification of emotions is the elaboration of categories of expectations and sanctions used to differentiate emotion labels.

Ortony et al. published their cognitive theory of emotions in 1988. They were a few of the first psychologists to recognize the importance of social events in elaborating emotion categories. Their categories included being pleased or displeased about *desirable* or *undesirable events.* These positive and negative sanctioning dimensions were used to define *joy* as Self being pleased about a desirable event and *distress* as Self being displeased about an undesirable event. Happy-for-other was defined as being pleased about a desirable event for Other and sorry-for-other as being displeased about an undesirable event for Other. Like Hochschild, they also elaborated emotion categories in terms of *approving* or *disapproving* of an individual's actions. They defined *pride* in terms of self-approving of one's own action and *shame* as self-disapproving of one's own action. When Self approves of someone else's action, they assigned the label *admiration*, and when Self disapproves of someone else's action, the label *reproach* was assigned.

They also noted to which actor an emotion was directed, to Self or to Other. The *directionality* dimension is one of their contributions for classifying emotions. Another is the categorization of emotions in terms of the extent to which actors approve of their and other actor's actions (meeting expectations) and defining events as desirable (receiving rewards) or undesirable. In addition, they believed that the emotion categories they generated provided a "meaning" for emotion labels and a basis for grouping them into "levels of differentiation," separating the higher orders of emotions from the elemental ones.

Turner's (1998, 2002) approach to classification included the assumption of a set of four primary emotions generally agreed upon by other scholars that had origins in the evolutionary natural selection process. He grouped these four primary emotions in terms of their intensity and then "mixed" the primaries into *first-order combinations* or *elaborations*. These elaborations involved the simultaneous activation of two primary emotions with one being more dominant. He demonstrated that the permutations of each set of 2 primary labels "produced" 12 first-order groupings of over 50 new emotion labels. More complex second-order emotion categories were then generated, each combining three of the four primaries. Just how he determined the labels for each of the categories generated is not clear, but their elaborations at different levels became a model for a more comprehensive system of classification. Perhaps Turner's most seminal contribution is his belief that sanctions and expectations were the "two critical dimensions of any interaction that constrained and circumscribed the valence and amplitude of emotions" (Turner 2002:83).

What each of these scholars had in common was a set of theoretical dimensions from which they deduced the meanings for emotion categories and for which they attached primary and secondary labels. The various dimensions and categories proposed by these scholars will be critical in outlining a new classification system.

RELEVANT FACTORS IN CLASSIFYING EMOTIONS

Before presenting a classification scheme, a brief definition of emotion is needed. From a sociological perspective, emotion, in general, concerns the way the body responds to environmental conditions. If emotions are responses to environmental events (Arnold 1970; Kagan 1958), they must be defined in terms of their behavioral and environmental preconditions (Thamm 1975). Even Plutchik (2001) conceded that emotions are reactions to situations usually of a social origin, such as a change in a social relationship.

The assumption from a sociological perspective not only precludes the existence of social stimuli that aids in the prediction of emotion states, but is also a cognitive appraisal of emotion-relevant social preconditions and states (Thamm 1992, 2004). The social appraisals (cognitive processing) then produce subsequent physiological responses (affective arousal). For this taxonomic exercise, *emotion* includes both the appraisal and social dimensions and is defined as the *process of actors appraising and responding to real or imagined focused social situations*.

CULTURE, STRUCTURE, AND APPRAISAL

Although the appraisal process is essential in understanding emotions, the immediate concern will be on the antecedent social conditions that, after being appraised, directly define the meaning of each emotion category. In this regard, the most vital question is, exactly which social dimensions are being appraised in focused emotion situations. There are 2 distinct social factors in the emotion causal chain: the *social content* factor and the subsequent *social structure* factor. It is important to distinguish between them, for it will be assumed in the classification model that the social structural factor is more effective in differentiating emotion categories.

Content versus Structure

From the constructionists perspective (e.g., Averill 1980; Harré 1986), the presence or absence of emotion depends on the nature of the *social context* (or *content*) in unique cultural settings, as well as on the cognitive constructions of perceivers of emotion events. However, philosophers of social construction have denied any "essence" to emotion that can be reidentified across time and culture. In fact, they have devoted a great deal of effort to show that there are no legitimate ways of grouping emotions that would allow them to be classified across cultural contexts. In this regard, Griffiths (1997) noted that Harre and other constructionists have greatly exaggerated the range of emotion phenomena that they can explain.

So, can culture-specific social *content* differentiate emotion categories? From a constructionist perspective, it seems difficult, in that social content connected to a given emotion varies from time to time and location to location. If emotions involve cognitive constructions derived from culture-specific events, then it would seem impossible to isolate and define universal emotion categories using this methodology. For example, the same social content producing the emotion labeled anger in one culture-specific social situation might not in another.

How then can universal structures of emotion categories be differentiated and classified if the content associated with each of them has so much intercultural variation? In this respect, the culture-specific *social content* approach hardly provides a foundation for classifying universal emotion categories. Cultural content in emotion instances, however, can be conceptualized as a necessary precursor to the structural appraisals of that content. Gordon (1990:157) recognized this blending of social content and structure in the understanding of emotions by mandating that an "analysis is needed of the *social structural* and *cultural* circumstances that are prerequisite to experiencing and expressing a particular emotion" (emphasis added). According to Gordon (1990), *social structure* refers to persisting patterns of social relationships that instigate emotions. In turn, these social structural variations are theoretically associated with definitions of specific emotion categories.

Social Structure and Appraisal

In the past, appraisals of *social content* have not shown to be productive in emotion differentiation. This is partly because there are literally millions of social content instances that might evoke any given emotion. Moreover, there are far fewer emotion categories than the almost infinite number of social content situations that can be used to predict each of them (Morgan and Heise 1988). This leads us to postulate that although the social content approach has failed to produce a viable paradigm for the classification of emotions, the social structural approach has promise.

However, how does the appraisal process of deriving emotion structures and categories from social content instances work? More specifically and significantly, what do these millions of specific emotion content instances have in common? For example, what do all anger-producing social situations have in common? Attempting to answer these questions requires a closer examination of the appraisal process. The key observation in this explanation centers around the notion that emotion appraisals are not of social content per se, as some constructionists believe, but, rather, of the *structure of the content*. Within an emotion-focused situation, the real-perceived or imagined social-action content is appraised in terms of its structural configurations. The structure of the content is the "essence" of emotion appraisal, not the content itself.

This distinction is important in that it is the variants of *structural configurations* that ultimately define each emotion category. More importantly, these structural configurations can be elaborated, independent of content. The construction of emotion categories requires no specific social content, in that the collectivity of thousands of diverse and sometimes conflicting social content exemplifications might all be members of the structure of a specific emotion category.

Once the appraisal of the structural emotion categories is made, the emotion follows, but the emotion categories exist independently, whether or not they were ever appraised in any social situation. In this sense, the appraisal process is redundant in elaborating emotion categories, for it is only the remaining structurally defined categories that serve as the bases for emotion differentiation and classification.

THE CLASSIFICATION SCHEME

The proposed strategy of classifying emotions is divided into three stages. The first stage is the formal construction of emotion categories. During this stage, there is little need to consider either the subsequent effects of emotions (e.g., physiological responses and behavioral expression of emotions) or the antecedent *social content* of perceived social-emotion situations. It only involves the elaboration of *social structural* conditions and states associated with each emotion category generated and provides, in a Linnaean-like model, for their levels of differentiation.

The second stage involves the labeling of emotion categories elaborated at stage one. A preliminary glossary of emotion terms is eminent at this stage. A possible third stage involves the formal mapping of emotion categories similar to the Mendelean periodic chart. Charting or mapping of emotions would be the final stage in understanding how structural emotions are classified. However, the focus in this chapter is the enactment of stage one.

"CLASSIC" CONSTRUCTION OF EMOTION CATEGORIES

The primary purpose in the first stage of the classification scheme is to outline a strategy for defining and differentiating a comprehensive range of emotion categories. This requires a *classic* elaboration of sets of necessary and sufficient conditions that define each category. These conditions, in a sense, constitute the meanings of emotion. As Clore and Ortony (1991:48) maintained, such an approach involves defining emotions in terms of the conditions that produce them, since "the central tenet of the classical view is that there are necessary and sufficient conditions by virtue of which something is a member of a category." This is not an easy task in the elaboration of emotion categories. Russell (1991) cautioned that although philosophers and psychologists have tried for centuries, no one has listed features for emotion that are commonly accepted as necessary and sufficient.

In understanding the specific conditions necessary to define each emotion category, *structural dimensions* found in the literature will be applied at several levels of emotion differentiation. Recent attempts to explain human emotions have produced valuable contributions in proposing these necessary structural dimensions. However, one persistent problem has been the *number of dimensions* required to span the domain of emotions adequately. Morgan and Heise (1988) noted that as many as 5–11 structural dimensions have been proposed.

According to them, much discussion and research in past decades has centered on the three semantic differential scales of "evaluation, potency and activity" (EPA) (Osgood 1969), and there is much support, especially among the affect-control theory group, that these three dimensions represent universal and comprehensive dimensions of emotion. Morgan and Heise (1988), for example, concurred in favoring this EPA "three-dimensional structure" originally proposed by Osgood. The inclusion of these three dimensions in the classification scheme is critical, but to incorporate *only* these three dimensions is quite limiting.

Plutchik (1980), on the other hand, has classified the emotions according to four additional dimensions. They included (1) positive or negative, (2) primary or mixed, (3) polar opposites, and (4) varying intensity. Among sociologists, Kemper (1978), in a multidimensional approach, classified emotions in terms of (1) their duration (long or short term), (2) their real, imagined, and anticipated outcomes in social relations, (3) whether they are structural, anticipatory, or consequent, (4) whether they are positive or negative, and (5) whether they are power or status related. From a different perspective, Thamm (1992) and Turner (2002) saw expectations and sanctions as essential dimensions in classifying emotions, and Stryker (2004) and others have proposed numerous additional dimensions as part of their emotion theories.

Some of these dimensions are widely reported in the literature, but they might not be sufficient in predicting and differentiating a wide range of emotion categories. There might be other more important, yet unreported dimensions that need to be taken into account. However, whichever known dimensions contribute to the effective differentiation of emotion categories also need to be incorporated into the scheme. One objective is to include as many of these reported dimensions as possible.

Emotion Categories

The purpose of categorization in the sciences is to group together things because of some underlying similarity-generating mechanism. According to Griffiths (1997:16), instances of the same chemical element, for example, resemble one another because of a "shared microstructure." The general purpose in classifying emotion categories is the same, except that instead of chemical elements, the intent is to group emotion instances in terms of their resemblances because of their *microsocial structures*.

In grouping emotion instances, Gordon asked which elements that form a particular emotion differentiate it from other emotions. He maintained that "an analysis is needed of the *social structural* and cultural circumstances that are prerequisite to experiencing and expressing an emotion" (emphasis added) (Gordon 1990:157). In examining these circumstances, the social structural conditions and states that define each emotion category need to be uncovered, elaborated, and formalized.

Formal Category Dimensions

The primary benefit of formalizing structures of emotion categories is providing a scheme in which complex structural configurations that predict each emotion can be easily summarized and illustrated in condensed symbolic notations. In this manner, a clear interpretation of complex structural conditions and states that define emotion categories can more easily be achieved.

To this end, various universal emotion structural dimensions will be incorporated and integrated into a formal system of notations, symbolic of the necessary and sufficient conditions and states that define each emotion category. The result is a rather complex but parsimonious formal paradigm for generating and classifying the meanings for a wide range of human emotions.

According to Russell (1991), to know the meaning of each emotion is to know, at least implicitly, a set of necessary and sufficient causal features. In addition, he proposed that membership in an emotion category "is determined by a set of common features. All members have all the defining features, all members are equal in membership, and members can be precisely distinguished from nonmembers" (Russell 1991:37–38). In defining emotion categories, the following propositions are offered in addition to Russell's criteria.

1. Elemental emotion categories are "pure," discrete, mutually exclusive, and nonoverlapping.
2. Compound emotion categories are overlapping and are not characterized by mutual exclusivity.
3. Emotion categories are exhaustive. Meaningful additional categories cannot be logically deduced.
4. Emotion categories can be classified according to various levels of differentiation, complexity, and generality.

These criteria are suggested as guidelines in the following classification process.

Levels, Dimensions, and Formalizations

The elaboration and inclusion of various emotion-relevant social structural dimensions are prerequisite to generating specific emotion categories. The general objective is to use these dimensions to devise a formal classification of emotion categories and to combine many dimensions proposed in the literature into multiple "levels of differentiation" (Ortony et al. 1988).

The general classification model will also utilize analogies to the classical Mendelean and Linnean systems. Such approaches heretofore have been advocated by many scientists. After citing a few of these scholars, Plutchik (1980) listed three arguments favoring the viability of analogical method: (1) The resemblance between the laws of a science and the laws of another science makes one of the two sciences serve to illustrate the other; (2) it permits the organization of a large body of phenomenology in a logically consistent way according to a previously investigated logical system; and (3) it is characteristic of human language in that it is made up of metaphors and analogies, which are a fertile ground for the exploration of ambiguity and the discovery of hidden likenesses.

The analogical scheme proposed below parallels the seven-level conceptual approach used by Linnaeus in categorizing living things. He classified plants and animals ranging from the most general level (kingdom) to the most specific level (species): kingdom, phylum, class, order, family, genus, and species. The classification system outlined below will generally be analogous to the logic, levels, and terminology applied by Linnaeus. Each of these Linnaean levels will include selected emotion-relevant structural dimensions as well as respective emotion categories generated within them.

LEVELS OF EMOTION DIFFERENTIATION

The classification scheme begins with elaborating the most general and least complex categories and ends with the most specific and most complex categories. The most general level of differentiation is presented first. It incorporates the dimension of *valences,* including positive, negative, and mixed emotion categories.

Level I. Positive and Negative "Kingdoms" of Emotions

The positive-negative polarity and the notion of opposites originally derived from the medieval church, which, in turn, traces its psychology back to Aristotle. Today, the concept of valence enters in virtually every theory of emotion in at least an indirect way. The reliance on valence pairs has a long history in psychology. "Since 1961, more than 600 published papers have explored and tested the concepts of positive and negative affect" (Solomon and Stone 2002:418).

Many scholars have argued for the centrality of a valence in grouping emotions. Aquinas, for example, used "good" and "evil" to classify emotions. More recently, Arnold (1970) expanded the criteria used by Aquinas as to whether an object is "good" or "bad." Russell (1980:1163) later suggested that one property of the cognitive representation of affect is the dimension of "pleasantness-unpleasantness," and Kemper (1978:47) argued that an emotion is "a relatively short-term evaluative response essentially positive or negative in nature." Kelley (1984) reviewed the early valence-oriented emotion theories of Abelson (1983), de Rivera (1977), Roseman (1979), and Wiener (1980) and concluded that one feature common to all the theories is the positive or negative (pleasant or unpleasant, wanted or unwanted) nature of the emotion experience.

Other theorists connect the valence dimension to a preferred selected second dimension. Shelly (2001), in his model of how sentiments lead to expectations, extensively used valences to represent task-outcome states in terms of success or failure, states of liking or disliking, and states of task ability. Clark (1990) used "positive other-emotions" and "negative other-emotions" in indicating inferiority and superiority in controlling the balance of emotional energy and eliciting a sense of obligation in relations, and Collins (1990) contrasted positive and negative "short-term emotions" in terms of how they are generated and expressed as levels of "emotional energy." Hammond (1990) saw positive and negative arousal in terms of pursuing "affective maximization," and according to Plutchik (1980), environmental stimuli are given a positive or negative valence.

Appraisal models commonly suggest that situations are judged positively or negatively and that these "definitions of the situation" are emotionally appraised and reappraised. Other models, such as those presented by Arnold (1970) and Lazarus et al. (1980), however, failed to specify what instances or events in the situation led to positive or negative appraisals. However, in any case, *valence* seems to be a most fundamental and most frequently applied dimension in grouping emotions and it also appears to be the most commonly discussed emotion dimension by theorists and researchers. Overall, emotion scholars in their conceptualizations seem to have little reservation in elaborating positive and negative categories and they proceed to list examples of emotion labels attached to each.

In the proposed classification scheme, the *kingdoms* of emotion will include the *positive*, *negative*, and *mixed* emotion categories. These categories will be notated with various configurations of positive [+] or negative [−] states.

Level II. Normal and Abnormal "Phyla" of Emotions

The *normality* of emotion is also a fundamental classification dimension. However, because this dimension is not generally discussed at length by theorists or researchers, there seems to be little concern about a formal distinction between normal and abnormal emotion categories. This difference, however, is apparent in the psychological academic community in the offering of specialized courses in "abnormal psychology" that generally have a psychoanalytic orientation. The abnormal emotions are commonly identified with emotional (mental) disorders and "imaginary" emotion experiences, whereas the normal emotions are considered those experienced in most "real" day-to-day social interactions.

The primary assumption in classifying the phyla of emotions is that *social content* of appraisals is altered when moving from the normal to abnormal, but *social structural forms* do not change. Actors, as they wander from social reality, recall, fantasize, or dream by reconstructing social content. This cognitive manipulation of *real* content provides actors with more idealized escapes and solutions to a "shame-based" past reality. Although the *content* of their imaginations can be considered abnormal, the *structures* of their "magically" created emotion instances take on the same social forms as are found in normal emotion situations and categories. If the structures of emotion categories are the same for normal (real) and abnormal (imagined) social situations, they both can be formalized using the same notation system. The only two differences include a formal notation change by circling or inflating the valence signs to indicate abnormal states and the use of different emotion labels for abnormal categories due to their unreal properties.

The classification of the two emotion phyla includes the *normal* emotion categories and the *abnormal* emotion categories, along with their respective conditions and states. The states for these two emotion branches are identified with a notation and a brief structural definition.

1. Pluses [+] and minuses [−] represent *normal* emotion conditions when appraised emotion states reflect *real* social situations.
2. Circled pluses [⊕] and minuses [⊖] represent *abnormal* emotions when appraised emotion states reflect *imaginary* social situations.

These distinctions are interesting in that, perhaps for the first time, the formalization and integration of psychoanalytic processes might be possible. An elaboration of the phylum of abnormal emotions is eminent, but far beyond the limitations and scope of this presentation. The uncircled plus and minus notations will be used throughout the remainder of the chapter to represent *normal* emotion states.

Level III. Static and Dynamic "Classes" of Emotions

There is a long-standing structural-functional theoretical tradition distinguishing the *static* from the *dynamic* aspects of social systems. The static is usually defined more in terms of social structural variations, whereas the dynamic is defined in terms of social change and social functions in interactions and institutions (e.g., Parsons 1951). These distinctions can be applied in differentiating the two *classes* of emotions. The class of *structural emotions* is represented by states that are relatively stable and fixed, whereas the class of *transition emotions* is represented by processes of social change, from a set of stable states to an opposite set, from positive to negative, or vice versa. As states on social structural conditions change, so do emotion appraisals, and these changing states define the class of transient emotion categories. Gordon (1985:136) supported this distinction in stating that structural change in society ultimately leads to change in the emotions, and "as social stimuli change, so must emotional responses change."

Kemper (1978) characterized "structural emotions" (static) as a point of equilibrium, as being relatively stable with little change from interaction episode to episode, and, in contrast, he saw "anticipatory emotions" (dynamic) as looking to the future of the relationship, the probable success or failure of the relation, as prospectively good or bad, and in terms of optimism or pessimism. Kemper implied that positive anticipations involve going from a negative structural assessment to a positive assessment of the situation and that negative anticipations involve going from a positive structural assessment to a negative. Such transitions generally describe the *classes* of dynamic anticipatory emotion categories, including the positive "hopes" and the negative "fears."

Kemper further noted that in popular discourse, one of the most common anticipatory emotions is anxiety. Accepting this, *general anxiety* seems a reasonable label for both the positive and negative anticipatory emotion categories. An elaboration of the two *classes* of emotion includes the *static, stationary*, or *structural* emotion categories, and the *dynamic, anticipatory*, or *transitional* emotion categories. The states for these two emotion dimensions are identified with a notation and a brief structural definition.

1. Plus [+] and minus [−] *structural* emotion states: When emotion appraisal conditions are constructed from positive or negative *stable or stationary* conditions.
2. Minus-to-plus [− +] and plus-to-minus [+ −] *transitional* emotion states: When emotion appraisal conditions are constructed from positive or negative *anticipatory* conditions.

The static notations will be used directly in outlining the class of structural emotions. Like the phylum of abnormal emotions introduced at Level II, an elaboration of the class of anticipatory anxiety emotions is beyond the scope of this chapter.

Level IV. Expectation and Sanctioning "Orders" of Emotions

Before considering the more complex orders of emotion categories, a model for elaborating their conditions and states is presented. The following paradigm is designed to formalize emotion structures with up to four emotion-relevant conditions. An exhaustive number of permutations will be generated from the paradigm, and each configuration will symbolize the conditions and states associated with a specific emotion category.

Formal notations of brackets, conditions, and states are introduced. The brackets are used to illustrate the parameters of each emotion category. Structural conditions are presented in quadrant form within each bracket. The location of four elementary structural conditions is assigned to respective quadrants, and states on relevant conditions are illustrated within the quadrants.

To begin the formalization, each structural emotion category is defined in terms of the number of relevant emotion conditions and the appraised states for each condition. The number of relevant conditions is determined by how many pluses and minuses are illustrated within each bracket. The state on each relevant condition is notated in terms of valence signs with either a positive $(+)$ valence or a negative $(-)$ valence.

1. Examples of one-condition categories: $[^+\quad]$ and $[\quad_-]$.
2. Examples of two-condition categories: $[^-_+\quad]$, $[_-{}_+]$, and $[_-{}^+]$.
3. Examples of three-condition categories: $[^-{}^-_+]$, $[^-_-{}_+]$, and $[_-{}^\pm]$.
4. Examples of four-condition categories: $[^+_+{}^+_+]$, $[^-_+{}^+_-]$, and $[^-_-{}^+_+]$.

Different structural dimensions and conditions occupy different locations in the paradigm and their meanings and formal notations, illustrated as emotion categories, are generated and differentiated.

EXPECTATION DIMENSIONS. The first major social dimension to be formalized using the notations outlined above pertains to the extent to which actors meet or do not meet expectations in emotion situations. Over the past few decades, expectation states theory (see Berger 1988) has played a major role in understanding the structure of emotions. The essential idea in this theory is that interaction is organized around expectations that constrain how individuals respond to each other (Turner 2002). Such theories, however, center on expectations of group members prior to meeting or not meeting them. The meaning of the concept of *expectation* in this theoretical literature is confusing, in that actors are "expected" to meet "expectations" in social situations. This statement seems to have a double meaning in that the "expected" outcome is a different concept than the "actual" outcome. The expected outcome is described in the literature in terms of a "potential," "likely," or "probable" outcome and is a function of the "ability" of the actor to successfully meet expectations.

Expectation states theory thus seems to be more concerned with predicting whether actors will potentially perform (meet expectations in the future) or not (not meet expectations in the future), compared to whether actors *did* in fact perform (met expectations) or did not perform (failed to meet expectations). This theory is more about the unknown *anticipated* outcome rather than the known structural outcome, as in "the actor is expected to win the race," contrasted to "the actor won the race." Because of the dynamic and anticipated nature of the "expected" conceptualization, its classification value is more in understanding *transition* emotion categories where outcomes are unknown, rather than *structural* categories where outcomes have already been determined. The structural dimension proposed in this classification system pertains only to the outcomes in relations, *after* the expectations are or are not met, and how these outcomes, when appraised, define emotion categories.

This structural expectation dimension also does not involve the *content* of subsequent actions or future evaluations made by the actors subsequent to the emotion event. To this extent, expectation states theory again fails to provide a viable model for the prediction of *structural* emotion variation, as it is more concerned with "social content" in the appraisal process rather than the consequences of social structural outcomes. More relevant to the proposed dimension, Gordon (1990) noted that emotions are commonly aroused when one's expectations are either fulfilled or violated.

From a slightly different perspective, Kemper (1978) introduced the concept of *agency*, whereby Self or Other is *responsible* for social structural variations in relations. If Self is the agent, the implication is that Self is "responsible" for the outcome. Following this logic, the responsible Self is to be blamed or praised for meeting or not meeting expectations and to subsequently receive appropriate rewards or punishments (sanctions). Weiner (1982) also thought along similar lines in identifying a dimension of emotion that he called "controllability." Controllability implies internal causation and is defined in terms of which actor (Self or Other) is attributed with the responsibility (blame or praise) for controllable causal conditions. Like Kemper, the notion of *responsibility* presented by Weiner helps define this emotion-relevant dimension of actors having met or not met expectations.

SANCTIONING DIMENSIONS. In learning theory, environmental events consist of rewards and punishments or "reinforcements" for appropriate or inappropriate actions. Reflecting this theoretical tradition, Gray (1971) noted that the common element binding emotions is that they all represent some kind of reaction to a reinforcing event. For example, Turner (2002) proposed that using negative sanctions invites negative emotional responses. In contrast, positive sanctions generate variants and elaborations of happiness. Roseman (1979) also associated specific emotions with situational sanctioning. Positive sanctioning is represented as the "occurrence of a desired event," and negative sanctioning is represented as the "occurrence of an undesired event." He maintained that actors experience joy when a desired event occurs and sorrow when a desired event does not occur, and distress when an undesired event occurs and relief when an undesired event does not occur. It goes almost without saying that rewards tend to make people happy and punishment makes people unhappy!

What is important in the classification process, however, is how rewards and punishments are distributed among actors in emotion situations. This is perhaps the most salient dimension, for what could be more central emotionally than appraisals of who received or did not receive rewards in social relations?

EXPECTATION-SANCTION DIMENSIONS. Social role-model theories of emotion (e.g., Averill 1980) have two variants: The first is that behavior is driven by attempts to conform to social roles (meeting expectations), and the second is that behavior is brought into conformity by patterns of reinforcement (positive sanctioning) (Griffiths 1997). Elaborating on this, Hochschild (1983) argued that emotions are about "expecting and wanting," and she went on to categorize 19 emotion labels by the individual's "momentary focus." They include categories of liking or disliking, approving and disapproving (expectation dimensions), having or not having, and wanting or not wanting (sanctioning dimensions). Such categories fit well into the expectation-sanctioning conceptualization being proposed.

According to Turner (2002) and Thamm (1992), sanctions and expectations are the primary mechanisms by which emotions are aroused in encounters. The significance of these dimensions cannot be overemphasized, and their inclusion is necessary in any comprehensive emotion categorization scheme.

DIRECTIONALITY DIMENSIONS. Sociologists of emotion have been interested in a vocabulary used to identify emotions directed to Self or Other or emotions directed to both Self and Other. For example, it is quite likely that anger and pity can be self-directed, as well as other-directed (Weiner 1982). Expanding on this, Kemper (1978) maintained that different emotions might be directed toward the different parties involved, including Self, Other, and a third party (if there is one). Therefore, emotion appraisal can focus either on the Self, Other, both, or on all three parties, as in the special case of jealousy.

Interaction theory also assumes the identities of both Self and Other, and as Goffman (1974) indicated, emotions occurs *between* persons. Thus, concern for others or one's relation to others is reflected in various appraisal dimensions and might give rise to many different emotions

(Manstead and Fischer 2001). In general, there is somewhat of a consensus among thinkers that the *directionality* of emotions is a necessary social dimension in elaborating emotion categories. The Self-Other dimension combined with the expectation-sanction dimension will account for the elemental emotion categories.

ELEMENTAL EMOTIONS. A controversy over the basic emotions has been ongoing for several thousand years. Although there is a vast literature on this subject, there is little agreement concerning how many basic emotion traits there are or what these traits are to be called (Weiner 1982). So are there basic emotions at all, and what is their number and identity, and why is there such disorder of various proposed lists? These questions signal some confusion in the search for basic emotions, and perhaps as Solomon (2002) concluded, no emotion deserves to be elevated over all the others as more basic. However, there does seem to be agreement that some emotions are more basic, primarily because they have less complex specifications and eliciting conditions than others (Ortony et al. 1988).

Finally, Gordon (1990) asked if there might be a set of sociologically basic emotions relevant to social interaction. In response to his question, it is proposed that there is such a set of basic emotions, and these categories will be the first elaborated. It is achieved by formally integrating the positive-negative, the expectation-sanction, and the Self-Other dimensions. The combinations of these dimensions will define the most elemental (and mutually exclusive) emotion categories, and from these, more compound categories will be generated at the next level.

FORMALIZATION OF ELEMENTAL EMOTIONS. The classification of the two emotion orders includes the *expectation emotion* and the *sanctioning emotion* categories. *Expectation* conditions and states will be notated on the top row within the paradigm brackets, with *sanctioning* conditions and states on the bottom row. Of the dimensionality categories, *Self's* emotion states are indicated in the left column and *Other's* emotion states in the right column.

Like atoms in the differentiation of chemical elements, valences are used to elaborate the structure of the eight elemental emotion categories. They include the following structural configurations and corresponding notations:

1. Self met expectations $[^+\quad]$, or Self did not meet expectations $[_-\quad]$.
2. Other met expectations $[\quad^+]$, or Other did not meet expectations $[\quad^-]$.
3. Self received rewards $[_+\quad]$, or Self did not receive rewards $[\quad^-]$.
4. Other received rewards $[\quad_+]$, or Other did not receive rewards $[\quad_-]$.

Other theorists have come to similar conclusions. Ortony et al. (1988) have listed structures paralleling the elemental emotion categories outlined above.

Approving of one's own act $[^+\quad]$.
Disapproving of one's own act $[^-\quad]$.
Approving of another's act $[\quad^+]$.
Disapproving of another's act $[\quad^-]$.
Pleased about a desirable event $[_+\quad]$.
Displeased about an undesirable event $[_-\quad]$.
Pleased about a desirable event for Other $[\quad_+]$.
Displeased about an undesirable event for Other $[\quad_-]$.

The one-condition elemental emotion categories can also be combined to form compound emotion categories. The two-condition compounds will be addressed next.

Level V. The Comparative "Families" of Emotions

Ortony et al. (1988) noted that the "levels of differentiation" indicate higher orders of emotions and they differentiate them from the elemental ones. At this level, 24 two-condition categories compare 2 elemental categories, and together they make up the attribution, distribution, and interaction *families* of emotions. These three dimensions and their variations will account for the classification of a large number of the most commonly experienced emotions.

MIXED VALENCES.   In addition to the "pure" and mutually exclusive elemental emotion categories, emotions can have mixed positive and negative components. Even the traditional approaches attempt to explain and classify emotions by labeling a certain number of "primary" emotions and then argue that these emotion "labels" are interconnected in some fashion. From these primary emotions, more complex, or blended, emotions could be derived (Russell 1991).

Many theorists had something to say about mixed emotions. In a positive vein, Averill (1975) proposed the construction of "compound" emotions, based on the more "elementary" ones. Ekman (1982), in confirming his studies of facial expression of emotions, concluded that emotions do "mix," and Plutchik (1962) spoke of "mixed states" of primary emotions, in that a small number of "pure" emotions could be combined into more uniquely specific "compound" and "complex" structures. In addition, Turner (2002) noted that one way to increase the emotional repertoire is to "mix" primary emotions.

Conversely, Ortony and Turner (1990) argued that the mixing of emotions is not helpful and has caused a lack of precision and clarity. Also, Weiner (1982) concluded that how complex emotions get built up from more basic ones is still a mystery. Hopefully, the proposed formal integration of these mixed valence emotion categories will help dispel such a mystery and such vagueness.

Before formally elaborating the 24 mixed emotion categories, a brief review of the three families of emotions is offered along with some theoretical implications. The attribution family will be addressed first, followed by the distribution and interaction families.

ATTRIBUTION EMOTION FAMILY.   Emotions can be attributed to either Self or Other, or to both. In this subsection, the comparative emotion attributions of Self and Other will be examined from identity theory and power-status theory perspectives. However, how expectations are related to sanctions in defining the compound attribution emotion categories will be examined first.

Some time ago, Durkheim (1938) asserted that expectations define punishments and rewards for various forms of behavior and specify social consequences for the person performing the action. More recently, Scheff (1990) discussed how conformity (meeting expectations) related to sanctioning. He argued that actors usually conform because they are likely to be rewarded when they do and punished when they do not.

Turner (2002) tied these dimensions to emotions in maintaining that "sanctions are used to assure that individuals do what they are supposed to do." Sanctions, according to Turner (1998:445), are "ultimately a response to expectations about proper conduct, and moral codes have no meaning unless they are imbued with emotional content." Turner (2002) further hypothesized that the more individuals receive positive sanctions and the more expectations are met, the greater will be the variants and elaborations of satisfaction-happiness (positive emotions), and the more individuals receive negative sanctions and the less expectations are met, the greater will be the variants and elaborations of assertion-anger, aversion-fear, and disappointment-sadness (negative emotions). In conclusion, Turner (2002:89) argued, "if negative sanctions and failures to meet expectations did not arouse emotion, humans would all be sociopaths; and as a result, the social order would not be possible."

Attribution Theory. Comparing the appraisals of meeting or not meeting expectations for an actor to the resulting sanctions defines Self's and Other's attribution emotion categories. Weiner (1982) stated that "attributional analysis" facilitates the understanding of emotional experiences and underlying dimensions of attributions are the significant determinants of affective reactions. Moreover, he contended that causal attributions appear to be sufficient antecedents for emotions elicitation, and the discovery of these causal dimensions is an indispensable requirement for the construction of a general attribution theory of emotion.

Attribution processes, according to Turner (2002), are also an important part of emotional reactions. When emotions are positive, individuals can *attribute* their success in meeting expectations and receiving positive sanctions to themselves, or to others, or to categories of others. In assessing attributions in relations, actors define themselves or others in terms of expectation-sanction emotion categories, and the Self or the Other can take on verified attribution configurations as part of an "identity standard" (Burke 2004).

Identity Theory. Smith-Lovin (1990:238) has suggested that a sociological theory of emotion should link emotional response to other aspects of social action, like identity, and Stryker (2004) noted that one element in identity theory thinking recognizes the import of affect. Stryker further argued that actors care whether expectations are met, and the success or failure to meet expectations generates more or less strong and diverse forms of affective expression. More specifically, expected behavior typically generates or reflects feelings.

In reviewing identity theories, Turner (1998:432) proposed that "emotions drive individuals to act consistent with *expectations*" and to "receive *positive reinforcement*." Performance (meeting or not meeting expectations) and sanctioning (receiving rewards or punishments) seem to be central dimensions in defining an individual's identities, and according to Turner (2002), expectations are key in the emotional reactions of individuals to self-verification. The relevance of the expectation-sanction dimension to identity theory is also discussed by Thoits (1985). She argued that in the process of self-labeling, actors are motivated to conform to social expectations and, from identity enactment, to obtain social rewards. Moreover, she argued that social rewards are presumed to encourage voluntary conformity to normative expectations. Thusly, she connects the self-labeling identity conceptualizations to the expectation and sanctioning dimensions outlined earlier for the differentiation of emotion categories.

Valence and Identities. Although identities can be defined in terms of expectation-sanctioning dimensions, how are such identities represented in terms of positive and negative states? Turner (2002:101) noted that "one does not have a view of self without emotional valences." He believes that it necessary to untangle the complexity of the emotional Self in analyzing emotional valences attached to varying cognitions that individuals have about themselves. The relation between identity and affect certainly needs more attention, and this is addressed in the next subsection, in which power-status and expectation-sanction dimensions are integrated and applied in the elaboration of attribution identity emotion categories.

Power and Status Identities. Kemper (1978) pointed to two underlying relational themes that have consistently emerged in prior theory and research efforts. He labeled these two dimensions *power* and *status*. Kemper and Collins (1990) also viewed these dimensions as critical and have articulated a strong defense for their application in understanding emotions. They, however, did not provide a mechanism by which these dimensions can be formally translated into expectation-sanction valence states, a necessary requirement for inclusion in this classification system.

Power and Status Valences.   Many theorists have offered definitions of power and status conceptualizations and have suggested distinctions between them. An extensive review of these definitions was conducted by Kemper (1978) in reviewing many theorists' conceptualizations, including Weber, Parsons, Homans, Blau, Osgood, Thibaut and Kelley, Heise, Kemper and Collins, Scheff, and several others.

In response to his review, Thamm (2004) entertained the possibility that power and status, as conceived by these many theorists, could be represented in terms of positive and negative valences and then further elaborated in terms of expectation and sanctioning states. These valences and definitions are summarized below in terms of power and status attribution emotion categories.

[$^+_+$] *High Status:* When Self did something positive and received something positive, or Self met expectations and received rewards.

[$^-_-$] *Low Status:* When Self did something negative and received something negative, or Self did not meet expectations and did not receive rewards.

[$^-_+$] *High Power:* When Self did something negative but received something positive, or Self did not meet expectations but received rewards.

[$^+_-$] *Low Power:* When Self did something positive but received something negative, or Self met expectations but did not receive rewards.

How, then, are power concepts generally differentiated from status concepts? It is apparent, as Kemper (1978:35) suggested, that rewards are not "the *differentia*." The condition that distinguishes power from status is not sanctioning, but it differentiates whether expectations were met in a given social situation. Both power and status suggest that actors were rewarded, but only power derives reward as a result of not meeting expectations, including "coercion," as Kemper argued. Status, conversely, requires compliance in meeting expectations, also argued by Kemper. Although Kemper elaborated an extensive emotion theory, he failed to define his power and status conceptualizations in terms of either expectation-sanctioning dimensions or in terms of valences. Expressing power and status dimensions as formal representations allows for their added meaning to the attribution emotion categories and provides for their more parsimonious classification.

Power- and Status-Identity Types.   In affect-control theory, the evaluation, potency, and activity (EPA) dimensions introduced by Osgood (1969) include "feeling good" or "feeling bad" about performing. The good-bad performance dimension (meeting or not meeting expectations) could also include feeling good or bad about receiving rewards or punishment in social situations, a sanctioning dimension. Feeling good or bad, as expectation and sanctioning dimensions, can then be applied in defining both power and status attributions.

Combining feeling good about both one's performance and one's rewards defines a *high-status attribution*; feeling bad about ones performance along with feeling bad about one's punishment would constitute a *low-status attribution*; feeling good about one's performance but bad about one's punishment would be a *low-power attribution*; and feeling bad about one's performance but good about one's rewards would be a *high-power attribution*. This elaboration expands the EPA dimensions to include power and status, where "evaluation" becomes a status dimension and "potency" becomes a power dimension, a conclusion initiated by Kemper (1978).

Long-term power and status attributions might also be used to profile "classic" identity or personality types, such as the case with "heroes and villains." Of course, heroes are the high performers and villains the low performers. The corresponding sanctioning terms include "suffering" (receiving punishment) and "conquering" (receiving rewards). In summary, high status $\left[{}^+_+\right]$ is represented by the "conquering hero" identity type, low status $\left[{}^-_-\right]$ by the "suffering villain," high power $\left[{}^-_+\right]$ by the "conquering villain," and low power $\left[{}^+_-\right]$ by the "suffering hero." Each of these attribution types, when experienced over the long term, could be implemented as a fundamental dimension in characterizing a person's emotion identity.

Another classic psychological "typing" parallels the power and status attribution dimensions, including the categories of "sweet grapes" $\left[{}^+_+\right]$ for high status, "sour lemon" $\left[{}^-_-\right]$ for low status, "sweet lemon" for high power $\left[{}^-_+\right]$, and "sour grapes" $\left[{}^+_-\right]$ for low power. Applying the "mixed valence" conceptualizations of power and the "pure valence" conceptualizations of status allows for their inclusion within the proposed scheme. One insight in using power and status valence structures in defining emotion categories is that the consequences of meeting expectations is not always rewarding and not meeting expectations is not always punitive.

DISTRIBUTION EMOTION FAMILY. Inequalities in the distribution of rewards are especially emotion relevant, as indicated by Marx and Engels in their structural theory of the alienation of labor. Other conflict theorists have added to the understanding of inequality in societies, including Dahrendorf, Coser, and Mills, among others. In combination, they have extensively critiqued the unequal and discriminating effects of centralized reward distributions in society.

However, their emotion concerns were with the macro and were general in scope, rather than with outlining microemotion categories (Scheff 2000). At the micro level, Hammond (1990:65) argued that inequality serves as one means to pursue what he called "affective maximization" for the individual. However, an affective maximization for the larger collectivity demands a different logic, where rewards or performances are decentralized and shared more equally among members.

Although much discussion in the literature concerns inequalities in the distribution of rewards, performance inequalities and their corresponding emotion categories are not widely considered. One explanation for this is that the distribution of performances is generally not as salient as the distribution of rewards in producing emotional reactions. The eight distribution emotion categories, however, reflect the inequalities in both actors' performances and actors' sanctioning.

INTERACTION EMOTION FAMILY. In the eight comparative interaction structures, only permutations of the two conditions in the diagonals of the brackets are elaborated, as they make up these categories. They each consist of the effectiveness or ineffectiveness of one actor's performance on the other actor's sanctioning as well as the contribution that one actor made to the other or the retribution that one actor received from the other.

These interaction categories can also be used to define both specific and general interaction identities. One example is of the "loving mother" as having a role-specific social *content identity*, as opposed to a generalized "giving person" as the corresponding *structural identity*. Another example is the "sadistic boss" confirmed as Self's role-specific identity and the "abusive person" as the corresponding general structural identity.

The eight two-condition comparative interaction emotion categories are listed at the end of this fifth level of differentiation. The complete interaction categories, including both the contribution and retribution structures and their exchange outcomes, will be discussed at Level VII, where the complete four-condition emotion syndromes are elaborated.

FORMALIZATION OF COMPARATIVE EMOTIONS.   The classification of the three comparative emotion families includes (1) the eight power and status identity *attributions* of Self and Other, (2) the eight *distributions* of performances and rewards between Self and Other, and (3) the eight contributive and retributive basic *interactions*. The categories for each of these 24 two-condition emotions are listed below with a brief structural definition.

Attribution Categories.   *Just* (deserving) and *unjust* (undeserving) attribution identities make up the structural definitions of these categories. Just structures are defined when the expectation sign is consistent with the sanctioning sign, and unjust structures are defined when the two signs are inconsistent. This distinction parallels Turner's (2002) conceptualization of justice and injustice in relations.

1. Self status-identity dimensions (just/deserving)
   a. $\left[{+\atop+}\right]$ Self high-status-identity outcomes
   b. $\left[{-\atop-}\right]$ Self low-status-identity outcomes
2. Self power-identity dimensions (unjust/undeserving)
   a. $\left[{-\atop+}\right]$ Self high-power-identity outcomes
   b. $\left[{+\atop-}\right]$ Self low-power-identity outcomes
3. Other status-identity dimensions (just/deserving)
   a. $\left[{+\atop+}\right]$ Other high-status-identity outcomes
   b. $\left[{-\atop-}\right]$ Other low-status-identity outcomes
4. Other power-identity dimensions (unjust/undeserving)
   a. $\left[{-\atop+}\right]$ Other high-power-identity outcomes
   b. $\left[{+\atop-}\right]$ Other low-power-identity outcomes

Distribution Categories.   Distribution emotion categories include the distribution of performances and the distribution of sanctions, between Self and Other. *Equal* distribution structures are defined when the two expectation signs are consistent, and *unequal* distribution structures are defined when the signs are inconsistent.

5. Performance-equality distribution dimension (equal/consistent signage)
   a. [+   +] Self and Other high-performance-equality outcomes
   b. [−   −] Self and Other low-performance-equality outcomes
6. Performance-inequality dimension (unequal/inconsistent signage)
   a. [+   −] Self performance-advantaged outcomes
   b. [−   +] Self performance-disadvantaged outcomes
7. Reward-equality dimensions (equal/consistent signage)
   a. [₊   ₊] Self and Other high-reward-equality outcomes
   b. [₋   ₋] Self and Other low-reward-equality outcomes
8. Reward-inequality dimension (unequal/inconsistent signage)
   a. [₊   ₋] Self reward-advantaged outcomes
   b. [₋   ₊] Self reward-disadvantaged outcomes

Interaction Categories.   Emotion categories generated by this dimension include *contributions* of Self-to-Other and *retributions* from Other-to-Self. *Effective* interaction structures are defined when the two signs are consistent, and *ineffective* interaction structures are defined when the two signs are inconsistent.

9. Effective contribution dimension (effective/consistent signage)
   a. $[^+\,_+]$ Self-rewarded-Other outcomes
   b. $[^-\,_-]$ Self-punished-Other outcomes
10. Ineffective contribution dimension (ineffective/inconsistent signage)
    a. $[^+\,_-]$ Self-failed-to-reward-Other outcomes
    b. $[^-\,_+]$ Self-failed-to-punish-Other outcomes
11. Effective retribution dimension (consistent signage)
    a. $[_+\,^+]$ Other-rewarded-Self outcomes
    b. $[_-\,^-]$ Other-punished-Self outcomes
12. Ineffective retribution dimension (inconsistent signage)
    a. $[_-\,^+]$ Other-failed-to-reward-Self outcomes
    b. $[_+\,^-]$ Other-failed-to-punish-Self outcomes

These 24 comparative emotion categories combine several dimensions including attribution-distribution/interaction, power-status, Self-Other, just-unjust, and social identities. The families of emotions are some of the most commonly apprised in normal day-to-day relations.

Level VI. The "Genera" of Subtle Emotions

The three condition categories constitute the most undifferentiated groupings of emotions. There is little if any discussion in the literature elaborating emotion categories where three of the possible four conditions in the expectation-sanction paradigm are known. This is probably because of the subtle distinctions and highly overlapping structures among the 32 possible permutations. For this reason, the process of differentiating and classifying these subtle and complex emotion categories is especially difficult. Perhaps only the complexity and subtleties in natural language can offer meaning for these emotion categories. This remains to be seen.

FORMALIZATION OF SUBTLE EMOTIONS. Each of the three-condition subtle emotion categories is composed of three two-condition categories, including one interaction, one attribution, and one distribution category, as well as three one-condition elemental categories.

Four of the three-condition categories make up a complete syndrome of four conditions. Each of the eight formal complete emotion syndrome categories is created below, including their respective four three-condition unique subsets. The structures are listed below in additive form, beginning with the eight four-condition syndrome categories.

$$\left[^{+\ +}_{+\ +}\right] = \left[^{+}_{+\ +}\right] + \left[^{+\ +}_{+}\right] + \left[^{+\ +}_{\ +}\right] + \left[_{+\ +}^{\ +}\right]$$

$$\left[^{-\ -}_{-\ -}\right] = \left[^{-}_{-\ -}\right] + \left[^{-\ -}_{-}\right] + \left[^{-\ -}_{\ -}\right] + \left[_{-\ -}^{\ -}\right]$$

$$\left[^{-\ -}_{+\ +}\right] = \left[^{-}_{+\ +}\right] + \left[^{-\ -}_{+}\right] + \left[^{-\ -}_{\ +}\right] + \left[_{+\ +}^{\ -}\right]$$

$$\left[^{+\ +}_{-\ -}\right] = \left[^{+}_{-\ -}\right] + \left[^{+\ +}_{-}\right] + \left[^{+\ +}_{\ -}\right] + \left[_{-\ -}^{\ +}\right]$$

$$\left[^{+\ -}_{+\ -}\right] = \left[^{+}_{+\ -}\right] + \left[^{+\ -}_{+}\right] + \left[^{+\ -}_{\ -}\right] + \left[_{+\ -}^{\ -}\right]$$

$$\left[^{-\ +}_{-\ +}\right] = \left[^{-}_{-\ +}\right] + \left[^{-\ +}_{-}\right] + \left[^{-\ +}_{\ +}\right] + \left[_{-\ +}^{\ +}\right]$$

$$\left[^{-\ +}_{+\ -}\right] = \left[^{-}_{+\ -}\right] + \left[^{-\ +}_{+}\right] + \left[^{-\ +}_{\ -}\right] + \left[_{+\ -}^{\ +}\right]$$

$$\left[^{+\ -}_{-\ +}\right] = \left[^{+}_{-\ +}\right] + \left[^{+\ -}_{-}\right] + \left[^{+\ -}_{\ +}\right] + \left[_{-\ +}^{\ -}\right]$$

A complete structural definition of each complex four-condition category can be achieved by adding their respective one-, two-, and three-condition structures. These elaborations are too extensive and complex to explore in this chapter.

Level VII. The "Species" of Emotion Syndromes

Lazarus et al. (1980) maintained that some emotions are components of others and that several emotions can occur simultaneously. He argued that certain more complex emotions are distinguished by different patterns of components, which is what urges the analogy to a syndrome. Emotion syndromes in this scheme are manifested when all four conditions and states are appraised and known.

POWER AND STATUS RELATIONS AND IDENTITIES.   Kemper (1978) identified structural emotion hierarchies in terms of power and status positions and believed that different outcomes of power and status in interaction predict specific emotions. He used the power and status dimensions to generate a set of relational structures and outcomes to predict certain emotions. These dimensions included Self or Other having varying amounts of power or status over the other. An actor might have an excess of power or status, an adequate amount of power or status, or insufficient power or status, compared to the other actor.

In terms of this classification scheme, Kemper's hierarchal arrangements are interpreted as an actor has (1) power advantage (excessive power) or (2) status advantage (excessive status). Of course, if one actor has an advantage, the other must have a disadvantage. In terms of disadvantaged relations, an actor might have (3) power disadvantage (insufficient power) or (4) status disadvantage (insufficient status) in the relation. In the remaining four elaborations of the power and status syndromes, actors have (5) high power equality (adequate power), (6) high status equality (adequate status), (7) low power equality (inadequate power), or (8) low status equality (inadequate status) in the relation. Applying these interpretations, the eight syndrome categories can be elaborated in terms of power and status advantages or disadvantages.

In reference to status distributions, Clark (1990) showed an interest in how actors establish "emotional place" in relations, where one actor stands in a relation compared to the other. Clark believed that knowing one's "place" in the relation is created "either by elevating oneself, or reducing the standing of the other." This creates identity positions of superiority, inferiority, or equality in standing. The strategies she outlines (Clark 1990:327) included "expressing negative other-emotions" or "expressing positive other-emotions" (to curry favor, promote one's own self-worth, or diminish others). Clark's categories parallel the status-advantaged (superiority), the status-disadvantaged (inferiority), and the status-equality structures in the scheme. Consistent with this thinking, Collins (1984) considered hierarchical versus egalitarian structures as a basis for differentiating emotions. Other research and theory dealing with power and status advantages in relations, and their correspondence to some of the proposed emotion categories, are discussed by Hegtvedt (1990).

EXCHANGE THEORY AND EMOTIONS.   Kemper (1978) has argued that a sociological theory of emotions must stand basically on a comprehensive model of interaction. Interactive relations commonly involve exchanges, and, as Clark (1990) noted, the act of giving might underscore or enhance the donor's social worth. It might also obligate the recipient to repay the social debt. She maintained that obligation is either an emotion or an emotional blend and that it is necessary to discover how feelings of obligation develop and are channeled in exchange relations.

Exchange theory was originally developed by Thibaut and Kelley (1959), Homans (1961), and Blau (1964). It was based on the simple principle that one actor's contribution to another in costs can be compared to the other actor's retribution to the first in profits when comparing the "costs" and "benefits" among actors in exchanging rewards. In applying these economic concepts, Homans (1961) was concerned with which emotions were produced when his principle of "distributive justice" was violated in social exchange. He linked alternative exchange structures with emotion labels and proposed that when a person's cost exceeded his or her profit, the person will display anger, and when the person's profit exceeded his or her cost, the person will display guilt. These principles are examples of unfairness in exchange relations. Fairness, on the other hand, occurs when a person's profits are equal to the investments (costs). The greater the investment (or contribution), the greater the profits (or retribution).

A simple definition of fairness is offered by Hegtvedt (1990). She maintained that fairness exists when what an individual receives from an exchange (the retribution inputs) in relation to what he or she contributes to the exchange (the outputs) is equivalent to the outcome/input ratio of his or her partner. Following these definitions, variations of fair and unfair exchange in interactions are considered highly emotion-relevant, and their corresponding emotion categories are formalized below.

FORMALIZATION OF EMOTION SYNDROMES. The eight syndromes include complete status and power self-identity emotion structures. The identity dimensions are complete in that they compare Self's identity to Other's identity, compare fairness to unfairness in exchange, and compare advantages and disadvantages in power and status relations. They are subdivided into either consensus or conflict relations. Structures represent consensus relations when the attribution signs for Self and Other are equal and represent conflict relations when they are unequal. Four of the eight emotion syndromes, including status-consensus and power-conflict syndromes, represent effective exchange relations between Self and Other, and the other four syndromes, including status-conflict and power-equality, define ineffective exchanges. Emotion structures are "fair" when the contribution-to-Other is equal to the retribution-from-Other, and they are "unfair" when the contribution-to-Other is unequal to the retribution-from-Other.

Status-Identity Syndromes. There are eight possible permutations of these dimensions and conditions. The four status-identity emotion categories, indicating either consensus or conflict in relations, are listed first, along with their structural definitions.

> *Status-consensus identity dimension* (fair/effective interactions)
>   1. $[\substack{+ \\ +}\substack{+}]$ High-status-consensus identity outcomes
>   2. $[\substack{- \\ -}\substack{-}]$ Low-status-consensus identity outcomes
> *Status-conflict identity dimension* (unfair/ineffective interactions)
>   3. $[\substack{+ \\ +}\substack{-}]$ Status-advantaged identity outcomes
>   4. $[\substack{- \\ -}\substack{+}]$ Status-disadvantaged identity outcomes

Power-Identity Syndromes. The four power-identity emotion categories, reflecting either consensus or conflict in relations, are listed below, along with their structural definitions.

> *Power-consensus identity dimension* (fair/ineffective interactions)
>   5. $[\substack{- \\ +}\substack{-}_{+}]$ High-power-consensus identity outcomes
>   6. $[\substack{+ \\ -}\substack{+}_{-}]$ Low-power-consensus identity outcomes
> *Power-conflict identity dimension* (unfair/effective interactions)
>   7. $[\substack{- \\ +}\substack{+}_{-}]$ Power-advantaged identity outcomes
>   8. $[\substack{+ \\ -}\substack{-}_{+}]$ Power-disadvantaged identity outcomes

Exchanges are more central and effective in the status-consensus and power-conflict structures where the interaction signs are consistent. They are less central and ineffective in status-conflict and power-consensus relations where the sanctioning signs are inconsistent with the expectation signs.

Below are a few examples of where the formal definitions of emotion categories might be applied to theoretical conceptualizations.

1. When actors have status discrepancies [$^+_+$ $^-$] or [$^-$ $^+_+$] there appears to be less intimacy and more distance (Brown 1965; Stets 2004). This might be due to the ineffective interactions in these syndromes [$^+$ $_-$] and [$_+$ $^-$] or [$^-$ $_+$] and [$_-$ $^+$].

2. The person who loves least (contributes the least [$^-$ $_-$]) usually maintains more power (has power-advantage [$^-_+$ $^+$]) in a relationship (Waller 1963).

3. Cohesive bonds [$^+_+$ $^+$] between actors are a consequence of mutually rewarding exchanges [$^+$ $_+$] and [$_+$ $^+$] (Lawler and Yoon (1998).

4. Those who elicit more emotion from others [$_+$ $^+$] than they invest [$^-$ $_-$], exercise control (power) [$^-_+$ $^+$] over the interaction (Clark 1990).

CONCLUSIONS

Categorical variations listed in Levels I to VII might well constitute an exhaustive accounting of normal structural emotions. In this regard, Kemper (1987) asked how many emotions there are. Accepting the permutations outlined above, there are 72 structural emotion categories. Perhaps the number of possible emotion categories is better limited to the number of social structural configurations generated in social relations rather than the number of emotion labels somewhat arbitrarily listed in the literature. Kemper (1978) has argued that a full set of structural combinations would lead to 3^4, or 81 categories. This estimate is not far from the 72 outlined above.

The primary objective in this chapter has been to design a formal classification system that differentiates a wide variety of emotion categories. A number of social dimensions proposed by psychologists and sociologists were integrated in a formal elaboration of the structural emotions. These dimensions included (1) positive versus negative, (2) Self versus Other, (3) expectation versus sanction, (4) attribution versus distribution, (5) contribution versus retribution, (6) mild versus intense, (7) power versus status, (8) just versus unjust, (9) deserving versus undeserving, (10) fair versus unfair, (11) equality versus inequality, (12) conflict versus consensus, (13) consistent versus inconsistent, (14) effective versus ineffective, (15) elemental versus compound, (16) one condition versus multiconditions, (17) structural versus transitional, and (18) normal versus abnormal. The unique structures of emotion categories were described in terms of these 18 dimensions. What remains is the process of uncovering the best fit of emotion term or label for each of them.

The final question of course is which scheme best elaborates and predicts a large number of diverse human emotions? Although Kemper, Turner, Plutchik, and others have effectively proposed comprehensive structural theories of emotion, two of the advantages of this taxonomy over theirs include the larger number of structural dimensions that are taken into account in deriving emotion categories and the formal parsimonious differentiation of each category from each of the others.

In this outline of emotion categories, contributions of numerous scholars have been overlooked. It would require several volumes to do them justice. Nevertheless, many of their theories and research have been critical, directly or indirectly, in designing the taxonomy. Contributions of those frequently cited were indispensable.

The scheme outlined is obviously incomplete and preliminary, but, then again, every classification system is incomplete. In order to explain anything, one must omit the pretense of explaining everything. As Kemper (1990:207) pointed out, "there are always unanswered questions, challenges from other theories, from disconfirming findings, and from possible failures in internal logic."

REFERENCES

Abelson, Robert P. 1983. "Whatever Became of Consistency Theory?" *Personality and Social Psychology Bulletin* 9: 37–54.

Arnold, Magda B. 1970. "Perennial Problems in the Field of Emotions." Pp. 169–186 in *Feelings and Emotions*, edited by M. B. Arnold. New York: Appleton-Century-Crofts.

Averill, James R. 1975. "A Semantic Atlas of Emotional Concepts." *JSAS Catalog of Selected Documents in Psychology* 5: 421.

———. 1980. "A Constructionist View of Emotion." Pp. 305–339 in *Emotion, Theory, Research, and Experience:* Vol. 1. *Theories of Emotion*, edited by R. Plutchik and H. Kellerman. San Diego: Academic Press.

Berger, Joseph. 1988. "Directions in Expectation States Research." Pp.   in *Status Generalization: New Theory and Research*, edited by M. Webster and M. Foschi. Stanford, CA: Stanford University Press.

Blau, Peter M. 1964. "Exchange and Power in Social Life." New York: Wiley.

Brown, Roger. 1965. *Social Psychology*. New York: Basic Books.

Burke, Peter J. 2004. "Identities, Events, and Moods." Pp. 25–49 in *Advances in Group Processes*, edited by J. H. Turner. San Diego: Elsevier.

Clark, Candace. 1990. "Emotions and Micropolitics in Everyday Life: Some Patterns and Paradoxes of the Place." Pp. 305–333 in *Research Agendas in the Sociology of Emotions*, edited by T. D. Kemper. Albany: State University of New York Press.

Clore, Gerald L., and Andrew Ortony. 1988. "The Semantic of the Affective Lexicon." Pp. 367–397 in *Cognitive Perspectives on Emotion and Motivation*, edited by V. Hamilton, G. H. Bower, and N. H. Frijda. Norwell, MA: Kluwer Academic.

———. 1991. "What More Is There to Emotion Concepts than Prototypes?" *Journal of Personality and Social Psychology* 60: 48–50.

Collins, Randall. 1984. "The Role of Emotion in Social Structure." Pp. 385–397 in *Approaches to Emotion*, edited by K. R. Scherer and P. Ekman. Hillsdale, NJ: Lawrence Erlbaum.

———. 1990. "Stratification, Emotional Energy, and the Transient Emotions." Pp. 27–57 in *Research Agendas in the Sociology of Emotions*, edited by T. D. Kemper. Albany: State University of New York Press.

Darwin, Charles H. 1872. *The Expression of the Emotions in Man and Animals*. New York: Appleton.

de Rivera, Joseph. 1977. "A Structural Theory of the Emotions." *Psychological Issues* 10: 1–178.

Durkheim, Emile. 1938. *The Rules of Sociological Method*, translated by Sarah A. Soloway and John H. Mueller. Chicago: University of Chicago Press.

Ekman, Paul. 1982. *Emotions in the Human Face*. Cambridge: Cambridge University Press.

Gardiner, Howard M., Ruth C. Metcalf, and John G. Bee-Center. [1937] 1970. *Feelings and Emotion*. Westport, CT: Greenwood.

Goffman, Irving. 1974. *Frame Analysis*. New York: Harper.

Gordon, Steven L. 1985. "Micro-Sociological Theories of Emotion." Pp. 33–147 in *Micro-Sociological Theory: Perspectives on Sociological Theory*, edited by H. J. Helle and S. N. Eisenstadt. Beverly Hills: Saga Publications.

———. 1990. "Social Structural Effects on Emotions." Pp. 145–179 in *Research Agendas in the Sociology of Emotions*, edited by T. D. Kemper. Albany: State University of New York Press.

Gray, Jeffrey A. 1971. *The Psychology of Fear and Stress*. New York: McGraw-Hill.

Griffiths, Paul E. 1997. *What Emotions Really Are*. Chicago: University of Chicago Press.

Hammond, Michael. 1990. "Affective Maximization: A New Macro-Theory in the Sociology of Emotions." Pp. 58–81 in *Research Agendas in the Sociology of Emotions*, edited by T. D. Kemper. Albany: State University of New York Press.

Harré, Rom. 1986. *The Social Construction of Emotions*. Oxford: Basil Blackwell.

Hegtvedt, Karen A. 1990. "The Effects of Structure on Emotional Responses to Inequality." *Social Psychology Quarterly* 53: 214–228.

Hochschild, Arlie R. 1983. *The Managed Heart*. Berkeley: University of California Press.

Homans, George. C. 1961. *Social Behavior: Its Elementary Forms*. New York: Harcourt Brace.

Kagan, Jerome. 1958. "The Concept of Identification." *Psychological Review* 65: 296–305.

Kelley, Harold H. 1984. "Affect in Interpersonal Relations." Pp. 89–115 in *Review of Personality and Social Psychology: Emotions: Relationships, and Health*, edited by P. Shaver. Beverly Hills, CA: Sage.

Kemper, Theodore D. 1978. *A Social Interactional Theory of Emotions*. New York: John Wiley and Sons.

———. 1987. "How Many Emotions Are There? Wedding the Social and Autonomic Components."*American Journal of Sociology* 93: 263–289.

———. 1990. "Social Relations and Emotions: A Structural Approach." Pp. 207–237 in *Research Agendas in the Sociology of Emotions*, edited by T. D. Kemper. Albany: State University of New York Press.

Kemper, Theodore D., and Randall Collins. 1990. "Dimensions of Microinteraction." *American Journal of Sociology* 96: 32–68.

Lawler, Edward J., and Jeongkoo Yoon. 1998. "Network Structure and Emotions in Exchange Relations." *American Sociological Review* 63: 871–894.

Lazarus, R. S., A. D. Kanner, and S. Folkman. 1980. "Emotions: A Cognitive Phenomenological Analysis." Pp. 189–218 in *Emotion: Theory, Research and Experience*, edited by R. Plutchik and H. Kellerman. New York: Academic Press.

MacKinnon, Neil J., and Leo J. Keating. 1989. "The Structure of Emotions: Canada-United States Comparisons." *Social Psychology Quarterly* 52: 70–83.

Manstead, Anthony, and Agneta H. Fischer. 2001. "Social Appraisal: The Social World as Object of and Influence on Appraisal Processes." Pp. 221–232 in *Appraisal Processes in Emotion*, edited by K. R. Scherer, A. Schorr, and T. Johnstone. Oxford: Oxford University Press.

Morgan, Rick L., and David R. Heise. 1988. "Structure of Emotions." *Social Psychology Quarterly* 51: 19–31.

Ortony, Anthony, Gerald L. Clore, and Allen Collins. 1988. *The Cognitive Structure of Emotions*. New York: Cambridge University Press.

Ortony, Anthony, and Terance J. Turner. 1990. "What's Basic About Basic Emotions?" *Psychological Review* 79: 315–331.

Osgood, Charles E. 1969. "On the Ways and Wherefores of E, P, and A." *Journal of Personality and Social Psychology* 12: 194–199.

Parsons, Talcott. 1951. *The Social System*. New York: Free Press.

Plutchik, Robert. 1962. *The Emotions: Facts, Theories, and a New Model*. New York: Random House.

———. 1980. *Emotion: A Psychoevolutionary Synthesis*. New York: Harper and Row.

———. 2001. "The Nature of Emotions." *American Scientist* 89: 344–350.

Roseman, Ira J. 1979. "Cognitive Aspects of Emotions and Emotional Behavior." Paper presented at the 87th Annual Convention of the American Psychological Association, New York.

Russell, James A. 1980. "A Circumplex Model of Affect." *Journal of Personality and Social Psychology* 39: 1161–1178.

———. 1991. "In Defense of a Prototype Approach to Emotion Concepts." *Journal of Personality and Social Psychology* 60: 37–47.

Scheff, Thomas J. 1990. *Microsociology*. Chicago: University of Chicago Press.

———. 2000. "Shame and the Social Bond: A Sociological Theory." *Sociological Theory* 18: 84–99.

Shaver, Phillip, Judith Schwartz, Donald Kirson, and Cary O'Connor. 1987. "Emotional Knowledge: Further Explanations of a Prototype Approach." *Journal of Personality and Social Psychology* 52: 1061–1086.

Shelly, Robert K. 2001. "How Performance Expectations Arise from Sentiments." *Social Psychology Quarterly* 64: 72–87.

Smith-Lovin, Lynn. 1990. "Emotion as the Confirmation and Disconfirmation of Identity: An Affect Control Model." Pp. 238–270 in *Research Agendas in the Sociology of Emotions,* edited by T. D. Kemper. Albany: State University of New York Press.

Solomon, Robert C. 2002. "Back to Basics: On the Very Idea of Basic Emotions." *Journal for the Theory of Social Behavior* 32: 115–144.

Solomon, Robert C., and Lori D. Stone. 2002. "On Positive and Negative Emotions." *Journal for the Theory of Social Behavior* 32: 417–435.

Stets, Jan E. 2004. "Emotions in Identity Theory: The Effect of Status." Pp. 51–76 in *Advances in Group Processes*, edited by J. H. Turner. San Diego: Elsevier.

Stryker, Sheldon. 2004. "Integrating Emotion into Identity Theory." Pp. 1–24 in *Theory Advances in Group Processes*, edited by J. H. Turner. San Diego: Elsevier.

Tenhouten, Warren D. 1995. "Dual Symbolic Classification of and Primary Emotions: A Proposed Synthesis of Durkheim's Sociogenic and Plutchik's Psychoevolutionary Theories of Emotions." *International Sociology* 10: 427–445.

———. 1996. "Outline of Socioevolutionary Theory of the Emotions." *International Journal of Sociology and Social Policy* 16: 190–208.

Thamm, Robert. 1975. *Beyond Marriage and the Nuclear Family*. San Francisco: Canfield Press, Harper and Row.

———. 1992. "Social Structure and Emotion." *Sociological Perspectives* 35: 649–671.

———. 2004. "Towards a Universal Power and Status Theory of Emotion." Pp. 189–222 in *Advances in Group Processes*, edited by J. H. Turner. San Diego: Elsevier.

Thibaut, John W., and Harold H. Kelley. 1959. *The Social Psychology of Groups.* New York: Wiley.

Thoits, Peggy A. 1985. "Self-Labeling Processes in Mental Illness: The Role of Emotional Deviance." *American Journal of Sociology* 91: 221–249.

Turner, Jonathan H. 1998. *The Structure of Sociological Theory.* Belmont, CA: Wadsworth Publishing Company.

———. 2002. *Face to Face: Towards a Sociological Theory of Interpersonal Behavior.* Stanford, CA: Stanford University Press.

Waller, Willard. 1963. *The Old Love and the New: Divorce and Readjustment.* Carbondale: Southern Illinois University Press.

Weiner, Bernard. 1980. "The Role of Affect in Rational Attributional Approaches to Human Motivation." *Educational Researcher* 97: 4–11.

———. 1982. "The Emotional Consequences of Causal Attributions." Pp. 185–209 in *Affect and Cognition*, edited by M. S. Clark and S. T. Fiske. London: Lawrence Erlbaum.

CHAPTER 2

The Neuroscience of Emotions

DAVID D. FRANKS

It is hard to imagine a field as different from sociology as neuroscience. The differences in theory, method, tradition, and practice could readily breed antagonism between any two fields. However, it is just because of these differences that neuroscience has been able to present important findings about covert brain processes that can expand sociological theory. Traditionally, sociological social psychology has focused on self-consciousness and language as primary mechanisms of human adaptation. This focus might be appropriate to the cerebral image of the human animal, but neuroscience has produced evidence that emotional capacities underlie the intelligence implied by this image and indeed make it possible (Carter and Pasqualini 2004; Damasio 1994).

Although this goes counter to old sociological assumptions devaluing emotion's role in the reasoning process, neuroscience frameworks have also challenged traditional psychological views on the very nature of emotion. Part and parcel of the evidence of the importance of emotion to rational decision-making is another challenge to sociological tradition—that emotional brain processes are much more typically unconscious than conscious. This focus on the covert has been honed and won in spite of resistance from experimental psychologists following the Jamesian insistence that emotion must, by definition, be a conscious bodily feeling. Of course, we *feel* our emotions, but for many neuroscientists, the covert processes that cause these feelings are now considered emotions. Neither of these reversals could have come about without the unique methods available to neuroscientists (e.g., their highly technical brain scans, electrical stimulation, and case studies of traumatized patients).[1]

Electrical stimulation of the mesencephalon in the brain stem of an otherwise healthy patient treated for Parkinson's disease instantly caused acute feelings of depression. Equally important, it also evoked remarkably stereotyped lines of language about her worthlessness and the futility

DAVID D. FRANKS • Professor Emeritus of Sociology, Department of Sociology, Virginia Commonwealth University, Richmond, VA 23284 of her life. Immediately after stimulation, the patient returned to normal (Damasio 2003). It is extremely difficult to find an empirical case of pure emotion because in any normal situation, emotion is inseparably intertwined with cognition. This case, limited as case studies are, nevertheless presents a rare example that clearly differentiates the two. There was no external perception to interpret cognitively—only the inner feeling. The case provides a stark illustration of emotion's capacity to precede and cause particular lines of thought.

The serious limitation of purely verbal, overt approaches to emotional processes is hinted at from within sociology by Katz's (1999) observation that words are the one thing that emotions are not. (Also see Turner, 1999, and Turner and Stets, 2005.) Emotion can be seen as the ineffable language of the body in contrast to the linguistic language of the mind.

Viewing emotion as "lived experience" purposely skirted the awkward definitional problems about what emotions were, but unavoidably kept sociological analysis on the phenomenological level of verbalized awareness. From the evolutionary perspective of current neuroscientists, however, the focus on overt emotional feelings leaves out just those covert emotional processes that these feelings are all about. Cognitively oriented sociologists need to know about covert emotions because they so often have causal effects on the directions that overt symbolic interpretations and perceptions take.

The emotional unconscious is important to social psychology for at least two additional reasons. Most important, the neuronal channels going up from the emotional centers of the brain to the more cognitive centers are denser and more robust than the cognitive centers going down to inhibit and control the emotional structures. Self-conscious efforts to avoid prejudice, fear, hatred, and depression are often rendered unsuccessful by this imbalance.

Second is the consistent finding that unconscious preferences and emotional leanings exert significantly more influence over our thoughts and behaviors than do conscious preferences. We cannot exert conscious controls over "things we know not of." This type of information is not merely of tangential interest to sociology. For example, another finding is that of the "mere exposure effect." Unbeknown to us, we tend to respond favorably to objects and statements simply because they are familiar to us. Power structures that communicate by means of constantly repeated messages might find that these exposure effects constitute reliable technological means of "hidden persuasion" and mind control (see LeDoux 1996:57).

A more than cursory look at the evidence from neuroscience is therefore needed to change long-held tenets and understand the potential contribution of neuroscience to the sociology of emotions. Some might not find this an attractive enterprise, but sociology's general reputation in academic circles will depend on being willing to do so. Massey (2002:25) summed this up in his presidential address:

> Because of our evolutionary history and cognitive structure, it is generally the case that unconscious emotional thoughts will precede and strongly influence our rational decisions. Thus, our much-valued rationality is really more tenuous than we humans would like to believe, and it probably plays a smaller role in human affairs than prevailing theories of rational choice would have it.

WHY THE EMOTIONAL BRAIN?

Massey's statement has strong confirmation from neuroscience and articulates an important reason why emotion has taken a central place in brain studies. Another reason is presented by sociologists Wentworth and Ryan (1992:38); in highlighting the embodied character of emotion, they described how emotions gain an "ego-alien" hold on us that cognitions characteristically do not. It is emotion that puts the compelling *imperative* into social duties, the *ought* into morality, the *feeling* into respect, and the *sting* into conscience. This observation is why Socrates argued to the affect that thought alone moves nothing. Serial killers have readily reported that they knew what they were doing was wrong, but they did not *feel* this wrong enough to have it inhibit their actions (Lyng and Franks 2002). Without appreciating the compelling nature of the *embodied* "role-taking emotions" of guilt, shame, and embarrassment, we lack a full theory that fuses self-control and social control of behavior in one process (Shott 1979). Thus, one reason why emotion is so critical to the study of the brain is that its embodiment moves us to action (see also Rolls 1999).

Directly relevant to "why the emotional brain" is LeDoux (2000:225) summation of the formative function of emotion:

> Emotional arousal has powerful influences over cognitive processing. Attention, perception, memory, decision-making and the conscious concomitants of each are all swayed in emotional states. The reason for this is simple: emotional arousal organizes and coordinates brain activity.

Finally, Tredway et al. (1999) have shown the priority of emotional brain processes in three other major areas. First is the historical priority of emotion to language in the evolutionary cognitive development of the species (see also Turner 2000); second is its critical role in laying down a firm foundation for childhood cognitive development; third is emotion's role in shaping the direction of the young self-system.

SOCIOLOGY AND THE NEUROSCIENCE DIVIDE

There are many reasons why some sociologists are hesitant to recognize the contributions of brain studies to their field. Several will be discussed here in hopes of opening what many sociologists still see as a closed door.

Evolution as a Narrative

Some sociologists might still reject neuroscience because it is based on evolutionary thinking, which, to them, is just another arbitrary narrative. Much of brain science, however, confirms the importance of narrative to the coherence of self and its tendency to create events as meaningful (LeDoux et al. 2003). We can hardly discard narratives because they tell a story. The knowledge one could learn about the brain without evolutionary thinking is so limited that it would be of little use to anyone. Evolution informs our thinking of the brain.

Lakoff and Johnson (1999) argued that because convergent evidence is produced by different methods and interests, our frameworks are prevented from being totally arbitrary narratives. This also minimizes the possibilities that researchers' assumptions will predetermine the results. For example, frameworks as different as traditional symbolic interaction and the more socially oriented neuroscientists have converged on important findings in spite of different methods and conceptual orientations (Franks 2003).

A New False Dualism: Reductionism versus Emergence

In neuroscience, this dichotomy is seen as "top-down" and "bottom-up" chains of causation. Both chains are usually accepted, although more researchers are comfortable with the traditional bottom-up approach.

It might come as a surprise that the Nobel Laureate Roger Sperry, mentor for Gazzaniga and LeDoux, proposed an even more radical form of causal emergence in biology. His "emergent mentalism" went so far as to contradict the axiom that physical action waited only on another physical action. Sperry's (1965) claim was that the *causal potency of an idea became just as real as that of a molecule, a cell, or a nerve impulse.* Consciousness plays a causal role in directing the flow pattern of cerebral excitation. Simply put, mind can move matter. As TenHouten (1999:44) concluded, "Sperry put mind into the brain of objective science and in position of top command." This is not a one-sided model, however. The emergent whole—the "weave of our lives"—can only arise from the parts because a *mutual* interaction exists between physiological and mental properties. Consistent with this statement, Tredway et al. (1999) warned that although we talk about the parts of the brain as if they are individual, self-moving cogs in a machine, we must remember that the brain actually acts holistically. Far from viewing the weave of our lives as reduced to neuronal firing, it is our mundane everyday living that engages the parts.

Brain studies indicate that the emergent "new" does not just pop up unrelated to its past. New parts of the brain carry some of the old parts with them. For example, Lakoff and Johnson (1999) argued that the emergent symbolic, so long seen as qualitatively distinct from animal gesture, is heavily dependent upon metaphors that arise from bodily movements and actions. This is not to minimize its distinctive novelty, but only to recognize that it is not totally free of its past.

There is another type of reductionism that many leaders of neuroscience go out of their way to deny: A philosophical reductionism that assumes that human experiences of love and hate, aspirations of all types, and so forth are essentially epiphenomenal. In the words of Francis Crick (1994:3), we "are nothing but a pack of neurons." This is not an empirically held belief because nothing of an empirical sort speaks to this issue. On the contrary, it is a philosophical question of ontology—what is assumed real. Murphy (2003) called it an *attitude*. LeDoux (2002:328) referred to this as an "absurd kind of reduction that we have to avoid." There is no lack of irony in the fact that some sociologists dismiss neuroscience because of its alleged reductionist tendencies, whereas it is precisely in this field that some of the most telling arguments for emergence can be found.

In sum, the above assumes a technical notion of the top-down, bottom-up causation model in neuroscience and suggests that we need both (Franks and Smith 1999). As Ten-Houten (1999) and many neuroscientists remind us, the existence of an overall emergent system does not stop with the individual, but must include the cultural and structural systems operating downward on each brain (see, e.g., Brothers 1997; Cacioppo et al. 2000; Panksepp 2000).

SOME GENERALIZATIONS ABOUT THE EMOTIONAL BRAIN

First, all academic fields have experienced difficulty in defining emotions as one general class of distinctive phenomenon. Scholars from psychology (Griffiths 1997), sociology (Scheff 1995), and history (Reddy 2001) have suggested that the term is not a unitary concept defining a single object of knowledge. Neuroscience, at least in the hands of LeDoux (1996), Panksepp (2000), and Brothers (1997, 2001), takes a similar stance. LeDoux (1996) warned that emotion is not something that the brain does or has. Terms like cognition, perception, memory, and emotion are necessary reifications for analytical purposes, but they do not have clear boundaries and do not have discrete, dedicated locations in the brain. Perception, for example, describes loosely what goes on in a number of systems. For LeDoux,

> The various classes of emotions are mediated by separate neural systems that have evolved for different reasons.... There is no such thing as the emotional faculty and there is no single brain system dedicated to this phantom function. We should not mix findings about different emotions all together independent of the emotion that they are findings about. (1996:16)

Second, the brain is highly reactive and needs to engage in actions within an environment to maintain itself and develop. Brain cells that are not used die. For example, children who are allowed to indulge in temper tantrums do not develop the neuronal pathways to control the robust circuits already existent in the structures involved in early emotion (Carter 1999). This leaves them without controls in their mature years. "Use it or lose it" is as true in childhood as it is in older age.

Third, the brain is a "tinkerer." Its relatively new structural features do not come out of the blue as perfect answers to its new tasks. Once again, the brain can only build on what the past allows, and its past is therefore a part of the new. For example, Wentworth and Yardley (1994) cautioned that we make a common mistake when we take the evolutionary youthfulness of the human neocortex and its comparatively large prefrontal lobes to mean that the neocortex alone reins the brain in queenly fashion—especially its older parts. We might fail to realize that the older emotional anatomy of the brain coevolved with the cortex. Nothing stays still. As a matter of fact, the development of human emotional capacities accelerated at a rate faster than did the neocortex, which is why emotional influences are causally favored over the cortex (Turner 2000). Contrary to common understanding, the old so-called limbic system, which was once considered the distinctive seat of emotion, has been decisively modernized. It is a full partner in whatever is distinctively and currently human.

Fourth, the brain has immense flexibility. Other structures do what they can to perform the function of traumatized structures. Related to this is the brain's "lateralization." Every structure in the brain is located on each hemisphere, with the exception of the pituitary gland and the corpus callosum. If a baby lost half of its brain, the other hemisphere would rewire itself to perform the tasks usually seen as the exclusive prerogative of one side. This firms up with age and myelinization—the hardening of the cover on nerve cells. Regardless of this lateralization, the left and right brains have different, but often complementary, styles and capacities, which will be discussed later.

Finally, neuroscience has driven a final stake into the heart of Locke's "tabula rasa" theory, wherein mind is conceived as an empty slate "writ" on by experience and passively mirroring "what is." According to Lakoff and Johnson (1999) correspondence theory is dead in the water. Our senses are transducers (Franks 2003). The brain and its senses must reconstruct incoming information, changing it to be "accommodatable" to the brain's capacity to process it. The brain consistently sees patterns where there are none, and much of it is designed to get the "gist of things" rather than precise details. Emotion is a pure, brain-given projection onto the world. It plays a significant role in what we remember, and it is now well accepted that memory is a highly edited and heavily revisionist capacity.

THE FUNCTIONAL ANATOMY OF EMOTION IN THE BRAIN

Structurally, the human brain is obviously an individual organ with discrete biological boundaries. Functionally, however, a *working* brain only operates in conjunction with other brains. For Brothers (1997:xii, 2001), who is probably the most socially minded of the neuroscience researchers, "cultural networks of meanings form the living content of the mind so that the mind is communal in its very nature."

The key to understanding the functioning human brain, even down to its genetic structure, is not solely an investigation of its self-contained parts but, rather, their relation and interaction in the brain as a whole. Furthermore, as Gazzaniga (1985) argued in *The Social Brain*, the left hemisphere's linguistically enabled "interpreter" plays an executive function attempting to pull together the many less analytical right-brained modules and their impulses into a nearly unified whole. Above all, the brain is a proactive and reactive organ. Any description of the individual brain's anatomy must be informed by the above.

The average brain is a 3-lb saline pool of brain cells called neurons that act like a conductor for electricity. It is only 2% or 3% of the individual owner's body weight, but it uses 25% of the body's oxygen. It takes up a full 50–55% of our genomes. The cerebral cortex covers the brain with convoluted folds and houses the "computation" part of the brain. This computational part is only one-fourth of the brain's functioning, the other parts being devoted to emotional, perceptual, motor, and maintenance tasks, among others. In short, within these 3 lbs of cells is a microscopic universe of incomprehensible expanse and complexity.

In a conservative estimate, Damasio (1994) writes that a brain contains several billion neurons. The number of synaptic connections formed by these neurons is at least 10 trillion. The timescale for neuronal firing is extremely short, on the order of tens of milliseconds, and the firing never rests. Within 1 s, the brain produces millions of firing patterns. Each neuron is supported by 10 glial cells that act as a nourishing glue that keeps the gelatinlike structure of the brain together. Recent speculation has it that glial cells also play a more substantive role. Given this complexity, caution about our understanding of the brain is in order. Although there have been important discoveries about the way the brain works, we should not deceive ourselves that we have anything but the most rudimentary knowledge of what there is to know.

Building Blocks of the Brain

At the center of each neuron is the *cell body*, which stores genetic instructions, performs house-cleaning, and makes protein and other molecules necessary for its functioning. Stretching out of the cell body in both directions are nerve fibers that look like tree trunks with thick branches that communicate with other neurons. The first type—axons—are transmitters that send signals away from the cell nucleus (output channels). Some axons stretch out several feet, ending in the lower spinal cord. The second type of fiber—dendrites—are shorter and act as receivers (input channels) of messages from axons.

Most neuronal cell bodies have only one axon, but on the branches of each axon are numerous swollen parts (terminals), allowing the axon to send messages to the dendrites of as many as 1000 other neurons (Kandel et al. 2000). The same neuron receives as many as 10,000 messages. Thus, through these branches each neuron is a receiver and sender of messages. At the terminals, gaps thinner than the ink on this paper exist between axons and dendrites of other neurons. This is referred to as a *synapse*. Chemicals from vesicles in the axon terminal called neurotransmitters are released into this synaptic space when the neuron fires. These chemicals trigger gated ion channels to open or close in the dendrite, making the receiving neuron more likely or less likely to fire. Activity within neurons is electrochemical, whereas communication between neurons is chemical.

A neuron initiates its signal by creating a rise in voltage of about 50 mV where the axon emerges from the cell body. This rise in voltage is called an *action potential*. It has little to do with action in the usual sense. Nor is its electricity like that running through a wire. It is more like a pulse or propagation moving down the axon in a "neurodomino" effect, producing similar changes in adjacent parts to the transmitting terminal (LeDoux 2002).

Transmission only occurs one way because the chemical storage sites for the neurotransmitters exist only in the transmitting terminal of the axon. Thus, we have electrical signals traveling down axons being converted to chemical messages that help trigger electrical signals in the next neuron. This picture of single neurons is deceptive, however. Many input signals arriving within milliseconds of one another are necessary to trigger a neuron to fire. It takes many action potentials arriving at about the same time from different transmitting neurons to make a dendrite actually receive it. The elements of such a flood must occur within milliseconds of each other. This electrochemical event forms the material basis for the constant conversation between neurons that make human hopes and fears, joys, and sorrows possible.

One Person, Two Brains: Lateralization

The brain has two hemispheres. "Lateralization" refers to the fact that each hemisphere specializes in different capacities. In right-handed people, the left side is usually involved in processing, cognition and language. It tends toward the lineal and analytic. Above all, it is interpretive, seeking meaning and sensibility. The right side is perceptual, characteristically more gestalt-driven and intuitive. Whereas the left brain puts experiences in a larger context and risks mistakes to create sensibility, the right brain typically remains more true to the perceptual aspects of stimulus. This tendency toward literalness can add needed correction to the interpretive tendencies of the left hemisphere. Like other executives, however, the interpreter has a tendency to "kill the messenger." Obviously, with such strengths and weaknesses, both sides are needed to complement each other.

Structures in the human right hemisphere have a disproportionate involvement in the basic processing of emotion, but there are many exceptions to this picture of the functioning of the two sides. Most probably, the contrast is significantly more subtle than usually depicted. Carter (1999:35) wisely warned against the "dichotomania" regarding brain hemispheres in the popular literature.

Split-brain research began in the 1960s when Sperry (1965) and Gazzaniga (1985, 1998a, 1998b) found that certain cases of epilepsy could be cured by severing the corpus callosum connecting the two lateralized hemispheres. This is a massive bundle of some 200 million fibers enabling the fully linguistic left brain (in right-handed people) to know what the largely mute right brain is doing.

Split-brain studies helped establish the modular organization of the brain. Modules perform very specific functions and are relatively autonomous. They are found beneath the cortex in the form of lumps, tubes, or chambers the size of nuts or grapes connected by crisscrossing axons. Each module is duplicated in the other hemisphere. Taken-for-granted perceptions such as facial recognition, the organization of space, or sequencing of events are dependent on modular functioning. Modules have their own intentions, behavioral impulses, emotions, and moods. The task of the executive left brain to organize all of these impulses into some semblance of unity is daunting. According to Gazzaniga (1985), these are often capricious, but the left-brain "interpreter," as he calls it, will manufacture a verbal "account" (Scott and Lyman 1968) to make it appear sensible and creditable. This discovery hinged on the fact that Gazzaniga and his co-workers could instruct the right brain to do things unknown to the subjects' conscious left brain. Nonetheless, the left brain reliably gave its contrived reasons to explain why they acted. As Gazzaniga (1998b:54) concluded,

> [t]he interpretive mechanism of the left hemisphere is always hard at work, seeking the meaning of events. It is constantly looking for order and reason even when there is none—which leads it continually to make mistakes. It tends to overgeneralize, frequently constructing a potential past as opposed to a true one.

When the left hemisphere is involved with emotion, affect is usually positive. The right hemisphere is more typically involved with negative emotion (Rolls 1999). This hypothesis derives from earlier studies showing that catastrophic levels of depression were found more often in stroke patients after damage to their left hemispheres than to the right. Electroencephalograph (EEG) recordings for depressed patients indicated more activation on the right hemisphere, and for positive emotional episodes, there is more activation on the left. In these cases, it is suggested that the left brain is not able to assert the usual controls on the negative feelings that germinate more typically in the right brain (Carter 1999; Davidson 1992; Rolls 1999). The arguments for the lateralization of emotion are complex but have to do with efficiency and the imperative of minimizing weight and size in the 3-lb brain. Thus, neurons of similar function tend to group together in one place rather than being spread out in both hemispheres (Rolls 1999). Other findings encourage further work on emotional lateralization, like the fact that right-hemisphere cortical damage impairs the patient's recognition of the expression of fear in others.

TOP TO DOWN BRAIN STRUCTURES

The Cerebral Cortex

The cerebral cortex is the top layer of the brain covering its top and sides with a layer of densely packed cell bodies known as the gray matter. Underneath this layer is another layer of axons that connects these neurons known as the white matter—white because of the myelin that insulates the axons and facilitates the flow of electricity (Carter 1999; Damasio 2003). According to Heilman (2000), the cerebral cortex analyzes stimuli, develops percepts, and interprets meaning preliminary to emotional responses.

The deep fissures and crevices of the cerebral cortex allow its sixteen-square-foot surface to be packed into the skull. Each infold is referred to as a sulcus and each bulge is a gyrus. Two-thirds of the cortical surface is hidden in the folds of the sulci. Large convolutions are called fissures and they divide the cerebrum into five lobes. Frontal lobes are involved in planning action and control of movement; the parietal lobe with sensation and forming body image; the occipital lobe with vision; the temporal lobe with hearing and through its deeper structures it is involved with aspects of emotional learning and memory (Figure 2.1).

Precise motor and sensory functions have been located and mapped to specific areas of the cerebral cortex. The frontal cortex does not lend itself to such precise mapping but includes areas of association that integrate different pieces of sensory information. It plays an important part in the conscious registration of emotion through messages sent from deeper structures (Carter 1999). The sensory cortex is an important part of the cerebral cortex running across the top of the brain from left to right. It receives information from sense organs. In front of that, also from left to right, is the motor cortex.

Neocortex

The external part of the cerebral cortex described above is the neocortex, so called because it is the gray matter of the cortex most recently acquired in evolution.[2] The neocortex is by far the largest component of the human brain, comprising 75% of its neurons. These neurons are arranged in six layers that vary in thickness in different functional areas of the cortex ranging from 2 to 4 mm thick (Kandel et al. 2000). The massive expansion of the human neocortex in the frontal lobes is considered critical to full consciousness, thinking, planning, and linguistic communication. It

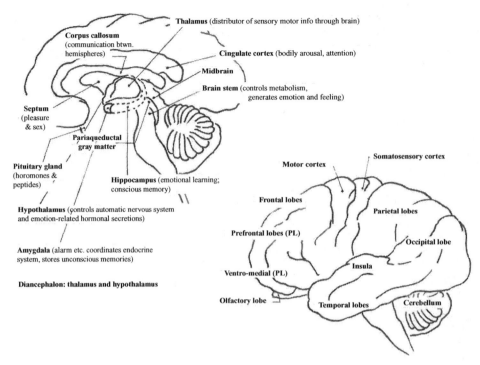

FIGURE 2.1. Emotion-Related Structures in the Brain

also houses its ample share of unconscious processes. Behind the prefrontal lobes, the neocortex also contains motor areas, the sensory cortex, and association cortexes (Turner 1999). It bears repeating that lower-level emotional structures powerfully bias and otherwise regulate higher neural structures. As one might suspect by now, the terms *cerebral cortex*, *cortex*, and *neocortex* are often used in overlapping ways.

LeDoux (1996) and a few other neuroscientists insist that the higher brain functions of the cortex are essential for the generation of emotional feelings. However, Panksepp (2000) pointed to the failure of direct neocortical stimulation to generate emotional states. It is clear, however, that the role of the cortex in lending sophisticated ways of controlling, inhibiting, and effectively organizing emotion is vital.

Cerebrum

The term *cerebrum* is used when the brain is looked at in terms of its two hemispheres separated by the longitudinal fissure. Damasio (2003) saw it as a synonym for brain, perhaps because it makes up 85% of the brain's weight and includes the cortex layers and their functions described above.

Cingulate Cortex

The cingulate cortex is a longitudinal strip running from front to back above the corpus callosum. The front of the cingulate cortex is especially implicated in emotion, including depression and transient sadness. The posterior is more associated with cognitive processes. This large area is an integral part of the somatosensory mapping system that creates bodily feelings or "arousals," from the chills created by music, to sexual excitement, and to bodily reactions to drug experiences (Damasio 2003). To be capable of feeling, the organism must not only have a body but also must be able to represent that body inside itself. One of the major characteristics of the human brain is that it is extremely nosey, and much of what it is nosey about is its self (Damasio 1994). The cingulate cortex plays a vital part of this representation. There is much more to emotion than feeling, but feeling is vital nonetheless. Experientially, without feeling from our bodies, emotions are indistinguishable from thoughts (Carter 1999). Damasio's "prefrontal" patients who can think of feelings but not feel them are vivid cases in point.

Intractable pain has been relieved by surgical destruction of the cingulate cortex (Berridge 2003). The recognition of emotional expression might involve its anterior regions. Pictures of happy faces have produced activation in the left side of this area. However, no cingulate involvement was found in response to sad faces. This asymmetry is considered consistent with Davidson's (1992) suggestion that the left hemispheric specialization elicits positive emotion and right specialization elicits negative emotion. It is one of the most consistently activated regions in patients with obsessive—compulsive disorder. Some suggest that the anterior cingulate acts as a bridge between emotion and attention. It is also described as being involved in the integration of visceral, attentional, and affective information necessary for self-regulation and, by implication, social control, as is the cortex as a whole. It is essential for integrating emotions with the forebrain (Turner 1999) and is also well connected with deeper structures.

Insula

The insula is another critical somatosensing region behind emotional feeling that Damasio (2003) considers underappreciated. It is tucked away deep inside the fold of the temporal lobe. In emotional feelings, signals from the entire body are conveyed from the brain stem to a dedicated nucleus of the thalamus and then to neural maps in the anterior and posterior insula. The insula, in turn, sends this on to the ventromedial prefrontal lobes and the anterior cingulate (Damasio 2003). The cingulate cortex and the insula are dominant sites of engagement in the feelings produced by ecstasy, heroin, cocaine, and marijuana. Damasio (2003) saw the body sensing regions such as the insula as the sites of neural patterns that are the proximate cause of feeling states.

Other Subcortical Structures

Lying deep within the cerebral cortex is the hippocampus and the amygdala. A small but very complicated collection of nuclei, the amygdala lies at the front of the long, horn-shaped hippocampus, whose tail end wraps around the thalamus. It is most known for being the brain's instantaneous alarm system. It monitors the external world for danger and enables instant fear and anger. Although it has many connections to the cortex, it can be engaged with minimum time-consuming cortical inputs. It is even important in *consolidating* memories—ensuring that emotionally significant memories will be well remembered (Kandel et al. 2000). It coordinates the autonomic and endocrine systems involved in emotions and is important for the ability to interpret others' emotions. According to Fellows et al. (2000), the amygdala also stores unconscious memories in much the same way as the hippocampus stores long-term explicit memories.

It is well known that emotional events facilitate such storage and are important in learning the lessons that life teaches. The pains and delights of emotional experiences make them vital as rewards and punishments in emotional conditioning. Thus, the role of the hippocampus in memory is crucial. Without memory, learning is severely limited and nothing approximating emotional intelligence will develop.

The hippocampus also works closely with the amygdala in context conditioning—the recognition and remembering of contexts that make objects dangerous or not. This enables us to be afraid of bears in the wild but not in the zoo.

It is well known that memory is enhanced by emotion. Memory "consolidation" depends on the hippocampus, which is connected to almost all of the cortex, making an elaborate flow of information between the two possible.[3] Consolidation means that the memories are arranged into one episode of many parts. Thus, remembering one part will often bring back the others.

Without an intact hippocampus, the person cannot incorporate anything new. The amygdala stores fearful covert past memories, but because cortical activity operates to depress amygdala activation, these memories cannot be voluntarily brought to consciousness. At later dates, when least expected, they might pop up as flashbacks. Long-term elevations of stress hormones as in childhood abuse and military actions can damage the hippocampus and literally shrink its tissues, causing the memory defects associated with posttraumatic stress disorder (Carter 1999).

Dienchephalon

The dienchephalon lies between the cerebral hemispheres and the midbrain. The latter is on top of the brain stem and continues to the spinal cord. This structure and the pituitary gland lying in front of it are mediators of sensory inputs that carry emotional charges (LeDoux 1996; Turner 1999). They also produce hormones and peptides critical to emotional responses. The diencephalon is composed of the thalamus and the hypothalamus, the latter lying in front of and below the thalamus. The thalamus is the large relay station for processing and distributing all sensory and motor information from the periphery going to the cerebral cortex. The emotional aspects of this information are regulated by the thalamus through its variety of connections to the cortex. More recently, it has been found that the thalamus determines whether this information reaches *awareness* in the neocortex (Kandel et al. 2000).

The pea-sized hypothalamus controls the autonomic nervous system and hormonal secretions by the pituitary gland. It has input and output connections to every region of the central nervous system crucial to emotional feeling. According to Damasio (2003), the hypothalamus is the master executor of many chemical responses that comprise emotion. For example, the peptides oxytocin and vasopressin, vital to attachment and nurturing, are released under its control with help from the pituitary gland. According to Kandel et al. (2000), it coordinates the peripheral expressions of emotional states. The hypothalamus is also involved in appetites, from hunger to sexual excitement. Finally, new areas of pleasure were apparently layered over the most ancient emotional centers—the amygdala and septum. The latter is located above the pituitary gland and is the repository of sexuality. Turner (2000) suggested that this might have heightened capacities for reciprocity and altruism in early *Homo sapiens*.

Brain Stem

The brain stem is a set of small nuclei and pathways between the diencephalon and the spinal cord. They are associated with the basics of life maintenance like metabolism. Because it is like the brain of current reptiles and formed around 500 million years ago, it is sometimes referred to as the reptilian brain. Emotion processes were an early evolutionary development taking place when brain organization was dominated by the brain stem, and present brain organization remains rooted in brain-stem neural systems.

Damasio (1999) and Panksepp (2000) viewed the brain stem as critical to mapping feelings because it is the conduit from the body to the brain and the brain to the body. Berridge (2003:36) reminded us that contrary to earlier understandings of the brain stem as merely reflexive, "almost every feeling of pleasure or pain felt by the forebrain must climb its way there through the brain stem."

According to Damasio (1999), areas of the brain stem work with the forebrain structures of the cingulate cortex and prefrontal cortex to generate consciousness, including emotional states. Damage to the brain stem most often causes the loss of all consciousness.

The midbrain rests on top of the brain stem and includes a group of nuclei called the pariagueductal gray area. Damasio (1999) saw this area as critical to high-order control of homeostasis and a major coordinator of emotion. According to Panksepp (2000), it releases opiod neurotransmitter receptors important to many emotional states. He suggested that it was this area that first allowed creatures to cry out in distress and pleasure, and he agreed that the brain stem is a subcortical contributor to conscious feeling.

THE DEBATE ABOUT THE LIMBIC SYSTEM

At the end of the nineteenth century when sensory perception and movement control were found located in specific areas of the neocortex, questions arose about the specific location of emotions in the brain. James (1884), of course, concentrated on conscious feelings as a result of the behavioral responses to "emotional stimuli." Emotion was then located in our sensory cortices that perceived bodily movements appropriate to gearing up for action in different situations. This precipitant movement produced the bodily feeling. We ran, not because of the emotion of fear; the feeling of fear was the sensation of the body in the preparation for the act of running. This was refuted by Cannon's (1927) demonstration that the removal of the neocortex failed to extinguish emotional responses.

This pushed the search down underneath the neocortex, ending with MacLean's (1949) proposal that such a place could be found in the "limbic system." This comprised a discrete network of primitive structures between the supposedly more recent neocortex and the brain stem. The neocortex was thought to have enabled the cognitive and learning capacities of mammals as opposed to reptiles. Structures usually associated with the limbic system include the hippocampus, thalamus, hypothalamus, and the amygdala. MacLean's limbic system was an update of his original idea of emotion in general as essentially involving our blind, visceral reactions to environmental stimuli. This dimension of mentality *"eludes the grasp of the intellect because its animalistic and primitive structure makes it impossible to communicate in verbal terms"* (LeDoux 1996:94, emphasis in original). Phylogenetically, humans have the reptilian brain, the paleomammalian brain, and the later more advanced neomammalian brain, which is shared with late mammals and other primates. All three are linked in humans, but they were thought to have retained their own very different kinds of intelligence, memory, and sense of time and space. Above all, MacLean's framework was an evolutionary theory of the localization of emotion processing in the old reptilian cortex. Clearly, all of this was a strong force in keeping alive the cultural devaluation of emotion as primitive and antithetical to reason.

As brain anatomy became better understood, the difference in these cortical areas became impossible to order phylogenetically and with it, the evolutionary backdrop to MacLean's proposal

(LeDoux 1996). As observational techniques improved, it turned out that primitive creatures had rudimentary cortices similar to the supposedly more advanced mammalian neocortex. They were just in different places and had escaped notice. Thus, there was no distinctively reptilian cortex in humans that has remained unchanged since primordial times and that exclusively housed emotional processing. The neocortex turned out not to be so new and the supposedly distinct reptilian cortex was not so distinct. As a result, the old/new cortex distinction broke down (LeDoux 2002).

MacLean (1949) defined the limbic system particularly in terms of its connection to the hypothalamus. As research techniques improved, it became evident that the hypothalamus connected to all levels of the nervous system, including the neocortex. If the limbic system is significantly connected to the entire brain, as its structures seem to be, its ability to localize emotion or anything else is lost. As we have observed in other cases of newer structures, the limbic area could not be seen as ancient and static in time, because all areas were so interconnected that they influence each other, resulting in the allegedly old structures having new properties and roles. Presumably, they retain aspects of old characteristics and tendencies, but taken as a whole, they are not what they used to be. One criterion for inclusion in the limbic system was proposed to be connection with the thalamus, but it was soon recognized that such connectivity included structures at all levels of the nervous system from the neocortex to the spinal cord (LeDoux and Phelps 2000).

According to LeDoux (1996), the popular theory of the limbic system finally broke down with the finding that its essential structures like the hippocampus were by no means dedicated to emotion and actually had a clearer involvement in cognitive processes like declarative memory (LeDoux and Phelps 2000). However, in spite of numerous critics, this expected rejection was not to be the case.

The reason why the concept has refused to die starts with the amygdala. Its deserved reputation for generating emotional judgments with minimal cognitive input also made it a gateway to the study of "pure" emotion in the brain. The amygdala has a very low threshold to electrical stimulation, which adds to its reputation for producing emotional quick triggers. This capacity, however, is because of only one of its major pathways. Granted that emotion here is relatively cognition free and offers a "limbic" gateway to researchers, but at other times and in different ways, the amygdala is driven by cognitive pathways in the neocortex and prefrontal lobes. Nonetheless, the amygdala remained at the forefront of research into the emotional brain and carried with it the related notion of the limbic system.

A balanced view of the amygdala must recognize that it can also receive significant input from sensory cortical regions involved in consciousness and is acted on by cognitive neuronal pathways that can inhibit its felt strength. Lesions to areas of the amygdala disrupt positive as well as negative emotional reactions. As we have seen, some of these disruptions include the ability to apprehend emotional implications of social situations and the ability to generate appropriate emotional responses to them. Covert memories involving fear are presumably stored in the amygdala rather than the cortex.

Within all of this complexity it is nonetheless clear that the amygdala is more consistently involved in emotion than any other area between the hypothalamus and the neocortex. However, it is not involved in all emotions and commonly draws from areas outside of the limbic system.

One of the reasons researchers think that it might be easier to glean emotion independent of cognitive aspects in the amygdala is because it is so closely connected to the thalamus that it can send noncognitive messages directly from the outside environment without time-consuming input from the more distant neocortex. However, this is only one of the pathways in its emotional functioning. When potentially fearful objects come to attention, *two* parallel tracks send information to the amygdala. Prior to engaging either track, data simplified by the senses are sent to the thalamus, where they are further sorted and sent to appropriate processing areas (Carter 1999). In the case of the sighting of a snake, the fearful message is sent on the fast route described above. This path takes milliseconds. The long path goes to the visual cortex at the back of the brain and takes twice as long. At the visual cortex, it is uncategorized raw data. Next it must be categorized as a snake with the memories that go along with that, and then an emotionally laden and cognitively appraised message is sent to the amygdala, which stirs the body proper into action.

In sum, the concept of the limbic system was originally intended to explain emotion in general and localize all emotion in a specific place in the brain. Emotions are involved in many areas of the human brain and are tightly interwoven with structures of cognition, memory, and motivation. There is much more to emotional processing than the amygdala or its adjacent "limbic" system. Berridge (2003) concluded that neural substrates of feeling and emotion are distributed throughout the brain, from front to back and top to bottom. LeDoux's criticisms are no doubt correct, and it would probably be more accurate to talk simply of the "emotional brain." However, Berridge (2003) and Panksepp (2000) suggested that once we are aware of the inadequacies of the limbic system as a concept, we might be prudent to tolerate its use. At this stage of neuroscience, the term is not really less vague than many current anatomical concepts, and in order to advance our knowledge, we might have to tolerate successive approximations.

NEUROSCIENCE AND UNCONSCIOUS EMOTION

As critical as consciousness is to being human, the vast majority of what the brain does is accomplished through unconscious processes that often affect the course this consciousness will take. This has been a major theme of neuroscience and of this chapter. According to Gazzaniga (1998a) and Lakoff and Johnson (1999), more than 95% of what the brain does is below consciousness and shapes conscious thought. Much of what goes into these estimates, however, should be considered evident. We cannot bring into consciousness the processes that enable this consciousness, much less those involved in facial recognition, memory retention, or a sneeze. Any single second of consciousness is the smallest iceberg tip in an infinite sea of involuntary synaptic processes sealed from awareness.

A less evident type of emotional unconscious has to do with *content* rather than processes. For example, Scheff (1990) discussed the negative effects of chronic, unacknowledged shame. One can suffer from guilt or anxiety so long that these feelings become part of the person's "assumptive emotional order" and are only recognized when they are lifted. Defense mechanisms like projection and reaction formation are often emotional in character, and when acknowledged, they lose their efficacy. Unfortunately, process and content are often conflated when discussing the emotional unconscious.

Unconscious emotions tend to spill over and become misattributed to objects unrelated to their origins. Also, as we have seen, the usual cortical controls of emotion are rendered useless when we are not aware that there is anything to control. Ironically it is this psychologically important meaning of unconscious emotional content that has proven the most controversial.[4]

The Appeal of "Mentalism" and Disentanglement from the Early Freud

One reason for the reluctance to accept the idea of unconscious emotions is that it goes counter to an important Western assumption about thought and action. Certainly, an important dimension of thinking is the self-conscious weighing of alternative courses of action and our ability to reflect on our motives before we act. People know what they are doing and know their reasons for doing so. In this view, consciousness is first and action follows (Öhman 1999). Actually, there was little question of the rather narrow validity of mentalism as far as it went; the limitation, as stated in the beginning of this chapter, was one of scope.

According to Öhman, it was not until the mid-1980s that experimental psychology began to recognize the converging evidence for the unconscious, although they preferred the term "implicit learning." Writers in the sociology of emotions have long recognized the inability of those expressing negatively sanctioned emotions to recognize them in themselves. Jealousy and envy are clear cases in point, and others' attempts at enlightenment are very frequently met with irritation. In a culture where it is important to appear as masters of our own fates and practitioners of agency, notions of the unconscious can be unwelcome. Scientists are no exception.

The problem was exacerbated by the legitimate concerns that academics had over the widely popular acceptance of Freud's fanciful early speculations on the unconscious id and superego that rendered the ego epiphenomenal.

Neuroscience contributions to the unconscious have little resemblance to Freudian views and arise from very different perspectives and methods. In terms of processes, it is generally recognized in neuroscience that by the time a person consciously initiates an action, the brain has already done its work (Libet 1996). For every subject intentionally initiating a particular motor movement, Libet found a prior electrophysiological neural potential causing the action 100 ms before the conscious decision. Similarly, with emotion as content, by the time we become conscious of our feelings, the brain, especially the amygdala, has also already done its work. This is a major theme in the writings of Damasio and LeDoux among others, as will be seen below.

The neuroscience readiness to accept the emotional unconscious must be seen in relation to the overwhelming evidence for the cognitive unconscious and dramatic denials connected with various medical maladies. Prosopagnosia, for example, is the lack of ability to recognize faces, even those of one's most intimate family members. However, patients do seem to exhibit "emotional blind sight" reliably responding with higher skin conductance responses to familiar persons than to nonfamiliar ones and making appropriate responses to them on unconscious levels (Lane et al. 2000). Ramachachandrun and Blakeslee (1998) saw the dynamics of Freud's defense mechanisms writ large in such blatant cases of unawareness, repression, and denial. A conscious defense mechanism is an anomaly—a failed psychological operation.

The New Separation of Emotion and Feeling: Disentangling from James

Along with LeDoux's first argument that the brain was essentially emotional, there was also a new separation of emotion (which was characteristically unconscious) from feeling (which was always conscious). Feeling, and the awareness of the body as in fear and trembling or the chill of goose bumps, had taken center stage in James's view of emotion. According to James (1884:193), "If we fancy some strong emotion and then try to abstract from our consciousness of it all the feelings of its characteristic body symptoms, we find that we have nothing left behind, no 'mind stuff' out of which the emotion can be constituted."

Wresting psychologists away from the plausibility of this argument has been helped by the unique outlook of current brain studies. However, James himself had hinted at the entry point for current neuroscience, namely that these very sensory feelings to which he gave such emphasis were themselves caused by *involuntary reactions to events*. Whereas James gave relatively little attention to this once it was said, Damasio and LeDoux focused on just this point—not that emotions cannot be to some extent manufactured, but to them the essential characteristic of basic emotions is their involuntaristic and automatic character. If emotions are equated with feelings, then emotions seem intuitively subjective and private. For Damasio (2003), emotions are objective and public; they occur in the face, posture, voice, and specific behaviors. They engage heart rates, blood pressure, skin conductance, and endocrine responses. The subject is unaware of most of these emotional processes.

Thus, LeDoux and Damasio turned the lived experience of emotion so popular in sociology on its head. They granted the importance of feeling and its feedback that affects the original emotion and the importance of feeling to what it is to be human. They also recognized the importance of Wentworth and Ryan's (1992) felt "limbic glow" to our apprehensions of self and, thus, social control. However, from an evolutionary point of view, emotion is the set of "mute survival mechanisms rooted in the body," which itself is not conscious feeling and thus not mental. The experienced feeling is seen as a "sophistication" of the basic unconscious brain mechanism turning us from danger and attracting us to things of benefit. LeDoux at one point calls feeling "a frill—the icing on the cake" (Carter 1999:82). In the final analysis, he saw it as a very important frill for much the same reasons sociologists do.

The Unconscious in Evolutionary Perspective

LeDoux (1996), like Damasio, argued that to understand emotion, we must go deeper than the behavioral and physiological responses described by James. The interest of both men is to probe the unconscious system that causes the feelings (like fear) before we even know that we are in danger. Damasio's (2003:30) answer to why emotion comes first and causes feelings later is "because evolution came up with emotions first and feelings later."

From the beginning of life on Earth, organisms have been endowed with mechanisms to automatically maintain life processes. These include immune responses, basic reflexes, and metabolic regulation that maintains interior chemical balance. Working up to the more complex of these devises are systems of pain and pleasure, which automatically determine what is to be sought and avoided. Further up this ladder are the appetites, including hunger, thirst, curiosity, and sex. The crown jewel of such life regulation is emotion. Above emotion is feeling, which is ultimately seamlessly connected and looping back on it. Although all of these homeostasis devices are present at birth, the more complex the system is, the more learning is required to engage it.

Consciousness, being a late development in evolution, came long after emotion. One would therefore expect that unconscious emotional systems and conscious feeling systems would exist in the brain, and although interrelated, they would be, in some meaningful sense, distinct. Jacoby et al. (1997) have provided consistent support for the hypothesis that conscious and unconscious processes are independent. The fear system, for example, is available to consciousness but operates independently of it, making fear a prototypical unconscious emotional system. Of course, whether and to what extent fear can be generalized to other emotions awaits further study (Brothers 2001).

A study described by Öhman (1999) demonstrated that fear responses do not require consciousness. Subjects were recruited from two groups: those who were very fearful of snakes but not fearful of spiders and those fearful of spiders but not fearful of snakes. The control group consisted of students who did not fear either one. Pictures of snakes, spiders, flowers, and mushrooms were then shown on slides significantly faster than possible for conscious perception. Nonetheless, when exposed to the imperceptible snake slides, those fearful of snakes had elevated skin conductance responses (SCR) to the snake slides but not those of the spiders. The participants fearful of spiders responded similarly to the spider slides but not those of the snakes. The control group had no elevated responses to any of the slides. In sum, with no consciousness of the slides' contents, subjects showed enhanced sympathetic, unconscious responses. After describing similar studies, Öhman (1999) concluded, in accordance with LeDoux, that aspects of an unconscious fear response are independent of conscious processes, although they can be consciously accessed.

More Evidence of Unconscious Emotion from Neuroscience

One early illustration of emotional memories beyond the patient's awareness might prove somewhat disconcerting to current sensibilities. In 1911, a doctor pricked a patient suffering from short-term memory loss with a pin, causing significant distress. The physician left the room until the patient regained her composure. Suffering from *source amnesia*, she had no way of recognizing the doctor when he came back in with his hand out in a gesture of greeting. Reasonably enough, but with no conscious recall of the first incident, she refused to shake his hand again. She explained that "sometimes people hide pins in their hands." Fortunately, more current case studies demonstrate progress in doctors' concern for their patients.

One such illustration comes from Damasio's (1999) traumatized patient David. His damaged hippocampus and amygdala resulted in the loss of all conscious memory. He could not recognize individuals because he could not remember them. Nonetheless, he did seem to gravitate to certain people and avoid others. To probe this further, David was placed in social situations with three different types of experimental accomplices. One was pleasant and rewarding and a second was neutral. The third was brusque and punishing. David was then shown four photos including the faces of the three accomplices and asked who he would go to for help and who was his friend. In spite of his inability to consciously remember any of them, he chose the pleasant accomplice.

David was quite capable of feeling preferences and related affect when it did not depend on short-term memory. Because he suffered significant destruction to his ventromedial cortexes, basal forebrain, and amygdala, Damasio surmised that these areas, as involved as they are in regular emotional life, were not necessary by themselves for either emotion or consciousness (Damasio 1999).

According to Kihlstrom et al. (2000), the evidence for this type of unconscious emotion is not limited to anecdotal case studies, although they describe other current experimental case studies like the one above by Damasio. For example, using the strategy of mere exposure effects, unconscious preferences for melodies were created in amnesic subjects who have no ability to remember the exposure.

Damasio's (2003) stronger argument for the unconscious nature of emotion as opposed to conscious feeling came from his own empirical study. A hypothesis was tested regarding the brain structures that would be activated by emotions of sadness, happiness, fear, and anger. Activation was measured by blood flow in the hypothesized regions as measured by positron-emission tomography (PET) scans. These brain areas included the cingulate cortex, two somatosensory cortices (including the insula), the hypothalamus, and several nuclei in the back of the brain stem (the tegmentum). PET scans reflect the amount of local activity of neurons and, thus, the engagement of these structures when emotions are felt. Next subjects were coached in theatrical techniques of reliving memories of experiencing the four emotions to the point of actually experiencing some degree of feelings for each. Preexperimental tests determined which of the four emotions subjects could enact the best for the final experiment. In the actual study, subjects were able to make themselves feel their assigned emotion with surprising intensity. They were asked to raise their hand when they started to feel this emotion. Heart rate and skin conductance were measured before and after the hands were raised.

In terms of results, all of the brain structures identified above became activated during the onset of emotional feeling. Furthermore, these patterns varied among the four emotions in expected ways. Most important for the purposes here, changes in skin conductance and heart rate always preceded the signal that the feeling was being felt; that is, they occurred *before* the subjects raised their hands. Damasio (2003) concluded that this was just another situation where emotional states came first and conscious feelings afterward.

Damasio also insisted that we must separate emotion, which is always unconscious, from feeling, which is always conscious. Although they might operate in close interaction with each other and in the final analysis might be seen as fused, he argued for a clear analytical distinction between the two *at this point*. In sum, Damasio (1999) argued strongly that the basic mechanisms underlying emotion proper do not require consciousness, although they may eventually use it.

In conclusion, it should be clear that inquiry into the unconscious is an important, although difficult area. The route to rational emotional control is not in resisting the unconscious because its reputation was tarnished by "Freudian misuse" or because it goes counter to common sense and cultural assumptions about agency. We need to use common sense to go beyond it. From the beginning, the course of empirical research into the unconscious aspect of emotion has been dictated by definitional assertions and semantics. Neuroscience has very recently played its part in cracking this resistance, first by case studies of patients that clearly indicated the existence and causal importance of unconscious content. Damasio, for one example, took the next critical step by using normal patients in testing his hypothesis concerning the causal priority of unconscious emotion to feeling.

ON THE RELATIONSHIP OF COGNITION AND EMOTION: THE INTERACTION OF COGNITIVE AND EMOTIONAL PROCESSES IN THE BRAIN

The fallacy of dualistic contrasts between emotion and cognition that pit each against the other as inevitable antagonists is a familiar theme. Certainly, the conflict is true at times, but more satisfactory comparisons will depend on describing how they can be inextricably linked while capable of being in tension. Researchers predisposed to one side often fail to retain this difficult balance by making epiphenomena of the other side (Lyng and Franks 2002).

Because definitions are frequently biased by preferences for one side or the other of the dualistic coin, it follows that they cannot be unreflectively taken for granted or as carved in stone. Rather, they need to be handled with awareness that they are our own theoretical products to be evaluated in terms of their consequences for the advancement of knowledge. We will see below that as important as the collection of data is to the research process, definitions will determine how these data are interpreted. As such, definitions are social constructions, basically matters of considered judgment, at times productive and at other times not.

Definitions of Emotion from Cognitive Psychology

It is not surprising, therefore, that when Damasio and LeDoux talked about emotion, they were thinking about something different from the cognitive psychologists and perhaps most sociologists. Neuroscientists might be somewhat more inclined to stress those definitions that highlight the mute character of emotions as expressions from the "theater of the body," whereas cognitively oriented thinkers are more interested in the intertwining of emotions and appraisals from the "theater of the mind." Both emphases are critical in eventually maintaining the balance necessary in avoiding dualistic dead ends. Clore and Ortony (2000), for example, pushed their cognitive preferences to the limit and neuroscientists do the same to retain the separability of emotion and cognition.

To Clore and Ortony (2000), the cognitive component of emotion is the *representation* of the emotional meaning. Their definition of the cognitive extends its reach to include perception, attention, memory, action, and, of course, appraisal, but stops after the representation. They do not include an emotion beyond its cognitive representation. On the other hand, for these authors, the cognitive belief that someone is cheating you and the resulting emotion are not causally arranged in that order. Rather, they are two separate and parallel ways of experiencing the "personal significance of the situation" (i.e., emotion). Both are different levels of appraisals—cognitive and emotional. Here it seems that their boundary is honored.

For those interested in keeping the integrity of emotion per se, like Zajonc (2001), a problem arises in Clore and Ortony's familiar definition of emotions as relational. Emotions are always "about," "over," "at," or "with" their object. In philosophical terms, this relational quality is referred to as *intentionality*.[5]

However, where does this leave affects caused by electrical stimulation that might be considered by some a prime example of pure emotion? Such stimulation, taken as the *initiation* of the emotional process, is patently not appraisal of any kind. We have discussed the temporary full-blown depression followed by the recognizable pattern of depressive cognitions caused by such stimulation. Similarly, a recent case was reported when the left cortex of an epilepsy patient was inadvertently electrically stimulated, causing robust laughter. Each time the doctor applied the current, the patient found something different and normally unfunny to laugh at. Whatever the definitional issues, this artificially stimulated arousal indicates the separable integrity of something we can call "pure emotion" or "affect." This has the advantage of allowing for tension between emotion and cognition that lived experience tells us exists.

Given Clore and Ortony's (2000) contention that emotions always include cognition, the authors handle the problem posed above by including reactions to the electrical stimulation under "affect" rather than full emotion, even though the above descriptions seem quintessentially emotional. Nonetheless, to these authors, affect is only an incomplete, "degenerate" form of fully blown, intentional emotion. If it is critical to retain the tension between emotion and thought while also seeing them as interactionally intertwined, their definition might seem too narrow. None of this causes insurmountable problems as long as we keep a critical perspective on definitions as tools created relative to our purposes.

A Neuroscience Approach to Cognitive and Emotional Interactions

LeDoux (1996) emphasized the separability and primacy of emotion by pointing out cases when subjects "evaluate" objects before identifying them. More important for the primacy of emotion is the fact, mentioned above, that connections from the subcortical emotional systems to the cognitive systems are stronger than connections from the cognitive systems to the emotional ones. LeDoux also stated that emotional feelings involved many more brain systems than thoughts. This is why emotions engulf and commit us so inflexibly while cognitively we can easily argue one position as well as another just for the sake of argument. Attempts at "emotion work," although sociologically important on the collective level, often meet with individual failure.

LeDoux (2000) admitted to more confusion than consensus about the relation between emotion and cognition. He attributed much of this to the fact that neither term refers to real functions performed by the brain but, instead, to collections of disparate brain processes. However, earlier, LeDoux (1996) made clear that emotion and cognition are best thought of as separate but interacting mental functions mediated by separate but interacting brain systems. When certain brain regions are traumatized, animals, including humans, lose the capacity to evaluate the emotional significance of particular stimuli but retain the cognitive ability to perceive and identify them. These processes are separately processed in the brain.

In line with the flexibility of cognition in contrast to emotion, systems involved in cognitive processing are not as closely connected with automatic response systems as those of emotion. Emotional meanings can begin formation before cognitive/perceptual mechanisms have completed their appraisals. Emotional and cognitive memories are registered, stored, and retrieved by different brain processes. Damage to emotional memory processes prevents an object with learned affective meaning (the sight of one's children or lover) from eliciting emotion. Damage to cognitive mechanisms prevents remembrance of where we saw the object, why we were there in the first place, and with we were whom.

Examples of Complex Interactions Between Cortical and Subcortical Regions of the Brain

Having made the argument that cognition and emotion are separate brain processes, LeDoux (2000) turned to listening to the interactions in the brain. Most of the interactions reported in his essay had to do with the amygdala and different cortical regions. However, one such study described a most curious feedback loop between these two.

We have seen that the overriding task of the amygdala is to scan the environment for danger, the quicker the better. We have seen that the thalamus gives it the quickest and most direct input for such assessment, and the slower but more "considered" inputs come from the numerous sensory cortexes. Thus, the amygdala is alert and active before these cortical messages arrive. This gives an opening in time for the alerted amygdala to project its quick and dirty "leanings" back into the early cortical processing. It then receives its own unconsidered biases mixed in with the final sensory cortical messages. Inputs from the thalamus, in contrast, are a one-way street contaminated by no such "regulation" from the amygdala. This leaves a quick, but most unreliable mechanism as both author and receptor of its cortical inputs—a most curious interaction.

According to LeDoux (2000:139) "amygdala regulation of the cortex could involve facilitating processing of stimuli that signal danger even if such stimuli occur outside of the (conscious) attentional field." No wonder that what we perceive most clearly and convincingly is our own fears and that scapegoating so often brings tragedy to innocent persons.

The Somatic Marker Hypothesis

There is a growing body of evidence that somatic states are involved in cognitive processes including learning (Carter and Pasqualini 2004). Damasio's (1994) somatic marker hypothesis, mentioned above, has been a major contribution to this development. Bodily feelings associated with emotional experiences are, figuratively speaking, "marked" and then retrieved when similar situations reoccur. These embodied markers are strongly connected with emotional systems of the brain.

Subjects for Damasio's first study comprised patients who, like the famous Phineas Gage, had damage to the ventromedial part of the prefrontal lobe. This is the area where cognition and the "secondary" emotions important to making social judgments are thought to be integrated.

Most of Damasio's patients scored highly on intelligence tests and even scored well on Kolberg's moral thinking test. They had been competent in their professions and social relationships. Like Phineas Gage, their lives unraveled socially and businesswise after their traumas. Four deficits destroyed their professional lives: they could not make decisions, they could not judge people, they were incorrigible at home, and they could not learn from previous emotional experiences.

More generally, they could not empathize even with themselves; they dispassionately told of their demise to interviewers who were themselves on the verge of tears. While looking at what they recognized readily as terrible pictures of car wreck victims and so forth, their bodies showed none of the skin conductance responses that are used to indicate emotional feelings.

When asked by the hospital staff when they wanted to make their next appointments, they would sit endlessly giving every possibility they could think of equal attention without any way to make a judgment. As de Sousa (1987:191) observes, "no logic sets *saliency*." In this regard the patients were remarkably like Pylyshn's (1987) purely rational robot made by the artificial intelligence workers. His story featured a completely objective robot that gave equal, unbiased attention to all conceivable consequences of its actions and therefore could not make the simplest decisions. This was because without emotional predispositions, it could not narrow down the infinite number of objective possibilities to those worth consideration. It is a matter of irony that the first scientists to discover the necessity of emotion to decision making were artificial intelligence workers.

The somatic marker hypothesis goes further to suggest that Damasio's "prefrontal" patients' major incapacity was an inability to fully embody secondary emotions relevant to complex social situations and thus learn by positive and negative previous experiences. Damasio is not suggesting that emotions are a substitute for reason, nor is he down-playing the fact that emotions can cloud thought. His conclusion is simply that a "selective reduction of emotion is at least as prejudicial for rationality as excessive emotion" (Damasio 2000:13).

Damasio's prefrontals lacked this ability to draw emotional feelings from their bodies and in so doing they lost the capacity for realistic choice making and learning. A game was devised referred to as the "Gambler" to test exactly where this deficit was in functional terms compared to normals. The basic assumption of the game was that if long-term values could not be felt somatically, players would bow to short-term decisions even when they were experienced as deadly in the long run. The game required the subliminal learning that some cards promised large financial rewards but also carried risks down the road that would destroy any chances of winning. The prefrontal patients could not learn to become suspicious or emotionally uneasy about these deceptive choices and invariably lost the game. Normal players intuitively caught on. Damasio concludes that without the help of their somatically marked thoughts, their images of the long run were weak and unstable. This lack of capacity does not have to be from medical trauma. Diagnosed sociopaths with criminal records acted much the same in similar games and Damasio (1994) does not rule out the effect of "sick" cultures on normal adult systems of reasoning.

As mentioned above, Carter and Pasqualini (2004) produced support for the external validity of Damasio's hypothesis when thirty normal women played the card game. Higher skin conductance responses to negative outcomes were strongly accompanied by more successful learning on the Gambler game. The opposite was true for those who lost. The hypothesized relationships were robust enough to show up clearly in a relatively homogeneous group of normal women.

Berridge (2003) cautions that loss of cognitive *integration* with emotion is not the same thing as lacking emotionality in general. Damasio's patients lacked the emotions that produce voluntary social control like guilt, shame, embarrassment, and empathy (Shott 1979). Berridge suggested that emotional *regulation* (emotion work) might be the most impaired in these subjects.[6]

CONCLUSION

A major theme of this chapter has been that emotion drives the brain. It was emotional long before its conscious cognitive powers developed and this character still permeates the brain. Emotion organizes its activity both enabling rational decisions and powerfully influencing cognition. LeDoux's (1996) challenge to cognitive science has advanced markedly in favor of the neurophysiological primacy of emotion, but closure is far away.

For LeDoux, higher brain functions are essential for the generation of conscious emotional feelings, but not for emotion per se. Direct neocortical stimulation does not promote affective states (Öhman 1999; Panksepp 2000). Damage to the cortex only limits *intensities* of emotion. Consensus among researchers does exist on the importance of the cortex in emotional regulation, although even here emotion has the advantage in having more plentiful neural pathways. Panksepp believed that more evidence exists that brain-stem areas, rather than the neocortex, mediate affect, as demonstrated with the electrical stimulation studies on depression and laughter. His is a strong argument for the primacy of emotion in the brain.

Despite the strategic importance of the establishment of pure emotion, the complementary interaction between emotion and cognition greatly predominates in the brain. None of its structures or regions are exclusively devoted to emotion or to cognition, instead, their respective systems most probably overlap. There is clear overlap between behavioral patterns and those representing emotion as well as cognition (Lane et al. 2000). To repeat LeDoux's (1996) conclusions, emotion and cognition are best thought of as separate but interacting mental functions mediated by separate but interacting brain systems. Lane et al. (2000) believed that emotional processes that are uniquely different from cognition have yet to be demonstrated. It is clear that on the neural level, they are the same. Perhaps emotion's simple embodiment—the autonomic, neuroendocrine, and musculoskeletal concomitants of emotional experience—will become what distinguishes it from cognition.

Neuroscience has brought back the unconscious in a very different guise from past renditions. Emotion and the unconscious characterize the brain. Once confused with feeling, emotion is now thought to be an involuntary, unconscious process involving behavioral tendencies that cause conscious feelings that then reverberate on the emotion. Even though fear, for example, can be accessed by consciousness, it operates independently of awareness. According to Öhman (1999), this explains why rational thought has little influence on strong fears.[7]

LeDoux has opted for a detailed analysis of fear as a possible prototype for other basic emotions, but how this can be generalized is not known. According to Brothers (2001), this strategy emphasizes one structure (the amygdala), one behavior (defense), and only one or two emotions (presumably fear and anger). Many researchers are dubious about finding principles of a general domain of emotion, expecting different mechanisms behind different emotions. Nonetheless, LeDoux's strategy was reasonable as a starter.

Although cognition is not free-floating, unconscious emotion like pathological affect can permeate experience like moisture or heat. It scatters and spills over to become attached to any stimulus often totally unrelated to its origins (see Zajonc 2001). There is a very strong convergence between neuroscience literature and those aspects of sociology emphasizing the power of emotionally driven cognition to interpret almost anything as true that supports one's predispositions or what is simply familiar to us.

We have emphasized that no satisfactory common thread is available that draws the myriad cultural emotional differentiations into one definitional basket. This is as recognized in the social sciences as in neuroscience, where many think taxonomies are premature. This problem with emotion as a general term does not apply to emotions like fear and shame that have been relatively thoroughly researched. Nonetheless, one stands on solid empirical ground by recognizing that emotion as a large category is necessary in balancing the still healthy cognitive bias in psychology and sociology. Many would think that this recognition is more important than the lack of closure produced by the definitional problem. It would be foolish to think that the lack of a common thread minimizes the functional importance of particular emotions to the brain and its mentality. Perhaps at this stage we can see emotion *in general* as a very important residual category in the sense that it is so often just what cognition is not. Rather than thinking categorically, it may be wiser to see emotion and cognition on a continuum with a very large middle ground. However that might be, we will learn more by putting aside for the moment the problems of emotions in general and investigating specific emotions with nontraditional empirical techniques tailored to the task. Panksepp (2000) suggested that because our ignorance concerning emotion so grossly outweighs our knowledge, we should minimize the emphasis on competing perspectives and concentrate more on integrative efforts, including biological and social constructionist positions.

Naive formulations of the rational capacities of humankind would benefit from a close look at neuroscience literature. Hopefully, more work will appear on the secondary emotions so intimately involved in social control and interpersonal relations.

NOTES

1. Various highly technical measuring scanners that are the hallmark of neuroscience do not dispel the fact that there is little unifying theory tailored distinctively to neurological processes that help interpret the data generated (Brothers 2001). Nor does magnetic imaging dispel the problems of spurious correlations and determination of cause. In our ever-so-familiar social world, we know that fire engines do not start fires and storks do not bring babies. Brain processes offer another world foreign to us and common sense is of little help in interpreting correlational findings. Thus, the vague term "mediates" frequently substitutes for more explicit causal descriptions.
2. White matter is more predominant in the right brain and the left has more gray. Right-brain white matter is made of neurons that have longer axons and, thus, can connect to several modules simultaneously, resulting in integrative but vague insights. Gray matter is composed of densely woven, shorter, left-brain neurons capable of intense, focused, logical operations.
3. See Carter (1999) for a description of how emotional long-term memories are laid down in the hippocampus and then relinquished to the cortex.
4. See Fellows et al. (2000) for the major complex nuclei of the amygdala and connections to other structures.
5. Psychologically, this stipulation is important. It separates emotion from pain or purely sensory feeling, both of which are self-contained. A bee sting is not "over" or "at" the bee. The stipulation also brings the perception of the object of emotion into the emotional process. This avoids a notion of emotions as self-contained entities in the brain divorced from pragmatic action on the world.
6. For a succinct discussion of brain structures and pathways involved in emotional control in murders, see Carter (1999).
7. Very likely this is why governments throughout the ages control the public through creating false fears.

REFERENCES

Berridge, Kent C. 2003. "Comparing the Emotional Brains of Humans and Other Animals." Pp. 25–51 in *Handbook of Affective Sciences*, edited by R. J. Davidson, K. R. Scherer, and H. H. Goldsmith. New York: Oxford University Press.
Brothers, Leslie. 1997. *Friday's Footprint: How Society Shapes the Human Mind.* New York: Oxford University Press.
———. 2001. *Mistaken Identity.* New York: State University of New York Press.

Cacioppo, John T., Gary G. Berntson, Jeff T. Larsen, Kisrten M. Poehlmann, and Tiffany A. Ito. 2000. "The Psychophysiology of Emotion." Pp. 173–191 in *The Handbook of Emotions*, edited by M. Lewis and J. M. Haviland-Jones. New York: Guilford.

Cannon, William B. 1927. "The James-Lange Theory of Emotions: A Critical Examination and an Alternative Theory." *American Journal of Psychology* 39: 106–124.

Carter, Rita. 1999. *Mapping the Mind*. Berkeley: University of California Press.

Carter, Sid, and Marcia C. Smith Pasqualini. 2004. "Stronger Autonomic Response Accompanies Better Learning: A Test of Damasio's Somatic Marker Hypothesis." *Cognition and Emotion* 18: 901–911.

Clore, Gerald L., and Andrew Ortony. 2000. "Cognition in Emotion: Always, Sometimes, or Never?" Pp. 24–61 in *Cognitive Neuroscience of Emotion*, edited by R. D. Lane and L. Nadel. New York: Oxford University Press.

Crick, Francis H. 1994. *The Astonishing Hypothesis: The Scientific Search for the Soul*. New York: Simon and Schuster.

Damasio, Antonio. 1994. *Descartes' Error: Emotion, Reason, and the Human Brain*. New York: Avon Books.

———. 1999. *The Feeling of What Happens: Body and Emotion in the Making of Consciousness*. New York: Harcourt Brace.

———. 2000. "A Second Chance for Emotion." Pp. 12–23 in *Cognitive Neuroscience of Emotion*, edited by R. D. Lane and L. Nadel. New York: Oxford University Press.

———. 2003. *Looking for Spinoza: Joy, Sorrow and the Feeling Brain*. New York: Harcourt Brace.

Davidson, Richard J. 1992. "Anterior Cerebral Asymmetry and the Nature of Emotions." *Brain and Cognition* 6: 245–268.

de Sousa, Ronald. 1987. *The Rationality of Emotion*. Cambridge, MA: MIT Press.

Fellows, Jean-Marc, Jorge L. Armony, and Joseph E. LeDoux. 2000. "Emotional Circuits." Pp. 398–401 in *The Handbook on Emotions*, edited by M. Lewis and J. M. Haviland-Jones. New York: Guilford.

Franks, David D. 2003. "Mutual Interests, Different Lenses: Current Neuroscience and Symbolic Interaction." *Symbolic Interaction* 26: 613–630.

Franks David D., and Thomas S. Smith. 1999. "Some Convergances and Divergenses between Neuroscience and Symbolic Interaction." Pp. 157–182 in *Mind, Brain and Society: Toward a Neurosociology of Emotion. Social Perspectives on Emotion*, edited by D. D. Franks and T. S. Smith. Stamford, CT: JAI Press.

Gazzaniga, Michael S. 1985. *The Social Brain*. New York: Basic Books.

———. 1998a. *The Mind's Past*. Berkeley: University of California Press.

———. 1998b. "The Split Brain Revisited." *Scientific American* (July) 279(1): 51–54.

Griffiths, Paul E. 1997. *What Emotions Really Are: The Problem of Psychological Categories*. Chicago: University of Chicago Press.

Heilman, Kenneth M. 2000. "Emotional Experience: A Neurological Model." Pp. 328–344 in *Cognitive Neuroscience of Emotion*, edited by R. D. Lane and L. Nadel. New York: Oxford University Press.

Jacoby, Larry I., Andrew P. Yonellinas, and Janine M. Jennings. 1997. "The Relation between Consciousness and Unconscious (Automatic) Influences: A Declaration of Independence." Pp. 13–48 in *Scientific Approaches to Consciousness*, edited by J. D. Cohen and J. W. Schooner. Hillsdale, NJ: Erlbaum.

James, William. 1884. "What is an Emotion?" *Mind* 9: 188–205.

Katz, Jack. 1999. *How Emotions Work*. Chicago: University of Chicago Press.

Kandel, Eric R., James H. Schwartz, and Thomas M. Jessell. 2000. *Principles of Neural Science*. New York: McGraw-Hill.

Kihlstrom, John F., Shelagh Mulvancy, Betsy A. Tobias, and Irene P. Tobias. 2000. "The Emotional Unconscious." Pp. 30–86 in *Cognition and Emotion*, edited by E. Eich. New York: Oxford University Press.

Lakoff, George, and Mark Johnson. 1999. *Philosophy in the Flesh: The Embodied Mind and Its Challenge to Western Thought*. New York: Basic Books.

Lane, Richard D., Lynn Nadel, and Alfred W. Kaszniak. 2000. "The Future of Emotion Research from the Perspective of Cognitive Neuroscience." Pp. 407–410 in *Cognitive Neuroscience of Emotion*, edited by R. D. Lane and L. Nadel. New York: Oxford University Press.

LeDoux, Joseph. 1996. *The Emotional Brain: The Mysterious Underpinnings of Emotional Life*. New York: Simon and Schuster.

———. 2000. "Cognitive-Emotional Interactions: Listen to the Brain." Pp. 129–155 in *Cognitive Neuroscience of Emotion*, edited by R. D. Lane and L. Nadel. New York: Oxford University Press.

———. 2002. *Synaptic Self: How Our Brains Become Who We Are*. New York: Penguin Group.

LeDoux, Joseph, Jacek Debiec, and Henry H. Moss. 2003. *The Self: From Soul to Brain*. New York: New York Academy of Sciences.

LeDoux, Joseph, and Elizabeth A. Phelps. 2000. "Emotional Networks in the Brain." Pp. 157–171 in *The Handbook of Emotions*, edited by M. Lewis and J. M. Haviland-Jones. New York: Guilford.

Libet, Benjamin. 1996. "Neural Time Factors in Conscious and Unconscious Mental Functions." Pp. 337–347 in *Toward a Science of Consciousness. First Discussions and Debates*, edited by S. R. Hameroff, A. W. Kaszniak, and A. Scott. Cambridge, MA: MIT Press.

Lyng, Stephen, and David D. Franks. 2002. *Sociology and the Real World*. New York: Rowman and Littlefield.

MacLean, Paul D. 1949. "Psychosomatic Disease and the 'Visceral Brain:' Recent Developments Bearing on the Papez Theory of Emotion." *Psychosomatic Medicine* 11: 338–353.

Massey, Douglas S. 2002. "A Brief History of Human Society: The Origin and Role of Emotion in Social Life." *American Sociological Review* 67: 1–29.

Murphy, Nancy. 2003. "What Ever Happened to the Soul? Theological Perspectives on the Self." Pp. 61–64 in *The Self from Soul to Brain*, edited by J. LeDoux, J. Debiec, and H. Moss. New York: New York Academy of Sciences.

Öhman, Arne. 1999. "Distinguishing Unconscious from Conscious Emotional Processes: Methodological Considerations and Theoretical Implications." Pp. 321–349 in *Handbook of Cognition and Emotion*, edited by T. Dalgleish and M. Power. New York: John Wiley and Sons.

Panksepp, Jaak. 2000. "Emotions as Natural Kinds within the Mammalian Brain." Pp. 137–156 in *The Handbook of Emotions*, edited by M. Lewis and J. M. Haviland-Jones. New York: Guilford.

Ramachachandrum, V. S., and Sandra Blakeslee. 1998. *Phantoms in the Brain: Probing the Mysteries of the Human Mind*. New York: William Morrow.

Reddy, William M. 2001. *The Navigation of Feeling: A Framework for the History of Emotions*. New York: Cambridge University Press.

Rolls, Edmund T. 1999. *The Brain and Emotion*. New York: Oxford University Press.

Scheff, Thomas J. 1990. *Microsociology: Discourse, Emotion, and Social Structure*. Chicago: University of Chicago Press.

———. 1995. "Review of Social Perspectives on Emotion, Vol. 2." *Contemporary Sociology* 24: 400–403.

Scott, Marvin, and Stanford Lyman. 1968. "Accounts." *American Sociological Review* 33: 46–64.

Shott, Susan. 1979. "Emotion and Social Life: A Symbolic Interaction Analysis." *American Journal of Sociology* 84: 1317–1334.

Sperry, Roger. 1965. "Mind, Brain and Humanistic Values." Pp. 588–590 in *New Values on the Nature of Man,* edited by J. R. Platt. Chicago: University of Chicago Press.

TenHouten, Warren D. 1999. "Explorations in Neurosociological Theory: From the Spectrum of Affect to Time Consciousness." Pp. 41–80 in *Mind, Brain and Society: Toward a Neurosociology of Emotions. Social Perspectives on Emotion*, edited by D. D. Franks and T. S. Smith. Stamford, CT: JAI Press.

Tredway, James V., Stan J. Napp, Lucile C. Tredway, and Darwin L. Thomas. 1999. "The Neurosociological Role of Emotions in Early Socialization, Reasons, Ethics and Morality." Pp. 109–156 in *Mind, Brain and Society: Toward a Neurosociology of Emotions. Social Perspectives on Emotions*, edited by D. D. Franks and T. S. Smith. Stamford, CT: JAI Press.

Turner, Jonathan H. 1999. "The Neurology of Emotion: Implications for Sociological Theories of Interpersonal Behavior." Pp. 81–108 in *Mind, Brain and Society: Toward a Neurosociology of Emotion. Social Perspectives on Emotion*, edited by D. D. Franks and T. S. Smith. Stamford, CT: JAI Press.

———. 2000. *On the Origins of Human Emotions: A Sociological Inquiry into the Evolution of Human Affect*. Stanford, CA: Stanford University Press.

Turner, Jonathan H., and Jan E. Stets. 2005. *The Sociology of Emotions*. New York: Cambridge University Press.

Wentworth, William, and John Ryan. 1992. "Balancing Body, Mind and Culture: The Place of Emotion in Social Life." Pp. 25–46 in *Social Perspectives on Emotion*, edited by D. D. Franks and V. Gecas. Greenwich, CT: JAI Press.

Wentworth, William, John Ryan, and D. Yardley. 1994. "Deep Sociality: A Bioevolutionary Perspective on the Sociology of Human Emotions." Pp. 21–55 in *Social Perspectives on Emotion*, edited by D. D. Franks, W. M. Wentworth, and J. Ryan. Greenwich, CT: JAI Press.

Zajonc, R. B. 2001. "Closing the Debate over the Independence of Affect." Pp. 31–58 in *Feeling and Thinking: The Role of Affect in Social Cognition*, edited by J. P. Forgas. New York: Cambridge University Press.

CHAPTER 3

Gender and Emotion

Stephanie A. Shields
Dallas N. Garner
Brooke Di Leone
Alena M. Hadley

In this chapter we consider the relation between gender and emotion, particularly as that connection is expressed in stereotyping, power relations, and sexuality. As we review pertinent research we strive to move beyond the conventional "gender differences" model that has tended to dominate the study of gender and emotion. We propose two useful theoretical frameworks for investigating the gender-emotion link. The first, *expectation states theory* (Berger et al. 1977; Ridgeway and Correll 2004), is useful in explaining the relation of gender-emotion beliefs to social roles and other social structural variables. The second, *doing emotion as doing gender* (Shields 1995, 2002), can be used to explain connections among beliefs about emotion, emotional experience, and a gendered sense of self.

We begin with the assumption that, whereas status-marked aspects of the self such as ethnicity, age, and economic status mutually constitute social identity (e.g., Baca Zinn and Dill 1996; Nakano Glenn 1999), gender has a distinctive relation to emotion within and across social groups. First, a number of beliefs about gender difference are grounded in beliefs about the emotional nature of each sex, particularly the way in which emotionality marks female/feminine as different from male/masculine. This strong association between emotionality and female/feminine is a common theme throughout Western history. Since the mid-nineteenth century the form it has taken emphasizes the comparatively ineffectual nature of women's emotion (Shields 2002). Second, the link between gender and emotion is apparent in the development of a gendered sense of self

Stephanie A. Shields, Dallas N. Garner, Brooke Di Leone, and Alena M. Hadley • Department of Psychology, Pennsylvania State University, University Park, PA 16802

(Shields 1995). Adolescence, for example, marks a period in which issues of emotion and gender converge in identity development (e.g., Polce-Lynch et al. 1998). Psychological measures that attempt to quantify femininity and masculinity as psychological attributes also illustrate how beliefs about emotion are reflected in definitions of gender (Shields 2002). For example, self-report inventories such as the Bem Sex-Role Inventory are heavily loaded with emotion-relevant items. Similarly, emotion beliefs, whether explicitly expressed in emotion stereotypes or more subtly transmitted, as in parent advice books (Anderson and Accomando 2002; Anderson et al. 2002; Shields and Koster 1989; Shields et al. 1995), define core qualities of "masculine" and "feminine."

In this overview, we focus on three areas in which the convergence of gender and emotion, especially the association between emotionality and female/feminine, serves as a medium for maintaining, reproducing, and sometimes subverting social structural inequities.

Beliefs About Gender and Emotion

Gender-emotion stereotypes are important because they pertain to ideas of appropriateness and legitimacy: Who is entitled to what emotion? Emotion stereotypes and their connotations of value and appropriateness are likely to depend on other aspects of social identity as well as gender, but the gender-emotion connection can be described as a kind of emotion "master stereotype" (i.e., she is emotional; he is not), which appears to reflect a notion of white, heterosexual gender differences (Fischer 1993; Shields 2002; Warner and Shields 2005). In addition to influencing people's evaluations of others, gender-emotion stereotypes can influence people's reports about their own experience, functioning as a heuristic guiding self-report (Robinson et al. 1998).

Power and Status

Power is a central theme in analyses of gender, particularly in those analyses concerned with the apparent capacity of gender inequities to be self-maintaining even when challenged. Power and status concerns are likewise central to understanding the micropolitics of emotion in every-day life—that is, judgments about and negotiations of emotion's legitimacy, authenticity, and appropriateness (Shields 2005).

Sexuality

Sexuality and scripts for intimacy, including sexual expression and romantic relationships, high-light connections between gender and emotion. The topic of intimate relationships is arguably one in which beliefs about gender differences in emotional needs and expressive behavior are articulated most strongly in everyday discourse. We cover each of these three themes in separate sections. Before turning to these topics, however, we provide a framework for our approach to understanding gender as it relates to emotion. Specifically, we replace the conventional enumeration of gender differences and similarities with an examination of the factors that exaggerate or attenuate these differences. By doing so, we move from the descriptive—Are there differences?—to the explanatory—What drives the extent to which differences are manifested?

A FRAMEWORK FOR STUDYING GENDER AND EMOTION

Much of social psychological research on everyday emotion, whether that research is concerned with specific emotions such as anger or global concepts such as emotionality, has framed the question simply as "Do women and men (or girls and boys) differ with respect to emotion?" as, for example, in reported experience of specific emotions. The too-common question of whether women "really are" more emotional than men exemplifies the differences approach. This focus on enumerating differences across individual studies tends to yield inconclusive results that fail to illuminate what causes, moderates, or maintains differences. A number of researchers have outlined the deficiencies of the differences approach (e.g., Bacchi 1990; Deaux and LaFrance 1998; Hare-Mustin and Marecek 1994); therefore, here we describe one alternative: investigating the contexts in which gender effects are evident. This approach requires a shift *from* describing differences, toward examining both what drives those differences and the social relationships that give differences meaning.

The growing empirical research on gender and emotion reveals a pattern showing that gender's greatest effect lies not in gender differences in knowledge about emotion, but in the way that knowledge is deployed. Gender differences in emotion-related beliefs and behavior are modality-specific and context dependent (Brody 1999; LaFrance and Banaji 1992; Shields 1991, 1995); that is, the extent to which differences are evident depends on what about emotion is measured and how the research context is framed. In the case of self-reports about emotion experience, for instance, gender effects more closely resemble stereotypes when reports are taken retrospectively than when reports are made online (Robinson et al. 1998).

As an alternative to the differences approach, we employ two theoretical perspectives as an explanatory framework. First, *expectation states theory*, as applied to gender, is useful in describing the processes through which groups reproduce existing disparities in status and power. This theory explains how macrolevel aspects of social context affect gender-emotion linkages. Second, *doing emotion as doing gender* captures the intimate connection between beliefs/stereotypes about gender and emotion and their psychological meaningfulness for the individual, the dyad, and the group. In tandem, these perspectives offer a way to explain the individual's participation in gender-relevant interpersonal interactions and how those interactions are "nested" in and sustain gender systems.

Expectation States Theory

Expectation states theory aims to explain how status beliefs operate to sustain social hierarchies. Specifically, expectation states theory begins with the premise that status beliefs, like stereotypes or norms, are widely shared cultural beliefs that express the status relationship between one social group and another within a given society (Ridgeway and Bourg 2004). Regardless of whether individuals are members of the advantaged or disadvantaged group, they endorse the reality of the status belief, if not its legitimacy.

Status beliefs, as construed by expectation states theory, are similar to stereotypes but not identical to them. Stereotypes are broader in that they can include descriptive characteristics that do not indicate status, such as certain appearance and behavior descriptors. Stereotypes of different groups vary, but all contain core status content that expresses the comparative value or standing of the group with respect to another group or groups. Expectation states theory asserts that specific skills associated with the status beliefs regarding one group compared to another reflect the history and social structural relationship of the groups; thus, they are both relatively stable, yet able to change over time.

Ridgeway and Bourg (2004) noted that consensual status beliefs (i.e., status beliefs shared within *and* across groups) are more likely to develop among groups whose members must regularly cooperate, such as employees of an organization. Consensual status beliefs, which maintain the illusion that the groups are simply different from one another, imply, rather than make explicit, status difference. In contrast, competitive in-group/out-group beliefs explicitly favor one group over the other, thereby creating the conditions for group conflict or self-segregation. Thus, minority/majority racial or ethnic groups would be susceptible to evolving a separatist or conflictual coexistence based on competitive in-group/out-group beliefs. Women and men within each of those groups, however, would be more likely to share status beliefs and so evolve a naturalized "separate-but-equal" set of beliefs about gender difference.

According to expectation states theory, shared status beliefs (in contrast to in-group/out-group beliefs) facilitate intergroup interactions, thereby creating conditions for reproducing status hierarchies. Shared status beliefs set up expectations regarding behavior within one's own group and between one's group and those higher and lower in the status hierarchy. Thus, status beliefs can foster the reproduction of the groups' hierarchical organization in that people look for cues to define the situation, guide their own behavior, and anticipate and interpret how others behave. In this way, heterogeneous groups composed of individuals who differ in status soon sort themselves in such a way as to reproduce the hierarchies reflected in status beliefs.

Ridgeway and her colleagues (Correll and Ridgeway 2003; Ridgeway 2001; Ridgeway and Bourg 2004; Ridgeway and Correll 2004) maintained that gender is particularly well suited for examination in terms of expectation states theory because of several characteristics that foster reliance on status beliefs. Women and men make up roughly equal parts of the population and interact frequently, often in situations that require cooperation and interdependence, as in work, family, and intimate heterosexual relationships. Gender thereby functions as a "background identity"— that is, an "implicit, cultural/cognitive presence that colors people's activities in varying degrees" (Ridgeway and Correll 2004:516) even when it is not the focus of the situation and quite powerfully when it is. Thus, gender beliefs are always available to bias interpersonal interactions and can do so even without the interaction participants' awareness of their operation.

Beliefs about emotion occupy a central place in gender stereotypes of the "generic" woman and man. In the stereotype of women, emotion is rendered both as good (e.g., warm; nurturing) and as bad (e.g., "too emotional"). Thus, gender as a background identity carries with it consensual status beliefs regarding emotion. Those beliefs are readily recruited to the foreground when emotion itself is an issue or emotional needs are a prominent concern. In mixed-sex dyads and groups, the qualities of emotion expertise and emotion-as-weakness lend themselves to reproducing gender hierarchies.

Doing Emotion/Doing Gender

West and Zimmerman's (1987) landmark paper proposed that gender can be understood by examining the work of being a gendered person. (See also Fenstermaker and West 2002; West and Fenstermaker 1995.) In other words, gender is not something one *has*, but it is something that one *does*. Even with unambiguous core gender identity, the markers of maleness/masculinity and femaleness/femininity that assure one (and others) of that identity are always being contested, disputed, and negotiated. In a sense, one is always practicing gender and comes to own the role in much the same way that an actor seems "naturally" the character that she or he plays. Unlike the actor, however, people move in and out of situations that might make gender "performance" more salient or that require them to improvise ways to meet the challenges of the situation while continuing to believe in the consistency and truth of their own gendered character. Much of the time, the practice of gender is unself-conscious. At other times, one is acutely aware of the demands of sustaining a coherent and believable gender self-presentation (to oneself and to others), as when reminded that big boys don't cry or that good girls are nice. It is important to point out that the interpretation of doing emotion as doing gender that we use here does not imply gender performance concerned primarily with appearances (Moloney and Fenstermaker 2002), but gender as deeply acted.

If gender is not an achieved state but something that is actively created through ongoing practice, it has a certain flexibility that enables adjustment of gender performance to meet the variation in demands across relationships and social contexts. At the same time, gender is never a finished product. One remains vulnerable as a gender performer as questions of whether one is a "real man" or "womanly enough" lurk at the borders of the secure sense of self.

Shared beliefs about emotion assist in defining and maintaining beliefs about gender and gender-as-difference (Shields 2002). Emotion is associated with doing gender in two pivotal ways. First, beliefs about emotion reveal the distinctive "how" of being a gendered person: Doing emotion (expressing emotional feelings and emotion values) signals one's genuineness as female or male, feminine or masculine. One might also self-consciously manipulate that gendered enactment (Worcel et al. under review). For example, because emotionally expressive behavior is gender-coded, an important component of a child's gender practice (i.e., enacting a gendered identity) involves practicing emotion—its expression, values, interests—as it befits gender. Doing gender through doing emotion encompasses not only emotional display but also emotion values (e.g., real girls value emotional self-disclosure) and beliefs about emotional experience (e.g., anger is appropriate only when one's rights are violated).

A second way in which emotion is implicated in doing gender is through the expression of how one thinks about oneself as a person. Deaux (1993) proposed that the individual's formulation and reformulation of identity is fashioned as a response to the events and circumstances of one's life. As a dimension of gender, emotion beliefs and values and their instantiation in emotion episodes provide a thread of continuity through formation and change in the individual's social identities.

In defining cultural representations of masculinity/femininity, emotion beliefs constitute a medium for practicing gender-coded emotional values and behavior in childhood and adulthood. Children have ample opportunity to learn and practice gender-coded emotion. The peer group is an especially potent medium for rehearsal of practicing and coming to understand emotion (e.g., Sheldon 1992; von Salisch 1997). For example, the emotional sharing that especially characterizes girls' friendships (Maccoby 1990) is part of learning how to "do girl" at a certain moment in development. This early experience with emotional sharing defines the parameters for when and how to engage in some kinds of emotional self-regulation. In the larger scheme of things, emotion beliefs are recruited to create and refine the definition of mature, appropriate behavior, both prescriptively (e.g., a "real man" responds appropriately with anger when he is deprived of what he is entitled to) and proscriptively (e.g., a "real man" does not cry).

In summary, emotion beliefs give one a position from which to assess one's own emotional life and, thereby, one's authenticity as a person. Gender performance verifies the authenticity of the self, and emotion performance is measured in terms of its authenticity. Therefore, successfully doing gender validates emotion at the same time as successfully doing emotion validates gender.

Investigation of beliefs about gendered emotion can reveal what gender means, how gender operates, and how gender is negotiated in relationships with others.

BELIEFS ABOUT THE GENDER-EMOTION CONNECTION

A stereotype is a "generalization about the shared attributes of a group of people" (Judd and Park 1993). Stereotypes can have a profound impact on how we treat others (Agars 2004) and how we make judgments about others (Cameron and Trope 2004). Beliefs about emotion are included in a number of stereotypes, including age (Fabes and Martin 1991), race (Popp et al. 2003), and weight (Klaczynski et al. 2004). Perhaps the most persistent and pervasive emotion stereotypes concern gender, especially those that involve beliefs about men's and women's expression of emotion (e.g., Gray and Heatherington 2003; Heesacker et al. 1999). In addition, the majority of research on gender and emotion shows that gender-emotion stereotypes are equally endorsed by both female and male participants (e.g., Knox et al. 2004; Robinson and Johnson 1997).

Studies on gender-emotion stereotypes rarely use targets that have an explicit racial identity. When researchers do not clearly define a target's race, participants might infer racial information about targets. Specifically, when participants are asked to evaluate targets described as the "average man" or "average woman," they likely assume that the target is a member of the dominant group, which, in the United States, leads participants to imagine a white target (Schneider 2004). The results of at least one study suggest that the race of a target can enhance or attenuate the effect of target gender in ratings of emotion expression. Shields and Crowley (2000) found a greater difference between beliefs about men's and women's behavior for white targets than for targets of other races. If college-age participants infer that a generic target belongs to the dominant group, most studies examining gender-emotion stereotypes are measuring responses to targets that are presumptively white, young, and heterosexual. The extent to which other facets of target identity, such as age and sexual orientation, affect participant evaluations of gendered emotion has yet to be investigated.

In this section we discuss research on the predominant gender-emotion stereotypes. We focus on how these stereotypes fall short of fully describing how women and men enact emotion by failing to include moderating factors, such as contextual demands. In addition, we examine the ways in which beliefs about gender and emotion can be self-perpetuating, as in the stereotype of female emotionality as well as through self-reports of past emotion experience. Finally, we discuss the connection between displays of emotion and displays of power.

The Contextual Nature of Gender-Emotion Stereotypes

Gender-emotion stereotypes are context dependent. For example, Kelly and Hutson-Comeaux (1999) studied the evaluations of extreme overreaction and underreaction described in vignettes concerning interpersonal (e.g., in a friendship) and achievement-related (e.g., at work) situations. They found that participants' beliefs about characteristic emotion behavior differed as a function of the interaction of target gender and context. Participants rated overreactions to happy and sad events in the interpersonal context as more characteristic of women, but judged overreactions to happy and sad events in the achievement context as more characteristic of men.

Studies that have examined more "average" displays of emotion also find evidence that context significantly affects ratings of emotionality (e.g., Robinson and Johnson 1997; Warner and Shields 2006). Johnson and Schulman (1988), for example, found that participants expected women to express more positive emotions (e.g., happiness) than men in an other-oriented situation (e.g., in personal relationships) while expecting men to express more positive emotions than women in a self-oriented situation (e.g., in achieving personal goals).

The findings discussed above are especially helpful in demonstrating the contradiction of the gender-emotion stereotype of female emotionality. This stereotype describes women in general as more emotional than men (e.g., Johnson and Schulman 1988; Petrides, et al. 2004; Timmers et al. 2003). Robinson and Johnson (1997), for example, found that participants described female targets as more "emotional" than male targets and male targets as more "stressed" than female targets. Given that participants believe men express anger more often than women (Timmers et al. 2003), believe men express powerful emotions more often than women (Fabes and Martin 1991), and believe men express positive emotions more often than women in certain contexts (Johnson and Schulman 1988), it seems contradictory that participants would also describe women as "more emotional" than men. Essentially, participants are labeling female, but not male, emotion expression as "emotional."

Ambiguity and Self-Report

Individuals are most likely to rely on stereotypes to guide judgments in hypothetical or ambiguous situations (e.g., Augoustinos and Walker 1995; Collings 2002). When individuals are asked to make judgments based on ambiguous information, such as facial expressions of mixed emotions, their judgments conform to gender-emotion stereotypes. Plant et al. (2000) found that participants rated ambiguous (a combination of angry and sad) faces in stereotypical ways, rating the male target as more expressive of anger and the female target as more expressive of sadness. However, when faces were unambiguous (more clearly either angry or sad), ratings were less likely to follow stereotypical patterns.

This phenomenon holds true for self-reports of one's own emotion experience as well. If asked about experiences after the fact, for example, participants' self-reports tend to follow the stereotypical pattern more than online reports of emotion experience do (e.g., Hess et al. 2000; LaFrance and Banaji 1992; Shields 1991). For example, Robinson et al. (1998) asked participants to make judgments about their own emotions immediately after playing a game, 1 week after playing a game, or while imagining themselves playing a game. All participants reported experiencing or expecting to experience emotions that were consistent with gender-emotion stereotypes (e.g., pride and anger for men; friendliness and guilt for women) except for those who made self-reports immediately after playing the game. Robinson et al. concluded that making judgments after a delay or without the benefit of actual experience to draw from reduces the accessibility of direct emotion experience information, leading to increased reliance on gender-emotion stereotypes as the basis for self-report.

In most research, ambiguous situations lead participants to rely on heuristics when making judgments about *others*. In studies on past emotion experience, participants also use heuristics to guide *self*-reports. Studies that ask men and women to describe past emotion experiences often conclude that men and women differ in their subjective experience of emotion. Studies using online reports of emotion experience, however, show diminished gender differences. Gender differences in self-report about emotion experience should, therefore, be understood as reflecting, to some degree, stereotypical beliefs about gender and emotion.

Emotions and Displays of Power

Both women and men report believing that women express sadness and fear more often than men and that men express anger and pride more often than women (e.g., Brody 1997; Fabes and Martin 1991). Reasoning that there is a connection between masculinity and the expression of power, Fischer (1993) proposed that gender-emotion stereotypes are founded on the belief that men express power*ful* emotion, whereas while women express power*less* emotions. Powerless emotions are those that imply vulnerability and are associated with positions of low power, whereas powerful emotions imply dominance and are associated with positions of high power (Brody 1997; Fischer 1993).

The association of specific emotions with displays of power or powerlessness, however, does not fully describe how women and men act or how their emotional displays are evaluated. As discussed above, women and men are sometimes expected to display specific emotions that would contradict this stereotype (e.g., expecting men to express sadness in achievement-related contexts). In addition, the expression of powerless emotions can be used as a powerful display, as in expressing controlled intense emotion (Shields 2002, 2005). Likewise, displays of powerful emotions can be seen as an expression of powerlessness when the emotion is perceived to be out of control. Rather than the type of emotion itself being an expression of power or powerlessness, it appears that the displays of emotion thought typical of each gender reflect beliefs about when, how, and by whom emotion can be an expression of power.

Controlled expressivity or "manly emotion," a term coined by Shields (2002), is a style of emotion expression that subtly conveys emotion while also displaying control over one's own emotion. Although both women and men are held to this standard of expression in certain circumstances, it is associated more with men's emotion expression and men might be more positively evaluated than women for adhering to it. A prime example of this expression style is seen in a specific type of crying, in which the individual merely tears up or has a moistened eye. This clear, controlled expression of emotion is viewed quite positively. Warner and Shields (2006) found that men who were described as tearing up in response to sad events were rated more positively than men and women who were described as crying and women who were described as tearing up. The moist eye enables one to display a "weak" emotion while also demonstrating emotional control.

Shields (2002, 2005) has identified a second expressive standard, termed *extravagant expressiveness*, which is an open style of experiencing and communicating emotion. Shields hypothesize that extravagant expressiveness is the form of emotion linked to expressions of intimacy in the United States and that it is the form of emotion expression expected in caregiving and close relationships. Although extravagant expressiveness is considered good nurturing behavior, it also implies a giving of the self to the other at the expense of power and control.

Problems and Suggestions

Regardless of whether others actually react negatively to counterstereotypical emotion displays, the anticipation of negative reactions can have an effect on the actor. Individuals might anticipate potential reactions to their displays of emotion and feel compelled to enact stereotypical emotion. For example, women report feeling pressured to restrict their competitiveness and to express positive emotions, such as happiness, toward others (Graham et al. 1981; Stoppard and Gunn Gruchy 1993). Men also fear that if they express certain emotions, such as fear or sadness, negative consequences might follow, including rejection and being called "unmanly" (Brody

1999; Timmers et al. 1998). Individuals might be aware of these potentially negative responses to gender nonconformity and so act in stereotypical ways to avoid those negative responses. Ironically, this strategy serves to perpetuate gender-emotion stereotypes.

As noted above, women and men rarely, if ever, differ in the degree to which stereotypes are evident in their ratings of targets. Thus, it appears that gender-emotion stereotypes function as consensual status beliefs to which both the higher- and lower-status groups subscribe. It is important for future research to further examine how these stereotypes operate as consensual status beliefs, especially in their impact on (1) labeling women's emotion expression—and not men's—as "emotional," (2) women feeling obligated to express emotions in a way that conveys vulnerability, and (3) believing that women's emotion displays are also displays of powerlessness. In the section that follows, we examine how power and status, as social cues apparent in most interactions, affect beliefs about gender and emotion.

POWER AND STATUS

Gender and emotion researchers have used the power/status lens to examine gender differences in smiling (Deutsch 1990; Dovidio et al. 1998; Hall and Friedman 1999; Hall et al. 2000; Hecht and LaFrance 1998), joking and teasing (Keltner et al. 1998, 2001; Robinson and Smith-Lovin 2001), experience and expression of anger (Kring 2000), and expectations for felt and displayed emotion (Conway et al. 1999; Kemper 1991; Tiedens et al. 2000). Power, status, and gender are all types of social information that individuals and groups use to socially rank themselves and others; their combined effects on emotion outcomes, however, are complex.

Within the field of social psychology, the terms *power* and *status* often are used interchangeably (Deaux 2000). Status, however, does not necessarily confer power, nor does power determine an individual's status. We define power as the ability and competence to control rewards and punishments, dominate resources, and influence others (Anderson and Thompson 2004; French and Raven 1959; Keltner et al. 2003) and define status as a social position accorded by others, dependent on perceptions of respect and prominence (Anderson and Berdahl 2002; Kemper 1990). In what follows, we separate the terms *power* and *status* where possible and only combine them when referring to both dimensions or in describing research that conflates the two terms.

In this section we review empirical research on the links among power, status, and gender, and the ways in which these links are evident in felt and displayed emotion. We focus on the processes of predicting emotion from power and status information and predicting power and status from emotion. In addition, we address anger as it relates to power, status, and gender. Finally, we highlight issues or problems with the existing empirical work on power, status, gender, and emotion and pose future directions for gender and emotion research using a power/status lens.

The Connection Among Power, Status, Gender, and Emotion

Power, status, and gender produce expectations for individual performance, including emotion performance, especially in the workforce and other contexts in which individuals must work as a group to achieve a specific goal. There is evidence that men and women display different types and amounts of expressive behavior; for example, women smile more often than men (Hall et al. 2000) and engage in more eye-gazing than men (Dovidio et al. 1998). One idea that has been widely debated is that power or status can explain gender differences in emotion-related nonverbal behavior.

Henley (1973) hypothesized that gender differences in nonverbal behavior could be attributed to status, a theoretical prediction sometimes referred to as the subordination hypothesis (LaFrance and Henley 1997). Henley argued that gender differences paralleled those of power/status—that women and men differed in ways that mirrored low and high power/status differences. According to the subordination hypothesis, women are more accurate than men in understanding others' nonverbal behavior because women's comparatively lower power and status, compared to men, necessitate greater vigilance regarding nonverbal cues. Fiske (1993) added that low-power people pay attention to those of higher power in an effort to more accurately predict high-power people's thoughts, feelings, and actions and, ultimately, to increase their own power.

Contrary to what the subordination hypothesis would predict, researchers have not found parallel effects of gender and power/status. Hecht and LaFrance (1998) examined smiling frequency in same-sex dyads. Within the unequal-power conditions, reward power was manipulated through randomly assigning participants to act as either an interviewer (higher power) or an applicant (lower power) for a clinical psychology research position. Within equal-power conditions, participants engaged in a conversation about their career plans, business skills, and work-related experiences. Hecht and LaFrance found no gender differences when power was unambiguous; however, when power was ambiguous (i.e., within dyads of equal power), gender differences in smiling emerged. Although women smiled more often than men overall, low-power individuals did not smile more often than high-power individuals, as the subordination hypothesis would have predicted. These effects held for both social smiles (smiles of "being pleasant") and smiles indicative of felt emotion. Hecht and LaFrance concluded that social power affects the propensity to smile—that high-power people are free to display positive emotion when they experience it, but low-power people might feel obligated to smile even in the absence of positive affect.

Hall and Friedman (1999) found similar results when they asked observers to rate actual employees' nonverbal behaviors in dyadic, videotaped interactions with randomly chosen co-workers. Hall and Friedman found that differences in status did not explain gender differences in nonverbal behavior. Across status conditions, gender differences remained constant; however, when they controlled for status, gender differences grew stronger. Hall and Friedman concluded that predicting nonverbal behavior from status might be unwise without considering other moderating variables (such as age, culture, values, and motives) that could have directed the employees in their study to behave differently. LaFrance and her colleagues' (2003) meta-analysis of gender and smiling found that for both social smiles and genuine smiles, women smile more often than men, but that the magnitude of this effect depended on participant characteristics (e.g., age, nationality, and ethnicity), norms for gender expressivity (e.g., culturally specific display rules), and situational demands (e.g., caretaker, flight attendant, or funeral director roles). LaFrance et al. (2003) concluded that in situations of unequal power/status, gender differences are small, but in more ambiguous situations of equal power/status, status beliefs appear to provide a gender-based guide for smiling and possibly other expressive behavior.

Power/Status as Predictors of Emotion

Apart from research on smiling, the effects of power and status on emotion have been investigated to the exclusion of gender. Empirical evidence shows that power and status influence expectations for the amount and kind of emotion felt and displayed by all individuals involved in a social interaction. In positive situations involving the achievement of a goal, high-status people are expected to be proud and low-status people to be appreciative (Tiedens et al. 2000). Negative situations involving failure are expected to elicit anger among high-status men and women (Conway et al. 1999; Tiedens et al. 2000) but sadness and guilt among low-status men and women. More specifically, low-status people are perceived as *feeling* more anger, disgust, sadness, and fear but *displaying* less anger and disgust and more sadness and fear than high-status people (Conway et al. 1999). One explanation for these results can be found in the subordination hypothesis. Specifically, low-status individuals should feel pressured to inhibit their negative and threatening feelings of anger and disgust, whereas less threatening emotions of sadness and fear can be felt and displayed without risk of disrupting the social order.

Expectations concerning emotion outcomes of social interactions can be used to make predictions from limited power and status information. If high power and status increase the possibility of an individual's experience and expression of positive affect and low power and status increase the likelihood of negative affect (Anderson and Berdahl 2002; Keltner et al. 2003; Robinson and Smith-Lovin 2001), then one should be able to predict the type of emotion felt and displayed by an individual, depending on her or his status. Kemper's (1991) study of emotion predictions found that participants were able to accurately predict emotions of happiness, anger, fear, and sadness well above chance levels after determining the correct power-status relationships between individuals in vignettes. The vignettes were self-reports of people's actual emotion experiences, and unless the situation was one in which gender was obvious, explicit gender information was omitted. Nevertheless, participants might have inferred gender on the basis of the power and status labels that they assigned to targets in the vignettes; therefore, their emotion predictions might have been influenced by gender-emotion stereotypes or status beliefs. Without teasing apart the effects of gender and power/status, one cannot draw conclusions as to the basis for participants' emotion predictions.

Displayed emotion can also be used to predict the power and status of individuals involved in a social interaction. As Clark (1990) observed, displayed emotion provides information about each individual's position in the social-ranking system. For example, a person expressing anger communicates a sense of violated entitlement; sadness, on the other hand, indicates feelings of helplessness and resignation. Emotional expressions convey messages that signify one's position of power and status in the social hierarchy.

Anger, Gender, and Power/Status

Although gender-emotion stereotypes identify women as more emotionally expressive than men (Fischer and Manstead 2000), expressions of anger are associated more with Western masculinity than femininity (Fabes and Martin 1991). Men's expressions of anger might also increase the amount of status conferral they receive. Tiedens (2001), for example, reported that displays of anger serve as indicators of perceived competence, which, in turn, determine status conferral. An alternative explanation would be that anger is associated with high status because the high-status individual is more likely to experience a sense of violated entitlement, which is the basis for anger. Shields (2002) thus argued that gender differences in experience of anger probably arise from differences in perceived entitlement. In general, men might have a stronger and broader sense of entitlement than women have, which would translate to more opportunities to encounter situations evoking feelings of violated entitlement. Thus, anger might be an outcome of status, rather than a source of status conferral.

Some researchers believe that expressions of anger by high power/status individuals are not the only means for reinforcing the social order. Expressions of humor and teasing (Keltner et al. 1998, 2001) can also decrease resistance to influence (Lovaglia and Houser 1996). Emotions associated with paternalism, such as love and sympathy, can be effective means for convincing others to oblige and might even be more effective than coercion. According to Jackman (1994), the dominant group's success is a reflection of the extent to which it can persuade, rather than force, subordinates to accept positions of low power/status. Through the use of coercive emotions, the dominant group can exert social control by maintaining close, seemingly positive relations with subordinates (Jackman 1994).

Problems and Suggestions

The literature on power, status, gender, and emotion is unsettling. We began this section by differentiating between the social dimensions of power and status, yet not all empirical research that we have covered actually separates these effects. Instead, power and status are sometimes conflated, as in Hall and Friedman's (1999:1082) definition of organizational status as "power and influence within a company." Different emotions might be more closely associated with power than with status. For example, the loss of power (i.e., losing control, dominance, and influence) might evoke anger; whereas the loss of status (i.e., losing a social position accorded by others) might induce sadness. Also, some researchers operationally define power as reward power, overlooking the other kinds of power (coercive, legitimate, referent, and expert power) described by French and Raven (1959). Dovidio et al. (1998) manipulated both reward and expert power and found that visual dominance was associated with men and women high in both types of power—a finding that indicates that when power is unequally distributed between men and women, gender differences in performance and competence expectations are derived from beliefs about status. Future research on gender and emotion should continue to address the separate effects of power and status as well as the various types of power. Through investigating the connections among power, status, gender, and emotion we can come to a better understanding of how gender-emotion stereotypes are implicated in maintaining (and occasionally challenging) the existing gender system.

SEXUALITY

Romantic and sexual relationships are fraught with emotional issues. Here we focus on one issue in which gender-emotion standards and stereotypes are central and for which the interconnections among power, emotion, and gender offer an explanatory framework. Specifically, we consider the emotional tensions surrounding the expression of sexual desire in heterosexual relationships, particularly in the earliest stages of a relationship or potential relationship.

Our definition of emotional expression in intimate relationships has several components. Emotional expression includes the exploration of the self through communication, ego support, comforting, and conflict management between the individual and her or his partner (Burleson 2003); therefore, emotional expression depends on conveying emotion as well as the partner's response to that communication. We define sexual desire as the subjective experience of being interested in sexual objects or activities or wishing to engage in sexual activities (Regan and Berscheid 1999).

In the United States, heterosexual women and men have similar attitudes about elements that comprise a fulfilling sexual relationship (Burleson 1997; Kunkel and Burleson 1998). Specifically, both report the desire to express their sexuality and emotional closeness within dating relationships (Carroll et al. 1985; Cohen and Shotland 1996; McCabe 1987; McCabe and Collins 1984; Oliver and Hyde 1993). Although women and men report wanting both of these characteristics in their romantic relationships, they report wanting them to different degrees. More specifically, men report placing a greater emphasis on *sexual desire* within dating relationships, whereas women report placing a greater emphasis on *emotional connectedness* (Carroll et al. 1985; Cohen and Shotland 1996; Hendrick and Hendrick 1995; Leigh 1989; McCabe, 1987; McCabe and Collins 1984; Oliver and Hyde 1993; Peplau, 2003).

In this section we focus on the tension between expressing emotion and sexuality that occurs in young adults' heterosexual relationships. We do not aim to provide a comprehensive account, but one that highlights a domain in which gender-emotion stereotypes play a role in the maintenance of systemic gender-based power inequities. We examine these conflicts in terms of sexual scripts (Simon and Gagnon 1986), which can be thought of as culturally sanctioned guidelines for doing emotion and gender in intimate relationships. Of course, women's and men's standards for a fulfilling sexual relationship vary across cultures and historical time. In addition, the scripts and conflicts that we focus on are likely to change with age and experience.

Emotion and the Male Sexual Script

Young men report a greater emphasis on the sexual desire aspect of dating relationships than do women. More specifically, men report expecting to engage in sex earlier in relationships (Byers and Lewis 1988; Cohen and Shotland 1996), expecting sex regardless of physical attractiveness of their partner and in the absence of emotional closeness (Cohen and Shotland, 1996), and desiring more frequent sexual activity than they are currently experiencing, particularly in the earlier stages of their relationships (McCabe 1987; McCabe and Collins 1984). This pattern suggests that although both men and women desire sexual activity within relationships, the script that young adults initially rely on emphasizes men's sexual interest over other factors, including emotional closeness, partner attractiveness, and length of the relationship.

One explanation for the apparent sex differences in the need for emotional connectedness within intimate relationships is that men, in general, are less able to express their emotions (Levant and Brooks 1997). According to this viewpoint, society expects men to suppress their need for sensual contact and encourages them to develop an emotionally stoic exterior and to be insensitive to emotional issues that might arise in relationships (Levant and Brooks 1997). Researchers posit that because of this socialization, many otherwise well-adjusted men develop a mild form of alexithymia, a disorder characterized by difficulty in describing or identifying one's own emotions (Levant and Brooks 1997). Proponents of this position cite studies of men's difficulty in expressing emotion in therapeutic settings (Brooks 1998; Robertson 2001; Scher 1981).

Other researchers, however, question the portrayal of emotional inexpressivity as normative masculinity and suggest that men's inexpressivity is more accurately explained as a disinterest in explicit talk about emotion. In fact, Shields (2002) pointed out that openly expressing a wide range of emotions is expected in many conventionally masculine domains, especially competitive sports. Shields further suggested that the idea of pathological inexpressivity as normative masculinity can be traced to a late 1960s and early 1970s response to second-wave feminism's disruption of gender-defined emotion boundaries, especially feminist appropriation of anger as an aspect of consciousness raising.

Nevertheless, male emotional inexpressivity is a theme that remains popular in the relationship literature. We suggest an alternate perspective, specifically one that employs doing emotion as doing gender. Several studies indicated that both women and men reported that affectively oriented expressive skills are important in close relationships (Burleson et al. 1996; Myers and Knox 1998; Westmyer and Myers 1996). Although men recognize the significant interpersonal dimension of emotion, emotional components of relationships might be less salient to them without prompting. Egerton (1988) individually interviewed women and men about their experience of anger and her results suggested that women and men might adopt different ways of viewing the relational nature of emotion. Women were more likely than men to anchor evaluations of their anger episodes in their relationships with others. Specifically, women were more likely to describe their experience of anger in terms of its connection to the relationship that gave rise to the anger, whereas men were more likely to describe anger as something that happened without a specific connection to their relationship.

Men's apparent inability or reluctance to make the connection between emotion and its inter-personal causes and consequences might account in part for the low priority they give to emotional aspects of casual sexual encounters. In established relationships, however, men do acknowledge the emotional aspects of their committed relationships. In addition, satisfaction with sexual ac-tivity is not, by itself, a function of the type of relationship (casual versus committed). Although men report significantly more positive feelings than women about casual sexual encounters, they endorse similar positive feelings about sexual activity within loving and committed relationships (Carroll et al. 1985; Cohen and Shotland 1996; Oliver and Hyde 1993; Sprecher 1989). As in other areas of emotion knowledge and expression, it appears that inattention to emotion in relationships is not a matter of men's lack of knowledge about emotion, but of their use of that knowledge.

Emotion and the Female Sexual Script

Women report desiring more affection from their partners during sexual encounters compared to men (Hatfield and Rapson 1987). Consistent with valuing affection, women report that emotional closeness is more important in deciding whether or not to engage in sexual activity than do men (Leigh 1989). Women, in comparison to men, also report being more committed to and invested in their relationships and endorse the importance of being loved, being deeply in love, and saying that love is important (Hendrick and Hendrick 1995). Women in lesbian relationships similarly emphasize the emotional component of relationships (Peplau 2003).

Hill (2002) found that women felt more comfortable engaging in sexual activity in the early stages of a relationship if they perceived their partners as displaying adequate emotional involve-ment. The link that women make between sexual activity and emotional connectedness might be a reflection of expressing an "authentic feminine self," one aspect of which involves valuing in-terpersonal warmth and an orientation toward maintaining close relationships (Wood et al. 1997). The norms for emotional expression within sexual relationships outline the script for doing gender, and adhering to the script requires some degree of conformity to conventional femininity. As the putative "emotion experts" in relationships, the burden on women is to define what constitutes the correct kind and level of "emotional involvement." They are expected to dictate the amount of ex-travagant expressiveness used in their relationships. Nevertheless, the other side of the emotional woman stereotype, that of "being emotional," calls into question the soundness of her judgment. The catch-22 for young women's authority on emotional matters in relationships is that the legit-imacy of their authority is undermined by the consensual status belief about their emotionality.

Although emotional engagement is one dimension of the conventional script, so is restraint of sexual desire. The sexual suppression aspect of the female sexual script reflects social norms that discourage women from admitting, recognizing, or acting on sexual impulses. Thus, the basis for the sexual double standard is the idea that men's sexual activity is tolerated and encouraged; women, on the other hand, are stigmatized for engaging in such behavior. Considering the double standard a form of consensual status belief offers a way to understand why women acquiesce to the double standard despite their dissatisfaction with it. Women believe that the sexual double standard exists today, but they do not endorse it (Aubrey 2004; Crawford and Popp 2003; Gentry 1998; MacCorquodale 1989; Milhausen and Herold 1999; Muehlenhard 1988). Nonetheless, women judge sexually active women more negatively than nonsexually active women (Gentry 1998; Milhausen and Herold 1999). The conflict between expressed attitudes and judgments of other women's behaviors might affect women's emotional responses to their own sexual behaviors.

According to Tolman (2002), the sexual double standard causes conflicting emotions in young women when they consider their own sexual behavior. Tolman suggested that young women have both positive and negative emotional responses to engaging in sexual behaviors. They believe that healthy sexuality means having sexual desires, yet they are under social pressure not to act on those desires; therefore, when young women do engage in sexual activity, they experience conflicting emotions. They report feeling desirable, and they appreciate the mutual connection that they have established with their partners, but they also worry about how society will judge them (Tolman 2002). Ambivalent feelings such as these show the power of the sexual double standard. Katz and Farrow (2000) studied female's views of their own sexuality and found that women believed they should be *both* more sexually conservative and more sexually open and passionate. This research demonstrates the existence of an emotional and moral conflict when women consider their own sexual behaviors. The pressure on women to suppress sexual expression might generate conflict between the desire to be sexual and external pressures to curb expression of desire.

Competing Scripts for Men and Women

Men and women experience between- and within-gender conflicts regarding emotional and sexual expression within intimate relationships. Although these conflicts might differ, the issues are closely interrelated. For example, men's acceptance of sex without emotional commitment can place further strains on women's conflict. Kane and Schippers (1996) found that although both men and women report believing that the other gender has more sexual power within society, men report being satisfied with the current structure, whereas women report that women are harmed by it. All of this takes place within a popular culture milieu that promotes the romantic script for young women and the sexualized script for young men. If anything, media aimed at the young adult male audience more often associates sexuality with violence than with emotional connection, as demonstrated in Oliver's (2000) analysis of media entertainment differentially enjoyed by male and female audiences. Sexualized images of female pop idols intended to appeal to young women promise freedom of sexual expression without acknowledging the ambivalence and consequent emotion that gives that promise its power. Kim and Ward (2004), for example, found that women who frequently read magazines that focus on women's beauty and success in relationships were less likely to equate sex with emotional risks than women who do not.

Young women are expected to be sexy but not sexual (Crawford and Popp 2003). When young women push limits of acceptable "feminine" sexual expression, they are at risk for negative emotional reactions from others and within themselves (Katz and Farrow 2000; Tolman 2002). Negative emotional experiences, in turn, justify the idea that such sexual experiences are unacceptable, which propagates the sexual attitudes, stereotypes, and status beliefs that men and women endorse.

Problems and Suggestions

It is important to remember that the sexual scripts we discussed in this section largely represent research on white college students. Studies comparing European, African, and Asian Americans have found differences in the reported value of explicit communication about emotion in close relationships. For example, Hammer and Gudykunst (1987) found that European Americans reported greater emotional disclosure than African Americans. Samter and Burleson (1998) found that African Americans reported less value than both Asian Americans and European Americans on emotionally expressive skills when interacting with close friends, and this was particularly the case for African American women. These studies caution against unwarranted generalizations about a single sexual script for either women or men. They further suggest that it is useful to problematize what "emotional expressivity" (e.g., ego support, comforting, and conflict management) encompasses, who is held responsible for monitoring expressivity in relationships, and the relationship consequences for deviation from expected standards of emotional sharing.

CONCLUSION

In this chapter we have given a brief overview of research on gender and emotion that has particular relevance for the sociology of emotion. We used work on gender-emotion stereotypes, power, and sexual scripts to explain how and why beliefs about gender and emotion operate so effectively to maintain existing gender systems. We relied on two theoretical perspectives: expectation states theory and doing emotion as doing gender. Expectation states theory is useful for explaining how gender-emotion stereotypes contribute to maintaining gender hierarchies and how they "naturally" emerge in novel, mixed-gender settings. Doing emotion as doing gender is a way to express why individual participation in gender hierarchies is so compelling; even when individuals try to resist the re-creation of gender boundaries in emotion-related behavior and feeling, they capitulate, motivated to do so both by the expectations and responses of others and by their own desire for self-consistency and feelings of authenticity. Through practicing "gender correct" emotion, beliefs about emotion—the language of emotion, social conventions regarding emotion, and the like—inscribe and reinscribe gender boundaries.

We hypothesize that the motivation for doing emotion the proper way (i.e., following gender prescriptions) stems from the connection that emotion and gender each have in the formation and maintenance of the individual sense of self. Gender figures in the individual's earliest self-representations and gender categorization pervade interpersonal interactions even before an individuated sense of self emerges developmentally. As for emotion, both the experience of emotion and its representation in language are taken to validate or challenge the individual's authenticity as a human being (Morgan and Averill 1992). Simply manipulating the appearance of emotion does not accomplish the same ends (Hochschild 1983). Emotion experience tells us that we are human; believing that others honestly and authentically experience emotion reassures us of their humanity as well.

The study of gender and emotion is a field ripe for further study. Our brief overview suggests several significant directions for future research; to conclude, we briefly note three: (1) How does the account of gender and emotion developed in this chapter map onto gender practices that aim to operate outside of the established gender system? For example, what role do beliefs about emotion, especially gendered emotion, play in the creation of queer or transgender identity? (2) Although "powerful" emotions are stereotypically associated with men, men can actually benefit from exhibiting "weak" emotion. For example, tears are not interpreted as a display of weakness if shed the "right way," but as something to be valued and even admired. When and why is appropriation of weak emotion effective in demonstrating legitimacy and authenticity? (3) The micropolitics of emotion have both a subtle and pervasive connection to gender systems. Further investigation of this connection can elucidate how power and status are maintained and challenged through the deployment of emotion, especially the judgment of emotion's legitimacy and social appropriateness: Whose emotion is valued? When is emotion acknowledged as a sign of legitimacy and truth of an utterance and when is it written off as "merely emotion"?

REFERENCES

Agars, Mark D. 2004. "Reconsidering the Impact of Gender Stereotypes on the Advancement of Women in Organizations." *Psychology of Women Quarterly* 28: 103–111.

Anderson, Cameron, and Jennifer L. Berdahl. 2002. "The Experience of Power: Examining the Effects of Power on Approach and Inhibition Tendencies." *Journal of Personality and Social Psychology* 83: 1362–1377.

Anderson, Cameron, and Leigh L. Thompson. 2004. "Affect from the Top Down: How Powerful Individuals' Positive Affect Shapes Negotiations." *Organizational Behavior and Human Decision Processes* 95: 125–139.

Anderson, Kristin J., and Christina Accomando. 2002. "'Real' Boys? Manufacturing Masculinity and Erasing Privilege in Popular Books on Raising Boys." *Feminism and Psychology* 12: 491–516.

Anderson, Kristin, J., Jessica George, and Jessica Nease. 2002. "Requirements, Risks, and Responsibility: Mothering and Fathering in Books about Raising Boys." *Analyses of Social Issues and Public Policy* 2: 205–221.

Aubrey, Jennifer S. 2004. "Sex and Punishment: An Examination of Sexual Consequences and the Sexual Double Standard in Teen Programming." *Sex Roles* 50: 505–514.

Augoustinos, Martha, and Iain Walker. 1995. *Social Cognition: An Integrated Introduction.* Thousand Oaks, CA: Sage.

Baca Zinn, Maxine, and Bonnie Thornton Dill. 1996. "Theorizing Difference from Multiracial Feminism." *Feminist Studies* 22: 321–331.

Bacchi, Carol Lee. 1990. *Same Difference: Feminism and Sexual Difference.* Boston: Allen and Unwin.

Berger, Joseph, M. Hamit Fisek, Robert Z. Norman, David G. Wagner, and Morris Zelditch, Jr. 1977. *Status Characteristics and Social Interaction.* New York: Elsevier.

Brody, Leslie R. 1997. "Gender and Emotion: Beyond Stereotypes." *Journal of Social Issues* 53: 369–394.

———. 1999. *Gender, Emotion and the Family.* Cambridge, MA: Harvard University Press.

Brooks, Gary R. 1998. *Group Therapy for Traditional Men.* New York: Wiley.

Burleson, Brant R. 1997. "A Different Voice on Different Cultures: Illusion and Reality in the Study of Sex Differences in Personal Relationships." *Personal Relationships* 4: 229–241.

———. 2003. "The Experience and Effects of Emotional Support: What the Study of Cultural and Gender Differences Can Tell us About Close Relationships, Emotion, and Interpersonal Communication." *Personal Relationships* 10: 1–23.

Burleson, Brant R., Adrianne W. Kunkel, Wendy Samter, and Kathy J. Werking. 1996. "Men's and Women's Evaluations of Communication Skills in Personal Relationships: When Sex Differences Make a Difference—and When They Don't." *Journal of Social and Personal Relationships* 13: 201–224.

Byers, E. Sandra, and Kim Lewis. 1988. "Dating Couples' Disagreements Over the Desired Level of Sexual Intimacy." *Journal of Sex Research* 24: 15–29.

Cameron, Jessica A., and Yaacov Trope. 2004. "Stereotype-Based Search and Processing of Information About Group Members." *Social Cognition* 22: 650–672.

Carroll, Janell L., Kari D. Volk, and Janet S. Hyde. 1985. "Differences Between Males and Females in Motives for Engaging in Sexual Intercourse." *Archives of Sexual Behavior* 14: 131–139.

Clark, Candace. 1990. "Emotions and Micropolitics in Everyday Life: Some Patterns and Paradoxes of 'Place'." Pp. 305–333 in *Research Agendas in the Sociology of Emotions,* edited by T. D. Kemper. Albany: State University of New York Press.

Cohen, Laurie L., and R. Lance Shotland. 1996. "Timing of First Sexual Intercourse in a Relationship: Expectation, Experiences, and Perceptions of Others." *Journal of Sex Research* 33: 291–299.

Collings, Steven J. 2002. "The Impact of Contextual Ambiguity on the Interpretation and Recall of Child Sexual Abuse Media Reports." *Journal of Interpersonal Violence* 17: 1063–1074.

Conway, Michael, Robert Di Fazio, and Shari Mayman. 1999. "Judging Others' Emotions as a Function of the Others' Status." *Social Psychology Quarterly* 62: 291–305.

Correll, Shelley J., and Cecilia L. Ridgeway. 2003. "Expectation States Theory." Pp. 29–51 in *Handbook of Social Psychology,* edited by J. Delamater. New York: Kluwer.

Crawford, Mary, and Danielle Popp. 2003. "Sexual Double Standards: A Review and Methodological Critique of Two Decades of Research." *Journal of Sex Research* 40: 13–26.

Deaux, Kay. 1993. "Reconstructing Social Identity." *Personality and Social Psychology Bulletin* 19: 4–12.

————. 2000. "Gender and Emotion: Notes from a Grateful Tourist." Pp. 301–318 in *Gender and Emotion: Social Psychological Perspectives*, edited by A. H. Fischer. Cambridge: Cambridge University Press.

Deaux, Kay, and Marianne LaFrance. 1998. "Gender." Pp. 788–827 in *The Handbook of Social Psychology*, edited by D. T. Gilbert, S. T. Fiske, and G. Lindzey. New York: McGraw-Hill.

Deutsch, Francine M. 1990. "Status, Sex, and Smiling: The Effect of Role on Smiling in Men and Women." *Personality and Social Psychology Bulletin* 16: 531–540.

Dovidio, John F., Steve L. Ellyson, Caroline F. Keating, Karen Heltman, and Clifford E. Brown. 1998. "The Relationship of Social Power to Visual Displays of Dominance between Men and Women." *Journal of Personality and Social Psychology* 54: 233–242.

Egerton, Muriel. 1988. "Passionate Women and Passionate Men: Sex Differences in Accounting for Angry and Weeping Episodes." *British Journal of Social Psychology* 27: 51–66.

Fabes, Richard A., and Carol L. Martin. 1991. "Gender and Age Stereotypes of Emotionality." *Personality and Social Psychology Bulletin* 17: 532–540.

Fenstermaker, Sarah, and Candace West. 2002. *Doing Gender, Doing Differences: Inequality, Power, and Institutional Change*. New York: Routledge.

Fischer, Agneta H. 1993. "Sex Differences in Emotionality: Fact or Stereotype?" *Feminism and Psychology* 3: 303–318.

Fischer, Agenta H., and Antony S. R. Manstead. 2000. "The Relation between Gender and Emotion in Different Cultures." Pp. 71–94 in *Gender and Emotion: Social Psychological Perspectives*, edited by A. H. Fischer. Cambridge: Cambridge University Press.

Fiske, Susan T. 1993. "Controlling Other People: The Impact of Power on Stereotyping." *American Psychologist* 48: 621–628.

French, John R. P., Jr., and Bertram Raven. 1959. "The Bases of Social Power." Pp. 150–167 in *Studies in Social Power*, edited by D. Cartwright. Ann Arbor: University of Michigan.

Gentry, Margaret. 1998. "The Sexual Double Standard: The Influence of Number of Relationships and Level of Sexual Activity on Judgments of Women and Men." *Psychology of Women Quarterly* 22: 505–511.

Graham, John W., Kevin W. Gentry, and Jane Green. 1981. "The Self-Presentational Nature of Emotional Expression: Some Evidence." *Personality and Social Psychology Bulletin* 7: 467–474.

Gray, Stephen M., and Laurie Heatherington. 2003. "The Importance of Social Context in the Facilitation of Emotional Expression in Men." *Journal of Social and Clinical Psychology* 22: 294-314.

Hall, Judith A., Jason D. Carter, and Terrence G. Horgan. 2000. "Gender Differences in Nonverbal Communication of Emotion." Pp. 97–117 in *Gender and Emotion: Social Psychological Perspectives*, edited by A. H. Fischer. Cambridge: Cambridge University Press.

Hall, Judith A., and Gregory B. Friedman. 1999. "Status, Gender, and Nonverbal Behavior: A Study of Structural Inter-actions between Employees of a Company." *Personality and Social Psychology Bulletin* 25: 1082–1091.

Hammer, Mitchell R., and William B. Gudykunst. 1987. "The Influence of Ethnicity and Sex on Social Penetration in Close Friendships." *Journal of Black Studies* 17: 418–437.

Hare-Mustin, Rachel T., and Jeanne Marecek. 1994. "Asking the Right Questions: Feminist Psychology and Sex Differences." *Feminism and Psychology* 4: 531–537.

Hatfield, Elaine, and Richard L. Rapson. 1987. "Gender Differences in Love and Intimacy: The Fantasy vs. the Reality." *Journal of Social Work and Human Sexuality* 5: 15–26.

Hecht, Marvin A., and Marianne LaFrance. 1998. "License or Obligation to Smile: The Effect of Power and Sex on Amount and Type of Smiling." *Personality and Social Psychology Bulletin* 24: 1332–1342.

Heesacker, Martin, Stephen R. Wester, David L. Vogel, Jeffrey T. Wentzel, Cristina M. Mejia-Millan, and Carl Robert Goodholm, Jr. 1999. "Gender-Based Emotional Stereotyping." *Journal of Counseling Psychology* 46: 483–495.

Hendrick, Susan S., and Clyde Hendrick. 1995. "Gender Differences and Similarities in Sex and Love." *Personal Relationships* 2: 55–65.

Henley, Nancy M. 1973. "Status and Sex: Some Touching Observations." *Bulletin of Psychonomic Society* 2: 91–93.

Hess, Ursula, Sacha Senecal, Gilles Kirouac, Pedro Herrera, Pierre Philippot, and Robert E. Kleck. 2000. "Emotional Expressivity in Men and Women: Stereotypes and Self-Perceptions." *Cognition and Emotion* 14: 609–642.

Hill, Craig A. 2002. "Gender, Relationship Stage, and Sexual Behavior: The Importance of Partner Emotional Investment within Specific Situations." *Journal of Sex Research* 39: 228–240.

Hochschild, Arlie R. 1983. *The Managed Heart*. Berkeley: University of California Press.

Jackman, Mary R. 1994. *The Velvet Glove: Paternalism and Conflict in Gender, Class, and Race Relations*. Berkeley: University of California Press.

Johnson, Richard A., and Gary I. Schulman. 1988. "More Alike than Meets the Eye: Perceived Gender Differences in Subjective Experience and its Display." *Sex Roles* 19: 67–79.

Judd, Charles M., and Bernadette Park. 1993. "Definition and Assessment of Accuracy in Social Stereotypes." *Psychological Review* 100: 109–128.

Kane, Emily W., and Mimi Schippers. 1996. "Men's and Women's Beliefs about Gender and Sexuality." *Gender and Society* 10: 650–665.

Katz, Jennifer, and Sherry Farrow. 2000. "Discrepant Self-Views and Young Women's Sexual and Emotional Adjustment." *Sex Roles* 42: 781–805.

Kelly, Janice R., and Sarah L. Hutson-Comeaux. 1999. "Gender-Emotion Stereotypes are Context Specific." *Sex Roles* 40: 107–120.

Keltner, Dacher, Lisa Capps, Ann M. Kring, Randall C. Young, and Erin A. Heerey. 2001. "Just Teasing: A Conceptual Analysis and Empirical Review." *Psychological Bulletin* 127: 229–248.

Keltner, Dacher, Deborah H. Gruenfeld, and Cameron Anderson. 2003. "Power, Approach, and Inhibition." *Psychological Review* 110: 265–284.

Keltner, Dacher, Randall C. Young, Erin A. Heerey, Carmen Oemig, and Natalie D. Monarch. 1998. "Teasing in Hierarchical and Intimate Relations." *Journal of Personality and Social Psychology* 75: 1231–1247.

Kemper, Theodore D. 1990. "Social Relations and Emotions: A Structural Approach." Pp. 281–304 in *Research Agendas in the Sociology of Emotions*, edited by T. D. Kemper. Albany: State University of New York Press.

———. 1991. "Predicting Emotions from Social Relations." *Social Psychology Quarterly* 54: 330–342.

Kim, Janna L., and L. Monique Ward. 2004. "Pleasure Reading: Associations between Young Women's Sexual Attitudes and Their Reading of Contemporary Women's Magazines." *Psychology of Women Quarterly* 28: 48–58.

Klaczynski, Paul A., Kristen W. Goold, and Jeffrey J. Mudry. 2004. "Culture, Obesity Stereotypes, Self-Esteem, and the 'Thin Ideal': A Social Identity Perspective." *Journal of Youth and Adolescence* 33: 307–317.

Knox, David, Marty E. Zusman, and Heather R. Thompson. 2004. "Emotional Perceptions of Self and Others: Stereotypes and Data." *College Student Journal* 38: 130–134.

Kring, Ann M. 2000. "Gender and Anger." Pp. 211–231 in *Gender and Emotion: Social Psychological Perspectives*, edited by A. H. Fischer. Cambridge: Cambridge University Press.

Kunkel, Adrianne W., and Brant R. Burleson. 1998. "Social Support and the Emotional Lives of Men and Women: An Assessment of the Different Cultures Perspective." Pp. 101–125 in *Sex Differences and Similarities in Communication*, edited by D. J. Canary and K. Dindia. Mahwah, NJ: Erlbaum.

LaFrance, Marianne, and Mahzarin Banaji. 1992. "Toward a Reconsideration of the Gender-Emotion Relationship." Pp. 178–201 in *Emotion and Social Behavior. Review of Personality and Social Psychology*, edited by M. S. Clark. Newbury Park, CA: Sage.

LaFrance, Marianne, and Nancy M. Henley. 1997. "On Oppressing Hypotheses: Or, Differences in Nonverbal Sensitivity Revisited." Pp. 104–119 in *Women, Men, and Gender: Ongoing Debates*, edited by M. R. Walsh. New Haven, CT: Yale University Press.

LaFrance, Marianne, Marvin Hecht, and Elizabeth Levy Paluck. 2003. "The Contingent Smile: A Meta-Analysis of Sex Differences in Smiling." *Psychological Bulletin* 129: 305–334.

Leigh, Barbara C. 1989. "Reasons for Having and Avoiding Sex: Gender, Sexual Orientation, and Relationship to Sexual Behavior." *Journal of Sex Research* 26: 199–209.

Levant, Ronald F., and Gary R. Brooks. 1997. *Men and Sex: New Psychological Perspectives.* New York: Wiley.

Lovaglia, Michael J., and Jeffrey A. Houser. 1996. "Emotional Reactions and Status in Groups." *American Sociological Review* 61: 867–883.

Maccoby, Eleanor E. 1990. "Gender and Relationships: A Developmental Account." *American Psychologist* 45: 513–520.

MacCorquodale, Patricia. 1989. "Gender and Sexual Behavior." Pp. 91–112 in *Human Sexuality: The Societal and Interpersonal Context*, edited by S. Sprecher and K. McKinney. Westport, CT: Ablex.

McCabe, Marita P. 1987. "Desired and Experienced Levels of Premarital Affection and Sexual Intercourse During Dating." *Journal of Sex Research* 23: 23–33.

McCabe, Marita P., and John K. Collins. 1984. "Measurement of Depth of Desired and Experienced Sexual Involvement at Different Stages of Dating." *Journal of Sex Research* 20: 377–390.

Milhausen, Robin R., and Edward S. Herold. 1999. "Does the Sexual Double Standard Still Exist? Perceptions of University Women." *Journal of Sex Research* 36: 361–368.

Moloney, Molly, and Sarah Fenstermaker. 2002. "Performance and Accomplishment: Reconciling Feminist Conceptions of Gender." Pp. 55–80 in *Doing Gender, Doing Difference: Inequality, Power, and Institutional Change*, edited by S. Fenstermaker and C. West. New York: Routledge.

Morgan, Charles, and James R. Averill. 1992. "True Feelings, the Self, and Authenticity: A Psychosocial Approach." Pp. 95–123 in *Social Perspectives on Emotion*, edited by D. D. Frances and V. Gecas. Greenwich, CT: JAI Press.

Muehlenhard, Charlene L. 1988. "'Nice Women' Don't Say Yes and 'Real Men' Don't Say No: How Miscommunication and the Double Standard Can Cause Sexual Problems." *Women and Therapy* 7: 95–108.

Myers, Scott A., and Ronda L. Knox. 1998. "Perceived Sibling Use of Functional Communication Skills." *Communication Research Reports* 15: 397–405.

Nakano Glenn, Evelyn. 1999. "The Social Construction and Institutionalization of Gender and Race: An Integrative Framework." Pp. 3–43 in *Revisioning Gender,* edited by M. M. Ferree, J. Lorber, and B. B. Hess. Thousand Oaks, CA: Sage.

Oliver, Mary B. 2000. "The Respondent Gender Gap." Pp. 215–234 in *Media Entertainment*, edited by D. Zillmann and P. Vorderer. Mahwah, NJ: Lawrence Erlbaum.

Oliver, Mary B., and Janet S. Hyde. 1993. "Gender Differences in Sexuality: A Meta-Analysis." *Psychological Bulletin* 114: 29–51.

Peplau, Letitia A. 2003. "Human Sexuality: How Do Men and Women Differ?" *Current Directions in Psychological Science* 12: 37–40.

Petrides, K. V., Adrian Furnham, and G. Neil Martin. 2004. "Estimates of Emotional and Psychometric Intelligence: Evidence for Gender-Based Stereotypes." *Journal of Social Psychology* 144: 149–162.

Plant, E. Ashby, Janet S. Hyde, Dacher Keltner, and Patricia G. Devine. 2000. "The Gender Stereotyping of Emotions." *Psychology of Women Quarterly* 24: 81–92.

Polce-Lynch, Mary, Barbara J. Myers, Christopher T. Kilmartin, Renate Forssmann-Falck, and Wendy Kliewer. 1998. "Gender and Age Patterns in Emotional Expression, Body Image, and Self-Esteem: A Qualitative Analysis." *Sex Roles* 38: 1025–1048.

Popp, Danielle, Roxanne A. Donovan, Mary Crawford, Kerry L. Marsh, and Melanie Peele. 2003. "Gender, Race, and Speech Style Stereotypes." *Sex Roles* 48: 317–325.

Regan, Pamela C., and Ellen Berscheid. 1999. *Lust: What We Know about Human Sexual Desire.* Thousand Oaks, CA: Sage.

Ridgeway, Cecilia L. 2001. "Gender, Status, and Leadership." *Journal of Social Issues* 57: 637–655.

Ridgeway, Cecilia L. and Chris Bourg. 2004. "Gender as Status: An Expectation States Theory Approach." Pp. 217–241 in *The Psychology of Gender*, edited by A. H. Eagly, A. E. Beall, and R. J. Sternberg. New York: Guilford.

Ridgeway, Cecilia L., and Shelly J. Correll. 2004. "Unpacking the Gender System: A Theoretical Perspective on Gender Beliefs and Social Relations." *Gender and Society* 18: 510–531.

Robertson, John M. 2001. "Counseling Men in College Settings." Pp. 146–169 in *The New Handbook of Psychotherapy and Counseling with Men: A Comprehensive Guide to Settings, Problems, and Treatment Approaches*, edited by G. E. Good and G. Brooks. San Francisco: Jossey-Bass.

Robinson, Dawn T., and Lynn Smith-Lovin. 2001. "Getting a Laugh: Gender, Status, and Humor in Task Discussions." *Social Forces* 80: 123–158.

Robinson, Michael D., and Joel T. Johnson. 1997. "Is It Emotion or Is It Stress? Gender Stereotypes and the Perception of Subjective Experience." *Sex Roles* 36: 235–258.

Robinson, Michael D., Joel T. Johnson, and Stephanie A. Shields. 1998. "The Gender Heuristic and the Database: Factors Affecting the Perception of Gender-Related Differences in the Experience and Display of Emotions." *Basic and Applied Social Psychology* 20: 206–219.

Samter, Wendy, and Brant R. Burleson. 1998. "The Role of Communication in Same-Sex Friendships: A Comparison Among African-Americans, Asian-Americans, and Euro-Americans." Paper presented at the International Conference on Personal Relationships, Saratoga Springs, NY, June.

Scher, Murray. 1981. "Men in Hiding: A Challenge for the Counselor." *Personnel and Guidance Journal* 60: 199–202.

Schneider, David J. 2004. *The Psychology of Stereotyping.* New York: Guilford.

Sheldon, Amy. 1992. "Conflict Talk: Sociolinguistic Challenges to Self-Assertion and How Young Girls Meet Them." *Merrill-Palmer Quarterly* 38: 95–117.

Shields, Stephanie A. 1991. "Gender in the Psychology of Emotion: A Selective Research Review." Pp. 227–245 in *International Review of Studies on Emotion,* edited by K. T. Strongman. New York: Wiley.

———. 1995. "The Role of Emotion Beliefs and Values in Gender Development." Pp. 212–232 in *Review of Personality and Social Psychology,* edited by N. Eisenberg. Thousand Oaks, CA: Sage.

———. 2002. *Speaking from the Heart: Gender and the Social Meaning of Emotion.* Cambridge: Cambridge University Press.

———. 2005. "The Politics of Emotion in Everyday Life: 'Appropriate' Emotion and Claims on Identity." *Review of General Psychology* 9: 3–15.

Shields, Stephanie A., and Jill L. Crowley. 2000. "Stereotypes of 'Emotionality': The Role of the Target's Racial Ethnicity, Status, and Gender." For the symposium The Influence of Beliefs Regarding Men's and Women's Emotions on the Perception and Self-Perception of Emotions, chaired by U. Hess and R. Kleck. Quebec City, August.

Shields, Stephanie A., and Beth A. Koster. 1989. "Emotional Stereotyping of Parents in Child Rearing Manuals, 1915–1980." *Social Psychology Quarterly* 52: 44–55.

Shields, Stephanie A., Pamela Steinke, and Beth A. Koster. 1995. "The Double Bind of Caregiving: Representation of Emotion in American Advice Literature." *Sex Roles* 33: 417–438.

Simon, William, and John H. Gagnon. 1986. "Sexual Scripts: Permanence and Change." *Archives of Sexual Behavior* 15: 97–120.

Sprecher, Susan. 1989. "Premarital Sexual Standards for Different Categories of Individuals." *Journal of Sex Research* 26: 232–248.

Stoppard, Janet M., and Carla Gunn Gruchy. 1993. "Gender, Context, and Expression of Positive Emotion." *Personality and Social Psychology Bulletin* 19: 143–150.

Tiedens, Larissa Z. 2001. "Anger and Advancement versus Sadness and Subjugation: The Effect of Negative Emotion Expressions on Social Status Conferral." *Journal of Personality and Social Psychology* 80: 86–94.

Tiedens, Larissa Z., Phoebe C. Ellsworth, and Batja Mesquita. 2000. "Stereotypes about Sentiments and Status: Emotional Expectations for High- and Low-Status Group Members." *Personality and Social Psychology Bulletin* 26: 560–557.

Timmers, Monique, Agneta H. Fischer, and Antony S. R. Manstead. 1998. "Gender Differences in Motives for Regulating Emotions." *Personality and Social Psychology Bulletin* 24: 974–985.

———.2003. "Ability versus Vulnerability: Beliefs about Men's and Women's Emotional Behaviour." *Cognition and Emotion* 17: 41–63.

Tolman, Deborah L. 2002. *Dilemmas of Desire: Teenage Girls Talk about Sexuality.* Cambridge, MA: Harvard University Press.

von Salisch, Maria. 1997. "Emotional Processes in Children's Relationships with Siblings and Friends." Pp. 61–80 in *Handbook of Personal Relationships,* edited by S. Duck. Chichester: Wiley.

Warner, Leah R., and Stephanie A. Shields. 2005. "'Manly Emotion' and Gendered Standards of Expressive Competence." In APA symposium *Gender and the Politics of Emotion in Everyday Life.* Washington, DC, August.

———.2006. "The Perception of Crying in Women and Men: Angry Tears, Sad Tears, and the 'Right Way' to Weep." In *Emotion Recognition across Social Groups,* edited by U. Hess and P. Phillipot. Cambridge: Cambridge University Press.

West, Candace, and Sarah Fenstermaker. 1995. "Doing Difference." *Gender and Society* 9: 8–37.

West, Candace, and Don H. Zimmerman. 1987. "Doing Gender." *Gender and Society* 1: 125–151.

Westmyer, Stephanie A., and Scott A. Myers. 1996. "Communication Skills and Social Support Messages across Friendship Levels." *Communication Research Reports* 13: 191–197.

Wood, Wendy, P. Niels Christensen, Michelle R. Hebl, and Hank Rothgerber. 1997. "Conformity to Sex-Typed Norms, Affect, and the Self-Concept." *Journal of Personality and Social Psychology* 73: 523–535.

Worcel, Sonia D., Wendy Smith, Stephanie A. Shields, and Brooke DiLeone. Under review. "The Development and Validation of the Self-styled Gender Scale (SSGS)."

THEORIES

CHAPTER 4

Power and Status and the Power-Status Theory of Emotions

Theodore D. Kemper

Power and status theory has an ancient provenance, extending back as far as pre-Socratic Greek philosophy. The power-status theory of emotions, a somewhat different matter, is modern, but depends, of course, on the earlier theory.

Power and status theory holds that when human actors orient their behavior to each other, two fundamental dimensions, namely power and status, are operative.[1] This is a bold statement and it took philosophical daring to assert it during its earliest incarnation. Fortunately, modern social science also provides strong support for the exclusiveness of the power and status dimensions in human social relations.

The power-status theory of emotions is a contemporary application of power and status theory. It takes seriously the claim that social relational behavior can be described and elaborated in two dimensions and derives from it a theory of how emotions result from outcomes of interaction in terms of those dimensions. In this chapter, we first discuss power and status theory and then the power-status theory of emotions.

POWER AND STATUS THEORY

Few nonspecialists read pre-Socratic Greek philosophy, but Freud did. "Empedocles," he wrote, "was my great predecessor" (1959:349–350). Writing a century or so before Plato, Empedocles was a typical thinker of his time in judging that the basic constituents of nature were earth, air, fire, and water. Like his contemporaries, he observed that these elements constantly changed their

Theodore D. Kemper • Department of Sociology, St. John's University, Jamaica, New York, 11439 state: Water evaporated into air; air condensed and became water; earth could be ignited into fire; and fire turned into smoke (air).

How can we explain this dynamic quality of nature? *Love* and *strife*, said Empedocles, produced the changes in nature's constituent elements. Love binds the elements together, making them cohere. However, strife inevitably arises to disintegrate the whole and reduce the elements to their prior state (Cleve 1969; Wright 1981). It was not a great leap for Freud to see that love and strife were cognate to his two basic forces: Eros and Thanatos, the instincts of life and death, respectively. Using modern methods, social scientists have more recently confirmed what Empedocles asserted.[2]

The contemporary version of love and strife, here named status and power, respectively, emerged during a period of methodological innovation and empirical investigation during and following World War II, when it was deemed important to understanding military leadership.

The principal tool of discovery was factor analysis, a mathematical technique for determining underlying patterns in large sets of correlated variables. Developed by psychologist Spearman (1904) and later refined by Thurstone (1934), it was used at first to study whether intelligence was unitary or composed of different basic "factors" (e.g., verbal intelligence, mathematical intelligence, and so on). Factor analysis soon became a leading method by which analysts in many sciences explored how many factors or basic dimensions underlay the data of their field.

The utility of such inquiry is manifest. In a field without a good grasp of its basic dimensions, the work is largely anarchic, responding often to idiocentric interests but rarely leading to a body of valid statements about the domain in question. On the other hand, if one can sensibly circumscribe the basic properties of one's field, then one can work on a set of questions whose answers might cumulate into a coherent body of findings and an overarching theory to account for those findings.

Factor analysis also allows work at the level of "theoretical constructs" as opposed to "observables" (Willer and Webster 1970). The latter are any set of indicators, such as demographic variables like age, sex, race, or religion or attitudes or behavior—whatever is subject to direct perception by observers or can be obtained through self-report. According to Willer and Webster, observables do not lead to cumulative theory. In an example, they translated the observables occupation and sex into the construct "status characteristic." Theory about status characteristics can be generalized to other observables that share the same underlying status property as occupation and sex. Factor analysis is one method for generating a smaller set of constructs from a larger set of observables.

With respect to power and status theory, Carter (1954) wrote perhaps the seminal paper. It confirmed and extended what *his* great predecessor, Empedocles, had discovered earlier, but with an important sociological extension. Carter (1954:487) asked, "What are the characteristics which can be evaluated by observing people interacting?" In his work with Couch (Couch and Carter 1952), he found that three dimensions accounted for the variance in ratings of the group behavior of college males on 19 variables. This was an interesting finding in itself, but it gained importance because it was the culmination of a line of corroborative research that began with the Office of Strategic Services (OSS) Assessment Staff (1948) study of OSS candidates, which was factor analyzed by Sakoda (1952), Hemphill and Coons's (undated) study of leadership, Wherry's (1950) study of army officers, and Clark's (1953) study of army rifle squads in Korea.

The important discovery was that each of these investigations, despite differences in group size, tasks, social locations of subjects, and types of measurement, had found essentially the same three factors or dimensions or theoretical constructs underlying the larger number of variables that were used in these studies. Carter named the three factors *Individual Prominence and Achievement*, *Group Goal Facilitation*, and *Group Sociability*. This was a rare convergence in social science, and modern power and status theory was essentially launched by this development.

Two issues arise from Carter's work. First, although power and status theory entails two factors, Carter found three. Second, there is the matter of definition: How do (two of) Carter's factors translate into power and status? On the two-versus-three factor question, it is useful to recognize that Carter's solution to the problem of dimensions is more sociologically comprehensive than the power-status approach. This can be seen as follows.

Where we try to imagine a starting point for sociological theory, it must inevitably be grounded in the fact that humans are an interdependent species and that this implies a division of labor. Reproduction requires two actors and the exigencies of human survival after birth also require other actors to nurture and care for the neonate. Added to the division of labor of reproduction and parenting is a partly efficiency-based, socially constructed further specialization of tasks, with wide variation between groups in the particulars. But whatever the details, whatever the local variations and whatever their origin, we can conclude without a sociological doubt that a division of labor is always present in human groups. Proceeding, we judge that the division of labor consists of a distribution of tasks, or what can be thought of as *technical activities*, assigned to different actors and designed *in toto* to accomplish the goals of the group: from simple survival, at one end of the scale of complexity, to the most recondite and arcane interests, such as are involved in modern science, at the other end.

If this sociological account of activity in human groups is adequate, we have a way of accounting for Carter's Group Goal Facilitation factor. The items that mark this factor support the analysis based on the division of labor. They include such traits and behaviors as: efficiency, cooperation, adaptability, pointed toward group solution, helpful, effective intelligence, and enable group members to recognize their function. These address the technical and task problems that the group confronts and indicate members' efforts to undertake and solve problems of that kind.

However, humans do more than task or technical activities. They also act toward each other—something we call social relations. This is the arena in which the details of who gets how much of the available rewards and benefits and by what means are settled. Social relations differ analytically, and usually empirically, from technical activity.[3] In terms of this chapter, social relations are constituted wholly by the power and status dimensions. We now offer a provisional definition of power and status.

Power

We deem it useful to use Weber's (1946:181) definition of power, namely when actors are able to "realize their own will . . . even over the resistance of others." Thus, to have power in a relationship is to be able to coerce others to do what one wants them to do even when they do not want to do it. When compliance is obtained, it is involuntary. When there is a relatively stable power structure—that is, a relationship in which one actor reliably has more or higher power than the other actor(s)—we can predict that this actor will be able to obtain his or her way more often and in more domains than the other actor(s).

The ability to coerce others in this way depends on an arsenal of power tactics, which range from the horrific to those that are so subtle that they remain largely out of sight. Killing is the ultimate power tactic, but it is a boundary condition because it terminates the relationship between the killer and the killed and, therefore, removes the possibility of compliance. However, killing serves as a manifest threat to others by showing what will be done to them if they refuse to comply.[4]

Proceeding in some rough order of intensity, at the extreme high end, we can think of the infliction of physical pain—beating, scourging, slapping. Next comes physical confinement, which includes the whole repertoire of limitations on free movement. Also included are various forms of short-term control of the individual's space—pushing, shoving, blocking access, and so on. Additional physical means of coercion include cutting off vital resources for survival, such as food or air or water.

Further down the power scale, we see emotional violence, including screaming and shouting, as one form, and verbal abuse as another form. The latter includes insults and depreciation of the individual or the individual's identity groups or valued group symbols or beliefs. Yet further along are deprivations of customary or promised benefits and rewards, such as the parent's "grounding" an offending offspring or the denial of sex to a spouse or intimate other. Less apparent, but still power moves, are such tactics of verbal behavior as interrupting, talking-over, ignoring the other's topic, and refusing to discuss what the other wishes to discuss. The "silent treatment," whether used as a calculated snub or as an emotional rejection of contact, is also a form of power exercise.

All the above tactics and others that are related to them may be either initiated or threatened. In either case, the object is to obtain compliance when it is not forthcoming. Once compliance is obtained, the relationship begins to stabilize in power terms. The actor with more power—however achieved—is known to be willing to employ one or another tool of power to subject the other actor(s) to his or her will.

Once a power relationship has stabilized, power acts per se are relatively rare. This is because it is clear to the actor(s) with less power that he or she will be punished for rebelling or refusing to comply when asked for something. Under these circumstances, the individual will usually comply, even against his or her will, rather than receive punishment for noncompliance. Except in the most egregious cases, there are supervening institutional limits on how much power can be employed. Thus, although a parent has the right to spank his or her child, the parent is proscribed from holding the child's hand over a fire to obtain compliance.

Power is often exercised after the fact, so to speak, as a punishment for noncompliance. Punishment is designed to inform the actor who disobeyed that equal or worse punishment will follow further disobedience. Power tactics are also designed to weaken the will to be disobedient or to rebel. A nasty retort to a spouse informs him or her that there is a price to pay for repeating what has evoked the retort.

To this point, we have described tactics of overt power. They directly confront the other actor. Indirect forms of power are also available. These include manipulations such as deception and outright lies, which bring about the actor's compliance voluntarily, but on a false basis. Gossip and rumor are kindred forms. They enlist others who then shun or scorn the actor, thus depriving him or her of allies. The target is now weakened and made more likely to conform to the wishes of the actor who initiated the manipulation.

Status

In addition to the involuntary compliance that marks the social relations of power, there is authentic voluntary compliance. Actors willingly and gladly defer to, accept, approve, support, respect, admire, and, ultimately, love others without compulsion or coercion. We call this status-conferral or status, in brief. An actor with high status is one who receives many benefits and rewards from the other actor(s) in the relationship. Although status differentiation is endemic, the smaller the group, the less likely there will be large status differences among members.[5] In large groups, to use Collins's (2004) terminology, there are "central" members and "peripheral" members. The former are the focus of group attention and receive the most rewards; the latter are almost invisible and exist in a penumbra on the margin of the group, with little attention or interest directed toward them. As is the case with power, stable status relations generate a structure in which actors give and receive status according to a settled pattern.

In sum, status and power embody Empedocles' love and strife, respectively. Heuristically, they constitute what actors do with, to, for, and against each other in social relationships. Enacting power and status and the activities related to them—such as status-claiming and power-building, as will be discussed below—comprise, along with technical activity, an asymptotically complete program of what goes on in social life.

We now return to the second issue arising out of Carter's work, namely the connection between Carter's factors, Individual Prominence and Achievement and Group Sociability, and power and status. Individual Prominence and Achievement is identified by such items as authoritarianism, aggressiveness, leadership, forceful, bold, not timid, and confidence. Additional items include quick to take the lead, initiation and organization, alertness, and competence. This list leads us to judge that this is the power factor. Group Sociability lends itself easily to identification as the status dimension. The items that define this factor include sociability, behavior which is socially agreeable to group members, genial, cordial, well liked, and pointed toward group acceptance. We have thus linked Carter's empirical results with the power and status conceptual domain, thus providing an empirical basis for what originated as a philosophical speculation.

Because of the way in which power and status emerge in factor analytic studies, the two dimensions can be represented as orthogonal axes in a two-dimensional space. Any-and-all power and status relationships can be depicted in the space. An example is shown in Figure 4.1, in which A and B are any two actors. P_a and P_b are A's and B's power, respectively, and S_a and S_b are A's and B's status, respectively. (A more complex depiction of power-status relationships will be offered in the discussion of love relationships.)

Beyond Carter's early support for power-status theory, there is an abundance of empirical work that supports the model of two dimensions: small-group interaction analysis, cross-cultural

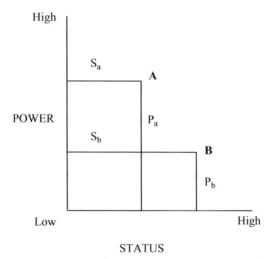

FIGURE 4.1. Power and Status Relationship Between Actors A and B.

studies of interaction and language, and semantic analysis. Details and supporting evidence are in Kemper (1978, 1990a, 1992) and Kemper and Collins (1990).

A continuing and encouraging source of support for power-status theory is featured in the work of two important and interlocked traditions of research in psychology: the Interpersonal Circle (IPC) and Five-Factor Model (FFM) approaches to personality. The IPC method (Freedman et al. 1951; Leary 1957) assesses personality in terms of two orthogonal dimensions, named Dominant-Submissive and Friendly-Hostile, both clearly cognate with power and status, respectively. Kiesler (1996) and Plutchik and Conte (1997) reviewed the broad range of IPC work.[6]

Five-factor model theorists declare five traits fundamental to human personality. They partition these into two that are interpersonal or social—Extraversion and Agreeableness—and three that are not deemed social—Neuroticism, Openness to Experience, and Conscientiousness (see McCrae and Costa 1989:586). Furthermore, the two social traits are considered equivalent to the IPC Dominance and Friendliness dimensions (Pincus et al. 1998) and, hence, also to power and status.

Going even further, McCrae (in Hofstede and McCrae 2004:74) asserted that the FFM "traits [including the power-status equivalents] are construed as *basic tendencies* that are rooted in biology" (emphasis in original). This reaches well beyond a sociologically less determinative view, but two bodies of collateral data cast some light here. First, given the evidence for specific physiological differences between different emotions (Funkenstein 1955; Gellhorn 1967, 1968) and given that power and status give rise to emotions (as will be detailed below), Kemper (1978) proposed that there is a necessary linkage between power and status, emotions and physiological processes, and thus a nexus between social relations and biology. Second, Chance (1976, 1988) and Waal (1982, 1988) have shown that power and status are fundamental in nonhuman primate behavior, thus providing a phylogentic ground for the biological anchorage of the power and status dimensions (see discussion in Kemper and Collins 1990).

Power and Status as Macrodimensions

Up to this point we have examined power and status as a model of microinteraction. Certainly, this is where power and status behavior are closest both to ordinary and scientific observations. However, power-status theory is applicable as well to large groups and to interaction between large groups and to the emotions generated both within and between large groups.

In order to achieve a better understanding of the power-status dimensions at the macrolevel, a change of terminology will be useful. At the societal level, we refer to power and status as issues of *freedom* and *justice*, respectively. These terms accommodate well to historical trends. Over a long period, as observed by Tocqueville (1945) and others, societies in the Western world and, increasingly, elsewhere have struggled toward the twin goals of moderating and regulating power (freedom) and providing for a just and equitable distribution of benefits (status). Social movements in fact are normally motivated by one or another of these interests (Kemper 2001). The intriguing question is whether or not such interests are reflected in the fundamental dimensions of societies.

Although there is not as much empirical work here as in face-to-face and other small-group settings, the results strongly suggest that the power and status dimensions are fundamental to interaction within any size group or between groups of any size. Kemper (1992) examined a set of studies dealing with fundamental dimensions of societies and of interaction between nation-states. Considerable complexity is observed at this level, but the essential technical activity and power (freedom) and status (justice) factors emerge. In sum, the power and status dimensions are grounded theoretically and empirically at both the microlevel and macrolevel.

Although technical activity, power acts, and status acts are the immediate "stuff" of social life, they do not fill up the whole social calendar. There are also metaprocesses devoted to gaining power or status and, sometimes, to reducing the other actor's power or status. We turn to some of these processes now.

RELATIONAL METAPROCESSES

In any given relationship, an actor might or might not be satisfied with his or her power or status standing vis-à-vis the other actor(s). When satisfied, the actor need only tread water, so to speak, to maintain that state. This may entail modest adjustments of conduct. When dissatisfied—this usually means a sense of insufficiency in the power or status dimensions—the actor is motivated to change either his or her standing or the standing of the other actor. This sets in motion processes for the enhancement (or reduction) of the power or status configuration of the relationship. These processes have not previously been identified as such,[7] but a review of some of them will reveal that they constitute what might be thought of as "social filler"—what individuals do in daily social interaction that is not task related or relational in the immediate sense (i.e., using power or conferring status).

Status Deficit

Probably the most frequent of the relational metabehaviors in social life is dealing with real or imagined status deficit. A status deficit refers to the feeling—it is an emotional state—that one is not receiving a suitable, appropriate, or deserved level of appreciation, respect, approval, acceptance, or love.[8] Depending on the institutional setting and its properties, the actor might engage in the following actions.

1. *Formal Attainment According to Universalistic Criteria.* In this option, the person seeks to enhance status through achievements that are universally regarded as deserving status. In modern societies, this would include obtaining educational credentials or other evidence of preparation for satisfactory or superior occupational performance. A bachelor's, graduate, or professional degree ensures higher status than lesser education in terms of more interesting work, higher pay, and acceptance into higher-prestige (status) circles. Correlative to this type of status attainment, the status level of the educational institution where one obtains one's credentials also matters. Schools with top standing confer their status on their graduates. More generally, any major occupational step-up or attainment—frequently marked by higher monetary reward—is a notice to others that one deserves more status, not only within the occupational setting but outside it as well. For example, because women in many cultures value male occupational achievement highly, such attainment has a sexual and reproductive payoff (Buss 1989). Because educational and occupational credentials often take years to acquire, to launch on such a path to improve one's status absorbs much interaction time.

2. *Normative Appeals.* In dealing with institutions, or in settings enduring long enough to develop an acknowledged tradition, the person with a felt status deficit may appeal to norms of fairness or justice. Formal or legal procedures might exist by which such claims can be adjudicated. In the United States, federal and state Equal Opportunity Commissions are vehicles through which normative claims of this kind can be pursued. However simple appeals—"That's not fair!"—addressed to group members or even superiors may be undertaken. All such appeals rely on the existence of accepted rules and guidelines for status conferral and for repair of deficits when they are brought to light.

However a different strategy might be called for in bureaucratic settings. Those who feel a status deficit might desist from pressing their case so as not to be viewed as "troublemakers" and thus even more likely to be denied deserved status in such settings.[9] The usual hope is that circumstances will change in some way—the boss might leave or have a heart attack and so pass out of the picture—so as to create an improved environment for status receipt.

3. *Extreme and Dangerous Attainments*. In informal groups, individuals who want to win more status might resort to extreme and often perilous gambits. This is a frequent tactic among adolescents who do not have the firm ground of high educational or occupational achievement to sustain their status ambitions. The wish to be found sexually attractive, a major status challenge, also fuels often unwise and sometimes fatal status-claiming actions.

4. *Claims to Insider or Expert Knowledge*. Anyone who can sustain a claim to inside knowledge about a topic of group interest is virtually guaranteed attention and appreciation for sharing that knowledge. The "inside dopester" of Riesman et al. (1952) amasses status capital in this way. The more private the knowledge, the better. Even if the individual lacks special knowledge, a mere stance of knowledge might suffice to earn some status. This is frequently established by the phrase "I know" when someone purports to share information presumably known only to the speaker. Even if this method does not earn status, it somewhat reduces the status of the speaker and thus keeps the status system more equilibrated according to the needs of the one who feels the deficit.

5. *Claims to Deep Experience*. The individual who can claim to have had a deep emotional experience is accorded a special regard. One simply raves about how good, great, excellent was the concert, the play, the movie, the restaurant, the trip, the date, the family occasion, and so forth or how deplorable, awful, lousy it was. Such expressions of extraordinarily deep feelings are often effective in gaining attention and regard. Sports talk, when not based on the "expert" enumeration of statistics about past performance, is often of this kind (e.g., "What a *great* play!") and is accompanied by the appropriate body language of amazement and intense appreciation.

6. *Early Adopter*. The person who is first to introduce a high-status fashion or practice into a group earns a certain standing. Leading others to what is becoming *au courant* is one version of this. Bolder, but more risky, is to stake out avant garde territory. Although this will certainly earn attention, it might also earn contempt from those whose status is invested in the status quo (no pun intended).

7. *Exemplary Conduct*. Each group has its purpose and its standards. To meet the standards in an exemplary way is to purchase status from group members. Those wishing to move up in standing often perfect their performance of group roles, removing any grounds for complaint and establishing their bona fides as devoted group members. This often involves outdoing other group members—a form of potlach.

8. *Humility*. A frequently successful tactic in gaining increased status is to desist from claiming it, despite the acknowledged or suspected legitimacy of the claim, thus indicating one's humility in the hope of being recognized for it. Humility also adds merit to support the original claim. Cinderella not only had the right-sized foot but also a history of uncomplaining dutifulness. Although the source of the deficit might be in a specific area—for example, one is not being recognized for one's talent—the status that is eventually earned might have to do with the humble character one presents. This is because groups ordinarily value outward harmony and undisturbed process and are willing to pay in status coin when someone with a legitimate complaint does not press that complaint, but waits for the group to come around on its own.

9. *Victimhood and Complaints*. In victimhood, the group is put on notice that it has a special case of deprivation that must be compensated. Such claims have their perils, especially if the putative victimizers are fellow group members, who might resist the designation and reduce the

putative victim's status even further. This metabehavior is more likely to succeed when the victim can claim to have been victimized by members of another group.

One of the most frequent vehicles for securing status is to voice complaints about an unfair, distressing, or terrible experience one had to endure at someone else's hands. It could be as banal as a traffic tie-up (Katz 1999) or as heartfelt as the rejection of one's pet ideas. What is sought is a sympathetic response from a listener (Clark 1997). Often the listener is a targeted person in this respect. It could be the spouse, who has the acknowledged role as emotional nurturer and fixer; or it could be a friend, with whom one exchanges roles, sometimes as complainer, sometimes as nurturer. Children seek this kind of solace from parents and, at a later point, from their friends. In fact, what marks a friend is precisely that one can reveal one's chagrin and status neediness to that person, who will, when the occasion presents itself, reciprocally avail himself or herself of the same privilege. In virtually all cases, the listener is a status-equal, as status superiors are likely to be uninterested and status inferiors likely to gloat.

10. *Jesting and Joking*. Some group members earn increments of status through entertaining the members with wit, jests, jokes, or humorous stories. Some of this might even be prepared in advance, the reverse of *esprit d'escalier*. Also, one might develop a reputation as a fount of humor. Although this might have nothing to do with the purpose of the group, it is often a highly desired social lubricant. Humor serves to bring all those who are entertained by it onto a more or less equal status plane for the moment while elevating the status of the person who can accomplish this (think of the jester in various Shakespeare plays). Although some levity is generally acceptable, some groups, taking themselves very seriously, deny status to anyone who attempts such status leveling.

11. *Nostalgia Retrieval*. One of the more enjoyable ways to pass time in social discourse is to retrieve the elements of a common past. These are fragments of shared biography that display ideal or idealized sectors of time. Recalling these in the company of those who were also there is to reexperience with them the features that contributed to their bond and, by recapturing those features, strengthen the bond in the present. As membership and solidarity mechanisms, they confirm the validity of the members' status. It works like a Durkheimian (Durkheim 1965) solidarity ritual, in the manner examined by Collins (2004).

12. *Games, Contests, and Recreational Activity*. Games, contests, and sports are simulacrums of social life. The elements of skill and contestation are played out in constructed settings where chance, as in real life, might also play a part. From chess to Scrabble, from baseball to tennis, from Monopoly to draw poker, players strive to win over other players. Gaining what?—status for being skilled and competent performers or for being extraordinarily favored by luck; that is, someone deserving status. When the game is played for real stakes, such as money, it is no longer a status exercise, but a power exercise.

13. *Boasting*. A dangerous route to status enhancement is through boasting of accomplishments or experiences that normally earn status, if true. Ordinarily, the boaster comes to be disbelieved and, hence, extruded from the group, except if membership is secure on other grounds (e.g., he is a member of the family).

Power Deficit

Power deficit is a threatening state, as can be surmised from the list of power tactics discussed earlier, to which one is vulnerable when one lacks sufficient power to defend oneself. It provokes metarelational activity to gain more power for the self or, what is essentially the same thing, reduce the power of the other.

1. *Dependency Reduction*. Emerson (1962) formulated a cogent statement of power and dependency: $P_{ab} = D_{ba}$ and $P_{ba} = D_{ab}$, which reads as follows: The power of *a* over *b* equals the dependency of *b* on *a* and the power of *b* over *a* equals the dependency of *a* on *b*. Although absolute independence is a theoretical option, it is not feasible, except in such fictions as *Robinson Crusoe*. Where a power-status structure exists, a reduction of dependency, by whatever means, leads to a reduction in the power of the other.

2. *Coalition-Building*. Where dependency reduction is not relevant or feasible, one can augment one's own power by recruiting allies who will either be guided by one's own strategies or will act independently against the one whose power is being opposed. Coalition partners can be variously motivated. When the potential partner has a grievance against a common enemy, the main task is to work out a satisfactory division of labor in conducting the struggle. However, when the potential partner has no prior interest in the conflict, the burden is to negotiate terms that will pay the partner enough to bring him or her into the fight. International diplomacy—including all those dinners—is substantially devoted to building and maintaining coalitions and power blocs.

3. *Bluffing, Propaganda, and Disinformation*. A common strategy when there is a power deficit is to attempt to deceive the other about one's true strength, making it seem as if one has more power than is the case. When successful, this nullifies some of the power of the other and can also be persuasive in recruiting coalition partners.

These examples of status claiming and power gaining by no means exhaust the field of such efforts. Taken together, these activities, which are separate from the direct enactment of power and status behavior, consume a sizable amount of interaction time that is also not technical or task oriented.

Provisionally, we have established a model of social relations both at the interpersonal and the intergroup levels, which is understandable in terms of power and status. Social life is also a fount of emotions, and an important benefit of power-status theory is that it enables us to predict the emergence and persistence of those emotions in terms of the dynamics of the two relational dimensions.

THE POWER-STATUS THEORY OF EMOTIONS

The power-status theory of emotions derives from the proposition that a "large class of emotions results from real, imagined or anticipated outcomes in social relationships" (Kemper 1978:43). Real outcomes are those that happen in "real time," so to speak (i.e., in the immediate framework of interaction, e.g., there is an insult and a consequent flare-up of anger). Imagined outcomes include those in fantasy scenarios of what-might-be or what-might-have-been or are recalled from past interaction (e.g., someone recollects a first kiss). Anticipated outcomes are those that are projected as a result of future interactions (e.g., tomorrow is my first day at a new job and I don't think the "old timers" will like me). Social relationships are power-status relationships—that is, actors who have a certain standing vis-à-vis each other in a space defined by the power-status dimensions.

We must now consider the matter of outcomes. What can occur when there is interaction in power-status terms? For simplicity, we will confine the analysis to the dyad. When actors A and B interact, 12 outcomes are possible: A's power can rise, decline, or remain the same; B's power can rise, decline, or remain the same; A's status can rise, decline, or remain the same; and B's status can rise, decline, or remain the same.

Given that both A and B have both a power and a status position, it should be apparent that any interaction between them will necessarily result in some combination of 4 of the 12 possible outcomes. For example, A's power might remain the same (0), A's status might decline (−), B's power might remain the same (0), and B's status might rise (+); or A's power might rise (+), A's status might remain the same (0), B's power might rise (+), and B's status might rise (+). For terminological purposes, we will refer to A's and B's power and status as relational channels.

Now combining and permuting the outcome possibilities among the 4 relational channels, we obtain a total of 81 possible sets of outcomes of social relations in any interaction episode, beginning with an increase in all 4 relational channels (+ + ++), through no change in any relational channel (0 0 0 0), and ending with decrease in all 4 relational channels (− − −−). By definition, 1 of the 81 possible outcomes will occur. This might seem a daunting number of outcomes to deal with and, thus, to inhibit work with such a theory of emotions. However, the following can be argued in mitigation.

First, if anyone has doubted that a "mere" two-dimensional model of social relations can handle the acknowledged complexity of human interaction and emotions, the multiplicity of outcomes just described should allay that concern. Second, given the complexity of interaction outcomes, the power-status model affords a useful entry point into the question of mixed emotions or mixed feelings. Not only is there an entry point but also, importantly, a theoretical explanation, namely the fact that interaction outcomes will always occur in four different relational channels and, thus, will always have the potential to produce four different emotions. Parenthetically, we note that one outcome is often regarded as dominant and hence reduces any interference, so to speak, from any less intense emotions that derive from what occurs in the other three relational channels. Third, as we will see below, emotions will be assigned to relational channel outcomes one relational outcome at a time; that is, each discrete emotion is assigned to a discrete outcome of a given relational channel. The link between relational channel outcome and emotion is stated unambiguously.[10]

Heuristically, we conceive of three types of emotion: *structural*, *anticipatory*, and *consequent*. We define structural emotions as those that result from a relatively stable power-status relationship, for example, as is usually the case between spouses or parents and children or between workers and their supervisors. This is not to say that such structures are frozen. Ongoing interaction will result in immediate outcomes that will tip the structure in one direction or another, but these will often be slight and only transient changes. For example, spouses might have an argument and their power-status positions might shift for a period, but then the couple will reconcile and return to the earlier structure. Thus, we can speak of structural emotions—those that prevail in relatively stable social relationships.

Anticipatory emotions result from contemplating future interaction outcomes. Such contemplation takes into account interactions of a similar nature in the past and especially their outcomes. This information will be factored into an appraisal of possible outcomes in the future interaction and an anticipatory emotion will result.

Consequent emotions result from immediate outcomes of ongoing interaction in power-status terms (e.g., an abusive spouse threatens his or her mate in an argument and the target feels fear). These emotions constitute the surface flux of emotional life, because they are often short term and most susceptible to change and variation with the ongoing flow of interaction.

Before turning to these three types of emotion, we introduce the concept of *agency*. Even given the complexity of 81 possible outcomes of any single interaction episode between actors A and B, the model thus far does not account for who is felt to be the party responsible for the outcome(s). We hypothesize three agents: *self*, *other*, and *third party*. Self and other are quite straightforward with regard to agency. Third party might be a person, or an abstraction, such as God, or fate, or luck, or "the way things are," thus indicating immutability or irremediability, as when someone dies. Emotions are likely to differ, as will be seen below, depending on who is regarded as the agent. The three possible agents also give us three possible directions for emotion: to self, other, and third party.

Structural Emotions

When there is a stable structure of social relations, we propose that there are also emotions that correspond to the position of the actors on the power-status dimensions. Here we do not speak of the outcome of interaction, as in the general presentation above, because the standing of the actors on the power-status dimensions is stable. To get at the emotions in this situation, we must formulate the question in terms of *excess*, *adequacy*, or *insufficiency*. This will allow us to offer hypotheses about the long-term emotions that are felt in stable social structures.[11] In dyadic interactions, each actor will have an emotion that derives from his or her own power, his or her own status, the other's power, and the other's status.

Power

Own Power Adequate.   When one is satisfied with the amount of one's own power, we hypothesize that the emotion is a feeling of *safety* or *security*. This has not been identified previously as a separate emotion and we propose that it is a subclass of the general sense of satisfaction or contentment. Contentment might not be consciously experienced and might only be detected or, better, recollected in the moment of its loss. Notwithstanding, having enough power to manage the relationship to one's satisfaction is one key to being content with the relationship. Importantly, one might not be content with the relationship overall because other relational channels are not satisfactory. Finally, with respect to the adequacy of one's own power, the notion of adequacy is relative and can be variably related to the absolute amount of power involved.

Own Power Excessive.   When one feels that one's own power is excessive, we hypothesize that the emotion is *guilt*. Guilt involves unpleasant feelings of ruefulness and remorse—a sense that one has wronged or oppressed another through one or another tactic of coercion. Moral standards from virtually all of the major religious traditions condemn transgressions that employ excess power—from killing to lying and cheating. Also, given that the moral sense, as used here, is often derived from a religious tradition, to violate the tradition and to experience guilt is to experience a desire for punishment as a means of atonement. Excess power can be exerted through any of the various power tactics discussed above.

Own Power Insufficient.   In a relationship in which one senses that one's own power is insufficient, we hypothesize that the emotion is *fear/anxiety*.[12] One is concerned that one cannot prevent the other from coercing one to do what one does not want to do. Given that the other might actually or potentially engage in such coercion, one's time horizon is importantly curtailed. "Anything can happen," because of one's weakness, and the sense of this augments fear/anxiety.

A realistic appraisal of this situation might suggest that other emotions are also likely in this situation (e.g., anger at the other and shame because of one's weakness). This is indeed true, but not accurately represented as stemming from the insufficiency of power; that is, anger and shame in such a situation derive not from the power dimension but from inadequacy in the status dimension. Because four relational channels are involved in every examination of emotion, we must include them all in order to understand the emotions that result from a given relationship structure. We will defer the discussion of anger and shame until we come to the status channel below.

Other's Power Excessive.   Although power is not entirely zero-sum, it frequently approximates such a condition. This allows us to see the level of other's power as reciprocal to the level of one's own power. Thus, the condition of other's power excessive is tantamount to own power insufficient. The emotion here would be *fear/anxiety.*

Other's Power Adequate.   On the basis of the reciprocity principle described above, other's power adequate is tantamount to own power adequate. The emotion would be *safety* or *security.* Because power is always a threat, it can be conjectured that there is a psychological disposition never to deem another's power adequate, but always, regardless of how much it is in absolute terms, excessive. Although this in fact may be a valid view, there are institutional frameworks that can impose normative standards and cause a reframing of what is considered adequate or excessive. For example, although employers might not care to have their workers represented by a union—a counterpower to their own power—they generally accept the union as a legitimate entity that has power to a certain degree in the employment setting.

Other's Power Insufficient.   The reciprocity principle makes other's power insufficient equivalent to own power excessive and the hypothesized emotion is *guilt.* Again, there might be some psychological resistance to such a notion, but the more or less zero-sum nature of power invites this rendering of the emotional landscape.

Status

Own Status Adequate.   When one senses that one's own status is adequate, one feels *satisfied,* *contented,* or *happy.* This might be a covert feeling that does not rise to consciousness, unless probed or attended to in reflection or in comparison with the emotional state of previous times or the emotional state of others in like situations. In relational terms, status adequacy means that one is receiving the amount of acceptance, regard, deference, and benefits that one feels one deserves.

Own Status Excessive.   When one senses that one's own status is excessive, we hypothesize that the emotion is *shame/embarrassment.* This must be understood as follows: As Goffman (1959, 1963) has well described, individual actors expend a fair amount of energy creating an image of themselves that will lead to acceptance in one group or another. The presented image constitutes, in our terms, a status claim (see discussion of metaprocesses earlier); that is, depending on how well polished and with what degree of éclat, it will earn deference, attention, approval, acceptance, and so on to a certain degree. As Goffman observed, group members are ordinarily prepared to accept each other's status claims more or less on faith because, in that way, the group can get on with its business without always having to check too deeply into members' credentials.

However, given that a status claim has been accepted, it is the member's duty to see that it is not tarnished by unworthy action. With respect to feeling that one has enjoyed excessive status, that clause has been violated. We speculate that shame/embarrassment might be an evolutionarily developed capacity to feel that one has wronged the group if one overvaluates oneself with other group members.

There are countless ways in which one can fall into shame/embarrassment: solecisms and faux pas, inadvertent revelation of discreditable information about oneself, failure to retort adequately to a jest at one's expense, being caught "backstage" (Goffman 1959) without one's pants on, so to speak, and so on.

We are now prepared to examine the difference between shame/embarrassment and guilt. The latter, as discussed above, is concerned with doing wrong to another via excess power, frequently in violation of a moral standard. The former is simply the sense that by acting as one did, one does not deserve to receive the amount of status one has claimed for oneself. In a given situation, one might feel one or the other of these emotions or both of them. However, it is important to keep them distinct, because they stem from different relational channels, and how one copes with these emotions might differ substantially.

Guilt, as indicated above, is absolved through punishment. Only when one has "paid for one's sins" can one feel that atonement has been made. In shame, on the other hand, one has acted discreditably. The solution here is not punishment (unless the incriminating act was also one of excess power), but compensatory action; that is, an act or actions that reinstate the person as one who deserves the amount of status originally claimed that has been lost. Thus, if someone acts in a cowardly manner and has thus brought shame on himself or herself, the solution usually is to engage in immoderately risky behavior to show that the act of cowardice was an aberration and not characteristic. The ultimate here is the Japanese response of *sepuku*.

Own Status Insufficient.   When one believes that one is not receiving one's status due from the other, the hypothesized emotion is a complex amalgam of *sadness-depression* and *anger*. In sadness-depression, one's focus is on the deprivation and one suffers from it in the same way that one suffers from a missed meal—hungry from the lack of sustenance. In anger, one's focus in on the unjustness of the deprivation and on the stupidity or malice of the other who deprived one of one's status deserts.

Whether sadness-depression or anger predominates is a matter of how agency or responsibility is assigned. This is to say, who is to blame for the insufficiency: self, other, or a third party? In the case of self as agent, the dominant emotion is sadness-depression. One simply could not "cut the mustard," as the expression has it. One failed to elicit status because one had not met the prevailing standards for status-conferral and it was one's own fault. When agency is assigned to the other—"he or she did this to me!"—the dominant emotion is anger. One's emotional force is directed toward the status-denier, the culprit. When third party is the agent and if the third party is another person or other social entity, then the resulting emotion is anger. If the third party is a condition, such as fate or any other irremediable situation, then the emotion is sadness-depression.

Other's Status Adequate.   Given the dyad, when other's status is adequate, it can only be because one is voluntarily according deference, benefits, attention, and so forth in sufficient amounts to the other. Of course, this is one's own judgment. The other might disagree. However, if this is the judgment, then one will feel *contented* or *satisfied*. As in the case of own status adequate, there will be no recognition of the emotion unless the matter is challenged in some way. Extending the setting beyond the dyad, we might suppose that if other members of the group are not according the target other his or her deserved status, then the fact that one is doing so might induce a certain invidious self-righteousness; that is, one is doing the "right thing" when others are not. If, on the other hand, one is giving less than others are, one might feel anger toward the others (third parties), who, by their acts, are impugning one's own status; that is, one is not acting in a status-worthy manner.

When modest amounts of status are involved, such as casual politeness according to the rules of manners or etiquette, very little is at stake. However when the amount of status is massive, as in the case of love (treated below), then contentment is too pale a version of what is felt; rather, delight and swooning at the opportunity to give to the other.

Other's Status Excessive. This would seem to be an odd and perhaps null category because, by definition, status is voluntarily given. We might suppose that uxoriousness partakes somewhat of the condition of excess status-conferral, or foolish doting. It is only by contrast with what is the usual amount of status conferred in such situations by others that one might come to judge one's own level as excessive. Here we might conjecture some internal debate as to whether, on the one hand, one is doing what one truly wants to do and that the amount one is conferring is truly deserved, and on the other hand, that one is somehow being coerced. This can be subtle. In the dyad, social relations require that if there is coercion, it came from the other. However, the actor himself or herself could be the coercer of himself or herself. Even without grounds, he or she might fear what the other might think or do if any lesser amount of status is given. Thus, the fear in this instance is the result of an imagined outcome. (See Kemper, 1978:381–382, for discussion of how any relational act may be partitioned between power and status components.)

Other's Status Insufficient. When other's status is insufficient, it is because one is not conferring it in adequate amounts. This can lead either to *guilt* or *shame/embarrassment*, or both. If the reason for the deprivation of the other is a power tactic by the self, it will lead to guilt. One has, after all, acknowledged that the other deserves more, but one has intentionally granted less. If the reason, on the other hand, for the deprivation is an inadequacy of the self, then the emotion is shame/embarrassment. The inadequacy here might be one of means (one simply does not have the resources) or of manners (e.g., one might be acting out of fear of what a third party will say if one conferred the proper and due amount of status on the other).

Anticipatory Emotions

Thinking, as Mead (1934) explained, involves a rehearsal of future events. When that future involves self and others in interaction, emotions are at least shadow outcomes of the interaction in the thought process. Because the actual interaction has not yet happened, there is a special set of emotions that reflects the fact of anticipation.

The anticipatory emotions are derived from two factors: *optimism-pessimism* and *confidence-lack of confidence*. Optimism-pessimism depends on the cumulation of all past experiences, especially outcomes of prior power-status interactions. A history of more or less successful interactions (i.e., where one has received status as desired and has had adequate power) leads to a general expectation of good outcomes, or optimism. Frequent failures in these areas lead to a general expectation of poor outcomes, or pessimism. Confidence depends on an appraisal of one's

TABLE 4.1. Anticipatory Emotions

Optimism		Confidence		Anticipatory emotion		Outcome	Emotion
						Favorable	Mild satisfaction
High	+	High	=	Serene Confidence	+		
						Unfavorable	Consternation
						Favorable	Strong satisfaction
High	+	Low	=	Guarded Optimism (anxiety)	+		
						Unfavorable	Mild disappointment
						Favorable	Mild satisfaction
Low	+	High	=	Grudging Optimism (anxiety)	+		
						Unfavorable	Mild disappointment
						Favorable	Astonishment
Low	+	Low	=	Hopelessness (anxiety)	+		
						Unfavorable	Resignation

resources in relation to the future interaction at issue. If the setting, the interaction partner, and other features augur success, then confidence ensues, otherwise, there will be lack of confidence. When the two variables are cross-classified, we postulate a set of anticipatory emotions, and when the actual outcome is factored in, the likely emotions at the end of the sequence. These are displayed in Table 4.1.[13]

Consequent Emotions

Consequent emotions result from immediate outcomes of interaction. A insults B and B feels anger. C compliments D and D feels happy; and so forth. However this is a deceptive simplicity. If A and B are in a relational structure in which A grants adequate status to B (from B's point of view) and B does not anticipate change, then B might be shocked by A's insult and the anger might be lessered while B tries to establish whether it actually was A's intention to be insulting. If C and D are in a relational structure in which D feels that C does not confer sufficient status and D does not anticipate a change, then the compliment might elicit satisfaction as well as astonishment and uncertainty as to its sincerity, which we consider to be a mild anxiety. Clearly, then, consequent emotions need to be considered as grounded in both structural and anticipatory emotions. This complicates the predictive task considerably.

Recall that we begin with 81 possible structural states of relationship between 2 actors. Then factor in the possible anticipatory emotional states, the possible states of agency, and the direction of the emotion (toward self, other, or third party). A complete theory must not shun any of these, but such a theory is presently out of reach. The measurement problem would be huge and to locate supporting evidence in the literature for a complete set of hypotheses is well nigh impossible.

As in all sciences, when such a degree of complexity is encountered, certain simplifying assumptions must be made. Kemper (1978) proposed several such shortcuts. One is to subsume the structural aspects of the relationship between the two actors under the rubric of a simple dichotomy: *liking* versus *disliking*. (Below we discuss liking in the context of love. Here it is sufficient to accept liking as a summary judgment on the felt adequacy of the overall power-status relationship as seen from the perspective of the focal actor with whom we are concerned.) This assumption reduces the number of emotional outcome cells by a factor of 4.

A second simplifying assumption is to accept the power-reciprocity principle discussed above, namely that an increase of one's own power is equivalent to a decrease in other's power and that a decrease in one's own power is equivalent to an increase in the other's power. This reduces by a quarter the remaining number of cells that must be addressed in hypothesizing consequent emotions.

A third simplifying assumption is to assume that under certain structural conditions, an outcome of interaction might not lead to a separate emotion, but only to an intensification or attenuation of the structural emotion already in place. For example, if one's status in the relationship is felt to be adequate, then an interaction outcome that continues the state of adequacy, without either gain or loss, could be expected to continue the satisfaction or contentment level already present. Gain would likely lead to an intensification of the prevalent emotion, whereas loss would lead to a different emotion. Parsing relational structures for these kinds of unremarkable outcome and excluding them further reduces the complexity of the predictive task.

Kemper (1978) provided hypotheses and supporting evidence for a reduced number of cells in a consequent-emotion matrix. The attempt establishes that although there is empirical work to support predictions for many cells in the matrix, numerous cells remain empty because there are no empirical findings to provide the basis for a hypothesis. Space does not permit more than a suggestion here of how this work is set up. The two examples given below, in which only the structural summary (indicated by the numbers 1 and 2) changes, display both the potential and the complexity of the analysis. The emotions proposed are hypotheses.

Relational Channel: *A's status*
B's Anticipatory Emotion: *Serene confidence*
Interaction Outcome: *Status loss by A*
Agent: *Third Party*
  1. Structural Summary: *Liking for A*
     B's consequent emotion directed to parallel: *Consternation, Sadness*
     B's consequent emotion directed to A: *Sympathy*
     B's consequent emotion directed to third party: *Anger*
  2. Structural Summary: *Dislike for A*
     B's consequent emotion directed to parallel: *Schadenfreude*
     B's consequent emotion directed to A: *Contempt*
     B's consequent emotion directed to third party: *Liking*

In order to obtain a full set of hypothesized consequent emotions, each of the defining conditions of structure—anticipation, relational channel, agency, and outcome—would need to be varied, and this is presently beyond our ability. Although the power-status theory of emotions begins with only two dimensions of relationship, the addition of only a few other elements takes the task of prediction to a high level of intricacy and specificity.

Love and Liking

Love and liking are elusive emotions—both in fact and in theory—and generally not addressed by sociological theories of emotions. Power-status theory is an exception.

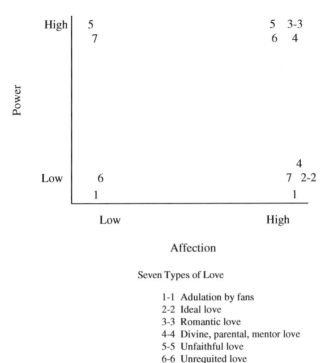

Affection

Seven Types of Love

1-1 Adulation by fans
2-2 Ideal love
3-3 Romantic love
4-4 Divine, parental, mentor love
5-5 Unfaithful love
6-6 Unrequited love
7-7 Parent-infant love

FIGURE 4.2. **Seven Types of Love Relationship.**

We begin with the recognition that love as an emotion stems from love as a relationship, which we define as follows: *A love relationship is one in which at least one actor gives, or is prepared to give, extreme amounts of status to another actor*. This definition says nothing about power, so we can assume that power can vary freely in love relationships. With this definition of a love relationship, we can generate seven ideal-typical versions of relationship in which at least one actor actually or potentially gives an extreme amount of status and power varies freely. The seven types are shown in Figure 4.2. We now label and discuss these briefly.

1. *Adulation by Fans.* In relationship 1-1, one actor gives extremely high status to another and neither has any power. This seems to approximate the swooning and adoration that fans lay on their icons. However it is also the way most love relationships begin; that is, one actor finds another actor worthy of receiving very large amounts of status. The other actor might not even be aware of the first.

2. *Ideal Love.* Relationship 2-2 shows that both actors are conferring extreme amounts of status upon each other and there is no power in the relationship. This is arguably the most blessed type of love, as each is voluntarily complying in the extreme with the other and there is no coercion. It is also a model for doctrinally inspired "brotherly (or sisterly) love" or for the vision of the peaceable kingdom, when the "wolf shall dwell with the lamb" (Isaiah 11:6). Whether this state can ever be attained as a general condition for humanity

is problematic. What is not problematic is that it is a transient state for two individuals. All who have experienced this state in a love relationship can testify that the bliss of this early stage does not last. It is no frivolity to assert that it is often a matter of moments and rarely lasts more than a few weeks.

3. *Romantic Love*. In relationship 3-3, we see the natural evolution of relationship 2-2, ideal love. Ideal love devolves into a relationship in which not only is there extreme mutual status-conferral, but also extreme power for both actors. We know that power enters love relationships when the actors feel that they cannot live without each other, that the other is not only a source of the greatest pleasure, but also often of the greatest pain.

   Ironically, power enters love relationships because of how good the actors feel in the ideal stage. Who would not want such delight to continue ad infinitum! Thus, one becomes dependent on the other for the continuation. However, as we know from Emerson's (1962) formulation, dependency on another puts one in the power of the other. Thus, the full-blown romantic love relationship entails both extremes of status-conferral and extremes of power. As with the ideal stage, relationships cannot remain forever at this stage. At best, the status-conferral remains high and the power decreases significantly, although probably not to zero.

   The adulation, ideal, and romantic types of love comprise the "attraction" phase of a long-term relationship. How the relationship develops from there and the problems—for now there *are* problems—that need to be addressed comprise the "maintenance" phase. Very specifically, fear and anger become more prominent and, sometimes, dominant emotions (see Kemper and Reid 1997).

4. *Divine, Parental, or Mentor Love*. In relationship 4-4, we find that both actors are receiving extreme amounts of status while one also has extreme power. This is the paradigm for a number of love relationships in which both actors give to the other, but only one is dependent on the other for what is given. Divine love is of such an order, in which although God loves humanity, God has all the power and the glory (status). On a less exalted plane, parenting, mentoring, and therapeutic relationships are of this type. In the best instances of these, the parent, mentor, or therapist loves the child, mentee, or client and the child, mentee, or client loves in return. However, the parent, mentor, or therapist holds power in the relationship because the other member of the dyad is dependent in an important way.

5. *Unfaithful Love*. In relationship 5-5, one actor retains extreme status and power while the other actor has only high power. This is one way in which a 3-3 romantic relationship can devolve. It is a model of infidelity, where the betrayed has (were all known) lost the status formerly given by the betrayer, who still receives high status. We know that the betrayed, despite the loss of status, has high power because the betrayer ordinarily wants to keep the infidelity secret, lest the betrayed use his or her power vengefully. If, in fact, the infidelity becomes known and the betrayed does not use his or her power, the relationship devolves even further and becomes the next type infatuation.

6. *Unrequited Love*. As shown in relationship 6-6, when one actor has all the power and status and other none, we can speak of infatuation. Against all sense or logic, the actor with no power or status continues to give (or is prepared to give) extreme amounts of status to the other, although there is little hope of recompense. This type of love is common among adolescents and also among adults with a pathological inability to seek satisfaction from someone who is likely to reciprocate.

7. *Parent-Infant Love*. Relationship 7-7 allows us to distinguish between two types of love involving parents. Prior to the kind of parent-child love that is modeled in relationship 4-4, there is parent-infant love. The neonate (and for some time after birth) receives extreme amounts of status. Whatever the infant needs for survival, at whatever cost, is given. However, the neonate gives nothing in return. Its cognitive and emotional capacities are too limited to recognize and to be grateful to the source of its survival. Although receiving no status, the parent has complete power over the infant and is capable of coercing the infant in any way the parent wishes; however, these "coercions" are usually for the infant's benefit.

These seven types of love relationship derive from power-status theory. They do not speak to the feeling or the "emotion" of love, to which we turn now. Because love involves the giving of extreme amounts of status, we must ask how that is possible, or why one would want to give anyone status in any amount, whether extreme or not.

Status, as defined, is voluntary compliance. Yet, in a manner that is not simply verbal byplay, voluntary compliance is *nonvolitional*. This conundrum can be explained as follows and depends on the seminal work of Hamblin and Smith (1966). These investigators studied the dynamics of status accorded to professors by students in academic departments. Their crucial finding was that when students held certain values or standards—for teaching, publication, mentoring, and so forth—and professors manifested excellence in these areas, students accorded them high status. However, the amount of status accorded followed the same mathematical model that accounts for nonvolitional psychophysiological responses. Hamblin and Smith daringly concluded that "having feelings of approval, respect or esteem for someone appears to be beyond the individual's direct choice" (p. 184). Importantly, this makes the psychological state behind status-conferral an emotion. Further, "as with all nonvoluntary responses, these feelings are presumably controlled by the unconditioned or conditioned stimuli which elicit them. Apparently, *an individual must provide the valued attributes and behavior which produce in the other the feelings of approval, respect or esteem; then and only then may these feelings be communicated as genuine status*" (p. 184, emphasis added).

In other words, if one has standards for certain behaviors, traits, or qualities, when another person displays these behaviors, traits, or qualities, the feeling of approval, esteem, and so forth comes automatically and nonvolitionally, unmediated by a process of choice. Thus, we have in Hamblin and Smith's approach a ground for understanding why any status in whatever amount is ever conferred at all. It is because someone displays a quality that matches a standard. Now we may ask how this applies to love, which entails the conferral of massive amounts of status.

We conjecture that standards are deeply held structural parts of personality and identity. They constitute us as actors in the world, providing us with evaluative guidelines so that we can measure experience and act in accordance with our valuations, whether it involves a matter of aesthetics, of culinary art, or of persons. By giving standards such an important place, we can better understand how individuals might respond with such enthusiasm and pleasure when standards are met.

When the standards are for beauty and character, they touch on fundamentals that are possibly evolutionary in origin and certainly culturally fostered from earliest childhood both by family models and by all of the agencies and media of socialization. What comprises and defines the attractive and good person, the one who promises to be an ideal mate or lover, is both an explicit and implicit topic in much informational and anecdotal talk and in literature, which depicts models of desirable and undesirable conduct.

Thus, armed with these standards, when we meet someone whose traits and qualities match those standards extraordinarily well, there is a nonvolitional response of approval, acceptance, respect, and so forth. The emotion has been described extensively in poetry. However, for present purposes, it can be understood as a certain *joy*, giddiness, or high spiritedness. It comes from having a rare experience, namely a match between oneself and the outer world. Consider that, ordinarily, we stand athwart the business and affairs of social life. There are misunderstandings, lack of consideration, indifference, failure to accommodate or acknowledge, cross-purposes, violence, and more. We are frequently rubbed the wrong way in all kinds of ways.

Then miraculously, it seems, someone appears who matches our standards for beauty, common sense, humor, ethics, and so on. How can we not respond! It is as if all contradictions are resolved, all contraries reconciled. The world is indeed a wonderful place if it has such people in it; and, *mirabile dictu*, he or she regards us in the same way. Joy! Joy! Joy! Thus, love is the status emotion carried to the extreme. We then voluntarily give, gratify, reward the other who has such qualities that match our standards so perfectly.

However, what of liking? Liking is often confused with love as if it were a lesser amount of the same commodity. However, it has long been recognized that there is another conundrum here, namely that one can love someone but not like him or her. This cannot be if liking is simply a lesser amount of love. The answer is that liking, like love, is also a status-related emotion, but, unlike love, it is not a response to the other's qualities, but *a response to the amount of status the other confers on us*. If someone pays us attention, esteems us, or rewards and gratifies us, it feels good. We want it to continue and we take pleasure in having that person near us. In sum, we "like" that person. We are pleased to have that person around us; we are available to him or her when he or she wants to see us. That person satisfies our need for attention and acceptance and we feel grateful. The emotion of gratitude in this incarnation is the feeling of liking. Of course, we can like someone without loving him or her, that is, their qualities do not match our standards (Kemper 1989).

We can love someone—because their qualities match our standards—but we might not like them, because they do not do much for us, literally. They do not reward or gratify us. However, because love is all about giving, it is indifferent to what one gets in return. It is important to understand that once love devolves into contingent reciprocity—one gives only if one gets—it is no longer love, regardless of the institutional formula or framework (e.g., marriage).

Postdicting Emotions

The power-status theory of emotions is couched in relatively plain language. This means that ordinary actors, without extensive training, can learn to examine their social encounters in power-status terms. Because everyone from an early age has used power (only saints have not) and has been on the receiving end of power, everyone is familiar with it. One has only to learn that the label applies to the structure of a relationship and to the range of behavior (the tactics) described above. Everyone is also familiar with status, often because of a felt sense of insufficiency of it. Thus, although power and status are technical terms in a scientific vocabulary, they are also easily accessible to anyone with a modicum of ability for abstraction and generalization.

Given that this is the case, we propose that the power-status theory of emotions is an easily acquired tool to help one better maneuver through the emotional shoals of social life. Here it is best to use the theory for predictive purposes; that is, in a Meadian type of rehearsal, one applies the theory to achieve or avoid specific interactional, ergo, emotional outcomes. Indeed, this is often a coping mechanism (Thoits 1990), although without benefit of a formal theory of emotions to guide the reflections. Often it is done exceedingly well and we praise the person who can do this. Of course, he or she is intuitively employing a theory of emotions to guide his or her examination of prospective behaviors and their probable outcomes. Presumptively, if the theory were made explicit, it would strongly resemble the power-status theory of emotions.

Often enough, we do not forecast events very well and there are emotional currents and outbursts that surprise us. We have somehow missed the cues or misunderstood them, either those of others or our own. We must now extricate ourselves from something of a mess; that is, at least for purposes of retaining our self-respect, we must understand what was going on and how it went wrong.

We propose that here, again, the power-status theory of emotions can be of use. It is a forward-running theory that links emotions to their social relational antecedents. However, there is no reason the theory cannot be run backward. If the emotion has already occurred, what was its social relational antecedent? What did you say or do or what did he or she say or do? What is the power-status structure within which what you said or did or what he or she said or did that conveyed a certain power or status implication and produced consequent emotions, the very ones that require explanation? Examples of this would be using the power and status dimensions to postdict emotions at the microlevel (Kemper 2004) and the macrolevel (Kemper 2002).

TESTS OF THE THEORY

Although the sociology of emotions has been prolific in producing theory, it has been scant in providing tests of theory. The power-status theory of emotions is not special in this regard. However, several tests have shown it to be nicely robust.

Kemper (1991) analyzed a portion of data collected in an eight-nation study of emotions by Sherer et al. (1986). These investigators asked subjects to describe the situations in which they had experienced four primary emotions: joy, sadness, fear, and anger. Respondents provided answers in the form of vignettes, varying in length from a few lines to a whole page. In two studies, Kemper tested the power-status theory of emotions with 48 cases from the West German sample.

In study one, two coders were trained in the power-status theory of emotions and given edited vignettes from which identifying labels or descriptions of the emotions themselves were removed; the coders only had before them the relational details of the situations that had produced the emotion. Their first task was to specify these details in power-status terms and then to identify the emotion. Although only four emotions were actually being reported in the data, the coders were encouraged to think that a full spectrum of emotions was involved. Altogether, the coders examined 192 vignettes (48 subjects times 4 emotions).

Twenty-two of the descriptions were judged nonsocial by one or both coders and these were omitted from coding.[14] An additional 8 situations were inadvertently omitted, leaving 162 situations. Using the known emotion to which the situations ostensibly pertained as the criterion, the two coders reached 74.6% and 69.7% accuracy in their judgments. Given that chance alone would have made for 25% accuracy, the results were highly encouraging.

Study two was undertaken in order to preclude the possibility that the coders had, entirely unaware, first detected the emotion in the episode and then translated it back into its theoretical power-status antecedents. A third coder was trained in power-status theory, without any intimation that it could be used to predict emotions. The coding task, in the 162 situations was simply to specify the power-status conditions there. In this "blind test," so to speak, the coder correctly specified 64.8% of the situations in power-status terms; that is, the coder identified the power-status conditions that theoretically should give rise to the emotion of the anecdote. Although the third coder's accuracy was slightly lower than that of the first two coders, it was sufficiently above chance to warrant the results as a successful test of the theory.

A second test of the power-status theory of emotions was undertaken by Simon and Nath (2004). Using a random sample of 1,346 cases from the emotions module of the 1996 General Social Survey (GSS), they undertook a competitive test between the power-status theory of emotions and the "normative" theory of emotions (Hochschild 1975, 1981). Simon and Nath derived hypotheses about males' and females' emotional experience based on the two approaches. The results were as follows: "Taken as a whole, our findings for emotional experience are more consistent with predictions based on Kemper's structural theory about emotion . . . than with Hochschild's normative theory about emotion" (p. 1168). The value of this confirmation of the power-status theory of emotions is that it demonstrates that the theory is sufficiently general to be applicable to domains other than what the theory specifically proposed.

A third investigation also supports the power-status theory of emotions in a competitive test—this time with Heise's (1979) Affect Control Theory (ACT). Although they are methodologically very different, the two theories share some common roots, principally the results obtained by the Semantic Differential (Osgood et al. 1957). The main substantive difference is that power-status theory relies on two factors and ACT relies on three. Power and status in the one theory is matched by potency and evaluation in the other. The third factor in ACT is activity, which we have suggested (Kemper 1978) might reflect the division of labor, but is not relevant for the prediction of emotions.

Robinson and DeCoster (1999) and Robinson (2002) compared predictions from the two theories, using a sample of undergraduate women who were asked to describe recent events that elicited a strong positive and strong negative emotion. The reported events were coded according to each theory and then the power-status codes were transformed into ACT codes in order to obtain a single coding metric. Results showed that both theories did well in predicting emotions, particularly along the potency and evaluation (i.e., power and status) scales. However, the two approaches also diverged, as follows: (1) ACT made predictions of all social events reported, whereas power-status theory had some missing cells according to the method employed in this analysis and therefore no predictions were available. (2) Where both approaches made predictions, power-status theory was somewhat more accurate, and this degree of accuracy did not depend on the subset of cases where ACT made predictions and power-status theory did not. As with the confirmatory findings of the Simon and Nath study, these results demonstrate that power-status theory can be adapted to research questions that are distant in type and approach from what the original statement of the theory proposes.

RESEARCH AGENDA

Kemper (1990a) proposed three items for a research agenda for the power-status theory of emotions that are of continuing interest: universality, social relational precedence, and sociophysiological integration.

Universality

A fundamental assumption of the theory is that the power-status antecedents of specific emotions apply universally across the spectrum of social and demographic categories (e.g., sex, race, ethnicity, social class, and so forth). Heuristically, it is plausible to think that at least what might be thought of as primary emotions—fear, anger, depression, and happiness-contentment—are connected in the same way to social relational outcomes in all social categories and groups. This position is based in part on the communication or signal function of emotions (Buck 1984).

Were the primary emotions to vary in their relational precursors, considerable social ambiguity would result. It would be hard to understand the social state and feelings of a person in a different social category from one's own, and this would make problematic which emotion might, in an evolutionary sense applying to all humans, have emerged. In addition, it would confute one of our best understandings of why emotion is expressed to a great extent by the face and in visible body movements.

Another reason to support the universality assumption is that virtually everyone has multiple memberships and identities; hence, each is a member of overlapping social categories—for example, a lower-class Italian white male, a middle-class English black female, and so forth. Were the emotional effects of power and status outcomes to vary greatly by social category, it would be difficult to reconcile the effect of different categories on the experience of emotion in given relational situations.

Social Relational Precedence

The assumption here is that emotions result from outcomes of power and status relations and not from cultural imposition. This means that when another person uses power against us, we are going to feel fear, even if cultural fiat were to dictate another emotion, such as joy. Although it might seem odd to contemplate that culture would somehow wish to substitute joy for fear—this is an extreme example—it is a fact that culture has sought to direct emotional response away from what power and status outcomes would entail *naturally*. Think of how a puritanical sex code can insist on disgust as a response to sexual stimuli. The work here must investigate whether and to what degree and with what consequences culture can mediate or transform emotions that would ordinarily arise from power-status outcomes.

Sociophysiological Integration

This assumption is that power and status are linked, via emotions, to underlying physiological processes, thus indicating a theoretical arc between the biological and the social. The research in this area needs to be directed to the general question of specificity of physiological patterns both in emotion and in the experience of power and status. Sociologists have in general shunned physiological issues, although see Robinson et al. (2004). A model for such work can be found in Kemper (1990b), in which outcomes in the power and status dimensions, renamed dominance and eminence, are seen to produce hormonal changes, specifically in testosterone levels.

CONCLUSION

Power-status theory is a deceptively simple formulation about what actors do to, with, for, and against each other in social interaction. However, from only these two dimensions, which have strong empirical support, it is possible to generate quite complex examinations of emotions across a very broad spectrum of social situations.

When power and status actions and outcomes stabilize into a continuing structure, we can assign what we call structural emotions, which are based on actors' power and status positions vis-à-vis each other in the structure. In the normal course of ongoing interaction, actors look ahead to the outcomes of future interactions and develop expectations, based on past power and status outcomes and future power and status contingencies. These expectations give rise to what we call anticipatory emotions. Structural emotions and anticipatory emotions provide an orienting context within which what we call consequent emotions occur. These are the emotions instigated by immediate interaction outcomes in power and status terms. Together, structural, anticipatory, and consequent emotions provide a comprehensive account of emotions in social life when looked at from a relational perspective.

NOTES

1. A third dimension, technical activity, is also present, but because it does not lead directly to the power-status theory of emotions, it will receive less attention in this chapter. Kemper (1995) contains an extended discussion of how technical activity, power and status, and other constructs contribute to a social psychological understanding of social structure.
2. Unlike Freud, no modern social scientist has acknowledged Empedocles' prior discovery.
3. Although technical activity, on the one hand, and power and status, on the other hand, are analytically distinct, there can be empirical overlap between the two. For example, a carpenter might ask a fellow carpenter for a tool in one of several ways: casually, politely, formally, peremptorily, and so on. This example is elaborated in Kemper and Collins (1990).
4. Although killing is usually dedicated to such power interests, at least one genocide, namely the Holocaust, was undertaken simply for an ideological purpose. It was not intended to prevent the Jewish victims from frustrating the Nazi drive to realize "their own will," nor even as a demonstration to cow other people into submission.
5. In a chilling rejection of what might be thought of as the most likely case of status equality, the French poet Charles Baudelaire (1983:23–24) wrote, "Love greatly resembles an application of torture or a surgical operation." Even if "two lovers love passionately and are full of mutual desire, one of the two will always be cooler or less self-abandoned than the other. He or she is the surgeon or executioner; the other, the patient or victim."
6. Although varying nomenclature is employed in different IPC studies, examination of the items that define the two dimensions supports their identification as power and status. Among them are assertiveness and likeability; control and affection; autonomy versus control and love versus hostility; dominance and friendliness; control and affection; interpersonal deprivation and interpersonal seeking; tendency to use socially unacceptable techniques and tendency to use socially acceptable techniques equal versus unequal and cooperative and friendly versus competitive and hostile; and up-down and positive-negative. Sources for these factor names can be found in Kemper (1991:333).
7. In fact, they might need a Goffman, as in his "Presention of Self in Everyday Life" (1959), to do them justice. His forte was to detect subtle nuances in social life.
8. The underlying emotions here are depression or anger. This is discussed in the power-status theory of emotions below.
9. Even if one tries the strategy of "exit" (Hirschman 1970), in relatively closed circles, such as academic departments in a given discipline, someone labeled as a troublemaker usually has difficulty obtaining a new post after being so labeled.
10. When multiple or mixed emotions occur, it is not clear how physiological processes accommodate this state.
11. Evidence for these hypotheses is cited extensively in Kemper (1978).
12. Although many investigators distinguish between fear and anxiety, we will not do so because the distinction is not germane here.
13. Table 4.1 is from Kemper (1978:75).
14. For example, more than a few respondents chose dangerous driving conditions (e.g., icy roads) for their fear situation.

REFERENCES

Baudelaire, Charles. [1930] 1983. *Intimate Journals*. Translated by Christopher Isherwood. San Francisco: City Lights.
Buck, Ross. 1984. *The Communication of Emotion*. New York: Guilford.

Buss, David H. 1989. "Sex Differences in Human Mate Preferences: Evolutionary Hypotheses Tested in Thirty-Seven Cultures." *Behavioral and Brain Sciences* 12: 1–49.

Carter, Launor F. 1954. "Evaluating the Performance of Individuals as Members of Small Groups." *Personnel Psychology* 7: 477–484.

Chance, Michael R. A. 1976. "Social Attention: Society and Mentality." Pp. 315–333 in *The Social Structure of Social Attention*, edited by M. R. A. Chance and R. R. Larsen. London: Wiley.

———. 1988. "Introduction." Pp. 1–35 in *Social Fabrics of the Mind*, edited by M. R. A. Chance. Hillsdale, NJ: Erlbaum.

Clark, Candace. 1997. *Misery and Company: Sympathy in Everyday Life*. Chicago: University of Chicago Press.

Clark, R. A. 1953. "Analyzing the Group Structure of Combat Rifle Squads." *American Psychologist* 8: 333.

Cleve, Felix M. 1969. *The Giants of Pre-Sophistic Greek Philosophy: An Attempt to Reconstruct Their Thought*. The Hague: Nijhoff.

Collins, Randall. 2004. *Interaction Ritual Chains*. Princeton, NJ: Princeton University Press.

Couch, Arthur, and Launor F. Carter. 1952. "A Factorial Study of the Rated Behavior of Group Members." Paper read at Eastern Psychological Association, Boston, MA.

Durkheim, Emile. [1912] 1965. *The Elementary Forms of the Religious Life*. New York: Free Press.

Emerson, Richard. 1962. "Power-Dependence Relations." *American Sociological Review* 40: 252–257.

Freedman, Mervin B., Timothy Leary, Abel G. Ossorio, and Hubert S. Coffey. 1951. "The Interpersonal Dimensions of Personality." *Journal of Personality* 20: 143–161.

Freud, Sigmund. [1937] 1959. "Analysis Terminable and Interminable." Pp. 316–357 in *Collected Papers*, Vol. V. Translated by Jon Riviere. New York: Basic Books.

Funkenstein, Daniel. 1955. "The Physiology of Fear and Anger." *Scientific American* 192: 74–80.

Gellhorn, Ernst. 1967. *Principles of Autonomic-Somatic Integration: Physiological Basis and Psychological and Clinical Implications*. Minneapolis: University of Minnesota Press.

———. 1968. "Attempt at a Synthesis: Contribution to a Theory of Emotion." Pp. 144–153 in *Biological Foundations of Emotion: Research and Commentary*, edited by E. Gellhorn, Glenview, IL: Scott, Foresman.

Goffman, Erving. 1959. *The Presentation of Self in Everyday Life*. Garden City, NY: Doubleday.

———. 1963. *Behavior in Public Places*. New York: Free Press.

Goldberg, Lewis R. 1990. "An Alternative 'Description of Personality': The Big-Five Factor Structure." *Journal of Personality and Social Psychology* 59: 1216–1229.

Hamblin, Robert L., and Carole R. Smith. 1966. "Values, Status and Professors." *Sociometry* 29: 183–196.

Heise, David R. 1979. *Understanding Events: Affect and the Construction of Social Action*. New York: Cambridge University Press.

Hemphill, John, and Alvin Coons. Undated. *Leadership Behavior Description*. Columbus, OH: Personnel Research Board, Ohio State University.

Hirschman, Albert O. 1970. *Exit, Voice and Loyalty: Responses to Decline in Firms, Organizations and States*. Cambridge, MA: Harvard University Press.

Hochschild, Arlie R. 1975. "The Sociology of Feeling and Emotion: Selected Possibilities." Pp. 208–307 in *Another Voice: Feminist Perspectives on Social Life and Social Science*, edited by M. Millman and R. M. Kantor. New York: Anchor Books.

———. 1981. "Attending to, Codifying, and Managing Feelings: Sex Differences in Love." Pp. 225–262 in *Feminist Frontiers: Rethinking Sex, Gender and Society*, edited by L. Richardson and V. Taylor. Reading, MA: Addison-Wesley.

Hofstede, Geert, and Robert R. McCrae. 2004. "Personality and Culture Revisited: Linking Traits and Dimensions of Culture." *Cross-Cultural Research* 38: 52–88.

Katz, Jack. 1999. *How Emotions Work*. Chicago: University of Chicago Press.

Kemper, Theodore. 1978. *A Social Interactional Theory of Emotions*. New York: Wiley.

———. 1989. "Love and Like and Love and Love." Pp. 249–268 in *Emotions, Self and Society: Essays and Research Papers in the Sociology of Emotions*, edited by D. Franks and E. D. McCarthy. Greenwich, CT: JAI Press.

———. 1990a. "Social Relations and Emotions: A Structural Approach." Pp. 207–237 in *Research Agendas in the Sociology of Emotions*, edited by T. D. Kemper. Albany, NY: State University of New York Press.

———. 1990b. *Social Structure and Testosterone: Explorations of the Socio-Bio-Social Chain*. New Brunswick, NJ: Rutgers University Press.

———. 1991. "Predicting Emotions from Social Relations." *Social Psychology Quarterly* 54: 330–342.

———. 1992. "Freedom and Justice: The Macro-Modes of Social Relations." *World Futures* 35: 141–162.

———. 1995. "What Does It Mean Social Psychologically to Be of a Given Age, Sex-Gender, Social Class, Race, Religion, etc.?" *Advances in Group Processes* 12: 81–113.

———. 2001. "A Structural Approach to Social Movement Emotions." Pp. 58–73 in *Passionate Politics: Emotions and Social Movements*, edited by J. Goodwin, J. Jasper, and F. Polletta. Chicago: University of Chicago Press.

————. 2002. "Predicting Emotions in Groups: Some Lessons from September 11." Pp. 53–68 in *Emotions and Sociology*, edited by J. Barbalet. Oxford: Blackwell/The Sociological Review.

————. 2004. "For a Good-Enough Theory of Emotions, Post-Diction Is Good Enough." Paper presented at August meetings of the American Sociological Association, San Francisco.

Kemper, Theodore, and Randall Collins. 1990. "Dimensions of Microinteraction." *American Journal of Sociology* 96: 32–68.

Kemper, Theodore D., and Muriel T. Reid. 1997. Love and Liking in the Attraction and Maintenance Phases of Long-Term Relationships." *Social Perspectives on Emotions* 4: 37–69.

Kiesler, Donald J. 1996. *Contemporary Interpersonal Theory and Research*. New York: Wiley.

Leary, Timothy. 1957. *The Interpersonal Diagnosis of Personality*. New York: Ronald.

McCrae, Robert R., and Paul T. Costa. 1989. "The Structure of Interpersonal Traits: Wiggins's Circumplex and the Five-Factor Model." *Journal of Personality and Social Psychology* 56: 586–595.

Mead, George H. 1934. *Mind, Self and Society*. Chicago: University of Chicago Press.

Office of Strategic Services Assessment Staff. 1948. *Assessment of Men*. New York: Rinehart.

Osgood, Charles H., George C. Suci, and Percy H. Tannenbaum. 1957. *The Measurement of Meaning*. Urbana: University of Illinois.

Pincus, Aaron L., Michael B. Gurtman, and Mark A. Ruiz. 1998. "Structural Analysis of Social Behavior (SASB) Circumplex Analysis and Structural Relations with the Interpersonal Circle and the Five-Factor Model of Personality." *Journal of Personality and Social Psychology* 74: 1629–1645.

Plutchik, Robert, and Hope R. Conte. 1997. *Circumplex Models of Personality and Emotion*. Washington, DC: American Psychological Association.

Riesman, David, Nathan Glazer, and Ruell Denny. 1952. *The Lonely Crowd*. Garden City, NY: Doubleday Anchor.

Robinson, Dawn T. 2002. "ACT and the Competition: Some Alternative Models of Emotion and Identity." Paper presented at the Conference on Research Agendas in Affect Control Theory, Highland Beach, Florida.

Robinson, Dawn T., and Vaughn A. DeCoster. 1999. "Predicting Everyday Emotions: A Comparison of Affect Control Theory and Social Interactional Theory." Paper presented at annual meetings of the American Sociological Association in Chicago.

Robinson, Dawn T., Christabel L. Rogalin, and Lynn Smith-Lovin. 2004. "Physiological Measures of Theoretical Concepts: Some Ideas for Linking Deflection and Emotions to Physical Responses During Interaction." *Advances in Group Processes* 21: 77–115.

Sakoda, James M. 1952. "Factor Analysis of OSS Situational Tests." *Journal of Abnormal and Social Psychology* 47: 843–852.

Sherer, Klaus R., Harld G. Wallbott, and Angela B. Summerfield. 1986. *Experiencing Emotion: A Cross-Cultural Study.* Cambridge: Cambridge University Press.

Simon, Robin W., and Leda E. Nath. 2004. "Gender and Emotion in the United States: Do Men Differ in Self-Reports of Feelings and Expressive Behavior?" *American Journal of Sociology* 109: 1137–1176.

Spearman, Charles E. 1904. "General Intelligence, Objectively Determined and Measured." *American Journal of Psychology* 15: 201–293.

Thoits, Peggy A. 1990. "Emotional Deviance: Research Agendas." Pp. 180–203 in *Research Agendas in the Sociology of Emotions*, edited by T. D. Kemper. Albany, NY: State University of New York Press.

Thurstone, Louis L. 1934. "The Vectors of the Mind." *Psychological Review* 41: 1–32.

Tocqueville, Alexis de. [1835] 1945. *Democracy in America*, Vol. 1. New York: Vintage.

Waal, Frans B. M. de. 1982. *Chimpanzee Politics: Power and Sex among the Apes*. London: Counterpoint.

————. 1988. "The Reconciled Hierarchy." Pp. 105–136 in *Social Fabrics of the Mind,* edited by M. R. A. Chance. Hillsdale, NJ: Erlbaum.

Weber, Max. 1946. *From Max Weber: Essays in Sociology*. Translated and edited by H. H. Gerth and C. W. Mills. New York: Oxford University Press.

Wherry, Robert J. 1950. *Factor Analysis of Officer Qualification Form QCL-2B*. Columbus, OH: Ohio State University Research Foundation.

Willer, David, and Murray Webster, Jr. 1970. "Theoretical Constructs and Observables." *American Sociological Review* 35: 748–757.

Wright, M. R. 1981. *Empedocles, the Extant Fragments*. New Haven, CT: Yale University Press.

CHAPTER 5

Cultural Theory and Emotions

GRETCHEN PETERSON

One defining element of the study of emotions has been the emphasis on the critical role of culture. From Goffman's (1961) early work on the encounter, through Hochschild's (1979, 1983) work on feeling rules and emotional labor and Gordon's (1990) work on emotional socialization, culture has been paramount to our understanding of emotions. Culture is an important element in definitions of emotions, emotional socialization, and emotional labor. The purpose of this chapter is to review cultural theorizing on emotions, discuss relevant research in this area, and provide direction for future work. The chapter begins by examining the critical role that culture plays in basic processes of labeling or defining our emotional experiences. In labeling our emotions, we must draw from our society's emotion culture. The next section of the chapter examines the concept of emotion culture and how people are socialized into their particular emotion culture. Even emotionally competent actors who have been socialized must still work at managing their emotions to fit with society's expectations. Following a discussion of emotional socialization is an examination of processes of emotion management and emotional deviance. Finally, the chapter concludes by examining how emotion management has moved into the arena of work and become part of our working lives. Throughout this chapter, it should be evident that much of our emotional experience is at the very least impacted, if not determined, by culture.

In recent work reviewing dramaturgical and cultural theorizing on emotions, Turner and Stets (2005) highlighted the work of Goffman (1961, 1983), Hochschild (1979, 1983), Rosenberg (1990, 1991), Thoits (1990), and Clark (1997). They further examined subsequent empirical work that utilized the concepts first introduced by these researchers. This chapter draws from Turner and Stets (2005), yet builds on their work by incorporating additional theoretical and empirical work relevant to cultural theorizing on emotions.

GRETCHEN PETERSON • Department of Sociology, California State University, Los Angeles, CA 90032

I would like to thank Jan Stets for her tremendous support and advice on this chapter. Her assistance and patience are both greatly appreciated.

DEFINING EMOTIONS

Culture is fundamental even to our understanding of what constitutes an emotion. Gordon (1981) distinguished between biological emotions and social sentiments. He referred to biological emotions as more of a psychological concept, which involves the bodily sensations and gestures in response to some emotional stimuli. On the other hand, a social sentiment introduces the importance of culture and is defined as "a socially constructed pattern of sensations, expressive gestures, and cultural meanings organized around a relationship to a social object, usually another person" (Gordon 1981:566). Social sentiments are thus more so a sociological concept because the sentiments are defined by culture and require socialization to be learned by individuals.

Both Gordon (1981) and Thoits (1990) described four components to an emotional experience. Gordon (1981) argued that emotions are composed of (1) bodily sensations; (2) expressive gestures; (3) social situations or relationships; and (4) emotion culture of a society. Along these same lines, Thoits (1990) described the components of an emotional experience as the appraisal of a situational stimulus, changes in bodily sensations, displays of expressive gestures, and cultural meanings. For both Gordon (1981) and Thoits (1990), the emotion culture or cultural meanings impacts each of the other three components.

In both of their conceptions, bodily sensations refer to physiological changes or feelings of arousal. These feelings of arousal are common across many emotions, so arousal alone is generally not sufficient to determine which emotion is being experienced. Cultural definitions come into play in defining how a particular pattern of arousal or physiological changes should be labeled. For example, cultural knowledge is important in determining whether a rapid heart rate is symptomatic of excitement or fear in a given situation.

The expressive gestures component is composed of facial expressions, bodily displays, and instrumental actions. As with changes in bodily sensations, expressive gestures can also be ambiguous. Although Ekman (1982) and Izard (1977) have described certain universal facial expressions for basic emotions, these universals do not exist for most emotions. Furthermore, the same expression might indicate different emotions. For example, a person might smile when he or she is nervous as well as happy. In addition to this ambiguity, there are also cross-cultural differences in expressive gestures. Wierzbicka (1999) described the differences between Polish and Americans in terms of expressions of sincerity. In the United States, people are expected to smile in general encounters. On the other hand, Polish people only expect smiling as a sincere expression of happiness. This example highlights the importance of culture in connecting an expressive gesture to its corresponding emotion.

THE SELF AND EMOTIONS

In his work on the looking-glass self, Cooley (1964) linked emotional reactions with the conception of the self. Cooley argued that feelings of pride or shame result from individuals' perceptions of how they appear to others and how others are believed to judge that appearance. Although Cooley did not explicitly deal with culture in his theory, his work sets the stage for later theorizing, which incorporates culture into understanding the link between emotions and the self.

This connection between the self and emotions is exemplified in the work of Rosenberg (1990, 1991). Rosenberg's discussion of reflexivity not only explains the self-emotion link but also explains the impact of culture on emotional identification and emotional displays. In terms of this self-emotion link, Rosenberg discussed the connection between reflexivity and emotions. Reflexivity involves the ability of individuals to see themselves as objects and act back upon themselves. Rosenberg emphasized two types of reflexivity as particularly important. The first type is cognitive reflexivity, and this involves bringing any type of cognition (memory, perception, and so forth) to bear upon the self as an object. The other type, reflexive agency, involves becoming an active agent in producing an outcome for the self.

Cognitive reflexivity can impact one's interpretation of the physiological arousal that accompanies emotional responses, and this cognitive reflexivity includes a strong cultural component. Rosenberg argued that because people's internal arousal is often ambiguous, they must look for clues from the external environment to make sense of their arousal. The same physiological responses can yield very different emotions, and it is also possible that individuals might experience multiple emotions simultaneously. Because of these ambiguities, people must think about their emotions, and this, of course, involves cognitive reflexivity. This cognitive reflexivity draws on causal assumptions, social consensus, and cultural scenarios as the content for the cognitions that impact emotional identification. These are essentially elements of a society's emotion culture, which are acquired through socialization and applied to our emotional experiences.

Although cognitive reflexivity is critical to emotional identification, the impact of reflexive agency is particularly evident in the management of emotional displays. In this case, reflexivity leads us to manage these displays using verbal devices, facial and physical expressions, and physical objects. This involves reflexive agency since an individual acts upon themselves or their environment to produce an emotion management outcome for the self. Rosenberg (1991) further argued that individuals have varied reasons for engaging in emotional display. The first reason is to demonstrate conformity with norms. This lends a moral character to our actions. Another reason for emotional display is as a means toward obtaining some outcome or goal. This lends a tactical element to some emotional displays. Overall, through its emphasis on cultural scenarios, Rosenberg's work supports the contention that culture is critical for understanding emotional experiences and their connection to the self.

CULTURAL CONTENT

Rosenberg's (1990, 1991) work establishes that culture is critical to identifying and displaying our emotions. The next issue that needs to be addressed is an examination of the structure of these cultural scenarios or cultural scripts. Turning now to the work of Goffman (1959, 1961, 1967) allows for a more thorough discussion of the elements that comprise a cultural script. Goffman's dramaturgical approach is an inherently cultural approach. Goffman compared much of social interaction and social life to a dramatic production. Actors put on a performance, which involves invoking cultural scripts in order to create their performance. Goffman's work also described how we use emotions as cues in analyzing interactions as well as how we react emotionally to an interaction.

Goffman's (1959) discussion of the presentation of self outlined not only the idea of interaction as theatrical production, but it also described the aspects of the situation that individuals examine when determining the appropriate cultural script. The four aspects of the situation that people look for when determining how an interaction will proceed include the conduct and appearance of people, the setting, what individuals say about themselves, and past experience with individuals. In other words, people look at the appearance and behavior of others in order to guide their interactions. One aspect of the appearance of others is their emotional displays. These displays are examined as a clue to understanding an interaction. Particularly in an unfamiliar setting, observing the behavior and emotional displays of others can provide essential information on the interactional dynamics expected in the particular situation. Additionally, the location of the interaction can be used to determine the interactional expectations. For example, in a university setting, one expects to encounter students, professors, and staff. Knowing this, a person can draw from their cultural scripts to engage in behavior appropriate to the people present in that location. Finally, as one has experiences with others in an interaction, others' vocalizations and our past experience with those others provide clues to the interaction. All of these factors guide people in their choice of cultural script for their interactions.

The cultural and emotional aspects of Goffman's work are also particularly evident in his discussion of the encounter. According to Goffman, an encounter involves the following elements:

> "(1) a single visual and cognitive focus of attention; (2) a mutual and preferential openness to verbal communication; (3) a heightened mutual relevance of acts; (4) an eye-to-eye ecological huddle that maximizes each participant's opportunity to perceive the other participants monitoring of him; (5) participants' presence tends to be acknowledged through expressive signs and a 'we rationale' is likely to emerge; (6) ceremonies of entrance and departure are likely to be employed; (7) a ritual and ceremonial punctuation of openings, closings, entrances, and exits; (8) a circular flow of feeling; and (9) procedures for corrective compensation of deviant acts" (1981:18).

Culture plays a role in each element of the encounter. It defines the focus of attention, it enables verbal communication, it delineates perceptions, it creates solidarity, it proscribes entry and exit rituals, and it constructs ritualized procedures concerning deviance. These cultural constructions also contribute to the emotional aspects of the encounter. The expressive displays of the encounter contribute to the feelings of solidarity. In addition, the encounter involves the flow of feelings among participants within the encounter.

Goffman's (1983) later work situated this focused encounter within larger cultural settings. Encounters are embedded within gatherings (assemblies of individuals within a space), which are embedded within social occasions. Within each level of interaction, cultural scripts serve to orient actors. These cultural scripts are composed of a number of dimensions: (1) form of talk; (2) use of rituals; (3) framing; (4) use of props; (5) categorization of the situation; (6) role-making; and (7) expressiveness. According to Goffman (1983), the cultural scripts utilized in interaction include proscribed emotions appropriate to the interaction. In particular, Goffman's inclusion of expressiveness among the dimensions of cultural scripts clearly demonstrates this connection between emotion and cultural scripts.

One element of the encounter tied to emotions that Goffman discussed is the ritualized procedures for pointing out and correcting deviant acts. Goffman's (1967) concept of facework elaborates these ritualized procedures. Goffman analyzed embarrassing situations and identified ritual elements to the restoration of face. According to Goffman, face is "the positive social value a person effectively claims for himself by the line others assume he has taken during a particular contact" (1967:5). The choice of face is determined by the situation and is thus determined by culture. When an actor's behavior falls out of line with his or her chosen face, the actor must work to ease embarrassment and restore face. Thus, cultural scripts are important not only in the choice of face but also in attempting to restore face.

Goffman described two general ways to restore face. The first way is to engage in avoidance. This preemptive facework involves avoiding people or situations that might threaten face. For example, when meeting the family of a significant other for the first time, an actor might avoid discussing certain topics in order to sustain a positive face. The second way to restore face is to engage in corrective facework. Corrective facework involves a ritual interaction order and is thus part of a cultural script. In the first step in corrective facework, a challenge is issued. Someone in the interaction lets the person know that he or she has done something that violates the accuser's face. In the second stage in the ritual, an offering is made. The person whose face is compromised offers some sort of apology or account to explain his or her behavior. Once the offering has been issued, it is then up to the person who issued the challenge to accept the offering. In the final step in the ritual sequence, the person whose face had been compromised expresses gratitude (Goffman 1967).[1] This formula for restoring face is one type of cultural script that is used in everyday interaction.

Whereas Goffman focused on cultural scripts that guide our interaction, Gordon (1981) emphasized emotion culture as a central element defining social sentiments. The importance of culture is particularly evident in emotion vocabularies, emotion beliefs, and emotion norms (feeling and expression rules). These three elements (vocabularies, beliefs, and norms) comprise the emotion culture of a society. Emotion vocabularies delineate categories of meanings that are used in describing our emotional experiences. Along with these vocabularies, individuals learn the general cultural beliefs about emotions as well as normative expectations regarding our emotions.

The normative expectations that Gordon (1981) discussed derive from Hochschild's (1979) work describing emotion culture as composed of the feeling rules and display rules for that culture. Feeling rules govern the intensity (strong versus weak), direction (positive versus negative), and duration (fleeting versus lasting) of an emotion. Display rules (also called expression rules) involve norms regarding how an emotion or feeling is to be expressed. Hochschild (1979) described feeling rules as the normative indicators of what is appropriate in a given situation regarding the experience and expression of feelings or emotion. Taken together, feeling and expression rules culturally define much of our emotional experiences. In addition to these two types of rules, Hochschild (1979) also argued for the existence of framing rules. Framing rules dictate the meanings that individuals should give to particular situations. These rules also exist as part of our emotion culture.

Essentially, the content of any emotion culture includes emotion vocabularies, beliefs, and norms (Gordon 1981). Although this provides a framework for understanding emotion culture generally, one must examine the specific content of a society's or group's emotion culture in order to develop a full understanding of the concept. Several researchers have taken this next step and examined the content of emotion culture for specific emotions. Lofland's (1985) work on grief and Clark's (1997) work on sympathy are examples where the emotion culture was analyzed for specific emotions. The works of Hochschild (1989) and Kemper (1990) analyzed how our relationships and changes in those relationships lead to particular emotional responses. These emotional responses also comprise the emotion culture of a society.

EMPIRICAL WORK ON EMOTION CULTURE

Lofland (1985) examined the specific content of U.S. emotion culture regarding grief. In particular, Lofland focused on the feeling and display rules and the experiential components that socially construct our experiences of grief. These four components are the level of significance of the other who dies, the definition of the situation surrounding death, the character of the self experiencing a loss through death, and the interactional setting in which the other three components occur.

Lofland identified a number of threads of connectedness that determine the level of significance of another person to us. These threads of connectedness include the roles we play, the help we receive, the wider network of others made available to us, the selves others create and sustain, the comforting myths others allow us, the reality others validate for us, and the futures they make possible. Each of these threads of connectedness indicates a way in which someone is involved in our lives. For example, the roles we play define significance because someone who is central to our lives will see us enacting many different roles. An acquaintance at work only sees us in our work role, whereas a spouse sees us in all of our different roles, including work and family roles. The help we receive establishes significance because allowing someone to help us leads to interactional consequences. In terms of the wider networks, a person who is significant in our lives will include us in their larger network by introducing us to their family and friends. Significant others will also enable us to create or sustain a certain self. A spouse might care for the children during final exam week so that a partner who is in school can focus on his or her studies. Additionally, significant others will allow us to maintain certain comforting myths but will also help us validate a particular reality.[2] These actions help us to sustain certain selves and contribute to our emotional well-being. Finally, the significance of another can be determined by the future he or she makes possible for us. This indicates that someone is expected to have an ongoing influence in our life. The greater the number of threads of connectedness between another and oneself indicates a greater degree of significance the other has in our life. Greater significance is expected to lead to stronger feelings of grief upon that person's death.

The second component affecting our experience of grief is the definition of the situation surrounding death. This component is culturally determined, as it involves philosophical or ideological variations in beliefs about death. Different religions have different conceptions of what happens after one dies and, thus, treat death differently. Some might view death as a time of great sadness because of the loss, whereas others might see it as a cause for celebration since a loved one is believed to have moved on to a better place. In addition, demographic variations have impacted our view of death. Given our longer life span, we now view the death of a spouse or loved one as unexpected and it hits us harder. In addition, changes in medical technology have allowed parents to see their babies even in the womb; thus, miscarriages are now seen as unexpected and tragic. Changes in medical technology and skills have altered our cultural expectations regarding when death is likely to occur. Because death is now more often viewed as unexpected, the feeling rules now require us to experience greater grief with each death.

The third component that shapes our experience of grief is also culturally defined, as it pertains to whether a person is allowed or even encouraged to express his or her feelings. An example of the variations in expression rules regarding grief is particularly evident when one considers gender differences in displays of grief. Even when facing the death of a loved one, men are expected to maintain subdued expressions of grief. Crying hysterically would be viewed as inappropriate for a man. Women, on the other hand, could cry hysterically due to grief and this would not likely be viewed as an inappropriate emotional expression. Lofland (1985) argued that our experience of grief is thus impacted by the culture's expression rules that allow some but deny others the right to express their grief.

Finally, the interactional setting component is culturally determined by whether the bereaved has the time or is given the opportunity to focus on his or her loss. In cultures where people live with their extended family, people lack the opportunity to focus on their loss because of the presence of others in the household. Historical changes in the structure of households as well as cross-cultural variations thus impact our experience of grief.

Whereas Lofland (1985) focused on the feeling and expression rules surrounding grief, Clark's (1997) work illustrated the importance of culture in defining appropriate emotional displays and reactions to such displays with regard to sympathy. Clark viewed the expression of sympathy as an exchange process that creates a socioemotional economy. Sympathy flows between actors within this socioemotional economy through reciprocal exchange relationships. When an actor engages in a sympathy exchange, he or she does not know whether or when the other will reciprocate. However, the exchange operates on the assumption that the other will eventually reciprocate. Clark argued that actors in a relationship maintain sympathy margins with one another. The degree of sympathy margin is defined by the type of relationship. Relationships involving significant others will include a greater sympathy margin. Claims for sympathy and expression of sympathy can impact this sympathy margin.

There are a number of cultural rules Clark (1997) described that dictate the exchange of sympathy and the functioning of the sympathy margin in these relationships. Some of these rules include the following: Do not make false claims to sympathy, do not claim too much sympathy, claim some sympathy, and reciprocate to others for the gift of sympathy. If discovered, making false claims to sympathy will hurt someone's credibility and damage the relationship. Claiming too much sympathy will exhaust a person's sympathy margin. Although claiming too much sympathy is considered inappropriate, claiming no sympathy at all is also problematic for a relationship. Accepting sympathy from someone indicates that a person values that relationship.[3] Thus, it is important to claim some sympathy. Finally, the expectation for the reciprocation of sympathy is critical to maintaining a relationship. As mentioned earlier, sympathy exchange is predicated on reciprocity, and a lack of reciprocity will likely result in the end of the relationship. These rules of sympathy exchange illustrate yet another aspect of our emotion culture and highlight how well defined the emotion culture is even though it is not explicitly stated.

A society's emotion culture is evident not only with regard to specific emotions but also in specific relationships. Hochschild (1989) studied marital roles and the gender ideologies associated with them. In her research, Hochschild interviewed 50 married couples and identified three main types of gender ideology relating to the household division of labor. The first type is traditional, in which the woman's place is in the home and the man's place is in the workplace. The second type is egalitarian, in which women and men are equally responsible for both the paid and unpaid labor. Finally, the transitional ideology views it as important that women work outside the home but that home is still primarily her responsibility.

Hochschild further found that feeling rules supported each of these ideologies. These feeling rules define such things as when a spouse should feel grateful for help with the household labor, whether spouses should identify themselves with the labor they perform at home or at work, and whether sharing in the household labor should be expected. Hochschild argued that the egalitarian ideology was supported by feeling rules that emphasized that men should want to share in the household labor and are not owed any gratitude for doing so. The feeling rules for this ideology further specify that women can identify themselves with labor performed out side the home. On the other hand, the traditional ideology includes feeling rules that specify that men should only identify themselves with labor performed in the workplace, women should only identify themselves with labor performed in the home, and that gratitude is owed to men who help with the household labor. These culturally defined feeling rules thus specify the emotional dynamics within intimate relationships.

When people's feelings deviated from their gender ideologies, they were left with the need to create a gender strategy. Gender strategies are persistent lines of feeling and action that reconcile feeling rules with situations. The couples that Hochschild studied developed family myths as ways of coping with a disjuncture between ideology and feeling. An example that Hochschild gave of a family myth was the "upstairs-downstairs" split. For one of the couples that Hochschild studied, the man was traditional and the woman was egalitarian in ideology. This disjuncture in their ideologies was putting considerable strain on their marriage. The couple eventually compromised by defining the upstairs portion of the house as the woman's responsibility and the downstairs areas as the man's responsibility. This sounds like an equal split except for the fact that the downstairs did not include any of the family's general living spaces. However, even though the division of labor was still unequal, this myth allowed each partner to reconcile the level of household labor with his or her gender ideology. In general, these family myths reflect a family's emotion culture.

A society's emotion culture defines the emotional reactions to aspects of intimate relationships. In the work of Kemper (1990), changes in the dynamics of our relationships impact our emotional reactions. Kemper's theory thus explains yet another aspect of a society's emotion culture. Cultural knowledge is critical to understanding how people evaluate changes in social relationships. Kemper (1990) illustrated how changes in power and status in a relationship lead to particular emotional reactions. According to Kemper, power is the ability to coerce another in order to get what one wants, and status is defined as a supportive behavior that involves deferring to another. In Kemper's theory, all relationships can be characterized in terms of power and status. The degrees of power and status that characterize a relationship are impacted by cultural constructions. For example, minorities in the United States are often at an interactional disadvantage in interracial interactions because discrimination has contributed to placing them into lower power and status positions. Thus, the relative power and status of participants in a relationship are impacted by cultural expectations.

According to Kemper, changes in either power or status will result in particular emotional responses. For example, an increase in one's own power or a decrease in a partner's power will result in feelings of security. Knowing that one is able to get what one wants or that a partner can no longer coerce one into action contributes to feelings of security. In the opposite case, a decrease in one's own power or an increase in a partner's power result in fear or anxiety because these changes mean one is more likely to be able to be coerced by a partner.

Because status involves a more positive behavior, changes in status in a relationship lead to different emotional responses. An increase in one's own or a partner's status results in feelings of satisfaction or happiness. As for a decrease in status, the resulting emotions depend on the cause of the decrease. A decrease in one's own status caused by a partner results in anger, whereas shame is the result when a status decrease is caused by self. If the status decrease is caused by fate or some other factor, then the resulting emotion is depression. The final potential change in a relationship described in Kemper's theory is a decrease in a partner's status. An intentional decrease in a partner's status leads to satisfaction and fear, whereas an unintentional decrease causes guilt or shame. The combination of satisfaction and fear results from successfully decreasing another's status (when it is done intentionally) while fearing potential consequences. Overall, Kemper's (1990) theory clearly illustrates how changes in relationships create emotional responses. The particular emotional responses that are expected to result are determined by a society's emotion culture.

The works of Lofland (1985), Clark (1997), Hochschild (1989), and Kemper (1990) illustrated small portions of the emotion culture in U.S. society. However, even taking this work into account, the specific content of emotion culture has not received enough attention. There still exist large gaps in our understanding of emotion culture. This is true even before considering the potential changes and variations in emotion culture.

VARIATIONS IN EMOTION CULTURE

As Gordon (1981) described, emotion culture is not static and there are changes in emotion culture across time. Cancian and Gordon (1988) examined the changes in emotion norms regarding love and anger in marriage. They used qualitative and quantitative analysis to examine messages conveyed in a sample of articles on marriage from popular women's magazines from 1900 to 1979. These popular magazine articles socialized their readers into the emotion culture of marital relationships. Cancian and Gordon argued that these articles provided readers with a vocabulary for their emotions, emotion scenarios, emotion norms, sanctions, management techniques, and justifying ideologies for their marriages. Their overall analysis found that the predominant messages in women's magazines have emphasized the suppression of anger and love as self-sacrifice. These messages place responsibility for relationships squarely on women's shoulders and thus maintain gender differences in emotional expectations and maintain women's powerlessness. However, more recent articles in these women's magazines have encouraged women to freely express their emotions, particularly their anger, and this openness encourages more equal relationships. Cancian and Gordon also found that changes in emotion norms and messages conveyed in these magazines were tied to historical transformations in political oppression and liberation as well as other structural events. Changes in emotion norms regarding love and anger in marriage were most evident following periods of social and political liberation (1920s and 1960s), during intellectual movements (1940s rise of psychotherapy), and during momentous historical events such as the Great Depression and World War II.

Cancian and Gordon's (1988) work also demonstrated how the documents of an emotion culture can be used as indicators of social structural changes. However, in the case of publications, there is a time lag between the historical event and its impact on documentation. Also, changes in documentation will be impacted by whether those changes suit the interests of those who control the mass media. Changes occur more quickly when they suit the controlling interests and more slowly when they suit the target audience. This has significant implications for research on the content of emotion culture. Careful consideration must be given to the documents being studied in terms of their origins and the timing of their dissemination.

Whereas Cancian and Gordon (1988) demonstrated how emotion culture varies over time, Wierzbicka (1999) illustrated how emotion culture varies across societies. In particular, Wierzbicka demonstrated how differences in emotion vocabularies, beliefs, and norms lead to differences in both experienced and expressed emotions across societies. In particular, language differences can lead to fundamental differences in our emotion vocabularies. Wierzbicka argued that language affects our emotions. She compared English and Russian in looking at sadness. In English, there is only one word for sadness, whereas in Russian there are two words that connote different types of sadness. Language also affects our emotional expression. Again comparing English and Russian, there are differences in how laughter is conceived. In Russian, there are two words for laughter, both of which mean hearty laughter. In English, there are a number of different words for different types of laughter ranging from chuckle and giggle to laugh. Finally, as discussed earlier, Wierzbicka also argued that culture affects our emotion norms. Wierzbicka's comparison of emotion norms between Polish and Anglo-Americans illustrated how emotion culture influences interactional dynamics.

LEARNING THE EMOTION CULTURE: EMOTIONAL SOCIALIZATION

The fact that society's emotion culture is nowhere explicitly stated and varies over time can make learning the content of the emotion culture difficult. Emotional socialization is the process whereby individuals come to learn their emotion culture. Given the importance of understanding emotion culture to engaging in daily interactions, emotional socialization is crucial to our development into emotionally competent actors.

In order to achieve emotional competence, children must be socialized into a society's emotion culture. According to Gordon (1990), children's cognitive constructions of emotions are impacted by several factors. These factors include differential exposure, diversity, and socialization sequence. In terms of differential exposure, the capacity to experience and observe particular emotions is dependent upon a person's position in the social structure. The emotion culture delineates that actors in different social structural positions experience different emotions both as an agent and target of emotions. Diversity impacts emotional socialization through experiences with multiple socializing agents. If these multiple agents hold different views of emotions, the children will be socialized to a wider spectrum of emotional experience. Socialization sequence refers to how society's emotion culture defines which emotions are appropriate for children at different ages. Expectations for emotional competence vary depending on children's ages and the socialization sequence that takes into account the timing of expectations for competence for each emotion.

Emotional socialization is not only impacted by external socializing agents but also can be impacted by an individual's self-locus. Drawing from Turner's (1976) ideas concerning the institutional versus impulsive locus for the self, Gordon (1989) expanded on this to consider institutional versus impulsive meanings of emotion. According to Turner, an institutional locus for the self is defined by adherence to societal norms, whereas an impulsive locus is defined by spontaneous action. When applied to emotions, institutional meanings are those that are seen when an individual controls his or her emotions in line with societal standards. The impulsive meanings of emotions are those spontaneous and uninhibited expressions of emotions. Thus, the meanings that emotions carry for people will depend on their self-locus and where they see themselves as "most real." These different emotion orientations further lead to the implication that the same emotion can have very different meanings depending on an individual's self-locus. Those individuals with an institutional self-locus will view emotional experiences that are in line with societal norms as most "real." Achieving emotional competence for these individuals will focus on learning to effectively manage one's emotions. Those with an impulsive self-locus will favor their "spontaneous" expressions of emotion, and emotion management will be less critical to their definition of emotional competence (Gordon 1981).

RESEARCH ON EMOTIONAL SOCIALIZATION

Research on emotional socialization has examined how particular socializing agents impact emotional socialization. Pollak and Thoits (1989) examined how adult caretakers in a therapeutic nursery teach children about emotional experiences. In general, they found adult caretakers do socialize children to identify and express their emotions. In order to teach children about emotions, the adult caretakers in these facilities made verbal connections among three of the aspects of emotional experience. They connected situational stimuli, expressive gestures, and emotion words. These experiences form a crucial part of a young child's socialization into the emotion culture. Parents also participate in children's emotional socialization, although their teachings are less deliberate than those of professional caretakers.

In contrast to Pollak and Thoits (1989), Leavitt and Power (1989) found that day care providers can actually fail to legitimize children's emotions when they focus solely on appropriate emotional display by the children in their care, not on what the children might actually be feeling. Children were thus taught early on about the importance of emotion management with the likely consequence that children's authentic feelings are suppressed and caregivers maintain an emotionally distant relationship with the children in their care. The differences between these two studies might be due to the differences between a therapeutic nursery geared to children who need emotional assistance and a general day care center.

Another type of socializing agent is a culture-making institution. Denzin (1990) examined the role of culture-making institutions in emotional socialization through his examination of movies and emotions. Culture-making institutions are those "groups or institutions explicitly oriented to the production of cultural meanings" (Denzin 1990:90). Although Denzin focused on the movies as a culture-making institution, other examples would include other forms of media,[4] the educational system, religious groups, and other support groups. Denzin argued that culture-making institutions such as the movies ideologically define emotionality. He further argued that the emotional practices represented in film are gender-specific and include representations of intimacy. Movies provide particular images of a romantic relationship. These images become integrated into a society's emotion culture and impact how love and intimacy are defined within the society. As Denzin (1990) argued, this study of emotionality must be grounded both historically and culturally for the culture-making institution must also be responsive to the larger social setting.[5] The sum of his argument is that emotional experiences are gender-specific and ideologically defined by the larger social order.

MANAGING EMOTIONS

Even with emotional socialization, individuals do not always experience the emotion that they are expected to experience. There will often be occasions when the individual will find it difficult to follow the feeling rules. Part of our emotional socialization includes learning to effectively manage one's emotions to fit expectations. This need to engage in emotion management is culturally proscribed and is a crucial interactional skill. Society expects an emotionally competent actor to fit his or her emotional experiences with the emotion culture. In order to do so, the individual will need to engage in emotion management.

Hochschild (1979:561) first introduced the concept of emotion management and defined it as "the act of trying to change in degree or quality an emotion or feeling." Emotion management, or emotion work, refers to the process a person undergoes in his or her efforts to follow the feeling rules. In everyday life, emotion work, or emotion management, is typically used to induce a proper state of mind in oneself. For example, if a person attends a funeral of a distant relative and is initially in a good mood that day because of some other positive event in his or her life (i.e., a job promotion), then that person will have to engage in emotion work once at the funeral in order to evoke feelings of sadness. In U.S. culture, the norm is that one should feel sad at funerals so if a person does not initially feel that way, then emotion work is performed and the person induces the appropriate emotion. Whether the individual is successful in changing the emotion is unimportant, simply the attempt at doing so defines the behavior as emotion management (Hochschild 1979). Individuals' attempts at emotion management are driven by their desire to follow the feeling rules and display rules that comprise the emotion culture.

In order to follow the display rules, individuals might only have to engage in surface acting. Surface acting simply involves changing one's outward expressions and appearance in order to follow the normative standards. This involves simply altering one's presentation to deceive others about one's feelings. In contrast, following the feeling rules might require deep acting. It is not enough to simply alter one's expressions; one must alter one's experience of emotions and that requires deep acting. Deep acting involves altering one's feelings by deceiving oneself about the nature or extent of one's feelings (Hochschild 1990).

A number of researchers have examined emotion management processes. Hochschild (1990) identified body work and cognitive work as general techniques for managing one's emotions. Body work involves changing the physiological aspects of an emotional experience, whereas cognitive work involves altering one's thoughts and ideas to bring about a change in one's emotional experience.[6]

Hochschild (1990) distinguished between two broad types of emotion work and among three techniques of emotion work. The two broad types involve evocation or suppression. In evocation, the focus is on trying to bring about a feeling that was initially absent. In suppression, the focus is on trying to diminish a feeling that was initially present. Both of these types involve attempts to follow the feeling rules by inducing or diminishing emotional reactions. The three techniques of emotion work that Hochschild describes are cognitive, bodily, and expressive. These three techniques map onto the components of an emotional experience described by Gordon (1990) and Thoits (1990).

Thoits's (1990) approach to emotion management uses the components of emotional experience and the modes for altering those experiences to identify a categorization of emotion management strategies. As discussed earlier, the four components of emotional experience that Thoits identifies are situational cues, physiological changes, expressive gestures, and emotional labels. Thus, whenever an individual experiences an emotional reaction, all four of these components are activated in some form. This means that there is a situational cue to trigger an emotion, an experience of physiological arousal, the labeling of the arousal as a particular emotion, and an emotional display (or expressive gestures. These four components are all interconnected so that a change in one of the components will trigger changes in the other components. This provides the basis for Thoits's typology of emotion management, which allows change directed at any one component to result in management of the emotional experience. The two modes through which an individual can alter an emotional experience are through the behavioral mode or the cognitive mode. In general, behavioral manipulations involve acting or avoiding some aspect of the emotional experience, whereas cognitive strategies focus on changing the meaning of the situation.

Thoits (1990) created a typology of emotion management that crosses these two modes of alteration with the four components of the emotion. Examples of cognitive strategies for each of the components of an emotion include reinterpreting a situation or distracting oneself, meditation or hypnosis, prayer, or reinterpreting feelings. Reinterpreting a situation and distracting oneself are cognitive, situation-focused strategies. These strategies involve thinking about the situation in a different way or thinking about other things in order to avoid thoughts related to the situation. Meditation and hypnosis are cognitive strategies geared toward altering one's physiological responses. To cognitively alter one's expressive gestures, one technique would be to pray. Finally, one can cognitively alter the cultural meanings given to an emotion by reinterpreting feelings.

Behavioral strategies can be used to alter the situational stimulus, physiological responses, or expressive gestures. Since cultural meanings are purely cognitive constructions, it is not possible to alter that component behaviorally. Examples of behavioral strategies include taking direct action or withdrawing, vigorous exercise or using drugs, or exhibiting a catharsis or hiding feelings. Taking direct action and withdrawing are situation focused because they involve physical motion to change or leave the situation. To alter one's physiological responses, an individual can engage in strenuous exercise or use drugs. Finally, behavioral strategies for altering one's expressive gestures include a catharsis where one releases pent up emotional expression in an outburst or hides one's feelings.

When an individual is unable to effectively manage his or her emotions, the result is emotional deviance. Thoits (1990:181) defined emotional deviance as the "experiences or displays of affect that differ in quality or degree from what is expected in a given situation." Thus, emotional deviance occurs when an individual's emotional reaction is not consistent with what is expected for the given situation. In order for a person to experience emotional deviance, they must be involved in a situation where there are clearly defined feeling rules that establish the emotional expectations for the situation. There are a number of factors in the social situation that can contribute to experiences of emotional deviance. Two conditions that can exacerbate difficulties in emotion management and lead to emotional deviance are the persistence of stressful situations and a lack of social support for one's feelings. Thoits (1985) argued that persistent emotional deviance contributes to a person self-labeling as mentally ill. This self-labeling then contributes to an increased likelihood of voluntary treatment seeking.

Although emotional deviance is characteristic of a number of mental illnesses, it is not uncommon for individuals who are not mentally ill to have emotional experiences that deviate from the feeling rules of a situation. This is more likely to happen under certain conditions. The first set of factors is from the emotional situation. The three factors that fall under this category include time, memory, and complex situational stimuli. Time can contribute to emotional deviance because although an individual can change settings quickly (with an accompanying change in feeling rules), he or she might not be able to change emotions as quickly. Our memories can also intrude upon us at an inopportune time, resulting in an emotional response to the memory that does not fit the feeling rules for one's current situation. Additionally, situations might have complexities that lead to multiple, even conflicting, feeling rules. Each of these situational factors can contribute to an inability to effectively manage our emotions.

In addition to situational stimuli, there are also structural conditions that can contribute to emotional deviance. Thoits (1990) identified four such conditions. First, when individuals find themselves in a situation of multiple role occupancy, there is greater likelihood of a discrepancy. Multiple roles can lead to contradictory feelings that can be difficult to reconcile. The second time when a discrepancy is likely to occur is in a situation of subcultural marginality. As with multiple roles, it can be difficult to reconcile competing demands of different subcultures. Emotional deviance can also occur during a situation of normative or nonnormative role transitions. Any type of role transition can increase stress and uncertainty, which can make it much more difficult for an individual to keep his or her emotions in line with the feeling rules. Finally, situations in which there are rigid rules associated with roles or rituals can lead to increased stress with even the most minor of deviations. All of these situations share a common ability to induce stress, which makes it much more difficult for an individual to bring his or her emotions in line with the feeling rules.

RESEARCH ON EMOTION MANAGEMENT

This typology of emotion management can be applied in many different settings. Stets and Tsushima (2001) examined how individuals cope with anger when they are occupying role-based identities versus group-based identities. In role-based identities (such as worker role), individuals are more likely to use situation-focused, behavioral strategies. In group-based identities (such as family), individuals are more likely to use cognitive, expressive strategies. These differences in the use of emotion management strategies are likely tied to the differences in identities. The role-based, worker identity is a task-oriented identity that would require task-focused action (in emotion management terms, situation-focused, behavioral) to manage emotions. In group-based, family identities, behavioral strategies might not be as appropriate given the ongoing, intimate connections among family. Instead, cognitive, expressive strategies are used in order to sustain (or at least not disrupt) the intimate connections within the family group.

Thoits (1990) found that the most commonly used emotion management techniques were catharsis (behavioral, expressive gestures), taking direct action (behavioral, situation focused), seeking support (behavioral, situation focused), hiding feelings (behavioral, expressive gestures), and reinterpreting the situation (cognitive, situation focused). Each of these techniques was also found to be among the most effective emotion management techniques. In general, it appears that behavioral strategies are used more often than cognitive strategies, and these behavioral techniques appear to be quite effective.

Cahill and Eggleston (1994) used the concept of emotion management to examine the specific case of wheelchair users who must manage both their own and others' emotions in public spaces. Through participant observation, interviews, and analysis of published accounts, Cahill and Eggleston derived three types of emotion management used by these wheelchair users. The first type of emotion management used by the wheelchair users is humoring embarrassment. In this situation, the wheelchair person attempts to use humor to defuse an otherwise embarrassing situation. This is emblematic of Goffman's (1967) discussion of the use of humor as a technique to defuse embarrassment. Cahill and Eggleston found that humor was both the most common and the most effective strategy employed by wheelchair users. The second type of emotion management is embarrassing anger. Wheelchair users often feel anger at their treatment as nonpersons. However, although this anger is often felt, it is not often expressed. Since the expression of anger can lead to an embarrassing public scene, wheelchair users often suppress their anger.

The final type of emotion management is ingratiating sympathy.[7] Because of the rules of sympathy etiquette (Clark 1997), wheelchair users are often torn about making demands for assistance from strangers. When this sympathetic assistance is granted, wheelchair users must respond with gratitude. Even when the assistance was unsolicited, gratitude is still expected. This gratitude thus situates the wheelchair user within the interactional setting, and if the wheelchair user attempts to withhold gratitude, they are perceived as uncivil. Although Cahill and Eggleston (1994) focused on the situation of wheelchair users in public places, their findings regarding emotion management among strangers hold more generally as well. In public, we all must manage our own emotions and must suppress anger, use humor to avoid embarrassment, and display gratitude for sympathy.

COMMERCIALIZATION OF EMOTION MANAGEMENT

Although emotion management is part of everyday life, research has also examined how businesses have co-opted and commercialized emotion management. Emotional labor is "labor requiring one to induce or suppress feeling in order to sustain the outward countenance that produces the proper state of mind in others" (Hochschild 1983:7). Although emotional labor is quite similar to emotion management, because both of these concepts rely on feeling rules to define normative emotional reaction, a key difference between emotional labor and emotion management is the target of the emotional control. Emotion management is solely focused on controlling one's own emotions for one's own benefit. Emotional labor, on the other hand, requires one to manage one's own emotions in order to influence the emotions of another person. Another difference between emotional labor and emotion management lies in the location where the emotional control is exercised. Emotional labor is performed in a work setting and is directed at a customer or client. Emotion management is performed in any location as a part of daily life. Hochschild initially identified three criteria of jobs that define them as emotional labor:

face-to-face or voice-to-voice contact with the public, production of an emotional state in another person, and employer control over employees' emotional activities. Thus, an emotional laborer is required to manage his or her own emotions in order to ensure that the customer has the appropriate reaction.

Regardless of one's conceptualization of emotional labor, the requirements of emotional labor are based on feeling rules. Feeling rules are important in emotional labor because they are the social guidelines that direct feeling (Hochschild 1979). Thus, feeling rules define the parameters for emotional labor because they delineate which emotions the emotional laborer is expected to experience in himself or herself in order to produce the proper emotion in others. For example, feeling rules establish that a flight attendant should act in a happy, mothering manner in order to make the customers feel like they are "at home" and comfortable (Hochschild 1983). The flight attendant who is successful in following this feeling rule will likely have convinced the customers to fly the same airline again (or so the airlines believe).

Hochschild (1983) clearly illustrated the role of the organization in teaching flight attendants the feeling rules that guide their interactions with customers. Rafaeli and Sutton (1987) expanded upon Hochschild's ideas about the sources of emotional labor expectations (or feeling rules) by introducing emotional transactions as an additional source of expectations for emotional labor (in addition to organizationally defined feeling rules). Emotional transactions describe the interaction loop whereby emotions are displayed, feedback is received, and emotions are readjusted within a particular situation. Thus, emotional laborers are guided by an organization's feeling rules as well as by the process of a particular interaction (Rafaeli and Sutton 1987). This means that the emotion culture determining emotional labor includes organizational culture as well as interactional dynamics.

Hochschild (1983) argued that the workers' emotional stamina is crucial to their proper performance as emotional laborers. Emotional stamina refers to "sustaining a particular controlled feeling for an extended period of time" (Turner and Stets 2005:39). Often, the emotional requirements of a job do not match what a worker might actually be feeling. Thus, workers are required to feign emotions during the time they are at work. In order to reduce the discrepancy between what the worker is feeling and what they are feigning, workers have two choices. They can change what they are feeling or they can change what they are feigning. Hochschild further argued that these requirements place a strain on individuals engaged in emotional labor. This strain can include feelings of self-estrangement, alienation, and inauthenticity (Hochschild 1983).

As with emotion culture generally, Hochschild (1983) contended that emotional laborers receive socialization as children, which prepares them for future jobs as emotional laborers. In essence, there is a reproduction of the social structure of emotional labor across generations. The argument is that through the family control system, some parents teach their children to value feelings, which prepares the child to become an emotional laborer. There are two types of family control system; the positional and the personal. In a positional control system, a child is taught to obey because of clear and formal rules and the focus is simply on the child's behavioral conformity. In a personal control system, the child is taught to obey because of persuasion and the focus is on the control of feeling (Bernstein 1971). More specifically, the personal control system involves teaching children three things. First, children are taught that the feelings of superiors are important. Second, children learn that their own feelings are important. Finally, children socialized under a personal control system learn that feelings should be managed (Hochschild 1983). It is this third lesson that is important for engaging in emotional labor.[8] Emotional laborers need to manage their own feelings, including the evocation of emotion as well as its suppression, in order to affect their customers' experiences.

RESEARCH ON EMOTIONAL LABOR

Since Hochschild's initial discussion of emotional labor, numerous researchers have proposed elaborations or changes to how the concept is viewed. More recently, Tolich (1993) argued for a new dichotomy of emotional labor based on whether the worker has control over his or her own emotional activities. In this typology, regulated emotional labor refers to emotional labor supervised by others (this is consistent with Hochschild's original definition of emotional labor). Autonomous emotional labor involves emotional labor that is controlled by the individual. Both types of emotional labor involve controlling one's own emotions in order to create an emotional state in another person. In Hochschild's original conceptualization, the third criterion that defined a job as emotional labor was that the worker was supervised for his or her emotional activities. Tolich's typology thus covers Hochschild's original conceptualization and labels those workers as regulated emotional laborers. Tolich's typology then extends Hochschild's conceptualization of emotional labor to include those workers who are not directly supervised for their emotional activities but, instead, who have control over their own emotional activities. Having control over one's emotional activities makes emotional labor a liberating experience because it is under one's own control. On the other hand, emotional labor that is regulated by others can be an alienating experience for the worker. The advantage of this dichotomy is that it provides an explanation for how emotional labor can be both alienating and liberating for different workers.

Paules' (1991) study of the waitresses at Route Restaurant provided a unique example of autonomous emotional labor in a job that would normally be considered regulated emotional labor. Because of a labor shortage in the area, the waitresses at this restaurant were able to resist management's attempts at imposing emotional labor demands. Corporate management attempted to impose a situation where the waitresses were defined as servants to customers. However, the waitresses had the power (due to the labor shortage) to construct their own emotional labor. The waitresses viewed themselves as entrepreneurs working for higher tips or as soldiers fighting the onslaught of rude customers. This construction allowed the waitresses to view their emotional deviance to the customers as part of their ability to get tips from customers. So, while the waitresses still engaged in emotional labor, it was under their own control. In this particular instance, the structural conditions of a labor shortage enabled the waitresses to autonomously construct their own emotional labor.

DeCoster (1997) differentiated between emotional control directed toward self or others. DeCoster argued that emotional labor is self-directed emotional control that is part of one's paid employment role. Emotion treating, in this typology, is emotional control directed toward another as part of one's paid employment. Thus, DeCoster argued for consideration of two types of job-related emotional control. On the one hand, workers might need to control their own emotions in order to display appropriate affect in the workplace. Additionally, workers might have to engage in emotion treating where they attempt to influence the emotional reactions of others in the workplace. DeCoster's typology of emotional labor and emotion treating thus broadens the conception of the range of emotional activities considered to be part of one's paid employment.

Morris and Feldman (1996) argued for the use of four distinct dimensions in describing the concept of emotional labor that focus on emotional display rather than emotion management or emotional control. Their four dimensions include "frequency of appropriate emotional display; attentiveness to required display rules; variety of emotions required to be displayed; and emotional dissonance generated as a result of having to express organizationally desired emotions not genuinely felt" (p. 987). This conceptualization presents emotional labor as a continuum where different occupations require more or less emotional labor. Focusing on these different dimensions increases our understanding of the complexities of emotional labor. This emphasizes how engaging in emotional labor involves generating different emotions with different frequencies and that there can be emotional consequences to performing emotional labor.

Ashforth and Humphrey (1995) emphasized a focus on emotional display instead of emotion management. They argued that it is important to focus on the display of emotions because it is the observable behavior that affects the interaction between an emotional laborer and a customer. Further, Ashforth and Humphrey argued that workers can conform to emotional display rules without engaging in emotion management. Thus, Ashforth and Humphrey essentially argued that emotional labor (as they defined it) is actually a type of impression management. Thoits's (1990) work discussed earlier argued that managing an emotional display was a technique that could be used to manage one's emotions. However, Ashforth and Humphrey raised the question of whether emotional display and emotion management can be separated. They argued that managing an emotional display can be done for its own sake and does not necessarily have to lead to emotion management.

Peterson (1998) found that having a mother who engages in regulated emotional labor makes a child more likely to become a regulated emotional laborer. However, the support for the idea that the social structure of emotional labor is reproduced across generations was limited to this one finding regarding the effects of mother's emotional labor. Peterson also demonstrated some initial support for the idea that the children of emotional laborers learn to value emotional labor, although support for this idea was also mixed. A father's emotional labor occupation was found to have significant effects on child's aspiration to an autonomous emotional labor occupation. Some researchers argued that male emotional laborers have a "status shield" that protects them from the harmful effects of emotional labor (Hochschild 1983). Thus, children whose fathers engage in emotional labor might not see any harmful effects from engaging in emotional labor and are more likely to aspire to autonomous emotional labor occupations.

One of the important aspects of Hochschild's discussion is the role the organization and earlier socialization play in preparing emotional laborers. Cahill (1999) examined the concept of emotional capital in the case of the professional socialization of mortuary science students who are required to develop an affective neutrality toward death and working with the dead. In essence, their education as mortuary science students normalizes the experience of death for these students. The three ways in which death becomes normalized are through normalizing scenes, normalizing associations, and normalizing talk. Scenes become normalized as students in these programs are surrounded by cadavers and busts on a regular basis. The normalizing associations occur because mortuary science students associate mainly, if not only, with other people in the business. The discomfort others have with death makes it difficult for people in this field to maintain relationships with those outside of the field. These insular networks with others who feel the same way about death truly normalize their experiences. Finally, normalizing talk involves the way instructors talk and the way students talk about death. They adopt an analytical perspective toward the bodies of the dead and this enables them to maintain their affective neutrality. As Cahill argued, this professional socialization in part depends on earlier socialization. The students who successfully complete the mortuary science program share a common biographical connection to death. Approximately two-thirds of the students are the children of funeral directors and the remaining have other connections to people who work in the business. Thus, childhood emotional socialization prepares many of these students for the secondary socialization that occurs at school. As Cahill (1999) described, these students develop emotional capital that involves professional detachment. This emotional socialization actually creates occupational exclusion.

Emotional detachment is also important for students preparing to become doctors. Smith and Kleinman (1989) examined the techniques used by medical students in managing the emotions that arise during their job. Medical students often face emotionally difficult situations and yet they are expected to severely limit any emotional displays. These medical students need to become emotionally socialized into the demands of their occupation. Thus, part of their training (although not necessarily an explicit part) involves learning new feeling rules and new emotion management techniques for conforming to those rules. Through such techniques as transforming contact into something different from personal contact, accentuating the positive aspect of finally practicing medicine, using the patient through empathizing or blaming them for inappropriate emotions, laughing about uncomfortable situations, and avoiding uncomfortable contact, medical students are able to manage the emotions that arise from the intimate body contact that is part of their profession. They are thus able to maintain emotional displays in line with cultural proscriptions considered appropriate for physicians.

A similar study by Arluke (1994) examined the techniques used by workers in an animal shelter. These animal lovers must often face the death or neglect of animals and yet must strive to maintain some emotional detachment. These shelter workers use such techniques as transforming shelter animals into virtual pets, empathizing with the animal, resisting and avoiding euthanasia, blaming the owner for neglecting the animal, and dealing with others by avoiding a discussion of their work.[9] As with the medical students, these techniques allow shelter workers to manage their emotional displays and effectively engage in emotional labor.

The requirement of emotional control as part of one's job is also evident in Pierce's (1995) work on the emotion labor in law firms. The gendered division of labor in these law firms leads to more men working as trial lawyers and more women working as paralegals. Even for these trial lawyers, there was an emotional dimension to their work. These "Rambo Litigators" engaged in displays of hypermasculinity. Their self-presentations involved displays of aggression, in order to intimidate, as well as "strategic friendliness."

The "mothering paralegals" in the firm were also required to engage in nurturing emotion work. The two main components of this nurturing work involved deference and caretaking. Even when men and women were in the same job, there were different emotion norms. The "Rambo Litigators" were part of the emotion norm for men, who were expected to be aggressive and manipulative. Women lawyers, on the other hand, were expected to be nonthreatening and kind. Women were thus faced with a double standard where the job was seen to require aggressive behavior, but they were expected to be kind. Pierce found that female litigators adapted to this situation in one of three ways: (1) They reshaped the adversarial role to fit their care orientation; (2) they acted using both an adversarial and care orientation; or (3) they adopted the adversarial role. Although the female lawyers struggled with these conflicting expectations, the male paralegals had an easier time. Their higher status as males along with the expectations for masculinity meant they were not held to the same emotional labor standards as the female paralegals and they were not even treated the same as female paralegals. Overall, Pierce demonstrated that even in the same position, women and men do different amounts and kinds of emotional labor. The maintenance of this gendered emotional division of labor maintains status differences within the workplace and reproduces the status hierarchy.

CONCLUSION

Overall, this chapter has demonstrated that culture is not only relevant but clearly very significant to a wide range of research topics within the study of emotions. Culture plays a role in defining our emotions, connecting emotions and our sense of self, dictating our interactional scripts, determining our emotional reactions to our relationships, using emotion management techniques, and performing emotional labor. The relevant cultural constructions must be learned as part of ongoing processes of emotional socialization. Despite this broad range of research connecting culture and emotions, a number of avenues remain to be explored in future research.

Within the area of emotional socialization, one of the inherent difficulties is that of conducting research on processes of primary emotional socialization. Although the studies mentioned in this chapter have managed to examine some aspects of emotional socialization in particular settings, our knowledge of processes of emotional socialization within other settings (such as the family) is limited. Thus, although there has been research on professional emotional socialization and even childhood emotional socialization performed by care workers, our understanding of emotional socialization processes within the family is still severely limited.

As this chapter has indicated, research has demonstrated that emotion management is utilized everyday in many of our interactions. The works of Hochschild (1979), Thoits (1990), and others have examined the techniques of emotion management in great detail. However, an avenue for further work on emotion management would be to consider how people choose particular emotion management techniques. Stets and Tsushima (2001) have taken an initial step in this direction with their research, but further consideration should be given to whether the choice of emotion management techniques are situationally defined or perhaps part of our emotion culture.

Further research on emotional labor could focus on broadening our understanding of emotional labor beyond studying specific occupations. The types of emotional labor required by a job as well as how workers learn the expectations for their particular jobs have been examined extensively. These studies have been almost exclusively qualitative, which has limited the research to particular organizations. In order to expand our understanding of emotional labor, research should look to expand analyses across organizations and occupations.

In her review chapter on the sociology of emotions more than 15 years ago, Thoits (1989) argued there were a number of areas within the realm of emotions that deserved further consideration. At that time, Thoits argued that the majority of work done on emotions had examined the micro level of interaction and very little consideration had been given to the macro level of analysis. Furthermore, emotions had been treated primarily as a dependent variable, and little research had yet considered its impact as an independent or intervening variable. Additionally, problems in measuring emotions loomed large in this area of research. Thoits also characterized work on emotions as lacking adequate discussion of the content of emotion culture.

In examining the status of cultural theorizing on emotions today, it is evident that many of Thoits's concerns are still relevant. Thoits's (1989) concern about the lack of research on the content of emotion culture is clearly still relevant. The works of Cancian and Gordon (1988), Clark (1997), and Lofland (1985) exemplified the excellent research that has been done on the content of emotion culture, but this research has barely scratched the surface. To achieve a fuller understanding of the emotion culture of society requires much more work geared toward increasing our understanding of the content of emotion culture.

The problem of measuring emotions and studying aspects of emotions still looms large even 15 years after Thoits (1989) discussed this. Understanding emotion culture requires developing an understanding of how people acquire their knowledge of the emotion culture. The difficulties discussed previously that are inherent to studying emotional socialization have limited our understanding of the processes of emotional socialization. Difficulties in measurement also make quantifying emotional variables difficult.

Despite this difficulty, another important avenue for future research would be to strive to achieve a balance between qualitative and quantitative research on cultural aspects of emotions. Using a greater range of methodological tools would allow for further development of cultural theory in emotions. One area in which the qualitative and quantitative could be bridged would be to draw more connections to affect control theory, which has successfully quantified the components of our sentiments through systematic research. Establishing links between the qualitative research that has characterized the study of emotional culture with the quantitative research that has characterized affect control theory might be an interesting avenue for furthering our understanding of emotion culture.

NOTES

1. Kemper's (1990) theory of how changes in relations effect emotional responses would also predict embarrassment or shame to result from challenges to one's face since this would decrease someone's status in a relationship. Thus, facework could be viewed as restoring status in a relationship as well as restoring face.
2. Hochschild's (1989) work on the second shift describes how couples create family myths as a way of dealing with their different expectations for the division of household labor. These family myths can be viewed as comforting myths, which then become a validated reality for these couples.
3. The sympathy we accept from others in Clark's (1997) work is similar to the help we receive described in Lofland's (1985) work on grief. The willingness to accept sympathy or help from someone indicates that a particular relationship is valued.
4. Cancian and Gordon's (1988) work on norms of marital love and anger in magazine articles is another example of research examining the impact of a culture-making institution on emotions.
5. Cancian and Gordon's (1988) work is an excellent example of a historically grounded analysis.
6. Rosenberg's (1990) work on reflexivity and reflexive agency discussed earlier clearly connects with the concept of emotion management. In addition, Rosenberg explicitly discussed cognitive work and bodily work as techniques for altering emotional experiences.
7. All three of these strategies would fall into Thoits's (1990) category of behavioral, expressive gesture-focused strategies.
8. These family control systems have implications for emotional socialization more generally, not just in terms of socializing emotional laborers.
9. These specific techniques can easily be connected to Thoits's (1990) typology of general emotion management techniques.

REFERENCES

Arluke, Arnold. 1994. "Managing Emotions in an Animal Shelter." Pp. 145–165 in *Animals and Human Society: Changing Perspectives*, edited by A. Manning and J. Serpell. New York: Routledge.

Ashforth, Blake E., and Ronald H. Humphrey. 1995. "Emotion in the Workplace: A Reappraisal." *Human Relations* 48: 97–125.

Bernstein, B. 1971. *Class, Codes, and Control*. New York: Schocken.

Cahill, Spencer E. 1999. "Emotional Capital and Professional Socialization: The Case of Mortuary Science Students (and Me)." *Social Psychology Quarterly* 62: 101–116.

Cahill, Spencer E., and Robin Eggleston. 1994. "Managing Emotions in Public: The Case of Wheelchair Users." *Social Psychology Quarterly* 57: 300–312.

Cancian, Francesca M., and Steven L. Gordon. 1988. "Changing Emotion Norms in Marriage: Love and Anger in U.S. Women's Magazines since 1900." *Gender and Society* 2: 308–342.

Clark, Candace. 1997. *Misery and Company: Sympathy in Everyday Life*. Chicago: University of Chicago Press.

Cooley, Charles Horton. 1964. *Human Nature and the Social Order*. New York: Schocken Books (original work published 1902).

DeCoster, Vaughn A. 1997. "Physician Treatment of Patient Emotions: An Application of the Sociology of Emotion." *Social Perspectives on Emotion* 4: 151–177.

Denzin, Norman. 1990. "On Understanding Emotion: The Interpretive-Cultural Agenda." Pp. 85–116 in *Research Agendas in the Sociology of Emotions*, edited by T. D. Kemper. Albany: State University of New York Press.

Ekman, P. 1982. *Emotion in the Human Face*. Cambridge: Cambridge University Press.

Goffman, Erving. 1959. *The Presentation of Self in Everyday Life*. Garden City, NY: Doubleday.

———. 1961. *Encounters: Two Studies in the Sociology of Interaction*. Indianapolis, IN: Bobbs-Merrill.

———. 1967. *Interaction Ritual: Essays on Face-to-Face Behavior*. Garden City, NY: Doubleday.

———. 1983. "The Interaction Order." *American Sociological Review* 48: 1–17.

Gordon, Steven L. 1981. "The Sociology of Sentiments and Emotion." Pp. 562–592 in *Social Psychology: Sociological Perspectives*, edited by M. Rosenberg and R. H. Turner. New York: Basic Books.

———. 1989. "Institutional and Impulsive Orientations in Selectively Appropriating Emotions to Self." Pp. 115–135 in *The Sociology of Emotions: Original Essays and Research Papers,* edited by D. D. Franks and E. D. McCarthy. Greenwich, CT: JAI Press.

———. 1990. "Social Structural Effects on Emotions." Pp. 180–203 in *Research Agendas in the Sociology of Emotions*, edited by T. D. Kemper. Albany: State University of New York Press.

Hochschild, Arlie R. 1979. "Emotion Work, Feeling Rules, and Social Structure." *American Journal of Sociology* 85: 551–575.

———. 1983. *The Managed Heart: Commercialization of Human Feeling*. Berkeley: University of California Press.

———. 1989. *The Second Shift: Working Parents and the Revolution at Home*. New York: Viking Press.

———. 1990. "Ideology and Emotion Management: A Perspective and Path for Future Research." Pp. 117–142 in *Research Agendas in the Sociology of Emotions*, edited by T. D. Kemper. Albany: State University of New York Press.

Izard, Carroll E. 1977. *Human Emotions*. New York: Plenum.

Kemper, Theodore D. 1990. "Social Relations and Emotions: A Structural Approach." Pp. 207–237 in *Research Agendas in the Sociology of Emotions*, edited by T. D. Kemper. Albany: State University of New York Press.

Leavitt, Robin L., and Martha B. Power. 1989. "Emotional Socialization in the Postmodern Era: Children in Day Care." *Social Psychology Quarterly* 52: 35–43.

Lofland, Lyn H. 1985. "The Social Shaping of Emotion: the Case of Grief." *Symbolic Interaction* 8: 171–190.

Morris, J. Andrew, and Daniel C. Feldman. 1996. "The Dimensions, Antecedents, and Consequences of Emotional Labor." *Academy of Management Review* 21: 986–1010.

Paules, Greta Foff. 1991. *Dishing It Out: Power and Resistance Among Waitresses in a New Jersey Restaurant*. Philadelphia: Temple University Press.

Peterson, Gretchen. 1998. "Reproducing the Social Structure of Emotional Labor: A Reformulation and Test of Hochschild's Argument." Pacific Sociological Association annual meetings, Portland, OR.

Pierce, Jennifer L. 1995. *Gender Trials: Emotional Lives in Contemporary Law Firms*. Berkeley: University of California Press.

Pollak, Lauren H., and Peggy A. Thoits. 1989. "Processes in Emotional Socialization." *Social Psychology Quarterly* 52: 22–34.

Rafaeli, Anat, and Robert I. Sutton. 1987. "Expression of Emotion as Part of the Work Role." *Academy of Management Review* 12: 23–37.

Rosenberg, Morris. 1990. "Reflexivity and Emotions." *Social Psychology Quarterly* 53: 3–12.

———. 1991. "Self Processes and Emotional Experiences." Pp. 123–142 in *The Self–Society Interface: Cognition, Emotion, and Action*, edited by J. A. Howard and P. Callero. New York: Cambridge University Press.

Smith, Allen C., and Sherryl Kleinman. 1989. "Managing Emotions in Medical School: Students' Contacts with the Living and the Dead." *Social Psychology Quarterly* 52: 56–69.

Stets, Jan E., and Teresa Tsushima. 2001. "Negative Emotion and Coping Responses within Identity Control Theory." *Social Psychology Quarterly* 64: 283–295.

Thoits, Peggy A. 1985. "Self-Labeling Processes in Mental Illness: The Role of Emotional Deviance." *American Journal of Sociology* 91: 221–249.

———. 1989. "The Sociology of Emotions." *Annual Review of Sociology* 15: 317–342.

———. 1990. "Emotional Deviance: Research Agendas." Pp. 180–203 in *Research Agendas in the Sociology of Emotions*, edited by T. D. Kemper. Albany: State University of New York Press.

Tolich, Martin B. 1993. "Alienating and Liberating Emotions at Work: Supermarket Clerks' Performance of Customer Service." *Journal of Contemporary Ethnography* 22: 361–381.

Turner, Jonathan H., and Jan E. Stets. 2005. *The Sociology of Emotions*. New York: Cambridge University Press.

Turner, Ralph H. 1976. "The Real Self: From Institution to Impulse." *American Journal of Sociology* 81: 989–1016.

Wierzbicka, Anna. 1999. *Emotions across Languages and Cultures: Diversity and Universals*. Cambridge: Cambridge University Press.

CHAPTER 6

Ritual Theory

ERIKA SUMMERS-EFFLER

Ritual theories assert that focused interaction, which these theories refer to as ritual, is at the heart of all social dynamics. Rituals generate group emotions that are linked to symbols, forming the basis for beliefs, thinking, morality, and culture. People use the capacity for thought, beliefs, and strategy to create emotion-generating interactions in the future. This cycle, interaction $\rightarrow$ emotions $\rightarrow$ symbols $\rightarrow$ interaction, forms patterns of interaction over time. These patterns are the most basic structural force that organizes society.

Durkheim (1995) was one of the first to put forward a strong theory of ritual and emotion, building his theory on ethnographic accounts of the ritual behavior of aborigines in central Australia. Durkheim investigated the mechanisms that held society together from many angles throughout his career; in *The Elementary Forms of Religious Life* he focused on religious ritual, ultimately arguing that ritual is the fundamental mechanism that holds a society together. Although the aspects of his arguments that rest on his assumption that aboriginal groups are examples of the most primitive human behavior are untenable, he provided a powerful theory of the role of ritual in group life. He illustrated how religious ritual leads to increased interaction, especially focused, intense, and rhythmic interaction.

Durkheim described how rituals generate emotional arousal, which he referred to as *collective effervescence*. Collective effervescence is experienced as a heightened awareness of group membership as well as a feeling that an outside powerful force has sacred significance. This sacred sentiment is attached to the symbols at the center of the group's ritual attention space. Through this association, the ritual symbols are made sacred in the interaction. Both the group and the sacred totem objects of the group have the capacity to arouse intense emotion that has a moral quality; those things that offer positive affirmation of the group and its sacred symbols are "good," whereas those that threaten the symbols or the boundaries of the group are "bad." Durkheim pointed out that groups must come together periodically to engage in ritual to renew both the sense of

ERIKA SUMMERS-EFFLER • Department of Sociology, University of Notre Dame, Notre Dame, IN 46556 group membership and the sacred symbols that represent the group, which are used as the moral foundation for group membership. The most powerful aspect of Durkheim's theory is his analysis of the mechanisms that generate the intense emotions at the foundation of solidarity and culture.

Durkheim (1995) suggested that his theory of religious ritual could be extended to secular life, and slightly less than 50 years later, Goffman (1959, 1967) took up this project. Rather than focusing on the formal interactions that we often think of as rituals, Goffman illustrated how all focused interactions, even passing greetings, had the ritual quality that Durkheim described. When two people exchange:

"How are you?"
"Fine, and how are you?"
"Fine. Thank you."

they are engaging in an informal interaction ritual. There is a shared focus of attention and the affirmation of solidarity and the symbols of that solidarity—the actors themselves. Goffman illustrated that informal interaction has a moral character that constrains behavior on the most microlevel.

Collins (1981, 1990, 2004) built on Goffman's theory and returned to the more mechanistic approach of Durkheim. Like Goffman, Collins argued that face-to-face focused interaction is the foundation of social life, but like Durkheim, he offered a mechanistic analysis of these interactions and generated a formal theory of ritual interaction. Collins argued that for a ritual to take place, there must be the following: two or more people in the physical presence of each other; a mutual awareness shared by participants and a common focus of attention, whether it is on the group itself, an activity, or a particular symbol; and a common emotional mood, although this mood can change or grow during the ritual itself. If all of these factors are present, actors are then in a position to engage in rhythmic coordinated behavior. If any of these factors are absent, the ritual will likely fail. Similarly, the range of these factors' intensity will also affect the intensity or success of the ritual. Intense involvement and focus result in intense ritual activity.

Focused rhythmic activity generates collective effervescence, which Collins suggested has two components: group-focused solidarity and individual-focused *emotional energy* (EE). Failed rituals generate negative emotions, primarily shame (Scheff 1990). The intensity of emotion varies with the intensity of focus. Symbols associated with ritual, generally the focus of attention during the interaction, are associated with feelings of solidarity and EE.

Polillo (2004) and Summers-Effler (2002, 2004a, 2004b, 2004c), both students of Collins, have continued to expand and develop ritual theories of emotion in interaction by further specifying social dynamics grounded in interaction ritual (process of the self and small groups specifically) and further detailing the dynamics of ritual involvement (see below).

THE INTERACTION ORDER

To be clear, in ritual theory the ritual interaction generates the emotions that are at the basis of social life. Durkheim (1995) argued that the realm of collective consciousness, the group's experience of itself as a group, is not a mere combination of individual consciousness but a *sui generis* form of consciousness. This realm of social life generates "feelings, ideas, and images that follow their own law once they are born" (Durkheim 1995:426). Society is not based in the propensity and capacity of the individual. Rather, symbols are formed in social interaction and then used by individuals (Durkheim 1995).

In ritual theory, properties often attributed to the self are attributed to the realm of the interaction. Both Goffman (1959) and Collins (2004) made it a theoretical priority to argue and empirically demonstrate that situations or encounters are the fundamental causal force on the microlevel of social life. Goffman stated clearly that the self is not derived from the individual, but from the encounter. If the encounter is carried off correctly, the audience members and participants of the encounter will attribute selves to the actors involved in the encounter (Goffman 1959).

The ritual theory perspective on the *sui generis* dynamics and constraints of the interaction order leads to a grammatical style in the theory that might appear to be nonspecific if misunderstood. Durkheim, Goffman, and Collins occasionally used the passive voice to describe mechanisms or give active capacity to interaction, encounters, or situations, and thus seemingly treat what is commonly thought of as intangible as though it were a concrete material thing. This is not accidental, but in fact captures the central assumption of the ritual approach—interactions are tangible entities that have active and compelling properties that are irreducible to individuals participating in them or more macro social dynamics.

INTERACTION ORDER DYNAMICS

Durkheim (1995:217) argued that the act of gathering is a powerful stimulant, generating a "sort of electricity" from mere closeness. When groups engage in ritual action, defined as intense, focused, and rhythmic behavior (Durkeim 1995), they experience the feeling of collective effervescence, which is highly enjoyable, and the development of the conscience collective, which is intersubjective thinking in which the group is perceived as a single entity. This emotional and cognitive state gives rise to the sensation and thought of the divine, which feels like and is perceived as a force outside the group. However, despite the external feel of the divine, the sensation is the experience of the group's own power. This sensation of the external divine is then attached to the symbols of the ritual—totems in the cases in which Durkheim builts his theory. The moral order is created in ritual practice; the totem, the ritual itself, and the boundaries of the group achieve a sacred status. Any transgression against these sacred elements is a moral transgression that engenders righteous anger. By coming together for ritual activity, groups reaffirm their boundaries, feelings of solidarity associated with the group, and the power of the sacred symbols that help to organize the group's activity outside of formal ritual activity (see Figure 6.1).

Rather than formal ritual, Goffman described the obligations each of us encounters when we enter into informal interaction with another. We must take up a line, which is a coherent approach

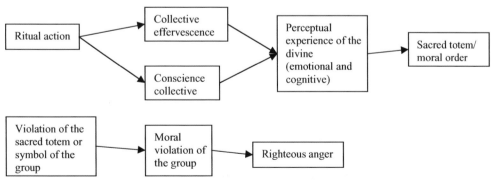

FIGURE 6.1. Durkheim's Theory Ritual Action and the Moral Order

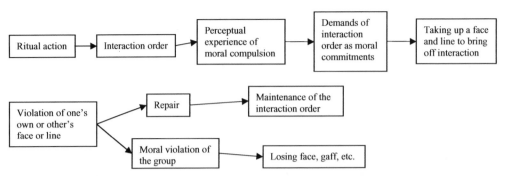

FIGURE 6.2. Goffman's Conception of the Interaction Order as a Moral Order

to communicating in the interaction that conveys our perspective on the situation, including ourselves and the other actors (Goffman 1967). By taking up a line, we claim a face, which is the positive social value that a person claims in an encounter (Goffman 1967). In order for an encounter to come off successfully, participants must work to preserve not only their own line and face but also those of the others involved. Because all participants' lines and faces must remain intact to bring off an interaction, when a person's line or face fails, the individual and his or her audience members will work to repair the interaction through a variety of techniques.

If interactions go well, attributions of selves will precipitate out of the interaction (Goffman 1959). In the interaction ritual, the line, face, and self are the sacred totemic symbols of the ritual. Goffman illustrated the moral obligation to preserve interaction. Emotion, in the form of moral compulsion, is central to his analysis of the interaction order. However, he did not analyze or theorize about the mechanisms that generate the interaction order, thus there is no clear picture of the role of emotion in creating the moral order (see Figure 6.2).

Collins formalized Goffman's work on interaction ritual. He put forth mechanisms that specify how interaction ritual produces the moral expectations of interaction order (Collins 1981, 1990, 2004). To create an interaction ritual, there must be two or more people who are physically close enough to become entrained in each other's actions. These people must share a mutual awareness in order for the ritual potential in such proximity to be realized. Participants must also share a focus of attention and a transient emotion, both of which allow for intersubjectivity. If these four requirements are met, they will create rhythmic entrainment, meaning that participants will begin to move in synch with each other, either in physically obvious ways or through micro-coordination below the level of conscious awareness that nonetheless can be detected by slowing down video or audio recordings (Collins 2004).

Entrainment and joint rhythmic activity generates what Durkheim described as collective effervescence, which Collins broke down into two emotions: group-focused solidarity, which is composed of positive, enthusiastic, and moral feelings toward the group that will change to righteous anger if the boundaries of the group are transgressed; and individual-focused emotional energy, which is a positive feeling of enthusiasm, confidence, and a willingness to initiate interaction. Rather than the more punctuated and disruptive transient emotions, such as joy or anger, EE (emotional energy) is experienced as a level that is carried from interaction to interaction, increasing when we engage in successful interaction ritual and depleting when rituals fail or when we go for too long without engaging in ritual activity. Conflict can also take the form of an intensely focused interaction, and Collins argued that these sorts of interaction will generate EE as well, but only for the victor (see Figure 6.3). Similarly, those who dominate, order givers, gain EE (or at least prevent EE loss), whereas those who are dominated, order takers, lose EE (Collins 2004).

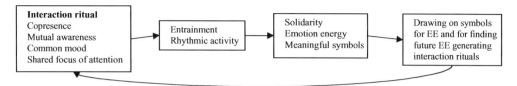

FIGURE 6.3. Collin's Model of Interaction Ritual

Collins argued that we are motivated to maximize our experience of EE and that this is the fundamental drive behind individual behavior, group activity, culture, and networks. Thus, all patterns of social activity, even the most macro, are traceable to the level of interaction where the goal of maximizing EE is realized and meaningful symbols are formed. We move from interaction to interaction, bringing the EE consequences and the symbols created in the interaction with us as we go. So whereas the interaction order has independent situational demands, past interaction determines the level of emotional energy and symbolic capital available to us to deal with these demands. The consequences of the interaction adjust our level of EE and our symbolic capital, which has consequences that reach into the future as we navigate our social world in response to that recent interaction and all the ones that have come before. As we move through time, we create chains of interaction rituals, each encounter linking us to the ones that came before and the ones that will follow. If you followed a single individual's chain over time, you would be able to see his or her level of EE fluctuate and the symbolic consequences of the EE—positive, negative, and neutral—interactions that make up the person's chain. Hypothetically, by accessing the history of their interaction ritual chain, you would be able to predict which interactions they would move toward and how they would draw on their store of symbols to negotiate their changing context (Collins 2004).

In recent work, Summers-Effler (2004c) further specified many of the claims Collins made about the interaction order, in some cases returning to Goffman's focus on the role of shared knowledge in pulling off interaction rituals. As stated above, Collins explained varying levels of emotional intensity generated in interaction by the varying levels of focused attention achieved in the interaction. Based on ethnographic observation of small activist groups, Summers-Effler (2004c) argued that shared uncertainty about interaction outcomes generates the most intense focus of attention, as participants must pay careful attention to the changing context to be able to negotiate the unfolding interaction. Thus, interaction rituals that involve group risks are likely to generate intense focus, intense emotion, and high levels of EE. Formal rituals create reliable patterns of engaging groups, securing at least some focused attention. However, they involve little to no risk, meaning that although they might be sure bets, they will have limited EE and solidarity payoffs compared to high-risk, and therefore more spontaneous and emergent, rituals.

Summers-Effler (2002, 2004c) also built on Collins's work to further specify the dynamics of power in interaction. Collins stated that individuals can gain access to EE through solidarity or power, but his illustrations of power in interaction primarily described how the powerless lose EE in interaction rather than how the powerful gain EE in interaction. Separating EE from solidarity is a theoretical challenge. Although a conflict can be an intimate and entraining interaction, the shared emotion is missing altogether or superficial at best. Hatfield et al. (1994) found that negative threatening emotions, like anger, engender reciprocal, not shared emotion. The dominated party or parties might *perform* shared emotion, but the solidarity would seem to only go as deep as the shared emotion. There remains the potential for solidarity through deep acting (Hochschild 1983), Stockholm syndrome would be an example of this effect, but in this case, it would seem that the interaction is actually transformed to a solidarity-based rather than power-based interaction.

Collins (2004) stated that there are two types of power: D power, which is power based in the ability to command deference, and E power, which is the power to get things done or to change the way that things are done. He suggested that D power is a microphenomenon, whereas E power is realized on the mesolevel of networks. I suggest that distinguishing these types of power by the social levels on which they are realized might not give us the most complete understanding of power dynamics in interaction. For example, we can think of charismatic power—the ability to mobilize initiative on the level of interaction—as a microform of E power. However, if we only focus on the microlevel, we miss how finite opportunities in any one network's attention space generate mesolevel competition for E power. Similarly we can think of a competition between athletes as a challenge for interactional dominance on a microlevel and an effort to create solidarity with a coach or teammates at a later time.

The multidimensional dynamics of power relationships suggests that the concept of an interaction chain might be too linear an image to illustrate the role of embeddedness in interactions. I suggest that a single moment usually plays a role in multiple embedded emotional histories. Although we can only be involved in one interaction at a time, the meaning of the interaction and the strategic reason behind the interaction might be situated in many interactions in the future, so that a single moment has not only a multiplicity of meanings but a multiplicity of emotional consequences for various series of interactions that unfold from a particular moment. Embeddedness is part of all but the most intense and overwhelming of interaction rituals that have the capacity to engulf us in their momentum and, by doing, so to narrow our focus to a single point of time.

SECOND-ORDER SYSTEM DYNAMICS

Despite his argument that ritual organizes social life, Durkheim understood that people live in a multicausal world. He acknowledged the interrelationship between basic material needs and sacred activity. Goffman recognized the significance of other levels of social life (Rawls 1987), but focused on describing how the interaction order is irreducible and articulating the dynamics of the interaction order. Collins has made the most assertive claim about the primacy of the interaction order, stating that all macropatterns are aggregates of interactions and that such macropatterns reflect the dynamics of face-to-face interactions. Although he has acknowledged that we live in a multicausal world, primarily in writings that demonstrate the applications of interaction ritual chain (IRC) theory to empirical problems, he focuses primarily on the basic motivating force of maximizing EE.

One direction to develop ritual theory is to look at performances as events belonging to semiautonomous realms (Alexander 2004). Another is to bring in systems logic, thus conceptualizing different levels of social life as emergent. Polillo (2004) and Summers-Effler (2004a, 2004b, 2004c) have been developing models of second-order systems that are interrelated with the interaction order but that have emergent properties of their own. Rather than a micro causing macro assumption, we present a picture of interlocking levels. Systems theory helps us to conceptualize how the levels relate to each other, explaining both direct effects and the dampening of effects between systems. With a systems approach, we can still offer predictive capacity, but at the expense of understanding that other levels of social life, although traceable to the interaction order, have emergent properties of their own that must be theorized. This is not to suggest that ritual theory is not crucial for gaining insight into all levels of social processes, but, rather, that there is much work to be done before it is fully a micro/macrotheory of social life.

THINKING AND THE SELF

Durkheim was primarily occupied with creating a gestalt shift where people saw society, rather than the individual, as the primary actor. Despite this focus, Durkheim did address thinking, which we can conceptualize as a particular process of the self. He distinguished between what we are able to sense and what we are able to think. Senses are based in the body. They are immediate, ever fluctuating, and tell us little that is meaningful outside the immediate experience (Durkeim 1995). Concepts, on the other hand, are based in ritual and are transpersonal. They resist change, changing only when they become problematic (Durkeim 1995). Durkheim (1995) described how, once formed through symbolic representation of emotional ritual, society gains the capacity to experience an indirect consciousness of itself through concepts (indirect because it is focused on the symbol rather than the ritual interaction that generated the meaning of the symbol). Because concepts grow out of group activity, they do not share the narrow self-oriented perspective of sensations. They enable a sense of the whole that is not connected to the body, and as such, they are the foundation for abstract and logical thought (Durkeim 1995). Durkheim argued that this capacity for abstract reasoning, so often attached to the individual, soul, or self, is only possible through social interaction.

Although Durkheim's agenda was to decenter the self as the primary social force, he does concede the relevance of individual dynamics, stating that once internalized, collective concepts tend to become individualized. He acknowledged that even though society is the basis for the creation of "our nature," once created this nature is no less real (Durkeim 1995). The individual plays some role in selecting relevant concepts, and thus over time, a personality develops as an autonomous source of action (Durkheim 1995). However, Durkheim specified neither the mechanisms by which this happens nor the secondary influence of the individual on the social order.

Goffman (1959) paralleled Durkheim's approach in his argument that interaction creates the self rather than the other way around, but Goffman's perspective is all the more striking because he focused specifically on the self. Goffman set the encounter and the causal dynamics of interaction order against our folk presumption that the self is the dominant causal force on the microlevel. People strategize, perform, and cooperate in teams in order to present a positive self. The person, who will either succeed or lose in his or her effort to generate a positive self-image, is merely "the peg on which something of collaborative manufacture will be hung for a time. Also, the means for producing and maintaining selves do not reside inside the pege" (Goffman 1959). The self is the sacred symbol of the interaction (Goffman 1959), and like Durkheim argues in *Elementary Forms of Religious Life*, the force that generates the symbol is attributed to the symbols that represent it once the symbols are formed. Agency is attributed the sacred self because it is the sacred symbol affirmed in the multiple interaction rituals that constitute our day-to-day lives.

Goffman, however, confused his argument through his complex and not entirely consistent use of the terms. Throughout *The Presentation of Self in Everyday Life* (Goffman 1959), the self is used to indicate the positive value an individual claims in an interaction, which Goffman (1967) referred to as *face* in later works. However, he also described strategizing individuals actively creating and vying for positive selves. We are left to ask, "if there is no self, who is doing this strategizing to bring off a positive presentation of self?" On the surface, Goffman dismissed the self altogether, but he was primarily arguing that we need to reconsider the notion of a self that is fixed and similar to our conception of a personality or a soul. Although arguing that the interaction order generates the capacity for becoming human, he concedes that a general capacity to be bound by moral rules belongs to the individual (Goffman 1967). He was not presenting a picture in which there are no relevant social processes or dynamics at work on the level of the individual. It is an oversimplification to suggest that his work supports the position that there is no self or that important social dynamics do not occur on the level of the self. Rather, he successfully decenters the self and points our attention toward the fundamental level of social life—the interaction order.

Goffman presented the individual as a strategist working to present a positive self, but he did not explain the mechanisms or capacity to strategize. Collins, on the other hand, accomplished the goal of developing a microsociological theory where the self plays only a minimal role as a third-order product of the primary interaction order. Collins (2004), like Goffman, argued that the self is a product rather than a cause of the situation. Through developing his theory of IRC, Collins connected thinking directly to network position rather than internal self-dynamics. Through individual IRCs people learn what interactions are likely to have the best EE payoffs. People operate within an EE market for interactions (Collins 2004), but they do not usually consciously strategize about interaction market choices. Rather the market *pulls* them toward the optimal interactions based on their IRCs (Collins 2004:144). Patterns of interaction create differing opportunities for interactions depending on where the individuals are positioned in the ongoing patterns of interaction.

From this perspective, rational choice theory is useful for understanding behavior as long as we understand both that EE is the common denominator that determines value and that maximization patterns appear on the network level (Collins 2004). Building on Durkheim's original point about the dynamics that give birth to meaningful symbols, Collins (2004) argued that symbols circulate through networks as a result of actors' attempts to match cultural capital in order to facilitate IRCs to generate EE. The patterns of symbolic circulation are the product, not the cause, of this symbolic matching process within EE markets; the symbols lag behind and reveal a history of interaction.

Internal dynamics of thinking mirror these external patterns. Collins (2004) argued, as the pragmatists have, that people proceed habitually until the actor encounters an obstacle; when habits fail, conscious thinking begins. Collins (2004) argued that even such an apparently individualist activity as thinking is a product of network position. Networks determine both access to symbols and level of EE, which is crucial, as high levels of EE are required to creatively integrate the symbolic potential represented in a network position (Collins 2004). Internal verbal thought is a third-order phenomenon based in the second-order networks in which we participate (Collins 2004). We use the symbols that circulate within our external networks for the internal process of thinking. Not only the symbolic content of networks but also the density and diversity of network formations affect patterns of thinking—looser and more diverse external networks generating more abstract and relativistic thinking, and denser and more homogeneous external networks generating narrower and more concrete thinking (Collins 2004).

Networks, rather than individual strategizers, play an essential role in organizing microdynamics, even the microdynamics of thinking, which are usually relegated to the self or the individual. The self has only a limited capacity to direct future scenarios, as levels of EE, cultural capital, and network position all have a more immediate impact. Therefore, past interactions are only consequential in terms of their immediate consequence for EE, cultural capital, and network position. This is a radical departure from the Freudian perspective that has been so dominant in our understanding of the individual (Collins 2004).

Summers-Effler builts on Durkheim's, Goffman's, and Collins's arguments for the primacy of the interaction order, but argued that the self is a level of social life with its own emergent properties that affect other levels of social life. In fact, Summers-Effler (2004a) argued that the self is the key to understanding the process of culture. The self is a system that emerges, over time, out of the competing push and pull of two other systems: the interaction order and the body.

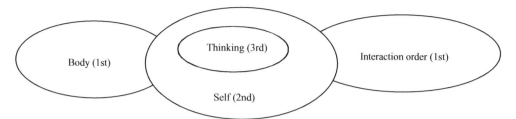

FIGURE 6.4. Self and Thinking as Emergent Systems

Culture is often understood in opposition to the biological processes of the body; it is assumed that our symbolic capacity separates humans from other animals that are more firmly grounded in their bodies. Alternately, Summers-Effler (2004a) argued that when we ground the potential for learning, and thus acquisition of symbolic meaning, in the body, we arrive at the most dynamic and flexible understanding of the self and culture (see Figure 6.4).

Although it has not been the central focus of ritual theory, theorists of ritual have recognized the role of the body and the biological forces in ritual life: Durkheim (1995), psychobiological forces; Goffman (1959), the role of basic drives for social contact and companionship; and Collins (2004), the coordination of bodies in interaction and the physiological arousal of bodies in the experience of emotional energy. Collins (2004) argued for a basic motivation to maximize emotional energy; Summers-Effler went further and demonstrated how and why this motivation is inborn. Summers-Effler (2004a) argued that although we are motivated by self-interest, this self-interest is tempered by reliance on groups. The development of a genetic drive toward social solidarity did not happen through the individual-level selection but a socially oriented selection whereby the group is the selection force for evolution at the individual level (Stevens and Fiske 1995); thus, the capacity to adapt to the group, regardless of specific group processes, has been genetically selected as advantageous for humans (Gopnik and Meltzoff 1997). Possessing a drive toward group membership and the capacity to be flexible in regard to group content means that a capacity for learning is closely tied to the drive for solidarity. Emotions are our primary tools in this learning process. This body-level process works in much the same way that Durkheim's theory of ritual works on the group level. Social conditions arouse adaptive bodily responses that are experienced as emotions (Brothers 1997; Damasio 1994; Schneider 1991).

Through parallel processing, symbols from the environment are attached to the bodily response and stored as somatic markers. These markers create "as if" loops (Damasio 1994:155). When we encounter the symbol again, either in the world or in our minds, the symbol activates neural connections that make us feel "as if" we are experiencing the interaction between our body and our environment that generated the meaning of the symbol (Summers-Effler 2004a). "As if" loops are the basis for learning that allows us to anticipate and navigate our social environment. By specifying the mechanism that generates symbols and claiming that they are, in themselves, strategies, not just tools for implementing the strategy, we not only have a foundation for a theory of how culture is formed but also how it changes, thus explaining the emergent properties of selves and culture without dismissing either the role of the biological body or the structural importance of the interaction order where the symbols are formed and modified.

Like Durkheim, Summers-Effler argued that there are two processes to the self: the sensing process of the self that experiences emotional reactions in response to environmental conditions, and the contextualizing process of the self that forms and updates "as if" loops. Whereas the sensing process of the self is anchored in a motivation to maximize EE, the contextualizing process lags behind as new information is reconciled with the old. Expectations for positive and negative interactions are built up over one's history. These expectations are not born of abstract understandings of cultural discourses but from patterns of interaction. In children we can see this process with little history, so that there is less stability and fluctuations are rampant. A best friend is subject to vicious hatred and anger if he or she does not behave as a child wishes, but the friendship is restored quickly once everyone returns to shared expectations. Maturity, consistency, loyalty, and commitment are born of a history of long-established patterns where the long haul is valued beyond short-run up and down fluctuations.

Undermining expectations renders "as if" loops useless and leaves us with no social bearing; thus there is a drive to build useful strategies. If we imagine that the self is the process of creating, reconciling, and updating all of the "as if" loops that connect the body to the continual unfolding of particular environmental contexts and that this process is organized to predict and achieve the greatest access to EE, we can see that although the self might be generated by the inborn motivation to maximize EE or integration into the group, once formed there is an emergent drive for self-consistency on the level of the self. The self is born of the drive to maximize EE, but the need to anticipate makes it conservative once formed. We will often hang on to strategies that only make sense within the context of our entire history rather than the immediate context. This is particularly the case for "as if" loops that were formed early and have been used to negotiate many of our interactions. Many of our more developed strategies are modifications of these initial orientations to the world. We can think of these older, more general, and most useful "as if" loops as personal style. As many of our more specific "as if" loops would be rendered useless if the more fundamental personal style were undermined, personal style is a particularly conservative force within the self.

When we update our "as if" loops in order to continue to seek EE, we are engaged in proactive strategizing. Because the goal is to achieve more EE, proactive "as if" loops are modified when there is any loss or unanticipated gain of EE. Because these associations are sensitive to shifts in the context and are easily modified, their development and modification are fluid processes. Alternately, when it seems that all avenues for building EE are closed off and we are forced to develop strategies to minimize loss, we engage in defensive strategizing (Summers-Effler 2004b). In these situations, efforts to control the emotional consequences of interactions are turned inward, and the focus is on controlling one's own behavior in a particular context rather than on moving through one's environment. Defensive "as if" loops anticipate EE loss, so they are unlikely to be updated even when there are significant losses. This means that these strategies tend to be far more durable than proactive strategies. Although all strategies lag behind the immediate context, defensive strategies persist long after they have outlived their usefulness. Summers-Effler (2004b) argued that defensive strategies are often the foundation of self-destructive behaviors (such as staying with abusive partners or eating disorders).

Defensive strategies generate a paradox of reflexivity. They tend to create a narrow focus on the self, but this narrow focus undermines the capacity to take in the subtle changes in context, which undermines the potential for identifying other options. Reflexivity is also diminished when internal representations of dominating others overwhelm internal conversation by shutting out weaker positions, which also limits one's capacity to conceive of all possible strategies of action. Because defensive strategies are born of a lack of positive choice, we could anticipate that those who are most systematically disadvantaged (those denied many EE maximization opportunities) would be most likely to develop defensive strategies. This suggests that disadvantaged network positions negatively affect not only immediate access to material resources and EE but also the potential for building strategies that would enable those at the margins to take advantage of situational opportunities when the opportunities arise (Summers-Effler 2002).

Two types of conflict can generate reflexivity about the normally unconscious proactive strategies. The first is when our "as if" loops fail to accurately predict an interaction and the interaction does not come off as well as planned. Small variations will bring about subtle modifications of existing "as if" loops, whereas substantial conflict between what was expected and what ensues requires the dismissal of old loops and the formation of new. This more drastic process is more likely to become conscious, although not necessarily verbal. As Collins (2004) and Turner (2000) pointed out, much of conscious thought is based in images rather than dialogue. Situations that call on competing or conflicting "as if" loops also generate conscious thought. Membership in multiple networks can often be sustained with few conflicts, but conflict ensues when membership in different networks demands different strategies. These conflicts are not so much about the failure of a prediction as they are about a history of IRCs that invoke conflicting strategies.

For example, consider women who may have "as if" loops associated with work situations and gender identity. In the event of becoming a mother, the chains will likely compete as past experience predicts conflicting scenarios for EE maximization and EE drains—the strategies for gender and work conflict. Although incompatible but potentially equally positive strategies can create conscious thinking, the most extensive and verbally based reflexivity is based in incompatible and potentially equally draining strategies—situations in which is seems that all roads lead to EE drain in one way or another.

The voices in thinking are representations of significant others or generalized others associated with the competing network positions. Although Mead (1934) and Wiley (1994) dedicated great effort to detailing the specific dynamics of internal conversation, I would suggest that the conversation and the grammar of the conversation is a product of the particular social context and history (context unfolding over time) that generated the situation. The more rigid grammar of internal conversation that the pragmatists depict does not capture the flexibility of the thinking process, in which much is visual, and the roles in the internal dialogue are significantly determined by the immediate context and particular history. We could imagine scenarios where the "I" would play a central role in discussion and others where the "I" would be entirely excluded. Network position determines the level of EE that one has available for the internal problem solving through internal dialogue and the cultural capital at one's disposal for solving the problem. This is in line with Collins' (1998) point that network position generates the potential for particular ideas to crystallize at particular times and in particular people.

Polillo (2004) has further specified the internal dynamics of the self. He built on pragmatists' work on the self, Wiley's (1994) semiotic self in particular, by imagining the parts of the self as a network with different temporal orientations. He incorporated Goffman's work on the interaction order and Collins' work on interaction rituals to analyze the EE potential of different network compositions within the self. He argued that internal networks that have developed strong ties among their components can result in essentialist perspectives on the self and one's personal identity, based on an idealization of the past or, at best, a strategy of day-to-day survival.

Such a perspective on the self limits the reflexive potential for envisioning alternative identities and social positions—a dynamic that is particularly damaging for those who occupy diminished social positions with oppressive social identities, especially when the external interactional environment binds the dominated to the dominant and leaves little structural space for the dominated to develop an oppositional identity. When internal network structures between positions within the self become less strongly tied to one another, a constructivist perspective on the self and the social conditions that shape the self is allowed. Whereas a strongly tied self looks to the past or, at best, to the present, it is the future that orients the self when it is embedded in a "cosmopolitan" external network. Again, this sort of internal network composition is particularly powerful for those who suffer from oppressive identities, as it enables them to envision alternatives, an ability that is central in the process of organizing to create those alternatives.

NETWORK PROCESSES

Durkheim focused on society as a whole, Goffman focused on the interaction order and Collins introduced the potential for ritual theory to connect all levels of social life, from face-to-face interaction to social patterns that emerge over many lifetimes. IRCs connect the interaction order to all larger patterns. Networks are a particular type of IRC in which types of interaction, thus particular transient emotions and symbols, are recycled among overlapping ties. Rather than connections between people, networks are connections between parts of the self that are activated in patterned situations. Network theory looks at the connection between people, but from an IRC perspective; network ties are between repeated significant social interactions (Collins 2004). Interactions within networks are primed through shared history or shared interaction patterns and symbols, so the network connections and symbols are self-reinforcing.

Ritual theory approaches provide the basic motivation behind the formation, destruction, and evolution of networks, thus theoretical insight into the unfolding of networks over time. Efforts to anticipate positive social interaction (see above section on the self) generate networks. If individuals were randomly put in a limited space with no preexisting ties, the process of people relying on anticipation as a tool to experience EE would result in patterns of interactions between people—networks born of individual efforts to anticipate interactions over time.

We can imagine IRCs as though they are time-lapsed photographs that capture the patterns of light made by automobiles at night. From the perspective of a single street, we would see a single stream of light made from cars on this particular street, but from above, we would see a grid of light that would reflect the paths available for cars rather than any particular route. From an IRC perspective, it is intuitive to focus on the larger pattern of interactions over an individual path. An individual at any given time appears as a crystallization of the larger pattern.

Why is the individual so entwined with the larger pattern of interactions? The competition for optimal positioning within the limited attention space that creates interaction markets shapes networks as well. Although the interactions themselves might be primarily focused on building solidarity, competition for limited attention space shapes the possibilities for building solidarity. Privileged network position is determined by early and enduring patterns of interactions with those who occupy a central position in a network. Once gained, central positions are maintained through enduring patterns of interaction with contemporaries who are similarly advantaged by early connections to preeminent figures in a network (Collins 1998). Parties illustrate this dynamic in concrete terms. If we are popular, we feel the burden of choice, as we cannot talk to everyone at once. If we are not popular, we feel the effort required to get ourselves into a conversation. From a more macroview, this dynamic crystallizes into status positions within networks and the law of small numbers that Collins (1998) described.

Although Collins illustrated the process of networks and the competition for attention space in the development of philosophy and prominent figures in philosophy, a process that involves patterns that unfold over many lifetimes, we could presume that the same process would unfold more quickly in other sorts of network. Newcomers to a social network who are able to build enduring patterns of interactions with those at the center of the social network will be ensured a better opportunity for taking up that central attention space. Once involved, sustaining relationships with others who have similarly privileged access helps to maintain one's position as a person hosts will invite to their parties. Philosophers with privileged positions have the potential to generate creative ideas that are meaningful for a large number of philosophers because they are exposed to multiple "hot" ideas and their position endows them with the EE necessary for combining these ideas in new and interesting ways (Collins 1998). Similarly, popular people have the potential to be funny or good conversationalists because they have access to the latest goings-on in the scene and their positions endow them with the EE to take risks and initiate interactions.

In ritual theory, networks are based in interaction, thus they have less of a thinglike quality than they do in other network approaches. The meaningful network for each moment is determined by the context of the interaction. Enemies in one situation become friends in others. New neighbors invited to a party might be at the periphery of a party until the activation of another network connection by a partygoer reveals the once outsider to be closer to the center of an entirely different but situationally relevant network. Histories of relationships and affiliations are network potential that might be realized in a particular interaction. Collins' (1998) example of how philosophers' preeminence is not only determined by the networks that they emerge out of, but the networks that flow out of them, illustrates the contingent interaction-bound quality of network relations.

Collins (2004:396) claimed that network analysis is "too glib about the content of ties" and argued that the patterns of EE that are associated with a tie are a much more powerful predictor of the social implications of the tie than just the presence or absence of a tie. For example, it is likely that the advantageous weak ties and ties that bridge structural holes (Burt 1992; Granovetter 1973) are high EE ties at the periphery of networks, between unlikely and infrequent connections, or over long distances (Collins 2004). Not only the emotional, but also the symbolic content of the tie is important. Collins argued that in most cases, symbols have little meaning other than as cultural capital that facilitates access to certain networks and certain types of interaction. I would add that this is mostly true for the center of the network. At the periphery, where network members encounter those outside the network, the cultural or ideological content associated with past affiliations can be a powerful force in shaping interactions. For example, although missionaries might be driven by indirect strategies to maximize solidarity with their sending community, their ideological commitments that embody that indirect drive toward solidarity become a determining force in missionaries' interactions, at least until their networks affiliation or position shifts. Thus, cultural dissemination is not just the product of network relations; at the periphery, symbolic content also shapes relations.

SMALL GROUPS

Goffman (1967) did not focus on the unfolding of the interaction order across situations. If he had, he would have had access to observing the dynamics of a particular type of network: the small group. Small groups are self-referential patterns of interaction that involve routine face-to-face interaction among more than two members. We can learn much about other levels of social life from observing groups because, like the interaction order, we can actually see the process of a group in action. We cannot see the self in operation except through introspection, which presents certain methodological limitations; for example, there is no way to gain similar access to other selves for the sake of comparison. Likewise, we cannot see networks directly; thus, when studying them, we have the same limitations that we encounter when we use survey data: We have to rely on theory and measurements to try to understand a reality that we can never directly see.

Groups, on the other hand, are processes that offer unparalleled opportunities for observation. Groups are a particular type of network, and, like the self, groups are systems that are grounded in the interaction order and emerge out of the history of interactions within the constraints of a changing environment over time. Thus, we can assume that groups share some of the same general dynamics as the self and other types of network. Rather than relying on pieced-together data from a series of moments or a single moment—methods that often lead us to more static views of social life—observing groups over time reveals highly dynamic processes. The theory Summers-Effler (2004c) generated out of her comparative ethnographic study of group dynamics highlights the role of change and movement in group processes, even in times of stability.

Groups are focused around activity, around doing and accomplishing things. We can think of the shared goal, implicit or explicit, as the everyday ideology of the group. The tasks might be focused on meeting the needs of family members, on organizing and carrying out social functions that keep group members together, or on meeting some external goal. Regardless of how abstract or concrete or how trivial or significant, shared ideological demands require groups to face the challenge of coordinating activity to accomplish tasks. A group's day-to-day ideological demands create a shared focus of attention. The environmental context of this focus filters the articulated abstract ideology of the group, so that a group's day-to-day goals are related directly to its environmental context and only indirectly to its abstract goals.

The day-to-day goals generate challenges and mundane responsibilities. When the challenges are met successfully, they lead to a sense of expansion and an increase in EE. The more intense challenges demand focus and are thus more emotionally intense. High-risk activity either culminates in success or failure or it can cause group burnout if consequences are indeterminate for extended periods of time. When goals are not met, the group fails, leading to a sense of contraction and a loss of EE. Mundane responsibilities also drain the groups, but in a less drastic way than do incidents of failure. The groups that Summers-Effler observed engaged in recovery rituals to maintain enthusiasm and minimize a sense of contraction. The groups' successes and failures were dramatic and attention grabbing, but the cycle of mundane drain and recovery rituals created the rhythm of everyday life. By looking at groups in this way, we can anticipate where and when the disruption of the continuity of involvement lays—during failure and mundane activity when enthusiasm is low and group members are more likely to be pulled into subgroups or competing groups (Summers-Effler 2004c).

The emotional consequences of successes, failures, and mundane drain mark symbols in their interactional environment with emotional significance. As with individuals, a group draws on these symbols to anticipate positive interactions and avoid draining interactions. Over time, a group develops shared expectations for future interactions. This is the group's style—its specific culture and emotional tone. Eliasoph and Lichterman (2003) defined group style as a group's shared grounds for interaction and suggested that rather than reflecting abstract commonly held values, group style emerges within the group. By looking at patterns of interaction and emotion within the two groups that Summers-Effler studied, she observed that ritual interaction is an important mechanism in the production of group style.

The shared expectations for future interaction, or group style, form a pattern that, although ever-changing in response to changes in the interaction environment, constitutes the rhythm of daily life within these groups. Similar to the way passengers in a car turning a corner all correct their balance at the same time to compensate for the change in the environment, group members learn to shift interactions in different ways in response to changes in their environment. Because it takes time to share enough history with the groups to learn this rhythm, these implicit shared expectations mark an invisible boundary between insiders and outsiders. The ways in which group members are with each other, in which they see, understand, and strategize in response to their environment, are constructed through shared history. This construction has objective roots in the direct relationship between the structure of interaction and emotional consequences. The development of meaningful symbols over time in the form of personal and group style renders this direct connection less direct. Although group style is directly responsive to the environment, it lags behind current contexts because it develops as an increasingly complex strategy until repeated harsh failure requires the complete dismissal of the strategy.

The groups' emotionally based shared expectations supported the groups in the face of their challenges and gave them tools for dealing with failure and mundane responsibilities. These expectations also fed back into the groups' larger ideologies and goals, although they were only indirectly connected to them. The symbols that a group can call on during an encounter come from its history of prior interactions. New symbols can also be created if an interaction is at least moderately successful (Collins 2004), but these new symbols are still tied to the history of interaction that has been experienced before. In order to anticipate a group's style, one would have to know far more than its ideological orientation and ultimate goal. Style emerges from interaction within a group's specific interactional environment. This does not mean that interactions and group styles are entirely unpredictable, only that one would need access to the group's interactional history in order to predict either.

If we look only at the content and not the dynamic process that generated the content, we learn primarily about the specific history of the group rather than understanding the continually adapting dynamic that will enable us to make predictions about how changes in the environment would affect the group. At any one given point, a similar group style in different groups might reflect different conditions, because where the groups come from affects when they stay and where they will go. Stability hides the fluidity of group style; changes in the environment might be dampened for a time by expectations. Only if we pay attention to the different dynamics that produce temporarily similar group styles will we be able to anticipate how and under what circumstances the styles of the groups are likely to diverge.

CONSTRAINTS ON THE INTERACTION ORDER

The interaction order is the only place where social life actually happens, so every other social dynamic can be traced back to this realm. Although asserting that the interaction order is primary, we have seen throughout this chapter that, once formed, systems that emerge out of tension between the interaction order and other constraining conditions loop back and constrain the interaction order. All other levels of systems are a function of time, so time is the most basic constraint on the interaction order. History is the principal artifact of time, and we can see that history ultimately structures the moment through shaping material and cultural conditions and limits as well as cycles of interaction. History matters because it brings us here, within these physical parameters, with these expectations, interacting with others who have expectations as well.

History determines our access to and reliance on particular material resources. Collins (2004) noted that there are often material conditions necessary for caring out IRCs. The availability of resources to bring people together, such as places to meet, money (Summers-Effler 2004c), and biological needs (Summers-Effler 2004a), all impinge upon the interaction order. Durkheim (1995) emphasized material constraints in the other direction, stating that people must break from sacred ritual activity to engage in the profane, mundane, and material activity required to physically sustain individuals and groups. Thus, despite the *sui generis* demands of the interaction order, material conditions can support or undermine the conditions that generate rituals and limit the capacity for individuals to remain involved in ritual activity.

We inherit not only our material conditions from history but our cultural conditions as well. Durkheim stated that beyond the emotional forces of collective effervescence there are forces embodied in the techniques we use: "We speak a language we did not create; we use instruments we did not invent; we claim rights we did not establish; each generation inherits a treasury of knowledge that it did not itself amass; and so on" (1995:214). Similarly, Rawls (1987) pointed out that whereas Goffman describes order as the product of commitment to a shared set of expectations, the expectations are obviously not all, or even primarily, generated by social structure. These shared expectations are in large part generated on a local level through a history of interactions. Collins (2004) detailed how cultural capital limits the potential for interaction ritual as relevant symbols must match up in order for the potential for an interaction ritual to develop. Summers-Effler (2004) argued that expectations generate a cultural lag, which generates history and limits the determining power of the situation. Thus, culture, in the form of symbols circulated in networks, groups, and minds, constrains the interaction order.

History not only constrains the interaction order through the material and cultural conditions that limit any particular interaction, but it also shapes the rhythm of interactions. If we take the microview, like Goffman, we see interactions. If we take a larger view, we see networks of interactions. If we watch the process of interaction in motion over time, we see cycles of focused ritual interaction. In their writing on ritual, Durkheim, Goffman, and Collins at least implicitly acknowledged that rituals have cycles: beginnings, peaks, and ends. Collins (2004) stated that we reach a satiation point and then lose focus and enthusiasm for the ritual. Goffman (1959) detailed the ways people begin and end ritual interactions, but Durkheim (1995) told us the most about why we move in and out of focused interaction. He states that although we are attracted to ritual, the need to tend to material concerns that require individual or unfocused interaction means that we must move between these sacred and profane times just as we move between sacred and profane activities.

My ethnographic observation of groups supports Durkheim's claims about the need for regular periods of mundane downtime to sustain groups. Groups are composed of an interaction cycle in which intense ritual is followed by periods of mundane unfocused activity, which, if the group is in a stable pattern, will be followed by a similar intense ritual period. Mundane backstage activity is the downside of the interaction cycle. Activities such as washing dishes, sealing envelopes, cooking dinner, and all types of backstage unfocused interaction (Goffman 1959, 1967), are examples of required mundane activity. In unfocused interactions people rely on already established expectations to lubricate the social interaction that is required but not the primary purpose or focus of group activity. During these times, people have to negotiate appropriate meanings because they are not completely pulled into the moment.

Other forces beyond material and mundane needs pull people out of ritual moments. The pattern-seeking orientation of selves and groups can conflict with particularly intense or excessive ritual involvement. As discussed above, selves and groups are not only EE seeking but also pattern seeking, for it is the ability to anticipate that enables purposeful action on both the individual and group levels. If rituals become too intense or last too long, they can undermine the history of expectations that brought the individual or group to the ritual in the first place. Individuals and groups seek a sense of expansion, but if a situation demands expansion that is too quick or too extensive, the self or the group itself is threatened. This point at which ritual begins to have diminishing returns is what Collins (2004) referred to as satiation and Scheff (1990) referred to as engulfment. Not only the push and pull of resources but also the limits of satiation and the motivation to avoid engulfment create a cycle between intense focused interaction ritual and backstage, unfocused, mundane activity.

The potential for positive interaction is not only measured by EE resources and correct match of cultural capital but also by timing, by being in a similar place in interaction cycles (Summers-Effler 2004c). Interaction is like successfully jumping into twirling double-dutch jump ropes. One needs to have more than the energy and knowledge; one must also have the appropriate timing to successfully enter. If you look at the *process* of interaction moving through time from a macroperspective, you see not only network connections but also that these network connections would be *pulsating* (Summers-Effler 2004c). At certain intervals, there are some connections, and at other, times there are others. The pulsing connections are the moments of interaction and the rhythm and emotion that hold the encounter together. The time in between the pulse is the downtime, when intensity is low, focus is diffuse, and people are running on past histories of solidarity and EE. The emerging context, determined by both past histories of interaction under varied conditions and the current conditions of the moment, determines whether the pulse will remain at the same rhythm with the same components or whether the components will be pulled toward other rhythms to create new systems of involvement.

You would also see the center setting the rhythm for a larger portion of the network than the periphery. A periphery position that begins to set the rhythm for a larger swath of interactions is in the process of creating a new network center. So, just as the connecting of emotion to symbols in rituals is the foundation for the diffusion of culture across networks, the role of rhythm is central not only for focusing attention and creating entrainment (Collins 2004) but for larger patterns of interaction timing on the level of interactions, groups, and networks (Summers-Effler 2004c).

Understanding the ritual cycles and more macrorhythms of interactions gives us a better picture of how networks, groups, and teams transform. Patterns do not shift or end only when symbols fail to match up or when EE levels are so low that potentially successful interactions are not initiated; they also shift with shifting rhythms of interaction cycles. In her research on groups, Summers-Effler (2004c) found that being out of sync is a major cause of interaction failure. People are embedded in multiple networks at once, and alternate patterns can temporarily or permanently exert more force, pulling one or more potential interactants out of sync with another. Those who are "on" when others are "off" can move toward other opportunities for "on" interaction, leading others into being "on," or they can be experienced as irritating and inappropriate by those who are in a down phase of the interaction cycle.

I have been discussing the self, networks, and small groups as systems that emerge from the primary level of social life—the interaction order that is organized by interaction rituals. Self-organizing systems arise from the interaction of a large number of factors. These systems are open, which means that they exchange energy, matter, or information with their environment. Systems that are open form patterns over time, but they interact with outside influences (Kelso 1995). If we are going to claim to understand how a pattern works (e.g., the relationship between ideology and daily practice), we have to be able to handle two problems: how a given pattern persists under various environmental conditions (its stability) and how it adjusts to changing internal or external conditions (its adaptability) (Kelso 1995).

Systems are composed of elements pulled into relationships with each other through the constraints of local contexts. Systems are only sustained in motion (in the social realm, the motivation to maximize EE provides this forward momentum), so fluidity and change are presumed. From this focus on dynamic processes of interaction patterns, a group, network, or even personality is not a stable structure that endures until it fails. Rather, all such entities are a product of continual creation that under certain conditions gives off the impression of stability. In reality, the process of change or failure is not fundamentally different from the process of stability; only the outcome is different.

Over time, systems learn by adjusting to their changing context. The longer the history of a system, the more nuanced the dynamics of interaction between component elements—in this case, the expectations for interaction. This complexity continues until the system blows apart and the elements are taken up by new systems. A systems is not static; it is only through the relationship between its component elements that a system has an emergent force of its own. The end of interaction between elements is the end of the emergent force. If we only look at particular substantive issues, we either see a stable system or how a stable system changes in response to a particular shift in context. Through comparison, however, we can gain insight into the basic processes of systems that organize many different substantive outcomes.

The boundaries of the systems are established by failures and the defensive strategies that result. Proactive strategies are eminently flexible and thus represent a good match between expectations and environment. The proactive response to unanticipated success or mild setbacks is loose, flexible, and open-ended. Alternately, defensive strategies are persistent unless radically ruptured (see above section on the self). As discussed above, they often endure beyond their usefulness. However, as Abbott (2001:277) pointed out, the entities that emerge from patterns with "thingness" properties do not need to be optimal or particularly functional. Because of their durability, defensive strategies offer the firmest foundation for the development of patterns. Defensive strategies derived from patterns of avoidance offer the greatest resistance to environmental conditions. I am suggesting that social entities, like groups or networks, are entities because they offer resistance in the flow of activity—they are eddies in the social stream. They become an obstacle in the structure from which they emerge. This is the reason why they have what Abbott (2001:277) referred to as "causal authority."

CONCLUSION

Ritual approaches to emotion place interaction rituals and their emotional consequences at the center of social life. Durkheim laid the framework for understanding the role of ritual in creating the emotional and cultural foundations of society. Goffman applied Durkheim's perspective to the level of face-to-face interaction in day-to-day life and illustrated how the same ritual forces create the interaction order. Collins built on Goffman by specifying the mechanisms that create rituals and the emotional and cognitive products of rituals. This enabled him to detail how interaction rituals form chains over time, a process that creates networks and more macropatterns of social life over time. In doing so, Collins generated one of the most promising visions for connecting microlevel and macrolevel of social life. Polillo and Summers-Effler have built on ritual theory to further specify the dynamics within the self, and Summers-Effler has also detailed the dynamics of small groups.

Using the past work specifying the properties and dynamics of rituals, recent work has examined how other emergent levels of social life constrain interaction rituals. Interaction markets constrain opportunities for interaction rituals and thus shape networks (Collins 2004). The rhythm of interaction, not just within rituals but between rituals, also shapes interaction opportunities, as do the demands and limits of material life (Summers-Effler 2004a, 2004c). The conservative pattern-seeking processes of the self, within-self dynamics, and the process of thinking generate culture and constrain interaction as well (Polillo 2004; Summers-Effler 2004a). Finally, by approaching the interaction order and the second- and third-order dynamics derived from the interaction order as emergent systems whose emergent patterns comprise elements of other levels of systems, we can develop predictive theory about causal relationships between social levels (Summers-Effler 2004c).

The work of understanding the role of time and history in interaction rituals has just begun. We still do not know much about the relationship among ritual intensity, the amount of EE generated, and the duration of EE. Nor do we know much about emotion and the experience of time. Because the other levels of social life that emerge out of the interaction order are generated through time, future work on the process of time and other levels of social life will no doubt inform each other. Because the primary focus up to now has been on the mechanisms of rituals, we have only just begun to explore the cyclical nature of social life. The image of network connections pulsing on varying cycles suggests that some connections are only intermittently possible or relevant, creating new problems for ritual theory to solve. We occupy multiple network positions; we are shy in some places, aggressively enthusiastic in others. This also complicates the image of a chain of interactions. Although the effects of one interaction carry over into the next interaction, we are also tied to history, anticipation, and particular contexts. Interaction ritual chains might be too linear an image to capture how contingent and embedded patterns of interaction emerge from the past and unfold into the future.

REFERENCES

Abbott, Andrew. 2001. *Time Matters: On Theory and Method*. Chicago: University of Chicago Press.

Alexander, Jeffery. 2004. "Cultural Pragmatics: Social Performance between Ritual and Strategy." *Sociological Theory* 22: 527–573.

Burt, Ronald. 1992. *Structural Holes: The Social Structure of Competition*. Cambridge: Harvard University Press.

Brothers, Leslie. 1997. *Friday's Footprint: How Society Shapes the Human Mind*. New York: Oxford University Press.

Collins, Randall. 1981. "On the Microfoundations of Macrosociology." *American Journal of Sociology* 86: 984–1014.

———. 1990. "Stratification, Emotional Energy, and the Transient Emotions." Pp. 27–57 in *Research Agendas in the Sociology of Emotions*, edited by T. Kemper. Albany State University of New York Press.

———. 1998. *The Sociology of Philosophies: A Global Theory of Intellectual Change*. Cambridge: Harvard University Press.

———. 2004. *Interaction Ritual Chains*. Princeton, NJ: Princeton University Press.

Damasio, Antonio R. 1994. *Descartes' Error*. New York: HarperCollins.

Durkheim, Emile. 1995 [1912]. *The Elementary Forms of Religious Life*. Translation by K. Fields. New York: Free Press.

Eliasoph, Nina, and Paul Lichterman. 2003. "Culture in Interaction." *American Journal of Sociology* 108: 735–794.

Goffman, Erving. 1959. *The Presentation of Self in Everyday Life*. New York: Doubleday.

———. 1967. *Interaction Ritual: Essays on Face-to-Face Behavior*. Chicago: Aldine.

Gopnik, Alison, and Andrew Meltzoff. 1997. *Words, Thoughts and Theories*. Cambridge: MIT Press.

Granovetter, Mark S. 1973. "The Strength of Weak Ties." *American Journal of Sociology* 78: 1360–1380.

Hatfield, Elaine, John T. Cacioppo, and Richard Rapson. 1994. *Emotional Contagion*. Cambridge: Cambridge University Press.

Hochschild, Arlie R. 1983. *The Managed Heart: Commercialization of Human Feeling*. Berkeley: University of California Press.

Kelso, Scott J. A. 1995. *Dynamic Patterns: The Self-Organization of Brain and Behavior*. Boston: MIT Press.

Mead, George Herbert. 1934. *Mind, Self, and Society*. Chicago: University of Chicago Press.

Polillo, Simone. 2004. "The Network Structure of the Self: The Effects of Ritual on Identity." Unpublished manuscript.

Rawls, Anne Warfield. 1987. "The Interaction Order Sui Generis: Goffman's Contribution to Social Theory." *Sociological Theory* 5: 136–149.

Scheff, Thomas J. 1990. *Microsociology: Discourse, Emotion, and Social Structure*. Chicago: University of Chicago Press.

Schneider, David J. 1991. "Social Cognition." *American Review of Psychology* 42: 527–561.

Stevens, Laura E., and Susan T. Fiske. 1995. "Motivation and Cognition in Social Life: A Social Survival Perspective." *Social Cognition* 13: 189–214.

Summers-Effler, Erika. 2002. "The Micro Potential for Social Change: Emotion, Consciousness, and Social Movement Formation." *Sociological Theory* 20: 41–60.

———. 2004a. "A Theory of Self, Emotion, and Culture." *Advances in Group Processes* 21: 273–308.

————. 2004b. "Defensive Strategies: The Formation and Social Implications of Patterned Self-Destructive Behavior."
    Advances in Group Processes 21: 309–325.
————. 2004c. "Humble Saints and Righteous Heroes: Sustaining Intense Involvement in Altruistic Social Movements."
    http://repository.upenn.edu/dissertations/AAI3138079/. Unpublished dissertation, University of Pennsylvania,
    Philadelphia.
Turner, Jonathan H. 2000. *On the Origins of Human Emotions: A Sociological Inquiry in the Evolution of Human Affect.*
    Stanford, CA: Stanford University Press.
Wiley, Norbert. 1994. *The Semiotic Self.* Chicago: University of Chicago Press.

CHAPTER 7

Symbolic Interactionism, Inequality, and Emotions

Jessica Fields
Martha Copp
Sherryl Kleinman

Emotions are central to everyday interactions. They motivate behavior, shape agency, contribute to self-control and social control, and bear the traces of systemic disadvantage. Our chapter explores the contributions of symbolic interactionism as a theoretical perspective in sociological studies of emotions. We focus on how an interactionist analysis of emotions has added immeasurably to our understanding of social interaction and, in particular, of social inequality. Not all interactionist research, including interactionist studies of emotion, focuses on inequality. However, in tracking the patterns of social interaction to their troubling consequences, we heed the advice of an early interactionist, Blumer (1969), who urged symbolic interactionist researchers to pay attention to the obdurate reality—the empirical patterns—going on around us. The obdurate reality that we observe is replete with examples of inequality and resistance in people's ongoing social interactions. Thus, our goal is to present an overview of the territory that symbolic interaction and sociological studies of emotions share and then analyze the most challenging direction for interactionist research: understanding the reproduction of inequality.

In the following pages, we locate symbolic interactionism in the field of sociology of emotions and explain the theoretical foundations and basic premises of symbolic interactionism. Using

Jessica Fields • Department of Sociology, San Francisco State University, San Francisco, CA 94132

Martha Copp • Department of Sociology and Anthropology, East Tennessee State University, Johnson City, TN 37614

Sherryl Kleinman • Department of Sociology, University of North Carolina, Chapel Hill, NC 27599

The authors thank Jan Stets, Jonathan Turner, and Valerie Francisco for their comments on earlier versions of this chapter.

examples from interactionist studies of emotion, we discuss what is unique about symbolic interactionism as a sociological perspective. We then show readers how the study of emotions is indispensable to symbolic interactionist work. We examine the key questions that symbolic interactionist researchers ask: Who are we? What do we believe? How do we act on our beliefs? What conditions shape our interactions with others? What are the consequences of our interaction for reproducing or challenging inequality in everyday life? We argue that to answer those questions, researchers must take emotions into account. Finally, we offer a pragmatic discussion of how one can profitably study emotions from a symbolic interactionist perspective in order to gain greater insight into the everyday experience and reproduction of inequality.

THEORETICAL FRAMINGS AND FOUNDATIONS

Symbolic interactionists' understandings of social inequality and emotions are grounded in the sociological challenge to conventional ideas about emotions as innate or universal responses to external stimuli. Most interactionists acknowledge the physiological aspects of emotion and feeling, but, as Franks (1987:231) has noted, they spend little time on their "bodily, social expressions." As McCarthy (1989:57) asserted, "My feelings are social, that is, they are constituted and sustained by group processes. They are irreducible to the bodily organism and to the particular individual who feels them." Thus, interactionists fix their analytical attention on social conventions and norms that shape the feelings that people typically experience and define as "natural" (see, e.g., Cahill 1995; Denzin 1984; Franks 2003; Hochschild 1990; Scheff 1988).

From this analytical stance, self and society are two sides of the same coin. Interactionists study the constraints of culture as well as how people use their agency to navigate those constraints. In studies of emotions, interactionists explore how individuals use their capacity for agency to bring their feelings in line with what is expected of them. As Hochschild (1979) put it, people can *work on* their feelings, trying to create within themselves the proper response to a situation. Our sense of proper responses reflects socially determined "feeling rules"—cultural norms for how we are supposed to feel in a situation. For example, we are expected to feel sad at a funeral and happy at the birth of a child. If we do not have the appropriate feelings, we will likely feel uncomfortable and try to change how we feel. We can also practice emotion work on others, trying to induce in them particular feeling states: for example, encouraging students to feel proud of their accomplishments or suggesting that a student who cheated should feel remorseful. That people can work on their own and others' feelings and *change* them indicates that emotions are not merely natural impulses. Rather, they are shaped by both culture (e.g., feeling rules) and our human capacity to react to and make sense of our feelings.

This "emotion work" is a central concern for interactionists whose work fits the tradition of the Second Chicago School of sociology (Fine 1995), our focus in this chapter. Such "realist tales" (Van Maanen 1988) about emotions attend to the names, histories, meanings, and consequences of emotion (Hochschild 1990:120). Work in this tradition addresses many aspects of Thoits's (1989:318) classic definition of emotion: "(a) appraisals of a situational stimulus or context, (b) changes in physiological or bodily sensations, (c) the free or inhibited display of expressive gestures, and (d) a cultural label applied to specific constellations of one or more of the first three components." Researchers illuminate, for example, the rubrics through which people claim and allot sympathy (Clark 1987), the ways people make sense of their bodily experiences of embarrassment (Cahill 1995), people's feelings of frustration and resentment when others ask them to relinquish racial and other social privileges (Frankenberg 1993), and the relationship between changing gender norms and shifting assessments of which behaviors in ourselves and others warrant gratitude (Hochschild 1989a, 1989b).

Regardless of their focus, symbolic interactionist studies of emotions are based in large part on the theories of Mead (1934), Blumer (1969), and Goffman (1959, 1963, 1967). In his posthumously published *Mind, Self, and Society*, Mead (1934) outlined how people learn to anticipate others' reactions to their behavior and take on these reactions as their own. A sense of self develops as people recognize that others in their society, culture, and subculture have particular expectations for and values attached to their actions, desires, and identities. Identification with the perspective of the community—what Mead called the "generalized other"—informs the development, institutionalization, and maintenance of social ties and groups. These ties and groups constitute society and its inequities; this is the context in which people develop and maintain their sense of self.

As self emerges in the context of social interaction, so society emerges through what Blumer (1969) called "joint action." Society refers to patterns of interaction made up of individuals signaling and interpreting each other's—and their own—actions. These interactions contribute to the simultaneous development of selves and society. Attention to joint action allows the symbolic interactionist to avoid reifying social structure and, instead, to examine the interactions that comprise and maintain social arrangements. Blumer (1969) offered three premises for the study of social reality: People act toward objects based on the meaning those objects hold for the actor; the meaning of objects is negotiated through social interaction; and, because the meaning of objects is subject to people's interpretive processes, meaning is mutable. Symbolic interactionism thus highlights individual accountability and agency and addresses structural, cultural, and material conditions as people experience and reproduce them in their day-to-day lives. Snow (2001:368) recently offered a broadened definition of symbolic interactionism, a definition with four "organizing principles" that Snow claimed Blumer implied but did not fully develop: "the principle of interactive determination, the principle of symbolization, the principle of emergence, and the principle of human agency." This articulation of symbolic interactionism's tenets highlights interactional (structural, cultural, and material) conditions, meaning-making processes, the dynamism of social life, and individual accountability and agency as people experience and reproduce social contexts and processes in their day-to-day lives.

Dramaturgical theory provides a third foundation for symbolic interactionist studies of emotion (Goffman 1959, 1967). Goffman's work explored people's active, consistent negotiation of meaning, social convention, and impression. People engage in "impression management," working to make positive impressions on others and to help others and ourselves save face when interaction goes awry. Loss of face is an emotional experience—we feel embarrassed, guilty, or ashamed when we make a bad impression on others or fail to uphold our end of the social pact. Working together to save face keeps social life moving and maintains social institutions and patterns of interaction. Inequities in social institutions and interactions often make it difficult for members of disenfranchised groups—for example, sexual nonconformists, women, people of color, poor people, people with disabilities—to avoid making a bad impression or to recover from the embarrassment or shame that the bad impression brings. Emotions thus guide our encounters with others and help to establish and maintain social arrangements, whether just or unjust.

The study of emotions entered sociology largely through these theoretical foundations and the perspective of symbolic interactionism. Emotions are central to symbolic interactionist understandings of social life: No treatment of either the sociology of emotion or symbolic interactionism is complete without the other (Franks 2003; Sandstrom and Kleinman 2005; Sandstrom et al. 2001). Also, as we discuss below, symbolic interactionism is increasingly fundamental to sociological understandings of social inequality (Schwalbe 2005a), helping us understand how emotion contributes to social hierarchies and plays a part in hampering efforts to effect social change.

LINKING THE EMOTIONAL AND THE SOCIAL

Symbolic interactionists insist that emotion is never separable from the social; indeed, it signals our engagement with others and our cultural and subcultural memberships (Clark 1997; Franks 2003). Emotions make our engagement with and accountability to others visceral, and they remind us through bodily sensation when we have transgressed the bounds of social expectations (Franks 2003:788–789) or when those expectations are oppressive and unjust (Lorde 1984). Claiming membership in a group signals that we are willing to adhere to that group's expectations, and emotions help us to measure the extent to which we embrace and meet those expectations. Do we resent the expectations of the group? Do we suffer embarrassment when we violate them? Do we take pleasure in satisfying them? How easily do we meet these expectations, and what effort does meeting them require of us?

Our emotions also help us locate our selves in the often stratified worlds in which we live: we assess who we are in relation to others, and, if we are unsatisfied with that assessment, we struggle, in part through our emotion work, to reposition ourselves. We rely on emotion cues and we exercise interactional strategies in the "emotional micropolitics" of day-to-day interactions to determine and claim our own and others' "place," or social status (Clark 1990). For example, we express contempt for those who we consider our inferiors or admiration for those with whom we hope to affiliate ourselves in efforts to recognize, assert, defend, and alter our status in the world.

Symbolic interactionists' concern with the processes of social organization, meaning-making, and social control has fostered a particular interest in what Shott (1979) has called "role-taking emotions," such as guilt, embarrassment, shame, and empathy. Role-taking emotions require a social self: we cannot feel shame without having developed a generalized other; guilt can wrack us even when no one is around because we feel accountable to societal prescriptions (Scheff 1988, 2000; Shott 1979). Role-taking emotions thus foster both self-control and social control. People feel or anticipate shame; usually, they then work to rid themselves of the emotion or avert it.

Role-taking emotions are not only coercive and controlling. For example, Cahill (1995) argued that shame and embarrassment have the positive consequence of promoting *self*-control (not only *social* control). This self-control encourages people to respect the bounds of propriety and, in doing so, helps to sustain the integrity of the social fabric:

> We must cease once and for all to describe the effects of embarrassment in only negative terms: it destroys; it disrupts; it damages. In fact, embarrassment produces; it generates self-regulation; it creates trust; it sustains public civility. (Cahill 1995:254)

The threat of embarrassment promotes social responsibility and enlists us in enforcing social order; experiences of embarrassment signal not only that one has violated social norms but also, and perhaps more important, that one recognizes the legitimacy of those norms. Contemporary symbolic interactionists interested in role-taking emotions explore the part feelings play in promoting and maintaining social organization. If that organization is unjust, so too will be the emotion work required to maintain it. Members of some groups may exert themselves to avoid the shame that others attribute to them: For example, low-income university students feeling the stigma of not having had the appropriate cultural experiences, or pregnant girls resisting shaming messages from both peers and adults. Social actors' role-taking and their efforts to avoid emotions like shame, guilt, and embarrassment reflect, create, and maintain social groups and hierarchies.

Indeed, emotions are central to social order and group membership. In her discussion of sympathy margins, Clark (1987) theorized a sort of bookkeeping through which social actors organize their offering and receiving of sympathy. Social actors keep mental "ledgers" in which they record withdrawals from and deposits to their store of sympathy. The goal is an account neither too large nor too small, but an account that is active. The collective keeping of sympathy margins allows the offering and gathering of sympathy to become a criterion of group membership. Sympathizing occurs within a social framework—sustained by social actors—that helps to define the proper amount to give and receive. Thus, a person can sympathize too much or too little, demand too much sympathy, or seem to be too little in need of it. Failure to keep an appropriately balanced and active account can result in expulsion from the group. Like other symbolic interactionists, Clark asserted a reciprocal and constitutive relationship between self and society in which social actors recognize and monitor their selves in light of a social framework that they have helped to create and sustain. This monitoring of oneself and others always contributes to the maintenance of social order, as Cahill and Clark argued. When that order is an unjust or oppressive one, that monitoring also helps to maintain social inequalities.

EVERYDAY EMOTIONAL PRACTICES AND CONTEXTS

A common criticism of symbolic interactionism and the sociology of emotions is that they are exceedingly "micro" in their focus. However, symbolic interactionist and emotions scholars analyze social institutions and trends that determine the material conditions of people's lives. Interactionist understandings of emotion build on Blumer's resistance to the reification of social institutions. Blumer argued that instead of using institutions (education, government, the family) as the units of analysis, sociologists should instead explore the joint actions of people who reproduce those institutions. In doing so, symbolic interactionists would better understand the conditions supporting the continuation of institutions and the day-to-day lives of those whom the institutions touch (Blumer 1969).

Other interactionists have embraced Blumer's model and analyzed emotions in institutional contexts. Barbalet (1992:152) asserted in his macrosociological analysis of class resentment that "emotion exists not simply as internal states of the individual but in the relationships between individuals and in the interaction between individuals and their social situations." In an early article, Maines (1977) argued that understanding the relationship between individual action and social institutions equips symbolic interactionists to explore "meso"-level analyses that bridge the macro and micro. Franks (2003:794) claimed that symbolic interactionist analyses have the potential to explore, on the one hand, how "micro level feelings of individuals radiate 'upward' to confirm, support, and continually recreate present social structures" and, on the other hand, "the 'downward' shaping of the individual's emotions by culture, structure and social institutions."

Emotional Experiences in Historical Context

Institutions are only one emotional context. Sympathy expectations, experiences of shame, and standards for public behavior also vary across historical and social contexts. As Hochschild (1998:7) explained, our understandings about what we should and should not feel reflect the prescriptions of an emotional "bible, a set of prescriptions embedded in the received wisdom of

[our] culture." These teachings from our emotional bible define how we should feel in response to situations and other people. We should be happy to see our families at holiday gatherings (but we are allowed to feel relief when they return home); we should mourn a lover's departure (but not for "too long"); we have the right to be angry when another driver cuts us off (but others will frown if we express that anger aggressively).

A number of interactionists have examined emotions in their historical context. For example, Lofland (1985:178) argued that experiences of and responses to death shift "across time and space." Similarly, in her analysis of 200 years of U.S. autobiographies, Bjorklund (1998) discussed how, over time, autobiographers honored different conventions in describing their feelings, expressions, and spontaneous actions; these changes signal shifts in "emotional culture" (widely held views about how people in a society should express and interpret situated emotions). Hochschild's (1989b; see also 1989a) study of the division of household labor among heterosexual couples actively explored changes brought on by the second wave of the U.S. women's movement. Hochschild found that as the "gender culture" shifts in the United States, so too does the marital baseline against which women and men measure, receive, and appreciate gifts.

According to Hochschild, a rich "economy of gratitude" depends on the existence of a shared marital baseline: Both partners need to recognize a dozen red roses, dropping the children off at day care, a note tucked into a lunch bag, or entertaining in-laws as "gifts." As more wives work outside the home and ask their husbands to assume housekeeping responsibilities, economies of gratitude are increasingly impoverished. Wives bring home paychecks and second incomes as, among other things, gifts to their husbands; their husbands find the need for a second check, let alone one that exceeds their own, an insult. Husbands wash dishes as a gift to their wives, and wives note simply that their husbands are doing their fair share of the housework. Thus, the power women may have gained in the economic sphere is often a liability in the familial settings that they share with men. Men may find their wives' financial success and power shaming and refuse to accept their paychecks as gifts (Hochschild 1989a, 1989b). Ironically, the gifts that generate the greatest gratitude in these unequal relationships may be (1) men's "tolerance" of their wives' earnings and (2) their willingness to let their wives be both income earner *and* housekeeper.

Hochschild (1989a:97) explained that power in heterosexual marriages reflects a "gender lag" at the turn of the twenty-first century. As gender roles strain and shift, so, too, does power and, with it, feelings. A woman's economic power might *dis*empower her in the home; yet, a husband's lack of economic power does not abolish his gendered power in a world still largely characterized by sexism. Hochschild's analysis of renegotiated and perhaps unfamiliar forms of power rests on classic symbolic interactionist principles. She explored how couples act toward women's power based on the meaning it held for them; she examined how the meaning of economic power changed as couples reacted to it as a liability; and, finally, she presented how culture- and marriage-level negotiations produce new and unstable conceptions of gender and power and, in turn, shift emotional experiences. Emotions provide people with a sense of who and where they are in the world. As feminists challenge sexist understandings of family, work, and home, understandings of gendered and economic power change. With these changes will also come changes in people's sense of themselves and of their emotional possibilities.

Hochschild's analysis of economies of gratitude focuses on historical change as women gain in earning power and expectations for intimate partners shift. However, even within a single historical moment, emotion cultures likely vary according to social status and location:

> Are the sensibilities of white, suburban teen-age girls like those of middle-aged, male salesmen or engineers who may be their fathers? What about middle-class black men compared to middle-class black women or [to low-income Blacks]? How does social place affect the emotions and strategies of, say, female clerical workers or elderly, working-class, Jewish men or [Latina] housewives? (Clark 1990:328)

Beliefs about gender, race, class, sexuality, age, occupation, and physical and mental ability shape our sense of place, agency, and self and thus may also inform our emotional experiences. Attention to these subcultures and social inequalities is crucial to symbolic interactionists' understanding of the relationship among emotions, identities, socially recognized differences, and often oppressive social conditions.

Emotions and Organizational Contexts

As people construct new meanings for themselves and others, their identities are anchored to belief systems. Often, these beliefs are tied to our membership in organizations or occupational groups. Shared emotion norms and emotion management techniques further organizations' goals and elevate members' social position in relation to others. In the world of medicine and related disciplines, for example, practitioners invoke the rhetoric of science to justify managing emotions through displays of rationality (Emerson 1970; Leif and Fox 1963; Smith and Kleinman 1989). Medical practitioners suppress most forms of emotional expression and exhibit "affective neutrality" (Parsons 1951). As students, they learn to focus on technical details, use scientific jargon rather than intimate or personalized language, and avoid unpleasant or disturbing contact. These techniques allow practitioners to manage their own emotions, assume a more powerful position vis-à-vis their emotionally expressive patients, and buttress their identities and authority as physicians (Smith and Kleinman 1989).

The appearance of rationality as a technique for impression management and emotion management has also proved useful to social movement activists in their efforts to legitimate their beliefs and challenge critics. Groves (1995, 1997) observed animal rights activists deploying an unemotional and rational front when dealing with audiences who sought to discredit them as "too emotional." In their public-speaking engagements, activists built the case for animal rights and justice by graphically describing inhumane animal treatment and invoking statistics on the frequency of animal abuse. Graphic imagery and quantitative rhetoric allowed them to turn science into a "cloak of competence" (Haas and Shaffir 1977) and to present themselves as legitimate, objective, factual, and unemotional while inducing strong emotional responses in listeners, an interpersonal emotion management technique (Francis 1994). Appearing ultrarational as they described people's disturbing treatment of animals, activists were able to strategically avoid the charge that they were overly emotional about this issue. Gender inequities informed these efforts, as women activists felt compelled to employ this technique more than did men: "Men's willingness to express their feelings was considered a sign of fearlessness, but in women it was a sign of weakness. . . . Men were praised for being both emotional and rational. But women were criticized if they were not rational all of the time" (Groves 1997:147–148).

Often, members of social movements, civic organizations, workplaces, and occupations contend with organizational cultures that promote competing sets of beliefs. Such conflicts are not unusual in a historical and cultural context with contradictory and often discriminatory belief systems, and many interactionist researchers focus on them, exploring the problems and consequences that they generate for participants. Participants frequently experience conflicting beliefs as emotional struggles—responding with anger, frustration, shame, or anguish—because in upholding one deep-seated belief, they fear they will be judged as failing to honor another belief and lose face. The drama of dealing with contradictory beliefs thus plays out emotionally, and participants typically employ emotion management strategies to handle the conflicts and inequities they impose.

For example, in Arluke's (1994) study of emotion management at an animal shelter, workers came to the shelter expecting to love and care for lost or unwanted animals, but once on the job, they learned to euthanize animals when they were not adopted, when cage space ran out, or when animals were ill or diseased. Animal shelter workers developed emotion management techniques to handle the contradictions in their organizational beliefs, frequently by selectively applying one set of beliefs to comply with another. For example, they took pains to minimize animals' distress (and to see themselves as showing care) while administering lethal injections. Their empathy distracted them from thinking about their actions as killing. Conversely, they compensated for their potentially inhumane belief in animal population control by repeatedly forming special attachments to animals, feeling persistently uneasy about the animals' chances for survival and railing against people in the community whose irresponsibility and cruelty set the whole animal shelter process in motion and left workers feeling powerless.

In settings in which participants organize to fight some form of inequality, emotions are one of the resources that group members and leaders mobilize to uphold organizational goals and principles. In their study of an established social movement organization, Smith and Erickson (1997) analyzed how leaders encouraged worker-activists to mobilize their emotions in pursuit of social and environmental justice. Senior management in the organization harnessed worker-activists' passion for environmental justice in order to feed the organization's continuous demand for fund-raising. Workers hired to canvass donors by telephone and to raise funds for the organization were trained to play up their enthusiasm for fighting environmental problems as a strategy to help them meet nightly telemarketing quotas. The workers sold to prospective donors "the potential ability of their organization to reverse and prevent environmental degradation" (Smith and Erickson 1997:325). Their emotion management enabled them to believe that they were following a higher calling than *selling* an environmental cause. Moreover, the environmental organization depended on and reaped the benefits of their emotional labor by encouraging them to feel strongly about environmental injustice—hoping that their urgency and conviction would come through on every phone call. Ironically, cracks in the organizational culture appeared when managers exhorted workers to "voluntarily" assist additional activist causes in their free time, without pay, which underscored "the reality that canvassing was a form of paid labor" (Smith and Erickson 1997:337).

Mobilizing emotions successfully—whether for individual or organizational gain—requires some social support. Institutional cultures may focus on challenging inequalities, but organizational conditions can make or break participants' efforts to mobilize and manage their emotions in a fight for equality. In Copp's (1998) study of a sheltered workshop for adults with developmental disabilities, nondisabled workers, called "floor instructors," were trained to believe that improvement was always possible—that developmentally disabled adults could gain the skills to succeed in competitive employment outside the workshop. The floor instructors were also expected to honor a hard-nosed factory culture, which demanded speed and accuracy from workers and led management to treat workers' boredom, frustration, and physical discomfort as signs of a poorly developed work ethic. The sheltered workshop's organizational conditions of chronically unskilled and developmentally disabled workers, repetitive work, low pay, and frequent downtime produced a situation in which the floor instructors could live out neither their belief in improvement nor their ideal of a fast-moving, profit-oriented factory. The floor instructors' emotion management strategies for handling these organizational problems pushed them toward more adversarial and infantilizing forms of control and weakened their ability to emotionally relate to trainee-clients either as respectful, positive disability advocates or as business-oriented supervisors. Yet both of these sets of beliefs (advocacy versus business) held sway over the floor instructors, and they continually tried to serve their institutional purpose: to encourage "defective" workers to transform themselves into effective and motivated employees. In the absence of favorable organizational conditions, the floor instructors became "burned out," experiencing "emotional deviance" (Thoits 1985)—the awareness of being unable to uphold emotion norms.

Even ostensibly supportive emotional norms can foster oppressive organizational conditions. At Renewal, the holistic health center that Kleinman (1996) studied, participants of unequal status engaged in an emotional subculture that reinforced their feelings of solidarity. Doing so masked inequalities between the mostly male practitioners (dominants) and the all-female staff (subordinates). Gathering in "circles" at the start of board meetings and at retreats generated a feeling of collective closeness and fostered members' belief that everyone held equal status *outside* the circle. When Renewal members "processed" tensions and conflicts, they could have exposed gender and occupational inequalities, but their folk theories about emotions—what causes conflicts and how to resolve them—made it difficult for the staff women to challenge the dominance of the mostly male practitioners. At Renewal, participants focused on personality characteristics, not structural arrangements. Members considered titles, money, and prestige as superficial matters that hid the "true self" and "real feelings." If, for example, a staff member were to say "I, as a staff member, resent you, as a practitioner," others would accuse them of hiding behind the mask of an organizational role. The norm of language-use about emotions—using "I" rather than "we"—also made it difficult for staff to organize resistance or to have practitioners take their concerns seriously. Without a "we," it became difficult, almost impossible, to recognize social divisions at Renewal and, thus, to analyze systematic inequality (Kleinman 1996:80).

Finally, organizational cultures can promote inequality by encouraging emotional detachment and obscuring the connections between groups of people. Cohn's (1987) research on defense intellectuals, for example, analyzed why and how members of this elite community failed to be troubled by the prospect of nuclear annihilation of human life. In listening "to men engage in dispassionate discussion of nuclear war," Cohn writes,

> I found myself aghast, but morbidly fascinated—not by nuclear weaponry, or by images of nuclear destruction, but by the extraordinary abstraction and removal from what I knew as reality that characterized the[ir] professional discourse. (Cohn 1987:688)

Her analysis of the language of defense intellectuals and the flawed abstractions on which it is based provides an example of emotional scripting (Zurcher 1985) as an organizational emotion management strategy. The defense intellectuals perfected the emotion management technique of performing rationality. Their "technostrategic" language (Cohn 1987:690) impeded the expression of particular emotions (fear, anxiety, vulnerability, compassion, or empathy) and promoted feelings of distance, power, and control in speakers. By focusing on weapons instead of victims, they denied the possibility that some emotions could be considered, let alone felt. Sympathy for human beings and any obligation to protect them were written out of the script.

However, not all emotions were banned from verbal expression. Cohn pointed out that defense intellectuals' discourse included

> currents of homoerotic excitement, heterosexual domination, the drive toward competency and mastery, the pleasures of membership in an elite and privileged group, the . . . meaning of membership in the priesthood, and the thrilling power of becoming Death, shatterer of worlds. How is it possible to hold this up as a paragon of cool-headed objectivity? (Cohn 1987:717)

By analyzing how the technical language of defense intellectuals reflects and guides their occupational assumptions, Cohn also showed how their beliefs could be used to regulate participants' emotions—both by expressing emotions that made them feel dominant and powerful and by effacing emotions and meanings that would open their worldview to fundamental challenges. Thus, the symbolic interactionist understanding that language shapes thought can be extended: Language can also shape speakers' feelings. The consequences for others are anything but benign. Indeed, organizations' calls for emotional desensitizing can contribute to a broad social desensitizing to violence, power, and domination. As we discuss below, organizations may inadvertently reproduce inequality yet another way—when members operate under the influence of widely held emotion norms at the cultural level that support gender, race, or class hierarchies.

WHO WE ARE, HOW WE FEEL: EMOTIONS, IDENTITY, AND BELIEFS

Symbolic interactionism can be distinguished from other sociological perspectives by the attention that scholars give to the construction of meaning and self. Meaning does not inhere in the individual or in objects, but is, instead, social; knowing what objects (self, others, relationships, and communities) mean to people illuminates how social actors live out the often unequal patterns and arrangements that we call "society." Emotions are integrally connected to and inform our actions; we feel and express emotions that comply with, resist, or transform emotion norms (Hochschild 1979; Thoits 1985) that, in everyday life, are just as consequential to the maintenance of social inequality as other normative patterns of interaction. As Hochschild (1990:117) wrote, "what we feel is fully as important to the outcome of social affairs as what we think or do." Our feelings about ourselves, others, relationships, and communities are central to the meanings we construct and to the consequences of our interactions over time. Thus, the construction and maintenance of meaning, and ultimately of social inequality, can be understood as an emotional, not just a cognitive, process.

Identity Work as an Emotional Process

Interactionists understand the self as the product of an ongoing social process (Mead 1934); social actors continually participate in a process of "becoming" that incorporates their interpretations of past social experiences into their sense of who they are. People attach multiple meanings to themselves and to others, using identity labels that signify "the powers, status, inclinations, and feelings—in short, the self—of the persons to whom they attach" (Schwalbe and Mason-Schrock 1996:115). Identities are not static, nor are they solely the product of individual agency; instead, people engage in a social process of "identity work" (Schwalbe and Mason-Schrock 1996; Snow and Anderson 1987) to give meaning to themselves and others.

The concept of "identity work" captures the work that people do individually and collectively to signify who they are, who they want to be, and how they expect others to treat them. This signaling allows people to engage in coordinated social interaction. Identity work is also an emotional process (Francis 1997; Wolkomir 2001a), as emotions provide a means to communicate our identity claims, our imputations of other people's identities, and our responses when our identity expectations are met, breached, or challenged under adverse conditions.

Identity work as an emotional process frequently occurs when people possess an identity that attracts either strong moral opposition or ardent public support. For example, in Wolkomir's (2001a, 2001b) study of the identity work of participants in gay and "ex-gay" Christian support groups, members struggled with the assumption that one could not be gay *and* Christian. To them, "being a 'good Christian' meant being heterosexual, getting married, and having children" (Wolkomir 2001a:311), and, based on their upbringing in conservative Christian churches, being gay meant evil, sinful, and unworthy of the heteronormative privileges of marriage and children.

Rather than reject their belief in Christianity, support group members redefined "what it meant to be a good Christian" and how to feel authentic doing so (p. 311).

Members of Accept, the gay Christian support group, sought to reject opponents' imputation of their identities as amoral or evil and, instead, to redefine gay as a "moral identity" (Katz 1975; Kleinman 1996) that is equal to others (heterosexuals) and, therefore, equally worthy of God's unconditional love. Members of Expell, a support group for ex-gay Christians, sought to equate the "sin" of homosexuality with other kinds of sin and to recast their effort to suppress homosexual desires (framed as resisting the temptation to sin) as a morally superior sacrifice. Wolkomir (2001a) analyzed the emotional process that newcomers to both groups experienced: After first attracting newcomers with the "emotional promise" that they would feel good about themselves and gain acceptance from others, seasoned group members monitored new members' emotional expressions, encouraged them to practice their new identity in group discussions, and rewarded them emotionally (with solidarity, fellowship, and warmth) when they modeled the emotion norms that each support group valued. Wolkomir argued that without such emotional mobilization, participants would be unable to renegotiate the meaning that they attached to themselves and their gay identities and desires. Her study demonstrated that emotions play a vital role in transforming the meaning of a stigmatized and marginalized identity; they are not merely a by-product of that transformation.

Members of Metro PAGE, a support group for parents of adult lesbian women and gay men, experienced a similar conflict between a morally valued identity and a stigmatized identity (Fields 2001). The parents engaged in both normalization (of their children's deviant sexual identities) and normification (of their own "courtesy stigma") (Goffman 1963) as they struggled with a status inconsistency: "they were simultaneously normal—straight, married, middle-class, and middle-aged women and men—and deviant—the mothers and fathers of lesbian and gay adults" (Fields 2001:166). Parents in the study, especially mothers (who contended with our culture's gendered convention of holding mothers responsible for children's sexuality), initially struggled with feelings of shame, disappointment, and grief because they failed to "successfully" produce heterosexual offspring. The parents who joined Metro PAGE wanted to feel good about themselves and their children, but more than that, they wanted to convince outsiders of this transformation and change their feelings about gay and lesbian sexuality, too. For their identity work to succeed, they needed others to acknowledge and support their identity cues and signs. To cultivate that support, the parents differentiated themselves from other parents who rejected their lesbian and gay children and they "established themselves as generous in their love for those whom others found unlovable" (Fields 2001:179). They adopted "women and men who identified as lesbian or gay [and] engaged in an ennobling of their parental identities" (p. 180). The parents' exemplary, yet heteronormative, expression of parental love through their actions and talk allowed them to reclaim parenthood as a moral identity and transform their shame into pride in themselves and in their children. This emotional reworking indicates that pride is a role-taking emotion (Shott 1979) that even members of stigmatized groups can use to announce that they have worthy identities.

These previous examples illustrate social actors' emotional efforts to resolve fundamental conflicts between valued and stigmatized identities—what Schwalbe and Mason-Schrock (1996:141) call "oppositional identity work." Acquiring valorized or culturally celebrated identities also involves an emotional process, as Adler and Adler's (1989) study of the "gloried self" indicated. Adler and Adler observed players on a top college basketball team take on self-aggrandizing identities in response to intoxicating public adulation and media capitalization of their athletic feats. Adler and Adler's work documented that an identity can prove so seductive and overwhelming that, in the end, it can "engulf" other identities that social actors previously maintained or hoped to hold in the future and constrict their sense of self. Increasingly seduced by the lure of professional stardom, the young male athletes (mostly African American and lower middle class) abandoned their pragmatic goals of getting college degrees and steady jobs. Their response shows how pursuing a seemingly positive and pleasurable identity—to the exclusion of other identities—can magnify existing social inequality in unforeseen, oppressive ways.

Managing either stigmatized or glorified identities entails emotion work, but a key problem is that people who occupy unequal positions in race, class, gender, and sexual hierarchies lack equal resources to manage them. As Snow and Anderson (1987) noted among homeless men and women, sometimes the only resource available for identity work is talk, and talk cannot overcome severe social and economic deprivation or minimize profound emotional pain. For example, even when homeless people embraced their role and occasionally extolled the virtues of homelessness, they grew even more isolated and displayed signs of social and psychological deterioration. Rather than find that substance abuse and mental illness "caused" homelessness, as the general public maintains, Snow and Anderson observed chronically homeless women and men increasingly turn to chemical or cognitive forms of escape to cope with their unforgiving situations. Thus, without resources to manage stigmatized identities, people some time engage in an emotional coping process that causes them further damage.

People try to fashion and then maintain identities that make them feel good, or at least better, about themselves, individually and collectively, even if they do not succeed in the end. These interactionist studies reveal the emotional underside of cognitive redefinitions of the self in the context of social inequalities.

Inequalities and Self in the Culture of Emotions

The culture of emotions refers to feeling and display rules (how people are expected to feel and show their emotions in particular situations) and shared ideas about how to interpret emotions. This culture reflects a broader gendered culture in which women are expected to take care of others' emotions at work and at home (Hochschild 1983). Women and men are also expected to do different kinds of emotional labor and emotion work: Women are supposed to display sympathy and nurturance and to elevate the mood, feelings, and status of others, whereas men are supposed to act in ways that suppress sympathy, harbor criticism, and deflate the feelings and status of others. Men and women can violate the display rules, but usually not without consequence.

Pierce's (1995) study of feeling rules and emotional displays among trial lawyers and paralegals illustrated that emotional labor, especially in its gendered forms, reproduces hierarchy. Lawyering is a cognitive game involves "highly emotional, dramatic, flamboyant, shocking presentations" designed to "evoke sympathy, distrust, or outrage" (Pierce 1995:53). Trial lawyers, most of whom are men, are expected to display aggression in most aspects of their work. They also learn to practice what Pierce called "strategic friendliness" (1995:71–82). Paralegals, most of whom are women, have the job of reassuring witnesses, a type of emotional labor that helps the attorneys with their cases. Paralegals' deferential and caretaking emotional labor and attorneys' adversarial emotional labor, then, "reproduce gender relations in the law-firm hierarchy" (Lively 2000; Pierce 1995:86).

As Pierce points out, female lawyers, whether or not they go along with the aggressive requirement of the role, are in a double bind (see Frye 1983). If they act aggressively, they can be accused of being too aggressive (for a woman); if they do not act like sharks, male attorneys can accuse them of being lousy lawyers. The women's performances of strategic friendliness are deprecated and trivialized at times by male attorneys as "feminine wiles," even as the males applaud their own strategic friendliness as clever accomplishments. In addition, female attorneys face sexism from clients and are left to deal with that on their own.

The culture of romance fosters other double standards that can prove dangerous for women. In her study of women who had been stalked by men, Dunn (2002) found that romantic feelings initially made women feel special, agentic, and empowered, but eventually led to disastrous results. The women in her sample had been stalked by former male intimates. When the man pursued his former partner, he instilled fear—threatening that he would hurt her if she did not return to him—as well as guilt and romantic feelings. As Dunn (2002:38) put it, "even unwanted attention, when it fits within cultural constructions of love, can be interpreted as flattering or romantic. This can occur even when avowals of love are intermingled with surveillance, threats, and violence." Some women were forgiving of their ex-husbands because they thought the man's love for her controlled him.

Once the women decided to leave and began seeking help from others in finding protection, they encountered enormous difficulties presenting themselves as victims to lawyers in the district attorney's office of domestic violence units. In their attempts to get the stalkers to leave them alone, the women often agreed to talk to them. The women hoped to calm the man down (a kind of emotion work) and to convince him, nicely, to move on with his life. However, lawyers interpreted the women's behaviors as *complicity*. Lawyers know that cases will not be convincing to juries if the woman has had contact with the stalker. The rules for emotional display in a stalking or rape case require a presentation of the woman as a convincing victim. At the same time, women receive so little help from lawyers or the police that their feminine emotion-work skills become their main resource. Some women end up returning to the relationship, an act that appears irrational, but makes sense from the point of view of people in a desperate situation who are not finding help. One woman explained:

> I was scared if I didn't [resume the relationship] that something would happen to me. I felt like he won't— he won't let me go. He's proven that . . . He won't get the message. I don't want him. He will not get on with his life. It was—it was hard to explain. It's hard to explain. . . . But the only reason I was with him was because I feared if I didn't then he would hurt me. The police were not protecting me, they didn't get there on time. I felt like that was the only thing I could do to protect myself and my son. (Dunn 2002:94)

Women's difficulty in dealing with both their stalker and the recalcitrant criminal justice system reveals how they struggle with an emotional double bind: The emotional culture of romance (that privileges their stalker) clashes with institutionalized emotion norms in the court system that constrain how victims should present themselves in the "game" of winning a case against stalkers. Women walk a fine line between proving to legal authorities that they are victims who should be protected from the stalker while also showing that they are not *too helpless* and thus incapable of helping win the case. However, if they aggressively pursue their case, legal authorities might perceive them as too much of a survivor and cut back their assistance. As Konradi (1999) also found in studying rape survivors' courtroom emotion management strategies, any aggression or explosive anger violates the gendered display rule for victims: If she's a real victim, how can she be so strong?

Rothenberg (2003) and Loseke (1992) likewise found that women whose male partners had beaten them but did not fit the "battered woman syndrome" had difficulty obtaining official help. Women who got angry with their partners did not fit the picture of "innocent" and were seen, instead, as provoking the man (and thus could not be a real victim). The gendered display rules of the culture of romance (a woman loving and having contact with the male ex-partner) contradicted the gendered display rules of victims in the legal system (shunning contact, showing fear and pain while suppressing anger). Mills and Kleinman (1988) examined the consequences of this kind of double bind in their study of emotions and reflexivity among battered women. They found that women might initially perform emotion work on their partners to contain abusive interactions, but, in repeatedly failing to end the abuse, they could lose their ability to manage their emotions. Most of the time, this meant becoming numb and zombielike; occasionally, it meant striking back spontaneously and violently, without self-control or awareness.

EMOTION, IDEOLOGY, AND SUSTAINED SOCIAL INEQUALITIES

As our previous discussion suggests, symbolic interactionist research offers the opportunity to move beyond the study of social patterns and what they mean to participants and toward a critical appreciation of their consequences for reproducing inequality. Social arrangements both reflect and reproduce inequalities; people tie meanings to an ideology that justifies the advantages of the most powerful and the disadvantages of the least powerful. Emotions play a pivotal role in sustaining these meanings, ideologies, and disadvantages. An ideology is not "effective" unless people have strong feelings about the ideas embedded in it. For example, in the United States, many schools and families teach children to feel proud of living in a society presumably organized around meritocratic and do-gooder principles. These lessons persist in the face of pervasive inequalities in gender, race, class, and sexuality (among others).

Understandably, many privileged people do not want to believe that they gain at the expense of others or that their privileges came unearned. They can fail to acknowledge their privileged status because privileges remain largely invisible to those who have them (McIntosh 1997). The meritocratic ideal allows people to assume that they earned their comforts and advantages. If they came to believe otherwise, they might feel guilty about the benefits they receive. In addition, if privileged people were to recognize their unearned advantages and become allies of subordinates, then they would have to confront their fear about fighting the very system that benefits them.

Those with fewer privileges and less power also want to feel good about themselves, although the ideology of "you can make it if you try hard" can bring shame and frustration if their struggles continue. In the case of some inequalities, particularly sexism, it is even possible for individuals in an oppressed category to accept or enjoy the very practices that maintain the disadvantages of the group. From home to work to leisure, meanings and emotions are crucial for understanding how inequality works in our day-to-day interactions.

Dominants and Emotions

When members of privileged groups interact with one another, they find ways to reinforce differences between themselves and the subordinate group that preserve their superiority. Their efforts produce powerful feelings of solidarity. Because members of the dominant group in an unequal society use difference to justify their dominance (Lorber 1995; Reskin 1988), the cultural content on which dominants base their solidarity often devalues and "others" the oppressed group (Schwalbe et al. 2000). Thus, solidarity-building is both part of the process and a product of reinforcing privilege and dominance over subordinates.

For example, in his study of locker room behavior among male college athletes, Curry (1991) found that players constantly competed with each other to obtain coveted positions on the team, undermining the feeling of team unity deemed necessary to win games. Rather than reject competition as harmful, the players crafted solidarity with each other as men (i.e., as members of the dominant group) by bragging about women as sexual conquests, policing one another's sexuality through homophobic remarks, and practicing their "game face" by maintaining a pose of invulnerability. To signify their identities as men, the players learned to suppress empathy for women and queer people and to conceal sadness or anxieties about themselves inside and outside the game. These emotional practices helped to produce feelings of solidarity and to reinforce hegemonic masculinity.

As Sattel (1976) has argued, men (especially white, middle-class men) learn as boys to stifle feelings of sadness and empathy. This translates into a kind of "emotional capital" (Cahill 1999) that men accumulate and use to justify their authority. Presumably, men can be trusted in high-level positions because they appear to be rational when making important decisions and conceal that their feelings might get in the way. This does not mean that men will display an unemotional front across all situations. Men, for example, might claim "rational" authority at work by suppressing role-taking emotions but practice seductive vulnerability or "sensitivity" with women in the private sphere, which continues to empower them as men (Sattel 1976).

Members of dominant groups often feel hostile—and inflict harm—when they perceive that they cannot control subordinates. Dominants may then use culturally available rhetorics to assert that members of the subordinate group have wronged them and thus justify their hostile feelings and actions. Arendell (1992, 1997), for example, found that 66 of the 75 divorced fathers she interviewed spoke against their ex-wives. These men held traditional views of gender, believing that inherent differences between men and women justify men controlling their families. Even in cases in which the men won custody of the children, having their relationship result in divorce represented both a loss of control (over their ex-wives and children) and an affront to their masculinity. The divorced fathers used these ideas to justify their angry feelings and aggressive behavior toward their ex-wives and children. In turn, this legitimating rhetoric functioned as a cover for restoring male privilege. The men's feelings of anger—a conventionally acceptable masculine emotion, unlike loss or grief—became legitimate, even heroic, as they fought against the perceived injustice of having their domination challenged.

In Dunn's (2002) study of stalkers, men used love and jealousy to justify the violent acts that they committed against their female ex-partners. As one defendant said about the woman he stabbed repeatedly:

> She was my girlfriend and I still love her. I was mad and jealous.... And I gave her some candies, and a rose.... I always gave her presents.... What she did to me felt bad and that's why, when I saw the hickies, I got mad, 'cause I love her a lot, well, I loved her, I still love her. (Dunn 2002:42)

This stalker's father echoed that sentiment: "He is just very intense and very serious, and he loved this girl too much" (Dunn 2002:42). A rhetoric of romance and intense feelings for the woman can serve to legitimize the harm the man inflicts on her. This framing of the problem also positions women as the *cause* of the man's emotional response and, in turn, his harmful behavior, an idea that permeates the rape culture (Scully and Marolla 1984).

What happens in arenas in which men are expected, even encouraged, to express sadness and hurt and to engage in expressive behavior thought of as "unmanly"? Do these expectations curtail the reproduction of gender inequality? Schwalbe (1996) found in his study of the mythopoetic men's movement that participants engaged in rituals that had them hugging, crying in front of other men, and revealing fears through talk (especially about their fathers). Although these kinds of talk, emotion work, and rituals are culturally associated with women and femininity in U.S. society, the men dissociated their practices from women and habitually emphasized that they were doing *men's work* and "getting in touch with one's deep masculinity." The mythopoetic men might have characterized their therapeutic identity work as "human work," thus putting gender itself into question. However, they did not. Rather, they reinstated their identity as men, an identity they did not want to relinquish because of its cultural value. Thus, even in a setting in which men tried to challenge the usual norms of masculinity and engage in emotional displays that are culturally associated with women, they framed and spoke about their emotion work in ways that maintained the higher status of men and masculinity. Without recognizing it, they reinforced the gender hierarchy.

The men who participated in the mythopoetic movement did not think of themselves as sexist, and their privileges as straight men made it possible for others to buttress their good feelings about themselves as fair people. Similarly, whites who consider themselves nonracist often find ways to keep themselves from making any changes in society that might challenge their race privilege while still feeling good about themselves. Wellman (1993), Bonilla-Silva (2003), and Frankenberg (1993) interviewed white people and discovered how whites find ways to defend their racial privilege and justify inequality but still believe they are not "explicitly contradict[ing] egalitarian ideals" (Wellman 1993:53). The white people used what Frankenberg (1993:142) called a color- and power-evasive strategy: They claimed not to see color. Yet, as the three authors argued, such rhetorics ignore not only a history of the oppression of people of color but also *continuing* inequalities in, for example, education, employment, and housing.

Bonilla-Silva (2003:28) discussed the strategies that white people use to feel good about themselves while arguing against institutional changes that would help people of color. The main strategy he discovered is "abstract liberalism":

> using ideas associated with political liberalism (e.g., "equal opportunity," the idea that force should not be used to achieve social policy) and economic liberalism (e.g., choice, individualism) in an abstract manner to explain racial matters. By framing race-related issues in the language of liberalism, whites can appear "reasonable" and even "moral," while opposing almost all practical approaches to deal with de facto racial inequality.

Abstract liberalism permits white people to feel sadness and sympathy toward people of color and to express generic disapproval of racism. They think of themselves as nonracist because "racist" brings to mind images of white people spewing hateful white supremacist beliefs or carrying out hate crimes. By rejecting racist violence, white liberals can view themselves as good people. These feelings also allow whites to believe that they understand the experiences of people of color. Yet, as Schwalbe (2005b) argued, dominants often know little about subordinates because they do not have to. Nor do dominants need to pay attention to the feelings of subordinates (Hochschild 1983). Subordinates, on the other hand, must attend to the feelings, moods, and behaviors of dominants; their livelihoods and lives depend on it (hooks 1992).

Bonilla-Silva, Frankenberg, and Wellman discovered that many whites are against affirmative action and use the language of abstract liberalism in their arguments against it. One of Frankenberg's (1993:149) interviewees put it this way, a typical response of white people in all three studies: "I resent it particularly because I feel that people should be considered for who they are as a human being and not as this, that, or the other—who you are, regardless of outside trappings—[there's an] inner person, shouting to get out." Appealing to humanism made it difficult for whites to recognize that affirmative action programs are meant to make up for years of structural inequality (Fish 1994). When there is a chance that (race) privilege is threatened, whites' feelings of sadness and sympathy turn quickly into resentment. They can still feel good about themselves as nonracists, even as they resent (some) people of color for getting what they see as special consideration. Thus, we see how ideology (in this case, abstract liberalism) legitimized dominants' negative feelings against the subordinate group while making it possible for dominants to believe and feel that they are fair and just.

Dominants also reinforce differences between themselves and subordinates in service work settings in which subordinates perform emotional labor for the benefit of dominants. In a study of Korean immigrant-owned nail salons, Kang (2003) found that "body labor"—a form of service work requiring both physical contact and emotional labor performed for a client—was most exploitive in a setting in which Korean immigrant women physically and emotionally pampered white, upper-class professional women who expected "caring and attentive service" and who held "high expectations regarding [hand and foot] massages, cleanliness, sensitive touch, and friendly conversation" (Kang 2003:835). When female Korean immigrant workers at a different salon served a predominately working-class and lower-middle-class African American and Caribbean clientele, they honored different expectations: communicating respectfulness, fairness, and efficiency in their transactions with customers and exercising creativity for customers who sought to distinguish themselves through unique nail designs. Kang's work demonstrated that performing emotional labor does not automatically magnify inequalities. Rather, we must ask who performs what for whom, under what conditions, and with what consequences?

Subordinates and Emotion

As Kleinman (2006) pointed out, researchers might find it difficult to recognize the harmful consequences of rituals and practices when members of the disadvantaged group say that they *enjoy* them. Fieldworkers probably have a healthy skepticism about the rationales and desires of the powerful while overempathizing with subordinates (Kleinman and Copp 1993). However, desires are a product of socialization and social control as much as they are of thoughts, behaviors, and ideologies and, thus, require interrogation. As we discuss below, researchers need to assume that members of subordinate groups are not always aware of, for example, how their individual desires affect their group as a whole.

Hooks (1989:130) has observed that patriarchy is the only system of oppression in which members of the disadvantaged group are meant to *love* their oppressors. As a result, women sometimes engage in practices that win men's approval but reinforce inequality for women as a *group*. Building on Hochschild's (1983) studies of emotion work in relationships, Bartky (1990) conceived of the emotion work enjoyed by many women in intimate relationships with men as false power. She argued that when emotion work is performed only or mostly by the woman (Hochschild 1983; Rubin 1983; Sattel 1976), she might feel good about her skilled work, but she is, in effect, making his feelings more important than her own. Bartky (1990:116) commented on the work of "feeding egos and tending wounds":

> [T]he *feeling* of out-flowing personal power so characteristic of the caregiving woman is quite different from the *having* of any actual power in the world. There is no doubt that this sense of personal efficacy provides some compensation for the extra-domestic power women are typically denied: if one cannot be king oneself, being a confidante of kings may be the next best thing. But just as we make a bad bargain in accepting an occasional Valentine in lieu of the sustained attention we deserve, we are ill advised to settle for a mere feeling of power, however heady and intoxicating it may be, in place of the effective power we have every right to exercise in the world.

Does examining the oppressive consequences of desire for the disadvantaged group ignore human agency? From the symbolic interactionist viewpoint, agency is a given and can range from resignation to rebellion. Once a child can see herself as an object, she can react to her own thoughts and respond to others (Blumer 1969; Mead 1934). However, what kind of object does she see herself as being? And how do others perceive her?

Interactionists studying emotions and inequality ask similar questions about subordinate groups' desires and analyze their consequences for reinforcing or challenging inequalities. Giuffre and Williams (1994) studied how female and male servers came to label, or failed to label, particular acts as sexual harassment. White female servers in the restaurants that Giuffre and Williams studied accepted touching, pinching, and sexually explicit talk from white male middle-class servers, but they considered the same behavior as sexual harassment when initiated by male Hispanic cooks. Similarly, straight male servers felt disturbed by gay men's sexual joking, but they relished their own "raunchy" sexual jokes. Giuffre and Williams (1994:399) concluded that current cultural ideas about feelings of pleasure "protect the most privileged groups in society from charges of sexual harassment and may be used to oppress and exclude the least powerful groups."

The emotional experiences of pleasure and romance can have adverse material consequences for women. At Renewal (Kleinman 1996), the women on staff enjoyed flirting with the higher-status male practitioners and had sexual-romantic relationships with them. This helped make it possible for the women to become the "housewives" of the organization, working for little or no pay and doing emotional labor for the men. Nanny-domestic workers, too, are expected by their employers to work more for love than money (Hondagneu-Sotelo 2001; Parrenas 2001).

This exploitation is possible, in part, because subordinates often find their experiences with dominants emotionally satisfying. In her study of strippers, Barton (2002) found that the women initially felt good about having men react to them as sexually attractive and paying for the show. As one stripper said: "Sometimes you feel like a goddess with all the men looking at you. It makes you feel good. I like being spoiled with attention. Attention you wouldn't get anywhere else. Any woman would" (Barton 2002:591). Sociologists of emotion ask: What cultural ideas underlie group members' feelings? Strippers could have internalized the idea that women fitting conventional standards of beauty is what turns them into "goddesses," or, as another woman put it, "takes the [men's] breath away, whether they're drunk or not" (Barton 2002:590). Yet, as the strippers Barton studied soon discovered, their male customers did not think of them only as beautiful objects, akin to appreciating a painting in a museum. Rather, "on the flip side of male worship lies contempt for women who have stepped outside the bounds of respectable femininity" (Barton 2002:591). As one stripper noted:

> The job is bad because you have to deal with customers who can be problematic and rude . . . they feel like the normal laws of etiquette that govern any other social or business interaction are suspended there. . . . They'll say, "Turn around bitch, I want to see your ass. I'm paying." . . . That's not something you have to contend with systematically in other jobs. (Barton 2002:592)

Even in those subcultures in which groups have fashioned new standards of attractiveness and new norms for sexual activity, practices that anchor a group's new identity in unconventional norms of sexual desire can ultimately sustain gender inequality. In a local Goth scene (Wilkins 2004), women considered themselves independent, sexually assertive, and in charge of their lives and the spaces in which they hung out. However, as Wilkins pointed out, women in this subsociety cannot choose to present themselves as anything *but* sexy. Similarly, Kleinman (1996) found that participants' belief that they were "doing something different" at the holistic health center made it harder for them to see their own sexist practices. To participants, working at an "alternative organization" meant that they were progressive. To acknowledge that they did anything that failed to live up to their ideals would have challenged their identity as good people, a central identity for participants and their work. This realization was too threatening to their self-image and their good feelings about themselves to acknowledge.

The works of Giuffre and Williams, Barton, Wilkins, and Kleinman suggest that the pleasure subordinates feel about themselves and dominants can obstacle to social change. If members of the subordinate group are emotionally attached to receiving the approval of dominants and if that approval is tied to practices that ultimately benefit dominants, then subordinates will lack the emotional mobilization to make change.

These studies highlight the emotion work of dealing with inequality (DeVault 1999) and show us how emotions are central to understanding inequality. For the status quo to be sustained, dominants must feel comfortable about their entitlement and not have too much sympathy for subordinates. Similarly, subordinates learn to blame themselves for their low position in a hierarchical system. In the case of some forms of inequality, particularly sexism, many subordinates have intimate relationships with dominants and thus become invested in seeing them as mere "individuals," not as members of a dominant *group*. Alternatively, subordinates might agree that the dominant group exists, but argue that the individual member is an exception. The beliefs of dominants and subordinates are tied to strong feelings about the self that make dominants unlikely to see their privileges and subordinates unlikely to see dominants as a part of their own problems.

METHODOLOGICAL PERSPECTIVES FOR INTERACTIONIST STUDIES OF EMOTION

How do interactionists go about studying emotions and their consequences? Symbolic interactionists' research agenda requires a range of methodologies. Affect control theorists (e.g., Heise and Weir 1999; Lively and Heise 2004) and identity theorists (e.g., Stets 2005; Stets and Tsushima 2001) rely on quantitative models and both experimental and survey designs to explore models of emotion. Smith-Lovin, for example, has explored extensively how emotional responses signal continuity or discontinuity between social identities and events and thus motivate social action (Dawn Robinson, Lynn Smith-Lovin, and Allison Wisecup in this volume; Smith-Lovin 1990). Other symbolic interactionists have used "autoethnography" to explore their own lives and emotions. Through "systematic sociological introspection," these interactionists examine, for example, their own and their partners' experiences of illness (Ellis 1991, 1995; Frank 1997) and their lives as writers and scholars (Richardson 1997). They seek to analyze intense feelings and deeper understandings of emotion that would be difficult to access via other research methods.

Most realist interactionist studies of emotion rely on the qualitative methods of ethnography, participant observation, open-ended interviewing, and content analysis. As Blumer (1969:1–60) established in his chapter on "The Methodological Position of Symbolic Interactionism," theory and methodology are intertwined. Because meaning emerges in social settings through interaction, researchers must enter those settings and observe interactions in order to understand the meanings people negotiate, experience, and attach to social life (see also Goffman 1989). This type of empirical observation has been at the foundation of some of the most influential studies of emotion. For example, Hochschild (1983, 1989b) conducted interviews and participant observation in her studies of flight attendants, bill collectors, and heterosexual married couples; these empirical works led to fundamental insights into the more general topics of emotion work, feeling rules, and emotional labor. Thoits (1996) explored the emotion work of managing others' emotions in her analysis of fieldnotes she took during a year with Sisyphus, an encounter group, in the mid-1970s.

At times, Blumer's (1969) call for interactionists to explore everyday life has presented sociologists of emotion with a particular challenge: Public accounts of people's emotional lives are often difficult to come by, particularly among disadvantaged or disenfranchised communities (Lofland 1985). Interactionists thus often rely in their studies on multiple and unconventional data sources. Lofland (1985) used historical accounts of mourners and mourning rituals in her study of grief. Clark's (1987) analysis of the feeling rules governing sympathy drew on textual sources ranging from greeting cards to song lyrics, fieldnotes from observations of sympathy interactions, interviews with adult respondents, survey responses, and ethnographic data reported by other sociologists.

Emotion is not only a substantive focus of symbolic interactionist research; it is also a methodological tool. As Kleinman and Copp (1993) noted, researchers who study others' emotions also have their own emotional reactions to the people they study and the setting in which they have immersed themselves. Kleinman and Copp urged fieldworkers not to stifle, silence, or ignore these reactions but, instead, to locate them in the social settings they are studying. Emotions become tools of symbolic interactionist analysis as researchers explore the insights implicit in their situated feelings. Those adopting this methodological stance ask, for example, what their experiences suggest about the setting's emotional culture and what cultural expectations their "outlaw emotions" (Jaggar 1989) violate. For example, Thoits (1996) found that her feelings of vulnerability in a psychodrama-based encounter group helped her appreciate how other members might have felt after group meetings. Her anger helped her recognize gender inequities in the encounter group.

Other interactionists have looked to respondents' emotional experiences of the research process as a source of further insight. In Arendell's (1997) interviews with recently divorced fathers, respondents' expressions of anger, concern, suspicion, frustration, and desire—and, at times Arendell's reactions to these emotions—helped to reassert the gender hierarchy at the center of the research question (see also Arendell 1992). Fields (2005) found in her study of a community engaged in debates about school-based sexuality education that respondents' apparent caution and suspicion when answering interview questions about race and sexuality pointed to emotion rules governing talk about race—again, the subject of the researcher's inquiry. As these studies suggest and as Scheff (2000) has noted, researchers who explore emotions—particularly emotions that people experience as painful—will need to study not only respondents' testimonies about their emotional experiences but also their emotional behavior and discourse. Even as symbolic interactionists continue to emphasize the social nature of emotions, they also attend to how people experience the social without awareness, through their bodies—"preobjective in expression and yet very social" (Franks 2003:803). Methodological innovations will help interactionists explore not only what people can articulate about their feelings but also what they cannot articulate and cannot feel.

CONCLUSION

Interactionists study and theorize about the core concerns of sociology, including social order and inequality (Horowitz 1997; Schwalbe et al. 2000). Symbolic interactionism, as we have argued, challenges micro/macro distinctions, positing the individual as neither an entity who stands apart from society nor a passive repository of culture. Social life—its organization, inequities, and history—cannot be understood without paying attention to group process and interaction, meaning, and feelings. In U.S. society, these terms bring to mind the individual; however, as Mead (1934) and Blumer (1969) wrote long ago, one cannot understand individual actions without also understanding shared meanings, social constraints, and context.

We would go further: The interactionists' goal is not to understand the individual. Rather, interactionists seek to understand processes within groups, organizations, cultures, and networks. Particulars matter to interactionists because they further efforts "to generalize about process, not populations" (Kleinman et al. 1997; Schwalbe et al. 2000:421; see Becker, 1990, for a discussion of analytic generalizability). In their efforts to understand social arrangements and inequities—what sociologists usually call "stratification"—symbolic interactionists argue that we cannot understand systems of inequality—or any other social system—without understanding what people think, feel, and do (see Anderson and Snow 2001). Schwalbe et al. (2000:420) put it well: "The idea that inequality cannot be understood apart from the processes that produce it is ... deeply rooted in the interactionist tradition, as is the idea that these processes must be examined directly."

What does this mean for the sociology of emotions? The methodological imperative that Blumer (1969) set forth directs fieldworkers to study participants' shared understandings and misunderstandings, social divisions and social cohesion, what members produce or fail to produce despite their best intentions, and the creation and consequences of their joint action. Thus, for interactionists, emotions, like everything else, are data that help them understand social reality. However, if we fail to study the inequality in our midst and ignore the emotions of dominants and subordinates, then we fail to analyze the obdurate reality that Blumer identified as fundamental to the symbolic interactionist perspective. We call on interactionists not only to bring emotions into their analyses, but also to examine how people produce selves and social arrangements in a society still characterized by inequity, injustice, and resistance.

REFERENCES

Adler, Patricia A., and Peter Adler. 1989. "The Gloried Self: The Aggrandizement and Constriction of Self." *Social Psychology Quarterly* 52: 299–310.

Anderson, Leon, and David Snow. 2001. "Inequality and the Self: Explaining Connections from an Interactionist Perspective." *Symbolic Interaction* 24: 395–406.

Arendell, Terry. 1992. "The Social Self as Gendered: A Masculinist Discourse of Divorce." *Symbolic Interaction* 15: 151–181.

———. 1997. "Reflections on the Researcher-Researched Relationship: A Woman Interviewing Men." *Qualitative Sociology* 20: 341–368.

Arluke, Arnold. 1994. "Managing Emotions in an Animal Shelter." Pp. 145–165 in *Animals and Human Society: Changing Perspectives*, edited by A. Manning and J. Serpell. New York: Routledge.

Barbalet, J. M. 1992. "A Macro Sociology of Emotion: Class Resentment." *Sociological Theory* 10: 150–163.

Bartky, Sandra L. 1990. *Femininity and Domination: Studies in the Phenomenology of Oppression*. New York: Routledge.

Barton, Bernadette. 2002. "Dancing on the Möbius Strip: Challenging the Sex War Paradigm." *Gender and Society* 16: 585–602.

Becker, Howard S. 1990. "Generalizing from Case Studies." Pp. 233–244 in *Qualitative Inquiry in Education: The Continuing Debate*, edited by E. W. Eisner and A. Peshkin. New York: Columbia University Press.

Bjorklund, Diane. 1998. *Interpreting the Self: Two Hundred Years of American Autobiography*. Chicago: University of Chicago Press.

Blumer, Herbert. 1969. *Symbolic Interactionism: Perspective and Method*. Englewood Cliffs, NJ: Prentice-Hall.

Bonilla-Silva, Eduardo. 2003. *Racism without Racists: Color-Blind Racism and the Persistence of Racial Inequality in the United States*. Lanham, MD: Rowman and Littlefield.

Cahill, Spencer E. 1995. "Embarrassability and Public Civility: Another View of a Much Maligned Emotion." Pp. 253–271 in *Social Perspectives on Emotion*, edited by M. Flaherty and C. Ellis. Stamford, CT: JAI Press.

———. 1999. "Emotional Capital and Professional Socialization: The Case of Mortuary Science Students (and Me)." *Social Psychology Quarterly* 62: 101–116.

Clark, Candace. 1987. "Sympathy Biography and Sympathy Margin." *American Journal of Sociology* 93: 290–321.

———. 1990. "Emotions and Micropolitics in Everyday Life: Some Patterns and Paradoxes of 'Place.'" Pp. 305–333 in *Research Agendas in the Sociology of Emotions*, edited by T. D. Kemper. Albany: State University of New York Press.

———. 1997. *Misery and Company: Sympathy in Everyday Life*. Chicago: University of Chicago Press.

Cohn, Carol. 1987. "Sex and Death in the Rational World of Defense Intellectuals." *Signs: Journal of Women in Culture and Society* 12: 687–718.

Copp, Martha. 1998. "When Emotion Work Is Doomed to Fail: Ideological and Structural Constraints on Emotion Management." *Symbolic Interaction* 21: 299–328.

Curry, Timothy Jon. 1991. "Fraternal Bonding in the Locker Room: A Profeminist Analysis of Talk about Competition and Women." *Sociology of Sport Journal* 8: 5–21.

Denzin, Norman K. 1984. *On Understanding Emotion*. San Francisco: Jossey-Bass.

DeVault, Marjorie. 1999. "Comfort and Struggle: Emotion Work in Family Life." *Annals of the American Academy of Political and Social Science* 56: 52–63.

Dunn, Jennifer. 2002. *Courting Disaster: Intimate Stalking, Culture, and Criminal Justice*. New York: Aldine de Gruyter.

Ellis, Carolyn. 1991. "Sociological Introspection and Emotional Experience." *Symbolic Interaction* 14: 23–50.

———. 1995. *Final Negotiations: A Story of Love, Loss, and Chronic Illness*. Philadelphia: Temple University Press.

Emerson, Joan P. 1970. "Behavior in Private Places: Sustaining Definitions of Reality in Gynecological Examinations." Pp. 74–97 in *Recent Sociology Number 2*, edited by H. P. Dreitzel. London: Macmillan.

Fields, Jessica. 2001. "Normal Queers: Straight Parents Respond to their Children's 'Coming Out.'" *Symbolic Interaction* 24: 165–187.

———. 2005. "Children-Having-Children: Racism, Innocence, and Sexuality Education." *Social Problems* 52: 549–571.

Fine, Gary Alan, ed. 1995. *A Second Chicago School? The Development of a Postwar American Sociology*. Chicago: University of Chicago Press.

Fish, Stanley. 1994. "Reverse Racism, or How the Pot Got to Call the Kettle Black." Pp. 60–69 in *There's No Such Things as Free Speech . . . And It's a Good Thing, Too*, edited by S. Fish. New York: Oxford University Press.

Francis, Linda E. 1994. "Laughter, the Best Mediation: Humor as Emotion Management in Interaction." *Symbolic Interaction* 17: 147–163.

———. 1997. "Ideology and Interpersonal Emotion Management: Redefining Identity in Two Support Groups." *Social Psychology Quarterly* 60: 153–171.

Frank, Arthur W. 1997. *The Wounded Storyteller: Body, Illness, and Ethics*. Chicago: University of Chicago Press.

Frankenberg, Ruth. 1993. *White Women, Race Matters*. Minneapolis: University of Minnesota Press.

Franks, David D. 1987. "Notes on the Bodily Aspect of Emotions: A Controversial Issue in Symbolic Interaction." *Studies in Symbolic Interaction* 8: 219–233.

———. 2003. "Emotions." Pp. 787–809 in *Handbook of Symbolic Interactionism*, edited by L. T. Reynolds and N. J. Herman-Kinney. Lanham, MD: Rowman and Littlefield.

Frye, Marilyn. 1983. *The Politics of Reality: Essays in Feminist Theory*. Trumansburg, NY: Crossing Press.

Giuffre, Patti A., and Christine L. Williams. 1994. "Boundary Lines: Labeling Sexual Harassment in Restaurants." *Gender and Society* 8: 378–401.

Goffman, Erving. 1959. *The Presentation of Self in Everyday Life*. Garden City, NY: Doubleday.

———. 1963. *Stigma: Notes on the Management of Spoiled Identity*. Englewood Cliffs, NJ: Prentice-Hall.

———. 1967. *Interaction Ritual: Essays on Face-to-Face Behavior*. Garden City, NY: Anchor Books.

———. 1989. "On Fieldwork." *Journal of Contemporary Ethnography* 18: 123–132.

Groves, Julian McAllister. 1995. "Learning to Feel: The Neglected Sociology of Social Movements." *Sociological Review* 43: 435–461.

———. 1997. *Hearts and Minds: The Controversy over Laboratory Animals*. Philadelphia: Temple University Press.

Haas, Jack, and William Shaffir. 1977. "The Professionalization of Medical Students: Developing Competence and a Cloak of Competence." *Symbolic Interaction* 1: 71–88.

Heise, David, and Brian Weir. 1999. "A Test of Symbolic Interactionist Predictions about Emotions in Imagined Situations." *Symbolic Interaction* 22: 129–161.

Hochschild, Arlie Russell. 1979. "Emotion Work, Feeling Rules, and Social Structure." *American Journal of Sociology* 85: 551–575.

———. 1983. *The Managed Heart: The Commercialization of Human Feeling*. Berkeley, University of California Press.

———. 1989a. "The Economy of Gratitude." Pp. 95–113 in *The Sociology of Emotions: Original Essays and Research Papers*, edited by D. D. Franks and E. D. McCarthy. Greenwich, CT: JAI Press.

———. 1989b. *The Second Shift: Working Parents and the Revolution at Home*. New York: Viking.

———. 1990. "Ideology and Emotion Management: A Perspective and Path for Future Research." Pp. 117–142 in *Research Agendas in the Sociology of Emotions*, edited by T. D. Kemper. Albany: State University of New York Press.

———. 1998. "The Sociology of Emotion as a Way of Seeing." Pp. 3–15 in *Emotions in Social Life: Critical Themes and Contemporary Issues*, edited by G. Bendelow and S. J. Williams. London: Routledge.

Hondagneu-Sotelo, Pierette. 2001. *Doméstica: Immigrant Workers Cleaning and Caring in the Shadows of Affluence*. Berkeley: University of California Press.

hooks, bell. 1989. *Talking Back: Thinking Feminist, Thinking Black*. Boston: South End Press.

———. 1992. "Representing Whiteness in the Black Imagination." Pp. 338–342 in *Cultural Studies*, edited by L. Grossberg, C. Nelson, and P. Treichler. New York: Routledge.

Horowitz, Ruth. 1997. "Barriers and Bridges to Class Mobility and Formation: Ethnographies of Stratification." *Sociological Methods and Research* 25: 495–538.

Jaggar, Alison M. 1989. "Love and Knowledge: Emotion in Feminist Epistemology." Pp. 145–171 in *Gender/Body/Knowledge: Feminist Reconstructions of Being and Knowing*, edited by A. J. Jaggar and S. R. Bordo. New Brunswick, NJ: Rutgers University Press.

Kang, Miliann. 2003. "The Managed Hand: The Commercialization of Bodies and Emotions in Korean Immigrant-Owned Nail Salons." *Gender and Society* 17: 820–839.

Katz, Jack. 1975. "Essences as Moral Identities: Verifiability and Responsibility in Imputations of Deviance and Charisma." *American Journal of Sociology* 80: 369–390.

Kleinman, Sherryl. 1996. *Opposing Ambitions: Gender and Identity in an Alternative Organization*. Chicago: University of Chicago Press.

———. 2006. "Feminist Fieldwork Analysis." Book Manuscript.

Kleinman, Sherryl, and Martha A. Copp. 1993. *Emotions and Fieldwork*. Newbury Park, CA: Sage.

Kleinman, Sherryl, Martha Copp, and Karla A. Henderson. 1997. "Qualitatively Different: Teaching Fieldwork to Graduate Students" *Journal of Contemporary Ethnography* 25: 469–499.

Konradi, Amanda. 1999. "'I Don't Have to Be Afraid of You': Rape Survivors' Emotion Management in Court." *Symbolic Interaction* 22: 45–77.

Leif, Harold, and Renee C. Fox. 1963. "Training for 'Detached Concern' in Medical Students." Pp. 12–35 in *The Psychological Basis of Medical Practice*, edited by H. Leif. New York: Harper and Row.

Lively, Kathryn J. 2000. "Reciprocal Emotion Management: Working Together to Maintain Stratification in Private Law Firms." *Work and Occupations* 27: 32–63.

Lively, Kathryn J., and David R. Heise. 2004. "Sociological Realms of Emotional Experience." *American Journal of Sociology* 109: 1109–1136.

Lofland, Lyn H. 1985. "The Social Shaping of Emotion: The Case of Grief." *Symbolic Interaction* 8: 171–190.

Lorber, Judith. 1995. *Paradoxes of Gender*. New Haven, CT: Yale University Press.

Lorde, Audre. 1984. "The Uses of Anger: Women Responding to Racism." Pp. 124–133 in *Sister Outsider: Essays and Speeches*, edited by A. Lorde. New York: Crossing Press.

Loseke, Donileen R. 1992. *Battered Women and Shelters: The Social Construction of Wife Abuse*. Albany: State University of New York Press.

Maines, David R. 1977. "Social Organization and Social Structure in Symbolic Interactionist. Thought." *Annual Review of Sociology* 3: 235–259.

McCarthy, E. Doyle. 1989. "Emotions are Social Things: An Essay in the Sociology of Emotions." Pp. 51–72 in *The Sociology of Emotions*, edited by D. D. Franks and E. D. McCarthy. Greenwich, CT: JAI Press.

McIntosh, Peggy. 1997. "White Privilege and Male Privilege: A Personal Account of Coming to See Correspondences through Work in Women's Studies." Pp. 291–299 in *Critical White Studies: Looking Behind the Mirror*, edited by R. Delgado and J. Stefancic. Philadelphia: Temple University Press.

Mead, George Herbert. 1934. *Mind, Self, and Society*. Chicago: University of Chicago Press.

Mills, Trudy, and Sherryl Kleinman. 1988. "Emotions, Reflexivity, and Action: An Interactionist Analysis." *Social Forces* 66: 1009–1027.

Parrenas, Rhacel Salazar. 2001. *Servants of Globalization: Women, Migration, and Domestic Work*. Stanford, CA: Stanford University Press.

Parsons, Talcott. 1951. *The Social System*. New York: Free Press.

Pierce, Jennifer L. 1995. *Gender Trials: Emotional Lives in Contemporary Law Firms*. Berkeley: University of California Press.

Reskin, Barbara F. 1988. "Bringing the Men Back In: Sex Differentiation and the Devaluation of Women's Work." *Gender and Society* 2: 58–81.

Richardson, Laurel. 1997. *Fields of Play: Constructing an Academic Life*. New Brunswick, NJ: Rutgers University Press.

Rothenberg, Bess. 2003. "'We Don't Have Time for Social Change': Cultural Compromise and the Battered Woman Syndrome." *Gender and Society* 17: 771–787.

Rubin, Lillian. 1983. *Intimate Strangers: Men and Women Together*. New York: Harper and Row.

Sandstrom, Kent, and Sherryl Kleinman. 2005. "Symbolic Interaction." Pp. 821–826 in *Encyclopedia of Social Theory*, edited by G. Ritzer. Thousand Oaks, CA: Sage.

Sandstrom, Kent, Dan Martin, and Gary Alan Fine. 2001. "Symbolic Interactionism at the End of the Century." Pp. 217–231 in *The Handbook of Social Theory*, edited by G. Ritzer and B. Smart. London: Sage.

Sattel, Jack. 1976. "The Inexpressive Male: Tragedy or Sexual Politics?" *Social Problems* 23: 469–477.

Scheff, Thomas J. 1988. "Shame and Conformity: The Deference-Emotion System." *American Sociological Review* 53: 395–406.

———. 2000. "Shame and the Social Bond." *Sociological Theory* 18: 84–98.

Schwalbe, Michael. 1996. *Unlocking the Iron Cage: The Men's Movement, Gender Politics, and American Culture.* New York: Oxford University Press.

———. 2005a. "Identity Stakes, Manhood Acts, and the Dynamics of Accountability." *Studies in Symbolic Interaction* 28: 65–81.

———. 2005b. *The Sociologically Examined Life.* New York: McGraw-Hill.

Schwalbe, Michael, Sandra Godwin, Douglas Schrock, Daphne Holden, Shealy Thompson, and Michele Wolkomir. 2000. "Generic Processes in the Reproduction of Inequality: An Interactionist Analysis." *Social Forces* 79: 419–452.

Schwalbe, Michael, and Douglas Mason-Schrock. 1996. "Identity Work as Group Process." *Advances in Group Processes* 13: 113–147.

Scully, Diana, and Joseph Marolla. 1984. "Convicted Rapists' Vocabulary of Motive: Excuses and Justifications." *Social Problems* 31: 530–544.

Shott, Susan. 1979. "Emotions and Social Life: A Symbolic Interactionist Analysis." *American Journal of Sociology* 84: 1317–1334.

Smith, Allen, and Sherryl Kleinman. 1989. "Managing Emotions in Medical School: Students' Contacts with the Living and the Dead." *Social Psychology Quarterly* 52: 56–69.

Smith, Deborah A., and Rebecca J. Erickson. 1997. "For Love or Money? Work and Emotional Labor in a Social Movement Organization." *Social Perspectives on Emotion* 4: 317–346.

Smith-Lovin, Lynn. 1990. "Emotion as the Confirmation and Disconfirmation of Identity: An Affect Control Model." Pp. 238–270 in *Research Agendas in the Sociology of Emotions*, edited by T. D. Kemper. Albany: State University of New York Press.

Snow, David A. 2001. "Extending and Broadening Blumer's Conceptualization of Symbolic Interactionism." *Symbolic Interaction* 24: 367–377.

Snow, David A., and Leon Anderson. 1987. "Identity Work Among the Homeless: The Verbal Construction and Avowal of Personal Identities." *American Journal of Sociology* 92: 1336–1371.

Stets, Jan E. 2005. "Examining Emotions in Identity Theory." *Social Psychology Quarterly* 68: 39–56.

Stets, Jan E., and Teresa Tsushima. 2001. "Negative Emotion and Coping Responses within Identity Control Theory." *Social Psychology Quarterly* 64: 283–295.

Thoits, Peggy A. 1985. "Self-Labeling Processes in Mental Illness: The Role of Emotional Deviance." *American Journal of Sociology* 91: 221–249.

———. 1989. "The Sociology of Emotions." *Annual Review of Sociology* 15: 317–342.

———. 1996. "Managing the Emotions of Others." *Symbolic Interaction* 19: 85–109.

Van Maanen, John. 1988. *Tales of the Field: On Writing Ethnography.* Chicago: University of Chicago Press.

Wellman, David. 1993. *Portraits of White Racism.* New York: Cambridge University Press.

Wilkins, Amy. 2004. "'So Full of Myself as a Chick': Goth Women, Sexual Independence, and Gender Egalitarianism." *Gender and Society* 18: 328–349.

Wolkomir, Michelle. 2001a. "Emotion Work, Commitment, and the Authentification of the Self: The Case of Gay and Ex-Gay Christian Support Groups." *Journal of Contemporary Ethnography* 30: 305–334.

———. 2001b. "Wrestling with the Angels of Meaning: The Revisionist Ideological Work of Gay and Ex-Gay Christian Men." *Symbolic Interaction* 24: 407–424.

Zurcher, Lou A. 1985. "The War Game: Organizational Scripting and the Expression of Emotion." *Symbolic Interaction* 8: 191–206.

CHAPTER 8

Affect Control Theory

Dawn T. Robinson
Lynn Smith-Lovin
Allison K. Wisecup

When David Heise (1977, 1979) published his early statements of affect control theory, contributing to the newly developing sociology of emotion was not his primary goal. The main objective of the theory was to explain behavior in the context of social interactions. Heise hoped to develop a formal framework that could describe both the routine, expected role behaviors that people enact under normal circumstances *and* the creative responses they generate when encountering noninstitutionalized or counternormative situations. He combined insights from a measurement tradition in psycholinguistics (Osgood 1962, 1966; Osgood et al. 1973, 1975), empirical studies of impression formation (Gollob 1968; Gollob and Rossman 1973; Heise 1969, 1970), and a cybernetic model of perception (Powers 1973) to create his new theory of social action.

Heise's work has become a central part of the new sociology of emotions for three main reasons. First, one of the theory's fundamental assumptions is that cognitive understandings of social interaction around us cannot be separated from our affective reactions to them. Every cognitive label—every way that we think or talk about our social life—brings with it an affective meaning. Affect is irrevocably linked to all of our thoughts, identities, and actions. Second, the core affect control principle is that people act to maintain the affective meanings that are evoked by a definition of the situation. Therefore, affect control theory makes the control of *affect* the key feature underlying social life. The theory is a new variant of symbolic interactionism, in that it stresses that social actors respond to a symbolically represented world and strive to maintain the meanings that are associated with the elements of that world. However, it turns the historically cognitive symbolic interactionist paradigm on its head, positing that the dynamics of affective processing underlie

Dawn T. Robinson • Department of Sociology, University of Georgia, Athens, GA 30602
Lynn Smith-Lovin and Allison K. Wisecup • Department of Sociology, Duke University, Durham, NC 27708

both routine role-taking behavior and creative, negotiated responses to nonroutine situations. Third, the affect control model was elaborated soon after it developed to conceptualize emotions as signals about self-identity meanings within a situation and how well those meanings were aligned with stable, fundamental self-conceptions. Basically, emotions were signals about how well the situation was maintaining self-identity meanings. Because of its formal mathematical model, affect control theory could be much more specific about this process than earlier formulations were.

In this chapter, we will first very briefly review the history of symbolic interactionist thought on emotions. We distinguish between *affect* and *emotion* as two separate phenomena in affect control theory. We then describe the basic structure of the theory, with an emphasis on the parts of the formal model that allow prediction of emotional responses to events. We briefly compare affect control theory to other symbolic interactionist approaches, pointing out where competing hypotheses are logically generated by the different approaches. Finally, we review the research literature and suggest fruitful avenues for future work.

SYMBOLIC INTERACTIONIST ROOTS OF
AFFECT CONTROL THEORY

Although Chapter 7 in this volume gives a more comprehensive treatment of symbolic interactionist thought, we begin with a brief review to highlight affect control theory's points of commonality and its distinctive features (see also Turner and Stets 2005:100–150). Mead's (1938) original statement of the interactionist perspective[1] focused on how gestures (words or behaviors) could operate as symbols for which people shared meanings. Such shared symbols allow social actors to take the role of another person and to understand how other people were experiencing the situation. The ability to think about social life with these symbols gives people the capacity to anticipate how other actors are likely to respond to possible actions. Mead divided the self into two elements—the *I* and the *me*—representing the agentic element that had impulses to act and the symbolic processor that generated the anticipated reactions of others, respectively. Mead concentrated exclusively on the cognitive meanings that actors shared; affect control theory, on the other hand, uses the *affective* meanings that symbols hold for actors to describe how they anticipate, plan, and react to events. As with Mead's original formulation, people process what happens in social interaction symbolically. How one reacts to a social interaction depends on how one labels who has done what to whom. Affect control theory also depends on the shared nature of these symbols. Without some shared symbols and meanings, interaction would be a confusing kaleidoscope of uninterpretable physical events (similar to listening to someone speaking in a foreign language without signs or context to help interpret his or her utterances). We must share some meanings even to have a meaningful conflict about events that we are jointly considering.

Mead thought social action was motivated by impulses generated by disequilibrium with the environment (see discussion in Turner and Stets 2005:103–106; Ward and Throop 1992). This assumption becomes the core principle of affect control theory—that people act to maintain an "equilibrium" in the meanings they assign to an interaction. Mead's conception of disequilibrium was rather general, however; he was primarily concerned with the ways that impulses focused attention on certain parts of the environment and motivated their manipulation to resolve the disequilibrium.

Cooley's (1964) concept of the looking-glass self made more explicit the aspect of disequilibrium that would become the focus of most symbolic interactionist research. Cooley suggested that people were especially concerned with their appearance in others' eyes. He was the first to bring emotions explicitly into symbolic interactionist thought, seeing shame and pride as responses to the sense of evaluation by others.[2] Since Cooley, most symbolic interactionist treatments of emotion have emphasized social actors' concern with maintaining their positive self-meanings and the negative emotions that result from failure to maintain these meanings (see summary in Turner and Stets 2006). As a version of symbolic interactionism, affect control theory shares this concern with the maintenance of symbolic meanings. It views disequilibrium in the social environment more generally, however. People respond not just to disequilibrium in how others view them but also to dislocations in other symbolic meanings (like those for others' identities and for social actions).

In the late 1970s, Shott (1979) added symbolic interactionist insights to the fast-developing new sociology of emotions. She built directly on Cooley's work, arguing that physiological emotional arousal was ambiguous enough to be labeled in a variety of ways. Shott followed Mead (1938) in assuming that social life was understood through symbolic representation; she applied this idea to emotions, arguing that emotional response was socially constructed by using cultural labels for emotional states and feeling rules about what emotions were normatively appropriate in situations. She thought that emotions were an important mechanism for social control because normative emotional responses led to negative emotions when institutional rules were violated. Therefore, social control became self-control after emotional socialization occurred.

Shott (1979) also developed the distinction between the general personal identities that people carried from interaction to interaction and the situational identities that designated who actors were within a particular social situation. Affect control theory does not take a strong position on the nature of physiological emotional response—it might be the ambiguous, diffuse arousal that Shott discussed, or an array of specific physiological responses as described by Kemper (1978, 1987) and Turner (2000). However, the theory shares with Shott the emphasis on the cultural labels for emotions and the meanings that they carry. Perhaps more important, it conceptualizes identities and actions as having both general, stable meanings and situated meanings that are created in the immediate social context. Indeed, it is the tension between these two types of meanings that gives the theory its dynamic character.

As implied above, affect control theory makes distinctions among concepts that are often lumped together in other symbolic interactionist theories. The theory's distinction is that it defines these concepts in precise, measurable ways. This feature permits the development of a formal model, including empirical estimates and mathematical statements of its theoretical principles. Therefore, we offer a few definitions before turning to the formal structure of the theory.

DEFINITIONS

The terms *affect*, *emotion*, *sentiment*, and *mood* are often used interchangeably in the emotions literature (see discussion in Smith-Lovin 1995). In affect control theory, they mean very different things.

Affect

Affect is the most general term. Traditionally, it refers to any evaluative (positive or negative) orientation toward an object. In developing affect control theory, Heise (1977, 1979) used a psychometric literature to talk about the *affective meaning* that cultural labels for identities and actions carried. In the 1950s, Osgood and his colleagues (1957) found that three abstract dimensions—evaluation (good versus bad), potency (powerful versus weak), and activity (lively versus quiet)—could represent people's reactions to a wide variety of concepts. Osgood called these dimensions "affective meaning" to distinguish them from the more denotative types of meaning that we find in dictionaries (e.g., a father is a man who contributes sperm in the creation of a biological offspring compared to an affective definition of a father as quite good, very powerful, and somewhat lively). Therefore, he expanded the definition of affect to include three fundamental dimensions of meaning. The fact that these three dimensions seemed to represent reactions in a wide variety of national cultures (Osgood 1962; Osgood et al. 1975) encouraged Heise (1977, 1979) to use them as an effective way to measure the symbolic meaning of social events.

Affect control theory recognizes the fundamental nature of affect and its link to the labeling process. The theory rests on the idea that all labelings evoke affect. It is this affect, rather than the specific labels themselves, that we try to maintain during interaction.

Sentiments

Affect control theory views these three fundamental dimensions of meaning as cultural abbreviations, acting as an abstract summary of social information about all elements of an interaction—including identities, behaviors, emotions, and settings—that are symbolically represented in our definition of a situation.

All labels for social concepts evoke a certain amount of goodness, powerfulness, and liveliness. These are referred to as sentiments in the theory. *Sentiments* are transsituational, generalized affective responses to specific symbols in a culture. They are more socially constructed and enduring than simple emotional responses.[3] Although the dimensions themselves are universal across cultures, symbol-specific sentiments are products of a culture. Fathers come in a wide variety of shapes, sizes, colors, ages, and demeanors. Individuals in a culture may widely vary in attitudes toward and understandings about their *own* fathers. Nonetheless, all of us in the middle-class U.S. culture basically agree that the abstract notion of a Father[4] as somewhat good, quite powerful, and moderately active. In contrast, our culturally shared sentiments about employees are more neutral on all three dimensions, and our image of child molesters is very negative indeed on the evaluation dimension. It is our agreement about the generalized meanings associated with specific symbols that allow us to communicate effectively with other members of our culture.

Transient Impressions

When we define a social situation using culturally meaningful labels, the affect generated by that definition does not remain static. Affect control theory assumes that people respond affectively to every social event (the *affective reaction principle*). The theory further presumes that affective responses can be indexed along Osgood's three dimensions of affect meaning—evaluation, potency, and activity. Picture a Boss with his Employee at an office Party. The sentiments generated by the labels, Boss, Employee, and Party will help us make sense of this situation and know what actions we might expect to follow. Now, imagine that we see an event that we label as the Boss Browbeating the Employee. Our feelings about that boss, that employee, that party and perhaps even what it means to browbeat someone, are altered somewhat from their generalized cultural meanings. In affect control theory, we call these situated meanings *transient impressions*. Impressions are contexutalized affective meanings that are generated by symbolic labels in specific social events.

Emotions

Emotion is another subset of affect. Emotional labels have the same kinds of affective meanings that identities and actions do: to be contented is to feel good, powerful (secure, in control), and quiet. To be elated is to feel good and powerful, but very activated/lively.

In affect control theory, emotions are the labels (with their associated cultural meanings) that are applied to the ways that we feel after an event has occurred (Smith-Lovin 1990). There is a formal, mathematical model that predicts what emotion we will experience after we have participated in a social interaction (Averett and Heise 1987); we describe this model in detail below. At this point, the important thing to recognize is that emotions are culturally given labels that we assign to experiences in the context of a social interaction that is self-referential. They are signals about how we feel within a situation and how that feeling compares to the stable affective meanings that are usually associated with our self-identity.

Emotions, like other elements in the theory, are indexed as three-number profiles that typify the amount of pleasantness, potency, and activation associated with the emotion. The distribution of these typifications in a particular language can reveal important information about the structure of emotions in that language culture (MacKinnon and Keating 1989). For example, in English, as in some other languages, there are words for pleasant emotions that vary substantially in activation (e.g., contrast peaceful with thrilled). In English, however, all pleasant emotion words are relatively powerful. Unpleasant emotions, on the other hand, can vary in their degree of both potency and activation. The English emotion lexicon contains labels for unpleasant emotions that are quiet and weak (sad), quiet and powerful (bitter), active and weak (panicked), or active and powerful (furious).

Affect control theory distinguishes between characteristic and structural emotions (MacKinnon 1994; Smith-Lovin 1990). *Characteristic* emotions are the kinds of emotions that individuals experience when performing a role perfectly. For example, Heise (2004) pointed out that when a minister role is perfectly confirmed, an actor in that role is predicted to feel generous, compassionate, and kind. *Structural* emotions refer instead to the recurrent emotions that individuals experience in the context of role relationships. Situations—and relationships—constrain the degree to which experiences can be perfectly confirming. So, when ministers interact with sinners, they are predicted to feel emotions such as lovesick, apprehensive, or overwhelmed. In the context of their relationship to God, in contrast, ministers will instead feel grateful, relieved, and sympathetic according to affect control theory predictions (Heise 2004). The model for these predictions is detailed below.

Moods and Traits

Emotions in affect control theory represent the feelings that are situated in the moment after an actor processes a social event and responds to it affectively. They are momentary feelings that reflect past interactions, but do not necessarily motivate future action. Sometimes, an emotion can become more enduring and continue to affect social interactions after it is experienced. In affect control theory, we can represent this by modifying an actor's role identity with a label that represents a lasting emotional state—a mood. So, instead of dealing with a Father after one returns home 2 hours after curfew, one might deal with an Angry Father. This combination of mood and identity would have a different cultural meaning (which can be predicted from the separate meanings of Angry and Father as cultural labels). It would be much more negative in evaluation (less nice), even more potent, and considerably more activated/lively. Our recognition of the mood and identity within the situation would lead us to predict and feel different things than we would of a normal Father.

Sometimes moods become so typical of a given social actor that we (and perhaps they) come to think of the mood as a characteristic one—that is, tied to a person across virtually all situations. This mood then becomes a trait that might be a part of a personal identity (cf. Shott 1979) that is part of how that person thinks of him- or herself and how others view him or her. In affect control theory, this trait might modify virtually all identities that one takes on in social situations. If I think of myself as a Kind person, then I will be a Kind Teacher, a Kind Wife, and perhaps even a Kind Customer. Again, the trait has a culturally given affective meaning (a Kind person is good, powerful, and fairly neutral on activity) that can be combined with the general, cultural meanings of the identities. When we expect someone in an identity to be kind (e.g., a kind benefactor), the trait may be fairly redundant and would not change its affective meaning very much. But if we do not expect the abstract role actor to be kind (e.g., a Kind Judge), the meaning might change more dramatically. In any case, the key distinction here is that moods may temporarily become part of a person's identity within a situation, and therefore the person might work to maintain that feeling, rather than just experience it as a flash of emotion. Or a stable, long-term orientation might come to be seen as a personality trait that is part of our sense of self and actively maintained by ourselves and others who know us.

THE FORMAL STRUCTURE OF THE THEORY

The basic definitions and theoretical principles above do not distinguish affect control theory from many other symbolic interactionist approaches. Along with most other symbolic interactionist approaches, it argues that:

1. Actors react to social situations in terms of symbols and the meanings that those symbols carry for them.
2. The meanings that symbols have are largely shared within a culture, leading actors to be able to role take, viewing the situation from the position of other actors and anticipating their reactions to the interaction.
3. Actors are motivated to maintain the meanings associated with the self.
4. Meanings can shift within situations as a result of one's own or others' actions.
5. Emotions act as signals about how events are maintaining or failing to maintain self-identities within an interpersonal situation.

The thing that really differentiates affect control theory from other forms of symbolic interaction is the fact that it measures cultural meanings in such a well-defined, abstract way. The three dimensions—evaluation, potency, and activity—obviously lose some information about social roles, behaviors, and settings. Things that are affectively similar (e.g., Winner and Hero) may have denotative differences. One becomes a Winner by besting others in a contest, while one becomes a Hero by rescuing others from potential trouble. But the fact we can characterize *all* symbolic elements of a situation on the *same* three dimensions allows affect control theorists to talk concretely about how events change meanings. We can track actors, actions, settings, emotions, moods, traits, and virtually anything that we can name by using the same three affective-meaning scales. Furthermore, we can use these three scales to measure both the enduring culturally given sentiments about the symbols *and* the transient meanings that they take on in the context of situations. By specifying how events change meanings, we can then specify what events will maintain or restore those meanings.

Impression Change

In order to understand affect control theory's model for predicting emotions, it is necessary first to understand the theory's general predictive model. Affect control theory uses this Actor-Behavior-Object (ABO) grammar to represent the simplest social event, *Actor Behaves* toward *Object*. Each of these event elements can be represented with a three-number profile that captures the fundamental sentiments it evokes in terms of evaluation, potency, and activity. The transient impressions evoked by a specific event can be measured by in-context ratings of those event elements. So, imagine an event: "Employee Corrects the Boss." Impressions of *that particular employee* are likely to be somewhat different from our generalized sentiments about all Employees. Heise (1969, 1970) adapted analytic tools developed by Gollob (1968) describing exactly how our affective meanings toward symbols change as a result of their coappearance in social events. We can regress our generalized sentiments about Employee, to Correct someone, and Boss on the situated impressions of that employee in order to learn more about how these social elements combine to form new impressions during social interactions.

$$A' = c + b_1 A + b_2 B + b_3 O \tag{1}$$

where A' stands for the predicted impressions actor (the Employee that we see Correcting the boss), A refers to the more stable sentiments we associated with Employees in general, B stands for the generalized sentiments about the behavior (to Correct someone), and O refers to the generalized sentiments toward the object (Boss, in our example). Heise (1969, 1970) made the important observation that when these simple event sentences described a social interaction, the resulting equations specified how that event changed impressions of the people and the actions involved in the situation.

When we expand this equation to include a specification of the actor, object, and behavior on all three affective dimensions we get an equation like the following from Smith-Lovin (1987):

$$
\begin{aligned}
A'_e = {}& -0.98 + .468A_e - .015A_p - .015A_a + .425B_e - .069B_p - .106B_a \\
& + .055O_e - .020O_p - .001O_a + .048A_eB_e + .130B_eO_e + .027A_pB_p \\
& + .068B_pO_p + .007A_aB_a - .038A_eB_p - .010A_eB_a + .013A_pB_e \\
& - .014A_pO_a - .058B_eO_p - .070B_pO_e - .002B_pO_a + .010B_aO_e \\
& + .019B_aO_p + .026A_eB_eO_e - .006A_pB_pO_p + .031A_aB_aO_a \\
& + .033A_eB_pO_p + .018A_pB_pO \tag{2}
\end{aligned}
$$

Equation (2) uses information about the sentiments associated with all of the elements in a social situation (A_e, A_p ... O_p, O_a) to predict the situated impressions of the goodness (evaluation) of the Actor (A'_e). A, B, and O represent the Actor, Behavior, and Object and the e, p, and a subscripts represent the evaluation, potency and activity of those event elements. Each of the coefficients in this equation captures something about the normative process of impression formation in our culture. Note that the largest predictor of how nice an Actor seems in a given situation is the generalized goodness normally associated with the identity of that Actor. So, our impressions about the niceness of the Employee who Corrected the Boss are largely shaped by how nice we think Employees are in general. This strong, positive A_e in this equation captures the idea that Actors seem nicer when they are occupying identities that the culture already sees as good. In contrast, someone occupying a negatively evaluated identity like Perpetrator might seem relatively nasty, no matter what he or she did and to whom. Similarly, the strong, positive B_e term reflects how much nicer an actor seems when he or she is behaving in nice ways. In general, people seem nicer when they Help someone (a very positively evaluated act) than when they Correct them (a mildly negative behavior). The smaller, positive O_e term reflects the idea that the niceness of our interaction partners rubs off on us a bit. We seem somewhat nicer when we act toward others who are good, and we seem a little less good when we interact toward those whose identities are generally considered bad in our culture (guilt by association). In keeping with traditional parental advice, our reputations depend partly on the company we keep. These last two effects are qualified, however, by a positive and sizable interaction between them, captured in the $B_e O_e$ coefficient. This interaction (called the *balance* term, after Heider's, 1958 balance theory) captures the idea that social actors seem especially nice when they behave nicely toward good others (or badly toward mean others); actors do not seem as good when they are either mean to good others or nice to bad others.

A full set of impression formation equations like Equation (2) predicts changes in the impressions of Actors, Behaviors, and Objects on evaluation, potency, and activity (A_e', A_p', A_a', B_e', B_p', B_a', O_e', O_p', O_a'), as a result of their combination in various social events. Taken as a set, these impression formation equations generate empirical summaries of basic social and cultural processes. They characterize how people's meanings change when they symbolically react to events, as well as capturing important descriptive information about the ways in which social events temporarily transform the local impressions of the symbolic labels that we use to define these events. Along with the sentiment dictionaries, these equations provide the empirical basis for the theoretical predictions made by affect control theory.

Currently, there are full sets of impression formation equations for the United States (Smith-Lovin 1987), Canada (MacKinnon 1994), Japan (Smith et al. 2001), and Germany (Schneider 1996). Researchers have done partial studies of affective change in working-class Catholic schools in Belfast, Northern Ireland (Smith-Lovin 1987) and among Lebanese and Egyptian students studying in the United States (Smith 1980).

Control Principle

Sentiments refer to the culturally shared, fundamental meanings that we associate with particular social labels. Impressions refer to the more transient meanings that arise as social interactions actually unfold. Discrepancies between sentiments and impressions tell us something about how well interactions that we experience are confirming cultural prescriptions. Following the pragmatic assumption that social actors strive to maintain their working definitions of social situations, affect control theory proposes that actors try to experience transient impressions that are consistent with fundamental sentiments. This proposition is called the *affect control principle*. Inspired by Power's (1973) work on perception control theory, Heise (1977, 1979) developed a control system theory to model this principle.

The core mechanism in a control system is that the current state of a system (e.g., the air temperature in a room) is compared to a reference level (e.g., a thermostat setting). The direction and size of the difference between the two guide the future behavior of the system. Modern control system theories of identity (most notably affect control theory and Burke's (1991) identity control theory) share a common image: Actors use identity meanings as a reference level to which they compare what is happening in the current social situation. The behavior of self and others is judged according to how well it maintains those reference level meanings. New actions are planned and carried out to maintain identities.

Affect control theory uses the fact that both cultural sentiments *and* transient impressions are measured in the same way, on the same dimensions, to develop a formal model of the meaning control process. Affect control theory defines *deflection* as the discrepancy between fundamental cultural sentiments and transient, situated impressions in the relevant semantic space (usually the three-dimensional evaluation, potency, and activity space). Mathematically, researchers usually operationalize this concept as the squared Euclidean distance between the sentiments and impressions (usually in evaluation-potency-activity space).[5] In a standard ABO event, deflection would therefore be operationalized as

$$D = (A'_e - A_e)^2 + (A'_p - A_p)^2 + (A'_a - A_a)^2 + (B'_e - B_e)^2 + (B'_p - B_p)^2$$
$$+ (B'_a - B_a)^2 + (O'_e - O_e)^2 + (O'_p - O_p)^2 + (O'_a - O_a)^2 \quad (3)$$

This equation can be used with the impression-change equations to implement the affect control principle. Notice that we can substitute the regression equation (e.g., Equation (2)) for each transient impression (e.g., A'_e) in Equation (3). This gives us a very long and complicated expression, but that expression is composed entirely of things that we can measure. In addition, because the elements that predict the situated impressions are all the same, many of the terms in the equations cancel each other out, simplifying the expression a great deal.

We can then solve for a set of three-number profiles for a behavior that minimizes deflection. These equations predict the optimal behavior (in the form of a three-number evaluation-potency-activity profile) for generating an event whose corresponding impressions are as close as possible to the initial sentiments. (All of these calculations are done automatically for researchers by the simulation program INTERACT.) As an example, the deflection generated by the event Employee Corrects Boss is 2.0, indicating a relatively low discrepancy between the situated impressions and our cultural sentiments about Employees, Bosses, and Correcting.[6] The profile for a behavior that would *optimally* confirm our sentiments is an evaluation of 1.84, a potency of 0.03, and an activity of 0.74, corresponding closest to actions like Agree with, Obey, and Speak to. After the Correcting, the Employee would have to do a new behavior with a cultural meaning like evaluation = 1.96, potency = −0.37, and activity = 0.86 (corresponding most closely to Admire) in order to bring situated impressions back into line with cultural sentiments. Alternatively, the Boss could Instruct, Reassure, or Counsel the Employee (optimal profile: evaluation = 1.46, potency = 1.34, activity = −0.49). These predicted actions represent minor "repair work" after the slight dislocation in state and power that the Correcting has caused.

Reconstruction Principle

Sometimes events produce deflections that are so large that it is difficult or impossible to find a behavioral approach for resolving them. No amount of repair work can restore our sense that the people are who we thought they were. Affect control theory's *reconstruction principle* states that inexorably large deflections prompt redefinition of the situation.

To implement this, we can use the same type of equation used to predict behavioral resolution of deflection, only solve instead for a new actor identity or a new object identity. Consider the following event: Nurse Abandons Patient. This event produces a deflection of 19.0. It yields no predicted behaviors because no behavior exists in the sentiment dictionary that could possibly resolve that amount of deflection. In other words, there is nothing that a Nurse can do after Abandoning a Patient that would fully resolve the deflection produced by that event. One way of thinking about this result is that there is nothing that a Nurse could do to restore our image of him or her as a responsible, professional occupant of that role identity; we continue to define the action as Abandoning. So, he or she must offer an account that will lead us to change our view of what happened: Was the act something other than Abandoning? Or, was the person who appeared to be a Patient actually someone else? To resolve our affective reaction to this untenable event, we have to do something to reframe our understanding of the situation.

Using affect control theory's mathematical model, we know what kinds of redefinition will fill the bill. If the Nurse makes no account for his or her behavior, we might relabel her. We can solve for the optimal actor identity that would minimize deflection. In this case, we get a new actor-identity evaluation, potency, and activity of -2.34, 0.001, -0.69, corresponding most closely to an identity of a Malcontent. Alternatively, if the Nurse (or someone else arguing for a more benign interpretation of events) *does* offer an account, affect control theory can anticipate what type of framing might undo the affective damage. For example, viewing the action as Accommodating $(2.02, 1.06, -0.17)$, the patient (who presumably wanted to be left alone) would make the Nurse's behavior seem more appropriate. Alternatively, we can solve for a new object identity. These labeling equations allow affect control theory to model processes like our tendency to "blame the victim" in the case of unusual events. Our example is so extreme that there is, in fact, no identity that would be appropriate for a Nurse to Abandon (the predicted solution is: -1.59, 1.96, 5.85 which is outside the range of logical possibilities for identity profiles), suggesting that Nurses would *never* be expected to abandon a patient, no matter who it was. If, however, we use considerable latitude on the activity dimension and search for the object identity *closest* to that profile, we get predictions like Outlaw, Gangster, and Mobster. So, although the affect control theory equations predict that nurses would never abandon a patient, the identities that would come closest to "deserving" such treatment would be these sorts of extremely bad, powerful, and lively actors.

Emotions

The impression formation equations characterize impressions that get generated by specific social events; the behavioral prediction equations use the affect control principle to tell us how actors are likely to behave, given specific definitions of the situation. The labeling equations tell us how we are likely to redefine actors, objects, or actions as a result of observed or experienced interactions. All these parts of the formal model show us how affective meanings serve to guide our actions and interpretations of social interaction. However, as we noted above, affect control theory distinguishes between affect and emotion. Although events that do not maintain affective meanings might seem unlikely, surprising, disturbing, or even unreal (in the case of extreme deflection), these do not necessarily imply negative emotions. They *do* motivate us to resolve the discrepancy—to reduce deflection—by restoring our affective meanings. In that sense, they might evoke some sense of stress or physiological reaction (Robinson et al. 2004); however, the theory distinguishes between this motivational state and emotion. Instead, affect control theory represents emotions, moods, and even personality traits that indicate typical emotional orientations through the use of identity modifiers.

If we take the same labeling equations described above and hold the actor's *identity* constant, we can solve for a modifier that can be combined with the actor identity in order to produce a combination modifier-identity profile that best confirms the event's sentiments.

Averett and Heise (1987) estimated equations of the form

$$C = c + b_1 I_e + b_2 I_p + b_3 I_a + b_4 M_e + b_5 M_p + b_6 M_a \tag{4}$$

where C is the evaluation, potency, or activity of a composite modifier and identity (e.g., an Angry Professor), I is the identity of the composite (Professor), and M is the modifier associated with that identity in the composite (Angry). Once we know what the C_e, C_p, and C_a should be in the event (by producing the actor profile that would "make sense" of the experience), we can solve for the T values in the equation; both the C's and the I's are known.[7]

Consider our event Employee Corrects Boss. What kind of an Employee would Correct his or her Boss? Affect control theory answers this question by first solving for the optimal actor identity for the event (Actor) Corrects Boss. Because affect control theory translates everything into affective meanings to calculate its answers to such questions, our answer comes in the form of a three-number profile: an Actor with an evaluation of -1.5, a potency of 0.0, and an activity of 0.37. Then, we can look up that three-number profile in a dictionary of affective meanings from some group in order to translate it into a symbolic label: the identity of Tease is closest to this profile in the U.S. undergraduate dictionary.

If the identity of the actor is well established by the institutional context or personal knowledge, however, we might want to hold that identity constant. We then hold the identity of Employee constant and solve for the trait with the three-number evaluation-potency-activity profile that, when combined with Employee, produces a combined profile that is closest to that optimal identity. These attribution equations tell us what kind of Employee would Correct his or her Boss (answer: a *Contemptuous* Employee).

The attribution equations solve for traits or characteristics that, when added to an identity, can make sense of observed behaviors. Heise and Thomas (1989) showed that we can use these same equations with a set of emotion words to make predictions about what kind of emotions actors and objects are likely to feel in social events. Using information about the original identity (I in the equations below; Employee in the example above) and the combined, transient identity (C in the equations below; Tease in the example above), we can solve for the particular emotion that would make sense of the event (E in the equations below).

$$E_e = 0.364 - .871I_e - .182I_p - .162I_a + 1.722C_e + .317C_p + .365C_a$$
$$E_p = 0.430 - .139I_e - 1.17I_p - .104I_a + .240C_e + 1.691C_p - 0.21C_a \quad (5)$$
$$E_a = 0.015 - .110I_e - .174I_p - .816I_a + .139C_e - .159C_p - 1.326C_a.$$

These equations reveal that emotions are a result of both the transient impressions produced by the event (the Cs) *and* the original identity meanings for the role identity that we occupy (Averett and Heise 1987). In other words, emotions reflect how a situation is making us feel (in the context of our role identity within the situation), as well as signaling to us how those feelings compare to our reference standard.

Looking at the evaluation dimension, we can see that the effects of the fundamental sentiments (I) is negative and roughly half the size of the effects of the transient impressions (captured by the predicted identity combination, C). This shows us that the positivity of emotion is predicted by the positivity of the transient impression (t), as well as the positivity of the deflection produced by that transient impression (t − f). In other words, nice events make us feel good. Events that are even better than our identities would lead us to expect feeling even better. Note further than when events are perfectly confirming (e.g., t = f), then the pleasantness of our emotion should roughly reflect the niceness of that fundamental identity. This suggests the *characteristic* emotion for a given identity should be evaluatively congruent with that identity:

$$(2t - f) = t + (t - f) \quad (6)$$

The potency and activity equations reveal similar dynamics. Both of those equations can be roughly reduced to

$$(1.5t - f) = .5t + (t - f). \tag{7}$$

As with emotion evaluation, we see that emotion potency and emotion activity are each influenced by both the deflection and the transient impressions. When events push us further upward in potency than our identities suggest, we experience more powerful emotions. Likewise, when events make us seem livelier than our identities suggest, we experience more active emotions. In the case of perfectly confirming events (when $t = f$), we experience a characteristic emotion, whose potency is roughly half of the potency associated with fundamental identity. The picture is roughly similar for predictions about emotion activation. The emotion and trait equations turn the basic A-B-O event in affect control theory into a M-A-B-M-O event, where M stands for an identity modifier (either a trait or an emotion).[8]

While we can use the modifier equations to predict emotional response, we can also use them to create "new" identities—either a mood that is embraced for a short period of time or a personality characteristic that is embraced transsituationally. If we combine a modifier with a role identity for a substantial period (e.g., an Angry Father), this combination is no longer a simple *result* of a specific situation, but a new temporary identity that is maintained over several rounds of interaction. Maintaining an identity like Angry Father will obviously lead to different actions than a nonangry Father.

Therefore, experiencing a mood has very different effects than a situated emotional response. Emotions, in affect control theory, do not *cause* actions; instead they indicate or signal how we are experiencing a situation. It is deflection, not emotion, that leads to restorative action. Emotions are reflexive, and to some extent we end up acting in ways that are opposite from the emotions that we experience. A Novice that feels Elated at the Compliment of an Expert might still act in a way to bring down the Expert's view of him or her to a level more consistent with the role identity of Novice. The positive emotion comes from the interactions that are experienced in the situation (which have moved the situated meanings above the reference level); actions will serve to counter-balance them and bring things back into line. On the other hand, a Cheerful Novice (i.e., one who is in a persistently good mood for several rounds of interaction) might act nicer than a Novice who is not in such a nice mood.

When people consistently have the same modifier attached to (virtually) all of their identities, that modifier might actually become part of a personal identity. Then it becomes a part of the reference level in all situations. So, such typical emotional states act in affect control theory like status characteristics or any other identity modifier that is permanently attached to all identities. Just as we can talk of a Female Judge having a somewhat different meaning than a (prototypically male) Judge, we can also say that a Depressed person might enact the role identities of Mother, Employee, Friend, and so forth all in the Depressed state. Combining the modifier with all identities shifts their meaning in a predictable direction, and it is the new meaning that is maintained through action and perception.

INTERACT

Both the logic and the substance of affect control theory are contained in its mathematical specification. The empirically estimated equations contain crucial information about affective processing that reflects basic social and cultural processes in patterns of attribution, social judgment, justice, balance, and response to deviance. The logic of the theory (for example, the affect control principle and the reconstruction principle) is implemented through mathematical manipulation of these equations to produce predictions about behaviors, emotions, and labelings during interaction. The equations and the dictionaries containing culture-specific sentiments in the form of evaluation, potency, and activity ratings of identities, behaviors, emotions, settings, and so on, are contained in a software program called INTERACT. The current version of the INTERACT software allows users to choose among eight sentiment dictionaries (U.S. 1979, U.S. 2003, Canada 1988, Canada 2002, Japan, China, Germany, Northern Ireland). This software provides a user-friendly interface that allows researchers and research consumers to work through implications of the theory.

Simulation results using this software can be taken as explicit predictions of the theory and thus subjected to testing through empirical investigation. The theory can generate several kinds of hypothesis:

1. It can predict characteristic emotions—which offer an epidemiology of social emotion, showing how occupants of different social positions *typically* feel in response to normal situations that maintain their role identities. Because we can set the transient, situated meanings in Equations (5) and (6) equal to the fundamental reference levels, we can make predictions about how those role occupants would usually feel under meaning maintenance.

2. It can predict emotional responses to specific events that fail to maintain meanings (e.g., underreward and overreward). If an Expert Flatters a Novice, we expect different emotions than if the predicted, identity-maintaining behavior (Instructs) occurs. This feature of the theory can be used to "predict" much of what we already know; that is, affect control theorists can use the control theory framework to interpret experimental and clinical phenomena that have been observed in other studies.

3. It can show how persistent mood states (or personality characteristics) can systematically alter the performance of a large number of roleidentities across situations. For example, a depressed individual might be affected by that mood state in a variety of role performances and so engage in interactions as a Depressed Teacher, a Depressed Mother, and a Depressed Wife.

4. At a more macrolevel, it can describe the feeling rules or emotion norms that come from prototypical events that lead to emotional response. Therefore, we can say that a Lover who has been Jilted has a "right" to feel Angry, in the same way that a Mother who has lost her Child is "supposed" to be Sad. Similarly, we can describe the systematic production of jointly experienced emotions by interaction ritual chains (Collins 2004).

EMPIRICAL STUDIES OF EMOTION USING AFFECT CONTROL THEORY

Because of the marked progress in the sociology of emotions during the past three decades (Smith-Lovin 1995; Turner and Stets 2006), many recent studies of affect control theory have focused on the emotions component of the model. However, in spite of the range of predictions possible (see the list above), there are two basic themes in most affect control research on emotions: (1) studies that use the theory to predict emotion reactions and (2) studies that show how emotions act as a signal about identities.

The first type of study shows that the theory does a good job of predicting what people will feel in what social circumstances. Robinson and Smith-Lovin (1992) began the experimental assessment of affect control prediction of emotional response to deflecting events. Following closely an experimental paradigm developed by Swann et al. (1987), Robinson and Smith-Lovin selected participants from an undergraduate psychology pool who had either very positive social self-esteem or relatively negative social self-esteem.[9] The participants then read a three-minute passage from *Jonathan Livingston Seagull* during which they thought their performance was being evaluated by two raters to develop a new communication coding scheme. The participants got feedback from the two raters (in counter-balanced order). Their emotional responses to the first feedback and their choice of which raters to interact with in the second part of the experiment were the dependent variables. The affect control hypotheses proposed a counter-intuitive pattern: that positive evaluation by a rater would create positive emotion for participants with both high and low social self-esteem, but that low social self-esteem participants would choose future interaction with those who *confirmed* their negative self-identities. The hypotheses were confirmed—positive evaluation led to positive emotion and negative evaluation led to negative emotion, but participants chose future interaction partners who confirmed their self-images even when that confirmation caused them to feel bad.

Although behavioral studies like Robinson and Smith-Lovin (1992) are the most compelling examples, they only deal with a very limited number of situations for practical reasons. Research using vignettes has demonstrated accurate prediction over a wider range of (imagined) situations. Heise and Calhan (1995) asked students to imagine themselves in 128 situations and report what emotion they felt. This study makes use of the fact that symbolic interactionist theories like affect control theory presume that events are processed symbolically—thinking about being in a situation is expected to arouse the same types of emotions that actually *being* in that situation would evoke (MacKinnon 1994). The students reported their emotions on a graphic emotion spiral that mirrored the structure that Morgan and Heise (1988) found: pleasant emotions (Happy, Proud) are at the top while unpleasant feelings (Annoyed, Disgusted) are at the bottom. Vulnerable (low potency) emotions like Scared and Ashamed are inside the spiral, while high potency emotions like Bitter and Angry are toward the inside. Lively versus quiet emotions (Excited versus Contented) are represented on the left/right axis. Half of the imagined situations had the student as the actor and in the other half, the student was the object. For example, students were asked to "Imagine that you are flattering a professor. How do you feel at the moment?" Alternatively, they might be asked "Imagine that an evangelist is condemning you? How do you feel at the moment?" The study supported the theory. When Heise and Weir (1999) examined scatter plots of distances from the affect control prediction and the frequencies with which the students chose an emotion, they found that the distributions typically fit the following generalizations.

1. The emotion that a person reports feeling in an event usually is close to the theoretical emotion predicted by affect control theory.
2. People rarely report feeling an emotion in an event that is far from the theoretical emotion predicted by affect control theory.

Since emotions indicate *how someone occupying an identity with a particular meaning* is responding to an event, people can use them as signals to help define ambiguous situations. Robinson, Smith-Lovin and Tsoudis (1994; Tsoudis and Smith-Lovin 1998, 2001; Tsoudis 2000a, 2000b) used this feature of the theory to explore how emotional displays impact judgments made about criminal defendants. The studies follow a common design: they present students with a description of a court case (either a criminal confession or testimony by the victim of a crime), varying the emotions displayed by the perpetrator or victim in the case.[10] INTERACT predicts that people occupying fundamentally good identities should feel remorse after they have committed a negative act toward a good person (e.g., injured an innocent during a drunk driving accident); actors who have fundamentally negative identities would experience more neutral emotions. Similarly, victims who occupy good identities should feel devastated by being the object of such an action, while those occupying stigmatized identities expect negative acts to be directed at them and show less emotional response. In the studies, students gave lighter sentences to and thought less negatively about perpetrators who showed the repentant emotions that INTERACT would predict of fundamentally good actors. They also used the emotional reactions of the victim to shape their sentences and degree of empathy with those who had been hurt in the crime.

This research on judgments about criminals focuses on expected emotional responses to bad behaviors. Affect control theory makes the more general prediction that one's emotions should be evaluatively congruent with one's actions (Heise and Thomas 1989). In order to examine this prediction, Robinson and Smith-Lovin (1999) conducted vignette experiments that systematically varied the niceness of an actor's behavior with the emotion displayed. These experiments demonstrated that not only can actors mitigate damage to an identity by displaying an appropriately negative behavior, as in the case of remorseful defendants, but they can actually contribute to a spoiled identity by not feeling appropriately happy when engaged in beneficent behaviors.

Since emotional experiences are crucial for understanding mental health, some affect control research has examined clinical issues. Francis (1997), for example, conducted a qualitative study of two support groups: a divorce group and a bereavement group. In both cases, people entered the groups with negative identities and the unpleasant, powerless, low activation emotions that we would expect those identities to evoke. Divorced people saw themselves as failing at marriage, and bereaved spouses felt responsible for their partners' pain and ultimate death. Since it was difficult to redefine the event (divorce or death), Francis (1997) found that support group leaders worked on the identities of the group members and their former partners. They reinforced the positively evaluated, potent, and activated identities that the group members could occupy that would generate positive feelings from new events. In addition, they helped relabel the former partners in a more negative way, giving them responsibility for the negative event (divorce or death). In effect, the event became "a bad person does something bad to a good person (the support group member)." Since even this event construction involves some deflection and negative emotion, the group leaders then encouraged the group members to forgive their former spouse—a good, deep act that helped to support their new positive identity. The most important finding from the Francis study is that the group leaders did *not* focus directly on the negative feelings that the group members had. Instead, they shaped the view of the situation—the identities of self and other—to generate a new set of emotions that would be more productive for continuing life.

EMOTIONS IN UNDERSTANDING SOCIAL MOVEMENTS AND POLITICS

Given the power of affect control theory to link the framing of a situation and the emotional experiences that the situation evokes, it is natural that the theory has found powerful applications to the framing of social movements. Heise (1998) pointed out that we develop emphatic solidarity with other groups if we find ourselves having the same emotional reactions that they have to the same events. Feeling chagrin and annoyance at Summers' remarks about women's potential at science and math indicates to us that we have some solidarity with women scientists who have spoken out against his views. Berbrier (1998) and Schneider (1999) have both discussed the framing and cultural meanings that neoconservative and white separatist movements use to support their positions.

Researchers have applied the theory to more traditional political processes as well. Troyer and Robinson (forthcoming) used INTERACT simulations to show how political advertisements and voting behavior can be modeled using affect control theory. MacKinnon and Bowlby (2000) used the theory, together with social identity theory (Abrams and Hogg 1990), to explore the affective dynamics of intergroup relationships and the stereotypes that people form about other groups.

While we may not think of nation-states as unitary social actors to which social psychological theories apply, Lerner and colleagues (Azar and Lerner 1981; Lerner 1983) have noted that the symbolic processing that affect control theory models *can* be used to interpret the cultural understandings that world leaders have about international events. When we process statements like "the United States attacks Iraq" or "the Soviet Union is an Evil Empire," we have affective reactions that guide our cognitive labeling of ambiguous actions, our policy preferences for future events, and our feelings of solidarity (or lack thereof) with other collective actors. Seeing Arab citizens rejoicing in the streets at an event that causes us great distress (e.g., the 9/11 attacks on the World Trade Center and Pentagon) creates a sense that these people view the world very differently from us and cannot be trusted to behave in a predictable, "moral" manner.

Of course, social movement activity can involve institution building as well as the framing or interpretation of political events. One example of a stigmatized group developing new institutions, interaction ritual chains, and shared symbolic meanings is Smith-Lovin and Douglass (1992). This study combines the quantitative measurement that is typical of affect control research with qualitative field observations in a study of two religious groups. Smith-Lovin and Douglass (1992) asked the question: How do gay people who occupy stigmatized identities in the mainstream culture develop a religious interaction ritual that consistently generates positive, rewarding emotions and subcultural support for being simultaneously gay and religious? The study contrasted a traditional (and relatively liberal) Unitarian church with the Metropolitan Community Church (MCC), a religious denomination explicitly developed to serve the gay community.

Using participant-observation, Smith-Lovin and Douglass first compiled a list of thirty social identities and thirty behaviors that were significant social labels in both religious groups. Church members then rated these concepts on the evaluation, potency, and activity dimensions. The data showed large differences between the two groups' ratings of religious and, especially, gay identities, but not for social actions.[11] Unitarians had much more negatively evaluated, impotent meanings associated with gay identities compared with the MCC (several were rated in the study). There were also big differences in the potency and activity meanings of the religious figures—both symbolic (God) and institutional (minister). Notice that in the MCC context, Gay Person and Worshiper have very similar profiles (with the Gay Person being quite a bit livelier), while in the Unitarian Church group, there is a large difference on all three dimensions, most notably on evaluation.

Smith-Lovin and Douglass used the fundamental sentiments that they had measured in the two congregations for simulations in INTERACT. These simulations produced hypotheses about the religious rituals expected in both institutional contexts and about the standard production of emotions that those interaction rituals (Collins 1990, 2004) would produce. The more potent, lively meanings associated with religious identities in the gay church led INTERACT to produce more dramatic, flamboyant interactions, which contrasted markedly with the more staid role relationships among religious figures in the Unitarian church. For example, the expected action of a Minister to a Worshiper in MCC had the affective profile ($e = 0.9$; $p = 1.7$; $a = 0.7$), with actualizations like Stroke, Visit, and Please. In the Unitarian group, the same role relationship was supported by an action with the profile ($e = 0.3$; $p = 1.0$; $a = 0.2$), implying actions like Appeal-to, Flatter, and Consult. But the institutionalized religious interactions in *both* congregations predicted deep, positive emotions for both groups: presumably an important part of the religious experience. The very different meanings associated with homosexual identities also generated very different simulations. Using the MCC sentiments about Gay Person, INTERACT predicted positive interactions among gays (e.g., Applaud, Play With, Court) and directed to a Gay Person from the Congregation (Court, Play With, Desire Sexually). By contrast, the Unitarian meanings led INTERACT to predict that homosexuals will experience negative, unhappy interactions with one another, with God, and with formal religious figures.

To validate their simulation results, Smith-Lovin and Douglas created sixty descriptions of social events, each specifying an interaction between gay and religious identities. They selected the behavior directed from one identity (actor) toward the other (object) in each event from one of three sets of behavioral predictions: (1) those produced by the MCC sentiments, (2) those produced by the Unitarian sentiments, or (3) those produced through random selection of behaviors from the INTERACT corpus. Seven judges from the MCC church then rated the likelihood of these events (twenty from MCC sentiments, twenty from Unitarian sentiments, and twenty with randomly chosen behaviors). This allowed them to test whether or not the perceived likelihood of events generated by one's own group's fundamental sentiments were higher than those produced by another group's meanings (or randomly selected behaviors). An ANOVA produced a significant result for the three-category grouping variable, and a follow-up test confirmed the investigators' prediction of a significant difference between the MCC and Unitarian events. MCC raters saw the events generated from the MCC sentiments as more likely than events generated from the Unitarian sentiments. Smith-Lovin and Douglass (1992:243) concluded from their analyses that affect control theory shows promise as a "generative model of culture."

Britt and Heise (2000) argue that social movement organizations seek to transform negatively evaluated emotions associated with a stigmatized or minority identity such as shame or depression into other, more active emotions such as pride in an attempt to incite and motivate individuals to participate in group activities. They state that a primary tactic used in gay identity politics is to instill fear in group members through discussions about homophobic reactions toward gays and lesbians, but as they point out, fear renders individuals vulnerable and is less likely to leave them feeling as though they should fight for the group cause. These feelings of vulnerability must then be transformed into more active emotions such as anger. Britt and Heise conclude that fear and anger can be viewed as emotional capital for social movements. These emotions provide an individual-level resource that, when properly transformed, leads to group solidarity and subsequently aid in the achievement of group goals.

Recent work by Lively and Heise (2004) indicates that the experiential structure of emotions is very similar to the meaning structure of emotions. Moreover, the findings of Lively and Heise indicate that the "emotional capital" discussed by Britt and Heise (2000) may not require an external catalyst for use by social movement organizations. Instead, Lively and Heise (2004) determined that the connections between emotions and action may be more closely linked to one another due to their relative proximity to one another as measured by a remoteness index.

Although a majority of the empirical evidence for affect control theory comes from U.S. populations, Schneider (1996) illustrates the utility of affect control theory, a formal statement of symbolic interactionism for understanding how cultural differences in meaning translate into differences in affective responses. Schneider conducted a cross-cultural comparison of a U.S. undergraduate sample and a German undergraduate sample for over 400 identities. His results indicate that American students systematically rated sexual-erotic identities as more negative and active compared to the German sample. The differences in meanings associated with role identities between the two samples resulted in substantial differences in the emotions associated with these identities. Although German students associated emotions of impression and passion with sexual-erotic identities, American students associated more deviant and violent emotions with these identities. Furthermore, the results of the Schneider study indicated that as agreement on the level of sexual eroticism of identities converged between the two cultures, the affective responses to the identities illustrated a pattern of dramatic divergence. Schneider's results illustrated not only the importance of the broader social context for establishing meaning, but also indicated how the formal statement of symbolic interactionism, in the form of affect control theory, permits an empirical investigation of cross-cultural comparisons.

A BRIEF COMPARISON WITH A CLOSE THEORETICAL COUSIN

Due in large part to common symbolic interactionist roots, affect control theory (Heise 1977, 1979) and identity control theory (Burke 1991) share many assumptions, principles, and propositions. Both theories take as a starting point the symbolic interaction principles of shared meanings and individual attempts to maintain those meanings. Shared meanings are not only a requirement for meaningful interaction (Mead 1938). The attempt to maintain these meanings is the cornerstone of the individual creation and re-creation of structure—a core symbolic interaction principle. Affect control theory and identity control theory also agree that individuals attempt to maintain meanings through the confirmation of identity meanings. Disconfirmation of meanings in both theories motivates the individual to affect his or her environment in such a way as to stabilize the interaction system at or near the reference level given by one's definition of the situation.

As previously mentioned, the control model used by Heise (1977, 1979) is not specific to affect control theory. Burke (1991) also incorporated Powers' (1973) control model into the conceptual and theoretical framework of identity control theory. Although both theories posit that social actors rely on this cybernetic control loop to guide interaction through the comparison of meanings to reference levels, Burke developed a specific version of the control model wherein individuals compare reflected appraisals to self-identity meanings in an attempt to maintain identity meanings. Conversely, affect control theory argues that individuals attempt to maintain the meaning of the situation, including the identity meanings of all actors, behaviors, and the setting. The control system incorporated into both theories moves the conceptualization of the individual beyond the oversocialized view of the social actor. The theories effectively permit individuals to act and react to novel and unexpected circumstances that disturb their understandings of what is happening in the social situation. For both theories, the emotions resulting from the comparison process represent signals regarding the maintenance of meaning; however, their specific emotional predictions vary.

The measurement of affective meanings represents an area of divergence between the two theories. Heise (1977, 1979) and Burke (1991) differentially incorporated the work of Osgood (Osgood et al. 1957, 1975) into their respective measurement strategies. Osgood and colleagues identified three central dimensions of meaning evaluation, potency, and activity that, when measured, captured the culturally defined affective orientation of all concepts. Conceptual measurements used semantic differential scales anchored by opposing adjectives (e.g., good versus bad, active versus passive). Heise drew more heavily from the psycholinguistic measurement literature (Osgood et al. 1957, 1975) and the psychology of impression formation (Gollob and Rossman 1973; Heise 1969, 1970), traditions that emphasized the ubiquity of transsituational meanings.

Burke, on the other hand, adhered more closely to the symbolic interactionist and identity theory traditions (Stryker 1980), stressing the importance of domain-specific meanings for individuals and the relative importance of identities within the salience hierarchy. As a result of these differences, affect control theory measures general meanings of identities and actions and identity control theory emphasizes the more personalized, institutionalized meanings of individuals for interaction outcomes.

Given their common conceptual ground, it is surprising that the two control theories produce rather disparate predictions regarding the production of emotion. On the other hand, theories sharing a common set of assumptions (as these do) are likely to generate truly competing hypotheses that allow empirical comparison. The differential predictions and competing hypotheses represent opportunities for exploring the strengths and weaknesses of both theories, leading to their future development.

Before we outline areas of divergence, we should note some broad areas of agreement in the prediction of emotion. Both theories predict that emotion results *both* from confirming and disconfirming situations. Likewise, affect control theory and identity control theory agree that negative emotions result when individuals in normal, positive identities do bad things or have bad things done to them.

The theories *do* differ in the types of emotion that are predicted under some fairly unusual circumstances. For instance, affect control theory would predict negative emotion resulting from the confirmation of a negative identity, whereas identity control theory argues that the confirmation of all types of identity (even negative ones) results in positive emotion. Similarly, identity control theory postulates that the disconfirmation of identities, resulting from a lack of support in the form of reflected appraisals or from overreward, is always stressful and produces negative emotions, whereas affect control theory emphasizes the valence of situated identity meanings and the direction of deflection in the production of emotion. For instance, a mother who is evaluated more positively than expected would be predicted, by identity control theory, to experience negative emotions (because of the disconfirmation), whereas affect control theory would predict more positive emotions than those typically associated with the confirmation of this positively evaluated identity. Because the identity is conceived of as a positive identity to begin with and the deflection in this situation would cause the transient sentiments of the identity to exceed those of the fundamental sentiment, the result would be a more positively evaluated emotion.

These points of divergence represent opportunities for critical tests of the two theories. However, very few tests of this sort have been undertaken, with the exception of Stets (2003, 2005) and Burke and Harrod (2005). The majority of normal, institutionalized identities are positively evaluated. In confirming situations, both theories make identical predictions regarding the positive emotions that result from occupying such identities. Similarly, the disconfirmation of such positively evaluated identities will most likely be in a negative direction (at least on the evaluation dimension), leading to a prediction of negative emotions for both theories. In these commonly observed situations, it is almost impossible to determine whether these negative emotions arise from identity disconfirmation or from downward identity deflection.

Therefore, much research in both traditions, investigating the emotional outcomes of disrupted identities, supports both theories. The general conclusions of these investigations indicate negative emotions are a likely product of situations wherein support for positive identities is lacking (Burke 1991) or those situations in which positive identities are disconfirmed (Robinson and Smith-Lovin 1992). Research has also demonstrated that positive emotions might result when individuals occupying positive identities are treated more positively than expected (Robinson and Smith-Lovin 1992). These findings provide empirical support for affect control theory's predictions regarding deflection and the interaction between the valence of an identity and the direction of the deflection. Recent work by Stets (2003, 2005) has provided further support for both theories, although some of the results of this work indicate that the predictions of affect control theory may be more accurate in situations of positive deflection. Stets (2003) found that when individuals were overrewarded, they experienced more positive emotions and those that were underrewarded experienced more negative emotions. Finally, Burke and Harrod (2005) demonstrated support for identity control theory in their analysis of survey data collected from married couples in the first years of marriage. The findings of this study indicate that positive evaluations of husbands and wives by their spouses, when those positive evaluations were higher than the spouses' self-image, produced more negative emotions or moods for the spouse. These results appear to conform to the general stress process outlined by Burke (1991) concerning the congruence of meanings and reflected appraisals. Specifically, Burke (1991) argued that any incongruence, regardless of the valence of the identity or the direction of the disturbance, is likely to produce stress, which is then translated into more negative emotions. Although both theories have enjoyed considerable empirical support, much more work needs to be done to investigate the competing hypotheses generated by the theories. We will now turn to outlining what we view as the important directions for future research for both theoretical traditions.

DIRECTIONS FOR FUTURE RESEARCH

As we noted at the beginning of this chapter, affect control theory differs from other symbolic interactionist theories in its view of emotions. Other symbolic interactionist theories regard failure to maintain an adequate presentation of self as negative. Even Burke's identity control theory, a perspective that shares much of affect control theory's cybernetic structure, regards disruption of identity meanings as leading to stress and unpleasant feelings (Burke and Harrod 2005; Stets 2003, 2005). In affect control theory, there is a real difference between the sense of unlikelihood, stress, and unreality that may come from deflection and the evaluative valence of emotion. We can be devastated that our interaction partners act negatively toward us (if we have a typically positive self-image), but we can also be dazed and elated by an unexpectedly good fortune (recall Equations (5)–(7), above). To assess which view is more accurate, we will need measures that can differentiate between deflection and emotion—a tall order. Physiological measures may offer some traction on this issue (Robinson et al. 2004), and research on under- and overreward represents an important substantive domain for its exploration (Stets 2003, 2005).

Related to this issue, we note that empirical affect control theory research to date has focused heavily on evaluation dynamics, almost to the exclusion of attention to potency and activity dynamics. This is particularly unfortunate because one of affect control theory's distinguishing features is its attention to all three of these fundamental dimensions of social meaning. The three-dimensional, circumplex structure of emotions (MacKinnon and Keating 1989) highlights the distinctive need for attention to potency and activity in the area of emotions because most of the interesting variation occurs in the potency and activity dimensions. The theoretical structure of affect control theory affords opportunities for making distinguishing predictions about power dynamics among identities in interaction and discriminating among emotions with different levels of intensity and expressivity. Investigation into these predictions would better capitalize on the full structure of the existing theory and facilitate the exploration of predictions that are unique to affect control theory and nonoverlapping with related theories (especially in terms of distinguishing emotion from deflection).

Finally, we note that affect control theory (and most other symbolic interactionist approaches) predicts emotional response *only* as a response to the situated and culturally given (fundamental) meanings associated with one's *own* identity. The empirical reality is that we often respond to the observation of others' situations, and often share their emotional reactions even when we are not directly involved in an interpersonal event. "I feel your pain" might be a cliché, but even very young infants have the ability to model the emotional responses of others. That simple empathic response develops into a much more refined sensibility as children develop and expand their ability to take the role of the other. Given how basic this process is to our understanding of the self from an interactionist perspective, affect control theory is strangely lacking a model of empathic emotional response. Clearly, theoretical work is needed in this domain.

NOTES

1. Blumer (1969) labeled Mead's ideas "symbolic interaction," the term that most scholars now use to refer to this theoretical tradition.
2. Goffman (1959, 1967), Scheff (1990), and Shott (1979) built directly on Cooley's insights to develop their own contributions to the sociology of emotions.
3. This definition follows Cooley's classic statement (1964) and Gordon's (1981:566–567) more modern definition of sentiments as "a socially constructed pattern of sensations, expressive gestures and cultural meanings organized around the relationship to a social object."
4. Here, we follow the affect control theory convention of capitalizing cultural labels that carry measured affective meanings.
5. Some writers refer to the mathematical operationalization of deflection as a definition of the concept. We distinguish here between the conceptual definition and the operationalization to allow for times when researchers are focused on different event elements (e.g., settings) or even different dimensions. The important point, however, is that the measurement of meanings in a systematic, abstract way *allows* the theory to specify deflection mathematically and to model its effects.
6. All simulation results presented here were obtained using female equations and dictionaries from the 2003 U.S. Project Magellon Data in Java INTERACT. www.indiana.edu/~socpsy/ACT/interact/JavaInteract.html (last updated April 23, 2005).
7. The I's are the cultural sentiments associated with the original actor identity—Employee, in this case.
8. The basic A-B-O grammar of affect control theory has been elaborated in other ways as well, but these elaborations remain largely underexplored. Behavior settings, behavioral modifiers, and self-directed actions can all be represented using simple event sentences (e.g., the Doctor Insulted a Patient at the Party or the Daughter Obeyed her Mother while Rolling Her Eyes).
9. This social self-esteem scale contains many items about public presentation of self and public speaking and is not correlated with general self-esteem or with depression.
10. The vignette stimuli are designed to correspond to actual court cases, but are modified to embed emotion cues that are supposedly transcribed from a videotape to help the research participant imagine the original video.
11. This pattern supports the common use of the U.S. (undergraduate) behavior dictionary for subcultural analyses and is consistent with Heise's (1966, 1979) suggestion that most social actions will not have different meanings across subcultures. As Kalkoff (2002) points out, it also gives greater specificity to the claim in the deviance/criminological literature (e.g., Wolfgang and Ferracuti 1967) that subcultures are only partially different from the larger, parent culture.

REFERENCES

Averett, Christine P., and David R. Heise. 1987. "Modified Social Identities: Amalgamations, Attributions and Emotions." *Journal of Mathematical Sociology* 13: 103–132.

Abrams, Dominic, and Michael A. Hogg. 1990. *Social Identity Theory: Constructive and Critical Advances.* New York: Springer-Verlag.

Azar, Edward E., and Steve Lerner. 1981. "The Use of Semantic Dimensions in the Scaling of International Events." *International Interactions* 7: 361–378.

Berbrier, Mitch. 1998. "'Half the Battle': Cultural Resonance, Framing Processes, and Ethnic Affectations in Contemporary White Separatist Rhetoric." *Social Problems* 45: 431–450.

Blumer, Herbert. 1969. *Symbolic Interactionism: Perspective and Method.* Englewood Cliffs, NJ: Prentice-Hall.

Britt, Lory, and David R. Heise. 2000. "From Shame to Pride in Identity Politics." Pp. 252–268 in *Self, Identity, and Social Movements,* edited by S. Stryker, T. J. Owens, and R. W. White. Minneapolis: University of Minnesota Press.

Burke, Peter J. 1991. "Identity Processes and Social Stress." *American Sociological Review* 56: 836–849.

Burke, Peter J., and Michael M. Harrod. 2005. "Too Much of a Good Thing?" *Social Psychology Quarterly* 68: 359–374.

Collins, Randall. 1990. "Stratification, Emotional Energy, and the Transient Emotions. Pp. 27–57 in *Research Agendas in the Sociology of Emotions,* edited by T. D. Kemper. Albany: State University of New York Press.

———. 2004. *Interaction Ritual Chains.* Princeton, NJ: Princeton University Press.

Cooley, Charles H. [1902] 1964. *Human Nature and the Social Order.* New York: Schocken Books.

Francis, Linda. 1997. "Ideology and Interpersonal Emotion Management: Redefining Identity in Two Support Groups." *Social Psychology Quarterly* 60: 153–171.

Goffman, Erving. 1959. *The Presentation of Self in Everyday Life.* Garden City, NY: Doubleday.

———. 1967. *Interaction Ritual: Essays on Face-to-Face Behavior.* Garden City, NY: Anchor Books.

Gollob, Harry F. 1968. "Impression Formation and Word Combination in Sentences." *Journal of Personality and Social Psychology* 10: 341–153.

Gollob, Harry F., and B. B. Rossman. 1973. "Judgments of an Actor's 'Power and Ability to Influence Others.' " *Journal of Experimental Social Psychology* 9: 391–406.

Gordon, Steven L. 1981. "The Sociology of Sentiments and Emotion." Pp. 551–575 in *Social Psychology: Sociological Perspectives,* edited by M. Rosenberg and R. H. Turner. New York: Basic Books.

Heider, Fritz. 1958. *The Psychology of Interpersonal Relations.* Hillsdale, NJ: Lawrence Erlbaum.

Heise, David R. 1969. "Affective Dynamics in Simple Sentences." *Journal of Personality and Social Psychology* 11: 204–213.

———. 1970. "Potency Dynamics in Simple Sentences." *Journal of Personality and Social Psychology* 16: 48–54.

———. 1977. "Social Action as the Control of Affect." *Behavioral Science* 22: 163–177.

———. 1979. *Understanding Events: Affect and the Construction of Social Action.* New York: Cambridge University Press.

———. 1998. "Conditions for Empathic Solidarity." Pp. 197–211 in *The Problem of Solidarity: Theories and Models,* edited by P. Doreian and T. Fararo. Amsterdam: Gordon and Breach.

———. 2004. "Affect Control Theory Tutorial: Emotions." www.indiana.edu/~socpsy/ACT/acttutorial/emotions.htm (updated February 16, 2004).

Heise, David R., and Cassandra Calhan. 1995. "Emotion Norms in Interpersonal Events." *Social Psychology Quarterly* 58: 223–240.

Heise, David R., and Lisa Thomas. 1989. "Predicting Impressions Created by Combinations of Emotion and Social Identity." *Social Psychology Quarterly* 52: 141–148.

Heise, David R., and Brian Weir. 1999. "A Test of Symbolic Interactionist Predictions about Emotions in Imagined Situations." *Symbolic Interaction* 22: 129–161.

Kalkhoff, Will. 2002. "Delinquency and Violence as Affect-Control: Reviving the Subcultural Approach in Criminology." *Electronic Journal of Sociology,* Vol. 6.

Kemper, Theodore D. 1978. *A Social Interactional Theory of Emotions.* New York: Wiley.

———. 1987. "How Many Emotions Are There? Wedding the Social and the Autonomic Component." *American Journal of Sociology* 93: 263–289.

Lerner, Steven Jay. 1983. "Affective Dynamics of International Relations." Ph.D. dissertation. University of North Carolina, Chapel Hill.

Lively, Kathryn J., and D. Heise. 2004. "Sociological Realms of Emotional Experience." *American Journal of Sociology* 109: 1109–1136.

MacKinnon, Neil J. 1994. *Symbolic Interaction as Affect Control.* Albany: State University of New York Press.

MacKinnon, Neil J., and Jeffrey W. Bowlby. 2000. "The Affective Dynamics of Stereotyping and Intergroup Relations." *Advances in Group Processes* 17: 37–76.

MacKinnon, Neil, and Leo Keating. 1989. "The Structure of Emotion: A Review of the Problem and a Cross-Cultural Analysis." *Social Psychology Quarterly* 52: 70–83.

Mead, George Herbert. 1938. *The Philosophy of the Act.* Chicago: University of Chicago Press.

Morgan, R., and David R. Heise. 1988. "Structure of Emotions." *Social Psychology Quarterly* 51: 19–31.

Osgood, Charles E. 1962. "Studies on the Generality of Affective Meaning Systems." *American Psychologist* 17: 10–28.

————. 1966. "Dimensionality of the Semantic Space for Communication via Facial Expressions." *Scandanavian Journal of Psychology* 7: 1–30.

Osgood, Charles E., George J. Suci, and Percy H. Tannenbaum. 1957. *The Measurement of Meaning*. Urbana: University of Illinois Press.

Osgood, Charles E., H. May William, and M. S. Miron. 1975. *Cross-Cultural Universals of Affective Meaning*. Urbana, IL: University of Illinois Press.

Powers, William T. 1973. *Behavior: The Control of Perception*. Chicago: Aldine de Gruyter.

Rashotte, Lisa Slattery. 2002. "What Does that Smile Mean? The Meaning of Nonverbal Behaviors in Social Interaction." *Social Psychology Quarterly* 65: 92–102.

Robinson, Dawn T., Christabel L. Rogalin, and Lynn Smith-Lovin. 2004. "Physiological Measures of Theoretical Concepts: Some Ideas for Linking Deflection and Emotion to Physical Responses During Interaction." *Advances in Group Processes* 21: 77–115.

Robinson, Dawn T., and Lynn Smith-Lovin. 1992. "Selective Interaction as a Strategy for Identity Maintenance: An Affect Control Model." *Social Psychology Quarterly* 55: 12–28.

————. 1999. "Emotion Display as a Strategy for Identity Negotiation." *Motivation and Emotion* 23: 73–104.

Robinson, Dawn T., Lynn Smith-Lovin, and Olga Tsoudis. 1994. "Heinous Crime or Unfortunate Accident? The Effects of Remorse on Responses to Mock Criminal Confessions." *Social Forces* 73: 175–190.

Scheff, Thomas J. 1990. "Socialization of Emotion: Pride and Shame as Causal Agents." Pp. 281–304 in *Research Agendas in the Sociology of Emotions*, edited by T. D. Kemper. Albany: State University of New York.

Schneider, Andreas. 1996. "Sexual-Erotic Emotions in the U.S. in Cross-Cultural Comparison." *International Journal of Sociology and Social Policy* 16: 123–143.

————. 1999. "The Violent Character of Sexual-Eroticism in Cross-Cultural Comparison." *International Journal of Sociology and Social Policy* 18: 81–100.

Shott, Susan. 1979. "Emotion and Social Life: A Symbolic Interactionist Analysis." *American Journal of Sociology* 84: 1317–1334.

Smith, Bernadette Pelissier. 1980. Impession Formation among Egyptians and Lebanese. PhD dissertation. Chapel Hill, NC: University of North Carolina.

Smith, Herman W., Jakanori Matsuno, and Shunichirou Ike. 2001. "The Affective Basis of Attributional Processes among Japanese and Americans." *Social Psychology Quarterly* 64: 180–194.

Smith-Lovin, Lynn. 1987. "Impressions from Events." *Journal of Mathematical Sociology* 13: 35–70.

————. 1990. "Emotion as the Confirmation and Disconfirmation of Identity: An Affect Control Model." Pp. 238–270 in *Research Agendas in the Sociology of Emotions*, edited by T. D. Kemper. Albany: State University of New York Press.

————. 1995. "The Sociology of Affect and Emotion." Pp. 118–148 in *Sociological Perspectives on Social Psychology*, edited by K. S. Cook, G. A. Fine, and J. S. House. Boston: Allyn and Bacon.

————. 2002. "Roles, Identities, and Emotions: Parallel Processing and the Production of Mixed Emotions." Pp. 125–1 in *Self and Identity: Personal, Social, and Symbolic*, edited by Y. Kashima, M. Foddy, and M. Platow. Mahwah, NJ: Lawrence Erlbaum.

Smith-Lovin, Lynn, and William Douglass. 1992. "An Affect Control Analysis of Two Religious Subcultures." Pp. 217–248 in *Social Perspective in Emotions*, edited by D. Franks and V. Gecas. Greenwich, CT: JAI Press.

Smith-Lovin, Lynn, and David R. Heise. 1988. *Analyzing Social Interaction: Advances in Affect Control Theory*. New York: Gordon and Breach.

Stets, Jan E. 1997. "Status and Identity in Marital Interaction." *Social Psychology Quarterly* 60: 185–217.

————. 2003. "Justice, Emotion, and Identity Theory." Pp. 105–122 in *Advances in Identity Theory and Research*, edited by P. J. Burke, T. J. Owens, R. T. Serpe, and P. A. Thoits. New York: Kluwer Academic/Plenum.

Stryker, Sheldon. 1980. Symbolic Interaction: A Structural Version. Palo Alto, CA: Benjamin/Cummings.

————. 2005. "Examining Emotions in Identity Theory." *Social Psychology Quarterly* 68: 39–56.

Swann, William B., John J. Griffin, Steven C. Predmore, and Bebe Gaines. 1987. "The Cognitive-Affective Crossfire: When Self-Consistency Confronts Self-Enhancement." *Journal of Personality Social Psychology* 52: 881–889.

Troyer, Lisa, and Dawn T. Robinson. Forthcoming. "From Self to Affect to Action and Back." In *Feeling Politics*, edited by D. Redlawsk. New York: Palgrave.

Tsoudis, Olga. 2000a. "Relation of Affect Control Theory to the Sentencing of Criminals." *Journal of Social Psychology* 140: 473–486.

————. 2000b. "The Likelihood of Victim Restitution in Mock Cases: Are the 'Rules of the Game' Different from Prison and Probation?" *Social Behavior and Personality* 28: 483–500.

Tsoudis, Olga, and Lynn Smith-Lovin. 1998. "How Bad Was It? The Effects of Victim and Perpetrator Emotion on Responses to Criminal Court Vignettes." *Social Forces* 77: 695–722.

————. 2001. "Criminal Identity: The Key to Situational Construals in Mock Criminal Court Cases." *Sociological Spectrum* 21: 3–31.

Turner, Jonathan H. 2000. *On the Origins of Human Emotions: A Sociological Inquiry into the Evolution of Human Affect.* Stanford, CA: Stanford University Press.

Turner, Jonathan H., and Jan E. Stets. 2005. *The Sociology of Emotions.* New York: Cambridge University Press.

————. 2006. "The Sociology of Emotions." *Annual Review of Sociology.* Vol. 32.

Ward, Lloyd G., and Robert Throop. 1992. "Emotional Experience in Dewey and Mead: Notes for the Social Psychology of Emotion." Pp. 61–94 in *Social Perspectives on Emotion*, edited by D. D. Franks and V. Gecas. Greenwich: JAI Press.

Wolfgang, Marvin E., and Franco Ferracuti. 1967. *The Subculture of Violence.* London: Tavistock.

CHAPTER 9

Identity Theory and Emotions

JAN E. STETS

Identity theory grows out of structural symbolic interaction (Stryker [1980] 2002). Two features that are particularly important in structural symbolic interaction are *society* and *self*. Society is viewed as a stable and orderly structure as reflected in the patterned behavior within and between social actors. When we look at the patterned behavior across social actors and see how these patterns fit with the patterns of other social actors, we find larger interindividual patterns that constitute the core of social structure. While actors are creating social structure, they are also receiving feedback from the social structure that influences their behavior. In this way, actors are always embedded in the very social structure that they are simultaneously creating.

Actors have a self. Having a self involves the ability to be reflexive. It includes being self-aware, judging oneself, and planning to bring about future states. Perhaps most important, it entails taking oneself as an object of attention. When social actors take themselves as an object, they are looking from the viewpoint of others with whom they interact. In seeing themselves as others see them, their responses become like others responses, and the meaning of the self becomes a shared meaning. In this way, the self emerges out of social interaction and the larger context of a complex, differentiated society. Further, as society is organized and differentiated, so too must the self be organized and differentiated. This reflects the dictum that "the self reflects society" (Stryker [1980] 2002).

The organization of the self can be conceptualized in terms of different parts or *identities* with each identity tied to a different aspect of the social structure. This idea follows from James' (1890) notion that there are as many selves as there are different positions that one holds in society and different groups that respond to the self. For Stryker ([1980] 2002:60), an identity is an "internalized positional designation" for each of the different positions or roles that a person holds in society. From this has developed the idea that people have *role identities*.

A role identity is the *meaning* that actors attach to themselves while enacting a role. The meanings are derived from culture because individuals are socialized into what it means to take on

JAN E. STETS • Department of Sociology, University of California, Riverside, CA 92521 particular roles—for example, the role of custodian or the role of parent. The meanings also are derived from individuals' own understandings as to what the role means to them. In this way, the meanings attached to roles have a normative or shared component and a unique or idiosyncratic component. McCall and Simmons (1978) noted that idiosyncratic meanings attached to roles will require negotiation in interaction because this is the nonshared component of role identity meanings.

Any role identity is always related to a counterrole identity (Burke 1980). For example, the role identity of parent has the corresponding role identity of child such that each role identity can only be understood as it relates to the other. Further, role identities generate a sense of efficacy in that what one *does* in that role is important.

Along with role identities, social actors have *social identities* and *person identities*. Social identities are the meanings that individuals attach to themselves as a member of particular categories such as being a female, an American, a Democrat, and so forth. In defining oneself as a member of a certain group, individuals see themselves as similar to in-group members and different from out-group members. The identification with in-group members leads to a similarity in perceptions and action among group members and a feeling of acceptance and social approval (Stets and Burke 2000). Social identities activate a sense of self-worth, or who *one is*.

Person identities are meanings attached to the self that define the individual as distinct from others. The meanings include one's unique values and goals along dimensions such as how much control a person desires—the control identity (Stets and Burke 1994)—and how the person sees himself or herself along the moral dimension—the moral identity (Stets and Carter 2006). Unlike social or role identities, these identities operate across various roles and situations. For this reason, they may figure prominently into many interactions because they are always on display (Burke 2004).

Role, social, and person identities do not exist in isolation. Rather, they operate simultaneously in situations. Within groups, there are roles, and within roles, there are persons who play out the roles differently. For example, the role of parent is within the larger group of the family, and some individuals are more dominant than others in the role of parent.

IDENTITY THEORY AND RESEARCH

In its current form, there have been two slightly different emphases of identity theory (Stryker and Burke 2000): one that focuses more on social structural aspects as seen in the work of Stryker and his colleagues (Serpe and Stryker 1987; Stryker [1980] 2002; Stryker and Serpe 1982, 1994),[1] and a perceptual control emphasis that focuses on the internal dynamics of the self in the work of Burke and his colleagues (Burke 1991, 1996, 2004; Burke and Reitzes 1991; Burke and Stets, 1999; Cast et al. 1999; Stets and Burke 1996). Another view of identity theory exists in the work of McCall and Simmons (McCall 2003; McCall and Simmons 1978), which focuses, more than the other two views of identity theory, on the importance of negotiation with others in a situation to obtain identity support and maintain one's identity. However, a strong program of research has not developed out of this third version.

In presenting identity theory, I will spend most of my time discussing the role that emotions play in the overall theory. I will also discuss empirical work on emotions that has developed from the theory. In general, most of this chapter will be devoted to discussing emotions using the perceptual control emphasis mentioned above, simply because this is where there have been the most advances as to the relationship between emotion and identity processes. In the last section of this chapter, I point to avenues for future research. Before reviewing the different emphases of identity theory and the role of emotion in each, I begin with a brief discussion on McCall and Simmons' identity theory. This view focuses on the accomplishment of identities in interaction. Although a clear program of research has not developed, the authors do make some important theoretical contributions to our understanding of identities and emotions.

George McCall and J. L. Simmons: The Interactional Emphasis of Identity Theory

McCall and Simmons (1978) are chiefly interested in role identities. The identity theory focus of Stryker ([1980] 2002), which is discussed below, focuses on the *conventional* meanings of role identities, that is, the expectations associated with positions that individuals hold in the social structure. McCall and Simmons are more likely to emphasize the *idiosyncratic* dimension of role identities or the unique interpretations that individuals bring to their roles, and how these identities are negotiated with others in interaction.

Both McCall and Simmons (1978) and Stryker ([1980] 2002) argued that individuals have multiple identities given the different positions they hold in society. McCall and Simmons organized these multiple identities into a *prominence hierarchy* and a *salience hierarchy*. The prominence hierarchy reflects the ideal self or which role identities are central, important, and enduring to actors. It represents actors' priorities that guide their behavior across situations and across time. The salience hierarchy reflects the situational self or what role identities are temporarily salient in a situation. It is based on predictions as to how persons will behave in specific situations. In general, McCall and Simmons argued that when individuals are given a choice as to which identity to enact in a situation, they will choose a more prominent identity. However, some situations do not permit the enactment of prominent identities because they do not yield rewards (e.g., support from others) in those situations. Thus, individuals become sensitive to what role identities should be played out in some situations but not others. These become the salient identities.

While an actor seeks to have a role identity supported in interaction, other actors in the situation are seeking the same thing (i.e., support of their own identity). For this reason, McCall and Simmons highlighted the importance of negotiation among actors so that mutually sustaining identities can be obtained. This negotiation is worked out through identities and their corresponding counteridentities—for example, a husband supporting his wife (the counteridentity to the husband identity) or a teacher instructing a student (the counteridentity to the teacher identity). Essentially, identities interrelate in a mutually supportive manner so that interaction can proceed smoothly.

In McCall and Simmons's (1978) view of identity theory, emotions emerge when a prominent identity is challenged in interaction, as when others do not support one's identity performance. This challenge produces negative emotions, and actors may employ any number of strategies to rid themselves of the negative feelings.[2] One strategy is relying on "short-term credit." Here, an identity behavior that is not being supported by others is temporarily accepted because the identity was supported in the past. Individuals draw upon this "line of credit" to "ride out" current, nonsupported behavior by others perceiving the behavior as a one-time occurrence. Another strategy is "selective perception," where individuals attend to cues that they think support their identity and ignore cues that they think do not support their identity. Closely related to this strategy is "selective interpretation," where actors interpret cues as confirming their identity when the cues are disconfirming their identity. Other strategies include blaming others in the situation for not confirming one's identity, criticizing and sanctioning these others for their lack of support, disavowing an unsuccessful identity performance by claiming it was not what was intended, switching to another identity that can be confirmed in the situation, or withdrawing from the interaction. In short, these strategies enable the actor to escape the painful feelings associated with identity disconfirmation.

Sheldon Stryker: The Structural Emphasis of Identity Theory

For Stryker ([1980] 2002), social actors assume multiple role identities in society because they are tied to diverse social networks, and these networks are premised on particular identities being maintained. Like McCall and Simmons (1978), these multiple identities are organized in a salience hierarchy. However, for Stryker, a salient identity is an identity that is more likely to be played out across different situations.[3] Stryker argued that more salient identities will be those in which (1) role performances are consistent with the role expectations tied to the identity, (2) situations are seen as the opportunity to enact the identity, and (3) actors seek out situations that provide the opportunity to play out the identity.

Another important factor that influences the salience of an identity is one's commitment to the identity, with commitment having *quantitative* and *qualitative* dimensions (Serpe and Stryker 1987; Stryker and Serpe 1982, 1994). The quantitative dimension involves the number of persons that one is connected to through an identity. The greater the number of people that one is tied to, given an identity, the greater the commitment to that identity. The qualitative dimension concerns the depth of the ties to which one is connected based on an identity. The stronger or deeper the ties, the greater the commitment to that identity. Thus, if being a professor involves having many ties to others who are also professors, and those ties to other professors are strong, then the professor identity will be high in the person's hierarchy of identity salience.

The qualitative dimension of commitment reveals the early recognition of emotion in identity theory. Alternatively labeled "affective commitment" compared to the alternative label of "interactional commitment" applied to the quantitative dimension, Stryker (1987a) emphasized the independent influence of affect in the hierarchical ordering of identities. When strong, positive feelings emerged among actors in a network based on an identity, the greater would be their commitment to that identity.

Recently, Stryker (2004) more fully discussed the role of emotion in identity theory. He developed a set of testable relationships (Stryker 2004:11–16) which I outline below.[4]

Given Stryker's emphasis that people occupy various roles in a network and that these roles carry meaning in the form of identities, he maintained that affect has an influence on the formation of social networks in the following way:

1. Persons with shared affective meanings will be more likely to enter social relationships with one another and maintain those relationships.
2. Sentiments will influence commitment to groups to the degree that sentiments are shared within the groups, despite the positive or negative quality of the sentiment.

Regarding the second point, Stryker maintained that emotions are both a cause and consequence of commitment in relationships:

3. Positive affect will lead to more interaction in role relationships, which will increase commitment to those role relationships; negative affect will have the opposite effect.
4. Greater commitment to role relationships will lead to greater positive affective commonality.

In social networks, individuals behave according to the expectations associated with the roles they are occupying, and according to Stryker, emotions influence role performance in this way:

5. Performances that meet role expectations will produce positive affect (respect and liking) from others and self-esteem for the self; failure to meet role expectations will produce negative affect (anger and disappointment) from others and lowered self-esteem.
6. When commitment is high, a greater discrepancy in failing to meet role expectations will result in a greater negative affective response.
7. When others fail to meet role expectations, this prevents individuals from meeting their own role expectations, which will intensify their negative affective responses to those others.
8. Intense positive affect will lead to role performance that confirms the identity; intense negative behavior will have the opposite effect.
9. Intense affect following from role performances will tell individuals that they are highly committed to that identity and that the identity is highly salient.

Because identities that are more salient are more likely to be invoked across situations and social networks, affect influences salient identities in the following manner:

10. More salient identities will have more intense affect attached to them, and a person will find them more difficult to ignore but easier to read.
11. A strong emotional response will influence the salience of an identity directly, and indirectly, through commitment.
12. Highly salient identities will heighten the positive response of role partners.

Finally, Stryker discussed the role of intense and uncontrollable emotions for the maintenance of identities, commitment, and identity salience:

13. Intense emotional responses occur when role partners behave in ways that contradict another's identity claims.
14. Intense emotional responses occur when structural or interactional barriers prevent the enactment of highly positive identities or the denial of highly negative identities; in turn, this influences commitment, increasing or decreasing it, depending on the valence of the emotional response.
15. An emotional response that emerges spontaneously and uncontrollably will influence commitment, increasing or decreasing it, depending on the valence of the emotional response.
16. An emotional response that emerges spontaneously and uncontrollably will influence identity salience, increasing or decreasing it, depending on the valence of the emotional response.

Stryker acknowledged that the relationships he hypothesized needed to be tested. He also acknowledged that he did not discuss how specific emotions such as love, guilt, embarrassment, anger, and so forth can be incorporated into identity theory. Both areas—theory testing and the development of specific emotions in identity theory—should be the focus of future work.

Research from the Interactional and Structural Emphases of Identity Theory

A good example of research testing the relationship between emotions and identity processes as discussed by McCall and Simmons (1978) and Stryker (2004) is a study by Ellestad and Stets

(1998). They investigated jealousy and its relationship to a prominent and salient mother identity. Jealousy is an emotion that is experienced when one perceives or actually experiences a threat or actual loss of a relationship to a third party, often perceived as a rival (Harter and Whitesell 1989). Implied in this is the idea that another is intruding into an arena that is valued. Applying this idea to the family, Ellestad and Stets surmised that the mother identity could become vulnerable to disruption when the father begins to take over the caretaker role that is traditionally relegated to the mother. Although a wife may not discourage her husband from becoming more involved in childrearing, she may be sensitive to how much he becomes involved, with greater involvement producing a greater threat to her primary role as caretaker, the power she garners in the home in having a monopoly on this role, and the identity that she has built up around her role as caretaker.

In the study, Ellestad and Stets (1998) anticipated that women with a more prominent mother identity (i.e., who highly value their identity as caretaker) would become threatened when their spouses became involved in areas traditionally reserved for her (e.g., nurturance, close attachment, and ongoing attention to a child) and which stand in contrast to the more typical father-child interactions revolving more around play than intimacy. In fact, children often regard fathers as good playmates. The threat that women experience would reveal itself in the emotion of jealousy.

They also examined the salience of the mother identity and how this relates to the jealous experience. They argued that because identity salience is related to the probability of engaging in behavior that is consistent with identity meanings, the more salient the mother identity, the more a woman would engage in coping strategies designed to reduce the negative affect of jealousy. Because coping strategies are designed to manage negative feelings (Lazarus and Folkman 1984), a mother might devise various strategies to reduce her unpleasant feelings, such as spending more time with her child. In doing this, she is attempting to reassert her role as the principal nurturer, thereby maintaining the mother identity.

Using a sample of parents of children at eight day care centers in two northwestern university towns, mothers and fathers responded to a series of vignettes in which the father intrudes into different mother-child interactions. The parents were asked to identify how the woman in the story would feel if this occurred and how she would respond given her feelings. The results provided strong support for the fact when the mother identity is more prominent for the respondent, she is more likely to report that the woman in the story would experience feelings associated with jealousy. Further, when the mother identity is more salient for the respondent, she is more likely to identify coping strategies that the woman in the story might use that were designed to reduce the negative feelings associated with the intrusion of the father.

Ellestad and Stets (1998) discussed the fact that while a prominent identity is linked to the internal, feeling states of an emotion that stem from that identity (e.g., whether jealousy will be felt for the mother identity), salience is reflected in individuals' overt behavior associated with managing the emotion. The coping strategies that women employ help to reassert their identity when it has been challenged. Negative emotions can indicate a lack of confirmation of a prominent identity. The salience of the identity helps to foster ways to reduce the negative affect associating disconfirmation with the result that the identity is reaffirmed in the interaction. The thesis that negative emotion stems from a lack of identity verification is clearly evident in Peter J. Burke's theoretical approach.

Peter J. Burke: The Perceptual Control Emphasis of Identity Theory

Whereas McCall and Simmons (1978) and Stryker ([1980] 2002) focused on the internal hierarchical arrangement of identities and the structural settings in which interaction occurs, Peter

Burke focused on the internal dynamics that operate for any one identity (Stryker and Burke 2000). Essentially, Burke theorized that identities operate as a perceptual control system (Burke 1991, 1996; Burke and Cast 1997; Tsushima and Burke 1999). Based on the work of Powers (1973), the idea is that actors control their perceptions of themselves in situations so that these perceptions match an identity standard that individuals hold for themselves and that guide their behavior.

Burke (1991) maintained that when an identity is activated (or becomes salient) in a situation, a feedback loop is established. This loop has (1) an identity standard or set of self-meanings for an identity, (2) perceptions as to how individuals see themselves in a situation, which is partly based on feedback from others in the situation in the form of reflected appraisals and partly based on one's own perceptions, (3) a comparison process that relates self-perceptions in a situation with the identity standard meanings, and (4) behavior that is a function of the comparison between self-perceptions and identity standard meanings.

The goal of the perceptual control system is to match self-perceptions with identity standard meanings in the situation. The identity system is attempting to control perceptions of the self rather than behavior. Behavior in the situation will change if self-perceptions do not match the internal identity standard. For example, if one sees herself as strong and she sees that others agree with this view of her, she will continue to act in a strong manner. If she sees that others view her as weak, she will increase the "strength" of her performance in order to maintain perceptions of herself as strong. Essentially, the goal in behavior change is to better align perceptions of the self in the situation with identity standard meanings. When such an alignment occurs, identity verification exists.

Burke and Stryker do not differ significantly in how they incorporate emotion into an analysis of identities. Burke (1991, 1996) argued that emotion signals the degree of correspondence between perceptions of the self in the situation and identity standard meanings. Continuous correspondence or identity verification produces positive emotion, and continuous noncorrespondence or identity nonverification produces negative emotions. This idea is similar to Stryker's (2004) view that role performances that meet the expectations of others will generate positive affect, and the failure to meet role expectations will generate negative affect. Thus, the lack of support from others can be viewed as nonverification. A difference between the views of Burke and Stryker is that while Burke claimed that negative emotions emerge even when self-perceptions in the situation exceed the meanings in the identity standard (i.e., nonverification in a positive direction), Stryker did not discuss this idea in his theory. He simply stated that role performance failure produces negative affect.

Burke (1991) maintained that when negative emotion is experienced, an individual cannot remain in this state indefinitely because it threatens the stability of the identity control system. Consequently, individuals will engage in various strategies to get out of the negative state, such as behaving differently in the situation or thinking about the situation in a different way. In later work, Burke (1996) referred to these various behavioral and cognitive strategies as coping responses. Again, the goal is to realign self-in-situation meanings with identity standard meanings so that one feels positive emotions.

Both Burke and Stryker discussed the intensity of emotions. Stryker (2004) maintained that intense emotions result when actors are not able to enact highly positive identities or deny highly negative identities. In turn, this influences commitment to that identity. Similarly, Burke (1991) argued that intense emotions result from the disruption of a more *salient* identity and also a more *committed* identity. A more salient identity is an identity that is more likely to be activated in a situation (and a more salient identity is more central and important to one), and a more committed identity is an identity on which an individual is more dependent. Activated identities and identities to which individuals are dependent on will produce greater negative arousal when they are not able to be verified. In addition to salient and committed identities, Burke (1991) discussed two other factors that influence more intense emotions. These include the *frequency* by which an identity is disrupted and the *significance of the source* of the disruption.

According to Burke (1991), frequent interruptions in the identity verification process will produce more intense negative affect compared to infrequent interruptions. This happens irrespective of whether the nonverification is in a positive direction (self-perceptions in the situation exceed the identity standard) or negative direction (self-perceptions in the situation fall short of the standard). The idea that more intense negative affect is associated with frequent interruption in the identity control system is borrowed from the interruption theory of stress (Mandler 1975). According to Mandler, distress is experienced when organized activity is interrupted. In identity control theory terms, this would mean when an identity is not verified. The distress that emerges from the interruption indicates that something is not right, and one responds by attempting to adapt to the interruption. The more repeated the interruption, the more the actor is unable to initiate and sustain organized activity, and the more distress will occur.

There are several different types of interruption that produce negative affect. One type of interruption occurs when one changes his or her behavior so that perceptions of the self in the situation are better aligned with identity standard meanings, but the behavior change does not have its intended effect. Others in the situation ignore one's efforts. Another type of interruption occurs when the behavior change has the intended effect of better aligning self-in-situation meanings with identity standard meanings, but the actor misreads these effects.

A third interruption occurs when multiple identities may be salient in a situation such that maintaining one identity simultaneously undermines the maintenance of another identity. For example, when an employer must discipline an employee who is also the employer's friend, the disciplinary action may support the employer identity but undermine the friend identity. A fourth type of interruption occurs when an identity is tightly controlled. Here, the meaning structure of the identity forms a deep, integrated system such that a failure to affirm one meaning in the structure casts doubt on the other aspects of the meaning structure. As a result, the slightest disruption to the flow of the identity control process becomes distressful. The distress associated with people who are perfectionists is a good example of what occurs with overcontrolled identities. Much attention is devoted to maintaining the identity at the specific level required, making the person somewhat intolerant to any feedback that departs from his or her identity standard.

Finally, there is the interruption that occurs for identities that are episodically invoked. Here, an individual does not have enough practice in presenting the identity that he or she has claimed. The behavior that is associated with the identity has not been fully rehearsed. Thus, when identity nonverification occurs, the person may not know how to respond in order to achieve identity verification. Closely related to this is the idea that distress can also emerge when feedback from others on one's identity is irregular, with the result that even though the identity is presented with some degree of frequency, the lack of consistent feedback from others deprives the actor from experiencing a smooth flowing control system.

The source of a disruption in the identity control system has also been discussed. Early on, Burke (1991) argued that an interruption from a significant other would lead to more intense negative affect than an interruption from a nonsignificant other. The idea is that significant others are those with whom one has built up a set of mutually verified expectations. Past interactions have supported each other's identity, and the meanings that have been built up form a tightly organized system. Also, more tightly organized identities will lead to greater negative affect, if interrupted. This is consistent with the assumption in interruption theory that the interruption of a more highly organized process will lead to higher levels of autonomic arousal (Mandler 1975).

More recently, Stets and Burke (2005b) have extended the analysis on the source of disruptions in the identity control system and its relation to emotions by discussing the role of (1) the self and others in the disruption and (2) the status and power of others in the disruption. In a general sense, it is easy to see how others in the situation can disrupt the identity control process for an actor, thereby generating negative emotion for the individual. For example, others can change the identity meanings in the situation such that they no longer correspond with the actor's identity standard, as when employees expect their female boss to be less feminine than how she defines herself in terms of her gender on the job. The employees may act on this, thereby changing situational meanings.

There are several ways in which the self is the source of his or her own disruption in the identity control system. One source is in individuals holding multiple identities such that the verification of one identity may cause, simultaneously, the nonverification of another identity. Another source is accidental actions in which the meanings are inconsistent with one's identity standard meanings, as when one acts ineptly, thereby disrupting the identity meanings of being a competent person. A third source is unintended consequences of intended actions, as when one attempts to control another, particularly by behaving aggressively, in order to get the other to verify who they are with the consequence that the aggression decreases the level of verification that the other eventually provides, over time (Stets and Burke 2005a).

Stets and Burke (2005b) discussed the emotional outcomes that ensue when the source of an identity discrepancy is the self or other and when the source of identity meanings is the self or other. In the latter, when the self is the source of identity standard meanings, actors have essentially built up a set of expectations that they hold for themselves while in that identity. The meanings may be unique to the actor or shared with others. In general, these meanings *belong to the self*. When others are the source of identity standard meanings, the identity standard meanings are defined by others. To illustrate, let me take the identity of professor. An identity standard that is defined by others might involve behaviors in which the meanings include carrying out an active research program, obtaining grants, and publishing papers. An identity standard that is defined by the self might involve behaviors in which the meanings involve being a good mentor to one's students. If the professor reads student evaluations that report that he or she is a nonsupportive teacher, then the source of the disruption is an identity standard that has been defined by the self. Alternatively, if the professor gets feedback that he or she is not getting grants or getting papers accepted for publication, then the source of the disruption is an identity standard that has been defined by others.

Stets and Burke (2005b) hypothesized that when we consider the source of the identity meanings (self versus other) and the source of an identity disruption (self versus other), actors will experience the following range of emotions from weak to strong:

1. When the source of identity meanings is the self and the source of the identity disruption is the self, the self will feel emotions ranging from disappointment to sadness.
2. When the source of the identity meanings is the other and the source of the identity disruption is the self, the self will feel emotions ranging from embarrassment to shame.
3. When the source of the identity meanings is the self and the source of the identity disruption is the other, the self will feel emotions ranging from anger to rage.
4. When the source of the identity meanings is the other and the source of the identity disruption is the other, the self will feel emotions ranging from annoyance to hostility.

Underlying the above hypotheses is an attribution process. When actors take responsibility for the identity disruption (an internal attribution), irrespective of whether the identity standard meanings are set by themselves or by others, they blame themselves for not being able to verify their identity standards. Thus, negative feelings are directed inward, and they feel emotions such as sadness and shame. When actors blame others for the identity disruption (an external attribution), irrespective of whether they or others are the source of the identity standard meanings, the negative feelings are directed outward onto others, and they express such emotions as rage and hostility.

As mentioned earlier, Burke (1991) hypothesized that more intense emotions will emerge from more salient, prominent, and committed identities. What Stets and Burke (2005b) add to this is the recognition that less intense emotions feel very different from more intense emotions, thus a different label should be used to describe the emotional state. For example, when the source of one's identity meanings is the self and the other is the source of one's identity disruption, the individual will feel anger when his or her identity is low in salience, prominence, and commitment, but the individual will feel rage when the identity is high in salience, prominence, and commitment.

To further develop the role of emotions in identity control theory, Stets and Burke (2005b) extended the conceptualization of the nature of an identity discrepancy by discussing how one's position in the social structure in terms of status (esteem and respect) and power (control of resources) serves to provide additional meanings that influence the emotional consequences of identity nonverification. They generate the following hypotheses:

5. When the self is the source of the identity disruption, the self will feel shame when the other in the situation has higher status than the self, embarrassment when the self and other have equal status, and discomfort when the other has lower status than the self.
6. When the other is the source of the identity disruption, the self will feel anxiety when the other in the situation has higher status than the self, annoyance when the self and other have equal status, and hostility when the other has lower status than the self.
7. When the self is the source of the identity disruption, the self will feel sadness when the other in the situation has higher power than the self, disappointment when the self and other have equal power, and displeasure when the other has lower power than the self.
8. When the other is the source of the identity disruption, the self will feel fear when the other in the situation has higher power than the self, anger when the self and other have equal power, and rage when the other has lower power than the self.

The emotions in hypotheses 5 and 7 result from the internal attribution process, while the emotions in hypotheses 6 and 8 result from the external attribution process. Additionally, the emotions are the strongest when the other in the situation is of higher status or power, and the feelings are the mildest when the other in the situation is of lower status or power. Indeed, there is more at stake whether the other has more status or power than the self compared to the self having more status or power than the other.

Once again, identity salience, prominence, and commitment influence the intensity of the emotional outcomes to identity nonverification. When these are brought into the analysis of status and power, Stets and Burke (2005b) mentioned a further differentiation on emotional states. For example, if another is the source of one's identity discrepancy, the other is higher in power then the self, and the disrupted identity is of high salience, prominence, and commitment to the self, then the self may feel terror—an emotion that is stronger than the feeling of fear. On the other hand, if the disrupted identity is of low salience, prominence, and commitment, then the self may simply feel somewhat scared.

Still another way in which to extend the analysis of emotions in identity control theory is to consider the different emotional outcomes that emerge for different types of identity that actors take on in interaction. Earlier I mentioned that actors have social identities given their membership in different groups, role identities given their participation in various role relationships, and person identities as they define themselves as a unique entity. Recall that when a social identity is verified, it leads to feelings of worth, acceptance, and inclusion by others in the group. When a role identity is verified, it signifies that the person is competent because the individual has met the expectations of self and other while in that role. Finally, when a person identity is confirmed, feelings of authenticity emerge because the individual is meeting his or her own expectations and aspirations. Stets and Burke (2005b) hypothesized that the following emotional reactions will occur when the different identities are not verified:

9. When a social identity is not verified, the self will experience emotions ranging from embarrassment to shame.
10. When a role identity is not verified, the self will experience emotions ranging from discomfort to guilt.
11. When a person identity is not verified, the self will experience emotions ranging from sadness to depression.

When a social identity is disrupted, there is the threat of rejection from the group. If the identity is low in salience, prominence, and commitment, the self will feel embarrassed, but if the identity is high in salience, prominence, and commitment, the self will feel shame. Both embarrassment and shame focus on a negative evaluation of the self for not meeting the expectations of others (Tangney and Dearing 2002; Tangney et al. 1996). In turn, the emotions encourage the self to do something about the identity disruption and obtain verification so that one remains a group member and is not excluded.

Since role identities pertain to what one does rather than who one is, the emotional outcomes should focus on having done something that disrupts the identity verification process. Indeed, guilt and its family of related emotions involve having done a bad thing (Tangney and Dearing 2002). Stets and Burke (2005b) anticipated that if the identity is low in salience, prominence, and commitment, the self will feel discomfort, and when the identity is high in salience, prominence, and commitment, the self will feel guilt. Recognizing one's role in the identity disruption process should motivate the actor to restore identity verification and prevent future disruptions from arising.

Finally, person identities relate to verifying the "real self." Like the other types of identity, higher identity salience, prominence, and commitment are related to stronger emotional responses to problems in verification. When the identity is low in salience, prominence, and commitment, occasional sadness should occur for identity nonverification, whereas depression should emerge when the identity is high in salience, prominence, and commitment. The inward focus of these emotions helps to motivate the changes in identities and behaviors that will result in future success in verification.

Stets and Burke (2005b) discussed the nature of identity discrepancies and the emotions that ensue in one final way. They examine identity discrepancies and their corresponding emotional outcomes given a context of "mutual verification." Mutual verification contexts involve two or more actors who mutually support each other by not only verifying their own identity, but in doing so, they help in the process of verifying the identities of others in the situation. For example, a married couple often develop a mutual verification context in which each partner not only verifies his or her own spousal identity, but in doing so, the partner helps to maintain his or her spouse's identity (Burke and Stets 1999). A mutual verification context results in positive emotions and feelings of trust and commitment (Burke and Stets 1999). A disruption can occur in a mutual verification context. Stets and Burke (2005b) offered the following emotional outcomes to small and large disruptions:

12. If identity discrepancies are small or nonpersistent in a mutual verification context, actors will feel annoyed.
13. If identity discrepancies are large or persistent and caused by another in the mutual verification context, the self will feel anger.
14. If identity discrepancies are large or persistent and caused by the self in the mutual verification context, the self will feel depression.

Underlying the last two hypotheses is the attribution process. When another is judged as responsible for the identity disruption, negative affect is directed outward toward the other. When the self is evaluated as responsible for the identity disruption, the negative emotion is directed inward against the self. The emotions of anger and depression are strong negative emotions because the mutual verification situation is a well-established identity process that has become interrupted, and the interruption of well-established identity processes is more distressful than interruption of less well-established processes (Burke 1991).

In general, there are several theoretical advances in Stets and Burke's (2005b) analysis that are important to point out. First, specific emotions are brought into identity theory by linking particular identity discrepancies to particular emotional states. Rather than discussing the conditions under which emotions become intense, a theme echoed in earlier work by Stryker and Burke (2000), Stets and Burke assumed that a less intense emotion will feel very different from a more intense emotion, thus we need to identify these different emotional states and connect them to different identity discrepancy conditions. For example, a less intense state of sadness is disappointment, and this feels very different compared to a more intense state of sadness such as depression. Stryker (2004) began to discuss the role of specific emotions in identity theory; for example, when actors meet the expectations associated with a role identity, they experience respect and liking (from others), whereas a failure to meet role expectations results in anger and disappointment (from others) and embarrassment and guilt (for the self). However, he concluded that he has little to say about the emergence of a multitude of specific emotions and how they can be informed by identity theory. Stets and Burke attempted to theoretically develop the theory by outlining the possible emotional states that might emerge.

Another important advance in Stets and Burke's (2005b) analysis is that social structural features are brought into identity control theory, which is needed to broaden the theory. The dimensions of status and power have been discussed in other theories on emotions (Kemper 1991; Lovaglia and Houser 1996; Thamm 2004), but Stets and Burke's application of these dimensions to emotions is different from previous work. For example, Kemper maintained that absolute changes in status or power in the situation result in particular emotional responses. However, Stets and Burke saw emotion as resulting from a change in status and power meanings in the situation relative to the status and power meanings that are held in the identity standard for the actor. Further, in keeping with the symbolic interactionist perspective of identity control theory in which interaction is always understood through the eyes of the actor, status is always relative to the actor's status and power is always relative to the actor's power. Therefore, we need to focus on relative status and power rather than absolute status and power in a situation.

Finally, Stets and Burke (2005b) brought attribution theory into identity control theory by discussing how the source of a discrepancy can be internal or external. Corresponding to this attribution process are specific emotions that are directed inward, because one is judged responsible for the identity disruption, or outward, because another is evaluated as responsible for the identity disruption. As Stets and Burke pointed out, the different emotional outcomes that emerge from the attribution process are important because they are conducive to reducing the likelihood of identity discrepancies in the future. For example, by turning negative affect inward, as in feeling shame when one is the cause of an identity discrepancy, motivates the individual to manage identities and behaviors in ways that reduce the likelihood of future identity discrepancies. Similarly, by turning negative emotion outward, as in expressing anger when another is the cause of an identity discrepancy, encourages others to be more likely to change their identities and behaviors to prevent future discrepancies for the individual.

Research Using the Perceptual Control Emphasis of Identity Theory

EARLY WORK: IDENTITY BASES AND EMOTION.   Early work that examined the role of emotion in identity control theory investigated anger in a national sample (Stets and Tsushima 2001). Because anger results from one's goals being blocked, Stets and Tsushima argued that anger likely emerges when one's identity is not verified. They examined two identities with respect to anger: the family (social) identity and worker (role) identity. Recall that social identities in which individuals define themselves as a member of a group such as the family meet our need to feel worthwhile and accepted. In contrast, role identities such as the worker identity meet out need to feel competent and effective. A further distinction between the family identity and the worker identity is that the former is based on close bonds where issues of harmony and solidarity are important, while the latter is based on less intimate ties where task behavior is enacted to achieve one's goals.

Stets and Tsushima (2001) theorized and found support for the idea that the nonverification of group-based identities, such as the family identity, affects individuals deeply given the strong ties among group members such that intense anger is likely to be felt by an individual when he or she is not supported in the family. Alternatively, the nonverification of role-based identities such as the worker identity does not affect a worker as strongly because the bond among co-workers is not as close; thus, less intense anger will be felt when one does not receive support from co-workers. The fact that more intense anger emerges in the family identity compared to the worker identity is consistent with Burke's (1991) idea that identity disruptions from significant others are more distressful. Group-based identities are rooted in ties with significant others whose views about the self are important to an individual. If the self is not verified, then the emotional response can be powerful.

Identities carry a certain amount of power in situations, and Stets and Tsushima (2001) examined how the status of an identity influenced the intensity and duration of anger in the family and at work. In the family, they investigated the intensity and duration of anger for those in the parent identity (high status), in the child identity (low status), and in the spouse identity (equal in status to its counterpart—the other spouse). In the workplace, they examined the intensity and duration of anger for those in the employer identity (high status), employee identity (low status), and co-worker identity (equal status). Consistent with past research (Cast et al. 1999), they theorized that those with a low-status identity would be less likely than those with a high-status identity to experience identity verification because they are not as influential in getting another to confirm his or her self-view. Because identity nonverification leads to negative emotion, those with a low-status identity should experience more intense anger of a longer duration than those with a high-status identity. Indeed, this is what they found in the data. Those with a low-status identity may be ignored or treated unfairly or may have less access to resources that could help them in the verification process. This may intensify the anger that they feel, and more intense anger is more likely to last longer.

Finally, Stets and Tsushima (2001) examined how individuals coped with their anger. If individuals attempt to modify how they act in the situation, these attempts are behavioral coping responses. Attempts to modify how they see the situation are cognitive coping responses. They investigated both family and worker identities. In the family identity, they found that individuals tended to cope through cognitive strategies, particularly praying to God. Asking for help from God may be a way in which family members manage their anger toward one another without disrupting the relationship. In the worker identity, individuals tended to cope by using behavioral strategies, particularly seeking out social support. Indeed, others may be an important source in how to manage one's emotions. They may provide useful advice such as encouraging the individual to reinterpret the situation, offering information on relaxation techniques, or reminding the individual that he or she has been deprived of sleep or exercise. In general, the findings on coping suggest that different types of identity may dominant different parts of the identity control system. Coping responses for group-based identities such as the family identity may operate more at the perceptual side of the identity control system where cognitive strategies are used, while role-based identities such as the worker identity may operate more at the behavioral side of the identity control system where individuals try to act differently.

LATER WORK: IDENTITY CONTROL THEORY PREDICTIONS ON EMOTION.   In later work, Stets (2003, 2005) tested three assumptions of emotional arousal in identity control theory: (1) Identity nonverification is associated with negative arousal; (2) frequent interruptions compared to infrequent interruptions in the identity verification process will lead to intense negative arousal; (3) intense negative arousal will occur when the source of identity nonverification is a significant other compared to a nonsignificant other. In the laboratory, Stets simulated a work situation that invoked the worker identity. After doing three simple tasks, workers received either (1) feedback that was expected given their work (identity verification), (2) feedback that was more positive than what they would expect (identity nonverification in a positive direction), or (3) feedback that was more negative than what they would expect (identity nonverification in a negative direction). All participants were told that they performed "average" work. Feedback on their work was in the form of points earned for their work. For nonverification in a positive direction, participants received more points than they expected for average work (150 points); for identity verification, they received the expected number of points for average work (100 points); and for identity nonverification in a negative direction, they received less points than expected for average work (50 points). Half of the participants received this feedback after each of the three tasks (the persistent condition), and the other half of the participants received this feedback after the third and final task (the nonpersistent condition). Stets examined the workers self-reported emotional responses to the different feedback conditions.

IDENTITY NONVERIFICATION AND EMOTIONAL AROUSAL.   In a test of the first assumption of emotional arousal in identity control theory, Stets (2003, 2005) found that the lack of verification in a positive direction does not lead to negative arousal. In fact, she found that identity nonverification in a positive direction is associated with significantly more positive emotions than identity verification (i.e., feedback that is expected). This finding was unexpected given Burke's (1991) prediction that negative emotions emerge even when feedback for the self in a situation exceeds identity standard expectations. Why the unexpected effect of positive emotions rather than negative emotions?

In the laboratory study, identity nonverification was operationalized by way of administering rewards or "goods" (in the form of points) rather than punishments or "bads." Goods inherently are positive, reinforcing, and gratifying. When individuals receive feedback that signals more of a "good," it implies that the recipient is "good." In other words, "good people get good things." When people's identity standards are exceeded with the receipt of an unexpected good, they may quickly adjust their standard to the new level and experience feelings of self-enhancement. This finding is consistent with the theoretical argument that when people find themselves in inequitable situations, they may engage in "psychological equity restoration," which involves distorting reality to conclude that things are equitable (Walster et al. 1978). Indeed, self-enhancement or people's pursuit of favorable information about who they are is considered one of the most powerful motives underlying people's quest for self-understanding, followed closely by self-verification or people's pursuit of information that confirms their preexisting self-view (Leith and Baumeister 1998). If people experience self-enhancement from an unexpected good, then positive feelings should emerge.

Although feedback that is more positive than one's standard is enhancing, it is nonetheless nonverifying. This meaning of nonverification competes with the self-enhancing meaning of the nonverification. At issue is why the negative effect of nonverification did not prevail over the positive effect of self-enhancement. As Stets (2003) suggested, individuals may have been responding to both the self-enhancing meaning and the nonverifying meaning of the identity discrepancy by shifting their identity standard up, and by doing this, remove some of the incongruence (between the feedback and their standard) and the negative feelings associated with it. This resolves the competing messages that positive nonverification produces. However, the fact remains that the feedback has exceeded the expected standard, and according to identity control theory, negative emotions should result. In later work, Stets (2005) offered additional explanations of why individuals did not negatively react to the positive nonverifying feedback.

Individuals may have responded rather immediately to the positive message of the feedback, ignoring the fact that the message was inconsistent with their identity standard. If participants were given more time to think about the meaning of the feedback and the fact that it was nonverifying, negative emotions might have emerged. This is consistent with the idea in self-verification theory that when people are not given sufficient time to compare the feedback they receive with their self-view, they will simply categorize the feedback as good or bad and emotionally react in a manner consistent with the feedback; if the feedback is good, they will respond positively, and if the feedback is bad, they will respond negatively (Swann et al. 2003). This is known as the *accessibility principle* in self-verification theory. Essentially, self-verification strivings will operate when individuals have the mental resources to access their self-view. If they are deprived of these mental resources, self-enhancing strivings will emerge. Thus, the self-enhancement process dominates immediate affective reactions to social feedback, and the self-verification process dominates less immediate, albeit cognitive reactions to feedback.

Another reason for the lack of negative emotions to identity nonverification in a positive direction may be the absence of commitment to the worker identity in the laboratory. Indeed, assigning participants the role of worker does not ensure their investment in the role, including taking on the meanings associated with the worker identity. In this situation, individuals may be more interested in feeling good about themselves than verifying themselves. This is consistent with another principle in self-verification theory, the *investment principle*, which maintains that strivings toward self-verification will emerge when individuals are invested in their self-views; otherwise, they are inclined toward positivity strivings (Swann et al. 2003).

Not surprisingly, Stets (2003, 2005) found that nonverification in a negative direction was associated with strong negative emotions. This is consistent with what is predicted in identity control theory. In comparison to the meaning of nonverification in a positive direction, which has a "double meaning" (it is enhancing but nonverifying), the meaning of nonverification in a negative direction is unambiguous. When an individual receives feedback that signals less of a good, not only is his or her identity not verified, but there is also an implication that the individual is "not a good person." In other words, "bad things happen to bad people." The lack of verification coupled with the message that lies behind it (one may "not be good") leads individuals to report only negative feelings revolving around anger. Because the disconfirmation is both nonverifying of an identity and nonenhancing, this dual message generates intense negative emotional arousal.

FREQUENCY OF IDENTITY INTERRUPTIONS AND EMOTIONAL AROUSAL. In Stets' (2003, 2005) laboratory study, the frequency of identity interruptions was operationalized through the persistence condition (nonverifying identity feedback after each of three tasks) and the nonpersistence condition (nonverifying identity feedback after the third and final task) (Stets 2003, 2005). Stets (2003, 2005) found that as the nonverification context was repeatedly experienced by participants, their negative emotions became less, not more, intense. This unexpected finding challenges Burke's (1991) assumption that frequent identity interruptions will heighten emotional arousal. Stets (2003) argued that this finding suggested that individuals are changing their standards, adjusting their standards to the level of rewards that they receive. Because a strong emotional reaction would signal a discrepancy between input meanings and standard meanings, a weaker emotional reaction over time suggests a closer correspondence between input and identity standard meanings. Stets (2005) offered several reasons for why people change their identity standards, as reflected in their weak emotional response to nonverification: (1) a low level of commitment to identities created in a short-term laboratory study, (2) a response to those in a position of power, (3) the inability to take corrective action to alter the feedback they receive, and (4) the stability of nonverifying feedback.

Laboratory studies have had success in changing a person's self-concept, unlike efforts to change individual self-conceptions in nonlaboratory settings. This may be due to individuals' reduced commitment to identities created in the lab, as mentioned earlier for the worker identity. Greater commitment to an identity leads individuals to maintain correspondence between self-in-situation meanings and identity standard meanings by trying to change the responses of others rather than by adjusting the identity standard up or down (Burke and Reitzes 1981). Rather than experiencing the weak emotions of the laboratory and shifting the identity standard in the direction of the feedback received, individuals in their natural environment experience much more intense emotions and work to sustain their identity, if they can. This is not to say that people do not take on identities to which they lack commitment, for they do. However, when this occurs and the identity is challenged, they may be more inclined to change the meanings of the identity and, correspondingly, show a less intense negative response.

Another explanation for the weak, negative emotional arousal to frequent interruptions in the identity verification process may be due to power differences in the situation. In the laboratory study, the manager (confederate) in the study was providing the persistent, nonverifying feedback to the worker (participant). Given that the manager was evaluating the worker's output, the manager had more power in the situation. The participant may have taken on the manager's negative attitude regarding his or her work; indeed, this would be consistent with prior work that weaker persons are more likely to take on the views of the more powerful in situations (Cast et al. 1999). In turn, this would explain participants' weaker negative emotional response to the frequent nonverifying feedback from the manager.

Still another reason for a weaker emotional response to nonverifying feedback may have to do with the individual's ability to take corrective action in a situation (Swann and Hill 1982). Swann and Hill found empirical support for the fact that if individuals receive feedback that is inconsistent with how they see themselves but are given no opportunity to refute this feedback, they are more likely to align their subsequent view of themselves to the feedback. Alternatively, if people receive feedback that is inconsistent with how they see themselves and are given the opportunity to refute the feedback through interaction with the other who provides the feedback, little self-concept change occurs. Essentially, by challenging the feedback and defending their self-view, people can ward off the influence of disconfirming feedback on their identity standards. Correspondingly, they would show intense negative affect.

In Stets' (2003, 2005) laboratory study, participants were not given the opportunity to refute the feedback they received on their performance. If they had been given the opportunity to interact with the manager and express how they felt about the feedback, they may not have adjusted their standard, and their emotional responses may have been much more intense. Still, identity control theory predicts that if people cannot change the meaning in the situation to match their standard, the standard and identity will change. However, change is, apparently, related to the ability of individuals to, in essence, fight back and maintain their identity standard by changing the responses of others.

Finally, intense emotional arousal to frequent nonverifying feedback may not occur if the feedback is stable and the individual knows that there is nothing that he or she can do to change the feedback. Indeed, in Stets' (2003, 2005) laboratory study, when participants received persistent, nonverifying feedback, that feedback was fixed—always being half of what was expected—no matter how hard the participant worked. In response to the nonverifying feedback, participants may have acclimated to the lower amount of points, thereby displaying a less intense negative emotional reaction. This is similar to a state of "learned helplessness" that individuals experience in which they passively resign when they are exposed to stable, uncontrollable events that block their goals (Peterson et al. 1993). It is not uncommon for individuals to resign themselves to situations in which they have no control and not react affectively. People routinely are underpaid or passed over for a promotion. If they do not remove themselves from such situations, they may, over time, come to see themselves as less competent and, therefore, deserving of the feedback. This is identity change.

SOURCE OF IDENTITY NONVERIFICATION AND EMOTIONAL AROUSAL. To operationalize the significance of the other in the laboratory, Stets (2005) gave a random half of participants the opportunity to get to know one another for 10 min in a "getting acquainted session" (familiar condition) before the study began. Although this is only a proxy for the significance of the relationship between actors in real-world settings and talking for a brief period of time is not the same as having a history of interaction, it, nevertheless, had an impact in this study. Compared to participants in the nonfamiliar condition, those in the familiar condition reported more liking for the other and saw the other as a potential friend (Stets 2005). Getting to know one another for even a short period of time is sufficient in formulating the expectation that the other will verify one's expectations. In general, the results of her study revealed that familiarity with another does produce more negative emotions, but only when nonverification occurs once or is nonpersistent and only when the direction of the nonverification is positive. Of course, since the "significance" of the other does not match what would be the case in a long-term relationship, it is interesting that even surface familiarity can generate more intense emotional reactions.

To examine in more detail how the source of identity nonverification is associated with emotional arousal, Stets (2004) investigated one's status: low or high. Such an investigation provides insight on how the external structure (one's position in the social structure) influences internal identity processes to produce emotions. This study used gender as an indicator of status. Because high-status persons (men) are more likely to experience identity verification than low-status persons (women) (Stets 2004), when identity nonverification occurs, high-status persons should be more likely to experience negative arousal. Additionally, when the nonverification is frequent, it should produce more negative emotions for men than women. Stets (2004) also examined how the significance of the source interacts with individuals' status to produce emotions when identity nonverification occurs. Because women more than men are oriented to relationships, including developing and sustaining them (Eagly and Karau 2002), women should react more negatively to identity nonverification from a familiar other. Further, when the nonverifying source is a familiar other of low status, women should respond more negatively than men.

Consistent with the above expectations, Stets (2004) found that high-status people (men) respond more negatively to identity disruptions from an unfamiliar, nonsignificant other, whereas low-status persons (women) respond more negatively to identity disruptions from a familiar other. Stets argued that this finding reflects the different self-orientations of men and women. Men are inclined toward an independent self, which makes them more likely to respond to feedback from strangers. In contrast, women tend toward an interdependent self that emphasizes personal relationships, thereby making them more sensitive to nonverification within a newly forged relationship.

What was most interesting about the findings, however, was how status and familiarity interacted when people's identities were not verified. If the person who is not verifying an identity is of high status (male) and familiar, people respond more negatively to this person than if the nonverifying source is an unfamiliar male. Stets (2004) also found that when a nonverifying source is of low status (female) and unfamiliar, people respond more negatively than if the nonverifying source is a familiar female. What both patterns reveal is the "cueing" of inconsistent messages that are linked to the source. As pointed out many years ago by the social psychologist Roger Brown (1965), people expect relations with high-status persons to be nonintimate and distant, while those with low status persons are more intimate and close. This propensity is reflected, for example, in how actors formally address high-status persons, compared to the informal address directed at low-status persons. In the laboratory study, when a high-status person becomes an acquaintance, or when a low-status person is distant, the disconfirming feedback on their identities becomes particularly distressful. Some of the distress is from the disconfirmation, but some of it may also come from responding to the source as "illegitimate," given the conflicting messages that the source is giving.

In general, the above findings from Stets' (2003, 2004, 2005) laboratory study revealed that predictions about the identity process and emotional arousal need further examination. The laboratory findings did not support the identity control theory prediction that negative emotions would emerge for identity nonverification in a positive direction. It also did not support the finding that intense negative emotions would result from frequent identity interruptions. Additionally, negative emotions did not uniformly emerge when the source of the identity nonverification was a significant other. The findings do suggest that contextual factors need to be considered when theorizing how emotions emerge in the identity control process; for example, how committed persons are to their identities, power relations in the situation, and the opportunity to counteract feedback likely intervene in the identity verification process to produce a particular emotional outcome.

FUTURE RESEARCH

Stets' empirical tests on the relationship between the identity control process and emotion as summarized above reveal that the role of emotion in identity control theory needs further investigation because it is far more complex and contextual than originally thought. First, we need to test Burke's (1991) predictions that the nonverification of highly salient and highly committed identities will produce greater emotional arousal than the nonverification of less salient and less committed identities. The results of the laboratory study suggest that individuals may be less committed to identities that are generated in the lab, as demonstrated by their weak emotional arousal to nonverification in a positive direction. Rather than challenging the nonverifying feedback, they were more likely to change the meaning of their identity standard in the direction of the nonverifying feedback. Thus, the nonverification of salient and committed identities may indeed influence a more negative emotional response.

Second, identity control theorists may need to create scope conditions for identity processes and emotions. For example, identity nonverification in a positive direction does not always lead to negative arousal, and an important factor conditioning this relationship may be the individual's salience and commitment to the identity that is being disrupted. Additionally, frequent interruptions in the identity control process do not always produce more intense negative arousal. The relationship may only occur for more salient identities, prominent identities, or identities to which one is committed, for those with low status in a situation, or when one does not have the ability to challenge or change the nonverifying feedback.

Third, identity theorists need to consider the fact that emotional arousal may emerge not only from the identity verification process but also from other things that are simultaneously occurring in the situation. For example, when Stets (2004) examined the role of the status of actors in a situation, both as the recipient and source of identity nonverification, she suggested that when individuals are acting in a manner that is discordant with their status (e.g., high-status actors behave as if they are "close associates" or low status actors act as if they are "distant"), this unexpected and nonnormative behavior may influence others in the situation to react negatively. If, in addition, these high- or low-status actors are also not verifying others' identities, the negative response from others may become all the more intense. Thus, in understanding affective responses in situations, identity theorists need to be sensitive to the multiple meanings that are being transmitted in situations.

Fourth, we need to test the hypotheses as proposed by Stets and Burke (2005b) regarding the relationship between particular identity discrepancies and particular emotional states. For example, when the source of identity meanings is the self and the source of the identity disruption is another, does the self feel emotions ranging from anger to rage? We also need to examine the relative status and power of actors in a situation and investigate how one's social structural position, combined with the attribution process, influences specific emotional outcomes. For instance, when the self is the source of the identity disruption, will the self feel shame when the other in the situation has higher status than the self and discomfort when the other has lower status than the self? Further, we need to test whether the nonverification of different identity bases (social, role, or person identities) results in different emotional reactions. For example, is nonverification of a social identity more likely to lead to feelings of shame, while the nonverification of a role identity is more likely to lead to feelings of guilt? Essentially, Stets and Burke's theoretical analyses provide fertile ground for empirical validation.

CONCLUSION

The role of emotions in identity theory, particularly identity control theory, is developing at an ever-increasing rate. Social structural features are being incorporating into identity control theory, thereby integrating the internal dynamics of the self with issues of a more macro concern such as one's position in the social structure. In making self and identity central to explaining emotions, identity theorists have advanced our understanding of emotions at the microlevel. I am hopeful that as identity theory continues to develop, the theory will sharpen and correspondingly deepen our understanding of the human being as an emotional being.

NOTES

1. Thoits's work (1983, 1991, 2003) also has a structural emphasis.
2. These *strategies* are analogous to Burke's (1996) *coping responses* in his perceptual control theory.
3. For McCall and Simmons (1978), the salience hierarchy helps predict an actor's behavior in the short run. Longer-run predictions are determined by the prominence hierarchy. Stryker's ([1980] 2002) salience hierarchy predicts longer-run behavior. In this way, it is more similar to McCall and Simmons prominence hierarchy because it captures the more enduring rather than fleeting source of behavior. However, while McCall and Simmons prominence hierarchy is one in which individuals are conscious (i.e., persons are self-aware) of more important identities compared to less important identities, the ranking of identities in Stryker's salience hierarchy is not that in which persons are self-aware, although their behavior would inform them of its ranking (Stryker and Serpe 1994).
4. This is Stryker's clearest and strongest statement to date on the role of emotion in identity theory. The ideas originally developed in the late 1980s (Stryker 1987b) but were never published. Over time, researchers were interested in having Stryker's ideas published. The opportunity arose (Stryker 2004), and this forms the basis of my discussion.

REFERENCES

Brown, Roger. 1965. *Social Psychology*. New York: Basic Books.
Burke, Peter J. 1980. "The Self: Measurement Implications from a Symbolic Interactionist Perspective." *Social Psychology Quarterly* 43: 18–29.
———. 1991. "Identity Processes and Social Stress." *American Sociological Review* 56: 836–849.
———. 1996. "Social Identities and Psychosocial Stress." Pp. 141–174 in *Psychosocial Stress: Perspectives on Structure, Theory, Life Course, and Methods*, edited by H. B. Kaplan. Orlando, FL: Academic Press.
———. 2004. "Identities and Social Structure: The 2003 Cooley-Mead Award Address." *Social Psychology Quarterly* 67: 5–15.
Burke, Peter J., and Alicia D. Cast. 1997. "Stability and Change in the Gender Identities of Newly Married Couples." *Social Psychology Quarterly* 60: 277–290.
Burke, Peter J., and Donald C. Reitzes. 1981. "The Link between Identity and Role Performance." *Social Psychology Quarterly* 44: 83–92.
———. 1991. "An Identity Theory Approach to Commitment." *Social Psychology Quarterly* 54: 239–251.
Burke, Peter J., and Jan E. Stets. 1999. "Trust and Commitment through Self-Verification." *Social Psychology Quarterly* 62: 347–366.
Cast, Alicia D., Jan E. Stets, and Peter J. Burke. 1999. "Does the Self Conform to the Views of Others?" *Social Psychology Quarterly* 62: 68–82.
Eagly, Alice H., and Steven J. Karau. 2002. "Role Congruity Theory of Prejudice toward Female Leaders." *Psychological Review* 109: 573–598.
Ellestad, June, and Jan E. Stets. 1998. "Jealousy and Parenting: Predicting Emotions from Identity Theory." *Sociological Perspectives* 41: 639–668.
Harter, Susan, and Nancy Rumbaugh Whitesell. 1989. "Developmental Changes in Children's Understanding of Single, Multiple, and Blended Emotion Concepts." Pp. 81–116 in *Children's Understanding of Emotion*, edited by C. Saarni and P. L. Harris. Cambridge: Cambridge University Press.
James, William. 1890. *Principles of Psychology*. New York: Holt Rinehart and Winston.
Kemper, Theodore D. 1991. "Predicting Emotions from Social Relations." *Social Psychology Quarterly* 54: 330–342.
Lazarus, Richard S., and Susan Folkman. 1984. *Stress, Appraisal, and Coping*. New York: Springer-Verlag.
Leith, Karen P., and Roy F. Baumeister. 1998. "Empathy, Shame, Guilt, and Narratives of Interpersonal Conflicts: Guilt-Prone People Are Better at Perspective Taking." *Journal of Personality* 66: 1–37.
Lovaglia, Michael J., and Jeffrey A. Houser. 1996. "Emotional Reactions and Status in Groups." *American Sociological Review* 61: 867–883.
Mandler, George. 1975. *Mind and Emotion*. New York: Wiley.

McCall, George J. 2003. "The Me and the Not-Me: Positive and Negative Poles of Identity." Pp. 11–25 in *Advances in Identity Theory and Research*, edited by P. J. Burke, T. J. Owens, R. T. Serpe, and P. A. Thoits. New York: Kluwer Academic/Plenum.

McCall, George J., and J. L. Simmons. 1978. *Identities and Interactions*. New York: Free Press.

Peterson, Christopher, Steven F. Maier, and Martin E. P. Seligman. 1993. *Learned Helplessness: A Theory for the Age of Personal Control*. New York: Oxford University Press.

Powers, William T. 1973. *Behavior: The Control of Perception*. Chicago: Aldine.

Serpe, Richard T., and Sheldon Stryker. 1987. "The Construction of Self and Reconstruction of Social Relationships." Pp. 41–66 in *Advances in Group Processes*, edited by E. Lawler and B. Markovsky. Greenwich, CT: JAI Press.

Stets, Jan E. 2003. "Justice, Emotion, and Identity Theory." Pp. 105–122 in *Advances in Identity Theory and Research*, edited by P. J. Burke, T. J. Owens, R. T. Serpe, and P. A. Thoits. New York: Kluwer Academic/Plenum.

———. 2004. "Emotions in Identity Theory: The Effect of Status." *Advances in Group Processes* 21: 51–76.

———. 2005. "Examining Emotions in Identity Theory." *Social Psychology Quarterly* 68: 39–74.

Stets, Jan E., and Peter J. Burke. 1994. "Inconsistent Self-Views in the Control Identity Model." *Social Science Research* 23: 236–262.

———. 1996. "Gender, Control, and Interaction." *Social Psychology Quarterly* 59: 193–220.

———. 2000. "Identity Theory and Social Identity Theory." *Social Psychology Quarterly* 63: 224–237.

———. 2005a. "Identity Verification, Control, and Aggression in Marriage." *Social Psychology Quarterly* 68: 160–178.

———. 2005b. "New Directions in Identity Control Theory." *Advances in Group Processes* 22: 43–64.

Stets, Jan E., and Michael J. Carter. 2006. "The Moral Identity: A Principle Level Identity." In *Purpose, Meaning, and Action: Control Systems Theories in Sociology*, edited by K. McClelland and T. J. Fararo. New York: Palgrave Macmillan.

Stets, Jan E., and Teresa Tsushima. 2001. "Negative Emotion and Coping Responses within Identity Control Theory." *Social Psychology Quarterly* 64: 283–295.

Stryker, Sheldon. 1987a. "Identity Theory: Developments and Extensions." Pp. 89–104 in *Self and Identity: Psychological Perspectives*, edited by K. Yardley and T. Honess. London: Wiley.

———. 1987b. "The Interplay of Affect and Identity: Exploring the Relationships of Social Structure, Social Interaction, Self, and Emotion." Presented at the American Sociological Association, Chicago.

———. [1980] 2002. *Symbolic Interactionism: A Social Structural Version*. Caldwell, NJ: Blackburn Press.

———. 2004. "Integrating Emotion into Identity Theory." *Advances in Group Processes* 21: 1–23.

Stryker, Sheldon, and Peter J. Burke. 2000. "The Past, Present, and Future of an Identity Theory." *Social Psychology Quarterly* 63: 284–297.

Stryker, Sheldon, and Richard T. Serpe. 1982. "Commitment, Identity Salience, and Role Behavior: A Theory and Research Example." Pp. 199–218 in *Personality, Roles, and Social Behavior*, edited by W. Ickes and E. S. Knowles. New York: Springer-Verlag.

———. 1994. "Identity Salience and Psychological Centrality: Equivalent, Overlapping, or Complementary Concepts?" *Social Psychology Quarterly* 57: 16–35.

Swann, William B., Jr., and Craig A. Hill. 1982. "When Our Identities Are Mistaken: Reaffirming Self-Conceptions Through Social Interaction." *Journal of Personality and Social Psychology* 43: 59–66.

Swann, William B., Jr., Peter J. Rentfrow, and Jennifer S. Guinn. 2003. "Self-Verification: The Search for Coherence." Pp. 367–383 in *Handbook of Self and Identity*, edited by M. R. Leary and J. P. Tangney. New York: Guilford.

Tangney, June Price, and Rhonda L. Dearing. 2002. *Shame and Guilt*. New York: Guilford.

Tangney, June Price, Rowland S. Miller, Laura Flicker, and Deborah Hill Barlow. 1996. "Are Shame, Guilt, and Embarrassment Distinct Emotions?" *Journal of Personality and Social Psychology* 70: 1256–1269.

Thamm, Robert. 2004. "Towards a Universal Power and Status Theory of Emotion." *Advances in Group Processes* 21: 189–222.

Thoits, Peggy A. 1983. "Multiple Identities and Psychological Well-Being: A Reformulation and Test of the Social Isolation Hypothesis." *American Sociological Review* 49: 174–187.

———. 1991. "On Merging Identity Theory and Stress Research." *Social Psychology Quarterly* 54: 101–112.

———. 2003. "Personal Agency in the Accumulation of Multiple Role-Identities." Pp. 179–194 in *Advances in Identity Theory and Research*, edited by P. J. Burke, T. J. Owens, R. T. Serpe, and P. A. Thoits. New York: Kluwer Academic/Plenum.

Tsushima, Teresa, and Peter J. Burke. 1999. "Levels, Agency, and Control in the Parent Identity." *Social Psychology Quarterly* 62: 173–189.

Walster, Elaine, George Walster, and Ellen Berscheid. 1978. *Equity Theory and Research*. Boston: Allyn and Bacon.

CHAPTER 10

Self Theory and Emotions

Howard B. Kaplan

There are few, if any, subjects in social psychology that do not implicate the reciprocal relationships between self and emotion (Kaplan 1986). This is all the more so when considering the sociology of emotions and the social psychology of self (Stryker 2004). In fact, it might be argued that the social psychology of self is a useful framework for organizing the theoretical and empirical literatures that compose the sociology of the emotions.

SELF THEORY AS AN INTEGRATIVE FRAMEWORK FOR THE SOCIOLOGY OF EMOTIONS

The sociology of emotions is a rich and varied literature that has produced a variety of theoretical paradigms and extensive empirical research. However, along with virtually all sociological subspecialties, it has not produced a coherent organizing framework within which these theoretical and empirical literatures fit. In the following pages, it will be suggested that the literature on self-referent responses has the potential for offering such a coherent organizing framework. It will become apparent that the self-referent constructs composing virtually every self-relevant theoretical orientation reflect the self-referent nature of emotions and the direct and indirect linear antecedents and consequences of emotional responses as well as the variables that moderate these relationships.

For present purposes, self theories will be thought of as those that address the antecedents, consequences, and interrelationships among four classes of self-referent (reflexive) constructs: (1) self-cognition (including conception, perception, awareness), (2) self-evaluation (a special case

HOWARD B. KAPLAN • Department of Sociology, Texas A&M University, College Station, TX 77843

This work was supported by research grants R01 DA 02497 and R01 DA 10016 and by a Career Scientist award (K05 DA 00136) from the National Institute on Drug Abuse.

of self-cognition in which the person perceives himself or herself as more or less approximating self-evaluative standards), (3) self-feelings, and (4) self-enhancing or self-protective responses (Kaplan 1986). Self theories, in addition to addressing the direct or indirect linear relationships among the antecedents and consequences of self-referent responses and the more or less direct linear relationships among the varieties of self-referent constructs, also consider the variables that moderate these linear relationships. To provide a baseline for consideration of the commonalities and differences among the self theories, one overarching theory is summarized as a reference for consideration of other selected frameworks.

Exemplar: A Social Psychology of Self-Referent Behavior

In Kaplan's (1986) *Social Psychology of Self-Referent Behavior*, the person (as a psychological structure) is viewed in terms of the profound influence exerted on him by his past and continuing participation in social systems. As a product of past and contemporary social influences, the person, in turn, behaves in ways that have consequences for the social system. Mediating the processes by which the person is influenced by his past and current participation in interpersonal networks and his behavior that has consequences for the social system in which he participates are the person's self-referent responses (i.e., his responses that are oriented toward his own person). The four categories of self-referent constructs are viewed as mediating the mutually influential personal and social structures.

SELF-COGNITION.   Self-awareness, self-conceiving, and other self-referent cognitive responses are viewed as being influenced by the person's actual socially derived traits, intrapsychic responses, behaviors, and experiences, the social context in which these are perceived, the system of concepts that structures the self-perception, and the person's self-protective/self-enhancing responses. The situational context also provides symbolic cues that specify the relevance of particular phenomena that become objects of cognition. The context provides a range and distribution of values along specific dimensions that permit and stimulate the person to identify the particular values along those dimensions that characterize the individual.

The person uses a relatively stable, shared system of concepts from which he selects and structures the perceptions of personal traits, intrapsychic responses, behaviors, and experiences. The system of concepts is influenced by stable personal characteristics and by social reinforcements that sanction the use of particular concepts.

The person's need for positive self-evaluation motivates her to be aware of those phenomena that are most relevant to self-evaluation, to self-perceive in ways that will elicit positive self-evaluative responses, and to behave in ways that in fact lead to the approximation of self-values and that stimulate self-referent cognitions in these terms.

SELF-EVALUATIVE RESPONSES.   Self-judgments of the extent to which the person embodies desirable states is a learned disposition that is stimulated by self-awareness, in general, or by self-conceptualization, in particular. The nature of the self-evaluative responses is a function of the person's specific self-referent cognitions and of the system of self-evaluative standards (self-values) that are the criteria for more or less positive self-evaluative judgments. The specific self-perceiving/self-conceiving responses, in conjunction with social situational cues, stimulate self-judgments of approximating or being distant from those self-evaluative standards that are personally defined as applicable in a particular situation. The most inclusive and superordinate self-value in the person's system of self-values is positive self-evaluation. The person's overall self-evaluation is a function of the frequency and duration of self-perceptions of approximating self-evaluative standards that are more or less salient in the personal hierarchy of values.

SELF-FEELINGS.   Self-feeling reflects the stimulation of need dispositions occasioned by self-evaluations of being more or less distant from self-values. Need dispositions are internalized self-values and, as such, imply a readiness to respond in ways that permit the person to approximate valued states and to distance himself from disvalued states. The intensity and more or less distressful nature of the self-feelings are influenced by the salience of the self-evaluative criteria and the judgment of being proximate to or distant from the valued or disvalued state.

SELF-PROTECTIVE/SELF-EVALUATIVE RESPONSES.   The intensification of self-feelings that are stimulated by self-evaluative judgments motivates the person to engage in self-protective or self-enhancing responses. These responses are more or less consciously oriented toward the goal of forestalling the experience of self-devaluing judgments and the consequent distressful self-feelings (self-protective patterns) or increasing the occasions for positive self-evaluations and self-accepting feelings (self-enhancing responses). The self-enhancing or self-protective mechanisms either directly influence change in self-feelings (emotional experiences) or indirectly influence self-feelings by (1) effecting changes in personal traits, behaviors, intrapsychic responses, or experiences that, in turn, influence self-conceiving, self-evaluation, and self-feeling, (2) causing distortions in self-conceiving, which, in turn, influence self-evaluation and self-feeling, or (3) motivating changes in self-values, which, in turn, affect self-feelings.

A variety of social influences directly affect each of the four categories of self-referent responses and moderate the influence of other social processes on these responses. These self-referent responses are mutually influential and moderate the nature of these linear influences.

The self-referent responses, in turn, influence the functioning of interpersonal systems, either because the self-referent behaviors are visible to others and stimulate responses on their part or because, even if the self-referent behaviors are not recognized by others, the behaviors influence functioning of others by facilitating or constraining their responses. In short, a social-psychological framework is presented in which self-referent behaviors are conceived of as mediating the influence of the person (as a social product) on the interpersonal and social systems in which the individual participates.

Commonalities and Differences in Self Theories

Virtually all theories dealing with the self or self-reflexive responses incorporate the same four categories of self-referent constructs that compose Kaplan's (1986) framework. *Self-perceptions* are evaluated against self-standards. Disjunctions between the self-perceptions and self-standards (*self-evaluative* judgments) evoke distressful *self-feelings* that motivate responses to restore or attain compatibility between self-perceptions and self-evaluative standards (i.e., *self-enhancing* or *self-protective mechanisms*). The differences between them are frequently largely a matter of emphasis, whether to focus on the relationship between self-concept and self-evaluation, between self-evaluation and self-feelings, between self-feelings and self-enhancing or self-protective responses, feedback loops from these responses, or any combination of the above. The theories differ also in terms of the dimensions of the self-concept that are juxtaposed with each other or with evaluative standards. Finally, self theories also differ with regard to whether it is the frustration of the need for positive self-evaluation or the need for self-consistency that evokes emotions and their action-oriented sequelae.

EMPHASIS ON SELF-REFERENT LINKAGES. Although most self theories encompass considerations of all theoretical linkages, they might be differentiated in terms of the emphasis that some place on one or another linkage. Thus, Higgins (1987; Higgins et al. 1987) focuses primarily on the relationship between the discrepancies between self-perceptions and self-guides, on the one hand, and distressful emotional sequelae, on the other hand (while recognizing the motivated responses to self-feelings). Baumeister (1997) tended to focus on the self-protective/self-enhancing functions of aggressive responses following failure-induced negative emotions, just as others are said to "emphasize the regulatory/action eliciting aspects of the self" (e.g., Cantor and Kihlstrom 1986; Markus and Nurius 1987; Scheier and Carver 1982) (Higgins 1987:333).

SPECIFICITY OF SELF-CONCEPT CONTENT. Theories of the self and self-referent constructs differ in terms of the generality and nature of the content of the self-concept from the perspective of the social psychology of self-referent behavior. Negative emotions are responses to any experiences of failure or rejection that threaten more or less highly placed self-evaluative criteria in the person's hierarchy of self-values (Kaplan 1986). Conversely, success and acceptance by significant others that signify approximation of higher-order values in the person's hierarchy of self-values would be expected to evoke positive emotions. Self-referent theories that embody these propositions at one level of abstraction relate to all experiences that threaten or permit approximation of highly placed self-evaluative criteria in the person's hierarchy of self-values (Kaplan 1986). More specifically, in identity theory, the evaluative hierarchy would be specified in terms of personal identities reflecting the degree of commitment that individuals have to various identities and the likelihood that the identity will be invoked in particular situations. Thus, perceived threats to more highly placed, central, or salient identities would evoke more intense negative self-feelings than threats to less highly placed, more peripheral, or less salient identities (Stryker 1968).

In some respects, Burke's (1991) identity control theory also might be considered a special instance of Kaplan's (1986) theoretical approach and (perhaps more aptly) as a special instance of self-verification theory (Swann 1983) in that self-identities are the salient features of self-concept. In Burke's (1991) identity theory, individuals are said to regulate their behavior toward the goal of matching self-concept with self-standards. An interruption in the congruity between self-perceptions and self-standards evokes autonomic nervous system arousal, which is reflected in negative emotion (Burke 1996). The important defining characteristics of the social situation are social identities. When a particular identity is evoked in a given situation, feedback loops are initiated. The meanings associated with a particular identity are compared with the self-perceptions of the individual in the situation (in part influenced by the way others are perceived as viewing one's self). If the self-perceptions are congruent with the "identity standard," the person will act so as to maintain the congruity. However, to the extent that self-perception is incongruent with the identity standard, the individual will act so as to restore congruence.

SELF-EVALUATION VERSUS SELF-VERIFICATION NEEDS. In the literature on self theories, two broad categories have been recognized that focus respectively on the need for self-approval and self-consistency. For some observers (Higgins 1987), the former is also an exemplar of theories that relate incompatible beliefs about the self to emotional responses. In the former case, the theories posit that perceived differences between self-perception and self-evaluative standards evoke a need for self-approval (for self-esteem in some formulations) that is reflected in negative self-feelings, which motivate responses to attain or restore self-approval and so assuage emotional discomfort. Kaplan's (1986) formulation is an exemplar of this type, as are many others. Duval and Wicklund's (1972) theory relating to *objective self-awareness* asserts that self-focused attention occasions increased awareness of differences between our real self and personal self-values that define appropriate traits and behaviors. *Self-affirmation* theory postulates the existence of a self-system for maintaining the perception of overall moral and adaptive adequacy (Steele 1988). Threats to self-image, whether from negative evaluations by others or from behavior that contravenes salient personal attitudes, evoke the operation of a self-affirming, image-maintaining process through which continual reinterpretation of both one's experiences and external reality lead to the restoration of self-image. The particular threat might be rationalized or other salient aspects of the self might be reaffirmed to help the goal of reinforcing overall self-adequacy. In Higgins's (1987) self-discrepancy theory, threats to salient self-evaluative standards frequently are conceived of in terms of the discrepancy between the self as it is perceived and self-evaluative standards. The discrepancies might be between the individual's self-concept and the ideal self (what the person would like to be) or between the self-concept and some normative standard (what the person believes he ought to be). In response to perceived discrepancies between the person's actual attributes, on the one hand, and either ideal self-states or ought self-states, on the other hand, the person will experience one or another type of discomfort. Discrepancies between actual and ought self-states appear to evoke agitation-related emotions exemplified by fear, apprehension, or edginess. Perceived differences between actual and ideal self-states reflect the absence of positive outcomes and, as such, tend to evoke emotions related to dejection, exemplified in dissatisfaction, disappointment, or sadness (Higgins et al. 1987).

As Higgins (1987) noted, in addition to theories that focus on the affective relevance of discrepancies between self-concept and self-evaluative standards, other formulations focus on the emotion-inducing circumstances occasioned by perceived inconsistencies between self-concepts and external evidence or between apparently contradictory traits. Inconsistency between self-concept and external evidence, whether provided by one's own behavior or the responses of others, are considered in, for example, Aronson's (1969) statement of *cognitive dissonance* theory. According to this version, behaviors by people that are inconsistent with the way they conceive of themselves lead to the experience of psychological distress. A case in point would be believing oneself to be honest while behaving in a way that is manifestly dishonest. Self-verification theory (Swann 1983) also argues that distress occurs in the face of feedback that is inconsistent with their self-concept, even when that feedback gainsays negative self-concepts. Thus, people will behave so as to confirm their view of themselves and to disconfirm experiences that are inconsistent with their self-concept. A person with a negative evaluation of one's self would seek the company of someone who thinks ill of them rather than someone who disconfirms their self-image by thinking positively of them. Another type of theory dealing with incompatible self-beliefs focuses on the need for a coherent/unified self-concept. When perceiving mutually exclusive/contradictory traits as part of the self-concept, the person experiences emotional distress (Epstein 1980; Harter 1986; Lecky 1961).

The view that it is incompatibility in beliefs about the self rather than the positive or negative evaluations of self that make a person vulnerable to distressful self-feeling, in the eyes of many, has been largely discredited (Jones 1973; Kaplan 1986). To be sure, a good deal of evidence might be offered that appears to support the self-consistency motive. Low-self-esteem individuals are less likely to justify their poor performance, are more accepting of unfavorable feedback and less accepting of positive feedback about personal traits, are less likely to offer compensatory self-enhancement in response to negative feedback, are more likely to have poorer performance following negative feedback, and, in general, are more willing to accept unfavorable information about themselves (Steele et al. 1993). However, critics of the self-consistency approach argue that such behaviors serve functions that are compatible with the self-enhancement motive. For example, rejection of positive information about oneself or eschewing the company of those who have higher expectations for you might serve the purpose of low-self-esteem individuals in keeping expectations of oneself low and so forestalling future judgments of failure to meet what are subjectively perceived as overly high standards.

It has been noted that theories relating incompatible self-beliefs to emotion often do not distinguish between incompatibilities of actual-self attributes and between actual-self attributes and self-guides (Higgins 1987). A case in point is the formulation of Cast and Burke (2002), who build on the identity control theory (Burke 1991, 1996) referred to previously. The situation is made even more complicated by the assertion that self-verification enhances self-esteem. Further, empirical findings frequently disconfirm the expectations of identity control theory. Thus, Stets (2005) found that in a simulated work situation in which worker role identity is invoked, identity nonverification in a positive direction (receiving more positive feedback than they would expect) results in positive rather than negative emotions. This result would be predicted by what might be called self-evaluation theory, but it is the reverse of what would be expected by identity control theory. At the very least, identity control theory requires the specification of contingencies under which lack of verification in a positive direction would result in negative emotions.

In any case, common to theories about the relationship between perceived discrepancies between self-concepts, on the one hand, and self-evaluative standards or other comparators, on the other, is the assumption that the self-perceptions are evaluatively significant. Self-concepts are evaluatively significant because they have an

> *inherent developmentally derived association with affect and motivation.* That is, what individuals believe about themselves matters in their lives more than other forms of knowledge, even if all types of knowledge were to be structurally equivalent. (Strauman and Higgins 1993:23, emphasis added)

For this reason and for the others to be discussed, all emotions can reasonably be treated and studied as self-referent responses.

EMOTIONS AS SELF-REFERENT RESPONSES

Within the context of self theories, emotions are regarded as self-referent responses in the following five senses:

1. As objects of self-cognition, the experience and expression of emotions evoke self-evaluative responses.
2. All self-evaluative responses to self-cognition (whether or not referring to the experience and expression of emotions) in varying degrees evoke emotional responses (i.e., self-feelings).
3. Emotional responses stimulate self-enhancing or self-protective responses.
4. Emotional responses often are themselves self-enhancing or self-protective patterns.
5. Emotional responses are direct or indirect consequences of (other) self-enhancing or self-protective responses.

The theoretical and research literatures relating to each of these self-referent aspects of emotion are considered in turn.

As suggested earlier, the literature on emotions and the literature on self-referent or reflexive human responses are coterminous in many ways. Indeed, it is suggested that the literature on the emotions could parsimoniously translate into the vocabulary and models from the literature on self-referent processes. It is suggested that emotional experiences are self-referent responses because they are (as objects of self-cognition) stimuli for self-evaluative responses, responses to self-evaluation, stimuli for self-enhancing or self-protective responses, exemplars of self-enhancing or self-protective mechanisms, or (in)direct consequences of self-enhancing or self-protective responses.

EMOTIONAL EXPERIENCES/EXPRESSIONS AS SELF-COGNITIVE STIMULI FOR SELF-EVALUATION

All self-cognition in conjunction with self-evaluative responses (as will be noted in the following section) evoke self-feelings (i.e., emotional responses). One important category of self-referent cognitions is the self-perceived experience and expression of emotions. Self-awareness of the experience and expression of emotions—in particular—social contexts—evokes self-evaluations of responding (in)appropriately and, accordingly, evoke more or less intense negative or positive self-feelings.

Self-Conception of Emotional Experiences/Expression

The individual's recall, awareness, anticipation, or imagination of emotional experiences or expressions become part of consciousness and are conceptualized the way they are because of the context in which they occur, the concepts that the person has learned to use to recognize and structure the emotional experiences, and the person's motivation to conceive of oneself in other than veridical fashion, such as selectively screening or otherwise distorting one's self-conception in order to serve the need to think of oneself in a more positive way. For example, the intrapsychic experience, or visible expression, of anger will become part of the self-concept contingent upon the context (directed toward a friend), the concepts learned in the course of socialization (the idea of anger), and the motivation to conceive of the event in ways that will satisfy important needs (conceiving of the anger as a justified rebuke to an unwarranted insult on the part of the friend, or screening out the emotional response as violating the need to conceive of one's self as a pacifist).

Emotional responses encompass both experiences and expressions of emotions. The expressions or experiences of emotions are the object of self-evaluations that, in turn, evoke emotional (i.e., self-feeling) responses. One feels guilty at having not experienced guilt in certain circumstances, or one feels ashamed at having unreservedly *expressed* pride when humility was required.

Emotional expressiveness, but not necessarily experience, implicates the conscious or unconscious communication of emotional experiences. Thus, a person might purposively communicate anger by staring hard at an individual or might involuntarily or unconsciously communicate the emotion of shame by blushing. Either the expression or experience of particular contextualized emotions evokes self-evaluative responses.

Self-Evaluation of Emotional Experiences/Expression

As with everything else, children internalize self-evaluative standards regarding the experience and expression of emotions. For example, children are socialized to feel that the expression of negative emotions is situationally (in)appropriate and sanctioned to the degree that they more or less conform to these expectations (Garside and Klimes-Dougan 2002). Rules regarding individual emotional performance become part of the person's self-concept. When self-concepts deviate from self-evaluative standards, self-devaluation follows. The self-evaluative standards derive from the normative contexts in which the person is socialized. Insofar as the individual perceives himself as deviating from normative judgments regarding appropriate experiences or expression, he will label himself as an emotional deviant (Thoits 1985).

A good deal of evidence regarding social influences on self-evaluations of emotional responses exists. For example, public reports of one's emotional reactions to deprivation are influenced by beliefs about others' emotional responses to deprivation (Olson et al. 2000); also, independent of hedonic tone and perceived arousal, self-reports of mode (as a measure of subjective emotional experience) are influenced by social desirability (Barrett 1996).

In sociology, observations of the normative structures that inform the socialization of emotional expression and coping responses to normative violations have their roots in the writing of Hochschild (1979, 1983), among others. This literature focuses in large measure on cultural and social identity influences on norms relating to emotional response.

CULTURAL VARIATION.   Cultural expectations exist regarding, for example, emotional displays, and these expectations influence the degree of self-control one exercises over displays of emotion (Fox and Calkins 2003). Kang and associates (2003) observed that cultural differences in emotional expressiveness have been observed due to the inhibitory influence in some cultures of "display rules" (Ekman and Friesen 1969), perhaps because collectivist societies socialize their members to maintain intergroup harmony through control of emotional expressions (Oyserman et al. 2002). This is in contrast to individualistic societies in which emotional expressiveness is proscribed.

SOCIAL IDENTITIES.   Standards for the nature and intensity of emotional expression as well as the precedence one should take over another are associated with virtually all of our social identities (Shields 2005). However, research on this subject is most evident for gender-differentiated social identities. Socializing agents tend to respond negatively to emotional expressiveness on the part of boys and men (Eisenberg et al. 1998); that is, there are "display rules" for who may appropriately express particular kinds of emotion in particular circumstances (Zeman and Garber 1996). Women were expected to react with sadness to adversity and, indeed, expected themselves to so react. Men, however, were expected by others to react and expected themselves to react with more positive emotional responses to negative emotional situations (Hess et al. 2000).

Ideological beliefs held by men regarding appropriate behavior, including the expression of negative emotions, lead them to devalue themselves when expressing such emotions and to invoke inhibitory responses to such emotional expressions (Jakupcak et al. 2003). In effect, the inhibition of negative emotions is a self-protective device for precluding self-rejecting feelings consequent on violation of the prohibition against men being emotionally expressive. For men characterized by traditional masculine ideology, the experience of emotion itself is a violation of self-evaluative criteria that stimulates negative emotional response.

Emotional Responses to Emotional Deviance

Among the circumstances that evoke self-devaluation are the experience of emotions themselves, as when people feel anger toward those who died and abandoned them, and then feel guilty about their anger toward those who died (McNally 1993). This sequence of events reflects what has been referred to as secondary emotional responding, as distinguished from primary emotional responding (Jakupcak et al. 2003 citing Greenberg and Safran 1987).

In general, conformity to self-evaluative criteria for self-approval evokes positive affect, whereas negative self-evaluations evoke distressful emotions. For example, in support of the hypothesis that the experience of emotions violates masculine-based self-evaluative criteria, a measure indicating the experience of stress in response to a violation of masculine-based norms is positively related to expressed fear of emotions (Jakupcak et al. 2003).

The experience of emotions becomes part of the self-concept of the individual and is subject to self-evaluation. To the extent that the individual perceives himself as experiencing more positively valued emotions, the individual will evaluate himself more positively and experience a greater sense of well-being. In support of this contention, it was observed that in the United States, where independence and interpersonal disengagement of the self are more highly valued, general positive emotions were more frequently associated with the reported frequency of interpersonally disengaged positive emotions such as pride. However, in Japan, where feelings associated with interpersonal engagement are more highly valued, the frequency of general positive emotions (such as calm or elation) was associated with the reported frequency of interpersonally engaged positive emotions such as friendly feelings (Kitayama et al. 2000).

In sum, one's emotional experience influences self-concepts regarding one's emotional self. The emotional self-conception, in turn, evokes self-evaluation of one's emotional self, and this evokes emotional responses (Fivush et al. 2003).

EMOTIONAL (SELF-FEELING) RESPONSES TO SELF-COGNITION-STIMULATED SELF-EVALUATIONS

In the context of self-theories, all aspects of one's self-concept (not merely self-awareness or self-conception of emotion-relevant experiences) evoke self-evaluations that, in turn, stimulate self-feelings. Within these frameworks, self-feelings are the functional equivalent of emotional experiences in general or of specific patterns of emotional response.

Self-Conception and Self-Evaluation

Self-awareness and self-conceptualization stimulate self-evaluation. The disposition to evaluate oneself is learned in the course of the socialization process when the person becomes aware of the functional value of self-evaluation from the perspective of others as prerequisite to responding in ways that will secure gratifying outcomes from others. Self-evaluation is made with reference to a personal self-value system—that is, a hierarchy of situationally appropriate self-values that are learned, and so are vulnerable to change, in the course of the socialization process.

The most inclusive value in the social hierarchy is that of positive self-evaluation. Positive self-evaluation is defined in terms of the degree of approximation of other more or less salient and situationally appropriate self-values in the system. To evaluate oneself positively overall is to perceive oneself as meeting the general/specific demands made on one, as these demands are reflected in the person's more or less salient and situationally relevant values that comprise the hierarchy of values. If the person evaluates himself as closely approximating the relatively highly placed values in the system, the individual will tend to have an overall positive evaluation of self. Conversely, to the extent that the individual perceives himself as failing to approximate relatively highly placed positive values (or approximating salient negative values) he will tend to have an overall negative valuation of self.

The stability of positive self-evaluation depends on the constancy with which the individual perceives himself as meeting the situationally relevant demands. Over time if the individual fails to meet those demands, he will come to have a relatively stable negative self-evaluation, reflected in the expectation of a continued inability to meet what he regards as legitimate demands. Conversely, if over time the individual consistently perceives himself as meeting the demands made on him by self and others, he will come to develop a relatively stable positive self-evaluation reflected in the expectation of continuing success in meeting those demands (Kaplan 1986).

SELF-VALUES. Self-values are, at the same time, symbolic representations of personally held goals and the standards against which we measure our degree of approximating those goals. The person's underlying system of personal values is organized along two dimensions: situational relevance and hierarchical salience. Regarding the *situational relevance*, certain values are relevant for self-evaluation in some circumstances but not in others. Self-evaluation of courage might be appropriate on the battlefield but not in family contexts, whereas emotional responsivity might be an appropriate criterion within interpersonal familial relationships, but not on the battlefield.

Hierarchical salience refers to the priority that is assigned to any value when it comes into conflict with other personally held values; that is, one value contributes more to a person's overall self-evaluation than another. It is more important to be a person, for example, self-evaluated as honorable in his dealings with others than to be successful in garnering material goods.

Self-related values are influenced by sociocultural contexts. Thus, honor-related values are more salient in Spain, whereas values relating to individualism are more important in the Netherlands, and these differences are reflected in the conceptualization of the emotions of shame and pride (Fischer 1999). As another example, consistent with expectations, the maintenance of good interpersonal relationships was associated with better self-esteem among Koreans and Chinese participants in a study, but not for Euro-Americans (Kang et al. 2003).

In some instances considered by self-discrepancy theory, it might appear that self-concept does not appear to be involved in self-evaluation at all, as when "some people's personal hopes and wishes for themselves are discrepant from some significant other's beliefs about the kind of person it is their duty or obligation to be" (Higgins 1987:334). However, insofar as an individual has internalized as a self-value the need to conform to significant others' expectations regarding the kinds of self-ideals the subject should hold, the person is in effect evaluating himself against an internalized self-value, the one relating to the approximation of important others' expectations; that is, the attribution to others of derogatory attitudes is itself an occasion for self-devaluation insofar as a self-evaluative standard is to gain the respect of others.

The degree to which individuals identify with groups that are extensions of their self-image reflects the self-evaluative significance of being a group member and of the various correlates of membership in that group. Thus, among people who strongly identify with a team, success of the team is associated with positive mood and higher levels of self-esteem, whereas failure by the team leads to negative mood and lower levels of self-esteem (Hirt et al. 1992). Similarly, the association between conformity and self-evaluation depends on group identification and other contingencies (Christensen et al. 2004).

THE ISSUE OF ULTIMATE SELF-VALUES. The diverse theories that implicate the relationship between self-conception and self-evaluation at first glance appear to differ in the nature of the ultimate self-values that take precedence over other values. In effect, the most salient self-evaluative standards in theories such as those of Kaplan (1986) and Higgins (1987) relate to overall positivity of the self-concept. The mechanism at work is the self-evaluative comparison of one's self-concept as approximating what are regarded as the most desirable characteristics, states, or experiences. When the aspects of the self-concept are regarded as approximating those ideal or obligatory values, the person feels good about herself, and when the self-concept is seen as deviating from those ideal or obligatory standards, the individual evaluates herself negatively and experiences distressful emotions.

For identity theories (e.g., Burke 1996), the ultimate value appears to be the compatibility or congruence or similarity between what one perceives himself as (the self-concept), which is taken as the self-standard (whatever is, is right), and one's own behaviors or experiences that are more or less congruent with those standards. If the cognition of the two being consonant holds sway, the individual judges himself more favorably and experiences positive emotions, and if the individual perceives cognitive dissonance between the self-concept and immediate experiences, then the individual will evaluate herself negatively and feel distressful emotions. However, from the exposition of Cast and Burke (2002), it would seem that the need for self-verification serves the need for, and so is subordinate to, the need for self-approval of approximating internalized self-values. The issue is resolved, in any case, if self-consistency is taken to be a self-value that (along with others) facilitates overall self-approval (i.e., self-esteem).

Self-Values, Needs, and Emotions (Self-Feelings)

From the perspective of self-theories, it is not possible to conceive of emotions as arising from any other circumstances than those that are related to the frustration or satisfaction of personal needs, as it is difficult to conceive of needs as other than internalized personal values. In essence, all emotions are self-referential because they are ineluctably tied to the person's need-value system in which self-values are the symbolic expression of personal needs, and needs are internalized self-values (Kaplan 1983, 1986).

SELF-VALUES AND NEEDS. *Needs* are internalized values. The person subjectively associates particular attributes, intrapsychic responses (cognitions, feelings), behaviors, and experiences with more or less distressing or pleasurable outcomes. The internalization of a value entails being conditioned to respond emotionally to the awareness and conceptualization of being more or less distant from the desirable state symbolized by the value (Kaplan 1986). The conceptual interdependence of needs and values is recognized by Rokeach (1983) as well. For him, values (i.e., "conceptions of the desirable" or "prescriptive-proscriptive beliefs about desirable end-states and desirable modes of behavior")

> become internalized as standards for judging one's own and others' competence and morality. We thus see that values serve a dual purpose: on the one hand they are the *cognitive representations of societal demands* for competence and morality; on the other, they are the cognitive representations of individual needs. (p. 175)

NEEDS AND SELF-FEELINGS. When a person recognizes that he or she is distant from valued states or approximate to disvalued states, the need disposition to approximate valued states or distance oneself from disvalued states is stimulated. The recognition takes the form of self-evaluative response. The need disposition to approximate salient self-values that is stimulated by self-evaluative response takes the form self-feelings that motivate responses intended to achieve valued ends and so satisfy the person's needs—most importantly, the need for self-esteem.

The need for self-esteem is acquired thorough a complex sequence of conditioned responses. Initially, the infant's subjective association of the presence of adults' with the satisfaction of physical needs leads the infant to acquire a need for the presence of adults, independent of the physical need-satisfying function of the adults. The infant, sensitive to the presence of adults, observes an association of satisfaction or frustration of physical needs with specific adult behaviors. This recognition leads to the acquisition of a need to behave in ways that will evoke the kinds of adult response that are associated with the satisfaction of needs and to avoid the kinds of adult response associated with frustration of needs.

In order to maximize the satisfaction of the acquired need to evoke certain kinds of adult response and to avoid negative responses, the child adopts the role of others and perceives, evaluates, and expresses attitudes toward himself from their point of view in order to provide guides for the child's own behaviors that he or she imagines will elicit the desired responses from others. The child then responds to his or her own imagined adult responses toward himself as if they were, in fact, the behaviors of others, with positive or negative affects depending on whether the behaviors were associated with need satisfaction or need frustration. Through the symbolic association of the imagined responses of others with the person's own attitudinal responses to himself, the child acquires the needs to behave in a way that will maximize the experience of positive and minimize the experience of negative self-evaluations. In short, the child has acquired the self-esteem motive—the need for positive responses to oneself (Kaplan 1986).

More generally, the experience of emotions is a primary consequence of the perception of threats to basic needs (Epstein 1993). However, from the perspective of self theories, all such needs are self-relevant and so all emotional responses to need frustration/satisfaction are self-feelings/emotions. The conception of self-feelings as equivalent to affective or emotional responses by a person to self-evaluations or personal traits, intrapsychic responses, behaviors, and personal experiences is reflected in a long history of theoretical contexts. Merely considering this past century, Cooley (1902) distinguished among three components of a "self-idea": a person's imagination of how the person appears to another person, the person's imagination of the other person's evaluation of that appearance, and "some kind of self-feeling" such as pride or mortification. Jourard (1957) viewed the congruence between real self and ideal self as influencing self-cathexis or self-feeling (i.e., affective investment in self). May (1980:241) appeared to equate self-feelings with the emotion of anxiety when he observed that threats to values that the person holds to be "essential to his existence as a self" causes anxiety.

The conceptualization of self-feeling as affect or emotion evoked by self-evaluation, and less directly by self-cognition (Kaplan 1972, 1975, 1980), is compatible with Denzin's (1983:404–405) assertion:

> [A]ll the emotional terms used in everyday language, including being angry, resentful, sad, fearful, joyful, depressed, hostile, enraged, ashamed, proud, affectionate, friendly, embarrassed, rejected, guilty, or in pain, refer to embodied feelings, mental states, interactional experiences, and judgments of others (real and imagined) that persons feel and direct (or have directed) toward self.

Self-Evaluation and Emotions

From the perspective of self theory, self-feelings or self-conscious emotions are not a subset of emotions that have the self as a reference. Rather, all emotions are self-referential. Emotions are either positive or negative affective responses to self-evaluative judgments of approximating or being distant from salient self-evaluative standards or are the motivations for responses that are intended or function to (more or less directly) increase positive self-feelings or decrease negative self-feelings. The distinction that is frequently drawn between self-relevant emotional states and non-self-relevant emotional states (Brown and Marshall 2001; James 1890) might well be a spurious one. It might be argued that all emotions have self as a reference point, but the reference might be more or less direct and might serve different functions such as an expressive affective response to negative self-evaluations, an expressive emotional response to self-devaluation caused by experiencing the distressful self-emotion, or an affective response that serves self-enhancing/self-protective functions in response to experiencing distressful emotions.

In any case, arguably, the largest portion of the literature on self-theory and emotion relates to theoretical statements and empirical reports of the relationship between self-evaluation and emotions. As Kaplan (1986) described, the sequence of linkages culminating in self-feelings is as follows: the person perceives, recalls, imagines, or anticipates personal traits, behaviors, or experiences. These self-referent cognitive responses stimulate self-evaluations of self-referent cognitions as (in)congruent with the person's self-values that are internalized as need dispositions. The self-evaluations stimulate the need dispositions, which are then experienced as self-feelings.

Although disagreement might exist as to whether emotions arise only in response to self-relevant threats, there is widespread agreement that self-relevant threats do eventuate in emotional responses. It is not only the contemporary self-devaluing experience that evokes emotional response. Recall or anticipation and, indeed, imagination of self-devaluing circumstances would evoke emotional response as well. Thus, in an examination of four dimensions of self-defining memories, memory contents (the types of event in memories) and affect (subjective emotion upon recall) predicted individuals' degree of subjective distress (Blagov and Singer 2004). Sometimes negative self-evaluations take the form of comparing recollections of adverse outcomes (failure and rejection) with what might have been (i.e., counterfactual thinking) (Mandel 2003). Thinking of how things might have been better tended to be associated with negative emotions—that is, guilt, shame, sadness, regret, and disappointment. This is particularly the case when the counterfactual thinking is self-focused—that is, thinking that addresses how the person could have changed an adverse outcome for the better.

EMPIRICAL SUPPORT.   In addition to sources previously cited and those that are yet to be cited in other connections, it is apparent that a vast amount of empirical support exists for the hypothesized relation between self-evaluation in relevant circumstances and subsequent emotional responses. Numerous experimental studies support the expectation that experiences of rejection would elicit negative emotions such as anger, sadness, and hurt feelings compared with experiences of acceptance. It appeared, however, that increases in, rather than levels of, rejection elicited stronger emotional reactions (Buckley et al. 2004). Under experiences of failure, individuals are more likely to manifest greater degrees of anger than following experiences of success (Stucke and Sporer 2002). Dunkley and Blankstein (2000) reported that self-critical perfectionism is related to the experience of distress, a relationship that is explainable by the intervening effect of maladaptive coping.

In general, the identity control literature suggests that congruence between self-perceptions and self-standards will be associated with positive emotions, whereas meaningful discrepancies between self-standards and self-perceptions relating to identities will be reflected in distressful emotions (Burke 1996; Burke and Stets 1999; Cast and Burke 2002). Such literature is relevant not only to predicting the valence (positive or negative) and nature (anger, depression, elation, and so forth) of emotional responses, but is relevant also in accounting for the intensity and duration of specific emotions. Thus, Stets and Tsushima (2001:283) found that "group-based identities, which are more intimate, are associated with more intense anger while role-based identities which are less intimate, are related to anger that lasts longer."

A group of panel studies report relationships between antecedent global self-evaluation and subsequent subjective distress. In a panel study of several thousand seventh-grade students interviewed annually up to three times during their junior high school years, a measure of self-rejection in the seventh grade was related to subsequent self-reports of indices of negative self-feelings in the ninth grade among students who denied the presence of the symptom in the eighth grade (Kaplan 1980). The negative self-feelings were expressed variously in terms of depressive affect, self-distress, and a wide variety of psychophysiological manifestations of anxiety.

The influence of self-evaluation on self-rejecting feelings has been observed over long periods of time. Individual who displayed higher scores on a measure of self-derogation in 1971 when they were seventh-grade students were significantly more likely to display higher scores on an index of psychological distress administered over 10 years later when they were young adults (Kaplan et al. 1983).

Empirical support for the hypothetical association between perception of threats to salient self-evaluative standards and the experience of distressful emotions is provided by psychophysiological studies, where psychophysiological responses can be taken as indicators of emotional response. One interesting set of studies permits the interpretation that self-feelings are associated with the performance of particular social roles that are defined in terms of salient social standards and under conditions in which the appropriate level of role performance is problematic. In this case, the roles in question are those in which the social identity requires the acceptance of responsibility for the safety of others. These studies suggest that individuals whose ability to fulfill the demands made on them in the situation in question will experience intensified self-feelings, as these are reflected in psychophysiological activation. Presumably, the individuals evaluate themselves according to the certainty with which they are able to fulfill the expectations made on them and the identities they now accept. Thus, student aviators attempting their first aircraft carrier landings had higher mean serum cortisol levels and higher levels of urinary excretion of cortisol and 17-OHCS (hydroxycorticosteroid) metabolites than the radar intercept officers in the rear cockpit, who had no flight control and had to rely completely on the pilots' skill (Rubin 1974). In another study, the only men in a special combat unit in Vietnam anticipating enemy attack who showed elevated levels of 17-OHCS were the two officers and the radio operator (Bourne et al. 1968).

Kiritz and Moos (1974) discussed studies in which the results reflected higher heart rates in pilots than in copilots—a difference that reversed itself when the individuals changed positions—a positive association between responsibility for other individuals and diastolic blood pressure; a greater amplitude of gastric contractions in subjects who were able to press a button to avoid strong auditory stimulus to both members of a pair than in the passive members of the pair, highest levels of 17-OHCS secretion in aircraft commanders, and sharp increases in heart rate of key NASA personnel when suddenly given additional responsibility. Thus, when the self-evaluative standard can be presumed to be important and when the approximation of the standard is problematic, the person will experience exacerbation of self-feelings, as these are taken to be reflected in psychophysiological activation.

PATHOLOGICAL EMOTIONAL RESPONSES. In extreme cases, emotional responses to intense threats to positive self-evaluation take pathological forms eventuating in anxiety, depression, posttraumatic stress disorder, and generally dysphoric states. Depression derives at least partly from disruption of one's self-image as an effective and worthy person (Blatt and Bers 1993). Depression in the latter analysis is the result of being unable to think well of oneself in the face of wanting to do so (Tesser 1986). Threats to one's self-concept characterize dysphoria, in general, and posttraumatic stress disorders, in particular, as discussed by McNally (1993:73), who reported:

Following a traumatic event, individuals may experience survivor guilt about emerging relatively unscathed when others did not. Conversely, they may feel guilty about their anger toward those who died and therefore abandoned them. Soldiers who kill noncombatants or participate in atrocities often experience intense guilt about performing acts profoundly inconsistent with their self-concepts as a moral being. (March 1990)

MODERATING INFLUENCES. As much of the foregoing literature review suggests, the strength of the association between self-evaluation and emotional response is moderated by a number of circumstances. Boldero and Francis (2000) reported complex moderating influences of self-guide importance, location relevance, and social self-domain centrality on the association between self-discrepancies and emotion.

Perhaps the greatest attention in the literature devoted to self and emotion is accorded to the importance of the self-evaluative standard in the person's hierarchy of self-values. The more salient the self-evaluative standard and the greater the degree of distance from that standard that is perceived, the greater will be the intensity of the emotional discomfort experienced (Higgins 1987; Kaplan 1986). Thus, Plant and Devine (1998) reported that discrepancies between self-concept and what other people thought the subject was obliged to do was related to agitation-related emotions only for individuals who indicated that they cared about whether they met the others' standard. Again, where salient self-evaluative standards relate to the physical self, it is to be expected that self-evaluation of the physical self would be closely associated with affective responses. Therefore, Roberts (2004:22) reported that the "women who internalize a more sexually objectified view of their physical selves have more negative attitudes and emotions, including disgust and shame, toward their own menstrual cycles."

That experiences of rejection and failure evoke negative self-evaluative emotions to the extent that the perceived basis for the failure and rejection is a significant part of the self-concept is illustrated by two studies reported by McCoy and Major (2003). They indicated that the relationship between perceived prejudice and self-evaluative emotions depends on the person's identification with the group that is the object of prejudice. The salient self-evaluative standards according to which people judge themselves vary across cultures. Within cultures, in identity theories, the salience of social roles informs the experience of emotions in part (Franks 2003).

Arguably, of equivalent influence to salience of self-evaluative standards as a moderating influence is whether the person *characteristically* has *high or low self-esteem* and whether the self-esteem reflects a veridical self-evaluation or a *defensive grandiosity*. Regarding the former, chronic self-esteem has frequently been recognized as a buffer of the distress that is associated with the failure to approximate self-evaluative standards. Thus, Cast and Burke (2002) viewed self-esteem as a resource that serves the function of forestalling being overwhelmed by negative emotions that follow disturbances in self-verification. Further, the effect of experiences of success and failure on emotions is moderated by self-esteem; that is, the less individuals think of themselves, evaluativly speaking, the more their experiences of failure will evoke distressful emotions (Brown and Marshall 2001). This interaction was observed for so-called self-relevant emotions but not for non-self-relevant emotions. In the latter case, however, a main effect was observed indicating that success was associated with positive affect, whereas failure was associated with negative affect. Thus, self-relevant experiences are related to all emotions. However, for the self-relevant emotions, the effect is much stronger for people who have negative self-evaluations.

Chronically low self-esteem is reflected in self-criticism and unrealistically high self-expectations. Consistent with this, it was observed that in response to recalled experiences of failure, individuals who were more characteristically self-critical were more likely to demonstrate self-contempt and self-disgust (Whelton and Greenberg 2005). Further, Kuiper and Olinger

(1989) observed that distressful emotions are frequently the outcome of excessively rigid and inappropriate rules for evaluating self-worth.

In contrast to reality-based self-esteem, a positive self-view might reflect a grandiose defensive response to self-devaluing attitudes. Thus, narcissists who have inflated views of themselves would experience greater variance between their self-concept and their negative self-evaluation than would be suggested by experiences of failure and rejection. In fact, narcissists display more anger and correlated aggression following the experience of social rejection than nonnarcissists (Twenge and Campbell 2003). Consistent with this, Stucke and Sporer (2002) proposed that a combination of grandiose self-image along with insecure and unstable self-esteem (low self-concept clarity) would predict negative emotions and consequent aggression in response to failure-induced threats to self-esteem. Rhodewalt and Morf (1998) reported that participants characterized as narcissistic manifested more lability in self-esteem and more anger and anxiety in response to failure than did other subjects. This was consistent with the conclusion that among narcissists in particular, anger represents a response to threats to the grandiose expectations imposed upon the self. Baumeister et al. (1996) also offered findings suggesting that an extremely positive self-image stimulates aggression as a response to ego threat. Presumably an extraordinarily positive self-image, when compared to the experience of rejection and failure, represents a greater threat to self-esteem and, therefore, a more intense motivation to enhance the self-image by derogating or punishing the perceived source of the failure and rejection (Baumeister 1997).

Other moderators might have been presented as well. A case in point is the subjective probability of attaining the self-evaluative standards (Higgins 1987). It is to be expected that the relationship between self-evaluation and emotional response will be weaker if the subject perceives that it is highly unlikely that he or she will approximate the standard or if approximation of the standard is inevitable. Consistent with this hypothesis, emotional responses to prejudice (sexism) are moderated by a pessimistic/optimistic outlook on life (Kaiser et al. 2004). Salience of self-evaluative standards and chronic self-esteem level are presented as only two (albeit important) exemplars of moderators of the relation between self-evaluation and emotion.

SELF-ESTEEM. In the literature on the self, it is frequently difficult to disentangle the several possible meanings of self-esteem, notably the distinction between self-perceptions of being close to or distant from self-evaluative standards, on the one hand, and self-feelings that are stimulated by these judgments, on the other. Unless self-esteem is generally conceptualized, explicitly or by implication, as a judgment about one's approximation to self-evaluative standard, it would not make sense to correlate self-esteem to other emotional states (unless self-esteem was defined as some general emotional state, in which case the general state was correlated with specific states). However, it would make sense for self-esteem to be correlated with emotional states if it was postulated that self-esteem represented a personal judgment (a subset of self-conception) about one's degree of approximation to more or less highly valued and situationally appropriate standards of excellence. Indeed, self-esteem has been related to various emotional states. Self-esteem

> has been linked to anxiety and depression in the clinical literature (Mineka, Watson, & Clark, 1998), to pride and shame in the developmental literature (Tangney & Fischer, 1995), to happiness and contentment in personality psychology (Diener & Diener, 1995), and to anger and hostility in social psychology (Bushman & Baumeister, 1998; Kernis, Grannemann, & Barclay, 1989) (Brown and Marshall 2001:575).

In any case, self-esteem is used here as a judgment, a self-conception of being distant from/proximate to (positive or negative) self-evaluative criteria, and is distinguished from the self-feelings that are evoked by this self-conception.

In response to recognition of the difficulties involved in measuring self-feeling in contradistinction to self-evaluation, some investigators over the years have moved from using measures such as a variant of Rosenberg's (1965) self-esteem scale to the use of latent constructs in which measures such as that scale were cojoined with indices of negative affect such as depression and anxiety. Thus, it was the confluence of these scales that was said to truly represent negative self-feelings (see, e.g., Kaplan and Lin 2000).

Qualitatively Distinct Emotional Responses

The literature reviewed to this point supports the contention that self-evaluation is related to emotional responses and that this relationship is moderated by a number of circumstances. However, this review has yet to address the relationship between self-evaluative circumstances and particular *kinds* of emotional response.

SELF-EVALUATIVE CIRCUMSTANCES.   Self-theories frequently speak to the kinds of self-evaluative circumstance that will evoke particular modes of emotional responses. Thus, specific forms of emotional response are consequences of different kinds of discrepancy between self-perceptions and ideal or normative standards. Guilt might be a consequence of disparities between self-perception and one's perception of what one should be, whereas shame is the consequence of a disparity between self-perception and the perception of others' ideal models of the self (Higgins 1987). Similarly, Kuiper and Olinger (1989:383) offered that the self-threatening nature of life circumstances will variously be expressed in different negative self-feelings such as anxiety or depression depending on a number of conditions. Anxiety is proposed to be more prevalent as long as the individual continues to actively cope with a threat and maintain some hope of avoiding the threatened outcome. In contrast, depression is likely to ensue when the individual begins to despair of the effectiveness of coping attempts and, therefore, loses hope of avoiding threat. For individuals with a large number of dysfunctional attitudes, perceived difficulty in meeting self-worth contingencies might, in the first instance, lead to increased anxiety. If the vulnerable individual begins to lose hope of being able to cope successfully and perceives that contingencies for self-worth have not been met, then the individual is likely also to experience feelings of depression. At mild to moderate levels of depression, there might still be a significant level of anxiety as the vulnerable individual fluctuates between perceptions of loss and threat.

Kaplan (1986:90) offered two circumstances that define the qualitative nature of specific self-feelings. The nature of the evaluative standard influences the kind of emotional response. The failure to be part of an interpersonal network might be experienced as loneliness, and the failure to evoke high regard from others might be experienced as shame. Another defining characteristic is temporal in nature. Anticipated failure is experienced as anxiety, whereas recollection of failure in one's duty is experienced as guilt.

Whether an individual experiences shame, embarrassment, or anger might depend on such circumstances as the sources of the evaluative judgment and the perceived legitimacy of that judgment. Thus, individuals would report feeling shamed if a flaw was exposed, embarrassment when another person could legitimately infer that such a flaw existed, and anger if the perceptions of a flaw by others was unjustified (Sabini et al. 2001).

Brown and Marshall (2001) noted, also, that different emotions might be evoked depending on the particular dimension of self-concept and the relevance of particular self-evaluative standards. Thus, interpersonal rejection might evoke loneliness, immorality might evoke guilt, and being the object of interpersonal insults might be associated with reactions of anger, particularly in the case of low-self-esteem subjects.

EMPIRICAL SUPPORT.   The research literature supports the associations that (1) qualitatively different emotional patterns are observable and (2) different self-evaluative circumstances are associated with particular emotional patterns.

The existence of *qualitatively distinct emotions* is supported by observations of emotion-specific autonomic nervous system patterning that distinguishes among amusement, anger, contentment, fear, and sadness, varying across the dimensions of valence and activation (Christie and Friedman 2004). Lewis and Ramsay (2002) distinguished between two different kinds of embarrassment variously reflecting negative self-evaluation and being the object of others' attention, with the former being associated with higher cortisol responses than the latter. Confirmatory factor analyses affirm support for the hypothesis that fear, anxiety, and depression are different (albeit correlated) components of negative emotions (Muris et al. 2001).

The *empirical association between particular self-evaluative circumstances and qualitatively distinct emotional responses* is observed by a number of investigators. Higgins (1987), for example, as noted earlier, reported support for predictions regarding the kinds of emotion that would be associated with particular kinds of self-discrepancy. Thus, discrepancies between one's own self-concept and one's own ideal self were associated with feeling disappointed, dissatisfied, and blameworthy, among other feelings. Discrepancy between self-concept and one's own felt obligations was associated with guilt, self-contempt, and agitation.

Among the characteristics of the self-concept that one becomes aware of are the various group memberships held by the individual. To the extent that these group memberships are more or less positively valued, they would be expected to evoke self-feelings that were more or less positive in nature. Thus, perceptions of membership groups that deviated greatly from ideal standards were associated with "dejection-related" emotions, and perceptions of membership groups that deviated from expectations of what they should be were linked to "agitation-related" emotions (Bizman et al. 2001).

Narcissistic defenses not only moderate the relationship between threats to the self and negative emotion, but indeed also moderate the relationship between self-threatening experiences and the kind of emotion that is experienced. Thus, Stucke and Sporer (2002) reported that people who are characterized as high-narcissism/low-self-concept clarity types respond to negative feedback with anger, whereas low-narcissism/high-self-concept clarity types respond with depression.

EMOTIONS AND SELF-ENHANCING/SELF-PROTECTIVE RESPONSES

The experience of distressful self-feelings or emotions (whether generated by perceived failure to approximate salient self-values or by the absence of self-verification) motivates responses that promise to attain or restore positive self-feelings (self-enhancing patterns) or to forestall the experience of negative self-feelings (self-protective patterns). Where the person experiences positive emotions (again whether due to perceived approximation to self-evaluative standards or to manifest self-verification), the individual is motivated to perpetuate the responses that eventuated in positive self-feelings.

In short, self-feelings or emotions, the experiences of needs, stimulate the person to behave in ways that will permit the individual to satisfy those needs. These responses function either to directly impact self-feelings or indirectly affect self-feelings by revising self-referent cognition, self-evaluation, or, even more indirectly, changing one's personal traits, behaviors, and experiences that (in turn) influence self-conceptualization and consequent self-evaluation and self-feelings. The responses take the form of attacks on the perceived sources of distressful self-relevant emotions, intrapsychic or interpersonal avoidance of such perceived sources, substitution of self-evaluative standards that are more easily approximated, or actions that permit conformity to self-expectations (Kaplan 1975, 1986, 1996).

Modes of Self-Enhancing or Self-Protective Responses

Any of a variety of responses could be employed in response to the experience of self-feelings and toward the goals of (1) restoring, attenuating, or reinforcing positive self-feelings or (2) assuaging negative self-referent emotions.

AGGRESSION.   Aggressive responses directed toward the perceived occasions for self-devaluation and consequent self-feelings potentially serve to devalue the validity of the standards according to which one was devalued and at the same time might establish the relatively greater potency of the aggressor. Thus, those who experience self-rejecting feelings in response to self-evaluations of failure or rejection would be disposed to respond negatively toward the perceived occasion for these experiences. This would be even more strongly the case for those who had a more intense need for self-validation (i.e., narcissists). If individuals need to think well of themselves and that need is frustrated, then it is to be expected that self-enhancing/self-protective mechanisms would be evoked toward the goal of fulfilling that need (Bushman and Baumeister 1998; Stucke and Sporer 2002).

AVOIDANCE.   Individuals who experience negative self-feelings in response to self-evaluations of failure and rejection are motivated to avoid future self-devaluation by influencing self-cognitions in a positive way, perhaps through self-deception. Self-deceptive beliefs are themselves greatly influenced by emotions and desires (Lazar 1999). They express the person's hopes and wishes; that is, people might perceive themselves as they need to think of themselves. A number of normal defense mechanisms permit self-serving self-cognition, including denial, isolation, and reaction formation (Baumeister et al. 1998). Self-cognition is influenced at the onset by avoidance of self-awareness. Thus, experiences of social exclusion prompt avoidance of self-awareness (facing away from a mirror) (Twenge et al. 2003). In addition to intrapsychic avoidance mechanisms, the experience of evaluation-induced distressful emotions motivates interpersonal avoidance of potentially self-devaluing circumstances (Arkin 1981).

REVISION OF SELF-VALUES.   When an individual is required to evaluate himself negatively when judged according to particular self-evaluative standards and so experiences distressful self-feelings, one of the strategies that might be motivated in order to assuage the negative emotions is to change the nature or order of the hierarchy of self-values in order to facilitate the approximation of those values. If people cannot change their behaviors in order to permit compatibility with their identity, "then the identity or standard of comparison itself may be changed" (Burke 1991: 845).

When circumstances that are threatening to one's self-image arise, as when athletes fall into a slump, they might tend to use self-handicapping strategies to legitimate their poor performance (Prapavessis et al. 2003). The affective significance of self-threatening circumstances is suggested by the association of self-handicapping tendencies and cognitive state anxiety prior to competition. In effect, the person implores himself and others to judge the person according to a new and less arduous set of standards that precludes judgment of failure and consequent distressful emotions.

The person displays "a reluctance to accept the risks and pressures of a highly positive self-image" (Baumeister 1993:217).

Collectively, negative emotions often motivate actions that take the form of social movements, which in themselves embody praiseworthy self-values. Indeed, the very act of participating in what is defined as a laudable social movement permits self-evaluation of having a worthy collective identity (Kaplan and Liu 2000; Kiecolt 2000; Taylor 2000).

Among the defenses called upon in response to negative self-feelings is narcissism. The narcissist needs continual shows of admiration to support a tenuous perception of self-worth (Giddens 1991). Defensively, the person changes the self-evaluation of "unworthy" to one of grandiose self-approval and so replaces (for the moment) distressful negative self-feelings with positive emotions.

APPROXIMATING SELF-VALUES. When individuals experience negative emotions in response to self-judgments of failure or rejection (or incongruity replaces lack of "a match"), one possible response is to take action to approximate the self-values (or to restore self-verification). This is perhaps more easily accomplished by high-self-esteem individuals. For example, Higgins (1987), citing Weiner (1986), noted that emotional reactions to performance might influence subsequent achievement motivation. The action taken to restore positive self-evaluations and to attain correlated positive emotional experiences might take the form of alternatively laudable actions. Thus, the experience of shame or guilt in response to negative self-evaluations might, in turn, stimulate responses that have redeeming social value and so would compensate for previous sins by evoking positive self-evaluations and positive self-feelings.

In the same way that personal guilt leads to compensatory efforts at restitution, personal guilt stemming from perceptions of white privilege and seeing European Americans as agents of racial discrimination anticipate support for compensatory affirmative action programs (Iyer et al. 2003). Group-based sympathy was more broadly predictive of a variety of affirmative action programs.

Among self-enhancing and self-protective mechanisms is the act of conforming to other people's expectations in order to avoid their disapproval. For example, Carlsmith et al. (1974) reported that when children were shown an anxiety-provoking film, unlike when they were shown an amusing film, the children were observed to comply more frequently with adult requests, particularly when the adult was presented as negative and threatening as opposed to being presented as warm and positive.

However, circumstances frequently lead people to eschew conventional adaptations in favor of deviant actions that approximate alternative (deviant) self-values. The adoption of deviant patterns is occasioned by the past failure of conforming patterns to assuage negative emotions that were consistently associated with conventional social contexts (Kaplan 1975, 1980, 1986, 1995, 1996).

Moderators of Self-Enhancing or Self-Protective Patterns

The nature of the self-enhancing or self-protective strategy that is motivated by self-feeling is contingent upon a number of circumstances, including the nature of the self-evaluative standard, the nature of the motivating self-feelings, and the person's characteristic self-evaluation.

The nature of the self-enhancing or self-protective mechanisms that are employed to either assuage negative emotions or to reduce the likelihood of negative self-evaluations that lead to negative emotional experiences apparently depends in part on the *nature of the discrepancy between self-concept and self-evaluative standard*. Thus, within the context of self-discrepancy theory (Higgins 1987), perceived discrepancies between one's self-concept and one's perception of duties and obligations incumbent upon the person influence cognitive strategies (including reduction of the subjective importance of the self-guide) toward the goal of reducing the experience of agitation-related emotions. In contrast, discrepancies between one's actual self-concept and one's hopes or aspiration might lead to the adoption of situational strategies, including redefining particular social domains as less central to one's self-concept or shifting to a location that is deemed less relevant to a domain-specific discrepancy, toward the goal of reducing the experience of dejection-related emotions (Boldero and Francis 2000).

The nature of the self-enhancing or self-protective mechanisms used is contingent on the particular *emotional pattern* that stimulates the coping response. Those who are particularly vulnerable to self-evaluation are more likely to use coping strategies that preclude negative social interaction in response to failure to meet self-worth contingencies (Kuiper and Olinger 1989). Depressed individuals are more likely to use coping mechanisms such as wishful thinking, distancing, self-blame, and self-isolation compared to normal controls. Individuals who are vulnerable but are not currently in a depressed state are differentiated from normal controls on the basis of coping through self-isolation.

Regarding *characteristic self-evaluation*, Stucke and Sporer (2002:530) report support for the position that:

> individuals with a very positive but unstable and insecure self-view are especially vulnerable to ego-threats. In contrast to people with a stable and somewhat neutral, or negative, self-view, who seem to direct their negative feelings toward themselves, they tend to show defensive reactions and try to re-establish their positive self-image by derogating the source of the ego-threat.

EMOTIONAL RESPONSES AS SELF-ENHANCING/ SELF-PROTECTIVE MECHANISMS

From the perspectives of the sociology of emotion and self-theory and emotion, a particularly interesting subset of self-enhancing/self-protective responses are themselves emotional reactions: Depression might reflect the repression of, or emotional withdrawal from, disquieting emotions; anger might reflect the symbolic destruction of the standards according to which the individual was judged to have failed, thus evoking negative self-feelings; anxiety might reflect sensitization to environmental threat and, therefore, the capability of avoiding the threat, having been forewarned; manic states might reflect a compensatory positive reaction to agitated depression.

For some purposes, depression and anger are of particular interest as self-enhancing or self-protective mechanisms. Regarding *depression*, maintaining a negative self-image serves to relieve the individual of apparently futile attempts to maintain a positive self-image. Negative self-views serve the function of forestalling future pain and disappointment. By keeping expectancies for positive outcomes low, disappointment is minimized. Therefore, circumstances that threaten the negative self-view (positive outcomes) might be anxiety inducing because an effective defense against future disappointment is obviated. Depression controls emotions rather than the circumstances that evoke these emotions by keeping expectations low and thus minimizing the possibility of future pain and disappointment.

Another interesting emotional self-protective mechanisms is the use of anger as a self-protective response against the feeling of shame:

> In our theory, rage is used as a defense against a threat to self, that is, feeling shame, a feeling of vulnerability of the whole self. Anger can be a protective measure to guard against shame, which is experienced as an attack on self. As humiliation increases, rage and hostility increases proportionally to defend against loss of self-esteem; . . . (Scheff et al. 1989:188)

In short, emotions not only reflect needs that are evoked by self-evaluation and motivate self-enhancing or self-protective responses, but they also frequently *serve* such functions.

SELF-ENHANCING/SELF-PROTECTIVE MECHANISMS AND SELF-FEELINGS (EMOTION)

Although it is apparent that experiences of emotions in response to self-evaluation motivate self-protective responses (some of which are themselves emotions), it remains to be considered what consequences these self-enhancing/self-protective mechanisms have for emotions. Both theoretical and empirical considerations suggest that the relationship between self-enhancing and self-protective mechanism, on the one hand, and emotions, on the other, is reciprocal. Negative self-feelings (whether chronic or acute) motivate responses that will assuage or forestall distressful emotional experiences. In turn, self-enhancing or self-protective mechanisms will influence the experience of distressful emotions by assuaging of forestalling negative emotions or increasing the experience of positive emotions that are self-relevant. Although the literature on the subject is far from definitive, it is highly suggestive of the conclusion that self-enhancing or self-protective mechanisms do have a self-regulating effect on emotions, although this effect is contingent on a number of variables.

People with high self-esteem are able to maintain their high self-esteem because when facing failure and rejection, they are able to employ self-enhancing or self-protective mechanisms that obviate the self-evaluative significance of these experiences. Brown and Marshall (2001) observed that people protect their feelings of self-worth when encountering failure by focusing on their strong points in other areas and using self-serving attributions or downward social comparison processes. Indeed, a defining characteristic of high-self-esteem individuals is a commitment to feel good about oneself by seeking until one finds a strategy that works to maintain a feeling of self-worth.

As noted earlier, the acceptance of negative information about oneself is also interpretable as a defensive response. Thus, Epstein (1993) asserted that the maintenance of negative views of self reduces the experience of pain by maintaining low expectancies about future success and acceptance in order to avoid or assuage the experience of failure and rejection. Negative self-evaluation, along with negative overgeneralization, following unfavorable outcomes "are motivated states in the service of maximizing a person's pleasure-pain balance under the circumstances as conceived by the individual's experiential conceptual system" (Epstein 1993:834). The maintenance of negative self-views assuages anxiety and reduces threats to the stability of a person's conceptual system once the person has acquired negative self-attributions.

Self-protective or self-enhancing mechanisms can act directly on the emotions as when repression allows a person to distance himself from the experience of psychologically threatening emotions. Indirectly, the same self-protective mechanism can affect emotions by permitting cognitive distancing from self-threatening ideas that might elicit negative self-feelings. Repression, then, from a cognitive perspective is a perceptual defense. Mendolia (2002:215) reported data demonstrating that "individuals regulate their autonomic activity, facial muscle activity, cognitive attention, and subjective experience during isolated and repeated exposures to self-threatening negative and positive emotional events." Thus, by affecting self-cognition and the self-evaluative responses to that cognition, repression indirectly affects the experience of distressful emotions. Consistent with this conclusion, the disposition to employ repressive defensiveness was observed to be associated with recall of fewer specific memories (Blagov and Singer 2004).

Self-enhancing or self-protective mechanisms are variable in the extent to which they directly assuage distressful emotions, or evoke positive emotions, or indirectly accomplish these ends by influencing self-concept and self-evaluative frameworks. Thus, in dealing with events that challenge positive self-evaluation (perceived negative social effects of having high ability), gifted adolescents employ any of a variety of coping strategies, females being more likely to deny giftedness and maintain high activity levels and males being more likely to employ humor (Swiatek 2001). In this instance, examining the association of the various response patterns with self-concept, emotion-focused, denial-based strategies would appear to be less effective than problem-focused social coping patterns.

It is possible that particular self-protective or self-enhancing mechanisms might be specific to particular emotion outcomes and to particular kinds of self-evaluative response. Thus, the expectation of rejection when attributed to prejudice results in a decrease in self-blame and anticipation of feeling less depressed. However, attribution of rejection to prejudice did not preclude feelings of hostility or anxiety (Major et al. 2003).

The hostility and anxiety are (perhaps) interpretable as other self-protective mechanisms. The hostility to those who are anticipated as being rejecting of them might be regarded as an attempt to "destroy" the basis of the person's self-rejection, and anxiety might be interpreted as a form of hypervigilance against rejection. However, such effects might be contingent on the degree of identification with the group.

Drawing favorable comparisons with another group frequently serves a self-enhancing function by allowing the person to more favorably evaluate themselves relative to others, thus decreasing the experience of distressful self-feelings. For example, Latino Americans who were informed of prejudice against an out-group reported less depressed self-feelings to the extent that they more strongly identified with their own minority in-group (McCoy and Major 2003). Similarly, among individuals who experienced negative evaluations by a sexist evaluator, those who thought it was less important being a woman were more protected from experiencing depression, and the more important that being a woman was to their self-concept, the less protected they were from experiencing depression in response to rejection by a sexist evaluator (McCoy and Major 2003).

As observed earlier, self-enhancing or self-protective mechanisms can range from the conventional to the deviant. A number of deviant mechanisms have been observed to be effective in regulating the valence of self-referent emotions. Some pathological defense mechanisms act directly on the experience of negative emotions, as when the "detached or schizoid person decreases his emotional or actual participation in life in order not to feel inadequate and injure his self-image" (Arieti 1967:732). Among deviant coping responses to negative self-feelings are self-injurious behaviors, one function of which is recognized as the regulation of emotions (Jeglic et al. 2005).

However, the emotional consequences of deviant patterns are variable. Thus, substance abuse appears to have short-term effects of reducing self-derogation and depression but long-term consequences of increasing these states (Bentler 1987; Newcomb and Bentler 1988). The momentary gratification assuages distressful emotions, but over the long term, the deviant pattern might have social consequences that increase social stigmatization and, thus, the need for the momentary reduction of negative self-feelings (Kaplan 1996).

In extreme cases, emotional responses, while they motivate self-enhancing or self-protective responses, often interfere with the effective use of such mechanisms. Thus, anxiety, an outcome of low self-esteem, is an emotional state that often precludes self-enhancement because it freezes the person's capacity to respond and take the role of the other (Hewitt 1991).

In short, a number of circumstances moderate the nature of self-enhancing consequences of deviant patterns. Kaplan (1980), for example, specified and tested a number of such contingencies, informed by his general theory of deviant behavior, including the ability to reduce normative patterns, vulnerability to adverse consequences of adopting deviant patterns, and definition of the acts as deviant.

RETROSPECT AND PROSPECT

The foregoing review of the very rich theoretical and empirical research literatures dealing with self and emotions has been organized according to, and affirmed, five general propositions:

1. The experience and expression of emotions become objects of self-awareness and self-conceptualization, and these self-cognitions, in interaction with personal systems of self-values and socionormative systems, evoke self-evaluative responses (and their sequelae).
2. Self-evaluative responses (in response to all self-cognitions, including self-awareness and self-conceptualization of emotional experiences) stimulate self-feelings (i.e., emotional responses).
3. Self-feelings/emotions stimulate (motivate) self-enhancing or self-protective responses.
4. Emotions/self-feelings are among the responses that (are intended to) serve self-enhancing or self-protective functions.
5. Putative self-enhancing or self-protective responses have consequences for the experience of emotions, depending on a variety of moderating circumstances.

However, although testifying to the breadth and complexity of the theoretical and research literatures dealing with self and emotions, the review has pointed out a number of lacunae and weaknesses that require attention. Among the more salient issues are the following.

First, theoretical assumptions regarding the roles that emotions or self-feelings play in relationship to other self-referent constructs frequently are only tested piecemeal. For example, research reporting negative feedback in relation to emotional response presumes, but does not evidence, the intervening process of self-evaluation that putatively occurs in response to the perception of failure and rejection signified by the negative feedback. Similarly, reports of a relation between being the object of rejection and the employment of self-protective mechanisms frequently do not demonstrate the intervening processes that are theoretically presumed to occur, namely the evocation of negative self-feelings in response to negative self-evaluations. Ideally, future research would demonstrate the linear relation between self-concept and subsequent self-evaluations moderated by the system of self-values, the relation between self-evaluation and consequent self-feelings, the relation between self-feelings and the adoption of self-protective mechanisms, and the effects of self-protective mechanisms on the experience of self-feelings, the revision of self-evaluative mechanisms, and changes in self-concept (including the expression of emotion), all within the same estimatable model.

Second, in view of the fact that so many studies of emotion depend on self-reports, it is difficult to distinguish between self-cognition or self-evaluation of emotions and the actual experience of emotions. Future research should take advantage of improvements in the measurement of neurophysiological aspects of emotional arousal in order to allow these determinations. For example, higher cortisol responses to stress were observed in the presence of self-conscious emotions of evaluative embarrassment and shame associated with negative self-evaluation than in response to simply being the object of others' attention (Lewis and Ramsay 2002). Further, emotional situations are associated with activation of the neural substrate. For example, recall of disgust situations (relative to recall of emotionally neutral situations) is associated with functional magnetic resonance imaging indications of activation of the insula, hippocampus anterior and posterior singulate cortex, basal ganglia, thalamus, and primary visual cortex (Fitzgerald et al. 2004).

Third, a review of the literature has made it abundantly clear that research will benefit greatly when it is guided by theoretically informed specification of moderators of putative linear relationships. The necessity of offering moderating variables is apparent in the case of Higgins' (1999) self-discrepancy theory, which hypothesizes that discrepancies between self-concept and ideal self-concept are associated with dejection emotions, whereas discrepancies between self-concept and perceived duties or obligations are associated with agitation emotions. In response to empirical studies that do not uniformly confirm these predictions (Tangney et al. 1998), Higgins offered four variables that moderate these relationships: the magnitude, accessibility, importance, and relevance of a self-discrepancy.

Fourth, future research should attempt to resolve the question, once and for all, regarding distress-inducing consequences of positive input for persons with negative self-concepts. Do such experiences lead to anxiety because they pose threats to self-evaluation, as some theorists indicate, or do such experiences evoke distressful emotions because they represent a kind of cognitive dissonance for the person? It should be possible to design studies in which mediating variables that reflect one or the other process could be interpolated so that the preponderance of evidence suggests either a self-protective function of self-criticism or a dissonance-producing consequence of the same situation—that is, perceiving esteem-signifying experiences by low-self-esteem individuals.

Fifth, the greater part of the literature on self and emotion, by far, deals with the antecedents and consequences of distressful self-feelings. In the future, more attention must be given to the circumstances leading to positive emotional response rather than simply the absence of negative emotional response. Is the emotion of joy, for example, predicted by the high subjective probability of imminent approximation of salient self-evaluative standards when it is generally perceived that the outcome is a relatively rare occurrence?

Sixth, and finally, although the literature on the effectiveness of self-enhancing and self-protective mechanisms for regulating the experience of emotions is informative and theoretically provocative, this area (perhaps more than any of the others specified above) requires specification of the theoretical conditions under which particular self-enhancing/self-protective mechanisms effect emotional experiences that are more or less subjectively desirable.

It is hoped that this presentation will suggest to some the utility of viewing the sociopsychology of self-referent behaviors as an organizing framework for the study of emotions that (1) systematically stimulates new research on the antecedents and consequences of emotional experiences and expressions and the moderators of these relationships and (2) provides an organizing framework for the incorporation of the ever-increasing body of theoretical statements and empirical research that are offered with regard to this subject of serious scholarly activity.

In the extreme, self theory(ies) would have it that all emotional states are responses to stimuli that have self-evaluative implications. All stimuli that elicit an emotional state are interpretable in terms of their self-evaluative meaning(s). Further, all emotions are self-referent because they motivate self-enhancing or self-protective responses. In response to negative emotions, individuals are moved (motivated) to respond intrapsychically or behaviorally in ways that directly assuage distress or that permit avoidance of, attacks upon, or reevaluation of the circumstances that instigated negative self-evaluations. Alternatively, the responses instigated by negative self-evaluations might motivate approximation of the self-values to a greater degree than was theretofore experienced. The negative emotions are self-referent, then, insofar as they evoke self-protective or self-enhancing responses.

Were it not for the possibility that such a gesture might be interpreted as a self-aggrandizing mechanism in response to negative self-feelings, one might be moved to challenge scholars in the area to consider whether all of the literature currently subsumed under the sociology of emotion was interpretable in terms of the self-evaluative significance of emotional experiences and expressions, emotional (self-feeling) responses to self-evaluation, emotional (self-feeling) instigation of self-enhancing/self-protective responses, or the consequences of self-enhancing/self-protective mechanisms for emotional self-regulation.

REFERENCES

Arieti, Silvano. 1967. "Some Elements of Cognitive Psychiatry." *American Journal of Psychotherapy* 124: 723–136.

Arkin, Robert M. 1981. "Self-Presentation Styles." Pp. 311–333 in *Impression Management Theory and Social Psychological Research*, edited by J. T. Tedeschi. New York: Academic Press.

Aronson, Elliot. 1969. "The Theory of Cognitive Dissonance: A Current Perspective." Pp. 1–34 in *Advances in Experimental Social Psychology*, edited by L. Berkowitz. New York: Academic.

Barrett, Lisa Feldman. 1996. "Hedonic Tone, Perceived Arousal, and Item Desirability: Three Components of Self-Reported Mood." *Cognition and Emotion* 10: 47–68.

Baumeister, Roy F. 1993. "Understanding the Inner Nature of Low Self-Esteem: Uncertain, Fragile, Protective, and Conflicted." Pp. 201–218 in *Self-Esteem: The Puzzle of Low Self-Regard*, edited by R. F. Baumeister. New York: Plenum.

———. 1997. *Evil. Inside Human Violence and Cruelty*. New York: W. H. Freeman.

Baumeister, Roy F., Karen Dale, and Kristin L. Sommer. 1998. "Freudian Defense Mechanisms and Empirical Findings in Modern Social Psychology: Reaction Formation, Projection, Displacement, Undoing, Isolation, Sublimation, and Denial." *Journal of Personality* 66: 1081–1124.

Baumeister, Roy F., Laura Smart, and Joseph M. Boden. 1996. "Relation of Threatened Egotism to Violence and Aggression: The Dark Side of High Self-Esteem." *Psychological Review* 103: 5–33.

Bentler, Peter M. 1987. "Drug Use and Personality in Adolescence and Young Adulthood: Structural Models with Nonnormal Variables." *Child Development* 58: 65–79.

Bizman, Aharon, Yoel Yinon, and Sharon Krotman. 2001. "Group-Based Emotional Distress: An Extension of Self-Discrepancy Theory." *Personality and Social Psychology Bulletin* 27: 1291–1300.

Blagov, Pavel S., and Jefferson A. Singer. 2004. "Four Dimensions of Self-Defining Memories (Specificity, Meaning, Content, and Affect) and Their Relationships to Self-Restraint, Distress, and Repressive Defensiveness." *Journal of Personality* 72: 481–511.

Blatt, Sidney J., and Susan A. Bers. 1993. "The Sense of Self in Depression: A Psychodynamic Perspective." Pp. 171–210 in *The Self in Emotional Distress: Cognitive and Psychodynamic Perspectives*, edited by Z. V. Segal and S. J. Blatt. New York: Guilford.

Boldero, Jennifer, and Jill Francis. 2000. "The Relation between Self-Discrepancies and Emotion: The Moderating Roles of Self-Guide Importance, Location Relevance, and Social Self-Domain Centrality." *Journal of Personality and Social Psychology* 78: 38–52.

Bourne, Peter G., William M. Coli, and William E. Datel. 1968. "Affect Levels of Special Forces Soldiers under Threat of Attack." *Psychological Reports* 22: 363–366.

Brown, Jonathon D., and Margaret A. Marshall. 2001. "Self-Esteem and Emotion: Some Thoughts about Feelings." *Personality and Social Psychology Bulletin* 27: 575–584.

Buckley, Katherine E., Rachel E. Winkel, and Mark R. Leary. 2004. "Reactions to Acceptance and Rejection: Effects of Level and Sequence of Relational Evaluation." *Journal of Experimental Social Psychology* 40: 14–28.

Burke, Peter J. 1991. "Identity Processes and Social Stress." *American Sociological Review* 56: 836–849.

———. 1996. "Social Identities and Psychosocial Stress." Pp. 141–174 in *Psychosocial Stress: Perspectives on Structure, Theory, Life Course, and Methods*, edited by H. B. Kaplan. Orlando, FL: Academic.

Burke, Peter J., and Jan E. Stets. 1999. "Trust and Commitment through Self-Verification." *Social Psychology Quarterly* 62: 347–360.

Bushman, Brad J., and Roy F. Baumeister. 1998. "Threatened Egotism, Narcissism, Self-Esteem and Direct and Displaced Aggression: Does Self-Love or Self-Hate Lead to Violence?" *Journal of Personality and Social Psychology* 75: 219–229.

Cantor, Nancy, and John F. Kihlstrom. 1986. *Personality and Social Intelligence*. Englewood Cliffs, NJ: Prentice-Hall.

Carlsmith, J. Merrill, Mark R. Lepper, and Thomas Landauer. 1974. "Children's Obedience to Adult Requests: Interactive Effects of Anxiety, Arousal, and Apparent Punitiveness of the Adult." *Journal of Personality and Social Psychology* 30: 822–828.

Cast, Alicia D., and Peter J. Burke. 2002. "A Theory of Self-Esteem." *Social Forces* 80: 1041–1068.

Chrisite, Isreal C., and Bruce H. Friedman. 2004. "Autonomic Specificity of Discrete Emotion and Dimensions of Affective Space: A Multivariate Approach." *International Journal of Psychophysiology* 51: 143–153.

Christensen, P. Niels, Hank Rothgerber, Wendy Wood, and David C. Matz. 2004. "Social Norms and Identity Relevance: A Motivational Approach to Normative Behavior." *Personality and Social Psychology Bulletin* 30: 1295–1309.

Cooley, Charles Horton. 1902. *Human Nature and the Social Order.* New York: Scribner's.

Denzin, Norman K. 1983. "A Note on Emotionality, Self, and Interaction." *American Journal of Sociology* 89: 402–409.

Diener, Ed, and Marissa Diener. 1995. "Cross-Cultural Correlates of Life Satisfaction and Self-Esteem." *Journal of Personality and Social Psychology* 68: 653–663.

Dunkley, David M., and Kirk R. Blankstein. 2000. "Self-Critical Perfectionism, Coping, Hassles, and Current Distress: A Structural Equation Modeling Approach." *Cognitive Therapy and Research* 24: 713–730.

Duval, Shelly, and Robert A. Wicklund. 1972. *A Theory of Objective Self-Awareness.* New York: Academic.

Eisenberg, Nancy, Amanda Cumberland, and Tracy L. Spinrad. 1998. "Parent Socialization of Emotion." *Psychological Inquiry* 9: 241–273.

Ekman, Paul, and Wallance V. Friesen. 1969. "The Repertoire of Nonverbal Behavior: Categories, Origins, Usage, and Coding." *Semiotica* 1: 49–98.

Epstein, Seymour. 1980. "The Self-Concept: A Review and the Proposal of an Integrated Theory of Personality." Pp. 82–132 in *Personality: Basic Aspects and Current Research,* edited by E. Staub. Engelwood Cliffs, NJ: Prentice-Hall.

———. 1993. "Coping Ability, Negative Self-Evaluation, and Overgeneralization: Experiment and Theory." *Journal of Personality and Social Psychology* 62: 826–836.

Fischer, Agneta H. 1999. "The Role of Honour-Related vs. Individualistic Values in Conceptualising Pride, Shame, and Anger: Spanish and Dutch Cultural Prototypes." *Cognition and Emotion* 13: 149–179.

Fitzgerald, Daniel A., Stefan Posse, Gregory J. Moore, Manuel E. Tancer, Pradeep J. Nathan, and K. Luan Phan. 2004. "Natural Correlates of Internally-Generated Disgust via Autobiographical Recall: A Functional Magnetic Resonance Imaging Investigation." *Neuroscience Letters* 370: 91–96.

Fivush, Robyn, Lisa J. Berlin, Jessica McDermott Sales, Jean Mennuti-Washburn, and Jude Cassidy. 2003. "Functions of Parent-Child Reminiscing About Emotionally Negative Events." *Memory* 11: 179–192.

Fox, Nathan A., and Susan D. Calkins. 2003. "The Development of Self-Control of Emotion: Intrinsic and Extrinsic Influences." *Motivation and Emotion* 27: 7–26.

Franks, David D. 2003. "Emotions." Pp. 787–809 in *Handbook of Symbolic Interactionism,* edited by L. T. Reynolds and N. J. Hermann-Kinney. Walnut Creek, CA: Altamira.

Garside, Rula Bayrakdar, and Bonnie Klimes-Dougan. 2002. "Socialization of Discrete Negative Emotions: Gender Differences and Links with Psychological Distress." *Sex Roles* 47: 115–128.

Giddens, Anthony. 1991. *Modernity and Self-Identity: Self and Society in the Late Modern Age.* Stanford, CA: Stanford University Press.

Greenberg, Leslie, S., and Jeremy D. Safran. 1987. *Emotion in Psychotherapy: Affect, Cognition, and the Process of Change.* New York: Guilford.

Harter, Susan. 1986. "Cognitive-Developmental Processes in the Integration of Concepts about Emotions and the Self." *Social Cognition* 4: 119–151.

Hess, Ursula, Sacha Senecal, Gilles Kirouac, Pedro Herrera, Pierre Philipot, and Robert E. Kleck. 2000. "Emotional Expressivity in Men and Women: Stereotypes and Self-Perceptions." *Cognition and Emotion* 14: 609–642.

Hewitt, John P. 1991. *Self and Society: A Symbolic Interactionist Social Psychology.* Boston: Allyn and Bacon.

Higgins, E. Tory. 1987. "Self-Discrepancy: A Theory Relating Self and Affect." *Psychological Review* 94: 319–340.

———. 1999. "When Do Discrepancies Have Specific Relations to Emotions? The Second-Generation Question of Tangney, Niedenthal, Covert, and Barlow (1998)." *Journal of Personality and Social Psychology* 77: 1313–1317.

Higgins, E. Tory, Ruth L. Klein, and Timothy J. Strausman. 1987. "Self Discrepancies: Distinguishing among Self-States, Self-State Conflicts, and Emotional Vulnerabilites." Pp. 173–186 in *Self and Identity: Psychosocial Perspectives,* edited by K. Yardley and T. Honess. New York: Wiley.

Hirt, Edward R., Dolf Zillmann, Grant A. Erickson, and Chris Kennedy. 1992. "Cost and Benefit of Allegiance: Changes in Fans' Self-Ascribed Competencies After Team Victory versus Defeat." *Journal of Personality and Social Psychology* 63: 724–738.

Hochschild, Arlie Russell. 1979. "Emotion Work, Feeling Rules, and Social Structure." *American Journal of Sociology* 85: 551–575.

———. 1983. *The Managed Heart.* Berkeley, CA: University of California Press.

Iyer, Aarti, Colin Wayne Leach, and Faye J. Crosby. 2003. "White Guilt and Racial Compensation: The Benefits and Limits of Self-Focus." *Personality and Social Psychology Bulletin* 29: 117–129.

Jakupcak, Matthew, Kristalyn Salters, Kim L. Gratz, and Lizabeth Roemer. 2003. "Masculinity and Emotionality: An Investigation of Men's Primary and Secondary Emotional Responding." *Sex Roles* 49: 111–120.

James, William. 1890. *The Principle of Psychology*. New York: Holt.

Jeglic, Elizabeth L., Holly A. Vanderhoff, and Peter J. Donovick. 2005. "The Function of Self-Harm Behavior in a Forensic Population." *International Journal of Offender Therapy and Comparative Criminology* 49: 131–142.

Jones, Stephen C. 1973. "Self- and Interpersonal Evaluations: Esteem Theories vs. Consistency Theories." *Psychological Bulletin* 79: 185–199.

Jourard, Sideny M. 1957. "Identification, Parent-Cathexis, and Self-Esteem." *Journal of Consulting Psychology* 21: 375–380.

Kaiser, Cheryl R., Brenda Major, and Shannon K. McCoy. 2004. "Expectations About the Future and the Emotional Consequences of Perceiving Prejudice." *Personality and Social Psychology Bulletin* 30: 173–184.

Kang, Sun-Mee, Phillip R. Shaver, Stanley Sue, Kyung-Hwan Min, and Hauibin Jing. 2003. "Culture-Specific Patterns in the Prediction of Life Satisfaction: Roles of Emotion, Relationship Quality, and Self-Esteem." *Personality and Social Psychology Bulletin* 29: 1596–1608.

Kaplan, Howard B. 1972. "Toward a General Theory of Psychosocial Deviance: The Case of Aggressive Behavior." *Social Science and Medicine* 6: 593–617.

———. 1975. *Self-Attitudes and Deviant Behavior*. Pacific Palisades, CA: Goodyear.

———. 1980. *Deviant Behavior in Defense of Self*. New York: Academic.

———. 1983. *Psychosocial Stress: Trends in Theory and Research*. New York: Academic.

———. 1986. *Social Psychology of Self-Referent Behavior*. New York: Plenum.

———. 1995. "Drugs, Crime, and Other Deviant Adaptations." Pp. 3–46 in *Drugs, Crime, and Other Deviant Adaptations: Longitudinal Studies*, edited by H. B. Kaplan. New York: Plenum.

———. 1996. "Psychosocial Stress from the Perspective of Self Theory." Pp. 175–244 in *Psychological Stress: Perspectives on Structure, Theory, Life Course, and Methods*, edited by H. B. Kaplan. San Deigo, CA: Academic.

Kaplan, Howard B., and Cheng-Hsien Lin. 2000. "Deviant Identity as a Moderator of the Relation between Negative Self-Feelings and Deviant Behavior." *Journal of Early Adolescence* 20: 150–177.

Kaplan, Howard B., and Xiaoru Liu. 2000. "Social Movements as Collective Coping with Spoiled Personal Identites: Intimations from a Panel Study of Changes in the Life Course Between Adolescence and Adulthood." Pp. 215–238 in *Self, Identity, and Social Movements*, edited by S. Stryker, T. J. Owens, and R. W. White. Minneapolis: University of Minnesota Press.

Kaplan, Howard B., Cynthia Robbins, and Steven S. Martin. 1983. "Antecedents of Psychological Distress: Self-Rejection, Deprivation of Social Support, and Life Events." *Journal of Health and Social Behavior* 24: 230–244.

Kernis, Michael H., Bruce D. Grannemann, and Lynda C. Barclay. 1989. "Stability and Level of Self-Esteem as Predictors of Anger Arousal and Hostility." *Journal of Personality and Social Psychology* 56: 1013–1022.

Kiecolt, K. Jill. 2000. "Self-Change and Social Movements." Pp. 110–131 in *Self, Identity, and Social Movements*, edited by S. Stryker, T. J. Owens, and R. W. White. Minneapolis: University of Minnesota Press.

Kiritz, Stewart, and Rudolph H. Moos. 1974. "Psychological Effects by Social Environments." *Psychosomatic Medicine* 36: 96–114.

Kitayama, Shinobu, Hazel Rose Markus, and Masaru Kurokawa. 2000. "Culture, Emotion, and Well-Being: Good Feelings in Japan and the United States." *Cognition and Emotion* 14: 93–124.

Kuiper, Nicholas A., and L. Joan Olinger. 1989. "Stress and Cognitive Vulnerability from Depression: A Self-Worth Contingency Model." Pp. 367–391 in *Advances in the Investigation of Psychological Stress*, edited by R. J. W. Neufeld. New York: Wiley.

Lazar, Ariela. 1999. "Deceiving Oneself of Self-Deceived? On the Formation of Beliefs 'Under the Influence'." *Mind* 108: 265–290.

Lecky, Prescott. 1961. *Self-Consistency: A Theory of Personality*. New York: Shoe String Press.

Lewis, Michael, and Douglas Ramsay. 2002. "Cortisol Response to Embarrassment and Shame." *Child Development* 73: 1034–1045.

Major, Brenda, Cheryl R. Kaiser, and Shannon K. McCoy. 2003. "It's Not My Fault: When and Why Attributions to Prejudice Protect Self-Esteem." *Personality and Social Psychology Bulletin* 29: 772–781.

Mandel, David R. 2003. "Counterfactuals, Emotions, and Context." *Cognition and Emotion* 17: 139–159.

March, John S. 1990. "The Nosology of Posttraumatic Stress Disorder." *Journal of Anxiety Disorders* 4: 61–82.

Markus, Hazel, and Paula Nurius. 1987. "Possible Selves." Pp. 157–172 in *Self and Identity: Psychosocial Perspectives*, edited by K. M. Yardley and T. M. Honess. New York: Wiley.

May, Rollo. 1980. "Value Conflicts and Anxiety." Pp. 241–248 in *Handbook on Stress and Anxiety*, edited by I. L. Kutash and L. B. Schlesinger. San Francisco: Jossey-Bass.

McCoy, Shannon K., and Brenda Major. 2003. "Group Identification Moderates Emotional Responses to Perceived Prejudice." *Personality and Social Psychology Bulletin* 29: 1005–1017.

McNally, Richard J. 1993. "Self-Representation in Post-Traumatic Stress Disorder: A Cognitive Perspective." Pp. 71–91 in *The Self in Emotional Distress: Cognitive and Psychodynamic Perspectives*, edited by Z. V. Segal and S. J. Blatt. New York: Guilford.

Mendolia, Marilyn. 2002. "An Index of Self-Regulation of Emotion and the Study of Repression in Social Contexts that Threaten or Do Not Threaten Self-Concept." *Emotion* 2: 215–232.

Mineka, Susan, David Watson, and Lee Anna Clark. 1998. "Comorbidity of Anxiety and Unipolar Mood Disorders." *Annual Review of Psychology* 49: 377–412.

Muris, Peter, Henk Schmidt, Harald Merckelbach, and Erik Schouten. 2001. "The Structure of Negative Emotions in Adolescents." *Journal of Abnormal Child Psychology* 29: 331–337.

Newcomb, Michael D., and Peter M. Bentler. 1988. *Consequences of Adolescent Drug Use: Impact on the Lives of Young Adults*. New York: Sage.

Olson, James M., Carolyn L. Hafer, April Couzens, and Inese Kramins. 2000. "You're OK, I'm OK: The Self-Presentation of Affective Reactions to Deprivation." *Social Justice Research* 13: 361–374.

Oyserman, Daphna, Heather M. Coon, and Markus Kemmelmeier. 2002. "Rethinking Individualism and Collectivism: Evaluation of Theoretical Assumptions and Meta-Analysis." *Psychological Bulletin* 128: 3–72.

Plant, E. Ashby, and Patricia G. Devine. 1998. "Internal and External Motivation to Respond Without Prejudice." *Journal of Personality and Social Psychology* 75: 811–832.

Prapavessis, Harry, Robert J. Grove, Ralph Maddison, and Nadine Zillmann. 2003. "Self-Handicapping Tendencies, Coping, and Anxiety Responses Among Athletes." *Psychology of Sport and Exercise* 4: 357–375.

Rhodewalt, F., and C. C. Morf. 1998. "On Self-Aggrandizement and Anger: A Temporal Analysis of Narcissism and Affective Reactions to Success and Failure." *Journal of Personality and Social Psychology* 74: 672–685.

Roberts, Tomi-Ann. 2004. "Female Trouble: The Menstrual Self-Evaluation Scale and Women's Self-Objectification." *Psychology of Women Quarterly* 28: 22–26.

Rokeach, Milton. 1983. "A Value Approach to the Prevention and Reduction of Drug Abuse." Pp. 172–192 in *Preventing Adolescent Drug Abuse: Intervention Strategeies. Research Monograph Series 47*, edited by T. J. Glynn, C. G. Leukefeld, and J. P. Ludford. Rockville, MD: National Institute on Drug Abuse.

Rosenberg, Morris. 1965. *Society and the Adolescent Self-Image*. Princeton, NJ: Princeton University Press.

Rubin, Robert T. 1974. "Biochemical and Neuroendocrine Responses to Severe Psychological Stress: 1. U.S. Navy Aviator Study, 2. Some General Observations." Pp. 227–274 in *Life Stress and Illness*, edited by E. K. E. Gunderson and R. H. Rahe Springfield, IL: Charles C Thomas.

Sabini, John, Brian Garvey, and Amanda L. Hall. 2001. "Shame and Embarrassment Revisited." *Personality and Social Psychology Bulletin* 27: 104–117.

Scheff, Thomas J., Suzane M. Retzinger, and Michael T. Ryan. 1989. "Crime, Violence, and Self-Esteem: Review and Proposals." Pp. 165–199 in *The Social Importance of Self-Esteem*, edited by A. M. Mecca, N. J. Smelser, and J. Vasconcellos. Berkeley: University of California Press.

Scheier, Michael F., and Charles S. Carver. 1982. "Cognition, Affect, and Self-Regulation." Pp. 157–183 in *Affect and Cognition: The Seventeenth Annual Carnegie Symposium on Cognition*, edited by M. S. Clark and S. T. Fiske. Hillsdale, NJ: Erlbaum.

Shields, Stephanie A. 2005. "The Politics of Emotion in Everyday Life: 'Appropriate' Emotion and Claims of Identity." *Review of General Psychology* 9: 3–15.

Steele, Claude M. 1988. "The Psychology of Self-Affirmation: Sustaining the Integrity of Self." Pp. 261–302 in *Advances in Experimental Social Psychology*, edited by L. Berkowitz. New York: Academic.

Steele, Claude M., Steven J. Spencer, and Michael Lynch. 1993. "Self-Image Resilience and Dissonance: The Role of Affirmational Resources." *Journal of Personality and Social Psychology* 64: 885–896.

Stets, Jan E. 2005. "Examining Emotions in Identity Theory." *Social Psychology Quarterly* 68: 39–56.

Stets, Jan E., and Teresa M. Tsushima. 2001. "Negative Emotion and Coping Responses Within Identity Control Theory." *Social Psychology Quarterly* 64: 283–295.

Strauman, Timothy J., and E. Tory Higgins. 1993. "The Self Construct in Social Cognition: Past Present and Future." Pp. 3–40 in *The Self in Emotional Distress*, edited by Z. V. Segal and S. J. Blatt. New York: Guilford.

Stryker, Sheldon. 1968. "Identity Salience and Role Performance: The Relevance of Symbolic Interaction Theory for Family Research." *Journal of Marriage and the Family* 30: 558–564.

———. 2004. "Integrating Emotion into Identity Theory." *Theory and Research on Human Emotions Advances in Group Processes* 21: 1–23.

Stucke, Tanja S., and Sigfreid L. Sporer. 2002. "When a Grandiose Self-Image Is Threatened: Narcissism and Self-Concept Clarity as Predictors of Negative Emotions and Aggression Following Ego Threat." *Journal of Personality* 70: 509–532.

Swann, W. B., Jr. 1983. "Self-Verification: Bringing Social Reality Into Harmony with the Self." Pp. 33–66 in *Social Psychological Perspectives on the Self*, edited by J. Suls and A. G. Greenwald. Hillside, NJ: Erlbaum.

Swiatek, Mary Ann. 2001. "Social Coping among Gifted High School Students and Its Relationship to Self-Concept." *Journal of Youth and Adolescence* 30: 19–39.

Tangney, June Price, and Kurt Fischer. 1995. *The Psychology of Shame, Guilt, Embarrassment, and Pride.* New York: Guilford.

Tagney, June Price, Paula M. Niedenthal, Michelle Vowell Covert, and Deborah Hill Barlow. 1998. "Are Shame and Guilt Related to Distinct Self-Discrepancies?: A Test of Higgin's (1987) Hypotheses." *Journal of Personality and Social Psychology* 75: 256–268.

Taylor, Verta. 2000. "Emotions and Identity in Women's Self-Help Movements." Pp. 271–299 in *Self, Identity, and Social Movements*, edited by S. Stryker, T. J. Owens, and R. W. White. Minneapolis: University of Minnesota Press.

Tesser, Abraham. 1986. "Some Effects of Self-Evaluation Maintenance on Cognition and Action." Pp. 435–464 in *Handbook of Motivation and Cognition: Foundations of Social Behavior*, edited by R. M. Sorrentino and E. T. Higgins. New York: Wiley.

Thoits, Peggy A. 1985. "Self-Labeling Processes in Mental Illness: The Role of Emotional Deviance." *American Journal of Sociology* 92: 221–249.

Twenge, Jean M., and W. Keith Campbell. 2003. "Isn't It Fun to Get the Respect that We're Going to Deserve?" Narcissism, Social Rejection, and Aggression." *Personality and Social Psychology Bulletin* 29: 261–272.

Twenge, Jean M., Kathleen R. Catanese, and Roy F. Baumeister. 2003. "Social Exclusion and the Deconstructed State: Time Perception, Meaninglessness, Lethargy, Lack of Emotion, and Self-Awareness." *Journal of Personality and Social Psychology* 85: 409–423.

Weiner, Bernard. 1986. "Cognition, Emotion, and Action." Pp. 281–312 in *Handbook of Motivation and Cognition: Foundations of Social Behavior*, edited by E. Tory Higgins and Richard M. Sorrentino. New York: Guilford.

Whelton, William J., and Leslie S. Greenberg. 2005. "Emotion in Self-Criticism." *Personality and Individual Differences* 38: 1583–1595.

Zeman, Janice, and Judy Garber. 1996. "Display Rules for Anger, Sadness, and Pain: It Depends on Who Is Watching." *Child Development* 67: 957–973.

CHAPTER 11

Emotion-Based Self Theory

DAVID BOYNS

The self has been a long-standing topic of investigation within sociology. Supported by the original work of Mead (1934), sociologists have sought to examine the self, its internal structure, and its relationship to interpersonal processes. Although significant progress has been made toward a rich understanding of the development and structure of the self, only in recent decades have emotions been significantly incorporated into these sociological investigations. The emergence of the sociology of emotions in the late 1970s has been a boom for the study of self. Although a comprehensive theory of the self has not yet been developed that incorporates emotions as a central component of self-based processes, advances in the study of emotions have provided the foundational groundwork necessary for such an endeavor.

This chapter reviews the growing body of investigations that have collectively begun to articulate theoretical links between emotional processes and the self and is organized into three sections. First, sociological perspectives of the self are outlined, highlighting the recent efforts to remedy the cognitive bias that has inhered in the study of the self. Second, the study of emotions is examined along two basic dimensions divided between intrapersonal-interpersonal and positivist-constructivist approaches. The unification of emotions and the self is described as emerging at the intersection of these two dimensions. Finally, an outline of the theoretical and empirical work in the study of emotions that has initiated a foundation for a comprehensive theory of emotions and the self is developed. These efforts are explored using the intrapersonal-interpersonal/positivist-constructivist framework articulated in the first section. Overall, it is contended that the study of emotional processes has revealed not only that emotional experiences are deeply related to the construction and organization of the self but, moreover, that the self has an intrinsically emotional foundation.

DAVID BOYNS • Department of Sociology, California State University, Northridge, CA 91330

SOCIOLOGICAL APPROACHES TO THE SELF

Sociological approaches to the self are largely indebted to the work of George Herbert Mead (1934). Premised on a conceptualization of the human being that is fundamentally social, Mead's theory describes a self that is intrinsically a product of social interaction. The symbolic interactionists that have followed Mead's approach (e.g., Blumer 1969; Burke 1991; Kuhn 1964; Rosenberg 1979, 1990, 1991, 1992; Stryker 1980, 1987, 1989, 1992; Wiley 1994) have developed and refined his theory of the self and, in doing so, have generally remained true to Mead's initial ideas. However, although Mead's theory has laid the groundwork for sociological understandings of the self, recent efforts have contested the overly cognitive nature of his approach. Some have sought to elaborate Mead's theory by incorporating the study of emotions as a unique dimension of social interaction (Collins 1981, 2004; Goffman 1967; Hochschild 1979, 1983; Shott 1979). Others have attempted to develop a theory of self that contains emotional processes as a central component (Burke 1991, 1996; Denzin 1983, 1984; Johnson 1992; Rosenberg 1990, 1991; Scheff 1983, 1988, 1990, 1996; Stryker 1987, 2004). Collectively, these efforts have steered sociological investigations toward the development of a theory of the self that is fundamentally emotional and have exposed important limitations in the history of sociological investigations that stem from Mead's original work.

Sociological Theories of the Self

Mead's (1934) theory of mind, self, and symbolic interaction has generally laid the foundation for sociological investigations into the self. Drawing on the idea that one of the primary markers of human evolution is the ability to create and exchange language and symbols, Mead's theory suggests that the development of linguistic faculties provides the basis for the human capacity to acquire a sense of self. Although Mead's insight that language is central to the development of the self has been roundly embraced within sociology, it has also led to an almost exclusive emphasis on cognition in the study of the self. In his theory, Mead clearly emphasized the cognitive capacity of human beings over their emotional facilities, asserting that "self consciousness rather than affective experience . . . provides the core and primary structure of the self, which is thus essentially a cognitive rather than an emotional phenomenon" (1934:173). Although Mead created many openings for the introduction of emotional dynamics into his general theoretical approach, particularly in his theory of the act (Mead 1895, 1938), his theory of the self is almost exclusively cognitive.

As Mead conceptualized it, the self has two primary dimensions. On the one hand, it is a reflexive process organized externally through reflective role-taking with others and is manifested internally in the course of self-based ruminative processes. This dimension of the self describes the cognitive dynamics through which individuals monitor the reflective appraisals of others and respond to them imaginatively by envisioning themselves from another's perspective and rehearsing alternative courses of action. On the other hand, the self also represents an individual's understanding of itself as a stable and coherent object in the world and as a sense of self-identity. Here, Mead suggested that individuals crystallize a set of self-conceptions that they acquire throughout the course of role-taking with others. In short, Mead's theory describes the self as both a reflexive process as well as a structured and internalized set of self-conceptions.

For Mead, reflexivity and the ability to create self-conceptions are intimately interrelated. Reflexivity is the basis from which the self can emerge and change through time, whereas self-conceptualization allows individuals to create a coherent sense of their "self" and provides an anchor from which self-reflexivity can occur. In Mead's theory, the self is a structured social process of self-conceptualization that takes shape as individuals develop the capacity for self-reflexivity, abstracting from and responding to themselves as objects. He summarized this point by suggesting that "the individual is not a self in the reflexive sense unless he is an object to himself" (Mead 1934:142). According to Mead, reflexivity and self-conceptualization are the central, socially acquired abilities that combine to provide the sociological architecture for the self.

Mead argued that these key aspects of the self-reflexivity and self-conceptualization are orchestrated through the interrelationship of two phases of the self, the "I" and the "me." On the one hand, the "me" is a cognitive sense of self-identity that characterizes how an individual comes to understand him or herself as an object in the world. On the other hand, the "I" is the unpredictable, active part of the self that is largely responsible for the emergence of social change and innovation in interaction. Whereas the "me" is the knowable self, the "I" is the "intra-personal blind spot" of the "me," and it is that aspect of the self which is of the immediate moment and not yet open to reflexive awareness (Mead 1934; Wiley 1994:45). Mead's theory of the alternating phases of the "I" and the "me" has produced a conception of self that embodies a duality of both process and structure.

The tension between process and structure in Mead's theory has created a fertile basis for the sociological study of the self. The "I" is conceptualized as the active self continually involved in a reflexive process that develops and changes through interaction (Mead 1934:136–137, 178). Alternatively, the "me" is the self as a "social structure" (Mead 1934:140, 144, 166) organized around a stable set of self-conceptions that combine to form a "unity of self." The development of the Chicago and Iowa traditions of symbolic interactionism—the former historically represented by the works of Blumer (1969) and the latter by the works of Kuhn (1964) and Stryker (1980)—have served to articulate these differences. Whereas Blumer has maintained that the self is a fluid, interpretive process that emerges through social interaction, Kuhn and Stryker have argued that the self is relatively stable, structured, and organized.

These processual and structural notions of the social self have resulted in the development of two interrelated but distinct traditions of theory and research. Some argue that individuals cultivate a much more fluid sense of self composed of the multiplicity of identities that emerge as a product of the unique situational expectations of a given social interaction (Alexander and Lauderdale 1977; Alexander and Wiley 1992; Blumer 1969; Goffman 1959; Wiley and Alexander 1987; Zurcher 1977). Others contend that individuals embody a transsituational "core-self" that is composed of hierarchically arranged social identities organized and structured in terms of salience, prominence, and commitment (Burke 1991, 1996; Kuhn and McPartland 1954; Rosenberg 1979; Serpe 1987; Stryker 1980, 1987, 1992; Stryker and Serpe 1982, 1994; Turner 2002). However, until the mid-1980s, both of these traditions of theory and research into the self echoed the cognitive bias inherent in Mead's approach. It has only been in recent decades that emotional processes have been directly and centrally integrated into the sociological investigations of the self.

The Cognitive Bias of Sociological Approaches to the Self

Contemporary sociologists have sought to reintegrate emotions into Mead's model of the self and social interaction. However, few have developed a theory that incorporates emotions as a central element of the self (for exceptions, see Burke 1991, 1996; Denzin 1983, 1984, 1985;

Gordon 1989; Johnson 1992; Scheff 1988, 1996; Stryker 1987, 2004; Turner 2002; Wiley 1994). The slow movement toward the development of a comprehensive theory of the self that centrally embodies emotional dynamics is likely the result of the wide range of sociological investigations that have drawn the analysis of emotions away from the subjective and corporal experience of the individual and into the arena of social interaction. Here, variables such as ritual (Collins 1981, 1984, 1990, 2004; Goffman 1967; Scheff 1977, 1979), status and power relationships (Kemper 1978, 1984, 1991; Kemper and Collins 1990), negotiation of the definition of the situation (Gordon 1992; McCarthy 1989; Shott 1979), emotional management and self-regulation (Hochschild 1979, 1983; Rosenberg 1991), and the evaluation, potency, and activity (EPA) of emotions (Heise 1979, 1987; Heise and Thomas 1989; Morgan and Heise 1988; Smith-Lovin 1991; Smith-Lovin and Heise 1988) have been analyzed to determine their effects on emotional states and responses.

By outlining the sociological processes that circumscribe emotions, sociologists have broadly increased knowledge about emotions and have largely avoided the reduction of the study of affect to physiological or subjective processes. However, such sociological efforts have also moved the study of emotions away from the individual and, by default, from the self as a locus of emotional investigation. Exceptions to this trend are found in the works of Scheff (1977, 1979, 1988, 1990, 1996) and Turner (2002), who have explored the intrapersonal dynamics of emotions from a sociological perspective. Scheff's psychodynamic approach has been the most relevant for interfacing emotional processes and the self, as he has elaborated the fine details of body-based affective expressions and unconscious emotional processes and their roles in the development of the self. His study of the dynamics of self-based emotions like pride and shame, has contributed considerably toward the establishment of an emotionally grounded notion of the self. Scheff's work, complemented by a growing number of investigations, demonstrates that individuals do not only make self-evaluations and assessments of their self-conceptions on a cognitive level but also evaluate and assess their identities and actions with respect to self-feelings. His theory, and those who have developed parallel arguments, has exposed an overly cognitive emphasis as one of most serious limitations of sociological theories of the self.

The excessively cognitive conceptualization of the self has been increasingly recognized by sociologists, with many identifying it as a result of the undertheorization of Mead's notion of the "I" and a complementary failure to expand upon Cooley's (1902) notion of "self-feeling" (Bolton 1981; Hochschild 1983; Lewis 1979; Wiley 1994). However, even those sociological theories of the self that reflect an explicit emphasis on the "I" (e.g., Blumer 1969) have also tended to embody an almost exclusively cognitive orientation.

Although most sociological theories of the self have adopted Mead's cognitive framework and emphasized his notion of the "me," insights from the sociology of emotions have begun to offset this cognitive emphasis and demonstrated that emotions play a central role in the process and structure of the self. Two strands of theory and research have helped to connect emotions to the sociological study of the self. The first has contended that language is not the only medium by which the self is reflexively organized and that emotions are also intimately related to the reflexive process of the self (Gordon 1989:115, 120–123; Rosenberg 1990; Scheff 1990; Shott 1979; Tangey and Fischer 1995; Wiley 1994). For example, a specific set of emotions (e.g., pride, shame embarrassment, vanity) has been identified as "self-conscious emotions" that are intrinsically interrelated with the self (Tangey and Fischer 1995). Shott (1979) has defined such emotions as "role-taking emotions," suggesting that they emerge as a result of emotionally reflexive assessments of the identities and actions of both self and other.

The second strand of theory has explored the organization of self-conceptions and has demonstrated that the internal composition of the self is not simply ordered through cognitive processes, but is also arranged with respect to emotional valences attached to cognitions (Burke 1991, 1996;

Stets 2004, 2005; Stryker 1987, 2004). For instance, research into identity theory (e.g., Stryker 2004) has revealed that emotions play a central role in the organization and verification of identities. Challenges levied against highly salient identities are found to be much more likely to produce negative emotional responses. Additionally, identity control theory has discovered that the interpersonal verification of salient identities is likely to produce positive affect, whereas nonverification results in negative emotions (Burke 1991, 1996).

Such studies have established a firm conceptual foothold for an elaboration of a sociological theory of the self that is centrally organized around emotional processes. Collectively, this work has been based on three premises: first, that a thorough-going theory of the self needs to embody both emotional and cognitive dimensions; second, that a sociological conception of the self should theorize the intimate interrelationships between the cognitive and emotional dimensions of the self in the study of both the reflexive construction of the self as well as the structure of self-conceptions; and finally, that the cognitive and emotional dynamics of the self should be seen as fundamental to both intrapersonal and interpersonal dimensions of human interaction. It is the idea of an emotional dimension to the self that seeks not only to enrich sociological investigations into self-based processes but also to enhance the study of emotions within sociology.

LOCATING THE EMOTION-BASED SELF IN THE SOCIOLOGY OF EMOTIONS

Approaches to the study of emotions generally fall along two different dimensions. The first dimension represents those works that have sought to answer the question of where emotions are to be found and to define the proper unit of analysis for their examination. Generally, these investigations emphasize either *intrapersonal*, psychological, and subjective processes, or *interpersonal*, cultural, and social dynamics. The second dimension characterizes works that have explored epistemological issues and addresses the problem of how emotions are to be conceptualized and investigated. Here, emotions are typically approached either from a *positivistic* perspective, which focuses on the invariant biological and social structural properties of emotional dynamics, or from a *constructivist* perspective, which describes emotions as cultural, interpersonal, and interpretive social constructions. In the discussion that follows, these two dimensions of emotions will be summarized, their intersections articulated, and their respective roles outlined in developing an understanding of an emotion-based self.

Analytic Dimensions of Emotions

There is a long-standing tradition of the theory and research into emotions that has emphasized psychological and intrapersonal processes like neurophysiology (Damasio 1994; Jauregui 1995; LeDoux 1996; Simonov 1986), cognition (Ortony et al. 1988), phylogenetic expression (Darwin 1872; Ekman 1973, 1982; Izard 1971), evolutionary history (Turner 1996, 2000; Wentworth and Yardly 1994), and subjective experience (Denzin 1984, 1985; James 1950; Sartre 1962). These investigations have explored emotions as body-based phenomena, with the biological individual as the primary locus of emotional processes, and have been traditionally established as the principal foundation for the study of emotions. However, recent efforts have sought to articulate the interpersonal aspects of emotional dynamics and have suggested that emotions are not uniquely reducible to intrapersonal, or bodily, phenomena but have a highly salient interpersonal dimension as well (e.g., Collins 1981, 1984, 1990, 1993, 2004; Goffman 1967; Heise 1979, 1987;

Hochschild 1979, 1983; Kemper 1978, 1991; Kemper and Collins 1990; Schachter and Singer 1962; Smith-Lovin and Heise 1988). Several theorists have highlighted the analytic tension between the intrapersonal and interpersonal dimensions of emotions (Gordon 1985; Scheff 1983, 1988), but few have sought to develop an approach that explicitly seeks to integrate the two.

In addition to the intrapersonal-interpersonal dimension, the study of emotions has been divided epistemologically in terms of the problem of how emotions are to be conceptualized. Here, the question has been posed as to whether emotions can be most effectively studied through *positivist* or *constructivist* approaches (Kemper 1981; see Ratner, 1989, and Scheff, 1988, for parallel distinctions). Those taking a positivistic perspective contend that emotions are primarily the product of the structure of social situations (Heise 1979, 1987; Kemper 1978, 1991; Kemper and Collins 1990; Smith-Lovin and Heise 1988) and are often conceptualized as expressions of innate primary emotions (Izard 1977; Kemper 1987; Plutchik 1991). Those following the constructivist approach suggest that there are culture-specific "feeling rules" that must be negotiated (Goffman 1959, 1967; Gordon 1989, 1990; Hochschild 1979, 1983), limiting the emotional responses that are deemed appropriate for expression in a given sociocultural context. Emotions, here, are seen as social constructions, the result of subjective as well as culturally circumscribed definitions of situations and appraisals (Arnold 1960; Denzin 1984, 1985; Gordon 1989, 1990, 1992; McCarthy 1989; Sartre 1962; Schachter and Singer 1962; Scherer 2001; Shott 1979).

These two dimensions, intrapersonal-interpersonal and positivist-constructivist, have established a categorical framework for conceptualizing the various approaches to emotions. Ideally, a comprehensive approach to the study of emotions would seek to incorporate synthetically both the intrapersonal-interpersonal and the positivist-constructivist dimensions, simultaneously conceptualizing emotions as outcomes of biological and social structural processes, as well as defining them as constructed through cultural and situational definitions. Figure 11.1 outlines the intersections of these dimensions of emotion and depicts some of the key works that have played a prominent role in articulating the central distinctions in the study of emotions.

As illustrated in Figure 11.1, the intersection of the intrapersonal-interpersonal and the positivist-constructivist dimensions produces four domains that provide a general map for the study of emotions: intrapersonal-positivist (Quadrant I), interpersonal-positivist (Quadrant II), intrapersonal-constructivist (Quadrant III), and interpersonal-constructivist (Quadrant IV). Typically, psychological approaches have emphasized the intrapersonal and subjective aspects of emotions (Quadrants I and III), whereas sociological approaches have focused on the interpersonal, structural, interpretive, and cultural aspects of emotions (Quadrants II and IV). It is at the central intersection point of the four quadrants that a theory of the self has begun to emerge that embodies emotions as a central dynamic.

Ideally, a comprehensive and inclusive theory of emotions and the self would find itself located in the middle of Figure 11.1, incorporating both the intrapersonal and interpersonal dimensions of emotions, as well as accounting for both positivist and constructivist approaches. Emotions are biological phenomena (Quadrant I) that are often circumscribed by individual interpretation (Quadrant III); they are also the products of the structure of social situations (Quadrant II), oftentimes negotiated by the actors involved and subject to the flexibility and variation expressed in the rules of different cultures of emotion (Quadrant IV).

Contemporary investigations into the sociology of emotions have begun to articulate a theory of the self as a theoretical linchpin that finds its expression at the intersection of these diverse dimensions of the study of emotion. Although sociological theories of the self have been clear in their examination of the interpersonal processes that circumscribe the formation and development of the self, they have only recently begun to incorporate emotions as a central, theoretical dimension. Encouraged by the observation that many emotions are clearly self-based processes,

POSITIVIST

(emotions as products of biological and social structural processes)

I.   II.

Damasio (1994, 1999)   Burke (1996)
Darwin (1872)   Collins (1981, 1984, 1990, 1993, 2004)
Ekman (1973, 1982)   Heise (1979, 1987)
Ekman et al. (1972)   Kemper (1978, 1984, 1987, 1991)
Izard (1971, 1977)   Kemper and Collins (1990)
LeDoux (1996)   Lawler (2001)
Plutchik (1991)   Smith-Lovin (1991)
Scheff (1977, 1979, 1983, 1988, 1996)   Smith-Lovin and Heise (1988)
Simonov (1986)   Stets (2004, 2005)
Turner (1996, 2000, 2002)   Stryker (1987, 2004)

─────────── the self ───────────

INTRAPERSONAL   **INTERPERSONAL**

Arnold (1960)   Armon-Jones (1985, 1986)
Denzin (1983, 1984, 1985)   Averill (1980)
Frijda (1986)   Goffman (1959, 1967)
Lazarus (1984)   Gordon (1989, 1990)
Ortony et al. (1988)   Harre (1986)
Ratner (1989)   Hochschild (1979, 1983)
Sartre (1962)   Markus and Kitayama (1991, 1994)
Schachter and Singer (1962)   McCarthy (1989, 1994)
Scherer (2001)   Shott (1979)
Wiley (1994)

III.   IV.

CONSTRUCTIVIST

(emotions as cultural and processual)

FIGURE 11.1. Dimensions of the Study of Emotions

recent investigations have established a strong theoretical interconnection between emotions and the self and have begun to weave a theory that unites the two. It is toward the conceptualization of this emotion-based self to which we now turn.

Intrapersonal-Positivist Dimensions of Emotions and the Self

The theory and research represented in this domain emphasize the biological, evolutionary, and psychodynamic dimensions of emotions. Following the early work of Darwin (1872), an impressive tradition of research has emerged that seeks to explain the evolutionary role that emotions play in human social interaction. These works are premised upon Darwin's postulate that there are a set of biologically innate emotions and has sought to examine these differentiated, primary emotions (Izard 1977; Plutchik 1991), their expressions in the human face (Ekman 1973, 1982; Izard 1971), and their role in the evolutionary history of human sociality (Turner 1996, 2000; Wentworth and Yardly 1994). Several theoretical efforts have been made toward delineating the number and nature of primary emotions and the larger function that they play in emotional processes. For instance, Kemper (1987) argued that there are 4 primary emotions (fear, anger, disgust, and satisfaction) Plutchik (1991) contended that there are 8 (fear, anger, sadness, joy, acceptance, disgust, anticipation, and astonishment), Ekman (1973) described 6 (fear, anger, sadness, happiness, disgust, and surprise), and Izard (1971, 1977) listed 10 (fear, anger, enjoyment, interest, disgust, surprise, shame, contempt, distress, and guilt). Furthermore, some argue that these sets of primary emotions are the building blocks for more elaborate and complex emotions (Kemper 1987; Plutchik 1991; Turner 1996, 2000) and can develop into "master emotions," like shame, that provide the essence of group bonds, social control, and social solidarity (Scheff 1983, 1988, 1990, 1996).

The driving force behind these investigations into primary emotions, however, is the premise that human beings are motivated by fundamental emotional processes that are evolutionarily innate (Darwin 1872; Turner 1996, 2000). Primary emotions, this tradition of research suggests, might also provide the foundation for cognitive processes, memory, and decision-making (Damasio 1994; Jauregui 1995; LeDoux 1996; Simonov 1986) and supply the evolutionary basis for a "deep sociality" (Turner 1996, 2000; Wentworth and Yardly 1994). Generally, this tradition of research examines the biological basis for human emotions and their physical expression, seeking to unravel the universal foundation of emotions as intrapersonal processes.

Such theoretical and empirical studies into the biological basis of emotional experience have provided compelling evidence for an interface between emotions and the self. Central to these investigations has been the collective conclusion that emotions are instrumental in the development and organization of cognitive processes (Damasio 1994, 1999; Jauregui 1995; LeDoux, 1996; Simonov 1986). On a general level, this body of work suggests that emotions provide the neurophysiological foundation for cognition, with both memory and self-consciousness being neurologically structured around emotional processes. The basic premises of these studies have been complemented by research in developmental psychology (Hobson 2004; Sroufe 1984, 1997; Trevarthen 1984) and exploratory theories of the evolutionary social history of human beings (Turner 2000; Wentworth and Yardly 1994). As a whole, these research efforts have revealed that the physiological basis of human emotions is a biological substrate for the social psychological development of infants and for the general emergence of human sociality.

The research within this intrapersonal-positivist domain has contributed significantly to the sociological understanding of the self by establishing empirical evidence for the idea that there is an emotional foundation for cognitive processes. For example, studies into evolutionary biology have demonstrated that the cerebral cortex, which organizes cognition and language-based reasoning, is an evolutionary extension of preexisting brain structures centered in the limbic system, that part of the brain that stores and regulates emotional processes (Damasio 1994; LeDoux 1996; Turner 1996, 2000). These insights have revealed not only that the cognitive processes of human beings are neurologically hardwired in the emotional organization of the brain but, moreover, that the linguistic faculties that Mead has argued are instrumental to the self are intrinsically interrelated with emotions.

Turner (2000) expanded this set of ideas and theorized that the history of human social organization is an extension of the evolutionary selection processes that favored those early hominids who were able to both expand and regulate the primary emotions necessary for survival (e.g., anger, fear, surprise) and develop the complex emotions (e.g., pride, shame, gratitude, remorse) central to maintaining group solidarity. He contended that emotions composed a fundamental aspect of the fabric of the group life of early hominids and that it is likely the first system of communication among the evolutionary ancestors of human beings was based on a language of emotion, not words. Turner argued that higher-order cognitive processes, like language, emerged as elaborations of a preexisting emotion-based language. Among early hominids, this emotional language not only provided a mechanism for communication, signaling systems, and ultimately survival, but it also created a "deep sociality" (Wentworth and Yardly 1994) among hominids that finds expression in a broad arrangement of the forms of human social organization.

Although Turner's argument was largely speculative, it does find some confirmation in the literature within developmental psychology that has investigated the role of emotions in establishing interpersonal bonds between infants and their primary caregivers. A growing body of research (e.g., Hobson 2004; Sroufe 1984, 1997; Trevarthen 1984) has demonstrated the existence of something like a "deep sociality" that appears to be hardwired into human infants and is manifest in the emotional interactions between neonates and adults. A number of studies have suggested that these emotional interactions have an interpersonal reflexivity that is the foundation for the development of social attachments between infants and caregivers (for examples, see Sroufe 1984; Trevarthen 1984). In addition, and perhaps more important, these studies also indicate that neonatal emotional relationships play a crucial role in the development of intersubjective awareness and, ultimately, in the acquisition of language.

Collectively, this research in developmental psychology has discovered that infants engage in what might be called a form of "primitive role-taking" through the reflexive exchange of emotions that orchestrate feeling-based communication with others. Trevarthen (1984:142) made this point explicit, writing that:

> detailed descriptions of the expressive behavior of infants in interaction with their mothers produce abundant evidence that both mother and infant are perceiving affect in each other, and that both of them also mirror what they perceive by complementary generation of affective responses within themselves.

He argued that these emotional exchanges, when enacted through time, not only come to define an infant's intersubjective relations with others but, also, reflect a more stable sense of self-identity (Trevarthen 1984:136). Such results have led to the inference that interactions between caregivers and infants are primarily emotion based and serve to facilitate the formation of secure relationships and social attachments later in life. Additionally, these conclusions suggest that not only do emotional interactions provide the foundation for the development of a sense of self, but, also, that in the process of the development of a consciousness of self, self-based feelings precede the development of self-conceptions (Sroufe 1984).

Damasio's (1994, 1999) work brings together these lines of research. He argued that emotional and cognitive processes are interdependent and that normal reasoning processes cannot occur unless they are underpinned by emotions. Here, Damasio suggested that emotions are the underlying foundation for memory, decision-making, and language and that the cognitive processes that inhabit the neocortex have a foundation in the emotion centers of the brain. His review of cases of brain abnormalities (due to accidents, disease, tumors, and so forth) that have resulted in damage to the regions of the brain that are primarily responsible for emotions provides compelling evidence for the interdependence of emotion and cognition and supports the conclusion that biologically based emotional processes are the foundation of cognition. Thus, Damasio argued that individuals who have impaired limbic systems have significant cognitive incapacities and frequently manifest that inability to use language and reason to make rational decisions.

However, Damasio took his argument further. He contended that not only is cognition intimately tied to emotion; the self is also fundamentally connected to body-based feelings. Damasio (1999) envisioned three "layers" to the self, which he respectively labeled the "proto-self," the "core self," and the "autobiographical self." The proto-self is the nonconscious dimension of the self (much like Mead's "I") that is characterized by the collection of feelings and neural reactions that an individual experiences at a given moment. Emotions play a significant role in the manifestation of the proto-self. Layered on top of the proto-self is the core self, a schematic, image-based but nonverbal dimension to the self that creates a conscious sense of awareness of an individual's state of being. The core self is derived from the feelings and reactions contained within the proto-self. Finally, the autobiographical self is an individual's self-constructed historical record of the self-based experiences that stem from the core self (much like Mead's notion of the "me"). The autobiographical self is organized around memories of past experience, facilitated through language, and predicated upon preexisting core self experiences. Damasio described these three layers of the self as hierarchically interdependent, with the proto-self providing the basis of the core self processes that are elaborated into the mnemonic and linguistic architecture of the autobiographical self. Because emotions provide the primary means by which body-based feelings are translated into self-conceptions, Damasio suggested that the development of self-consciousness—and, by implication, self-conception—is predicated upon emotional processes.

Taken together, the study of emotion within the intrapersonal-positivist domain has led to conclusions that provide significant evidence for intrinsic links between emotions and the self. Not only does this work articulate the interconnections between the experience of the self and the hardwired neurophysiological processes of the human body, but it also suggests that emotions are likely the foundation for the development and experience of selfhood. Panksepp (1994:397) summarized this point nicely:

> Emotional feeling without some type of self-referencing seems impossible. I suspect that when we begin to fathom the nature of internal affective representations, we may be close to cracking the codes for some basic forms of self-consciousness that may be the root processes for all higher forms of self-awareness. In general, I suspect that we will make the most progress in understanding the basic nature of the primal forms of consciousness if we start by modifying Descartes' famous epithet: "I think, therefore I am" to "I feel, therefore I am," and then proceed to probe the neural nature of feelings.

As Panksepp suggested, one of the central blind spots of contemporary approaches to the self is the Cartesian emphasis on disembodied and emotionless cognition. Studies that have revealed an emotional foundation to both cognition and sociality have sought to rectify this disparity and have established an interrelationship between emotions and the self that requires significant consideration from sociologists. In fact, those sociologists whose work falls into the interpersonal-positivist domain have begun to produce a series of complementary studies that move the examination of the links between emotions and self into the interpersonal realm.

Interpersonal-Positivist Dimensions of Emotions and the Self

The tradition of research exemplified by this domain emphasizes human emotions as an emergent property of the structure of social situations. Here, emotions are identified primarily as interpersonal phenomena, and this work has been concerned with drawing out the structural properties of social interaction that produce specific emotional expressions, feeling states, self-evaluations, and relationships. In these efforts, emotions are conceptualized as social facts that are orchestrated by sociological forces external to individual actors and are derivative of social structural conditions. Variables such as status and power relationships (Kemper 1978, 1984, 1991; Kemper and Collins 1990), successful ritual exchanges of emotional and cultural resources (Collins 1981, 1984, 2004; Lawler 2001), the verification and salience of identities (Burke 1991, 1996; Stets 2004, 2005; Stryker 1987, 2004), and the evaluation, potency, and activity (EPA) of emotions (Heise 1979, 1987; Heise and Thomas 1989; Morgan and Heise 1988; Smith-Lovin 1991; Smith-Lovin and Heise 1988) are typically explored to assess the relevance of interpersonal processes to emotions. In the investigation of emotions as interpersonal phenomena, this tradition of work has conceptualized emotions as central to the dynamics of social interaction and has sought to specify the social conditions under which emotions are most likely to be experienced, manifested, shaped, and expressed.

Several strands of theory exemplify the general orientation of the work in this quadrant. For instance, affect control theory (Heise 1979, 1987; MacKinnon 1994; Smith-Lovin 1991) is premised on the idea that the means by which individuals define social situations is instrumental in producing emotional responses and that if individual interpretations of situations are at odds with more fundamental, culturally prescribed sentiments, emotional discordance will develop, creating pressures to generate new situational definitions. Likewise, interaction ritual theory (Collins 1981, 2004) has also contributed to this domain of investigation, suggesting that social life is composed of a vast number of emotional exchanges fueled by the drive for the acquisition of emotional energy. Successful interaction rituals result in the emergence of emotionally charged symbols that represent group membership and become the primary source of both social solidarity and motivation toward interaction. Finally, identity theory (Burke 1991, 1996; Stets 2004, 2005; Stryker 1987, 2004) has argued that interpersonal processes are instrumental in determining the salience and verification of identities and it provides the emotional context for the development of an individual's self-conceptions. Collectively, these strands of theory emphasize the role that social structural conditions play in shaping emotional life.

Although investigations into the biological basis of human emotions have established connections between the development of the self and emotion-based cognition, sociologists have explored the structural dynamics of social situations that are instrumental in understanding the links between emotions and self. Research in the interpersonal-positivist domain has explicitly investigated the relationship between self-conceptions and self-feelings and how they are modified by interpersonal processes (Burke 1991, 1996; Stets 2004, 2005; Stryker 1987, 2004; Turner 2002). In general, and like the research in the intrapersonal-positivist domain described above, this body of work has begun to conceptualize the dynamics of the self as intimately tied to emotions. However, in place of a focus on the emotional underpinnings of cognition, these approaches have sought to reconceptualize the sociological study of the self in terms of the interpersonal dynamics of emotions. Here, a novel understanding of the self has emerged that is premised upon an intrinsic interrelationship between self-conception and self-feeling. Although sociological approaches have typically emphasized the self as organized around cognitive processes like language, recent efforts have modified these approaches by recasting the self as structured by emotional experiences and characterized by self-conceptions that are organized emotionally.

The introduction of a link between the emotional and conceptual aspects of the self has had important implications for the current theories of the self, especially those that have investigated the structural dynamics of self-conceptualization. Drawn primarily from identity theory, these efforts have developed an approach that envisions the self as composed of a set of self-conceptions that are arranged in terms of a hierarchy of identities (Burke 1991, 1996; Kuhn and McPartland 1954; McCall and Simmons 1978; Rosenberg 1979; Serpe 1987; Stryker 1980, 1987, 1989, 1992; Stryker and Serpe 1982, 1994). Here, the self is generally conceptualized as a structured set of identities hierarchically organized in terms of the salience, commitment, and prominence that individuals attribute to the various social roles that they perform. Central to these approaches has been the specification of the sociological dynamics that affect an individual's hierarchical ordering of the multiple identities that he or she performs. Collectively, these studies revealed that those identities that have greater importance for an individual are also those that are most significantly affected by interpersonal processes. Social situations that confirm identities are most likely to reaffirm and support the existing structure of the self; those situations that disconfirm identities (either in a positive or negative direction) are likely to provoke emotional reactions and cause adjustments in identity salience.

Although empirical tests of identity theory have revealed a number of insights about the nature of self-conceptualization, recent efforts have discovered that emotions play an important role in the establishment and maintenance of an individual's salience hierarchy of identities (Burke 1991, 1996; Stets 2004, 2005; Stryker 1987, 2004). For example, Stryker (2004) argued that emotional responses are crucial aspects of the verification processes of identities. Those identities that are highly salient to an individual are also likely to have high emotional involvement and provoke strong emotional reactions when they are disconfirmed. According to Stryker, emotional expressions are important markers of the practicability of identity in a situation and illustrate the overall salience of that identity to an individual. Similarly, Burke's (1991, 1996) identity control theory suggests that interruptions of the feedback processes by which identities are normally verified (i.e., those social interactions that contribute to the creation and maintenance of identities) are met with emotional responses that are concomitant in intensity with the salience of the disconfirmed identities. Although identity control theory has argued that the nonverification of an identity typically results in negative emotions, recent work (Stets 2005) has revealed that nonverification in a positive direction creates positive emotional experiences connected to the positively nonverified identity.

The results of the research supporting identity theory have important implications for understanding the links between emotions and the self. As identity theory suggests, the sociological architecture of self-conceptualization is not simply composed of conceptions of self but, moreover, of conceptions of self that are interlaced with emotional valences. In fact, it is not too much of a stretch to envision the structure of self-conceptions as organized around a foundation of emotional self-feelings. If the internal structure of systems of identity salience are composed of self-conceptions tagged with self-feelings, then the greater the level of affect connected to any one self-conception, the higher its ranking will be in the salience hierarchy of identities. It might be that the self-feelings connected to self-conceptions are the driving dynamics of identity processes and the primary motivational forces behind self-conceptualization. Such a point serves to offer explanatory power to what is commonly referred to as the "self-consistency motive" in social psychological research (Rosenberg 1979:53–62; Swann 1983, 1990; Swann and Read 1981), whereby individuals come to maintain a relatively stable self-conception through time (either positive or negative) even when confronted with self-disconfirming information. If emotions provide the basic organization of the self, then self-consistency is not merely an attempt to maintain a stable self-conception, but it also involves negotiations on an emotional level. These emotions not only give shape to organization of the self but also likely form an emotional center to the "core self" and provide its organization and stability through time.

Turner (2002) has perhaps provided the strongest theoretical argument toward linking the results of identity theory with the idea of an emotional core to the self. He argued, like Damasio (1999), that it is useful to understand the structure of the self as a series of layers. At the core of the self are a series of self-feelings that generally shape how individuals experience themselves as beings in the world. Layered above the core self-feelings are subidentities that mark the general roles that individuals inhabit in the social world (e.g., family member, worker, citizen, and so forth). Finally, subidentities are transcended by role identities at the outermost layer that indicate the specific roles that individuals enact in their daily lives. In Turner's theory, core self-feelings provide the overall salience for both subrole and role identities and organize the respective needs for the verification of specific identities. Identities that are most closely connected to core self-feelings (i.e., those identities that identity theory describes as being of high salience) are those that are likely to be subject to more inflexible verification processes and to be a more accurate approximation of an individual's most fundamental sense of self.

The idea of emotional center to the self is also consistent with the tradition of theory derived from what Collins (1981, 1989, 1993, 2004) called "interaction ritual chains." Although Collins rarely discussed the self, his ideas can be extended to support the conception of an emotional foundation to the self. In his theory, Collins argued that individuals move through social interactions by the exchange of two primary resources that have been accumulated from previous encounters: cultural capital and emotional energy. In social situations, individuals seek to initiate interactions with others by exchanging cultural capital in order to maximize their gain of emotional energy. Successful exchanges of cultural capital subsequently result in acquisitions of emotional energy that mark the solidarity felt between those individuals during the interaction. Solidarity will be enhanced if individuals gain emotional energy from the interaction and will decrease if emotional energy is lost. Collins suggested that emotional energy is frequently attached to the symbols involved in the exchange in order to preserve it from situation to situation. For Collins, emotional energy exchanges are the essence of social interaction and provide the "electric current" that charges up social situations.

A weakness of Collins' theory, however, is his failure to specify where and how emotional energy is stored within individuals. Although Collins does not attempt to provide answers to these questions, it is likely that something like Turner's (2002) notion of the emotional core to the self offers an answer. Collins suggested that emotional energy is the driving force for social interaction, yet it is also probable that it provides the motivational basis for the emotional dynamics of the self. The specification of self-based emotional energy dynamics not only serves to enhance Collins' own theory, but it also provides key insight into the emotional organization of the self.

If the self is theorized as a primary focus of social interaction, a point that is consistent with Goffman's (1967) dramaturgical model of the self, it can then be conceptualized as one of the primary symbols toward which emotional energy is directed. Social interaction, thus, not only serves to charge up the individuals within a particular encounter but also creates an emotional effervescence that is attached to and circulated through the selves of those present. Here, as identities become charged with emotional energy, the self becomes a portable container for emotional energy that allows individuals to move from situation to situation carrying a complex of interrelated self-conceptions interlaced with self-feelings. In this sense, the self is both an "emotional battery" for social rituals and an organizational mechanism for arranging the emotionally salient identities that are described within identity theory. Although Collins' theory outlines the interpersonal dynamics that create collective emotion, identity theory describes the organizational dynamics by which the emotions are linked to the self and become a reservoir of affect for future social interaction and self-verification.

Intrapersonal-Constructivist Dimensions of Emotions and the Self

Perhaps the most contested investigations have been those that focused on emotions as social constructions, the product of cognitive appraisals and subjective definitions of social situations. Here, emotions are conceptualized as a second-order process that result from a preliminary cognitive awareness, appraisal, and definition of a body-based state. The most famous work in this tradition is that undertaken by Schachter and Singer (1962), who contended that emotional experiences are not contingent on the biological or social structural processes but on cognitive definitions of affective experience. Here it is argued that the development of emotional states begins with the emergence of undifferentiated affect that later crystallizes into emotions as it is defined and labeled through cognitive interpretation. Although this research has been widely criticized (for examples, see Kemper 1978; Scheff 1979), suggesting that cognitive definitions are only likely to be instrumental in labeling affective states that are of low intensity, it is still commonly cited and embraced by those who support the subjectivist and constructivist position of emotions (Ortony et al. 1988; Ratner 1989).

This social constructivist argument has also been echoed in phenomenological approaches that investigate emotions as "lived experiences" (Denzin 1983, 1984, 1985; Sartre 1962) and maintain that an understanding of emotions cannot be divorced from an individual's immediate, interpretive engagement of both their environment and themselves. Additionally, psychologists have reframed the constructivist position and have explored the role of cognitive appraisals in creating, interpreting, and managing affective states (Arnold 1960; Frijda 1986; Lazarus 1984; Scherer 2001). Here emotions are not necessarily pure social constructions, but are largely organized with respect to cognitive assessments and labels of body-based feelings.

In general, the intrapersonal-constructivist tradition of research suggests that emotional experiences are essentially cognitive constructions that develop from the interpretive evaluations that individuals generate in the course of understanding their personal, affective experience. Such approaches to emotions have also raised important issues that are central to the sociological study of self. Although both the intrapersonal and interpersonal positivist approaches outlined above have respectively examined the biological and sociological links between emotion and the self, investigations in the intrapersonal-constructivist domain have highlighted the role that the ruminative and reflexive processes of internal conversations play in the constitution and interpretation of the self (Wiley 1994). Generally, these approaches adopt a theory of the interpretative process that is consistent with Mead's theory of the internal conversation. For Mead, "self-talk" is a fundamental aspect of self-based processes and is one of the primary means by which individuals establish and maintain a sense of self. However, Mead's theory of the mind is premised on the same cognitive bias that is present throughout his treatment of the self (Collins 1989, 2004; Wiley 1994). Contemporary sociological investigations into the internal conversation have endeavored to reframe Mead's theory by incorporating emotion as a key component of self-consciousness. Because recent investigations into cognition have revealed explicit interdependencies between cognition and emotion, they suggest that Mead's theory of the subjective organization of self requires significant revaluation.

Mead's model of the internal conversation might be useful in describing some aspects of the subjective organization of the self, but it is far too simplistic to capture the broad range of processes by which the self is intrapersonally ordered. In fact, some of the recent and innovative theoretical work on the self suggests that cognitively organized internal conversations, like those described by Mead, are not the only or even the primary mechanism through which self-based information is processed. Instead, recent studies suggest that the self is organized schematically, articulated into self-schemas that are composed of interrelated cognitive maps of meaning about the self as a social object (Howard 2000; Markus 1977; Markus and Nurius 1987; Markus and Sentis 1982; Morgan and Schwalbe 1990; Nurius 1991). Explicitly, sociological approaches to self-schemas argue that the origin of the schematic content of the self stems directly from interpersonal interaction and forms loosely organized gestalts that are typically not accessible to an individual through the syntax and structure of conventional language (Howard 2000; Morgan and Schwalbe 1990; Stryker 1991).

These new theoretical efforts introduce not only novel means for articulating the structure and dynamics of the self but also open new possibilities for a theory of the self that moves beyond the cognitive model articulated by Mead. Although some dimensions of self-consciousness clearly proceed through self-talk, as Mead suggested, most self-reflexive activity is experienced as a blur of image-based gestalts that are not easily put into words—much like that of the proto-self described by Damasio (1999). There is a lived experience to the self that is largely fluid and significantly emotional (Denzin 1984, 1985). From this perspective, the process of self-reflexivity is not simply structured in terms of the internalized linguistic patterns of conversations, but, more accurately, it is organized in terms of a flow of experience. The schematic models of the self articulate a similar model of human cognition and are premised on an understanding of the subjective experience that is much more loosely organized than that described by Mead. However, like Mead's theory, the schematic model of the self must also be pushed toward the incorporation of emotions. If the lived experience of the self is intrinsically constructed out of self-conceptions and self-feelings, self-schemas cannot simply be loosely organized cognitive information about the self. Because cognition and emotion are neurologically fused, it is probable that the self-conscious, lived experience of the self is organized around cognitive schemas that are interlaced with emotion, with some schematic elements carrying greater affective charges than others.

A schematic theory of self that builds on the insight that cognition and emotion are interlinked allows sociological models of mind and self to be extended beyond the framework outlined by Mead. Not only does such a perspective expand an understanding of self-conscious processes beyond the Meadian model of the internal conversation, but it also helps explain when self-talk is likely to occur and how it can be utilized in constructing a sense of self. If the self is a lived experience of which emotions are an intrinsic aspect (Denzin 1983, 1984), then the baseline state of the self is most likely akin to the "stream of consciousness" described by James (1950). Individuals are likely to apprehend the self as a stream of self-consciousness until their experience is interrupted. When this occurs, an individual's apprehension of self shifts and becomes more explicitly self-conscious.

Shibutani (1961) described this process as the result of a "blockage" of action and suggested that individuals are most likely to become manifestly conscious of the self when their actions in the world are disrupted, a process that almost always results in the evocation of both self-talk and emotional reactions. Burke (1991) applied a similar idea directly to the organization of the self, arguing that the interruption of the processes by which identities are controlled causes the self to become a central object of an individual's attention and motivates attempts to ameliorate the effects of the disruption. In a Meadian sense, this kind of explicit self-consciousness moves an individual's subjective experience of self away from a level of the lived experience of schematic self-impressions and into self-talk. Thus, self-talk is not a baseline state of self but is, instead, an outcome of the interruption of an identity and a means by which an individual performs the work necessary to reestablish and stabilize the self and reenter the stream of self-consciousness. Here, self-talk emerges as a means of reducing the discrepancies that result from blockages in one's stream of experience, where the greater the affect attached to the identity that is interrupted, the more emotionally animated the self-talk is likely to be.

Sociological investigations into the dynamics of the internal conversation have further explicated the interrelationships between the self, self-talk, and emotions. For example, Wiley (1994) argued that the internal conversation is a central means for constructing and maintaining a coherent sense of self-feeling through the development of an "intrapersonal solidarity" among the self's component identities. In addition, Collins (1989, 2004) contended that self-talk is more accurately understood as an internalized conversation that serves to revivify those social interactions that resonate with a significant emotional charge.

Collins did not directly connect his "neo-Median" theory of the mind to the self, but it is easy to see how one might do so. If the self is a storehouse of self-concepts interlaced with self-feelings, self-talk emerges as an internalized interaction that serves to reverberate the positive affect acquired during social exchanges or to adjust the interruptions that occur in identity processes. Thus, an individual who has experienced a prideful or emotionally exhilarating situation might use self-talk to maintain this emotion by "imaginatively rehearsing" these experiences over and over; in addition, an individual who has experienced a shameful or embarrassing social encounter might engage in self-talk to reconstruct a baseline set of self-conceptions and self-feelings. It can be hypothesized that the greater the self-feeling attached to a particular identity, the more emotionally resonant will be the self-talk with respect to that identity.

Of course, not all self-talk is explicitly about the self (some self-talk is clearly about others, events, and activities). However, the self is frequently one of the central symbolic objects of internal conversations (Burke 1991; Mead 1934; Wiley 1994). When the self emerges as an object of subjective interpretation, such reflexive evaluations are made not only based on who individuals think they are but also on how they feel about themselves. The lived experience of the self is one of a constellation of thoughts and feelings, with self-conceptions that resonate with greater affect being more central to the mind. The research in the intrapersonal-constructionist domain suggests that the subjective constitution of the self is intrinsically premised on both self-conceptions and self-feelings. The ability to construct and subjectively manage a sense of one's self allows an individual to not only locate himself or herself appropriately within a social situation but also to subjectively define who he or she is both cognitively and emotionally.

Interpersonal-Constructivist Dimensions of Emotions and the Self

Finally, the fourth domain of theory and research conceptualizes emotions primarily as interpersonal constructs that are culturally malleable, irreducible to biology, fluid products of cultural frameworks, and the dynamics of social interaction. Here, emotions are analyzed as "social emergents" (McCarthy 1989, 1994), which are plastic interpersonal phenomena linked to transitory social roles, mediated by situational expectations and cultural definitions (Armon-Jones 1985, 1986; Averill 1980; Goffman 1959, 1967; Harre 1986; Shott 1979), and circumscribed by normatively organized "emotion cultures" and "feeling rules" (Gordon 1989, 1990; Hochschild 1979, 1983).

Research within this tradition conceptualizes emotions as the outcome of social interaction negotiated by individuals within a culturally predefined framework, which is exemplified by McCarthy's (1989) proclamation that "emotions are social things." In this respect, emotions are not merely constructed through individuals' subjective interpretations, but are more enduring and stable phenomena often differentially shaped and experienced with respective to specific sociocultural conditions. Thus, it is not only the case that individuals interpretatively construct their emotional experiences; societies and cultures also create filtering mechanisms through which emotional experiences are sorted.

An interesting body of work has emerged to explore the confluence of culture and emotion. This work has investigated the "emotional cultures" and "feeling rules" that circumscribe emotional responses and their expressions in diverse cultural contexts. Some have delineated the dramaturgical dimensions of emotional expressions (Goffman 1959, 1967; Hochschild 1979, 1983), whereas others have described the cross-cultural differences in the expressions of emotions (Markus and Kitayama 1991, 1994). Collectively, these studies have suggested that both emotional expression and experience are subject to significant cultural variation, and although some affective responses might be tied to physiological processes, their manifestation is delimited by the rules of emotional management prescribed within a given sociocultural context.

Although intrapersonal-constructivist research has emphasized the subjective nature of self-reflexivity, investigations in the interpersonal-constructivist dimension have explored the cultural and situational dynamics that shape an individual's constitution and reflexive interpretation of self. Central to these investigations is a theory that conceptualizes the self as sociologically malleable, a product of dramaturgical and cultural conditions. Here, self-feelings are seen as constructed out of an interface between individuals and the social contexts they inhabit. The harbinger of these approaches is found in the work of Goffman (1959, 1967), who argued that the self is a theatrical performance that emerges within a social situation. For Goffman, the self-reflexive process involves a continual monitoring of behavior, thoughts, and feelings to ensure that they are in accord with the codes of deference and demeanor outlined by the cultural script of a given situation. Any deviation from the script, according to Goffman, is likely to result in the manifestation of self-based emotions, like embarrassment, among those who have fallen out of character. If a breach of the script cannot be repaired and the emotional equilibrium of the interaction rectified, Goffman suggested that the situation is subject to potential collapse and the selfhood of all participants is liable to be compromised.

Goffman's theory of the self is strikingly interpersonal. Although individuals might commit blunders in the course of their dramaturgical performances, the emotions experienced are typically framed as group phenomena. One individual's self-embarrassment has consequences for the performance of his or her role, the ability of others to perform their roles, the success of the interaction, and, ultimately, for the cohesion of the group. In Goffman's work, emotional experiences do not resonate with deep intrapersonal meaning; instead, emotions are sociological phenomena that are primarily played out within the dynamics of group life. Emotions only become significantly attached to the self at the extremes, when an individual's ability to perform as self is compromised through the acquisition of stigmatized or deviant identities (Goffman 1963).

Hochschild (1979, 1983) has meaningfully expanded Goffman's work, providing both analytic depth to the dramaturgical model of the self and exploring the means by which the "feeling rules" that circumscribe emotional expressions affect an individual's construction of self. Hochschild argued, like Goffman, that individuals are frequently confronted with "feeling rules" that they must follow in managing their emotions. Such emotion management is typically accomplished in public life, at work, and in other places where an individual must routinely don a "mask" and play a "character." According to Hochschild, emotion management is accomplished at two levels, through both surface and deep acting. In surface acting, individuals manipulate the impressions that they make on others without internalizing the sincerity that they hope to convey by their performance, whereas deep acting requires a more complete embodiment of role performance and a genuine assimilation of the thoughts and feelings required by the role. Hochschild argued that specific cultural scripts compel individuals to manage their emotions differently and require them to construct a sense of self in distinct ways. Most important are those situations that involve a great deal of "emotion work," especially those entailing emotional displays that are at odds with an individual's authentic self-feelings, as they are the most likely to have lasting effects on an individual's sense of self-feeling. If individuals are embedded in emotionally disingenuous situations over an extended period of time, Hochschild argued that it is possible for them to become estranged from their authentic feelings and to develop a false and emotionally alienated sense of self.

Other works (Gordon 1989; Markus and Kitayama 1991, 1994) complement Hochschild's approach and also help to remedy the emotionally surface-level orientation of Goffman's theory. For example, Gordon (1989) argued that different social contexts are circumscribed by unique emotion cultures that have important consequences for how individuals attach emotions to the self. Some contexts emphasize the institutional control over emotions, whereas other stress a more impulsive and spontaneous orientation to emotional expression. The development of the self within these two contexts occurs differently. On the one hand, those individuals who identify with institutional contexts will be more likely to manage their emotional expressions and identify the self-control of their emotion as a sign of their authentic self; here, an impulsive outburst of emotion is seen as an anomaly. On the other hand, individuals who locate their self-conceptions in the impulsive expression of emotion will identify the expression of an authentically felt emotion as an aspect of their true self, whereas institutionally controlled emotions are viewed as expressions of self-hypocrisy and disingenuousness. In a similar way, Markus and Kitayama (1994) contended that the interconnections between emotions and the self are differently constructed between cultures that emphasize independent or interdependent understandings of the self. They argued that individuals in cultures that stress self-independence are much more likely to attach positive feelings to self-conceptions that highlight autonomy and attach negative feelings to those that indicate dependence; the opposite is found among individuals in cultures with an interdependent orientation who tend to attach positive feelings to self-conceptions that underscore relationships and attach negative feelings to those that stress egoism.

Collectively, the works in the interpersonal-constructivist domain suggest that the cultivation of self-feelings is a process that is significantly circumscribed by sociocultural context. Assessments of self-feeling are not simply products of subjective interpretation but are also constructed out of the reflexive engagement of emotion cultures and feeling rules. Although emotions might be a key organizational force for the constitution of the self, a point suggested by the works in the previous three domains, the perspective outlined here maintains that the self is a product of the attunement of self-feelings and sociocultural expectations for emotional expression. Following Shott (1979), these efforts have revealed that the reflexive process of role-taking, by which individuals imaginatively interpret the situational and cultural perspectives of the larger social world, is not just a cognitive process but one that is inherently emotional as well.

CONCLUSION AND FUTURE DIRECTIONS

The investigations outlined in this chapter suggest that the study of emotions has provided sociology with a richer and more sophisticated understanding of the self. The conception of the self revealed by these efforts has several implications. First, the reflexive process that is traditionally identified as the mechanism of self-constitution is organized by both cognition and emotion. Second, an individual's sense of self is composed not only of self-conceptions but also of interrelated self-feelings. Third, the structure of internalized identities is organized based on emotional valences that articulate the salience of identities with respect to one another. Fourth, the internal conversation through which a sense of self is often interpretatively constructed is only one means of subjective self-constitution; "self-talk" emerges out of interruptions of the self and is both circumscribed and mediated by emotional dynamics. Fifth, it is likely that the self has an emotional core that provides the organizational architecture for both self-conceptions and internal conversations. Sixth, selfhood is constituted out of the continual negotiation of the sociocultural dynamics of feeling rules and emotion cultures. Finally, the collective message of these implications points to the premise that emotional processes are not only intrinsic to the self but that they likely provide the foundation for its structure and reflexive organization.

Future theory and research are required to explore these implications. The sociological understanding of the self is likely to benefit from concerned efforts directed toward specifying the relationships between emotions and the self, investigating the role of emotions in both self-reflexivity and self-conceptualization. Clearly, there are many questions that remain unanswered concerning the link between emotions and the self. The sociological study of microprocesses has much to gain by exploring the emotional dimension of the self, and such efforts will not only further the understanding of the self but also enhance the sociological study of emotions.

REFERENCES

Alexander, C. Norman, Jr., and Pat Lauderdale. 1977. "Situated Identities and Social Influence." *Sociometry* 40: 225–233.

Alexander, C. Norman, Jr., and Mary Glenn Wiley. 1992. "Situated Activity and Identity Formation." Pp. 269–289 in *Social Psychology: Sociological Perspectives*, edited by M. Rosenberg and R. H. Turner. New Brunswick, NJ: Transaction Publishers.

Armon-Jones, Claire. 1985. "Prescription, Explication and the Social Construction of Emotions." *Journal for the Theory of Social Behavior* 15: 1–22.

———. 1986. "The Thesis of Constructivism." Pp. 32–56 in *The Social Construction of Emotions*, edited by R. Harre. Oxford: Basil Blackwell.

Arnold, Magda B. 1960. *Emotion and Personality: Psychological Aspects*. Oxford: Columbia University Press.

Averill, James R. 1980. "A Constructivist View of Emotion." Pp. 305–339 in *Emotion: Theory, Research, and Experience*, Volume 1: *Theories of Emotion*, edited by R. Plutchik and H. Kellerman. New York: Academic.

Blumer, Herbert. 1969. *Symbolic Interaction: Perspective and Method*. Englewood Cliffs, NJ: Prentice-Hall.

Bolton, Charles D. 1981. "Some Consequences of the Meadian Self." *Symbolic Interaction* 4: 245–259.

Burke, Peter. 1991. "Identity Process and Social Stress." *American Sociological Review* 56: 836–849.

———. 1996. "Social Identities and Psychosocial Stress." Pp. 141–174 in *Psychosocial Stress: Perspectives on Structure, Theory, Life Course, and Methods*, edited by H. B. Kaplan. Orlando, FL: Academic.

Collins, Randall. 1981. "On the Microfoundations of Macrosociology." *American Journal of Sociology* 86: 984–1014.

———. 1984. "The Role of Emotion in Social Structure." Pp. 385–396 in *Approaches to Emotion*, edited by K. R. Sherer and P. Ekman. Hillsdale, NJ: Lawrence Erlbaum.

———. 1989. "Toward a Neo-Meadian Sociology of Mind." *Symbolic Interaction* 12: 1–32.

———. 1990. "Stratification, Emotional Energy, and the Transient Emotions." Pp. 27–57 in *Research Agendas in the Sociology of Emotions*, edited by T. D. Kemper. New York: State University of New York Press.

———. 1993. "Emotional Energy as the Common Denominator of Rational Action." *Rationality and Society* 5: 203–230.

———. 2004. *Interaction Rituals Chains*. Princeton, NJ: Princeton University Press.

Cooley, Charles Horton. 1902. *Human Nature and the Social Order*. Glencoe, IL: Free Press.

Damasio, Antonio R. 1994. *Descartes' Error: Emotion, Reason, and the Human Brain*. New York: Putnam.

———. R. 1999. *The Feeling of What Happens: Body and Emotion in the Making of Consciousness*. New York: Harcourt.

Darwin, Charles. 1872. *Expression of the Emotions in Man and Animals*. London: John Murray.

Denzin, Norman. 1983. "A Note on Emotionality, Self, and Interaction." *American Journal of Sociology* 89: 402–409.

———. 1984. *On Understanding Emotion*. San Francisco: Jossey-Bass.

———. 1985. "Emotions as Lived Experiences." *Symbolic Interaction* 8: 223–240 [Special Issue on the Sociology of Emotion].

Ekman, Paul. 1973. *Darwin and Facial Expression: A Century of Research in Review*. New York: Academic.

———. 1982. *Emotions in the Human Face*. Cambridge: Cambridge University Press.

Frijda, Nico H. 1986. *The Emotions*. Cambridge: Cambridge University Press.

Goffman, Erving. 1959. *The Presentation of Self in Everyday Life*. New York: Doubleday.

———. 1963. *Stigma: Notes on the Management of Spoiled Identity*. Englewood Cliffs, NJ: Prentice-Hall.

———. 1967. *Interaction Ritual: Essays on Face-to-Face Behavior*. New York: Doubleday.

Gordon, Steven L. 1985. "Micro-Sociological Theories of Emotion." Pp. 133–147 in *Micro-Sociological Theory: Perspective on Sociological Theory*, Volume 2, edited by H. J. Helle and S. N. Eisenstadt. Thousand Oaks, CA: Sage.

———. 1989. "Institutional and Impulsive Orientations in Selectively Appropriating Emotions to Self." Pp. 115–135 in *The Sociology of Emotions: Original Essays and Research Papers*, edited by D. D. Franks and E. D. McCarthy. Greenwich, CT: JAI Press.

———. 1990. "Social Structural Effects on Emotions." Pp. 145–179 in *Research Agendas in the Sociology of Emotions*, edited by T. D. Kemper. Albany: State University of New York Press.

———. 1992. "The Sociology of Sentiments and Emotion." Pp. 562–592 in *Social Psychology: Sociological Perspectives*, edited by M. Rosenberg and R. H. Turner. New Brunswick, NJ: Transaction Publishers.

Harre, Rom. 1986. "Outline of the Social Constructionist Viewpoint." Pp. 2–14 in *The Social Construction of Emotions*, edited by R. Harre. Oxford: Basil Blackwell.

Heise, David R. 1979. *Understanding Events: Affect and the Construction of Social Action*. New York: Cambridge University Press.

———. 1987. "Affect Control Theory: Concepts and Model." *Journal of Mathematical Sociology* 13: 1–34.

Heise, David R., and Lisa Thomas. 1989. "Predicting Impressions Created by Combinations of Emotion and Social Identity." *Social Psychology Quarterly* 52: 141–148.

Hobson, Peter. 2004. *The Cradle of Thought: Exploring the Origins of Thinking*. Oxford: Oxford University Press.

Hochschild, Arlie. 1979. "Emotion Work, Feeling Rules and Social Structure." *American Journal of Sociology* 85: 551–575.

———. 1983. *The Managed Heart: Commercialization of Human Feeling*. Berkeley: University of California Press.

Howard, Judith. 2000. "Social Psychology of Identities." *American Sociological Review* 26: 367–393.

Izard, Carroll E. 1971. *The Face of Emotion*. New York: Meredith.

———. 1977. *Human Emotions*. New York: Plenum.

James, William. [1890]1950. *Principles of Psychology*, Volumes 1 and 2. New York: Dover.

Jauregui, Jose Antonio. 1995. *The Emotional Computer*. Oxford: Blackwell.

Johnson, Cathryn. 1992. "The Emergence of the Emotional Self: A Developmental Theory." *Symbolic Interaction* 15: 183–202.

Kemper, Theodore D. 1978. *A Social Interactional Theory of Emotions*. New York: Wiley.

———. 1981. "Social Constructivist and Positivist Approaches to the Sociology of Emotions." *American Journal of Sociology* 87: 336–362.

———. 1984. "Power, Status, and Emotions: A Sociological Contribution to a Psychophysiological Domain." Pp. 369–383 in *Approaches to Emotion*, edited by K. R. Sherer and P. Ekman. Hillsdale, NJ: Erlbaum.

———. 1987. "How Many Emotions Are There? Wedding the Social and the Autonomic Components." *American Journal of Sociology* 93: 262–289.

———. 1991. "Predicting Emotions from Social Relations." *Social Psychology Quarterly* 54: 330–342.

Kemper, Theodore D., and Randall Collins. 1990. "Dimensions of Microinteraction." *American Journal of Sociology* 96: 32–68.

Kuhn, Manford H. 1964. "Major Trends in Symbolic Interaction Theory in the Past Twenty-Five Years." *Sociological Quarterly* 5: 61–84.

Kuhn, Manford H., and Thomas S. McPartland. 1954. "An Empirical Investigation of Self-Attitudes." *American Sociological Review* 19: 68–76.

Lawler, Edward J. 2001. "An Affect Theory of Social Exchange." *American Journal of Sociology* 107: 321–352.

Lazarus, Richard S. 1984. "Thoughts on the Relations between Emotion and Cognition." Pp. 247–257 in *Approaches to Emotion*, edited by K. R. Sherer and P. Ekman. Hillsdale, NJ: Erlbaum.

LeDoux, Joseph E. 1996. *The Emotional Brain: The Mysterious Underpinnings of Emotional Life*. New York: Simon and Schuster.

Lewis, J. David. 1979. "A Social Behaviorist Interpretation of the Median 'I'." *American Journal of Sociology* 85: 261–287.

MacKinnon, Neil J. 1994. *Symbolic Interaction as Affect Control*. Albany: State University of New York Press.

Markus, Hazel. 1977. "Self-Schemata and Processing of Information about the Self." *Journal of Personality and Social Psychology* 35: 63–78.

Markus, Hazel, and Shinobu Kitayama. 1991. "Culture and the Self: Implications for Cognition, Emotion and Motivation." *Psychological Review* 98: 224–253.

———. 1994. "The Cultural Construction of Self and Emotion: Implications for Social Behavior." Pp. 89–130 in *Emotion and Culture: Empirical Studies of Mutual Influence*, edited by S. Kitayama and H. Markus. Washington, DC: American Psychological Association.

Markus, Hazel, and Paula Nurius. 1987. "Possible Selves: The Interface between Motivation and the Self-Concept." Pp. 157–172 in *Self and Identity: Psychosocial Perspectives*, edited by K. Yardley and T. Honess. New York: Wiley.

Markus, Hazel, and Kenneth Sentis. 1982. "The Self in Social Information Processing." Pp. 41–70 in *Psychological Perspectives on the Self*, edited by J. Suls. Hillsdale, NJ: Erlbaum.

McCall, George, and J. L. Simmons. 1978. *Identities and Interactions: An Examination of Human Associations in Everyday Life*, Revised Edition. New York: Free Press.

McCarthy, E. Doyle. 1989. "Emotions Are Social Things: An Essay in the Sociology of Emotions." Pp. 51–72 in *The Sociology of Emotions: Original Essays and Research Papers*, edited by D. D. Franks and E. D. McCarthy. Greenwich, CT: JAI Press.

———. 1994. "The Social Construction of Emotions: New Directions from Culture Theory." *Social Perspectives on Emotions* 2: 267–279.

Mead, George Herbert. 1895. "A Theory of Emotions from the Physiological Standpoint." *Psychological Review* 2: 162–164.

———. 1934. *Mind, Self, and Society*. Chicago: University of Chicago Press.

———. 1938. *The Philosophy of the Act*. Chicago: University of Chicago Press.

Morgan, David L., and Michael Schwalbe. 1990. "Mind and Self in Society: Linking Social Structure and Social Cognition." *Social Psychology Quarterly* 53: 148–164.

Morgan, Rick L., and David R. Heise. 1988 "Structure of Emotions." *Social Psychology Quarterly* 51: 19–31.

Nurius, Paula. 1991. "Possible Selves and Social Support: Social Cognitive Resources for Coping and Striving." Pp. 239–258 in *The Self-Society Dynamic: Cognition, Emotion, and Action*, edited by J. A. Howard and P. L. Callero. Cambridge: Cambridge University Press.

Ortony, Andrew, Gerald L. Clore, and Allan Collins. 1988. *The Cognitive Structure of Emotions*. New York: Cambridge University Press.

Panksepp, Jaak. 1994. "Evolution Constructed the Potential for Subjective Experience with the Neurodynamics of the Mammalian Brain." Pp. 396–399 in *The Nature of Emotion: Fundamental Questions*, edited P. Ekman and R. J. Davidson. New York: Oxford University Press.

Plutchik, Robert. 1991. *The Emotions*. New York: University Press of America.

Ratner, Carl. 1989. "A Social Constructionist Critique of the Naturalistic Theory of Emotion." *Journal of Mind and Behavior* 10: 211–230.

Rosenberg, Morris. 1979. *Conceiving the Self*. New York: Basic Books.

———. 1990. "Reflexivity and Emotions." *Social Psychology Quarterly* 53: 3–12.

———. 1991. "Self-Processes and Emotional Experiences." Pp. 123–142 in *The Self-Society Dynamic: Cognition, Emotion, and Action*, edited by J. A. Howard and P. L. Callero. Cambridge: Cambridge University Press.

———. 1992. "The Self-Concept: Social Product and Social Force." Pp. 593–624 in *Social Psychology: Sociological Perspectives*, edited by M. Rosenberg and R. H. Turner. New Brunswick, NJ: Transaction Publishers.

Sartre, Jean Paul. 1962. *Sketch for a Theory of the Emotions*. London: Methuen.

Schachter, Stanley, and Jerome Singer. 1962. "Cognitive, Social, and Physiological Determinants of Emotional State." *Psychological Review* 69: 379–399.

Scheff, Thomas. 1977. "The Distancing of Emotion in Ritual." *Current Anthropology* 18: 483–490.

———. 1979. *Catharsis in Healing, Ritual and Drama*. Berkeley: University of California Press.

———. 1983. "Towards Integration in the Social Psychology of Emotions." *Annual Review of Sociology* 9: 333–354.

———. 1988. "Shame and Conformity: The Deference-Emotion System." *American Sociological Review* 53: 395–406.

———. 1990. *Microsociology: Discourse, Emotion, and Social Structure*. Chicago: University of Chicago Press.

———. 1996. "Self-Esteem and Shame: Unlocking the Puzzle." Pp. 143–166 in *Individuality and Social Control: Essays in Honor of Tamotsu Shibutani*, edited K. M Kwan. Greenwich, CT: JAI Press.

Scherer, Klaus R. 2001. "The Nature and Study of Appraisal: A Review of the Issues." Pp. 369–391 in *Appraisal Processes in Emotion: Theory, Methods, Research*, edited by K. Scherer, A. Schorr, and T. Johnstone. Oxford: Oxford University Press.

Serpe, Richard T. 1987. "Stability and Change in Self: A Structural Symbolic Interactionist Explanation." *Social Psychology Quarterly* 50: 44–55.

Shibutani, Tamotsu. 1961. *Society and Personality: An Interactionist Approach to Social Psychology*. Englewood Cliffs, NJ: Prentice-Hall.

Shott, Susan. 1979. "Emotion and Social Life: A Symbolic Interactionist Analysis." *American Journal of Sociology* 84: 1317–1334.

Simonov, P. V. 1986. *The Emotional Brain: Physiology, Neuroanatomy, Psychology, and Emotion.* New York: Plenum.

Smith-Lovin, Lynn. 1991. "An Affect Control View of Cognition and Emotion." Pp. 143–169 in *The Self-Society Dynamic: Cognition, Emotion, and Action,* edited by J. A. Howard and P. L. Callero. Cambridge: Cambridge University Press.

Smith-Lovin, Lynn, and David R. Heise, eds. 1988. *Analyzing Social Interaction: Research Advances in Affect Control Theory.* New York: Gordon and Breach.

Sroufe, L. Alan. 1984. "The Organization of Emotional Development." Pp. 109–128 in *Approaches to Emotion,* edited by K. R. Sherer and P. Ekman. Hillsdale, NJ: Erlbaum.

———. 1997. *Emotional Development: The Organization of Emotional Life in the Early Years.* Cambridge: Cambridge University Press.

Stets, Jan E. 2004. "Emotions in Identity Theory: The Effects of Status." *Advances in Group Processes* 21: 51–76.

———. 2005. "Examining Emotions in Identity Theory." *Social Psychology Quarterly* 68: 39–74.

Stryker, Sheldon. 1980. *Symbolic Interactionism: A Social Structural Version.* Menlo Park, CA: Benjamin/Cummings.

———. 1987. "Identity Theory: Developments and Extensions." Pp. 89–103 in *Self and Identity: Psychosocial Perspectives,* edited by K. Yardley and T. Honess. New York: Wiley.

———. 1989. "Further Developments in Identity Theory: Singularity versus Multiplicity of Self." Pp. 35–57 in *Sociological Theories in Progress: New Formulations,* edited by J. Berger, M. Zelditch, Jr., and B. Anderson. Newbury Park, CA: Sage.

———. 1991. "Exploring the Relevance of Social Cognition for the Relationship of Self and Society: Linking the Cognitive Perspective and Identity Theory." Pp. 19–41 in *The Self-Society Dynamic: Cognition, Emotion, and Action,* edited by J. A. Howard and P. L. Callero. Cambridge: Cambridge University Press.

———. 1992. "Symbolic Interactionism: Themes and Variations." Pp. 3–29 in *Social Psychology: Sociological Perspectives,* edited by M. Rosenberg and R. H. Turner. New Brunswick, NJ: Transaction Publishers.

———. 2004. "Integrating Emotion into Identity Theory." *Advances in Group Processes* 23 :1–23.

Stryker, Sheldon, and Richard T. Serpe. 1982. "Commitment, Identity Salience, and Role Behavior." Pp. 199–218 in *Personality, Roles, and Social Behavior,* edited by W. Ickes and E. Kerchoff. Greenwich, CT: JAI Press.

———. 1994. "Identity Salience and Psychological Centrality: Equivalent, Overlapping, or Complementary Concepts?" *Social Psychology Quarterly* 63: 284–297.

Swann, William B., Jr. 1983. "Self-Verification: Bringing Social Reality into Harmony with the Self." Pp. 33–66 in *Psychological Perspectives on the Self,* edited by J. Suls and A. G. Greenwald. Hillsdale, NJ: Erlbaum.

———. 1990. "To Be Adored or to Be Known? The Interplay of Self-Enhancement and Self-Verification." Pp. 408–450 in *Handbook of Motivation and Cognition,* edited by E. T. Higgens and R. M. Sorrentino. New York: Guilford.

Swann, William B., Jr., and S. J. Read. 1981. "Self Verification Process: How We Sustain Our Self-Conceptions." *Journal of Experimental Social Psychology* 17: 351–372.

Tangey, June Price, and Kurt W. Fischer. 1995. "Self-Conscious Emotions and the Affect Revolution: Framework and Overview." Pp. 3–22 in *Self-Conscious Emotions: The Psychology of Shame, Guilt, Embarrassment, and Pride,* edited by J. P. Tangey and K. W. Fischer. New York: Guilford.

Trevarthen, Colwyn. 1984. "Emotions in Infancy: Regulators of Contact and Relationships with Persons." Pp. 129–157 in *Approaches to Emotion,* edited by K. R. Sherer and P. Ekman. Hillsdale, NJ: Lawrence Erlbaum.

Turner, Jonathan H. 1996. "The Evolution of Emotions in Humans: A Darwinian-Durkheimian Analysis." *Journal for the Theory of Social Behavior* 26: 1–34.

———. 2000. *On the Origins of Human Emotions: A Sociological Inquiry into the Evolution of Human Affect.* Stanford, CA: Stanford University Press.

———. 2002. *Face to Face: Toward a Sociological Theory of Interpersonal Behavior.* Stanford, CA: Stanford University Press.

Wentworth, William M., and D. Yardly. 1994. "Deep Sociality: A Bioevolutionary Perspective on the Sociology of Human Emotions." Pp. 21–55 in *Social Perspectives on Emotion,* edited by D. D. Franks, W. M. Wentworth, and J. Ryan. Greenwich, CT: JAI Press.

Wiley, Mary Glenn, and C. Norman Alexander. 1987. "From Situated Activity to Self-Attribution: The Impact of Social Structural Schemata." Pp. 105–117 in *Self and Identity: Psychosocial Perspectives,* edited by K. Yardley and T. Honess. New York: Wiley.

Wiley, Norbert. 1994. *The Semiotic Self.* Chicago: University of Chicago Press.

Zurcher, Louis. A., Jr. 1977. *The Mutable Self: A Self-Concept for Social Change.* Beverly Hills, CA: Sage.

CHAPTER 12

Psychoanalytic Sociological Theories and Emotions

Jonathan H. Turner

Relatively few sociologists analyzing emotions have sought to draw from the legacy of Freud and more recent work in the psychoanalytic tradition. This neglect is somewhat surprising in light of the fact that Freud, more than any other figure in the early twentieth century, drew attention to emotional dynamics. True, many of his constantly evolving ideas have not been supported by subsequent research and practice, but the general argument that humans activate defense mechanisms to protect ego in the face of negative emotions is certainly correct in its essentials. Yet, sociologists tend to adopt gestalt ideas about cognitive consistency and balance rather than repression and other defense mechanisms when explaining human emotional dynamics, and as a result, sociological theories miss a set of important leads in understanding emotions. Still, in going back to Freud (1900, 1923, 1938), we need to be selective in what we adopt and reject in his approach.

FREUD'S THEORY IN A MORE SOCIOLOGICAL GUISE

We begin this study with Freud's conception of libido, the energy driving mental processes. The libido as the source of psychic energy in a person is reducible in Freud's scheme to two sources: instincts for self-preservation and instincts for self-destruction. These two sources of libido energy are ultimately tied to biological origins that are primarily sexual in nature. Over the years, Freud successively expanded the idea of sexual energy to include drives for pleasurable sensations. Freud's views were obviously biased by the clinical nature of his data—people with anxiety disorders related to repressed sexual desires—but as he expanded the notion of libido, it

JONATHAN H. TURNER • Department of Sociology, University of California, Riverside, CA 92521 became, in essence, a view that individuals seek pleasure and positive emotional energy, and this drive structures the mental life of all individuals.

Freud saw the mental life of a person as divided into three domains. First, the conscious domain consists of those modes of thought about which an individual is aware and that order a person's actions. Conscious mental life is constantly altered as circumstances in the external world change and as pressures from the other two domains of mental life—the preconscious and unconscious—push upon reflective thought. The preconscious domain is available to a person when needed. Although Freud carefully distinguished this domain from the conscious and unconscious, it was not a prominent process in his conceptualization. Rather, it is the unconscious—perhaps Freud's most important insight—that is the key domain of mental life. For Freud, the unconscious is the most extensive part of mental life, consisting of emotions, desires, instincts, contradictions, fantasies, and other nonlogical mental elements. Freud saw this domain of mental life, as it surfaced in dreams and other overt manifestations, as the "primary" mental process, with consciousness viewed as a "secondary" process. Thus, libido energies work through unconscious, preconscious, and conscious thoughts, but often in distorted forms because the unconscious is often difficult to express through standard modes of reasoning (e.g., language, time, and logic). The energy flowing through the unconscious is pliable and can be molded by conscious processes, but the unconscious itself is not ordered by rules.

Freud's theory becomes more sociological with his famous tripartite division of personality into id, ego, and superego (and, later, ego-ideal). The id, ego, and superego are not parts of personality; they are *processes* that feed off one another. Id is the channeling of libido impulses, especially sexual energy, broadly defined as needs for love, affection, approval, positive emotions, and, of course, sex. Libido thus exerts influence on a person's behavior via id impulses as they filter through the unconscious, preconscious, and conscious domains of mental life. As these impulses arise, they activate ego processes which, in Freud's terms, constitute "the reality principle" or the capacity of a person to take cognizance in conscious thought of the realities of the external world. This external world consists of the physical environment, interpersonal relations, social structures, cultural prescriptions and proscriptions and, most important, a person's sexual identity. Sexual identity for Freud represents more than a gendered conception of oneself, although this is an important part of anyone's identity. It also consists of an individual's emotionally valenced cognitions of self as a certain kind of person. Much like William James, George Herbert Mead, Charles Horton Cooley, and John Dewy working in the pragmatist tradition, Freud viewed ego processes as directed in large part by the capacity to see oneself as an object in the environment (through ego processes and conscious thought). Superego processes invoke cultural codes—values, beliefs, norms, ethics, and other evaluative codes in a society's culture—and force ego to reconcile id impulses with the proscriptions and prescriptions contained in cultural codes. These codes can be internalized via socialization, and they often become part of an ego-ideal in which the group's goals and norms to realize these goals are also internalized and become a motive force in an individual's consciousness. There is not a great deal of difference between Durkheim's (1984) conception of the "collective conscious" or Mead's (1934) notion of the "generalized other" and Freud's conception of the superego and ego-ideal. As cultural dictates are internalized, they constitute a person's "conscience" and drive superego and ego-ideal processes as they impinge upon conscious deliberations by ego processes. When individuals are able to perceive that they act in accordance with superego processes and effectively channel their id impulses in socially acceptable ways, they experience pleasure and positive emotions, whereas when they perceive that they have violated cultural prescriptions and proscriptions, they experience pain and, more specifically, guilt.

Ego is always under strain trying to reconcile id impulses and unconscious processes with external reality, especially the reality embodied in identity and superego processes. At times, this strain intensifies into high levels of anxiety and leads to what Freud termed *ego defenses*, whereby ego processes disguise reality and objects in reality. In so doing, ego works to reduce the tension between id and superego by deceiving both through distortions of the external environment. Ego defenses not only distort reality, but they operate on an unconscious level, making the person unaware of what is being done to protect self.

Once operative, ego defenses distort both internal and external reality; the individual may not acknowledge a particular id impulse or some external object. The goal of ego defenses is to reduce the anxiety that comes from tensions between id and superego. In Freud's earlier works, the notion of repression is virtually coextensive with ego defense, but, over time, Freud and later Anna Freud (1946) expanded the list of defenses to include displacement, projection, reaction formation, sublimation, and denial. It is not entirely clear if repression activates these other defenses or is just one of several defenses, but my reading of Freud leads to the conclusion that repression initiates the process of ego defense, with other defenses following repression to complete the ego's defense.

For Freud, repression is the expulsion of painful cognitions from consciousness, making them a part of the unconscious and, hence, not directly accessible to reflective thought. When repressed, the impulses leading to the repression may stay in the unconscious and only surface when the ego defenses are down, as is the case in dreams or slips of the tongue. Yet, even though conscious thought cannot gain full access to repressed impulses, these impulses continue to exert pressure on a person, leading not only to the activation of other defense mechanisms but also pathological behaviors arising from repressed anxiety. Indeed, Freud implied in his clinical work that, once repressed, the emotions surrounding unacceptable impulses build in intensity and increasingly distort the worldview and actions of an individual. Even when the source of the id impulses causing anxiety is removed, Freud appeared to argue that, once repressed, the id impulse and its distortion in the subconscious continue to exert pressure on ego, thus maintaining the distortion and its pathological consequences. Moreover, individuals can get in a vicious cycle of repression of an id impulse leading to periodic leakage of the impulse to consciousness and pathological behavior that, in turn, leads to further repression in an escalating cycle ultimately resulting in severe behavioral pathology.

Displacement was often discussed by Freud in connection with repression. Freud argued that the psychic energy of a repressed impulse continues to circulate in the mind, often finding a "safe" outlet on another person. For instance, repressed anger at another individual, such as one's father, will be of such high intensity that it emerges as displaced hostility toward another male, perhaps a brother. Projection is the process of seeing one's own repressed impulses as residing in the character and behavior of others. Such projection allows the impulse to surface, but on a safe target: another person instead of self. In the case of reaction formation, the polarity of the repressed impulses is reversed, causing an individual to express in thought and behavior the exact opposite of the repressed impulse. For instance, hatred of father can lead to overly expressive proclamations of love for father. Denial involves ignoring the presence of an object, including oneself as an object, that poses a threat to ego processes. The person simply denies that there is an object or event that causes anxiety, often keeping the person "in denial" as a means for avoiding the pain of anxiety associated with an object or event. Finally, sublimation rechannels energy from unacceptable impulses into more acceptable behavior, and in fact, Freud believed that the creative energy of people is fueled by sublimated energy from repressed impulses.

Although Freud's model is clearly skewed by his database—neurotic individuals need-ing therapy—his approach adds something that is often missing in sociological and social psychological analyses of behavior. As noted earlier, there is a kind of cognitive bias in much psychology and sociology that sees individuals as trying to maintain consistency and congruity between self-conceptions and identities, on the one side, and behavioral outputs, reactions of others, and interpretations, on the other (e.g., Burke, 1991; Heise, 1977, 1979). When self is not verified, individuals will change their behavior, try to get others to respond differently, avoid others who do not confirm self, or shift identities or elements of a broader self-conception. In this way, self, behavioral outputs, and responses of others are seen to converge as gestaltlike processes for cognitive consistency. Freud's approach offers an alternative scenario: Individuals will often-times protect ego by activation of defense mechanisms, first through repression and then through other ego defenses. In the more standard sociological accounts of emotions, individuals experience distress and other negative emotions that lead them to make the cognitive and behavioral adjustments to achieve cognitive consistency (Burke 1991). In contrast, Freud's model argues that consistency arising from anxiety is often achieved by the activation of defense mechanisms, and once activated, cognitions and behaviors can become distorted. Moreover, the emotions that are repressed—for Freud, anxiety and guilt being the most prominent—can be transmuted into different emotional expressions through the ego defenses enumerated above. The emotional dynamics for persons and those in interaction change, and dramatically so, once we allow Freudian processes to enter analysis.

REDIRECTION OF PSYCHOANALYTIC THEORY AND RESEARCH

One of the centerpieces of Freudian psychology was the guilt that patients feel over their hostile feelings toward like-sexed parents, with this guilt being repressed and, eventually, causing what today are called anxiety disorders. Freud's model is attuned to guilt because he saw the psychic conflict as occurring primarily between id impulses and the dictates of superego. When individuals experience impulses that violate morality, they feel guilty, and in order to eliminate the anxiety associated with this guilt, repression and other ego defenses are activated. Lewis (1971) offered a useful corrective to Freud's and subsequent psychoanalysts' overemphasis on guilt. In her review of transcripts from therapy sessions, including her own work as a therapist, Lewis coded shame rather than guilt as the most common emotion. Moreover, she felt that therapists often conflated shame and guilt, seeing episodes of shame as guilt. Although an individual can often feel shame and guilt at the same time, Lewis emphasized that these are two very different emotions. Shame is directed at the person's global self—self-conception or prominent identities in sociological terms—whereas guilt is directed at specific behaviors that are perceived by a person to be wrong. Shame makes a person feel small, unworthy, powerless, and in disfavor with others, whereas guilt makes an individual feel that he or she has behaved badly or done a bad thing that separates behavior from an evaluation of the global self. Because shame attacks a person's identity and self, it is much more likely to activate defense mechanisms because it is so painful, whereas guilt is likely to motivate persons to engage in corrective actions to alleviate their guilt. Shame is an emotion that motivates withdrawal, escaping, hiding, and, when repressed, striking back at others who have made a person feel shame. Thus, the emotional dynamics of shame and guilt are very different (see Tangney and Dearing, 2004, for a review of the literature on shame and guilt).

Lewis (1971) argued that individuals employ at least two mechanisms for denying their shame. One is "overt, undifferentiated" shame, whereby a person experiences painful feelings but does not denote these feelings as shame. The shame is disguised as other affective states that are often expressed verbally, and in this manner, a person is able to avoid acknowledging the real source of his or her pain: shame. The other mechanism of denial is to "bypass" the shame before it surfaces in consciousness. The most common techniques are rapid speech and thought as well as body movements that keep the individual from recognizing any emotions, much less the shame that drives his or her hyperactivity.

Shame that is denied, or repressed, reduces interpersonal attunement. Shamed individuals are consumed with protecting self and, as a result, become less able to take on the perspective of others—or to "role take," in Mead's terms. Moreover, shamed individuals will often exhibit aggression toward others in ways that allow them to vent their negative emotional arousal and gain a sense of efficacy and control over feeling small and unworthy. Indeed, individuals can become locked into shame-anger cycles in which inappropriate anger leads to repressed shame, more episodes of anger, new layers of shame, and so on in a cycle that can lead to severe behavioral pathology. These pathological outcomes can be avoided, Lewis (1971) argued, if individuals can remain conscious of their shame, acknowledge the shame, and engage in corrective behaviors to reestablish shame-free social relations. The problem, of course, is that shame is painful and will likely activate ego defenses.

Thus, Lewis (1971) took the basic model provided by Freud and redirected inquiry to shame as opposed to guilt. In so doing, she recast Freudian psychoanalytic theory into a more sociological guise. Therefore, it should not be surprising that sociologists picked up on her work and incorporated it into sociological models of emotional dynamics.

SOCIOLOGICAL THEORIES OF PRIDE AND SHAME

Cooley (1964) viewed humans as being in a constant state of self-feeling. Individuals gaze into the "looking glass" created by the responses of others and derive an image of themselves that always involves a sense for how others are evaluating their behaviors. When the evaluation of others is perceived as positive, persons feel pride, and when the evaluation of others is seen to be negative, individuals experience shame. Even when individuals are not in direct interaction with others, they can imagine how others perceive them, thereby generating either pride or shame. When individuals feel pride, they give off positive emotions to others and, in so doing, increase the level of interpersonal solidarity.

Scheff (1988, 1994, 1997) melded the ideas of Cooley with Lewis to produce a new theory of emotions. Scheff argued that most of the time, pride and shame operate at low levels. In fact, given the negative sanctions that individuals are likely to receive by displaying high levels of these emotions, pride and shame are virtually invisible. Thus, to some degree, pride and shame are repressed. Still, they are the gyroscope guiding human actions. When an individual receives a lack of deference and respect from others, self will be negatively evaluated, leading the person to experience shame. If the shame is acknowledged and used to readjust behaviors in ways to increase interpersonal attunement and mutual respect with others, shame operates as an effective mechanism of social control and increases social solidarity. However, if the shame is denied through what Scheff calls either "overdistancing" or "underdistancing," it leads to hostility toward others, which will decrease interpersonal attunement and break bonds of solidarity.

Overdistancing is the same as Lewis's (1971) overt, undifferentiated shame, where the shame is not isolated from other emotions, whereas overdistancing corresponds to Lewis's concept of bypassed shame, where the shame is completely denied and hidden from self through hyperspeech and body movements. Once denied or repressed, shame can lock people into shame-anger cycles in which the repressed shame leads to outbursts of anger that generate shame that must be denied, only to come out again as anger. These shame-anger cycles can be part of the biography of a person, causing an individual to display a diffuse level of anger and aggression. Moreover, the cycle can be passed down across generations because as parents vent their anger on their children and cause them to experience shame that must be repressed, the children will grow up with diffuse hostility, vent their anger on their children, and thus keep the intergenerational shame-anger cycle going.

Of particular interest is Scheff's (1994) analysis of how macrostructural events can be shaped by population-level shame and anger. Societies revealing taboos against the expression of pride and shame will be characterized by encounters in which shame cannot be acknowledged, leading to repeated denials among many individuals over their lifetimes. This repression leads to a widespread lack of interpersonal attunement across a large segment of the population, which, in turn, will increase the likelihood that shame will be repressed on a population-level scale. As a result, members of the population will reveal diffuse hostility that becomes a potentially volatile force for collective mobilization by political leaders. For example, Scheff as well as Scheff and Retzinger (1991) analyzed the rise of Hitler and the initiation of World War II in these terms. Partly because of the hierarchical culture of Germany, coupled with the humiliation codified in the terms of their defeat in World War I and the degradations of the Great Depression, the population engaged in denial of shame, leading to diffuse hostility that was effectively channeled and targeted by Hitler to the "enemies" of Germany—Jews and other nations.

Scheff's (1994) theory brought the psychoanalytic tradition squarely into symbolic interactionism. Both Scheff and I were trained by Tamotsu Shibutani who, at Berkeley and Santa Barbara, taught a famous course on social control where the ideas of the pragmatists, especially George Herbert Mead and Freud as well as others in psychiatry like Harry Stack Sullivan, were juxtaposed and integrated. Thus, it is not surprising that the two sociologists working with psychoanalytic ideas in the sociology of emotions have a common origin, albeit a short generation apart.

EXPANDING THE THEORY OF EMOTIONS: A NEW KIND OF SYNTHESIS BETWEEN SOCIOLOGY AND PSYCHOANALYTIC IDEAS

Core Elements of the Theory

For well over a decade, I have sought to develop a general theory of interpersonal behavior, beginning with a simple model of emotions that emphasized anxiety reduction as the driving emotional force in social life—an emphasis obviously taken from Freud and the psychoanalytic tradition (Turner 1987, 1988). As I increasingly came to realize, it would be necessary to expand the theory to account for more than anxiety; as I read Scheff's (1988) and Lewis's (1971) theories, I also came to believe that it would be essential to develop a theory that could explain more than the dynamics of pride and shame. As a theorist, trained early in symbolic interactionism but later in virtually all theoretical traditions, the theory that I have developed, thus far, represents a blend of psychoanalytic and symbolic interactionists ideas, but it also incorporates important pieces of the puzzle from many different theoretical traditions in both sociology and psychology.

I began introducing psychoanalytic ideas in the late 1980s to a conceptualization of motivation. I argued that humans have fundamental needs that they seek to meet in every episode of face-to-face interaction (Turner 1987, 1988, 1999, 2002). This list of need states has changed somewhat, but the essentials have remained the same and now include the following:

1. *Needs to verify self.* Humans always attempt to verify their self in interaction. Over the years, I have come to conceptualize self as operating at three levels: (a) transsituational

core self or the mix of cognitions and emotions that people have about themselves as person and that they carry into *every* interaction; (b) subidentities about who one is in institutional spheres (e.g., work, family, community, school); and (c) role identities about who one is or wants to be in a particularly role. Depending on the situation, the salience of these dimensions of self will vary. When salience is high, the emotional stakes are high, and the more core self is on the line in an interaction, the more intense will be the emotional reaction when self is confirmed or disconfirmed by others. In my scheme, verification of self is the most powerful of all transactional needs, with the other needs in their order of importance for the emotional well-being of individuals listed below. When self is verified, positive emotions will be experienced, and the more verification of core self is verified, the more positive will be the emotions felt. Conversely, the less self is verified and the more toward the core-self feelings this lack of verification extends, the more negative will be the level of emotional arousal.

2. *Needs to have profitable exchange payoffs.* Individuals always seek to derive a profit in the exchange of resources with others. Resources can be material or nonmaterial, with positive emotions directed at self being particularly valuable to all persons. Profit is implicitly calculated by (a) the value of resources received, (b) the costs (resources given up) and investments (accumulated costs) incurred to receive resources, (c) the extent to which various levels of self are subject to verification by resources received, (d) the standards of justice employed, and (e) the comparison of the net payoffs to self (less costs and investments) to the payoffs to others (less their costs and investments). When individuals perceive that their payoffs exceed their costs and investments, they will experience positive emotions, and particularly so if resources received also serve to verify self. Conversely, when payoffs to individuals fall below their perception of costs and investments, they will feel negative emotions, and especially so if the failure to have profitable exchange payoffs involves resources needed to verify self.

3. *Needs for group inclusion.* People have a need to sense that they are part of the ongoing flow of interaction. They do not necessarily need to feel high levels of solidarity with others, but they always want to perceive that they are part of the encounter. When they feel included, individuals will experience positive emotions, and particularly so if self is highly salient in the encounter; conversely, they will experience negative emotions when not feeing included, and even more so if self is on the line in an encounter.

4. *Needs for trust.* Humans have needs in all situations to perceive that (a) the behaviors of others are predictable, (b) the responses of others are in synchronization with behaviors of self, (b) the responses of others are sincere, and (d) the responses of others mark respect for self. When persons realize these elements of trust in an encounter, they will experience mild positive emotions, and if self is on the line, they will experience more intense positive emotions. Conversely, when people do not realize these elements of trust, they will experience mild negative emotions, which become more intense to the extent that self, and particularly core self, is salient.

5. *Needs for facticity.* Individuals need to feel that the gestures of others in an encounter signal that (a) the person and others are experiencing a common, intersubjective world, (b) the situation is as it appears, and (c) the reality experienced by self and others has an obdurate character. When individuals sense an underlying facticity in an encounter, they will experience mild positive emotions, whereas they experience mild negative emotions when not feeling this sense of facticity, with the intensity of the negative emotional arousal increasing to the degree that self is salient, and especially so if core self is on the line in an encounter.

In my original model, I saw individuals as experiencing anxiety when what I now call transactional needs (Turner 2002) are not met. Individuals are motivated to avoid anxiety; thus they always seek to verify self, receive positive exchange payoffs, feel part of the group, experience trust, and perceive facticity. It is obvious that there are many more negative emotions than anxiety, as I explore with Stets in Chapter 23 on moral emotions. Three of the primary emotions are negative: sadness, fear, and anger. Each of these has many variants and combinations with other emotions (see Tables 23.1 and 23.2 in Chapter 23; and retain markers for future reference in this chapter, or consult the composite of these in Table 12.1). Thus, anxiety is simply one variant of fear, and it is clear that Freud's emphasis on this emotion as an outcome of repressed guilt was too narrow. Similarly, Lewis's (1971) and Scheff's (1988) emphasis on shame is too restrictive, but shame, like guilt, is a combination of all three negative emotions—what I have termed (Turner 2000) second-order elaborations of primary emotions (also see Chapter 23). Shame is perhaps one of the most important emotions because it attacks self, especially the global or core-self conception of an individual, but it is not the only negative emotion that is relevant to a sociologically oriented psychoanalytic theory. However a new theory needs to specify in greater detail *which* negative and *which* positive emotions will be aroused under *what* specific conditions.

As I expanded this narrow theory of human motivation to a more general theory of emotions, and even more general theory of interpersonal processes (Turner 2002), it became clear that interaction is guided by expectations, as the vast literature on states of expectation so clearly documents (see Berger and Webster, 2006, for a review). When expectations are realized, individuals experience positive emotions. Need states represent one source of expectation states; people always develop expectations for how they can realize the five transactional needs enumerated above. When expectations are clear and high for realization of need states, especially for verification of self and exchange payoffs, the emotional reactions will be more intense. However, increasingly I have come to realize that just about any force operating in an encounter can be a source of expectation states. This realization—which is so obvious that it is amazing that I did not hit upon it earlier—led me to conceptualize what I call "forces." A force is what drives the formation of social reality, and I see forces as very much like those in physics (e.g., gravity) or biology (e.g., natural selection). Thus, transactional needs are one microlevel force because each drives what transpires during the course of interaction. Emotions are another force because they, too, shape the flow of interaction. The other microdynamic forces, listed in Table 12.2, also drive the formation of an encounter. These set up expectation states, and, depending on the degree to which these expectations are realized, people's emotional reactions will vary.

In addition to expectations, the other key process influencing emotional arousal in situations is sanctioning. Sanctions can be negative or positive, with positive sanctioning arousing positive emotions and the converse for negative sanctioning. Hence, there are two basic processes determining the level of emotional arousal in humans—expectations and sanctions—and these are linked to the five basic forces driving all encounters (see Turner, 2002, for the more general theory of microdynamics). The forces driving encounters are unique to face-to-face interaction; other forces drive mesolevel and macrolevel domains of social reality. A critical point in my approach is that social reality unfolds at a microlevel, mesolevel, and macrolevel and that each level has its own forces determining the formation of structures at this level. At the microlevel, the forces listed in Table 12.2 shape the flow of interaction in encounters as the most elemental structural unit; at the mesolevel, the forces of segmentation, differentiation, and integration direct the formation of corporate units (revealing a division of labor for achieving ends) and categoric units (marking social differences and distinctions among individuals); and at the macrolevel, population, production, reproduction, regulation, and distribution drive the formation of institutional domains (composed of corporate units) and stratification system (composed of categoric

TABLE 12.1. Variant and Elaborations of Primary Emotions

Emotion	Variations			First-order emotions	Second-order emotions
	Low intensity	Moderate intensity	High intensity		
Satisfaction-happiness	Content, sanguine, serene, gratified	Cheerful, buoyant, friendly, amiable, enjoyable	Joy, bliss, rapture, jubilant, gaiety, elation, delight, thrilled, exhilarated	+ Fear: wonder, hopeful, gratitude, prided + Anger: vengeance, appeased, calmed soothed, relish, triumphant, bemused + Sadness: nostalgia, yearning, hopefulness	
Aversion-fear	Concern, hesitant, reluctance, shyness	Misgivings, trepidation, anxiety, scared, alarmed, unnerved, panic	Terror, horror, high anxiety	+ Happiness: awe, reverence, veneration + Anger: revulsed, repulsed, dislike, envy, antagonism + Sadness: dread, wariness	
Assertion-anger	Annoyed, agitated, irritated, vexed, perturbed, nettled, rankled, piqued	Displeased, frustrated, belligerent, contentious, hostile, ire, animosity, offended, consternation	Dislike, loathing, disgust, hate, despise, detest, hatred, seething, wrath, furious, inflamed, incensed, outrage	+ Happiness: snubbing, mollified, rudeness, placated, righteousness + Fear: abhorrence, jealousy, suspicion + Sadness: bitterness, depression, betrayed	
Disappointment-sadness	Discouraged, downcast, dispirited	Dismayed, disheartened, glum, resigned, gloomy, woeful, pained, dejected	Sorrow, heartsick, despondent, anguished, crestfallen	+ Happiness: acceptance, moroseness, solace, melancholy + Fear: forlornness, remorsefulness, misery + Anger: aggrieved, discontent, dissatisfied, unfulfilled, boredom, grief, envy, sulleness	+ Fear, anger: guilt + Anger, fear: shame

TABLE 12.2. Microlevel Forces

1. Emotional forces	The level and type of emotion experienced by self and displayed toward others, and the reactions of others and self to emotions.
2. Transactional forces	The needs of individuals with respect to (a) confirming self, (b) receiving positive exchange payoffs, (c) trusting others, (d) sustaining a sense of group inclusion, and (e) sensing facticity.
3. Symbolic forces	The texts, technologies, values, beliefs/ideologies, and norms guiding (a) the categorization of persons and situations, (b) the frames delimiting what materials are to be included and excluded, (c) the modes of communication to be employed, (d) the types of rituals to be emitted, and (e) the nature, intensity, and timing of emotions to be displayed.
4. Role forces	The mutual emission and interpretation of configurations and syndromes of gestures signaling the likely courses of behavior of individuals toward (a) each other, (b) others, and (c) broader cultural and social contexts.
5. Status forces	The placement of individuals in positions, revealing different characteristics, power, and prestige, as well as varying patterns of network relations.
6. Demographic/ecological forces	The number of individuals co-present, the distinctions among them, the distribution of individuals in space, the use of stages and props, and the movement of individuals.

units) as well as societies and intersocietal systems. Definitions of these forces are listed in Table 12.3.

The fact that social reality unfolds at three levels and is driven by distinct forces operating at each level highlights the *embeddedness* of social phenomena. From a top-down perspective, encounters are embedded in corporate and categoric units; corporate units are embedded in institutional domains and categoric units are embedded in stratification systems and institutional domains; institutional domains and stratification systems are embedded in societies, which, in turn, are embedded in systems of societies. From a bottom-up perspective, mesostructures are produced and reproduced by iterated encounters, whereas institutional and stratification systems are built from corporate and categoric units: Societies are ultimately given their form by the nature of institutional domains and stratification systems, and intersocietal systems are driven by the particular societies connected to one another (typically via various institutional systems).

Embeddedness is important to a general sociological theory of emotions because the emotions aroused at the level of the encounter are constrained by the mesolevel structures in which an encounter is embedded. As we will see, emotions are often directed at mesostructures and, at times, at institutional and stratification systems as well as societal and even intersocietal systems. Indeed, by introducing the dynamics outlined in psychoanalytic theory, links among levels of social reality can be seen as a result of the nature of emotional arousal and the targets of the emotional energy generated in encounters.

Thus, my theory views emotional arousal as directly influenced by expectations and sanctioning occurring at the level of face-to-face interaction in encounters that are embedded into ever more mesostructures and macrostructures. Expectations are constrained, to a degree, by the embedding of encounters in mesostructures and macrostructures as they circumscribe the microdynamics forces listed in Table 12.1. Similarly, emotions are influenced by the patterns of sanctioning at the level of the encounter and the mesostructures and macrostructures in which encounters are embedded. These emotional reactions can be directed at a delimited number of potential targets: self, other(s), local encounter, corporate unit, categoric unit, and, in some cases, institutional domain, stratification system, society, or intersocietal system. The intensity, type, and

TABLE 12.3. Macrolevel and Mesolevel Forces

Macrolevel forces	
1. Population forces	The absolute number, rate of growth, composition, and distribution of people.
2. Production forces	The gathering of resources from the environment, the conversion of resources into commodities, and the creation of services to facilitate gathering and conversion.
3. Distribution forces	The construction of infrastructures to move resources, information, and people in space as well as the use of exchange systems to distribute resources, information, and people.
4. Regulation forces	The consolidation and centralization of power along its four bases (coercion, administrative structures, manipulation of material incentives, and symbols) in order to control and coordinate members of a population.
5. Reproduction forces	The procreation of new members of a population and the transmission of culture to these members as well as the creation and maintenance of sociocultural systems that sustain life and social order.
Mesolevel forces	
1. Segmentation forces	The generation of additional corporate units organizing activities of individuals in the pursuit of ends or goals.
2. Differentiation forces	The creation of new types of corporate unit organizing activities of individuals in pursuit of ends or goals and new categoric units distinguishing people and placing them into socially constructed categories.
3. Integration forces	The maintenance of boundaries, the ordering of relations with corporate and categoric units, and the ordering of relations among corporate and categoric units.

target of emotion are not only influenced by expectations and sanctions, along with embedding, but also by defense mechanisms.

Repression is the master defense mechanism. Whatever we call it—bypassing, overdistancing, underdistancing, or denial—humans are predisposed to push negative emotions, to varying degrees, from consciousness. The more negative the emotions and the more they are associated with a failure to verify self, the more probable is repression. Once negative emotions have moved out of full conscious awareness, the more likely are they to increase in intensity and force ever greater amounts of cognitive control. Most important, the more emotions are repressed, the more they will be transmuted into new kinds of emotional responses. Moreover, the intensified or transmuted emotions will seek different targets, depending on conditions that we should be able to specify, at least in general terms. One of these conditions involves expectations and sanctions associated with transactional needs; another involves the expectations and sanctions associated with the other forces driving encounters; another involves the nature of the original negative emotion that is repressed; another involves the structure of the corporate and categoric units in which encounters are generally embedded; and, finally, yet another involves the defense mechanisms employed. We should, I think, be able to be more precise about the nature of the emotions aroused, repressed, transmuted, and displayed toward self, others, and various levels of social structure.

Some Provisional Generalizations

The intensity of the emotional reaction of individuals to meeting (or failing to meet) expectations and to positive (or negative) sanctions varies considerably under different conditions. To specify these conditions, we need to begin with transactional needs and then move successively through the nature of the emotions aroused, the type of defenses (or lack of defenses) employed by a person, the mesostructures in which an encounter is embedded, and the targets of repressed and transmuted emotions.

TRANSACTIONAL NEEDS. The most emotionally laden transactional need is to verify self, and the more sanctions and expectations revolve around core self conceptions, the greater is the potential for emotional arousal. The more sanctions and expectations focus on subidentities, the less is the emotional reaction compared to core-self conceptions but the greater the emotional reactions compared to role identities. All levels of self, when verified or not verified by others, will cause emotional arousal, but as one moves from role identity to core self, the potential for emotional arousal increases. In general, when a person realizes expectations of any level of self and receives positive sanctions for the self presented to others, the individual will experience mild positive emotions such as satisfaction, contentment, and gratification. If the individual had some fear about whether self would be verified and positively sanctioned, then the first-order emotion of pride (mostly happiness, mixed with some fear) will be felt. When expectations for self-verification are not met or individuals perceived that the self presented is subject to negative sanctions, many variants and elaborations of anger, fear, and sadness are possible. If all three are experienced simultaneously as a second-order elaboration, then a person will experience shame and perhaps guilt for not living up to expectations about how self should be received.

As we will see later, the precise valence of an emotion and its intensity not only vary with which level of self is salient but also with the nature of the negative emotions repressed, the mechanisms used in repression, and the target of repressed and transmuted emotions. For the present, we can conclude that the more individuals perceive that self is not verified and the more this perception moves toward the core-self conception, the more intense will be the negative emotional arousal and the more likely will the negative emotions be repressed, transmuted, and targeted to others and various levels of social structure. Also, true to my symbolic interactionist roots, I should emphasized again that verification of self is the most powerful transactional need, arousing the most powerful emotions—both positive and negative.

The next most powerful transactional need is for positive exchange payoffs. When individuals receive payoffs that they see as proportionate to their costs and investments relative to the costs and investments of others, they will experience mild positive emotions, such as satisfaction. If they receive more than they expected, they will experience more intense positive emotions such as elation, cheerfulness, and delight; however, at some point of "overreward," they will potentially experience guilt, although the overreward will have to be high and potentially involve negative sanctions from others or the perception that a person's overreward leads to underreward for others (Hegtvedt 2006; Jasso 2006). If individuals had fear that they would not receive expected (hoped for) payoffs or that they could not avoid negative sanctions, they will experience pride, and particularly so if self is salient, as they receive profitable exchange payoffs. When an individual does not receive expected rewards or receives sanctions for efforts to receive rewards, or both, this person will experience variants of anger and, potentially, first-order elaborations of anger such as jealousy (anger plus fear), envy (sadness plus anger), or bitterness and betrayal (anger plus sadness). If self is salient and payoffs are seen to be markers of self, then second-order elaborations like shame might be experienced. It takes far less underreward to arouse negative emotions than overreward (Jasso 2006), and so, individuals are attuned to their payoffs relative to others. The more they define payoffs in terms of justice and other moral symbols, the more intense will be the negative emotional arousal. Again, we will need to wait to say more about the specific emotions until the nature of the units in which exchanges occurs, the defense mechanisms employed, and the units targeted are examined.

Group inclusion is the next most powerful transactional need. When individuals feel included, they experience mild positive emotions like satisfaction, but if self-verification is at stake in feeling included and if the person has some fears about meeting expectations for inclusion, then more intense positive emotions like elation or first-order elaborations such as pride will be experienced. When individuals do not feel included, they will experience variants and elaborations of the three negative primary emotions. The exact emotion will, as we will see, be determined by not only the salience of self but also the attributions made.

Trust is the next most powerful transactional need, and depending on whether expectations for trust are met or go unmet, relatively low-intensity positive or negative emotions ensue. If, however, trust becomes conflated with exchange payoffs or self-verification, the emotional reactions— whether positive or negative—will intensify. Pride will be more likely if individuals were initially uncertain about trust that was successfully attained, and variants and elaborations of the three negative primary emotions will be felt and expressed when trust is not achieved. The valence and intensity of the negative emotions are determined by the external attributions made and the relative power of those who did not meet expectations for trust.

Finally, facticity is the least powerful transactional need, leading to mild positive emotions when realized and low-intensity variants of anger when not achieved. Individuals rarely blame self for a failure to achieve facticity; instead, they will blame others and sanction them negatively.

OTHER MICRODYNAMIC PROCESSES.   I cannot outline my entire theory of microdynamics here (see Turner 2002), but let me review some of the key generalizations. By reading down Table 12.2, the substance of each microdynamic force is reviewed. Turning first to the symbolic force, this force pushes individuals to normatize an encounter by developing expectations for categories, frames, modes of communication, rituals, and feelings. When an encounter is successfully normatized along these lines, individuals experience mild positive emotions, but when it is not normatized along any or all dimensions of normatization, individuals will generally feel variants of fear and anger. People become angry at what they perceive to be others' violation of key norms as well as at the extra interpersonal work in renegotiating normative agreements, and they may experience fear that the interaction is coming unraveled. If self is salient or if valued exchange payoffs are on the line, the emotional intensity will increase. Individuals will generally blame or fear others when normatization is unsuccessful, but other kinds of attribution are possible, as I will explore later.

Turning to role dynamics, individuals have conceptions of roles in their stocks of knowledge; and through role-taking, they read the gestures of others and scan their stocks of knowledgeability to discover the role that others are playing. People pay particular attention to the extent that others' self-concept and subidentities are tied up in a role. Conversely, people seek to make a role for themselves in situations (R. Turner 1962) and have others verify this role. The more core self and subidentities are invested in a role, the greater will be the potential for intense emotional reactions. When individuals have a role verified, they experience mild positive emotions, and when they had some fear about successfully getting others to verify a role, they will experience pride if they perceive others as confirming the role, and especially so if self is salient in the role. However, when a role is not verified and when self is tied into this role, individuals can experience the full range of negative emotional arousal. They can be angry at others or the social unit; they can be fearful about what the failure to verify means; and they can be sad about not having a key role confirmed. Also, if all three negative emotions are experienced simultaneously, persons will experience shame for not meeting expectations or receiving negative sanctions from others about their role, and they might even experience guilt if they defined the need to verify a role in moral terms. The level of repression, transmutation, and externalization of these emotions will shift the emotional dynamics, as I will examine shortly.

Status dynamics revolve around the distribution of prestige and power in networks of varying degrees of density. The greater the inequality in the distribution of prestige and power, the more hierarchical will be the status system; and the more hierarchical the system, the more clear-cut expectations for performances and the more likely negative sanctions will ensue when individuals do not meet expectations. As long as expectations are met, individuals experience mild positive emotions; however, when expectations for performance are not realized, a variety of negative emotional dynamics are potentially unleashed. Individuals who do not meet expectations will be sanctioned negatively, as will individuals who challenge the status order and thereby violate expectations for their place in this order. The exact negative emotions that arise will also be influenced by the attributions made for breaches in the status order and the units perceived to be responsible for the breach—topics that I explore below.

Finally, expectations develop over the demography and ecology of encounters. As long as individuals abide by these expectations, they all experience mild positive emotions; however, if these expectations are violated, anger generally ensues, and those perceived to violate understandings are sanctioned negatively. At times, if violations occur by powerful individuals, the valence of the negative emotions turns to fear, and on those occasions when a person perceives that he or she is the cause of the violation, sadness and mild forms of shame, such as embarrassment, are likely.

THE EMBEDDING OF ENCOUNTERS.   The arousal of emotions in the first place and the targets of these emotions when they do arise are very much influenced by the nature of mesolevel units in which an encounter is embedded. In turn, the properties of the mesolevel units are constrained by the culture and structure of the macrolevel units (institutions, stratification systems, societies, and intersocietal systems) in which mesolevel units are embedded. In Table 12.4, I outline some key properties of corporate units and categoric units. These properties affect the nature of emotional arousal in encounters embedded in mesolevel units. With respect to corporate units, clearly bounded corporate units revealing a formal structure and an explicit division of labor (horizontal and vertical) will operate to establish unambiguous expectations for individuals in encounters. As a consequence, individuals are likely to know how and in what ways they are to realize transactional needs, what role they can make for themselves, what their status is vis-à-vis other status positions, how they can normatize the situation, and what ecology and demography mean. When individuals can be clear on expectations, they are more likely to behave in ways that allow them to experience mild positive emotions, unless the vertical division of labor leads those in higher positions to impose costs on those in lower positions and to violate expectation states

TABLE 12.4. **Key Properties of Corporate and Categoric Units**

Corporate units	Categoric units
1. Size of unit	1. Homogeneity of members in unit
2. Integrity of boundaries	2. Discreteness of features defining membership
3. Formality of structure	3. Differential value or rank of categories
4. Explicitness and scope of horizontal division of labor	4. Correlation among categoric units
5. Explicitness and scope of vertical division of labor	5. Correlation of categoric units with division of labor in corporate units

TABLE 12.5. Repression, Defense, Transmutation, and Targeting of Emotions

Repressed emotions	Defense mechanism	Transmutation to:	Target
Anger, sadness, fear, shame, and guilt	Displacement	Anger	Others, corporate units, and categoric units
Anger, sadness, fear, shame, and guilt	Projection	Little, but some anger	Imputation of anger, sadness, fear, shame, or guilt to dispositional states of others
Anger, sadness, fear, shame, and guilt	Sublimation	Positive emotions	Tasks in corporate units
Anger, sadness, fear, shame, and guilt	Attribution	Anger	Others, corporate units, or categoric units

for how superordinates are to behave. Under these latter conditions, individuals will experience anger, fear, and perhaps sadness if the violation of expectations and negative sanctions from superordinates are chronic. If these emotions become repressed, they are often transmuted into alienation from the corporate structure and, at times, anger for the larger corporate unit.

With respect to categoric units (right column in Table 12.4), homogeneity of categoric unit membership among participants to an encounter increases the likelihood that each individual will experience mild positive emotions. When participants to an encounter come from different categoric units, expectations will be more explicit if the units are discrete, differentially valued, and correlated with each other (i.e., membership in one categoric unit predicts membership in another, thus doubling the expectations and differential evaluation). Also, when membership is correlated with the division of labor in a corporate unit, expectations will be unambiguous and carry the weight of both the status structure of the corporate unit and the differential evaluation of the categoric unit. Under these conditions, individuals know what to expect and will, therefore, generally behave in ways that allow for the arousal of mild positive emotions from having their expectations realized and from positive sanctioning. However, those who are members of less valued categoric units will often experience variants of fear (anxiety, stress), anger, and sadness, as individuals treat them as less worthy. As a consequence, these emotions may be suppressed, transmuted, and projected outward. Yet, even among those in categoric units that are given less value, clarity of membership establishes clear expectations, and when expectations are unambiguous, individuals usually follow them because to do otherwise invites negative sanctioning, which can be even more costly than being a member of a less valued categoric unit. Still, if individuals repress negative emotions arising from their low evaluation, then the emotional dynamics of the encounter change.

THE ACTIVATION OF DEFENSE MECHANISMS. Table 12.5 outlines the emotions that are likely to arise from the activation of various defense mechanisms. Negative emotions are repressed, and depending on the mechanism—projection, displacement, sublimation, or attribution—the emotional dynamics will vary. The repressed emotions are likely to be variants of anger, fear, sadness, as well as first-order and second-order emotions, particularly shame and guilt (shame more than guilt because the latter often leads to efforts at repair). If displacement of these emotions occurs, they are almost always transmuted into anger and vented on safe objects that cannot easily fight back and negatively sanction a person (e.g., a lower ranking person, the situation, the corporate unit, or members of categoric units). If projection is employed, transmutation is less likely because the emotion—whether fear, anger, sadness, shame, or guilt—is imputed to another person. If sublimation is the ego defense, then the emotion is transmuted into positive emotional energy for tasks performed by the persons alone or in their roles within the status structure of corporate units. However, sublimated emotions often come out when the positive glow of energy is relaxed or when fatigue sets in. Indeed, virtually all repressed individuals will often reveal intense spikes of negative emotions—anxiety and fear, sadness, anger, shame, or guilt—when the cortical censors are relaxed, as they are with fatigue or alcohol use.

The bottom of Table 12.5 lists the defense mechanism of attribution, which I think is the most important defense mechanism for sociological analysis. When individuals do not repress fear, anger, sadness, shame, or guilt, they will experience the full emotion if they make a self-attribution; that is, if self is considered to be responsible for failing to meet expectations or for receiving negative sanctions, then the person will experience shame or guilt (which are the second-order elaborations of anger, fear, and sadness). The emotion is not transmuted, and as a result, it can serve to bring individuals back into line through apologies and repairs to breaches in interaction. Once repressed, however, the emotion generally is transmuted into anger at external objects that are seen to be the cause of the failure to meet expectations or the receipt of negative sanctions. If the attribution is to another person, then variants of anger (e.g., annoyed, piqued, displeased, offended, loathing, wrath) or first-order elaborations of anger with other emotions (e.g., dislike, antagonism, righteousness, abhorence, bitterness, betrayal, aggrieved) are the most dominant emotions directed at this person. If the other person is powerful, then displacement might accompany attribution, and the original emotion will be transmuted to anger, directed at safer targets such as the structure of a corporate unit or members of a categoric unit.

As attributions shift to corporate and categoric units, the emotional intensity will often increase to emotional states like vengeance and other high-intensity first-order elaborations (generally, anger mixed with a sense of happiness at doing harm to "enemies"). Moreover, the emotions will typically be codified into prejudicial beliefs about the negative qualities of those social units seen as causing negative emotional arousal. Terrorism, for example, is driven by hatred and a desire for vengeance against whole populations, societies, and systems of societies; and the biographies of many terrorists, I suspect, reveal a history of shame transmuted into anger and externalized as an attribution to, and prejudicial beliefs about, safe targets. As individuals reveal anger at corporate and categoric units, they will also have their sadness and anger transmuted into a sense of alienation from social structures.

Attribution is thus more than a cognitive process of assigning causality to events; it is also a part of ego's defense system to protect self from painful negative emotions, particularly shame. It is what generates aggression toward, prejudices about, and alienation from social structures. Conversely, if attributions to social structures are made for positive emotions (from meeting expectations and receiving positive sanctions), then attribution is the process that generates attachments to social structures and solidarity with those incumbent in these structures. External attributions thus operate as an emotional switching station, pushing both negative and positive emotions outward toward social structures, typically mesolevel corporate and categoric but at times the macrostructures in which these mesolevel units are embedded.

Negative emotions reveal, as Lawler (2001, 2006) has argued, a distal bias, which I see as an outcome of repression and external attributions to others, corporate units, and categoric units. Conversely, positive emotional arousal reveals a proximal bias, with individuals making attributions to meet expectations and receive positive sanctions to self or, typically, others in the local situation. Thus, negative emotional energy tends to move toward social structures, whereas positive emotional energy tends to stay local (self, others, the encounter, and perhaps to categories of others in the encounter). Given these biases, it is not difficult to see why legitimization of macrostructures is difficult to achieve because individuals must make external attributions for their success in meeting expectations and positive sanctions across a range of encounters to institutional domains, stratification systems, societies, and even systems of societies. Conversely, the operation of defense mechanisms and external attributions moves negative emotions outward and, potentially, toward macrostructures that maintain social order. Thus, built into the very nature of defense mechanisms is a bias for delegitimization of mesostructures and potentially macrostructures. Once large numbers of individuals cannot realize expectations and they receive negative sanctions in encounters lodged in mesostructures that are, in turn, embedded in institutional domains, stratification systems, whole societies, and systems of societies, the external attributions can move immediately outward to ever more macrostructures, thus leading to delegitimization. Embedding thus provides the conduit for negative emotional energy—as intensified and transformed by defense mechanisms, transmutation, and external attributions—to target larger-scale social structures. Indeed, these defense mechanisms can translate negative emotions experienced at the level of the local encounter into heat-seeking missiles that target and try to destroy macrostructures.

This movement outward of negative emotional energy is accelerated with emotions activated when the two most powerful transactional needs—for self-confirmation and exchange payoffs—are not realized. Individuals will try to protect self and immediately activate ego defenses, and they will generally see the failure to receive expected resources in terms of codified norms/beliefs about justice and fairness, which, in turn, activate another level of anger on top of the shame-anger cycle for transmuted shame. However, unlike a shame-anger cycle that is directed at others who can sanction a person negatively (thus increasing shame), the shame that is transmuted into anger and directed at more remote social structures does not lead to more shame, but to more anger. Hence, the control functions inherent in interpersonal shame are sidestepped in what can be a very deadly expression of extreme anger. People rarely feel shame when they express anger toward remote social structures. To the degree that this anger is consistently fueled by shame about self and anger because of a failure to receive an exchange payoff at the level of local encounters, this individual can protect self from shame by making causal attributions about mesostructures and macrostructures, without fear of negative interpersonal sanctioning.

CONCLUSION

This chapter outlines some of the generalization that I have developed over the past few years—generalizations that incorporate the useful elements of psychoanalytic theory. This effort represents a work in progress, but my goal should be clear: to develop a theory of emotions that ties psychodynamic processes to social structural conditions. Emotions are aroused under particular conditions, and they are directed at a delimited range of targets: self, others, an encounter, corporate units, categoric units, institutional domains, stratification systems, societies, and intersocietal systems. As long as emotions are examined only in the microcontext and as operating under gestalt principles of balance, congruity, and consistency, the sociological analysis of emotions will remain limited. Taking key insights from the psychoanalytic tradition represents one important strategy for expanding analysis. Connecting this blend of traditions to the nature of social structure represents another useful way to extend the sociology of emotions.

Another point that I have emphasized is that emotions must be conceptualized in a more robust fashion than currently employed in most sociological approaches (with obvious exceptions such as Thamm's typology developed in Chapter 1). Too often, a few master emotions like shame and pride are emphasized to the exclusion of the full range of variation of first- and second-order elaborations. Moreover, although emotions do valence on a negative to positive pole, the nature of the negative or positive emotions *does make a difference* in the experiences of individuals, the ego defenses employed, the behaviors of individuals and their reactions to others, the emotions they feel for others, and for encounters in mesostructures and macrostructures. Psychoanalytic theory opens some new doors and provides new leads that can make sociological theories of emotions more robust.

My movement into the sociology of emotions still comprises well under a decade of exploration, although I did posit almost 20 years ago a simple view of motivation as directed by efforts to avoid anxiety (Turner 1987, 1988). As I have spent time in the field, it is clear to me that only sociology is positioned to analyze the full range of human emotions because so much of what transpires at the level of the encounter is influenced by people's location in embedded social structures. The next step in theorizing is to be even more specific than I have been in this chapter on which emotions are aroused under certain social structural conditions to produce particular effects on behavior and orientation to social structures. I have offered only a glimpse of what is possible, as have others in this volume. However, there is much more work to be done, and more will be accomplished if we supplement the dominant gestalt assumptions in many sociological approaches with those from the psychoanalytic tradition while trying to factor in how social structure (and the attendant culture of social structures) shapes and is shaped by emotional arousal among individuals in face-to-face encounters.

REFERENCES

Berger, Joseph, and Murray Webster. 2006. "Expectations, Status, and Behavior." Pp. 268–300 in *Contemporary Social Psychological Theories*, edited by P. J. Burke. Stanford, CA: Stanford University Press.

Burke, Peter J. 1991. "Identity Processes and Social Stress." *American Sociological Review* 56: 836–849.

Cooley, Charles Horton. [1902] 1964. *Human Nature and the Social Order*. New York: Schocken.

Durkheim, Emile. [1893] 1984. *The Division of Labor in Society*. New York: Free Press.

Freud, Anna. 1946. *The Ego and the Mechanisms of Defense*. New York: International Publishers.

Freud, Sigmund. 1900. *The Interpretation of Dreams*. London: Hogarth.

———. 1923. *The Ego and the Id*. London: Hogarth.

———. 1938. *An Outline of Psychoanalysis*. New York: Norton.

Hegtvedt, Karen. 2006. "Distributive Justice." Pp. 46–69 in *Contemporary Social Psychological Theories,* edited by P. J. Burke. Stanford, CA: Stanford University Press.

Heise, David R. 1977. "Social Action as the Control of Affect." *Social Psychology Quarterly* 56: 100–119.

———. 1979. *Understanding Events: Affect and the Construction of Social Action*. Cambridge: Cambridge University Press.

Jasso, Guillermina. 2006. "The Theory of Comparison Processes." Pp. 165–193 in *Contemporary Social Psychological Theories*, edited by P. J. Burke. Stanford, CA: Stanford University Press.

Lawler, Edward J. 2001. "An Affect Theory of Social Exchange." *American Journal of Sociology* 107: 321–352.

———. 2006. "The Affect Theory of Social Exchange." Pp. 244–267 in *Contemporary Social Psychology Theories*, edited by P. J. Burke. Stanford, CA: Stanford University Press.

Lewis, Helen Block. 1971. *Shame and Guilt in Neurosis*. New York: International Universities Press.

Mead, George Herbert. 1934. *Mind, Self, and Society*. Chicago: University of Chicago Press.

Scheff, Thomas. 1988. "Shame and Conformity: The Deference-Emotion System." *American Sociological Review* 53: 395–406.

———. 1994. *Bloody Revenge: Emotions, Nationalism and War*. Boulder, CO: Westview Press.

———. 1997. *Emotions, the Social Bond, and Human Reality*. New York: Cambridge University Press.

Scheff, Thomas, and Suzanne M. Retzinger. 1991. *Emotions and Violence: Shame and Rage in Destructive Conflicts*. Lexington, MA: Lexington.

Tangney, June Price, and Ronda L. Dearing. 2004. *Shame and Guilt*. New York: Guilford.

Turner, Jonathan H. 1987. "Toward a Sociological Theory of Motivation." *American Sociological Review* 52: 15–27.

———. 1988. *A Theory of Social Interaction*. Stanford, CA: Stanford University Press.

———. 1999. "Toward a General Sociological Theory of Emotions." *Journal for the Theory of Social Behavior* 29: 132–162.

———. 2000. *On the Origins of Human Emotions: A Sociological Inquiry into the Evolution of Human Affect*. Stanford, CA: Stanford University Press.

———. 2002. *Face-to-Face: Toward a Sociological Theory of Interpersonal Behavior*. Stanford, CA: Stanford University Press.

Turner, Ralph. 1962. "Role-Taking: Process versus Conformity." Pp. 20–40 in *Human Behavior and Social Processes*, edited by A. M. Rose. Boston: Houghton Mifflin.

CHAPTER 13

Social Exchange Theory of Emotions

Edward J. Lawler
Shane R. Thye

Emotions are likely to be produced when two or more people exchange valued outcomes (i.e., goods, rewards, payoffs). Emotions are internal events that occur within an actor and that stem from conditions or events external to the actor (e.g., the behavior of others, results of exchange, social context). These may take various forms, including general feelings of pleasure/satisfaction or displeasure/dissatisfaction or more specific feelings of anger, shame, pride, gratitude, and so forth. It is reasonable to presume that any emotions felt by actors due to their exchange could have important effects on their future exchanges and their relationships. For example, if the exchanges make them feel good or feel gratitude toward each other, their inclination to exchange should increase and they may develop a stronger relationship over time. On the other hand, if they feel anger or shame after concluding an exchange, their inclination to exchange in the future should decrease and a relationship may not develop at all. This chapter reviews theoretical and empirical work bearing on how and when emotions or feelings from social exchange affect the development and strength of social relations and groups.

One would not expect to find a large amount of work on emotion within social exchange theorizing, given the underlying assumptions of this tradition. Social exchange theories assume an instrumental view *of actors* (i.e., they are self-interested and oriented to increasing if not

Edward J. Lawler • Department of Organizational Behavior, School of Industrial and Labor Relations and Department of Sociology, Cornell University, Ithaca, NY 14853
Shane R. Thye • Department of Sociology, University of South Carolina, Columbia, SC 29208

The research underlying this chapter has been supported by four NSF grants over the past 12 years, and the authors express appreciation to Jeongkoo Yoon, who has been heavily involved in the research.

maximizing rewards) and *of social units* (i.e., relations and groups form and persist because they provide rewards or protect against punishments). Two guiding principles are as follows: (a) behaviors that generate rewarding consequences for the actor are repeated; and (b) actors stay in relations and groups from which they receive rewards that are comparatively better than rewards available elsewhere (e.g., Emerson 1972a; Molm and Cook 1995; Thibaut and Kelley 1959). Relations, groups, and larger social units are *means* for generating individual rewards (Hechter 1987), not ends in themselves. An important implication is that, in social exchange theory, social units (relations, groups, organizations) are precarious and unstable, because members come and go as changes occur in structural opportunities, incentives, values, or preferences. This makes social order at the microlevel or macrolevel problematic because it is contingent on stable structures and incentives that motivate and shape repetitive patterns of behavior and interaction. We propose that emotional processes in exchange can "solve" this social order problem by generating affective attachments to social units, rendering those units salient and objects of value in their own right.

There are currently two microfoundations for social exchange theorizing, each reflecting a different variation on the above instrumental theme: reinforcement or operant theory (Emerson 1972a; Homans 1961) and rational-choice theory (Elster 1986; Molm and Cook 1995; Willer 1999). An important difference between these two microfoundations is that, in a reinforcement framework, actors are assumed to "look backward" (i.e., orient their behavior to past experience), whereas in a rational-choice framework, actors are assumed to "look forward" (i.e., orient their behavior to future states of affairs or goals) (see Macy 1993). Exchange theories typically are built on one or both of these metatheoretical frameworks, implicitly or explicitly. Interestingly, based on some psychological theory and research (Izard 1991), "looking backward" and "looking forward" produce distinct emotional responses—looking backward may produces joy and comfort, whereas looking forward may produces interest and excitement. Thus, these different temporal perspectives (backward or forward) may have different consequences for relations and groups based on social exchange.

Exchange-theoretic actors are decidedly unemotional or emotionally vacuous (Lawler and Thye 1999). In exchange theory, actors process information, interpret others' intentions, and respond to rewards, but the fact that they also emote is generally neglected in the literature (see Homans, 1950, for a notable exception). One obvious reason for this neglect is that exchange theorists generally are inclined to eschew "internal states" in lieu of structural and behavioral explanations (Emerson 1972a, 1972b; Willer 1999). Cognitive notions of risk and trust have been borrowed from psychology and economics (e.g., Cook 2001; Molm 1997; Yamagishi and Yamagishi 1994) and used mainly to round out and deepen instrumental explanations of behavior. Yet, even here there are potentially relevant emotions, such as fear, confidence, gratitude, or anger, that could be important to understanding risk and trust. The purpose of this chapter is to theorize emotions in social exchange, develop the implications for relations and groups, and selectively review empirical literature.

THE PROBLEM

The core problem addressed by this chapter is to examine and explain the "order-producing" effects of emotions in social exchange. We assume that a social structure is the prime context within which actors may or may not exchange; exchange is voluntary and actors engage in a process of interaction that may or may not produce an exchange. We posit that individuals respond emotionally to the "results" of a social exchange (i.e., to the fact of exchange and to the rewards received). The emotions involve general positive or negative feelings—"feeling good" or "feeling bad." Key issues include how and when such feelings are produced by social exchange, and how and when individually felt emotions generate affective attachments to their relational or group affiliations. Person-to-group attachments would produce greater order and stability, because actors then would be more likely to stay in the relation or group, develop a collective orientation that moderates narrow self-interest, and trust others within the relation or group. Person-to-unit ties with an affective basis transform relations or groups into expressive objects of value in and of themselves.

A Social Formations Approach

In an earlier paper, Lawler and Thye (1999) analyzed a wide range of theoretical ideas that can be applied to emotions in social exchange. The purpose was to explore different points or places where emotions are important. Some of these ideas were from social exchange theory; however, most were from other areas of sociology and psychology. More specifically, Lawler and Thye offered a framework that identifies three junctures in social exchange at which emotions play an important role: (1) as integral elements of the *social context* of social exchange; (2) as features of the *processes* of exchange; and (3) as results of the *outcomes* of social exchange. *Social context theories* analyze norms about what emotions to feel or express in a given situation (Hochschild 1979, 1983), and why status/power differentiation generates different emotional responses from higher and lower power or status actors (Kemper 1978, 1987; Ridgeway and Johnson 1990). *Process-oriented theories* emphasize the signaling effects of emotions—to self (Heise 1987) and to others (Frank 1988)—and how emotions modify cognitions (Bower 1991; Isen 1987). *Outcome-oriented theories* examine the emotional effects of achieving an exchange and the impact of these emotions on personal commitment (Molm 2003a) or commitment to the relation or group itself (Lawler et al. 2000; Lawler and Yoon 1996). Lawler and Thye (1999) refer to the latter as the "social formations" approach because it addresses the conditions under which social exchanges create, sustain, or undermine social formations or social units. The larger issue is to understand how social exchange contributes to the creation of social order (Lawler 2002).

This chapter emphasizes and elaborates the social formations approach—in particular, when and how emotional responses to outcomes of social exchange strengthen or weaken relations and groups. Because of this focus, the chapter should not be interpreted as a comprehensive review but, rather, a selective treatment of emotions, focused on our own line of research over the past 10–15 years (Lawler 2001, 2002, 2003; Lawler and Thye 1999; Lawler et al. 2000; Lawler and Yoon 1993, 1996, 1998; Thye et al. 2002). This focus also reflects the fact that whereas emotions play different roles at different junctures in exchange (see Lawler and Thye 1999), social exchange is fundamentally an *outcome-oriented* theory. If we can show that exchange outcomes produce emotions and these emotions affect order (i.e., cohesion, commitment, and solidarity) in relations and groups, this adds an important dimension to extant exchange theorizing. Because emotions can be associated with different social objects (e.g., self, other, relation, group), we need to explain when emotions are attached to social units whether the social unit is a relationship, group, network, organization, community, or society.

Concept of Emotion

A standard definition of emotions is that they are positive or negative evaluative states with physiological, neurological, and cognitive components (Izard 1991). Emotions are internal states of the human organism, reflecting the organism's response to external stimuli. The neurological correlates are homeostatic mechanisms often ascribed to the evolutionary adaptation of the species (Pinker 1997; Turner 2000). Damasio (1999) made an important distinction between "feelings" and "feeling feelings." The former entail neurological states of the organism, wired, learned, and unconscious; the latter are feelings that the individual is aware of in some minimal sense, at least aware of their bodily organism's response (i.e., the feeling of a feeling). A unique feature of emotions is that they induce organismwide neurological effects (e.g., Damasio et al. 2000); that is, emotions activate chemical secretions that produce organismwide states. When an actor feels good, she feels good all over; when an actor feels bad or depressed, she feels bad all over. In part because of this, Damasio argued that "feeling feelings" is the most fundamental basis for consciousness—in particular the sense of a distinction between the internal states of the person as an organism (now felt) and stimuli external to the person (external environment). In this sense, the experience of feelings implies a rudimentary sense of self, juxtaposed to the external objects or events that are emotion-producing (Damasio 1999).

This chapter makes a case for treating emotions as central features of social exchange (i.e., as a third microfoundation, along with reinforcement and rational choice). Recent research of neuroscientists adds empirical weight to this point of view. There is strong evidence that elements central to social exchange theory (i.e., rewards and punishments) produce emotional counterparts (i.e., neurological or chemical manifestations) in the human brain. Rewarding stimuli activate certain emotional regions of the brain, and the regions of the brain activated by rewards versus punishments are different (e.g., Blood and Zatorre 2001; Damasio 1999; Damasio et al. 2000; Small et al. 2001). Damasio et al. (2000) observed different brain activation patterns for feelings of happiness and sadness and suggested that the subjective feeling of an emotion by an actor is correlated with changing internal states within the brain. Ashby et al. (1999) also showed that both reward and positive affect generate dopamine secretions in particular regions of the brain, and these secretions enhance cognitive flexibility, such as the capacity to look at stimuli from different perspectives. Negative affect, in turn, is mediated by different neural pathways and fosters less cognitive flexibility. By implication, if rewards and punishments generate emotional responses that impact neurological pathways in such fundamental ways, it is reasonable to argue that emotions and feelings are as central to social exchange as behaviors and cognitions are. It is also reasonable to propose that emotions have distinguishable effects on social formations, apart from other internal states (cognitions).

SOCIAL EXCHANGE THEORIES: BACKGROUND

Homans (1950, 1961) offered the first systematic social exchange theory, and the first to include emotion in a systematic way. In Homans's (1950) work on the human group, he theorized that any social context can be analyzed in terms of what *activities* are undertaken, how often *interaction* occurs between or among given individuals, and what *sentiments* develop among those that interact frequently. Sentiment here refers to "internal states of the human body," including affection, sympathy, antagonism, and liking/disliking. The focus is solely interpersonal, person-to-person rather than person-to-unit, sentiments. Homans used interaction frequency and sentiments (emotions) to explain the formation and strength of social relations. An external context or structure generates activities (e.g., tasks) within which individuals interact regularly; more frequent interaction tends to generate positive sentiments between the actors (interpersonal), and this underlies the strength of their relationship. In the *Human Group*, Homans (1950) placed an *interaction-to-emotion-to-relation* process at the center of his analysis, and this is an important backdrop for recent work on exchange and emotion (see Lawler 2006). To him, task activity, self, and other are the primary social objects. To us, social units also are important objects in exchange contexts and processes. We subscribe to Parsons's (1951) view that person-to-person and person-to-unit ties are fundamental to questions about social order.

In Homans' (1961, 1974) later work, he reinterpreted interaction and its effects on sentiment in reinforcement (operant psychology) terms. The focus turned to how rewards that A gives to B shape B's behavior in social interaction or exchange and vice versa (see also Emerson 1972a). Here, sentiments refer to "spontaneous" emotional responses that are felt immediately as a result of reinforcement or punishment. If repeated, they produce consistent patterns of behavior and can be interpreted in the context of the other more basic behavioral propositions (see Homans 1961, 1974; Lawler 2006). As part of his theoretical framework, Homans offered an "aggression-approval proposition" indicating that rewards or punishments, if unexpected, produce pleasure and anger. The "if unexpected" provision reflects the fact that these emotional responses are particularly useful to account for unusual circumstances or exceptions, rather than being at the center of his propositional framework. In operant-psychology terms, external reinforcements and punishments generally are sufficient to explain behavior, and sentiments or emotions are generally epiphenomenal. We adopt the idea that emotions are internal rewards and punishments, a view echoed by more recent work of psychologists (Izard 1991; Stets 2003), but we treat emotions as distinct stimuli, rather than subsuming them under standard rubrics of external reinforcement or punishment (see Damasio 1999).

The most precise of early exchange theories was offered by Thibaut and Kelley (1959). The theory focuses on dyads and suggests that social comparisons guide exchange behaviors. It presumes that individuals evaluate a dyadic relationship against an internal standard called a comparison level (CL) and, further, that individuals assess the attractiveness of other potential relations by comparing their focal relationship to the benefits expected from others (CL_{ALT}). Consistent with Homans' focus on reward contingencies, the theory defines the power of actor A over B as A's ability to affect the quality of outcomes attained by B. There are two ways that this can occur. *Fate control* exists when actor A affects actor B's outcome by changing her (A's) own behavior, independent of B's action. For example, if B is more heavily rewarded when A chooses one behavior over another, then A has fate control over B. *Behavior control* exists when the rewards obtained by B are a joint function of both A's and B's behavior. In either case, whether A has fate control or behavior control, B is dependent on A for valued rewards and, thus, A has some power over B. Other exchange theories that emerged during that same time frame echo the importance of social comparison, valued goods, and dependence. Emotions were simply not part of the theoretical landscape.

A major theoretical shift occurred in the early 1970s, with the development of Emerson's *power dependence theory* (Emerson 1972a, 1972b). Unlike previous theorists, Emerson cast exchange processes in broader terms. He put forth the notion that relations between actors are part of a larger set of potential exchange relations (i.e., an exchange network). Thus, in analyzing a dyad, he asserted that it is important to consider its broader connection to other dyads—the larger network in which it is embedded. Emerson considered two kinds of connection. A *negative connection* exists when interaction in one dyad reduces interaction in another. A *positive connection* exists when interaction in one dyad promotes interaction in another. The focus on connectedness across dyadic sets gave Emerson's theorizing a decidedly structural theme; his were network-embedded dyads.

As with other exchange theorists of the time, dependence is the centerpiece of Emerson's theory (Emerson 1972b). He coined his approach "power dependence theory" and anchored this theory in operant psychology (see Emerson 1972a), relying heavily on the concepts of reward and cost. The key assumption of the theory claims that the power of actor A over actor B is equal to the dependence of B on A, summarized by the equation $P_{AB} = D_{BA}$. In turn, dependence is a function of two factors: the availability of alternative exchange relations and the extent to which the actors value those relations. To illustrate, imagine a computer manufacturer (A) that must purchase specialized parts from a dealer (B). When the needed parts are not widely available from other suppliers, but computer manufacturers are abundant, then A is more dependent on B than B is on A ($D_{AB} > D_{BA}$) due to availability. When the manufacturer values parts more than the supplier values customers, then again A is more dependent on B ($D_{AB} > D_{BA}$). In both cases, the theory predicts B has power over A. Emotions, in power dependence theory, simply would be the by-product of the rewards and costs incurred by individuals as they exchange with others.

Nature of Social Exchange

In the most general sense, there are three kinds of relation at the heart of exchange theory, defined by the kinds of sanctions transmitted in each (Willer 1999). A *sanction* is simply any action transmitted from one individual and received by another that has positive or negative consequences. *Conflict* exists when A and B each transmit negative sanctions (e.g., when disgruntled lovers insult each other). *Coercion* occurs when a negative sanction (or threat thereof) is transmitted for a positive sanction (e.g., as when a loan shark threatens bodily harm to induce repayment). *Exchange* occurs when A and B mutually transmit positive sanctions (e.g., I mow the yard, you do the dishes). An *exchange relation* exists when two individuals repeatedly transmit positive sanctions within a larger context of opportunities and constraints (Emerson 1972b; Willer 1999). Structures and interdependencies set the stage for exchange transactions by shaping who can exchange with whom and by incorporating incentives that make some exchanges likely to yield better payoffs than others. At issue is whether to transact and in what amounts.

Social exchanges are transactions in a network that have relational consequences. Figure 13.1 captures the fundamental sequence assumed by contemporary social exchange theorizing. Social structures generate a set of interdependencies among actors, and these interdependences are the basis for who actually exchanges with whom and on what terms. The structure and interdependencies instantiate the opportunities and incentives for exchange, and the patterns of repeated exchange indicate what exchange relations actually form and are likely to be sustained as long as the structurally based opportunities and incentives remain constant (e.g., Cook and Emerson 1978; Markovsky et al. 1988; Willer 1999).

Social exchange is inherently a *joint* task. This point is implied by the role of interdependence in exchange theories (Emerson 1972b; Thibaut and Kelley 1978). Homans' (1950) concept of "activities" as a fundamental dimension in interaction or group settings implicitly poses the issue of how joint are the activities in which individuals engage. Examples of joint tasks are a merger of two organizations, two parents deciding how to raise a child, or a homeowners association deciding whether to undertake the repair of common property. Exchanges occur presumably because doing something jointly with another is likely to yield better rewards or payoffs than acting alone or not acting at all. Although all exchange—or social interaction, for that matter—entails a degree

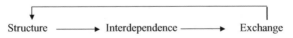

Structure ⟶ Interdependence ⟶ Exchange

FIGURE 13.1. Standard Social Exchange Model

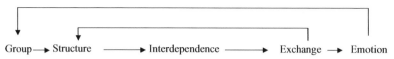

FIGURE 13.2. Modified Social Exchange Model

of jointness, this varies with the social structure. An important theoretical question for us is: What structural conditions vary the degree of jointness in the exchange tasks? We argue that emotions generate "order-producing" consequences, especially when exchange tasks are high in jointness.

The theoretical and empirical works reviewed in subsequent pages are guided by three orienting ideas or assumptions. First, social exchange is inherently a joint task in which actors have a common focus and engage in a "shared" activity (Lawler 2001, 2002). This is implicit in most social exchange theorizing (Emerson 1972b; Homans 1961; Thibaut and Kelley 1959; Willer 1999). Second, joint activities generate or amplify emotional responses (e.g., uplift or excitement/enthusiasm from doing things jointly with others, from affirming a common identity or affiliation, or from achieving some success with others). Durkheim (1915) suggested this in his analysis of religious ritual, and Collins (1981) developed the idea further in his theory of "interaction ritual chains." Third, the emotions that individuals experience as a result of a joint task are likely to be perceived as jointly produced. This makes relational or group affiliations a prospective source or cause of the emotions felt. These orienting ideas suggest some additions to the structure-interdependence-exchange process (see Figure 13.1) underlying standard exchange theory formulations. Figure 13.2 shows the modifications. The implications of Figure 13.2 are as follows: (1) Interaction or exchange has emotional effects on individual actors; (2) the emotions affect the strength of their group affiliations or attachments; and (3) these group affiliations are the context for structures that generate interdependencies (joint tasks) and patterns of exchange in the future. The next section presents a framework for theorizing emotions and emotional processes.

EMOTION AND EMOTIONAL PROCESSES

Emotional states, at the level of immediate experience, are not under the control of actors. They essentially "happen to people" (Hochschild 1983). However, once they happen, other social processes begin to emerge. If the emotions are positive, presumably actors wish to repeat the experience; if they are ambiguous, people interpret their meaning for self, other, and the situation. The experience of emotions also has a social and cultural component, beyond the neurological bases or correlates, which leads to a number of difficult conceptual issues: Are some emotions more fundamental than others? Are some universal and some cultural? When are emotions socially constructed and when are they innate? How do emotional expressions connect to the underlying internal states (feelings)? These issues have been subjected to considerable dialogue and debate in psychology and sociology (e.g., Hochschild 1983; Izard 1991; Kemper 1978, 1987; Lutz 1988; Schachter and Singer 1962; Scheff 1990; Scherer 1984; Watson et al. 1984).

One approach of psychologists has been to conceptualize and measure emotions with reference to the words people use to interpret or describe their own feelings and those of others (see Lawler and Thye 1999). This "psychometric approach" has assessed whether there are a small number of fundamental, distinct dimensions or emotion categories that capture the feeling states underlying the variety of words actors used to describe themselves and others in given contexts or situations. The "circumplex model" arranges the universe of emotion words on a circle around two cross-cutting (perpendicular) bipolar dimensions: pleasure/displeasure and the level of arousal (high/low) (see Russell et al. 1989; Watson et al. 1984). The form and intensity of the emotions is contingent on where they are located around this circle. There is substantial empirical evidence in support of such a formulation, although differences remain on how best to characterize or define the dimensions, especially the arousal dimension (Haslam 1995; Larsen and Diener 1992; Russell 1980, 1983). One implication is that although many different languages, words, or concepts are used by human actors to describe their emotional experiences, these boil down to a few underlying dimensions (see Heise, 1987, for a three-dimensional solution).

An alternative approach to emotions, "differentiated emotions theory," questions the premise that emotions are continuous or dimensional in favor of the view that they are discrete, discontinuous, and differentiated qualitatively (Clore et al. 1987; Ekman 1980; Izard 1991; Kemper 1987; Wierzbicka 1992). Anger is qualitatively different from sadness, happiness or joy from excitement, and so forth. For example, sets of qualitatively different emotions tend to include the following: fear/anxiety, joy/pleasure/happiness, sadness/depression, anger, and shame (e.g., Izard 1991; Kemper 1987). With the circumplex model, anger and fear are similar, but a differentiated model takes into account the fact that anger and fear often lead to very different behaviors (i.e., fight versus flight). Some research also indicates that different emotions activate different degrees of action readiness (Frijda 1986), and this also tends to support the differentiated model or theory of emotions.

Based on the evidence, it is not possible to claim that one approach is necessarily better or more accurate than the other. The intensity and type of emotions, as experienced, may fall along two or three dimensions as proposed by the circumplex model; and, at the same time, different emotions may produce different types of behavioral responses, as proposed by the differentiated model. The choice of approach is contingent on the theoretical or research problem to be addressed. For our theoretical purposes, we have developed a simple scheme for analyzing emotions in social exchange, borrowing both from the circumplex and differentiated models, as well as Weiner's (1986) "attribution theory of emotion."

From Weiner's (1986) formulation, we theorize a distinction between global emotions or feelings (Weiner terms these "primitive") and specific emotions (see Lawler 2001). Global emotions are positive or negative internal states produced by task activity and task success. These emotions entail immediate, involuntary responses and take the form of "feeling good" or "feeling bad." According to Weiner, these global or primitive emotions do not involve cognitive interpretations or emotion attributions. Specific emotions, in contrast, arise from the experience of the primitive or global feelings and are mediated by cognition or attribution (Weiner 1986). Weiner provided a useful way to distinguish immediate, automatic, nonvoluntary emotional responses from those that are stimulated by cognitive work and are socially constructed.

Global emotions can be likened to Damasio's (1999) notion of feeling of feelings; in this sense, we construe them as reflecting the person's (i.e., organism's) overall response to success or failure at the exchange task. Global emotions are special classes of reinforcement and punishment, being internal and correlated with neurological processes. They are primary motivational forces, relatively diffuse and ambiguous, but when activated, they organize interaction and generate cognitive work to interpret and understand where the feelings come from (i.e., what external objects or events cause them). This cognitive work is tied to actors' efforts to repeat their experiences of positive emotions (an internal reinforcement) and avoid a repeat of their experiences of negative emotions (an internal punishment). Specific emotions directed at social objects in the situation are a result of these cognitive interpretations.

Emotions and Social Objects

Whereas global emotions emerge from task activity, specific emotions are directed at social objects. Table 13.1 contains a classification scheme that identifies a specific emotion for each of the four objects of import in a social exchange context: task, self, other, and social unit. Self and other face an exchange task in the context of one or more social units (relation, network, and group). Pleasantness/unpleasantness is the overarching global emotion, generated by success or failure at the exchange task. The idea here is that success at the joint task generates an "emotional buzz," whereas failure generates an "emotional down." Lawler and Yoon (1996) distinguished two variants of global emotions—pleasure/dissatisfaction and interest/excitement—which were designed in part to correspond to the two primary dimensions of the circumplex model (pleasure and arousal). The sense of comfort from satisfaction is more "backward looking," and the sense of anticipation from interest/excitement is more "forward looking."

The specific emotions take different forms, contingent on the object perceived as causing the global feelings. If global positive feelings are attributed to self, the specific emotion is pride; if global positive feelings are attributed to the other, the specific emotion is gratitude. In a parallel way, if global negative emotions are attributed to self, the specific emotion is shame; if global negative emotions are attributed to the other, the specific emotion is anger. The emotions associated with the social unit are affective attachment or detachment. If positive emotions (global or specific) are attributed to the social unit, the affective attachment to that unit is increased; if negative emotions are attributed to the social unit, affective detachment is increased. These six emotions and the associated objects represent distinct interpretations for pleasant or unpleasant feelings (i.e., feeling good, feeling bad). To the extent that the social unit is perceived as the context for or source of positive emotions and feelings, it becomes an object of value in its own right, and actors are inclined to engage in collectively oriented behavior (e.g., staying in the social unit despite equal or better alternatives, giving rewards to others unilaterally and without strings attached, and cooperating in a social dilemma).

There are alternative explanations for such collectively oriented behavior that reflect the different microfoundations for social exchange. A rational-choice interpretation is that the relation or group becomes a part of the actor's utility function. A reinforcement explanation is that the relation or group becomes a discriminative stimulus, learned through repeated experiences within that group. A third interpretation is that the relation or group becomes an expressive object, symbolic of an affiliation with others, and an important source of social or personal identity (Collins 1981; Lawler 2001, 2003). These interpretations are not contradictory. All three processes could generate stable relations and groups in a complementary way. These alternative explanations reflect different ways an emotional/affective process can contribute to explanations of how and when social exchange generates social order.

TABLE 13.1. Emotions Directed at Each Object

Social Object	Valence of Emotion	
	Positive	Negative
Task	Pleasantness	Unpleasantness
Self	Pride	Shame
Other	Gratitude	Anger
Social unit	Affective attachment	Affective detachment

Source: Reprinted from Lawler 2001.

We argue, therefore, that the attribution of emotion to social units is central to understanding how social formations develop and are sustained by social exchange. However, the focus of attribution theory and research in psychology is on inferences *about individuals* from those individuals' behavior (Jones and Davis 1965; Kelley 1967; Weiner 1986). Social units are not viewed as possible objects of attribution. The key comparison is between internal or dispositional attributions and situational or external attributions of the individual's behavior. Our theory indicates that social unit attributions are possible and particularly important when individuals are engaged in a joint task such as social exchange.

A key finding and principle of attribution research—namely that attributions are self-serving—suggests that social unit attributions are likely to be uncommon and rare. Individuals are prone to give themselves credit for success at a task and blame others or the situation for task failure, regardless of interdependencies or task jointness. The premises of social exchange theory (i.e., actors are self-interested and instrumental) resonate with this attribution principle. From standard exchange theory notions, one would expect actors to credit self primarily when they succeed at the exchange task and blame the partner or situation when they fail. With reference to the emotions in Table 13.1, pride in self and anger toward the other would be more common in social exchange than shame in self and gratitude toward the other. In the next subsection, we theorize conditions under which the jointness of exchange promotes jointness of responsibility and a sharing of credit/blame for success/failure at exchange.

Theoretical Assumptions

The assumptions of our theorizing capture many of the underlying themes in the above discussion. Specifically, there are five assumptions (see Lawler 2001:327): First, social exchange produces global emotions and feelings (along a positive or negative dimension). Second, global emotions constitute immediate, internal, reinforcing or punishing stimuli. Third, given reinforcement and rational choice principles, actors strive to reproduce positive emotions and avoid negative emotions. Fourth, global emotions from exchange trigger cognitive work to identify the sources (causes) of global emotions and feelings. Fifth, actors interpret and explain their emotions partly with reference to social units (e.g., relations, groups, networks) within which the emotions are felt.

The first two assumptions indicate that social exchanges generate global feelings and that these are special classes of reinforcement and punishment. The third and fourth assumptions portray global emotions as motivational forces (Izard 1991). When activated, they unleash cognitive efforts to interpret where they come from, with the potential sources being self, other, and the social unit. The fifth assumption indicates that in the context of joint tasks, actors interpret global emotions as produced in part by social units, and this is the foundation for stronger or weaker affective attachments to those units (e.g., relations, groups, networks, organizations). These assumptions flesh out the reasons for the modifications of the standard exchange theory position portrayed in Figure 13.2 (i.e., the addition of an exchange-to-emotion link and an emotion-to-group link).

Next, we present two theories that are informed by the above emotions framework and assumptions: *relational cohesion theory* (Lawler and Yoon 1996; Thye, Yoon, and Lawler 2002) and the *affect theory of social exchange* (Lawler 2001). Some of the above theoretical assumptions (especially the second and fifth) were implicit and undeveloped when relational cohesion theory was formulated and tested (see Lawler and Yoon 1996, 1998). The affect theory of exchange (Lawler 2001) made these assumptions explicit and jumped off from the fifth assumption.

Relational cohesion theory addresses the question of how and when power dependencies produce relational or group commitments through an emotional/affective process. The affect theory of social exchange develops broader principles for analyzing structural conditions under which actors attribute their emotions to social units and, therefore, develop stronger person-to-unit ties and greater group solidarity.

RELATIONAL COHESION THEORY

Exchange is historically a theory about both *transactions* and *relations*. Exchange theories explain patterns of social interaction and relations in terms of transactions (i.e., the flow of benefits between actors); transactions are explained in terms of the relations or networks within which these are embedded (Emerson 1972b, 1981; Willer 1999). Emerson (1981), in fact, defined an "exchange relation" as a pattern of repetitive transactions among the same actors over time. He posited further that dyadic exchanges must be understood in the context of networks of exchange opportunities. Three or more interconnected actors are the minimal theoretical unit of analysis for Emerson. In the vast body of research on exchange networks over the past 20 years, repetitive or frequent exchange among the same pairs of actors is generally assumed; what is problematic is the division of payoffs. Thus, the development or strength of exchange relationships has received relatively scant attention, with the exception of more recent theory and research on commitment and trust (Buskens 2002; Cook and Emerson 1984; Kollock 1994; Molm 2003a).

Relational cohesion theory changes the emphasis of theorizing. First, the "fact" of exchange (frequency) is conceptually and empirically distinguished from the nature of exchange (i.e., the division of profits) and is important in its own right. Second, the key problematic is reaching agreement in exchange and, thus, the primary dependent variable is repetitive exchange (frequency). Third, exchange frequencies are construed as the principal basis for the formation and resiliency of exchange relations (Collins 1981; Homans 1950). Fourth, the focus is on when people become committed to their relation. Commitment is defined as an attachment to a social unit (i.e., relation, group, organization, community, or society) (Kanter 1968). The standard exchange theory explanation for commitment is uncertainty reduction or trust; that is, repeated exchange with the same partners makes them more predictable and, potentially, more trustworthy. Reduced uncertainty or increased trust generates a "bias" toward exchanging with the same partners one has successfully exchanged with in the past (Buskens 2002; Cook 2001; Kollock 1994; Molm 2003b). Relational cohesion theory proposes an emotional/affective explanation for such commitment. The theory is intended to complement, not displace, uncertainty reduction explanations (Lawler and Yoon 1996, 1998).

Relational cohesion theory developed from a line of theory and research on power dependence in bargaining and negotiation (Bacharach and Lawler 1981). That work distinguished zero-sum and nonzero dimensions of power, capturing these with concepts of relative and total power. Relative power is the comparison of each actor's power in a relationship vis-à-vis the other (the zero-sum dimension), and total power refers to the sum or average of both actors' power in the relation. Power dependence theory (Emerson 1972b) implies that both dimensions are important because mutual dependencies or interdependencies in a relationship can vary, as can the distribution of power across actors. Total power captures an integrative dimension of power (i.e., an aspect of power that promotes collaboration, cooperation, and cohesion). With this integrative dimension of power, it is a short step to posing the questions: Will some power dependence conditions promote relational commitments more than others and through what process might this occur? These questions motivated the development of relational cohesion theory.

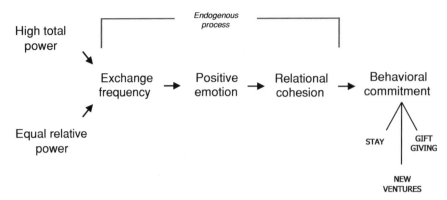

FIGURE 13.3. Relational Cohesion Theory.

Source: Reprinted from Lawler and Yoon 1996

The theoretical model in Figure 13.3 captures the main ideas of relational cohesion theory. The overall message is that exogenous structural power (dependence) conditions generate relational commitments *indirectly* through an endogenous process. Emotions are central to that process. The two power dependence dimensions include relative power (equal-unequal) and total (average) power in the relation (Bacharach and Lawler 1981; Molm 1987). Higher total power reflects greater interdependence, and equal power reduces the problems posed by equity and justice issues in the exchange process. These power conditions determine the frequencies of exchange in any given dyad. The core of the theory is the endogenous process, the *exchange-to-emotion-to-cohesion* sequence in the model that indirectly links structural power to behavioral commitment. Specifically, more frequent exchange generates (global) positive emotions and feelings, and positive emotions, in turn, produce cohesion (i.e., the perception that the relation is a unifying force in the situation). The result is various forms of commitment behavior: staying in the relation despite equal or better alternatives, providing benefits unilaterally and without explicit expectations or contingencies, undertaking new ventures in the context of a social dilemma and therefore the potential for malfeasance.

Empirical Evidence on Relational Cohesion Theory

Evidence bearing on the emotional mechanism of relational cohesion theory actually predates the theory's 1996 original publication date. In 1993, Lawler and Yoon published experiments designed to evaluate the impact of agreement frequency on positive emotions and commitment. These experiments involved two actors who could negotiate with one another under various conditions of power and exchange. In each condition, one individual was attempting to buy both iron ore and zinc from another individual who supplied these resources. Thus, the issues at stake were simply the price of iron ore and the price of zinc. The subjects occupied separate rooms, and each was instructed to maximize his or her benefit in the relation. In the event that subjects could not reach an agreement on one of the issues, each subject automatically earned some level of profit from a "standing alternative partner" that was in fact a simulated other.

The primary independent variables were power/dependence (equal versus unequal) and the type of bargaining (integrative versus distributive). Power/dependence was manipulated by varying whether the amount of profit available from the standing alternative partner was the same for both partners (equal power) or not (unequal power). The kind of bargaining was manipulated by varying whether the two products, ore and zinc, were worth the same to both individuals (distributive) or different, which would make trade-offs possible (integrative). At issue is whether or not conditions of equal power and integrative bargaining produce higher agreement frequency, positive emotions, and commitment behavior (i.e., gift giving and staying in the focal relationship despite exit options).

The results of the experiment affirm the importance of emotions in producing commitment. Under conditions of equal relative power and integrative bargaining, subjects were more likely to reach agreement with one another. In turn, agreement frequency was significantly related to interest/excitement though not related to pleasure/satisfaction (the nonfinding for pleasure/satisfaction has rarely occurred since this investigation). Finally, the data verify that positive emotion in the form of interest/excitement indeed predicted commitment behavior (both staying in the relation despite alternatives and gift giving). Overall, this was the first published evidence in support of the linkage among exchange frequency, positive emotion, and commitment behavior.

In 1996, Lawler and Yoon published the first tests designed specifically to evaluate the theory of relational cohesion, as portrayed by Figure 13.3. This project entailed three distinct experiments, each addressing a different form of commitment behavior (i.e., gift giving, stay behavior, and contribution to a joint venture involving a two-party social dilemma). As before, all sessions involved two subjects who negotiated exchange from separate rooms, each attempting to buy some resource possessed by the other. In accord with Figure 13.3, the experiment manipulated conditions of total power (high versus low) and relative power (equal verses unequal). The experimental setting simulated negotiations across a number of "years" or episodes. At select points in the study, as specified by the theoretical model (Figure 13.3), measures of key concepts were taken. These measures included (a) agreement frequency, (b) positive emotions in the form of interest/excitement and pleasure/satisfaction, (c) relational cohesion, and (d) commitment behavior. The temporal sequence specified by the theory was created in the experimental context, and the research tested the set of relations predicted by the model.

The results of the study provided strong and consistent support for the theory (Lawler and Yoon 1996). Conditions of high total power and equal relative power tended to produced more frequent agreement between the individuals. In turn, frequent exchange had a positive direct effect on both pleasure/satisfaction and interest/excitement, as predicted. Also, as predicted, positive emotions had a positive direct effect on relational cohesion. Finally, there was uniform support for the notion that relational cohesion is the proximate cause of commitment. In fact, with all variables in the model included (see Figure 13.3), relational cohesion was the strongest and most significant predictor across all three forms of commitment—stay behavior, gift giving, and contribution to a joint venture. The theory makes strong claims about the sequence of indirect steps through which structural power conditions promote commitment, and these were confirmed at each step by the research.

There is an interesting affinity between our findings on positive emotion and the broader sociology of emotions literature. The theory of relational cohesion focuses explicitly on two dimensions of positive emotion: pleasure/satisfaction and interest/excitement. Empirically, Lawler and Yoon's 1996 study showed that both dimensions have direct positive effects on relational cohesion when *each* emotion was included as the sole predictor of relational cohesion. However, when *both* emotions were included simultaneously to predict relational cohesion, only pleasure/satisfaction was significant. Since then, pleasure/satisfaction consistently has played a stronger role in predicting relational cohesion (Lawler et al. 2000; Lawler and Yoon 1998). This pattern might suggest that pleasure/satisfaction is a more prominent emotion flowing from exchange. In fact, pleasure/satisfaction was treated as one of four "primary" emotions by Kemper (1987), a distinction that is echoed in Turner's (2002) scheme of basic emotions and by psychologists (Ekman and Freisen 1975; see also Stets 2003). In the context of these theories and their evidentiary basis, the fact that pleasure/satisfaction plays a stronger role may reflect its more "basic" or fundamental nature.

To summarize, the theory and research on relational cohesion identify an *endogenous* process through which structures of dependence affect relational commitments. This process begins with the frequency of exchange; the second step is the occurrence of positive emotions, and the third is a perception of the relation as a cohesive object. These three moments are tied together, forming a conceptual unit. By implication, a structural condition that changes the frequency of exchange should correspondingly change the strength of this endogenous process; moreover, a structural condition under which exchanges do not produce positive emotions should inhibit or prevent the process from operating, and if the emotions experienced are not attributed in part to the relation, they will not generate perceptions of cohesion. This conceptual unit can be used to understand how relations within a network (or the same relation over time) stabilize to produce social order at the microlevel.

EXTENSIONS OF RELATIONAL COHESION THEORY

Since the basic series of tests in 1996, several other projects have sought to expand the basic theory and scope of application. Here we review two lines of work. First, in 1998, Lawler and Yoon studied whether dyads embedded in a larger social network would become committed to one another. Whereas previous work explicitly focused on a single dyadic exchange relation, the move to "network embedded" dyads broadened the scope of the theory and forged deeper connections to other branches of exchange theory (e.g., Cook and Emerson 1978; Cook et al. 1983; Markovsky et al. 1988) and to social identity theory (Rabbie and Horowitz 1988; Tajfel and Turner 1979, 1986). The question was whether "pockets of relational cohesion" would develop in exchange networks, particularly for dyads that have the highest frequency of exchange. Pockets of cohesion should fragment the network.

This extension dealt with dyadic-level commitments in two networks: the branch and the stem (see Figure 13.4). In the Figure 13.4 networks, each letter represents a person and each line represents an exchange relation. When each position can make only one exchange per round, the branch is a *strong-power* network because A can never be excluded while two of the more peripheral actors (B, G, or D) always are. This causes the low-power actors to make increasingly favorable offers to A to avoid exclusion, and as such, the central actor enjoys large profit advantages over time. Overall, the branch can be seen as a network consisting of three dyadic relations (A-B, A-G, and A-D) in which A has a relative power advantage.

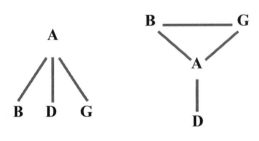

Strong Power—Branch   **Weak Power—Stem**

FIGURE 13.4. Branch and Stem Networks

In contrast, the stem is a *weak-power* network because no single individual must be excluded (Markovsky et al. 1993; Thye et al. 1997). Weak-power networks are characterized by more moderate profit differentiation. Studies show that the stem tends to "break" into two distinct exchange relations: an equal power dyad (B-G) and an unequal power dyad (A-D). Thus, the stem represents a network that contains both equal and unequal relative power dyads embedded in the same social context; thus, relational cohesion predicts a pocket of cohesion in the structurally equal power relation. At issue is how *network-based* power in each network alters the relational cohesion process.

A second aim in this project was to determine how the relational cohesion process is affected by an overarching group identity. Research in the identity tradition finds that when social identities are activated in a group context, a variety of pro-social behaviors are likely to ensue. For instance, individuals sharing a common group identity are more likely to be cooperative, collectively oriented, altruistic, and responsive to group goals rather than to purely egoistic ones. Relational cohesion in dyads should be weaker if actors in a network share a common group identity and, by implication, so should the network-fragmentation effects. In the branch network, an overarching group identity should reduce exploitation by the central, powerful actor.

Lawler and Yoon (1998) tested these ideas using four experimental conditions in which subjects negotiate exchange in either the branch or stem network, with or without a common group identity. The theory predicts that all relations in the branch will be used with equal frequency and, thus, no differences in cohesion and commitment should occur. However, exchange in the B-G relation of the stem was predicted to occur with greater frequency than A-D. The more frequent exchange along B-G should, according to the chain logic of relational cohesion theory, produce greater positive emotion, stronger relational cohesion, and higher behavioral commitment relative to A-D. To implement this idea, in half of the experimental sessions the members of the network were portrayed as "departments" within a larger organization. In the other half, the participants were simply told that they were competitors with an interest in trading with others (Lawler and Yoon 1998).

The results support the theory. First, there were no differences in exchange frequencies across any dyadic relations in the strong-power branch. However, when the members of the branch shared an exogenous group identity, profit taking by the central actor was reduced. Thus, as predicted, it appears that a common group identity may induce more pro-social behavior. With respect to the stem, as predicted, actors in the equal power B-G relation reached agreement more frequently than actors in the unequal power A-D relation. Further, actors in B-G experience greater pleasure/satisfaction, interest/excitement, and relational cohesion compared to the actors in the A-D relation; that is, the endogenous process operated more strongly for the equal power dyad (B-G) than for the unequal power dyad (A-D), and these effects were not weaker when network actors shared a group identity. Further analysis of A-D showed that the endogenous process breaks down at the very first moment or step in the theory: Frequent exchange did not produce positive emotions. This affirms the importance of the exchange-to-emotion process that is central to the theory (see Figure 13.3).

The next significant development in the relational cohesion research program came 2 years later, with a project that simultaneously expanded the theory along two fronts (Lawler et al. 2000). First, the theory was tested in a new *productive exchange* context. Productive exchange is one of four basic forms of exchange identified by exchange theorists (Emerson 1981; Molm and Cook 1995). The other forms include negotiated, reciprocal, and generalized exchange (see below for details). The second contribution of this research was to compare empirically the emotional-affective process of relational cohesion theory to an *uncertainty reduction* process (Lawler et al. 2000). The traditional exchange theory explanation for commitment is that frequent exchanges reduce uncertainty (Cook and Emerson 1984); that is, actors who exchange frequently should learn more about one another, come to find one another's behavior more predictable, and come to learn that they are similarly oriented to the exchange (Cook and Emerson 1984; Emerson 1981; Kollock 1994, 1999). Building on this idea, we expanded the relational cohesion model to test whether uncertainty reduction is a distinct, yet complementary, pathway to commitment vis-à-vis emotion. In other words, we incorporated uncertainty reduction in the theoretical model (Figure 13.3) as a second intervening pathway leading from exchange to cohesion.

The two endogenous paths reflect different phenomena. The *frequency-to-emotion-to-cohesion* pathway reflects a *social bonding* process. The positive emotion from frequent exchange can be construed as "rewards" generated by the exchange and completion of joint activity. As such, actors should strive to reproduce these rewards and also think about their proximate causes. To the extent that the group is perceived as a cause of the positive emotional experience, the group itself should come to take on expressive value in its own right (Tyler 1990, 1994). In contrast, the *frequency-to-uncertainty reduction-to-cohesion* pathway can be construed as a *boundary-defining* process wherein exchange partners become salient, distinctive, and set off relative to other potential partners. Social identity theorists frequently use this term to describe in-group versus out-group distinctions, and we adopt their terminology. At issue was whether the two processes were complementary explanations or if one had greater explanatory power.

A modification to the basic experimental setting was required to create a productive exchange context. Here, three actors faced a task in which they could produce greater joint benefits if they all collaborated than if they operated alone or worked with another group. The exchanges were structured such that (a) actors in this context were deciding whether to engage in a single collaborative effort that would produce a pool of joint profit; (b) for an exchange to be consummated, all actors had to agree to the exchange; (c) the exchange would allocate the pool of profits across actors; and (d) offers were made simultaneously and independently, which posed significant coordination problems. Overall, joint collaboration produced profits at the group level (actor-to-group flow of benefits) that benefited each of the actors (group-to-actor flow of benefits).

As with earlier tests, structural power conditions were manipulated by varying the relative (equal versus unequal) and total (high versus low) dependence of each member on the group (see Lawler et al. 2000), and dependence was operationalized as the quality (expected value) of a fixed outside offer that could be accepted in the event that the focal group did not reach agreement. Under these conditions, subjects exchanged for a total of 16 episodes. At select points, measures were taken of exchange frequency, positive emotion, predictability, and relational cohesion. Additionally, two kinds of commitment behavior were studied. After episode 13, subjects could either give one another small token gifts as a symbol of their relationship (i.e., gifts of small pieces of candy) or they could invest some of their earnings in a new joint venture that involves considerable risk but could provide substantial benefits (i.e., investment in a three-person prisoner's dilemma game).

Overall, the data clearly support the relational cohesion theory account of commitment in exchange. First, as predicted, the data indicate that structural power conditions significantly impact exchange frequency. Under conditions of high total dependence (i.e., the expected payoff from the alternative group is smaller than the expected payoff from the focal group) and equal relative dependence (i.e., the expected payoff from the alternative group is the same for each member of the focal group), more exchanges were consummated in the three-actor setting. In turn, frequent social exchange had a significant direct effect on *both* positive emotion and uncertainty reduction (i.e., predictability). These findings are important because they replicate and further verify the emotional effects of frequent exchange, and they support the hypothesis that exchange also generates uncertainty reduction or predictability. The latter finding is consistent with standard exchange-theoretic explanations for commitment and supportive empirical tests (e.g., see Kollock 1994).

The next step in the causal chain suggests that both uncertainty reduction and positive emotion increase perceptions of group cohesion. The results indicate that positive emotion has a significant effect on perceptions of group cohesion, as hypothesized, but uncertainty reduction does not. In short, it seems that when both theoretical constructs are included to predict the development of cohesion, positive emotion simply carries more explanatory power. This does not necessarily mean that uncertainty reduction is unimportant, but whatever impact it has on commitment is operating through paths separate from perceptions of cohesion. In short, the emotional affective process at the core of relational cohesion theory receives significant support. The role of uncertainty reduction is clarified below.

Finally, the theory predicts that group cohesion is the proximate cause of gift giving and contributions to a social dilemma—our measures of commitment. The results for this prediction are mixed, but, interestingly, help clarify the unresolved role of uncertainty reduction. Consistent with virtually all research in the relational-cohesion program, perceived cohesion had a significant effect on gift giving. However, group cohesion did not significantly affect the propensity of actors to invest in a new venture (i.e., cooperate in the social dilemma). In previous work on dyads, relational cohesion effects have been found for this form of commitment behavior (Lawler and Yoon 1996). The difference could be due to the fact that the obstacles to cooperation are known to be more difficult in a three-person prisoners' dilemma than in a two-person prisoners' dilemma. The addition of a third person heightens uncertainty and makes trust more difficult for actors under these conditions. At the outset of the project, we anticipated that this would make it even more likely that uncertainty reduction would be related, directly or indirectly, to this form of commitment behavior. Given that the indirect relationship was not observed, we suspected that a direct relationship might be present.

To investigate this, we changed the original theoretical model to include several new pathways suggested by prior theory and by our data. The results revealed a direct effect of perceived predictability on the investment form of commitment. Thus, uncertainty reduction does operate in the productive exchange context, but not in the way that we originally theorized. It is important to note that this alternative pathway to commitment can be interpreted in terms of trust. *Trust* is defined as the expectation of cooperation by others (Pruitt and Kimmel 1977) and is one of the best predictors of whether and how individuals resolve social dilemmas (Axelrod 1984; Kollock 1994, 1999; Komorita and Parks 1996; Yamagishi 1986). To be trusted, one must first be predictable, so in this regard, predictability can be construed as a necessary (though not sufficient) condition for the emergence of trust. If so, we should observe a direct relationship between predictability and investment, as we did.

To summarize, this project suggests that dual processes operate to produce commitment behavior. The data indicate that emotional affective and uncertainty reduction mechanisms promote different forms of commitment behavior. Of particular importance for relational cohesion theory is that the emotional/affective process operates as a separate and independent mediating process leading to commitment behavior. Other processes such as uncertainty reduction, trust, and norm formation have been emphasized in research on exchange, contracting, and social dilemmas (e.g., Cook and Emerson 1984; Macy and Skvoretz 1998; Williamson 1981; Yamagishi 1986). Relational cohesion theory, with its emphasis on the emotional-affective consequences of exchange, provides explanatory power above and beyond these alternative approaches.

AFFECT THEORY OF SOCIAL EXCHANGE

The *affect theory* of social exchange proposes that the *jointness* of the exchange task determines whether actors perceive the social unit as a source of global emotions (Lawler 2001). The main idea is that individuals attribute their individually felt emotions to their relation or group affiliation if the task is high in jointness. The jointness of the tasks likely varies, objectively and subjectively. For example, an organization may define the tasks of a work group in individual or joint terms and, in the process, highlight individual or collective responsibility for the results. A series of objectively individual tasks may be defined in more joint or collective terms within an overarching organizational framework. Both the objective task conditions and the subjective definitions put forth are important. To concisely address this issue, the affect theory of social exchange proposes a fundamental structural (objective) and cognitive (subjective) condition for social unit attributions.

The structural dimension is the degree that individual contributions to task success (or failure) are separable (distinguishable) or nonseparable (indistinguishable). This contrast is from Williamson's (1985:245–247) analysis of work structures. He argued that, in a work setting, when contributions are nonseparable, employees cannot assign individual credit or blame to one another for work group success or failure; such *task jointness* generates "relational teams" as a governing mechanism. Relational teams are structures of informal control that develop if the shared responsibility for group success is more salient to employees than their individual responsibility. The affect theory of social exchange adopts this as a fundamental principle for analyzing how social structures shape individual emotions and their consequences for relations, groups, and networks. Implied here is an underlying macro-to-micro and micro-to-macro process (Lawler 2002).

The cognitive dimension of jointness is the degree to which the exchange task promotes the sharing of responsibility for success at exchange. Our argument is that if exchange generates a sense of shared responsibility, actors are more likely to interpret their individual feelings as jointly produced in concert with others and, therefore, more likely to attribute those feelings to relationships with those others or to common group affiliations. Thus, if employees perceive a shared responsibility for group performance, a work group should generate greater emotion-based cohesion, group commitment, and group solidarity. Overall, additive tasks strengthen the sense of individual responsibility, whereas conjunctive tasks strengthen the sense of shared responsibility. Discrete, specialized, independent roles draw attention to individual responsibility; whereas overlapping, collaborative roles highlight shared responsibility (see Lawler 2003). The theory suggests an emotional affective explanation for the fact that systems of accountability that "target" individual performance have different consequences for group-level collaboration than systems of accountability that "target" group performance.

Based on the above reasoning, the core propositions of the affect theory of social exchange (Lawler 2001) are as follows:

> *Core Proposition 1*: The greater the nonseparability of individuals' impact on task success or failure, the greater the perception of shared responsibility.
>
> *Core Proposition 2:* The greater the perception of shared responsibility for success or failure at a joint task, the more inclined actors are to attribute resulting global and specific emotions to social units.

The key implication is that a sense of shared responsibility generates relational or group attributions of emotion and these, in turn, foster stronger person-to-social-unit affective attachments. In addition, these core propositions imply particular relationships among the specific emotions (see Table 13.1). To the degree that individuals attribute their emotions to joint activities, they can both feel pride in self and gratitude toward the other (e.g., "When we get together, good things happen)." Giving gratitude to the other does not reduce the sense of pride or vice versa. If failure occurs in this context, individuals feel anger toward the other but also shame in self; thus, each emotion moderates the other, which is a potential basis for a collective response to failure. On the other hand, if members of a work group attribute positive emotions to their own individual contributions, they feel pride in self but little gratitude toward others, reducing cohesion or solidarity effects (e.g., "I did most of the work and made this happen"). If they fail at a group task, they may direct anger toward others and direct little shame at self (e.g., "They didn't do their part").

In sum, the sign of the relationships among specific emotions is determined by the relative weight or strength of social unit and self-serving attributions. Social unit attributions generate positive relationships between self-other emotions, whereas individual attributions generate negative relationships. In the context of joint tasks and social unit attributions, positive experiences (task success) would have an even stronger effect on cohesion and group commitment than otherwise, whereas negative experiences (task failure) would have a less detrimental effect on cohesion and group commitment. Applying the theory's above core propositions, social unit attributions are most likely to occur when the structure of exchange entails high nonseparability and fosters a strong sense of shared responsibility. Social structures determine whether social exchanges entail nonseparability and, therefore, are likely to generate a sense of shared responsibility. The core propositions should apply to any structural dimension that varies the degree that individual efforts and contributions are nonseparable (Williamson 1985).

To date, the affect theory of social exchange has focused on two structural dimensions: the *form* of social exchange between actors and the *network connections* between exchange pairs. The structural form of exchange refers to the way that the behaviors of individuals are interconnected (e.g., negotiated versus reciprocal exchange). Network connections refer to the connections between different dyadic exchanges or prospective relations in a network (e.g., positively or negatively connected). These are basic structures in the social exchange tradition (e.g., Molm and Cook 1995). Theoretical predictions for each are detailed below.

Structural Forms of Exchange

There are four structural forms of exchange and two types of network connection analyzed in the original formulation of the affect theory of social exchange (Lawler 2001). The forms of exchange are as follows: productive, negotiated, reciprocal, and generalized (Emerson 1981; Molm 1994; Molm and Cook 1995). Productive exchange is a context in which actors coordinate their behaviors to generate a joint, private good. Examples are a business partnership or co-authors on a paper or book. Negotiated exchange is a context in which actors form an explicit agreement that specifies the terms of a trade (i.e., who gives and receives what and how much). Reciprocal exchange involves sequential giving of rewards (unilaterally), essentially becoming interconnected and expected over time. Finally, generalized exchange occurs when actors give and receive benefits from different partners. Overall, productive exchange is person to group, whereas negotiated and reciprocal exchanges are direct, person to person. Generalized exchange has been termed indirect and impersonal (Emerson 1981; Molm and Cook 1995). The analysis of the theory (see Lawler 2001) indicate that the degree of jointness varies across these four forms of exchange as follows: productive > negotiated > reciprocal > generalized.

Thus, the theory makes the following predictions for forms of exchange:

Prediction 1: Productive exchange generates stronger perceptions of shared responsibility and stronger global emotions than direct or generalized exchange.

Prediction 2: Direct exchange produces stronger perceptions of shared responsibility and stronger global emotions than generalized exchange.

Given the above predictions and core propositions;

Prediction 3: The strength of person-to-group attachments (solidarity) is ordered as follows across forms of social exchange:

productive > negotiated > reciprocal > generalized

Prediction 4: Direct exchange structures—negotiated and reciprocal—generate stronger dyadic relations than group relations, whereas productive or generalized exchange generates stronger group relations than dyadic relations.

Prediction 1 is based on the fact that productive exchange is the most cooperative and group-oriented exchange structure. Each of the other structures has mixed motive interests or a significant trust problem. Prediction 2 assumes that in direct exchange relations, the person-to-person feature enables actors to solve trust problems more readily than generalized exchange. This proposition contradicts Ekeh's (1974) idea that generalized exchange generates the greatest group solidarity, but we argue that Ekeh's prediction assumes an already existing group (see Lawler 2001:339). Generalized exchange entails a high separation of individual "contributions" and (*ceteris paribus*) generates lower shared responsibility and affectively based solidarity; at the same time, the solidarity that does occur will be at the group level, as prediction 4 indicates. Prediction 3 stems from the notion that shared responsibility promotes relational or group attributions of emotion. Prediction 4 is based on the notion that, in direct relations, emotion is attributed to the exchange relation, whereas in productive or generalized exchange, emotion is attributed to the network or group.

Types of Network Connection

Emerson (1972b) distinguished two types of connection: positive and negative. Assume a four-actor box network—A, B, C, D—in which each actor can exchange with two of the others. If the network is positively connected, then an exchange between A and B increases the probability that A and B will also exchange with the others (C and D). If the network is negatively connected, an exchange between A and B excludes the possibility that A or B will exchange with any others. These two forms of connection involve different structural incentives to exchange with one or more partners in the network.

Willer (1999) clarified and specified the incentives underlying different network connections by proposing a tripartite distinction among exclusive, inclusive, and null connections. Exclusive connections are similar to Emerson's negative connections (i.e., an exchange of any two excludes exchange with others). Inclusive and null connections are two versions of what Emerson would term "positive connections." With inclusive connections, all exchanges that are possible must be completed in order for any given exchange to yield rewards for partners. Thus, in the four-actor box network, all possible exchanges in the network would have to occur in order for an exchange between A and B to yield benefits. A "null" connection signifies that there is no prior relation between exchange in one relation and exchange in another; transactions in the two relations are independent. Actors have an incentive to exchange with as many others as possible in the network. If actors want to exchange with all others in an exclusively (negatively) connected network, they have to do it sequentially across transaction periods, but they have no structural incentive to do so. With a null connection, they can exchange within the same transaction period and, in fact, have an incentive to do so. The overall implication is that at the network level, the jointness of the exchange task is highest in an inclusively connected network and lowest in an exclusively connected network.

A null-connected network would be in between. This has important implications for the emotional effects of exchange and for the transformation of networks into tacit or explicit groups.

The explanation for network-level effects is that emotions diffuse across relations in a network (Lawler, 2001, 2002, 2003; Markovsky and Lawler 1994). In a three-person network (A, B, C), if A feels good from an exchange with B and then enters an exchange with C, A's positive feelings from A-B spread to the A-C interaction; if A feels bad from an exchange with B and then exchanges with C, A's negative feelings spread. This assumption is plausible, given that considerable psychological research on affect and mood shows that global, diffuse feelings (good or bad) from interaction with one person carry over to interaction with others, even if there is no connection or similarity between the situations or persons (Isen 1987). Moreover, those in a positive mood are likely to cooperate more, use more inclusive categories for others, take more risks, and employ heuristics in processing information (Bless 2000; Forgas 2000; Isen 1987). Because positively connected networks promote exchanges with as many others as structurally possible, positive emotions in each relation reinforce and strengthen those in other relations. The main implications are as follows:

> *Prediction 5*: In positively connected exchange networks, dyadic exchanges generate group formation at the network level and strengthen affective attachments to this unit; in negatively connected networks, exchanges in dyads generate the pockets of cohesion in exchange relations and strengthen affective attachments to the relation rather than the network or group.
> *Prediction 6*: Cohesion and solidarity at the network level will be ordered as follows across the three types of network connection: inclusive > null > exclusive.

Evidence Bearing on the Affect Theory

To date there are no direct tests of the affect theory, although we are currently in the process of collecting experimental data that will do just that. Even so, there are a number of theoretical and empirical studies that bear on the underlying logic of the theory. For example, the affect theory indicates that structural conditions that give actors a sense of shared responsibility for the collective result should trigger positive emotions and person-to-group attachments. The most immediate unit in any two-party exchange is the relation itself, but insofar as there is common activity and experience across interdependent dyads in a broader network, the emotions should make salient the *group attachments across the entire network*. Thus, the theory has implications for when individuals comprising an exchange network come to view themselves as members of a common group and behave with regard for one another.

One recent study took up the question of when and how networks of individual agents come to see themselves as belonging to a common group and behave in pro-social ways (Thye and Lawler 1999). We have developed a concept of *network cohesion* that captures two such network conditions: (a) the proportion of relations within a network that are equal in power and (b) the degree of relational density in the network (Thye and Lawler 1999). The main assertion is that exchange networks containing a high degree of equal power relations and many direct ties among actors will unleash the endogenous process of relational cohesion theory at the *network level*. As such, we predicted that individuals exchanging within highly connected networks composed of many equal power relations should be more likely to sense a common experience and shared responsibility with the others, even if they interact and exchange with select partners. The results of this new study were supportive. In networks with high network cohesion, dyadic exchanges generate positive feelings, and these promote group formation at the network level. From the perspective of the affect theory, the underlying reason is that such networks promote a sense of common experience, interdependence, and a corresponding sense of shared responsibility.

In terms of the strength of person-to-group attachments, recall that the affect theory orders the four forms of exchange as follows: productive > negotiated > reciprocal > generalized. This stands in contrast to Ekeh's (1974) theory, which asserts that generalized exchange is a fundamental basis for social order at the macrolevel because it creates obligations to the larger collectivity. Ekeh argued that in systems of generalized exchange, wherein individuals are unilaterally giving to (and reaping benefits from) others in the system, *trust* is likely to emerge and become normative. Trust, as such, should encourage pro-social behavior and regulate the temptation to act out of self-interest. However, as Lawler (2001) noted, Ekeh's analysis centered more on the consequences of generalized exchange provided that it has emerged and is part of the normative context. The affect theory focuses more on the fact that generalized exchange entails distinct individual contributions and, thus, is fragile. As such, the theory predicts that it is less likely to have the emotional consequences of direct exchange and promote perceptions of shared responsibility.

On a related note, the order specified for negotiated versus reciprocal exchange is controversial (see Molm 2003a). An argument can be made that commitment and cohesion, all else being equal, will be greater in reciprocal rather than negotiated exchange because reciprocal exchange involves greater risk and a more serious trust problem (Molm 2003a, 2003b). The issue of risk and trust in reciprocal exchange comes down to the following: When one actor gives unilaterally, he or she has no assurance that the other will reciprocate. Negotiated exchange typically involves binding agreements, which, by definition, resolve the trust problem and minimize risk. The key obstacle in negotiated exchange is to balance ones motive to profit against the fear of being excluded. Experiments by Molm et al. (1999) have found that reciprocal exchange produces more positive affect directed at the exchange partner and more commitment to that partner relative to negotiated exchange.

However, it should be noted that prediction 3 of the affect theory is based *solely* on the presumption that jointness is more salient in negotiated than in reciprocal exchange. Our focus is on the development of *person-to-unit* affective attachments, which we believe are theoretically driven by jointness of task and perceptions of shared responsibility. In contrast, Molm and colleagues (1999) have theorized and studied *person-to-person* processes involving the development of trust, risk aversion, and perceptions of fairness. Molm has shown empirically that these processes operate differentially across negotiated and reciprocal exchange contexts and, thus, clarifies some of the theoretical differences across these forms of exchange (see Molm, 2003b, for a review). In short, the two theoretical research programs address different conceptual and empirical issues. Taken together, they offer complementary perspectives that promise to illuminate important differences across these (and other) forms of exchange.

CONCLUSION AND FUTURE DIRECTIONS

Since the early 1950s, with rare exception, the actors of traditional social exchange theory have been portrayed as calculating and unemotional beings. The emphasis has been on theorizing purely instrumental actors that are either backward looking agents driven by environmental reinforcement schedules or forward looking agents who rationally calculate the potential to maximize gains and avoid losses. Our research program introduces a new kind of social actor: one who interacts with others lodged in a social structure, experiences and seeks to understand her or his emotional reactions, and attributes these emotions to self, other, or the larger social unit. The primary aim is to understand how, in the latter case, exchange processes trigger emotions and attributions that render dyads, networks, and groups as expressive objects of value.

Over time, our theoretical research program has evolved from one concerned with dyadic encounters (Lawler and Yoon 1993, 1996) to a broader emphasis on exchange within social networks (Lawler and Yoon 1998) and fundamental links to the varieties of social exchange and the nature of commitment (Lawler 2001; Lawler et al. 2000). In many regards, the research program is a textbook example of cumulative theory growth in that the questions and problems addressed by the program today emerged directly from those of yesterday. Although we have made substantial progress in understanding the emotional underpinnings of commitment and solidarity, there are a number of questions that still remain. In closing, we review some of the general implications of our work and how these connect to broader literature.

A recurrent theme in our research is that people experience emotions from accomplishing or not accomplishing an exchange task, and these trigger efforts to understand the emotions. We agree with Hochschild (1979) that emotions are involuntary reactions that simply "happen to people," but what is most important is not *that* emotions happen, but *to what* they are attributed (i.e., task, self, other, or social unit). Our research calls attention to the fact that under certain exchange conditions, positive emotions will be attributed to the social unit, resulting in affective attachment to that unit. The forms of exchange most likely to produce affective attachments are those in which the task success is not clearly attributed to one actor or the other but, instead, to the joint activity, and perceptions of shared responsibility are high.

The emotional processes at the center of our research are distinct, yet complementary, to the rational-choice and behavioral orientations that are fundamental to exchange theory. Our research has implications for the relationship of social exchange and social order, even when such order seemingly contradicts otherwise rational action. To illustrate, consider combat units in the armed services that depend on social order among rank-and-file soldiers to effectively implement military strategies. Social order, in this context, depends on individual soldiers who obey commands, even when those commands fly in the face of their immediate self-interest (i.e., advancing on the enemy when there is some probability that you yourself could be shot). Our theory and research program suggests that order will be established and maintained to the extent individual soldiers possess strong affective ties to social units (i.e., company, brigade) in which they frequently interact and exchange items of value. If strong enough, such ties regulate self-interest and provide a common emotional/affective basis for coordinated social action (see also Collins 1989). From our work, this is most likely to occur when task success depends on the existence of joint activities for which there are perceptions of shared responsibility.

In closing, the theoretical research program reviewed here uniquely emphasizes the role of emotions in social exchange and focuses on the processes through which social structures strengthen or weaken affective attachments to relations, networks, and groups. In comparison to other exchange-based theories, our work brings together the rational and emotional consequences of social interaction. The incentives lodged within social structures provide rational incentives for agents to interact and exchange with one another so that they can jointly accomplish tasks that are otherwise unobtainable. However, such interaction carries emotional consequences, and these determine when individuals come to see the relation, network, or group as an expressive object of value in its own right. Implicit in this approach is that micro social encounters create affective ties to more macrounits (i.e., groups, networks, communities), which, in turn, provide a basis for solidarity, stability, and social order.

REFERENCES

Ashby, F. Gregory, Alice Isen, and U. Turken. 1999. "A Neuropsychological Theory of Positive Affect and Its Influence on Cognition." *Psychological Review* 106: 529–550.

Axelrod, Robert. 1984. *The Evolution of Cooperation.* New York: Basic Books.

Bacharach, Samuel B., and Edward J. Lawler. 1981. *Bargaining: Power, Tactics, and Outcomes.* San Francisco: Jossey-Bass.

Bless, Herbert. 2000. "The Interplay of Affect and Cognition: The Mediating Role of General Knowledge Structures." Pp. 201–222 in *Thinking and Feeling: The Role of Affect in Social Cognition*, edited by J. Forgas. Cambridge: Cambridge University Press.

Blood, Anne J., and Robert J. Zatorre. 2001. "Intensely Pleasurable Responses to Music Correlate with Activity in Brain Regions Implicated in Reward and Emotion." *Proceedings of the National Academy of Sciences USA* 98: 11,818–11,823.

Bower, George H. 1991. "Mood Congruity of Social Judgments." Pp. 31–53 in *Emotion and Social Judgments*, edited by J. Forgas. Oxford: Pergamon.

Buskens, Vincent. 2002. *Social Networks and Trust.* Boston: Kluwer.

Clore, Gerald L., Andrew Ortony, and Mark A. Foss. 1987. "The Psychological Foundations of the Affective Lexicon." *Journal of Personality and Social Psychology* 53: 751–766.

Collins, Randall. 1981. "On the Microfoundations of Macrosociology." *American Journal of Sociology* 86: 984–1014.

———. 1989. "Toward a Neo-Meadian Sociology of Mind." *Symbolic Interaction* 12: 1–32.

Cook, Karen S. 2001. *Trust in Society.* New York: Sage.

Cook, Karen S., and Richard M. Emerson. 1978. "Power, Equity, and Commitment in Exchange Networks." *American Sociological Review* 27: 41–40.

———. 1984. "Exchange Networks and the Analysis of Complex Organizations." Pp. 1–30 in *Research on the Sociology of Organizations*, edited by S. B. Bacharach and E. J. Lawler. Greenwich, CT: JAI Press.

Cook, Karen S., Richard M. Emerson, Mary R. Gillmore, and Toshio Yamagishi. 1983. "The Distribution of Power in Exchange Networks: Theory and Experimental Evidence." *American Journal of Sociology* 89: 275–305.

Damasio, Antonio. 1999. *The Feeling of What Happens.* New York: Harcourt Brace.

Damasio, Antonio R., Thomas Grabawski, Antoine Bechara, Hanna Damasio, Laura L. B. Ponto, Josef Parvizi, and Richard D. Hichwa. 2000. "Subcortical and Cortical Brain Activity during the Feeling of Self-Generated Emotions." *Nature Neuroscience* 3: 1049–1056.

Durkheim, Emile. 1915. *The Elementary Forms of Religious Life.* New York: Free Press.

Ekeh, Peter. 1974. *Social Exchange Theory: The Two Traditions.* Cambridge, MA: Harvard University Press.

Ekman, Paul. 1980. *The Face of Man: Expressions of Universal Emotions in a New Guinea Village.* New York: Garland STMP Press.

Ekman, Paul, and Wallace V. Friesen. 1975. *Unmasking the Face: A Guide to Recognizing Emotions from Facial Cues.* Oxford: Prentice-Hall.

Elster, Jon. 1986. "Introduction." Pp. 1–33 in *Rational Choice*, edited by J. Elster. Albany: New York University Press.

Emerson, Richard M. 1972a. "Exchange Theory Part I: A Psychological Basis for Social Exchange." Pp. 38–57 in *Sociological Theories in Progress,* edited by J. Berger, M. Zelditch, Jr., and B. Anderson. Boston: Houghton Mifflin.

———. 1972b. "Exchange Theory Part II: Exchange Rules and Networks." Pp. 58–87 in *Sociological Theories in Progress,* edited by J. Berger, M. Zelditch, Jr. and B. Anderson. Boston: Houghton Mifflin.

———. 1981. "Social Exchange Theory." Pp. 30–65 in *Social Psychology: Sociological Perspectives*, edited by M. Rosenberg and R. H. Turner. New York: Basic Books.

Forgas, Joseph. 2000. "Affect and Information Strategies." Pp. 253–280 in *Thinking and Feeling: The Role of Affect in Social Cognition*, edited by J. Forgas. Cambridge: Cambridge University Press.

Frank, Robert H. 1988. *Passions within Reason: The Strategic Role of Emotions.* New York: W. W. Norton.

Frijda, Nico H. 1986. *The Emotions.* Cambridge, MA: Cambridge University Press.

Haslam, N. 1995. "The Discreteness of Emotion Concepts: Categorical Structure in the Affective Circumplex." *Personality and Social Psychology Bulletin* 21: 1012–1019.

Hechter, Michael. 1987. *Principles of Group Solidarity.* Berkeley: University of California Press.

Heise, David R. 1987. "Affect Control Theory: Concepts and Model." *Journal of Mathematical Sociology* 13: 1–33.

Hochschild, Arlie R. 1979. "Emotion Work, Feeling Rules, and Social Structure." *American Journal of Sociology* 85: 551–575.

———. 1983. *The Managed Heart: Commercialization of Human Feeling.* Berkeley: University of California Press.

Homans, George L. 1950. *Human Group.* New Brunswick, NJ: Transaction Publishers.

———. 1961. *Social Behavior: Its Elementary Forms.* New York: Harcourt Brace Jovanovich.

———. 1974. *Social Behavior: Its Elementary Forms*. New York: Harcourt Brace Jovanovich.

Isen, Alice M. 1987. "Positive Affect, Cognitive Processes, and Social Behavior." Pp. 203–253 in *Advances in Experimental Social Psychology*, edited by L. Berkowitz. New York: Academic.

Izard, Carroll E. 1991. *The Psychology of Emotion*. New York: Plenum.

Jones Edward E., and Keith E. Davis. 1965. "From Acts to Dispositions: The Attribution Process in Person Perception." Pp. 219–266 in *Advances in Experimental Social Psychology*, edited by L. Berkowitz. New York: Academic.

Kanter, Rosabeth M. 1968. "Commitment and Social Organization: A Study of Commitment Mechanisms in Utopian Communities." *American Sociological Review* 33: 499–517.

Kelley, Harold H. 1967. "Attribution Theory in Social Psychology." Pp. 220–266 in *Nebraska Symposium on Motivation*, edited by D. Levine. Lincoln: University of Nebraska Press.

Kelley, Harold H., and John W. Thibaut. 1978. *Interpersonal Relations: A Theory of Interdependence*. New York: Wiley.

Kemper, Theodore D. 1978. *A Social Interactional Theory of Emotions*. New York: Wiley.

———. 1987. "How Many Emotions Are There? Wedding the Social and the Autonomic Components." *American Journal of Sociology* 93: 263–289.

Kollock, Peter 1994. "The Emergence of Exchange Structures: An Experimental Study of Uncertainty, Commitment, and Trust." *American Journal of Sociology* 100: 315–345.

———. 1999. "The Production of Trust in Online Markets." *Advances in Group Process* 16: 99–123.

Komorita, Samuel S., and Craig D. Parks. 1996. *Social Dilemmas*. Boulder, CO: Westview.

Larsen, Randy J., and Edward Diener. 1992. "Promises and Problems with the Circumplex Model of Emotion." Pp. 25–59 in *Emotion*, edited by M. S. Clark. Newbury Park, CA: Sage.

Lawler, Edward J. 2001. "An Affect Theory of Social Exchange." *American Journal of Sociology* 107: 321–352.

———. 2002. "Micro Social Orders." *Social Psychology Quarterly* 65: 4–17.

———. 2003. "Interaction, Emotion, and Collective Identities." Pp. 135–149 in *Advances in Identity Theory and Research*, edited by P. J. Burke, T. J. Owens, R. T. Serpe, and P. A. Thoits. New York: Kluwer Academic/Plenum.

———. 2006 "Exchange, Affect and Group Relations." Pp. 177–201 in *George C. Homans: History, Theory, and Method*, edited by J. Trevino. Boulder, CO: Paradigm.

Lawler, Edward J., and Shane R. Thye. 1999. "Bringing Emotions into Social Exchange Theory." *Annual Review of Sociology* 25: 217–244.

Lawler, Edward J., Shane R. Thye, and Jeongkoo Yoon. 2000. "Emotion and Group Cohesion in Productive Exchange." *American Journal of Sociology* 106: 616–657.

Lawler, Edward J., and Jeongkoo Yoon. 1993. "Power and the Emergence of Commitment Behavior in Negotiated Exchange." *American Sociological Review* 58: 465–481.

———. 1996. "Commitment in Exchange Relations: Test of a Theory of Relational Cohesion." *American Sociological Review* 61: 89–108.

———. 1998. "Network Structure and Emotion in Exchange Relations." *American Sociological Review* 63: 871–894.

Lutz, C. 1988. *Unnatural Emotions: Everyday Sentiments on a Micronesian Atoll and Their Challenge to Western Theory*. Chicago: University of Chicago Press.

Macy, Michael W. 1993. "Backward-Looking Social Control." *American Sociological Review* 58: 819–836.

Macy, Michael W., and John Skvoretz. 1998. "The Evolution of Trust and Cooperation Between Strangers: A Computational Model." *American Sociological Review* 63: 638–660.

Markovsky, Barry, and Edward J. Lawler. 1994. "A New Theory of Group Solidarity." *Advances in Group Processes* 11: 113–134.

Markovsky, Barry, John Skvoretz, David Willer, Michael J. Lovaglia, and Jeffery Erger. 1993. "The Seeds of Weak Power: An Extension of Network Exchange Theory." *American Sociological Review* 58: 197–209.

Markovsky, Barry, David Willer, and Travis Patton. 1988. "Power Relations in Exchange Networks." *American Sociological Review* 53: 220–236.

Molm, Linda D. 1987. "Extending Power Dependency Theory: Power Processes and Negative Outcomes." *Advances in Group Processes* 4: 178–198.

———. 1994. "Dependence and Risk: Transforming the Structure of Social Exchange." *Social Psychology Quarterly* 57: 163–189.

———. 1997. *Coercive Power in Social Exchange*. Cambridge: Cambridge University Press.

———. 2003a. "Power, Trust, and Fairness: Comparisons of Negotiated and Reciprocal Exchange." *Advances in Group Processes* 20: 31–66.

———. 2003b. "Theoretical Comparisons of Forms of Exchange." *Sociological Theory* 21: 1–17.

Molm, Linda, and Karen Cook. 1995. "Social Exchange and Exchange Networks." Pp. 209–235 in *Sociological Perspectives on Social Psychology*, edited by K. S. Cook, G. A. Fine, and J. S. House. Boston: Allyn and Bacon.

Molm, Linda, Gretchen Peterson, and Nobuyuki Takahashi. 1999. "Power in Negotiated and Reciprocal Exchange." *American Sociological Review* 64: 876–890.

Parsons, Talcott. 1951. *The Social System*. New York: Free Press.

Pinker, Steven. 1997. *How the Mind Works*. New York: W. W. Norton.

Pruitt, Dean J., and M. J. Kimmel. 1977. "Twenty Years of Experimental Gaming: Critique, Synthesis and Suggestions for the Future." *Annual Review of Psychology* 19: 172–202.

Rabbie, Jacob M., and Murray Horowitz. 1988. "Category versus Groups as Explanatory Concepts in Intergroup Relations." *European Journal of Social Psychology* 19: 172–202.

Ridgeway, Cecilia, and Cathryn Johnson. 1990. "What Is the Relationship between Socioemotional Behavior and Status in Task Groups?" *American Journal of Sociology* 95: 1189–1212.

Russell, James A. 1980. "A Circumplex Model of Affect." *Journal of Personality and Social Psychology* 39: 1161–1178.

———. 1983. "Pancultural Aspects of the Human Conceptual Organization of Emotions." *Journal of Personality and Social Psychology* 45: 1281–1288.

Russell, James A., Anita Weiss, and George A. Mendelsohn. 1989. "Affect Grid: A Single-Item Scale of Pleasure and Arousal." *Journal of Personal and Sociology Psychology* 57: 493–502.

Schachter, Stanley, and Jerome E. Singer. 1962. "Cognitive, Social and Physiological Determinants of Emotional State." *Psychology Review* 69: 379–399.

Scheff, Thomas J. 1990. *Microsociology: Discourse, Emotion and Social Structure*. Chicago: University of Chicago Press.

Scherer, Klaus R. 1984. "Emotion as a Multicomponent Process: A Model and Some Cross-Cultural Data." *Review of Personality and Social Psychology* 5: 37–63.

Small, Dana M., Robert Zatorre, Alain Dagher, Alan C. Evans, and Marilyn Jones-Gotman. 2001. "Changes in Brain Activity Related to Eating Chocolate: From Pleasure to Aversion." *Brain* 124: 1720–1733.

Stets, Jan E. 2003. "Emotions and Sentiments." Pp. 309–335 in *Handbook of Social Psychology*, edited by J. DeLamater. New York: Kluwer Academic/Plenum.

Tajfel, Henri, and John C. Turner. 1979. "An Integrative Theory of Intergroup Conflict." Pp. 33–47 in *The Social Psychology of Intergroup Relations*, edited by W. G. Austin and S. Worchel. Monterey, CA: Brooks/Cole.

———. 1986. "The Social Identity Theory of Intergroup Behavior." Pp. 7–24 in *Psychology of Intergroup Relations*, edited by S. Worchel and W. G. Austin. Chicago: Nelson-Hall.

Thibaut, John W., and Harold H. Kelley. 1959. *The Social Psychology of Groups*. New York: Wiley.

Thye, Shane R., and Edward J. Lawler. 1999. "Collaborative Research on Social Exchange and Network Cohesion." Proposal to the National Science Foundation (funded May 15, 1999).

Thye, Shane R., Michael J. Lovaglia, and Barry Markovsky. 1997. "Responses to Social Exchange and Social Exclusion in Networks." *Social Forces* 75: 1031–1047.

Thye, Shane R., Jeongkoo Yoon, and Edward J. Lawler. 2002. "The Theory of Relational Cohesion: Review of a Research Program." *Advances in Group Process*es 19: 139–166.

Turner, Jonathan H. 2000. *On the Origins of Human Emotions*. Stanford, CA: Stanford University Press.

———. 2002. *Face-to-Face: Towards a Sociological Theory of Interpersonal Behavior*. Stanford, CA: Stanford University Press.

Tyler, Tom R. 1990. *Why People Obey the Law: Procedural Justice, Legitimacy, and Compliance*. New Haven, CT: Yale University Press.

———. 1994. "Psychological Models of the Justice Motive: Antecedents of Distributive and Procedural Justice." *Journal of Personality and Social Psychology* 67: 850–863.

Watson, David, Lee Anna Clark, and Auke Tellegen. 1984. "Cross-Cultural Convergence in the Structure of Mood: A Japanese Replication and a Comparison with U.S. Findings." *Journal of Personality and Social Psychology* 47: 127–144.

Weiner, Bernard. 1986. *An Attributional Theory of Motivation and Emotion*. New York: Springer-Verlag.

Wierzbicka, A. 1992. "Defining Emotion Concepts." *Cognitive Science* 16: 539–581.

Willer, David. 1999. *Network Exchange Theory*. Westport, CT: Praeger.

Williamson, Oliver E. 1981. "The Economics of Organization: The Transaction Cost Approach." *American Journal of Sociology* 87: 549–577.

———. 1985. *The Economic Institutions of Capitalism*. New York: Free Press.

Yamagishi, Toshio. 1986. "The Provision of a Sanctioning System as a Public Good." *Journal of Personality and Social Psychology* 51: 110–116.

Yamagishi, Toshio, and Midori Yamagishi. 1994. "Trust and Commitment in the United States and Japan." *Motivation and Emotion* 18: 129–166.

CHAPTER 14

Emotion in Justice Processes

Guillermina Jasso

Every day humans experience a wide range of emotions—the joy of the sunrise, the disappointment of a nonexistent closed-form expression, the consolation of a beautiful theorem, the thrill of tasty food, the pleasure of a deep friendship, the unbearable sadness of another's lost love (weeping for Dido, as the young Augustine), the peace of a day well worked.

Meanwhile, every day the human sense of justice is at work. Humans form ideas about what is just, and they make judgments about the justice or injustice of the things they see around them. Both the ideas of justice and the assessments of injustice set in motion a train of individual and social processes, touching virtually every area of the human experience, from love to gifts to crime, from disaster to war to religion.

Justice and emotions overlap, for at every step of a justice process, the sense of justice triggers emotion. Thus, understanding the operation of the sense of justice and the special sentiments it arouses is important to the project of understanding human emotion.

In this chapter I focus on three basic kinds of justice reflection and the accompanying sentiments—justice in how we see ourselves, justice in how we see others, justice in how others see us. In reflexive justice, humans form ideas about what they think are their own just rewards, and they assess the justice or injustice of their actual rewards. In nonreflexive justice, humans form ideas about what they think are the just rewards for others, and they assess the justice or injustice of others' actual rewards. Of course, if everyone is engaged in both reflexive and nonreflexive justice, there might be a discrepancy between what an individual thinks is just for self and what others think is just for this individual. Thus, there is a third reflection: the individual contrasting his or her own with others' ideas of what is just for self.

The emotions released at the various steps of a justice process might be characterized in a number of ways. They might be solitary or a set, positive or negative, experienced or expressed. They vary in intensity. They might be momentary or persistent; as Aristotle (*Nicomachean Ethics*,

---

Guillermina Jasso • Department of Sociology, New York University, New York, NY 10012

Book I, Chapter 7) observed in discussing happiness, "One swallow does not make a summer, nor does one day." They might be drawn from among the large palette of emotions, including primary and secondary emotions. My task here is to search for the underlying principles that generate this vast diversity. In this endeavor, I build on the literature on emotions and the growing literature on emotion in justice processes (Hegtvedt and Killian 1999; Homans 1961, 1974; Jasso 1993; Kemper 1978; Stets 2003; Turner 2000, 2005; Turner and Stets 2005).

Careful examination of justice yields a coherent and testable portrait of the emotion dimension. This portrait yields many new insights and new questions. For example, it broadens the idea of impartiality to include two new types of impartiality—framing-impartiality and expressiveness-impartiality—which I empirically investigate in this chapter, asking the questions: (1) When individuals judge the fairness of another's reward, do they frame the reward uniformly or do they frame the reward as a good for some and a bad for others? (2) When individuals judge the fairness of another's situation, do they display impartiality in their emotional reactions or does their emotion display vary across the judged others? As well, the methodological knowledge gained can be put in the service of other processes, providing an orderly way to assess the emotion dimension in all sociobehavioral processes, a project I sketch in barest outline at the end of the chapter. As will be seen, all of the major questions about the emotion dimension—how many emotions, what valence, what intensity, and so on—can potentially be addressed via a simple and rigorous framework that links them tightly to the sociobehavioral processes triggering emotion.

Along the way, we take some risks. It is too early to guess which elements will survive unrejected by empirical test and which will be rejected and discarded. However, whatever better portraits emerge, they will share with this one a measure of parsimony and that hallmark of a useful synthesis, in Samuel Smiles' words: "A place for everything, and everything in its place."

JUSTICE ANALYSIS: UNDERSTANDING THE OPERATION OF THE SENSE OF JUSTICE

Justice analysis begins with *four central questions* (Jasso and Wegener 1997):

1. What do individuals and societies think is just, and why?
2. How do ideas of justice shape determination of actual situations?
3. What is the magnitude of the perceived injustice associated with given departures from perfect justice?
4. What are the behavioral and social consequences of perceived injustice?

Justice analysis addresses the four central questions by developing three elements: *framework for justice analysis, theoretical justice analysis*, and *empirical justice analysis* (Jasso 2004). Developing the framework entails analyzing each of the four central questions, identifying the fundamental ingredients in justice phenomena, and formulating a set of fundamental building blocks—the fundamental actors, quantities, functions, distributions, matrices, and contexts. Theoretical justice analysis focuses on building theories, both deductive and nondeductive, with each theory addressing one of the central questions and using as a starting premise one of the building blocks provided by the framework. Empirical justice analysis spans testing the implications derived from deductive theories and the propositions suggested by nondeductive theories as well as carrying out measurement of the justice quantities, estimation of the justice relations, and inductive exploration.

In general, justice analysis encompasses all justice domains. However, for simplicity and concreteness, I focus here on the distributive-retributive domain. In this domain, the archetypal situation involves personal amounts and levels of goods and bads—beauty, income, punishments, taxes, and so on. The domain, however, also includes amounts and levels of goods and bads in collectivities—resource endowment and income inequality, for example. Moreover, the tools developed for this domain can be straightforwardly applied to some cases of procedural justice, such as those involving quantifiable attributes (e.g., duration of deliberations and number of persons consulted).

Emotion is generated at every step. As is amply noted in the literature and as will be seen below, there is emotion in the activities addressed in each of the four central questions listed above.

Overview of the Framework for Justice Analysis

The archetypal situation that awakens the sense of justice in the distributive-retributive domain involves a person who receives or is assigned a specified amount or level of a benefit or a burden. Examples include earnings, income, beauty, intelligence, or athletic skill. Reasoning about the four central questions leads quickly to a set of fundamental ingredients—the fundamental actors, quantities, functions, distributions, matrices, and contexts. These fundamental ingredients, in turn, become the building blocks of theoretical and empirical justice analysis.

Fundamental Actors

Although in general there is one fundamental actor—the *observer* who forms ideas of justice and judges the justice or injustice of actual situations—in the distributive-retributive domain, there are two fundamental actors. The new fundamental actor in the distributive-retributive domain is the *rewardee*, the person who receives an amount or level of a benefit or burden. The rewardee could be the observer himself or herself. When the observer and the rewardee are the same, the situation is termed *reflexive*; otherwise, it is termed *nonreflexive*.[1]

Thus begin the three justice reflections we highlight. The first is reflexive, where the actor, operating as both observer and rewardee, judges the fairness of his or her own attributes and possessions. The second is nonreflexive, where the actor, operating as observer, judges the fairness of others' attributes and possessions. The third is a hybrid, where the actor operates as rewardee and reacts to others' nonreflexive judgments of the fairness of his or her situation.

A basic principle, proposed by Hatfield and amply supported empirically, is that of *observer independence of mind*: "[E]quity is in the eye of the beholder" (Walster et al. 1976:4).

Immediately, two new emotion questions arise: Does the nature or intensity of emotion differ between reflexive and nonreflexive justice situations? Within nonreflexive justice situations, does emotion differ across different others? Below I formalize these and other questions.

Fundamental Quantities

The things that awaken the sense of justice in the distributive-retributive domain are *quantitative characteristics*, like intelligence and wealth. Quantitative characteristics are of two kinds: *cardinal*, such as income and land, and *ordinal*, such as beauty and intelligence. Quantitative characteristics of which more is preferred to less are called *goods*; quantitative characteristics of which less is preferred to more are called *bads*.

Goods and bads form two of the three fundamental quantities in the distributive-retributive domain. These are the rewardee's actual amount or level of a good or a bad, called the *actual reward*, and the observer's idea of the just amount or level of a good or a bad for the rewardee, called the *just reward*. The third fundamental quantity is the observer's assessment that the rewardee is justly or unjustly rewarded, called the *justice evaluation*.

The actual reward, denoted A, and the just reward, denoted C, are measured in the reward's own units, if the reward is cardinal, and by relative ranks, if the reward is ordinal. This is the basic measurement rule proposed in Jasso (1980). The formula for relative ranks is given by $i/(N+1)$, where i denotes the raw rank and N denotes the group size. In some justice situations involving additive and transferable cardinal goods and bads, the individual may care about a share; in such case, the *actual share* and *just share* are defined and measured as the actual or just reward divided by the total amount of the cardinal thing in a comparison group.[2]

The justice evaluation, denoted J, is represented by the full real-number line, with zero representing the point of perfect justice, negative numbers representing unjust underreward, and positive numbers representing unjust overreward. Thus, a justice evaluation of zero indicates that the observer judges the rewardee to be perfectly justly rewarded. The closer a value of the justice evaluation to zero, the milder the injustice it indicates; the farther away from zero, the greater the injustice. A justice evaluation of -7 and a justice evaluation of -13 both indicate that the observer judges the rewardee to be unjustly underrewarded, with the rewardee associated with the -13 judged to be more underrewarded than the rewardee associated with the -7. Similarly, a justice evaluation of 8 and a justice evaluation of 12 both indicate that the observer judges the rewardees to be unjustly overrewarded, with the rewardee accorded the 12 judged to be more overrewarded than the rewardee accorded the 8.

The justice evaluation variable has twin roots in Homans' (1961, 1976) and Berger et al.'s (1972) idea of a three-category variable and Jasso and Rossi's (1977) nine-category fairness rating, emerging as a continuous variable on the full real-number line with Jasso's (1978) introduction of the justice evaluation function.

The just reward and the justice evaluation are always observer-specific and rewardee-specific. The actual reward is, of course, rewardee-specific, but might be observer-specific if there are perceptual errors or distortions, such that different observers perceive different actual rewards for the same rewardee. The justice quantities are instantaneous, individuals forming many distinct just rewards and experiencing many distinct justice evaluations.

As will be formalized below, emotion might differ across different rewards and across justice evaluations, depending on reflexivity, as already mentioned, and on the particular good or bad. For example, a justice process involving beauty might trigger less intense emotion than a justice process involving earnings or vice versa. Also, a justice process involving own earnings might trigger more intense emotion than a justice process involving another's earnings or vice versa.

Fundamental Functions

Each of the fundamental questions is addressed by a fundamental function: the *just reward function*, the *actual reward function*, the *justice evaluation function*, and the *justice consequences function*, respectively. The fundamental functions are generalized functions encompassing a variety of special cases, and the functions also give rise to new quantities and new functions.

The just reward function (JRF) is amenable to representation in several versions. This is because the observer's idea of the just reward can have a multiplicity of sources. It might be a past own reward, an imagined reward, another person's reward, a function of another person's reward, a location parameter of the distribution of that reward in a group, a reward in a referential structure, and so on. In one version, paralleling the attainment functions of sociology and economics, such as the Mincer-type earnings function, the just reward is expressed as a function of rewardee characteristics. This function is called the BZAC JRF, after Berger, Zelditch, Anderson, and Cohen (1972), whose ideas it represents. Two versions directly involve reference group concepts, as discussed by Merton and Rossi (1950): a version in which the just reward is (a function of) the reward of a reference individual, and a version in which the just reward is (a function of) a location parameter (e.g., mean or median) of the reward distribution in a reference group. For example, the just income might be equal to the expected value of actual income, as in $C = E(A)$, where lowercase letters indicate the individual's holding and uppercase letters indicate the variable.[3] Following Brickman et al. (1981), parameters of the BZAC version of the JRF provide estimates of the *principles of microjustice.*

The justice evaluation function (JEF) combines the actual reward and the just reward to produce the justice evaluation. It plays a critical role in both theoretical justice analysis and empirical justice analysis. For example, in theoretical justice analysis, it serves as the first postulate of several theories, including justice-comparison theory, yielding testable implications for many disparate domains of sociobehavioral phenomena. In empirical justice analysis, the JEF makes it possible to obtain estimates of the experienced justice evaluation and of the true just reward. Accordingly, we take a closer look at it below.

To illustrate a justice process, consider the following sequence. Guided by the considerations embedded in the JRF, the observer forms an idea of the just reward. The observer can then use this idea of the just reward to affect the rewardee's actual reward, via the actual reward function (ARF). Of course, the just reward is only one argument in the ARF; as was noted by Leventhal (1976), an allocator's decision-making process might include not only considerations of justice but also other considerations (see also Jasso and Webster 1997). A given observer might vote, say, in ways that depart from his or her ideas of justice, doing so to pursue other ends. In any case, the rewardee receives an actual reward, and the stage is set for the justice evaluation. The observer then judges the justice or injustice of the rewardee's actual reward, reaching a judgment that the rewardee is justly or unjustly rewarded and, if unjustly rewarded, whether underrewarded or overrewarded, and to what degree. Finally, the observer might take action in response to the justice evaluation. Of course, any action depends not only on the justice evaluation but also on other factors. For example, a worker's decision to strike depends not only on the justice evaluation but also on family and economic factors.

Note that the first and third functions—the JRF and JEF—describe ideas and judgments in the observer's head, whereas the second and fourth functions describe behaviors that depend, in part, on the outcomes of the JRF and JEF, respectively. Further, note that each step involves emotion, as will be formalized below.

Fundamental Matrices

Each of the three fundamental quantities—actual reward, just reward, justice evaluation—can be arrayed in an observer-by-rewardee matrix, as depicted in Table 14.1. These matrices are used in both theoretical and empirical justice analysis. For example, the justice evaluation matrix is the starting point for one of the techniques of derivation in theoretical justice analysis (the matrixmodel).

Each matrix collects and exemplifies the three justice reflections I highlight in this chapter. The first justice reflection is represented by the main diagonal of the matrix, which contains each observer's actual reward as well as the just reward and justice evaluation for self. The second

TABLE 14.1. Observer-by-Rewardee Matrices of the Just Reward, the Actual Reward, and the Justice Evaluation

1. Just Reward Matrix

$$C = \begin{bmatrix} c_{11} & c_{12} & c_{13} & \cdots & c_{1R} \\ c_{21} & c_{22} & c_{23} & \cdots & c_{2R} \\ c_{31} & c_{32} & c_{33} & \cdots & c_{3R} \\ \vdots & \vdots & \vdots & \ddots & \vdots \\ c_{N1} & c_{N2} & c_{N3} & \cdots & c_{NR} \end{bmatrix}$$

2. Actual Reward Matrix

$$A = \begin{bmatrix} a_{11} & a_{12} & a_{13} & \cdots & a_{1R} \\ a_{21} & a_{22} & a_{23} & \cdots & a_{2R} \\ a_{31} & a_{32} & a_{33} & \cdots & a_{3R} \\ \vdots & \vdots & \vdots & \ddots & \vdots \\ a_{N1} & a_{N2} & a_{N3} & \cdots & a_{NR} \end{bmatrix}$$

If there are no perception errors, the actual reward matrix collapses to a vector:

$$a_j = \begin{bmatrix} a_{.1} & a_{.2} & a_{.3} & \cdots & a_{.R} \end{bmatrix}$$

3. Justice Evaluation Matrix

$$J = \begin{bmatrix} j_{11} & j_{12} & j_{13} & \cdots & j_{1R} \\ j_{21} & j_{22} & j_{23} & \cdots & j_{2R} \\ j_{31} & j_{32} & j_{33} & \cdots & j_{3R} \\ \vdots & \vdots & \vdots & \ddots & \vdots \\ j_{N1} & j_{N2} & j_{N3} & \cdots & j_{NR} \end{bmatrix}$$

Note: Observers are indexed by $o = 1, \ldots, N$; rewardees are indexed by $r = 1, \ldots, R$. Thus, c_{or}, a_{or}, and j_{or} represent the observer-specific/rewardee-specific just reward, actual reward, and justice evaluation, respectively.

justice reflection is represented by the rows of the matrix (minus the terms on the main diagonal); each row contains each observer's justice terms for everyone in the collectivity. The third justice reflection is represented by the columns of the matrix (again minus the terms on the diagonal); each column contains all the justice terms for each rewardee. Thus, an actor generates a row, which includes both the reflexive terms for self and the nonreflexive terms for others, and reacts to a column, which contains others' justice terms about him or her. The matrices set the stage for the questions that we will ask pertaining to emotion differences across self and other.

Fundamental Distributions

Each of the three fundamental quantities gives rise to three kinds of distributions: the observer-specific distribution, the rewardee-specific distribution, and the reflexive distribution. The distributions are visible from the matrices in Table 14.1. The observer-specific distribution is represented by the rows of the matrix (one row per observer); the rewardee-specific distribution is represented by the columns of the matrix (one column per rewardee); and the reflexive distribution is represented by the main diagonal of the matrix. Of course, there is also a global distribution, which consists of all the entries in the entire matrix.

Some of these distributions play important parts. For example, following Brickman et al. (1981), parameters of the observer-specific just reward distribution provide estimates of the *principles of macrojustice*. Variability in the observer-specific just reward distributions (rows) provides a measure of how much inequality each observer regards as just. Variability in the rewardee-specific just reward distributions (columns) provides a measure of the degree of consensus (or, alternatively, Hatfield's independence of mind).

As with the principles of microjustice, new functions arise that specify determination of the principles of macrojustice. Similarly, the reflexive justice evaluation distribution is the starting point for one of the strategies of derivation (the macromodel). Further, special sentiments accompany each of the three kinds of distribution.

Fundamental Contexts

All of the quantities and functions can differ systematically across a range of contexts, currently thought to include the benefit or burden under consideration, the social context, and the time period. Combining these with the observer and rewardee already identified gives rise to five contexts, conveniently represented by five subscripts with the mnemonic *brots* (*b* for the benefit or burden, *r* for the rewardee, *o* for the observer, *t* for the time period, and *s* for the society).

These contexts light the way in our search for the operation of emotion, for, as will be discussed below, emotion could be context-specific. Moreover, I assess empirically the possibility that emotion display is rewardee-specific.

A CLOSER LOOK AT
THE JUSTICE EVALUATION FUNCTION

Justice Evaluation Function: General Function

The justice evaluation arises from the comparison of the actual reward to the just reward. This comparison can be stated as a general function: The justice evaluation is a function of the actual reward and the just reward, such that, in the case of a good, the justice evaluation increases with the actual reward and decreases with the just reward, and such that when the actual reward equals the just reward, the justice evaluation equals zero, the point of perfect justice. The general justice evaluation function, for both goods and bads, is written as follows:

$$
\begin{aligned}
J &= \theta[J(A, C)], \\
&\partial J / \partial A > 0, \partial J / \partial C < 0, \\
&\theta > 0 \text{ for a good}, \theta < 0 \text{ for a bad}, \\
&J(a_0 = c_0) = 0
\end{aligned}
\tag{1}
$$

where J denotes the justice evaluation, A denotes the actual reward, C denotes the just reward, and θ denotes the signature constant. The sign of θ is called the *framing coefficient*, because it embodies the observer's framing of the reward as a good or as a bad (negative for a bad, positive for a good), and the absolute value of θ is called the *expressiveness coefficient*, because it transforms the observer's experience of justice into the expression thereof.

The framing and expressiveness coefficients play important parts in understanding emotion. In particular, an important source of variability in emotion might arise from differential framing and expressiveness in reflexive and nonreflexive justice and, within nonreflexive justice situations, across different others. Below, we assess empirically differential framing and expressiveness across different others.

Justice Evaluation Function: Specific Function

Further reasoning about the JEF—in particular, reasoning about the properties of a desirable functional form—leads to a new specific form: the logarithmic-ratio specification of the JEF.[4] In this form, the justice evaluation varies as the natural logarithm of the ratio of the actual reward to the just reward, in the case of a good, and in the case of a bad, it varies as the logarithm of the ratio of the just reward to the actual reward. Thus, the JEF is parsimoniously written

$$J = \theta \ln\left(\frac{A}{C}\right) \tag{2}$$

Properties of the Justice Evaluation Function

The logarithmic-ratio specification imparts several good properties to the JEF. The first three noticed were (1) exact mapping from combinations of the actual reward and the just reward to the justice evaluation, (2) integration of two rival conceptions of J as a ratio (Homans 1961) and as a difference (Berger et al. 1972), and (3) deficiency aversion, namely, deficiency is felt more keenly than comparable excess (and loss aversion; viz. losses are felt more keenly than gains). These properties were quickly discussed (e.g., Wagner and Berger 1985) and remain the most often cited (Turner 2005; Whitmeyer 2004).

However, as will be seen below, a new theory for which the JEF served as first postulate was yielding a large number of implications for a wide variety of behavioral domains, and a stronger foundation was needed. In the course of scrutinizing the JEF, two new properties emerged: (4) additivity, such that the effect of the actual reward on J is independent of the level of the just reward, and conversely, and (5) scale invariance (Jasso 1990). In fact, in the case of a cardinal reward, the log-ratio form is the only functional form that is both additive and scale-invariant (Jasso 1990).

Six years later, two other desirable properties were noticed (Jasso 1996): (6) symmetry, such that interchanging A and C changes only the sign of J, and (7) the fact that the log-ratio form of the JEF is the limiting form of the difference between two power functions:

$$\lim_{k \to 0} \frac{A^k - C^k}{k} = \ln\left(\frac{A}{C}\right) \tag{3}$$

where k is a positive constant. This last result not only strengthens integration of the ratio and difference views of the justice evaluation but also integrates power-function and logarithmic approaches. More recently, an eighth (almost magical) property has come to light, linking the JEF and the Golden Number: $(\sqrt{5} - 1)/2$ (Jasso 2005).

Experienced and Expressed Justice Evaluation Functions

As hinted above, the *experienced JEF* is defined as the log of the ratio of A to C, multiplied by the framing coefficient:

$$\text{experienced } J = [\text{sgn}(\theta)] \ln\left(\frac{A}{C}\right) \tag{4}$$

The experienced JEF releases emotion, variously imagined as an explosion when the logarithm of the A/C ratio is taken or when $\ln(A)$ confronts $\ln(C)$.

The *expressed JEF* is defined as the experienced JEF multiplied by the expressiveness coefficient:

$$\text{expressed } J = [|\theta|](\text{ experienced } J). \tag{5}$$

The expressiveness coefficient governs the style of expression, including emotion display (Jasso 1993).

Justice Evaluation Across Contexts

Of course, not only is the justice evaluation specific to observer and rewardee combinations, but it might also vary systematically across reward domains and across societies and over time. These context-specific effects, which also extend to the signature constant, are represented by the *brots* subscripts introduced earlier, producing the context-sensitive expression of the JEF:

$$J_{brots} = \theta_{brots} \ln\left(\frac{A_{brots}}{C_{brots}}\right) \tag{6}$$

which can be reexpressed to highlight the separate operation and contextual variability of the framing and expressiveness coefficients:

$$J_{brots} = [\text{sgn}(\theta)]_{brots} [|\theta|]_{brots} \ln\left(\frac{A_{brots}}{C_{brots}}\right) \tag{7}$$

Expression (7) is the basic representation of the JEF that alerts to variation in emotion across justice processes and helps test for it.

Absolute Value of the Justice Evaluation

In some situations, the behaviorally relevant justice evaluation does not distinguish between underreward and overreward, collapsing both into a single type of injustice. For these situations, a new quantity, the *absolute value of the justice evaluation,* $|J|$, is defined (Fararo and Skvoretz 1993:447–448; Jasso 1986, 1999). Note that emotion might differ across the justice evaluation and its absolute value.

Reference Groups in the Justice Evaluation Function

A reference group (more accurately, a *comparison group*) is required in two cases: when the reward is ordinal and when the just reward is a (function of) a parameter of a group. In other cases, no comparison group is required. As formalized in the contexts, the emotion triggered by a justice evaluation might differ across comparison groups and might differ between situations with and without a comparison group.

Connections and Decompositions

The JEF also generates several useful connections: (1) a link between justice and inequality, such that as inequality increases, injustice increases, something widely believed and often asserted but for which no proof previously existed (Jasso 2002); (2) a link with ideology, via the *justice index* JI1 (the arithmetic mean of J), which can be decomposed into the amount of overall injustice due to reality and the amount due to ideology; (3) a link with poverty and inequality, via another decomposition of the justice index into the amount of overall injustice due to poverty and the amount due to inequality (Jasso 1999); and (4) a decomposition into subgroup-specific justice indexes (Jasso 2004). As well, the JEF connects the two great literatures in the study of justice: the literature on ideas of justice and the literature on reactions to injustice.

Justice Evaluation and Relations Between Actors

To characterize relations between actors, new quantities are defined, such as the difference between the reflexive justice evaluations of two actors and the average of their reflexive justice evaluations (i.e., operations on quantities in the justice evaluation matrix shown in Table 14.1). These new quantities exemplify the classical insight that interaction between actors can be represented by interaction between selected aspects of actors (Smelser 1967). In the study of justice, it has long been thought that when the sense of justice is activated, interaction can be modeled as a meeting of justice sentiments (Jasso 1980).

Multiple Simultaneous Justice Evaluations

There might be multiple justice evaluations at the same time. For example, an observer might simultaneously judge the fairness of own and others' rewards, as shown in Table 14.1. Configurations of justice evaluations might produce distinctive behaviors and emotions. For example, Jasso (1993:243) proposed that the combination of negative reflexive justice evaluations and positive nonreflexive justice evaluations triggers revolution, and Hegtvedt and Killian (1999:276) proposed that the combination of a positive reflexive justice evaluation and a negative nonreflexive justice evaluation triggers guilt.

Levels and Changes in the Justice Evaluation

Justice analysis distinguishes between the instantaneous justice evaluation and the *change in justice evaluation*. In theoretical work, one of the four major techniques of theoretical derivation, the micromodel, begins with the change in the justice evaluation from Time 1 to Time 2 due to changes in the constituent factors of the justice evaluation (e.g., the amount of the actual reward or the population size). The new variable, CJ, could be negative, zero, or positive, depending on whether the justice evaluation decreases, remains the same, or increases, respectively. For example, in an application to gifts, the change in J due to receiving a gift is positive, and the change in J due to being a member of a group in which another member receives a gift is negative. Note that the change is independent of the level. An actor might experience a positive change, where both the Time 1 and the Time 2 magnitudes of J are negative; similarly, an actor might experience a negative change, where both the Time 1 and Time 2 magnitudes of J are positive.

Justice Profile

Finally, the *justice profile*—the time series of J—permits assessment of the relative importance in a person's life of goods, bads, groups, self, others, of justice itself, as well as enabling analysis of location, scale, extreme values, drop-offs, and so forth.

THE LONG REACH OF JUSTICE:
THEORETICAL JUSTICE ANALYSIS

The many quantities, functions, matrices, and distributions identified in the framework for justice analysis can serve as postulates for justice theories. The JEF has proved exceptionally fruitful in generating testable implications (Jasso 1988, 2001a, 2001b). The early question, "If I know the distribution of the actual reward, what does the distribution of J look like?" was soon answered and joined by new questions and new answers (Jasso 1980, 1988).

As noted earlier, the problem of how to calculate J when rewards are ordinal (for everyone understood that all quantitative characteristics can arouse the sense of justice, not only cardinal things like money but also ordinal things like beauty and intelligence) led to a new rule, "Cardinal rewards are measured in their own units, ordinal things as relative ranks within a group," a rule that would have profound substantive consequences, including the prediction that the most beautiful person in a collectivity experiences less overreward than the wealthiest. The rule for ordinal things also joined the case in which the just reward arises from a parameter of a distribution (e.g., mean wealth) in securing within justice theory a place for *qualitative characteristics*, thereby providing yet another instance of the pervasive import of the distinction pioneered by Blau (1974, 1977a, 1977b).

The problem of how to represent the just reward led to an identity, with roots in Merton and Rossi's (1950) work on reference groups, in which C is replaced by the product of the average A and an idiosyncrasy parameter denoted by $\phi : c = \phi E(A)$. Average A was, in turn, replaced by its constituent factors in the cardinal and ordinal cases, enabling, for example, in the cardinal case, derivation of predictions about the effects of group size and group affluence.

Theoretical derivation is, of course, not automatic, especially if the goal is the "marvelous deductive unfolding," which not only yields a wealth of implications but also reaches novel predictions (Popper 1963:221, see also 117, 241–248). In this endeavor, mathematics is the power tool, enabling long deductive chains that take the theory "far afield from its original domain" (Danto 1967:299–300). Purely verbal arguments tend to tether the deduced consequences to overt phenomena in the assumptions, constraining fruitfulness and destroying the possibility of novel predictions. Instantiation, for example, cannot produce novel predictions, for novel predictions are novel precisely because nothing superficially evident in the assumptions could lead to them.

Four main techniques of theoretical derivation have developed, called the micromodel, the macromodel, the mesomodel, and the matrixmodel. They have different starting points (e.g., J, change in J, distribution of J) and use different mathematical approaches.

Examples of testable predictions derived include the following:

1. A thief's gain from theft is greater when stealing from a fellow group member than from an outsider, and this premium is greater in poor groups than in rich groups.
2. Parents of two or more nontwin children will spend more of their toy budget at an annual gift-giving occasion than at the children's birthdays.
3. Blind persons are less at risk of eating disorders than are sighted persons.
4. In a materialistic society, social distance between subgroups always increases with inequality.
5. The parent who dies first is mourned more.
6. Veterans of wars fought away from home are more vulnerable to posttraumatic stress disorder than veterans of wars fought on home soil.
7. Antitheft norms do not arise spontaneously in a society but must be imposed from outside (or above).
8. In a society with warring subgroups, the direction of the effect of the subgroup's relative size on conflict severity depends on whether the society values cardinal or ordinal goods and, if cardinal, on the shape of the distribution.
9. It is unwise to entrust delicate groupwide missions to the best and the brightest, for in a time of crisis, they will prove more loyal to themselves than to the group.
10. There are beneficial effects of playing games of chance.
11. The public benefit of religious institutions is an increasing function of income inequality.
12. Whether a society has emigration from the bottom, from the top, or from both depends on the valued goods and, if cardinal, on their distributional form.
13. In a workplace group in which all the members value cardinal goods, making a new top appointment generates a loss in well-being among all the members except the appointee.

As well, justice theory provides interpretations of rare events, such as the invention of mendicant institutions in the thirteenth century and of detective fiction in the nineteenth. It also suggests the existence of fundamental constants, including a constant governing the switch between valuing cardinal and ordinal goods.

Note that each deduced implication involves a new set of emotions, distinct from the emotions in the initiating justice evaluation(s). Thus, the emotion triggered by the sense of justice is even more diverse and substantial than at first appears.

EMOTION IN JUSTICE PROCESSES: BASIC FRAMEWORK AND NEW EXTENSIONS

We begin with a few simple propositions, which are testable and which will enable precise understanding of emotion in justice processes:

1. *Experienced and Expressed Emotion.* This is a fundamental distinction in the study of emotion. In the study of justice, it arises naturally in the JEF, as described above. The expressiveness coefficient (the absolute value of the signature constant θ in the JEF)

transforms the experienced justice evaluation into the expressed justice evaluation (see Equations (4) and (5)).

2. *Triggers of Experienced Emotion.* Every quantity generated in the justice process except the expressiveness coefficient potentially triggers emotion. These quantities include the just reward, the JRF (including all of the specific versions, such as the BZAC JRF and the JRF in which the just reward is a function of a parameter of the actual reward distribution), the principles of microjustice, the principles of macrojustice, the experienced justice evaluation, the framing coefficient, the justice indexes JI1 and JI2, the components of JI1, and all of the phenomena in the deduced predictions, including gift giving and receiving, theft, disasters, religious institutions, conflict between subgroups, loyalty to self versus subgroup versus group, bereavement, and so forth. The principal *immediate* justice quantities generating emotion are, however, the experienced justice evaluation J and the change in the experienced justice evaluation CJ, together with the framing coefficient.

3. *Valence Matching in Experienced Emotion.* The valence of the triggered emotion matches the valence of the experienced justice evaluation J and the change in the experienced justice evaluation CJ. This proposition has far-reaching consequences. It means, for example, that the condition of perfect justice generates neutral emotion, a state of quiescence, of perfect tranquillity. Homans (1961) and others have argued that perfect justice produces positive emotion and, thus, the stage is set for empirical test of these opposing views.[5]

4. *Intensity Matching in Experienced Emotion.* The intensity of the triggered emotion matches the intensity of the experienced justice evaluation J and the change in the experienced justice evaluation CJ. For example, the intensity of the emotion triggered by an experienced justice evaluation of $+7$ is greater than the intensity of the emotion triggered by an experienced justice evaluation of $+5$, and the intensity of the emotion triggered by an experienced justice evaluation of -13 is greater than the intensity of the emotion triggered by an experienced justice evaluation of -6.

5. *Framing Coefficient and Types of Experienced Emotion.* The specific emotion triggered depends, in part, on framing. Thus, two experienced justice evaluations of magnitude $+4$ both generate positive emotion of equal intensity, but the specific emotion generated depends on whether the reward is a good or a bad—say, earnings or time in prison.

6. *Contexts and Types of Experienced Emotion.* The specific emotion triggered depends, in part, on the context. For example, two experienced justice evaluations of the same good and the same magnitude both generate emotions of the same valence and of equal intensity, but the specific emotion generated differs for self and other, or across social contexts, or across the life span.

7. *Simple and Mixed Experienced Emotions.* A single experienced justice evaluation J or change in the experienced justice evaluation CJ generates a simple emotion. Multiple experienced justice evaluations or changes in the experienced justice evaluation generate mixed emotions; the particular mixture reflects the configuration of the justice quantities (as well as the underlying framing).

8. *Expressiveness Coefficient and Emotion Display.* Emotion display triggered by an experienced justice evaluation is governed by the expressiveness coefficient. Display of emotion triggered by a change in experienced justice evaluations is governed jointly by the expressiveness of the Time 1 and Time 2 justice evaluations underlying the change.

9. *Sources of the Just Reward and Types of Emotion.* The type of emotion triggered by an experienced justice evaluation J or a change in the experienced justice evaluation CJ

depends, in part, on the sources of the just reward(s) in the JEF, as discussed by Turner (2005). For example, although the magnitude of the justice evaluation and the valence and intensity of the triggered emotion are the same whenever the justice evaluation is the same (as when the actual reward is 10 and the just reward is 15), the type of emotion triggered will differ depending on whether the just reward was drawn from a neighbor or a vision or one's past or a radio report on average wages, and so forth.

10. *Emotion and the Justice Reflections.* By noting the effect of context, we have already distinguished between the first two justice reflections: justice for self and justice for others. What remains to be made explicit is the special emotion generated by the third justice reflection: the hybrid reflection in which an actor reacts to the justice quantities (just rewards and justice evaluations, both experienced and expressed) that others produce for him or her. This third justice reflection is the justice of reputation, and special emotions arise to celebrate or safeguard a good reputation or fight a bad one, as in the processes of Burke's (2004) identity control theory. In this case, a new set of variables is generated, each expressing the difference between the justice quantity generated by the actor for self and (1) the justice quantities generated by individual others for him or her (collected in the rewardee-specific column of the justice matrices in Table 14.1) and (2) parameters (e.g., mean or median) of the rewardee-specific justice distribution (in the column of the justice matrices in Table 14.1). Each variable can assume negative, zero, or positive values. As with the justice evaluation and the change in justice evaluation, valence matching operates so that the valence of the emotion matches the valence of the discrepancy variables.

11. *Emotion Management.* Building on Hochschild's (1979) pioneering idea of emotion management, all of the justice quantities can be used as elements in strategies to achieve, for self or other, an emotion or emotion-related goal. Examples of such strategies are discussed in Jasso (1993) and include gift giving, switching goods in justice evaluations, switching ideas of justice, changing the subject in a conversation, and inheritance rules. For example, to prevent sadness among young children, parents might spend more of their toy budget at an annual gift-giving occasion (such as Christmas) rather than at the children's birthdays.

A NEW EXTENSION:
IMPARTIALITY IN THE JUSTICE PROCESS

In this section we examine differential framing and expressiveness across rewardees—both across self and other and also across different others. These are new types of impartiality; they broaden current notions of impartiality that highlight impartial assignment of just rewards or, equivalently, universalistic application of the JRF and the principles of justice. Thus, these new types of impartiality—*framing-impartiality* and *expressiveness-impartiality*—go beyond impartiality in the first central question of justice (highlighting just rewards) to impartiality in the third central question (highlighting justice evaluations).

The basic framework for justice analysis (sketched above) permits differential framing and expressiveness across rewardees and provides special subscripts to enable modeling and testing these effects. However, no empirical study has ever assessed differential framing and expressiveness, and they have been little discussed.

Framing-Impartiality: Differential Framing of Goods and Bads for Self and Others

In this subsection I combine two ideas of justice analysis to produce a new extension, one that links the first and second justice reflections—the reflexive and nonreflexive justice reflections. First, as described above, the rewards that awaken the sense of justice are framed by the observer as goods or bads. It has long been known that two observers can frame the same thing differently. As Lucretius observed, "What is food to one, is to others bitter poison."[6] In justice analysis, individuals who differ from most of their fellows have been called *contrarian* (e.g., persons who regard earnings as a bad or time in prison as a good). Second, justice analysis encompasses and distinguishes between justice ideas and judgments about self and other—the reflexive and nonreflexive just rewards and justice evaluations in the first and second justice reflections.

Now consider the notion of "fellow-feeling," what is classically called sympathy. In some justice situations, the observer "feels with" the rewardee, perhaps even imagining that he or she is indeed the rewardee. In such a situation, the observer will frame things as goods or bads for others in the same way that he or she frames them for self. In other situations, however, the observer does not see the rewardee as a fellow and does not frame things the same way.

Think of Aristotle's (Rhetoric II, 4) definition of friendship: "We may describe friendly feeling towards any one as wishing for him what you believe to be good things." It is evident that if one believes that a thing is a good, one wishes it for oneself; to wish it also for another is to hold a "friendly feeling" for him or her. Or think of Christ's extraordinary second commandment, "Love your neighbor as yourself," and consider a new application: "Frame things for others as you would frame them for yourself."

What was once viewed as pure framing can now be seen to encompass a basic way of regarding the other—as self or as not-self, with sympathy or with dyspathy. To illustrate, consider time in prison. A recent study estimates framing coefficients for several sets of observers judging the fairness of the prison sentences of convicted offenders (Jasso 1998). The study found that among a representative sample of the general population, 2% view time in prison as a good; the remainder viewing it as a bad. This result was interpreted as indicating that, as with earnings, 2% of the population seem to be contrarians. However, a new and different interpretation is now possible. The observer might frame time in prison for self as a bad, but time in prison for a convicted offender as a good. In the latter case, there is no fellow-feeling; the observer benefits from the alien stranger being in prison.

In the case of earnings, an observer who frames earnings as a good for self and who is sympathic will frame earnings as a good for the other; the higher the other's earnings, the better for the observer. However, a dyspathic observer who also frames earnings as a good for self will frame earnings as a bad for the other; the higher a neighbor's earnings, the worse for the observer.

Thus, there are two operations involved in framing. In the first, the observer frames a thing as a good or a bad for self. In the second, the observer frames the thing for other in either the same or the opposite way as for self (i.e., either sympathically or dyspathically). Table 14.2 depicts the four possibilities that ensue.

Of course, the justice process does not end with framing. Framing is only the beginning, as it were. The main event is the justice evaluation. Holding everything constant for both self and other—that is, same actual reward and just reward—the justice evaluation of the sympathic observer will be the same for self and other, but in the dyspathic situation, the justice evaluation will be oppositely signed for self and other. Table 14.3 portrays the combinations of outcomes

TABLE 14.2. **Sympathy and Dyspathy in Framing**
of Goods and Bads for Self and Other

	Other	
Self	Goods	Bads
Goods	Sympathy	Dyspathy
Bads	Dyspathy	Sympathy

TABLE 14.3. **Sympathy and Dyspathy in the Justice Evaluation**

	Other		
Self	Unjust Underreward	Perfect Justice	Unjust Overreward
Unjust underreward	Sympathy	NA	Dyspathy
Perfect justice	NA	Sympathy	NA
Unjust overreward	Dyspathy	NA	Sympathy

Note: NA = not applicable.

in the sympathy and dyspathy situations. Figure 14.1 provides the graphs of the partial functions of the justice evaluation on the actual reward, for goods and bads. Accordingly, a sympathic individual will have the same graph for self and other (whether for a good or for a bad), but the dyspathic individual's justice evaluations will have both graphs—one for self and a second for other. Note that the same observer might be sympathic in some situations and dyspathic in others, or sympathic toward some nonself rewardees and dyspathic toward other rewardees. No empirical study has ever assessed framing-impartiality.

The Effect on Deficiency Aversion of Sympathy and Dyspathy

The graphs in Figure 14.1 immediately suggest an important consequence of sympathy and dyspathy. Among sympathic individuals, the deficiency aversion that characterizes goods extends from

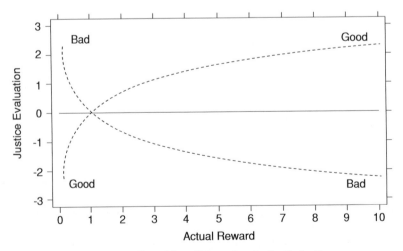

FIGURE 14.1. **Effect of Actual Reward on Justice Evaluation**

self to others. However, among dyspathic individuals, the opposite occurs; deficiency aversion for self becomes excess aversion for others. A small increase in the good received by another produces a larger justice evaluation than a comparable decrease.

Expressiveness-Impartiality: Differential Expressiveness Across Self and Others

As discussed above, the justice evaluation function permits the just reward and the signature constant θ (and both the framing coefficient and the expressiveness coefficient) to vary across five general contexts, abbreviated by the mnemonic *brots*. The just reward and the signature constant might obviously vary across observers and they might also vary across rewardees, reward, time period, and society. All empirical studies that have estimated signature constants have tested for interobserver differences, and, in fact, one of the most robust findings pertains to the uniqueness of the signature constant, as the name implies. However, although it has been suggested that the observer's expressiveness might differ across self and other, no model or study has analyzed within-observer differential expressiveness across a set of rewardees.

A New Research Design for Studying Impartiality in Framing and Expressiveness

A new design based on work by Evans (1989), Kelley and Evans (1987), and Jasso and Webster (1999) enables estimation and testing of framing-impartiality and expressiveness-impartiality. Independently, they developed procedures that can be used to estimate a version of the signature constant that is not only observer-specific but also rewardee-specific.

Evans (1989) developed a procedure for measuring just earnings for self, in which each respondent was given five hypothetical earnings amounts for self and asked to judge the fairness or unfairness of each. This procedure was first applied in the 1987 round of the International Social Science Survey/Australia (Kelley and Evans 1987).

Jasso and Webster (1999) developed a variant of the research design formulated by Jasso and Rossi (1977), with the aim of sharpening procedures for indirect estimation of the true just reward. The just reward in the JEF formula (2) is used to generate the justice evaluation and, hence, has come to be called the "true just reward" (Jasso and Wegener 1997). It can be expressed as

$$C = A \exp(-J/\theta) \tag{8}$$

A challenge is how to estimate it. Of course, respondents can be directly asked what they think is just, as in the International Social Justice Project (Jasso 1999). The possibility remains, however, that the response—called the "disclosed just reward"—differs from the true just reward, incorporating such mechanisms as socialization, rhetorical influences, response sets, and the like (Jasso and Wegener 1997). Equation (2), together with Rossi's factorial survey method (Jasso and Rossi 1977; Rossi 1979), points the way to a new technique for estimating the true just reward: Ask respondents to rate the justice or injustice of the actual reward among a large set of rewardees (i.e., obtain expressed J for rewardees with prespecified A), estimate the signature constant θ, and then use Equation (8) to estimate C. This procedure yields the estimated true just reward, which substantively is free of disclosure mechanisms and statistically is biased but, by Slutsky's theorem, consistent (Jasso 1990).

The new procedure developed by Jasso and Webster (1999) differs from the original Jasso and Rossi (1977) procedure in that each respondent is asked to rate the fairness of multiple hypothetical rewards for each rewardee, rather than only one hypothetical reward per rewardee, as in the original design. Thus, Jasso and Webster's (1999) new procedure is squarely in the spirit of the Evans (1989) and Kelley and Evans (1987) procedure. Jasso and Webster (1999) implemented the new procedure in a study of earnings fairness, assigning 7 hypothetical actual earnings amounts to each of 10 fictitious workers.

Jasso and Webster (1999:379) also noticed that it was possible to estimate a different signature constant for each rewardee and, of course, to test for within-respondent/interrewardee differential expressiveness. To set up the model for such a test, we begin with the JEF in Equation (2), which represents the process whenever a respondent judges the fairness or unfairness of a fictitious worker's actual earnings, and write it in the difference form amenable to statistical estimation:

$$J = \theta \ln(A) - \theta \ln(C) \tag{9}$$

Next we rewrite the justice evaluation equation to include an error term, as no empirical situation is without the operation of chance:

$$J = \theta \ln(A) - \theta \ln(C) + e \tag{10}$$

Finally, we write the two models we will test. The equation will be specified for a single respondent and will include all the ratings for all rewardees ($7 \times 10 = 70$). In both models, we assume that the just reward is specific to the rewardee; that is, given that the 10 fictitious workers differ in age, schooling, etc., the respondent will have a different idea of the just reward for each worker.[7] In the first model, we specify the same signature constant for all rewardees:

$$J_{vr} = \theta \ln(A_{vr}) - \theta \ln(C_r) + e_{vr} \tag{11}$$

whereas in the second, we specify a different signature constant for each rewardee:

$$J_{vr} = \theta_r \ln(A_{vr}) - \theta_r \ln(C_r) + e_{vr} \tag{12}$$

where r denotes the rewardee, of whom there are 10, and v denotes the vignette representing each of 7 hypothetical actual earnings for each rewardee.

Thus, in each respondent's equation, there are 70 observations, with 70 actual rewards and 70 realizations of the error term. In both equations, there are 10 just rewards. The two equations differ, however, in that the first has a single signature constant for all 10 rewardees, whereas the second allows the signature constant to vary across rewardees (as indicated by the subscripts).

Because the just reward C is unobserved and is in the respondent's head, the two equations are rewritten in the estimable forms:

$$J_{vr} = \theta \ln(A_{vr}) + \alpha_r + e_{vr}, \tag{13}$$

where there are 10 intercepts, one for each rewardee, each of the form $-\theta \ln(C_r)$, and

$$J_{vr} = \theta_r \ln(A_{vr}) + \alpha_r + e_{vr} \tag{14}$$

where, again, there are 10 intercepts, each of the form $-\theta_r \ln(C_r)$.

Thus, both models are differential-intercept models, with a unique intercept for each re-wardee. As noted, they differ, however, in that the first one has a single slope θ, whereas the second has a different slope θ for each rewardee. Because the first model is nested within the second model, estimation of the second model enables a test of homogeneity of the slope. If the homogeneity hypothesis is rejected, we can infer that the respondent displays different signature constants across the fictitious workers.

Estimates of Equation (14) immediately enable assessment of framing-impartiality across the fictitious workers. If the signs of the signature constants do not differ, then the slope homogeneity test immediately provides a test of expressiveness-impartiality.

Substantively, differential framing and expressiveness strike at impartiality. Perfect impartiality with respect to the principles of justice and the ensuing just reward does not exhaust the demands of impartiality. Framing rewards differently across rewardees and displaying more emotion about some rewardees than others signal a lack of this final kind of impartiality.[8]

EMPIRICAL ASSESSMENT OF IMPARTIALITY

Research Design

To explore impartiality empirically, I carried out a factorial survey study of the justice of earnings using the new multiple-rewards-per-rewardee design. As in all factorial surveys (Jasso 2006a) the design has three main elements: a rewardee sample, a rating task, and a respondent sample.

REWARDEE SAMPLE.   The study used two of the four vignette decks constructed by Jasso and Webster (1999), the two that are mirror images of each other with respect to gender. Fictitious workers are described by their gender, age, educational attainment, and occupational title; each description of a worker is accompanied by seven hypothetical actual earning amounts. In Jasso and Webster's (1999) full study, with 4 decks of vignettes, the vignette combinations were fully crossed based on 10 levels of age, 4 levels of education, and 10 occupational titles, and the earnings randomly drawn from a set of 15 amounts (Jasso and Webster 1999:369–370). The 2 decks used in the present study represent 6 levels of age (from 23 to 58), all 4 educational levels (completion of eighth grade, graduation from high school, graduation from college, and postgraduate degree), 6 occupational titles (cashier, grade school teacher, laundry worker, physician, shoe repair person, and telephone operator), and 14 levels of annual earnings (ranging from $5,000 to $85,000).

As in all factorial survey justice studies, impossible combinations of characteristics were deleted from the vignette population, and the samples presented to respondents were randomly drawn from the adjusted population. Intercorrelations of vignette characteristics are at a minimum.

The pack presented to each respondent included 10 fictitious workers, each associated with 7 hypothetical earnings amounts.

RATING TASK.   Unlike Jasso and Webster (1999), who employed a line-matching technique in their study, this study used a number-matching technique, also part of the set of magnitude estimation procedures developed by Stevens (1975). The usual protocol for factorial survey justice studies was followed. The instructions were read aloud, examples provided, and questions answered. The instructions, in addition to describing the justice evaluation rating task, highlight the randomness of the attached hypothetical actual earnings and make explicit mention of fractions and decimals to activate the full real-number line. The appendix to this chapter provides a facsimile of the instructions and one vignette.

RESPONDENT SAMPLE.   The respondent sample consisted of undergraduate students enrolled in a required core-curriculum course at a large U.S. university. The instrument was administered early in the semester to preclude familiarity with the fairness literature.

Results

Forty-four students were given the instrument, with each of the two vignette decks randomly assigned to half of the students. All 44 students returned the completed instrument. One worker was left unrated by 1 respondent, so that of the 3,080 possible ratings, a total of 3,073 were obtained.

To test for framing-impartiality across the 10 rewardees, the justice of whose earnings was judged by each respondent, I estimated the 439 respondent-specific/worker-specific regressions. Every one of the 439 slopes is positive. Every respondent frames earnings as a good for every worker. Thus, this sample is characterized by complete framing-impartiality.

To test for expressiveness-impartiality across the 10 rewardees, we estimate, for each of the 44 respondents separately, the differential-intercept/differential-slope model in Equation (14), followed by a statistical test for slope homogeneity. All but 1 of the 44 regressions has 70 observations and yields estimates of 20 parameters—10 intercepts and 10 slopes; the F-test for slope homogeneity has 9 intercepts and 50 degrees of freedom. The regression for the one respondent who left a worker unrated has 63 observations and yields 18 estimated parameters—9 intercepts and 9 slopes; the F-test for slope homogeneity has 8 intercepts and 45 degrees of freedom.

Inspection of the regression estimates and F-tests for slope homogeneity among each of the 44 respondents indicates that in 31 out of 44 respondents, slope homogeneity is unambiguously rejected, based on a 95% statistical level of significance. Additionally, there are two cases with borderline probability values of .0513 and .0529. Thus, we conclude that 70% of the respondents lack expressiveness-impartiality, and this proportion could go as high as 75%.

To provide a flavor for the test protocol, we report in Figure 14.2 the quantile function of the distribution of probability levels in the respondents' F-tests. Each respondent is represented by a circle. The grid includes a horizontal line at the value .05 and a vertical line at the median. As

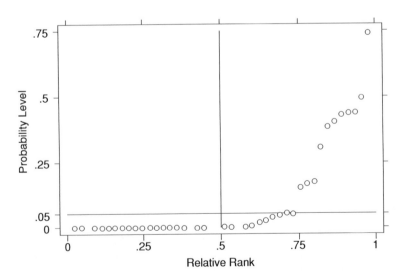

FIGURE 14.2. Distribution of Probability Levels in Impartiality Test

shown, a large subset is close to zero, indicating high statistical significance. The median value is .0185. The plot is approximately horizontal until about the 60th percentile, where the probability level jumps from .0059 to .0202. After the second borderline value of .0529, the values jump again to .152.

If this result is replicated in other samples, then an important question involves the determinants of expressiveness-impartiality or lack of it. Are personal characteristics such as age or gender a factor? Is there an association with field of study or, among the adult population, occupation or other endeavors? If so, is there selection or socialization? Finally, does this measure of expressiveness-impartiality signal a broader emotional stance? Does it correctly identify persons whose emotion display differs across the rewardees they judge?

EMOTION IN A NEW UNIFIED THEORY
OF SOCIOBEHAVIORAL PROCESSES

There are three basic justice reflections. However, justice is not the only sociobehavioral engine. Accordingly, I close with a brief look at the outlines of a possible new unified theory. The theory highlights three basic sociobehavioral engines called primordial sociobehavioral outcomes (PSOs). Justice (together with its sibling comparison processes, such as self-esteem) is one of the three PSOs. The other two are status and power. Although each has three lines of development—corresponding, as with justice, to a reflexive, nonreflexive, or hybrid focus—here I restrict attention to the first reflexive line, leaving for future work the task of working out the second and third lines for the other two PSOs and the requisite new vocabulary.

The basic ideas outlined here might be regarded as the "text" accompanying the new theory. The new theory itself has a parsimonious structure. Its first postulate presents the mathematical formulas for the three PSOs, such as the justice evaluation function and the status function. Its second postulate mirrors that in justice theory, stating the measurement rule for cardinal and ordinal things, which is applicable to justice and power. Theoretical derivation has begun, and results highlight the not inconsiderable effects of caring about one or the other of the three PSOs.

The ideas listed here place the unified theory in the larger context of the study of human behavior, as well as include some starting propositions that might well turn out to be incorrect—for example, the notion that because there are three possible rates of change, there must be three PSOs, and the consequent notion that power processes must be linear. These and other features here collected have the potential to affect the emotion dimension.

1. *Fundamental Forces*. All observed phenomena are the product of the joint operation of several basic forces. For elaboration and a list of candidate forces, see Jasso (1988, 2003).
2. *Midlevel Forces*. The basic forces generate midlevel forces, in the spirit of Merton's theories of the middle range.
3. *Primordial Sociobehavioral Outcomes, Goods/Bads, and Groups/Subgroups*. The primordial sociobehavioral outcomes are generated by quantitative characteristics within the groups formed by categories of qualitative characteristics; this is the fundamental template for a midlevel sociobehavioral force. For goods, the PSOs increase with the characteristics. Qualitative characteristics provide the groups for calculating relative ranks and distributional parameters and generating subgroup structures.
4. *Three Rates of Change and Three PSOs*. Because there are three possible rates of change, a useful starting point posits the existence of three midlevel sociobehavioral forces.
5. *Justice, Status, and Power*. As Homans (1976:231) appears to have come to believe late in his life, justice, status, and power are the three prime candidates for midlevel forces

(Jasso 2006b). Justice increases at a decreasing rate, and status increases at an increasing rate (Goode 1978; Sørensen 1979; Jasso 2001c). Although the rate of change in power processes has not been directly addressed, the reasoning here suggests that power must increase at a constant rate.

6. *Identity*. Each instantaneous combination of a PSO, a quantitative characteristic, and a qualitative characteristic is an identity, consistent with the tenets of both sociological and psychological theories of identity (Stryker and Burke 2000; Tajfel and Turner 1986).

7. *Persons*. A person is a collection of identities. This classic idea in identity theory is also a generalization to all three PSOs of the justice profile.

8. *Personality*. Persons can be characterized by the configuration of quantitative characteristics, qualitative characteristics, and PSOs in their identities. Some might be dominated by one of the three elements or, within an element, by one particular realization. Examples include the status-obsessed, the race-conscious, the beauty-fixated. The distinctive configuration constitutes the individual's personality.

9. *Groups*. A group is a collection of persons. This is a classic idea in identity theory.

10. *Culture*. Groups can be characterized by the configuration of quantitative characteristics, qualitative characteristics, and PSOs in the identities of their members. Groups, too, might be dominated by one or another element. Examples include materialistic society, status society, jock culture, and nerd group. The constellation constitutes the group's culture.

11. *Subgroups, Preexisting and Emergent*. There are two kinds of subgroups. Preexisting subgroups arise from the categories of personal qualitative characteristics (e.g., gender-based or race-based subgroups). Emergent subgroups arise from the operation of PSOs (e.g., the overrewarded, the fairly rewarded, and the underrewarded).

12. *Theoretical Derivation of Predictions*. The four techniques developed in justice theory—the micromodel, macromodel, mesomodel, and matrix model—are used to derive predictions for all three PSOs. Novel predictions include those concerning the competition among PSOs and the effects of the relative importance of the PSOs in the group culture. For example, an early prediction is that in a justice group, each person is closer to the neighbor above than to the neighbor below, whereas in a status group, each person is closer to the neighbor below than to the neighbor above, and in a power group, each person is equally close to the neighbors above and below—a consequence of the distinctive rates of change.

13. *Emotions*. Emotion is released by the PSOs and by change in PSO. The valence of the emotion matches the valence of the PSO or the change in PSO. Justice always releases both positive and negative emotions. Status releases only positive emotions, although intensity might be very low. Change in PSO can, of course, be positive or negative for all PSOs.

14. *Inequality*. Inequalities of interest include both inequality in quantitative characteristics and inequality in PSOs. A new question immediately arises: Is inequality greater in the good or in the PSO? For example, in a situation where wealth generates status, which is greater, wealth inequality or status inequality?

15. *Happiness*. Happiness is produced by the individual's PSO profile. New questions that can be posed and precisely answered include questions about the effects on happiness of changes in income inequality, changes in valued goods and bads, and changes in dominant PSO.

Finally, we can envision carrying intact into the new unified theory the framework for studying the emotion dimension in justice processes presented earlier in this chapter. Thus, it will be straightforward to explore the nature, types, valence, and intensity of the emotion triggered by status and power. Accordingly, it will be possible to examine the distinctive operation of emotion across the three primordial sociobehavioral engines, thereby achieving a deeper understanding of emotion and its manifestations when humans reflect on self, others, and others' reflections of self.

APPENDIX

Facsimile of Rating Instructions in Multiple-Rewards-per-Rewardee Study of Justice of Earnings

SURVEY OF JUDGMENTS ON THE JUSTICE OF EARNINGS

To the Respondent:

People and their jobs differ in a lot of ways. We have made up descriptions of different kinds of people and jobs. All the persons described work full time; and all have worked continuously and full time since finishing school. Each person is randomly assigned several hypothetical earnings amounts. We would like to know what you think about whether, at each earnings amount, each person is fairly or unfairly paid, and, if you think that a person is unfairly paid, whether you think the person is paid too much or too little.

We would like you to use numbers to represent your judgments. Let zero represent the point of perfect justice. Let negative numbers represent degrees of underreward, and positive numbers represent degrees of overreward. The greater the degree of underpayment, the larger the absolute value of the negative number you choose (for example, if two earning amounts receive ratings of -68 and -23, the earnings amount receiving the -68 is viewed as greater underpayment than the earnings amount receiving the -23). Similarly, the greater the degree of overpayment, the larger the positive number (for example, an earnings amount receiving a rating of $+200$ is viewed as greater overpayment than an earnings amount receiving a rating of $+75$). In other words, mild degrees of underreward and of overreward are represented by numbers relatively close to zero; larger degrees of underreward and of overreward are represented by numbers farther away from zero.

The justice evaluation scale may be visualized as follows:

Underbenefit   Overbenefit

0

Overburden   Perfect Justice   Underburden

When you read each description of a person and an earnings amount, please write the number that best matches your judgment about the fairness or unfairness of that earnings for that person. There is no limit to the range of numbers that you may use. For example, some respondents like to map their personal scale to the numbers from -100 to $+100$; others prefer to use smaller regions, and still others, larger regions. Of course, you may choose any real number (for example, decimals and fractions as well as whole numbers) to represent a judgment.

You may change any of your ratings.
Your responses are completely confidential.
Thank you very much for your participation.

Facsimile of Vignette in Multiple-Rewards-per-Rewardee Study of Justice of Earnings

A MAN 43 YEARS OLD,
WHO COMPLETED 16 YEARS OF SCHOOL,
GRADUATING FROM COLLEGE WITH A B.A. DEGREE.
HE IS A GRADE SCHOOL TEACHER.

ANNUAL EARNINGS	YOUR RATING
$12,500	_____
15,000	_____
20,000	_____
25,000	_____
30,000	_____
55,000	_____
70,000	_____

NOTES

1. In some situations, there is a third fundamental actor: the *allocator*.
2. For example, the share terminology is applicable to wealth and taxes but not to time in prison.
3. Comprehensive exposition of these versions of the just reward function is found in Jasso (1980, 1983, 2000) and Jasso and Wegener (1997).
4. We are following a logical sequence from general to specific function. In point of fact, the logarithmic-ratio specification of the JEF was proposed before the general JEF was formulated.
5. Note that if the valence matching proposition turns out to be correct, the choice of numbers to represent sociobehavioral variables such as justice or status is far from inconsequential (for a discussion, in the justice context, of the problem of choosing numbers to represent a variable, see Jasso 1996:263–265).
6. Or, as Beaumont and Fletcher put it over 1600 years later, "One man's poison . . . is another's meat."
7. This proposition is routinely tested and egalitarianism (assigning the same just reward to all rewardees) is seldom found.
8. Note that this possibility implies the multidimensionality of impartiality, there being at least four kinds of impartiality: with respect to the principles of justice, the just reward, framing, and emotion display. Note also that there might be further kinds of impartiality, for example, in the behavioral consequences of the justice evaluation (the fourth central question), if the decision to take action, net of the magnitude of the justice evaluation, varies across rewardees.

REFERENCES

Aristotle. 1952. *The Works of Aristotle*. Chicago: Britannica.

Berger, Joseph, Morris Zelditch, Jr., Bo Anderson, and Bernard P. Cohen. 1972. "Structural Aspects of Distributive Justice: A Status-Value Formulation." Pp. 119–246 in *Sociological Theories in Progress*, edited by J. Berger, M. Zelditch, Jr., and B. Anderson. Boston: Houghton Mifflin.

Blau, Peter M. 1974. "Presidential Address: Parameters of Social Structure." *American Sociological Review* 39: 615–635.

———. 1977a. *Inequality and Heterogeneity*. New York: Free Press.

———. 1977b. "A Macrosociological Theory of Social Structure." *American Journal of Sociology* 83: 26–54.

Brickman, P., R. Folger, E. Goode, and Y. Schul. 1981. "Micro and Macro Justice." Pp. 173–202 in *The Justice Motive in Social Behavior*, edited by M. J. Lerner and S. C. Lerner. New York: Plenum.

Burke, Peter J. 2004. "Identities and Social Structure: The 2003 Cooley-Mead Award Address." *Social Psychology Quarterly* 67: 5–15.

Danto, Arthur C. 1967. "Philosophy of Science, Problems of." Pp. 296–300 in *Encyclopedia of Philosophy*, edited by P. Edwards. New York: Macmillan.

Evans, M. D. R. 1989. "Distributive Justice: Some New Measures." Presented at the meeting of the International Sociological Association's Research Committee 28 on Social Stratification and Mobility, Stanford, California.

Fararo, Thomas J., and John Skvoretz. 1993. "Methods and Problems of Theoretical Integration and the Principle of Adaptively Rational Action." Pp. 416–450 (references, pp. 491–494) in *Theoretical Research Programs: Studies in the Growth of Theory*, edited by J. Berger and M. Zelditch, Jr. Stanford, CA: Stanford University Press.

Goode, William J. 1978. *The Celebration of Heroes: Prestige as a Control System*. Berkeley: University of California Press.

Hegtvedt, Karen, and Caitlin Killian. 1999. "Fairness and Emotions: Reactions to the Process and Outcomes of Negotiations." *Social Forces* 78: 269–302.

Hochschild, Arlie Russell. 1979. "Emotion Work, Feeling Rules, and Social Structure." *American Journal of Sociology* 85: 551–575.

Homans, George Caspar. 1961. *Social Behavior: Its Elementary Forms*. New York: Harcourt, Brace, and World.

———. 1974. *Social Behavior: its Elementary Forms*. New York: Harcourt, Brace, Jovanovich.

———. 1976. "Commentary." Pp. 231–244 in *Advances in Experimental Social Psychology*, edited by L. Berkowitz and E. Walster. New York: Academic.

Jasso, Guillermina. 1978. "On the Justice of Earnings: A New Specification of the Justice Evaluation Function." *American Journal of Sociology* 83: 1398–1419.

———. 1980. "A New Theory of Distributive Justice." *American Sociological Review* 45: 3–32.

———. 1983. "Fairness of Individual Rewards and Fairness of the Reward Distribution: Specifying the Inconsistency between the Micro and Macro Principles of Justice." *Social Psychology Quarterly* 46: 185–199.

———. 1986. "A New Representation of the Just Term in Distributive-Justice Theory: Its Properties and Operation in Theoretical Derivation and Empirical Estimation." *Journal of Mathematical Sociology* 12: 251–274.

———. 1988. "Principles of Theoretical Analysis." *Sociological Theory* 6: 1–20.

———. 1990. "Methods for the Theoretical and Empirical Analysis of Comparison Processes." *Sociological Methodology* 20: 369–419.

———. 1993. "Choice and Emotion in Comparison Theory." *Rationality and Society* 5: 231–274.

———. 1996. "Exploring the Reciprocal Relations between Theoretical and Empirical Work: The Case of the Justice Evaluation Function." *Sociological Methods and Research* 24: 253–303.

———. 1998. "Exploring the Justice of Punishments: Framing, Expressiveness, and the Just Prison Sentence." *Social Justice Research* 11: 397–422.

———. 1999. "How Much Injustice Is There in the World? Two New Justice Indexes." *American Sociological Review* 64: 133–168.

———. 2000. "Some of Robert K. Merton's Contributions to Justice Theory." *Sociological Theory* 18: 331–339.

———. 2001a. "Comparison Theory." Pp. 669–698 in *Handbook of Sociological Theory*, edited by J. H. Turner. New York: Kluwer Academic/Plenum.

———. 2001b. "Formal Theory." Pp. 37–68 in *Handbook of Sociological Theory,* edited by J. H. Turner. New York: Kluwer Academic/Plenum.

———. 2001c. "Studying Status: An Integrated Framework." *American Sociological Review* 66: 96–124.

———. 2002. "Mapping the Exact Relations Between Justice and Inequality." Presented at the biennial conference of the International Society for Justice Research, Skovde, Sweden.

———. 2003. "Basic Research." Pp. 52–53 in *The Sage Encyclopedia of Social Science Research Methods*, edited by M. Lewis-Beck, A. Bryman, and T. F. Liao. Thousand Oaks, CA: Sage.

———. 2004. "The Tripartite Structure of Social Science Analysis." *Sociological Theory* 22: 401–431.

———. 2005. "Theory Is the Sociologist's Best Friend." Plenary address presented at the annual meeting of the Swedish Sociological Society, Skövde, Sweden.

———. 2006a. "Factorial Survey Methods for Studying Beliefs and Judgments." *Sociological Methods and Research* 34: 334–423.

———. 2006b. "Homans and the Study of Justice." Pp. 203–227 in George C. Homans: History, Theory, and Method, edited by A. Javier Treviño. Boulder, Colorado: Paradigm Press.

Jasso, Guillermina, and Peter H. Rossi. 1977. "Distributive Justice and Earned Income." *American Sociological Review* 42: 639–651.

Jasso, Guillermina, and Murray Webster, Jr. 1997. "Double Standards in Just Earnings for Male and Female Workers." *Social Psychology Quarterly* 60: 66–78.

———. 1999. "Assessing the Gender Gap in Just Earnings and Its Underlying Mechanisms." *Social Psychology Quarterly* 62: 367–380.

Jasso, Guillermina, and Bernd Wegener. 1997. "Methods for Empirical Justice Analysis: Part I. Framework, Models, and Quantities." *Social Justice Research* 10: 393–430.

Kelley, Jonathan, and Mariah D. R. Evans. 1987. "IsssA: International Social Science Survey/Australia: Ideology of Inequality 1987–88: Questionnaire." International Survey Centre and Research School of Social Sciences, Australia National University.

Kemper, Theodore. 1978. *A Social Interactional Theory of Emotions.* New York: Wiley.

Leventhal, Gerald S. 1976. "The Distribution of Rewards and Resources in Groups and Organizations." Pp. 91–131 in *Equity Theory: Toward a General Theory of Social Interaction,* edited by L. Berkowitz and E. Walster. New York: Academic.

Merton, Robert K., and Alice S. Rossi. 1950. "Contributions to the Theory of Reference Group Behavior." Pp. 40–105 in *Continuities in Social Research: Studies in the Scope and Method of "The American Soldier,"* edited by R. K. Merton and P. Lazarsfeld. New York: Free Press.

Popper, Karl R. 1963. *Conjectures and Refutations: The Growth of Scientific Knowledge.* New York: Basic Books.

Rossi, Peter H. 1979. "Vignette Analysis: Uncovering the Normative Structure of Complex Judgments." Pp. 176–186 in *Qualitative and Quantitative Social Research: Papers in Honor of Paul F. Lazarsfeld,* edited by R. K. Merton, J. S. Coleman, and P. H. Rossi. New York: Free Press.

Smelser, Neil J. 1967. *Sociology: An Introduction.* New York: Wiley.

Sørensen, Aage B. 1979. "A Model and a Metric for the Analysis of the Intragenerational Status Attainment Process." *American Journal of Sociology* 85: 361–384.

Stets, Jan E. 2003. "Emotions and Sentiments." Pp. 309-335 in *Handbook of Social Psychology,* edited by J. DeLamater. New York: Kluwer Academic/Plenum.

Stevens, S. S. 1975. *Psychophysics: An Introduction to Its Perceptual, Neural, and Social Prospects,* edited by G. Stevens. New York: Wiley.

Stryker, Sheldon, and Peter J. Burke. 2000. "The Past, Present, and Future of an Identity Theory." *Social Psychology Quarterly* 63: 284–297.

Tajfel, Henri, and John C. Turner. 1986. "The Social Identity Theory of Intergroup Behavior." Pp. 7–24 in *The Psychology of Intergroup Relations,* edited by S. Worchel and W. G. Austin. Chicago: Nelson-Hall.

Turner, Jonathan H. 2000. *On the Origins of Human Emotions: A Sociological Inquiry into the Evolution of Human Affect.* Stanford, CA: Stanford University Press.

———. 2005. "Justice, Injustice, and Emotional Arousal." Presentation at the Social Justice Conference, University of Bremen, Germany.

Turner, Jonathan H., and Jan E. Stets. 2005. *The Sociology of Emotions.* New York: Cambridge University Press.

Wagner, David, and Joseph Berger. 1985. "Do Sociological Theories Grow?" *American Journal of Sociology* 90: 697–728.

Walster, Elaine, Ellen Berscheid, and G. William Walster. 1976. "New Directions in Equity Research." Pp. 1–42 in *Equity Theory: Toward a General Theory of Social Interaction,* edited by L. Berkowitz and E. Walster. New York: Academic.

Whitmeyer, Joseph M. 2004. "Past and Future Applications of Jasso's Justice Theory." *Sociological Theory* 13: 432–444.

CHAPTER 15

Expectation States Theory and Emotion

Cecilia L. Ridgeway

One of the enduring observations of human life is that when people come together to accomplish a shared goal, be it choosing a sofa for the living room or drafting a policy for national defense, a social hierarchy soon emerges among the participants in which some have more social esteem and influence in the situation than do others (Bales 1950; Lonner 1980). Everyday experience with such *status hierarchies* suggests that they are fraught with feeling. Yet, how exactly is emotion intertwined with the dynamics of social status in groups? This is the question I will address in this chapter. I will do so through the lens of *expectation states theory*, which is the most systematic and empirically well-documented theory of status processes in groups currently available (Berger et al. 1974, 1977; Correll and Ridgeway 2003; Wagner and Berger 2002). Although expectation states is a theory of status, not emotion, it provides a framework in relation to which research on emotion in hierarchies can be articulated to understand how status affects emotion and emotion shapes status in interpersonal contexts.

The affective dimension of social life covers a range of experiences from intense but transient flashes of feeling, such as rage, joy, or shame, to more enduring evaluative attitudes toward another, such as liking. In this chapter, *emotion* will refer to the actual experience of feeling in a situation. Emotions vary in intensity and duration but are accompanied by changes in bodily sensation and tend to be relatively transitory (Thoits 1989; Stets 2003). *Sentiments* are more stable affective appraisals of a person, relationship, or group (Gordon 1981; Ridgeway 1994). As attitudes, sentiments summarize past feelings and reflect expectations for future feelings. In addition to the emotions and sentiments that an individual subjectively experiences in group contexts, this person might also engage in observable behavioral displays of emotions or sentiments, typically referred to as *expressive* or socioemotional behavior. Such expressive behavior might or might not directly

Cecilia L. Ridgeway • Department of Sociology, Stanford University, Stanford, CA 94305 reflect an individual's feelings. In this chapter, we are interested in the relation between status and affect, understood as encompassing emotions, expressive behavior, and sentiments toward group members and the group itself.

There is every reason to anticipate that interpersonal status hierarchies will have powerful affective implications for their participants. Working together with others in groups has been fundamental to human survival over the ages (Brewer 1997; Turner 2000). Given the importance of group life for people's ability to obtain what they want and need, from the basics of food, shelter, and security to social recognition and achievement, it is reasonable to expect that groups and people's standing within them will have substantial emotional significance for them (Spoor and Kelly 2004). Indeed, Turner (2000) has argued that people's ability to experience, cognitively control, and socially shape a broad pallet of emotion developed in response to their need to coordinate interpersonal behavior in a changing environment. Kemper (1978, 1990) and Collins (1990) similarly have argued that people's positions of power and regard in social groups and changes to those positions are basic determinants of the emotions they feel.

This chapter begins its examination of status and affect with a review of an influential set of early studies. These studies framed the initial questions that have driven the contemporary study of status and affect and set the stage for the development of expectation states theory's account of status. A brief review of expectations states theory itself follows. Then I turn to current research on status and affect, beginning with a set of studies that asks whether status processes themselves inherently create affective dynamics in groups, and if so, what the characteristic forms of these dynamics are. The legitimacy of the status hierarchy turns out to be a key determinant of the affective dynamics it provokes, and so I consider that next. After this examination of how status creates affect, I turn to research that addresses the reciprocal question: how preexisting affective relations among people shape status hierarchies. Finally, I turn to the role of the status hierarchy in creating shared feelings among members and group solidarity.

EARLY STUDIES OF STATUS AND AFFECT

The modern study of status and affect in interpersonal groups began with Bales's (1950, 1970) functionalist analysis of group development and the detailed observational studies of group interaction that he used to support this analysis. All groups must address two basic problems to survive, according to this analysis. They must develop a means for accomplishing their shared goals and dealing with their surrounding environment. They must also achieve bonds among the group members that are sufficiently positive to keep members in the group and willing to work toward shared goals.

Bales' observations as well as his theoretical analysis suggested that status hierarchies arise primarily out of members' efforts to address their group task or goals. In the course of task discussions, however, Bales argued that disagreements inevitably develop and create social tensions that must be resolved if group solidarity is to be maintained. These tensions are resolved, he argued, through positive "socioemotional" behaviors such as seeming friendly, or supportive, or in some way expressing positive evaluative feelings toward another (Bales 1970). Positive and negative (e.g., criticizing or seeming unfriendly) socioemotional behaviors not only express and resolve interpersonal tension, Bales argued. These behaviors also act as rewards or punishments that encourage or discourage the task behaviors that immediately precede them. Consequently, the task behaviors out of which status hierarchies arise and the socioemotional behaviors by which solidarity is maintained are inherently interconnected, according to Bales. However, they have compensatory, somewhat competing effects on group dynamics that force the group to balance among them (Bales 1950, 1953).

Bales and Slater (1955; Slater 1955) developed the implications of these ideas further in a pair of well-known studies of leadership in male discussion groups. The studies showed that the highest status member, ranked the "best idea man," had the highest rate of task behavior and overall participation. However, this task leader also engaged in more negative socioemotional behavior and was not always the best liked. The number two member in participation was the best liked in the group and was higher in positive socioemotional behavior. Bales and Slater (1955) argued from these findings that task leadership requires disagreements and negative evaluations of others, creating some negative feelings toward the task leader. As a result, the second in status takes on the role of socioemotional leader to maintain solidarity.

Although Bales and Slater's (1955) idea of separate task and socioemotional leaders in groups gained popular attention, it also raised problematic theoretical questions about whether goal-oriented groups develop two separate status hierarchies, one based on task contributions and the other on popularity, or sentiments, as we would term them. Subsequent studies challenged the idea of separate status hierarchies. Reanalyses of Bales and Slater's data raised questions about whether separate leaders had actually reliably emerged in the groups that they observed (Bonacich and Lewis 1973; Riedesel 1974). Other studies show that high-status group members can sometimes be seen as attractive and likable (Suls and Miller 1978). Additional studies show that only when task leaders lack legitimacy in the group do separate socioemotional leaders clearly develop (Burke 1967, 1971).

These studies suggest that task and affective demands in groups do not inherently or even typically lead to separate, specialized status hierarchies. In general, groups seem to develop a single hierarchy that organizes their members' behavior and, as we will see, is based primarily on task-oriented behavior. Yet, these early studies did show that status hierarchies are deeply involved in the affective dynamics in groups. The extent to which the status hierarchy and the inequalities that it entails are affectively accepted in the group depends on its legitimacy for the members. Furthermore, even when legitimate, these early studies suggest that the hierarchy might provoke distinctive affective reactions and behaviors in high- and low-status members. The exact nature of these connections between status and affect, however, remained unclear. Work in the tradition of Bales and Slater, then, raised important questions about status, sentiments, and expressive behavior but did not resolve these questions. To make further progress, a more explicit theory of interpersonal status hierarchies was needed.

EXPECTATION STATES THEORY

Expectation states theory (Berger et al. 1974, 1977; Wagner and Berger 2002) developed as an effort to formally account for the status hierarchies observed by Bales (1950, 1970) and others (see Burke 2003; Correll and Ridgeway 2003). Bales' studies show strong empirical correlations among four types of behavior: the opportunities a person receives to participate, the person's task-related suggestions and contributions, others' evaluative reactions to those contributions, and the influence the person achieves in the group, as indicated by the extent to which others change to adopt the person's ideas. Berger and his colleagues argued that these behaviors are highly correlated because they are all observable indicators of a single phenomenon: the group's "power and prestige" or status structure.

Expectation states theory argues that the extent to which group members engage in these "power and prestige" behaviors is determined by the expectations that each forms for his or her own task performance in comparison to the others (Berger et al. 1974, 1977). These *performance expectations* are implicit, not necessarily conscious, guesses about group members' relative competence at the group's particular task or goal. They are anticipations of the likely usefulness of one person's task contributions compared to another's.

People form performance expectations, according to the theory, in order to decide how to act in the group situation: whether to speak up firmly with their own opinions or hold back and wait for others to begin and whether to give in or persist when others disagree with them. The lower the performance expectations that actors hold for themselves compared to another, the less likely they are to speak up with their own suggestions, the more likely they are to ask for the other's opinions, the more likely they are to positively evaluate the other's suggestions, and the more likely they are to grant the other influence by changing to agree with him or her. In this way, self-other performance expectations give rise to and control the "power and prestige" or status hierarchy in the group.

Actors form performance expectations by reading social cues about the other group members compared to themselves. Quite often, members of interpersonal groups differ in social attributes, such as gender, age, education, race, occupation, formal rank, or socially recognized skills that act as status characteristics in the surrounding society. An attribute is a status characteristic for people if widely held beliefs in their society associate people in one category of that attribute (e.g., whites, men, professionals) with greater social esteem and competence than those in another category of the attribute (people of color, women, service workers) (Berger et al. 1977). Status characteristics become salient in the situation for group members when the members differ on the characteristic or it is culturally perceived to be relevant to their group task.

The theory argues that when status characteristics are implicitly salient in the situation, they shape actors' performance expectations whether or not the characteristics are logically relevant to the shared task. However, the more relevant to the task a status characteristic is perceived to be, the stronger is its impact on performance expectations. Because people differ in multiple ways at once, several status characteristics are often salient in a given situation (e.g., gender, occupation, and formal rank). The theory argues that people combine the positive and negative competence implications of each characteristic, weighted by its relevance to the group task, to form an aggregated performance expectation for self compared to each other in the group (Berger et al. 1977; Correll and Ridgeway 2003).

When status characteristics are salient among a group of actors, the aggregated self-other performance expectations they create largely drive the actors' agentic, task-related behaviors in a self-fulfilling manner, so that the hierarchy of influence and esteem that develops corresponds to the actors' relative status characteristics (Berger et al. 1977; Webster and Foschi 1988). These agentic, task-related behaviors include not only Berger's original, largely verbal "power and prestige" behaviors (opportunities to participate, participation, evaluation, and influence). As subsequent research has shown, they also include nonverbal and paraverbal cues that communicate confidence and agency in the United States and are typically read as indicating competence (Ridgeway 1987; Ridgeway et al. 1985). Examples include a confident tone of voice, verbal fluency, more direct eye gaze, taking the head seat, having a relaxed, more expansive body posture, and so on.

Occasionally, however, members of goal-oriented groups are peers in that they do not initially differ in obvious external status characteristics. This was the case for Bales' groups of Harvard sophomore men. In such homogeneous groups, expectation states theory argues that participants form performance expectations from the behavioral interchange patterns that develop among them, often in the first moments of interaction. For whatever reason, someone speaks up and another agrees with him or her, and this exchange repeats so that a pattern of assertion and deference develops between the actors that implicitly activates the participants' cultural ideas of leader-follower behavior and causes them to form higher performance expectations for the assertive actor compared to the deferential one (Berger et al. 1974; Fisek et al. 1991). In homogeneous groups, then, patterns of assertive and deferential task-related behaviors, both verbal and nonverbal, create self-other performance expectations that then drive actors' subsequent behaviors so that a hierarchy of influence and esteem emerges.

Several decades of research in the expectations states tradition has provided a large body of empirical support for this account of the emergence of status hierarchies among actors who are faced with a shared goal or task (for reviews, see Correll and Ridgeway 2003; Ridgeway 2001; Wagner and Berger 2002). How, then, are the task-related status processes that expectation states theory describes related to patterns of emotion, sentiment, and expressive behavior in such groups? In its initial formulation, expectation states theory acknowledged the presence of affective dynamics in groups, but classified them as outside the scope of the theory. Instead, the theory was limited to the task-related behaviors that lie at the core of status processes, although the theory recognized that the task itself might sometimes have an affective character, as in a support group (Berger et al. 1974). Subsequent expectation states researchers, however, have sought to move beyond this initial position to bring emotion, sentiment, and expressive behavior back into a systematic account of interpersonal status processes. It is to this research that I turn now.

IS AFFECT INHERENT IN STATUS PROCESSES?

Bales (1950, 1970) argued that affect is inherent in status processes because efforts to address the task, out of which status emerges, inevitably cause disagreements that result in social tensions. Ridgeway and Johnson (1990) returned to the exchange of agreements and disagreements in task discussions as a crucial site at which status processes and affective dynamics meet in groups. They drew on expectation states theory and advances in the study of emotion to reanalyze these exchanges' impact on actors' emotions and socioemotional behavior in groups. The intent was not only to reask the question of whether status processes inherently create affective dynamics but also to account for established empirical evidence about typical patterns of socioemotional behavior in goal-oriented groups.

Studies using Bales' (1950, 1970) coding system to record task and socioemotional behavior in groups ranging from student discussion groups and simulated juries to husbands and wives, labor mediation groups, and therapy groups all show certain general patterns of task and social emotional behavior (Anderson and Blanchard 1982; Bales 1970; Bales and Hare 1965). Typically, about two-thirds of behaviors in goal-oriented groups are task behaviors out of which the status hierarchy emerges, such as offering task suggestions or asking task-related questions. The next most common behaviors are positive socioemotional behaviors, which, in turn, are about twice as prevalent as negative socioemotional behaviors. Finally, high-status actors are more likely than low-status members to express negative socioemotional behaviors (Bales 1970; Wood and Karten 1986). These are the patterns that Ridgeway and Johnson (1990) sought to explain with a systematic account of status, emotion, and expressive behavior.

Ridgeway and Johnson (1990) began with the assumption that group members were initially neutral in their feelings toward one another and were simply working together to accomplish a shared goal. Because status hierarchies typically emerge in the first few moments of interaction (see Ridgeway, 2001, for a review), they also assumed that group members had formed initial performance expectations for themselves compared to each other in the group.

When group members offer task suggestions under these conditions, Ridgeway and Johnson (1990) reasoned, they are trying to make sense of the task and exercise mastery or competence over it. Evidence marshaled by Kemper (1978, 1990) suggests that efforts to exercise mastery in interaction with the environment elicit pleasurable emotions in people when they seem successful but result in negative feelings when they are blocked or frustrated. Another's agreement with one's task suggestion confirms its competence and so should trigger pleasurable feelings. Another's disagreement with that task suggestion, however, draws the actor up short, eliciting frustration and negative feelings. Even when purely task oriented in intent, other group members' agreements and disagreements with an actor's task suggestions evoke in the actor diffuse positive and negative emotional responses.

This suggests that task agreements and disagreements play a dual role in goal-oriented groups. As essential behaviors in the evaluation of task ideas and the development of influence, they are central to status processes. However, as elicitors of positive and negative emotions, they inevitably set in play affective dynamics in the group. Here, then, is a location at which status structures and affective processes necessarily connect in groups.

Drawing on evidence that people's causal analysis of the event precipitating an emotional reaction is essential to the precise emotion they experience, Ridgeway and Johnson (1990) argued that what actors make of the diffuse, positive, and negative "gut" reactions elicited by agreements and disagreements depends on their cognitive appraisal of the situation. Appraisals, in turn, are shaped by self-other performance expectations.

Consider first the case of disagreements. Why has another disagreed with an actor's suggestion? If the actor attributes it to his or her own failings (the task suggestion was flawed), the actor is likely to experience depression or sadness. If the actor attributes the disagreement to the others' failings (the other doesn't get it), the actor is likely to experience annoyance or anger toward the other. If an actor's performance expectation for self is equal to or higher than that for the disagreer, Ridgeway and Johnson (1990) argued that the actor will attribute the disagreement to the others' failings and experience annoyance. If the actor's performance expectation for self is lower than that for the disagreer, the actor will assume that he or she must be wrong and feel depressed.

The emotions of annoyance and depression, although both negative, motivate the actor to respond to the disagreer in very different ways, Ridgeway and Johnson (1990) argued. Annoyance encourages the actor to express negative socioemotional behavior, such as a critical glance or unfriendly tone, toward the other in an effort to discourage further annoying disagreements. If the actor feels depressed, on the other hand, it makes no sense to express negative behavior toward the other because the disagreement was the actor's own fault. As a result of the way that self-other performance expectations shape actors' emotional reactions to disagreements, then, higher status actors are more likely to express negative socioemotional behavior in groups than are lower-status actors, as the data indeed show (Bales 1970; Wood and Karten 1986).

The expressive implications of agreements are a bit simpler, according to Ridgeway and Johnson (1990). Actors with equal or higher performance expectations for self than the other are likely to attribute the other's agreement to themselves and experience satisfaction or pride. Actors with lower expectations for self than the other might attribute the agreement to the other and feel gratitude. However, both pride and gratitude are pleasurable emotions, that motive the actor to express positive socioemotional behavior toward the other in order to encourage further pleasurable agreements. As a result, the status order does not inhibit the expression of positive socioemotional behavior as it does negative behavior. Indeed, Ridgeway and Johnson argued that once one group member expresses friendly behavior toward another, that other is likely to reciprocate in kind because positive behavior (smiling, expressions of support) serves as a reward that actors seek to encourage. Agreements, then, can set off chains of positive socioemotional exchanges that encourage the development of group solidarity by creating for the actors an association between the group and the exchange rewards. In effect, chains of positive socioemotional exchange encourage actors to form a positive sentiment toward the group.

By Ridgeway and Johnson's (1990) account, then, affect is indeed inherent in status processes. Even purely task-oriented agreements and disagreements evoke emotional reactions and create characteristic patterns of positive and negative socioemotional exchange. Although the status hierarchy does not block the exchange of positive behaviors, it reduces the occurrence of negative behaviors by encouraging low-status members to feel depressed rather than angered by disagreements. The reduction of negative socioemotional behavior in the group is especially large because high-status members, who are more likely to react to disagreements with negative behavior, are less likely to be disagreed with in the first place. The status hierarchy, then, is one mechanism that accounts for the empirical predominance of positive over negative socioemotional behaviors in goal-oriented groups. The prominence of positive over negative behavior, in turn, increases the likelihood that the group will be able to achieve and maintain solidarity. Note that these effects of the status hierarchy that control negative behavior and promote solidarity come at the expense of low-status members, who experience more negative self feelings in the group than do high-status members.

CULTURAL SCHEMAS OF STATUS AND EMOTION

To answer the question of whether status processes necessarily evoke emotion and expressive behavior, Ridgeway and Johnson (1990) made their argument *de novo*, without assumptions that actors bring to the group prior cultural assumptions about the emotions associated with high or low status. Yet, if affect is in fact inherent in status processes, as their account suggested, it is reasonable to expect that people's everyday experience with status hierarchies would lead to shared cultural schemas (i.e., stereotypes) of the characteristic emotions and expressive behavior associated with high-status and low-status, leader-follower positions. This is exactly what more recent research shows.

Tiedens et al. (2000) used vignettes to ascertain people's emotional expectations of high- and low-status actors. In accord with expectation states theory, Tiedens et al. argued that people expect high-status actors to be more agentic and competent than low-status actors and to feel emotions that correspond to that agency. They found, in confirmation of Ridgeway and Johnson's (1990) analysis, that when high- and low-status actors were confronted with a negative, problematic situation, people expected the high-status person to blame the low-status person more than himself or herself and to feel more angry than guilty or sad. The low-status person, on the other hand, was expected to blame himself or herself more and feel sad and guilty rather than angry. When presented with a positive situation, people thought that the high-status actor would feel pride and the low-status actor would feel appreciation, again as Ridgeway and Johnson (1990) predicted. In an even clearer indication that people hold stereotypes about status and emotions, Tiedens et al. (2000) found as well that when people did not know the status of actors in vignettes, they inferred it from the emotions that the actors displayed. Angry or proud actors were presumed to be high status, whereas sad, guilty, or appreciative actors were assumed to be low status.

Lovaglia and his colleagues argued and provided evidence that high status positions are culturally considered to be "compatible" with the experience of more positive emotions whereas low-status positions are compatible with more negative emotions (Houser and Lovaglia 2002; Lovaglia and Houser 1996; Lucas and Lovaglia 1998). This assumption is consistent with Ridgeway and Johnson's (1990) argument that, compared to low-status members, high-status members receive more attention, agreements, and positive evaluations of their ideas, all of which elicit pleasurable emotions. As a result, high-status people experience more elicitors of positive emotion and fewer elicitors of negative emotions than do low-status people, even though high-status people are freer to respond with anger to those negative events that they do experience.

Research by Conway et al. (1999) indicated that people's expectations for those in high- and low-status positions reflect these emotional and expressive consequences of status. They found that people judge low-status individuals to be more likely to experience circumstances that elicit negative emotions such as sadness, fear, anger, and disgust and less likely to experience elicitors of happiness than high-status people. People further expected low-status members of a hypothetical society to feel more sadness, fear, and anger and less happiness than high-status members. Importantly, however, people also expected these low-status members to actually *display* less anger and disgust than high-status members. Cultural schemas, then, appear to recognize the way that the status hierarchy constrains low-status members' expression of agentic negative emotions such as anger or disgust. Conway et al. also found that low-status members were expected to display more unagentic negative emotions such as sadness and fear and less happiness than high-status members.

These studies suggest that people hold shared, systematic expectations for high- and low-status members that reflect the emotional ironies created by status hierarchies. Backed by presumptions of their greater competence in the situation, high-status members are seen as experiencing more self-focused positive emotions but directing more critical, affectively negative behavior toward others. Low-status members receive more criticism and experience more negative self-focused emotions, but express more agreements and positive, supportive behavior toward higher-status members than they receive. In an example of how such emotional expectations play out in the workplace, Pierce (1995) described how female legal assistants are expected to remain calm and supportive in the face of angry outbursts from the trial lawyers for whom they work.

The emotional and behavioral profiles created by status hierarchies are also reflected in cultural schemas of the personality traits thought to be characteristic of high- and low-status actors, according to Conway et al. (1996). In their vignette studies, actors who differed in status based on occupation, gender, and standing in a hypothetical tribal society were all similarly perceived to be more agentic, but less considerate, when high status and less agentic but more communal when low status. Studies of the emergence of new status beliefs about social differences show the same pattern (Jost and Burgess 2000; Ridgeway and Erickson 2000). At least in North America, people expect members of high-status groups to be more competent and agentic but less considerate. Those in low-status groups are expected to be less competent but more considerate, cooperative, and nice. Note that by being cast into the position of reacting to and being dependent on presumably more competent high-status others, low-status members are expected to be more "other focused," responsive, and "nice" than high-status members. Although the processes by which this occurs follow a different logic than that suggested by Bales and Slater (1955), the result, as they suggested, is indeed a cultural expectation that low-status members will be more communal than high-status members.

There is good evidence, then, that people have shared cultural schemas or stereotypes of high-status and low-status actors that include not only differences in agentic, task-oriented behaviors and competence but also the characteristic emotional responses and expressive displays that accompany these actors' positions in the hierarchy. In effect, these culturally expected emotional responses and expressive displays are the "feeling rules" and "display rules" of status in North American society (Hochschild 1979, 1983). Because these emotion norms are part of the implicit cultural rules for enacting or performing interpersonal status, actors should be able to turn this around and use a behavioral display of these emotions as part of an effort to claim status in an interpersonal context (Clark 1990). Especially in homogeneous groups where performance expectations and status differences emerge from behavioral interchange patterns, accompanying task behaviors with the expression of confident, agentic emotions, such as positive self-feeling and critical reactions to challenges from others, should increase the likelihood that an actor creates the appearance of competence and elicits deference. Accompanying task behaviors with a display of negative self-feeling and an excessive responsiveness to the feelings of others, however, could undermine the appearance of competence and the attainment of status. Other factors equal, then, the more closely a behavioral claim to status corresponds to the emotion rules as well as the task behavior rules of status, the more successful it is likely to be.

LEGITIMACY DYNAMICS, EMOTIONS, AND
THE CONTAINMENT OF CONFLICT

We have seen that the emergence of the status hierarchy from group members' efforts to grapple with their task inherently gives rise to emotional dynamics in the group. Once the status hierarchy emerges, its perceived *legitimacy* for its members becomes an important regulator of their emotional reactions to subsequent status dynamics in the group. The legitimacy of the status hierarchy affects emotional reactions to the directive behaviors of high-status members and the efforts of lower status members to rise in the hierarchy. Legitimacy also affects the development of emotionally laden events such as conflict and status struggles within the group. To understand how this works, we first need a better understanding of the nature and sources of legitimacy in status hierarchies.

Legitimacy

A status hierarchy is legitimate for is members when they accept it as implicitly normative and, therefore, subject to sanction when violated (Zelditch and Walker 1984). As Zelditch and Walker (1984; Walker and Zelditch 1993) have shown, perceived legitimacy depends not only on a member's personal sense that the hierarchy is as it should be and "proper" but also on the sense that others in the group support it and that it is consistent with or backed by sources of authority in the surrounding environment.

Expectation states research has shown that the basic norms that legitimate interpersonal status hierarchies dictate that deference is exchanged for apparently more competent task efforts so that the collective goal can be achieved (Ridgeway 1993; Ridgeway and Berger 1986). Research suggests that these norms emerge because, although members might personally wish to claim status regardless of their ability to contribute to the group task, they want all others in the group to be granted influence and status only on the basis of competence so that the group's task efforts will be successful (Ridgeway and Diekema 1989). As group members pressure others to defer on the basis of apparent competence, others pressure them to defer on that basis as well, creating normative enforcement of the exchange of status for apparent task competence. As a result of these legitimating norms, actions by either high- or low-status members to claim status or to direct the behavior of others that do not appear to be justified by performance expectations or necessary for the task effort will seem illegitimate and be subject to sanction. An interesting implication of this argument is that in goal-oriented groups, efforts to seize status through purely intimidating, fear-inducing dominance behavior without efforts to show competence typically fail, as experiments show, because other members intervene to attack the attacker so that the dominator loses influence (Ridgeway and Diekema 1989).

Research has shown, then, that the backing of performance expectations is essential for status to be perceived as legitimate in goal-oriented groups. However, performance expectations are not the only determinant of legitimacy. Group members' sense that their fellow members support the hierarchy and that it is supported by outside authority structures are also important factors. Expectation states theory has shown that status characteristics like race, gender, occupation, or formal title not only shape performance expectations but also create expectations about the social appropriateness of members for high-status positions in the group (Ridgeway and Berger 1986; Berger et al. 1998). In a sense, advantaging status characteristics, say those of a man in a group of women, provide outside cultural support or authorization for a group member's candidacy for high status. Such apparent authorization, in turn, encourages those within the group to endorse that member's candidacy as well. As a result, holding performance expectations constant, high-status members who have advantaging status characteristics (a male boss with female subordinates) are more likely to be treated as legitimate and complied with rather than resisted than are high-status members who are not supported by advantaging status characteristics (a female boss with male subordinates) (Ridgeway et al. 1994).

The Emotional Consequences of Legitimacy

Perceived legitimacy regulates the extent to which the inequalities between high- and low-status members in the positive and negative emotions that they experience in the group lead to behavioral displays of conflict and to resistance to the hierarchy. Perhaps this is the most fundamental emotional consequence of legitimacy in groups. Legitimacy also affects how group members react to a low-status member's effort to rise in the hierarchy.

Bales (1950, 1970) argued, as we know, that the directive, sometimes critical behaviors that are necessary to the exercise of influence over the group's task efforts inevitably give rise to tensions in the group. We have seen, however, that high-status members' directive or critical task behaviors, although they might evoke self-focused feelings of sadness in lower-status members, do not necessarily provoke feelings or expressions of conflict and tension in the group. Whether they do depends on how legitimate the members feel the status hierarchy is (Burke 2003; Johnson et al. 2000). As a consequence, Ridgeway and Johnson's (1990) and Tiedens and her colleagues's (2000) evidence that low-status members are more likely to feel sad than angry in the face of negative reactions actually depends on the assumption that low-status members implicitly accept that they are less competent at the task than the high-status members. These emotional reactions, in other words, will only be typical when low-status members accept the underlying legitimacy of the status hierarchy as properly based on performance expectations.

To the extent that low-status members begin to doubt that high-status members actually are more competent, their sadness at the negative responses they receive is likely to shade into the more agentic emotions of resentment or anger. Indeed, Conway et al. (1999) found that people expect low-status actors to experience not only sadness and fear but also anger even if people expect low-status actors not to display that anger. This could reflect a social recognition that status hierarchies do not always seem perfectly legitimate to their low-status members. As Lovaglia and Houser (1996; Houser and Lovaglia 2002) pointed out, when low-status members resent high-status members, they are more likely to resist the high-status members' influence attempts and essentially reduce those members' status.

In addition to each group member's personal acceptance of the performance expectations on which the status hierarchy rests, its perceived legitimacy is also affected by the extent to which it appears to be endorsed by their fellow group members. Johnson et al. (2000) used vignettes to examine how this element of legitimacy affects subordinates' emotional reactions to a superior's inequitable and possibly conflict-inducing action. They found that even an inequitable action was less resented from an endorsed, highly legitimate superior, but feelings of anger and resentment grew when endorsement was low. Even then, however, if the subordinate was highly dependent on the superior for valued outcomes, the subordinate was perceived as unlikely to actually express his or her anger or resentment to the superior. Note that if resentment is not expressed, collective efforts among low-status members to change the hierarchy are unlikely to develop (Lawler 1975). Interestingly, Johnson et al. (2000) found that reactions of anger and resentment at the superior's inequitable action were especially low when both the superior and subordinate were highly dependent on each other to achieve good outcomes. This suggests that greater task dependence among actors, although it fosters the inequalities of the status hierarchy, nevertheless facilitates conciliation and cooperation in the face of conflicts.

The appearance of outside cultural support for the status hierarchy that occurs when high-status members are advantaged by external status characteristics similarly increases lower-status members' willingness to comply with high-status members' directives. Such compliance effects are particularly apparent when the high-status member goes beyond persuasion to exercise directive, authoritative power over lower-status members. An example is when high-status members direct dominance behavior toward a lower-ranking member. Dominance is not merely assertive or confident behavior, but behavior that attempts to control through actual or implied threat (Ridgeway 1987). Examples are commanding rather than requesting, treating another dismissively, and shouting at or interrogating someone.

As expectation states theory predicts, Ridgeway et al. (1994) found that high-ranking members who were advantaged by external status characteristics were able to direct dominance behavior toward a lower-ranking member and receive compliance even though this behavior reduced liking for the high-ranking member. However, when equally high-ranking members, whose status was based on high ability despite lower external status characteristics, used similar dominance behavior, they were not only disliked but resisted by lower-ranking members. As a result of their lesser legitimacy, then, the influence of these "meritocratic" high-ranking members over the group was more circumscribed than was that of high-ranking members whose social characteristics carried higher status in the surrounding society. These legitimacy effects provide an explanation for the resistance and hostility socially atypical leaders and managers such as women and people of color sometimes encounter when they attempt to exercise directive authority over subordinates (Butler and Geis 1990; Eagly and Karau 2002; Rudman and Glick 2001).

The legitimizing effects of external status characteristics also affect how group members react to a low-status member who attempts to improve his or her position in the status hierarchy. Low performance expectations generated by disadvantaging status characteristics might initially cast a woman or a person of color into a position of low influence and esteem in a decision-making group of white men. However, what if that person knows that she is actually highly competent at the group task and speaks up assertively and confidently to offer task suggestions and gain influence? Evidence suggests that other group members are likely to react with annoyance and disapproval to this assertion, seeing it as a violation of the legitimate status order. As a result, the low-status person's influence attempt might fail (Cohen and Roper 1972; Ridgeway 1982; Shackelford et al. 1996).

An assertive influence attempt from someone who group members presume is not very competent seems to them to be a selfish and illegitimate grab for power (Ridgeway 1982). They begin to dislike the person and see him or her as "pushy." As a consequence of its perceived illegitimacy, then, this effort to change the status order triggers negative emotions, hostile expressive behavior, and the formation of negative sentiments that are used to punish the ambitious low-status member and preserve the status quo.

There is, however, a way around this unfortunate "backlash" effect. Research shows that the low-status member can mitigate the perception of her influence attempt as selfish and illegitimate if she accompanies her assertive task suggestion with positive socioemotional behavior that suggests that she is not selfishly motivated but only trying to cooperatively help the group's task efforts

(Carli 2001; Ridgeway 1982). It is a tricky balancing act to appear sufficiently agentic to be convincingly competent but also sufficiently cooperative and friendly to appear group oriented. Also, this effort only works if the low-status person really does have competent suggestions to offer. However, if the low-status person can succeed in managing this atypical display of competent, assertive task behaviors and positive socioemotional behaviors, she can raise the performance expectations held for her and her status in the group.

Taken together, then, the evidence suggests that the legitimacy of a status hierarchy affects its affective dynamics in two ways. First, legitimacy contains conflict and the development of overt status struggles by reducing the low-status members' emotional feelings of resentment and anger over their treatment by higher-status members, by further restraining their expression of such feelings in the group, and by ensuring their compliance even when high-status members are not well liked. Second, by making the status hierarchy normative, legitimacy empowers group members to use negative expressive behavior (critical comments or looks, sarcasm) to sanction members who violate the established status order.

The affective consequences of legitimacy provide some explanation for evidence that overt status struggles in interpersonal status hierarchies, although not rare, are also not common (Mazur 1973). They also suggest why the development of status inequalities does not automatically engender resentment and tension and are not inherently inconsistent with either positive sentiments among the members or cohesiveness (e.g., Tiedens and Fragale 2003). Affective dynamics, then, form an important part of the process by which legitimacy maintains the stability of status hierarchies. These affective dynamics are among the more formidable challenges that must be overcome by those who wish to change a status order.

HOW DO EMOTIONS AND SENTIMENTS SHAPE STATUS?

Until this point, I have focused primarily on how the status hierarchy creates and shapes emotions, expressive behavior, and sentiments. Many of the status-driven analyses reviewed so far take as a starting point that actors are emotionally neutral toward one another when they begin working on their shared goal (e.g., Bales 1970; Ridgeway and Johnson 1990). This starting point is a logical one to answer the question of whether status processes themselves inherently create affective dynamics in interpersonal groups. However, it leaves unaddressed the question of whether members' preexisting feelings and sentiments toward one another shape the development of the status hierarchy. If emotions and sentiments do affect status, what is the nature of their impact? After all, although some workplace groups and committees do begin with affective neutrality, many goal-oriented groups in all aspects of life do not. It is not uncommon for people to have developed sentiments of liking or disliking for individuals with whom they find themselves cooperating with to attain a shared goal. How might such sentiments and the emotions associated with them shape the development of status relations among those individuals?

Several early writers who considered these questions suggested that, all other things equal, people would be more willing to accept influence from those they like and less willing to accept influence from those they dislike (e.g., Bales 1953; Berkowitz 1957). When considered in relation to recent research on sentiment and status, this general suggestion leads to two more specific questions that guide the discussion below. First, to what extent does evidence suggest that people are indeed more willing to accept influence from those they like than dislike and in what contexts does this occur? For instance is it limited to peer relations or status differentiated relations? Second, if liking does directly impact influence and status, how can we explain this effect? In particular, how can this effect be related to expectation states theory's well-documented account of status processes?

Expectation states researchers have suggested two possible models for how sentiment relations might affect status processes (Bianchi 2004; Driskell and Webster 1997; Fisek and Berger 1998). In the *constitutive* model, sentiments act like status characteristics that cause people to evaluate task performances by people they like more positively and to presume them to be generally more able than people they do not like. In this way, sentiments act like other status information that directly shapes performance expectations and influence by implying competence. The constitutive model implies that whenever sentiments are salient among a group of actors, they will systematically affect influence and status by modifying performance expectations. In the *moderator* model, sentiments do not shape performance expectations directly, but act as a situational parameter that modifies the extent to which people rely strictly on performance expectations in granting influence to another. The moderator model implies that salient sentiments affect influence under some circumstances, such as when nothing much is at stake in the group decision, but might not affect influence in a crisis when task competence seems all important to group members. Thus, the question is not only whether evidence documents that sentiment shapes influence and status, but whether it does so in a way that seems to support either the constitutive or moderator account of how this occurs.

In recent years, several researchers have turned their attention to the impact of sentiment relations on status. The research area is relatively new, however, and perhaps as a result, it is fraught with conceptual inconsistencies and methodological differences that make comparisons of findings difficult. As a result, strong conclusions about the research findings in this area are premature, but I will attempt a general review and assessment of the current state of knowledge. I begin by considering some of the conceptual issues involved in linking sentiment relations to status and then turn to an evaluation of the research evidence.

Linking Sentiment Relations to Status

What is the logic by which sentiments of liking or disliking might lead to status? Considering this question illustrates some of the conceptual complexities in this area of research. Shelly (2001) argued that when we like someone, we think well of them, and thinking well of someone in contemporary society means seeing them as competent among other positive attributes. Using vignettes to tap cultural schemas of liked others, Shelly (2001, study 2) asked people to rate two individuals in terms of competence and personality, one presented as a person they liked and the other as someone they disliked. Liked others were seen as more competent and intelligent, among other traits, suggesting that we think of ourselves as liking more competent others.

What is not clear from Shelly's results, however, is whether we think of liked others as more or less competent than ourselves. As a result, the implications of these results for status relations between self and the liked other are unclear. In fact, there is considerable evidence that liking is powerfully predicted by perceived similarity (Berscheid and Reis 1998). As a consequence, many studies use perceived similarity between a study participant and another to manipulate liking. In the absence of other information about self and other, however, liking based on similarity would appear to imply equal competence and, therefore, equal status between self and other (Shelly 1993).

This suggests that for a status hierarchy to develop between self and other, the parties would have to acquire additional information about each other that differentiates their performance expectations for one another beyond the initially egalitarian competence implications of liking.

Liking, however, might cause people to treat another in a manner that allows such differentiating information to emerge. Shelly (1993, 2004) suggested that liked others are given more opportunities to participate, and Ridgeway and Johnson (1990) speculated that people pay more attention to what liked others say, increasing the likelihood that they become influential.

The logic linking negative sentiments to status is more straightforward. Because a disliked other is presumably perceived as dissimilar from self and, according to Shelly's (2001) results, of lesser competence, negative sentiments relations imply that the other will be treated as lower status, other things equal. This suggests that positive and negative sentiments might have differing impacts on the development of status hierarchies and might affect status processes in different ways.

Another difficult question that arises when considering how sentiments might lead to status is what is meant by a sentiment relation. In most actual interpersonal groups, sentiment relations involve some degree of *mutual* liking or disliking among individuals. Thinking about the implications for the development of status hierarchies of research on liking and influence, as a consequence, requires careful consideration of how patterns of relative liking lead to self-other *differences* in the acceptance of influence, not just to higher or lower levels of mutual influence.

Does Sentiment Alone Create a Status Hierarchy?

With these considerations in mind, I turn to the question of whether preexisting sentiments among actors are sufficient in themselves to create a status hierarchy among them. This question is the reverse of our earlier consideration of whether status inherently creates affect. To investigate this question in its simplest form, I begin with studies of group members who do not differ in status characteristics and have no specific knowledge about each other's task competence, but do know that they like or dislike one another.

Driskell and Webster (1997) gave participants in an experiment a purported personality test and then told them that their partners were either similar or dissimilar from them so that they were likely to either like or dislike their partners. This manipulation did indeed cause participants to report more liking for their partners in similarity rather than dissimilarity conditions. When participants worked with their partners on a decision task, however, there were no differences in their willingness to accept influence from a liked or disliked partner. There were also no differences in the participants' measured performance expectations for a liked or disliked partner. This study suggests that sentiment alone is unlikely to lead to a clear status hierarchy and raises questions about whether people are always more willing to accept influence from those they like. One must keep in mind, however, that the "sentiments" created in an experiment like this are weak, and it is possible that stronger feelings would have clearer effects.

In a rather different study, Shelly (1993) used perceived similarity to manipulate mutual liking between pairs of actors in three-person groups such that one person was more "popular," in that he or she liked and was liked by two others while the other actors were each liked by only one other. Reasoning that liked others would be given more opportunities to participate, which, in turn, would make them appear more competent, Shelly argued that a status hierarchy would emerge in each triad that favored the most popular member. Codings of open interaction among group members, however, showed no significant differences in the observable power and prestige behaviors (task suggestions, evaluations, and so forth) between the most popular member and others, although the differences were in the predicted direction (Shelly 1993; Shelly and Webster 1997).

Shelly's study is suggestive, but like Driskell and Webster's (1997), it provides no clear evidence that sentiment alone is sufficient to create a predictable status hierarchy. I suspect that stronger manipulations of similarity-based sentiments might show that actors are more willing to grant influence to a highly similar and well-liked other than to a dissimilar and less liked person. However, liking alone would not determine whether the actor allowed the similar and well-liked other to become more influential and higher status than himself or herself.

Does Sentiment Modify the Hierarchies That Develop from Other Status Information?

Although sentiment on its own has not yet been shown to create status, there is some evidence that prior sentiments or emotions do modify the status hierarchy that would otherwise result from group members' status characteristics and task competence. The modifying effects of sentiments in these situations appear to be noticeably weaker than the impact of other factors like task skill, that are directly related to status, as Shelly (2004) argued is predictable. Also, in general, the effects are stronger for negative than positive emotions and sentiments. It is clearest to consider the modifying effects of liking and positive emotion separate from those of disliking and negative emotion.

POSITIVE SENTIMENTS AND EMOTIONS.   In a set of experiments that are distinctive for their focus on positive and negative emotions rather than sentiments, Lovaglia and Houser (1996) differentiated participants and their partners on status characteristics, induced positive and negative emotions by having the partner either reciprocate a gift exchange with a friendly note or refuse to reciprocate with a hostile note, and examined the impact on acceptance of influence from the partner. Positive emotions tended to increase acceptance of influence for both high- and low-status participants, although the effects were not always significant. As Bianchi (2005) commented, however, it is unclear in these studies whether influence was affected by the induced positive emotion or by the reciprocal exchange itself.

Two studies examined the effects of liking on low-status actors' acceptance of influence from higher-status actors. Driskell and Webster (1997) found that low-status participants' liking for their partner did not increase their willingness to accept influence from that partner. Shelly (2001, study 3) used vignettes to put participants in what was, in effect, a low-status position in which they picked between two possible "advisors" to help them study for an exam. The advisors' status characteristics and task competence were the most important determinants of participants' choices, but holding these factors constant, liking increased the likelihood that a given advisor would be chosen.

Evidence about how liking affects high-status members' willingness to accept influence from lower-status others comes from Shelly and Webster's (1997) studies of interaction in triads, in which one member is more "popular" than the others. When a member who was advantaged over the others in status characteristics was also the most popular member, his or her advantage in task behaviors and influence tended to be intensified. Lovaglia and Houser (1996; Houser and Lovaglia 2002) suggested that a high-status member's positive emotions toward lower-status members should moderate the status hierarchy. However, Shelly and Webster's (1997) data show that the opposite might occur if liking is mutual between high- and low-status members and there are more low- than high-status members in the group.

Finally, Bianchi (2005) examined the effect of similarity-based liking on influence when participants and their partners were both equally and highly competent at the task. Liking only affected influence when the participant's decisions had little impact on the group's task accomplishment and, interestingly, it reduced willingness to accept influence. It was as if the participant felt that when it was not all that important and both were competent, the liked other could be counted on to "understand" if the participant did not change to agree with the other.

Taken together, these studies suggest that there is no simple, across-the-board effect of liking on the status hierarchies that form when participants have other status information about self and other. The effects that occur are weak and vary in direction depending on contextual factors such as whether liking is mutual, the status of the other relative to self, and the task significance of the decision. Again, of course, it is possible that stronger sentiment ties than those created in these studies would produce more powerful effects. My guess, however, is that even such more powerful effects would remain contextually sensitive.

NEGATIVE SENTIMENTS AND EMOTIONS.   There is clearer and more consistent evidence that dislike and negative emotion modify the influence that actors attain based on other status factors. Lovaglia and Houser (1996) found that angry, negative emotion significantly reduced both high- and low-status members' willingness to accept influence from the other. Note that this angry emotion was elicited by others' illegitimate violations of routine norms such as reciprocity. Thus, the loss of influence here is comparable to the hostile reactions and loss of influence that we saw for the illegitimate exercise of authority. Driskell and Webster (1997) also found that a low-status member's dislike for a higher-status partner reduced the partner's influence. Shelly's (2001, study 3) vignette study similarly showed that dislike reduced the extent to which participants chose and deferred to an otherwise competent advisor. Finally, Bianchi (2004) found that dislike reduced a participant's willingness to accept influence from an equally and highly competent partner, but only when the decision did not affect the group's task success. Thus, the effects of disliking are stronger than those of liking and, for both high- and low-status actors, consistently reduce the disliked other's influence.

Are Sentiments and Emotions Constituents or Moderators of Performance Expectations?

Despite weak manipulations and not always comparable methods, the above studies indicate that sentiments do modify the formation of status hierarchies to some degree. How, then, do they do so? By acting as one more factor that shapes performance expectations or by acting as a situational parameter that affects how strictly group members adhere to assumptions about competence in granting influence? The latter, "moderator" approach assumes that people routinely form expectations about the competence of the other that are independent of their sentiments for that person and, so, could easily say, "I don't like him but he is competent." The former, "constitutive" model assumes that sentiments and assessments of competence are typically blended evaluations because liking creates performance expectations.

The strongest evidence in favor of the constitutive model comes from Shelly's (2001) vignette studies in which he found that liked others were not only presumed to be more competent, but also that ratings of the others' competence did not load on different factors in factor analysis from ratings of their other evaluative qualities. Shelly interprets these results as showing that sentiments and performance expectations are not separate, independent evaluations. Lovaglia and Houser (1996) as well interpreted their results as more consistent with a constitutive approach, although alternative explanations cannot be ruled out. Neither of these studies directly tests one model against the other in a context of self-other influence, however.

Studies that pit the models against one another vary the importance of the participants' decisions for the groups' task success because if sentiment acts as a moderator, its effects on influence should decline or disappear when important outcomes are at stake. If sentiment is a constituent of performance expectations, variations in task dependence should not affect its impact. Driskell and Webster (1997, study 1) reported a first study of this sort that produced weak results in favor of the moderator model. Bianchi (2004) conducted a stronger study like this using negative sentiments and found an effect for these sentiments when the participant's decision was unimportant for group outcomes but no effect when the group outcome depended on the participant's decision, supporting the moderator model. A replication of this study with positive sentiments again showed no support for the constitutive model and some support for the moderator model (Bianchi 2005). This issue is not yet resolved, but, thus far, evidence is slightly stronger for the moderator approach.

Final Thoughts on How Sentiments and Emotions Shape Status

In my view, whether sentiments directly create performance expectations or just modify their impact on status processes might not be a simple, either-or matter. The process might begin much as described by the constitutive model. It might indeed be that when we perceive others to be similar to us and like them, we implicitly presume them to be more competent in comparison to those toward whom we have neutral or negative feelings. In goal-oriented contexts, we might indeed give liked others more opportunities to express their opinions and listen more closely to what they have to say, increasing the likelihood that they will influence us (Ridgeway and Johnson 1990; Shelly 1993, 2004). In contrast, we respond less carefully and more critically to the suggestions of disliked others, allowing them little opportunity to influence us.

What happens, however, when in the typical course of task discussion, disagreements develop with the liked other and choices must be made between views? Here, I argue that the need to implicitly decide whether the liked other is not only more competent than neutral or disliked others, but also more or less competent than self leads people to look past liking for more specific information on the other's competence. They might more closely scrutinize the content and behavioral style of the others' task suggestions, for instance.

As differentiated performance expectations emerge for the liked other compared to self, sentiments and performance expectations begin to separate in the group and the process begins to resemble the moderator account. For a similar divergence to occur between an actor's sentiments and performance expectations for a disliked other, it might be necessary for clear outside information about that other's positive competence to be introduced into the situation. Once the actor is able to distinguish implicitly between liking or disliking for the other and conceptions of the other's competence, however, the importance of the task and its dependence on the actor's decisions determine the extent to which his or her willingness to accept influence from the other is biased by his or her liking for the other.

This analysis suggests that prior sentiments among group members have an impact on the initial status structures that develop, but sentiment relations and status tend to become somewhat independent of one another over time so that sentiment never fully drives the status hierarchy. In fact, for status relations, the most important affective assessment of another might not be liking or positive or negative emotion but the perception of the other as group- or self-oriented. When people defer to another in a goal-oriented context, they do so on the assumption that the other will use his or her competence to help the group achieve it goals rather than simply for self-interest (Ridgeway 1982). A competent but not group-oriented other cannot be trusted with status and influence over the group. In general, similar or liked others might be presumed to be more group-oriented. If evidence contradicts this assumption, however, I suggest, it is apparent group orientation rather than liking that will be most important for status. Dissimilar or disliked others might be presumed not to be group-oriented unless there is evidence to the contrary, and indeed, strong negative affect could cause the group to redraw its boundaries so that the disliked other is no longer a member.

FEELING WITH THE GROUP AND SOLIDARITY

Because status is a system of differentiation among group members, I have so far examined how it leads to or is affected by corresponding differentiations in group members' sentiments and emotions toward one another. Affect in groups not only differentiates members, however, it can also cause them to feel in concert with one another. As we noted at the onset, displays of emotion are among the means people use to communicate with one another in groups, coordinate their responses, and mobilize their efforts toward their goal (Spoor and Kelly 2004). There is a variety of evidence that experiences in which group members' emotions converge with one another increase group solidarity (see Spoor and Kelly 2004). Lawler (2001) has shown that shared successful task activities create a positive emotional "buzz" for group members, which increases their commitment to the group, whereas shared failures undermine it. We can speculate that the positive emotional "buzz" from successful joint activity might be especially important for binding low-status members to the group, as these members' routine interactions within the group generate fewer positive emotions for them than are generated for high-status members.

There is also evidence that high-status members act as the principal coordinators of shared emotion in groups. That is to say, one of the implications of status is that low-status members are more susceptible to regulation of their emotions and mood in the group than are high-status members. As a result, high-status members intentionally or unintentionally set the emotional tone of the group as low-status members accommodate to the high-status members' affective mood rather than vice versa (Anderson et al. 2003). Finally, to the extent that the status hierarchy succeeds in efficiently coordinating group activity, that coordination itself generates positive affect among the members and promotes positive sentiments among the members (Spoor and Kelly 2004; Tiedens and Fragale 2003). The experience of positive affect in the group, in turn, is a major contributor to group cohesiveness (Kelly and Barsade 2001; Ridgeway and Johnson 1990).

CONCLUSION

Although researchers have been concerned with status and affect for decades, it is only in the past two decades that detailed empirical studies have begun to appear. These more recent studies have been facilitated by the prior development of expectation states theory, which offers a well-documented theory of status in relation from which to study affect. Nevertheless, it is clear that at present what we do not know about status and affect outweighs what we do know. Still, some things can now be said. Although status processes arise out of efforts to coordinate behavior in regard to a shared goal or task, they give rise to characteristic emotions, expressive displays, and sentiments that become the "feeling rules" of high and low status. As a result, these emotions and displays are part of the culturally expected performance of high and low status. The perceived legitimacy of the status hierarchy further regulates the experience of resentment or anger at the actions of high-status members or toward challengers to the hierarchy. Thus, affective dynamics play a substantial role in maintaining the stability of the status order. An interesting implication is that status hierarchies, because of the way they regulate emotion, do not inherently undermine solidarity and cohesiveness in groups and sometimes contribute to it.

Although there is good evidence that status processes drive emotions and expressive displays in interpersonal groups, evidence is less clear about the reverse process. Status hierarchies do not seem to emerge systematically from sentiment relations alone, but emotions and sentiments nevertheless have some impact on the formation of status relations in combination with more directly related status information. Negative sentiments have stronger effects than positive ones and reduce the influence of the disliked other. These and other effects of sentiments on status appear to vary by context, however. Although emotions and sentiments might sometimes shape the performance expectations on which status is based, most evidence suggests that they are not usually at the core of the status process, but typically act as situational factors that modify influence processes when less is at stake and recede in impact when shared goal attainment becomes paramount. It appears, then, that status and affect are entwined in groups but are also, to some degree, separate processes.

REFERENCES

Anderson, Cameron, Dacher Keltner, and Oliver P. John. 2003. "Emotional Convergence Between People Over Time." *Journal of Personality and Social Psychology* 84: 1054–1068.

Anderson, Lynn R., and P. Nick Blanchard. 1982. "Sex Differences in Task and Social-Emotional Behavior." *Basic and Applied Social Psychology* 3: 109–139.

Bales, Robert F. 1950. *Interaction Process Analysis: A Method for the Study of Small Groups*. Cambridge, MA: Addison-Wesley.

———. 1953. "The Equilibrium Problem in Small Groups." Pp. 111–161 in *Working Papers in the Theory of Action*, edited by T. Parsons, R. F. Bales, and E. A. Shils. Glencoe, IL: Free Press.

———. 1970. *Personality and Interpersonal Behavior.* New York: Holt, Rinehart, and Winston.

Bales, Robert F., and A. Paul Hare. 1965. "Diagnostic Use of the Interaction Profile." *Journal of Social Psychology* 67: 239–258.

Bales, Robert F., and Phillip E. Slater. 1955. "Role Differentiation in Small Decision-Making Groups." Pp. 259–306 in *The Family, Socialization and Interaction Processes*, edited by T. Parsons and P. E. Slater. Glencoe, IL: Free Press.

Berger, Joseph, Thomas L. Conner, and M. Hamit Fisek. 1974. *Expectation States Theory: A Theoretical Research Program*. Cambridge, MA: Winthrop.

Berger, Joseph, M. Hamit Fisek, Robert Z. Norman, and Morris Zelditch, Jr. 1977. *Status Characteristics and Social Interaction*. New York: Elsevier.

Berger, Joseph, Cecilia L. Ridgeway, M. Hamit Fisek, and Robert Z. Norman. 1998. "The Legitimation and Delegitimation of Power and Prestige Orders." *American Sociological Review* 63: 379–405.

Berkowitz, Leonard. 1957. "Liking for the Group and the Perceived Merit of the Group's Behavior." *Journal of Abnormal and Social Psychology* 54: 353–357.

Berscheid, Ellen, and Harry T. Reis. 1998. "Attraction and Close Personal Relationships." Pp. 193–281 in *The Handbook of Social Psychology*, edited by D. T. Gilbert, S. T. Fiske, and G. Lindzey. New York: McGraw-Hill.

Bianchi, Alison J. 2004. "Rejecting Others' Influence: Negative Sentiment and Status in Task Groups." *Sociological Perspectives* 47: 339–370.

———. 2005. "Sentiments and Status Processes: News from the Front." Paper presented to the annual meeting of the North Central Sociological Association, Pittsburgh, PA.

Bonacich, Philip, and Gordon H. Lewis. 1973. "Function Specialization and Sociometric Judgment." *Sociometry* 36: 31–41.

Brewer, Marilynn B. 1997. "On the Origins of Human Nature." Pp. 54–62 in *The Message of Social Psychology*, edited by C. McGarty and A. Haslam. Oxford: Blackwell.

Burke, Peter J. 1967. "The Development of Task and Social-Emotional Role Differentiation." *Sociometry* 30: 379–392.

———. 1971. "Task and Socio-Emotional Leadership Role Performance." *Sociometry* 34: 22–40.

———. 2003. "Interaction in Small Groups." Pp. 389–410 in *Handbook of Social Psychology*, edited by J. Delamater. New York: Kluwer/Plenum.

Butler, Dore, and Florence L. Geis. 1990. "Nonverbal Affect Responses to Male and Female Leaders: Implications for Leadership Evaluations." *Journal of Personality and Social Psychology* 58: 48–59.

Carli, Linda. 2001. "Gender and Social Influence." *Journal of Social Issues* 57: 725–743.

Clark, Candace. 1990. "Emotions and Micropolitics in everyday Life: Some Patterns and Paradoxes of 'Place'." Pp. 305–333 in *Research Agendas in the Sociology of Emotions*, edited by T. D. Kemper. Albany: State University of New York Press.

Cohen, Elizabeth G., and Susan S. Roper. 1972. "Modification of Interracial Interaction Disability: An Application of Status Characteristics Theory." *American Sociological Review* 37: 643–657.

Collins, Randy. 1990. "Stratification, Emotional Energy, and the Transient Emotions." Pp. 27–57 in *Research Agendas in the Sociology of Emotions*, edited by T. D. Kemper. Albany: State University of New York Press.

Conway, Michael, Roberto DiFazio, and Shari Mayman. 1999. "Judging Others' Emotions as a Function of the Others' Status." *Social Psychology Quarterly* 62: 291–305.

Conway, Michael, M. Teresa Pizzamiglio, and Lauren Mount. 1996. "Status, Communality, and Agency: Implications for Stereotypes of Gender and Other Groups." *Journal of Personality and Social Psychology* 71: 25–38.

Correll, Shelley J., and Cecilia L. Ridgeway. 2003. "Expectation States Theory." Pp. 29–52 in *Handbook of Social Psychology*, edited by J. Delamater. New York: Kluwer/Plenum.

Driskell, James E., Jr., and Murray Webster, Jr. 1997. "Status and Sentiment in Task Groups." Pp. 179–200 in *Status, Network and Structure: Theory Construction and Theory Development*, edited by J. Szmatka, J. Skovertz, and J. Berger. Stanford, CA: Stanford University Press.

Eagly, Alice H., and Stephen J. Karau. 2002. "Role Congruity Theory of Prejudice Towards Female Leaders." *Psychological Review* 109: 573–598.

Fisek, M. Hamit, and Joseph Berger. 1998. "Sentiment and Task Performance Expectations." Pp. 23–41 in *Advances in Group Processes*, edited by J. Skvoretz and J. Szmatka. Stamford, CT: JAI Press.

Fisek, M. Hamit, Joseph Berger, and Robert Z. Norman. 1991. "Participation in Heterogeneous and Homogeneous Groups: A Theoretical Integration." *American Journal of Sociology* 97: 114–142.

Gordon, Steven L. 1981. "The Sociology of Sentiments and Emotion." Pp. 562–592 in *Social Psychology: Sociological Perspectives*, edited by M. Rosenberg and R. H. Turner. New York: Basic Books.

Hochschild, Arlie R. 1979. "Emotion Work, Feeling Rules, and Social Structure." *American Journal of Sociology* 85: 551–575.

———. 1983. *The Managed Heart: The Commercialization of Human Feeling*. Berkeley: University of California Press.

Houser, Jeffrey A., and Michael J. Lovaglia 2002. "Status, Emotions, and the Development of Solidarity in Stratified Task Groups." Pp. 109–138 in *Advances in Group Processes*, edited by S. Thye and E. J. Lawler. New York: Elsevier.

Johnson, Cathryn, Rebecca Ford, and Joanne Kaufman. 2000. "Emotions Reactions to Conflict: Do Dependence and Legitimacy Matter." *Social Forces* 79: 101–138.

Jost, John T., and Diana Burgess. 2000. "Attitudinal Ambivalence and the Conflict Between Group and System Justification in Low Status Groups." *Personality and Social Psychology Bulletin* 26: 293–305.

Kelly, Janice R., and Sigal Barsade. 2001. "Emotions in Small Groups and Work Teams." *Organizational Behavior and Human Decision Processes* 86: 99–130.

Kemper, Theodore D. 1978. *A Social Interactional Theory of Emotions*. New York: Wiley.

———. 1990. "Social Relations and Emotions: A Structural Approach." Pp. 207–237 in *Research Agendas in the Sociology of Emotions*, edited by T. D. Kemper. Albany: State University of New York Press.

Lawler, Edward J. 1975. "An Experimental Study of Factors Affecting the Mobilization of Revolutionary Coalitions." *Sociometry* 38: 163–179.

———. 2001. "An Affect Theory of Social Exchange." *American Journal of Sociology* 107: 321–352.

Lonner, Walter J. 1980. "The Search for Psychological Universals." Pp. 143–204 in *Handbook of Cross-Cultural Psychology*, edited by H. C. Triandis and W. W. Lambert. Boston: Allyn and Bacon.

Lovaglia, Michael J., and Jeffrey A. Houser. 1996. "Emotional Reactions and Status in Groups." *American Sociological Review* 61: 867–883.

Lucas, Jeffrey, and Michael J. Lovaglia. 1998. "Leadership Status, Gender, Group Size, and Emotion in Face-to-Face Groups." *Sociological Perspectives* 41: 617–637.

Mazur Allan. 1973. "Cross-Species Comparison of Status in Established Small Groups." *American Sociological Review* 38: 111–124.

Pierce, Jennifer L. 1995. *Gender Trials: Emotional Lives in Contemporary Law Firms*. Berkeley: University of California Press.

Ridgeway, Cecilia L. 1982. "Status in Groups: The Importance of Motivation." *American Sociological Review* 47: 76–88.

———. 1987. "Nonverbal Behavior, Dominance, and the Basis of Status in Task Groups." *American Sociological Review* 52: 683–694.

————. 1993. "Legitimacy, Status and Dominance Behavior in Groups." Pp. 110–127 in *Conflict Between People and Groups*, edited by J. Simpson and S. Worchel. Chicago: Nelson-Hall.

————. 1994. "Affect." Pp. 205–230 in *Group Processes: Sociological Analyses*, edited by M. Foschi and E. Lawler. Chicago: Nelson-Hall.

————. 2001. "Social Status and Group Structure." Pp. 352–375 in *Blackwell Handbook of Social Psychology: Group Processes*, edited by M. A. Hogg and S. Tindale. Maulden, MA: Blackwell.

Ridgeway, Cecilia L., and Joseph Berger. 1986. "Expectations, Legitimation, and Dominance Behavior in Task Groups." *American Sociological Review* 51: 603–617.

Ridgeway, Cecilia L., Joseph Berger, and LeRoy Smith. 1985. "Nonverbal Cues and Status: An Expectation States Approach." *American Journal of Sociology* 90: 955–978.

Ridgeway, Cecilia, and David Diekema. 1989. "Dominance and Collective Hierarchy Formation in Male and Female Task Groups." *American Sociological Review* 54: 79–93.

Ridgeway, Cecilia L., and Kristan G. Erickson. 2000. "Creating and Spreading Status Beliefs. *American Journal of Sociology* 106: 579–615.

Ridgeway, Cecilia L., and Cathryn Johnson. 1990. "What Is the Relationship Between Socioemotional Behavior and Status in Task Groups?" *American Journal of Sociology* 95: 1189–1212.

Ridgeway, Cecilia L., Cathryn Johnson, and David Diekema. 1994. "External Status, Legitimacy, and Compliance in Male and Female Groups." *Social Forces* 72: 1051–1077.

Riedesel, Paul L. 1974. "Bales Reconsidered: A Critical Analysis of Popularity and Leadership Differentiation." *Sociometry* 37: 557–564.

Rudman, Laurie. A., and Peter Glick. 2001. "Prescriptive Gender Stereotypes and Backlash Toward Agentic Women." *Journal of Social Issues* 57: 743–762.

Shackelford, Susan, Wendy Wood, and Stephen Worchel. 1996. "Behavioral Styles and the Influence of Women in Mixed Sex Groups." *Social Psychology Quarterly* 59: 284–293.

Shelly, Robert K. 1993. "How Emotions Organize Interaction." Pp. 113–132 in *Advances in Group Processes*, edited by E. Lawler, B. Markovsky, K. Heimer, and J. O'Brien. Greenwich, CT: JAI Press.

————. 2001. "How Performance Expectations Arise from Sentiments." *Social Psychology Quarterly* 64: 72–87.

————. 2004. "Emotions, Sentiments, and Performance Expectations." Pp. 141–165 in *Advances in Group Processes*, edited J. H. Turner. New York: Elsevier.

Shelly, Robert K., and Murray Webster. 1997. "How Formal Status, Liking, and Ability Status Structure Interaction." *Sociological Perspectives* 40: 81–107.

Slater, Phillip E. 1955. "Role Differentiation in Small Groups." *American Sociological Review* 20: 300–310.

Spoor, Jennifer R., and Janice R. Kelly. 2004. "The Evolutionary Significance of Affect in Groups: Communication and Group Bonding." *Group Processes and Intergroup Relations* 7: 398–412.

Stets, Jan E. 2003. "Emotions and Sentiments." Pp. 309–338 in *Handbook of Social Psychology*, edited by J. Delamater. New York: Kluwer/Plenum.

Suls, Jerry, and M. Miller. 1978. "Ability Comparison and its Effects on Affiliation Preferences." *Human Relations* 31: 267–282.

Thoits, Peggy A. 1989. "The Sociology of Emotions." *Annual Review of Sociology* 15: 317–342.

Tiedens, Larissa Z., Phoebe C. Ellsworth, and Batja Mesquita. 2000. *Personality and Social Psychology Bulletin* 26: 560–575.

Tiedens, Larissa Z., and Alison R. Fragale. 2003. "Power Moves: Complementarity in Dominant and Submissive Nonverbal Behavior." *Journal of Personality and Social Psychology* 84: 558–568.

Turner, Jonathan H. 2000. *On The Origins of Human Emotions*. Stanford, CA: Stanford University Press.

Wagner, David G., and Joseph Berger. 2002. "Expectation States Theory: An Evolving Research Program. Pp. 41–76 in *New Directions in Contemporary Sociological Theory*, edited by J. Berger and M. Zelditch. New York: Rowman and Littlefield.

Walker, Henry A., and Morris Zelditch. 1993. "Power, Legitimacy, and the Stability of Authority: A Theoretical Research Program." Pp. 364–384 in *Theoretical Research Programs: Studies in the Growth of Theory*, edited by J. Berger and M. Zelditch. Stanford, CA: Stanford University Press.

Webster, Murray, Jr., and Martha Foschi, eds. 1988. *Status Generalization: New Theory and Research*. Stanford, CA: Stanford University Press.

Wood, Wendy, and Steven J. Karten. 1986. "Sex Differences in Interaction Style as a Product of Perceived Sex Differences in Competence." *Journal of Personality and Social Psychology* 50: 341–347.

Zelditch, Morris, Jr., and Henry A. Walker. 1984. "Legitimacy and the Stability of Authority." Pp. 1–27 in *Advances in Group Processes*, edited by E. J. Lawler. Greenwich, CT: JAI Press.

CHAPTER 16

Evolutionary Theory and Emotions

Michael Hammond

Darwin himself began the investigation into the relationship between emotions and evolution with *The Expression of the Emotions in Man and Animals* in 1872. However, unlike most of Darwin's other work, this area of inquiry lay dormant for almost 100 years. Even when Wilson tried to restart interest in the possible linkages between evolution and social life with his publication of *Sociobiology* in 1975, there was virtually no analysis of emotions. Sociologists like Van Den Berghe (1975), who took up the evolutionary cause in the 1970s, also paid scant attention to emotions. Thus, it has been only in the past two decades that some sociologists have begun to focus analysis specifically on emotions and evolution.

The theoretical models of emotions and evolution divide into weak and strong programs regarding the depth of sociological implications of emotions forged in our distant past. The leading representatives of the weak program perspective are William Wentworth and his colleagues (Wentworth and Ryan 1992; Wentworth and Yardly 1994). They argue that it is important to understand the evolution of emotions, but only insofar as evolution sets the stage at the beginning of the play and moves off stage once the play is in motion. Then, historical, cultural, and social factors take over prime importance in understanding emotions. Emotions were part of the evolutionary cauldron of humanity, but emotions play no important causal role in shaping our later history. The leading representatives of a stronger theoretical program are Turner (2000) and Hammond (2003, 2004). They argued that it is indeed important to understand the evolutionary origin of emotions, but it is also important to recognize how the early development of emotions continues to impact social change in later history.

Both the strong and weak sociological models for linking emotions and evolution share certain characteristics and common starting postulates. All agree that getting the very beginning right is crucial to sociology. Most sociological analysis has paid virtually no attention to our context of origin (Massey 2002). However, if we do not get the start right in our analysis, we

MICHAEL HAMMOND • Department of Sociology, University of Toronto, Toronto, Ontario, Canada M5S 2J4 are unlikely to get later developments right. Take the example of astrophysics. Why are those scientists so interested in the first minutes or even the first seconds of the universe? This is not simply some strange academic obsession. It is a belief that if we could just figure out the start, many of the problematical qualities of the present would no longer be so mysterious. Sociologists studying emotions and evolution also believe that a solid beginning will dramatically improve the theoretical strength of our modeling of later developments.

All of the models analyzed here also agree that there is no strong biogrammar or bioprogramming that details the behavioral specifics for human social interaction. In popular vocabulary, there is not much in the way of a "gene for" some social action. There are no hard-wired instructions, but there are some tools that predispose humans to pursue sociality in particular ways. Emotions are part of this tool kit. All models agree that emotions permeate every aspect of social life, including the so-called rational-choice decisions in our lives. Increased emotionality is at the heart of the biological evolution of the species, and this emotionality has left its mark everywhere in our lives.

In addition, all of the theoretical models analyzed here have some element of a "just so" narrative, referring to Kipling's famous stories such as "How the Leopard Got His Spots" and "How the Camel Got His Hump." Kipling's fanciful stories of how things in the world came to be as they are stand as classic models of stories that begin at the end and work backward in a more or less plausible fashion to a beginning. Evolutionary analysis often cannot avoid taking on this form of argument, because we are at the end and the beginning is so distant that it cannot be studied directly. While recognizing the limitations in this kind of reconstruction, these evolutionary stories can be important in focusing our attention on just how certain mechanisms or behavioral patterns evolved and continue to operate today (Turner 2000).

In order to select issues relevant to most sociologists, many aspects of the relationship between evolution and emotions will not be considered here. For instance, there are competing models tracing the origin of emotions in terms of reactions to stimuli and in terms of reactions to the appraisal of those stimuli. Thus, Rolls (1998) and Damasio (1994) take up once again the James-Lange-Cannon struggle over the true nature of emotions. There are also different models concerning the origin of the role of emotions in facilitating the storage and retrieval of memories in the evolutionary expansion of human cognitive capacities (Rolls 1998). These are important issues, especially in relation to basic definitions of emotions and feelings, but they do not necessarily have major sociological implications.

EVOLUTIONARY EXISTENTIALISM

For Wentworth and his colleagues (Wentworth and Ryan 1992; Wentworth and Yardly 1994), the primary importance of an evolutionary perspective on emotions is to understand how they frame the basic parameters of the human condition. Evolution itself, or the biology of emotions, is ultimately secondary in relation to the comparative impact of the social construction of emotions in specific circumstances. Still, it is our evolutionary past that sets the stage for any such construction. First, emotions serve as a bridge between motivational systems based on hard-wired instructions for social behavior to systems based on learning and flexibility. We did not evolve from instinctually driven beings to rational cognitive beings. We evolved into emotional beings with amazing cognitive capacities, but, nonetheless, our "deep sociality" is emotional at the core. This is the same basic idea that Collins (1993) refers to in his classic analysis of the limitations of the rational-choice theoretical model. We may be rational in our pursuit of certain goals or values, but those ends only have an impact because of the emotional release associated with them.

Given the paucity of our instinctual heritage, even though emotions can be unsettling and disruptive, we are helpless without them. Without emotions, we cannot evaluate options in even the most mundane of circumstances. For Wentworth, complex emotionality is the key to rapid and relevant information processing. Emotions connect different levels of the brain processing information. Emotions facilitate learning and memory storage. This is the same idea that the neuroscientist Damasio (1994) made so forcefully in his famous attack on the Cartesian separation of mind and emotion marking so much of Western intellectual history. As Damasio was able to show with his brain-damaged patients who did not have normal access to affective responses, even something as simple as choosing among alternative times and dates for a doctor's appointment becomes an overwhelmingly complex undertaking. Strong emotions, and especially strong negative emotions, can bring decision-making to a halt. However, the lack of even the most basic emotional response has the same consequence. Without emotional weighting, the efficient sorting and recall of complex information is simply not possible. So much of this occurs unconsciously that we are often unaware of these processes at work, but when something such as a car accident or other trauma cuts off emotional responsiveness, then we can see clearly the essential role of emotions in the everyday structure of our cognitive task performance. In Damasio's now famous phrase, reason is nowhere pure.

For evolutionary existentialists, emotions sort out behavioral options into meaningful categories that carry rewards for following one path of action as opposed to another. Emotions provide the physiological impact that can give real weight to a conscience or a moral imperative. Shame and guilt are the prime examples of this moralizing role for emotions. They can give gravity to any social construction to which individuals are emotionally tied. They can transform an ultimately arbitrary rule of behavior into something that appears very meaningful to the individual bathed in the emotional release tied to obeying or disobeying that rule.

For Wentworth, emotions are also a basic form of communication among humans. It was in part this communication role that sparked the original interest of Darwin in emotions. The psychologist Ekman (1982) spent his lifetime demonstrating how finely tuned the human face is for exhibiting emotions in all kinds of social interaction. Wentworth believes that reading facial emotions actually predated the emergence of complex spoken communication in humans, and that the development of more complex forms of language and social structure was only possible with a parallel development in emotions and emotional sophistication. Ekman felt that the study of the face and emotions might cast light on the evolutionary origin of basic emotions universal to all human cultures. He rejects a radical constructionist position that sees all emotions as being wholly shaped by specific social conditions. As an evolutionary thinker, Ekman opposes this extreme cultural relativism, and he argues that facial analysis points to six primary emotions: happiness, fear, anger, sadness, surprise, and disgust. Wentworth recognizes that there are some basic emotions, but their range is small, and their release is more a matter of culture than biology. Primary emotions might provide a basis for the elaboration of secondary emotions and even more complex emotions built upon this deep foundation, but the foundation itself is of secondary importance in comparison to the social factors shaping the expression and interpretation of emotions. Once again, evolution sets the stage and then basically plays no further important role in the human drama.

THE EVOLUTIONARY BIOLOGY OF EMOTIONS

Turner (2000) took a much more ambitious approach to the study of emotions and evolution. He too is interested in the existential framing of human behavior by emotions, but he also believes that much more can be learned from an investigation into the specifics of the evolution of emotions in our distant past. Most important, he tries to show how the evolution of emotions led to a situation in which we have two competing sets of emotionally loaded activity patterns rooted in our context of origin and still shaping behavior today. Reflecting our general origins among the great apes and our own specific context of origin, we are a compromise species, craving strong emotional attachments and, at the same time, bridling against the constraints in closed social circles laid out by these strong interpersonal ties. This two-sidedness is rooted deeply in our biology, and it is not just the product of historically specific ideologies and social structures.

Turner (2000) argues that it is illusory to try to detach human biology from the modern sociocultural world because our world is made possible by our hominoid neuroanatomy and is constrained by this biological legacy. He roots this argument in the work of Maryanski (1992, 1993) on the differences in social structures between apes and monkeys and on the likely social characteristics of the last common ancestor to great apes and humans. Maryanski concludes that apes demonstrate more degrees of freedom, individualism, and mobility than monkeys, as well as demonstrating more relaxed status hierarchies and kinship networks. She also concludes that this was roughly the same pattern of the last common ancestor for the great apes and for humans. Given these loose-knit social patterns, when forced to move out of the forest, most apes were not well suited for adapting to a savanna ecological system, but humans were. What changes made this adaptation possible for one line of the great ape tradition and not others?

Turner (2000) argues that one of the key adaptations was to rewire the hominid brain to make emotions increasingly central to social life. With such a rewiring, humans could form stronger bonds than the more loose-knit bonds of apes and, with such bonds, increase the complexity of social organization. Turner (2000: 43–62) presents a detailed analysis of the many transformations required in such a shift, but perhaps the clearest evidence are some fascinating data on changes in the relative size of parts of the brain related to cognition and emotion in apes and humans when adjusted for general body size. The neocortex shows the greatest change in the evolution of humans, but there are also striking changes in the subcortical areas tied to emotion. Most of these subcortical areas are at least two times as large as those in apes. The result was a species with the tools to solve some of the social organization problems inherent in our origin as a low-sociality primate.

Turner (2000: 43–62) reverses the normal way that selection pressures are envisioned by arguing that there was a sociology of natural selection in terms of the problems of transforming a low-sociality animal. He argues that selection worked on six basic paths: mobilization of emotional energy, attunement of interpersonal responses, sanctioning, moral coding, valuing and exchanging resources, and rational decision-making. For instance, take the issue of selection pressure and moral coding. There is no morality without emotion. After all, how else could an abstract system of rules not backed up by a hard-wired biogrammar have an impact on social life itself? Adherence to moral codes and support for sanctions against breaking those codes are directly related to the emotional weight of those codes. This impact involves both positive and negative emotions and mixes of the two. Without a brain tuned to complex and subtle emotions, moral codes rooted in emotions could not approach the complexity of social organization required by humans in even the smallest of populations.

Similarly, thinking and decision-making become selection pressures for increased emotionality. Turner agrees with Damasio (1994) that there is no cognitive processing possible in the prefrontal cortex without emotions from the subcortical areas of the brain. If there is a selective advantage to an increased capacity in thinking and decision-making, there must also be an advantage to an increased capacity for emotions. Turner also stresses that the elaboration of emotions as a basis for social solidarity could only occur among highly self-aware individuals. Without strong bioprogramming, the selective pressure would be for individuals who could see themselves as objects and who could self-evaluate the consequences of their actions, both positive and negative. This self-awareness would give them a significant degree of self-control.

Turner's approach is similar to the evolutionary psychology of Tooby and Cosmides (1990), who posit "modules" in neurophysiology shaped by evolution to solve certain problems. For Tooby and Cosmides, natural selection is a hill-climbing feedback mechanism based on functional success in problem solving. Emotions solve different adaptive problems occurring repeatedly in our context of origin. One of the most important functions for emotion is mechanism orchestration, which coordinates different components of action into the right configurations at the right time. Guilt, fear, sexual jealously, and other emotions are part of our environment of evolutionary adaptedness (EEA). Each should have some hard wiring that can be isolated to some extent and explained in terms of natural selection. Of course, these modules continue to operate even as humans leave their EEA and move into other social worlds.

For Turner (2000: 72–79), there are four basic emotions with deep neurological modules shaped by natural selection: satisfaction-happiness, assertion-anger, aversion-fear, and disappointment-sadness. Three of the four are negative. There are then a number of variants on primary emotions. Turner organizes these variants in terms of low, moderate, and high intensity. For instance, low-intensity satisfaction-happiness leads to contentment, moderate-intensity to cheerfulness, and high-intensity to joy. In addition, there are emotions that combine different primary emotions. For instance, shame and guilt are crucial social emotions because they predispose individuals to monitor their actions in terms of negative consequences and to correct such actions if they in fact occur. Second-order emotions like guilt and shame combine first-order emotions like disappointment-sadness with aversion-fear and assertion-anger. They draw upon all three negative emotions, and that is one of the reasons why they can be so potent for shaping social behavior in a species with weak social bioprogramming. Also, there are important solidarity enhancing emotions that combine positive rewards with one or more negative emotions. For instance, mixing first-order emotions like satisfaction-happiness with aversion-fear can lead to second-order emotions like wonder and pride. Mixing satisfaction-happiness with disappointment-sadness can produce nostalgia and hope. These second-order emotions can be used to help forge stronger social ties between individuals and to group symbols such as those used in religion.

Turner further argues that these second-order emotions are so important that they probably have some specific wiring in the modules of the brain evolved for different emotion sets. Turner goes beyond Kemper's (1987) classic sociological model of the socially emergent quality of second-order emotions rooted in a small number of biologically based first-order emotions. Turner (2000) believes that complex emotions like guilt, shame, delight, depression, and nostalgia are more hard wired than constructed. As more and more high-technology research is being done on emotions, it already appears that Turner is at least partially correct. For instance, one study using functional magnetic resonance imaging demonstrated how one area of the brain lights up when individuals experience social rejection (Eisenberger et al. 2003). This suggests that there is at least some hard wiring for this socially important behavioral outcome. Turner (Turner and Maryanski 2005) has continued this line of investigation in regard to the possibility that there is some hard wiring for negative emotions to react to specific behaviors such as incest.

From the point of view of a deep structure approach, Turner (2000: 126–128) sees emotions as similar to Chomsky's model for language. There are some universal, pan-human modules in the human brain, giving humans emotional abilities similar to those for language. There are also some hard-wired aspects that make emotion and language learning comparatively easy, especially in the younger years, and there are grave consequences if these emotions are not expressed early. Thus, emotions should have a deep neurological substrate, not just for a few primary emotions shared by all primates but also for some more complex emotions that were crucial to the emergence of the human primate, such as shame and guilt. Like Wentworth, Turner believes that emotions as a mode of communication preceded spoken languages, and it was the elaboration of emotions that facilitated the elaboration of language and social organization. Thus, as neuroscientists come to possess more sophisticated technologies to study complex emotions, sociology will be left out in the cold if it does not find the means to link its analysis to deep, hard-wired aspects of emotion.

Furthermore, if emotions are like language in having a deep structure, these elements do not simply disappear in any particular social circumstance. The deep structure puts limits on the degree of relativism that is likely to appear. This is one of the reasons why Turner (2002) is not attracted to postmodernist theory. Postmodernism stresses the fragile nature of all social constructions and, hence, that there is a great deal of relativity in historical patterns. Turner is not a nineteenth-century-like linear theorist of social evolution, but his model of deep structure in emotions reveals that history is not a blank slate on which we can write most anything we want as soon as we realize that we are existentially free to do so.

Despite all the cognitive and motivational changes in the evolutionary emergence of the human species, Turner notes that we still possess the behavioral propensities of our distant common ancestor with the great apes. The Last Common Ancestor was mobile, individualistic, and autonomous, had low sociality, and was not prone to common pursuits (Turner 2000: 12–13). Because ancient tendencies for weak ties and autonomy were not extinguished, but instead were supplemented by new cognitive and affective capacities, humans can lay claim to two emotion reward systems. It was in regard to the new solidarity-enhancing systems that the most selective pressures were in play. However, those ancient systems are still there and capable of generating rewards for certain kinds of behaviors.

It is not surprising that since our species is something of a compromise between two evolutionary pasts, there is always some tension or even outright conflict between the individual and the collective. Given our dual natural history, ambivalence is going to be part of the human condition. Wentworth also draws attention to the intrinsic affective conflict between the individual and society, but this is only of passing interest in his modeling. For Turner, this ambivalence is more deeply grounded and more important in considering the implications of our complicated evolutionary past.

It should be noted that this ambivalence is not Freudian. Freud was very interested in human evolution, and, in part, his focus on sex was rooted in late nineteenth-century considerations of the role of reproductive success in human evolution (Sulloway 1979). After all, the practical expression of reproductive success was sex, and for a psychobiologist like Freud, his focus on sex was part of the greatest scientific revolution of the late nineteenth and early twentieth centuries, namely the science of evolution. In his own "just so" re-creations of our distant origins, Freud tried to trace the origins of contemporary ambivalence about sex to the first struggles over sexual access in the mists of prehistory. Turner's conception of the ambivalent nature of the imprint of the past on the present is much broader and more grounded in paleoanthropology, but it is part of the same analytical tradition dating back to Darwin and Freud.

Social Caging

How does this deep structure play itself out in our history? Maryanski and Turner (1992) argue that much of that history involves an increasing tension between our biological heritage and our social constructions. The hunting and gathering form of social organization was closest to that of our context of origin. Even though contemporary hunters and gatherers might somewhat distort those origins, it is clear that their loose and fluid structures, having a strong collective life mixed with a considerable degree of autonomy and freedom, have tremendous emotional appeal and staying power. Indeed, as we learn more about our distant past, it is evident that we could have left the foraging life long before we did. It seems that only when population pressure finally forced us to alter our production systems and settle down in order to support more individuals did we reluctantly alter our social world. The horticultural societies that first emerged after our exodus had significant social tensions in comparison to the world we had left behind. Humans are not hardwired collectivists, like a social herd or pack of animals. With horticulture, they found themselves increasingly locked in a cage of kinship. It was perhaps not as bad as the cage of power that would follow in the agrarian world, but it was difficult enough (Maryanski and Turner 1992: 91–95).

From this perspective, Turner objects to what he sees as the overidealization of preindustrial social life. Given our deep emotion structure, there was no easy transition from one cultural form to another. The first structures to emerge used kinship in an elaborate and highly restrictive manner in order to organize these larger populations. Residence, conjugal options, defense obligations, economic cooperation, and religious symbols were framed in terms of kinship and locked most individuals into a tight system. This rigidity facilitated the rise of special individuals to key positions in their organizational groupings. Power become more focused in the hands of a smaller part of the population. The status of women declined. Force and coercion became more a part of social life, involving both internal and external structures. Indeed, Turner argues that the intense emotional rituals so common to these societies, and so admired by many sociological theorists of solidarity like Durkheim, actually demonstrate how difficult things were. Only a culture under constant stress would need such intensive ritualization.

Turner argues that the emergence of warfare, territorial strife, and often bloody power succession struggles do not indicate that human biology is marked by an aggression gene or a territory gene. Even the concept of the selfish gene does not explain much about the emergence of these patterns. (Maryanski and Turner 1992: 110–112). Instead, Turner believes that this emergence is rooted in the contradiction between emotional rewards for fluid decentralist tendencies from our most distant biological past and the exigencies of more social organization with the exodus from our context of origin. These elements can never be fully reconciled, and it is no wonder that the resulting emotional dynamics have such wild swings and feed warfare and competition.

Turner does not deal directly with one aspect of this emergence. Hunting and gathering societies show many examples of the successful resistance to escalating inequality. For instance, as Boehm (1999) argues, there are clear emotional rewards for resisting the growth of inequality and maintaining a higher degree of freedom and autonomy. However, these rewards seem sufficient only under a very strict set of constraining conditions. Thus, even hunting and gathering societies with food storing and semipermanent living conditions demonstrate the beginnings of inequality inflation. In terms of emotional rewards, the questions are, given our early history in successfully resisting such dominance: Why should humans subordinate themselves with even moderate increases in social scale? What was handicapping their resistance compared to similar efforts in smaller-scale social worlds? As noted below, I try to extend this part of Turner's analysis by considering the emotional reward dynamics of long-term resistance to inflated inequality after the exodus.

Agrarian societies create the second cage, as power replaces kinship as the primary organizational principle for human groups. The agrarian social scale is larger in terms of population, urbanization, and surplus production, but the core dynamics of power concentration are the same as the kinship cage. As we move to an even larger social scale, kinship itself appears to be too constraining, and the state becomes the institution for the consolidation of power. Specific dynasties may collapse, but they are simply replaced by clone structures. Furthermore, once resources become concentrated, they are used to accumulate yet more, producing a self-escalating cycle.

Although Turner does not deal directly with the emotional rewards that may be at the core of this self-escalation, I take up this issue in the next section.

Turner's (2000) model of the contradictory elements in human nature produces a different vision of industrialization than that found in other stage models of evolution (Maryanski and Turner 1992: 139–146). Turner challenges the Weberian tradition of a third cage, the "iron cage" of rational-legal authority. Although clearly acknowledging the negative aspects of industrialization, especially early industrialization, he also notes that even these early systems were, comparatively speaking, less confining, more individualistic, more mobile, and freer. Thus, there were many emotional characteristics of the individual in the industrial world that were actually closer in form to the role of the individual in hunting and gathering societies. Kinship began to return to a model more like our context of origin, with a more mobile and egalitarian nuclear family. The fragmentation of these complex industrial cultures created many niches where individual autonomy could thrive. Ironically, many of these were in the massive urban assemblies that were so hated by many critics of industrialization. In the city, the air was freer, even if it was also polluted. The monetization of everything made it virtually impossible to impose the same kind of cultural conformity that could exist in earlier postexodus societies.

Thus, with industrialization, history came partially back to where it started. However, this is not the return seen by Marx in his stage model of communism, fulfilling the social evolutionary destiny of primitive communism after the long march in the postexodus wilderness. Given our deep biology, there is no room for utopian thinking in Turner's vision of evolution and emotion. Still, given our ape ancestry, Turner argues that there is reason to assume that most individuals will adapt satisfactorily to the developments of the so-called postmodern world based on less hierarchical production units, more flexible roles, and more indirect social relations. For the most part, these changes are extensions of long-term trends in industrialization that, as a by-product, return us to many of the basic emotional patterns of our evolutionary context of origin.

A wide variety of researchers should find Turner's model very useful. The problems at the heart of much sociological research are the same basic problems that humans faced in their context of origin. Take for example Turner's (2000) list of six paths of evolution in hominids moving to higher degrees of sociality and requiring an elaboration of emotionality in order to make that change. Mobilization of emotional energy, attunement of interpersonal responses, sanctioning, moral coding, valuing and exchanging resources, and rational decision-making are both ancient and current problems. Turner presents an elaborate reconstruction that will have insights for anyone studying these core issues in a more contemporary setting. Similarly, the dual-heritage model of social evolution serves well to make us think twice about the adaptability of humans to changing social circumstances. Anyone studying long-term change in response to different social structures in different times and circumstances will gain much from considering their specific problem in terms of its relation to the evolutionary origins of our species.

EMOTIONS AND SOCIAL EVOLUTION

For Turner, in the postexodus world, there is a fundamental tension between two aspects of our evolutionary history, and it is in part this tension that drives social evolution. For Hammond (1999, 2003, 2004), there is a different tension in postexodus conditions. Hammond's model focuses on emotions as motivational rewards, particularly in terms of Turner's description of the positive side of the continuum of primary emotions and the variants and elaborations of those emotions. The model posits two tracks of preconscious emotional reward rules. One set of rules limits rewards and dampens the extension of interest. For instance, they are at the heart of habituation to familiar arousers and of diminishing marginal utility that discounts the emotional rewards for additional arousers. The second set of rules pushes against those limits and heightens interest by providing a reward bonus for special qualities such as elevated contrasts and novelty. Hammond believes that in the evolutionary origin of humanity, there was an imbalance in favor of special arouser packages with interest-extending bonuses over otherwise attractive packages lacking these enhanced qualities. The selective logic of this long-term imbalance was to predispose humans to create special social structures such as religion that could produce these enhancements on a regular basis. He also believes that the enhancement favoring imbalance in this push-pull of arousal release rules created some emotion reward windows that mark social constructions along the historical path from the exodus to the present. From this perspective, when even partially released from the constraints of our earliest history, inflated social inequality was, unfortunately, the emergent social structure most able to take advantage of these emotion reward bonuses. Thus, emotional factors do not just frame these developments, but they play a causal role in their emergence.

Hammond (2003, 2004) begins with an analysis of the role of evolution and emotions in the emergence of religion. As Maryanski and Turner (1992) emphasize, it was crucial for early humans to expand the size and reliability of their social networks in order to survive in a wider range of ecological circumstances. Hammond (2003) notes that such expansion could be done on a tie-by-tie basis. This did occur to some extent, but in terms of time and effort, this is an expensive way to expand networks. However, there was an alternative way to expand networks through triangulation. If a number of individuals all have a deep emotional commitment to a common arouser package, then there is a framework to exchange a wide variety of goods and services based on this common linkage, rather than on more personal linkages. The network of trustworthy exchanges could, therefore, be expanded.

The question becomes how to get humans interested in creating such bridges for expanded social networks. One means would be to redirect preconsciously some emotional rewards already established for personal attachments to these additional objects. However, how would we encourage this redirection? Hammond (2003) posits a model of preconscious arousal release rules with an imbalance in favor of the interest-heightening rules over interest-dampening rules like variety discounting. This push-pull would make the creation of an additional set of attachments irresistible.

Variety discounting limits the rewards that otherwise might occur from having additional attractive arousers available. This pattern has been studied most extensively in neurophysiological experiments on such activities as eating. For example, Rolls (1998) and his colleagues (Rolls et al. 1981, 1986) have shown clearly some of the neurophysiological changes in discounting that occur when a variety of foods are offered to monkeys. Variety increases the interest in food, but not on a proportionate basis. Instead, the variety is depreciated, and the rate of discounting increases as the total amount of variety increases. Thus, offering five different kinds of attractive food increases food interest, but does not produce 5 times the interest. Offering 10 different foods extends interest once again, but not by doubling the interest produced by 5 foods. Instead, there is some declining marginal utility with each increase in food offering. This volume discounting is a very general pattern that has appeared in species after species, and the selective advantage appears to go to arousal release patterns that are generous in rewarding variety, but not too generous.

We do not have the neurophysiological tools to study emotion rewards in humans in the same manner that we can study neurons and synaptic alteration in rewarding food preferences in other species, but the assumption here is that the general patterns of rewards are going to be much the same. Rewards are rewards, and once natural selection had created a useful set of rules for appetite and hedonistic activities, it is most plausible that the same small bag of tricks will be used again in regard to emotional rewards.

To counter dampening rules, there are also many circumstances in which it is advantageous for individuals to pursue additional variety. From the point of view of natural selection, an interest in variety has to have some flexibility of outcome built into it. To encourage this flexible pursuit, a number of bonus reward mechanisms are possible. Humans exhibit at least three means to slow the volume discounting of rewards by providing some arousal release bonuses.

First, there is the elevated contrast bonus. If attractive arousers with higher-contrast qualities can be found, then additional rewards can be triggered. This was evident in Rolls et al.'s (1981, 1986) studies of variety food preferences. Even if it occurred later in an interest curve, when general interest was in decline, the presentation of a higher-contrast arouser produced a spike that slowed discounting. The more elevated contrast spikes an individual can use, the more interest can be extended when fueled by these rewards.

Second, there is the variety spacing bonus. Extensive variety can make possible the spacing of the reappearance of any one arouser, and this allows for more time for resensitization. Repetition produces desensitization (Mullen and Linz 1995). The longer that repetition can be delayed by having alternative arousers available, the more likely it will be that an attractive arousal spike occurs with the reappearance of the stimulus.

Third, there is the novelty bonus. Novel arousers can also produce an additional rewarding arousal spike, at least until habituation sets in with repetition and growing familiarity for the stimulus. Altogether, arouser packages offering high contrasts, wide variety, and novelty are going to be the most effective in triggering the maximum rewards. Each offers an attractive arousal bonus that can be very appealing and extend interest fueled by such rewards.

Although there do not exist at present the technical means to demonstrate these patterns directly in positive emotion rewards, the assumption is that the same bonuses exist for those rewards as for other rewards that we are able to study. It is important to note that many emotional reward dynamics are based on preconscious processes. Natural selection is unlikely to favor complete conscious control of these rewards, even in a species as intelligent as ours. For a species with many interests that must be regularly met, it is simply too risky to have an open-ended reward system that individuals could consciously control and perhaps limit. Habituation is the most common example of this preconscious discounting. Faced with the repetition of even the most attractive novel arouser, rewarding arousal release begins to decrease, and even the awesome cognitive capacities of our species can do little to stop this discounting. The same is true for the volume discounting limiting the rewards for arouser additions. Of course this means that the antidiscounting arousal bonuses also have an important preconscious element. If they were under more conscious control, then there would be virtually no limits to the ways in which humans took advantage of those rewards. Metaphorically speaking, natural selection does not seem to be attracted to no limit games.

This preconscious discounting also raises the issue of what costs an individual might consciously be willing to bear in order to gain access to additional arousers. If these additions are discounted, then individuals are not going to be eager to put out the same time and effort or face the same negative emotions or risks that they might have paid for the initial arousers. If five times the variety produces only two times the rewards, most will be unwilling to pay five times the costs for five times the variety. If costs are not controlled or reduced, then individuals will eventually decide that the additional costs are just not worth the depreciated rewards. The best situation in this regard is to have some form of cost savings; that is, the additional arousers must become available without a parallel addition in access costs. Most species have little control over arouser packaging, but humans have more options in this regard. These considerations are particularly important in regard to antidiscounting bonuses such as extra variety, regular novelty, elevated contrasts, and access to cost savings. Hammond (2003) labels these special arouser combinations as enhancements, offering some additional arouser quality without a parallel increase in access costs. Of course in the real world, all of these different bonuses are not available all of the time, but these elements are always there as a potential influence on human actions fueled by emotional rewards.

The Enhancement Imperative

What evidence is there that these emotional reward rules do in fact operate so as to make it imperative that humans seek out a special set of additional arousers offering these bonus reward possibilities? Hammond (2003) argues that high-technology neurophysiological studies of arousal release in religion appear to demonstrate this very phenomenon (Joseph 1996; Newberg et al. 2001; Saver and Rubin 1997). There does not appear to be separate reward wiring for religious stimuli. Instead, they appear to piggyback other reward releasers, such as neurotransmitters associated with positive emotional arousal in personal attachments (Kirkpatrick 2004). How could natural selection facilitate such a piggybacking without creating too much confusion among the different arouser packages using part of the same reward systems? The answer is to use a classic variety depreciation rule and begin discounting early for additions with the same general characteristics, such as those possessed by other human beings. Reward a small number of such personal ties, but even with significant rewarding arousal release still in reserve, begin to erode the rewards for yet more similar ties. With many attractive rewards still available, this early screening shifts the balance of interest in favor of somehow finding additional enhanced arousers with sufficient bonuses to counter this dampening. For instance, since there are no great natural differences among individuals, humans would then be predisposed to seek out another set of high-contrast arousers that could tap these additional rewards.

In our evolutionary context of origin, with small and dispersed populations using simple technologies, where could such contrasts be found except in imaginary social constructions like religion? With the addition of sacred beings and spirits who have enough humanlike qualities to use the personal attachment reward system, but who also have some extraordinary qualities that humans can only dream of, these extraordinary arousers could then piggyback the reward systems originally evolved for interpersonal ties. Since these stimuli would be most powerful when constructed by a group of individuals working together, such arousers could also provide the basis for a triangulation of attachments and network expansion.

Such a social construction is also appealing in terms of the access cost issues for an increasing variety of arousers. After all, in the face of variety discounting of rewards, it is not as if this additional arousal release is going to be greater than that for strong personal ties. If costs such as time, effort, information gathering and processing, negative emotions, or risk escalate as attractive contrasts escalate, and if the rewards remain significant but still the same in total intensity, then individuals will be paying more for something that they received elsewhere for less. This is not an attractive option in the long run. The solution is to offer an enhancement (i.e., to offer high-contrast stimuli without a parallel increase in access costs). Once again, religion is ideal for enhancements, because the imaginary beings created in religion are just that—imaginary. We can use our expanded cognitive capacities to create another package of rewarding attachments without too great an expansion of costs. The same logic applies to the anthropomorphizing of the natural world in religion. By recasting that world in human terms, another set of striking stimuli is created that can piggyback on the reward systems for attachment and not require too many costs for such additions.

All of these arouser additions could also provide yet more arousal spikes by making it possible to space the reappearance of any one stimulus such that repetition is reduced. This would allow more time for resensitization to occur and for further bonus arousal spikes to be added to the reward package. These arousal add-ons provide another opportunity for humans to reshape their social world in order to squeeze out some additional benefits. Of course, since these spacing bonuses are significant but generally modest in nature, the access costs that individuals would be willing to pay for these spikes are also limited. Once again, the best add-ons would offer attractive arousal release without a parallel increase in access costs. This is just what enhancement packages in religion provide.

Natural selection can work on areas like synaptic alteration in the electrochemical transmission of neural messages, as well as on hormone and other neurochemical releases to shape the rules for rewarding arousal release (Carlson 1995). Natural selection can also favor individuals seeking enhanced arouser variety on a dual track of emotion rewards, and in our context of origin, individuals would have little choice of where else to turn except to the construction of social structures offering arouser variety such as found in religion. Individuals who take part in these social creations would have larger and more reliable networks and, hence, more successful reproduction rates. Metaphorically speaking, natural selection has no interest in religion per se, but only in its role as a network extender. There is no need to have, in popular terms, a religion gene. Using preconscious arousal release rules to make it a virtual imperative that humans find some such network extender, religion is the most likely creation to emerge in our context of origin. It offers the best ratio of high-contrast attractive arouser additions without a parallel increase in access costs. Since these religious arousers piggyback on personal attachment rewards, they will feel every bit as real as ties to actual human beings. Natural selection has little interest in correcting such illusions because they have a selective value for an individual. The piggybacking is not always neat and clean because natural selection is not interested in neatness, but, rather, in mixes and compromises that produce regular benefits more often than not.

Inequality and Emotion Rewards

What other structures might extend social networks using enhanced arouser packages? Hammond (2004) argues that ascriptive inequality appears to be another candidate. For instance, gender solidarity groups would be most useful in our context of origin, especially among males. Given our distant evolutionary origins in the great apes, male-male competition should be a regular occurrence, but the cooperative hunting of humans requires different patterns of behavior. How do we limit such competition? Once again, as in the case of religion, we shape preconscious emotion release rules so as to make something like male gender solidarity appealing. Scientists are not as advanced in their studies of the neurophysiology of status rewards as they are in the study of attachment dynamics, but there is some interesting evidence in monkeys tying successful status acquisition to neurotransmitters like serotonin, which, in turn, has been associated with positive emotional arousal (Bramer et al. 1994; Knutson et al. 1998). The assumption is that neuroscientists will eventually unravel the technical specifics of status rewards, just as they are doing with so many other reward systems in humans and nonhumans.

Male ascriptive inequality requires the cooperation of lower- and higher-status males so that imputed differences do not have to be actually demonstrated in each and every case. For such inequality, there are a number of options with regard to the natural selection of emotion reward rules favoring such cooperation. One possibility is that there was volume discounting with early screening of basic variety rewards for status differentiation among all individuals. This would quickly depreciate the value of additional status rewards, offering the same ratio of attractive qualities to costs and shifting the balance of interest to enhanced-status arousers; that is, additional status contrasts would have to be offered without a parallel increase in access costs. This is precisely what ascription offers to males in these circumstances. Males are awarded extra status, but they are not required to actually demonstrate that they merit such additions in a full and open competition with females. Instead, females are ascriptively excluded from status competition that would be potentially costly for males. After all, since there is only moderate sexual dimorphism in humans compared to our evolutionary cousins, a full and open competition would mean that many males would not be awarded extra status or that their status awards would be diluted by the increased competition.

Another option to make gender solidarity appealing was to use the variety-spacing bonus; that is, natural selection could have made use of the extra rewarding release that is possible when arousers can be spaced sufficiently to allow for extensive resensitization to occur. The addition of ascriptive arousers could mean that any specific arouser did not have to be repeated as often when seeking status rewards. With less repetition, there was less desensitization and more rewards could be reaped. Since these ascriptive differences were moderate in most hunting and gathering cultures, individuals would not be predisposed to incur significant costs to access these additions; but as noted above, this is just what ascription provides: some nice status variety additions with a spacing bonus and without too great a cost.

Like many questions about our distant evolutionary past, we may never be able to sort out fully the beginnings of the emergence of these social patterns. However, whatever the bonus rewards were at the beginning, the long-term consequences are the same. It is the enhanced arouser packages that will be the most appealing and that will predominate. Once again, because these ascriptive additions can be piggybacked on classic status differentiation rewards, they will seem real. The preconscious nature of these rewards means that individuals will be attracted to such additions without having a complete understanding of their actions. It is not that individuals are somehow aware that a social constructionlike ascriptive inequality is really a false front, but it is so appealing that they go along willingly with this illusion. Humans, therefore, create ideologies that provide a rationalization for their actions. However, it is the underlying emotion reward dynamics that are driving these creations and make these creations feel so real.

In comparison to religion, status rewards are somewhat more complicated within a population, since there is always a zero-sum element to status competition. Individuals are rewarded for successfully differentiating themselves from others, but there are also rewards for limiting the potential dominance that others might have over an individual (Boehm 1999). In most of our earliest history, these emotional rewards have effectively limited the expansion of inequality. Of course, enhancements could be created that magnify differences among all individuals, thereby escalating the rewards for those successful in demonstrating their superiority in one manner or another. For instance, male-male differentiation could be inflated, and there would be emotional release rewards for those males successful in dominating such an escalation of inequality. However, there is bound to be resistance to this particular inflation, since it necessitates that most males lose relative status, along with most females. Gender ascription offers some enhancements, but it spreads these rewards over a greater percentage of the population. Thus, it is the most likely enhancement to emerge in our context of origin when resistance to overly inflated differentiation is usually successful.

Natural selection must also have had a role in shaping the temporary escalation of inequality in our distant past. These elevated contrasts are seen in the emergence of leaders during temporary assemblies of normally nomadic populations, as well as in the emergence of war captains in periods of strife (Keeley 1996). Both of these circumstances create situations in which there is likely to be decreased resistance to escalated status differentiation by some individuals, at least in the short term. For instance, in times of warfare, even small differences among individuals in such areas as physical skills or tolerance of risk take on extra importance and make it possible to extract extra status rewards in crisis situations. These kinds of circumstances must have occurred regularly enough to be a factor in the biological evolution of emotional rewards for expanded status. Natural selection would create the capacity to make these extra rewards temporarily available from time to time. Once again, this could be done through reward bonuses for elevated contrasts and for additional arouser spacing.

The Exodus and Emotion Rewards

All of these changes set the stage for other linkages of evolution and emotions when the exodus from our context of origin makes possible permanent rather than temporary status escalations. If human populations began to abandon the nomadic life and settle down, it would become possible to have a regular, long-term accumulation of social, material, and sexual resources that could not occur with nomadism. Settling down would erode the role of dispersal and fissioning as a response to social strains, such as the attempt by some to increase their relative status at the expense of others. After the exodus, what would happen with preconscious emotion reward rules that were forged in our context of origin? Hammond (2004) argues that these rules would shift interest toward the pursuit of additional status differentiation and, simultaneously, they would handicap resistance to such an expansion.

A few could acquire an extensive variety of status arousers useful in countering the volume discounting of emotion release rules. Using bonuses from the second track of emotion rules, they could attack depreciation rules in a way not regularly possible in our context of origin. They could take more regular advantage of the use of high-contrast additions to counter the impact of arousal discounting. Similarly, they could more regularly use the variety spacing and even regular novelty add-ons to slow depreciation. The additions do not all have to be high intensity in terms of their impact. Most will be of low or moderate intensity, but their appeal is still great because of the total arousal release made possible over time. Of course, those able to tap these emotion bonuses could also use their position to limit the costs of such actions. They could seek out a multiple-status differentiation without paying a parallel increase in access costs; that is, they would be fueled by another set of enhanced arousers. The emergence of the "big man" and then the chief, as well as the ideologies surrounding these creations, can be seen as partly rooted in these emotion release dynamics.

Indeed, the "big man" appears as one of the first examples of individuals using emergent social structures to accumulate as large an arouser package as is possible and to use that package in one way or another to counter variety discounting. The "big man" not only seeks out magnified status differentiation but also a whole host of add-ons that accompany this role. The accumulation of material goods, even if it is temporary, can be very appealing in terms of antidiscounting bonuses; so too can the accumulation of sexual partners. The advantage of magnified differentiation is that it makes possible arouser accumulation without a parallel increase in access costs. Demand 5 or 10 times the status and put out some additional effort and time, without 5 or 10 times the access costs. This is in part possible because with inflated inequality, it is other individuals who are bearing some or even most of the costs of such positions. In one way or another, a few can take advantage of the labor of many to create these special arouser packages. The larger the social scale, the greater the cost savings for any individuals able to sit atop that social world.

The exodus from our context of origin facilitating the emergence of these inflated-status figures also handicaps a parallel increase in resistance to such a development. The problem is that whereas status accumulation can pick up a host of bonus add-ons, it is difficult for antiaccumulation resistance to acquire the same bonuses. This is not too important in normal hunting-gathering circumstances, where dispersal and fissioning provide a low-cost means of resistance to those trying to escalate inequality. However, with permanent settlements and the erosion of this dispersal option, the balance of arousal rewards between status accumulation and resistance to such accumulation begins to erode. The motivational edge fueled by emotion reward bonuses begins to shift more and more toward the inflation of inequality and away from long-term resistance to such changes. There could be virtually constant short-term resistance, but that is not going to reverse the basic status-inflation package. Thus, once again, there seems to be two emotion reward packages in play. One is fed by the pursuit of inequality, and the other is fed by successful efforts in resisting dominance. In our context of origin, the balance was only slightly in favor of the former, but with the exodus, the imbalance continued to grow. Altogether, the focus on the differential capacities of different interests to pile on additional emotion rewards casts a new light on the classic exodus problem of explaining just why humans seemed to lose their long-demonstrated capacities to resist status inflation.

The first stage of social evolution rooted in emotional reward dynamics should see the emergence of social structures that make permanent the inflated differences that were previously only temporarily available. This emergence is not a product of natural selection itself but, rather, a by-product of rules established through natural selection in another set of circumstances. It is social evolution, not biological evolution. Just as there is no "territory" gene behind the emergence of territorial social structures, there is also no "power" gene that was a part of human nature laying dormant for most of our early history. It is not necessary to postulate an innate human desire for power and control, as Sanderson (2001) does in order to fuel his vision of social evolution. Instead, power is an emergent need providing a means to extend rewarding arousal release in the face of strong reward limitation rules. The trail of social evolution should be marked by structures fueled in part by emotion release triggered by the regular provision of enhanced packages offering some high-contrast, widely spaced, and sometimes novel arousers. The historical path is not that wide because there is only a rather narrow range of structures that can offer such a potent combination of permanence, cost savings, variety, contrast, and novelty.

From this perspective on the relationship of emotions and evolution, status inflation should continue to expand as social scale expands. Increased scale would make greater and greater arouser contrasts possible, even as habituation erodes the long-term impact of those contrasts, hence leading to a need for yet more contrasts. Without the constraints of our context of origin, self-escalation is virtually built into arousal release bonuses like elevated variety and novelty. For instance, if novelty becomes even a small part of an arousal reward package, there is a self-escalating quality. The most common form of novelty is much more of something that an individual already values. As habituation erodes any particular novelty bonus, the individual most likely seeks after another bonus; but to be truly novel and have a major reward release, something extra special is going to be required. Once that plateau is reached, habituation sets in again, and so does the escalation. If individuals begin to rely on novelty, then novelty is quickly going to be tied to elevated contrasts. Of course, paying full price for such a ladder of novel arousers is not a good strategy, since habituation demands more arouser contrasts for the same rewarding release. Inflated inequality is the ideal vehicle to deflect these costs to others, but this requires an increasing concentration of power and centralization of resources. Thus, the patterns driven in part by these rewards, such as the increasing concentration of power and the centralization of resources, should be marked by self-escalation.

Only another enhancement engine could reverse this inflation. For individuals in the pursuit of enhanced arousers, high technology is like inflated inequality, offering unequaled opportunities to exploit these preconscious release rules. By having machines absorb much of the effort costs, technology too can offer permanent enhanced arouser packages with high contrasts, wide variety, and regular novelty. These additional rewards would also shift the dynamics in opposition to the hyperinequality of agrarian systems. Resisting dominance would now have its own emotional rewards, plus numerous add-ons that would come with any success in such resistance that made available more access to technologically enhanced production and consumption.

An understanding of these preconscious emotion-release rules in action could, in turn, help us to understand a variety of phenomena in the modern world. Take the example of the exploding area of happiness studies. One of the few consistent findings in this research is that general measures of happiness tend to increase up to a certain level of per capita income and then level off. Further increases in per capita income have little or no effect on the overall reporting of happiness (Easterbrook 2003). This is what should occur if individuals are using income not just to purchase the basics necessary to life itself but also to add as much arouser variety as possible in order to tap the bonus emotion release rules. Once again, just as in the case of power and inequality, emotional bonuses for happiness are self-escalating. This means that more will be required over time just to have the same amount of rewarding release, a total that is topped with bonuses for escalating contrasts, variety spacing, and novelty. Once the expected total regularly includes these add-ons, habituation sets in, and then only more add-ons can maintain the same elevated level of rewards. This is what appears to be happening in general happiness-level surveys. This dual-track model also indicates why having more, and even having a great deal more, of something does not necessarily mean that a feeling of scarcity disappears. Elevated emotion release levels generate constant scarcity in the face of preconscious volume discounting.

It is a truism that humans always seem to want more, but it is important that social scientists make efforts to specify just how such a need emerges. Hammond's (2003) model demonstrates that the distant origins of this desire for more were in part rooted in the natural selection of arousal release rules that favored the creation of an additional special class of arousers, even when other arousers existed that had already demonstrated their attractiveness. The extension of an attachment interest into religion was the archetypal example of the origin of the need for more. More personal ties to other human beings were simply not enough for our species. Preconscious emotional reward release rules were set such that the balance of interest pushed individuals beyond the alternative of more personal ties. The range of interests touched by this imbalance would grow and multiply with the exodus, and humans would come to want more and more for more and more interests.

Hammond's (2004) also suggests that some interests are going to expand more than others because they are better vehicles for emotion bonuses. Just as the dual track of dampening and heightening emotion rewards has a differential impact on the appeal of inflated inequality and on the appeal of avoiding such inequality, it should have an unbalanced impact on altruistic and more self-interested behavior. Once again, emotion bonuses for altruism, just like add-ons for inequality resistance, will normally be harder to accumulate than extra rewards for more self-centered behaviors. As social scale grows, the imbalance between these behaviors should also grow. Similarly, the material expression of interests through high-technology enhancements in mass production and consumption should be very appealing in terms of possible reward add-ons, and these enhancements should eventually conquer emotional alternatives based on simpler technologies. The investigation of these patterns can proceed without having to posit some fixed biogrammar or some hard-wired interest to cover each of these emergent phenomena. If some emotions regularly serve as rewards and if these emotion rewards are governed by the same rules as other rewards, then these rules should be a key part of the deep structure in the pattern of social evolution. Indeed, one of the sociologically most important parts of our biological heritage is a dual-track package of interest-dampening and interest-extending emotion reward rules forged in our context of origin, but still operating today.

CONCLUSION

There is a continuum of models linking evolution and emotions, moving from the weak-impact model of Wentworth to the stronger models of Turner (2000) and Hammond (2003). Despite their many differences, all of these models stress the importance of understanding the earliest origins of emotions in human social life. Without such a perspective, it is easy to underestimate the wide impact of emotions on shaping all aspects of our social life. Whatever problem sociologists of emotion decide to study, they should make one part of their analysis an investigation of the evolutionary history of that problem. Has it always been a part of human social interaction and, therefore, a possible factor in the evolutionary origins of our species? If so, what can an appreciation of this evolution add to the analysis? If it appears to be emergent, then what aspects of our most distant past might still have an impact on that emergence? All three models considered here have offered a number of suggestions and conjectures rooted in the common belief that evolution and emotions are inseparable, and there should almost always be some additional insights that can be gained by a consideration of this tangled past.

REFERENCES

Boehm, Christopher. 1999. *Hierarchy in the Forest: The Evolution of Egalitarian Behavior*. Cambridge, MA: Harvard University Press.

Bramer, Gary, Michael Raleigh, and Michael McGuire. 1994. "Neurotransmitters and Social Status." Pp. 75–91 in *Social Stratification and Socioeconomic Inequality*, edited by L. Ellis. Westport, CT: Praeger.

Carlson, Neil. 1995. *Foundations of Physiological Psychology*. Boston: Allyn and Bacon.

Collins, Randall. 1993. "Emotional Energy as the Common Denominator of Rational Action." *Rationality and Society* 5: 203–230.

Damasio, Antonio. 1994. *Descartes' Error: Emotion, Reason, and the Human Brain*. New York: Putnam.

Darwin, Charles. 1872. *The Expression of the Emotions in Man and Animals*. London: Oxford University Press.

Easterbrook, Gregg. 2003. *The Progress Paradox*. New York: Random House.

Eisenberger, Naomi, Mathew Lieberman, and Kipling Williams. 2003. "Does Rejection Hurt? An MRI Study of Social Exclusion." *Science* 302: 290–292.

Ekman, Paul. 1982. *Emotions in the Human Face*. Cambridge: Cambridge University Press.

Hammond, Michael. 1999. "Arouser Depreciation and the Expansion of Social Inequality." Pp. 339–358 in *Mind, Brain, and Society: Toward a Neurosociology of Emotions*, edited by D. Franks and T. Smith. Stamford, CT: JAI Press.

———. 2003. "The Enhancement Imperative: The Evolutionary Neurophysiology of Durkheimian Solidarity." *Sociological Theory* 21(4): 359–374.

———. 2004. "The Enhancement Imperative and Group Dynamics in the Emergence of Religion and Ascriptive Inequality." *Advances in Group Processes* 21: 167–188.

Joseph, Rhawn. 1996. *Neuropsychiatry, Neuropsychology, and Clinical Neuroscience*. Baltimore: Lippincott, Williams & Wilkins.

Keeley, Lawrence. 1996. *War Before Civilization*. New York: Oxford University Press.

Kemper, Theodore. 1987. "How Many Emotions Are There? Wedding the Social and Autonomic Components." *American Journal of Sociology* 87: 336–362.

Kirkpatrick, Lee. 2004. *Attachment, Evolution, and the Psychology of Religion*. New York: Guilford.

Knutson, B., O. Wolkowitz, S. Cole, T. Chan, E. Moore, R. Johnson, J. Terpstra, R. Turner, and V. Reus. 1998. "Selective Alternation of Personality and Social Behavior by Serotonergic Intervention." *American Journal of Psychiatry* 155: 373–379.

Maryanski, Alexandra. 1992. "The Last Ancestor: An Ecological-Network Model on the Origins of Human Sociality." *Advances in Human Ecology* 2: 1–32.

———. 1993. "The Elementary Forms of the First Proto-Human Society." *Advances in Human Ecology* 2: 215–241.

Maryanski, Alexandra, and Jonathan H. Turner. 1992. *The Social Cage: Human Nature and the Evolution of Society*. Stanford, CA: Stanford University Press.

Massey, Douglas. 2002. "A Brief History of Human Society: The Origin and Role of Emotion in Social Life." *American Sociological Review* 67: 1–29.

Mullin, Charles, and D. Linz. 1995. "Desensitization and Resensitization to Violence Against Women." *Journal of Personality and Social Psychology* 69: 449–459.

Newberg, Andrew, E. d'Aquili, and V. Rause. 2001. *Why God Won't Go Away: Brain Science and the Biology of Belief.* New York: Ballantine.

Rolls, B. J., E. A. Rowe, E. T. Rolls, B. Kingston, A. Megson, and R. Gunary. 1981. "Variety in a Meal Enhances Food Intake in Man." *Physiology and Behavior* 26: 215–21.

Rolls, E. T., E. Murzi, S. Yaxley, S. J. Thorpe, and S. J. Simpson. 1986. "Sensory-Specific Satiety: Food-Specific Reduction in Responsiveness to Ventral Forebrain Neurons After Feeding in the Monkey." *Brain Research* 368: 79–86.

Rolls, Edmund. 1998. *The Brain and Emotion.* Oxford: Oxford University Press.

Sanderson, Stephen. 2001. *The Evolution of Human Sociality.* Lanham, MD: Rowman and Littlefield.

Saver, Jeffrey, and John Rubin. 1997. "The Neural Substrates of Religious Experience." *Journal of Neuropsychiatry* 9: 495–499.

Sulloway, Frank. 1979. *Freud: Biologist of the Mind.* Cambridge, MA: Harvard University Press.

Tooby, John, and Leda Cosmides. 1990. "The Past Explains the Present: Emotional Adaptation and the Structure of Ancestral Environments." *Ethology and Sociobiology* 11: 375–424.

Turner, Jonathan H. 2000. *On the Origins of Human Emotions.* Stanford, CA: Stanford University Press.

———. 2002. *Face-to-Face: Towards a Sociological Theory of Interpersonal Behavior.* Stanford, CA: Stanford University Press.

Turner, Jonathan H., and Alexandra Maryanski. 2005. *Incest: Origins of the Taboo.* Herndon, VA: Paradigm.

Van den Berghe, Pierre. 1975. *Man in Society: A Biosocial View.* New York: Elsevier.

Wentworth, William, and John Ryan. 1992. "Balancing Body, Mind, and Culture: The Place of Emotion in Social Life." Pp. 25–46 in *Social Perspectives on Emotions*, edited by D. Franks and V. Gecas. Greenwich, CT: JAI Press.

Wentworth, William, and D. Yardly. 1994. "Deep Sociality: A Bioevolutionary Perspective on the Sociology of Human Emotions." Pp. 21–55 in *Social Perspectives on Emotions*, edited by D. Franks, W. Wentworth, and J. Ryan. Greenwich, CT: JAI Press.

Wilson, Edward O. 1975. *Sociobiology: The New Synthesis.* Cambridge, MA: Harvard University Press.

SECTION III

SELECT EMOTIONS

CHAPTER 17

Love

Diane H. Felmlee
Susan Sprecher

What's love, but a second-hand emotion?
—Tina Turner

Love is a topic of considerable import and fascination in virtually every society. In Western cultures, love is claimed as the grounds for mating and dating and as the basis for family bonding. On a cultural level, love is one of the most frequently discussed literary topics. It is the repeated focus of philosophers, poets, novelists, musicians, artists, playwrights, and screen writers; there is no question that love preoccupies us as a society. For at least two decades, social scientists also have been adding to the burgeoning cornucopia that represents the production of knowledge on love. Research on the topic of love has expanded at an impressive pace, and there is no slowdown in sight. Yet, as we will see, despite the near-universal attraction of the subject of love, scholars rarely agree on first principles or stray beyond their disciplinary boundaries.

A scholarly approach to love is not always appreciated. Former U.S. Senator William Proxmire criticized funding research on love, arguing that love is not a science and that "200 million other Americans want to leave some things in life a mystery" (cited in Hatfield and Walster 1978:viii). Nonetheless, much can be learned from an application of the rigorous and critical eye of the social scientist to love. Serious social problems abound surrounding love and intimacy in our society, with the high divorce rate being only one crude barometer. Why study love then? One reason is that it is simply a topic of fascination, even to those in the most ivory of towers. In addition, there is the possibility that scholarly work might have something to say that could have

DIANE H. FELMLEE • Department of Sociology, University of California, Davis, CA 95616
SUSAN SPRECHER • Department of Sociology and Anthropology, Illinois State University, Normal, IL 61790

We express appreciation to Scott Gartner, Liz Sweet, and Richard Novak for their comments on our work.

an impact, no matter how modest, on a society at the crossroads of crisis and confusion regarding this intimate and, yes, mysterious emotional experience.

The main purpose of this chapter is to review the latest social scientific literature on the topic of love and, in particular, to draw together work from both psychological and sociological perspectives. Although there is a number of extensive reviews of the literature on love from the field of psychology (e.g., Aron et al. 2006; Hendrick and Hendrick 2000; Noller 1996), there appears to be little to no work integrating research and theory on love within the discipline of sociology. Furthermore, we know of no attempts to address both streams of the psychology and sociology literatures on love in the same venue. We believe that there is much to be gained by examining work from both disciplines and attempting to explicate points of common agreement and those of departure. Because love is wildly varied in its expression and its experience, its study can readily benefit from both the incisive and rigorous magnifying glass yielded by psychologists and the wide-angle, social, cultural, and historical lens employed by sociologists.

In the first section of the chapter, we address a fundamental and controversial question: Is love an emotion? In the second section, we summarize the main, classical theories and approaches to love within the field of psychology. Third, we discuss the major conceptual approaches to love that appear in the sociological literature. Finally, we describe avenues for future research, noting the strengths and weaknesses of the existing literature. We particularly call for more work that is truly multidisciplinary, incorporating concepts, themes, and approaches from both of these major fields.

We caution that by no means will we be able to discuss every conceptual approach, or mention of love, within the literature. In order to narrow our focus, we will concentrate primarily on broad theories, and less on the expansive, empirical literature on love that is developing, especially within the field of close relationships. Moreover, we will focus on major psychological and sociological approaches to love; contributions to the literature on love emanating from several related disciplines, such as communication, family studies, and anthropology, are beyond the scope of the current chapter. We should note, too, that many works that we review are not easily classified into one major approach or subarea. Psychologists occasionally address questions that are typically sociological in nature, and sociologists also sometimes engage in psychological work. Furthermore, within one field, it can be challenging to develop firm boundaries between genres of theoretical work. Sociological perspectives can be particularly difficult to pigeonhole, in part because they are often broadly philosophical in nature and also because they tend to draw on multiple paradigms within the same work. Thus, our typologies are meant to be a guide to the major themes that arise within approaches to the study of love, rather than a foolproof, exclusionary, classificatory schema. With these caveats aside, we believe that our assessment reveals critical areas of agreement and divergence among the literature as well as avenues for fruitful future research.

IS LOVE AN EMOTION?

What is love? This is a question pondered persistently by philosophers, poets, musicians, scholars, and popular culture. Within the scholarly literature, in particular, there is an ongoing debate regarding whether love is an emotion. The emotional status of love is an issue worth addressing for a number of reasons, one of which is that the answer to this question points us in the direction of what types of theory might be useful in explaining and understanding love—theories of emotions, attitudes, or motivation. Next, we present both sides of the debate, evidence of lay perspectives, and then our assessment of the arguments.

Love Is Not an Emotion

A number of emotion theorists and some scholars of love maintain that love is not an emotion because it is omitted from the lists of many contemporary emotion theorists (e.g., Ekman 1992; Kemper 1987; Oatley and Johnson-Laird 1987). There is a number of reasons for this omission, including the argument that, unlike the basic emotions of anger, disgust, fear, joy, sadness, and surprise, there is no distinctive universal facial expression associated with the state of love (e.g., Ekman 1992). Other reasons given for excluding love as an emotion include the following: it is an attitude (Rubin 1970), a "plot" (Ekman 1992), a sentiment (Turner 1970), a culturally constructed, emotional syndrome (Averill 1985), it needs an "object" (Oatley and Johnson-Laird 1987), and it is a mixture of several other emotions, such as joy and anxiety (Izard 1992).

Recently, some scholars have argued that love is a goal-oriented motivational state rather than an emotion. They claim that love resembles our basic drives, such as hunger, thirst, and sleep (Aron and Aron 1991). Rempel and Burris (2005:299), for example, defined love as "a motivational state in which the goal is to preserve and promote the well-being of the valued object." The argument that love is not an emotion is supported further by research concluding that individuals associate the experience of love with many more emotions of opposite valences than they do for the experience of presumably more basic emotions such as happiness, sadness, fear, or anger (Acevedo and Aron 2004). In addition, recent research using physiological data gathered from functional magnetic resonance brain imaging (fMRI) contends that when participants gaze at pictures of beloved partners, activation occurs in regions of the brain that are associated with the motivation to obtain rewards (areas of the brain that can induce euphoria) (Bartels and Zeki 2000). Additional fMRI research suggests that romantic and maternal love activate similar brain regions in the reward system and, at the same time, lead to suppression of both negative emotions and the critical assessment of other people. Neurologically, in other words, "love is blind," and it has the power to overcome social distance and bond individuals through its ability to motivate and induce euphoria (Bartels and Zeki 2004).

Love Is an Emotion

A number of scholars also argues that love is indeed an emotion (e.g., Gonzaga et al. 2001), and, in particular, an emotion that occurs within a relationship (Kemper 1989). Sociological treatments of love that we discuss later tend to refer to love as an emotion (e.g., Goode 1959; Hochschild 2003). Some psychologists consider love to be one of the primary emotions (e.g., Epstein 1984; Scott 1980). Shaver and colleagues (1987, 1996) argued that love is a basic emotion, particularly if one focuses on the immediate short-term moments of love, or "love surges," rather than the long-term disposition of love. In support of this position, there is a good deal of evidence for the universality of romantic love across cultures, across historical time, and among all age groups (Jankowiak and Fischer 1992). Research also suggests that there might be universal nonverbal signs of love, similar to what occurs with other basic emotions. These signs include soft and tender facial expressions (Hatfield and Rapson 1993), mutual gazing (Rubin 1973), and a host of other behaviors, including hugging and kissing, that are common in all societies.

Finally, findings discussed earlier from recent fMRI studies regarding the nature of love remain controversial. For example, research shows that regions in the brain associated with euphoria are stimulated when an individual is gazing at photos of the person they love (Bartels and Zeki 2000), which suggests the participants are undergoing an emotional, not simply a motivational, experience. On the other hand, the situation in which a person views a picture of a loved one while lying down in a noisy fMRI scanner might not always engender an immediate "love surge" in the participants, the type of romantic love most closely thought to be a basic emotion. Furthermore, theorists maintain that emotions in general are a motivating force, in which individuals experiencing emotions are mobilized and pushed in various ways (Turner and Stets 2005). A fearful individual, for example, is apt to be motivated to flee a threatening situation. Thus, the argument that love is associated with motivational regions of the brain does not rule out the possibility that it is still an emotion.

A Layperson Approach

Although theorists on emotions and theorists on love are not able to agree on whether love is an emotion, research clearly establishes that people *believe* that love is an emotion and there are emotional components to love. For example, in a study by Fehr and Russell (1984), participants were given the word "emotion" and asked to list examples. Love was the fourth most commonly listed type of emotion, behind only happiness, anger, and sadness. In a follow-up study, Fehr and Russell (1984) asked participants to rate several emotions identified in the first study in terms of the degree to which they were good examples of emotion. Of the emotions provided, participants indicated that love was the best example. Similar results were found by Shaver et al. (1987), who provided participants with several terms that could refer to emotions and asked them to indicate the degree to which they would call each an emotion. Love received the highest mean rating, followed by anger, hate, fear, happiness, and sadness.

People also believe that emotional states coexist with love. For example, in a study by Lamm and Wiesmann (1997), participants were asked the open-ended question "How can you tell that you love someone?" (They were also asked a similar question about liking someone and being "in love" with someone.) A positive mood was the most commonly mentioned feature for love; 53% of the participants reported that being in a positive mood when in the other's presence or when thinking about the other was a good indicator of love. Positive mood was also a common indicator for the sentiments of being in love and liking. Interestingly, a negative mood also was rated by at least a proportion of the respondents as a common indicator of both love and being in love. In additional analyses, Lamm and Wiesmann (1997) categorized the indicators provided by the participants for each sentiment into three categories: cognitive, affective (emotional), and behavioral. Of the indicators provided by the participants in the free-list format, a greater proportion was affective (emotional) than cognitive or behavioral. In addition, in research by Aron and his colleagues (Acevedo and Aron 2004; as reported in Aron et al. 2006), participants were asked to indicate which emotions they felt when experiencing love or a specific subtype of love, such as passionate love. Participants in their study chose a greater variety of specific emotions for love than they did for fear, anger, sadness, and happiness.

In sum, although emotion theorists do not always include love as one of the basic emotions, individuals believe that it is one of the best examples of emotions. In addition, people believe that love is characterized by emotional states.

Certainly, research on the definition of love is just the beginning, and our guess is that the controversy over love's origins will not be over shortly. However, to the best of our knowledge, no one denies that emotions are associated with love or that love has motivational dimensions. Furthermore, it is clear that emotions and motivation are closely linked in the human animal. What we might have here is a "chicken and egg" dilemma. For our purposes, the most important point is that love should not be ignored when discussing emotions. Regardless of whether love is a truly basic emotion or an emotion-laden motivated goal, it is clear that love is a central aspect of the emotional backdrop of social interaction and a topic worthy of serious, scholarly scrutiny.

CLASSIC PSYCHOLOGICAL APPROACHES TO LOVE

The identification of different categories or types of love represents a major thrust of the readily expanding psychological research and theory on love over the past two decades. Although most types of love we describe below typically address the varieties of love experienced in adult intimate relationships, some types of love can also be experienced for others, such as friends and family members. We focus on the classic, and most influential, categorization schemes for love in the psychological literature. For each approach, we highlight the particular type(s) or subtype(s) of love that is more likely to be experienced as a "surge of emotion," in contrast to others that better fit the definition of love as a disposition. In developing schemas of love, however, one of the first tasks is to distinguish love from closely related concepts, such as liking and attraction, and thus we turn first to a discussion of such conceptual distinctions.

Love versus Liking and Other Sentiments

In some typologies, love is distinguished from a less intense sentiment directed toward others, such as *liking*. Many years ago, Rubin (1970) distinguished liking from love and developed scales to measure each. Liking included the themes of similarity, respect, and positive evaluation. The dimensions of love were dependency, caring, and exclusiveness. Rubin developed scales to measure both liking and love for another and found that they were only moderately correlated. The distinction between liking and love remains in the literature (e.g., Lamm and Wiesmann 1997), although rarely is liking assessed in research on relationships.

Love is also distinguished from *attraction*. Within the discipline of social psychology, a major subarea that emerged in the 1970s and that predated a social psychological emphasis on love was interpersonal attraction (Byrne 1971, 1997). Attraction is a positive attitude directed toward another person (e.g., Berscheid 1985) and, thus, is related to, although less intense than, love.

Love is also compared to, or studied in conjunction with, other constructs that assess the "pulse of a relationship," including commitment, satisfaction, respect, and intimacy (Orbuch and Sprecher 2003). However, of these various "pulse" measures, love is most often referred to as an emotion. Laypersons generally do not characterize other indicators of the quality of the relationship (e.g., satisfaction) as good examples of emotions (Fehr and Russell 1984; Shaver et al. 1987).

Companionate Love versus Passionate Love

In early scientific writing on love, social psychologists distinguished between passionate love and companionate love (Berscheid and Walster 1978; Walster and Walster 1978). Companionate love is the affection two people feel for each other when their lives are intertwined. Passionate love is "a state of intense longing for union with another" and associated with "fulfillment and ecstasy" when the love is reciprocated and with "anxiety and despair" when it is not (Hatfield and Rapson

1993:5). Thus, passionate love is much more emotionally intense than companionate love. The emotional intensity of passionate love led Berscheid and Walster (1974) to apply Schachter's (1964) two-component theory of emotion to passionate love. They argued that passionate love can be more intense when there is physiological arousal and there is a reason that the arousal can be labeled as passionate love or lust for the other. (For indirect support that an intense emotion for another can sometimes occur due to a misattribution of physiological arousal caused by another source, see Dutton and Aron (1974) and White et al. (1981).)

Passionate love also is distinguished from companionate love in its fragility and in its connection with sexual desire. Passionate love is presented as the less enduring but more sexually intense type of love. Some evidence exists for the theoretical differences between passionate love (often measured by Hatfield and Sprecher's (1986) Passionate Love scale) and companionate love (often measured by a subset of items for the Rubin's (1970) Love scale), although the differences are not substantial. For example, both passionate and companionate love are linked to the experience of various positive emotions in the relationship, but generally are not associated with negative emotions (Regan et al. 1998; Sprecher and Regan 1998). One exception is jealousy, typically considered to be a negative emotion, which is positively associated with passionate love (Regan et al. 1998; Sprecher and Regan 1998). Although Walster and Walster (1978) originally speculated that passionate love exists early in the relationship and then evolves into companionate love, both types of love tend to coexist in romantic relationships (Hatfield 1988; Hendrick and Hendrick 1993). The combination might be most supportive of the maintenance of long-term relationships such as marriage (Noller 1996).

A dichotomous distinction akin to the companionate love/passionate love distinction is that between *loving* someone versus "*being in love*" with someone (Meyers and Berscheid 1997). The state of being in love is more intense and less common than love, and it is associated with sexual desire (Regan 1998; Regan et al. 1998), an increase in self-esteem (Hendrick and Hendrick 1988), and enhancement of self-concept (Aron et al. 1995), especially when love is reciprocated. In fact, the process of "falling in love," which is a common cultural phenomenon (Hendrick and Hendrick forthcoming), might represent "being in love" at its emotional peak.

Love Styles

A particularly influential categorization schema distinguishes among six "styles of loving." This typology of love styles was originally developed by a sociologist, John Lee (1973, 1977), based on interviews conducted with married individuals. The six love styles or types are eros (intense, passionate love), ludus (game-playing love), storge (friendship love), pragma (practical love), mania (obsessive, dependent love), and agape (selfless love). Whereas, initial research with the love styles focused on the development of the scales and establishing their psychometric properties (e.g., Hendrick and Hendrick 1986, 1990; Hendrick et al. 1984, 1998), more recent research examines how the love styles predict relationship outcomes and are associated with individual characteristics (for a review, see Hendrick and Hendrick 1992; Hendrick and Hendrick forthcoming).

Some of the love styles, at least based on the content of the items used to measure them (e.g., Hendrick et al. 1984), are more emotionally intense than others. In fact, Hendrick and Hendrick (1986) characterized love styles based on the degree of their emotional intensity. Eros and mania are the most emotionally intense, agape is average in emotional intensity, and ludus, storge, and pragma are low in emotional intensity. In general, however, the love styles reflect more "love as sentiment" than "love as an upsurge in emotion" in the distinction that we referred to earlier. Hendrick and Hendrick (1986, forthcoming) referred to the love styles as a combination of enduring personality attributes and attitude/belief complexes.

Triangular Theory of Love

Sternberg (1986, 1988) described love as having three primary components: intimacy, passion, and commitment (pictorially represented as a triangle). Each component (triangle side) can range from low to high so that a number of different triangle shapes and sizes are possible. In addition, passion, commitment, and intimacy can differ between partners within the same relationship and between one's current relationship and what ideally one would want. Intimacy is the emotional or affective component and refers to warmth, understanding, caring, support, and connection. Passion represents a motivation characterized by physical attraction and arousal. Commitment is cognitive and refers to the decision to stay in the relationship and maintain it. Although Sternberg described intimacy as the emotional component, both intimacy and passion have emotional dimensions, as reflected in the content of the scale items to measure these different components (e.g., Sternberg 1997).

The triangular model of love yields eight different love types ranging from nonlove (no intimacy, no passion, and no commitment) to consummate love (high on all three components). The types of love that include both passion and intimacy could be considered more emotionally intense than the others. These types include romantic love (intimacy + passion) and consummate love. The least emotional kind of love, other than nonlove, would be empty love, which consists only of commitment. However, the lack of a strong measure for this particular love typology impedes research, due to problems of discriminant validity (Aron et al. 2006).

Love as a Story

Sternberg (1996, 1998) presented a new approach to love that departs dramatically from that of his previous framework discussed above. This perspective represents a social constructionist view to love, as reflected in narrative autobiographies, and frames love as a story. He argued that people develop stories about love based on socialization experiences with parents, media, and others and that individuals attempt to act out these love stories in their own lives. Thus, each story shapes the choice of a partner and the eventual course of a relationship. Although people might have multiple stories, they prefer some narratives more than others. Typical themes include that of a couple growing closer over time as they continually tend to their relationship and the story of a couple constantly struggling with each other. Sternberg identified 25 common love stories, and among those that appear to be more likely to have emotions as part of the story plot are the following: the addiction story (strong, anxious attachment), the gardening story (relationship needs nurturance), the horror story (relationships thrive on one or both partners terrorizing each other), and the war story (love is a series of battles).

The love story approach is the "new kid on the block" when it comes to psychological classification schemes for love, and it is deserving of further empirical examination. One question worthy of attention is the extent to which this perspective's numerous love types relate to, or differ from, those of prior schemas. One broad difference is that, unlike previous approaches, this new conceptualization refers to the interdependent roles of two partners in each individual's type of love.

The Prototype Approach to Love

The above approaches, even though informed by ordinary people's love experiences, focus on experts' definitions and measurements of love. The prototype approach, however, examines laypersons' experiences with, and meanings given to, love, and as we referred to in a prior section, it finds that people believe that love is a prototypical emotion (e.g., Fehr and Russell 1984). Studies in this genre also examine what features people associate with love. Some (e.g., Fehr 1988) establish that characteristics such as trust, caring, intimacy, respect, and friendship are considered most central to love. Other research (e.g., Fehr and Russell 1991) investigates which types of love people assume are more prototypical and finds that ordinary people regard maternal love, parental love, and friendship love to be the best examples of love; romantic love is fifth. Recent analyses also consider the relationship outcomes of having different conceptions of love. For example, Fehr and Broughton (2004) found that those couples who conceptualize love in prototypical terms experience greater love and liking for their partner than those who conceptualize love in a less prototypical manner.

Other Approaches to Love

Although the above approaches concentrate on enumerating different types of love, other scholars focus in depth on a particular type of love, including unrequited love (e.g., Baumeister et al. 1993), limerence or an intense type of love (Tennov 1979), lust (Regan and Berscheid 1999), friendship love (Grote and Frieze 1994), compassionate love (Sprecher and Fehr 2005), and love as a theme of relationship development distinct from conflict/negativity, ambivalence, and maintenance behaviors (Braiker and Kelley 1979). Although the various types of love might have some similarities, they also have unique correlates and consequences. For example, feeling unrequited love can lead to a decrease in self-esteem (Baumeister et al. 1993), which might not be characteristic of other types of love. Compassionate love might be especially predictive of engaging in socially supportive behavior (Sprecher and Fehr 2005).

A limited amount of research also investigates cultural and subcultural differences in love types and experiences. Do people love in relationships in similar ways regardless of cultural background and ethnicity and social class? What about differences between men and women? Cross-cultural studies of these questions find relatively modest differences (e.g., Sprecher et al. 1994), and some scholars conclude that there is evidence for the cultural universality of romantic love (Hatfield and Rapson 1993). Research also finds some discrepancies between ethnic and social classes within the United States (e.g., Contreras et al. 1996). Modest gender differences do occur consistently, however, especially in love styles. For example, men rate higher in eros and ludus, whereas women tend to report higher levels of storge, pragma, and mania (Hendrick and Hendrick 1986).

Certain general theories of human behavior also pertain to the study of love. For example, Aron and Aron's (1996) self-expansion theory maintains that people develop love and the desire to enter a relationship with a particular other because they want to include the other in the self and experience self-expansion. In addition, attachment theory (e.g., Bartholomew 1990; Bowlby 1973; Hazan and Shaver 1987) is a developmental theory applied to love. Hazan and Shaver (1987) argued that adult romantic love develops out of human attachment, caregiving, and sexuality systems and that adults vary in their relationship attachment styles, in part as a function of formative experiences with caretakers. For a recent review of the voluminous research in this area, see Feeney et al. (2000). Finally, another general theory that is applied at least indirectly to love is evolutionary theory (e.g., Buss 1988, 1995). This perspective focuses on how behaviors and feelings might have evolved over time and served an evolutionary, reproductive value. For example, as noted by Hendrick and Hendrick (2000:207), a passionate form of love might have helped "to drive males and females into reproduction" and a companionate form of love might have provided the "contact for the survival of the relationship and the offspring produced from it." This theory also predicts gender differences in preferences for a love partner and the mate strategies engaged in to attract a love partner. In addition, Buss (1988) argued that "love acts" (actions displayed toward the other) exist because of their association with reproductive success.

In sum, in this section, we referred to several classic, psychological approaches to love and began by describing theories that address the question "What is love?" We see that there are many different types and subtypes of love, most of which have corresponding, validated, and well-developed scales. Some types of love are more emotionally intense than others, including passionate love, Eros, and falling in love. Theories of related concepts also help to explicate an aspect of love, such as the motivation for entering love relationships. In the next section, we turn to sociological approaches to love.

SOCIOLOGICAL PERSPECTIVES ON LOVE

Traditionally, sociological theories and research do not focus on love, and sociologists are apt to view love as the domain of psychology and other more individualistic, or philosophical, scholarly domains. Yet, scholars from this discipline have made theoretical contributions to the study of love, particularly in recent years. Sociologists who write on the topic tend to focus on the broad, societal, cultural, and institutional patterns that relate to love. The study of love has much to gain from the application of the "sociological imagination" (Mills 1959)—that is, the ability to "think ourselves away" from the routine of our daily lives and examine our social world in a new light. Such a focus contends that the social and cultural milieu shapes fundamentally the individual experience of love and that this social nature of love must not be ignored.

In the following subsection, we review several main works on love developed by sociologists. We group them into four clusters: structural, historical, cultural, and social inequality. These groupings are loose, and there is overlap between the clusters; yet, we believe that these categories represent major themes in the literature.

Social Structural Perspectives

Social structure refers to persistent patterns of social relationships among actors over time. These patterns operate at the macrolevel and microlevel. We review one macrolevel structural perspective on love, which considers the implications for human attachment of broad, societal structures, such as the institution of marriage. We also examine a second structural perspective, at the microlevel of social organization, in which an individual's status position within a social structure is of relevance.

MACRO-LEVEL SOCIAL STRUCTURE. Love has considerable macrolevel, social structural implications for societies, according to one of the initial sociological treatments of love. In "The Theoretical Importance of Love," Goode (1959) defined love as a strong emotional attachment. He maintained that this psychological "cathexis" is of crucial significance to the study of societal-level phenomena. In particular, Goode discussed the power of love and its potential to disrupt social structure, class systems, and kinship lineages within society. Love is often the basis for marriage and mating, and mate choice connects two kinship groups. "Both mate choice and love, therefore, are too important to be left to children," according to Goode (1959:43). Random mating would involve fundamental transformations in a society's existing social structure and stratification system.

Societies control love through a variety of methods. For example, in certain cultures, social institutions constrain mating by mechanisms such as the physical and social segregation of females from males and the arrangement of marriages by kin. In Western society, love and mate choice are presumably free, and yet social control abounds via individuals' peer groups, who provide constant feedback regarding a partner, and parents. In order for their children to develop "appropriate" companions, parents in the United States structure the environment by moving to particular neighborhoods, choosing the correct schools, socializing with the appropriate groups, and so on. On a more direct level, parents "threaten, cajole, wheedle, bribe, and persuade their children to 'go with the right people'" (Goode 1959:45). Greater social control is exerted by the upper, as compared to the lower, classes, because those from the upper ranks of society have more to lose as a result of unconstrained love choices on the part of their offspring. Thus, Goode's argument suggests that this phenomenon of love is fundamentally linked to societal functioning at a broad, macrolevel.

MICRO SOCIAL STRUCTURE.   Kemper (1987, 1989) argued that love is a social relationship, as well as an emotion, and that it is shaped by two principles: power and status. Love is simultaneously both the emotional experience of a sense of harmony and the desire to accord status to the object of one's love. Loving differs fundamentally from liking, because liking is an emotion evoked by the rewards, or status, we receive from another. Romantic love arises when both the loved person and the lover experience relatively high levels of both status/affection and power in their relationship (Kemper and Reid 1997). During the romantic love stage, lovers display extreme degrees of affection, but intense pain also can be inflicted upon one another because of the heightened fear of relationship loss. "We are in the grip of a passion and feel we have no choice," noted Kemper and Reid (1997:45). The paradox of love, hence, is that it is both voluntary, or unforced, and nonvolitional, seemingly not under one's control.

Historical Social Transformations

Sociologists also focus on filling in the gaps in the developmental, historical side of human social life. They trace societal shifts and movements, such as feminism, that mold the experience and expression of love in our culture.

THE RISE OF CONFLUENT LOVE.   Giddens (1992) discussed societal trends in sexuality, love, and intimacy over time, and his perspective suggests that love is a social construction that evolves historically. In his work on love, he drew eclectically from a range of theories, including feminist psychoanalytical perspectives and his own "structuration" perspective, in which individuals are seen as influencing their social world while being shaped by society. Giddens described the revolutionary changes in our society, particularly for women, that resulted from the relatively recent historical development of the separation of sexuality from marriage and reproduction. He traced the rise of romantic love following the Middle Ages and argued that this ideology of romance propagates masculine values and helps to keep women "downtrodden." On the other hand, he discussed the recent development of "confluent love," love that presupposes equality between partners in both emotional and sexual expression, a type of love that occurs in what Giddens termed the "pure relationship." He contrasted confluent love with that of romantic love, love that idealizes the other and projects a "fantasy" narrative into the future. Giddens envisioned the possibility of a continued radical transformation of intimacy and love in this society, due in large part to the disengaging of sexuality from reproduction. This transformation is one toward equality and democracy. He argued that women and homosexual relationships are the "emotional revolutionaries" behind this societal shift away from romantic love and toward the democratization of intimacy.

FEMINIZATION OF LOVE. Love is feminized in our society, according to Cancian (1987), who traced developmental themes over time regarding love and also spoke to issues of gender inequality. Today, love is strongly associated with women and with the expression of feelings and other traditionally feminine aspects of relationships, she argued. For example, scholars of love usually define love in terms of emotional intimacy and they often focus on communication and self-disclosure in relationships as measures of love. There is a tendency to ignore the more material and practical dimensions of love, such as the provision of money, sex, and practical assistance, that are more typically viewed as masculine. The feminization of love encourages women to focus their energies on love, intimate relationships, and the family, with a concomitant loss of power. For example, popular magazines since 1900 continue to direct marital advice toward women, not men (Cancian and Gordon 1988). Self-development, on the other hand, is masculinized and associated with separation, independence, and, ultimately, power.

Cancian (1987) claimed that a blueprint for love is emerging in contemporary society that emphasizes interdependence between women and men, rather than either independence or traditional gender roles. It is based on an androgynous image of love, in which prominence is given to flexible, mutual love and, at the same time, self-development. Love and self-development are viewed as mutually reinforcing, rather than contradictory, as is often assumed. She viewed this new blueprint for love as a promising possibility for societal change in the future.

Cultural Construction

A recent shift in the discipline of sociology has been a "turn to culture," and major recipients of this relatively new focus are the topics of love, intimacy, and caregiving. Cultural theorists tend to examine the ideology, values, norms, and material goods that a society creates and the manner in which these cultural products shape and constrain an individual's behavior and emotions. According to this theoretical perspective, love is a fundamentally cultural construction.

INDIVIDUALISM AND LOVE. One aspect of culture that receives considerable attention is the ideology of individualism. In particular, recent societal critiques in the social science literature bemoan the overemphasis on individualism in U.S. culture (e.g., Putnam 2000). In *Habits of the Heart*, Bellah and colleagues (1985) developed the argument that the intense cultural focus on individuality and the individual pursuit of happiness and success conflict deeply with ideals of love. Contemporary society presents two contrasting views of love, according to findings from these authors' interviews with varied groups of Americans. One view is based on religious ideals of obligation, in which love is largely a matter of will and action, as opposed to spontaneous feeling, a stance that is particularly common among the evangelical Christians they studied. The other is a "therapeutic" view that is much more widespread among middle-class society, according to the authors. The "therapeutic" image is one in which deeply committed love is seen as developing only from "self-actualization" and from having confronted one's own individual feelings honestly. This clinical picture of love reinforces the individualistic strains in our culture, and it can create a paradox in which there is a contradiction between self-development and visions of love.

CULTURAL REPERTOIRE AND LOVE.   Swidler (2001) examined the ways in which Americans rely on cultural tools to develop "narratives of love" in their everyday lives. Using evidence from a sample of 88 middle-aged, middle-class white residents in the San Jose, California area, she noted that these middle-aged adults actively embrace and reject aspects of a vast cultural repertoire regarding love. Two love myths proliferate when people talk about love, according to Swidler's findings—the first of romantic love and the second of a more practical, "real" love. Romantic love is based on the notions of a clear choice of a unique partner, in which the choice is often made in defiance of social forces and a choice that portends an individual's destiny. Prosaic, or "real," love, on the other hand, is not sudden, but grows slowly. In the cultural icon of "real" love, there is no "one true love." Love depends, instead, on practical, compatible traits and it does not always last forever.

Individuals do not necessarily passively accept the cultural symbols available to them, especially those of romantic love, and many remain highly skeptical. Yet, images of romantic love continually reappear in even some of the most "rational" individuals' interviews. Swidler maintained that the power of the romantic love myth is reinforced in our society by the structural reality of the institution of marriage, in which individuals choose one partner with the intent that the liaison last forever. "The social organization of marriage makes the mythic image true experientially, whatever the facts" (Swidler 2001:121).

Social Inequality

Sociologists point to the enduring inequities inherent in the experience of love in our society. This perspective represents a powerful critique of our societal structure and the obstacles inherent in experiencing love in such a milieu.

PATERNALISM.   Feminists paint romantic love, in particular, as a societal ideology that leashes women to the home (e.g., Ehrenreich 1983). More generally, Jackman (1994) maintained that dominant societal groups, whether on the basis of gender, race, or social class, prefer to maintain power not by means of force, but by the more subtle means of affection. Exploitation is better undertaken by "sweet persuasion" than by hostility and, thus, the preferred tool of dominant groups, such as men, whites, and the upper class, is paternalism. Supported by findings from national attitudinal surveys, Jackman argued that affection is the emotion that dominants want to feel toward groups that they exploit. In the process of preserving the privileged status of dominants, "love and affection offer a coercive energy and a soothing balm that cannot be matched" (Jackman 1994:383). Thus, love is a major tool that aids in expropriative social arrangements, and the bonds of this "conditional love" are insidious and destructive.

THE COMMODIFICATION OF LOVE.   An additional theme regarding inequality and love in the sociological literature is the argument that our capitalist society "commodifies" love (Fromm 1956). Hochschild, in a series of essays from her newest book *The Commercialization of Intimate Life* (2003), built on this theme in a discussion of the everyday conflicts between love and work in modern capitalism. In particular, Hochschild maintained that the concepts of care and love are devalued in our society, and her argument is, in part, bolstered by findings from an examination of popular advice books. Trends toward a "cooler" and more rational society have led to the adoption of "male rules" of love, with a corresponding deemphasis on love, a separation of love from sex, and fewer sanctions on adultery.

According to Hochschild (2003), one emotion management strategy in adapting to the unstable realities of our capitalist society is to invest less and less in emotions, such as that of love. Likewise, we commodify and depersonalize the loving and caring tasks traditionally performed by a wife or a mother. The bakery provides bread for the family, for instance, child care is for hire, and even the various traditional functions of a wife can be purchased. Yet, paradoxically, our society also idealizes love and expects it to be increasingly expressive and fulfilling. Hochschild argued that our modern culture places a heightened importance on the caring, maternal image, perhaps due to a harsh external, market environment. There also is increased pressure put on the intimate pair to fulfill all of the communal functions once enacted by a host of family and community connections. Hochshild called for a societal revolution to address this major social problem that would entail love and care being rewarded as much as market success.

In sum, sociological approaches place love in its structural, historical, cultural, and societal context. We see the ways in which cultural ideologies of love develop and shift over time and the manner in which societies constrain and control the experience of this emotional connection. These approaches raise our awareness of the invasive presence of societal inequality and capitalism. Love is socially, and culturally, constructed. In the next section, we discuss avenues for future research and, in particular, turn to an approach that attempts to bridge the gap between the sociological and the psychological.

THE FUTURE OF SCHOLARSHIP ON LOVE

There are numerous avenues for additional scholarship on love, which is not surprising given the multidimensional nature of this elusive construct. We will discuss those that are of particular relevance to us as social psychologists and as relationship scholars. In our reading of the literature, we note that there is relatively little work on love at the particular intersection of psychology and sociology that is referred to as sociological social psychology. Put differently, there is a relative neglect of the immediate situation (Goffman 1964). From psychology, we have microlevel, detailed typologies and carefully, categorized schemes for love. From sociology, we have a range of macrolevel societal perspectives. What is missing is at the middle range of theorizing and research—in particular, the study of love within the context of the couple and the immediate social environment. In this section, we discuss three avenues for future scholarship on love that fall in this interface between sociology and psychology. First, we encourage more research on the dyadic nature of love. Second, we recommend the consideration of love beyond the pair, as a network phenomenon. Finally, we call for more scholarship on love that combines different levels of analysis so that fundamental aspects of love from an individual perspective are considered while wider societal influences are taken into account.

Love as a Couple-Level System

One of the unique aspects of love as an emotion is that it is apt to be intensely dyadic. However, scholars generally study love as if it exists in a situational vacuum, and most theories of love do not consider the existence of an active, engaged partner (Felmlee and Sprecher 2000). Ironically, in this sense, both psychological and sociological approaches to theorizing are relatively individualistic, rather than dyadic. There are exceptions, of course; there are interactionist elements to various theories both from psychology and sociology, including Sternberg's (1998) "love is a story" and Kemper's (1987) power and status perspective. Simmel (1984; see also Oakes 1989) employed a couple-level, rather than individualistic, approach when he touched on the topic of love and discussed the reciprocal relationship between actor and object.

Several traditional approaches to love would benefit from greater attention to how the responses of one partner sculpt the shape that love takes for the other. First, classic psychological perspectives that refer to myriad types of love need to consider further the manner in which one's primary way of loving (e.g., manic love style, secure attachment, passionate love) may depend on the behavior and emotions of one's partner. Love styles may vary between pairs involving the same individual, for example. With a particular partner, one might tend to be passionate and intense; later with a different person one might be primarily storgic. Psychological classification schemes also suggest that individuals often possess a single type of love, a love style, or a love story, that is apt to be relatively stable over time. With some exceptions, there is little discussion of the ways in which partners might influence the shifting form that love between the same two individuals takes over time. A young couple might start out with an erotic love style, or romantic love story, which they transform over time into an agape style, or a relatively stable, companionate story.

Typologies of love could focus on the patterns of love types for couples in addition to those at the individual level. Relationships, instead of individuals, could be manic, passionate, or companionate. Furthermore, the way in which love for a pair evolves may depend on each partner's love type or style, as well as the manner in which each individual responds to the other's expression of love. Interdependence between partners can produce numerous possible paths over time, depending on whether the pair responds in either cooperative, individualistic, or reactionary ways to each other (Felmlee 2006; Felmlee and Greenberg 1999).

Scholars who take a cultural perspective to love would also benefit from focusing on love from a couple-level perspective. Researchers (e.g., Swidler 2001) argue that individuals have a variety of cultural tools, that is, aspects of ideology from which they choose and mold their experience of love. However, how do individuals choose which tools to rely on in a particular situation? How do they interpret the meaning of those cultural ideas? We maintain that these processes evolve first and foremost in the day-to-day interaction with the one who is the object of one's affection. Two partners are often exposed to the same cultural symbols and images because of the time they spend together. Therefore, they are likely to create similar narratives of love.

In the study of the link between love and inequality, a pair-level perspective also needs to be considered. Our society is riddled with inequalities. It is racist, sexist, homophobic, and class based, to name only a few of the "isms" that haunt our social world. Yet, how are these disparities experienced? How are they realized and confronted on a day-to-day basis, and, in particular, how do they influence feelings of love? In romantic love, individuals are apt to encounter inequality within their relationships. For example, one actor might earn more income, make more of the decisions, have a greater ability to veto outcomes, exert more influence, and, in general, have more power. Many times, these inequities are apt to reflect those of society, with, for instance, males and whites having more power in a romantic dyad than females and persons of color. On the other hand, a particular pair might defy typical forms of stratification. The wife might occupy a more prestigious and lucrative occupation than that of her husband, or the couple might be of the same gender. Are such liaisons able to challenge traditional forms of paternalism and commodification, or do power inequities reassert themselves in other ways? In short, we see a need for more theoretical and empirical work on love at its dyadic, relationship foundations, in work on inequality, as well as in other areas such as culture and psychology.

Love from a Social Network Perspective

Interaction between partners is not the only interactive influence on love. In romantic love, for example, each partner's wider social network also shapes the course of love that emerges between two partners. Individuals' primary style of love and cultural ideas and tools are likely to be affected by their larger social circle of family and friends. In addition, the social network is likely to affect the course of love over its various developmental stages, including its initiation, maintenance, and termination. Networks can influence all aspects of love.

First, in order for a couple to love one another, the two individuals need to meet. Social networks shape the environment in which individuals are apt to contact a potential loved one. As suggested by Goode (1959), some parents choose neighborhoods and schools, at least in part, so that their children will be likely to meet the "right" kind of friends and potential mates. Moreover, across social classes, parents and other family members are likely to shape the mate and friendship choices of their offspring.

Social networks also likely influence the type of love that an individual seeks, or expects to experience. Western culture propagates various love myths, and it champions sometimes contradictory notions of individualistic, feminine, and masculine love. To what extent is an individual influenced by one myth or one particular cultural image of love? An individual's immediate social milieu is apt to be one of the main conveyors and interpreters of cultural symbols and messages. Furthermore, individuals seek a partner to play out their particular love story, whether it is a garden, mystery, or horror theme. We might learn more about the factors affecting these choices by investigating a couple's broader social environment.

Once a relationship is under way, a couple's immediate social situation continues to affect love between the pair. Support and approval from a couple's social network predicts enhanced feelings of love and relationship endurance over time (e.g., Felmlee 2001; Felmlee et al. 1990; Sprecher and Felmlee 2000). Yet, we know little about the intervening processes that produce these network effects.

Why might approval from one's social surrounding enhance feelings of love and increase relationship stability? Having supportive friends and family members provides a ready-made safety net for couples over time, a source of instrumental and emotional support that enables love to take root and develop. For example, many young couples need practical and financial help in order to buy a house, raise children, manage a household, and maintain employment. Emotional advice and support is also required to keep many relationships going. On the other hand, it remains plausible that, in some instances, network opposition toward a couple's relationship could enhance, rather than dampen, feelings of love between partners. Parental opposition to a pair's involvement, rather than extinguishing the flames of desire, might act as fuel on the fire; this is the theme of various Western plays and movies. There is only limited evidence for such a "Romeo and Juliet" effect (Driscoll et al. 1972); however, and the overall role of network support and opposition in shaping a couple's love remains controversial and deserving of more attention.

A couple's relationship cannot last forever; it ends via breakup, divorce, or, if it survives such pitfalls, death. Such a time of loss can be revealing with respect to the nature of a social bond (Lofland 1982). What happens to love, therefore, at this type of key juncture? There is little research on the topic, but it seems likely that an individual's social environment plays a part in the emotional course that ensues.

Finally, almost no scientific attention has been given to how love for nonromantic close others (family members, friends) interferes with, enhances, or changes the love experienced for a romantic partner and vice versa. Scholarship on love is dominated by a focus on romantic love in adult, heterosexual couples, rather than love among families and other network members. Furthermore, these couple and familial social dynamics are apt to vary among different cultures; therefore, we need to expand research beyond the borders of the United States in order to investigate such issues.

Integration of Literature

Third, we would like to see more integration of the two strands of social scientific research on love: the psychological and the sociological. In general, neither camp refers to the work of the other. In fact, within the sociological (but not psychological) literature, it is not uncommon to cite little or no prior research or theories on love. There are problems that stem from this lack of integration of scholarly work; for example, there is a proliferation of terms for love in the literature, and it seems that every scholar who writes on the topic generates a "new" type of love. For a list of the main varieties and typologies of love discussed in this chapter, see Table 17.1. One implication of the propagation of terms for love, and the lack of integrated literature, is that there is not a clear research agenda for the accumulation of knowledge regarding this noteworthy concept, certainly not one that crosses disciplinary boundaries.

There is bound to be a good deal of overlap among the countless terms and schemas for love generated by multiple disciplines. We note that confluent love (Giddens 1992), for instance, has much in common with consummate love (Sternberg 1986). The typology of love into two types, romantic and "real," identified by Swidler (2001), is similar in many ways to the dichotomy of passionate and companionate love originally suggested by Berscheid and Walster (1978). More generally, note that some version of romantic love occurs in the large majority of categorization schemes (e.g., passionate, "being in love, Eros, romance story, *love*). Many of the remaining

TABLE 17.1. **Main Types and Typologies of Love Taken from Psychology and Sociology**

Types and Typologies	Author(s)
Passionate and companionate	Berscheid and Walster 1978
"Loving" versus "being in love"	Meyers and Berscheid 1997
Eros, ludus, storge, pragma, mania, agape	Lee 1973;
	Hendrick and Hendrick 1986
Nonlove, liking, infatuated, empty, romantic, companionate, fatuous, consummate	Sternberg 1986
Garden, travel, mystery, addiction, horror, war, art, romance (and 17 others)	Sternberg 1998
Maternal, parental, friendship, romantic, and others	Fehr and Russell 1991
Love, like, and *love*	Kemper 1989
Confluent versus romantic	Giddens 1992
Feminized versus androgynous	Cancian 1987
Obligation versus "therapeutic"	Bellah et al. 1985
"Real" versus romantic	Swidler 2001
Paternalism (conditional)	Jackman 1994
Commodified	Hochschild 2003

terms for love also incorporate romantic notions (e.g., feminine, paternalism, commodification). Romantic love, or its equivalent, is typically contrasted with other types of affection that are not romantic and are either more companionate and friendship based (e.g., storge, "real" love, garden story) or "newer" and more egalitarian (e.g., confluent, androgynous).

Another difficulty is that there are seemingly contradictory statements about love in the literature. For instance, Cancian (1987) argued that our culture "feminizes" love, with its emphasis on emotional expressivity, whereas Hochschild (2003) decried its "masculine" dimensions, such as a deemphasis on intimacy and the separation of love from sex. Another case is clashing definitions of love. Kemper (1989) defined love as a relationship, whereas Rempel and Burris (2005) maintained that love is *not* a relationship. Greater mixing of literatures could help to resolve such possible inconsistencies and help us to move beyond these and other debates such as whether love is an emotion.

Given the complexity of love, it is not surprising that there is a lack of consensus on its nature. We are reminded of the words of the philosopher Finck (1902:1), over a century ago: "Love is such a tissue of paradoxes, and exists in such an endless variety of forms and shades that you may say almost anything about it that you please, and it is likely to be correct." Nevertheless, the tendency within sociology and across disciplines to ignore other scholars' opinions on the issue is disconcerting. We will learn the most about love from a social scientific approach when research is interactive and cumulative, rather than disjointed and idiosyncratic.

An additional problem is that researchers from one field sometimes ignore entire conceptual approaches to love that might be important to consider in developing a more complete theory. For example, sociologists tend to avoid biological perspectives, in any of their forms, when discussing love (or other topics). A number of psychologists employ evolutionary approaches, and several also directly examine brain and body functioning. With a human experience as basic as love, it seems likely that biology and evolution are relevant. It will no doubt prove worthwhile to take these fundamental processes into account in the development of comprehensive theoretical frameworks. Psychology, on the other hand, often pays little attention to the societal embeddedness of love. Social factors emphasized by sociologists, such as gender inequality, the institution of marriage, and cultural ideology, are apt to vastly influence couples' love styles and other aspects of love studied by psychologists. Conceptual development would benefit from a wider focus that includes the social and cultural milieu of love.

Moreover, sociological research tends to be broadly theoretical and philosophical, and it relies on very little data for its arguments. Psychologists are more narrow in scope, but they are more apt to subject their arguments to empirical investigation. From our vantage point, it appears that the sociologists need to gather more data. Psychological work, on the other hand, might stand to gain from a broader, theoretical focus. Once again, we believe that the two perspectives could profit from each other's strengths.

CONCLUSION

Reflecting on its status in society at large, love remains a controversial, yet captivating topic to social science scholars. To begin with, theorists disagree on a number of definitional issues. One bone of contention is whether love is an emotion, although laypersons are in wide agreement that it is a, if not *the*, central emotion. Psychological research highlights the multidimensional nature of love, using several classification schemes, the most fundamental of which distinguishes between passionate and companionate love. Sociological work points to extensive structural, cultural, and historical influences on love. Perhaps the most important point is that the experience of love is not individually determined, but that it is fundamentally immersed in a societal backdrop. We also call for more research at the intersection of the two fields of psychology and sociology, noting that love is a dynamic emotion that develops in a socially interactive sphere.

Finally, as noted at the beginning of this chapter, for some it seems as if the scientific study of love represents an oxymoron. Thus, we ask the question: Is there anything we have said here that could not be expressed better by Shakespeare, Emily Dickinson, Monet, or even the Beatles? Perhaps not. Social science research to date generates multiple classification schemes, contradictory conclusions, and unresolved conflicts. When the dust settles on the scholarship we have reviewed here, love still remains a mystery. However, that is not uncommon for relatively new scholarly endeavors. Moreover, social scientific endeavor has in no way affected, nor do we anticipate it will affect, the depth of experience of which love is capable, an experience that might be better represented by art. Yet, we believe that the research we reviewed here demonstrates that the social scientific enterprise has its own rightful place in the panoply of work on love, expanding our understanding of this salient, interpersonal phenomenon.

REFERENCES

Acevedo, Bianca, and Arthur Aron. 2004. "On the Emotional Categorization of Love and Beyond." Paper presented at the International Association for Relationship Research Conference, Madison, WI.

Aron, Arthur, and Elaine N. Aron. 1991. "Love and Sexuality." Pp. 25–48 in *Sexuality in Close Relationships*, edited by K. McKinney and S. Sprecher. Hillsdale, NJ: Erlbaum.

Aron, Elaine N., and Arthur Aron. 1996. "Love and Expansion of the Self: The State of the Model." *Personal Relationships* 3: 45–58.

Aron, Arthur, Helen E. Fisher, and Greg Strong. 2006. "Romantic Love." Pp. 595–614 in *The Cambridge Handbook of Personal Relationships*, edited by A. Vangelisti and D. Perlman. New York: Cambridge University Press.

Aron, Arthur, Meg Paris, and Elaine N. Aron. 1995. "Falling in Love: Prospective Studies of Self-Concept Change." *Journal of Personality and Social Psychology* 69: 1102–1112.

Averill, James R. 1985. "The Social Construction of Emotion: With Special Reference to Love." Pp. 89–109 in *The Social Construction of the Person*, edited by K. J. Gergen and K. E. Davis. New York: Springer-Velag.

Bartels, Andreas, and Semir Zeki. 2000. "The Neural Basis of Romantic Love." *NeuroReport* 11: 1–6.

———. 2004. "The Neural Correlates of Maternal and Romantic Love." *NeuroImage* 21: 1155–1166.

Bartholomew, Kim. 1990. "Avoidance of Intimacy: An Attachment Perspective." *Journal of Social and Personal Relationships* 7: 147–178.

Baumeister, Roy F., Sara R. Wotman, and Arlene M. Stillwell. 1993. "Unrequited Love: On Heartbreak, Anger, Guilt, Scriptlessness, and Humiliation." *Journal of Personality and Social Psychology* 64: 377–394.

Bellah, Robert N., Richard Madsen, William M. Sullivan, Ann Swidler, and Steven M. Tipton. 1985. *Habits of the Heart: Individualism and Commitment in American Life*. Berkeley: University of California Press.

Berscheid, Ellen. 1985. "Interpersonal Attraction." Pp. 413–484 in *The Handbook of Social Psychology*, edited by G. Lindzey and E. Aronson. New York: Random House.

Berscheid, Ellen, and Elaine H. Walster. 1974. "A Little Bit about Love." Pp. 355–381 in *Foundations of Interpersonal Attraction*, edited by T. L. Huston. New York: Academic.

———. 1978. *Interpersonal Attraction*. Reading, MA: Addison-Wesley.

Bowlby, John. 1973. *Attachment and Loss*. Vol. 2. *Separation: Anxiety and Anger*. New York: Basic Books.

Braiker, Harriet B., and Harold H. Kelley. 1979. "Conflict in the Development of Close Relationships." Pp. 135–168 in *Social Exchange in Developing Relationships*, edited by R. L. Burgess and T. L. Huston. New York: Academic.

Buss, David M.. 1988. "Love Acts: The Evolutionary Biology of Love." Pp. 100–117 in *The Psychology of Love*, edited by R. J. Sternberg and M. L. Barnes. New Haven, CT: Yale University Press.

———. 1995. "Evolutionary Psychology: A New Paradigm for Psychological Science." *Psychological Inquiry* 6: 1–30.

Byrne, Donn. 1971. *The Attraction Paradigm*. New York: Academic.

———. 1997. "An Overview (and Underview) of Research and Theory within the Attraction Paradigm." *Journal of Social and Personal Relationships* 14: 417–431.

Cancian, Francesca. 1987. *Love in America: Gender and Self-Development*. New York: Cambridge University Press.

Cancian, Francesca M., and Steven L. Gordon. 1988. "Changing Emotion Norms in Marriage: Love and Anger in U.S. Women's Magazines since 1900." *Gender and Society* 2: 308–342.

Contreras, Raquel, Susan S. Hendrick, and Clyde Hendrick. 1996. "Perspectives on Marital Love and Satisfaction in Mexican American and Anglo Couples." *Journal of Counseling and Development* 74: 408–415.

Driscoll, Richard, Keith E. Davis, and Milton E. Lipetz. 1972. "Parental Interference and Romantic Love: The Romeo and Juliet Effect." *Journal of Personality and Social Psychology* 24: 1–10.

Dutton, Donald G., and Arthur P. Aron. 1974. "Some Evidence for Heightened Sexual Attraction under Conditions of High Anxiety." *Journal of Personality and Social Psychology* 30: 510–517.

Ehrenreich, Barbara. 1983. *The Hearts of Men*. New York: Doubleday.

Ekman, Paul. 1992. "An Argument for Basic Emotions." *Cognition and Emotion* 6: 169–200.

Epstein, Seymour. 1984. "Controversial Issues in Emotion Theory." Pp. 64–88 in *Review of Personality and Social Psychology*, edited by P. Shaver. Beverly Hills, CA: Sage.

Feeney, Judith A., Patricia Noller, and Nigel Roberts. 2000. "Attachment and Close Relationships." Pp. 185–201 in *Close Relationships: A Sourcebook*, edited by C. Hendrick and S. S. Hendrick. Thousand Oaks, CA: Sage.

Fehr, Beverley. 1988. "Prototype Analysis of the Concepts of Love and Commitment." *Journal of Personality and Social Psychology* 55: 557–579.

Fehr, Beverley, and Ross Broughton. 2004. "Conceptions of Love: Implications for Thoughts, Feelings and Behavior in Close Relationships." Unpublished manuscript, University of Winnipeg.

Fehr, Beverley, and James A. Russell. 1984. "Concept of Emotion Viewed from a Prototype Perspective." *Journal of Experimental Psychology: General* 113: 464–486.

———. 1991. "The Concept of Love Viewed from a Prototype Perspective." *Journal of Personality and Social Psychology* 60: 425–438.

Felmlee, Diane H. 2001. "No Couple Is an Island: A Social Network Perspective on Dyadic Stability." *Social Forces* 79: 1259–1287.

———. 2006. "Application of Dynamic Systems Analysis to Dyadic Interactions." In *Handbook of Methods in Positive Psychology*, edited by A. D. Ong and M. van Dulmen. New Yark: Oxford University Press.

Felmlee, Diane H., and David F. Greenberg. 1999. "A Dynamic Systems Model of Dyadic Interaction." *Journal of Mathematical Sociology* 23: 155–180.

Felmlee, Diane, and Susan Sprecher. 2000. "Close Relationships and Social Psychology: Intersection and Future Paths." *Social Psychology Quarterly* 63: 365–376.

Felmlee, Diane, Susan Sprecher, and Edwin Bassin. 1990. "The Dissolution of Intimate Relationships: A Hazard Model." *Social Psychology Quarterly* 53: 13–30.

Finck, Henry T. 1902. *Romantic Love and Personal Beauty: Their Development, Casual Relations, Historic and National Peculiarities*. London: Macmillan.

Fromm, Erich. 1956. *The Art of Loving*. New York: Harper.

Giddens, Anthony. 1992. *The Transformation of Intimacy: Sexuality, Love and Eroticism in Modern Societies*. Stanford, CA: Stanford University Press.

Goffman, Erving. 1964. "The Neglected Situation." *American Anthropologist* 66: 133–136.

Gonzaga, Gian C., Dacher Keltner, Esme A. Londahl, and Michael D. Smith. 2001. "Love and the Commitment Problem in Romantic Relations and Friendship." *Journal of Personality and Social Psychology* 81: 247–262.

Goode, William J. 1959. "The Theoretical Importance of Love." *American Sociological Review* 24: 38–47.

Grote, Nancy K., and Irene H. Frieze. 1994. "The Measurement of Friendship-Based Love in Intimate Relationships." *Personal Relationships* 1: 275–300.

Hatfield, Elaine. 1988. "Passionate and Companionate Love." Pp. 191–217 in *The Psychology of Love*, edited by R. J. Sternberg and M. L. Barnes. New Haven, CT: Yale University Press.

Hatfield, Elaine, and Richard L. Rapson. 1993. *Love, Sex, and Intimacy: Their Psychology, Biology, and History*. New York: HarperCollins.

Hatfield, Elaine, and Susan Sprecher. 1986. "Measuring Passionate Love in Intimate Relationships." *Journal of Adolescence* 9: 383–410.

Hatfield, Elaine, and G. William Walster. 1978. *A New Look at Love*. Reading, MA: Addison-Wesley.

Hazan, Cindy, and Phillip R. Shaver. 1987. "Romantic Love Conceptualized as an Attachment Process." *Journal of Personality and Social Psychology* 52: 510–524.

Hendrick, Clyde, and Susan S. Hendrick. 1986. "A Theory and Method of Love." *Journal of Personality and Social Psychology* 50: 392–402.

———. 1988. "Lovers Wear Rose Colored Glasses." *Journal of Social and Personal Relationships* 5: 161–183.

————. 1990. "A Relationship-Specific Version of the Love Attitudes Scale." *Journal of Social Behavior and Personality* 5: 239–254.

————. Forthcoming. "Styles of Romantic Love." In *The Psychology of Romantic Love*, edited by R. Sternberg and K. Weis. New Haven, CT: Yale University Press.

Hendrick, Clyde, Susan. S. Hendrick, and Amy Dicke. 1998. "The Love Attitudes Scale: Short Form." *Journal of Social and Personal Relationships* 15: 147–159.

Hendrick, Clyde, Susan S. Hendrick, Franklin F. Foote, and Michelle J. Slapion-Foote. 1984. "Do Men and Women Love Differently?" *Journal of Social and Personal Relationships* 1: 177–195.

Hendrick, Susan S., and Clyde Hendrick. 1992. *Romantic Love.* Newbury Park, CA: Sage.

————. 1993. "Lovers as Friends." *Journal of Social and Personal Relationships* 10: 459–466.

————. 2000. "Romantic Love." Pp. 203–215 in *Close Relationships: A Sourcebook*, edited by C. Hendrick and S. S. Hendrick. Thousand Oaks, CA: Sage.

Hochschild, Arlie Russell. 2003. *The Commercialization of Intimate Life: Notes from Home and Work.* Berkeley: University of California Press.

Izard, Carroll E. 1992. *Human Emotions.* New York: Plenum.

Jackman, Mary. 1994. *The Velvet Glove: Paternalism and Conflict in Gender, Class, and Race Relations.* Berkeley: University of California Press.

Jankowiak, William R., and Edward F. Fischer. 1992. "A Cross-Cultural Perspective on Romantic Love." *Ethnology* 31: 149.

Kemper, Theodore D. 1987. "How Many Emotions Are There? Wedding the Social and Autonomic Components." *American Journal of Sociology* 93: 263–289.

————. 1989. "Love and Like and Love and *Love*." Pp. 249–268 in *The Sociology of Emotions: Original Essays and Research Papers*, edited by D. D. Franks and E. D. McCarthy. Greenwhich, CT: JAI Press.

Kemper, Theodore D., and Muriel T. Reid. 1997. "Love and Liking in the Attraction and Maintenance Phases of Long-Term Relationships." *Social Perspectives on Emotions* 4: 37–69.

Lamm, Helmut, and Ulrich Wiesmann. 1997. "Subjective Attributes of Attraction: How People Characterize Their Liking, Their Love, and Their Being in Love." *Personal Relationships* 4: 271–284.

Lee, John A. 1973. *Colours of Love: An Exploration of the Ways of Loving.* Toronto: New Press.

————. 1977. "A Typology of Styles of Loving." *Personality and Social Psychology Bulletin* 3: 173–182.

Lofland, Lyn H. 1982. "Loss and Human Connection: An Exploration into the Nature of the Human Bond." Pp. 219–242 in *Personality, Roles, and Social Behavior*, edited by W. Ickes and E. S. Knowles. New York: Springer-Verlag.

Meyers, Sarah A., and Ellen Berscheid. 1997. "The Language of Love: The Difference a Preposition Makes." *Personality and Social Psychology Bulletin* 23: 347–362.

Mills, C. Wright. 1959. *The Sociological Imagination.* New York: Oxford University Press.

Noller, Patricia. 1996. "What Is This Thing Called Love? Defining the Love that Supports Marriage and Family." *Personal Relationships* 3: 97–115.

Oakes, Guy. 1989. "Eros and Modernity: Georg Simmel on Love." Pp. 229–247 in *The Sociology of Emotions: Original Essays and Research Papers*, edited by D. D. Franks and E. D. McCarthy. Greenwich, CT: JAI Press.

Oatley, Keith, and Phillip N. Johnson-Laird. 1987. "Toward a Cognitive Theory of Emotions." *Cognition and Emotion* 1: 29–50.

Orbuch, Terri L., and Susan Sprecher. 2003. "Attraction and Interpersonal Relationships." Pp. 339–362 in *Handbook of Social Psychology: Sociological Perspectives*, edited by J. DeLamater. New York: Kluwer/Plenum.

Putnam, Robert D. 2000. *Bowling Alone: The Collapse and Revival of American Community.* New York: Simon and Schuster.

Regan, Pamela C., 1998. "Of Lust and Love: Beliefs about the Role of Sexual Desire in Romantic Relationships." *Personal Relationships* 5: 139–157.

Regan, Pamela C., and Ellen Berscheid. 1999. *Lust: What We Know about Human Sexual Desire.* Thousand Oaks, CA: Sage.

Regan, Pamela C., Elizabeth R. Kocan, and Teresa Whitlock. 1998. "Ain't Love Grand! A Prototype Analysis of Romantic Love." *Journal of Social and Personal Relationships* 15: 411–420.

Rempel, John K., and Christopher T. Burris. 2005. "Let Me Count the Ways: An Integrative Theory of Love and Hate." *Personal Relationships* 12: 297–313.

Rubin, Zick. 1970. "Measurement of Romantic Love." *Journal of Personality and Social Psychology* 16: 265–273.

————. 1973. *Liking and Loving: An Invitation to Social Psychology.* New York: Holt, Rinehart, and Winston.

Schachter, Stanley. 1964. "The Interaction of Cognitive and Physiological Determinants of Emotional State." Pp. 49–80 in *Advances in Experimental Social Psychology*, edited by L. Berkowitz. New York: Academic.

Scott, John P. 1980. "The Function of Emotions in Behavioral Systems: A Systems Theory Analysis." Pp. 35–56 in *Emotion: Theory, Research, and Experience*, edited by R. Plutchik and H. Kellerman. New York: Academic.

Shaver, Phillip R., Hillary J. Morgan, and Shelley Wu. 1996. "Is Love a 'Basic' Emotion?" *Personal Relationships* 3: 81–96.

Shaver, Phillip, Judith Schwartz, Donald Kirson, and Cary O'Connor. 1987. "Emotion Knowledge: Further Explorations of a Prototype Approach." *Journal of Personality and Social Psychology* 52: 1061–1086.

Simmel, Georg. 1984. "On Love (A Fragment)." Pp. 153–192 in *On Women, Sexuality, and Love*. Translated and edited, with an introduction, by Guy Oakes. New Haven, CT: Yale University Press.

Sprecher, Susan, Arthur Aron, Elaine Hatfield, Anthony Cortese, Elena Potapova, and Anna Levitskaya. 1994. "Love: American Style, Russian Style, and Japanese Style." *Personal Relationships* 1: 349–369.

Sprecher, Susan, and Beverley Fehr. 2005. "Compassionate Love for Close Others and Humanity." *Journal of Social and Personal Relationships* 22: 629–652.

Sprecher, Susan, and Diane Felmlee. 2000. "Romantic Partners' Perceptions of Social Network Attributes with the Passage of Time and Relationship Transitions." *Personal Relationships* 7: 325–340.

Sprecher, Susan, and Pamela C. Regan. 1998. "Passionate and Companionate Love in Courting and Young Married Couples." *Sociological Inquiry* 68: 163–185.

Sternberg, Robert J. 1986. "A Triangular Theory of Love." *Psychological Review* 93: 119–135.

———. 1988. "Triangulating Love." Pp. 119–138 in *The Psychology of Love*, edited by R. J. Sternberg and M. L. Barnes. New Haven, CT: Yale University Press.

———. 1996. "Love Stories." *Personal Relationships* 3: 59–79.

———. 1997. "Construct Validation of a Triangular Love Scale." *European Journal of Social Psychology* 27: 313–335.

———. 1998. *Love Is a Story*. New York: Oxford University Press.

Swidler, Ann. 2001. *Talk of Love: How Culture Matters*. Chicago: University of Chicago.

Tennov, Dorothy. 1979. *Love and Limerence: The Experience of Being in Love*. New York: Stein and Day.

Turner, Jonathan H., and Jan E. Stets. 2005. *The Sociology of Emotions*. Cambridge: Cambridge University Press.

Turner, Ralph H. 1970. *Family Interaction*. New York: Wiley.

Walster, Elaine, and G. William Walster. 1978. *A New Look at Love*. Reading, MA: Addison-Wesley.

White, Gregory L., Sanford Fishbein, and Jeffrey Rutstein. 1981. "Passionate Love: The Misattribution of Arousal." *Journal of Personality and Social Psychology* 41: 56–62.

CHAPTER 18

Jealousy and Envy

Gordon Clanton

Human emotions are socially constructed (Berger and Luckmann 1966). Emotions are shaped by social processes and social forces. Emotions are social as well as psychological phenomena, responses to social situations that are shaped by social learning. However useful it may be to consider emotions as physiological or as psychological events, the sociological study of emotions draws attention to often-overlooked *social* aspects of emotions, including the situations that provoke them, the social learning by which they are shaped, their historical and cross-cultural variability, their social usefulness, their contribution to social conflict, and the social arrangements that humans set up to manage them. To paraphrase Mills (1959), the private emotions of individuals are shaped by public issues of social structure.

Emotions are shaped by society. Private experiences of emotion are embedded in history, culture, and social structure. Not only our feelings, but also our feelings about our feelings are shaped by psychological, philosophical, and theological frameworks that are institutionalized in social life. Thus, patterns of emotional experience change in response to changes in society and culture.

Emotions cannot be fully understood without some attention to the social forces that influence them. Emotions reflect the norms, attitudes, and values of groups as well as individuals; they are useful and dangerous for groups as well as individuals. As Collins (1975:92) observed, it is through emotional behavior that humans "exercise power, create religions and works of art...and enact bonds of solidarity among family and friends." Shalin (2004) argues that politics is fueled by emotions, economics feeds on moral feelings, and democracy is an embodied process that binds affectively as well as rhetorically.

Emotions are shaped by the beliefs, attitudes, and values that individuals acquire in the course of their socialization. The experience and expression of emotions depend on what one "knows," what one believes to be true. The private experience of love depends in part on beliefs about sex and its social regulation. The private experience of jealousy depends in part on beliefs about

---

GORDON CLANTON • Department of Sociology, San Diego State University, San Diego, CA 92182

marriage (and relationships leading to marriage), threats to marriage, and appropriate ways of protecting a marriage that is threatened by a third party. The private experience of envy depends in part on beliefs about wealth, status, and power and how they should be distributed. Love is about sex; jealousy is about adultery; envy is about justice and injustice.

Emotions are important as motives for human action. Both words, *emotion* and *motive*, are derived from the same Latin root, *movere*, to move. The word *emotion* refers mostly to inner feelings, to disturbances of the conscious or unconscious mind, typically involuntary and often leading to complex bodily changes and forms of behavior. The word *motive* refers to that which produces motion or action. Emotions are inner states that move individuals to action in the social world. Anger can be a motive for aggression. Guilt can be a motive for making restitution or atonement. Grief can be a motive for doing something to honor the departed.

A discussion of some social aspects of jealousy and envy may be useful for illustrating a sociological approach to emotions and demonstrating the importance of the meso- and macrolevel social forces that are omitted from many discussions of emotions. Microsociology reveals that emotions are learned through interaction. Emotions reflect the life experience of the individual. Mesosociology reveals that emotions are socially useful, indeed indispensable, to social order. Emotions reflect the institutional settings in which they are experienced. Macrosociology reveals that emotions are shaped by society and culture. Emotions reflect the history and the values of a people, and the relevant values vary from time to time and place to place.

The neglect of emotions by sociologists is partially explained by the historic reluctance of sociologists since Durkheim to look at phenomena that appear to be "psychological" in nature (Manning 2005). In fact, emotions are inescapably *social*, important to the understanding of social interaction, social institutions, and society and culture.

RECOGNIZING JEALOUSY AND ENVY

Jealousy and envy are separate and distinct emotions, but they are confused with each other in ordinary speech. Clarity about the distinction between jealousy and envy is a key to understanding either emotion and the necessary foundation for their scientific study. Both empirical research and therapeutic intervention are compromised by language that confuses the two emotions.

It is widely believed that jealousy and envy are the same emotion. In ordinary American English usage, the word "jealousy" is applied to both emotions (Parrott and Smith 1993). Envy is routinely referred to as "jealousy," and both are associated with the "green-eyed monster." In fact, although jealousy and envy often are mixed together in real life, they are responses to quite different situations.

Jealousy is a protective reaction to a perceived threat to a valued relationship or to its quality (Clanton and Smith 1998). The protective reaction can involve thoughts, feelings, or actions. Although jealous behaviors sometimes damage relationships, the *intention* of jealousy is the protection of the relationship or the protection of the ego of the threatened partner. Jealousy typically involves an attempt to protect a valued relationship (especially marriage) from a perceived threat (especially adultery). As Goffman (1967) notes about embarrassment, jealousy is not an irrational impulse breaking through socially prescribed behavior, but part of this orderly behavior itself.

Although jealousy may be experienced in many types of relationship, including the Oedipal triangle, sibling rivalry, and jealousy of nonsexual friendships, the focus of this analysis is the adult jealousy that arises in romantic relationships and in marriage. Adult jealousy typically results when a person believes that a marriage or romantic relationship is threatened by a real or imagined third party.

An individual's jealousy is likely to be strongest in those situations where the attributes or behaviors of others threaten the individual's own self-definition (Ellestad and Stets 1998; Salovey and Rodin 1989; Salovey and Rothman 1991). Jealousy is felt in regard to what matters most to an individual, and marriage and marital fidelity matter very much to most people. Jealousy may reflect an erosion of one's social position. An experience of jealousy tips one off to one's own need to be recognized for certain attributes that one possesses. For example, a woman who is beautiful will be more likely to feel jealous of another beautiful woman, because she knows that she herself is valued for beauty. A woman who is not beautiful, who does not compete on that level because she cannot, probably will not manifest a jealous response. She has simply given up and will not act jealously, although she may become depressed.

Whereas jealousy is rooted in the desire to hold on to what one has, envy begins with the wish for something desirable that one does not have (Foster 1972). Whereas jealousy may occur when a person fears losing, or already has lost, an important relationship with another person to a third party, envy may occur when a person lacks what another has and wishes that the other did not have it (Parrott 1991).

Envy is hostility toward superiors, a negative feeling toward someone who is better off (Scheler 1961; Schoeck 1970). In other words, envy is resentment toward someone who has some desirable object or quality that one does not have and cannot get. Any quality or achievement that provokes admiration also is likely to provoke some envy. These include wealth, status, power, fame, success, talent, good health, good grades, good looks, and popularity.

Envy is *not* the wish for the object or advantage that provoked the envy. Rather, envy is the much darker wish that the superior would *lose* the object or advantage. Envy is the perverse pleasure, the malicious joy (*Schadenfreude*) that is felt when the superior fails or suffers. The most common outward expression of envy is gossip (Foster 1972).

Most people with whom I have discussed jealousy and envy are unclear about the distinction. I have asked hundreds of people over the course of 30 years about the difference between these emotions. Many say, "I thought they were the same." Many others say, "Jealousy is about people, and envy is about things." Neither of these responses captures the difference between jealousy and envy. In my experience, however, Europeans and people from the third world are much more likely than Americans to be able to articulate the difference.

My students delight in finding examples in speech and in the media of envy being called "jealousy" or otherwise mislabeled. For example, "The other players on the team were *jealous* of the star's huge salary," or "I'm *jealous* because you were honored and I was not," or "Some of the other performers were *jealous* of her obvious talent." In each of these cases, the emotion being reported is *envy*, not jealousy.

Because envy is a completely negative emotion, it usually is repressed, denied, disguised, and relabeled. For this reason, it is difficult to observe and almost impossible to assess through self-report. Having defined jealousy and envy, making clear the distinction between them, we turn now to further analysis of the two emotions in turn.

JEALOUSY

Here we consider the social usefulness of jealousy, its cross-cultural variations, how it changed because of the sexual revolution and the women's movement, and some implications for psychotherapy and self-understanding. The findings are summarized so as to dispute ten dangerous misconceptions about jealousy that prevail in U.S. society in the early 21st century.

The Social Function of Jealousy

Although it often is dismissed as "the useless emotion," jealousy is useful to individuals, couples, and society as a whole. By protecting marriage from the betrayal of adultery, jealousy helps to preserve social order (Davis 1936). Jealousy serves to maintain traditional social roles. For example, a mother's jealousy over her husband's attentions to their child causes her to protect her turf as nurturer by allowing the father to have only or primarily the playmate role (Ellestad and Stets 1998).

In every culture, people form valued relationships in accordance with prevailing norms. Jealousy protects whatever kinds of relationships cultures teach people to value. As Davis (1936:400) notes:

> Where exclusive possession of an individual's entire love is customary, jealousy will demand that exclusiveness. Where love is divided, it will be divided according to some scheme, and jealousy will reinforce the division.

The protective function of jealousy also is noted by Pines (1992, 1998) and Buss (2000).

Specific jealous behaviors vary enormously across cultures because of the great diversity of human beliefs about relationship boundaries, threats, and protection. The experience and the interpretation of jealousy change as beliefs about these matters change. The cross-cultural and historical variability of jealousy will be discussed below.

Jealousy, which often is described as a triangle, is, in fact, a quadrangle. The fourth party is the community. Jealousy is approved by the community when the third party is viewed as a trespasser, but disapproved when the third party is viewed as a legitimate rival (Davis 1936).

The analysis offered here is consistent with that of Davis in his 1936 article "Jealousy and Sexual Property," but I have deliberately avoided the metaphor of property, because contemporary connotations of the term "property" distract from Davis's point and from mine. One need not "treat one's mate as property" (in the contemporary pejorative sense of the word) in order to feel jealous. The Davis article is about rules of sexual access (especially marriage rules) and their impact on the experience of jealousy.

Whereas conventional wisdom, borrowing from biology and psychology, sees jealousy as a universal instinct that requires the invention of marriage rules, sociological analysis reveals that, without marriage rules, individuals would not know when to be jealous. Thus, it is not jealousy that produces marriage rules. Rather, marriage rules produce jealousy. Despite variations, jealousy is universal because every society values marriage and prohibits extramarital sex.

Society shapes jealousy by defining what constitutes a marriage, what constitutes a threat to marriage, and how to protect a marriage that is threatened by a third party. The experience of jealousy in an individual is shaped by the marriage rules and the adultery taboo of the community and society. Jealousy is the declaration of one's rights within a particular system of marriage rules.

The social usefulness of jealousy is easily overlooked in contemporary U.S. society because of the prevailing view, encouraged by the sexual revolution, that jealousy is a useless emotion that grows out of the insecurity or low self-esteem of the jealous individual. These matters are further discussed below.

A Comparative View of Jealousy

Jealousy is universal, but jealousy is different in different societies (Ford and Beach 1951; Hupka 1981; Malinowski 1929; Mead 1931). Among the Yurok Indians of Northern California, if a man asked another man's wife for a cup of water, this was considered an inappropriate overture and the husband would become jealous. By way of contrast, in some Eskimo societies men lend their wives to overnight guests, apparently without jealousy. The Yurok people appears to be "more jealous" than most Americans of our own time, and the Eskimo "less jealous." Similarly, the Toda people of South India, who practiced polygamy for both genders and tolerated affairs as well, strike us as much "less jealous" than the Samoan wife who, upon discovering that a woman was having an affair with her husband, was expected to seek out the rival and bite her on the nose. Surely these differences are best explained in terms of cultural variations in the marriage rules rather than in terms of biology or psychology. Cross-cultural surveys confirm that, in general, societies with relatively restrictive sexual norms provide more occasions for jealousy and value it more highly than societies with more permissive norms.

Culture shapes the experience of jealousy through the life cycle (Mead 1931). The Dobuans, Pacific islanders east of New Guinea, had very permissive rules about premarital sex. At age 12 or 13 boys were turned out of their family hut at night in the expectation that they would wander about and, eventually, have sex with most of the girls in the locality. These liaisons generated virtually no jealousy. When Dobuans married, however, they fell under the sway of marriage rules characterized by a very strict adultery taboo. Not surprisingly, adult Dobuans appear to be highly jealous and inordinately suspicious, to the point of recruiting kinspeople to follow and spy on the spouse as a deterrent to adultery. Adult Dobuans are much "more jealous" than adolescent Dobuans because of culture, not because of biology or psychology.

American Indian cultures reflect the great human diversity in such matters. If a Zuni wife suspected that her husband were having an affair, she had a culturally prescribed way of communicating her displeasure to her husband and to the community: She refused to do his laundry and, instead, dumped it on the ground in front of her home. Among the Apache, the code of honor required that the husband of a woman who committed adultery should mutilate his wife by cutting off her nipples or the tip of her nose. In some Native American cultures, the wedding ceremony included the father of the bride giving to the groom a special arrow, with which he must kill his wife if she betrays him.

The particulars of the adultery taboo are different in different cultures. Some cultures are more tolerant of affairs than others—the Toda, the Mehinaku Indians in Brazil (Collins and Gregor 1995; Gregor 1985), and perhaps the French. Many cultures are characterized by a double standard, by which women's infidelities are more severely punished than men's.

Culture influences an individual's interpretation of an event as threatening or not threatening to a valued relationship. Similarly, culture prescribes behaviors designed to protect the relationship by preventing the intrusions of the rival, punishing an aberrant mate or the rival, compensating an aggrieved mate, restoring one's standing in the eyes of others, and so forth (Hupka 1981). For example, in the case of a man who finds that his wife has been sexually involved with a neighbor, a particular culture may prescribe one or more of several responses: killing the spouse or the rival with the approval of the community; fighting the rival until one combatant is seriously wounded or killed, mock combat supervised by friends and relatives of the rivals so that neither is likely to be seriously wounded or killed; loud, abusive arguing; a debate or formal insult match; a drum match or other musical competition, among others. Most cultures provide several possible solutions so a jealous person may choose a reaction that fits his or her disposition.

The jealousy between wives in polygynous households in Nigeria is not principally sexual jealousy. It is part of a competition to secure maximum access to scarce economic resources. Favoritism between wives produces friction because the husband is likely to follow sexual favors with economic benefits (Ware 1979).

In contrast with hunting and gathering societies, industrial societies are characterized by pluralism and rapid social change. Since the 1960s, swingers and practitioners of sexually liberal lifestyles have emerged as subcultures in which much more permissive marriage rules prevail

(Berger 1981; Buunk 1981; Gilmartin 1998; Kinkade 1972; Pines and Aronson 1981; Smith and Smith 1974). Swingers, for example, do not view sexual exclusiveness as a necessary condition for a happy marriage and so appear to be without jealousy in situations that would make most people jealous. Apart from swinging, some couples agree to permit a measure of freedom or at least agree to a don't-ask-don't-tell policy. People in various sexually liberal lifestyles, however, constitute a very small proportion of marriages and other committed relationships. Adultery is much more common than swinging. Cheating is much more common than the negotiated "arrangement."

Even among more conventional couples in which no one is cheating, substantial differences are observed in definitions of appropriate and inappropriate behavior, with younger, urban, secular, and better-educated individuals typically being more permissive and more tolerant of "innocent flirtation" than older, rural, religious, and less well-educated individuals. Disagreements about such boundaries within a couple often become a source of conflict. For all this diversity, however, the overwhelming majority of married Americans feel strongly that their mates should not have sex or deep emotional involvement with others, and they are apt to become very upset (jealous) if this happens. For the vast majority, the expectation of sexual exclusivity is a defining characteristic of a committed relationship. Salovey and Rodin (1985) found that survey respondents who placed great value on their current relationships and on the importance of exclusivity were more prone to feel jealous.

Many people with whom I have discussed these matters say they felt powerful jealousy for the first time when they reached the point in the development of a romantic involvement where they were ready for an exclusive relationship and did not want this other person to have sex with anyone else. Many of these relationships turned into marriages. Jealousy, in other words, was the signal that one desired a committed relationship with another.

Because of the impact on American culture of the sexual revolution, popular conversation often neglects the still quite strong adultery taboo. Although the norms regarding premarital sex have become much more permissive since the 1960s, disapproval of extramarital sex remains very strong for the vast majority. The influence of the sexual revolution on the experience, expression, and interpretation of jealousy is considered in the next section.

Jealousy and Social Change

Although jealousy protects marriage from adultery in all societies, Western history reveals that jealousy has protected various kinds of valued relationships across the centuries (Clanton 1984, 1987; Coontz 2005; Goode 1959, 1963; Hunt 1959). In classical Greek culture, jealousy protected the homoerotic relationships of men with teenage boys. In the Middle Ages, jealousy protected the tender, extramarital flirtations of Roman Catholic lords and ladies whose ideal was to love "pure and chaste from afar." But in those days romantic love had nothing to do with marriage, because marriages were arranged by the parents of the bride and groom. Following the Protestant Reformation, jealousy protected Puritan marriage, a new kind of man-woman relationship that attempted for the first time to combine sex, love, and companionship in marriage. The Protestant Reformation and the Industrial Revolution weakened the ancient custom of arranged marriage and encouraged the modern practice of choosing one's own mate on the basis of love.

Jealousy in the United States: 1945 to 2005

The contemporary experience and understanding of jealousy have been shaped by the dramatic changes in matters of sex, love, marriage, and the family that began in the 1960s (see Clanton

1984; Clanton and Downing 1975). As Berger and Berger (1984) later noted, Americans have been involved since the 1960s in a cultural war over the family, a vociferous and value-loaded debate over the history, present condition, prospects, and human and societal value of the family. Americans remain sharply divided over issues such as birth control, abortion, sex education, unmarried cohabitation, single parents, and homosexuality. Jealousy becomes especially salient when sexual norms and gender roles are in flux.

An analysis of articles in popular magazines reveals that the experience, expression, interpretation, and treatment of jealousy have changed substantially in the United States since World War II. Prior to the late 1960s, the prevailing view of marriage emphasized commitment and "togetherness," so jealousy (within appropriate limits) was widely viewed as a natural emotion, as evidence of love, and as good for marriage. Women's magazines told readers that they should be flattered if their husbands were a little jealous.

Beginning in the late 1960s, as the sexual revolution and the women's movement introduced a new concern with personal freedom, jealousy came to be viewed by many as a learned emotion, as evidence of some personal defect such as "low self-esteem," and as bad for marriage and other intimate relationships. By the early 1970s, women's magazines reflected the new view of jealousy as a useless emotion that is out of place in a world of "liberated" relationships. Changes in society and culture produced changes in the private emotional life of individuals (Clanton 1989; Clanton and Smith 1998).

From the end of World War II until the late 1960s, virtually all of the articles in popular magazines said that a certain amount of jealousy was natural, proof of love, and good for marriage. The reader (typically a woman) was advised to keep her jealous feelings "under control" and to avoid the "unreasonable" jealousy that is marked by suspicion, hostility, accusations, and threats. The woman was told to avoid situations that might make her husband jealous, but to interpret his expressions of jealousy as evidence of love. Accounts of such efforts suggest the necessity of "emotion work," active attempts to manage our emotions by evoking desirable ones and suppressing undesirable ones (Hochschild 1983; Thoits 1984). If jealousy threatened the stability of the marriage, the reader was advised to seek professional help.

By about 1970, magazine articles began to question the appropriateness of jealous feelings in love relationships. Many people no longer assumed that jealousy was evidence of love. For the first time, guilt about jealousy became an issue. According to the emerging view, jealousy was not natural; it was learned. Jealousy was no longer seen as proof of love; it was, rather, evidence of a defect such as low self-esteem or the inability to trust. Thus, jealousy was not seen as good for relationships; it was bad for them. From this it followed that one could and should seek to eradicate every trace of jealousy from one's personality.

The change in the understanding of jealousy was accompanied by semantic shifts, changes in language that reflected new beliefs. Whereas in the 1950s the word "jealousy" was often used to describe normal and possibly beneficial feelings and behaviors, by the early 1970s the word increasingly was used primarily with reference to inappropriate, unconstructive, and even pathological reactions such as suspiciousness, paranoia, and violence. In the common speech of the 1970s, the jealous person often was characterized as unduly possessive, insecure, suspicious, and suffering from low self-esteem.

Social Sources of the New View of Jealousy

The new view of jealousy that arose in the late 1960s was encouraged by a larger shift in the shape of love relationships in the United States. The 1950s and early 1960s were characterized by an emphasis on relationship commitment or "togetherness." There was almost no talk about personal freedom in marriage. The sexual revolution and the women's movement were not yet topics of conversation. In such a time, jealousy was seen as a natural proof of love and as good for marriage.

In contrast, in the late 1960s and early 1970s, many individuals sought to enhance personal freedom in relationships, often at the cost of the forms of commitment characteristic of earlier times. Cohabitation became much more common. Women demanded fairness. The divorce rate rose. The media reported on nude beaches, communes, and gay pride. The book *Open Marriage* (O'Neill and O'Neill 1972) topped the best-sellers list for over a year in 1972. For discussion of these trends, see Clanton (1984), Gagnon (1977), Lawson (1988), and Swidler (1980).

As a result of these and other manifestations of concern for more personal freedom in love relationships, jealousy came to be viewed by many as a personal defect. If one emphasizes freedom in relationships, one will see jealousy as inappropriate and undesirable.

The quest for more personal freedom in love relationships and in marriage was part of a larger trend in favor of more freedom, more experimentation, and a more positive view of pleasure. These qualities often are associated with the youthful counterculture of the late 1960s, but, in fact, various manifestations of these themes diffused through the whole culture in the 1970s and 1980s. By the 1980s, even such a conventional voice as the advice columnist "Dear Abby" embraced the view that the jealous person is suspicious, insecure, and in need of counseling. The view of jealousy as a personal defect remains strong today.

To summarize: Jealousy is a consequence of social organization and will vary as forms of social organization vary. The sexual conservatism of the period before about 1965 produced a relatively positive view of jealousy, while the liberalization of the late 1960s and early 1970s produced a negative appraisal of jealousy.

Stearns (1990) demonstrates that the understanding of sibling jealousy (sibling rivalry) also changed in the twentieth century. Before the 1920s, neither experts, nor advice-givers, nor parents expressed much concern about sibling jealousy, but from about 1925 onward, child-rearing manuals routinely included dire and lengthy warnings about sibling rivalry, and parents came to note the issue as a major concern. Various strategies were recommended to reduce tension between siblings and to reassure children that they were loved. Some factors that contributed to this shift include smaller family size, which heightened actual sibling rivalry over previous levels; expert reassessment of early childhood as a time of emotional turmoil; and a growing desire to produce smooth, conflict-free personalities to fit into a more managerial, service-oriented economy.

Understanding and Managing Jealousy

Although sociology is not a clinical method, the sociological study of emotions has clinical implications. A sociological view of jealousy can facilitate better self-understanding and more effective therapy. Sociology encourages a focus on normal jealousy rather than pathological jealousy.

Sociological analysis suggests that most jealousy is best understood as a relationship problem rather than a personal problem rooted in the psychological inadequacies of one individual. The reduction of painful jealousy may depend more on negotiation between the partners than on the eradication of some weakness in one partner. If professional help is sought, marriage counseling or relationship therapy may be more helpful than individual psychotherapy. By concentrating so narrowly on the individual, psychotherapy sometimes exacerbates relationship problems. Furthermore, when an individual enters private psychotherapy because of relationship problems, divorce is a likely outcome, especially if the therapist is also divorced and remarried. Helping professionals who work with jealous couples should give more attention to the social forces bearing upon them, especially the life cycle of the couple, their economic circumstances, and the changing cultural environment, especially recent and ongoing changes in sexual rules and gender roles.

Jealousy and Self-Esteem: A Misunderstood Relationship

Today it is fashionable to assume that low self-esteem is a major cause of jealousy and that raising one's self-esteem is a good way to reduce or "cure" jealousy. Sociological analysis calls this view into question. The sociology of knowledge (Berger and Luckmann 1966) encourages a search for the social roots of this assumption.

Explanations of jealousy as evidence of low self-esteem are part of the larger tendency since the 1970s to view a wide range of personal failures and problems as caused by low self-esteem. This view is widely taken for granted by both helping professionals and lay people. It is, nevertheless, erroneous and dangerous. In fact, one may have high self-esteem in general but still be uncertain and vulnerable in some situations. One may have high self-esteem but still experience jealousy if a valued relationship appears to be threatened.

Although it enjoys the status of a "scientific" principle of great therapeutic usefulness, the notion that emotional upsets are caused mostly by low self-esteem is, in fact, an erroneous extension of the commonsense principle that success is associated with self-confidence and with liking oneself and that failure is associated with lack of self-confidence and not liking oneself (i.e., low self-esteem).

Explanations of human behavior often assert that low self-esteem causes failure, but it is at least as true that failure causes low self-esteem (or, that the relationship is reciprocal). Thus, most statements in the popular psychological literature about the relationship between low self-esteem and various personal failures or inadequacies are at best circular and at worst backward. That is, such statements either say nothing beyond the truism that successful people feel better about themselves than do failures, or, worse, they actually invert the causal relationship and view low self-esteem as the cause of failure when, in fact, failure is more often the cause of lowered self-esteem.

Reflecting this viewpoint, a psychotherapist told me, "I have never had a jealous patient who was not also suffering from low self-esteem." She was puzzled when I asked her which caused which. Like many others, she *assumed* that the low self-esteem caused the jealousy. It is at least as plausible that the jealousy caused the low self-esteem. That is, individuals' experiences of jealousy resulted in their feeling less good about themselves, a tendency encouraged by the new view, which sees jealousy as a personal defect. As Ellis and Weinstein (1985) point out, after an intrusive episode that provokes jealousy, one can no longer take for granted the partner's commitment. This undercuts one's sense of self. The jealous person must be on guard against threats to self as well as against the possible loss of the partner. Similarly, Buunk and Bringle (1987) conclude that the experience of jealousy results in loss of self-esteem.

If an experience of jealousy routinely causes low self-esteem, how can low self-esteem be the principal cause of jealousy? If an experience of jealousy reflects a relationship problem, how can the jealousy be reduced solely through the enlargement of the self-esteem of one individual? As Durkheim (1995) noted, whenever a social fact is explained in terms of a psychological fact, we can be certain the explanation is false. For thoughtful sociological analysis of popular self-help movements, see Hochschild (2003) and Irvine (1995).

Leaving aside the methodological problems that characterize many studies of jealousy and self-esteem, several kinds of evidence suggest that low self-esteem is not the principal cause of jealousy.

1. Cross-cultural surveys reveal that low self-esteem plays little or no role in explanations of jealousy in various cultures (Hupka 1981). In all cultures, jealousy is provoked by perceived violations of marriage rules, by real events in the social world, not by personal defects in isolated individuals (Davis 1936).

2. The "low self-esteem" explanation for jealousy is not found in the popular media in the United States before the late 1960s. If it were a timeless truth, you would expect someone would have written about it earlier.

3. Empirical research has not found a consistent correlation between low self-esteem and jealousy. Kosins (1983) reviewed the literature and found five studies that reported modest correlations and five more that found no significant correlation. Hansen (1985) cited one study that finds a negative relationship between self-esteem and jealousy for both men and women, one that finds this relationship only for men, and three that find no relationship between the two variables. In his own research, Hansen (1985) found low self-esteem to be associated with jealousy for females but not for males. Furthermore, most studies do not address the question of causation at all.

4. Kosins (1983; Clanton and Kosins 1991) tested the psychoanalytic speculation that early conflicts with parents and siblings make an individual more likely to experience intense jealousy in adult relationships. The research found no statistically significant relationships between a subtle measure of jealousy and several developmental variables including childhood conflicts with siblings, separations and losses during childhood, harshness of parental discipline, quality of early parent-child relations, and emotional support from peers in childhood. Furthermore, there was no significant difference in the intensity of jealousy reported by college students (representing the "normal" or nonclinical population), psychotherapy outpatients, and a small group of psychiatric inpatients. These surprising findings suggest that jealousy is not best viewed primarily as an emotional disorder and that therapists treating clients with jealousy problems ought not assume that jealousy always is rooted in disrupted attachment history and early sibling conflicts. Although this study is a modest one and further research is needed, these findings call into question the popular view that all or most jealousy is caused by personal deficiencies such as low self-esteem.

5. Those who assume that low self-esteem causes jealousy also are likely to assume that low self-esteem causes delinquent behavior in young people. Contrary to this expectation, McCarthy and Hoge (1984) found that the effect of self-esteem on subsequent delinquent behavior is negligible. Instead, they found consistent but weak negative effects of delinquent behavior on subsequent self-esteem. In other words, low self-esteem does not cause delinquency, but delinquency tends to lower self-esteem. Furthermore, it is reasonable to assume that delinquent behavior sometimes *raises* self-esteem for persons who can find no other route to "success." This study challenges the assumption that low self-esteem is the cause of delinquency, and it provides a basis for questioning the assumption that low self-esteem is the cause of jealousy.

6. In his introduction to a collection of articles on self-esteem and social problems, sponsored by the California Task Force to Promote Self-Esteem and Personal and Social Responsibility, Smelser (1989) notes that most of the social problems under consideration were assumed by the researchers to be caused by low self-esteem, not the other way around. Smelser notes, however, that in some cases this assumption is only half-plausible.

For example, because so much unemployment is involuntary and so many of the unemployed are chronically dependent on welfare, we should not conclude from a correlation of dependence and low self-esteem that the dependence is caused by low self-esteem. We know that diminished self-esteem often is the product of something outside the individual.

Smelser (1989) concludes that one of the most disappointing aspects of every chapter in the anthology is how low the associations are between self-esteem and its alleged consequences. In a few cases, consistent relationships are found. For example, high self-esteem is associated with the use of contraceptives by teenage girls, and measures of high self-esteem correlate positively with academic achievement. Children with alcoholic parents have lower self-esteem than other children. Children who have been abused by their parents show low scores on self-esteem measures. In some cases, however, the associations run in unexpected directions. For example, the use of psychoactive drugs seems to have a positive effect on self-esteem, and one study appears to suggest a positive association between high self-esteem and child abuse!

The most consistently reported finding, however, is that the hypothesized associations between self-esteem and its expected consequences are mixed, insignificant, or absent (Smelser 1989). The absence of correlation holds in important areas such as teenage pregnancy, child abuse, and most cases of alcohol and drug abuse. If the association between self-esteem and behavior is so weak, even less can be said for a causal relationship between the two.

Although jealousy may be exacerbated by the personal weaknesses and pathologies of individuals, sociological analysis suggests that most jealousy is best understood as a relationship problem that requires the attention of both members of the couple. As Margolin (1981) has noted, jealousy is an interactional problem more often than it is an individual problem. Jealousy is often a reflection of larger issues of relationship satisfaction and dissatisfaction. Questionnaire data from 66 married individuals found marital satisfaction to be negatively correlated with jealousy (Guerrero and Eloy 1992).

Jealousy and Power: A Neglected Relationship

The key to understanding jealousy is not the low self-esteem of the jealous individual (a psychological fact), but rather the imbalance of power within the couple (a social fact). I devised the Relationship Assessment Scale to measure power differences in love relationships, including dating, cohabitation, engagement, and marriage. Partners respond separately and without consultation to ten questions such as: Who makes more money? Who has more professional prestige? Who loves the other more? Who would find a new partner quicker if you broke up? Who desires sex with the other more? Who is more articulate, more persuasive? In most relationships, one partner will be more powerful in some areas and the other in others.

My hypothesis holds that the greater the imbalance of power within the couple, the greater the likelihood of problems with jealousy. Conversely, the more equal the balance of power, the less jealousy. Movement toward equality of power in a relationship may be useful for preventing and reducing painful jealousy (White and Mullen 1989).

Within a couple, the less powerful partner is more likely to become jealous. Insofar as women are usually less powerful than men, they are more likely to appear jealous. The societal trend in the direction of greater gender equality probably has the effect of reducing jealousy generally, especially among women. This reduction in women's jealousy is reflected in higher divorce rates (which leveled off around 1980) and higher rates of unmarried mothers (which continue to rise). Since the 1960s, women have been less likely than their mothers and grandmothers to protect their relationships with men at all costs, less likely to forgive betrayal, less likely to tolerate excessive possessiveness and the double standard, less likely to tolerate physical abuse, and less likely to sacrifice for the sake of the marriage.

Ten Dangerous Misconceptions about Jealousy

Much of what sociology reveals about jealousy contrasts sharply with American conventional wisdom and popular psychology since about 1970. It is useful, therefore, to summarize the sociological findings so as to challenge ten dangerous misconceptions about jealousy that are widespread in late twentieth- and early twenty-first-century American culture. These misunderstandings threaten the happiness and well-being of those who hold them and thus have implications for education, marriage, law, psychotherapy, and self-understanding, as well as for further development of the sociology of emotions. What we feel (emotions) depends on what we know (beliefs).

THE SOCIAL USEFULNESS OF JEALOUSY.

1. It is widely believed that jealousy is a useless emotion. In fact, jealousy often is useful for individuals, couples, community, and society. The largely overlooked social function of jealousy is the protection of love, marriage, and other valued relationships. By protecting marriage, jealousy contributes to solidarity and social order (Davis 1936). Jealousy may be defined as a protective reaction to a perceived threat (especially adultery) to a valued relationship (especially marriage or a relationship that leads to marriage) or to its quality. The usefulness of jealousy is easily overlooked in our culture because of the readiness to assume that jealousy is always a bad thing and that the jealous person is overly sensitive and probably suffering from low self-esteem. The sexual revolution of the 1960s and 1970s encouraged the more negative view of jealousy that now prevails in the United States.

JEALOUSY AND ENVY.

2. It is widely believed that jealousy and envy are the same emotion. In fact, although jealousy and envy often are mixed together in real life, they are responses to quite different situations. Jealousy always involves an attempt to protect a valued relationship (especially marriage) from a perceived threat (especially adultery). Envy is resentment toward someone who has some desirable object or quality that one does not have and cannot get. Envy, in other words, is hostility toward superiors, a negative feeling toward someone who is better off. Envy is not the wish for what one does not have. It is the much darker wish that the superior should lose the advantage that provoked the envy or otherwise should suffer.

LEARNING TO BE JEALOUS.

3. It is widely believed that jealousy is an instinctive biological reaction that humans share with lower animals. People often speak of the jealousy exhibited by pets, suggesting thereby that human jealousy is all or mostly "instinctive." In fact, adult jealousy

in humans is learned as other things are learned through modeling, practice, and feedback. Jealousy is learned as individuals internalize marriage rules, the adultery taboo, and strategies for the protection of threatened relationships. Because these arrangements vary across cultures, jealousy is learned differently in different times and places. Monogamous and polygamous cultures produce different patterns of jealousy. Extramarital sexual activities that provoke intense jealousy in most Americans may provoke little or no reported jealousy among wife-lending Eskimos, the sexually permissive Toda, or contemporary swingers, assuming that the ground rules of each culture or subculture were honored.

THE PSYCHOLOGY OF JEALOUSY.

4. It is widely believed that jealousy is usually a personal problem, rooted in the inadequacies of the jealous individual. In fact, jealousy is usually a relationship problem. Its solution requires the involvement of both partners. The unit of analysis should be the couple, not the individual. Attention should be devoted to communication and negotiation. Most jealousy problems that require professional help call for couple therapy or marital counseling rather than individual psychotherapy.

5. It is widely believed that all or most jealousy results from low self-esteem in the jealous individual. In fact, although low self-esteem can exacerbate jealousy, most jealousy results from an imbalance of power between the partners (Clanton 1989). Thus, movement toward equality of power within a relationship may reduce the potential for jealousy.

6. It is widely believed that women are more jealous than men. In fact, there is no consistent evidence to indicate that either gender is more jealous than the other (Clanton and Smith 1998). Women, however, are more willing to acknowledge jealousy (and to blame themselves for the problem), while men are more likely to deny or relabel jealousy (and to blame the woman and others for the problem). Women's greater willingness to admit to jealousy is consistent with women's greater willingness to talk honestly about feelings and to take responsibility for how a relationship is going. Kosins (1983) found that women's slightly higher scores on a measure of jealousy were roughly proportional to women's lower scores on a measure of social desirability.

7. It is widely believed that adult jealousy is rooted in disrupted attachment history and the emotional conflicts of the early years. In fact, adult jealousy shows no strong association with early conflicts (Clanton and Kosins 1991). Experiences of romantic love and loss of love in adolescence and young adulthood probably are more important than early childhood experiences in contributing to a propensity toward adult jealousy.

8. It is widely believed that jealousy is associated with neurosis or mental illness. In fact, a comparison of patients in a mental hospital, psychotherapy outpatients, and a control group (neither hospitalized nor in therapy) found no significant differences in the amount and intensity of jealousy (Clanton and Kosins 1991). The view of jealousy as rooted simply in a psychological weakness of the jealous person is a reflection of the negative view of jealousy that emerged at the time of the sexual revolution.

MANAGING JEALOUSY.

9. It is widely believed that jealousy should be repressed and denied. Indeed, the repression and denial of negative emotions is characteristic of American, English, and other Northern European Protestant cultures. The repression and denial of jealousy are often

accompanied by a conscious or unconscious reduction of commitment in a relationship: To avoid being hurt, one may withdraw from a relationship. In fact, jealousy should be acknowledged, expressed, and analyzed in the context of negotiations aimed at improving relationship quality. The denial of jealousy is no guarantee that it is absent.

10. It is widely believed that an individual's goal should be the complete eradication of jealousy. In fact, one's goal should be appropriate jealousy, constructively expressed. We should attempt to minimize inappropriate jealousy and destructive expressions of jealousy. But the complete absence of jealousy sometimes reflects indifference (Buss 2000). As Kris Kristofferson warned, sometimes "freedom's just another word for nothing left to lose."

The Further Sociological Study of Jealousy

Although observation and survey research are desirable, both are problematic, because jealousy is usually denied, repressed, and relabeled. Observational research requires a keen sense of what jealousy is, how it is likely to be expressed, and by what means it is likely to be hidden from view. Survey research and attempts to measure jealousy in individuals require unobtrusive measures, probably connected to descriptions of possible jealousy-producing vignettes (Ellestad and Stets 1998), and avoid the use of the term *jealousy*. It is meaningless to ask subjects how jealous they are when they probably are unclear about what jealousy is and they are very likely to deny being jealous (Clanton 1981).

Historical and cross-cultural research holds great promise for advancing our understanding of jealousy. All societies, past and present, are available to us as case studies in the production and management of jealousy. As Durkheim (1995) extracted lessons about religion from anthropological accounts of hunting and gathering cultures, we can extract lessons about jealousy from a vast trove of historical and comparative materials. Sociological accounts of jealousy must move beyond psychometrics and therapeutic concerns to reveal the overlooked larger social implications of jealousy and, by extension, the social implications of emotions in general.

Sociology and Psychology

Sociological analysis challenges some elements of the psychological view of jealousy that prevails in the "therapeutic culture" in which Americans live (Rieff 1966). The psychological framing of life experience is encouraged by the excessive individualism that characterizes American culture (Bellah et al. 1985). Sociological consideration of jealousy and other emotions draws attention to the influence of society and culture on the private emotions of individuals and to the hidden social usefulness of emotions. The sociological view tends to destigmatize the jealous individual and to break the cycle of blaming the victim, which is encouraged by the widespread but erroneous view that jealousy is caused primarily by the personal inadequacies (especially the low self-esteem) of the jealous person. Sociology is useful in the education of psychotherapists as an antidote to the tendency of clinicians to neglect social forces and concentrate too narrowly on the early experiences and the inner life of the individual and on the dysfunctional aspects of jealousy and other emotions.

This analysis of jealousy is intended to demonstrate the usefulness of the sociology of emotions and to provide a framework for the sociological study of other emotions. As Durkheim (1951) sought to demonstrate the power of sociology by explaining the solitary act of suicide in terms of the influence of group membership, this chapter follows Davis (1936) in seeking to demonstrate the power of sociology by explaining the private emotion of jealousy in terms of the influence of social learning, social institutions, and society and culture.

ENVY

Here we distinguish envy from other emotions with which it often is confused. We note the universality of envy, its cross-cultural variability, its overlooked social usefulness, the strategies by which societies attempt to reduce and manage it, and the political implications of envy management.

The Neglect of Envy by the Social Sciences

As both Scheler (1961) and Schoeck (1970) have noted, despite its considerable social significance, envy largely has been neglected as a topic of social scientific inquiry. Jealousy has received more attention than envy (Parrott 1991). Salovey (1991:xi), in the preface to *The Psychology of Jealousy and Envy*, chronicles the emergence of jealousy research in the 1970s and 1980s and concludes that after decades of neglect, "jealousy and envy . . . have certainly emerged as legitimate topics of scientific inquiry." However, of the 12 chapters in the Salovey book, 9 are about jealousy, only 1 is about envy, and 2 are about both emotions. Envy remains the most neglected emotion and the least well understood.

Discovering Envy

Here we revisit and extend the definition of envy and note the difficulty of studying an emotion that routinely is denied, repressed, and relabeled. As noted above, envy is hostility toward superiors, a negative feeling toward someone who is better off (Scheler 1961; Schoeck 1970). In other words, *envy* is resentment toward someone who has some desirable object or quality that one does not have and cannot get.

Envy is *not* the wish for the object or advantage that provoked the envy. Rather, envy is the much darker wish that the superior would *lose* the object or advantage. Envy is the perverse pleasure, the malicious joy (*Schadenfreude*), that is felt when the superior fails or suffers.

The envious person rarely resorts to violence against the superior and rarely seeks to seize or to win the desired object through direct competition (Schoeck 1970). Often the envious person takes no action, but instead merely wishes that the other would lose the advantage that provoked the envy or otherwise would suffer. And the envious person may quietly celebrate any such loss or suffering that may befall a superior. Most often, such dark feelings are contained within the individual. Occasionally, they may be voiced to others: "I'd like to see him get what's coming to him," "Serves them right," or "How the mighty have fallen."

The most common outward expression of envy is gossip (Foster 1972). Recall, for example, the deprecating labels your high school peers used to describe the student with the best grades ("teacher's pet" and worse), the best football or basketball player ("dumb jock"), and the beauty queen ("stuck up"). Any quality or achievement that provokes admiration also is likely to provoke some envy.

An individual's envy is likely to be strongest when the advantage of the superior is in an area of importance to the individual's own self-definition. As James (1983:296) observed, he might envy another person whose knowledge of psychology exceeded his own, but he would be unlikely to envy someone whose knowledge of Greek exceeded his own.

> I, who for the time have staked my all on being a psychologist, am mortified if others know much more psychology than I. But I am contented to wallow in the grossest ignorance of Greek. My deficiencies there give me no sense of personal humiliation at all. Had I "pretensions" to be a linguist, it would have been just the reverse.

Following James, Salovey and his associates (Salovey and Rodin 1989; Salovey and Rothman 1991) have argued that envy is most likely to be felt when comparisons are made in domains that are especially important to how we define ourselves. We only truly care about our performance in a limited number of life domains. This "domain relevance hypothesis" holds that envy is most likely to be experienced when comparisons with another person are negative for the self, and these comparisons are in a domain that is especially important and relevant to self-definition.

Conceptually speaking, one cannot envy "down." By definition, the envied must be better off than the envier. In real life, however, it is possible to be simultaneously better off than another in some ways but less well off in other ways. For example, younger people may envy older people for their wealth and power, but older people with wealth and power may envy younger people for their health and good looks. The unemployed youth who is going fishing may envy the bank president because of his wealth, but the bank president may envy the unemployed youth because of his freedom to go fishing.

Envy, like all emotions, is a feeling within an individual. But envy may also prevail between groups, classes, and whole societies. Poor individuals may envy the rich as a whole. Losers in competitions envy winners in general. (This may account in part for the tendency of some sports spectators, when they do not care strongly which team wins, to root for the underdog.) The New York Yankees and the Los Angeles Lakers have been described by numerous sportswriters as "the most hated team in America," the result of long histories of success and glamour. Likewise, New Yorkers and Californians often are targets of envy from people who live in other parts of the country. Americans are targets of envy from people who live in other parts of the world. Following the attacks of September 11, 2001, even in nations friendly to the United States, some individuals voiced the idea that Americans previously had been spared such attacks on their own soil but now must come to terms with loss and vulnerability such as other nations know.

The Denial of Envy

Because envy is a completely negative emotion, it usually is repressed, denied, disguised, and relabeled. To admit straightforwardly to envy is to declare oneself to be inferior to another and hostile toward that person (or class of persons) because of the inferiority.

Because of repression, individuals are usually unaware of their own envy and so are not reliable informants about their own envy. In a review quoted on the cover of Helmut Schoeck's 1966 book *Envy*, anthropologist George Murdock writes: "Schoeck has accomplished something comparable to what Freud did, namely to uncover and reveal the social implications of a deeply repressed motive." Freud argued that many social institutions are designs for the management of unconscious sexuality and the propensity toward violence. Schoeck shows that many social institutions are designs for the management of unconscious envy. Although many sociologists have an aversion to Freud and to the notion of the unconscious mind (Manning 2005), the study of envy clearly represents an area of inquiry in which a full understanding of the phenomenon in question requires both sociological and psychological sensitivities.

Envy often is mislabeled as "jealousy," thus making it less likely that we will understand it and deal with it constructively. Conversely, jealousy is almost never mislabeled as "envy." This pattern of usage suggests that envy is more negative, more shameful, and more deeply repressed than jealousy, even if we are not sure why. Envy is one of the seven deadly sins, but jealousy is not (Lyman 1978).

As an example of the confusion surrounding jealousy and envy, the 2004 comedy film *Envy* was promoted by HBO thus: "Jealousy rears its ugly head in *Envy*." A TV guide listed the film as follows: "*Envy* (2004, Comedy) A man becomes jealous of his wealthy friend." Although this film is clearly about *envy*, these two different descriptions of the film use the word "jealousy." Thus, the popular media both reflect and contribute to the confusion of jealousy and envy.

Some academic writing also contributes to the confusion. Mead (1931), toward the end of a classic article on jealousy, begins discussing envy, without ever using the word "envy" and without realizing that she has switched topics. DeSwann (1989) titles his inquiry "Jealousy as a Class Phenomenon: The Petite Bourgeoisie and Social Security," but the article is clearly about envy, not jealousy.

Because envy is repressed, denied, and relabeled, it is difficult to observe and almost impossible to assess through self-report. To study envy by observation, we must look for it in the situations in which it is likely, and we must watch for the disguises in which it often appears.

Situations in which envy is likely include the following: Your best friend wins a coveted scholarship or award. A neighbor wins the lottery. A co-worker gets a raise or a promotion, but you do not. Another woman becomes pregnant when you cannot. The star of the team gets a huge salary and most of the press attention. In a crowded parking lot, another driver finds a parking place when you cannot. In each case, if you could be 100 percent happy for the other with no qualifications or second thoughts, you would be without envy. But to whatever degree you find yourself, even for a moment, thinking the other does not deserve the good fortune or wishing that the other would lose his or her advantage or otherwise suffer that is a measure of your envy.

The great stories of Western civilization include many examples of envy. The Egyptian god Osiris is killed and dismembered by his brother Seth, who is envious of his radiant attractiveness, power, and success. Othello is brought down by the envious Iago, who, by the way, uses Othello's propensity to jealousy against him. Salieri hates Mozart because he is more talented and his work as a composer is so effortless. Sailor Billy Budd, adored by the crew for his innocence and natural charisma, becomes the victim of the envy of the ship's master-at-arms John Claggart, who falsely accuses Billy of conspiracy to mutiny.

Although no one likes to admit to envy, especially when we are clear about what it is, it is hard to imagine any human being completely without envy. Some individuals, of course, are, for whatever reasons, much more or less envious than others. But all humans who have not yet achieved moral perfection probably experience some envy.

The common disguises (indirect expressions) of envy include attempts to shift a comparison from areas in which one compares poorly with another to areas in which one looks good, attempts to provoke envy in others, to project envy and greed onto others, excessive admiration, or attempts to share the glory of another. Common verbal formulas for expressing envy include "If I can't have/do X, then no one else should either," "It's not fair that they have X and I/we don't," and, in Oscar Wilde's famous variation, "It is not enough for me to succeed; my friends must also fail."

One of my students showed that she understood what envy is when she put this note at the end of her final paper in our course:

> When I was in high school I knew this girl named Kim. I hated her to the point I avoided her in the halls. She was everything I hated in a person. She was popular, pretty (well not all that pretty), had big boobs (but they sagged), intelligent, and stuck up. It hit me in class after your envy lecture that I was envious of her.

Not only is this an example of envious resentment of the superiority of another, the envy is still active, as indicated by the tendency, years later, to gossip about the superior.

What Envy Is Not

To be clear about what envy is, it is useful to differentiate it from several other emotions and conditions with which envy often is confused in ordinary speech.

JEALOUSY. Most important here is that envy is *not* the same as jealousy. As noted above, jealousy is a protective reaction to a perceived threat to a valued relationship or to its quality (Clanton and Smith 1998). Envy is hostility toward superiors, negative feelings toward someone who is better off. Whereas jealousy typically involves three people, envy involves only two. Not only are the two emotions distinct in terms of the situations that give rise to them, an experimental study (Parrott and Smith 1993) revealed qualitative differences between them. Jealousy was characterized by fear of loss, distrust, anxiety, and anger. Envy was characterized by feelings of inferiority, longing, resentment, and disapproval of the emotion.

AN INNOCENT WISH. Envy, as noted above, is not an innocent wish for what one does not have. Envy is the darker wish that a superior should lose or suffer. Envy takes delight at the downfall of a superior. Of course, a wish for an object or advantage may be accompanied by unconscious envy.

ADMIRATION. Although the two often are mixed together in real life, envy is different from admiration. In ordinary speech we may say that we "envy" someone's ability as a public speaker. This is technically a misuse of the word "envy," because we presumably are not consciously wishing that the speaker in question will embarrass himself before an audience or get laryngitis before a big speech. Instead, we are expressing admiration for this person's skill, and the admiration may or may not be mixed with unconscious envy.

Advertisers often play on the fact that if one is admired, one also might be envied. A recent print ad for a German luxury car trumpets: "More Horses. Bigger Engine. Increased Envy." Another luxury car ad promises, "Once again envy will be standard equipment." An expensive men's fragrance is called Envy. A recent print ad for diet pills shows a photo of a newly slim celebrity model with the caption, "Be envied." A long-running ad for a line of hair products showed beautiful women with great hair and the caption: "Don't hate me because I'm beautiful." Advertising, which is the consumer culture's version of mythology, promises the pleasure that comes from being envied by others. As Aeschylus noted, "He who goes unenvied shall not be admired."

EMULATION. Envy is different from emulation. In ordinary speech, we may say that "envy" is a good thing because it motivates people to work harder to get for themselves what they envy others for having. Rather than envy the owner of a fine automobile, we should emulate her. This presumably means that we should work hard, make a lot of money, and buy such a car for ourselves. Our capitalist ethos encourages us to convert our envy into emulation, thus reducing the risk that the envious have-nots will demand redistribution of wealth and privilege. Because much envy is stimulated by differences that cannot be relieved by emulation, this advice is hollow. Some envy can be converted into emulation with a resulting increase in productivity, but a great deal of envy is the result of enduring inequalities that cannot be eliminated through hard work.

Distinguishing envy from jealousy, innocent wishes, admiration, and emulation helps us to see that envy, unlike these others, is a thoroughly negative experience for both the envier (because no one enjoys contemplating his or her own inferiority and hostility toward others) and the envied (because no one likes being hated and gossiped about by friends, associates, and the general public). Although one may momentarily celebrate being envied as a mark of one's success, no one really wants others to, day in and day out, wish that one would fail, lose, or suffer—and celebrating when one does.

THE UNIVERSALITY OF ENVY.   Envy is rooted in comparison: To be envious, one must first compare oneself with another person or persons who are judged to be better off in some way that is important. Because comparisons with others are inescapable in social life, *envy is a universal potential*. In every society, envy is a possible response in a vast range of social interactions between and among persons and groups of unequal wealth, status, power, fame, success, health, talent, grades, looks, and popularity. Envy is potential in virtually all human interactions. Indeed, envy would be a *likely* outcome in most social situations were it not for social conventions designed to reduce envy.

A Comparative View of Envy

Although envy is universal, it varies across cultures and over time (Foster 1972). Sociological understanding of envy is facilitated by the comparison of envy in the simplest tribal societies and in complex industrial societies such as the United States.

In simple societies, the awareness of envy is high. Tribal people know what envy is and anticipate it in every situation in which it is potential. In industrial societies, awareness of envy is low. As noted above, most Americans are unclear about what envy is. The denial of envy is largely effective. Most Americans, most of the time, do not think of themselves as being envious, and most do not consciously anticipate being the target of envy in situations where it is potential.

In simple societies, the fear of envy is very high. Tribal people believe that they will be hated (envied) by their neighbors for any advantage they may gain, and they are likely to believe that the hostile wishes of their neighbors can harm them, bring bad health to their families, and cause their gardens to wither and their goats to die. Compliments are largely absent in tribal and peasant societies (Foster 1972:173).

In industrial societies, conscious fear of envy is low. Americans worry much less about provoking envy than tribal people. We are much less likely to turn down an opportunity to minimize the envy of others. We are much less fearful about being the target of envy and less fearful of compliments in part because we mostly do not believe, as tribal people do, that the hostile wishes of an envious neighbor have the power to harm us.

A cross-cultural comparison of jealousy and envy (Hupka et al. 1993) found that conceptual distinctions between the two emotions overlapped strongly in the United States, weakly in Germany, and not at all in Russia. In other words, Americans (living in the most advanced, most capitalist industrial society) are least clear about the difference between envy and jealousy, Russians (living in the least advanced industrial society, with a long history of forced collectivism) most clear, and Germans somewhere in between.

Because of the very high awareness and fear of envy, simple societies have low levels of economic productivity that remain unchanged for many generations (Foster 1972; Schoeck 1970). Tribal people are reluctant to invent new and more efficient technologies, and they are reluctant to accumulate any benefits that might come from improved efficiency because of the fear of being envied and because of the belief that the envious wishes of others can bring harm to oneself and one's family.

Because of the low awareness and fear of envy, industrial societies have high levels of economic productivity and enjoy dramatic economic growth across the generations. Americans are more likely than tribal people to innovate and accumulate wealth because we are not much inhibited by the fear of being envied and because we do not believe the envious wishes of others can harm us.

Because of high fear of envy, people in simple societies attempt to manage envy by protecting themselves from envy as expressed in witchcraft, curses, and the "evil eye." As Foster (1972:174) notes:

> The evil eye is the most widespread of cultural definitions of the situation in which envy is present, and where its harmful effects must be guarded against. Although children are the prime targets of the "eye," other valued property such as animals and crops may be damaged.

Because of low awareness and fear of envy, people in industrial societies manage envy in the face of great inequality of wealth and power by doing their best to ignore the differences that might provoke envy and by rationalizing (explaining away) those differences they cannot ignore.

Awareness and fear of envy are higher in preindustrial than in industrial societies, higher in rural than in urban communities, and higher in recently arrived immigrant groups than among native-born Americans. The fear of envy is higher in poor communities than in the middle class and above and higher for nonwhite minorities than for most whites.

A major cultural constraint on higher education for disadvantaged minorities is the high level of envy in the communities from which many minority students come. If very few in the community have gone to college, there will be more who wish others from the community should also not go to college. In some immigrant communities, it is assumed that kids who go to college will move away from the neighborhood, and the prevailing sentiment is, "It's a stupid man who makes his son better than he is." This is similar to the Italian peasant proverb, "Never educate your children beyond yourself." Blacks sometimes refer to black communities as "crabs in a barrel," suggesting that anyone who is about to climb out of the disadvantaged neighborhood will be pulled down by others. A black student who speaks standard correct unaccented English often will be put down by other blacks as "talking white." Hispanic students, especially females, often face strong family pressure to drop out of college, being told they are "selfish" to want what their parents did not have. American Indian students are influenced by tribal cultures in which high awareness and fear of envy make individuals reluctant to achieve what their neighbors do not have. For all disadvantaged minorities and for poor whites as well, educational achievement and upward mobility are inhibited by the fear of being envied in communities from which few have gone to college.

Avoiding Envy

The important differences in envy-management between simple and complex societies can be illustrated by comparisons of their respective strategies by which an individual may avoid the envy of others (Foster 1972). In every society, four main strategies of envy-avoidance are employed, always in the same order, because each strategy reduces envy while giving up less than the strategy that follows it. The strategies are concealment, denial, symbolic sharing, and true sharing or redistribution.

CONCEALMENT. In simple societies, a person may hide surplus food or hide from view a healthy child (or goat) in order to avoid being envied by a neighbor, especially by one who has no food or whose own child (or goat) is sick or has died. Concealment was difficult in tribal societies, where everyone lived in an open camp and privacy was unknown. In industrial societies, class segregation allows the rich to conceal their advantage from the nonrich in residential enclaves, country clubs, private schools, and exclusive entertainments.

DENIAL.   In simple societies, a person who is found to have surplus food may reduce the envy of neighbors by claiming that the food is rotten or otherwise inedible. A person may claim that his or her child (or goat) is sick and could die at any time. In industrial societies, a polite person is expected to minimize his or her own achievements, to deflect compliments, to exhibit modesty, to deny, in other words, that he or she has done anything that should result in being envied. Winners of Oscars and MVP awards reduce envy by being modest and by sharing the glory with associates.

SYMBOLIC SHARING.   If neither concealment nor denial is successful, the next step is to seek to reduce the envy of the other by giving up some part of that which provoked the envy or by sharing the glory in some way. In some tribal societies, new fathers leave a phallic gift of a baton at the door of each other husband in the village, as though to say, "Don't hate me for fathering a healthy child. You too can do this." In industrial societies, new fathers give a phallic gift of a cigar to other men whom they meet but without a clear sense of why. The ancient tradition of bringing food to the home where someone had died is another form of symbolic sharing that originated as an envy-avoidance mechanism.

The tip or gratuity is another modern form of symbolic sharing (Foster 1972:181), an envy-avoidance mechanism that says, "Here is some money. Don't hate me for enjoying this fine meal while you must serve me." In most European languages, the word for the tip means "drink" or "drink money" (the French *pourboire*, the German *Trinkgeld*). The English word "tip" probably derives from the older word *tipple*, meaning to drink. The tip is only enough money to buy a drink. It is only a small part of the cost of the meal that the diner has enjoyed.

Much contemporary philanthropy may be understood as symbolic sharing. Through their public generosity, the very rich are able to reduce their tax burdens and, more important, head off any popular movement in the direction of progressive taxation (Slater 1980).

TRUE SHARING.   If symbolic sharing is unsuccessful, one usually can reduce envy by sharing equally with the other the object that provoked the envy. Such redistribution reduces envy, but at a very high cost to the person who is the target of the envy. In simple societies, the fear of envy is so great that no one seeks to gain anything that the neighbors do not have. Among tribal people, wealth taboos to reduce envy ensure that everyone remains poor. Anyone who comes into any extra food or wealth is required by tribal custom to provide a feast for his neighbors (the potlatch) or otherwise to give away his advantage. The Lakota call such redistribution "the giveaway."

In industrial societies, taxation is the means by which wealth is redistributed so that envy is reduced. Contending approaches to tax policy reflect the range of economic and political options within a society. The political right seeks to reduce envy by means of class segregation and, especially, by means of rationalizations of existing inequality. The political left seeks to reduce envy by reducing the inequalities of wealth and power that cause envy. The politics of envy will be further discussed below.

Envy and Social Order

Envy, paradoxically, both threatens and helps to preserve social order (Schoeck 1970). Envy is both dysfunctional and functional. Envy threatens social order by stimulating interpersonal hostility that might lead to conflict, by inhibiting the innovation and accumulation of wealth that are necessary for prosperity, and by stirring the have-nots to revolution that overthrows the existing order. Thus, the management of envy is a universal social problem.

All societies prohibit envy; all moral systems condemn it as a violation of the highest values. In hunting-and-gathering societies, everyone remains poor because of the fear of being envied. In agricultural and industrial societies, various rationalizations of inequality are employed to reduce envy (Schoeck 1970). The Greeks explained success that otherwise might provoke envy in terms of luck; the Roman Catholics, in terms of the will of God; the Protestants, in terms of the work ethic. All three rationalizations are commonly used to reduce envy in contemporary American society.

Envy also helps to preserve social order. The social usefulness of envy lies primarily in its contribution to social control (Schoeck 1970). Fear of being envied provides one motive for conformity to necessary norms: We conform rather than be hated for our nonconformity by those who do conform. Fear of being envied protects private property: One motive for reporting a car thief is the envious feeling that "he has no more right to that car than I do." Fear of being envied encourages fairness: We are less likely to cheat on an exam or to take a favor from a judge, because we know that we would be hated and perhaps reported to authorities by those who did not cheat or receive favors.

More generally, fear of being envied reduces injustice in society (Smith 1991). Following Rawls (1971), Smith distinguishes between *resentment*, which grows out of a legitimate perception of being treated unfairly, and *envy*, in which one is unable to show that the other's advantage results from unfair circumstances or improper actions. For Rawls, resentment is a moral emotion and envy is not. Hostility is a typical response to perceived injustice, so perceptions of unfairness are very important to the understanding of envy.

Some envy can be turned into emulation of those who are more successful. This, presumably, would increase productivity, thus benefiting both the individual and the group. In all but a few cases, however, it is not possible for the nonrich to become rich simply by "working harder." By exaggerating the payoff for hard work, the capitalist prescription that envy be converted into emulation helps to rationalize and preserve existing inequalities.

Envy, then, is double-edged. It is necessary to society because it inhibits dangerous deviance, but it also threatens society, especially by inhibiting innovation, depressing productivity, and discouraging accumulation of wealth. Thus, the management of envy requires that a balance be struck. From the point of view of the political right, the goal of envy management in society is that there should be enough envy to encourage the masses to conform to necessary rules, but not so much envy as to hold back the most talented individuals (Schoeck 1970). From the point of view of the political left, the goal of envy management is that there should be not only enough envy to encourage conformity to necessary norms, but enough additional envy to inspire demands for some redistribution of wealth and power (Slater 1980). The right is concerned that too much envy would prevent the rich from becoming even richer. The left is concerned that too little envy would make it impossible to narrow the gap between the rich and the nonrich. Thus, the right seeks to conceal, minimize, and rationalize existing inequality, while the left seeks to reveal, publicize, and dramatize existing inequality.

The Management of Envy in Society

Because envy threatens social order, its management is a universal social problem. As Foster (1972:175) noted:

> All societies appear to have cultural forms, attitudinal norms, and cognitive outlooks that serve to reduce the fear of the consequences of envy, thereby contributing to the stability of the social group as well as to the psychological well being of the individual.

Envy is reduced by its prohibition in combination with one of two political strategies: shared poverty or rationalizations of inequality.

PROHIBITIONS OF ENVY. Envy is prohibited in all known societies (Foster 1972; Lyman 1978; Schoeck 1970). Every religious and ethical system condemns envy. The Ten Commandments of the Jews and Christians include, "Thou shalt not covet (envy) . . . anything that is thy neighbor's." Buddhism teaches that a virtuous person will wholeheartedly celebrate the good fortune of a neighbor. Such celebration would be the opposite of envy, in which one would begrudge the neighbor's good fortune.

The prohibition of envy, alas, is not sufficient to eradicate it from society, just as universal prohibitions of murder and adultery do not wipe out these behaviors. The universal prohibition of any attitude or behavior, especially when the prohibition is part of the highest religious and ethical principles of a people, is good evidence that the attitude or behavior is not only bad for society but also that it is potentially widespread and, by its nature, difficult to suppress. There would be no reason for such rules unless the prohibited attitudes and behaviors are likely to occur.

Because the prohibition of envy does not result in its eradication, every society must take additional measures to reduce envy. Two strategies are available, shared poverty (typical of simple tribal societies) and rationalizations of inequality (typical of agricultural and industrial societies).

SHARED POVERTY. In simple societies, where the awareness and fear of envy are high, everyone remains poor in order to reduce envy (Foster 1972). Envy, presumably, is reduced by the forced equality of shared poverty. If everyone is poor, then no one can be hated for having more than others. Such poverty probably was functional for hunting-and-gathering peoples living marginally in the face of unyielding nature: If anyone took ten times the resources of others, some members of the group probably would die. Thus, the wealth taboos of tribal peoples require that one quickly share with others any surplus one may gain. As noted above, the tribal obligation of true sharing or radical redistribution reduces the incentive for hard work, innovation, and accumulation. In this way, high fear of envy inhibits economic productivity.

Among the aboriginal people of Australia, for example, a person is required to share what he has with appropriate relatives as prescribed by kinship rules. Thus, if by working in the white economy, an aborigine obtains extra food or money or a cassette recorder, he may be required to give it away. The kinship rules are such that each individual is related to a very large number of others; so, the demands made upon the aborigine who is successful in Western terms can be very great. Frequently, the earnings of such a person become exhausted; so, there is less motivation for working hard in a competitive environment in order to earn more. Why should an individual work for the whites to earn money to buy a cassette recorder if it must be shared equally with all of one's many cousins, one of whom is likely to lose or break it? Kinship obligations such as these originated in ancient hunting-and-gathering societies. Resources were scarce and perishable, and in such situations, one finds security in the widest possible definition of mutual obligation.

But wealth taboos do not eliminate envy. In fact, tribal societies, despite their shared poverty, are marked by much more envy than is found in agricultural and industrial societies. Although tribal people are roughly equal in economic terms, they find other things to be envious about (Schoeck 1970). In such societies, where any small or temporary advantage makes one the target of a lot of envy (hatred, hostile wishes, gossip, witchcraft) from the neighbors, any attempt to improve one's situation (including traveling, moving away, learning a new skill, getting an education) would be strongly discouraged.

RATIONALIZATIONS OF INEQUALITY. In complex societies, where the awareness and fear of envy are low, it is possible to achieve or obtain more than one's neighbor without becoming the target of a lot of envy. In such societies, envy is reduced by means of *rationalizations of inequality*, socially constructed explanations that make it all right for some to have more and do better than others. Such explanations legitimize existing patterns of inequality, thus reducing the risk that one will be hated for doing better than others. Three rationalizations of inequality that are important in Western culture are the Greek concept of luck, the Roman Catholic belief in the will of God, and the Protestant work ethic (Schoeck 1970).

The Greek concept of luck (or chance or fate or fortune) is one of the most important cultural inventions in history because it freed humans from the inhibitions that resulted from envy and, thus, made possible all of the cultural inventions that followed (Schoeck 1970). By explaining one's own success as the result of good luck, one reduces the likelihood that another will be made envious by that success. Similarly, by explaining one's own failure as a result of bad luck rather than some malicious act by another, one reduces the tendency to envy those who have done better and reduces the threat that one's envy might pose to those who have done better. The concept of luck greatly reduces the power of envy to inhibit innovation, productivity, and the accumulation of wealth, status, and power.

The Roman Catholic Church taught that differences in wealth, status, power, and achievement are the result of the will of God. One ought not hate (envy) those who are better off in any way, because everyone's situation is an assignment from God and, thus, not to be questioned. If a poor person believes that his poverty is the will of God, he is less likely to hate (envy) the rich. Even more important, if a rich person knows that the poor believe his wealth is the will of God, he has less to fear from their envy and he is less apt to be inhibited from accumulating more. Roman Catholic belief in the will of God thus serves to reduce envy in society and to legitimize and preserve existing inequalities. Belief in the divine right of kings, for example, helped to preserve monarchies and to prevent the rise of democracy. Super-rich Protestant John D. Rockefeller claimed, "God gave me my money."

As Weber (1996) notes, the official teaching of the Roman Catholic Church was that poverty was noble and that wealth was morally suspect. In practice, the church sanctioned the existing inequalities of wealth and poverty as "God's will," collaborated with the ruling classes of Europe in supporting the divine right of kings, formally opposed democratic government in principle until the 1960s, and, of course, accumulated vast wealth of its own. More recently, the Catholic Church condemned the liberation theology of those priests and theologians in Latin America who engaged in political action to reduce inequality and injustice among the people to whom they minister. Pope Benedict XVI, in his previous role as the chief enforcer of Vatican policy, was the principal agent of the Catholic Church in the suppression of liberation theology.

More important than these particulars of Roman Catholic history is the church's role as the main carrier of Western culture from the fall of the Roman Empire until the Renaissance and the Reformation and beyond. We ought not let the foibles or failures of the Catholic Church or our modern secular sensibilities blind us to the social and cultural importance of the church. Monasteries preserved ancient writings that otherwise would have been lost during the Dark Ages (Cahill 1995). The Catholic Church contributed to the rise of feudal society, which replaced the chaotic warlordism of the Dark Ages. The Catholic Church established libraries, patronized the arts, and founded the first universities in Europe. The Catholic Church trained two priests, Martin Luther and John Calvin, who broke from the Catholic Church and launched the Protestant Reformation, which, according to Weber (1996), encouraged industrialization, the rise of capitalism, the possibility of democracy, the dominance of bureaucratic administration, and other aspects of modernization.

As the main carrier of Western civilization, the Roman Catholic Church provided the vocabulary and imagery for using "God's will" as a rationalization of an inequality that might otherwise stimulate envy. But this socially useful concept is much broader than Catholicism or, more generally, Christianity. Not only Orthodox and Protestant Christians, but also Jews and Muslims attribute inequalities of outcome, including the deaths of loved ones, to God's will, whether God be called Yahweh or Allah. Eastern religions, although not monotheistic, also have the notion that one's social rank and one's personal triumphs and losses are related to larger forces or higher powers. Even modern people with a secularist bent are likely, under the stress of setback, misfortune, or loss, to refer to God or to appeal to God as a way of coping.

Although Protestant Christians also use the will of God as a rationalization of inequality that reduces envy, the Protestants developed a further explanation for why some individuals have more wealth, status, and power than others—the work ethic. As Weber (1996) argued, the Protestants, especially the Calvinists, saw work in this world as a religious duty and, in time, came to believe that material success as a result of hard work and thrift is a probable sign that one is among the elect (that one is saved and likely to go to heaven).

The notion that prosperity is evidence of one's salvation was not part of the official teaching of Protestantism. The belief emerged as part of the popular religion, Weber argues, as a response to the Calvinist doctrine of predestination, the belief that God knows in advance who will be saved. Whereas Catholics were assured that they would go to heaven if they were baptized and if they participated in the important rituals of the Catholic Church, the doctrine of predestination left Protestants uncertain of their salvation. To compensate, Weber argues, the Protestants developed the idea that prosperity resulting from hard work in a vocation (any legitimate occupation) was a sign that one was among the elect.

In contrast to earlier Christian teaching that wealth is an obstacle to salvation, the Protestant work ethic made it morally acceptable to become rich. As John Wesley, the founder of Methodism, later put it (Weber 1996:175): "We ought not to prevent people from being diligent and frugal; we must exhort all Christians to gain all they can, and to save all they can; that is, in effect, to grow rich." By the time of Benjamin Franklin (1700s), who for Weber was an important exemplar and popularizer of the work ethic, the religious roots of the obligations of hard work and frugality had been largely forgotten. A secularized work ethic now prevails, sustained by the economic productivity of the capitalist system and routinized by bureaucratic administration.

To sum up: Envy is reduced by its prohibition, by the shared poverty of simple tribal societies, and by socially constructed rationalizations of inequality, especially luck, the will of God, and the Protestant work ethic. All three rationalizations, especially the work ethic, make it possible for individuals to gain wealth, status, power, and other advantages without being held back by the envy of the less fortunate. Thus, all three rationalizations, especially the work ethic, are fundamental underpinnings of industrial capitalism and its handmaiden, bureaucratic administration. The work ethic legitimizes the inequality that earlier moral systems condemned.

The Politics of Envy Management

The management of envy is inescapably political. Every political system is an arrangement for the management of envy (Yamaguchi 1997). The debate between the political left and right may be understood as a disagreement as to how envy should be managed.

Conservatives, reactionaries, and libertarians (defenders of capitalism, including most Republicans) see inequality as inevitable and prescribe class segregation, emulation, and rationalizations of inequality in order to reduce envy. From the point of view of the political right, the chief concern is that the rich and talented should not be held back by the envy of the poor masses (Novak 1988; Schoeck 1970). The right is concerned that too much envy would prevent the rich from becoming even richer. As conservative columnist George Will puts it, "Egalitarianism is envy masquerading as philosophy."

Progressives, reformers, and democratic socialists (critics of capitalism, including most Democrats) see much inequality as resulting from unfairness and prescribe progressive taxation in order to reduce the inequality that is at the root of envy. From the point of view of the political left, the chief concern is that the envy of the have-nots should be sufficient to fuel demand for reform (Slater 1980). The left is concerned that too little envy would make it impossible to narrow the gap between the rich and the nonrich.

The right seeks to conceal and minimize existing inequality, while the left seeks to reveal and dramatize existing inequality. With some justification, the right accuses the left of stirring up the envy of the masses (Novak 1988; Schoeck 1970). With some justification, the left accuses the right of dampening and diverting the envy of the masses as a way of protecting the rich from taxation (Slater 1980).

Defenders of capitalism advise the have-nots to convert their envy into emulation (Schoeck 1970). Rather than hating and pulling down those who have what you do not, you should do what they did: Work hard so that you can get the desired object for yourself.

Critics of capitalism argue that most of the envy provoked by gross inequality cannot be converted into emulation. Most nonrich people cannot reasonably hope to become very rich simply by "working harder." The capitalist advice to convert envy into emulation is largely a scam, a way of cooling out the mark, a way of thwarting progressive taxation and other reforms.

Defenders of capitalism endorse the three historic rationalizations of inequality discussed above: luck, the will of God, and the work ethic. For the right, the rich have been lucky, they have been blessed by God, or they have worked hard. Wealth is seen as nature's reward for talent and hard work. The rich are, therefore, entitled to what they have, and they ought not be hated (envied) or pulled down by those who have less (Novak 1988; Schoeck 1970). Schoeck (1970) goes further, arguing that the rich are entitled to *much more* than they have now—and that they have been blocked by the pervasive envy of the have-nots and the willingness of politicians of the left to inflame and manipulate that envy.

Critics of capitalism reject the idea that inequality is best explained in terms of luck, God's will, and the work ethic. For the left, the rich have *not* been luckier, more richly blessed, or harder-working. Great wealth, when it is not inherited, often is gained through greed, ambition, sharp dealing, cheating, and exploitation. The rich, therefore, are *not* entitled to what they have, and they should be the object of resentment (envy) by the masses and of political action that leads to greater fairness in the distribution of wealth and power (Slater 1980).

The management of envy in capitalist society involves the social construction of the approval of greed, what Slater (1980) calls "wealth addiction." Where greed is generally approved, there will not be much demand for reform. Thus, it is in the interest of the rich and powerful that the masses of the people should believe that "everyone wants to be rich." Greed stimulates little indignation, because most Americans feel that they would do the same if they could. Ordinary people come to admire the rich rather than resent them. The rich become celebrities, TV stars, and icons. The nonrich, blinded by the unrealistic hope that they someday will be wealthy, tend to protect the prerogatives of the rich rather than use their numerical majority to demand progressive reform. "Don't tax the rich," they say, "I may hit the lottery someday, and I wouldn't want the government to get any of that money." Those who think that they can beat the system seldom try to change the system. The rich, says Slater (1980), are wealth addicts. The nonrich are "closet addicts," whose unrealistic dreams of wealth tend to thwart reform and preserve the advantage of the rich.

A certain amount of envy is inevitable in the face of great and growing inequality. Defenders of capitalism see the envious as whining low achievers who ought not be allowed to pull down those who have achieved success and accumulated wealth (Schoeck 1970). Those who seek the progressive reform of capitalism see envy as a legitimate form of protest against the greed and unfairness of American capitalism (Slater 1980).

The Further Sociological Study of Envy

Although observation and survey research are desirable, both are problematic because envy is usually denied and repressed. Observational research requires a keen sense of what envy is, how it is likely to be expressed, and by what means it is likely to be hidden from view. Survey research and attempts to measure envy in individuals require unobtrusive measures, probably connected to descriptions of possible envy-producing situations and avoidance of the use of the terms *jealousy* and *envy.* It is meaningless to ask subjects how envious they are when they probably are unclear about what envy is and they are very likely to deny being envious.

Historical and cross-cultural research holds great promise for advancing our understanding of envy. The societies of the world, past and present, are available to us as case studies in the production and management of envy. The accounts of historians and anthropologists provide a vast database for the study of envy, even if these scholars did not set out to focus on envy. As Durkheim (1995) extracted lessons about religion from anthropological accounts of hunting-and-gathering cultures, we can extract lessons about envy from a vast trove of historical and comparative materials.

Envy must be studied in the real-life situations where it arises—in the workplace, competitive sports, politics, the worlds of theater and film, the circle of close friendships, and the family. Envy touches every area of life. Many of the institutions and social processes studied by social scientists are influenced by envy or by systems that evolved to reduce the social harm of envy. Sociological accounts of envy must move beyond psychometrics and therapeutic concerns to reveal the overlooked larger social implications of envy and, by extension, the social implications of emotions in general. By revealing these larger patterns, sociology can contribute to the management of envy in the individual and the management of envy in groups and societies.

Envy in Society: Two Examples

Envy is influenced by history and culture, economics, politics, and religion. Not only micro- but also meso- and macrolevel sociological tools must be employed for a full understanding of this dark, elusive emotion. Two examples will be considered here: the Russian culture of envy and the Rwandan genocide of 1994.

THE RUSSIAN CULTURE OF ENVY.   Compared with other industrial societies, Russia is a high-envy society. The journalist Hedrick Smith (1990:200), reporting from the Soviet Union in what proved to be its last days, writes:

> Traveling around the country, I came to see the great mass of Soviets as protagonists in what I call the culture of envy. In this culture, corrosive animosity took root under the czars in the deep-seated collectivism in Russian life and then was cultivated by Leninist ideology. Now it has turned rancid under the misery of everyday living.

The prevalence of envy in Russian society also has been noted by Hochschild (1994) and Shogren (1992). Shalin (1995) has commented on the pervasive emotional violence of Russian society, characterized by anger, self-hatred, and emotional overloading akin to posttraumatic stress syndrome.

Envy in Russian society has been exacerbated by the market reforms introduced by Gorbachev, which continue to our own time. The envy of the rank and file is aimed at anyone who rises above the crowd, anyone who gets ahead, even if the gains are honestly earned. In 1990, Gorbachev warned that the culture of envy would snuff out initiative, deter new entrepreneurs, and cripple hopes of real economic progress (Smith 1990).

One Russian TV journalist told Smith that if an American sees someone with a shiny new car, he will think, "Maybe I can get that someday for myself." But if a Russian sees someone with a new car, he will think, "This bastard with his car. I would like to kill him for living better than I do" (Smith 1990:203f). A reformist deputy in the Supreme Soviet told Smith (1990:204), "Our people cannot endure seeing someone else earn more than they do." An American correspondent observed, "In America, it's a sin to be a loser, but if there's one sin in Soviet society, it's being a winner" (Smith 1990:203).

In Russia, envy toward the elite, the *vertushka*, is further encouraged by the prevailing corruption. Russians often make up for poor pay by stealing from the state. As almost everyone engages in illegal acts to enrich themselves, it is assumed that those who have done well have done so by means of massive cheating and stealing rather than through hard work, and this assumption undermines the work ethic.

Successful Russians try to hide their good fortune. Smith observed that, when Americans meet and ask each other, "How are things?" both will say, "Fine," even if one's mother died the day before. When Russians meet and ask each other how they are, they will say, "Normal," or "So-so." Even if things are good, you do not want people to think things are great, because they might be envious, and there is no telling what they might do.

The historical roots of the Russian culture of envy run deep. Russia was among the last European nations to industrialize, so many Russians lived in rural, peasant communities through much of the twentieth century. As previously noted, awareness and fear of envy are stronger in rural than urban societies. Russian villagers often repeat the aphorism, "The tallest blade of grass is the first to be cut down by the scythe," clearly a warning about the danger of trying to stand above the crowd. This is similar to the Japanese saying discouraging flamboyance: "The nail that sticks up shall be hammered down." Likewise, in Canada and the upper Midwestern United States, one hears variations of the saying, "Don't stick your head above the herd. You'll get it chopped off."

In an old Russian tale, God comes to a lucky peasant and offers him any wish, but God adds, "Whatever you choose, I will give twice as much to your neighbor." The peasant is stumped, because he cannot bear to think of his neighbor being better off than he. Finally, he tells God, "Strike out one of my eyes and take out both eyes of my neighbor." In another version of this story, the peasant asks that God take one of his testicles.

Since medieval times, Russian peasants lived in a world of collective rather than private enterprise. In czarist times, most Russians lived in small clusters of homes, close to one another, not in single homesteads scattered independently across the plains. After serfdom was abolished in 1861, the peasants banded together and worked the land together. After 1917, communism forced further collectivization and taught that individual profit is immoral.

Jacoby (1973) demonstrated that, despite great shifts in the political structure of Russia, an undemocratic bureaucratic structure evolved and became stronger over hundreds of years. Prior to the Tatar invasion of 1240, most Russians lived in small villages. The central government was weak, and many decisions were made locally by assemblies of the people called *Veche*. The Tatar conquest resulted in the establishment of an administration to collect taxes and supervise the drafting of Russian recruits. In the 1400s, the Tatars deputized a Muscovite grand duke to administer the payment of tribute, an important step toward making Moscow a central and dominating power. The Tatars were defeated in 1522, but the czars, rather than dismantling the bureaucracy the Asian conquerors had brought, turned the system to their own purposes, while strengthening it with the addition of a secret police apparatus. When the czars were replaced by the communists after 1917, the new rulers again chose not to dismantle the bureaucracy but rather to adopt it and strengthen it through the increased use of terror toward opponents of the regime. By the time of the fall of the Soviet Union in 1991, despite two historic upheavals, the Russian people had lived under increasingly despotic bureaucratic regimes for more than 700 years. As a result, the envious resentment of their rulers and of the newly rich has very deep roots.

THE RWANDAN GENOCIDE.   Envy played a part in the Rwandan genocide of 1994 (Taylor 1999). Rwanda was colonized by Germany beginning in 1890. The population was composed of three ethnic groups: the more numerous Hutu, the historically dominant Tutsi, and the pygmoid Twa, a very small, marginalized group. These ethnic groups share a common language and culture. Before 1994, both Rwanda and neighboring Burundi were characterized by a similar ethnic mix of approximately 80–85 percent Hutu, 15–20 percent Tutsi, and less than 1 percent Twa. Under Belgian colonial rule, ambiguities about ethnic group membership were settled by an economic criterion: those with ten or more cows were classified as Tutsi, those with fewer, as Hutu (de Waal 1994).

Because the Tutsi were politically dominant in the areas with which the German colonizers had the most experience, and because the Tutsi had a strong monarchy with a somewhat centralized administration, the Germans decided to administer the region indirectly through the Tutsi (Taylor 1999), much as the Tatars administered Russia through the grand duke of Moscow. When Germany was defeated in World War I, the League of Nations awarded the territory to Belgium, under whose administration the Tutsi continued to be favored. Resentment built up among the Hutu. After 1926, the Belgians required Rwandans to carry an identity card, indicating the person's ancestry (de Waal 1994). Like the Germans, the Belgians helped their Tutsi allies to expand their control into peripheral regions. Over time, power came to be concentrated in the hands of a relatively small clique of Tutsi administrators and a handful of Belgian colonial officials.

Taylor (1999) shows how the resentment was exacerbated by the European belief that the Tutsi were more attractive than the Hutu. Many Tutsi are taller and thinner than Hutu and have longer and thinner arms and legs. Furthermore, the Tutsi have a face shape that is more attractive to Europeans. Many European men married Tutsi women, further strengthening the control of Tutsi over Hutu and adding to the Hutu envy of the Tutsi. Many upper-class Tutsi understood that it was to their advantage to reinforce European perceptions of their natural superiority, and they obliged with pseudohistorical fabrications extolling their intellectual, cultural, and military achievements.

Hutu dissatisfaction with the system grew during World War II. Hutu protest became more vocal following the war and into the 1950s. The Rwandan Catholic Church, which had evangelized large numbers of Rwandans, began to shift its support from the Tutsi elite toward the Hutu masses, who comprised a majority of the converts. This shift was encouraged by the fact that more and more of the missionary priests were recruited from blue-collar, Flemish-speaking areas of Belgium and fewer from the French-speaking elite.

Amid the anticolonial rhetoric of the time and fearing a leftward shift by their Tutsi allies, Belgian administrators shifted to support what had become the safer group, the Hutu. Violence between Hutu and Tutsi political groups broke out in 1959, and many Tutsi fled the country or were expelled. The more numerous Hutu won a United Nations–sponsored election and took control of the government when Rwanda gained its independence in 1962.

Hutu presidents of Rwanda exploited lingering fear of the Tutsi for their own political purposes. Although a quota system based on population was adopted, Tutsi were never given their allotted portion (9 percent) of state jobs or places in schools and universities, and the Twa were given nothing. After decades of civil war, a multiparty government was established in 1993, but hostilities resumed following the 1994 assassination of the Hutu president of Rwanda.

A radio propaganda campaign that appealed to Hutu envy of the Tutsi encouraged the Hutu to kill their Tutsi neighbors. The Tutsi were compared to cockroaches or rats to be exterminated. The Tutsi were portrayed as foreign invaders, intent on turning the Hutu into slaves, and the Hutu were reminded that the Tutsi had ruled over them for centuries. The Hutu government passed out machetes and told their people, "It's time to go to work," meaning that it was time to go out and kill the Tutsi. The Hutu referred to Tutsi survivors as "those not finished off." The Hutu government did nothing to protect the Tutsi, and the United States and the United Nations did not intervene to stop the killing.

The resulting genocide took the lives of almost one million people, about one-seventh of the population of Rwanda. About 80 percent of the Tutsi population died. Rwanda's infrastructure was left in ruins, and most of the intelligentsia (Hutu and Tutsi) were dead or no longer living in the country.

Other factors contributed to the Rwandan genocide. Rwanda is the smallest and most densely populated nation in sub-Saharan Africa, with over 250 inhabitants per square kilometer, but its per capita GDP is one of the lowest in the world. Rwanda's population growth rate is one of the highest in the world. Lack of available land contributed to the political tensions that led to the genocide. Virtually all the arable land in the country is under intensive cultivation.

Clearly, however, the Rwandan genocide was fueled in part by what Taylor (Personal Communication 2005) calls the passions of nationalism, including envy, especially Hutu extremist envy of alleged Tutsi intelligence and beauty. This envy was exacerbated by the resentments born of long-standing Tutsi dominance, despite their smaller numbers, in both precolonial and colonial periods.

CONCLUSION

A sociological approach focuses on neglected social aspects of emotions, including their historical and cross-cultural variability, their hidden social usefulness, their relationships to social conflict and change, and their relationships to social institutions. Emotions are responses to social situations that are shaped by social interaction and social learning.

Jealousy is a protective reaction to a perceived threat to a valued relationship or to its quality. Jealousy protects marriage from adultery, thus contributing to social order. Jealousy is learned differently in different cultures because of variations in marriage rules, adultery taboos, and gender roles. Prior to about 1965, jealousy was viewed positively in Americal society. The sexual revolution and the women's movement encouraged a more negative view of jealousy, which was blamed on the low self-esteem of the jealous individual. This makes it difficult for contemporary Americans to see the social usefulness of jealousy.

Envy is hostility toward superiors. Envy is not the wish for an object, but rather the wish that the superior would lose his advantage. Because envy threatens social order, envy is prohibited in all societies. In hunting-and-gathering societies, fear of envy is high and everyone remains poor so as to avoid being the target of the envy of neighbors. In industrial societies, fear of envy is low because of rationalizations of inequality. Envy is reduced if differences in wealth, status, and power are rationalized as the result of luck, the will of God, and hard work. Although it is negative for both the envier and the envied, envy is socially useful because fear of being envied provides an additional motive for complying with necessary norms. Envy management is inescapably political. The right seeks to reduce envy by ignoring and justifying existing inequality. The left seeks to reduce envy by reducing inequality through progressive taxation.

REFERENCES

Bellah, Robert N., Richard Madsen, William M. Sullivan, Ann Swidler, and Steven M. Tipton. 1985. *Habits of the Heart: Individualism and Commitment in American Life.* Berkeley: University of California Press.

Berger, Bennett M. 1981. *The Survival of a Counterculture: Ideological Work and Everyday Life among Rural Communards.* Berkeley: University of California Press.

Berger, Brigitte, and Peter L. Berger. 1984. *The War over the Family: Capturing the Middle Ground.* New York: Anchor/Doubleday.

Berger, Peter L., and Thomas Luckmann. 1966. *The Social Construction of Reality: A Treatise in the Sociology of Knowledge.* Garden City, NY: Anchor/Doubleday.

Buss, David. 2000. *Dangerous Passion.* New York: Free Press.

Buunk, Bram. 1981. "Jealousy in Sexually Open Marriages." *Alternative Lifestyles* 4: 357–372.

Buunk, Bram, and Robert G. Bringle. 1987. "Jealousy in Love Relationships." Pp. 123–148 in *Intimate Relationships: Development, Dynamics, and Deterioration,* edited by D. Perlman and S. Duck. Beverly Hills, CA: Sage.

Cahill, Thomas. 1995. *How the Irish Saved Civilization.* New York: Anchor.

Clanton, Gordon. 1981. "Frontiers of Jealousy Research." *Alternative Lifestyles* 4: 259–273.

———. 1984. "Social Forces and the Changing Family." Pp. 13-46 in *Marriage and Family in the Year 2020,* edited by L. A. Kirkendall and A. E. Gravatt. Buffalo, NY: Prometheus.

———. 1985. "Love, Jealousy, and Envy: A Course in the Sociology of Emotions." *ASA Teaching Newsletter* 10: 4.

———. 1986. "Teaching Sociology of Emotions." *Sociology of Emotions Newsletter* 1: 4.

———. 1987. "A Historical Sociology of Sex and Love." *Teaching Sociology* 15: 307–311.

———. 1989. "Jealousy in American Culture, 1945–1985: Reflections from Popular Culture." Pp. 179–193 in *The Sociology of Emotions: Original Essays and Research Papers,* edited by D. D. Franks and E. D. McCarthy. Greenwich, CT: JAI Press.

———. 1996. "A Sociology of Jealousy." *International Journal of Sociology and Social Policy* 16: 171–189.

Clanton, Gordon, and Chris Downing, eds. 1975. *Face to Face to Face: An Experiment in Intimacy.* New York: Dutton.

Clanton, Gordon, and David J. Kosins. 1991. "Developmental Correlates of Jealousy." Pp. 132–145 in *The Psychology of Jealousy and Envy,* edited by P. Salovey. New York: Guilford.

Clanton, Gordon, and Lynn G. Smith, eds. [1977] 1998. *Jealousy.* Lanham, MD: University Press of America.

Collins, Jan C., and Thomas Gregor. 1995. "Boundaries of Love." Pp. 72–92 in *Romantic Passion: A Universal Experience?* edited by W. Jankowiak. New York: Columbia University Press.

Collins, Randall. 1975. *Conflict Sociology: Toward an Explanatory Science.* New York: Academic.

Coontz, Stephanie. 2005. *Marriage, A History: From Obedience to Intimacy, or How Love Conquered Marriage.* New York: Viking.

Davis, Kingsley. 1936. "Jealousy and Sexual Property." *Social Forces* 14: 395–405.

De Swann, Abram. 1989. "Jealousy as a Class Phenomenon: The Petite Bourgeoisie and Social Security." *International Sociology* 4: 259–271.

de Waal, Alex. 1994. "Genocide in Rwanda." *Anthropology Today* 10: 1–2.

Durkheim, Emile. [1897] 1951. *Suicide: A Study in Sociology.* Translation by J. A. Spaulding and G. Simpson. New York: Free Press.

———. [1912] 1995. *The Elementary Forms of Religious Life.* Translation by K. Fields. New York: Free Press.

Ellestad, June, and Jan E. Stets. 1998. "Jealousy and Parenting: Predicting Emotion from Identity Theory." *Sociological Perspectives* 41: 639–668.

Ellis, Carolyn, and Eugene Weinstein. 1985. "Jealousy and the Social Psychology of Emotional Experience." *Journal of Personal and Social Relationships* 3: 3.

Ford, Clellan S., and Frank A. Beach. 1951. *Patterns of Sexual Behavior.* New York: Harper and Row.

Foster, George M. 1972. "The Anatomy of Envy: A Study in Symbolic Behavior." *Current Anthropology* 13: 165–186.

Gagnon, John H. 1977. *Human Sexualities*. Glenview, IL: Scott-Foresman.

Gilmartin, Brian G. [1977] 1998. "Jealousy among the Swingers." Pp. 152–158 in *Jealousy*, edited by G. Clanton and L. G. Smith. Lanham, MD: University Press of America.

Goffman, Erving. 1967. *Interaction Ritual*. Garden City, NY: Doubleday.

Goode, William J. 1959. "The Theoretical Importance of Love." *American Sociological Review* 24: 38–47.

———. 1963. *World Revolution and Family Patterns*. New York: Free Press.

Gregor, Thomas A. 1985. *Anxious Pleasures*. Chicago: University of Chicago Press.

Guerrero, Laura K., and Sylvie V. Eloy. 1992. "Relational Satisfaction and Jealousy across Marital Types." *Communication Reports* 5: 23–31.

Hansen, Gary L. 1985. "Perceived Threats and Marital Jealousy." *Social Psychology Quarterly* 48: 267–268.

Hochschild, Adam. 1994. *The Unquiet Ghost: Russians Remember Stalin*. Boston: Houghton Mifflin.

Hochschild, Arlie Russell. 1983. *The Managed Heart: Commercialization of Human Feeling*. Berkeley: University of California Press.

———. 2003. *The Commercialization of Intimate Life: Notes from Home and Work*. Berkeley: University of California Press.

Hunt, Morton M. 1959. *The Natural History of Love*. New York: Grove Press.

Hupka, Ralph B. 1981. "Cultural Determinants of Jealousy." *Alternative Lifestyles* 4: 310–356.

Hupka, Ralph B., Jurgen Otto, Nadia V. Tarabrina, and Lucy Reidl. 1993. "Cross-Cultural Comparisons of Nouns Associated with Jealousy and the Related Emotions of Envy, Anger, and Fear." *Cross-Cultural Research* 27: 181–211.

Irvine, Leslie J. 1995. "Codependency and Recovery: Gender, Self, and Emotions in Popular Self-Help." *Symbolic Interaction* 18: 145–163.

Jacoby, Henry. 1973. *The Bureaucratization of the World*. Berkeley: University of California Press.

James, William. [1890] 1983. *The Principles of Psychology*. Cambridge, MA: Harvard University Press.

Kempton, Murray. 1990. "The Party of Envy." *The New York Review of Books*, February 15.

Kinkade, Kathleen. 1972. *A Walden Two Experiment: The First Five Years of Twin Oaks Community*. New York: William Morris.

Kosins, David J. 1983. "Developmental Correlates of Sexual Jealousy." Ph.D. dissertation, California School for Professional Psychology, San Diego.

Lawson, Annette. 1988. *Adultery: An Analysis of Love and Betrayal*. New York: Basic Books.

Lyman, Stanford M. 1978. *The Seven Deadly Sins: Society and Evil*. New York: St. Martin's Press.

Malinowski, Bronislaw. 1929. *The Sexual Life of Savages*. New York: Harcourt Brace.

Manning, Philip. 2005. *Freud and American Sociology*. Cambridge, England: Polity.

Margolin, Gayla. 1981. "A Behavioral-Systems Approach to the Treatment of Jealousy." *Clinical Psychology Review* 1: 469–487.

McCarthy, John D., and Dean R. Hoge. 1984. "The Dynamics of Self-Esteem and Delinquency." *American Journal of Sociology* 90: 396–410.

Mead, Margaret. 1931. "Jealousy: Primitive and Civilized." Pp. 35–48 in *Woman's Coming of Age*, edited by S. Schmalhausen and V. F. Calverton. New York: H. Liveright.

Mills, C. Wright. 1959. *The Sociological Imagination*. New York: Oxford University Press.

Novak, Michael. 1988. "Politics of Resentment Is Sign of Desperate Left." *Los Angeles Times*, January 13.

O'Neill, Nena, and George O'Neill. 1972. *Open Marriage: A New Life Style for Couples*. New York: M. Evans.

Parrott, W. Gerrold. 1991. "The Emotional Experiences of Envy and Jealousy." Pp. 3–30 in *The Psychology of Jealousy and Envy*, edited by P. Salovey. New York: Guilford.

Parrott, W. Gerrold, and Richard H. Smith. 1993. "Distinguishing the Experiences of Jealousy and Envy." *Journal of Personality and Social Psychology* 64: 906–920.

Pines, Ayala M. 1992. *Romantic Jealousy: Understanding and Conquering the Shadow of Love*. New York: St. Martin's Press.

———. 1998. *Romantic Jealousy: Causes, Symptoms, Cures*. London: Routledge.

Pines, Ayala, and Elliot Aronson. 1981. "Polyfidelity: An Alternative Lifestyle Without Jealousy?" *Alternative Lifestyles* 4: 373–392.

Rawls, John. 1971. *A Theory of Justice*. Cambridge, MA: Harvard University Press.

Rieff, Philip. 1966. *The Triumph of the Therapeutic: Uses of Faith after Freud*. New York: Harper and Row.

Salovey, Peter, ed. 1991. *The Psychology of Jealousy and Envy*. New York: Guilford.

Salovey, Peter, and Judith Rodin. 1985. "The Heart of Jealousy." *Psychology Today* 19: 22–25, 28–29.

———. 1989. "Envy and Jealousy in Close Relationships." Pp. 221–246 in *Review of Personality and Social Psychology: Close Relationships*, edited by C. Hendrick. Newbury Park, CA: Sage.

Salovey, Peter, and Alexander J. Rothman. 1991. "Envy and Jealousy: Self and Society." Pp. 271–286 in *The Psychology of Jealousy and Envy*, edited by P. Salovey. New York: Guilford.

Scheler, Max. [1912] 1961. *Ressentiment*. New York: Free Press.

Schoeck, Helmut. [1966] 1970. *Envy: A Theory of Social Behavior*. Translation by M. Glenny and B. Ross. New York: Harcourt, Brace, and World.

Shalin, Dmitri. 1995. "Emotions and Democracy." *Sociology of Emotions Newsletter* 8: 4.

———. 2004. "Liberalism, Affect Control, and Emotionally Intelligent Democracy." *Journal of Human Rights* 3: 107–128.

Shogren, Elizabeth. 1992. "In Russia, New Rich Flaunt It." *Los Angeles Times*, May 25.

Slater, Philip. 1980. *Wealth Addiction*. New York: Dutton.

Smelser, Neil J. 1989. "Self-Esteem and Social Problems: An Introduction." In *The Social Importance of Self-Esteem*, edited by A. Mecca, N. J. Smelser, and J. Vasconcellos. Berkeley: University of California Press.

Smith, Hedrick. 1990. *The New Russians*. New York: Random House.

Smith, James R., and Lynn G. Smith, eds. 1974. *Beyond Monogamy: Recent Studies of Sexual Alternatives in Marriage*. Baltimore: Johns Hopkins University Press.

Smith, Richard H. 1991. "Envy and the Sense of Injustice." Pp. 79–99 in *The Psychology of Jealousy and Envy*, edited by P. Salovey. New York: Guilford.

Stearns, Peter N. 1990. "The Rise of Sibling Jealousy in the Twentieth Century." *Symbolic Interaction* 13: 83–101.

Swidler, Ann. 1980. "Love and Adulthood in American Culture." Pp. 120–147 in *Themes of Work and Love in Adulthood*, edited by N. J. Smelser and E. H. Erikson. Cambridge, MA: Harvard University Press.

Taylor, Christopher C. 1999. *Sacrifice as Terror*. Oxford: Berg/Oxford International.

———. 2005. Personal Communication.

Thoits, Peggy A. 1984. "Coping, Social Support, and Psychological Outcomes: The Central Role of Emotion." Pp. 219–238 in *Review of Personality and Social Psychology*, edited by P. Shaver. Beverly Hills, CA: Sage.

Ware, Helen. 1979. "Polygyny: Women's Views in a Transitional Society, Nigeria 1975." *Journal of Marriage and the Family* 41: 185–195.

Weber, Max. [1905] 1996. *The Protestant Ethic and the Spirit of Capitalism*. Translation by Talcott Parsons; Introduction by Randall Collins. Los Angeles: Roxbury.

White, Gregory L., and Paul E. Mullen. 1989. *Jealousy: Theory, Research, and Clinical Strategies*. New York: Guilford.

Yamaguchi, Masao. 1997. "Envy and the Social Construction of Political Reality in Communities." *Semiotica* 117: 227–230.

CHAPTER 19

Empathy

MARK H. DAVIS

What is empathy? Although seemingly simple, this question has proven surprisingly difficult to answer. For over 200 years, thoughtful people have tried to understand the general phenomenon in which one individual, through observation of another, comes to experience some change in his or her thoughts or feelings. These efforts have typically fallen into one of two broad categories. One approach has been to consider empathy an essentially emotional phenomenon, with the defining feature of the empathic experience consisting of observers either coming to *share* the target's emotional state (e.g., Eisenberg and Strayer 1987) or to experience some emotional state in *response* to the target's (e.g., Batson 1991). The other approach has been to consider empathy an essentially cognitive phenomenon, with the defining feature of the experience consisting of observers coming to discern accurately the target's internal state, but without necessarily experiencing any emotional change themselves (e.g., Wispe 1986).

Recent years have seen growing acceptance of a third approach, which is to explicitly treat empathy as a multidimensional phenomenon that inevitably includes both cognitive and emotional components (e.g., Davis 1983; Hoffman 1984). In this vein, I have previously proposed a model designed to organize all of these approaches into a comprehensive treatment of the empathy phenomenon (Davis 1994); Figure 19.1 contains a somewhat revised and updated version of this model. In contrast to much previous work, the spirit of this model is deliberately inclusive, designed to emphasize the connections between these constructs. Thus, empathy is broadly defined here as a set of constructs that connects the responses of one individual to the experiences of another. These constructs specifically include both the *processes* taking place within the observer and the affective and nonaffective *outcomes* that result from those processes. Based on this definition, the model conceives of the typical empathy "episode" as consisting of an observer being exposed in some fashion to a target, after which some response on the part of the observer—cognitive, affective, motivational, or behavioral—occurs. Four related constructs can be identified within this prototypical

MARK H. DAVIS • Department of Psychology, Eckerd College, St, Petersburg, FL 33711

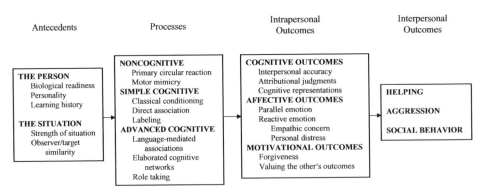

FIGURE 19.1. Organizational of Model of Empathy-Related Constructs

episode: *antecedents*, which refer to characteristics of the observer, target, or situation; *processes*, which refer to the particular mechanisms by which empathic outcomes are produced; *intrapersonal outcomes*, which refer to cognitive, affective, and motivational responses produced in the observer that are not necessarily manifested in overt behavior toward the target; and *interpersonal outcomes*, which refer to behavioral responses directed toward the target. One critical feature of this model is that it considers both cognitive and affective outcomes to be part of empathy.

Because of its breadth and versatility, in this chapter I will use the model as a framework for selectively presenting and discussing past and current work on the general topic of empathy. At the conclusion of the chapter, I will offer some suggestions regarding promising areas for future research. To begin, however, let us consider in more detail the various elements contained within this model.

EMPATHY: AN ORGANIZATIONAL FRAMEWORK

Antecedents

The first component of this framework encompasses antecedent factors—features of the observer, target, or the situation that might influence, in some way, the subsequent empathy episode.

THE OBSERVER.   All observers possess certain characteristics that have the potential to influence the empathy episode. One of these is the *biological capacity* for empathy-related processes and outcomes. Almost all members of our species possess these capabilities, although sometimes serious deficiencies do occur in the ability to imagine other perspectives (e.g., autism) or to experience compassion for distressed others (e.g., sociopathy). Of more importance for the purposes of this chapter are the *individual differences* that exist in nonclinical populations in the tendency to engage in empathy-related processes or to experience empathic outcomes. A variety of individual difference measures has been developed over the years for the purpose of assessing the dispositional tendency to engage in empathy-related processes such as perspective taking (e.g., Hogan 1969) or to experience empathy-related affective responses (e.g., Mehrabian and Epstein 1972). Of special note here are individual differences in the tendency to experience two particular affective reactions to the distress of others. Specifically, the tendency to experience feelings of sympathy for a person in distress and the tendency to experience personal unease in such cases are especially important antecedent characteristics that have considerable relevance for social interactions.

THE SITUATION.   All responses to another person, whether cognitive or affective, emerge from some specific situational context, and these contexts vary along certain dimensions. One such dimension is the *strength of the situation*, defined as its power to evoke an emotional response from observers. For example, a situation that includes a clear display of negative emotion by a weak or helpless target is particularly able to engender powerful observer emotions and would be classified as a "strong" situation. In contrast, situations lacking such evocative emotional cues would be characterized as relatively weak. A second situational feature is the *degree of similarity* between the observer and target. Although similarity is, of course, affected by characteristics of the observer, it is really a joint function of the target *and* observer and is thus considered a feature of the situation.

Processes

The second major construct within the framework consists of the specific processes that generate empathic outcomes in the observer. Based on the work of Hoffman (1984) and Eisenberg et al. (1991), the model identifies three broad classes of empathy-related processes, chiefly distinguished from one another by the degree of cognitive effort and sophistication required for their operation. In a sense, it is potentially misleading to characterize these processes in terms of dimensions like "cognitive" and "affective." It is really the *outcomes* of these processes that can be more clearly identified in this way, and each process is capable of producing both cognitive and affective outcomes. However, given the clear differences in the level of cognitive sophistication required for their operation, it seems reasonable to use this dimension to describe these three broad classes.

NONCOGNITIVE PROCESSES.   Some processes that lead to empathic outcomes require very little cognitive activity. The apparently innate tendency for newborns to cry in response to hearing others cry, which Hoffman (1984) refers to as the *primary circular reaction*, is one example. Another noncognitive process is *motor mimicry*, the tendency for observers automatically and unconsciously to imitate the target. Although early conceptions of mimicry viewed it as a somewhat deliberate strategy for "feeling into" the other (e.g., Lipps 1903), more recent approaches (e.g., Hatfield et al. 1994; Hoffman 1984) have treated it as a relatively automatic, largely noncognitive process.

SIMPLE COGNITIVE PROCESSES.   In contrast, other processes require at least a rudimentary cognitive ability on the part of the observer. *Classical conditioning* is an example; if an observer has previously perceived affective cues in others while experiencing that same affect (perhaps because both observer and target are simultaneously exposed to the same unpleasant stimulus), then the affective cues of targets could come to evoke that emotional state. Similar processes of comparably modest sophistication—*direct association* (Hoffman 1984) and *labeling* (Eisenberg et al. 1991)—have also been proposed.

ADVANCED COGNITIVE PROCESSES.   Finally, some processes require rather advanced kinds of cognitive activity. One example is what Hoffman refers to as *language-mediated association*, in which the observer's reaction to the target's plight is produced by activating language-based cognitive networks that trigger associations with the observer's own feelings or experiences. For example, a target who says "My manuscript has been rejected" might exhibit no obvious facial or vocal cues indicating distress, but an observer might respond empathically because her relevant memories (perhaps of an especially undiplomatic review) are activated by the target's words. The *elaborated cognitive networks* of Eisenberg et al. (1991) refer to a very similar process. The most advanced process, however, and the one that has received the most empirical attention, is *role-taking* or *perspective-taking*: the attempt by one individual to understand another by explicitly imagining the other's perspective. It is typically considered an effortful process, involving both the suppression of one's own egocentric perspective on events and the active entertaining of someone else's.

Intrapersonal Outcomes

The model's third major construct deals with *intrapersonal outcomes*—the cognitive, affective, and motivational responses of the observer that result from exposure to the target. These outcomes are thought to result primarily from the various processes identified at the previous stage in the model.

COGNITIVE OUTCOMES.   One cognitive outcome is *interpersonal accuracy*—the successful estimation of other people's thoughts, feelings, and characteristics; typically, such interpersonal judgments have been viewed as resulting to a considerable degree from role-taking processes (e.g., Dymond 1950). Empathy-related processes have also been implicated in affecting the *attributional judgments* offered by observers for targets' behavior (e.g., Regan and Totten 1975). More recently, perspective-taking has been linked to changes in the *cognitive representations* that perceivers form of targets—in particular, the degree to which these representations resemble the cognitive representations of the self (Davis et al. 1996).

AFFECTIVE OUTCOMES.   This category consists of the emotional reactions experienced by an observer in response to the observed experiences of the target and is further subdivided into two forms: parallel and reactive outcomes. A *parallel emotion* might in a sense, be considered the prototypical affective response: an observer's actual reproduction of the target's feelings. This sort of emotional matching has clearly been the focus of several historical approaches (McDougall 1908; Spencer 1870). *Reactive emotions*, on the other hand, are defined as affective reactions to the experiences of others that differ from the observed affect. They are so named because they are empathic reactions *to* another's state rather than a simple reproduction of that state in the observer. One response that clearly falls into this category is the feeling of compassion for others referred to variously as sympathy (Wispe 1986), empathy (Batson 1991), and *empathic concern* (Davis 1983); another example would be *personal distress*: the tendency to feel discomfort and anxiety in response to needy targets.

MOTIVATIONAL OUTCOMES.   A third category of intrapersonal outcomes, somewhat related to the second, are motivational states produced in the observer by empathy-related processes. For example, *forgiveness* is often conceptualized as a transformation of motivation toward a transgressing partner in which desires for revenge are reduced and desires for reconciliation are increased (McCullough et al. 1997). More generally, empathic processes have also been linked to increased motivation to *value the other's outcomes* (Batson et al. 1995).

Interpersonal Outcomes

The final construct in the model encompasses *interpersonal outcomes*, defined as behaviors directed toward a target that result from prior exposure to that target. The outcome that has attracted the most attention from empathy theorists and researchers is *helping behavior*; both cognitive and affective facets of empathy have long been thought to contribute to the likelihood of observers offering help to needy targets. *Aggressive behavior* has also been linked theoretically to empathy-related processes and dispositions, with the expectation that empathy will be negatively associated with aggressive actions. The effect of empathy on behaviors that occur within *social relationships*—a topic that has only recently begun to attract consistent research interest—also falls into this category.

RESEARCH EVIDENCE RELEVANT TO THE MODEL

It should be apparent from this brief overview that this model aspires to incorporate most, if not all, of the social psychological research carried out in the name of empathy. Thus, it is well suited for use as an organizing device, and in this section I will selectively discuss past and contemporary research on empathy, using the organizational model as a framework. The goal is to provide some sense of the history of research efforts in each area, but to also highlight some of the most interesting and provocative lines of research currently under way.

Antecedents

As Figure 19.1 suggests, there are several ways to think about the antecedents of empathic processes and outcomes. At one level, explanations might focus on the inherent human capacity for empathic responding that grapple with the issue of why such capacities would evolve in humans at all. At another level, explanations might focus on our dispositional tendencies to utilize the capacities we possess. Finally, explanations focusing on empathy as it occurs within specific situations must examine features of both the particular setting and of the individuals involved. At each level of analysis, of course, it will be important to carefully distinguish among the various kinds of cognitive and affective process and outcome.

EVOLUTIONARY ORIGINS OF EMPATHY.   The idea that an empathic capacity might have its roots in humans' evolutionary history has been around for some time. The earliest impetus for such thinking came from theoretical attempts to reconcile altruistic behavior with evolutionary theory. Self-sacrificing behavior, which on the surface seems incompatible with the notion that we are all engaged in a struggle for survival, has been found in many species and has been explained by such additions to evolutionary theory as inclusive fitness (Hamilton 1964), genetic similarity theory (Rushton et al. 1984), and reciprocal altruism (Trivers 1971). Each of these approaches accounts for altruistic behavior by arguing that the genes contained within an individual "benefit" from behavior that increases their survival chances. This holds true even if we are talking about identical genes residing in others—especially close relatives. Thus, a genetic tendency to offer help—even costly help—to those who share our genetic make-up can be evolutionarily advantageous.

Empathy comes into this discussion because of the need for some proximate mechanism to produce altruistic behavior. It is one thing to say that genes "for" altruism produce altruistic behavior, which, in turn, leads to greater survivability for those genes in the population. However, the altruistic behavior is still undertaken by the *individual organism* and not the gene; some mechanism must exist within that individual—between the gene level and the behavioral act—to prompt the individual to act against its own short-term interest. Hoffman (1978) has made the case for empathy's role by arguing that any mechanism responsible for producing altruism in humans must be reliable, but also flexible; that is, it should not be so automatic in operation that behavior could not be modified as a result of environmental conditions. In particular, the mechanism should allow the behavior to be affected by judgments regarding costs to the individual and benefits to the recipient(s). Thus, Hoffman argued that what must have been selected for during evolution was a biologically based *predisposition* to act altruistically, but one that was still subject to control by cognitive processes. In his view, empathy, defined as a vicarious affective response to the experiences of others, meets these criteria. This analysis therefore suggests that the empathic response selected for by eons of evolutionary pressure is the sharing of negative affect.

INDIVIDUAL DIFFERENCES IN EMPATHY.   Another way to think about the antecedents of empathy is to focus on individual differences in empathy-related constructs—that is, the degree to which individuals possess the ability or the motivation to think, feel, or act in an empathic fashion. Several approaches have been taken in attempts to measure these differences. One early and influential technique was that of Dymond (1950), who defined empathy in terms of the accurate transposition of the self into the thinking, feeling, and acting of others. Thus, her method consisted of assessing the accuracy with which observers could estimate how targets describe themselves on trait-rating scales. Unfortunately, high levels of accuracy in this technique can result from several different factors, most of which have nothing to do with empathy (Cronbach 1955; Gage and Cronbach 1955). Once this was recognized, this method rapidly fell from favor.

The most widely used contemporary measure based on a cognitive definition of empathy is, no doubt, Hogan's (1969) empathy scale, which was developed based on a definition of empathy that emphasized the intellectual attempt to imagine another's point of view *without* experiencing any affective response. The 64-item scale is made up of items drawn from other psychological instruments (e.g., the Minnesota Multiphasic Personality Inventory (MMPI) and the California Psychological Inventory (CPI)). Just as Hogan's scale is the most widely used measure employing a purely cognitive definition of empathy, the Questionnaire Measure of Emotional Empathy (QMEE; Mehrabian and Epstein 1972) has been the most widely utilized instrument adopting an affective definition. The QMEE was designed explicitly to assess the chronic tendency to react emotionally to the observed experiences of others. Its 33 items assess the likelihood of experiencing such affective responses in a variety of contexts.

In addition to those instruments based on cognitive *or* affective definitions of empathy, one measure based explicitly on a multidimensional view of empathy has also been developed. The Interpersonal Reactivity Index (IRI; Davis 1980, 1983) takes as its starting point the notion that empathy consists of a set of separate but related constructs and seeks to provide measures of dispositional tendencies in several areas. The instrument contains four, seven-item subscales, each tapping a separate facet of empathy. The *perspective-taking* (PT) scale measures the reported tendency to spontaneously adopt the psychological point of view of others in everyday life. The *empathic concern* (EC) scale assesses the tendency to experience feelings of sympathy and compassion for unfortunate others. The *personal distress* (PD) scale taps the tendency to experience distress and discomfort in response to extreme distress in others. The *fantasy* (FS) scale measures the tendency to imaginatively transpose oneself into fictional situations. In recent years the IRI has become increasingly popular, and in the sections that follow, some of the research using this instrument will be mentioned.

CHARACTERISTICS OF THE SITUATION.   A third approach to the question of antecedents has been to focus not on the empathizer but on characteristics of the situation—in particular, the target, or the relationship between the target and observer. Much less systematic study has been devoted to this approach, and the issue that has received the most study is probably the *degree of similarity* between observer and target.

Early investigations of this question tended to support the link between similarity and empathic responding (Krebs 1975; Stotland 1969; Stotland and Dunn 1963). For example, Krebs (1975) manipulated observer-target similarity and found that observers who believed that they were similar to the target displayed heightened skin conductance and vasoconstriction when the target appeared to receive shocks; they also reported feeling worse during the procedure. However, not all investigations have supported the notion that similarity produces affective reactions in observers (Gruen and Mendelsohn 1986; Marks et al. 1982). Most recently, Batson et al. (2005) found in two studies that observer-target similarity produced no reliable increase in reported sympathy for a distressed target. Given the somewhat inconsistent prior evidence for the role of similarity in producing affective responses, Batson et al. interpreted the results of their investigations as consistent with the view that similarity does not have the impact on empathic processes and outcomes that is often supposed.

Processes

The second major component of the organizational framework is concerned with the processes that take place within an observer during an empathy episode—in short, the actual mechanisms that bring about changes in thoughts, emotions, or behavior. It is possible to identify a number of such processes that vary in terms of the cognitive complexity required for their operation (see Figure 19.1). To date, however, there has been considerable variation in the degree to which these processes have been studied, and some have received almost no systematic investigation at all. Two of these processes, though, have generated a considerable literature.

MOTOR MIMICRY. Motor mimicry refers to the fact that observers often imitate (usually unconsciously) a wide variety of behaviors observed in others. This tendency appears early in life—infants will imitate the facial expressions of adults (Meltzoff and Moore 1977)—and does not seem to abate over the life span. Indeed, adults have been shown to mimic not only the facial expressions of their interaction partners but also body posture, gestures, and vocal characteristics (see Hatfield et al., 1992, for a fuller description).

What implication does such mimicry have for empathy-related outcomes? One possibility is that it allows observers to more accurately infer targets' internal states, and in fact Lipps (1903) and Titchener (1909) both argued that such imitation was at the heart of our ability to "feel into" another person. In recent years, however, research has focused less on the issue of accuracy and more on delineating how mimicry can lead observers to experience emotional responses similar or identical to those of the target.

One approach has been taken by Hatfield et al. (1992, 1994), who have termed this general phenomenon *emotional contagion*. In order for such emotional contagion to occur, two separate processes must unfold. First, it is necessary that observers mimic the behavior of targets and, second, that this mimicry produces in the observers an emotional state that parallels that of the targets. Evidence for the first process (mimicry) is plentiful, as noted above. In addition, considerable research supports the conclusion that this mimicry of others produces in observers emotional states consistent with the observed affect (e.g., Adelmann and Zajonc 1989).

Recent work by neuropsychologists has begun to identify the neural mechanisms that might underlie these processes. Evidence suggests that humans, along with other primate species, possess specialized neurons that are activated both when we engage in a certain action (e.g., grasping a tool) and when we simply observer that action carried out by someone else (Gallese 2003). Because these "mirror neurons" respond in the same way whether an action is carried out by the self or other, the implication is that we are, in a sense, *primed* for behavioral mimicry. Preston and Dewaal (2001) have argued that the fundamental mechanism underlying empathy is this perception action mechanism (PAM)—a biological tendency, when observing the state of another, to automatically activate one's internal representations of that state, which, in turn, generate autonomic and somatic responses in the observer.

Given the considerable evidence that mimicry can produce parallel emotional states in observers, what is the effect of this emotional synchrony between observer and target? The most socially important outcome seems to be greater feelings of rapport between the target and observer—variously operationalized as feeling "in step," involved, or compatible with the other person. Lafrance (1979), for example, found that when participants in an interaction had greater liking for one another, they also displayed greater posture similarity. Chartrand and Bargh (1999) manipulated mimicry by having confederates mimic (or not) the physical actions of their partner during a 15-min interaction; those in the mimicking condition reported greater liking for the confederate and a stronger perception that the interaction had gone smoothly. Most recently, Van Baaren et al. (2004a) found that people who have been mimicked during a brief interaction are more willing later to help not only the mimicker but unrelated individuals as well. Thus, growing evidence supports the view that the net effect of emotional synchrony is to increase feelings of closeness with, and goodwill toward, other people.

Although the ubiquity and automaticity of mimicry suggests that it is part of our biological heritage, it also appears that mimicry is more likely for some people and in some situations. Chartrand and her colleagues have found that mimicry is at least sometimes more likely among individuals who are high in self-monitoring (Cheng and Chartrand 2003), who have a field-dependent cognitive style (Van Baaren et al. 2004b) or who come from a culture with a more interdependent construal of self (Van Baaren et al. 2003). In addition, Bavelas et al. (1987) have found that mimicry is more frequent and pronounced when observers are *aware* that the targets will perceive the mimicked expressions, a pattern consistent with the view that one purpose of mimicry is to direct an affective message to the target. Thus, although mimicry appears to frequently occur outside of conscious awareness, it might also be sensitive to more strategic concerns.

PERSPECTIVE-TAKING. At the other end of the continuum of cognitive sophistication is perspective-taking: the deliberate attempt to imagine the internal state of another person. Historically, the concept of perspective-taking can be traced back to Smith *in the eighteenth century*, and somewhat more recently to Mead (1934), who argued specifically for the importance that role-taking ability has in allowing humans to effectively perform in society. According to Mead, perspective-taking allows us to overcome our usual egocentrism, tailor our behaviors to others' expectations, and, thus, make satisfying interpersonal relations possible. The capacity to engage in role-taking has also been theoretically linked to the development of moral reasoning (Kohlberg 1976), altruism (Batson 1991; Eisenberg and Miller 1987), and a decreased likelihood of inter-personal aggression (Feshbach 1978; Richardson et al. 1994). In each of these cases, the ability to entertain the psychological points of view of other people is said to result in some outcome that elevates—relative to one's own self-interest—the interests of the other person.

The empirical evidence gathered by social psychologists over the past 35 years has been broadly consistent with this theoretical view. In particular, research has convincingly documented two fundamental phenomena that result when an observer actively attempts to entertain the per-spective of another person. First, perspective-taking makes the observer more likely to offer causal attributions for the target's behavior that resemble the target's own—that is, attributions that emphasize situational factors relative to dispositional ones (e.g., Regan and Totten 1975). In essence, active role-taking has the effect of reducing or eliminating the usual actor-observer difference (Jones and Nisbett 1971). Second, when observers engage in perspective-taking while exposed to a needy target, their affective reactions also change. In general, role-taking observers become more likely to experience two affective states: feelings of sympathy and compassion for the target (e.g., Batson et al. 1989) and feelings of personal unease and distress (e.g., Betancourt 1990). Thus, consistent with theory, empirical investigations also support the view that perspective-taking provides a kind of "favored" status for the person whose perspective is being taken; observers explain the target's behavior in a way that resembles explanations for the observers' *own* behavior, and observers are more likely to experience emotions congruent with the target's own.

In addition to the large number of studies that have examined the consequences of perspective-taking, in recent years modest but increasing attention has been given to the actual mechanisms underlying perspective-taking. In short, what do people *do* when they attempt to imagine another's perspective? One approach to this question can be seen in Karniol's (1986) model that describes perspective-taking as a process by which people choose and employ "transformation rules" in order to move from observable behaviors and reactions by a target to an inference about the target's internal states. These rules reflect different ways that observers access and use existing knowledge to make such predictions. Karniol and Shomroni (1999) predicted and found that high school students high in dispositional perspective-taking made use of a greater variety of transformation rules when attempting to imagine the perspective of a dissimilar target.

It also appears that not all forms of perspective-taking are alike. For example, Batson et al. (1997a) have demonstrated that what might appear to be relatively small differences in perspective-taking instructions can produce significantly different outcomes in observers. They instructed some observers to "imagine how the target feels" before exposing them to a distressed target, and they instructed others to "imagine how you would feel" in the target's situation. Compared to a control condition, both instructional sets produced increased levels of sympathy for the target. However, the "imagine self" instructions also produced an increase in *personal* discomfort that the "imagine target" instructions did not. Clearly, something was different about the cognitive processes engendered by these two instructional sets. Davis et al. (2004) further demonstrated that these two sets also produce different kinds of thought in observers: those receiving "imagine self" instructions report more self-related thoughts than target-related thoughts, whereas those receiving "imagine target" instructions display the reverse pattern.

As with the research on mirror neurons, recent work by neuropsychologists has also begun to identify specific structures associated with perspective-taking. Evidence suggests that the brain activity that occurs when imagining another person's point of view is different from the activity that accompanies imagining one's own perspective: imagining another's perspective is associated with increased activity in the right inferior parietal lobe and the frontopolar cortex, whereas taking one's own perspective increases activity in the somatosensory cortex (Ruby and Decety 2003, 2004). Thus, it appears that both mimicry and perspective-taking—empathic processes that vary considerably in their cognitive complexity—are reliably associated with specific neural structures.

Intrapersonal Outcomes

The next component in the organizational framework consists of intrapersonal outcomes, defined as changes within the observer that result from exposure to the target. These outcomes might in turn, contribute to overt behavior toward the target, but they do not necessarily have this effect. There are at least three distinguishable categories of such outcomes: cognitive, emotional, and motivational.

COGNITIVE OUTCOMES.   A variety of cognitive outcomes has been linked to empathic processes. Taking the perspective of a target, for example, has been found to alter the type of causal attributions that observers make for the target's behavior, generally leading observers to make attributions for the target that mirror the kind of attributions observers usually make for their own behavior (e.g., Regan and Totten 1975). In recent years, perspective-taking has also been found to influence the cognitive representations that observers form of targets, and, again, the effect of perspective-taking is to lead observers to construct representations of the target that more closely resemble their own self-representations (Davis et al. 1996; Galinsky and Moskowitz 2000).

However, the cognitive outcome that has received the most attention is undoubtedly *interpersonal accuracy*, the degree to which the observer comes to have an accurate knowledge of the target. This is certainly an important outcome, and a desire for such accuracy is probably the primary reason that observers attempt to imagine the target's perspective in the first place. Early research in this tradition often attempted to identify the characteristics of "good judges"—that is, highly accurate observers. It typically assessed accuracy by having observers estimate how targets would evaluate themselves on a series of trait-rating scales. Unfortunately, this method for assessing accuracy had some significant problems, and with the publication of several critiques of this method, especially that of Cronbach (1955), things came to a rather abrupt halt. The problem was that accuracy in the rating-scale method is made up of several different constructs, some of which seem to be the result of judge or target response sets (e.g., a tendency to use the midpoint of the rating scale) rather than any kind of empathic transposition. As a result, accuracy scores based on this method contain an unknown amount of statistical confounding.

With increases in methodological sophistication, however, there has been a growing realization that accuracy can be studied in ways that avoid the problems described by Cronbach (e.g., Funder 1987; Kenny and Albright 1987). As long as the undesirable components of accuracy can be removed from the total accuracy score, or eliminated through the use of other techniques, it is possible to assess accuracy in a meaningful way. The result of this realization has been a growing number of studies that address interpersonal accuracy in a methodologically sound fashion.

Perhaps the most intriguing research in this modern tradition is Ickes' empathic accuracy (EA) paradigm (Ickes 1997, 2003). Ickes et al. (1990) reported the first use of this interesting and relatively naturalistic procedure. Mixed-sex dyads made up of unacquainted undergraduates were secretly videotaped during a 6-min period as they sat waiting for an experiment to "begin." Later, each participant separately viewed the tape and systematically indicated the specific thoughts and feelings that he or she recalled having at specific points throughout the 6-min period. Finally, the participants individually viewed the tapes a second time, with the experimenter stopping the tape at every point where their dyad partners had reported having a specific thought or feeling; the subjects then estimated their partners' thoughts/feelings at each point. Accuracy was indexed by the frequency with which subjects were able to estimate successfully the dyad partner's thoughts and feelings. This basic technique has now been used in numerous investigations, both by Ickes and his colleagues and by independent researchers (see Ickes, 2003, for a review). Observers in these investigations consistently exceed chance accuracy levels, and there appear to be reliable individual differences in performance.

From where does this accuracy come? The evidence from a number of investigations suggests two possible answers. The first is that accuracy results from the observer and target having some shared knowledge and experience. For example, EA studies often find evidence for an "acquaintance effect" such that dyads made up of friends or romantic partners display greater accuracy than dyads made up of strangers (e.g., Stinson and Ickes 1992). Although accuracy is certainly possible when predicting a stranger's responses, greater levels of EA are more likely when predicting someone with whom you have shared prior experiences.

The second answer is that EA is, to a considerable degree, the result of a strong motivation to be accurate; for example, Klein and Hodges (2001) found that the EA of observers can be enhanced by offering monetary incentives for better performance and Graham and Ickes (1997) have also found that men and women typically display equivalent accuracy levels—unless attention is called to the nature of the task so that women see it as relevant to the female sex role (e.g., more socially sensitive). In these cases, women outperform men, suggesting that the improved performance is due to increased motivation to do well. On the other side of the coin, Simpson et al. (1995) found that in certain circumstances (e.g., when one's dating partner is interacting with an attractive member of the opposite sex), the motivation to be accurate is diminished and, as a result, accuracy declines.

AFFECTIVE OUTCOMES. Although the study of cognitive outcomes—especially accuracy—has a long history, recent years have seen a greater emphasis on the affective changes that exposure to a target can produce in an observer. One type of emotional response to a target is to experience parallel affect, and a substantial number of investigations have examined potential influences on such responses. We have already considered one important mechanism by which parallel responses are generated—motor mimicry. As noted earlier, considerable evidence supports the notion that mimicry produces a convergence of affect between observers and targets.

Another empathic process described earlier—perspective-taking—has also been linked with parallel affective responding. In this research, role-taking has typically been manipulated by providing observers with instructional sets explicitly directing them to adopt the psychological perspective of the target. Two variants of these instructions, both initially developed by Stotland (1969), have been commonly employed: *imagine-self* and *imagine-the-other* instructions. Most investigations employing either of these instructional sets also include a "control" set that directs the observer to simply observe the target carefully, noting and remembering audio or visual details with as much clarity as possible.

Both types of perspective-taking instruction seem to increase parallel responding. Stotland (1969), for example, exposed observers to a target undergoing a diathermy (heat) treatment described as either painful or pleasurable. Observers receiving either instructional set exhibited more arousal than control subjects—albeit on different physiological measures—when the treatment was thought to be painful. Aderman and colleagues (1974; Aderman 1972) found that imagine-self observers were more likely to experience affect consistent with a distressed target. Batson et al. (1989, study 3) provided observers with imagine-the-other or control instructions and then exposed them to an audiotaped depiction of a female college student trying to support her family following the death of her parents; those attempting to imagine the other's feelings reported more sadness than did the control subjects.

There is another kind of affective reaction as well. In contrast to parallel emotions, reactive emotional responses do not match those of the target, but are, in some sense, a reaction *to* the target's situation. Although this in theory could encompass a wide variety of emotions, practically speaking, only two reactive responses have received much sustained research attention. The first of these is *empathic concern*—the other-oriented emotional response of compassion for the target; the second is *personal distress*—the self-oriented response of discomfort and anxiety to another's misfortune (Davis 1994).

Most of the investigations examining empathic concern's antecedents have focused on role-taking and have used instructions to induce a role-taking set toward the target. Moreover, virtually all of the studies have employed one type of instruction: the imagine-the-other instructional set. Following delivery of the instructional set, subjects in these studies were typically exposed to a target in some distress. One frequently used target is "Katie Banks," originally introduced by Coke et al. (1978). In this paradigm, subjects listen to an audiotape in which the plight of a young college student—Katie—is described. Following the recent death of her parents, Katie is struggling to support her younger brother and sister while finishing school. After listening to this tape, participants typically complete a questionnaire containing the empathic concern items. Other commonly used paradigms have exposed observers to targets who were injured in an automobile accident, who were experiencing college-related stress, who needed volunteers for a research project, or who were receiving painful electric shocks (see Batson 1991). The vast majority of these investigations, whether using "Katie Banks" or some other target, have found imagine-the-other instructions to produce significantly greater feelings of sympathy for the target than control instructions.

The other reactive emotional response to have received substantial research attention is personal distress. Because contemporary theorizing has so frequently focused on the contrasting motivational properties of empathic concern and personal distress, almost every study explicitly addressing the antecedents of personal distress has simultaneously examined empathic concern; thus, many investigations mentioned in the previous paragraph on empathic concern also address the issue of personal distress. One consequence of this is that virtually the same experimental procedures and targets have been employed in investigations of both affective states. In contrast to the pattern found for empathic concern, however, the effect of these instructions on feelings of personal distress is not quite as reliable. As Davis (1994) noted at the time that he reviewed this literature, imagine-the-other instructions produced heightened empathic concern in over 80% of the investigations, but had such an effect on personal distress only 50% of the time.

MOTIVATIONAL STATES.   A third intrapersonal outcome of empathy-related processes is some change in the motivational state of observers—that is, in their internal desires, needs, and concerns. In some ways, of course, this outcome resembles the previous one—affective states—because of the link that often exists between emotion and motivation. How can these be distinguished? One important difference between them, at least insofar as this chapter is concerned, is that motives and emotions frequently operate at somewhat different levels of specificity, with motivations typically being more general and emotions more specific. For example, the presence of a given motive (e.g., a general need for achievement) might give rise to a variety of specific emotional states (e.g., satisfaction following success; shame following failure).

One example of an empathy-mediated effect on motivation comes from the burgeoning literature on forgiveness. The past decade has seen an increasing amount of attention paid to this important interpersonal phenomenon (e.g., Enright et al. 1992; McCullough et al. 2000). Although a variety of definitions have been advanced, one influential approach is that of McCullough et al. (1997), who defined forgiveness as a set of motivational changes characterized by lowered desires to retaliate against and maintain estrangement from an offending relationship partner and a heightened desire for conciliation. Thus, forgiveness at its heart is a set of changes in the *motivations* of the offended party.

What is empathy's role? McCullough et al. (1997) have proposed a model that identifies empathic concern for the transgressor (which they simply term "empathy") as the most important cause of forgiveness following a transgression. Only to the extent that wronged parties feel empathic concern (perhaps as a result of an apology by the transgressor) do they experience a motivational change that replaces desire for revenge or estrangement with a wish for reconciliation. Considerable recent evidence supports this model. In a pair of investigations, McCullough et al. (1997) found that feelings of empathy, as hypothesized, were associated with greater forgiveness for a transgressor; moreover, forgiveness was then associated with less avoidance and greater conciliation. McCullough et al. (1998, study 4) reported similar findings in an investigation that examined two distinct behavioral responses to being wronged by another: avoidance and revenge. Feelings of empathy for the transgressor were associated with decreased motivation for both behaviors. In a sample of Italian married couples, Fincham et al. (2002) found the same pattern: More tolerant attributions for a partner's misbehavior led to feelings of empathy, which, in turn, led to increased forgiveness. Finally, in a pair of longitudinal studies, McCullough et al. (2003) repeatedly queried individuals for weeks after they suffered an interpersonal transgression. In both studies, empathy at the time of the transgression was significantly related to immediate forgiveness but was much less likely to predict additional forgiveness over time. Thus, it might be that empathic concern has its greatest effect on the motivation to forgive in the immediate aftermath of another's misbehavior.

Interpersonal Outcomes

The end point in the organizational model is an overt behavioral act by the empathizing individual. Unsurprisingly, much of the past research on empathy has consisted of attempts to discover which empathy-related antecedents or processes are reliably associated with specific behavioral outcomes. A number of such outcomes has been studied over the years, but these can largely be subsumed by three categories: helping behavior, aggression, and a more general category of social behavior. By far the most studied of these areas is the first.

EMPATHY AND HELPING. The evidence is convincing that a dispositional tendency to engage in perspective-taking—the relatively nonemotional facet of empathy—is associated with greater helpfulness (Eisenberg and Miller 1987). However, most recent attempts to examine the empathy/helping connection have focused on the more clearly affective elements in the organizational framework.

One way that empathically created affect can lead to helping is straightforward. If seeing another in distress leads observers to experience parallel affect and if that affect is experienced as unpleasant, then helping might result simply to reduce this undesirable state. Because the ultimate goal in such a sequence is to improve the well-being of the observer, such helping seems clearly egoistic. This logic underlies a variety of social psychological theories of helping; one good example is the negative state relief (NSR) model (Cialdini et al. 1973; Cialdini and Kenrick 1976).

Another mechanism by which empathy-related affect can lead to helping is not through parallel emotions but through some form of reactive affective response. In particular, considerable research has investigated the role of *empathic concern* in promoting helping behavior. Batson (1991) has been the primary advocate of this approach, and he has made the argument that helping motivated by feelings of empathic concern (simply termed "empathy" in his approach) might be considered truly altruistic—that is, not motivated by any desire to reduce one's own distress or to enhance one's own well-being. In a set of studies, Batson and colleagues (1981, 1983) attempted to demonstrate the existence of altruistic helping by constructing an experimental design that contrasts the effects of a truly altruistic motivation with those of an egoistic arousal reduction motivation. To do so, they made use of the differential impact that ease of escape should have on the behavior of those motivated by egoistic versus altruistic motives.

**TABLE 19.1. Batson's Experimental Design:
The Effect of Empathic Emotion and Ease
of Escape on Helping Behavior**

	Predominant Emotional Response	
	Distress	Concern
Ease of escape		
Easy	Escape	Help
Difficult	Help	Help

Consider for a moment an observer who is experiencing a high degree of personal distress while in the presence of a needy target. The observer's high level of aversive arousal creates in her a motivation to reduce it. If physically escaping from the situation is difficult for some reason, then this high level of arousal will probably lead her to help as a means of eliminating the source of the arousal; on the other hand, if escape from the situation is easy, then she might well choose that option instead. Therefore, the behavior resulting from this egoistic motivation depends on the ease or difficulty of escape. In contrast, consider a situation in which the observer is predominantly experiencing empathic concern for the target. In this case, the ease or difficulty of escape is *irrelevant* to her goal of reducing target distress; as a result, she is likely to help whether escape is easy *or* difficult. If this logic is correct and feelings of personal distress and empathic concern really do produce egoistic and altruistic motivational states, respectively, then an experiment producing the four conditions displayed in Table 19.1 should produce levels of helping that conform to the one versus three (personal distress/easy escape versus all other combinations) pattern depicted there.

This is precisely the pattern that has emerged in number of studies (Batson et al. 1981, 1983; Toi and Batson 1982). In each of these investigations, a comparison was made between subjects predominantly experiencing empathic concern and those predominantly experiencing personal distress. In some cases, these emotional reactions were produced through experimental manipulations, and in others, the predominant emotional response was simply assessed via questionnaire. In every instance, the observers who were experiencing empathic concern provided relatively high levels of help, regardless of ease of escape. Observers who were primarily experiencing personal distress displayed the predicted sensitivity to the ease of escape manipulation; when escape was difficult, they helped at the same level as those experiencing empathic concern, but when escape was easy, the level of helping dropped dramatically. Importantly, this pattern held over a variety of different need situations. Based on these investigations, a convincing case can be made that empathic concern and personal distress are two distinctly different affective reactions, that the motivation associated with personal distress is clearly egoistic in nature, and that the motivation associated with empathic concern is not egoistic in nature.

This conclusion is not universally accepted. Cialdini and colleagues (1997), in particular, have argued that the helping associated with empathic concern is in fact egoistic and, thus, does not constitute evidence for "true" altruism (Maner et al. 2002). The crux of their argument is that the same factors that cause feelings of empathic concern in observers (e.g., perspective-taking instructions; relationship closeness) will often engender self-oriented states as well. In particular, they argued that one such state is a feeling of shared identity or "oneness" with the target. This sense of oneness in a way constitutes a merging of self and other, and this "confusion" of self and other means that actions carried out to help the target are, in a sense, carried out to help the self and are, therefore, egoistic in nature. Maner et al. (2002) conducted a study explicitly designed to evaluate this possibility and reported results supporting their arguments—feelings of empathic concern were associated with greater helping for a needy target, but this association disappeared once the effects of more egoistic states, including oneness, were controlled.

One other recent approach to the question of empathy and helping merits discussion. The kind of helping that often occurs in the laboratory research cited thus far is spontaneous and unplanned, with the opportunity to help typically coming without warning. In such research the focus is usually on single acts that take place in response to the presence of a clear and present victim. However, a tremendous amount of helping does not occur in this fashion. Community volunteering, for example, often represents a long-term commitment rather than a single act, and the decision to volunteer is not typically made spontaneously, but as a result of careful and deliberate thought. Consequently, the initiation and maintenance of volunteer activity might be governed by different variables than those that control spontaneous single acts of helping.

To examine this issue, Omoto and Snyder (1995) studied volunteerism using an approach that they termed the "volunteer process model"—a framework that conceives of *antecedent* factors (characteristics of the volunteer or the volunteer setting), volunteer *experiences* such as satisfaction or integration into the volunteer organization, and *consequences* of volunteering such as persistence or attitude change. Using a sample of AIDS volunteers, Omoto and Snyder found that personality measures of a "helping disposition" (nurturance, empathic concern) were not directly related to greater persistence, but were related to higher satisfaction with one's volunteer work and to greater integration into the volunteer organization. Greater satisfaction, but not integration, was, in turn, positively associated with longer persistence as a volunteer. Penner and Finkelstein (1998) also evaluated the volunteer process model, again making use of a sample of AIDS volunteers. Like Omoto and Snyder, Penner and Finkelstein found that at least one measure of the helping personality (other-oriented empathy) displayed positive associations with volunteer satisfaction, although these associations were not consistently significant. As in the earlier study, volunteer satisfaction was positively, albeit modestly, related to greater persistence.

Using a slightly revised version of the volunteer process model, Davis et al. (2003) studied community volunteers during their first year of service. Volunteers were contacted four times during this year and queried regarding their emotional reactions (sympathy, distress) and satisfaction. Consistent with the revised model, feelings of sympathy and distress were substantially predicted by antecedent factors, especially dispositional empathic concern and the emotional intensity of the work itself. Also consistent with the revised model, volunteer involvement (number of hours per week volunteered) was predicted by satisfaction, although volunteer persistence over time was not. These findings, as well as others (Bekkers 2004; Stolinski et al. 2004), strongly and consistently implicate one empathy-related construct in particular: the dispositional tendency to experience empathic concern for needy targets. This disposition was associated in each investigation with at least one important aspect of the volunteer experience.

EMPATHY AND AGGRESSION. The role of empathy in reducing aggressive behavior has not received the same degree of research attention as the empathy-helping link but has nonetheless prompted some investigation. There are at least two primary mechanisms by which empathy can regulate hostile or aggressive behaviors. The first possibility is that observers' emotional responses to the distress of others might lessen their likelihood of aggressing against those others. This might happen, for example, if observing the victim's distress cues leads to a sharing of the victim's distress. To escape this vicarious distress, the aggressor stops or reduces the aggression (e.g., Feshbach 1964). Victim distress cues can also produce the reactive emotion of empathic concern in perpetrator-observers, and these feelings of sympathy might then lead the observer to stop or reduce the aggression (Miller and Eisenberg 1988). In both cases, however, it is the observers' affective response that is responsible for inhibiting aggression. Evidence reviewed by Miller and Eisenberg (1988) suggests that for adults there is in fact a reliable association between dispositional emotional empathy and aggressive behavior. Across the nine studies using adult samples included in that review, greater dispositional empathy was, for the most part, reliably associated with less aggressive behavior. Studies conducted since that time (Davis 1994; Richardson et al. 1994) have found a similar pattern.

The second mechanism by which empathy might reduce the occurrence of aggressive actions is through the process of perspective-taking; that is, adopting the point of view of a person who acts in a potentially provoking way might lead to a more tolerant perception of that person's actions, which can consequently reduce the likelihood that retaliation will occur. A number of studies have examined this possibility and found evidence consistent with it.

Davis and Kraus (1991) reported, in two samples of adolescent and preadolescent boys, a significant negative correlation between dispositional perspective-taking and their self-reported number of fights and arguments over the previous 2 years. Two investigations (Richardson et al. 1994, 1998) examined the link between dispositional perspective-taking and actual verbal aggression in a laboratory setting and found evidence that high perspective-takers were less likely to retaliate against opponents who had mildly provoked them; this held true even if the opponents increased the magnitude of their provocation across trials. Finally, Giancola (2003) examined the effect of provocation, alcohol consumption, and dispositional empathy (both perspective-taking and empathic concern) on actual aggression (administering electric shocks). Using a sample of "healthy social drinkers," he found that alcohol increased aggressive responding, but that this was especially true for those who were lowest in dispositional empathy. Thus, not only does perspective-taking seem to make hostile responding less likely in general, it might also serve a buffering function by diminishing the harmful effects of other variables such as alcohol consumption. It should also be noted here that some of the effects of perspective-taking on aggression might be due to emotional responses produced by taking the perspective of the provoker. Given the well-documented links between perspective-taking and emotional reactions, it is likely that affective states such as empathic concern and personal distress often accompany perspective-taking and that they mediate—at least to some degree—the apparent influence of perspective taking on hostility.

EMPATHY AND SOCIAL BEHAVIOR.   The idea that social intercourse is significantly influenced by the capacity for empathy is certainly not new. Smith (1976) and Spencer (1870) have both argued that important social consequences flow from our tendency to "sympathize" with others' experiences—that is, to share a "fellow-feeling" with them. Theorists with a decidedly more cognitive view of empathy (Mead 1934; Piaget 1932) also hold that possessing such a capacity will improve the social climate. What both approaches have in common, although perhaps more clearly with regard to the role-taking argument, is the recognition that empathy in some guise is necessary to help us deal with the fundamental obstacle in social life, namely other people. Because other people commonly have needs, desires, and goals that differ from our own and because the attainment of their goals is frequently incompatible with ours, a powerful tendency toward conflict is inherent in all social life, resulting in high levels of conflict and disagreement. More accurately, the result *can* be such a conflict-filled existence if no mechanism—such as empathy—is available to interrupt this sequence. Over the past two decades, the possible role of empathy within social relationships has been examined in a variety of ways.

One approach has been to examine the association between dispositional empathy and overall relationship satisfaction, and several studies have adopted this strategy (Fincham and Bradbury

1989; Franzoi et al. 1985; Long and Andrews 1990; Rusbult et al. 1991). Although the precise pattern of results varied somewhat from study to study, each investigation found at least some significant positive association between perspective-taking and satisfaction for at least one member of the romantic relationship and often for both. Thus, taking your partner's perspective—or having a partner who takes yours—is associated with greater personal satisfaction with the relationship.

Another approach to the question of empathy's role in social relationships has been to consider its influence on specific behavioral patterns that occur within relationships. One such pattern is the use of a *considerate social style,* defined here as displaying tolerance, cooperation, active support for others, and a general lack of egocentrism in thought and deed—characteristics that all reflect sensitivity to the other person's needs and desires. Four studies using college populations have examined associations between dispositional empathy and measures of a considerate style. Davis and Oathout (1987, 1992) had college students report the frequency with which they engaged in a number of considerate behaviors toward their romantic partners, including "warmth" (acting in affectionate and supportive ways) and "positive outlook" (being friendly, positive, and dependable). In both studies, dispositional empathic concern was significantly and positively related to both kinds of behavior; although the pattern was not as consistent, dispositional personal distress was generally related to considerate behavior significantly but *negatively.* Trobst et al. (1994) measured college students' dispositional empathy and also assessed their willingness to offer social support to both friends and strangers; in both cases, dispositional empathic concern was related to offering more support. Thus, the evidence suggests that empathic concern is positively and substantially related to a considerate style and that personal distress is more weakly and generally negatively associated with such a style.

The Rusbult et al. (1991) investigation cited earlier approached this question from a slightly different angle, through their focus on accommodation in close relationships. They assumed that when one partner in a close relationship behaves badly, the initial impulse of the other partner is typically to retaliate. In many instances, however, such retaliation never takes place; instead, the wronged party inhibits the immediate impulse and, instead, acts in a constructive fashion, perhaps ignoring the transgression or treating it as only a minor annoyance. Rusbult et al. termed this constructive reaction *accommodation,* and it seems reasonable to consider it part of the considerate social style. Rusbult et al. presented subjects with a series of hypothetical destructive acts that could be committed by one's partner (e.g., criticizing you) and asked them to report their most likely response to such acts. The tendency to make accommodating responses was most powerfully influenced by the subjects' *commitment* to the relationship: those more committed to the relationship were more likely to accommodate. Above and beyond the effect of commitment, however, a greater self-reported tendency to take the partner's perspective was also associated with greater accommodation.

Another positive behavioral pattern is *good communication,* and several studies indicated that dispositional empathic concern has a constructive effect on social relationships. One set of studies (Davis and Franzoi 1986; Franzoi and Davis 1985) examined the link between high school students' dispositional empathy and self-disclosure to peers; personal distress was not related, but empathic concern for both male and female students was significantly and positively related to disclosure *to females.* In two investigations mentioned previously, Davis and Oathout (1987, 1992) asked college students about the degree to which they "opened up" and "readily listened" to their romantic partner. For both men and women, empathic concern scores were significantly and positively associated with higher scores on this communication index; for women only, personal distress scores were negatively associated.

FUTURE DIRECTIONS

This somewhat selective presentation of past and contemporary empathy research provides an overview of the current state of the field, at least as it is typically studied by social psychologists. Based on the picture that has emerged, I conclude this chapter by offering some suggestions regarding two interesting and potentially important directions for future empathy research.

Studying Perspective-Taking for Its Own Sake

Perspective-taking occupies a central place within the empathy framework. It has long been recognized as a uniquely important cognitive skill—in fact some approaches have essentially equated perspective taking with empathy. Even those who have favored an affective definition of empathy have seen perspective-taking as one of the most important methods for inducing such emotional responses. However, one fact that becomes apparent when examining previous research is that the focus has almost exclusively been on perspective-taking as a means to an end; that is, most research by contemporary social psychologists has been interested in perspective-taking, either measured as a disposition or situationally induced, because of its ability to influence some other phenomenon in which they were *more* interested: causal attributions, affective states, helping, accuracy in person perception, forgiveness, and so on. There is nothing wrong with such a strategy, but, as a consequence, surprisingly little attention has been devoted to the study of perspective taking per se.

As mentioned previously, however, there has recently been an increased interest in such questions. The work of Batson et al. (1997a), comparing the effects of imagine-self and imagine-the-target instructional sets on observers' affective responses, and the work of Davis et al. (2004), examining the effect of such sets on self-reported thoughts, both place more focus on perspective-taking as a process of interest for its own sake. Davis (2005), moreover, has argued for an even more systematic approach to the study of perspective-taking based on identifying its essential constituents. In particular, he has argued that perspective-taking attempts all have some *aim* (what the observer is trying to achieve), *information used* (the particular kind of information used in the perspective-taking attempt), *process employed* (the particular process or processes used in the attempt), and *outcome* (the end result of the perspective-taking attempt). Thinking about perspective-taking in such a systematic way leads to some interesting questions. The following are three of them.

First, *is taking the perspective of others in everyday life "natural"?* In other words, is our usual response to adopt the point of view of other people (to empathize with them, in the broadest terms), or does this kind of response usually require some kind of additional prompt from the environment? Very preliminary evidence suggests that at least when faced with someone not too dissimilar, the kinds of thought that naturally occur are very similar to those that result when explicitly instructed to imagine the target's point of view (Davis et al. 2004). In fact, the results of that investigation suggested that it might take the presence of empathy-*inhibiting* instructions to disrupt the "default" thought pattern. The finding that neural structures predispose us to respond to the activities of others as though we had performed the activities ourselves is also tantalizingly consistent with the notion that we are in a sense "primed" to empathize. However, given the near-total absence in empathy research of the truly "neutral" instruction condition employed by Davis et al., there is little research to date that allows an evaluation of this question. Thus, it is far too early to conclude that empathizing is our default orientation.

Second, and relatedly, *is perspective taking as effortful a process as is typically assumed?* Virtually all theoretical accounts of perspective-taking conceive of it as a controlled, effortful process (Hoffman 1984; Eisenberg et al. 1991), especially as compared to other empathy-related processes like mimicry. Although this assumption is plausible, it is also possible that the matter might not be so simple. In the one investigation to date that has explicitly addressed this question, Davis et al. (1996) found evidence that although some effects of perspective-taking instructions were reduced or eliminated by the presence of a competing task, not all were. (Finding that some mental process is diminished by the presence of a competing task suggests that the process in question is effortful, requiring some mental resources.) Specifically, evidence from that investigation indicated that the general tendency to ascribe a greater number of traits to a novel target was increased by perspective-taking instructions and that the presence of a competing task eliminated this effect. The specific tendency to ascribe *self*-related traits to the target was also increased by perspective-taking, but it is not clear that this tendency was reduced by the presence of a competing task. Thus, one interesting possibility is that perspective-taking might involve a family of different responses to the target—some intentional and some not, some effortful and some not—and that these responses might have different effects on later outcomes.

Finally, a third potentially useful avenue for future research is to *distinguish between the intended and unintended effects of perspective-taking.* This refers to the fact that when considering the history of social psychological research on perspective-taking, it turns out that, to a considerable degree, what social psychologists have studied for the past three decades are really the *unintended* effects of perspective-taking; that is, when we explicitly consider the aim of most perspective-taking efforts, it is clear that what is being sought by the observer is usually some kind of accuracy. What observers *desire* is some better insight into the internal state of targets—their thoughts, or motives, or goals.

However, when social psychologists have studied the consequences of perspective-taking, a huge proportion of this work has had nothing to do with this kind of accuracy. Dozens of investigations have been carried out to determine the effect of perspective-taking on observers' emotional reactions, attributions, helping behavior, aggression, stereotype use, and so forth. As interesting and important as all of these phenomena are, they are also *not* typically the aim of real-world observers. Although it is not impossible that such observers sometimes have aims such as "behaving less aggressively" or "reducing stereotype use" when they engage in perspective-taking, it seems more likely that their usual goal is to gain some accurate insight into the target.

This somewhat surprising realization leads to some interesting questions. To take just one example, how frequently do people engage in perspective-taking for their own accuracy-oriented reasons but end up with some unintended consequence instead? For example, can an observer take the target's perspective in order to defeat him in a negotiation and, instead, begin to experience sympathy or an increased sense of oneness with that target? For those with a taste for the ironic, this is a very interesting possibility; in fact, hints of it can be seen in some research by Batson et al. (1997b), in which observers who were led to take the perspective of an unsavory target (e.g., a convicted murderer) came to hold more favorable attitudes—not only toward that particular target but also toward the entire stigmatized class to which he belonged! It seems likely in this case that these more tolerant attitudes toward murderers as a class were an unintended outcome of perspective-taking; whether this also happens in more natural settings remains to be seen, but the possibility seems worthy of examination.

The Practical Uses of Empathy

A second promising avenue for future research is in some ways the opposite of the first. In addition to studying empathy-related processes like perspective-taking for their own sakes, there is also value in making a more careful study of what might called the *practical* uses of empathy. An example of this kind of approach can be seen in the work described earlier on empathy and volunteering. This research has typically examined community volunteers within their organizational settings and has sought to answer such practical questions as why people volunteer in the first place, what they seek and what they obtain from their work, what determines their satisfaction with the volunteer experience, and what affects volunteer persistence over time. All of these are questions of considerable practical importance for organizations that make heavy use of volunteers, and continued efforts in this area hold much value.

Another practical issue that seems ripe for serious attention is the question of *empathy training*. Given the widely recognized importance of empathy in many walks of life, one longstanding assumption has been that it is possible to develop methods for increasing empathic responding, however this might be defined. Thus, programs have been designed to increase the empathy of widely varying populations—psychiatric patients (Lomis and Baker 1985), delinquents (Pecukonis 1990), bullies (Eslea and Smith 1998), and parents (Gordon 2003), among others.

What has not yet been done is to subject such programs to a systematic and rigorous examination in an effort to determine what works and what does not. This task will not be easy. Training attempts have been carried out in so many different ways, using so many different definitions of empathy, with so many different goals, and with so many different populations that simply organizing them in a meaningful way will be a considerable undertaking. However, the benefits of such an effort could also be considerable. It seems likely, for instance, that a systematic review will reveal some forms of empathy training, or some components of such training, to be relatively ineffective; it is to be hoped, however, that others *will* turn out to be generally effective, at least under some circumstances. Such an identification of successful empathy training's "active ingredients" will be of tremendous importance for those designing, implementing, or funding such programs.

CONCLUSION

Empathy occupies a strategically crucial location in modern social psychology; it lies at the border that separates the individual from the other, ego from alter. The capacity to set aside egocentric concerns and entertain the point of view of other people provides a kind of bridge that links otherwise isolated persons; it allows those separate entities, at least for a time, to share thoughts, feelings, and goals. This sharing makes possible some of the most admirable human activities—those that raise our motivations from the purely selfish to the selfless and that give us the occasional opportunity to display a true nobility of purpose. The possession of such empathic capacities does not, of course, ensure such nobility; evidence of that is all too obvious. Our capacity for other-oriented thinking and acting, however, makes it *possible*, and this makes the study of empathy and related phenomena a most worthy one for sociologists and psychologists alike.

REFERENCES

Adelmann, Pamela K., and Robert B. Zajonc. 1989. "Facial Efference and the Experience of Emotion." *Annual Review of Psychology* 40: 249–280.

Aderman, David. 1972. "Elation, Depression, and Helping Behavior." *Journal of Personality and Social Psychology* 24: 91–101.

Aderman, David, Sharon S. Brehm, and Lawrence B. Katz. 1974. "Empathic Observation of an Innocent Victim: The Just World Revisited." *Journal of Personality and Social Psychology* 29: 342–347.

Batson, C. Daniel. 1991. *The Altruism Question: Toward a Social-Psychological Answer.* Hillsdale, NJ: Erlbaum.

Batson, C. Daniel, Judy G. Batson, Cari A. Griffitt, Sergio Barrientos, J. Randall Brandt, Peter Sprengelmeyer, and Michael J. Bayly. 1989. "Negative-State Relief and the Empathy-Altruism Hypothesis." *Journal of Personality and Social Psychology* 56: 922–933.

Batson, C. Daniel, Bruce D. Duncan, Paula Ackerman, Terese Buckley, and Kimberly Birch. 1981. "Is Empathic Emotion a Source of Altruistic Motivation?" *Journal of Personality and Social Psychology* 40: 290–302.

Batson, C. Daniel, Shannon Early, and Giovanni Salvarani. 1997a. "Perspective Taking: Imagining How Another Feels versus Imagining How You Would Feel." *Personality and Social Psychology Bulletin* 23: 751–758.

Batson, C. Daniel, David A. Lishner, Jennifer Cook, and Stacey Sawyer. 2005. "Similarity and Nurturance: Two Possible Sources of Empathy for Strangers." *Basic and Applied Social Psychology* 27: 15–25.

Batson, C. Daniel, Karen O'Quin, Jim Fultz, Mary Vanderplas, and Alice Isen. 1983. "Influence of Self-Reported Distress and Empathy on Egoistic versus Altruistic Motivation to Help." *Journal of Personality and Social Psychology* 45: 706–718.

Batson, C. Daniel, Marina P. Polycarpou, Eddie Harmon-Jones, Heidi J. Imhoff, Erin C. Mitchener, Lori L. Bednar, Tricia R. Klein, and Lori Highberger. 1997b. "Empathy and Attitudes: Can Feeling for a Member of a Stigmatized Group Improve Feelings Toward the Group?" *Journal of Personality and Social Psychology* 72: 105–118.

Batson, C. Daniel, Cynthia L. Turk, Laura L. Shaw, and Tricia R. Klein. 1995. "Information Function of Empathic Emotion: Learning that We Value the Other's Welfare." *Journal of Personality and Social Psychology* 68: 300–313.

Bavelas, Janet B., Alex Black, Charles R. Lemery, and Jennifer Mullett. 1987. "Motor Mimicry as Primitive Empathy." Pp. 317–338 in *Empathy and Its Development*, edited by N. Eisenberg and J. Strayer. Cambridge: Cambridge University Press.

Bekkers, Rene. 2004. "Giving and Volunteering in the Netherlands: Sociological and Psychological Perspectives." Ph.D. dissertation. Department of Sociology, Utrecht University, The Netherlands.

Betancourt, Hector. 1990. "An Attribution-Empathy Model of Helping Behavior: Behavioral Intentions and Judgments of Help-Giving." *Personality and Social Psychology Bulletin* 16: 573–591.

Chartrand, Tanya L., and John A. Bargh. 1999. "The Chameleon Effect: The Perception Behavior Link and Social Interaction." *Journal of Personality and Social Psychology* 76: 893–910.

Cheng, Clara M., and Tanya L. Chartrand. 2003. "Self-Monitoring without Awareness: Using Mimicry as a Nonconscious Affiliation Strategy." *Journal of Personality and Social Psychology* 85: 1170–1179.

Cialdini, Robert B., Stephanie L. Brown, Brian P. Lewis, Carol Luce, and Steven L. Neuberg. 1997. "Reinterpreting the Empathy-Altruism Relationship: When One Into One Equals Oneness." *Journal of Personality and Social Psychology* 73: 481–494.

Cialdini, Robert B., Betty L. Darby, and Joyce E. Vincent. 1973. "Transgression and Altruism: A Case for Hedonism." *Journal of Experimental Social Psychology* 9: 502–516.

Cialdini, Robert B., and Douglas T. Kenrick. 1976. "Altruism as Hedonism: A Social Development Perspective on the Relationship of Negative Mood State and Helping." *Journal of Personality and Social Psychology* 34: 907–914.

Coke, Jay S., C. Daniel Batson, and Katherine McDavis. 1978. "Empathic Mediation of Helping: A Two-Stage Model." *Journal of Personality and Social Psychology* 36: 752–766.

Cronbach, Lee J. 1955. "Processes Affecting Scores on Understanding of Others and Assuming 'Similarity'." *Psychological Bulletin* 52: 177–193.

Davis, Mark H. 1980. "A Multidimensional Approach to Individual Differences in Empathy." *Journal Supplemental Abstract Service Catalog of Selected Documents in Psychology* 10: 85.

———. 1983. "Measuring Individual Differences in Empathy: Evidence for a Multidimensional Approach." *Journal of Personality and Social Psychology* 44: 113–126.

———. 1994. *Empathy: A Social Psychological Approach.* Boulder, CO: Westview.

———. 2005. "A 'Constituent' Approach to the Study of Perspective Taking: What Are Its Fundamental Elements?" Pp. 44–55 in *Other Minds: How Humans Bridge the Divide Between Self and Others*, edited by B. Malle and S. Hodges. New York: Guilford.

Davis, Mark H., Laura Conklin, Amy Smith, and Carol Luce. 1996. "Effect of Perspective Taking on the Cognitive Representation of Persons: A Merging of Self and Other." *Journal of Personality and Social Psychology* 70: 713–726.

Davis, Mark H., and Stephen L. Franzoi. 1986. "Adolescent Loneliness, Self- Disclosure, and Private Self-Consciousness: A Longitudinal Investigation." *Journal of Personality and Social Psychology* 51: 595–608.

Davis, Mark H., Jennifer A. Hall, and Marnee Meyer. 2003. "The First Year: Influences on the Satisfaction, Involvement, and Persistence of New Community Volunteers." *Personality and Social Psychology Bulletin* 29: 248–260.

Davis, Mark H., and Linda A. Kraus. 1991. "Dispositional Empathy and Social Relationships." Pp. 75–115 in *Advances in Personal Relationships* Vol. 3, edited by W. H. Jones and D. Perlman. London: Jessica Kingsley Publishers.

Davis, Mark H., and H. Alan Oathout. 1987. "Maintenance of Satisfaction in Romantic Relationships: Empathy and Relational Competence." *Journal of Personality and Social Psychology* 53: 397–410.

———. 1992. "The Effect of Dispositional Empathy on Romantic Relationship Behaviors: Heterosocial Anxiety as a Moderating Influence." *Personality and Social Psychology Bulletin* 18: 76–83.

Davis, Mark H., Tama Soderlund, Jonathan Cole, Eric Gadol, Maria Kute, Michael Myers, and Jeffrey Weihing. 2004. "Cognitions Associated with Attempts to Empathize: How Do We Imagine the Perspective of Another?" *Personality and Social Psychology Bulletin* 30: 1625–1635.

Dymond, Rosalind F. 1950. "Personality and Empathy." *Journal of Consulting Psychology* 14: 343–350.

Eisenberg, Nancy, and Paul A. Miller. 1987. "Empathy and Prosocial Behavior." *Psychological Bulletin* 101: 91–119.

Eisenberg, Nancy, Cindy L. Shea, Gustavo Carlo, and George P. Knight. 1991. "Empathy-Related Responding and Cognition: A 'Chicken and the Egg' Dilemma." Pp. 63–88 in *Handbook of Moral Behavior and Development* Vol. 2: *Research*, edited by W. Kurtines and J. Gewirtz. Hillsdale, NJ: Erlbaum.

Eisenberg, Nancy, and Janet Strayer. 1987. "Critical Issues in the Study of Empathy." Pp. 3–13 in *Empathy and Its Development*, edited by N. Eisenberg and J. Strayer. Cambridge: Cambridge University Press.

Enright, Robert D., Elizabeth A. Gassin, and Ching-Ru Wu. 1992. "Forgiveness: A Developmental View." *Journal of Moral Development* 21: 99–114.

Eslea, Michael, and Peter K. Smith. 1998. "The Long-Term Effectiveness of AntiBullying Work in Primary Schools." *Educational Research* 40: 1–16.

Feshbach, Norma D. 1978. "Studies of Empathic Behavior in Children." Pp. 1–47 in *Progress in Experimental Personality Research*, edited by B. A. Maher. New York: Academic.

Feshbach, Seymour. 1964. "The Function of Aggression and the Regulation of Aggressive Drive." *Psychological Review* 71: 257–272.

Fincham, Frank D., and Thomas N. Bradbury. 1989. "Perceived Responsibility for Marital Events: Egocentric or Partner-Centric Bias?" *Journal of Marriage and the Family* 51: 27–35.

Fincham, Frank D., Giorgia Paleari, and Camillo Regalia. 2002. "Forgiveness in Marriage: The Role of Relationship Quality, Attributions and Empathy." *Personal Relationships* 9: 27–37.

Franzoi, Stephen L., and Mark H. Davis. 1985. "Adolescent Self-Disclosure and Loneliness: Private Self-Consciousness and Parental Influences." *Journal of Personality and Social Psychology* 48: 768–780.

Franzoi, Stephen L., Mark H. Davis, and Richard D. Young. 1985. "The Effects of Private Self-Consciousness and Perspective Taking on Satisfaction in Close Relationships." *Journal of Personality and Social Psychology* 48: 1584–1594.

Funder, David C. 1987. "Errors and Mistakes: Evaluating the Accuracy of Social Judgment." *Psychological Bulletin* 101: 75–90.

Gage, Nathaniel L., and Lee J. Cronbach. 1955. "Conceptual Methodological Problems in Interpersonal Perception." *Psychological Review* 62: 411–422.

Galinsky, Adam D., and Gordon B. Moskowitz. 2000. "Perspective-Taking: Decreasing Stereotype Expression, Stereotype Accessibility, and In-Group Favoritism." *Journal of Personality and Social Psychology* 78: 708–724.

Gallese, Vittorio. 2003. "The Roots of Empathy: The Shared Manifold Hypothesis and Neural Basis of Intersubjectivity." *Psychopathology* 36: 171–180.

Giancola, Peter R. 2003. "The Moderating Effects of Dispositional Empathy on Alcohol-Related Aggression in Men and Women." *Journal of Abnormal Psychology* 112: 275–281.

Gordon, Mary. 2003. "Roots of Empathy: Responsive Parenting, Caring Societies." *Keio Journal of Medicine* 52: 236–243.

Graham, Tiffany, and William Ickes. 1997. "When Women's Intuition Isn't Greater Than Men's." Pp. 117–143 in *Empathic Accuracy*, edited by W. Ickes. New York: Guilford.

Gruen, Rand J., and Gerald Mendelsohn. 1986. "Emotional Responses to Affective Displays in Others: The Distinction Between Empathy and Sympathy." *Journal of Personality and Social Psychology* 51: 609–614.

Hamilton, William D. 1964. "The Genetic Evolution of Social Behavior." *Journal of Theoretical Biology* 7: 1–51.

Hatfield, Elaine, John T. Cacioppo, and Richard L. Rapson. 1992. "Emotional Contagion." Pp. 151–177 in *Review of Personality and Social Psychology: Emotion and Social Behavior*, edited by M. S. Clark. Newbury Park, CA: Sage.

———. 1994. *Emotional Contagion*. Cambridge: Cambridge University Press.

Hoffman, Martin L. 1978. "Psychological and Biological Perspectives on Altruism." *International Journal of Behavioral Development* 1: 323–339.

———. 1984. "Interaction of Affect and Cognition in Empathy." Pp. 103–131 in *Emotions, Cognition, and Behavior*, edited by C. E. Izard, J. Kagan, and R. B. Zajonc. Cambridge: Cambridge University Press.

Hogan, Robert. 1969. "Development of an Empathy Scale." *Journal of Consulting and Clinical Psychology* 33: 307–316.

Ickes, William. 1997. *Empathic Accuracy*. New York: Guilford.

———. 2003. *Everyday Mind Reading: Understanding What Other People Think and Feel*. Amherst, NY: Prometheus.

Ickes, William, Linda Stinson, Victor Bissonnette, and Stella Garcia. 1990. "Naturalistic Social Cognition: Empathic Accuracy in Mixed-Sex Dyads." *Journal of Personality and Social Psychology* 49: 730–742.

Jones, Edward E., and Richard E. Nisbett. 1971. *The Actor and the Observer: Divergent Perceptions of the Causes of Behavior*. Morristown, NJ: General Learning Press.

Karniol, Rachel. 1986. "What Will They Think of Next? Transformation Rules Used to Predict Other People's Thoughts and Feelings." *Journal of Personality and Social Psychology* 51: 932–944.

Karniol, Rachel, and Dorith Shomroni. 1999. "What Being Empathic Means: Applying the Transformation Rule Approach to Individual Differences in Predicting the Thoughts and Feelings of Prototypic and Nonprototypic Others." *European Journal of Social Psychology* 29: 147–160.

Kenny, David A., and Linda Albright. 1987. "Accuracy in Interpersonal Perception: A Social Relations Analysis." *Psychological Bulletin* 102: 390–402.

Klein, Kristi J. K., and Sara D. Hodges. 2001. "Gender Differences, Motivation, and Empathic Accuracy: When It Pays to Understand." *Personality and Social Psychology Bulletin* 27: 720–730.

Kohlberg, Lawrence. 1976. "The Cognitive-Developmental Approach to Moral Education." Pp. 31–53 in *Moral Development and Behavior: Theory, Research and Social Issues*, edited by T. Lickona. New York: Holt, Rinehart and Winston.

Krebs, Dennis L. 1975. "Empathy and Altruism." *Journal of Personality and Social Psychology* 32: 1134–1146.

Lafrance, Marianne. 1979. "Nonverbal Synchrony and Rapport: Analysis by the Cross-Lag Panel Technique." *Social Psychology Quarterly* 42: 66–70.

Lipps, Theodor. 1903. "Einfuhlung, Inner Nachahmung, und Organempfindaungen." *Archiv fur Die Gesamte Psychologie* 2: 185–204.

Lomis, Marsha J., and Linda L. Baker. 1985. "Microtraining of Forensic Psychiatric Patients for Empathic Counseling Skills." *Journal of Counseling Psychology* 32: 84–93.

Long, Edgar C., and David W. Andrews. 1990. "Perspective Taking as a Predictor of Marital Adjustment." *Journal of Personality and Social Psychology* 59: 126–131.

Maner, Jon K., Carol L. Luce, Steven L. Neuberg, Robert B. Cialdini, Stephanie Brown, and Brad J. Sagarin. 2002. "The Effects of Perspective Taking on Motivations for Helping: Still No Evidence for Altruism." *Personality and Social Psychology Bulletin* 28: 1601–1610.

Marks, Edward L., Louis A. Penner, and Anthony V. W. Stone. 1982. "Helping as a Function of Empathic Responses and Sociopathy." *Journal of Research in Personality* 16: 1–20.

McCullough, Michael E., Frank D. Fincham, and Jo-Ann Tsang. 2003. "Forgiveness, Forbearance, and Time: The Temporal Unfolding of Transgression-Related Interpersonal Motivations." *Journal of Personality and Social Psychology* 84: 540–557.

McCullough, Michael E., Kenneth I. Pargament, and Carl E. Thoresen. 2000. "The Psychology of Forgiveness: History, Conceptual Issues, and Overview." Pp. 1–14 in *Forgiveness: Theory, Research, and Practice*, edited by M. E. McCullough, K. I. Pargament, and C. E. Thoresen. New York: Guilford.

McCullough, Michael E., K. Chris Rachal, Steven J. Sandage, Everett L. Worthington, Jr., Susan W. Brown, and Terry L. Hight. 1998. "Interpersonal Forgiving in Close Relationships II: Theoretical Elaboration and Measurement." *Journal of Personality and Social Psychology* 75: 1586–1603.

McCullough, Michael E., Everett L. Worthington, Jr., and K. Chris Rachal. 1997. "Interpersonal Forgiving in Close Relationships." *Journal of Personality and Social Psychology* 73: 321–336.

McDougall, William. 1908. *An Introduction to Social Psychology*. London: Methuen.

Mead, George H. 1934. *Mind, Self, and Society*. Chicago: University of Chicago Press.

Mehrabian, Albert, and Norman Epstein. 1972. "A Measure of Emotional Empathy." *Journal of Personality* 40: 525–543.

Meltzoff, Andrew N., and M. Keith Moore. 1977. "Imitations of Facial and Manual Gestures by Human Neonates." *Science* 198: 75–78.

Miller, Paul A., and Nancy Eisenberg. 1988. "The Relation of Empathy to Aggressive and Externalizing/Antisocial Behavior." *Psychological Bulletin* 103: 324–344.

Omoto, Allen M., and Mark Snyder. 1995. "Sustained Helping without Obligation: Motivation, Longevity of Service, and Perceived Attitude Change among AIDS Volunteers." *Journal of Personality and Social Psychology* 68: 671–686.

Pecukonis, Edward V. 1990. "A Cognitive/Affective Empathy Training Program as a Function of Ego Development in Aggressive Adolescent Females." *Adolescence* 25: 59–76.

Penner, Louis A., and Marcia A. Finkelstein. 1998. "Dispositional and Structural Determinants of Volunteerism." *Journal of Personality and Social Psychology* 74: 525–537.

Piaget, Jean. 1932. *The Moral Judgment of the Child* (Trans. Marjorie Gabain). London: Kegan Paul, Trench, Trubner.

Preston, Stephanie D., and Frans B. M. Dewaal. 2001. "Empathy: Its Ultimate and Proximate Bases." *Behavioral and Brain Sciences* 25: 1–72.

Regan, Dennis T., and Judith Totten. 1975. "Empathy and Attribution: Turning Observers into Actors." *Journal of Personality and Social Psychology* 32: 850–856.

Richardson, Deborah R., Laura R. Green, and Tania Lago. 1998. "The Relationship Between Perspective-Taking and Nonaggressive Responding in the Face of an Attack." *Journal of Personality* 66: 235–256.

Richardson, Deborah R., Georgina S. Hammock, Stephen M. Smith, Wendi Gardner, and Manuel Signo. 1994. "Empathy as a Cognitive Inhibitor of Interpersonal Aggression." *Aggressive Behavior* 20: 275–289.

Ruby, Perrine, and Jean Decety. 2003. "What You Believe versus What You Think They Believe: A Neuroimaging Study of Conceptual Perspective-Taking." *European Journal of Neuroscience* 17: 2475–2480.

———. 2004. "How Would *You* Feel versus How Do You Think *She* Would Feel? A Neuroimaging Study of Conceptual Perspective Taking with Social Emotions." *Journal of Cognitive Neuroscience* 16: 988–999.

Rusbult, Caryl E., Julie Verette, Gregory A. Whitney, Linda F. Slovik, and Isaac Lipkus. 1991. "Accommodation Processes in Close Relationships: Theory and Preliminary Empirical Evidence." *Journal of Personality and Social Psychology* 60: 53–78.

Rushton, J. Phillipe, Robin J. H. Russell, and Pamela A. Wells. 1984. "Genetic Similarity Theory: Beyond Kin Selection." *Behavior Genetics* 14: 179–193.

Simpson, Jeffry A., William Ickes, and Tami Blackstone. 1995. "When the Head Protects the Heart: Empathic Accuracy in Dating Relationships." *Journal of Personality and Social Psychology* 69: 629–641.

Smith, Adam. 1976. *The Theory of Moral Sentiments*. Oxford: Clarendon.

Spencer, Herbert. 1870. *The Principles of Psychology*. London: Williams and Norgate.

Stinson, Linda L., and William Ickes. 1992. "Empathic Accuracy in Interactions of Male Friends versus Male Strangers." *Journal of Personality and Social Psychology* 72: 787–797.

Stolinski, Amy M., Carey S. Ryan, Leslie R. M. Hausmann, and Molly A. Wernli. 2004. "Empathy, Guilt, Volunteer Experiences, and Intentions to Continue Volunteering among Buddy Volunteers in an AIDS Organization." *Journal of Applied Biobehavioral Research* 9: 1–22.

Stotland, Ezra. 1969. "Exploratory Investigations of Empathy." Pp. 271–314 in *Advances in Experimental Social Psychology* Vol. 4, edited by L. Berkowitz. New York: Academic.

Stotland, Ezra, and Robert E. Dunn. 1963. "Empathy, Self-Esteem, and Birth Order." *Journal of Abnormal and Social Psychology* 66: 532–540.

Titchener, Edward. 1909. *Elementary Psychology of the Thought Processes*. New York: Macmillan.

Toi, Miho, and C. Daniel Batson. 1982. "More Evidence that Empathy Is a Source of Altruistic Motivation." *Journal of Personality and Social Psychology* 43: 281–292.

Trivers, Robert. 1971. "The Evolution of Reciprocal Altruism." *Quarterly Review of Biology* 46: 35–57.

Trobst, Krista K., Rebecca Collins, and Jayne M. Embree. 1994. "The Role of Emotion in Social Support Provision: Gender, Empathy, and Expressions of Distress." *Journal of Social and Personal Relationships* 11: 45–62.

Van Baaren, Rick B., Rob W. Holland, Kerry Kawakami, and Ad Van Knippenberg. 2004a. "Mimicry and Prosocial Behavior." *Psychological Science* 15: 71–74.

Van Baaren, Rick B., Terry G. Horgan, Tanya L. Chartrand, and Marit Dijkmans. 2004b. "The Forest, the Trees, and the Chameleon: Context Dependence and Mimicry." *Journal of Personality and Social Psychology* 86: 453–459.

Van Baaren, Rick B., William W. Maddux, Tanya L. Chartrand, Cris De Bouter, and Ad Van Knippenberg. 2003. "It Takes Two to Mimic: Behavioral Consequences of Self-Construals." *Journal of Personality and Social Psychology* 84: 1093–1102.

Wispe, Lauren. 1986. "The Distinction between Sympathy and Empathy: To Call Forth a Concept, a Word Is Needed." *Journal of Personality and Social Psychology* 50: 314–321.

CHAPTER 20

Sympathy

Christopher S. Schmitt
Candace Clark

[P]erhaps, gratitude may serve as the pennies, sympathy as the dimes, and love as the quarters. It is in [the socioemotional] economy, [a] more-or-less orderly exchange system, that people give and withhold emotional resources, form social bonds and divisions, negotiate microhierarchical arrangements, and derive identity and self-worth. (Clark 2004:406)

Emotions were long treated by Westerners as animalistic, antithetical, and inferior to rational thought, not quite a fit topic for scholarly research. No longer. Over the past quarter century or so, both the general public and the academic community have begun to conceive of human emotion and cognition as two inseparable, interdependent, and important modes of experience. Physiological and psychological approaches to human emotionality have tended to define emotions in neurobiological and chemical terms and to emphasize such issues as facial expressions, brain physiology, the effects of substances such as oxytocin and serotonin, and the search for "real" or "core" emotions (Buck 1988; Ekman and Rosenberg 2005; Ekman et al. 1972; Panksepp 1998; Preston and de Waal 2002; Wood et al. 2005). At the same time, anthropological (Lutz and Abu-Lughod 1990), historical (Stearns and Stearns 1986), economic (Frantz 2000; Robison et al. 2002; Sally 2000, 2001, 2002a), legal (Maroney 2006), business (Dutton and Ragins 2004; Kanov et al. 2004), philosophic (Kahan and Nussbaum 1996; Nussbaum 2001; Solomon 1994), criminal justice (Goodrum and Stafford 2003; Katz 1988; Kenney 2002), and sociological approaches such as those represented in this volume have taken a wider perspective. They examined the social roots and consequences of specific emotions, as well as the individual's constant stream of emotionality and have insisted on the social shaping of emotions within the centrifuges of culture, organizations, social structure, and stratification.

CHRISTOPHER S. SCHMITT • Department of Sociology, University of California, Riverside, CA 92521
CANDACE CLARK • Kure Beach, NC 28449

Also, a great deal of cross-fertilization of these approaches (see e.g., Buck 1988, Franks this volume; Leach and Tiedens 2004; Manstead et al. 2004; Wentworth and Yardley 1994) has led to the awareness that biological and social understandings of emotions are not incompatible. Humans' basic brain processes do not predetermine the experiences we think of as emotions, but rather signal people to interpret, integrate, and construct their experience, which they do in line with language, tradition, and social structural forces. As social psychologists Leach and Tiedens (2004:3) argued:

> [We must] start considering [emotion] as a bridge between the individual and the world that blurs the boundaries between individuals and their contexts.... [E]motions are one channel through which the individual knows the social world, and the social world is what allows people to know emotion.

Although it seems obvious that studying emotions can help us understand human biology and psychology, it might be less apparent that studying emotions can help us understand basic sociological questions. At the societal level of analysis, the enduring paradox is the relatively peaceful coexistence of social division and social cohesion. Both division and cohesion, and their coexistence as well, are in part the products of patterned and often ritualized *interchanges* of human emotions. That is, in many ways, interchanging emotions—particularly social emotions (Shott 1979, 1981)—glue us together, albeit in unequal arrangements. Our efforts in this chapter are directed toward unraveling this paradox of social life by examining the value and meanings of sympathy. Although sympathy receives less attention than emotions such as love or anger, it is scarcely possible to imagine a society—human or chimp—surviving without it.[1] Here we show how sympathy give and take reinforces and creates social bonds and divisions.

Sympathy exists only as an embedded and negotiated process that is "triply social" (Clark 1987:290). First, it involves a sympathizer feeling sad or concerned "with or for another," the sympathizee (Clark 1987:290). For sympathizers, there are both interior aspects, such as empathy and sentiment, as well as exterior aspects, such as expression and display. Second, a symbol-laced language and myriad "feeling rules" (Hochschild 1983) steer all these processes and generate complicated symbolic meanings. The parties to a sympathy interchange often perceive and evaluate events in different ways and, therefore, engage in a "coordination game of meaning" (Sally 2002b). If sympathizees are aware of sympathizers' thoughts and sentiments, they may either accept or reject sympathy (and its attached symbolic messages). Third, sympathy give and take establishes or strengthens relationships and the unequal relations of power within them (Kemper 1978).

So many factors influence the flow of sympathy give and take that it seems at times impossible to predict who will sympathize with whom under what conditions, whether a sympathetic message will be received with gratitude or with ire, or how a group's sympathy rules change. Indeed, the improvisational and highly complex character of social interaction (Scheff 1990) ensures this state of affairs. Yet, complexity makes the study of sympathy interesting, and researchers have been able to discern some basic patterns and alternatives.

We first frame sympathy within an interactionist perspective that draws on the historical literature on gift giving and social exchange (Cushman 2003; Gouldner 1960, 1973; Levi-Strauss 1969, 1974; Mauss 1954; Schwartz 1967; Simmel 1950) before delving into research that specifically addresses sympathy from an in-depth, interpersonal perspective (Clark 1997, 2004; Karp 2001). To integrate these ideas, we introduce the concept of *socioemotional economy* (Clark 1997; see also Collins 1981, on emotional economy). Newer sympathy research and theorizing will be presented throughout. Some questions asked almost 20 years ago (Clark 1987) will be taken up in terms of those recent findings; others have yet to be addressed. Last, we discuss what we hope will be some of the most promising directions for new research to take in order to better understand the many roles that sympathy plays in groups, communities, nations, and the global order.

SYMPATHY CONCEPTUALIZED

We define sympathy in line with everyday speech: feeling sorry, genuinely or otherwise, for another's plight. The other might be an intimate, a co-worker, an acquaintance, a stranger, or even a social category (e.g., the poor or victims of a natural disaster). At sympathy's core lie three basic elements: empathy, sentiment, and display (Clark 1987, 1997; see also Kanov et al. 2004 for a similar conceptualization of compassion).[2] *Empathy* refers here to taking the "attitude," or role, of another (Mead and Morris 1934), envisioning the other's perceptions and likely responses.[3] *Sympathy sentiment* is an experience of emotions similar to another's or on behalf of the other. *Display* refers to appropriate and discernible behavior that conveys sadness or concern for another's plight. When people use the term "sympathy" in everyday conversation, they are usually talking about sympathy sentiment, sympathy display, or both.

Empathy is a necessary prerequisite for both sympathy sentiment and display, but it does not guarantee either one. Feelings about others that accompany role-taking can vary widely: from malicious glee (*Schadenfreude*, e.g., a politician gloating over an opponent's gaffe), to placid disregard (urbanites passively glancing at homeless people on the streets), to couvades (husbands experiencing sympathetic morning sickness, weight gain, and birth pains along with their pregnant wives). We can distinguish analytically, if not in practice, among several ways in which empathy can arise. *Cognitive* empathy is merely an awareness that another person is having difficulties. *Physical* empathy is a painful sensation such as one might feel when viewing another's deplorable surroundings or evidence of severe bodily suffering, as Ko (2003) documented among Western museum-goers observing the outcome of foot binding. *Emotional* empathy is the apprehension of another's situation *through* feelings such as indignation, sadness, or alarm. For example, discussing what we are calling here emotional empathy, the eighteenth-century economic philosopher Adam Smith (1759) contended that a child's cries trigger the sympathy of even the most hardened criminal.

Comprehending another's plight moves a person partway toward sympathy. To take the next step, one's sentiments must mirror the emotions of others or entail feelings for the other's emotions. In other words, "[s]ympathy sentiment is the counterpart in one person of another's sense of discomfort, loss, sorrow, and the like" (Clark 1987:295). Of course, one's own sympathy sentiment resonates with another's emotion based on the degree and type of empathy one experiences. Beyond empathy but before sympathy sentiment, potential sympathizers make many judgments and attributions, some of which concern the other's degree of responsibility for bringing about or not coping with her or his plight.

In Western culture, a sympathy-worthy plight is typically the result of "bad luck". It is neither good nor merely trivial, but bad; and it results from forces beyond one's control and one's own responsibility. If, for example, a family member is fired from her job because of substance abuse, other family members might determine that the plight is "bad" but not the result of "luck," unless perhaps they have adopted a medicalized view of substance abuse as an illness outside of individual control. A potential sympathizer's perceptions and responses depend greatly on their attributions of how responsible others are for their own plights. Victims of natural disasters such as fires, tsunamis, hurricanes, or earthquakes evoke immediate sympathy sentiments and displays, as no one can be held accountable. Victims of man-made disasters, on the other hand, invite both blame and sympathy. For instance, the attacks on the World Trade Center and Pentagon in 2001 produced a worldwide torrent of sympathy for those who died and for the United States in general, including pro-U.S. fatwas, or religious edicts, from several Muslim leaders (Kurzman 2003); however, sympathy was accompanied by blame for the perpetrators or for U.S. policies that had incited such measures.

A large body of research on Weiner's "attribution (responsible/not responsible)-emotion (anger/sympathy)-action (helping/not helping)" model of helping behavior, based primarily on studies using hypothetical scenarios, is relevant to this point (Rudolph et al. 2004; Struthers et al. 1998, 2001; Weiner 1980, 1991). As MacGeorge (2003:175) summarized:

> [H]elp seekers who are perceived as more responsible for their problems evoke more anger and less sympathy from others . . . . These effects of perceived responsibility . . . have been observed across different populations, types of problems, [and] relationships between helper and help seeker.

For instance, AIDS researchers (O'Hea et al. 2001) found that their respondents were less sympathetic toward HIV-infected women who had injected drugs or engaged in unprotected sex with multiple partners than toward monogamous women whose partners had infected them. Similarly, Li (2001) found that Indonesians did not hold responsible and sympathized with indigenous people whose land was seized; however, when financial opportunists and protesters wrangled over the rights of the indigenous people, the public's sympathy or blame for them was based on appraisals of responsibility. Further, results of several studies in the attribution and helping literature have indicated the importance of another perceptual influence on helping behavior: effort attributions (MacGeorge 2003). In sympathy judgments as well, social actors are unlikely to sympathize with people in plights whom they believe were not making efforts to extricate themselves. For example, during the 2005 Hurricane Katrina disaster in New Orleans, many U.S. citizens and public officials became angry with residents who refused to leave their homes and pets. With regard to the murder of homosexual Matthew Shepard, Quist and Wiegand (2002) found that the conservative press had little sympathy for Shepard or for gays in general because it viewed homosexuality as a controllable condition that could be overcome with some effort. More generally, Clark (1987) found that some potential sympathizers found it hard to empathize with people facing problems like their own, whom, they believed, could have put more effort into overcoming adverse situations as they had done themselves.

Yet, judgments about what constitutes bad luck are not solely based on perceptions and attributions of responsibility and effort, nor do they occur in a vacuum. *Sympathy entrepreneurs* (Clark 1997:243), such as the Society for the Prevention of Cruelty to Children, the Hallmark greeting card company (Clark 1997; McGee 1980), Internet-based (Mooney and Brabant 1998) greeting card/flowers/candy sympathy industry, prisoners' rights organizations, *Ms.* magazine, Mothers Against Drunk Driving (Gusfield 1980), the American Medical Association (Conrad and Schneider 1980), social workers (Forte 2002), and countless others instruct the public as to *which* plights are sympathy-worthy for the particular culture or historical period. They often parlay their sympathy work into successful businesses (manufacturing greeting cards or providing expert testimony), international organizations (Amnesty International), and social movements (indigenous rights).

Historian Clark (1995), for example, concluded that writers of literature and narratives about the antebellum American South played an important role in spreading sympathy for the plights of animals, slaves, and women. Similarly, Mulcahy (2005) found that the legal arguments leading to the ban on slavery in the eighteenth-century British Caribbean created a more sympathetic climate for indigenous hurricane victims than had previously existed. Today, the pervasive mass media amplify sympathy entrepreneurs' messages, extending sympathy processes to local, national, and international issues and audiences. The Internet (Coffey and Woolworth 2004), "blogs" (web logs), and podcasters make possible the instantaneous transmission of information that molds sympathy. In nanoseconds, images of suffering, framed by a wide array of sympathy entrepreneurs from tsunami relief agencies to Al Qaeda, flash across televisions and computers across the world. The indefinite Other takes on the face of a deserving associate or vice versa. At the same time that entrenched disparities of resources reinforce the inequality of social relations among interest groups and nations, ongoing changes in access to media and other resources create contradictions, new definitions of social problems, and new means to solve them.

In addition to sympathy entrepreneurs who make general claims to sympathy for victims of certain plights, at times a *sympathy broker* (Clark 1997:42), such as a close friend or defense attorney, a public official, or news commentator, tries to present a particular *person* or *group* as sympathy-worthy. Successful sympathy brokers can alter the course of events with great consequence; for example, Marc Antony, in a classic plea intended to paint Julius Caesar as a "sympathetic character" while damning Caesar's enemies with faint praise, pointed out the former's generosity and sacrifice and the latter's bloody deeds. The mob of people gathered around Caesar's corpse becomes increasingly sympathetic and indignant on Caesar's behalf and eventually drives his enemies from the city (Bevington 1980). Still today, when sympathy brokers lend their standing and explanatory skills to another's cause, audiences may be more convinced to sympathize than if the person had made his or her own sympathy claim. The mass media are eager to provide platforms for selected sympathy brokers (Nacos 2002); in fact, the content of political talk shows is often nothing more than adversarial sympathy brokers spinning sympathy and blame for public figures.

In some cases, sympathy entrepreneurs simultaneously serve as sympathy brokers. For instance, every holiday season (Thanksgiving through January) from 1912 to 1972, the *New York Times'* Neediest Cases Appeal printed the sad stories of actual people, carefully vetted for deservingness. The Appeal cast both specific plights and the particular people in them as sympathy-worthy. It urged readers to offer consolation personally to Mr. X or Mrs. Y or to contribute specific amounts of money for food, coal, medicine, and the like, which the newspaper would then disburse to the likes of the "five Parker orphans" or the widowed mother whose husband was killed by a falling crane. The Appeal evoked readers' sympathy sentiment and provided precise directions for displaying sympathy; it also served as a go-between. Other appeals such as those used in court trials provide excellent examples of how sympathy entrepreneurs and brokers attempt to assess, influence, and manipulate sympathizers' judgments and displays, and we will discuss them in more detail in a later section.

Sympathy entrepreneurs not only set out general criteria for sympathy-worthy plights, they also tailor bad-luck principles to particular social statuses. This is because to be sympathy-worthy, a plight must be "bad or unlucky for those with the person's particular set of gender, age, social class, and other characteristics" (Clark 1997:82). According to the *special deprivation* principle, people who are typically identified with one aspect of life (e.g., women with relationships, and men with work) are especially damaged when troubles arise in that area and thus more deserving of sympathy than people not so identified. The *special burden* principle connects sympathy worthiness with socially valued or inherently difficult pursuits (e.g., fighting fires or wars). Following the *balance of fortune* principle, privileged members of a society are already sufficiently cushioned or insulated so that their occasional reverses do *not* constitute grounds for sympathy. The *vulnerability* principle applies to societal members perceived as fragile, weak, or even helpless, for example, children, women, the elderly, the alter-abled, and indigenous persons (Wallerstein 2004). By extension, those who *lack* vulnerability may be held to higher levels of accountability for their plights. For instance, MacGeorge (2003) found that men were likely to attribute responsibility for their plights to other men, and they reacted with anger rather than sympathy, especially when they perceived that the others had made little effort to remedy their situations. People follow the *potential* principle when they sympathize with those who either have not yet had the opportunity for life accomplishments (e.g., infants and children suffering from life-threatening diseases) or have had their options suddenly foreshortened (e.g., "youthful" accident victims such as actor Christopher Reeve). The *special responsibility* principle holds that individuals in some social categories possess greater knowledge or awareness of potential threats and therefore should have greater responsibility to avoid problems; thus, physicians who smoke cigarettes cannot attribute their lung cancer to ignorance or bad luck, and enlisted personnel who are harmed in war "knew what they were getting into." Last, the *social worth* principle applies to people whom society perceives to be especially deserving of sympathy by dint of their particularly valuable contributions, such as Mother Teresa (Clark 1997).

Sympathizers may focus on a combination of different bad-luck principles in any given case. The far-reaching public outpouring of sympathy at the death of Britain's Princess Diana helps to illustrate how various principles can interact, taking an additive form in this case (special deprivation, balance of fortune, potential, plus social worth). In modern Western societies, several principles (vulnerability, potential, and *lack* of special responsibility) generally apply to infants and children, making them especially sympathy-worthy (Sudnow 1967). However, when children such as Lizzie Borden, the more recent Columbine High School shooters, or sniper Lee Malvo are responsible for horrific deeds, attributions of responsibility expand to include them. Additionally, sometimes a combination of applicable principles produces ambivalence or mixed emotions. For instance, elderly crime victims may elicit some sympathy because of their plights, but forfeit some because of their lack of potential. Also, children who deliberately misbehave evoke varying degrees of sympathy and blame from their mothers (Graham et al. 2001). Furthermore, observers may differ in the principles they follow. For example, some onlookers blamed former president Bill Clinton for his sexual misconduct, which they felt fell short of a president's special responsibility to behave in a dignified manner. Others sympathized with Clinton because they viewed that same behavior as a "common" foible (Rojek 2002) and the proposed penalty, removal from office, excessive. When highly paid celebrity athletes face problems, social actors adhering to the balance of the fortune principle feel little sympathy, whereas others following the social worth principle are more sympathetic.

In addition to considering these principles based on cultural capital, people also make judgments of sympathy worthiness on the basis of social capital (Bourdieu 1986; Farr 1978). Actors earn social capital by observing interactional rules for proper decorum and deportment, by having charisma, by being "nice" or "fun to be around," by bestowing gifts on others, by honoring obligations, and the like. For instance, researchers (Follingstad et al. 2001) have found sympathy levels for abused women to be an interactive function not only of their lack of responsibility for the abuse (external "locus of control") and their justification for staying in abusive relationships but also of their positive social traits. People are less apt to sympathize with the quarrelsome, the miserly, the mean, and the disreputable—those whose social capital is meager.

Societally speaking, displaying sympathy is the most important aspect of sympathy. In Clark's (1997:56–57) words, "Without display, the emotion is a social outcome but not a social force." Goffman (1967:95) noted that as Western societies have shifted away from communal bases, the individual has become "a deity of considerable importance. He [*sic*] walks with some dignity and is the recipient of many little offerings." Changing manners over the past half millennium reflect an increasing concern individuals and their sensibilities and problems (Elias 1982, 1994). In today's "civil religion of self," a sympathy display serves as one of many "little offerings" that affirm the recipient's social worth, smooth human interactions, and strengthen social bonds.

To gauge the appropriate type and amount of offering, social actors again make appraisals whose rapidity belie their complexity. The display must occur without any apparent hesitation, lest the delay itself devalue the legitimacy of the offering (Bourdieu 1977:3–8). Sympathizers must deftly match status, plight, and setting using selections from among a large constellation of display modes and "sign vehicles" (Goffman 1967): Tone, body posture, facial expressions, choice of phrase, touch, civil inattention to faux pas, greeting cards, financial contributions, and offers of help are but a few possibilities. The delivery must be as "natural" as the timing, and the amount must be suited to the magnitude of the plight. As Hochschild (1983) argued, the display must appear to be "sincere" even if it is not. When people fail to follow these rules for sympathy display, they could face criticism, as the Bush administration learned after Hurricane Katrina.

Time and context also condition sympathy displays. The ranks of sympathizers swell during holidays, after deaths (DiGirolamo 2002), and with the onset of illness (Karp 2001). Sympathy displays also follow their own time line within both annual cycles (Bunis et al. 1996) and across decades, life spans, or historical periods (Clark 1997; Clark 1995; Mulcahy 2005; Okabayashi et al. 1995; Rai 2002; Twomey 1999).

Social settings often include expectations that actors "owe" sympathy or should "pay" their respects to other actors who deserve sympathy. However, a person's sympathy sentiments may not always measure up. Although sympathy displays with authentic sentiment are common, "there are few signs that cannot be used to attest to the presence of something that is not really there. Also, it is plain that many performers have ample capacity and motive to misrepresent the facts" (Goffman 1967:58). Observing the bare minimum of interactional proprieties, feigning sympathy ("surface acting"), and even "deep acting" (Hochschild 1983:49) to produce genuine feeling are all forms of display that strengthen social bonds in a way that the mere recognition and acknowledgment of another's plight does not.

As Hochschild (1983) pointed out, women often specialize in emotional display, and such is the case with sympathy. In Clark's (1997) research, qualitative and quantitative approaches unearthed little disparity in empathy and sympathy sentiment between men and women; however, a different picture emerged with regard to display. Women tended to take a more pro-active approach to sympathy, constantly scanning family and friends for evidence of need and concerning themselves with display (see also Gilligan 1982; Jaffee and Hyde 2000); men took a more reactive approach and conceived of sympathy primarily as an interior phenomenon. For example, women buy and send more sympathy cards than do men (Mooney and Brabant 1998) and are likely to spend more time discussing others' problems (Basow and Rubenfeld 2003) and offering help. In line with several generations of researchers, Karp (2001) found considerable evidence of the gendered nature of caregiving. Other research from the criminal justice field has found that "counselors who were predominantly female did the bulk of the system's emotion work, and they protected detectives and prosecutors who were predominantly male from this work" (Goodrum and Stafford 2003:179). The preponderance of a very large body of literature supports the notion that women perform the bulk of sympathy work.

The sympathizer's perceptual path from empathy to sympathy sentiment to display is at times almost instantly accomplished; at other times, it is a recurring, long-term process. Even the briefest and smallest offering has some mental, emotional, monetary, or physical costs, and the costs of long-term and extended sympathy can be enormous. Therefore, although feeling rules call for sympathy in certain circumstances, and potential sympathizees might feel that sympathy is owed to them, social actors should not presume upon each other's sympathy. This is because sympathy falls in the realm of gifts, and it is subject to the cultural rules for gift giving.

DIMES OF SYMPATHY: EMOTIONAL GIFTS, EXCHANGE, AND MICROPOLITICS

Hochschild introduced the term "feeling currency" in her early work on the rising number of jobs requiring emotional labor (Hochschild 1983:18). This term emphasizes the fact that emotions and emotional displays can be both costly to the donor and quite valuable to the recipient. Hochschild also saw that, in everyday life, the flow of feeling currency among social actors follows exchange principles. Sympathy is one of the recognized and negotiable feeling currencies that people and their societies use as resources in social exchanges. We will outline several basic principles that help explain exchanges involving sympathy.

We first posit that sympathy is an interactional gift with significant social value. Not only does it cost the sympathizer, it also rewards the sympathizee. Sympathy attends plights, and plights could instead call forth others' blame. In fact, social psychologists studying labeling and the "belief in a just world" (Lerner and Simmons 1980) have found that mental processes such as cognitive dissonance or cognitive-emotional dissonance tend to predispose people toward blaming "innocent" people for their "fates" rather than sympathizing with them. When a person feels or displays sympathy, the sympathizee may experience rewards: exemption from normal role expectations, closeness to the sympathizer, and enhanced social worth. As Offer (1997) argued in his analysis of the "economy of regard," people in plights value not merely sympathetic words and deeds, but, more important, the regard that such a gift symbolizes (see also Nussbaum 2001). Borrowing from early anthropologist Malinowski's (1923) theory of pathic communication, we could say that the mere fact of offering sympathy, as a social act, conveys regard. Receiving others' regard helps actors verify their identities, especially their "friend" identities (Stets and Harrod 2004), which could be especially important in times of trouble. What is more, sometimes the "guilty," who have broken rules, acted irresponsibly, or brought on their own troubles, receive sympathy rather than blame. In these cases, sympathy is an even more valuable gift.

A second postulate is that people do not have the time, energy, or inclination to give limitless sympathy. To do so can lead to "compassion fatigue," as Link and associates (1995) found when considering sympathy for the homeless, or a sympathy "burden," as Karp (2001) found among family members of the depressed. Fortunately, cultural rules and social logics set limits on when and how we give sympathy. Emergency workers and ambulance drivers have to develop "rules of rescue" for whom they should tend to first (McKie and Richardson 2003), and everyday actors, as well, need their own rules for sympathy triage. Sympathy is scarce, and scarcity adds to its already considerable value.

A third postulate is that all relationships are to some degree stratified, and all gift giving—including emotional gift giving—reflects, reinforces, generates, or modifies the unequal relationships among the parties. At any given point in time, each actor occupies a "place" (Goffman 1951) that is "one-up" or "one-down"—or even two-up or three-down—in relation to the other actors in the arena. Such "microhierarchical arrangements" (Clark 1997) are akin to, somewhat dependent on, but more fragile and fluid than societal stratification systems. Rules for gift giving take microhierarchies into account, and actors learn that gifts carry meanings that subtly or not so subtly signify the recipients' place. If the donor is a "superior," the gift's meaning might be: " 'I know what you need and what's good for you,' 'If I give you a gift first, you can never overcome the fact that you are indebted to me,' and 'My gift shows that I have more resources than you do' " (Clark 2004:404). If the donor is an "inferior" who accepts that place: "My small and humble offering attests to your importance." If the donor dislikes her or his inferior place: "My gift just might undercut your claims to superiority."

Also, the timing of gift giving can convey as much meaning as the type of gift. As Bourdieu (1977) contended, donors demonstrate consideration and respect for recipients by making appropriately measured and timed gifts. However, appropriately measuring a gift but deliberately offering it late points to the donor's "superiority" to a greater degree than if the donor's appropriately measured gift is accidentally late. The size, timing, and delivery of sympathy donations help to create a context that donors and recipients use to shape its meanings and interpretations.

In continuous negotiation, social actors make presentations that "claim a place" in microhierarchical arrangements, sometimes by *displaying* emotions such as anger, scorn, or tolerance. They also *experience* emotions such as smugness, awe, or humiliation—"place markers"—that contribute to a *felt sense of place*. This sense of one's place in a microhierarchy is the "momentary consciousness of 'who I am and how I can act at this moment in this encounter'—part of the situated self" (Clark 1997:230). Social actors who know intuitively that emotions can serve as "place claims" and "place markers" can consciously or subconsciously use emotions micropolitically to gain, enhance, reinforce, and sometimes cede place. "Nice," humble people acting as "You First" micropoliticians use emotions to enhance others' place and minimize their own (Clark 2004). In contradistinction, "Me First" micropoliticians use emotions strategically to lower others' place or elevate their own. In her research on law firms, Pierce (1995) provided examples of micropolitics and gender in the workplace. Attorneys (who were usually men) could use Me First emotional micropolitics, shouting and cursing at paralegals (who were usually women), but not vice versa. To ward off the place-marking emotion of humiliation, paralegals had to establish or gain place by "keeping their cool" and adopting a "professional" demeanor.

The Socioemotional Economy

From internal dialogues with imaginary others, to turn taking between infant and parent, to international money markets, every kind of interaction entails an exchange of some sort or another. As Karp (2001:15) concluded, "[n]early every general theory concerned with understanding social order assumes that expectations of reciprocity and exchange constitute the essential foundation of society." The modern-day money-goods-and-services economy—a highly stylized, rationalized, and "sedimented" (Fine 1991) exchange system—is but one example. Alongside and usually commingled with the money-goods-and-services economy, the *socioemotional economy* operates as an informal but relatively orderly system in which people exchange social and emotional currencies. These currencies take the form of material or nonmaterial and intrinsic or extrinsic "goods": assistance, compliments (Rodriguez et al. 1998), attention (Derber 1979), gratitude (Hochschild 1989), love, tolerance, caregiving, respect, sympathy, and the like. Each socioemotional exchange, framed by language and culture, establishes or reestablishes a connection or division that speaks to the participants' social capital. This is because, as Robison et al. (2002) argued, socioemotional goods are products of one's social capital, and social capital is generated and "resides" in interactions and relationships. Socioemotional goods, like physical goods and services, have value as does the social capital that is engaged in their production.

When people bestow social and emotional gifts, cultural rules lead them to expect returns of some sort (see Blau 1964; Gouldner 1960; Homans 1984; Lawler 2001; Lawler et al. 2000; Levi-Strauss 1974; McCall and Simmons 1978; Simmel 1950; Stauth and Turner 1988). Returns do not have to be immediate or precisely commensurate; they do not even have to be given to the donor, but could instead, be presented to the donor's intimates or even to strangers in the community at large. However, those who accept socioemotional resources without reciprocating in any way are usually sanctioned or even shunned.

The sociological "problem" of socioemotional exchange is to determine the principles, or "social logics" (Davis et al. 1941), on which exchanges proceed. A social logic is a collectively based "if-then" assumption, such as "If I bestow sympathy on you, then you will feel supported enough to overcome your plight." As Gouldner (1973) explained, several principles can underpin exchange. First, the logic of *complementarity* posits that if each actor adequately fulfills a complementary role, everyone's needs will be met. This logic typically applies in traditional, reciprocal-role relationships such as husband and wife, student and teacher, or employer and employee. In traditional societies, exchange imbalances resulting from a superior's failure to honor his or her role requirements are often ignored, whereas imbalances resulting from an inferior's failures can elicit harsh reprisals. Second, the logic of *reciprocity*—epitomized in the money-goods-and-services economy—requires actors to discharge their obligations to repay upon or soon after receiving a good: a "back-scratching" or "pay-as-you-go" understanding. Third, the logic of *beneficence* embodies the Golden Rule: At all times, do unto others as you would have them do unto you.

Of course, these three ideal types of exchange are rarely found in pure form. Rather, social actors concoct and negotiate *blended logics* to guide their interchanges, in part because cooperative exchange strategies that, in theory, should provide advantages to all the parties are, in everyday practice, subject to problems with free riders, defections, and changing "contractual" conditions. Clark (2004:409) observed that a blended logic of *reciprocal complementarity* is most likely for socioemotional exchanges among family members and close friends: "I will fulfill my obligations to you, but only so long as you fulfill yours to me." Socioemotional exchanges with nonkin and nonintimates depend more on *reciprocal beneficence*, the understanding that one actor will provide resources when needed, but only so long as the recipient does the same.

Embedded in the overall socioemotional economy are many smaller subeconomies, including an "economy of regard" (Offer 1997) and an "economy of gratitude" (Hochschild 1989). Each shares the rules and logics of the socioemotional economy, and each has its own somewhat unique rules and logics. We turn now to the particulars of the "economy of sympathy."

Principles of Sympathy Exchange in the Socioemotional Economy

Within the broader socioemotional economy, sympathy give and take between and among social actors tends to follow an exchange or "market" logic (see Berezin 2005; Offer 1997; Robison et al. 2002; Sally 2001). The most successful market arrangements follow from particular guidelines based on desirable resource distribution. If capitalism promotes competition for maximum profit in a zero-sum game, and socialism seeks a better balanced distribution through beneficence, then the economy of sympathy lies somewhere in between. As a socially constructed emotional bond, sympathy usually flourishes under conditions of reciprocity and beneficence and withers in zero-sum climates. Adapting the concept of social margins (see Wiseman 1979) to sympathy helps explain when and why it flourishes or withers.

SYMPATHY MARGIN. Each social actor is entitled to a limited account of sympathy credits, or a "sympathy margin," with each of the many other actors in his or her network. An actor can claim, replenish, or entirely use up the credits in a particular sympathy margin. Usually, sympathy margins are not simply wide open, with an infinite number of sympathy credits, or closed, with none. They vary in width, spreading over a small or large number of plights, and depth, consisting of few credits or many. Initially, one enjoys minimum margins, or "account balances," as a right of group membership. Intimates typically have the benefit of wider and deeper margins than do acquaintances or strangers. Furthermore, social actors pay attention to others' cultural capital (education, occupation, gender, age, and the like), social capital (e.g., niceness, commitment, and likeability), and microhierarchical place when they are considering the width and depth of the sympathy margins they make.

SYMPATHY PROTOCOLS. Over time, both access to sympathy margins and the number of credits available are subject to revision and ongoing negotiation by donors and recipients alike. Too-frequent searches for sympathy can drain one's account with some donors, but not others. Some sympathizers may comply, some may "tune out," might others and become irritated instead of sympathetic. Rejected claims highlight the limits of sympathy-as-resource: There is only so much to go around. Social actors' *sympathy biographies*—that is, their histories or records of claiming and repaying sympathy—develop and flesh out over time. Experience and shared narratives bring to light the actors' records of past adherence to what Clark (1987:292) referred to as four sympathy-claiming rules. These protocols guide sympathy exchanges for both recipients and, by logical extension, donors as well: "1) do not make fraudulent claims to sympathy; 2) do not claim too much sympathy or accept it too readily; 3) claim some sympathy to keep accounts open; and 4) reciprocate for gifts of sympathy." A sympathy biography that honors these rules makes for larger sympathy margins; a sympathy biography that includes many "transgressions" makes for restricted or closed accounts.

FRAUDULENT CLAIMS. Legitimate sympathy claims are neither pretense nor exaggeration, nor do they stem from deliberately placing oneself in harm's way. Trust issues stand at the heart of this rule. Sympathizers want to be sure that a potential sympathizee is trustworthy and will reliably uphold the culture's sympathy rules. Shams and pretenses violate that trust, as the following urban legend illustrates:

> In a classified ad for Super Bowl tickets, a father posted that his son had visited a medical clinic recently and the doctor had told them he "had no idea how long the boy would live." The little boy's dream was to see the Super Bowl ... would any Good Samaritan step forward and donate two tickets? An anonymous donor sympathized with the boy's plight and donated the two tickets, only to learn later that the boy was not actually dying. The father defended his ad, saying that he had not lied; nobody, including the doctor knew how long the boy had to live. The ticket donor was understandably outraged and humiliated by his betrayed trust and misplaced sympathy.

Yet, cultural rules for false claims appear to be changing, at least with regard to falsely "calling in sick." A recent Internet survey (Hirsch 2005) found that about a third of U.S. workers admitted to making such a false claim at least once within the previous year; bosses tended to grant leeway to high-performing workers, but they penalized "chronic offenders." It would seem then that the meaning of false sick claims is under negotiation.

Exaggerated claims on sympathy accounts also offend potential sympathizers. People who describe minor troubles using the words, tones, and gestures usually reserved for catastrophes can anger co-workers, friends, and even family members, especially if it becomes a habit. Those who deliberately take risks and court trouble usually perplex or annoy potential sympathizers. All of these types of fraudulent claims change the trust equation and compromise the legitimate right to sympathy. Sympathizers are apt to temporarily close or even permanently shut down the sympathy margins of those who betray trust. A pointed example comes from France. In a period of high unemployment, the French government gave emergency funds to citizens on the basis of letters they wrote explaining why they deserved the money. Some letters successfully engendered sympathy and funds, but those who exaggerated their problems received lower aid amounts that the government calculated in order to send them a "message" (Fassin 2003).

Not Too Much.   If Aesop's fable of the boy who cried wolf amply illustrates the previous point, then Goldilocks and the Three Bears serves the purpose here. The amount of sympathy claimed and accepted has to be "just right." Sympathizees should solicit only the amounts of sympathy that appropriately correspond to their plights. Sympathizers expect to provide larger amounts for grievous situations and much less for petty grievances, and sympathizees should tailor their claims accordingly. They must only accept what is both needed (lest they seem to exaggerate) and well deserved (just right). An actor who accepts sympathy too readily can be seen as needy, dysfunctional, or irresponsible—certainly not brave.

In addition, even when a person has legitimate grounds for sympathy, if the plight is too brief (e.g., an injection) or persists too long (a chronic illness), others tend to offer minimal sympathy. Sympathizers perceive a brief plight as not "bad" enough for much sympathy. A prolonged plight calls for sympathy negotiations on the part of both sympathizers (Karp 2001) and sympathizees (Charmaz 1980, 1991) to keep accounts open, but at some point, sympathy margins can run dry. Thus, the duration of plights affects sympathy in a curvilinear fashion: Donors offer markedly less sympathy with plights of very short and very long durations. In between lie difficulties varying in severity, but lasting for an intermediate amount of time. In such cases, we find more protracted and extensive sympathy exchanges; for example, recovering from a serious operation, a failed love affair, or the death of a spouse provides justification for more prolonged and substantial donations.

Yet, in these situations as well, sympathy margins can erode if sympathizees continue their claims beyond the amounts or time period deemed culturally fitting to the plight. On the occasions when a group member seeks more and more sympathy, peers or intimates may still provide some, but an employer or other nonintimate, on the other hand, might provide less, given that the sympathizer has consistently overdrawn the entire group's "pool of sympathy."[4] Persistent plights that others perceive as inherently minor call for smaller and smaller donations of sympathy as time goes on. That is, people will tolerate listening to others' problems over time, but they become inured when they hear the same complaint time and again. They might say (aloud or to themselves), "If it's that bad, why don't you do something about it?" If a sufferer cannot do anything about a situation, others often come to ignore or even resent sympathy claims as presumptuous and expect the sufferer to minimize complaints.

In his work on the family members of people suffering from mental illness, Karp (2001) has provided important insights into how social actors define the limits to empathy and sympathy. With appropriate amendments and specifications, Karp's model of how sympathizers enter and eventually leave their role should be applicable to a wider variety of plights and in many broader contexts. Individual and public sympathies for family crises, social movements, disaster-stricken regions, or even celebrities charged with crimes involve the need to resolve sympathy quandaries, and exiting is one such solution. We turn briefly to Karp's model.

Before a person suffering with depression is diagnosed, caregivers experience what Karp (2001:74) called "emotional anomie": "sheer bewilderment of a life that has quickly changed from coherence and predictability to chaos and disorder." This uncomfortable state is somewhat remedied by a diagnosis that provides a medical frame and thereby permits the emergence of caregiving and sympathy (p. 75). "Heroic measures are more easily undertaken at the onset of a catastrophic illness because sympathy margins remain wide and caregivers often believe that once an emotionally ill person realizes how much he or she is cared about, they will get better"

(p. 51). No boundaries are established at this point because caregiving is embraced "fully and optimistically."

However, sympathy margins began to drain if the ill person failed to "respond" appropriately or quickly enough. "Once it becomes clear that a family member's illness is chronic and probably unsolvable, the kinder emotions of sympathy and concern typically recede and darker feelings of frustration, anger, and resentment surface." These unwelcome feelings lead sympathizers to undertake even more deliberate emotion work and management in an attempt to work up more sympathy sentiment (Karp 2001:106, 90–91, respectively).

In the end, caregivers often came to consider exiting the sympathizer role. They "articulated three fundamental criteria that might require exiting—the realization that their efforts to care are ineffective, feeling that their own health is seriously jeopardized by caring, and believing that their self or identity is in danger of obliteration because of their relationship." Further, if caregivers believed the depressed person was not following medical advice, they focused their strategies on obtaining compliance, because "everyone interviewed agreed that they [the ill person] must bear significant responsibility for getting well" (Karp 2001:66, 59, respectively). Absent compliance, these family members' claims outstripped their margins, and sympathizers felt less guilt when they exited. It is likely that the process of entering and exiting the sympathizer role covers a narrower time span with nonintimate sympathizees, who can more easily claim too much sympathy.

If sympathizees must judge the right amount of sympathy to *claim*, sympathizers also must determine just the right amount of sympathy to *give*, which necessitates making a series of delicate judgments. In a particular encounter, a sympathizer can offer too much sympathy or too little depending on the merit of the plight, the sympathizee's current circumstances relative to one's own, situational or time constraints, the actor's sympathy biography, and the recipient-donor relationship and place configuration. Setting and time also play a part in what is too much or too little sympathy to give (Goffman 1967). The amount and type of sympathy offered in backstage versus frontstage settings usually differ widely. For example, although a woman who has been sexually assaulted might very much appreciate consolation from any number of people, she might not feel the same about receiving it in a public setting, such as on the front steps after church. Timing is also important (Bourdieu 1977). Offering sympathy too quickly in an encounter can send the message that the sympathizer is trying to "butter up" the sympathizee or wants to be considered more intimate than is the case. Too late an offer lessens its impact, perhaps calling the relationship into question, especially if it serves as a painful reminder of the sympathizee's plight. Once again, social actors must choose settings, occasions, and timing that are "just right."

We are not suggesting that people coolly and methodically calculate each of these factors in turn to arrive at entries in some bookkeeper's double-entry log (Frantz 2000). Rather, we are acknowledging the significant efforts people make through a well-practiced iterative process of abduction (see Scheff 1990).

Not Too Little: Keeping Accounts Open. Although extending sympathy to others might seem an obvious strategy for maintaining one's sympathy accounts, accepting sympathy also serves to keep them open. If too much time elapses between an actor's sympathy claims, the strength of previous emotional bonds weakens. Also, just as first-time borrowers discover, those who never need or claim sympathy and have no history of repaying donors may have no sympathy credits. Strictly one-way flows create obligations that recipients simply cannot discharge; thus, they remain in a one-down position relative to the sympathizer and their gratitude may turn to either apathy or resentment. Accidentally or otherwise, rebuffing an offer of sympathy delegitimizes the gift and quite possibly destabilizes the relationship itself. Denying the need for sympathy can be as damaging to sympathy margins as ingratitude or constant, overbearing claims. Others may view a person who denies needing sympathy, like Scrooge, as too lofty or too faultless to befriend.

Reciprocate.   Because sympathy is both an emotion and a gift, feeling rules *and* exchange logics call for reciprocity. Sympathizers are to offer suitable, timely donations that recipients are expected to receive with relief and gratitude. The amount of each should be in proportion to the other: pennies of gratitude as token repayment for dimes of sympathy. If the microhierarchical gap between the parties is especially great, nickels of deference are more appropriate repayment.

Important as they are, these small, immediate repayments of gratitude or deference are not sufficient to replenish sympathy credits. Recipients should also respond in kind when their "turn" to sympathize comes. Sympathizees, especially insistent and "repeat" sympathizees, who ignore their sympathizers' current or future plights usually overdraw their accounts.

Again, timing is an important consideration. Not only must sympathy and gratitude be exchanged in a timely fashion, but also repayments of sympathy should not be too long in coming. Appropriately timing exchanges between donors and sympathizees helps to demonstrate one's level of caring and sincerity. Too quick an offer of repayment might bespeak manipulation; too late an offer can convey lack of concern or insincerity. Thus, the timing between plight, sympathy, gratitude, plight, and sympathy is as much a part of the perceptual reckoning as the amounts involved.

As we saw with violations of the previous rules, sympathizees who fail to reciprocate appropriately risk their sympathy margins. An example from the international arena illustrates this point: Citizens and leaders of many other nations expressed sympathy for the United States after the 2001 highjackings, but within a short time that sympathy evaporated and cooperation with U.S. leaders lessened. Although some observers doubted the sympathy had been sincere in the first place (Krauthammer 2003), many blamed U.S. politicians for squandering it by making further demands on sympathizers without offering sufficient gratitude and respect. Bokszanski (2002) has suggested that one nation's sympathy offerings to another are based on its *expectations* of the amount of sympathy the other nation would give back if conditions called for it. These expectations are based on past performance.

The way social actors (including nations) deal with these four rules over time—their "sympathy biographies"—has important consequences for future interaction. Putting together the reciprocity rule with the claim-some-sympathy rule, we see that sympathy margins must be extended both ways: Every sympathizer must at some point be a recipient, and every sympathizee a donor. Nations, like people, establish sympathy biographies over time that color future exchanges among them.

SYMPATHY AND MICROPOLITICS.   As is the case with other gift givers, sympathizers typically gain micropolitical power or enhance their place vis-à-vis sympathizees, temporarily or over the long run. Intentionally or not, they underscore their own generosity and generate feelings of obligation in the recipients. Sympathizers often feel a mix of emotions such as sorrow, annoyance, self-congratulation, and moral worth. Sympathizees usually feel some combination of regard, reprieve, closeness, gratitude, and obligation. Experiencing these emotions helps social actors define the relationship's microhierarchy for each other and for themselves.

Additionally, because sympathy only arises when someone has problems, the micropolitical uses of sympathy are somewhat unique compared to other emotions. All gifts both reward the recipient and engender obligation, but a gift of sympathy has the additional potential to spotlight the recipient's problems, lowering his or her place even further. Because social actors are not likely to sympathize with someone if their own problems are greater, giving sympathy implies that the recipient is "damaged," "troubled," or "not normal" compared to the sympathizer. Thus, a gift of sympathy inherently contains special messages of asymmetricality that can result in sympathizees feeling belittled.

Sympathy giving can carry such different meanings that social actors employ it in both You First and Me First micropolitics. Donors use sympathy offers as a You First strategy when their manner and gestures convey messages of genuine consolation and closeness that can mitigate hierarchical or moral differences, minimize sympathizees' guilt or shame or sympathizers' self-aggrandizement, and otherwise avoid win-lose social scenarios. If such a message "works" as a claim to a more equal place, the sympathizee's place-marking emotions will include a sense of social worth. However, when donors use sympathy as a Me First strategy, their demeanor can underscore their own virtue at the cost of another's, promote themselves in the eyes of superiors, inflict guilt in others over their inadequacy, and create other situations beneficial to their place. In these cases, sympathizees are likely to experience place-marking emotions of resentment, shame, and perhaps confusion over the fact that what was supposed to be a gift caused them to feel resentment or shame. Thus, anger is not an uncommon reaction to receiving sympathy, especially among men, who may be more sensitive than women to having their place called into question (Basow and Rubenfeld 2003; Jaffee and Hyde 2000; Michaud and Warner 1997; Tannen 1990). Anger can lead to counter-claims to place through additional micropolitical wrangling. It is considerations such as these that led Berezin (2005:126) to conclude that "sympathy is about place and position . . . and not charity."

Many of the sympathy roles and processes described above feature prominently in courtroom trials. Trials feature sympathizers, sympathizees, and sympathy entrepreneurs and brokers. They illustrate the improvisation of meaning, attribution, framing, and exchange, as well as the importance of sympathy biographies and margins and micropolitics. We tend to think of the processes that lead to sympathy and blame in everyday life as constitutionally different from the law and the courthouse. However, courtroom trials are merely formalized, objectivated public arenas for making sense of people's plights. Chinese codes of law require that every legal decision include the universal human quality Confucianism calls *jen*: benevolence and sympathy for one's fellow humans. Although U.S. codes disavow sympathy and explicitly warn jurors against it, there, too, the search for procedural, distributive, and restorative justice almost invariably entails sympathy.

COURTROOM TRIALS

Perhaps more pointedly than in everyday settings, the trial's adversarial system pits the victims/plaintiffs' plights against defendants' plights, forcing participants and onlookers to divide their sympathies and their blame as they seek to properly distribute justice. When the American mass media spotlight a celebrity trial (e.g., O. J. Simpson, Bill Clinton, Martha Stewart, or Michael Jackson), they pull millions of viewers into the arena.

Of course, defendants play the starring role in trials. Their plight is, in part, being accused of wrongdoing when they are presumed innocent. If their innocence is not easy to demonstrate, they rarely try to represent themselves in court, but rely on sympathy brokers—attorneys—to present them in a manner that convinces jurors to grant them sympathy margins and perhaps sympathy. To keep those margins open throughout the trial, defendants must pay careful attention to their demeanor lest they violate any of the four rules of sympathy etiquette outlined above.

Courtroom actors also include jurors and judges, whose task is to balance law against considerations less easily codified. Social and cultural understandings of sympathy and responsibility condition those gray areas, and negotiations over meaning ensue. Jurors' and judges' sympathy for defendants depends on the latter's sympathy biographies, ascribed and achieved statuses, and the degree of responsibility attributable to them (Haegerich and Bottoms 2000). In one mock-trial study (Robinson et al. 1994), when "defendants" took responsibility and showed remorse for their deeds, mock jurors were more likely to sympathize. Sympathy somehow permeates the codified and, especially in cases of jury nullification, provides the means to arrive at a "just" verdict despite the constraints of the letter of the law.

Trials also concentrate attention on the plights of victims, who, as Kenney's (2002) analysis indicates, themselves face a labeling process parallel to that for perpetrators. Family, friends, acquaintances, and the community at large attribute varying degrees of sympathy worthiness and blameworthiness to victims. For instance, Dunn (2001) found that, to avoid blame, women victimized by stalkers were compelled to enact demeanors and behaviors of the victim role. Accomplishing and sustaining the victim identity was the clearest path to securing court sympathy and legal protection. The same difficulties apply to women victimized by rape. Pervasive cultural rape myths (e.g., "She dressed that way because she wanted it") can convert "victimization by violence" into "consensual rough sex." Defense attorneys and also news reporters (Meyers 1997) often attribute tainted identities to rape victims. Women can thus be victimized repeatedly, by an individual, a legal process, and then the media coverage of the event (Ardovini-Brooker et al. 2002). Women of color and other feminized minorities are subjected to multiple forms of oppression (Hill-Collins 1991) that only exacerbate these kinds of blame attribution.

Not only victims of sex crimes, but all victims are vulnerable to having their personal lives scrutinized and labeled as blameworthy. When the victim is a faceless corporate or government entity such as an insurance company (Brune 2003) or the IRS, jurors and observers might accord them less sympathy. Instead, they might view rule breakers as fellow underdogs and moderate the degree of blameworthiness they attribute to them.

Prosecutors and defense attorneys, whose occupations require them to steer courtroom negotiations, act as sympathy brokers who compete for the judge's or jury's sympathy. These brokers often begin their sympathy work with the jury-selection process, sometimes hiring consultants to assess what types of juror are most likely to be sympathetic to people with the defendant's or victim's traits. However, research findings on jurors' sympathy are far from straightforward. On the one hand, Clark and Carpenter (1997) reported that basic demographic factors such as race, age, gender, income, and education have been shown to be influential factors in sympathy. However, researchers Hans and Vidmar (1986) concluded that only slight differences in sympathy are associated with gender, age, and occupation. Evidence does point to an interactive effect of juror's and defendant's race with regard to jurors' attitudes, sympathy, and resulting trial outcomes (Bottoms et al. 2004; Brewer 2004).

Furthermore, although survey data (Clark 1997:201) have shown that sympathy for hypothetical "rule breakers" is strongly correlated with recommendations of leniency, sympathy may not trump the facts (see Haegerich and Bottoms 2000). DecisionQuest, the firm that handled the jury-selection coaching for O. J. Simpson's defense attorneys, summarized: "Our work on hundreds of such cases shows no automatic link between sympathy and verdict. In fact, it is clear, jurors conduct a more sophisticated attributional analysis" comparing "the relative amounts of knowledge [about risks] and control [over events] possessed by the key actors in the case" (DecisionQuest 2005a). In an illustrative case, a child visiting a neighbor tipped over a coffee urn that the neighbor had connected, contrary to the products' instructions, with an improper cord. The child was burned, and attorneys filed suit against the coffeepot manufacturer. Jurors sympathized with the child, but attributed responsibility for the situation to the neighbor, who was informed of the risk and in control of attaching the improper cord, rather than blaming the manufacturer.

In addition to or instead of relying on jury selection, attorneys broker sympathy at trial. To point out their clients' worth, vulnerability, special burdens, potential, and acceptable sympathy biographies, attorneys open windows into their clients' personal situations as well as those of their family, friends, and acquaintances. Understanding that gifts of sympathy convey moral worth, defense attorneys in Clark's study (1997) advised clients to dress "respectfully" (some had closets of conservative clothing in various sizes at the ready in their offices), control their demeanor, and come to court with family members and friends in order to merit jurors' regard. Attorneys might make blatant claims to sympathy by, for instance, exhibiting gruesome crime scene photos, leading a defendant through a tearful disclosure of past abuse, or enlisting a witness as a fellow sympathy broker to describe a victim's plight. They might also use subtler micropolitical strategies that manipulate defendants' and plaintiffs' "face" (Goffman 1967) and "place" (Goffman 1951). By directing emotions such as anger, concern, disdain, impatience, and respect at jurors, judges, defendants, plaintiffs, witnesses, and opposing attorneys, they can enhance or belittle the face or place of the parties concerned to their best advantage. Taking into consideration their own place and their client's place vis-à-vis each of these social actors helps attorneys select appropriate opening gambits and exert continued control over the interaction. Attorneys also hire "expert witnesses" to serve as (well-paid) sympathy entrepreneurs who can lend legitimacy to claims that defendants' actions are the result of sympathy-worthy conditions (e.g., battered wife syndrome, PMS, racial discrimination, and even "Twinkies"). One example that reflects our increasingly globalized world involves "a culture defense of provocation ... a crime committed by a person who in anger kills someone for gravely insulting him, his family, or his cultural community" (Torry 2001:311). Torry (2001:311–312) concluded that jurors are apt to feel "sympathy for defendants who: 1) belong to marginalized aboriginal populations; 2) are minority culture newcomers to a foreign land; or 3) hail from a mainstream enclave of society steeped in cultural values and practices condemned by the law."

In light of the growing importance of the media and growing media attention to trials, attorneys must also broker sympathy between their clients and the public. Watson (2002:77) noted that there is now "a basis in contract and malpractice law for requiring attorneys to tend to their clients' interests in the court of public opinion as zealously as they do in courts of law." Managing sympathy toward one's clients is no longer just a matter of social grace or a tacit expectation of the attorney's job (Hochschild 1983); it has now entered the realm of legal obligation.

High-profile cases and highly mediated events such as those involving Supreme Court nominee Clarence Thomas, Princess Diana, Rodney King, Scott Peterson, Robert Blake, and Michael Jackson are bellwethers for our understanding of sympathy processes. One example is the O. J. Simpson trial, which occurred in the wake of the Rodney King case in which the centrality of race and power had been captured on video in the police beating of a black man. Simpson's trial generated a tremendous amount of public interest and media coverage. Much of the interest in this case derived from the cross-cutting nature of Simpson's many statuses: a famous, wealthy, allegedly abusive African American athlete and father accused of murdering his white ex-wife and her suspected lover in a fit of jealous rage. Observers had a welter of contradictory bases for creating or closing sympathy margins.

If social scholars have traditionally been reluctant to recognize that the "irrational" social emotion of sympathy guides "rational" social actors, trial attorneys do not share that reluctance. Both the plaintiffs and the defendant in the Simpson case hired jury-selection professionals to help choose jurors sympathetic to their clients. The fact that one juror disclaimed any role of sympathy in the group's verdict (Lowe 1995) might have been a case of protesting too much. Sympathy for Simpson varied as an interactive function of several demographic characteristics. For instance, Enomoto's (1999) public survey data during the trial indicate that whites and older, more educated, and wealthy men had the least sympathy for Simpson; women tended to have more sympathy than males; and blacks were most sympathetic of all. (Although Enomoto's data included respondents' judgments about Simpson's guilt or innocence, unfortunately he did not search for associations between sympathy and these judgments.)

Once at trial, consultants at DecisionQuest advised Simpson's attorneys to broker sympathy in an indirect manner. Rather than attempting to evoke sympathy directly (a strategy that had failed to produce a favorable outcome for the plaintiff in the coffeepot case), attorneys can ultimately influence how much sympathy jurors feel for a key actor by strategically portraying the *other* key actor(s) in the case as having greater knowledge about risks and control over events (DecisionQuest 2005b).

Like Simpson, Michael Jackson represents a hodge-podge of social statuses and possible grounds for sympathy, and the parallel between the manufacturer in the coffeepot case and Jackson in his child-molestation trial is striking. Wondering aloud how a child could repeatedly spend the night with an adult stranger, one juror in the Jackson trial asked: "What mother in her right mind would allow that to happen?" (Harris 2005). Although jurors certainly had sympathy for the child involved with Jackson, they perceived that the mother (similar to the homeowner in the coffeepot case) had placed the child in harm's way; thus, the mother was culpable because of her knowledge of risks and control over events. Jurors were not sympathetic to Jackson or to the coffeepot manufacturer, but neither did they attribute responsibility to them.

Celebrity trials also make us aware that sympathy not only ties one donor to one recipient, it also arises from and can create group bonds. Hundreds of people stood watch for Michael Jackson every day on the courthouse steps, thousands camped out and wore "Free OJ" T-shirts during Simpson's trial, and thousands more visited Martha Stewart's website to leave messages of sympathy during her trial and incarceration. For every active participant, perhaps thousands of others felt tied to a community through the media. Such communities of sympathy arise in many other situations and circumstances as well.

COMMUNITIES OF SYMPATHY

As funerals illustrate, common sympathies often serve to bind together not only families and friends but also other interest groups. For instance, in the late nineteenth century, when a news boy died, other newsboys banded together to pay their respects (DiGirolamo 2002). Similarly today, motorcycle riders organize rides (Corrigan 1994) and surfers stage "paddle outs" (Staff 2005) for fallen members. These collective sympathy rituals provide both evidence of group cohesion and occasions to reinforce that cohesion.

Encouraged by sympathy entrepreneurs who bring new plights to public attention and sympathy brokers who organize soup kitchens, Meals on Wheels volunteers, and neighborhood crime watches, new groups and networks develop where none had existed before.[5] Sharing a focus with other sympathizers creates commonality, and commonality can create community. Especially when participants are linked by the same ideology, similar communities of sympathy form and endure across virtual spaces. If people learn through the media that others share their sympathies, they may feel part of a larger group or community even though they have no contact with its "members." If they interact through call-ins, e-mails, chat rooms, or "blogs," they experience their membership in the community more keenly. Of course, real and virtual communities of sympathy can be very short-lived, ebbing and waning as calamities emerge and resolve, as the media's lenses refocus to incorporate or exclude particular plights or populations, or feeling rules change.

In addition, changing economic and social conditions can create or fragment communities of sympathy. After German reunification, many West Germans felt guilty for their good fortune relative to that of East Germans and developed sympathy for and a bias toward East Germans (Schmitt and Maes 2002). However, rather than producing such an outgroup bias or "unification," abolition in the antebellum South left poor whites feeling their elevated status in relation to slaves keenly threatened, and they became distinctly unsympathetic toward the outgroup of former slaves (van den Berghe 1967).

Similar reactions to economic and social changes appear to be influencing the sympathy of many U.S. citizens today. The invisible privileges of a white majority are now "menaced" by immigration, job flight, and other aspects of fading U.S. hegemony in an increasingly globalized and "colorized" world. Policies unsympathetic to the plights of immigrants and minorities have proliferated.

For example, in the years following the North American Free Trade Agreement, Californians passed Proposition 187 to deny social, educational, and medical benefits to undocumented immigrants, Proposition 209 to roll back affirmative action policies for state contracting in employment and education, and Proposition 227 to ban bilingual education in public schools. Also, anger over attacks on U.S. soil and fear of future attacks led to the Patriot Act and to anti-Arab sentiment and violence. If increased well-being and freedom from subsistence serve to free mental and emotional energy for sympathizing with more plights and more groups (Clark 1997), a diminished sense of well-being does the opposite. Further, the perceived or actual loss of privilege and safety can coalesce into feelings of sympathy for other in-group members and, thus, lead to collective solidarity. By the same token, the racially oppressed often develop bonds of sympathy that lead to collective racial identities and minority solidarity (Shelby 2002). Once again, sharing sympathy engenders cohesion and feelings of belonging.

CONCLUSION

The forms and functions of social emotions like sympathy remain as pervasive as they are variable, much akin to changing manners over the past 500 years (Elias 1982, 1994) or the varying forms that discipline and punishment have taken (Foucault 1977). That people exchange sympathy so ubiquitously and with such nicety attests to deep-rooted cultural norms and social practices born of sympathy's central role in human interaction. We can observe sympathy's pervasive effects—as a social emotion, social capital, a gift, an insult, negotiation, leverage, collateral (Biggart and Castanias 2002), a bond, a catalyst, and as divisive force—across the global landscape. These sometimes conflicting effects help shape human societies. Just as emotions themselves have gained acceptance in the field of sociology, so too has the importance of sympathy solidified its foothold in the social world. Not only individuals but also attorneys, corporations (Dutton and Ragins 2004; Kanov et al. 2004), social movements (Goodwin and Jasper 2004; Goodwin et al. 2001), and nations increasingly acknowledge the importance of sympathy processes and put to use its micropolitical strategies and tactics. The conception of emotions as irrational is giving way to the conception of the socioemotional economy as a central system operating alongside and within more material human exchange systems.

As awareness of the importance of sympathy grows, the need for further investigation becomes more obvious. The ideas presented in this chapter point to several promising directions for new sympathy research at both the micro and macro social levels. One such area already investigated by Karp (2001) is how people enter and exit the sympathizer role, or what might be termed sympathizer careers. Another concerns the parallel and intermingled labeling processes involving rule-breakers and victims (Kenney 2002). As this issue illustrates, group-level sympathy practices merit much additional sociological attention. For example, researchers might apply Whyte's (1943) methods of observing and mapping group members with an eye to events involving sympathy and blame. Doing so could provide information on a multitude of questions about how people divide sympathy among group members, how groups divide sympathy work, how sympathy exchanges play out, and the consequences of both sympathizing and blaming for the group's character and membership.

Focusing on how organizations deal with sympathy processes, members of the Compassion Lab at the University of Michigan School of Business (see e.g., Kanov et al. 2004) have begun exploring how organizations create cultures and climates that encourage or discourage sympathy claims and displays. For instance, Kanov et al. (2004) reported that the CEO of Cisco Systems implemented a policy that supervisors must inform him within 48 hours of a death or serious illness in any employee's family so that he can express his sympathy in a timely fashion. This kind of policy might set a tone that encourages people to talk about troubles and claim sympathy, and it might result in people spending more time sympathizing. In such a context, what group processes arise to handle sympathy sentiment and display? Do some workers (e.g., women) become sympathy specialists who take on the group's sympathy work, or do all workers display more caring and concern for each other? What emotion work is required to "work up" sympathy to fit new rules of compassion, and how much emotion work is avoided by not having to "work down" sympathy under the old rules? Do sympathy exchange processes create greater solidarity? Are all group members more attuned to each other's plights and problems? Does attunement carry over into other arenas? Are newly "sympathized" workers more or less productive than previously? Are job dissatisfaction levels and employee turnover rates lower?

At a more macro social level, sociologists must explore the potent influence on sympathy processes of the rapidly transmuting mass media. "The media," "the networks," and "the Internet" fit Fine's (1991) criteria for "collective actors": "[c]rucial actors who set agendas for people's behavior" in large part because they have a collective character. "That people never interact with collective actors is literally true, but ignores that they so interpret their interactions" as they "attempt to introject the institutional order into cognition, affect, and behavior. The [resulting] consequential character of the external world prevents decisions from being idiosyncratic and provides a ground for the *collective character of knowledge*" (Fine 1991:171, emphasis in original).

The media instruct sympathizers and sympathizees in rules (through advertising, human interest stories, spreading news of whom celebrities sympathize with—Band Aid, Farm Aid, the One Campaign—and the like), provide rewards and punishments (fame and infamy in inches of print) for those who enact sympathy roles properly (saints) or poorly (Scrooge), and provide a stage for sympathy entrepreneurs and brokers. The media also keep hard copies of sympathy biographies in archives that can combed for evidence that, say, a political figure did or did not express appropriate gratitude for past sympathy. The media use micropolitical tactics to influence an audience's sympathies ("You, audience, are so dumb/smart that you . . ."). Additionally, the media point up breaches of the social logics that guide the socioemotional economy. Most obviously, the media frame plights as sympathy worthy or blameworthy.

Sympathy comes with plights, plights make for drama, and the media use drama to attract audiences and sell advertising. Nacos (2002) contended that because acts of political violence make for good "infotainment," they get extensive news play, thereby offering social actors such as Osama bin Laden and Timothy McVeigh many opportunities to put their causes before the global public in hopes of garnering sympathy. The news also presents audiences with many, many victims of political violence, natural disasters, crime, abuse, poverty, and other plights. The sheer volume of suffering and trouble that the media make available has its own consequences for sympathy that illustrate its limits. To combat sympathy fatigue, coverage must be more and more dramatic (Moeller 1999). Sensational presentations intended to call forth observers' sympathy can reach a point of diminishing returns; the viewing of media violence has been linked to a lessening of sympathy for victims (Cantor 2000). On the other hand, the global scope of today's media engenders cosmopolitanism, which, in turn, could promote sympathy for wider sets of circumstances and wider populations (Nash 2003). Again, these social processes beg for research.

Yet another area ripe for study is the effect of globalization on sympathy processes. We have little understanding of cultural differences in sympathy forms, functions, and processes. We know even less about how sympathy practices are changing with today's multilevel border crossings and the growing integration of the world economy. The globalization of the media only increases the complexity. Corporate consumerism and profiteering in the guise of branding and logos (Klein 2000; Ritzer 2004) could spread the "punitive" consumer culture that generates pervasive insecurities (Sznaider 2000), and its resulting narcissism might create a disregard for "distant suffering" (Cushman 2003). Still, future researchers might find that these outcomes are not inevitable: "The process of consumption, of expressing our identity through tastes and possessions, changes the entire field of interaction. It makes possible new kinds of social identity. It also makes possible new forms of social integration, based on individuation and sympathy" (Vaughan 2002:195).

NOTES

1. de Waal (2004) and his colleagues in primate research have repeatedly documented fairly complex patterns of sympathy giving and getting among chimpanzees. The researchers concluded that sympathy plays an important evolutionary role by promoting social bonds and group solidarity.
2. Compassion is a closely related concept. As Eisenberg et al. (1989) viewed it, compassion is an extension of sympathy because it stems from the misery of another, but it also entails a need or desire to relieve that suffering. For discussions of compassion, see Wuthnow (1991) on interaction and Kanov et al. (2004) on work organizations.
3. For another sociological approach to empathy, see Davis, this volume. For similar psychological models of "empathy" see Preston and de Waal (2002) and Prinz (1997).
4. Thanks to Liliane Floge and Kimberly E. Noon for this observation. See also Kanov et al. (2004).
5. Numerous sociologists speak to this topic in terms of social networks or virtual communities (see Lawler 2001; Lawler et al. 2000; Lawler and Yoon 1998; Waskul et al. 2000; Waskul and Lust 2004; Wellman 1998; Wellman and Haythornwaite 2002).

REFERENCES

Ardovini-Brooker, Joanne, and Susan Caringella-Macdonald. 2002. "Attributions of Blame and Sympathy in Ten Rape Cases." *Justice Professional* 15: 3–18.

Basow, Susan A., and Kimberly Rubenfeld. 2003. "'Troubles Talk': Effects of Gender and Gender-Typing." *Sex Roles* 48: 183–187.

Berezin, Mabel. 2005. "Emotions and the Economy." Pp. 109–130 in *Handbook of Economic Sociology*, 2nd ed. edited by N. J. Smelser and R. Swedberg. New York, Princeton, NJ: Russell Sage Foundation Princeton University Press.

Bevington, D. M. 1980. *The Complete Works of Shakespeare*. edited by D. M. Bevington. Glenview, IL: Scott, Foresman.

Biggart, Nicole Woolsey, and Richard P. Castanias. 2002. "Collateralized Social Relations: The Social in Economic Calculation." *American Journal of Economics and Sociology* 60: 472–502.

Blau, Peter M. 1964. *Exchange and Power in Social Life*. New York: Wiley.

Bokszanski, Zbigniew. 2002. "Poles and Their Attitudes toward Other Nations: On the Conditions of an Orientation toward Others." *Polish Sociological Review* 3: 255–274.

Bottoms, Bette L., Suzanne L. Davis, and Michelle A. Epstein. 2004. "Effects of Victim and Defendant Race on Jurors' Decisions in Child Sexual Abuse Cases." *Journal of Applied Social Psychology* 34: 1–33.

Bourdieu, Pierre. 1977. *Outline of a Theory of Practice*. New York: Cambridge University Press.

———. 1986. "The Forms of Capital." Pp. 241–258 in *Handbook of Theory and Research for the Sociology of Education*, edited by J. G. Richardson. New York: Greenwood.

Brewer, Thomas W. 2004. "Race and Jurors' Receptivity to Mitigation in Capital Cases: The Effect of Jurors', Defendants', and Victims' Race in Combination." *Law and Human Behavior* 28: 529–545.

Brune, C. 2003. "Survey Uncovers Sympathy for Fraudsters." *Internal Auditor*, 1: 18–19.

Buck, Ross. 1988. *Human Motivation and Emotion*. New York: Wiley.

Bunis, William K., Angela Yancik, and David A. Snow. 1996. "The Cultural Patterning of Sympathy toward the Homeless and Other Victims of Misfortune." *Social Problems* 43: 387–402.

Cantor, Joanne. 2000. "Media Violence." *Journal of Adolescent Health* 27: 30–34.

Charmaz, Kathy. 1980. "The Social Construction of Self-Pity in the Chronically Ill." *Studies in Symbolic Interaction* 3: 123–145.

———. 1991. *Good Days, Bad Days: The Self in Chronic Illness and Time*. New Brunswick, NJ: Rutgers University Press.

Clark, Candace. 1987. "Sympathy Biography and Sympathy Margin." *American Journal of Sociology* 93: 290–321.

———. 1990. "Emotions and Micropolitics in Everyday Life: Some Patterns and Paradoxes of 'Place'." Pp. 305–333 in *Research Agendas in the Sociology of Emotions*, edited by Theodore D. Kemper. Stony Brook: Suny Press.

———. 1997. *Misery and Company: Sympathy in Everyday Life*. Chicago: University of Chicago Press.

———. 2004. "Emotional Gifts and 'You-First' Micropolitics." Pp. 402–421 in *Feelings and Emotions: The Amsterdam Symposium: Studies in Emotion and Social Interaction*, edited by A. S. R. Manstead, N. H. Frijda, and A. Fischer. New York: Cambridge University Press.

Clark, Elizabeth B. 1995. " 'The Sacred Rights of the Weak': Pain, Sympathy, and the Culture of Individual Rights in Antebellum America." *Journal of American History* 82: 463–493.

Clark, Marcia, and Teresa Carpenter. 1997. *Without a Doubt*. New York: Viking.

Coffey, Brian, and Stephen Woolworth. 2004. "'Destroy the Scum, and Then Neuter Their Families': The Web Forum as a Vehicle for Community Discourse?" *Social Science Journal* 41: 1–14.

Collins, Randall. 1981. *Sociology Since Midcentury: Essays in Theory Cumulation*. New York: Academic.

Conrad, Peter, and Joseph Schneider. 1980. *Deviance and Medicalization: From Badness to Sickness*. St. Louis, MO: Mosby.

Corrigan, Don. 1994. "Bikers Protest KSD-TV Coverage." *St. Louis Journalism Review* 23: 9.

Cushman, Thomas. 2003. "Is Genocide Preventable? Some Theoretical Considerations." *Journal of Genocide Research* 5: 523–542.

Davis, Allison, Burleigh B. Gardner, Mary R. Gardner, and W. Lloyd Warner. 1941. *Deep South; a Social Anthropological Study of Caste and Class*. Chicago: University of Chicago Press.

DecisionQuest. 2005a. "Beware the Stupid Jury Theory." http://www.decisionquest.com/litigation_library.php?NewsID= 153 (accessed September 10, 2005).

———. 2005b. "Everything Is Evidence." http://www.decisionquest.com/litigation_library.php?NewsID=165 (accessed September 10, 2005).

Derber, Charles. 1979. *In Pursuit of Attention: Power and Individualism in Everyday Life*. Boston: G. K. Hall.

de Waal, Frans B. M. 2004. "On the Possibility of Animal Empathy." Pp. 381–401 in *Feelings and Emotions: The Amsterdam Symposium* edited by A. S. R. Manstead, N. H. Freida, and A. Fischer. Cambridge: Cambridge University Press.

DiGirolamo, Vincent. 2002. "Newsboy Funerals: Tales of Sorrow and Solidarity in Urban America." *Journal of Social History* 36: 5–30.

Dunn, Jennifer L. 2001. "Innocence Lost: Accomplishing Victimization in Intimate Stalking Cases." *Symbolic Interaction* 24: 285–313.

Dutton, Jane, and Belle R. Ragins. 2004. *Exploring Positive Relationships at Work: Building a Theoretical and Research Foundation*. Mahwah, NJ: Erlbaum.

Eisenberg, Nancy, Paul A. Miller, Mark Schaller, Richard A. Fabes, Jim Fultz, Rita Shell, and Cindy L. Shea. 1989. "The Role of Sympathy and Altruistic Personality Traits in Helping: A Reexamination." *Journal of Personality* 57: 41–67.

Ekman, Paul, Wallace V. Friesen, and Phoebe Ellsworth. 1972. *Emotion in the Human Face: Guidelines for Research and an Integration of Findings*. New York: Pergamon.

Ekman, Paul, and Erika L. Rosenberg, ed. 2005. *What the Face Reveals: Basic and Applied Studies of Spontaneous Expression Using the Facial Action Coding System (FACS)*. New York: Oxford University Press.

Elias, Norbert. 1982. *The History of Manners*. New York: Pantheon.

———. 1994. *The Civilizing Process*. Cambridge, MA: Blackwell.

Enomoto, Carl E. 1999. "Public Sympathy for O. J. Simpson: The Roles of Race, Age, Gender, Income, and Education." *American Journal of Economics and Sociology* 58: 145–161.

Farr, James. 1978. "Hume, Hermeneutics, and History: A 'Sympathetic' Account." *History and Theory* 17: 285–310.

Fassin, Didier. 2003. "Justice Principles and Judgment Practices in Allotting Emergency State Financial Aid in France." *Revue française de Sociologie* 44: 109–146.

Fine, Gary Alan. 1991. "On the Macrofoundations of Microsociology: Constraint and the Exterior Reality of Structure." *Sociological Quarterly* 32: 161–177.

Follingstad, Diane R., Margaret M. Runge, April Ace, Robert Buzan, and Cindy Helff. 2001. "Justifiability, Sympathy Level, and Internal/External Locus of the Reasons Battered Women Remain in Abusive Relationships." *Violence and Victims* 16: 621–644.

Forte, James A. 2002. "Not in My Social World: A Cultural Analysis of Media Representations, Contested Spaces, and Sympathy for the Homeless." *Journal of Sociology and Social Welfare* 29: 131–157.

Foucault, Michel. 1977. *Discipline and Punish: The Birth of the Prison*. New York: Pantheon.

Frantz, Roger. 2000. "Intuitive Elements in Adam Smith." *Journal of Socio-Economics* 29: 1–19.

Gilligan, Carol. 1982. *In a Different Voice: Psychological Theory and Women's Development*. Cambridge, MA: Harvard University Press.

Goffman, Erving. 1951. "Symbols of Class Status." *British Journal of Sociology* 2: 294–304.

———. 1967. *Interaction Ritual: Essays on Face-to-Face Behaviour*. New York: Doubleday Anchor.

Goodrum, Sarah, and Mark C. Stafford. 2003. "The Management of Emotions in the Criminal Justice System." *Sociological Focus* 36: 179–196.

Goodwin, Jeff, and James M. Jasper. 2004. *Rethinking Social Movements: Structure, Meaning, and Emotion*. Lanham, MD: Rowman and Littlefield.

Goodwin, Jeff, James M. Jasper, and Francesca Polletta. 2001. *Passionate Politics: Emotions and Social Movements*. Chicago: University of Chicago Press.

Gouldner, Alvin W. 1960. "The Norm of Reciprocity: A Preliminary Statement." *American Sociological Review* 25: 161–177.

———. 1973. *For Sociology: Renewal and Critique in Sociology Today*. London: Allen Lane.

Graham, Sandra, Bernard Weiner, Maisha Cobb, and Tina Henderson. 2001. "An Attributional Analysis of Child Abuse among Low-Income African American Mothers." *Journal of Social and Clinical Psychology* 20: 233–257.

Gusfield, Joseph. 1980. *The Culture of Public Problems: Drinking-Driving and the Symbolic Order*. Chicago: University of Chicago Press.

Haegerich, Tamara M., and Bette L. Bottoms. 2000. "Empathy and Jurors' Decisions in Patricide Trials Involving Child Sexual Assault Allegations." *Law and Human Behavior* 24: 421–448.

Hans, Valerie P., and Neil Vidmar. 1986. *Judging the Jury*. New York: Plenum.

Harris, Hamil R. 2005. "Jury Acquits Jackson on All Charges." *Washington Post*, June 14.

Hill-Collins, Patricia. 1991. *Black Feminist Thought: Knowledge, Consciousness, and the Politics of Empowerment*. New York: Routledge.

Hirsch, Stacey. 2005. "Called Out on Calling in Sick." *Wilmington (Delaware) Star News*, July 25.

Hochschild, Arlie Russell. 1983. *The Managed Heart: Commercialization of Human Feeling*. Berkeley: University of California Press.

———. 1989. *The Second Shift: Working Parents and the Revolution at Home*. New York: Viking Penguin.

Homans, George C. 1984. *Social Behavior: Its Elementary Forms*. New York: Harcourt Brace Jovanovich.

Jaffee, Sara, and Janet S. Hyde. 2000. "Gender Differences in Moral Orientation: A Meta-Analysis." *Psychological Bulletin* 126: 703–726.

Kahan, Dan M., and Martha C. Nussbaum. 1996. "Two Conceptions of Emotion in Criminal Law." *Columbia Law Review* 96: 269–374.

Kanov, Jason M., Sally Maitlis, Monica C. Worline, Jane E. Dutton, Peter J. Frost, and Jacoba M. Lilius. 2004. "Compassion in Organizational Life." *American Behavioral Scientist* 47: 808–827.

Karp, David Allen. 2001. *The Burden of Sympathy: How Families Cope with Mental Illness*. New York: Oxford University Press.

Katz, Jack. 1988. *Seductions of Crime: Moral and Sensual Attractions in Doing Evil*. New York: Basic Books.

Kemper, Theodore D. 1978. *A Social Interactional Theory of Emotions*. New York: Wiley.

Kenney, J. Scott. 2002. "Victims of Crime and Labeling Theory: A Parallel Process?" *Deviant Behavior* 23: 235–265.

Klein, Naomi. 2000. *No Logo: Taking Aim at the Brand Bullies*. New York: Picador.

Ko, Dorothy. 2003. "Footbinding in the Museum." *Interventions* 5: 426–439.

Krauthammer, Charles 2003. "To Hell with Sympathy." *Time*, November 17.

Kurzman, Charles. 2003. "Pro-U.S. Fatwas." *Middle East Policy* 10: 155–166.

Lawler, Edward J. 2001. "An Affect Theory of Social Exchange." *American Journal of Sociology* 107: 321–352.

Lawler, Edward J., Shane R. Thye, and Jeongkoo Yoon. 2000. "Emotion and Group Cohesion in Productive Exchange." *American Journal of Sociology* 106: 616–657.

Lawler, Edward J., and Jeongkoo Yoon. 1998. "Network Structure and Emotion in Exchange Relations." *American Sociological Review* 63: 871–894.

Leach, Colin W., and Larissa Z. Tiedens. 2004. "Introduction: A World of Emotion." Pp. 1–16 in *The Social Life of Emotions*. Cambridge: Cambridge University Press.

Lerner, Melvin J., and Carolyn Simmons. 1980. *The Belief in a Just World: A Fundamental Delusion*. New York: Plenum.

Levi-Strauss, Claude. 1969. *The Elementary Structures of Kinship*. Translated by J. H. Bell, J. R. von Sturmer, and R. Needham. Boston: Beacon.

———. 1974. "Reciprocity, the Essence of Social Life." Pp. 3–12 in *The Family: Its Structures and Functions*, edited by R. L. Coser. New York: St. Martin's Press.

Li, Tania M. 2001. "Masyarakat Adat, Difference, and the Limits of Recognition in Indonesia's Forest Zone." *Modern Asian Studies* 35: 645–676.

Link, Bruce G., Sharon Schwartz, Robert Moore, Jo C. Phelan, Elmer Struening, Anne Stueve, and Mary. E. Colten. 1995. "Public Knowledge, Attitudes, and Beliefs about Homeless People: Evidence for Compassion Fatigue." *American Journal of Community Psychology* 23: 533–555.

Lowe, Karen 1995. "Jurors Tell Why They Acquitted Simpson." *The Australian*, October 6.

Lutz, Catherine A., and Lila Abu-Lughod. 1990. *Language and the Politics of Emotion*. New York: Cambridge University Press.

MacGeorge, Erina L. 2003. "Gender Differences in Attributions and Emotions in Helping Contexts." *Sex Roles* 48: 175–182.

Malinowski, Bronislaw. 1923. "The Problem of Meaning in Primitive Languages." Pp. 451–510 in *The Meaning of Meaning; A Study of the Influence of Language Upon Thought and of the Science of Symbolism*, edited by C. K. Ogden, I. A. Richards, B. Malinowski, F. G. Crookshank, and J. P. Postgate. New York: Harcourt, Brace.

Manstead, A. S. R., Nico H. Frijda, and Agneta Fischer. 2004. *Feelings and Emotions: The Amsterdam Symposium*. New York: Cambridge University Press.

Maroney, Terry A. 2006. "Law and Emotion: A Proposed Taxonomy of an Emerging Field." *Law and Human Behavior*.

Mauss, Marcel. 1954. *The Gift: Forms and Functions of Exchange in Archaic Societies*. Translated by I. Cunnison. Glencoe, IL: Free Press.

McCall, George J., and J. L. Simmons. 1978. *Identities and Interactions: An Examination of Human Associations in Everyday Life*. New York: Free Press.

McGee, Marsha. 1980. "Faith, Fantasy, and Flowers: A Content Analysis of the American Sympathy Card." *Omega* 11: 25–35.

McKie, John, and Jeff Richardson. 2003. "The Rule of Rescue." *Social Science and Medicine* 56: 2407–2419.

Mead, George Herbert, and Charles W. Morris. 1934. *Mind, Self and Society from the Standpoint of a Social Behaviorist*. Chicago: University of Chicago Press.

Meyers, Marian. 1997. *News Coverage of Violence against Women: Engendering Blame*. Thousand Oaks, CA: Sage.

Michaud, Shari L., and Rebecca M. Warner. 1997. "Gender Differences in Self-Reported Response to Troubles Talk." *Sex Roles* 37: 527–540.

Moeller, Susan D. 1999. *Compassion Fatigue: How the Media Sell Disease, Famine, War, and Death*. New York: Routledge.

Mooney, Linda, and Sarah C. Brabant. 1998. "Off the Rack: Store Bought Emotions and the Presentation of Self." *Electronic Journal of Sociology* 3. http://www.sociology.org/content/vol003.004/mooney.html (accessed September 10, 2005).

Mulcahy, Matthew. 2005. *Melancholy and Fatal Calamities: Hurricanes and Society in the British Greater Caribbean*. Baltimore: Johns Hopkins University Press.

Nacos, Brigitte L. 2002. *Mass-Mediated Terrorism*. Lanham, MD: Rowman and Littlefield.

Nash, Kate. 2003. "Cosmopolitan Political Community: Why Does It Feel So Right?" *Constellations* 10: 506–518.

Nussbaum, Martha Craven. 2001. *Upheavals of Thought: The Intelligence of Emotions*. Cambridge: Cambridge University Press.

Offer, Avner. 1997. "Between the Gift and the Market: The Economy of Regard." *Economic History Review* 3: 450–476.

O'Hea, Erin L., Sara E. Sytsma, Amy Copeland, and Phillip J. Brantley. 2001. "The Attitudes toward Women with HIV/Aids Scale (ATWAS): Development and Validation." *AIDS Education and Prevention* 13: 120–130.

Okabayashi, Hideki, Naoko Ooi, and Kazuo Hara. 1995. "Chronological Changes in College Students' View of Life." *Kyoiku Shinrigaku Kenkyo/Japanese Journal of Psychology* 66: 127–133.

Panksepp, Jaak. 1998. *Affective Neuroscience: The Foundations of Human and Animal Emotions.* New York: Oxford University Press.

Pierce, Jennifer L. 1995. *Gender Trials: Emotional Lives in Contemporary Law Firms.* Berkeley: University of California Press.

Preston, Stephanie D., and Frans B. M. de Waal. 2002. "Empathy: Its Ultimate and Proximate Bases." *Behavioral and Brain Sciences* 25: 1–20.

Prinz, Wolfgang. 1997. "Perception and Action Planning." *European Journal of Cognitive Psychology* 9: 129–154.

Quist, Ryan M., and Douglas M. Wiegand. 2002. "Attributions of Hate: The Media's Causal Attributions of a Homophobic Murder." *American Behavioral Scientist* 46: 93–107.

Rai, Amit. 2002. *Rule of Sympathy: Sentiment, Race, and Power, 1750–1850.* New York: Palgrave.

Ritzer, George. 2004. *The McDonaldization of Society.* Thousand Oaks, CA: Pine Forge Press.

Robinson, Dawn T., Lynn Smith-Lovin, and Olga Tsoudis. 1994. "Heinous Crime or Unfortunate Accident? The Effects of Remorse on Responses to Mock Criminal Confessions." *Social Forces* 73: 175–190.

Robison, Lindon J., A. Allan Schmid, and Marcelo E. Siles. 2002. "Is Social Capital Really Capital?" *Social Economy* 60: 1–21.

Rodriguez, Noelie, Alan L. Ryave, and Joseph Tracewell. 1998. "Withholding Compliments in Everyday Life and the Covert Management of Disaffiliation." *Journal of Contemporary Ethnography* 27: 323–345.

Rojek, Chris. 2002. "The Post-Auratic President." *American Behavioral Scientist* 46: 487–500.

Rudolph, Udo, Scott C. Roesch, Tobias Greitemeyer, and Bernard Weiner. 2004. "A Meta-Analytic Review of Help Giving and Aggression from an Attributional Perspective: Contributions to a General Theory of Motivation." *Cognition and Emotion* 18: 815–848.

Sally, David. 2000. "A General Theory of Sympathy, Mind-Reading, and Social Interaction, with an Application to the Prisoner's Dilemma." *Social Science Information/Information sur les Sciences Sociales* 39: 567–634.

———. 2001. "On Sympathy and Games." *Journal of Economic Behavior and Organization* 44: 1–30.

———. 2002a. "Two Economic Applications of Sympathy." *Journal of Law, Economics, and Organization* 18: 455–487.

———. 2002b. "'What an Ugly Baby!': Risk Dominance, Sympathy, and the Coordination of Meaning." *Rationality and Society* 14: 78–108.

Scheff, Thomas J. 1990. *Microsociology: Discourse, Emotion, and Social Structure.* Chicago: University of Chicago Press.

Schmitt, Manfred, and Jurgen Maes. 2002. "Stereotypic Ingroup Bias as Self-Defense against Relative Deprivation: Evidence from a Longitudinal Study of the German Unification Process." *European Journal of Social Psychology* 32: 309–326.

Schwartz, Barry. 1967. "The Social Psychology of the Gift." *American Journal of Sociology* 73: 1–11.

Shelby, Tommie. 2002. "Foundations of Black Solidarity: Collective Identity or Common Oppression?" *Ethics* 112: 231–266.

Shott, Susan. 1979. "Emotion and Social Life: A Symbolic Interactionist Analysis." *American Journal of Sociology* 84: 1317–1334.

———. 1981. "A Social Interactional Theory of Emotions." *American Journal of Sociology* 86: 928–929.

Simmel, Georg. 1950. *The Sociology of Georg Simmel.* Translated and edited by K. T. Wolff. New York: Free Press.

Smith, Adam. 1759. *The Theory of Moral Sentiments.* London: A. Millar.

Solomon, R. 1994. "Sympathy and Vengeance: The Role of the Emotions in Justice." Pp. 291–312 in *Emotions; Essays on Emotion Theory (Festschrift for Nico Frijda),* edited by S. van Goozen, N. de Poll, and J. Sergeant. New York: Erlbaum.

Staff. 2005. "Obituary for Justin Lee Kelley." *The Island Gazette,* July 20.

Stauth, Georg, and Bryan S. Turner. 1988. *Nietzsche's Dance: Resentment, Reciprocity, and Resistance in Social Life.* New York: Blackwell.

Stearns, Carolun Zisowitz, and Peter N. Stearns. 1986. *Anger: The Struggle for Emotional Control in America's History.* Chicago: University of Chicago Press.

Stets, Jan E., and Michael M. Harrod. 2004. "Verification across Multiple Identities: The Role of Status." *Social Psychology Quarterly* 67: 155–171.

Struthers, C. Ward, Deborah L. Miller, Connie J. Boudens, and Gemma L. Briggs. 2001. "Effects of Causal Attributions on Coworker Interactions: A Social Motivation Perspective." *Basic and Applied Social Psychology* 23: 169–181.

Struthers, C. Ward, Bernard Weiner, and Keith Allred. 1998. "Effects of Causal Attributions on Personnel Decisions: A Social Motivation Perspective." *Basic and Applied Social Psychology* 20: 155–166.

Sudnow, David. 1967. *Passing On: The Social Organization of Dying.* Englewood Cliffs, NJ: Prentice-Hall.

Sznaider, Natan. 2000. "Consumerism as a Civilizing Process: Israel and Judaism in the Second Age of Modernity." *International Journal of Politics, Culture and Society* 14: 297–312.

Tannen, Deborah. 1990. "Gender Differences in Topical Coherence: Creating Involvement in Best Friends' Talk." *Discourse Processes. Special Issue on Gender and Conversational Interaction* 13: 73–90.

Torry, William I. 2001. "Social Change, Crime, and Culture: The Defense of Provocation." *Crime, Law and Social Change* 36: 309–325.

Twomey, Christina. 1999. "Courting Men: Mothers, Magistrates and Welfare in the Australian Colonies." *Women's History Review* 8: 231–246.

van den Berghe, Pierre L. 1967. *Race and Racism: A Comparative Perspective*. New York: Wiley.

Vaughan, Barry. 2002. "The Punitive Consequences of Consumer Culture." *Punishment and Society* 4: 195–211.

Wallerstein, Immanuel Maurice. 2004. *World-Systems Analysis: An Introduction*. Durham, NC: Duke University Press.

Waskul, Dennis, Mark Douglass, and Charles Edgley. 2000. "Cybersex: Outercourse and the Enselfment of the Body." *Symbolic Interaction* 23: 375–397.

Waskul, Dennis, and Matt Lust. 2004. "Role-Playing and Playing Roles: The Person, Player, and Persona in Fantasy Role-Playing." *Symbolic Interaction* 27: 333–356.

Watson, John C. 2002. "Litigation Public Relations: The Lawyers' Duty to Balance News Coverage of Their Clients." *Communication Law and Policy* 7: 77–103.

Weiner, Bernard. 1980. "A Cognitive (Attribution)-Emotion-Action Model of Motivated Behavior: An Analysis of Judgments of Help-Giving." *Journal of Personality and Social Psychology* 39: 186–200.

———. 1991. "Metaphors in Motivation and Attribution." *American Psychologist* 46: 921–930.

Wellman, Barry. 1998. *Networks in the Global Village: Life in Contemporary Communities*. Boulder, CO: Westview.

Wellman, Barry, and Caroline A. Haythornthwaite. 2002. *The Internet in Everyday Life*. Malden, MA: Blackwell.

Wentworth, William M., and Darrell Yardley. 1994. "Deep Sociality: A Bioevolutionary Perspective on the Sociology of Human Emotions." Pp. 21–55 in *Social Perspectives on Emotions*, Vol. 2, edited by W. M. Wentworth and J. Ryan. Greenwich, CT: JAI Press.

Whyte, William Foote. 1943. *Street Corner Society: the Social Structure of an Italian Slum*. Chicago: University of Chicago Press.

Wiseman, Jacqueline P. 1979. *Stations of the Lost: The Treatment of Skid Row Alcoholics*. Chicago: University of Chicago Press.

Wood, Richard, James K. Rilling, Alan G. Sanfey, Z. Bhagwagar, and Robert D. Rogers. 2005. "The Effects of Altering Dietary L-Tryptophan on the Performance of an Iterated Prisoner's Dilemma (PD) Game in Healthy Volunteers." Presented at European College of Neuropharmacology in Nice, Italy.

Wuthnow, Robert. 1991. *Acts of Compassion: Caring for Others and Helping Ourselves*. Princeton, NJ: Princeton University Press.

CHAPTER 21

Anger

Scott Schieman

Almost everyone at some time experiences anger in some form or another. Most of us have played the role of the angry actor, been the target of someone else's anger, or witnessed expressions of anger between other individuals in real life, on stage, or in the media. Anger provides drama; rage enlarges and expands it. Thus, it is hardly surprising that many television programs, cinema, and live theater utilize variants of anger as script elements. "Reality" television programs often instigate anger among "actors," letting their viewers witness its psychosocial effects. Anger can be personally and socially destructive, but it can also inspire, mobilize, and propel individuals to alter the undesirable circumstances of their lives. In addition, anger provides us with explanations for other people's behavior—especially intensely shocking acts; for example, on May 30, 2005, a 9-year-old girl in East New York, Brooklyn, stabbed an 11-year-old girl in the chest with a steak knife. The headline for the story in the *New York Times* read "Neighbors Saw Anger in Girl, 9, Accused in Killing."

A central question for sociologists is: What can we learn about social life by studying anger? The focus on anger (versus other emotions such as sadness) provides unique knowledge about social relationships and conditions, the norms and expectations that occur within those domains, and dynamics in the wider society. This chapter explores those issues in three main sections: (1) the conceptualization of anger from a variety of perspectives; (2) a summary of the core "sites of anger provocation" in social contexts; and (3) a review of studies of the social distribution of anger processes. I also briefly discuss the complex associations among power, the sense of control, and anger processes—identifying the *utility* of anger. In each section, I summarize the main findings and a research agenda for the sociological study of anger. My orientation is guided by an interest in the integration of approaches in the sociologies of emotions and mental health; in that effort, I also seek to apply tenets of stress process theory to define anger's role in stress-related processes and its relationship to other forms of emotionality.

SCOTT SCHIEMAN • Department of Sociology, University of Toronto, Toronto, Ontario, Canada M5S 2J4

CONCEPTUALIZATION OF ANGER

Scholars of emotions assert that anger is among the "basic" emotions (Ekman 1994a; Izard 1977; Turner 2000), although there is debate on this issue. In Kemper's (1987) view, anger is a "primary" emotion because it has evolutionary value, is present early in life, has cross-cultural universality, and has differentiated autonomic patterns from other emotions. Likewise, Scherer (1994:28) asserts that frustration is "universal and ubiquitous" because "all organisms, at all stages of ontogenetic development, encounter blocks to need satisfaction or goal achievement at least some of the time." Irrespective of its status as a basic emotion, anger is one of the most commonly experienced and recognized emotions in the United States and other Western societies (Averill 1982; Ekman et al. 1987; Scherer and Tannenbaum 1986; Scherer and Wallbott 1994). Surveys show that Americans report feeling anger on average of 1 or 2 days a week, whereas the milder variants of anger are much more common (Mirowsky and Ross 2003a; Schieman 1999; Schieman et al. 2005a). The milder variants of anger, such as feeling annoyed or rankled, intensify to fury and wrath as the provoking stimuli become increasingly more central to the actor's concerns.

What exactly *is* anger? Despite a long tradition of inquiry by philosophers, psychologists, sociologists, and others, the conceptualization of anger still remains fuzzy. In my judgment, anger—perhaps more than other emotions—is an "I know it when I feel (or see) it" emotion. Most people are able to delineate anger from other emotions, such as fear, sadness, and happiness (Russell and Fehr 1994). From an emotion-prototype perspective, the "anger script" is typically marked by uncomfortable cognitions and affect and by unique triggers, physiological reactions, expressions, and social consequences (Fehr and Baldwin 1996). According to Kassinove and Sukhodolsky (1995:7), anger is

> [A] negative, phenomenological (or internal) feeling state associated with specific cognitive and perceptual distortions and deficiencies (e.g., misappraisals, errors, and attributions of blame, injustice, preventability, and/or intentionality), subjective labeling, physiological changes, and action tendencies to engage in socially constructed and reinforced organized behavioral scripts.

These definitions provide a complicated picture because they include an array of components of *anger processes*. The conceptualization of anger is further clouded by the fact that some scholars have defined anger in terms of its subcategories, blending "angerlike" emotions of different forms and intensities. Ellsworth and Scherer (2003:575) state that "rather than a single emotion of anger, there can be many varieties of 'almost anger' and many nuances of the anger experience." Likewise, Spielberger and his colleagues (1985:28) described anger as "an emotional state that consists of feelings of irritation, annoyance, fury, or rage and heightened activation or arousal of the autonomic nervous system." Social cognitive perspectives of anger identify four angerlike emotions, including "frustration emotions (involving undesirable outcomes), resentment emotions (involving the outcomes received by others), reproach emotions (involving the attribution of blame), and anger emotions (involving both undesirable outcomes and blame)" (Clore et al. 1993:68). Debate continues as to whether anger includes or is conceptually distinct from emotions like frustration, reproach, and resentment (Berkowitz and Harmon-Jones 2004; Smith and Kirby 2004).

Facial expressions, autonomic specificity of emotions, and neurological substrates can further distinguish anger from other emotions. Research has identified typical anger-related facial actions such as lowering and knitting the brow, tightening the eyelids, raising the mound of the chin and lower lip upward, and tightening and narrowing the lips (Marsh et al. 2005:75). Moreover, some scholars argue that the facial expressions of anger convey *similar* social messages across different cultures (Darwin 1965; Ekman 1994b; Izard 1994). There is evidence of distinctive patterns of autonomic nervous system activity for anger (Ekman 1994a), although the autonomic specificity and neural substrates that distinguish anger from other emotions are not clearly demarcated and are actively being investigated in the affective sciences (Elliott and Dolan 2003; Levenson 2003; Ketter et al. 2003). Irrespective of the physiological processes, neurological pathways, or facial expressions that distinguish anger, sociologists are usually interested in the *perceptual differences* that individuals make with respect to anger. Therefore, despite the complexity and "fuzziness" of anger as a concept, sociologists who study anger typically rely on individuals' self-reports of anger. For example, in recent studies, anger is operationalized in terms of feelings that range from mild to more severe (e.g., annoyed, angry, outraged) and behavioral expression (e.g., yelling at someone) (Mirowsky and Ross 2003a; Schieman 1999, 2005a).

Social contexts influence the conceptual parameters and processes associated with any emotion (Thoits 1989), and anger is no exception. Uncomfortable cognitions and affect, physiological reactions or bodily sensations, and expressions or gestures are all elements of anger processes. However, language and the contextual factors that envelope situational stimuli provide the meanings and cultural labels that enable actors to identify an emotional experience as "anger." Therefore, even if researchers in the burgeoning area of affective neuroscience discover that dimensions of anger processes are the product of genetic heritage and preprogrammed into human brains, the social situations and structural arrangements of individuals' lives will remain relevant because they provide the contexts that provoke or confine anger in patterned, systematic ways; that is, social conditions cause, mediate, and modify the evocation and expression of "hard-wired" emotions. As sociologists, our aims entail the description of those social conditions and their roles in the activation, course, expression, and management of anger *as a process*.

SOCIAL CAUSES OF ANGER PROCESSES

Why do people get angry? Scholars from an array of disciplines have compiled theories and evidence about the "sites of anger provocation" (Canary et al. 1998). A general consensus emerges from those summaries: Anger is a highly *social* emotion. Common elicitors of anger involve actual or perceived insult, injustice, betrayal, inequity, unfairness, goal impediments, the incompetent actions of another, and being the target of another person's verbal or physical aggression (Berkowitz and Harmon-Jones 2004; Izard 1977, 1991). One of the most prominent reasons for anger involves direct or indirect actions that threaten an individual's self-concept, identity, or public image (Cupach and Canary 1995); insults, condescension, and reproach represent these threatening actions (Canary et al. 1998). Collectively, these sites of anger provocation involve the perceptions of social conditions or actual, objective circumstances. Major institutionalized social roles embedded in work and family contexts provide structure and organization for the conditions that expose individuals to the sites of anger provocation and pattern anger processes across core social statuses such as gender, age, and social class.

Social Contexts and the Sites of Anger Provocation

Work and family contexts represent intermediate social structures that channel the effects of macrolevel social structures on emotions (Gordon 1990). In addition, a growing body of literature identifies the importance of neighborhood contexts for emotions (Mirowsky and Ross 2003a). In my judgment, there is a compelling parallel in the processes associated with the sites of anger provocation and the most common sources of chronic stress in work, family, and neighborhood life. A long-standing cornerstone of the sociology of mental health literature, the "stress process model," proposes that chronic stressors account for a substantial portion of social variation in psychological functioning (Pearlin 1999). Chronic stressors often involve demands, threats, conflicts, complexity, underreward, and structural constraints (Wheaton 1999). These stressors are classified as *chronic* because of their association with enduring, persistent, and structured experiences in work, family, and neighborhood domains. Similarly, studies from different countries and cultures indicate that the bulk of emotion-related experiences—both positive and negative—are often associated with relationships in work or family roles (Scherer and Tannenbaum 1986; Scherer et al. 1986). The most *intense* experiences of many different emotions are likely to occur in close, intimate relationships because individuals tend to be highly invested in those relations (Carstensen et al. 1996). This makes work and family contexts ideal and accessible social contexts for sociologists who study emotions, especially anger.

THE WORK CONTEXT.   Occupations connect individuals to macrolevel systems of inequality and stratification. Moreover, they structure individuals' activities for substantial tracts of time over most of the adult life course. In 1844, Karl Marx (1983:140) theorized about the psychosocial impact of the social organization of work, asserting that

> [A] direct consequence of man's alienation from the product of his labor, from his life activity, from his species-being, is the *alienation of man* from *man*. . . . What is true of man's relationship to his work, to the product of his work, and to himself, is also true of man's relationship to the other man. (italics in original)

Marx contended that the social structural arrangements of people's lives, as reflected by their location within the means of production, contribute to "hostile and alien" affect. His ideas have yielded a tradition of inquiry. In particular, Kohn and Schooler's (1973) research has underscored the psychological effects of the "structural imperatives of the job," especially position in the organizational structure, self-directed work, and job pressures.

Among the potentially relevant structural conditions of the workplace, job authority is one of the most prominent (Smith 2002). Well-paid professionals with higher levels of authority often experience other higher-status work conditions, especially greater job autonomy and nonroutine work (Reskin and Ross 1992; Ross and Reskin 1992). Despite the benefits of job authority, it contributes to exposures to the sites of anger provocation because of its association with complex interpersonal dynamics (Schieman 2005a). For example, workers with more authority are often required to maintain supportive relations to complete tasks and achieve goals (Hodson 2001). Workers in these positions tend to have more responsibility for the vital operations that shape the course and success of the organization. Moreover, job authority often affords sanctioning, supervising, and decision-making control over others (Smith 2002), as well as the power to hire and fire others and influence other workers' rate of pay (Elliot and Smith 2004). Possessing power to distribute rewards and punishments in the workplace is likely, at some point or another, to evoke strong emotions among subordinates. Although subordinates often cannot not *directly* express anger to a superordinate, there are a multitude of methods for instigating disorder in the workplace (i.e., gossip, sabotage, passive-aggressive forms of incivility, and incomplete or inadequate work performance) (Andersson and Pearson 1999; Glomb 2002). These ideas imply that anger is a mediating link between being the target of anger and an array of personal, social, and organizational outcomes.

Mirowsky and Ross (2003b:123) assert that "decision-makers often feel apprehension about how things will turn out and tension about resolving the conflicting interests of others higher and lower in the organization." Interpersonal dynamics within authority structures may contribute to discord because of their links to power and status differentials. Workers with higher levels of authority sometimes confront resistance, noncompliance, and unsatisfactory performance, and they are often in charge of managing it (Hodson 2001). For these reasons, I contend that interpersonal dynamics associated with job authority are likely to be associated with different dimensions of anger processes, including the activation, course, expression, and management of anger. Understanding the links between job authority and anger would help define a general *utility* of anger (described later). Moreover, we might also examine the ways that episodic anger contributes to mental health problems, including other forms of distress. Few inquiries have sought to tackle these issues, so they represent rich zones for innovative theoretical and empirical advances.

The dynamics associated with job authority highlight the relevance of interpersonal conflicts for anger processes. Although it is well established that the workplace provides an important context for supportive social bonds (Hodson 2001), it is also a major source of interpersonal conflict (Schieman 2005a). The frequency of incivility, resistance, and negotiation makes the workplace one of the most interpersonally frustrating role contexts (Fitness 2000). For example, in a diary study, Schwartz and Stone (1993) found that 75% of all potentially harmful work-related episodes involve conflict with co-workers, supervisors, and clients or customers. Others have described the occurrence of anger among customers and its implications for thoughts (or acts) of violence against the service provider (Bougie et al. 2003). Although it is beyond the scope of this chapter, it is also worth considering the ways that interpersonal conflict and anger are relevant for emotional labor and its psychosocial consequences (Hochschild, 1979, 1983; Wharton 1999).

Given the complexity of social relations in the workplace, it is unsurprising that people identify the workplace as a major source of angerlike emotions. However, little is known about the nature and extent of interpersonal conflict with respect to *position* in the workplace authority structure; therefore, a comprehensive focus on the role-set would generate new insights into those dynamics. The role-set, as Merton (1968) defines it, involves clusters of related roles that entail different forms of social interaction (i.e., worker-supervisor, worker-client/customer). The growing shift toward team-oriented forms of organization across economic sectors amplifies the importance of the workplace role-set (Smith 1997; Vallas 2003). Team-oriented structures enhance efficiency and competitiveness, but they also necessitate more complex forms of interaction and interdependence among co-workers (Hodson 2002). Greater interdependence in the workplace role-set implies that one worker's incivility or anger can erode trust, cooperation, and organizational effectiveness (Neuman and Baron 1997; Rusbult and Van Lange 2003). Prior research has established that individuals may seek support from or solidarity with other co-workers in response to frequent altercations with superordinates, subordinates, or customers (Hodson 2001). Therefore, the workplace role-set contains a multifaceted constellation of supportive social bonds *and* the sites of anger provocation—but what is the interplay between them? Analyses of these interpersonal processes would address what Kohn (1990) referred to as an "unresolved issue" in research on work and psychosocial functioning. We might also learn a great deal more about anger processes and their distinctions from other emotions.

Nonroutine work and job autonomy are other prominent workplace conditions that may influence anger processes. Boring, routine jobs with little autonomy are often associated with unfavorable emotional outcomes, usually depressive affect (Mirowsky and Ross 2003a). By contrast, workers with nonroutine, autonomous work tend to possess higher levels of psychosocial resources such as self-esteem, the sense of control, and supportive co-worker relations (Ross and Wright 1998; Schieman 2002). By extension, it is plausible that nonroutine and autonomous work conditions have beneficial implications for different dimensions of anger processes; for example, workers in nonroutine jobs may have a variety of tasks and problems to solve—conditions that keep their work fresh, interesting, and engaging. Likewise, workers with more autonomy tend to have fewer encounters with supervisors or managers and their associated demands and expectations. Taken together, these elements of nonroutine, autonomous work likely reduce the risk of exposure to the sites of anger provocation or, if anger is aroused, help to modify the intensity, duration, expression, and social consequences of anger.

On the other hand, work that is nonroutine and autonomous may be associated with higher-status positions in the workplace that entail responsibilities and obligations—and more complex forms of social interdependence. Nonroutine work presents more challenges to individuals and increases the level of expectations for goal attainments, whereas repetitive, boring work with little challenge may be more depressing than it is anger-provoking. Likewise, workers with greater autonomy have greater decision-making authority over others in the workplace. Although workers with autonomy typically enjoy freedom from direct supervision, they often must still deal with an array of interpersonal problems such as incompetent subordinates or workers who fail to complete assigned tasks. A 2005 survey of U.S. working adults found that "someone else at work did not complete the work that needed to be done" is the most frequent interpersonal problem in the workplace (Schieman 2005a). Likewise, Kohn and Schooler (1973:109) alluded to the potential "costs" of higher-status positions, stating that "an increased risk of being held responsible for things outside one's control is the price one pays for holding an interesting and responsible job." Collectively, these ideas imply that although higher status work conditions yield many personal benefits, they often also require more sophisticated socioemotional skills to navigate chronic stressors and the elicitors of anger.

Noxious physical environments represent another relevant workplace condition. Workplaces that are noisy, dirty, and dangerous potentially expose workers to pain and threat. Experimental studies document that physical discomfort or pain can cause anger (Anderson et al. 1995). In fact, pain is considered one of the classic triggers of anger (Berkowitz and Harmon-Jones 2004); threat is another (Canary et al. 1998). Applying the stress process model, which identifies noxious job conditions as an important chronic strain, prior evidence confirms the distressing effects of noxious workplace conditions (Pearlin and Schooler 1978; Schieman et al. 2003). However, given the theoretical plausibility of their effects on anger processes, we might also expect noxious conditions to influence the activation, course, and management of anger in the workplace role-set.

Perceived inequity is one of the core sites of anger provocation. According to equity theory, perceptions of inequality in social roles foster feelings of frustration and anger (Ross and Van Willigen 1996). Getting less than one feels that he or she deserves is an unfair or unjust state of affairs (deCarufel 1979). Feeling underpaid probably yields some of the highest levels of anger, especially the type of anger that persists over time and contributes to both episodic anger *and* angry moods that may contribute to other mental health outcomes like depression. This is an important path for research because most prior evidence about the effects of feeling underpaid focus primarily on depression not anger (Mirowsky and Ross 2003a). Moreover, a 2005 survey of U.S. adults shows that the *majority* of workers report feeling underpaid (Schieman 2005a).

Coser (1974) describes work as a "greedy institution" that exacts effort and energy from its workers, especially workers in higher-status positions (Hodson 2004). In general, being the target of another's greed likely spawns unpleasant emotions, including variants of anger. Moreover, work often contains intricate social arrangements that provide the fuel for a substantial portion of our affective life. Collectively, these ideas identify the work context as an ideal domain for analyses of anger processes and their links to social structure and organization.

THE FAMILY CONTEXT.   Outside the workplace, people tend to spend a good deal of time engaged in activities associated with family roles. As I have already mentioned, some of the most intense experiences of emotion occur in close, intimate bonds. For many individuals, marriage represents "the highest emotional highs and the lowest emotional lows experienced in adult life" (Carstensen et al. 1996:233). Likewise, parenting is linked to an array of positive and negative emotions, although anger is especially salient. According to Dix (1991:3), "average parents report high levels of anger with their children, the need to engage in techniques to control their anger, and fear that they will at some time lose control and harm their children." By extension, family roles provide ample opportunities for exposure to the sites of anger provocation (Carpenter and Halberstadt 1996; Scherer and Tannenbaum 1986).

Stress research has documented the effects of marital and parental roles on emotional distress, especially depression and anxiety (Mirowsky and Ross 2003a). Although the evidence about family context and anger is limited, some studies show that adults who reside in households with children under the age of 18 years (Ross and Van Willigen 1996; Simon and Nath 2004) or with coresidents *of any age* tend to have a higher level of anger (Schieman 1999). These findings are consistent with the notion that anger is a highly social emotion—it takes two (usually) to spark anger. Individuals who live together tend to share finite amounts of space and resources. To some degree, then, interpersonal conflict with members of the household is inevitable. Incompatibilities emerge in expectations and behaviors, from the trivial annoyances (i.e., dishes left in the sink) to the more serious violations that incite anger (i.e., playing loud music at 3 A.M.). By extension, this is fertile terrain for the most common sites of anger provocation like inequity, unfairness, goal impediments, and so on. In addition, the unequal distribution of responsibilities for household duties reflects a more structural source of strife. The division of household labor is often unequal, with women absorbing the bulk of housework and parenthood duties (Bird 1999; Fuma 2005). Equity theory predicts that inequity in the division of household labor should generate feelings of irascibility, frustration, and anger (Ross and Van Willigen 1996). Likewise, the parenthood role entails responsibilities that tax energy and time and increases the likelihood of affective exchange, frustration, and anger provocation (Pearlin and Turner 1987). Although parenthood provides opportunities for many positive emotions, like love and joy, there are other elements that likely activate annoyance and anger (Dix 1991). Nagging about chores, disagreement about freedoms, and the highly emotional act of discipline are only a few. Moreover, gender variations in anger may be partly attributable to the amount of time women spend with their children. Recent evidence from the Panel Study of Income Dynamics shows that mothers engage in active care with their children an average of 24 hours per week, whereas fathers average about 5 weekly hours (Folbre et al. 2005). Therefore, simply by spending more time with children, women are probably exposed to a higher level of anger-eliciting events.

In family contexts, money issues are also especially relevant for the sites of anger provocation (Carpenter and Halberstadt 1996). Financial issues are interpersonal issues, especially when linked to marital and parenting roles, because they often require planning, sharing, negotiation, and reconciliation. Money may not be able to buy happiness, but *not* having enough money to pay for basic needs or desired objects probably contributes to aggravation and dissatisfaction. Moreover, when times are tight, the lack of money may feel like the root of all anger. Economic hardship can diminish one's sense of identity as a "good provider" for the family, especially for men in more traditional households (Pleck 1977). Because of its connection to social and economic disadvantage, sociologists have long recognized economic hardship as one of the most powerful predictors of anxiety or depression (Mirowsky and Ross 2003a). However, theoretical ideas about anger also underscore the potential effects of economic hardship because of its unique connection to goal impediments, injustice, inequity, and threats to identity. Despite the theoretical plausibility of such linkages and the few studies that link economic hardship (Ross and Van Willigen 1997) or greater dissatisfaction with their finances (Schieman 1999) to anger, the associations between economic hardship and anger processes—especially in the family context—have yet to be fully investigated.

Anger processes may also mediate the negative effects of economic hardship on marital quality and stability. Conger and his colleagues (1990) found that hostile, irritable affective responses contributed to the link between economic hardship and negative outcomes in marital dyads, especially for men. Criticism, anger, and threatening gestures in marital interactions ultimately influence perceptions about the quality of marriage and thoughts about marital dissolution and potentially escalate into more serious forms of violence. Some scholars suggest that economic hardship increases the risk for domestic violence (Straus et al. 1980). Collectively, these processes can also influence the well-being of children. Perceptions of hostile, overt conflict between parents (Gerard and Buehler 1999) or between a parent and the youth (Harold and Conger 1997) play a part in the development of young adults' problem behaviors.

Family relations contain expectations about being loved, valued, and esteemed. What happens when these expectations are unrealized? Social psychologists have examined the extent to which the lack of identity verification in close, intimate relationships contributes to negative emotions such as depression and hostility (Burke and Stets 1999). These issues are especially relevant in the family context, and they gel with theories of anger that underscore the importance of perceived threats to identity; for example, Stets and Burke (2005) describe a process in which threats to identity meanings raise the likelihood that one partner in an intimate relationship will seek to exert control over the partner in order to restore identity verification. Control over one's partner compensates for one's own diminished sense of control. This wielding of power is also designed to prompt the other to verify one's identity. Power generally allows individuals to control another person, forcing actions in another that would otherwise not have occurred (Homans 1974). However, when the reassertion of control is unsuccessful and deficits in identity verification remain, the risk increases for physical aggression "as a last resort" to reestablish control (Stets and Burke 2005). Actors use *interpersonal* control to reestablish identity verification and aggression to regain a sense of *personal* control (in the generalized sense).

Johnson and Ferraro (2000) identify the need for greater theoretical understanding of interpersonal aggression in domestic situations, underscoring the potential influence of interpersonal control as a critical factor. Family arguments may spawn domestic violence, especially if the urge for control prompts an actor to "lash out" with aggression that "usually is relatively mild, and injury is not serious" (Stets and Burke 2005:164). Variants of anger play important roles in these processes. For example, an actor may feel anger at the lack of identity verification in the intimate dyad. As I have mentioned, threats to the self-concept or identity are among the principal elicitors of anger. Therefore, anger *precedes* the assertion of interpersonal control, functioning as a motivator of action. Anger has interpersonal utility as a means of communication and control; its expression helps actors establish positions about objects and ideas (including identities) in social relations (Levenson 1994). Feelings of power and self-assurance often accompany anger (Izard 1991), so individuals may use anger as a *means* of interpersonal control in order to reestablish a desired goal, such as identity verification.

Alternatively, anger could be an outcome instead of aggression. Aggression that is relatively mild and yields nonserious injury may simply be one "notch" above intense anger that generates a form of verbal aggression. Therefore, verbal aggression that is laced with intense anger might be a substitute for physical aggression. Pushing, hitting, or breaking things are not necessary in order to expel force or influence. Expressed anger can create an interpersonal climate in which interpersonal control processes yield the desired outcomes. However, little is known about these interpersonal dynamics and their implications for anger processes or *mild* aggression. How is the verbal expression of intense anger, rage, or fury different from or intertwined with mild aggression in form and consequence? In my judgment, Stets and Burke's (2005) depiction of the interplay between interpersonal control, the generalized sense of control (self-efficacy), and aggression generates provocative questions about the complex links between control and anger. The fact that the sense of personal control is rooted in objective and subjective levels of power in social roles and social conditions reinforces the linkages among structural arrangements, psychosocial resources, and "everyday" emotions like anger.

There is an overlooked dimension of the processes described above: being the target of another's attempts at interpersonal control or aggression. Goal impediments are critical elements here because of the centrality of interpersonal control, which restricts another's activity and is generally oppressive. These are quintessential triggers of anger. Interpersonal control is a basic element of most forms of social exchange, so people may expect it to some degree, although such expectations are largely shaped by context (Goffman 1959). If a "certain amount" of interpersonal control is expected, then anger could be especially strong when an actor attempts to wield interpersonal control beyond an expected or acceptable amount (or in an inappropriate social context). In such instances, interpersonal control may evoke resistance and anger in the target and, in turn, modify the intensity, expression, and consequences of anger for both parties.

Although work and family contexts provide ample opportunities for anger independently of each other, conflicts *between* those contexts are also common stressors (Bellavia and Frone 2005). Such conflicts represent a form of chronic stress because of their enduring, repetitive nature and its link to major institutional roles of work and family (Pearlin 1983). Role strain theory posits that demands, responsibilities, and expectations in multiple roles vie for one's time, attention, and energy (Frone 2003). Interference between work and nonwork domains potentially undermines the capacity for individuals to adequately perform role-related duties. The incompatible demands related to family-role and work-role obligations likely contribute to goal impediments, feelings of unfairness or inequity, and threats to identity or self-concept. The subsequent implications for anger processes remain unknown because, as I have reported for other chronic stressors, most research on the effects of work-family conflict focuses on depression or anxiety (Schieman et al. 2003).

THE NEIGHBORHOOD CONTEXT. Work and family domains are intricately connected to a third relatively unexamined social context: the neighborhood. The social, economic, and interpersonal dimensions of neighborhood domains evoke an array of affective responses in everyday life. There are two main reasons that neighborhood contexts might influence anger: the presence of neighborhood problems and the quality of social relations in neighborhoods. These are not separate issues because the quality of neighborhood conditions is relevant for the quality of relationships among neighbors, as well as the perceptions that neighbors have of each other.

The subjective appraisal of neighborhood problems and objective indicators of socioeconomic disadvantages (i.e., the percentage of households in poverty in a census tract) are the most commonly studied aspects of neighborhood context (Schieman 2005b). Perceived neighborhood problems reflect the observable signs of social disorder and physical decay that residents encounter in their daily pursuit of activities in work, family, leisure, and informal relationships. Neighborhood problems include ambient hazards such as noise, trash, graffiti, dilapidated or run-down buildings, and so on (Ross and Mirowsky 1999). Some scholars have referred to these problems as "social and physical incivilities" (LaGrange et al. 1992). The associations between neighborhood problems and depression or mistrust are well documented (Mirowsky and Ross 2003a). Likewise, neighborhood problems are associated negatively with neighborhood satisfaction (Guest and Lee 1983; Herting and Guest 1985) and the desire to purchase a house in the neighborhood (Emerson et al. 2001). However, the effects of neighborhood problems on anger processes remain unclear.

Sociologists who have examined associations between neighborhood racial composition and residential preferences or neighborhood evaluations describe the effects of neighborhood contexts on residents' choices, attitudes, and behaviors (Bobo and Zubrinksy 1996; Harris 2001). Perceived threats in the neighborhood shape people's perceptions of race, neighborhood disadvantages, and patterns of residential choice, evaluation, mobility, and segregation (Chiricos et al. 1997). Studies of residential preferences and neighborhood evaluations imply that residing near blacks is stressful, especially for whites, who feel that they are part of the racial minority (Chiricos et al. 2001). This is a dimension that remains largely unacknowledged in the residential preferences and neighborhood evaluation literatures. For some residents, racial composition represents a chronic *stressor* either indirectly because of its association with other community-level disadvantages such as crime and poverty or directly because of its link to racial prejudice (Clark 1992; Farley et al. 1994; Harris 1999, 2001). As I have mentioned, perceived threat is a core form of chronic stress *and* a site of anger provocation. Therefore, the exploration of the connections among those neighborhood processes, perceived threat, and anger would provide new insights that distinguish anger processes from other emotional experiences, especially anxiety (fear) or depression; for example, to what extent do anger, fear, and depression contribute to individuals' motivation to leave neighborhoods once the presence of a recognizable minority group exceeds a particular threshold? Anger potentially mediates the association between neighborhood problems and levels of dissatisfaction with neighborhood or the desire to relocate.

Another potential source of anger related to neighborhood context and stress processes involves role captivity (Pearlin 1983). Some residents may feel trapped in the role of "resident" in their neighborhood. They wish to relocate but possess insufficient resources to do so; this represents a chronic stressor. The combination of role captivity and high levels of neighborhood problems could exacerbate feelings of anger. Black individuals experience this form of adversity more often because of barriers associated with racial discrimination (South and Crowder 1998; South and Deane 1993). Residential segregation and discrimination represent core sites of anger provocation because they involve goal impediments, injustice, unfairness, and threats to identity, among other things. The discussion of racial segregation and discrimination raises important questions about race patterns in anger. In their analysis of the 1996 General Social Survey (GSS), Mabry and Kiecolt (2005) found that blacks did not report a higher frequency of anger than whites, nor were there differences in the expression of anger. Space limitations restrict a broader and more complete discussion of race and anger, although most of the differences probably depend on race-linked variations in exposure to the sites of anger provocation.

Sociologists, especially those focusing on the form and consequences of urban life, have long been interested in the ways that macrolevel structures influence the "social fabric" of community life and levels of "community attachments" (Kasarda and Janowitz 1974). However, there are numerous and complex microlevel dimensions consisting of both supportive and conflictive social ties that coalesce to create the overall social climate of communities (Schieman 2005b). Levels of community attachment could be a function of, among other things, an individual resident's affective bonds to other residents, the place itself, and his or her involvement in social roles in the community. The specific human relationships in the community probably contain mostly positive affect, although negative forms are also plausible. With respect to levels of "community attachment," it is likely that the quality and extent of actual human attachments in the community contribute to the more general level of attachment to the broader community or neighborhood. According to the systemic view of community social organization, individuals are embedded within a complex web of social relations that involve mutual obligations, responsibilities, and expectations (Sampson 1988). Likewise, Putnam's (2000) concept of "bonding social capital" identifies the importance of strong social ties that connect individuals to friends, relatives, and neighbors. However, where there are opportunities for mutual obligations, trust, and reciprocity, there are also chances for mistrust, inequity, and irresponsible or unreliable behavior—all sites of anger provocation.

Neighborhood disadvantages also highlight inequalities in neighborhoods. Long ago, Marx identified the psychological impact of disadvantaged socioeconomic comparisons, asserting that one's "house may be large or small; as long as the surrounding houses are equally small, it satisfies all social demands for a dwelling. But let a palace arise beside the little house, and it shrinks from a little house to a hut" (Marx 1933:33). Visible inequalities reflect unremitting cues that some residents have more property, status, and power, thereby fostering conditions of perceived relative deprivation, injustice, resentment, and anger. These ideas are consistent with a strand of social comparison theory that involves perceptions of relative deprivation and explicitly predicts anger as an outcome of perceived inequality. According to Singer (1982:88):

> [T]he essence of both relative deprivation and the deprivational form of inequality is that a person (group) wants X; does not have it; and feels entitled to it—that is, expects to get it—on the basis of comparison with similar others...or on the basis of awareness of the norms governing the situation....The outcome of such feelings of inequality or relative deprivation is a sense of injustice, perhaps accompanied in our society by anger."

Neighborhoods provide a context for the visible disparities between individuals, reminding residents that some individuals have received greater material rewards or possess higher levels of status in society. Moreover, residents also possess values and standards about the quality of neighborhood life. Community- or individual-level conditions that violate or threaten those standards might evoke anger, although those effects likely vary across levels of objective socioeconomic standing. Some evidence shows that individuals who experience improving personal circumstances feel the angriest about lingering inequities (deCarufel 1979; Olson and Hazlewood 1986). Visible disparities among residents provide chronic reminders that some people possess more than others, yielding feelings of injustice and anger.

In sum, other than the workplace and household, neighborhoods represent another of the most potentially frustrating interpersonal domains in social life; for example, if some residents have expectations about desirable noise levels or the appearance of property, then there will undoubtedly be instances in which those expectations are violated either by other residents or, depending on the location of one's home, outsiders. What are the emotional effects of the violation of expectations? If someone defines having a "quiet neighborhood" as a central goal, then noise represents a goal impediment (especially if one is trying to sleep). If having a tidy front yard is a priority, then excessive clutter will disturb some residents. If having clean streets is an important standard, then excessive litter is a violation. These are classic sites of anger provocation that will likely yield some degree of strife among people sharing the same space, making it all the more difficult to "love thy neighbor."

THE SOCIAL DISTRIBUTION OF ANGER

In a classic volume that defined a research agenda for the emerging *Sociology of Emotions* area, Gordon (1990:161) claimed that an individual's position in the social structure shapes the "type, frequency, and intensity of emotions that will be directed toward him or her or aroused in him or her." Sociologists who study emotions have sought to document and describe the emotional correlates and consequences of social stratification (Smith-Lovin 1995), contributing to an "epidemiology" of emotions (Thoits 1989). A parallel interest exists in the sociological study of mental health. Many researchers have explored ways that socially structured inequality shapes an array of emotional/mental health outcomes, usually depression or anxiety (McLeod and Nonnemaker 1999; Turner et al. 1995) and, more recently, anger (Ross and Van Willigen 1996, 1997; Schieman 1999). There is an essential difference between anger and other emotions that surfaces here: Most analyses of depression and anxiety focus on their *frequency* only; by contrast, anger "straddles" the sociologies of emotions and mental health because inquiries often extend beyond the frequency of anger to elements such as the course, management, expression, and consequences of anger as a process (Schieman 2000; Simon and Nath 2004; Stets and Tsushima 2001). Sociologists of mental health have used the stress process model as a guiding framework because it posits that stressors are distributed unequally across core social statuses, especially gender, age, and social class (Pearlin 1999). Likewise, sociologists who study emotions could apply this perspective to understand emotions like anger.

Gender

Stereotypes about gender differences in emotions imply that women experience emotions more frequently and have less of a capacity for self-control (Shields 1986), whereas men tend to "lace up" their feelings in a process that Jansz (2000) refers to as "restrictive emotionality." However, *anger may be the exception*. Lay and clinical views label anger an "acceptable male emotion," suggesting that men are more comfortable with anger (Kring 2000). Stereotypes of anger as a masculine emotion legitimate it as assertive or powerful, whereas traditionally feminine nurturing roles discourage anger among women (Mirowsky and Ross 1995). Consistent with those stereotypes, gender socialization processes tend to encourage qualities that are congruous with male anger, such as competitiveness and combativeness (Ross and Van Willigen 1996).

As a status characteristic, gender molds relational conditions and behavioral expectations (Ridgeway 1993). Gender ideologies sustain "gender strategies" or enduring scripts that shape emotional regulation (Hochschild 1990). Strachan and Dutton (1992:1721) assert that "behavioral expectations based on gender encompass many aspects of interpersonal relationships including rules that govern gender-appropriate affect." By extension, display rules dictate that if women get angry, they are expected *not* to show it (Brody 1999). If women *do* express anger, they risk being labeled "hostile," "neurotic," or "unladylike" (Sharkin 1993; Tavris 1989). Moreover, women often fear that anger expression will exact a cost to their sense of self and their relationships (Egerton 1988). Some evidence suggests that people are likely to rate male leaders as less effective when they express sadness, but rate female leaders less effective if they express sadness *or* anger (Lewis 2000). Likewise, Hess et al. (2005:534) assert that "women who appear too affiliative may encounter social disapproval when showing anger." However, the nature and consequences of these dynamics for anger processes will likely vary across role contexts, like work and family, because of variations in the relevance of those role identities for one's sense of self-worth (Stets and Tsushima 2001).

Studies about individuals' *perceptions* of gender and emotion support the view that women experience and express emotions more often and intensely than men (Johnson and Shulman 1988). However, anger is the exception. For example, adults perceive men as expressing anger more often (Fabes and Martin 1991). Moreover, stereotypes imply that men should report more frequent anger. Are the stereotypes accurate? Some studies show that women tend to report a greater frequency of anger (Ross and Van Willigen 1996; Schieman 2005a; Strachan and Dutton 1992). By contrast, analyses of the 1996 GSS did not find gender differences in the frequency of anger (Schieman

1999). Others document that men express anger more frequently (Fischer 1993) or fail to detect gender differences in expression (Averill 1982; Kopper and Epperson 1991). Another analysis of the 1996 GSS found that, once angered, women think about the anger more, talk to the person they feel angry with more, and take longer to stop feeling angry (Schieman 2000). Mirowsky and Ross (1995) found that women are more likely than men to express their anger by yelling. In addition, although people tend to *perceive* that men's anger is more intense (Kring 2000), women tend to report more intense anger than men (Simon and Nath 2004; Stets and Tsushima 2001). In sum, gender differences in the frequency of anger are less clear than the quality, perceptions, or interpersonal consequences of anger experiences. People have many opinions about gender and patterns of anger, but the evidence does not consistently corroborate those opinions.

Age

Age is a fundamental marker of social status, stratification, and position across the life course. As such, it provides a basis for expecting systematic variations in anger processes in accordance with age-linked life events, social relationships, role incumbencies and qualities, and possession of psychosocial resources. The few studies of age patterns in anger document a negative association between age and the frequency of anger (Carstensen et al. 2000; Mirowsky and Ross 2003a; Schieman 1999; Schieman et al. 2005b). In addition, analyses of the 1996 GSS indicate that older adults are less likely to agree with the statement "when I am angry I let people know" (Schieman 2000). Moreover, when angered, older adults are *less likely* than younger adults to talk to the target of their anger, try to think differently about the anger-provoking situation, try to change the situation by doing something, drink alcohol or take pills, or talk to someone else about the anger. Although older people report less intense anger, there are no age differences in the average duration of anger or the perception about the appropriateness of the anger response (Schieman 2000; Simon and Nath 2004).

Little is known about the reasons for the negative association between age and the frequency of anger, the potential mediating and moderating factors, and the age-related changes in anger. Here, the application of stress process and life course theories can guide our thinking because these paradigms underscore age-correlated role stressors and psychosocial resources (Pearlin and Skaff 1996; Schieman et al. 2001). Age-linked patterns in the structural and subjective organization of people's lives provide a basis for suspecting systematic age variations in exposures to the sites of anger provocation. As described above, work and family roles generate ample opportunities for such exposures. Life course theory illustrates the ways that age influences the content, configuration, and meaning of social roles; for example, young adulthood often involves initial entry into the labor force and the encounter of novel workplace experiences, including the sometimes complex interpersonal dynamics associated with job authority. By contrast, older workers have likely spent much of their lives in the workforce; some may have even spent most of their working lives in the same place of employment so they may have long acclimated to work-related stressors (Schieman et al. 2005b). Moreover, many older adults are preparing to or already have left the labor force via retirement. Although retirement is not necessarily a "stress-free" period (Ross and Drentea 1998), most feel released from the demands, conflicts, and interpersonal strife of workplace settings and, by extension, the elicitors of anger.

Young adulthood is often a time of budding intimate relationships, family formation, and the establishment of a household. By contrast, these patterns change in later life as older adults encounter death of friends and relatives, the exit of children from the household and the "empty nest" period, and the death of a spouse or partner. Likewise, the fact that marital quality tends to increase during the early years of marriage, declines until midlife, and then rises steadily in the later years may be related to the rise and fall of role-related responsibilities and stressors (Orbuch et al. 1996). Older people are less likely to have children or teenagers living in their home—often a primary source of anger (Dix 1991; Schieman 1999). Therefore, in addition to fewer exposures to anger elicitors associated with childcare, older adults are less likely to have parental responsibilities that absorb their time and attention, leaving more time for other activities such as leisure. These processes may contribute to some of the decrease in marital dissatisfaction among older adults (White and Edwards 1990).

Disengagement theory summarizes these processes by predicting that the elderly are more likely to exit salient social roles and their associated expectations, obligations, and responsibilities (Cumming and Henry 1961). Although disengagement theory has its critics, the contention that role exits liberate individuals from the potential exposure to sites of anger provocation is worth consideration. Disengagement might more appropriately refer to freedom from social roles that are associated with stressors. It is clear that age-related shifts or losses in work and family roles reduce the number and intensity of close social bonds (Carstensen et al. 1996; Havighurst et al. 1996). Although role changes sometimes evoke "withdrawal" or "aversion" emotions, such as sadness or fear, the likelihood of anger should decrease if those role changes reduce exposure to the core sites of anger provocation in work and family contexts.

Psychosocial resources also vary with age, thus potentially reducing the experience of some negative emotions like anger; for example, Mirowsky and Ross's (1992) view of "age as maturity" posits that with advancing age, people become better equipped to cultivate more stable intimate relationships that contain fewer conflicts. Although those authors applied this view to predict a negative association between age and depression, it is also relevant for anger. Age affords time and experience to "weed out" social relations that contain high levels of incompatible beliefs, values, attitudes, and lifestyle choices (Keltner 1996; Neugarten 1996). According to Birditt and Fingerman (2005), older adults tend to be better at regulating their behavioral responses to inter-personal conflicts than their younger peers. These ideas are consistent with Carstensen's (1992) "social-emotional selectivity" theory, which predicts that adults in late life are more effective than younger adults at conserving their emotions, possess more self-control, and have a greater capacity for tolerance, even in circumstances that present conflict. Age itself affords time and experience that can enhance the ability to manage emotional responses to frustrating and unpredictable features of daily life (Keltner 1996). Collectively, these ideas support the view that older people should report less anger. However, rising levels of physical impairment and lower levels of personal control in late life potentially offset some of the other conditions that diminish anger. In addition, the paradox of higher levels of depression and lower levels of anger in late life might offer new insights into the processes associated with these different emotions (Mirowsky and Ross 2003a; Schieman 1999; Schieman et al. 2001).

Social Class

Education level, occupation, and income reflect sources of status, inequality, and resources that link individuals to forms of social organization and culture that, in turn, influence emotional life. It is well established that education level and income are associated negatively with depression and anxiety (McLeod and Nonnemaker 1999). However, the associations between dimensions of social class and anger processes are less clear (Schieman 2000). In a 1990 survey of U.S. households, for example, Mirowsky and Ross (1995) found that education level is associated negatively with sadness, anxiety, malaise, and aches and positively with happiness, but *unrelated* to anger. However, they found that education level is related negatively to the behavioral dimension of anger: yelling at someone. Others have found that education level is unrelated to (Schieman 1999) or associated negatively with the frequency of anger (Ross and Van Willigen 1996). Yet, summarizing the education-anger association beyond the *frequency* of anger is complex for two reasons: (1) the multifaceted nature of education's link to status, power, personal resources, and stratification and (2) the complexity of anger processes.

Education level is a component of socioeconomic status and a reflection of status credentials (Ross and Mirowsky 1999). Moreover, it is a pathway to higher-status attainments associated with occupational and financial domains across the life course (Schieman et al. 2005b). However, education's benefits extend beyond these status attainments to a variety of psychosocial benefits. Education challenges individuals with a variety of social and intellectual problems, providing opportunities for the development of cognitive abilities such as the sense of control (Mirowsky and Ross 2003b). From a human capital perspective, education also symbolizes competence, potential, and persistence—traits that are often highly valued in the labor market (Becker 1993). Moreover, education's structural benefits are also apparent in the fact that the well educated are less likely to have jobs that are routine, dangerous, and lack autonomy (Ross and Van Willigen 1997; Schieman 2002).

Theoretically, the psychosocial and occupational benefits of education should shield the well educated from the sites of anger provocation and provide resources to manage the course, expression, and consequences of anger; however, evidence has not substantiated this claim. The higher-status elements of education might increase some workplace stressors that off-set its overall emotional benefits; for example, as a "status credential," education increases the likelihood of having a job with more job authority and pay, which, in turn, often in-creases levels of expectations, responsibilities, and time commitments (Mirowsky and Ross 2003b). Taken together, then, higher levels of education, income, and job authority are in-dicators of higher status in the workplace that might elevate the risk for anger provocations. These positions afford more opportunities to *express* variants of angerlike emotions toward oth-ers in the workplace role-set without fear of retribution. According to Conway and colleagues (1999:292), "people who occupy higher status can effectively claim such status with displays of anger and disgust aimed at low-status others." In that respect, anger is an assertion of sta-tus, power, and authority—conditions that are distributed unequally across social class. To date, the nature of these interrelationships remains unknown, providing abundant paths for future analyses.

POWER, THE SENSE OF CONTROL, AND THE UTILITY OF ANGER

The sense of control (or mastery) involves the extent to which one feels in control of events and outcomes in everyday life (Pearlin and Schooler 1978). It reflects the self as a causal agent (Gecas and Burke 1995). People with a high sense of control disagree with the notion that they have little power or influence over the things that happen to them. They reject the claim that fate or luck determines their course through life. Although there is a long tradition of inquiry of the relationship between perceived control and depression (Mirowsky and Ross 2003a), its associations with anger processes remain relatively unexplored. Given the personal resource elements of personal control, it is plausible that people with a high sense of control experience less frequent anger. The evidence is mixed: An analysis of the 1996 GSS found a negative association between the sense of control and the frequency of anger (Schieman 1999), whereas another U.S. survey found no association

(Ross and Van Willigen 1997). The sense of control's association with other aspects of anger processes is also unclear, although its links to power and status provide provocative ideas about its effects on anger expression and the utility of anger.

The general sense of control is associated positively with the extent to which people possess power or potency in actual, objective conditions (Mirowsky and Ross 2003a). Power, in addition to being a critical element of the sense of control, is deeply embedded in the concept of anger. In fact, anger is a *power* emotion. Kemper (1991:334) contends that anger "helps the organism mobilize to resist deprivation of vital resources." Shaver and colleagues (1987:1078) found that people who felt angry also felt themselves "becoming stronger (higher in potency) and more energized in order to fight or rail against the cause of anger." Moreover, people often report that they feel powerful and potent when they experience or express anger (Berkowitz and Harmon-Jones 2004). Anger helps people move against others or unfavorable conditions.

Emotional displays also convey messages about one's status and power in structural arrangements (Clark 1990). Individuals tend to perceive anger as powerful and indicative of status (Tiedens 2001; Tiedens et al. 2000) and associate angry facial expressions, relative to sad faces, with more powerful positions (Keating 1985). The expression or communication of anger contributes to the *social* significance of any specific anger episode (Canary et al. 1998). However, the degree to which anger is regarded as a high-potency emotion may vary according to one's position in different social contexts. As I discussed above, such contexts are defined by major institutionalized social roles and the broader dimensions of social stratification that characterize them. Status and power in role domains are associated positively with the sense of personal control (Mirowsky and Ross 2003a) and, in turn, increase the likelihood of "status assertion anger" (i.e., anger that is felt and expressed as a means for the actor to display status or exert power over others). Under conditions of high personal control, anger has utility—at *appropriate* levels of intensity and duration—in motivating or coercing others to act in a desired manner. Here, anger is different from other emotions in that actors often ask: "Was my anger appropriate?" Although this might also occur for other emotions, it is likely more common with respect to anger (a hypothesis worth testing). Moreover, the actor's perceived appropriateness of anger influences the perception of its *usefulness* (Weber 2004).

Power, status, and authority contribute to the utility of anger. Anger may occur more often in situations in which individuals wish to be perceived by others as dominant (Canary et al. 1998). Currents of power flow through this form of anger. Moreover, anger reinforces and energizes that power. According to some appraisal theories of emotions, the display of anger is associated with perceived and actual power, or a "power potential" (Frijda 1986; Scherer 1999). Averill (1997) contends that power is an essential requirement of anger display because it lends an air of legitimacy to the actor who is displaying anger. Someone who expresses anger in order to deal with the anger-provoking event risk being viewed by the target as a fraud if he or she does not possess the necessary level of power for such actions. Status legitimizes the assertion of anger because people in higher-status positions have a "right" to use some variant of anger to achieve their aims. Anger ultimately might be a means of social control. Therefore, it is not surprising that some people use anger as a means to control others (Fitness 2000; Glomb 2002).

Collectively, these ideas identify a central role for power and status in anger processes—extending Kemper's ideas about the ways that power and status shape the elicitation of anger and contributing to the distinctions between anger and other emotions such as depression or anxiety. However, there is another side of the power dynamic to consider. Power involves relations in which one individual achieves desired outcomes or responses from another even when the other resists. The weaker party in the power dynamic is overcome and complies with the assertion of power in an involuntary manner. According to Kemper (1991:332):

[P]ower consists of all the actions that can be taken to gain, assert, and maintain power, including actual and threatened physical force, confinement or blocking freedom of movement, deprivation of valued objects, symbolic debasements such as insults and other verbal abuse, withdrawal of previously given rewards, sensory intrusions such as screaming and shouting, ignoring or dismissing the other's initiatives such as interrupting speech, or failing to recognize the other's proactions, and the like.

Kemper refers to these as the "everyday means and devices of coercion" that have as their central goal the compliance of an otherwise obstinate individual. Assertions of power may take potentially destructive forms that include fraud, manipulation, deception, and so on. Ultimately, then, anger processes can occur on both ends of this power dynamic. The asserter of power uses anger to get another to do what he or she would otherwise not do. However, as mentioned above, being the target of another's anger or aggression is a classic trigger of anger. It is clear that interpersonal control and dominance flow through these social exchanges—but little is known about the ways that a generalized sense of control and anger processes influence (and are influenced by) power dynamics.

People with a low sense of personal control tend to blame external sources for the events and outcomes in their lives (Mirowsky and Ross 2003a). In the case of anger, attributions matter for the activation, course, and expression of anger. Kemper's (1990, 1991) power-status theory of emotion predicts that anger is an outcome in circumstances in which an individual loses power and status, the situation is deemed as remediable, and *the other actor is perceived as responsible* for that loss. The notion of blameworthiness reflects a long-standing debate in psychology about the importance of cognitive appraisals for anger processes (Clore and Centerbar 2004; Smith and Kirby 2004). In cognitive appraisals, the self is viewed as a potent agent with some degree of control over events or outcomes in the specific situation (Berkowitz and Harmon-Jones 2004). Expectations of control and the associated feelings of potency enable anger when events or outcomes deviate from a desired or anticipated path (and another person is blameworthy).

Research in this area could further distinguish anger processes from other emotions, especially sadness, because the relevance of the sense of control likely varies depending on the dimension of anger processes under review—the frequency, intensity, duration, expression, and the consequences of these dimensions of anger processes within different role contexts. Future research might also explore the extent to which people in different positions of authority in the workplace role-set experience the utility of anger; that is, they feel that they have to express annoyance, irritation, or anger at others in the role-set in order to get them to do something. This would shed light on the complex interplay among objective levels of power, subjective dimensions of generalized control, the assertion of interpersonal control, and anger processes. These same processes might be contrasted with power and status in other social contexts as well.

CONCLUSION

Anger is a social emotion and a power emotion. In my judgment, it is more useful to approach anger as a set of processes, including the activation, course, management, expression, and consequences. To some degree, this sets anger apart from other emotions. We rarely discuss the suppression of depression, the intensity of shame, the duration of surprise, the management of happiness, or the consequences of disgust. Anger is unique in this regard because these elements have special relevance for the experience of anger as a process. I believe we can learn a great deal about social life by studying anger processes. Sociologists can contribute to the "affective sciences," more generally, by documenting and describing anger processes as they exist in socially patterned forms of social organization—work, family, neighborhood, and so on. Unfortunately, because of space limitations, I was unable to examine other potentially important areas, including (but not limited to) the effects of friendships, different forms of religiosity and anger processes, and the more political/social movement elements of anger.

The inclusion of questions about anger processes in the 1996 General Social Survey has inspired a growing number of scholars to pursue novel research questions about anger. In addition, the burgeoning interest in pursuing the synergy between the sociologies of emotions and mental health will likely promote a more comprehensive agenda for sociologists specializing in both arenas, contributing to the discovery of the ways that emotions like anger connect with the focal outcomes linked to mental health. Moreover, the cross-fertilization of theoretical and empirical perspectives will further explicate and refine our understanding about the ways that social structure and organization influence the affective experiences in everyday life.

REFERENCES

Anderson, Craig A., William E. Deuser, and Kristina M. DeNeve. 1995. "Hot Temperatures, Hostile Affect, Hostile Cognition, and Arousal: Tests of a General Model of Affective Aggression." *Personality and Social Psychology Bulletin* 21: 434–448.

Andersson, Lynne M., and Christine M. Pearson. 1999. "Tit for Tat? The Spiraling Effect of Incivility in the Workplace." *Academy of Management Review* 24: 452–471.

Averill, James R. 1982. *Anger and Aggression: An Essay on Emotion.* New York: Springer-Verlag.

———. 1997. "The Emotions: An Integrative Approach." Pp. 513–541 in *Handbook of Personality Psychology*, edited by R. Hogan, J. A. Johnson, and S. R. Briggs. San Diego: Academic.

Becker, Gary S. 1993. *Human Capital.* New York: Columbia University Press.

Bellavia, Gina M., and Michael R. Frone. 2005. "Work-Family Conflict." Pp. 113–148 in *Handbook of Work Stress*, edited by J. Barling, E. Kevin Kelloway, and M. R. Frone. Thousand Oaks, CA: Sage.

Berkowitz, Leonard, and Eddie Harmon-Jones. 2004. "Toward an Understanding of the Determinants of Anger." *Emotion* 2: 107–130.

Bird, Chloe E. 1999. "Gender, Household Labor, and Psychological Distress: The Impact of the Amount and Division of Housework." *Journal of Health and Social Behavior* 40: 32–45.

Birditt, Kira S., and Karen L. Fingerman. 2005. "Do We Get Better at Picking Our Battles? Age Group Differences in Descriptions of Behavioral Reactions to Interpersonal Tensions." *Journals of Gerontology: Psychological Sciences* 60: 121–128.

Bobo, Lawrence, and Camille L. Zubrinsky. 1996. "Attitudes on Racial Integration: Perceived Status Differences, Mere In-Group Preferences, or Racial Prejudice?" *Social Forces* 74: 883–909.

Bougie, Roger, Rik Pieters, and Marcel Zeelenberg. 2003. "Angry Customers Don't Come Back, They Get Back: The Experience and Behavioral Implications of Anger and Dissatisfaction in Services." *Journal of the Academy of Marketing Science* 31: 377–393.

Brody, Leslie R. 1999. *Gender, Emotion, and the Family.* Cambridge, MA: Harvard University Press.

Burke, Peter J., and Jan E. Stets. 1999. "Trust and Commitment through Self-Verification." *Social Psychology Quarterly* 62: 347–360.

Canary, Daniel J., Brian H. Spitzberg, and Beth A. Semic. 1998. "The Experience and Expression of Anger in Interpersonal Settings." Pp. 189–213 in *Handbook of Communication and Emotion: Research, Theory, Applications, and Contexts*, edited by P. A. Andersen and L. K. Guerrero. San Diego: Academic.

Carpenter, Sandra, and Amy G. Halberstadt. 1996. "What Makes People Angry? Laypersons' and Psychologists' Categorizations of Anger in the Family." *Cognition and Emotion* 10: 627–656.

Carstensen, Laura L. 1992. "Social and Emotional Patterns in Adulthood: Support for Socioemotional Selectivity Theory." *Psychology and Aging* 7: 331–338.

Carstensen, Laura L., Jeremy Graff, Robert W. Levenson, and John M. Gottman. 1996. "Affect in Intimate Relationships." Pp. 227–248 in *Handbook of Emotion, Adult Development, and Aging*, edited by C. Magai and S. H. McFadden. San Diego: Academic.

Carstensen, Laura L., Monisha Pasupathi, Ulrich Mayr, and John R. Nesselroade. 2000. "Emotional Experience in Everyday Life Across the Adult Life Span." *Journal of Personality and Social Psychology* 79: 644–655.

Chiricos, Ted, Michael Hogan, and Marc Gertz. 1997. "Racial Composition of Neighborhood and Fear of Crime." *Criminology* 35: 107–129.

———. 2001. "Perceived Racial and Ethnic Composition of Neighborhood and Perceived Risk of Crime." *Social Problems* 48: 322–340.

Clark, Candace. 1990. "Emotions and Micropolitics in Everyday Life: Some Patterns and Paradoxes of 'Place.'" Pp. 305–333 in *Research Agendas in the Sociology of Emotions*, edited by T. D. Kemper. Albany: State University of New York Press.

Clark, William A. V. 1992. "Residential Preferences and Residential Choices in a Multiethnic Context." *Demography* 29: 451–466.

Clore, Gerald L., and David B. Centerbar. 2004. "Analyzing Anger: How to Make People Mad." *Emotion* 4: 139–144.

Clore, Gerald L., Andrew Ortony, Bruce Dienes, and Frank Fuijita. 1993. "Where Does Anger Dwell?" Pp. 57–87 in *Advances in Social Cognition: Perspectives on Anger and Emotion*, edited by R. S. Wyer Jr. and T. K. Srull. Hillsdale, NJ: Erlbaum.

Conger, Rand D., Glen H. Elder Jr., Frederick O. Lorenz, Katherine J. Conger, Ronald L. Simons, Les B. Whitbeck, Shirley Huck, and Janet N. Melby. 1990. "Linking Economic Hardship to Marital Quality and Instability." *Journal of Marriage and the Family* 52: 643–656.

Conway, Michael, Roberto Di Fazio, and Shari Mayman. 1999. "Judging Others' Emotions as a Function of the Others' Status." *Social Psychology Quarterly* 62: 291–305.

Coser, Lewis A. 1974. *Greedy Institutions*. New York: Free Press.

Cumming, Elaine, and William Henry. 1961. *Growing Old: The Process of Disengagement*. New York: Basic Books.

Cupach, W. R., and Daniel J. Canary. 1995. "Managing Conflict and Anger: Investigating the Sex Stereotype Hypothesis." Pp. 233–252 in *Gender, Power, and Communication in Human Relationships*, edited by P. Kalbfleisch and M. J. Cody. Hillsdale, NJ: Erlbaum.

Darwin, Charles. [1872] 1965. *The Expression of the Emotions in Man and Animals* (rev. ed.). Chicago: University of Chicago Press.

deCarufel, Andre. 1979. "Pay Secrecy, Social Comparison, and Relative Deprivation in Organizations." Pp. 181–200 in *Relative Deprivation and Social Comparison: The Ontario Symposium*, Vol. 4, edited by J. Olson, P. Herman, and M. Zanna. Hillsdale, NJ: Erlbaum.

Dix, T. 1991. "The Affective Organization of Parenting." *Psychological Bulletin* 110: 3–25.

Egerton, Muriel. 1988. "Passionate Women and Passionate Men: Sex Differences in Accounting for Angry and Weeping Episodes." *British Journal of Social Psychology* 27: 51–66.

Ekman, Paul. 1994a. "All Emotions Are Basic." Pp. 15–19 in *The Nature of Emotion: Fundamental Questions*, edited by P. Ekman and R. J. Davidson. New York: Oxford University Press.

———. 1994b. "Strong Evidence for Universals in Facial Expressions: A Reply to Russell's Mistaken Critique." *Psychological Bulletin* 155: 268–287.

Ekman, Paul, Wallace V. Friesen, Maureen O'Sullivan, and Anthony Chan. 1987. "Universals and Cultural Differences in the Judgments of Facial Expressions of Emotion." *Journal of Personality and Social Psychology* 53: 712–717.

Elliot, James R., and Ryan A. Smith. 2004. "Race, Gender, and Workplace Power." *American Sociological Review* 69: 365–386.

Elliot, Rebecca, and Raymond J. Dolan. 2003. "Functional Neuroimaging of Depression: A Role for Medial Prefrontal Cortex." Pp. 117–130 in *Handbook of the Affective Sciences*, edited by R. J. Davidson, H. Goldsmith, and K. R. Scherer. New York: Oxford University Press.

Ellsworth, Phoebe C., and Klaus R. Scherer. 2003. "Appraisal Processes in Emotion." Pp. 572–595 in *Handbook of the Affective Sciences*, edited by R. J. Davidson, H. Goldsmith, and K. R. Scherer. New York: Oxford University Press.

Emerson, Michael O., George Yancey, and Karen J. Chai. 2001. "Does Race Matter in Residential Segregation? Exploring the Preferences of White Americans." *American Sociological Review* 66: 922–935.

Fabes, Richard A., and Carol Lynn Martin. 1991. "Gender and Age Stereotypes of Emotionality." *Personality and Social Psychology Bulletin* 17: 532–540.

Farley, Reynolds, Charlotte Steeh, Maria Krysan, Tara Jackson, and Keith Reeves. 1994. "Stereotypes and Segregation: Neighborhoods in the Detroit Area." *American Journal of Sociology* 100: 750–780.

Fehr, Beverly, and Mark Baldwin. 1996. "Prototype and Script Analyses of Lay People's Knowledge of Anger." Pp. 219–246 in *Knowledge Structures in Close Relationships: A Social Psychological Analysis*, edited by G. J. O. Fletcher and J. Fitness. Hillsdale, NJ: Erlbaum.

Fisher, Agneta H. 1993. "Sex Differences in Emotionality." *Feminism and Psychology* 3: 308–318.

Fitness, Julie. 2000. "Anger in the Workplace: An Emotion Script Approach to Anger Episodes between Workers and their Superiors, Co-Workers and Subordinates." *Journal of Organizational Behavior* 21: 147–162.

Folbre, Nancy, Jayoung Yoon, Kade Finnoff, and Allison Sidle Fuligni. 2005. "By What Measure? Family Time Devoted to Children in the United States." *Demography* 42: 373–390.

Frijda, Nico H. 1986. *The Emotions*. Cambridge: Cambridge University Press.

Frone, Michael R. 2003. "Work-Family Balance." Pp. 143–162 in *Handbook of Occupational Health Psychology*, edited by J. C. Quick and L. E. Tetrick. Washington, DC: American Psychological Association.

Fuma, Makiko. 2005. "Macro-Level Gender Inequality and the Division of Household Labor in 22 Countries." *American Sociological Review* 69: 751–767.

Gecas, Viktor, and Peter J. Burke. 1995. "The Self-Concept." Pp. 41–51 in *Sociological Perspectives on Social Psychology*, edited by K. S. Cook, G. A. Fine, and J. S. House. New York: Allyn and Bacon.

Gerard, Jean M., and Cheryl Buehler. 1999. "Multiple Risk Factors in the Family Environment and Youth Problem Behaviors." *Journal of Marriage and the Family* 61: 343–361.

Guest, Avery M., and Barrett A. Lee. 1983. "Sentiment and Evaluation as Ecological Variables." *Sociological Perspectives* 26: 159–184.

Glomb, Theresa M. 2002. "Workplace Anger and Aggression: Informing Conceptual Models with Data from Specific Encounters." *Journal of Occupational Health Psychology* 7: 20–36.

Goffman, Erving. 1959. *The Presentation of Self in Everyday Life*. Garden City, NY: Doubleday.

Gordon, Steven L. 1990. "Social Structural Effects on Emotions." Pp. 145–179 in *Research Agendas in the Sociology of Emotions*, edited by T. D., Kemper. Albany: State University of New York Press.

Harold, Gordon T., and Rand D. Conger. 1997. "Marital Conflict and Adolescent Distress: The Role of Adolescent Awareness." *Child Development* 68: 333–350.

Harris, David R. 1999. "'Property Values Drop When Blacks Move in, Because...': Racial and Socioeconomic Determinants of Neighborhood Desirability." *American Sociological Review* 64: 461–479.

———. 2001. "Why Are Whites Averse to Black Neighbors?" *Social Science Research* 30: 100–116.

Havighurst, Robert J., Bernice L. Neugarten, and Sheldon S. Tobin. 1996. "Disengagement, Personality, and Life Satisfaction in the Later Years." Pp. 281–287 in *The Meanings of Age*, edited by D. A. Neugarten. Chicago: The University of Chicago Press.

Herting, Jerald R., and Avery M. Guest. 1985. "Components of Satisfaction with Local Areas in the Metropolis." *Sociological Quarterly* 26: 99–115.

Hess, Ursula, Reginald B. Adams, Jr., and Robert E. Kleck. 2005. "Who May Frown and Who Should Smile? Dominance, Affiliation, and the Display of Happiness and Anger." *Cognition and Emotion* 19: 515–536.

Hochschild, Arlie Russell. 1979. "Emotion Work, Feeling Rules, and Social Structure." *American Journal of Sociology* 85: 551–575.

———. 1983. *The Managed Heart*. Berkeley: University of California Press.

———. 1990. "Ideology and Emotion Management: A Perspective and Path for Future Research." Pp. 117–142 in *Research Agendas in the Sociology of Emotions*, edited by T. D. Kemper. Albany: State University of New York Press.

Hodson, Randy. 2001. *Dignity at Work*. New York: Cambridge University Press.

———. 2002. "Demography or Respect?: Work Group Demography versus Organizational Dynamics as Determinants of Meaning and Satisfaction at Work." *British Journal of Sociology* 53: 291–317.

———. 2004. "Work Life and Social Fulfillment: Does Social Affiliation at Work Reflect a Carrot or a Stick?" *Social Science Quarterly* 85: 221–239.

Homans, George C. 1974. *Social Behavior: Its Elementary Forms*. New York: Harcourt.

Izard, Carroll E. 1977. *Human Emotions*. New York: Plenum.

———. 1991. *The Psychology of Emotions*. New York: Plenum.

———. 1994. "Innate and Universal Facial Expressions: Evidence from Developmental and Cross-Cultural Research." *Psychological Bulletin* 115: 288–299.

Jansz, Jeroen. 2000. "Masculine Identity and Restrictive Emotionality." Pp. 166–186 in *Gender and Emotion: Social Psychological Perspectives*, edited by A. H. Fischer. Cambridge: Cambridge University Press.

Johnson, Joel T., and Gregory A. Shulman. 1988. "More Alike Than Meets the Eye: Perceived Gender Differences in Subjective Experience and its Display." *Sex Roles* 19: 67–79.

Johnson, Michael P., and Kathleen J. Ferraro. 2000. "Research on Domestic Violence in the 1990s: Making Distinctions." *Journal of Marriage and the Family* 62: 948–963.

Kasarda, John D., and Morris Janowitz. 1974. "Community Attachment in Mass Society." *American Sociological Review* 39: 328–339.

Kassinove, Howard, and Denis G. Sukhodolsky. 1995. "Anger Disorders: Basic Science and Practice Issues." Pp. 1–26 in *Anger Disorders: Definition, Diagnosis, and Treatment*, edited by H. Kassinove. Washington, DC: Taylor and Francis.

Keating, Caroline F. 1985. "Human Dominance Signals: The Primate in Us." Pp. 89–108 in *Power, Dominance, and Nonverbal Behavior*, edited by S. L. Ellyson and J. F. Dovidio. New York: Springer-Verlag.

Keltner, Dacher. 1996. "Facial Expressions of Emotion and Personality." Pp. 385–401 in *Handbook of Emotion, Adult Development, and Aging*, edited by C. Magai and S. H. McFadden. San Diego: Academic.

Kemper, Theodore D. 1987. "How Many Emotions Are There? Wedding the Social and Autonomic Components." *American Journal of Sociology* 93: 263–289.

———. 1990. "Social Relations and Emotions: A Structural Approach." Pp. 207–237 in *Research Agendas in the Sociology of Emotions*, edited by T. D. Kemper. Albany: State University of New York Press.

———. 1991. "Predicting Emotions from Social Relations." *Social Psychology Quarterly* 54: 330–342.

Ketter, Terence A., Po W. Wang, Anna Lembke, and Nadia Sachs. 2003. "Physiological and Pharmacological Induction." Pp. 930–962 in *Handbook of the Affective Sciences*, edited by R. J. Davidson, H. Goldsmith, and K. R. Scherer. New York: Oxford University Press.

Kohn, Melvin L. 1990. "Unresolved Issues in the Relationship between Work and Personality." Pp. 36–68 in *The Nature of Work: Sociological Perspectives*, edited by K. Erikson and S. P. Vallas. New Haven, CT: ASA Presidential Series and Yale University Press.

Kohn, Melvin L., and Carmi Schooler. 1973. "Occupational Experience and Psychological Functioning: An Assessment of Reciprocal Effects." *American Sociological Review* 38: 97–118.

Kopper, Beverly A., and Douglas L. Epperson. 1991. " Women and Anger: Sex and Sex-Role comparisons in the Expression of Anger." *Psychology of Women Quarterly* 15: 7–14.

Kring, Ann M. 2000. "Gender and Anger." Pp. 211–231 in *Gender and Emotion: Social Psychological Perspectives*, edited by A. H. Fischer. Cambridge: Cambridge University Press.

LaGrange, Randy L., Kenneth F. Ferraro, and Michael Supancic. 1992. "Perceived Risk and Fear of Crime: Role of Social and Physical Incivilities." *Journal of Research in Crime and Delinquency* 29: 311–334.

Levenson, Robert W. 1994. "Human Emotions: A Functional View." Pp. 123–126 in *The Nature of Emotion: Fundamental Questions*, edited by P. Ekman and R. J. Davidson. New York: Oxford University Press.

———. 2003. "Autonomic Specificity and Emotion." Pp. 212–224 in *Handbook of the Affective Sciences*, edited by R. J. Davidson, H. Goldsmith, and K. R. Scherer. New York: Oxford University Press.

Lewis, K. M. 2000. "When Leaders Display Emotion: How Followers Respond to Negative Emotional Expression of Male and Female Leaders." *Journal of Organizational Behavior* 21: 221–234.

Mabry, J. Beth, and Jill K. Kiecolt. 2005. "Anger in Black and White: Race, Alienation, and Anger." *Journal of Health and Social Behavior* 46: 85–101.

Marsh, Abigail A., Reginald B. Adams, and Robert E. Kleck. 2005. "Why Do Fear and Anger Look the Way They Do?" *Personality and Social Psychology Bulletin* 31: 73–86.

Marx, Karl. [1844]1983. "Economic and Philosophic Manuscripts of 1844." Pp. 131–146 in *The Portable Karl Marx*, edited by E. Kamenka. New York: Penguin.

———. 1933. "Wage-Labor and Capital." Pp. 5–48 in *Marxist Library*, vol. 37. New York: International Publishers.

McLeod, Jane D., and James M. Nonnemaker. 1999. "Social Stratification and Inequality." Pp. 321–344 in *Handbook of the Sociology of Mental Health*, edited by C. S. Aneshensel and J. C. Phelan. New York: Kluwer Academic/Plenum.

Merton, Robert K. 1968. *Social Theory and Social Structure*. New York: Free Press.

Mirowsky, John, and Catherine E. Ross. 1992. "Age and Depression." *Journal of Health and Social Behavior* 33: 187–205.

———. 1995. "Sex Differences in Distress: Real or Artifact?" *American Sociological Review* 60: 449–468.

———. 2003a. *Social Causes of Psychological Distress*. Hawthorne, NY: Aldine De Gruyter.

———. 2003b. *Education, Social Status, and Health*. Hawthorne, NY: Aldine De Gruyter.

Neugarten, Bernice L. 1996. "Time, Age, and the Life Cycle." Pp. 114–127 in *The Meanings of Age*, edited by D. A. Neugarten. Chicago: University of Chicago Press.

Neuman, Joel H., and Robert A. Baron. 1997. "Aggression in the Workplace." Pp. 37–65 in *Antisocial Behavior in Organizations*, edited by R. A. Giacalone and J. Greenberg. Thousand Oaks, CA: Sage.

Olson, James M., and Douglas J. Hazlewood. 1986. "Relative Deprivation and Social Comparison: An Integrative Perspective." Pp. 1–16 in *Relative Deprivation and Social Comparison: The Ontario Symposium*, Vol. 4, edited by J. Olson, P. Herman, and M. Zanna. Hillsdale, NJ: Lawrence Erlbaum Associates.

Orbuch, Terri L., James S. House, Richard P. Mero, and Pamela S. Webster. 1996. "Marital Quality over the Life Course." *Social Psychology Quarterly* 59: 162–171.

Pearlin, Leonard I. 1983. "Role Strains and Personal Stress." Pp. 3–32 in *Psychosocial Stress: Trends in Theory and Research*, edited by H. Kaplan. New York: Academic.

———. 1999. "The Stress Process Revisited: Reflections on Concepts and Their Interrelationships." Pp. 105–123 in *Handbook of the Sociology of Mental Health*, edited by C. S. Aneshensel and J. C. Phelan. New York: Kluwer.

Pearlin, Leonard I., and Carmi Schooler. 1978. "The Structure of Coping." *Journal of Health and Social Behavior* 19: 2–21.

Pearlin, Leonard I., and Marilyn M. Skaff. 1996. "Stress and the Life Course: A Paradigmatic Alliance." *Gerontologist* 36: 239–247.

Pearlin, Leonard I., and Heather A. Turner. 1987. "The Family as a Context of the Stress Process." Pp. 143–65 in *Stress and Health: Issues in Research Methodology*, edited by S. V. Kasl and C. L. Cooper. New York: Wiley.

Pleck, Joseph H. 1977. "The Work-Family Role System." *Social Problems* 24: 17–27.

Putnam, Robert D. 2000. *Bowling Alone: The Collapse and Revival of American Community*. New York: Simon and Schuster.

Reskin, Barbara F., and Catherine E. Ross. 1992. "Jobs, Authority, and Earnings among Managers: The Continuing Significance of Sex." *Work and Occupations* 19: 342–365.

Ridgeway, Cecilia L. 1993. "Gender, Status, and the Social Psychology of Expectations." Pp. 175–197 in *Theory on Gender/Feminism on Theory*, edited by P. England. New York: Aldine De Gruyter.

Ross, Catherine E., and Patricia Drentea. 1998. "Consequences of Retirement Activities for Distress and the Sense of Personal Control." *Journal of Health and Social Behavior* 39: 317–334.

Ross, Catherine E., and John Mirowsky. 1999. "Disorder and Decay: The Concept and Measurement of Perceived Neighborhood Disorder." *Urban Affairs Review* 34: 412–432.

Ross, Catherine E., and Barbara F. Reskin. 1992. "Education, Control at Work, and Job Satisfaction." *Social Science Research* 21: 134–148.

Ross, Catherine E., and Marieke Van Willigen. 1996. "Gender, Parenthood, and Anger." *Journal of Marriage and the Family* 58: 572–584.

———. 1997. "Education and the Subjective Quality of Life." *Journal of Health and Social Behavior* 38: 275–297.

Ross, Catherine E., and Marylyn P. Wright 1998. "Women's Work, Men's Work, and the Sense of Control." *Work and Occupations* 25: 333–355.

Rusbult, Caryl E., and Paul A. M. Van Lange. 2003. "Interdependence, Interaction, and Relationships." *Annual Review of Psychology* 54: 351–375.

Russell, James A., and Beverly Fehr. 1994. "Fuzzy Concepts in a Fuzzy Hierarchy: Varieties of Anger." *Journal of Personality and Social Psychology* 67: 186–205.

Sampson, Robert J. 1988. "Local Friendship Ties and Community Attachment in Mass Society: A Multilevel Systemic Model." *American Sociological Review* 53: 766–779.

Scherer, Klaus R. 1994. "Toward a Concept of 'Modal Emotions.'" Pp. 25–31 in *The Nature of Emotion: Fundamental Questions*, edited by P. Ekman and R. J. Davidson. New York: Oxford University Press.

———. 1999. "Appraisal Theory." Pp. 637–663 in *Handbook of Cognition and Emotion*, edited by T. Dalgleish and M. J. Power. Chichester: Wiley.

Scherer, Klaus R., and P. H. Tannenbaum. 1986. "Emotional Experiences in Everyday Life: A Survey Approach." *Motivation and Emotion* 10: 295–314.

Scherer, Klaus R., and Harald G. Wallbott. 1994. "Evidence for Universality and Cultural Variation of Differential Emotion Response Patterning." *Journal of Personality and Social Psychology* 66: 310–328.

Scherer, Klaus R., Harald G. Wallbott, and A. B. Summerfield. 1986. *Experiencing Emotion: A Cross-Cultural Study*. Cambridge: Cambridge University Press.

Schieman, Scott. 1999. "Age and Anger." *Journal of Health and Social Behavior* 40: 273–289.

———. 2000. "Education and the Activation, Course, and Management of Anger." *Journal of Health and Social Behavior* 41: 20–39.

———. 2002. "Socioeconomic Status, Job Conditions, and Well-Being: Self-Concept Explanations for Gender-Contingent Effects." *Sociological Quarterly* 43: 627–646.

———. 2005a. "The Social Distribution of Interpersonal Conflict at Work in the United States." Paper presented at the Second ICOH International Conference on Psychosocial Factors at Work in Okayama, Japan.

———. 2005b. "Residential Stability and the Social Impact of Neighborhood Disadvantage: Gender- and Race-Contingent Patterns." *Social Forces* 83: 89–122.

Schieman, Scott, Debra Branch McBrier, and Karen Van Gundy. 2003. "Home-to-Work Conflict, Work Qualities, and Emotional Distress." *Sociological Forum* 18: 137–165.

Schieman, Scott, Leonard I. Pearlin, and Rachel Eccles. 2005a. "Anger and the Stress Process." Paper presented at the American Sociological Association conference in Philadelphia.

Schieman, Scott, Leonard I. Pearlin, and Kim Nguyen. 2005b. "Status Inequality and Occupational Regrets in Late Life." *Research on Aging* 27: 692–724.

Schieman, Scott, Karen Van Gundy, and John Taylor. 2001. "Status, Role, and Resource Explanations for Age Differences in Psychological Distress." *Journal of Health and Social Behavior* 42: 80–96.

Schwartz, Joseph E., and Arthur A. Stone. 1993. "Coping with Daily Work Problems. Contributions of Problem Content, Appraisals, and Person Factors." *Work and Stress* 7: 47–62.

Sharkin, Bruce S. 1993. "Anger and Gender: Theory, Research, and Implications." *Journal of Counseling and Development* 71: 386–389.

Shaver, P., J. Schwartz, D. Kirson, and C. O'Connor. 1987. "Emotion Knowledge: Further Exploration of a Prototype Approach." *Journal of Personality and Social Psychology* 52: 1061–1086.

Shields, Stephanie A. 1986. "Women, Men, and the Dilemma of Emotion." Pp. 229–250 in *Review of Personality and Social Psychology*, Vol. 7, edited by P. Shaver and C. Hendrick. Newbury Park, CA: Sage.

Simon, Robin, and Leda E. Nath. 2004. "Gender and Emotion in the United States: Do Men and Women Differ in Self-Reports of Feelings and Expressive Behaviors?" *American Journal of Sociology* 109: 1137–1176.

Singer, Eleanor. 1982. "Reference Groups and Social Evaluations." Pp. 66–93 in *Social Psychology: Sociological Perspectives*, edited by M. Rosenberg and R. H. Turner. New Brunswick, NJ: Transaction Publishers.

Smith, Craig A., and Leslie D. Kirby. 2004. "Appraisal as a Pervasive Determinant of Anger." *Emotion* 4: 133–138.

Smith, Ryan A. 2002. "Race, Gender, and Authority in the Workplace: Theory and Research." *Annual Review of Sociology* 28: 509–542.

Smith, Vicki. 1997. "New Forms of Work Organization." *Annual Review of Sociology* 23: 315–339.

Smith-Lovin, Lynn. 1995. "The Sociology of Affect and Emotion." Pp. 118–148 in *Sociological Perspectives on Social Psychology*, edited by K. S. Cook, G. A. Fine, and J. S. House. Boston: Allyn and Bacon.

South, Scott J., and Kyle D. Crowder. 1998. "Leaving the 'Hood: Residential Mobility between Black, White, and Integrated Neighborhoods." *American Sociological Review* 63: 17–26.

South, Scott J., and Glenn D. Deane. 1993. "Race and Residential Mobility: Individual Determinants and Structural Constraints." *Social Forces* 72: 147–167.

Spielberger, C. D., E. Johnson, S. Russell, R. Crane, G. Jacobs, and T. Worden. 1985. "The Experience and Expression of Anger: Construction and Validation of an Anger Expression Scale." Pp. 5–30 in *Anger and Hostility in Cardiovascular and Behavioral Disorders*, edited by M. A. Chesney and R. G. Rosenman. New York: Hemisphere.

Stets, Jan E., and Peter J. Burke. 2005. "Identity Verification, Control, and Aggression in Marriage." *Social Psychology Quarterly* 68: 160–178.

Stets, Jan E., and Teresa M. Tsushima. 2001. "Negative Emotion and Coping Responses within Identity Control Theory." *Social Psychology Quarterly* 64: 283–295.

Straus, Murray A., Richard J. Gelles, and Suzanne K. Steinmetz. 1980. *Behind Closed Doors: Violence in the American Family*. Garden City, NJ: Anchor Press/Doubleday.

Strachan, Catherine E., and Donald G. Dutton. 1992. "The Role of Power and Gender in Anger Responses to Sexual Jealousy." *Journal of Applied Social Psychology* 22: 1721–1740.

Tavris, Carol. 1989. *Anger: The Misunderstood Emotion*. New York: Simon and Schuster.

Thoits, Peggy A. 1989. "The Sociology of Emotion." *Annual Review of Sociology* 15: 317–342.

Tiedens, Larissa Z. 2001. "Anger and Advancement versus Sadness and Subjugation: The Effect of Negative Emotion Expressions on Social Status Conferral." *Journal of Personality and Social Psychology* 80: 86–94.

Tiedens, Larissa Z., Phoebe C. Ellsworth, and B. Mesquita. 2000. "Stereotypes of Sentiments and Status: Emotional Expectations for High and Low Status Group Members." *Personality and Social Psychology Bulletin* 26: 560–575.

Turner, Jonathan H. 2000. *On the Origins of Human Emotions*. Stanford, CA: Stanford University Press.

Turner, R. Jay, Blair Wheaton, and Donald A. Lloyd. 1995. "The Epidemiology of Social Stress." *American Sociological Review* 60: 104–125.

Vallas, Steven P. 2003. "Why Teamwork Fails: Obstacles to Workplace Change in Four Manufacturing Plants." *American Sociological Review* 68: 223–250.

Weber, Hannelore. 2004. "Explorations in the Social Construction of Anger." *Motivation and Emotion* 28: 197–219.

Wharton, Amy S. 1999. "The Psychosocial Consequences of Emotional Labor." *Annals of the American Academy of Political and Social Science* 561: 158–176.

Wheaton, Blair. 1999. "The Nature of Stressors." Pp. 176–197 in *A Handbook for the Study of Mental Health*, edited by A. V. Horwitz and T. L. Scheid. New York: Cambridge University Press.

White, Lynn, and John N. Edwards. 1990. "Emptying the Nest and Parental Well-Being: An Analysis of National Panel Data." *American Sociological Review* 55: 235–242.

CHAPTER 22

Grief

KATHY CHARMAZ
MELINDA J. MILLIGAN

In Western societies, most people define grief as the emotion elicited by involuntary loss. Loss gives rise to grief and the varied emotions included in grief. We associate grief with death of a person with whom the individual has intimate ties; however, people may grieve over other kinds of losses and, in some situations and societies, death of a close friend or family member does not always elicit grief.

This chapter explores varied social constructions of grief and identifies points at which a sociology of emotions critiques or informs these constructions. We locate grief in its contested definitions and ground it in a sociological description of the experienced emotion that readers can juxtapose against dominant psychological theories of grief. We find evidence that challenges these psychological theories in historical and cross-cultural studies as well in as sociological studies of social movements. Because any experience of grief takes place in specific social structures at particular times, we describe how modernist perspectives and practices structure social roles in professional and personal relationships and shape metaphors for understanding grief. Sociologists challenge conventional modernist views and metaphors of both "normal" grief and legitimate survivors through the concept of "disenfranchised grief" and renewed examination of loss and bereavement. Our study of grief brings us to a sociological analysis of attachments and opens possibilities for a renewed study of social bonds.

Western understandings of grief largely emerged from institutionalized medicine and have been granted considerable generality and universality. To paraphrase Walter's (1993:269) statement about death and pin it to grief, we might say: If at the public level grief has been medicalized, at the private level it has been individualized. At both levels, psychological perspectives have dominated understandings of grief and framed it as an illness to ameliorate by going through

KATHY CHARMAZ AND MELINDA J. MILLIGAN • Department of Sociology, Sonoma State University, Rohnert Park, CA 94928 a "normal" progression of stages. These notions of grief are historically and culturally specific, as Volkart and Michael (1977) pointed out decades ago. However, relocating grief to reflect its specific historical, cultural, and situational conditions has only begun (see, e.g., Irish 1997; Lofland 1985; Scheper-Hughes 1992). Sociological studies contribute to this relocating of grief, but few of them have drawn upon the sociology of emotions. The sociology of emotions can provide a powerful critique of earlier grief scholarship both through its general theories and through specific theorizing about grief.

Grief plays a limited role in general sociological theories of emotions. Theorists interested in categorizing emotions as primary and secondary inevitably include sadness (Turner 2000) or depression (Kemper 1987) as a primary emotion, but it remains unclear if grief is merely a variation on sadness or a more socially constructed, higher-order secondary emotion. Using the terminology of general theories of emotions, we can characterize grief as a socially constructed sentiment based on an individual's interpretation of a situation (Gordon 1981, 1990), as a variation of the primary emotion of sadness (Turner and Stets 2005), as a reactive emotion that always has an object (Averill and Nunley 1993; Jasper 1998), and as a negative emotion (Burke 1991; Goodwin et al. 2001; Turner 2000).

Explicit theorizing about grief within the sociology of emotions falls within the areas that Turner and Stets (2005:26, 100) call "dramaturgical and cultural theorizing on emotions" and "symbolic interactionist theorizing on emotions." Similarly, through our assessment of the grief literature, we find these perspectives the most fruitful for understanding grief. Charmaz (1980, 1997) supports theorizing grief as a complex emotion (rather than as primary or secondary) because experiencing grief is inseparably linked with a range of other emotions and it varies widely in length and intensity. For Lofland (1985), grief is likely universal, but varies across time and space in how people experience it, not simply in its display.

Studying grief contributes to understanding how unruly emotions are socially shaped and controlled and explicates which attachments are recognized and valued. At the individual level, studying grief not only offers a fresh understanding of emotional experience but also provides a window to look at disrupted lives and meanings of lost attachments and, by extension, the social bonds in which they are embedded (Lofland 1985).

In short, developing a sociology of emotions of grief offers untapped ways to theorize the nature of social bonds in contemporary society. To envision studying grief from this perspective, we must first review the major ideas in the extant literature—a task we undertake in this chapter. Throughout our discussion, we point out its convergence with the sociology of emotions and sites of contested meanings and, subsequently, begin a new conversation about directions for future research.

POSITIONING THE LITERATURE ON GRIEF

For the most part, the literature on grief focuses on loss of close attachments or relationships, an emphasis we will echo here. We take the following positions: (1) Grief is an emotion; (2) grief consists of varied feelings, both transitory and relatively enduring; (3) grief is socially shaped and controlled but individuals as well as collectivities interpret and enact it; (4) current cultural and professional practices reduce grief to an individual problem; and (5) contemporary definitions and debates about grief are social constructions meriting sociological scrutiny in their own right.

Despite its widespread definition as an individualized experience, grief is a contested emotion because scholars disagree about its basic meaning. Contested views of grief arise from four sources. First, various scholars disagree about the particular characteristics of grief: What grief is, when someone experiences it, where its locus resides, whether, when, and to what extent it is a universal part of human experience, and whether scholars should view it as an emotion at all are contested notions. Even when scholars agree that a given individual's emotion represents grief, they may disagree about what "type" of grief it represents and what it portends, such as whether it is "normal" or "pathological" grief (Stroebe et al. 2001).

Second, the literature on grief emerges from several disciplines and, thus, its scholars adhere to divergent assumptions about the meaning, character, emergence, and implications of emotions, in general, and of grief, in particular. Most scholars (see, e.g., Rando 1984; Catherine Sanders 1999; Worden 1991) have focused on grief as an object of clinical work, and Freudian assumptions permeate their conceptions of grief. Social constructionist ideas have emerged and reconstructed these conceptions (Averill and Nunley 1993; Charmaz 1980, 1997; Lofland 1982, 1985; Stearns 1994), and poststructuralist views exert some current influence, particularly among British sociologists (Seale 1998; Small 2001; Walter 1999a, 2000). Social constructionist and poststructural views have taken the study of grief out of the clinic and addressed how people experience it.

Third, because much discussion of grief has developed from clinical concerns rather than systematic qualitative and quantitative research, narrow views of grief, its meaning, and consequences have arisen and been reified as real and treated as though universal. Sociologists and historians (see, e.g., Charmaz 1980, 1997; Currer 2001; Doka 1989, 2002a, 2002b; Fraser 1997; Lofland 1982, 1985; Seale 1998; Stearns 1994; Walter 1997, 1999a) have challenged clinical views of grief, although an explicit sociology of emotions has influenced only a few of them.

Fourth, definitions of grief, mourning, and bereavement are often mixed and add to the confusion and the contested nature of grief. Similar to the definitions of grief, bereavement, and mourning offered by Stroebe et al. (2001:6), we define grief as the subjective emotional response to loss with mental, physical, and social manifestations. Grief consists of the person's distressing subjective feelings and physical sensations that emerge in response to loss.

In contrast, bereavement is the survivor's objective status following collective acknowledgment of the loss with expectations that he or she will grieve. Bereavement depends more on the person's direct relationship with the deceased than on attachment to the deceased, and in Western societies, this relationship tends to be narrowly defined. A person holds a special status in bereavement. Typically, scholars refer to bereavement in relation to loss through death and treat it as time limited, rather than as encompassing accumulated losses (Katz 2001). Even so, not everyone's grief is acknowledged; hence, bereavement may not occur. Alternatively, not every survivor who is defined as bereaved feels loss and subsequently experiences grief. For example, when notified of her husband's death in a traffic accident, a young wife said, "It couldn't have happened to a nicer guy and I'm not sorry" (Charmaz 1980:185).

Mourning consists of the practices in which people engage following a death or loss and reflects institutionalized traditions or individualized innovations. Survivors may follow mourning rituals without experiencing grief or may experience grief without having individual or collective rituals through which to mark and channel it. Because scholars do not entirely share definitions of grief, bereavement, and mourning, what we treat as grief, other scholars sometimes call bereavement or mourning (see, e.g., Catherine Sanders 1999).

WHAT IS GRIEF?

Grief is the emotion felt in the face of irretrievable loss. In the West, grief is a negative emotion not merely because it connotes suffering and sadness but also because it is enshrouded by death.

Grief can range in strength from weak to intense. When grief is weak, a person may experience unsettled mixed feelings of sadness, regret, and anxiety and, likely, sympathy for those for whom the loss extracts a greater toll, if he or she defines feeling grief at all. Intense grief, however, elicits considerable mental and physical distress; it is a searing disruption that not only inundates the bereaved person's emotions but also destablizes his or her life and self (Charmaz 1997). Consider the following statement by a 72-year-old widower:

> On February 18 my wife and I were in an automobile accident in which she was crushed and I did not get a scratch. To this day I'm haunted by the lingering sense of shock, loss, and memory of her poor little limp body, broken and bleeding, lying in the wreck. That hundreds of others are going through this experience right now does not help me.
>
> Daily, I go over a litany of a thousand "ifs," any one of which would have saved her life—a deadening treadmill. I was driving—thus a sense of guilt. When death is a murderer, there is no preparation for a shock like this. My hand-in-hand companion of 45 years, torn from me in one awful wrench. We were very close and sentimental. The loneliness is spiritually devastating. (Catherine Sanders 1999:211)

This man's statement hints of the multifaceted dimensions of intense grief (Hogan et al. 1996). From the perspective of a sociology of emotions, grief is a complex emotion constructed from multiple other emotions. In contrast, Bonnano (2001) argues that grief is not an emotion because he defines an emotion as ephemeral, unidimensional, immediate, and evoking instantaneous coping responses that sociologists would view as feeling states or, perhaps, a basic emotion. Experiencing intense sorrow combined with other feelings makes grief a complex emotion. Bonnano is correct on two points: Grief lasts and it consists of numerous feelings. It is not a transitory feeling, although transitory feelings are part of grief.

When we say that grief lasts, we mean that it reemerges and floods the person—again and again for moments, hours, and days. Pining and searching for the deceased are common responses. Grief, however, does not constitute the emotional entirety of bereavement. During this period, survivors may also experience moments of exquisite pleasure as they remember happy times with the deceased or feel pride about how they are handling their loss. The emotions felt depend on the nature of the attachment and the culturally prescribed experience of grief.

Which emotions are experienced during grief? In addition to the depth of sorrow we typically attribute to it, grief encompasses uncontrollable feelings of shock, disbelief, numbness, and overwhelming sorrow and suffering may alternate with fear, remorse, anger, anxiety, and depression, and be punctuated with moments of envy, self-pity, relief, and shame. After his wife's expected death, C. S. Lewis (1994:1) wrote, "No one ever told me grief felt so much like fear." He also recounted his feelings of numbness, disorganization, alienation from self and others and difficulty breathing at night.

Guilt and anger are common feelings in grief and can have spiraling effects. The widower above talked of guilt because of feeling responsible for his wife's death. Guilt may also arise over anger toward the deceased for his or her prior actions. Walter's (1999a) interview of Fiona, a 34-year-old woman, speaks to this point.[1] Fiona's mother had died when she was ten and her beloved father died three years later. Fiona said, "I did feel guilty about being angry at my dad for leaving me. ... 'Why did you leave me?! Why didn't you know this was going to happen? Why didn't you go to the doctor? You are the adult, you were the grown-up! You should have gone to the doctor' " (p. 11).

The turmoil of intense grief includes disquieting somatic changes such as loss of appetite, disturbed sleep, feelings of weakness, feeling disoriented, and experiencing difficulty in concentrating, breathing, and talking. Specifying how situations, feelings, and physical distress are linked in grief is one area that sociologists of emotion could pursue. Defining such connections can bring the body into a central position in the discourse on grief without pathologizing either the body or mind. Rather, this approach can integrate them.

Intense grief causes persistent suffering. The survivor feels that nothing will ease the pain. Initially, the person not only feels the void of loss but also the lack of its reality. Consistent with other life disruptions, the survivor's world has irrevocably changed (Becker 1997), yet the deceased remains present in consciousness and expectation despite his or her irrevocable physical absence. As Parkes (2000:326) states, grief "arises from an awareness of a discrepancy between the world that is and the world that 'should be'." A 50-year-old man whose mother died when he was 12 said: "I felt that my world had ended. My mother was the central person in my life. . . . I remember total, chaos, complete chaos. How are we going to get by? What is going to happen?" (Davidman 2000:99).

What people experience as grief intertwines with its chronology. Immediate feelings of intense grief differ from the prolonged sadness of lasting grief. In particular, the disbelief and numbness associated with news of the loss fade, but the sadness remains as well as other intermittent feelings that the bereaved person experienced earlier. The emotions of grief are fluid and usually begin with a definitive event when the death or life disruption occurred. The event marks the beginning of grief; its ending or perhaps resolution is often much less clear and may never occur.

Grieving is a process but is seldom linear; it ebbs and flows. Typically, sorrow, sadness, and suffering are most intense in the weeks and months after the loss, with feelings of distress and sorrow lessening over time. What were long periods of painful feelings and pining for the lost attachment become "pangs of grief" (Parkes 1972:39) that emerge with memories of shared moments or better times. Bereaved persons experience such pangs as episodic suffering, a temporary inability to handle immediate activities, uncontrollable feelings of sadness, fear, or remorse, and often a loss of composure.

Death expectations—or their absence—matter. A sudden, unexpected death intensifies survivors' feelings of disbelief. An expected death reduces the sense of disbelief, distress, and disorientation of family members except when the major caregiver's most significant attachment was to the deceased, and he or she had been engulfed in the dying person's care and feels a great loss.

The characteristics of grief that we outline do not necessarily mean that these responses reflect universality. Rather, they reflect the ways that Westerners define and act toward loss and, therefore, construct the experience of grief. Averill and Nunley (1993) not only view grief as a social construction to act on, but also as a role. We see grief as an experienced emotion that can lead to *assuming* a role, whether survivors embrace that role or have it foisted upon them. The feelings and defined emotion may differ from the role. A person may be denied the role as Doka (1989, 2002a) and Fowlkes (1990) inform us. We cannot separate a survivor's role or prescribed roles from the structural and situational conditions of his or her life. Studying intense grief gives clues to relationships between an individual's emotions and self-concept, significant attachments, and social structure and culture.

PSYCHOLOGICAL THEORIZING:
ATTACHMENT AND IDENTIFICATION

The dominant theoretical perspectives on grief derive from psychology and psychiatry and are rooted in the institution of medicine. These theories purport to identify what the bereaved individual feels, why these feelings arise, and what should be done about them. These theories center on the individual's response to loss, rather than on relationships with the deceased, the web of relationships that association with the deceased may have engendered, and the structural and situational conditions in which individuals define and express grief. This form of analysis assumes applying a medicalized interpretation of the survivor's grief and, hence, starts with professionals' external definitions rather than systematic inquiry building on survivors' views and actions.

An emphasis that culminates in clinical interventions for the survivor is not surprising because clinicians have made substantial contributions to the research and discussions on grief. This literature deals with the *consequences* of grief more than theorizing grief as an emotion, likely because of the degree of disruption that grief elicits and the subsequent implications for professional practices in dealing with such disruption.

Two major perspectives on grief have psychoanalytic antecedents: (1) attachment theory (Bowlby 1980; Freud 1957) and (2) projective identification (Klein 1984). Attachment refers to the binding emotional investment in the other person, animal, or object and can vary in intensity (Shaver and Tancredy 2001). Projective identification means attributing aspects of self to another person. In psychoanalytic views, the purpose of grief is to detach the projected attributes from the deceased and reintegrate them into self. Thus, many scholars who adhere to attachment theory assume the following: (1) Grief should be resolved, (2) detachment from the deceased represents its successful resolution, and (3) survivors must work through grief to accomplish this detachment.

Loss of emotional attachment and loss of identification with the deceased inform sociological conceptions of grief. Social psychologists have emphasized that the degree of attachment results in the magnitude of the loss and, therefore, the extent of grief. People tend to identify closely with others to whom they are attached. Intense emotional attachment—whether of love or hate—links the bereaved individual to the deceased. These bonds of attachment shape the kind of grief the person experiences, often its duration, its characteristics, and the social context in which it occurs.

HISTORICAL AND CROSS-CULTURAL STUDIES: EVIDENCE FOR THE SOCIAL AND CULTURAL CONSTRUCTION OF GRIEF

From sociological conception, emotions are rational and socially constructed, a challenge to the everyday view of emotions as irrational and natural. The best empirical support, for the argument that emotions are socially constructed stems from research on the emotional cultures of other times and places: historical and cross-cultural studies of emotions. To the extent that such research can document differences in felt emotion, not simply displayed emotion, it suggests that emotions are not universally or biologically defined.

The constructionist perspectives on emotion emphasize that both felt and expressed emotions result from an individual's socialization into the emotional culture of a given group. Expressed (or displayed) emotions are clearly constructed: The culture of any group contains norms of emotional display. Felt (or experienced) emotions are also constructed. Historical and cross-cultural studies tell us that (1) similar events evoke different emotions across time and culture and (2) the emotions felt across time and culture are not the same: Individuals in different cultures experience different emotions.

What do historical and cross-cultural studies tell us about the universality of grief? First, much of this work has been done within the social history of emotions and the anthropology of emotions, rather than within the sociology of emotions. These three fields both draw on and critique each other. Social historians Stearns and Stearns (1986:7) argue that anthropological studies of emotion tend to take a static, snapshot approach, rather than demonstrating causality by examining change over time. In addition, they also critique constructivist psychologists and sociologists who, they claim, acknowledge the cultural context of emotions, but need to show "how this cultural context develops or how and why it changes" (p. 6). Second, even historical and cross-cultural studies might be limited by their authors' assumptions regarding grief. Rosenblatt et al. (1976), once aimed to study grief comparatively in 78 cultures, but framed their study using a Western, medicalized definition of grief (as something to be "worked-through," etc.). More recently, Rosenblatt (2001) examined grief from a more explicitly constructionist perspective and noted growing challenges to the belief in the universality of grief.

Historical Support for the Constructionist View

Lofland (1985) argues that we have relatively little evidence about the actual experience of grief in other times and places. We know much about mourning rituals and the expression of grief, but little about what people actually felt. She argues that it makes sense to assume that grief was and is experienced differently because varied circumstances of everyday life (and death) should logically lead to variations in felt emotion. Using historical evidence, Lofland argues that four factors likely lead to variation in the experience of grief across time and culture. As these factors vary, so does the felt experience of grief. First, the level of significance of specific relationships is culturally and temporally specific; as it changes, so would grief in response to loss. Second, the definition of the situation of death (philosophically and demographically) varies; exposure to frequent death likely weakens the experience of grief. Third, the character of the self varies; the modern focus on self-reflection and emotional self-understanding likely leads to an intense experience of grief. Fourth, interactional settings vary; modern sustained grief requires control over space and time, access to privacy, and time for self-reflection.

Historical studies provide much additional empirical evidence for Lofland's claims (e.g., see Carroll 2000; Simonds and Rothman 1992; Strange 2002). Stearns (1987) notes that historical studies of emotions have detailed clear changes in Western emotional standards (emotional displays) and emotional experiences over the past 400 years due to the rise of industrialization and the decline of community ties, including changes in grief. Stearns's (1994) study of twentieth-century emotional culture details changes in the culture of grief at length. American middle-class Victorians saw grief as an inevitable and consuming emotion, but one to be embraced and celebrated as a vigorous and vital experience. By the middle of the twentieth century, however, Americans saw grief as "unpleasant, potentially overwhelming, lacking in any positive function" (p. 163). Stearns emphasizes the dominance of therapeutic approaches to grief in more contemporary times: Grief becomes something to be avoided, minimized, and recovered from, as well as affecting the individual alone.

Cross-Cultural Support for the Constructionist View

Lutz (1988:11) reminds us that Briggs's (1970) work on Eskimos initiated the social construction of emotions perspective in anthropology and "demonstrate[s] that learning about the emotional worlds of other societies involves more than the simple one-to-one matching of emotion vocabularies between language groups." The following three classic anthropological studies of emotion hold special relevance to viewing grief as socially and culturally constructed (see also Catlin 1993; Klass 1996, 2001; Woodrick 1995).

Western conceptions of emotion often treat "private" or "backstage" emotional displays as more authentic than "public" ones (Goffman 1959; Hochschild 1983), a distinction that, in fact, often holds. Anthropologist Abu-Lughod (1985) details how Egyptian Bedouins invoke two conflicting public and private discourses of emotion in response to loss, which she calls "the dual patterning of the expression of sentiment" (p. 249). Rather than one of these two being the more "authentic" display, Abu-Lughod suggests that both are authentically felt and the division illustrates cultural regulation of sentiments. The Bedouin culture's code of honor prescribes that, in public, the response to loss be one of indifference, denial, blame, or anger, although in private, extreme sadness, grief, and pain are acceptably expressed through song poems. Abu-Lughod argues that her findings challenge theories of universal responses to death and loss (pp. 256–257) because culture influences both felt and displayed emotions.

Lutz (1988) records how South Pacific Ifaluk constructions of emotions contrast with Western ones. The Ifaluk locate both thought and emotion in the gut. (Lutz says the precise terms come closer in meaning to thought/emotion and will/emotion/desire.) They treat emotional distress and physical illness as similar and believe a person risks physical illness if they do not express or "throw out" both thoughts and emotions. After their expression, however, the person must forget about them; to not do so will risk illness (pp. 98–100). Grieving should be intense, but brief. The Ifaluk encourage the bereaved to "scream and wail for the twenty-four hours of the funeral and then stop thinking about the deceased" (p. 100). The emotion the Ifaluk most associate with death is *fago* (compassion/love/sadness); however, they also commonly feel *fago* in situations in which an individual (e.g., a child) is believed to be in need, not only in response to loss. Lutz demonstrates that emotions themselves differ across cultures, as well as that people feel them in response to different situations and express them in different ways.

Scheper-Hughes's (1992) ethnographic study of Brazilian peasant women presents a rich example of cross-cultural variation in the experience of emotion. She shows how major human events do not engender "similar" emotional responses across cultures because of different structural circumstances. Specifically, a mother's love for her children and grief over their deaths, emotions thought to be "natural" in contemporary middle-class North American culture, do not generally occur among the Alto women of Brazil, a group with very high rates of infant and child mortality. First, the women tend not to become attached to their offspring (to feel "mother love") until they live well into childhood. Second, the women tend to not grieve over the deaths of their infants or young children. Scheper-Hughes argues that the displayed and felt emotions of the Alto women correspond: not only do they not display love or grief for their children, but they do not feel these emotions either. She concludes that "emotions do not precede or stand outside of culture; they are a part of culture ... without our cultures, we *simply would not know how to feel*" (p. 431, emphasis in original).

EMOTIONS AND SOCIAL MOVEMENTS: THE PLACE OF GRIEF

The emotion of grief is particularly relevant to and discussed in studies of social movements and emotions, an increasingly well-established area. Jasper (1998) claims social movement theorists must often justify the "rationality" of the movements they study and, in doing so, ignore the centrality of emotions. He notes that most researchers who study political action tend to characterize emotionality as the opposite of rationality. Therefore, they view emotions as "psychological" and thus irrelevant to "macrolevel" movement processes. According to Jasper, emotions are relevant to the study of social movements in two ways: First, movement goals often include the desire to change cultural standards regarding the acceptability and display of certain emotions and, second, movement dynamics are often fundamentally tied to emotions. Goodwin et al. (2001) continue the argument by describing both reciprocal (felt by movement members toward each other) and shared (felt by movement members toward something outside the group) emotions as collective emotions central to social movements.

These social movements theorists argue that grief is especially significant for two reasons.[2] First, both personal and collective experiences of grief have the potential to motivate people to either join an existing movement or form a new movement. For example, experiencing a person's death might lead an individual to join the hospice or right to die movement, whereas the loss of a place might lead one to join the environmental movement. Maxwell (1995) identifies personal loss and vulnerability as the main incentives for active participation in antiabortion activist groups. Second, the desire to prevent loss and to avoid grief—to prevent proposed change—is often an explicit movement goal. Milligan (2005) argues that historic preservationists are motivated both by past loss experiences and by the desire to avoid future loss. One committed preservationist said, "I feel very sad when I see . . . that another house is going and that eventually there will be nothing left of these beautiful structures in New Orleans" (Milligan 2005). Third, grief is a central part of movement dynamics. It might be more reactive and temporary (e.g., grief in response to the loss of a pivotal "battle"), such as the failure of a particular piece of legislation, or it might be more long term (e.g., in response to the overall failure of a movement to achieve its goals).

Both Jasper (1998) and Goodwin et al. (2001) suggest that many major concepts within the social movements literature involve emotions even though social movement theorists do not theorize emotions. Grief is often a key motivator in movement recruitment and ongoing movement participation through its role in causing moral shocks, situations in which "an unexpected event or piece of information raises such a sense of outrage in a person that she becomes inclined toward political action" (Jasper 1998:409). Movements in which grief serves a mobilizing force include the Irish land movement (Kane 2001), peasant political mobilization in El Salvador (Wood 2001), militant AIDS activism (Gould 2001), Nicaraguan protests over "disappeared" children (Thornton 2000; Tully 1995), and Israeli protests over occupation (Gabriel 1992).

Ongoing movement dynamics often involve establishing display and feeling rules for movement participants, as well as claiming the right to such displays and feelings as central movement goals. Whittier (2001) details the collectively organized feeling and display rules of the child abuse survivor movement by arguing that the movement regulates both emotions of trauma (grief, fear, shame, and helpless anger) and emotions of resistance (pride, happiness, love, love/confidence, and righteous anger). Emotions of trauma may well always involve grief in that they are a response to some sort of loss. Such activists promote displays of grief to accomplish movement goals at the internal and external levels, both during movement events and in legislative/courtroom situations.

Grief also shapes collective memory and memorialization, although researchers tend to position these topics within the sociology of culture rather than within the sociology of emotions. The notions of cultural definitions of loss and the negotiation of responses to it are inherent in these literatures because most commemorations and memorializations involve a shared grief over a loss. Whittier (2001:239) states that public memorials such as the Clothesline Project, which memorializes survivors of sexual abuse and violence, and the Names AIDS Memorial Quilt (see also Lewis and Fraser 1996) elicit grief in movement members and draw in additional supporters through promoting collective emotional expressions of grief. Importantly, for those with direct experience of the loss in question, the presence of the memorial is meant also to convey the sympathy, appreciation, and grief of others and reinforces the loss as legitimate at the public level (see, e.g., Wagner-Pacifici and Schwartz 1991). At times, memorials are formal, planned constructions, but at other times they emerge in an apparently spontaneous display of collective public sentiment over shared loss as public shrines at the sites of perceived tragedies (e.g., Jorgensen-Earp and Lanzilotti 1998). In some instances, the formal and spontaneous commemorations merge; for example, witness the extreme nature of the public grieving over the death of Princess Diana (Walter 1999b).

SITUATING GRIEF IN SOCIAL STRUCTURE

Modernity and Grief

Sociological conceptions of grief take into account the social structures in which attachments are situated. The social structures of modernity transformed how people dealt with death and ultimately experienced grief (Stearns 1987). Beginning in 1912 with Durkheim (1965) to the present, structural conceptions address norms that prescribe or proscribe grief and *constitute* its content. Grief does not simply reside in the bereaved individual because it emerges from relationships, attachments, expectations, and obligations. It is embedded in social life and situational location. How, when, and to what extent individuals express grief all reflect this social fabric.

Modernist institutions have constructed grief as an emotion that simultaneously separates the survivor from others and, however fleetingly, integrates this person in collective life through shared mourning rituals. Despite the weakening of modernist mourning rituals and their often tight control of expressed grief, emotional contagion may arise (Durkheim 1965; see also Kemper 1984).

The separation of bereaved persons' grief from other people reflects modernist social structural imperatives. Which social institutions support such separation? How is it enacted within the institution? By looking at empirical findings, we can gain important clues. Not only has the medical institution structured how survivors experience grief, but also economic institutions shape the expression of it; and both institutions affect bereaved families. Pratt's (1994) study of 40 businesses uses historical and survey data to show that most company policies framed their worker's bereavement solely in temporal terms—"time-off"—and only three days for the death of a close relative.

Pratt argues that business policies *lead* rather than reflect societal views of grief and practices toward it. Stringent requirements for bereavement leave from work limit the number of survivors who participate in mourning practices and share the grief. Here again, modernist institutional practices affect how survivors experience grief by restricting with whom they can experience it and by inhibiting the reaffirmation of social bonds. Pratt contends that as business limits involvement in mourning, the nuclear family simultaneously takes it over from the collectivity, or we might say, as the collectivity—if there is one—abandons participation in mourning. As a result, brief, privatized rituals, grieving, and efficient disposal of the body all occur under the assumption of individual rather than collective feeling and responsibility.

Studies of the workplace reveal social control at the institutionalized level and interactional constraints at individual level and, therefore, support Small's (2001) point that modernity shapes the way we think about grief and act toward it (see also Hazen 2003; Lofland 1985; Rowling 1995). Westerners treat grief as nonroutine and irrational and then minimize and bureaucratize it.

Structuring Roles

Structural analyses link individuals to society through their roles. How does grief influence roles? Where does grief fit in relation to social structure? Roles emerge in social contexts and implicate other social actors as well as the bereaved, such as workplace associates or professionals. When the bereaved are cast into a grieving role of some sort, health professionals assume roles that complement whatever grieving role the bereaved have been expected to take.

Survivors' roles are often curtailed and sharply controlled in both public and private arenas. The permissible limits of emotional expression and the efficient completion of immediate tasks or interactions underlie the construction of roles in grief and fulfill institutional prescriptions of modernity. Control over the roles of bereaved individuals raises intriguing analytic and experiential issues. Who has this control? Under which conditions does an individual or organization control roles? How does the individual(s) in control establish and use it? What latitude, if any, do the bereaved have in this unwelcome role foisted involuntarily upon them? Examining the construction of their roles brings up central issues in the sociology of emotions and indicates relationships between actors' imputations about these roles, the unfolding interaction, and what kind of emotions they purport to feel, and which, if any, they express. When survivors do not question institutional practices and their roles within them, the bureaucratization of grief can be efficiently accomplished.

Social institutions prescribe roles to bereaved persons; however, the newly bereaved might challenge them—loudly. The newly bereaved signify potential trouble because they might cause disruptive scenes and interfere with the work at hand. The institution of medicine, however, is perfectly organized to minimize such disruption. Awoonor-Renner (2000), a mother whose teenage son died in an accident, speaks to the silent power of the medical institution to control her. She writes, "What I desperately needed was to see my son. But it was explained that I couldn't see him until I had been interviewed by the coroner's officer, who, not knowing I was to arrive, was somewhere else. Eventually he arrived. By now I was getting nicely institutionalized. I was behaving myself" (p. 348). After staff refused Awoonor-Renner's several requests to see her son, they gave her permission on the condition that she "didn't do anything silly." Awoonor-Renner recounts:

> Timothy was my child; he had not ceased to be my child. I desperately needed to hold him, to look at him, to find out where he was hurting. These instincts don't die immediately with the child. The instinct to comfort and cuddle, to examine and inspect the wounds, to try to understand, most of all, to hold. But I had been told, "not to do anything silly." And they were watching me to see that I didn't. So I couldn't move the purple cloth. I couldn't find his hand by lifting the cloth. I couldn't do anything. I betrayed my instincts and my son by standing there "not doing anything silly." Because I knew that if I did my watchers would come in immediately, constrain me, and lead me away. (p. 348)

In the case above, staff monitored and managed Awoonor-Renner's behavior. When physicians deal with survivors, they control the scene, scripts, and timing to establish "proper" roles and can insist supporting actors to underscore their definition of the situation. Beyond any potentially disruptive encounters, routine medical work teaches physicians how to control conversations. As evident in Maynard's (2003) work, physicians can then control announcements of bad news. They can also manage survivors' response to prevent a time-consuming outpouring of grief—as well as questions about their medical judgment (Charmaz 1980). Other death workers, such as coroners' deputies, lack a physician's mantle of professional authority as well as the dramaturgical props to establish control over roles and expression of grief (Charmaz 1975).

Hockey (1993) explicitly moves her analysis of death work among the British clergy into the sociology of emotions. This clergy attended to the bereavement literature and specialized in creating services to console the bereaved and allow expression of grief. The ministers expressed commitment to supporting "natural" emotional expression, but Hockey found that they "made distinctions between acceptable and unacceptable forms of emotional response" (p. 134). These clergy members controlled the form and extent of expressed grief to keep survivors in a manageable role and, thus, to get through their work efficiently and protect the bereaved from potential embarrassment. One minister said:

> I wouldn't encourage them to cry. . . . I just encourage them to be natural about their grief and there are limits . . . there has to be limits. I mean, I will not allow people, after a certain length of time anyway, to cling uncontrollably to the coffin as it's disappearing down the hatch. I mean that it's not on. For everybody it's not on. (pp. 134–135)

The Medical Model of Grief in Practice

The dominance of the medical institution in defining and dealing with grief necessitates taking a close look at the medical model of illness and care. With several exceptions (e.g., Roos 2002; Rosenblatt 2001; Small 2001; Stephenson 1985), scholars and heath professionals invoke assumptions of the medical model and treat intense grief as a troublesome emotion. Implicit assumptions and explicit practices separate grief from collective life and set it apart from "normal" (i.e., usual) emotions. Researchers and lay persons often view grief as an emotion that should be ameliorated, resolved, and recovered from, similar to a physical illness (see, e.g., Catherine Sanders 1999). Yet, amelioration, resolution, and recovery are not construed as automatic or spontaneous outcomes of a major loss; rather, such grief has to be *acted* upon. Who does the acting? Certainly expectations arise for the bereaved person to do something about his or her grief, but also intimates, psychological professionals, and pastoral counselors get involved.

In the medical model, grief resembles an illness from which one should recover (see also Stroebe 1997). Taken together, Goffman's (1961) depiction of medicine as a "tinkering trade" and Parsons's (1953) concept of the "sick role" delineate crucial characteristics of the medical model. The medical model assumes an expert professional serving an inexpert patient or client and thus relies on a hierarchical relationship based on special knowledge. The bereaved client assumes a quasi or actual patient role, resembling someone who suffers from an acute illness and seeks expert treatment for it. The bereaved person presents mental and physical "symptoms" to the professional for care.

The medical model focuses on atomized individuals, places them in a clinical setting, and separates them from their social, cultural, and historical contexts. A survivor's social locations and cultural understandings fade when viewed out of context through the lens of the medical model. Active professionals draw upon their special knowledge to assess and make sense of a passive patient's symptoms. In the medical model, definitions of grief flow from professionals' assumptions and stock of knowledge and are imposed *on* the client's experience rather than being constructed *from* it. Practitioners who invoke a medical model see intense grief as rendering the bereaved person emotionally vulnerable, which justifies paternalistic authority. Their solutions to the problems that grief causes are frequently narrow medical treatments—drug prescriptions.

The professional's technical expertise legitimizes medicalizing grief, a process that has gained strength and credibility since psychiatrist Lindemann (1944) outlined how survivors experienced grief after the 1944 Coconut Grove nightclub fire. Prior to the fire, Lindemann had worked with patients who had facial disfigurements or had lost body parts. In his 101 interviews of survivors of the fire, he discovered that their responses of grief bore striking similarities to his patients' responses to disfigurement. These survivors' physical and emotional responses formed a predictable pattern including physical distress, preoccupation with thoughts of the deceased, guilt, irritability, distancing from others, and feelings of disorientation. Lindemann defined effective "grief work" as determining the duration of grief and its successful outcome, which connotes intervention and recovery.

The medical model of grief began with Freud and gained momentum as psychiatrists Linde-mann (1944), Bowlby (1980), and Parkes (1972) contributed foundational studies and psychologists, counselors, and social workers built on them. Several social scientists have collaborated with physicians on classic studies (see, e.g., Glick et al. 1974; Parkes and Weiss 1983) and other social scientists invoke medical metaphors and logic when studying grief. Sociologists Leming and Dickinson (1998) present coping strategies informed by Kavanaugh (1972) and stress the tasks of Worden's (1982) psychological grief work. Stroebe et al. (2001) address "normal" and "pathological" grief. Currer (2001), a sociologist and social worker asks, "Is Grief an Illness?" as she attends to cultural variation and notes that "professional wisdoms are taken as universal and given" (p. 52). Fried (1963) and Marris (1974) both assume medical definitions of grief, but apply sociological insights to their analyses of the socially structured nature of actual grief experiences.

As Currer's comment implies, the medical model has limitations. As early as 1980, Charmaz pointed out that empirical studies of survivors' experiences contradict conceptions of grief as a disease to be "worked out" and "gotten over," like recovery from an acute illness. Grief may never be wholly resolved, and the survivors may never recapture the selves they had been before the loss (Charmaz 1980:283). Walter (1997) argues that talking about grief helps biographical reconstruction but does not help to work through grief to achieve "adjustment" or "recovery" from it. Psychologists and counselors still attempt to distinguish "normal" from "pathological grief" and look for problems such as "inhibited grief," although now they may shy away from terms like recovery. Those who do not, like Balk (2004), may receive criticisms for using the dated concepts of "recover" and "recovery" as indicating human resilience (pp. 262–263). Bereavement researchers and practitioners now favor "manage," "adapt," "adjust," and "cope" (p. 262) because these terms allow for possible lack of closure after loss.

The medical model of grief informs most lay persons' view of grief. They see it as analogous to an illness from which the bereaved should get over in due time and something to be contained until then. Self-help groups and self-appointed experts in counseling the bereaved invoke assumptions of the medical model. Wambaugh (1985) found that members of a widows' self-help group adopted and reified Kübler-Ross's (1969) stages of dying and then applied them concretely to group members' experience. By doing so, the group enforced certain emotional responses and their timing as signifying "appropriate" ways to grieve and negated others as invalid. Their actions reproduced the rigid application of Kübler-Ross' stages that health and social service professionals embraced at that time and that still permeate the wider society.

Empirical Questions and Structural Critique

The medical model with its corresponding psychological theories of grief advanced modernist views of grief and practices for managing it. Modernist practices have removed grief from the public arena and relegated it to individual experience.[3] However, the extent to which psychological theories of grief fit with individual experience remains contested (Brabant 2000; Charmaz 1980, 1997; Stephenson 1985). In her study of widows, Lopata (1996) found that neither notions of recovery nor progressive detachment from the deceased fit these women's experience. Walter's (1996:7) personal experience of grief led him to challenge psychological models of grief that assume the survivor should "leave the deceased behind and form new attachments."

Walter (1996) raises his personal reflections on grief to a theoretical critique of how modernity constricts grief and mourning. Like Lopata's widows, Walter aims to retain the deceased in life. Rather than idealize the deceased, Walter calls for retaining the dead in collective memory and tradition and challenges modern conceptions of the purpose of grief and practices concerning it. Instead of concentrating on his feelings with lessening investment in the deceased, as typically occurs in bereavement counseling, he wanted to talk about who the dead were and piece together a "secure place" (p. 14) for them.

To take Walter's (1996) logic one step further, the modern gaze toward the future and its devaluation of the past do not support keeping deceased individuals alive in memory and tradition. Nor do social institutions offer collective ways of maintaining shared memories and traditions in smaller social units such as the community and extended family. Historians select public figures and events to memorialize and a few address how people grieved at a particular historical juncture, but remembering and memorializing one's family history remain individual pursuits.

The extent of social separation of survivors from the deceased—and each other—complicates grief and indicates how contemporary life fragments relationships. Survivors may not be able to piece together the deceased's multiple identities to reconstruct a coherent image of him or her to live on in memory. Walter (1996) suggests possible reasons why contacting other people who knew the deceased, much less as oneself knew him or her, becomes problematic: (1) obfuscation of aspects of the deceased's identify because of lack of a full explanation of the cause of death, (2) different ways and rates of grieving among key individuals, (3) inconsistent religious and generational norms for talking about death, (4) lack of knowledge of the deceased's significant persons and sites for identity, (5) separation from the deceased due to longevity and/or geographical mobility, and (6) lack of shared, consistent knowledge about the deceased and of his or her multiple selves (pp. 15–17).

In essence, Walter (1996) argues that modernity inhibits even intimate survivors from having known the deceased in all of his or her many facets. For him, the purpose of grief is to engage in honest talk with reflexive monitoring of relationships with the deceased and to puncture the idealizations and platitudes that commonly enshroud talking of the dead. Walter states that his own memories of Corina, a former lover, alone would not have permitted him to construct an accurate image of her. He writes:

> What helped me were not *"internal"* dialogues with a deceased person" but *external* dialogues with *others who knew her.* These were what, as Stroebe *et al.* put it, helped me "clarify thoughts, deal with unfinished business and prepare for the future." Nor was it a matter, as the bereavement literature so often portrays, of friends "supporting" the bereaved, but of a number of bereaved persons working out together who Corina was and what she meant to them. (p. 13, emphasis in original)

The structure of modern life may leave survivors with nagging identity questions about who the deceased was and had become that, can, in turn, raise troubling questions about their own identities and intentions. No doubt Walter's (1996) approach might help when the survivor had an unsettled relationship with the deceased; however, talk—honest or not—emerges in interaction and serves situational as well as personal purposes. In addition, the talk of the deceased reconstructs and accounts for the past from the vantage point of the present (Mead 1932).

RECONCEPTUALIZING GRIEF

Framing Grief in Metaphor

Consistent with Jasper's (1998) logic about the framing of emotions in social movements, how people frame a death or loss gives rise to the kinds of emotions felt about it. In this case, the type and quality of grief depend on how the person or persons frame the loss, or whether they can place a frame around it. Devastating losses such as loss of community, culture, and family may, for a period, lie beyond an individual's ability to comprehend. Thus, it becomes impossible to place a frame on such a massive assault on one's being in the world and ways of knowing the world in a similar way as individuals frame the loss of a partner or child.

The way in which people think about grief shapes how they act toward it. The dominant clinical terms of "normal" and "pathological" grief and its correlates—"neurotic," "abnormal," "dysfunctional," and "maladaptive" grief—imply judgments of the bereaved's behavior and functioning, although no clear criteria exist for these types of grief. "Delayed," "unresolvable," "chronic," and "inhibited" grief also allude to the bereaved's state of mind and suggest that his or her grieving is going amiss. An implicit notion of "feeling rules" (Hochschild 1979) resides in these metaphors because they contain rules that inform what the timing of grief should be and how to handle it.

Because concepts of "traumatic" or "complicated" grief take into account the circumstances of the death and the situation of the bereaved, they contain fewer pejorative judgments than the litany of pathological types of grief above. Doka's (1989, 2002b) concept of disenfranchised grief and Charmaz's (1997) depiction of "entitled grief" speak to issues of rights and deservingness that remain problematic in American life. Concepts of grief take their place in the language of property and rights—consistent with Western notions of legal status of possessions and citizenship. Such metaphors link emotional experience to current cultural conditions.

Not surprisingly, professional and lay concepts about grief reflect dominant metaphors in the medical model and are embedded in assumptions about illness, individual responsibility, work, legitimacy, achievement, and amelioration. For many professionals and bereaved persons, grief is work: Clients must work their way through and out of grief. Thus, the metaphor of "grief work" informs what people do and influences their actions. For Worden (1991), a leading proponent of grief counseling, the bereaved have tasks to work on in conjunction with their counselors. Grief becomes something to "handle," "manage," and "resolve," and grief work demystifies the grief process and makes it amenable to rational intervention.

Charmaz (1980, 1997) points out that in North America "work is the metaphor and guiding logic for resolving grief" (1997:230). The dominant way of framing grief and of understanding how to think, act, and feel about it hearkens back to our Protestant heritage (Charmaz 1980, 1997). Grief work with its attendant tasks reflects Protestant values of stoicism, individualism, rationality, privacy, progressive improvement, and systematic hard work. Styles of handling grief may change, but criteria endure for evaluating how survivors manage their grief. Bereaved persons may have once been lauded for stoicism and silence in the face of loss. The cultural influence of the medical model and widespread acceptance of psychological precepts has altered earlier silences at the individual level for some people. These individuals are now rewarded for their emotional expressivity and willingness to talk about the deceased, as long as other people view their grief as legitimate. Residuals of the Protestant ethic flicker in cultural imperatives to grieve according to rules and schedules. Grief work encourages survivors to aim toward future goals, avoid dwelling on the past, adopt a utilitarian stance, and assume individual control for resolving grief (Charmaz 1997).

The Protestant ethic encourages judgments of success and failure, of social and self-worth, and of diligence and deservingness. The following assumptions about grief flow from this ethic: (1) Some bereaved individuals are more deserving of sympathy and support than others, (2) coping with grief is a private matter, (3) the bereaved individual needs to work at resolving grief, (4) lack of will and work can cause the bereaved to fail at grief work, and (4) not everyone's grief is acceptable. These taken-for-granted assumptions are played out as unexamined truths in definitions of grief and practices toward it.

Sociological Contributions to Concepts of Grief

Sociological concepts of grief have expanded understandings of grief and taken them beyond the lexicon of pathology. Charmaz's (1997) concept of entitled grief emphasizes its conferred legitimacy and the bereaved's deservedness. Entitled grief is not without obligations, however. It demands expected, and, typically, obligatory sorrow over loss from the bereaved. Entitled grief affords its possessor priority concern; it confers a special status because it is deemed appropriate as to relationship, time, and type of death. In short, entitled grief fits the objective assessment of a "suitable" relationship, the ending of which merits acknowledgment and support.

The concept of anticipatory grief has long held significance in the bereavement literature. Fulton and Fulton (1971) define anticipatory grief as emotional preparation for an expected death that reduces grief after it occurs. Anticipatory grief has been sustained as an explanatory concept without substantial empirical examination. How it applies to actual situations remains ambiguous, and whether it lessens grief is debatable and perhaps untestable. The concept of anticipatory grief assumes attachment to the deceased weakens or ends. What then, if anything, distinguishes it from social death or abandonment?[4] Surely social death is a precursor of anticipatory grief, yet the literature on anticipatory grief does not interrogate the meaning, extent, and circumstances of social death. Mulkay (1993) argues, however, that long years of widowhood in Britain results in years of "increasing personal emptiness and declining social involvement" (p. 41) and thus leads to social death. Expecting a death allows the dying person and his or her survivors time to prepare for death, whereas an unexpected major loss can overwhelm survivors and render them unable to function (Rando 1984).

Perhaps the major sociological contribution to the scholarship on grief is Doka's (1989, 2002b) concept of disenfranchised grief. He defines this grief as occurring when the loss cannot be acknowledged or publicly mourned—survivors lack the right to grieve. These bereaved individuals' grief remains silent, silenced, and unsupported: it is disenfranchised. Doka's (see especially 2002b) emphasis on grieving rules brings his concept into the sociology of emotions. He observes that in the United States, grieving rules limit grief to family members and enforce specified ways of grieving. Similarly, Fowlkes (1990) argues that moral definitions of an intimate relationship regulate legitimate access to the grief role.

Doka points out that disenfranchised grief results from unrecognized relationships, losses, and grievers. In the first instance, when the relationship is unrecognized, the griever may also be unknown. The relationship may be known but not sanctioned, such as an extramarital love affair or homosexual partnership, or reside in the past, such as between ex-spouses. Losses such as through abortion, adoption, or death of a pet usually remain unrecognized. The characteristics of the grieving individual may result in him or her being unrecognized. Elders and children fall into this category. Disenfranchised grief complicates and intensifies grief and mourning and simultaneously limits the possibilities for obtaining support through the process because of its lack of legitimacy (Corr 1998–99; Sklar 1991–92). Legitimacy is revocable. Charmaz (1997) argues that when grief stretches over time, every form of grief becomes disenfranchised.

Rando (1992–93), a psychologist, has integrated sociological ideas in developing her concept of complicated grief, which refers to any psychological, behavioral, social, or physical symptom(s) that interferes with recognizing the loss, responding to it, remembering the deceased, relinquishing the attachment, moving into a revised world, and investing in it. Rando's approach emphasizes a linear progressive model of grieving, but she intends to shed complicated grief of the pejorative judgments inherent in categorizations that pathologize grief.

As a concept, complicated grief is significant because it takes into account the situations in which the survivor exists. Complicated grief not only emerges in the aftermath of a troubled relationship, but also remains connected to age, the deceased person's dying and death, and the character of interactions and relationships following the death. According to Rando (1992–93), a sudden, unexpected death complicates grief, particularly when it is violent, traumatic, or mutilating. In addition, the survivor's perceived preventability of the death complicates grief, as does prolonged dying or an untimely death. Davidman (2000) reveals how the death of one's mother at an early age may become a complicated grief made inaccessible through enforced silences. She wrote:

> This book, on growing up motherless, forces me to probe my memories and confront my feelings about my mother's death and its impact on my life, a subject which has been deeply repressed by me and my family. The silences around my mother's sickness and death began when she became ill. I was not told what was wrong with her, and when I guessed it with cancer (what else was un-nameable in the late 1960s?), my father and aunt denied it. . . . Needless to say, I was shocked when she died. The silences surrounding her illness and death have continued until very recently; my brothers and I have almost never discussed our mother, nor was it a topic I brought up even with my closest friends. (p. 8)

Clearly, what caused the death or came before it affects the quality of experienced grief and can complicate grief. The relative intensity of grief, its recognition, timing, duration, and emotional content can all vary. Survivors may underestimate their grief (see Ryan 1989), particularly when the relationship was ambiguous or untested.

If certain conditions produce complicated grief, what might make grief less disruptive? Which conditions might foster bereaved individuals experiencing grief with less despair? Survivors report fewer problems when they shared a valued relationship with the deceased person and felt that they acted appropriately during the deceased's life and—time permitting—while he or she was dying (see, e.g., Van Den Hoonard 1999). Although these survivors grieve the death, they regret neither the relationship nor their own actions and, thus, do not suffer lingering feelings of guilt and remorse that other survivors may experience.

LOSS OF SELF

From the earliest empirical studies of grief (e.g., Fried 1963; Marris 1958) to the present, the grieving survivor's feeling of loss of wholeness and new sense of uncertainty are resounding themes. The disruption of death and forced changes in life undermine the self and may elicit an existential crisis.

Losing a beloved partner or child may mean loss of a way of life, loss of shared understandings about the world, and loss of a valued identity (Charmaz 1980; Ellis 1995; Lofland 1982; Lopata 1973, 1996). After her 87-year-old husband's death, Flora implied that her marriage took an investment of self and spoke of losing part of herself: "You have put so much in . . . the other is like part of you dying too. I'm such a feisty individual that it was hard for me to even accept that" (Walter 2003:73).

Because grief arises from loss of attachment, it indicates the form and relative intensity of the attachment. Charmaz (1980, 1997) contends that intense grief is a crisis of the self because attachments that constitute the self have been broken. She argues that the radical individualism in Western society precludes us from seeing or acknowledging the depth and meanings of our attachments. Note that even after a long and happy marriage, Flora voiced her resistance to seeing her husband as part of herself. By muting awareness of attachments, individualism also supports suppressing grief and fosters accumulating it as losses accrue. As a consequence, an individual may become saturated with grief and overwhelmed by a later loss because it carries the weight of earlier losses. Charmaz (1997:233) maintains that individualism leads to the following:

- an exaggerated notion of one's separation from other people
- an overwhelming experience of grief when an exceedingly significant person dies
- a heightened sense of bewilderment and self-blame for being unable to cope with intense grief or for not being able to move on after the death.

In this view, the self is inherently social and predicated on attachments and their assumed continuity, as well as the resulting continuity of self. Yet, if individuals do not recognize the nature or extent of their attachments, then they are unlikely to realize the locus of their "real" selves (Turner 1976). When they view themselves as separate from other people, they experience bewilderment about their distressing, unsettled feelings when a significant person in their life dies.

Lofland (1982) states that attachments exist in the threads of connection shared with other people. By losing the person, however, the survivor loses more than the shared attachment per se; he or she also loses the part of self reflected by this attachment. The broken thread of connection means that the survivor faces the following kinds of loss: a role partner, a private self, links to other people and social worlds, a source of affirmation and trust, a shared reality, a projected future, and a mutual past. These threads of connection may have sewn lives together but may not have woven a tight fabric. More often, as Lofland points out, they consist of vulnerable strings to one person. Subsequently, loss of this individual shakens or shatters the self as well as the structure of everyday life.

In contemporary Western societies, people often have few close relationships at any given time. In the 1950s, Volkart and Michael (1977) contended that a small family bred overidentification and overdependence and resulted in ambivalence and hostility. Volkart and Michael observed that people shift their primary attachment from their family of orientation to one of procreation. Today, people might shift their attachment to partners and subsequent family arrangements several times without examining what each family—and each shift—means to them. Shifting commitments likely come at a cost of weakened attachments and decreased awareness of interdependence, and thus they fuel further individualism. Doka (1989, 2002b) and Rando (1984, 1992–93, 1993) provide particularly instructive indicators of how individuals experience a complicated grief after the deaths of people whom they believed they had left behind. In addition to the nature of the attachment, the speed of contemporary events and routine demands can preclude broadening deep attachments; the structure of daily life militates against it. When individualism increases, people have fewer close ties and likely experience a disruptive grief when they underestimate or do not recognize their past or present attachments.

The research on grief strongly indicates that survivors integrate aspects of the deceased in themselves as they assume his or her roles, act like him or her, and invoke his or her views as standards to measure their own behavior (see, e.g., Glick et al. 1974; Lopata 1973, 1996; Parkes 1972). When and how these aspects of self change is less clear. The bereaved may gradually change because new experiences bring them into a different present and anticipated future than they shared with the deceased. Walter (2003) tells of Kristin, a 29-year-old woman whose husband, Carl, died in an auto accident. At the time of the interview, Kristin was forming a new identity that built on her experiences with Carl's death, her past identity, and her present involvements. Walter states:

Kristen spoke of how she has integrated her memories of Carl into her new life. At about 20 months following Carl's death, Kristen started to feel better. "When I think of Carl now, I can think of happy memories. I am not really angry anymore . . . there's some days now I realized I go to bed and I like, 'Wow, I didn't even relate something to Carl today.' My parents believed that after Carl died, a filter got put on my thought process that was just Carl. Everything I did, everything I said, everything I experience had to go through that Carl filter. And it's not there anymore. Maybe it's still there, but some stuff goes around it."

> Kristin speaks about relocating Carl's memory in a place where it is accessible to her. "I think he'd be OK. I think he would have said a long time ago, 'Come on now, get on with it,' but I really wasn't ready." (p. 45)

Life consists of process and change. Grief changes people. Marris (1974) describes grief as always leaving a scar; even in cases of "recovery," people are changed permanently by grief. How they change varies. Some individuals may look back to the past and never "recover" from grief. Still, the search into the past has consequences for who they are and become. Other people may be forced to move into an unanticipated future and to reconstruct a self for the unfolding events they experience. Experiencing intense grief engenders more than a change of social identity. Rather, a changed self emerges.

RESEARCH ON VARIATIONS IN THE EXPERIENCE OF GRIEF

Studies of grief often focus on documenting and describing how the experience and expression of grief varies based on (1) the type of loss experienced and (2) the social characteristics of the person experiencing the loss. This research gives insight into how grief might vary; however, it seldom theorizes about the nature of grief itself. These studies tell us about the grief associated with a specific type of loss or type of person experiencing loss, but they should be not interpreted in an essentialist fashion.

Categories of Loss

Loss of any sort has the potential of eliciting grief, as long as the person believes an attachment has broken or ended. Disruption of continuity leads to loss (Davis 1979; Marris 1974; Milligan 2003a; Silver 1996; Strauss 1997), which then results in grief. Change of any sort involves loss because the old is lost as a part of the transition to the new (Marris 1974). Categories, or types, of loss include (1) animate objects such as persons and animals and (2) inanimate objects such as artifacts and places.[5]

Loss of Animate Objects: Persons and Pets

Contemporary Western people feel and claim "legitimate" grief in response to the loss of a close family member, although grief varies based on the social categories into which the lost person (or pet) is placed: child or parent or beloved companion animal. The loss of a child typically results in extreme grief (Knapp 1986; Rosenblatt 2000) because it involves the end of a fundamental attachment and the loss of seeing the child mature into adulthood, and it often evokes parental guilt about not preventing or forestalling the death. Researchers note historical variations in the definitions of such loss (e.g., among others, Klass 2001; Simonds and Rothman 1992), in addition to differences in parental grief as influenced by gender (Sidmore 1999–2000) and the child's age;

for example, the perceived "unnatural" death of an adult child (Tully 1995) may be especially traumatic.

Parental grief becomes potentially more ambiguous, disenfranchised, and less entitled when an infant dies, rather than a child (Dyregrov and Matthiesen 1987). A miscarriage makes legitimate grief difficult to claim due to the unclear status of the fetus at the time of its death. Women and their male partners can experience grief quite differently (Stinson et al. 1992), with paternal grief after a miscarriage often defined by others as relatively illegitimate (McCreight 2004; Puddifoot and Johnson 1997). An elective abortion elicits an even more ambiguous grief that is often substantially delayed (Peppers 1987–88). Also, parents may experience premature birth as a loss and grieve over not having a normal birth even when an infant survives (Golish and Powell 2003).

People grant children's grief over the loss of a parent as comparably legitimate to parental grief over the loss of a child, but expect an adult child's grief after a parent's death to be less acute when the parent is elderly (Rosenblatt and Elde 1990). Research on children's grief frames grief as an illness from which one must recover. They see children as particularly vulnerable to suffering negative consequences from loss and as having a much more difficult time "recovering" from it than adults. Riches and Dawson (2000) argue, for example, that girls whose mothers have died cannot grieve appropriately if their fathers remarry "early." Davidman (2000) finds that young girls often idealized their deceased mothers, sometimes despite having had experiences that contradict their idealized images. This concern with children's recovery abilities extends into research on other types of loss; for example, inner-city youth who experience frequent losses subsequently suffer grief well into adulthood (Kelly 2001).

The death of pets or companion animals elicits grief more similar to the loss of people than to that of inanimate objects. Dog owners often see their pets as "people" with whom they hold a reciprocal relationship (Irvine 2004; Clinton Sanders 1999) and grieve their loss accordingly. The ambiguous social position of the companion animal, however, means that different people will interpret the loss of such an animal in varied ways. Alternatively, some owners find that others do not define their grief over losing a pet as particularly legitimate (Meyers 2002). Close attachment to a pet (Irvine 2004) leads to correspondingly intense grief over its death.

Loss of Inanimate Objects: Places and Artifacts

Studies of the consequences of the loss of a place or artifact more often explicitly theorize about the nature of place attachment, rather than grief, but contain an implicit notion of grief. Fried's (1963) classic piece, "Grieving for a Lost Home," however, emphasizes and analyzes the grief of residents relocated as part of a slum clearance in Boston's West End. He finds a clear link between the degree of an individual's attachment and the intensity of his or her grief. Fried distinguishes between attachment to the built environment and attachment to people (the community relationships of the old neighborhood) and concludes that, although related, they are distinct. In addition, Marris (1974) used slum clearance and forced relocation as central evidence to theorize that displacement and other forms of spatial change have the potential to evoke intense loss and life disruption.

The concepts of place attachment, nostalgia, and the loss associated with displacement explain human-environment bonds at a range of scales, including dwellings (Cuba and Hummon 1993), neighborhoods and communities (Anderson 1990; Kasinitz and Hillyard 1995; Smith and Belgrave 1995), towns and settlements (Hummon 1990; Erikson 1976), hangouts (Anderson 1976), and immigrant homelands (Lomsky-Feder and Rapoport 2000). Milligan (1998, 2003a,

Kathy Charmaz and Melinda J. Milligan

2003b) examines organizational loss (the displacement of employees whose place of work relocated to a new site) as a means to demonstrate the existence and meaningfulness of place attachments as sites of identity. Even small artifacts such as stuffed animals and compact disks often function as identity anchors, facilitating a sense of identity continuity in the face of change (Silver 1996).

Survivors' Social Characteristics

The experience of grief varies based on the social characteristics of the individual experiencing loss (age, race/ethnicity, gender, etc.), in addition to the category, or type, of loss. Although people may experience comparable loss situations quite differently, these differences stem from learned conceptions emanating from people's social locations and the meaning of relationships based on these conceptions, as well as from the structural differences in contemporary cultures (e.g., gendered differences in access to power, resources), rather than due to innate differences.

Grief varies with age and position within the life course. However, many grief researchers base their conceptions of "normal" grief on loss experienced during midlife and late middle age and compare it to grief at other ages as more or less "typical" in form, duration, and so forth. Thus, children, adolescents, and elders complicate the medical model of grief and assumptions of "normal recovery" from grief. Children and adolescents, for example, raise concerns that failure to recover appropriately might negatively impact the remainder of their lives. The experiences of elders present another variation on the "normalcy" of grief during midlife. Interestingly, studies of elders often emphasize the extent to which long-term grief fails to follow the medical model. Field (2000) found the existence of strong and continued grief for losses experienced in childhood and early adulthood, rather than recovery from them, and McCandless and Conner (1997) discovered ongoing grief over the loss of reproductive capacities in late middle age.

An individual's race or ethnicity can lead to variation in experiencing grief because of cultural or structural circumstances typically linked to living as a member of a racial or ethnic category. A substantial literature on grief and violence emphasizes that African Americans live in communities where violent deaths are common (e.g., see Dixon 1997; Jenkins 2002; Stillion and Noviello 2001); thus, grief is a frequent occurrence (although perhaps less severe because of its familiarity). Understandings linked to ethnic cultures can alter the experience of grief and practices of mourning; for example, Grabowski and Frantz (1992–93) find that Latinos experience much more intense grief than Anglos after both expected and unexpected deaths. Many studies that focus on variations by race actually reveal social class variations (but see Strange 2002).

Grief tends to be a gendered emotion. In studying the experience of spouses caring for a husband or wife with dementia, Rudd et al. (1999) find that caregiving wives experienced significantly higher levels of anxiety, sadness, and anger than did caregiving husbands. Karp (2001) documents that women feel a stronger sense of obligation toward mentally ill family members and, thus, experience more grief over the myriad forms of loss the illness entails. The right to claim sympathy for one's loss varies substantially by gender (Clark 1997). In particular, men and women are held to different cultural standards when it comes to grief's feeling and display rules (Hochschild 1983). Hockey (1997) notes the inconsistencies between the limited public displays of grief allowed of contemporary women and the frequent representation of such public displays in paintings, photos, and written accounts. These cultural artifacts portray grief as a public emotion, although actual emotion rules constrain its display to the private sphere. Others argue that masculine socialization limits displays of grief and disadvantages men (Clark

1997; Lister 1991), especially in situations in which men's feelings do not match their displayed emotions.

Standards for masculine feeling and display of grief have changed and thus provide additional evidence for viewing grief and emotions, as a whole, as socially constructed. Walter (2000) suggests that cultural changes linked to the women's liberation movement have made men more comfortable discussing personal grief. Although standards for masculine expression of grief might have varied historically, they often remain linked to patriarchal social structures and continue to reinforce male privilege. Carroll (2000) argues that spiritualist men of the Victorian middle class felt that public displays of private grief would positively influence cultural conceptions of masculinity in the face of the ideology of domesticity, and, consequently, reaffirm male power. Women appear more willing than men to display grief in public as a means to a political end and are more successful in calling attention to their causes by doing so. Public displays of grief seem more acceptable for women due to their "naturally" more emotional nature, especially when women emphasize their role as mothers as a justification to demand political action (e.g., Damousi 1999; Gabriel 1992; Tully 1995).

CONCLUSION

The multidisciplinary literature on grief has attempted to define this emotion, its implications, and resolution. With few exceptions (Charmaz 1997; Doka 2002a; Lofland 1982, 1985), the sociology of emotions has largely remained absent in this literature, with its main roots in clinical practice and death education. The study of grief largely emerged from psychiatry and psychology and focused on grief as an individual phenomenon. Much of the interview and anecdotal material that permeates the literature on grief remains remarkably under analyzed or unanalyzed. Major arguments have arisen out of personal experience or limited systematic research. Like our analysis above, we believe that these arguments provide a site to begin inquiry that might lead *to* theorizing rather than a site *of* theorizing.

Insights from the sociology of emotions are beginning to emerge and advance the study of grief. Sociologists of emotions have the tools to place grief in its structural, interactional, and situational contexts. In this way, sociologists can move the study of grief away from its reductionist antecedents.

A sociological view of grief can take us back to attachments and forward into an analysis of social bonds. This approach underscores placing grief within its social context and looks for both agency and social constraint. Adopting such an approach when conducting empirical research fosters developing nuanced studies that can help us sort out diversity in grief and universality, if present, in human experience. In addition, sociological researchers can delineate how social structures and situations call for certain emotional responses in individuals and ignore or proscribe others. Through comparative study, researchers can address the conditions in which grief arises, is defined—or not—and changes. We can provide a vital link between social structure and individual experiences.

From a sociological standpoint, emotions arise under particular conditions and have consequences. Although the literature on grief still contains a strong emphasis on recovery and detachment from the lost other, changes are occurring. Scholars who focus on grief now give increasing credence to the existence of continuing attachment and mute pejorative treatment terms with concepts such as "healing," "coping," and "adaptive mourning." A growing number of practitioners and researchers seek to remove grief from the realm of pathology and focus on meaning and process.

This focus creates an opening for sociologists of emotions to advance the study of grief and emotions simultaneously. Reductionist, individualistic views of grief permeate much of North American culture. We propose that certain attachments can be much greater than acknowledged or permitted and grief much greater than defined or expressed. Other attachments are more contingent, revocable, and replaceable than are socially prescribed. The combination of individualistic conceptions of grief and ambivalence about attachment complicates grief and raises questions in the minds of the bereaved. Thus, the sociology of emotions can advance knowledge of the nature of attachment in contemporary society.

NOTES

1. Walter (1999a) explicitly stated that the interview illustrates major themes but may not reproduce Fiona's feelings from 21 years ago.
2. Jasper (1998) categorizes grief as a "primarily reactive" emotion, which makes sense because grief is a response to loss. Similarly, Goodwin et al. (2001) characterize grief as shorter term and as having a specific object. Although grief is reactive and has a specific object, these theorists do not give sufficient weight to the potential for grief to be a long-term, if not permanent, response to loss.
3. Howarth (2001) challenges the notion that death and grief have been moved into the private sphere, as those who critique modernity contend. She argues that sudden or violent death alters cultural imperatives for private expression of grief and states that the coroner's inquest in Britain has become a new site for public mourning. Perhaps in the United States, the television news interviews of survivors of victims of disasters, grisly accidents, wars, or murders provide a site for public grieving for some survivors.
4. Social death refers to treating a person as though he or she were incapable of social interaction or already physically dead.
5. It is also possible to experience grief over the loss of nonphysical objects such as language, culture, or ideals. Bostock (1997) finds that grief over actual or anticipated language loss is a potentially central, but often ignored, explanation for ethnic conflict.

REFERENCES

Abu-Lughod, Lila. 1985. "Honor and the Sentiments of Loss in a Bedouin Society." *American Ethnologist* 12: 245–261.
Anderson, Elijah. 1976. *A Place on the Corner.* Chicago: University of Chicago Press.
———. 1990. *Streetwise: Race, Class, and Change in an Urban Community.* Chicago: University of Chicago Press.
Averill, James R., and Elma P. Nunley. 1993. "Grief as an Emotion and as a Disease: A Social Constructionist Perspective." Pp. 77–90 in *Handbook of Bereavement: Theory, Research, and Intervention,* edited by M. S. Stroebe, W. Stroebe, and R. O. Hansson. New York: Cambridge University Press.
Awoonor-Renner, Sheila. 2000. "I Desperately Needed to See My Son." Pp. 347–349 in *Death, Dying and Bereavement,* edited by D. Dickenson, M. Johnson, and J. S. Katz. London: Sage.
Balk, David E. 2004. "Recovery Following Bereavement: An Examination of the Concept." *Death Studies* 28: 361–374.
Becker, Gay. 1997. *Disrupted Lives: How People Create Meaning in a Chaotic World.* Berkeley: University of California Press.
Bonanno, George A. 2001. "Grief and Emotion: A Social Functional Perspective." Pp. 493–515 in *Handbook of Bereavement Research,* edited by M. S. Stroebe, R. O. Hansson, W. Stroebe, and H. Schut. Washington, DC: American Psychological Association.
Bostock, William W. 1997. "Language Grief: A 'Raw Material' of Ethnic Conflict." *Nationalism and Ethnic Politics* 3: 94–112.
Bowlby, John. 1980. *Attachment and Loss: Sadness and Depression.* New York: Basic Books.
Brabant, Sarah. 2000. "A Closer Look at Doka's Grieving Rules." Pp. 23–38 in *Disenfranchised Grief: New Directions, Challenge, and Strategies for Practice,* edited by K. J. Doka. Champaign, IL: Research Press.
Briggs, Jean. 1970. *Never in Anger: A Portrait of an Eskimo Family.* Cambridge, MA: Harvard University Press.
Burke, Peter J. 1991. "Identity Processes and Social Stress." *American Sociological Review* 56: 836–849.

Carroll, Bret E. 2000. "'A Higher Power to Feel': Spiritualism, Grief, and Victorian Manhood." *Men and Masculinities* 3: 3–29.

Catlin, George. 1993. "The Role of Culture in Grief." *Journal of Social Psychology* 133: 173–184.

Charmaz, Kathy. 1975. "The Coroner's Strategies for Announcing Death." *Urban Life* 4: 296–316.

———. 1980. *The Social Reality of Death*. Reading, MA: Addison-Wesley.

———. 1997. "Grief and Loss of Self." Pp. 229–241 in *The Unknown Country: Death in Australia, Britain and the U.S.A.*, edited by K. Charmaz, G. Howarth, and A. Kellehear. London: Macmillan; New York: St. Martin's.

Clark, Candace. 1997. *Misery and Company: Sympathy in Everyday Life*. Chicago: University of Chicago Press.

Corr, Charles. 1998–1999. "Enhancing the Concept of Disenfranchised Grief." *Omega* 38: 1–20.

Cuba, Lee, and David M. Hummon. 1993. "A Place to Call Home: Identification with Dwelling, Community, and Region." *Sociological Quarterly* 34: 111–131.

Currer, Caroline. 2001. "Is Grief an Illness? Issues of Theory in Relation to Cultural Diversity and the Grieving Process." Pp. 48–60 in *Grief, Mourning, and Death Ritual*, edited by J. Hockey, J. Katz, and N. Small. Buckingham, UK: Open University Press.

Damousi, Joy. 1999. "Private Loss, Public Mourning: Motherhood, Memory and Grief in Australia during the Inter-War Years." *Women's History Review* 8: 365–378.

Davidman, Lyn. 2000. *Motherloss*. Berkeley: University of California Press.

Davis, Fred. 1979. *Yearning for Yesterday: A Sociology of Nostalgia*. New York: Free Press.

Dixon, Patricia. 1997. "Death of Significant Others and Unresolved Grief among a Population of African American Male Crack Cocaine Users." *Journal of African American Men* 3: 33–48.

Doka, Kenneth J. 1989. "Disenfranchised Grief." Pp. 3–12 in *Disenfranchised Grief: Recognizing Hidden Sorrow*, edited by K. J. Doka. Lexington, MA: Lexington Books.

———. 2002a. "How We Die: Stigmatized Death and Disenfranchised Grief." Pp. 323–336 in *Disenfranchised Grief: New Directions, Challenge, and Strategies for Practice*, edited by K. J. Doka. Champaign, IL: Research Press.

———. 2002b. "Introduction." Pp. 5–22 in *Disenfranchised Grief: New Directions, Challenge, and Strategies for Practice*, edited by K. J. Doka. Champaign, IL: Research Press.

Durkheim, Emile. [1912]1965. *The Elementary Forms of Religious Life*. New York: Free Press.

Dyregrov, Atle, and Stig Berge Matthiesen. 1987. "Similarities and Differences in Mothers' and Fathers' Grief Following the Death of an Infant." *Scandinavian Journal of Psychology* 28: 1–15.

Ellis, Carolyn. 1995. *Final Negotiations: A Story of Love, Loss, and Chronic Illness*. Philadelphia: Temple University Press.

Erikson, Kai T. 1976. *Everything in Its Path: Destruction of Community in the Buffalo Creek Flood*. New York: Simon and Schuster.

Field, David. 2000. "Older People's Attitudes towards Death in England." *Mortality* 5: 277–297.

Fowlkes, Martha R. 1990. "The Social Regulation of Grief." *Sociological Forum* 5: 635–652.

Fraser, Mary 1997. "The Legacy of Suicide: The Impact of Suicide on Families." Pp. 58–71 in *The Unknown Country: Death in Australia, Britain and the U.S.A.*, edited by K. Charmaz, G. Howarth, and A. Kellehear. London: Macmillan; New York: St. Martin's.

Freud, Sigmund. [1917]1957. *Mourning and Melancholia*. Pp. 152–170 in *The Standard Edition of the Complete Psychological Works of Sigmund Freud*, Vol. 14, edited by J. Strachey. London: Hogarth.

Fried, Marc. 1963. "Grieving for a Lost Home." Pp. 151–171 in *The Urban Condition*, edited by L. J. Duhl. New York: Simon and Schuster.

Fulton, Robert, and Julie Fulton. 1971. "A Psychosocial Aspect of Terminal Care: Anticipatory Grief." *Omega* 2: 91–100.

Gabriel, Ayala H. 1992. "Grief and Rage: Collective Emotions in the Politics of Peace and the Politics of Gender in Israel." *Culture, Medicine and Psychiatry* 16: 311–335.

Glick, Ira O., Robert S. Weiss, and Colin M. Parkes. 1974. *The First Year of Bereavement*. New York: Columbia University Press.

Goffman, Erving. 1959. *The Presentation of Self in Everyday Life*. New York: Doubleday Anchor.

———. 1961. *Asylums*. Garden City, NY: Doubleday Anchor.

Golish, Tamara D., and Kimberly A. Powell. 2003. "'Ambiguous Loss': Managing the Dialectics of Grief Associated with Premature Birth." *Journal of Social and Personal Relationships* 20: 309–334.

Goodwin, Jeff, James M. Jasper, and Francesca Polletta. 2001. "Introduction: Why Emotions Matter." Pp. 1–24 in *Passionate Politics: Emotions and Social Movements*, edited by J. Goodwin, J. M. Jasper, and F. Polletta. Chicago: University of Chicago Press.

Gordon, Steven L. 1981. "The Sociology of Sentiments and Emotion." Pp. 562–595 in *Social Psychology: Sociological Perspectives*, edited by M. Rosenberg and R. H. Turner. New York: Basic Books.

————. 1990. "Social Structural Effects on Emotions." Pp. 145–179 in *Research Agendas in the Sociology of Emotions*, edited by T. D. Kemper. Albany: State University of New York Press.

Gould, Deborah. 2001. "Rock the Boat, Don't Rock the Boat, Baby: Ambivalence and the Emergence of Militant AIDS Activism." Pp. 135–157 in *Passionate Politics: Emotions and Social Movements*, edited by J. Goodwin, J. M. Jasper, and F. Polletta. Chicago: University of Chicago Press.

Grabowski, Jo-Anne, and Thomas T. Frantz. 1992–1993. "Latinos and Anglos: Cultural Experiences of Grief Intensity." *Omega* 26: 273–285.

Hazen, Mary Ann. 2003. "Societal and Workplace Responses to Perinatal Loss: Disenfranchised Grief or Healing Connection." *Human Relations* 56: 147–166.

Hockey, Jenny. 1993. "The Acceptable Face of Human Grieving? The Clergy's Role in Managing Emotional Expression during Funerals." Pp. 129–148 in *The Sociology of Death*, edited by D. Clark. Oxford: Blackwell.

————. 1997. "Women in Grief: Cultural Representation and Social Practice." Pp. 89–107 in *Death, Gender and Ethnicity*, edited by D. Field, J. Hockey, and N. Small. London: Routledge.

Hochschild, Arlie Russell. 1979. "Emotion Work, Feeling Rules, and Social Structure." *American Journal of Sociology* 85: 551–575.

————. 1983. *The Managed Heart: Commercialization of Human Feeling*. Berkeley: University of California Press.

Hogan, Nancy, Janice M. Morse, and Maritza Cerdas Tasón. 1996. "Toward an Experiential Theory of Bereavement." *Omega* 33: 43–65.

Howarth, Glynnis. 2001. "Grieving in Public." Pp. 247–255 in *Grief, Mourning, and Death Ritual*, edited by J. Hockey, J. Katz, and N. Small. Buckingham, UK: Open University Press.

Hummon, David. 1990. *Commonplaces: Community Ideology and Identity in American Culture*. Albany: State University of New York Press.

Irish, Donald P. 1997. "Diversity in Universality." Pp. 242–256 in *The Unknown Country: Death in Australia, Britain and the U.S.A.*, edited by K. Charmaz, G. Howarth, and A. Kellehear. London: Macmillan; New York: St. Martin's.

Irvine, Leslie. 2004. *If You Tame Me: Understanding Our Connection with Animals*. Philadelphia: Temple University Press.

Jasper, James M. 1998. "The Emotions of Protest: Affective and Reactive Emotions in and around Social Movements." *Sociological Forum* 13: 397–424.

Jenkins, Esther J. 2002. "Black Women and Community Violence: Trauma, Grief, and Coping." *Women and Therapy* 25: 29–44.

Jorgensen-Earp, Cheryl R., and Lori A. Lanzilotti. 1998. "Public Memory and Private Grief: The Construction of Shrines at the Sites of Public Tragedy." *Quarterly Journal of Speech* 84: 150–170.

Kane, Anne. 2001. "Finding Emotion in Social Movement Processes: Irish Land Movement Metaphors and Narratives." Pp. 251–266 in *Passionate Politics: Emotions and Social Movements*, edited by J. Goodwin, J. M. Jasper, and F. Polletta. Chicago: University of Chicago Press.

Karp, David A. 2001. *The Burden of Sympathy: How Families Cope with Mental Illness*. Oxford: Oxford University Press.

Kasinitz, Philip, and David Hillyard. 1995. "The Old-Timers' Tale: The Politics of Nostalgia on the Brooklyn Waterfront." *Journal of Contemporary Ethnography* 24: 139–164.

Katz, Jeanne. 2001. "Introduction." Pp. 1–15 in *Grief, Mourning, and Death Ritual*, edited by J. Hockey, J. Katz, and N. Small. Buckingham, UK: Open University Press.

Kavanaugh, Robert. 1972. *Facing Death*. Baltimore: Penguin.

Kelly, Victor L. 2001. "The Cycle of Loss, Grief, and Violence as Exhibited in the Lives of Inner-City Youth." *Illness, Crisis and Loss* 9: 284–297.

Kemper, Theodore D. 1984. "Power, Status, and Emotions: A Sociological Contribution to a Psychophysiological Domain." Pp. 369–383 in *Approaches to Emotion*, edited by K. Scherer and P. Ekman. Hillsdale, NJ: Erlbaum.

————. 1987. "How Many Emotions Are There? Wedding the Social and the Autonomic Components." *American Journal of Sociology* 93: 263–289.

Klass, Dennis. 1996. "Ancestor Worship in Japan: Dependence and the Resolution of Grief." *Omega* 33: 279–302.

————. 2001. "Continuing Bonds in the Resolution of Grief in Japan and North America." *American Behavioral Scientist* 44: 742–763.

Klein, Melanie. [1975]1984. *Love, Guilt, and Reparation, and Other Works, 1921–1945*. New York: Free Press.

Knapp, Ronald J. 1986. *Beyond Endurance: When a Child Dies*. New York: Schocken.

Kübler-Ross, Elisabeth. 1969. *On Death and Dying*. New York: Macmillan.

Leming, Michael, and George E. Dickinson. 1998. *Understanding Dying, Death, and Bereavement*. Fort Worth, TX: Holt Rinehart and Winston.

Lewis, C. S. [1961]1994. *A Grief Observed*. San Francisco: HarperCollins.

Lewis, Jacqueline, and Michael R. Fraser. 1996. "Patches of Grief and Rage: Visitor Responses to the NAMES Project AIDS Memorial Quilt." *Qualitative Sociology* 19: 433–451.

Lindemann, Erich. 1944. "Symptomatology and Management of Acute Grief." *American Journal of Psychiatry* 101: 141–148.

Lister, Larry. 1991. "Men and Grief: A Review of Research." *Smith College Studies in Social Work* 61: 220–235.

Lofland, Lyn H. 1982. "Loss and Human Connection: An Exploration into the Nature of the Social Bond." Pp. 219–242 in *Personality, Roles and Social Behavior*, edited by W. Ickes and E. S. Knowles. New York: Springer-Verlag.

———. 1985. "The Social Shaping of Emotion: The Case of Grief." *Symbolic Interaction* 8: 171–190.

Lomsky-Feder, Edna, and Tamar Rapoport. 2000. "Visit, Separation, and Deconstructing Nostalgia: Russian Students Travel to Their Old Home." *Journal of Contemporary Ethnography* 29: 32–57.

Lopata, Helena Z. 1973. *Widowhood in an American City*. Cambridge, MA: Schenkman.

———. 1996. *Current Widowhood: Myths and Realities*. Thousand Oaks, CA: Sage.

Lutz, Catherine A. 1988. *Unnatural Emotions: Everyday Sentiments on a Micronesian Atoll and Their Challenge to Western Theory*. Chicago: University of Chicago Press.

Marris, Peter. 1958. *Widows and Their Families*. London: Routledge, Kegan Paul.

———. 1974. *Loss and Change*. New York: Pantheon.

Maxwell, Carol J. C. 1995. "Coping with Bereavement through Activism: Real Grief, Imagined Death, and Pseudo-Mourning among Pro-Life Direct Activists." *Ethos* 23: 437–452.

Maynard, Douglas W. 2003. *Bad News, Good News: Conversational Order in Everyday Talk and Clinical Settings*. Chicago: University of Chicago Press.

McCandless, N. Jane, and Francis P. Conner. 1997. "Older Women and Grief: A New Direction for Research." *Journal of Women and Aging* 9: 85–91.

McCreight, Bernadette Susan. 2004. "A Grief Ignored: Narratives of Pregnancy Loss from a Male Perspective." *Sociology of Health and Illness* 26: 326–350.

Mead, George Herbert. 1932. *Philosophy of the Present*. LaSalle, IL: Open Court Press.

Meyers, Barbara. 2002. "Disenfranchised Grief and the Loss of an Animal Companion." Pp. 251–264 in *Disenfranchised Grief: New Directions, Challenges, and Strategies for Practice*, edited by K. J. Doka. Champaign, IL: Research Press.

Milligan, Melinda J. 1998. "Interactional Past and Potential: The Social Construction of Place Attachment." *Symbolic Interaction* 21: 1–33.

———. 2003a. "Displacement and Identity Discontinuity: The Role of Nostalgia in Establishing New Identity Categories." *Symbolic Interaction* 26: 381–403.

———. 2003b. "Loss of Site: Organizational Moves as Organizational Deaths." *International Journal of Sociology and Social Policy* 23: 115–152.

———. 2005. "Ambivalent Passion and Passionate Ambivalence: Emotions and the Historic Preservation Movement." Presented at the annual meeting of the American Sociological Association, Philadelphia, PA.

Mulkay, Michael. 1993. "Social Death in Britain." Pp. 31–49 in *The Sociology of Death*, edited by D. Clark. Oxford: Blackwell.

Parkes, C. Murray. 1972. *Bereavement: Studies of Grief in Adult Life*. New York: Basic Books.

———. 2000. "Bereavement as Psychosocial Transition." Pp. 325–331 in *Death, Dying and Bereavement*, edited by D. Dickenson, M. Johnson, and J. S. Katz. Sage: London.

Parkes, C. Murray, and Robert S. Weiss. 1983. *Recovery from Bereavement*. New York: Basic Books.

Parsons, Talcott. 1953. *The Social System*. Glencoe, IL: Free Press.

Peppers, Larry G. 1987–1988. "Grief and Elective Abortion: Breaking the Emotional Bond?" *Omega* 18: 1–12.

Pratt, Lois. 1994. "Business Temporal Norms and Bereavement Behavior." Pp. 263–287 in *Death and Identity*, 3rd ed., edited by R. Fulton and R. Bendiksen. Philadelphia: Charles Press.

Puddifoot, John E., and Martin P. Johnson. 1997. "The Legitimacy of Grieving: The Partner's Experience at Miscarriage." *Social Science and Medicine* 45: 837–845.

Rando, Therese A. 1984. *Grief, Dying, and Death: Clinical Interventions for Caregivers*. Champaign, IL: Research Press.

———. 1992–1993. "The Increasing Prevalence of Complicated Mourning: The Onslaught Is Just Beginning." *Omega* 26: 43–59.

———. 1993. *Treatment of Complicated Mourning*. Champaign, IL: Research Press.

Riches, Gordon, and Pam Dawson. 2000. "Daughters' Dilemmas: Grief Resolution in Girls Whose Widowed Fathers Remarry Early." *Journal of Family Therapy* 22: 360–374.

Roos, Susan. 2002. *Chronic Sorrow*. New York: Brunner-Routledge.

Rosenblatt, Paul C. 2000. *Parent Grief: Narratives of Loss and Relationship*. Philadelphia: Brunner/Mazel.

————. 2001. "A Social Constructionist Perspective on Cultural Differences in Grief." Pp. 285–300 in *Handbook of Bereavement Research*, edited by M. S. Stroebe, R. O. Hansson, W. Stroebe, and H. Schut. Washington, DC: American Psychological Association.

Rosenblatt, Paul C., and Carol Elde. 1990. "Shared Reminiscence about a Deceased Parent: Implications for Grief." *Family Relations* 39: 206–210.

Rosenblatt, Paul C., R. Patricia Walsh, and Douglas A. Jackson. 1976. *Grief and Mourning in Cross-Cultural Perspective*. New Haven, CT: Human Relations Area Files Press.

Rowling, Louise. 1995. "The Disenfranchised Grief of Teachers." *Omega* 31: 317–329.

Rudd, Marilyn G., Linda L. Viney, and Carol A. Preston. 1999. "The Grief Experienced by Spousal Caregivers of Dementia Patients: The Role of Place of Care of Patient and Gender of Caregiver." *International Journal of Aging and Human Development* 48: 217–240.

Ryan, Dennis Raymond. 1989. "Raymond: Underestimated Grief." Pp. 127–134 in *Disenfranchised Grief: Recognizing Hidden Sorrow*, edited by K. J. Doka. Lexington, MA: Lexington Books.

Sanders, Catherine. 1999. *Grief the Mourning After*. 2nd ed. New York: Wiley.

Sanders, Clinton. 1999. *Understanding Dogs: Living and Working with Canine Companions*. Philadelphia: Temple University Press.

Scheper-Hughes, Nancy. 1992. *Death without Weeping: The Violence of Everyday Life in Brazil*. Berkeley, CA: University of California Press.

Seale, Clive. 1998. *Constructing Death: The Sociology of Dying and Bereavement*. Cambridge: Cambridge University Press.

Shaver, Phillip R., and Caroline M. Tancredy. 2001. "Emotion, Attachment, and Bereavement: A Conceptual Commentary." Pp. 63–88 in *Handbook of Bereavement Research*, edited by M. S. Stroebe, R. O. Hansson, W. Stroebe, and H. Schut. Washington, DC: American Psychological Association.

Sidmore, Kimberly Varney. 1999–2000. "Parental Bereavement: Levels of Grief as Affected by Gender Issues." *Omega* 40: 351–374.

Silver, Ira. 1996. "Role Transitions, Objects, and Identity." *Symbolic Interaction* 19: 1–20.

Simonds, Wendy, and Barbara Katz Rothman. 1992. *Centuries of Solace: Expressions of Maternal Grief in Popular Literature*. Philadelphia: Temple University Press.

Sklar, Fred. 1991–1992. "Grief as a Family Affair: Property Rights, Grief Rights, and the Exclusion of Close Friends as Survivors." *Omega* 24: 109–121.

Small, Neil. 2001. "Theories of Grief: A Critical Review." Pp. 19–48 in *Grief, Mourning, and Death Ritual*, edited by J. Hockey, J. Katz, and N. Small. Buckingham, UK: Open University Press.

Smith, Kenneth, and Linda Liska Belgrave. 1995. "The Reconstruction of Everyday Life: Experiencing Hurricane Andrew." *Journal of Contemporary Ethnography* 24: 244–269.

Stephenson, John. 1985. *Death, Grief, and Mourning*. New York: Free Press.

Stearns, Carol Z., and Peter N. Stearns. 1986. *Anger: The Struggle for Emotional Control in America's History*. Chicago: University of Chicago Press.

Stearns, Peter N. 1987. "The Problem of Change in Emotions Research: New Standards for Anger in Twentieth-Century American Childrearing." *Symbolic Interaction* 10: 85–99.

————. 1994. *American Cool: Constructing a Twentieth Century Emotional Style*. New York: New York University Press.

Stillion, Judith M., and Susan B. Noviello. 2001. "Living and Dying in Different Worlds: Gender Differences in Violent Death and Grief." *Illness, Crisis and Loss* 9: 247–259.

Stinson, Kandi M., Judith N. Lasker, Janet Lohmann, and Lori J. Toedter. 1992. "Parents' Grief following Pregnancy Loss: A Comparison of Mothers and Fathers." *Family Relations* 41: 218–223.

Strange, Julie-Marie. 2002. "'She Cried a Very Little': Death, Grief and Mourning in Working-Class Culture, c. 1880–1914." *Social History* 27: 143–161.

Strauss, Anselm. 1959. *Mirrors and Masks: The Search for Identity*. Blencoe, IL: Free Press.

Stroebe, Margaret. 1997. "From Mourning and Melancholia to Bereavement and Biography: An Assessment of Walter's New Model of Grief." *Mortality* 2: 255–262.

Stroebe, Margaret, Robert O. Hansson, Wolfgang Stroebe, and Henk Schut. 2001. "Introduction: Concepts and Issues in Contemporary Research on Bereavement." Pp. 493–515 in *Handbook of Bereavement Research*, edited by M. S. Stroebe, R. O. Hansson, W. Stroebe, and H. Schut. Washington, DC: American Psychological Association.

Thornton, Sally Webb. 2000. "Grief Transformed: The Mothers of the Plaza de Mayo." *Omega* 41: 279–289.

Tully, Sheila R. 1995. "A Painful Purgatory: Grief and the Nicaraguan Mothers of the Disappeared." *Social Science and Medicine* 40: 1597–1610.

Turner, Jonathan H. 2000. *On the Origins of Human Emotions: A Sociological Inquiry into the Evolution of Human Affect*. Stanford, CA: Stanford University Press.

Turner, Jonathan H., and Jan E. Stets. 2005. *The Sociology of Emotions*. New York: Cambridge University Press.

Turner, Ralph H. 1976. "The Real Self: From Institution to Impulse." *American Journal of Sociology* 81: 989–1016.

Van Den Hoonard, Deborah Kestin. 1999. "No Regrets: Widows' Stories About the Last Days of Their Husbands' Lives." *Journal of Aging Studies* 11: 59–72.

Volkart, Edmund H., and Stanley T. Michael. [1957]1977. "Bereavement and Mental Health." Pp. 195–215 in *Understanding Death and Dying*, edited by S. G. Wilcox and M. Sutton. Port Washington, NY: Alfred.

Wagner-Pacifici, Robin, and Barry Schwartz. 1991. "The Vietnam Veterans Memorial: Commemorating a Difficult Past." *American Journal of Sociology* 97: 376–420.

Walter, Carolyn Ambler. 2003. *The Loss of a Life Partner: Narratives of Grief*. New York: Columbia University Press.

Walter, Tony. 1993. "British Sociology and Death." Pp. 264–295 in *The Sociology of Death*, edited by D. Clark. Oxford: Blackwell.

———. 1996. "A New Model of Grief: Bereavement and Biography." *Mortality* 1: 7–25.

———. 1997. "Letting Go and Keeping Hold: A Reply to Stroebe." *Mortality* 2: 263–266.

———. 1999a. *On Bereavement: The Culture of Grief*. Buckingham, UK: Open University Press.

———, ed. 1999b. *The Mourning for Diana*. Oxford: Berg.

———. 2000. "Grief Narratives: The Role of Medicine in the Policing of Grief." *Anthropology and Medicine* 7: 97–114.

Wambaugh, J. A. 1985. "The Grief Process as a Social Construct." *Omega* 16: 201–211.

Whittier, Nancy. 2001. "Emotional Strategies: The Collective Reconstruction and Display of Oppositional Emotions in the Movement against Child Sexual Abuse." Pp. 233–250 in *Passionate Politics: Emotions and Social Movements*, edited by J. Goodwin, J. M. Jasper, and F. Polletta. Chicago: University of Chicago Press.

Wood, Elisabeth Jean. 2001. "The Emotional Benefits of Insurgency in El Salvador." Pp. 267–281 in *Passionate Politics: Emotions and Social Movements*, edited by J. Goodwin, J. M. Jasper, and F. Polletta. Chicago: University of Chicago Press.

Woodrick, Anne C. 1995. "A Lifetime of Mourning: Grief Work among Yucatec Maya Women." *Ethos* 23: 401–423.

Worden, J. William. 1982. *Grief Counseling and Grief Therapy: A Handbook for the Mental Health Practitioner*. New York: Springer-Verlag.

———. 1991. *Grief Counseling and Grief Therapy: A Handbook for the Mental Health Practitioner*. 2nd ed. New York: Springer.

CHAPTER 23

Moral Emotions

Jonathan H. Turner
Jan E. Stets

The "moral emotions" are often considered to be shame, guilt, sympathy, and empathy (Tangney and Dearing 2002), and, to a lesser degree, contempt, anger, and disgust (Rozin et al. 1999), but a moment of reflection reveals that this view is far too narrow. The palate of human emotions is much larger and diverse than this short list of moral emotions; and since human capacities for emotion evolved to increase moral commitments to others, social structures and culture, many more emotions have moral effects. For example, righteousness, awe, veneration, joy, happiness, remorse, vengeance, and even sadness can mark emotional arousal over moral issues, as we hope to demonstrate. Moreover, as the literature makes clear, the arousal of emotions like shame and guilt can set into motion cognitive and psychodynamic processes such as attribution, expectation states, repression, displacement, or projection that transmute the initial arousal of an emotion like shame into anger, fear, disgust, and hatred (Lewis 1971; Scheff 1990; Turner 2002). These and other emotional states are ultimately connected to morality, even if a person and others do not fully recognize this connection. Thus, from a sociological perspective, the study of moral emotions soon brings into play a much larger array of human emotions. The goal is to understand both the sociocultural dynamics and psychodynamics by which emotional arousal is fueled by considerations of morality.

WHAT IS MORALITY?

To talk about moral emotions, we need a provisional definition of what morality is. From a sociological perspective, morality ultimately revolves around evaluative cultural codes that specify what is right or wrong, good or bad, acceptable or unacceptable. Moral codes vary, however, in

Jonathan H. Turner and Jan E. Stets • Department of Sociology, University of California, Riverside, CA 92521

Intensity of
evaluative content

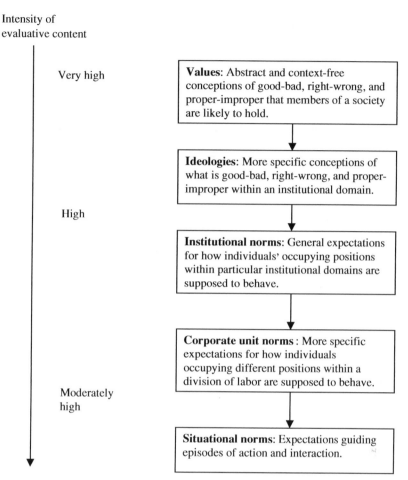

Very high

Values: Abstract and context-free conceptions of good-bad, right-wrong, and proper-improper that members of a society are likely to hold.

Ideologies: More specific conceptions of what is good-bad, right-wrong, and proper-improper within an institutional domain.

High

Institutional norms: General expectations for how individuals' occupying positions within particular institutional domains are supposed to behave.

Corporate unit norms: More specific expectations for how individuals occupying different positions within a division of labor are supposed to behave.

Moderately
high

Situational norms: Expectations guiding episodes of action and interaction.

FIGURE 23.1. Levels of Moral Codes

how much moral content they contain. Figure 23.1 outlines a simple conceptualization of various levels of moral coding.

At the societal level, there are typically highly abstract, yet general values that are context-free but that, nonetheless, articulate what is good-bad, proper-improper, and right-wrong in *all* social contexts. Values generally carry the highest level of moral content. Societies differ considerably in how much consensus individuals reveal over core values, but all individuals generally hold some core values, even if their values differ from those of others in a society. For example, Williams (1970) has classified American values along several dimensions such as achievement (it is "good" to try to do well), mastery (it is "good" to try to control situations), efficiency (being rational in the use of means to ends), individualism (relying upon self to achieve goals), progress (improving self and the broader world), materialism (acquiring objects to mark success), and a number of generalized codes for what is right, proper, and good. When individuals do not realize these values, they are likely to experience guilt because values are internalized early, and they direct virtually all actions and self-evaluations of persons.

When values are translated into moral codes for broad institutional domains—family, economy, polity, education, science, religion, and so forth—they become ideologies about what is right, proper, and appropriate for individuals operating within a domain. In essence, ideologies specify how individuals are supposed to realize values within a domain. For example, general values may specify that a person should try to make progress, while the ideology of the kinship institutional domain will specify just *how* this value is to be realized. The value of progress in the domain of kinship specifies that parents, if they are to be "good parents," are to help their children mature and grow up to be responsible individuals.

At the level of institutional domains, norms emerge; and these too carry evaluative content from the ideologies, and by extension, the broader core values. Institutional norms are general, and they indicate, in broad strokes, how a person is to act in key roles. For instance, a worker is to be industrious, a mother is to be nurturant, a worshiper is to be reverent, and a student is to be studious.

Most actions occur within corporate units (groups, organizations, and communities) revealing a division of labor, and inherent in any division of labor are even more specific norms directing behaviors of those at different positions. Because most corporate units, such as a company, are embedded within an institutional domain in the economy, many norms directing the division of labor carry moral content from the ideology of the institutional domain.

Finally, there are norms that form within encounters of face-to-face interaction. At a minimum, these norms are moral because they specify courteous conduct, such as waiting your turn in line, but they also often carry moral overtones by virtue of being embedded in a corporate unit that, in turn, is embedded in an institutional domain within a particular society. Relatively few encounters are isolated. Most occur within a group, organization, or community that is part of an institutional system. Because of this embedding, moral content filters down to each episode of action and interaction. Indeed, individuals not only evaluate each other with reference to moral codes, but they also evaluate themselves from a yardstick composed of normative instructions laced with elements of morality.

When individuals violate norms, they generally experience some form of shame such as embarrassment at the low-intensity end of the shame continuum and humiliation at the high-intensity end of the shame spectrum. The more ideological and value content embodied in norms, the more individuals will feel not only shame but guilt as well. Since institutional norms carry the most evaluative content (because they specify society's core values with highly evaluative ideologies), individuals will experience more intense forms of shame and guilt when violating institutional norms. For example, one may experience intense shame and guilt when violating norms associated with parenthood, being a scientist, or religious leader.

Thus, any cultural code is moral *to the extent* that it carries evaluative elements that specify what is good-bad, right-wrong, and proper-improper. Indeed, it is rare to find a norm that does not carry at least some moral content because virtually all norms guiding behavior and face-to-face interaction are embedded in corporate units, which are embedded in institutional domains (and the ideologies of these domains), which, in turn, are embedded in a society and its core values. We use the term "moral codes" as a convenient gloss for the obviously complicated relationships among various levels of cultural coding as outlined in Figure 23.1.

A BIOLOGY OF MORALITY?

It is now clear that emotional reactions to behaviors are not solely the result of violating the moral rules of culture. There is a growing body of evidence that moral emotions have a hard-wired basis in a least two senses. First, and less controversial, moral emotions are generated by the body systems—neurotransmitters and neuroactive peptides, hormones, and the autonomic nervous and musculoskeletal systems. Natural selection clearly worked on the hominid ancestors of humans to expand dramatically the range and potential intensity of emotional arousal (Turner 2000). Without this capacity, the large palate of emotions that are in play among humans would not exist (Turner and Stets 2005). Second, and more controversial for sociologists who appear to fear biology, is that certain affective responses that fall under the rubric of "moral" also appear to be hard wired. For example, higher primates all reveal a tendency for reciprocity in that favors given by one lead to favors given in return, and when there is a failure to reciprocate, negative emotions like anger are aroused (de Waal 1996).

Even more interesting is the clear sense of justice that monkeys and, no doubt, apes display when their payoffs in a situation do not correspond to their costs and the cost-benefits of others. Capuchin monkeys, for instance, can be conditioned to engage in behaviors that bring them rewards, but when they see another monkey receiving more rewards for the same level of behavioral output, they will cease exchanging with experimenters until they get the same level of reward (de Waal 1996). Thus, primates evidence a hard-wired tendency to assess costs and benefits relative to the costs and benefits of others in a clear comparison dynamic (Jasso 1980). More generally, de Waal's (1996) analysis of apes and monkeys reveals that they evidence characteristics indicative of being moral. They show signs of attachment, emotional contagion, and cognitive empathy; they are sensitive to prescriptive social rules and internalize rules and anticipate punishment; they have a clear concept of giving and a propensity for revenge when reciprocity rules are violated; and there is a community concern, maintenance of good relationships, and avoidance of conflict.

Turner (2000) went further than the hard wiring of reciprocity and justice. He contended that moral emotions such as shame and guilt are hard-wired capacities, forged into hominid neuroanatomy by natural selection. In his argument, shame and guilt are "second-order" emotions in that they involve combing the three negative primary emotions—anger, fear, and sadness—in different rank orderings. The dominant emotion in shame and guilt is sadness, and it is the relative amounts of fear and anger that produce shame or guilt. For shame, the dominant emotion of sadness is followed by anger (at self), and then fear of the consequences (to self) for one's actions. For guilt, the ordering is the reverse: Sadness is followed by fear about the consequences (to self) for one's actions, and then anger (at self).

Turner argued that shame and guilt are ways that natural selection worked to mitigate the power of the three negative primary emotions while producing emotions that keep individuals in line with cultural codes. As social organization had fitness-enhancing value for hominids, natural selection found a way to reduce the potentially disruptive effects of the three negative primary emotions by "combining" them into moral emotions. In a study of monozygotic and dizygotic twins, researchers found a strong genetic and weak environmental (socialization) effect for shame responses, whereas the opposite was found true for guilt: a weak genetic effect and a strong environmental effect (Zahn-Waxler and Robinson 1995). Thus, shame may be more hard wired than guilt, with the latter needing activation (much like language) through guilt-inducing experiences.

Naturally, the elaboration of culture leads to complex interaction effects between biology and culture. Larger brains allow humans to remember who has reciprocated and who has not over prolonged periods, to articulate what is just and transform this into cultural codes, and to convert expectation states into norms. Still, there is a biological basis for this morality. The emotions that humans experience when violating moral codes are not only the product of socialization into a moral culture; they also represent elaboration of hard-wired propensities of humans for reciprocity, justice, shame, and guilt.

Thus, it is important to avoid the sociologist's tendency to see all culturally directed behavior as socially constructed. The bias of culture toward expounding morality began with natural selection biasing hominid and then human neuroanatomy toward moral behaviors. Culture and socialization simply expanded the range of situations activating the moral emotions. The capacity and, indeed, the propensity to emit moral emotions are probably much more hard wired than most sociologists are willing to acknowledge.

THE MORAL SELF

Moral emotions connect a person to social structure and culture through self-awareness. This awareness is codified in a more general, transsituational self-conception of a person as well as more situational identities tied to roles in institutional systems (Turner 2002). An individual's transsituational self-conception and more situational identity are both cognitive and emotional constructs. They involve conceptions of who a person is, how others should respond to self, and valenced emotions about the characteristics of self in several or particular roles.

Most sociological conceptions view self as organized into different parts or *identities*, with some identities more prominent or salient than others in the overall hierarchy of identities (McCall and Simmons 1978; Stryker 2002). Those identities higher in the hierarchy are more likely to direct behavior. Individuals seek to verify their identities in all episodes of interaction, and when identities are verified, they feel positive emotions. When there is a failure to verify identities, individuals experience negative emotions. In response to the negative emotions, persons seek to restore verification by, for example, modifying how they are behaving or selectively attending to the feedback of others in the situation.

Because self is emotionally valenced, it can potentially become moral. Recently, it has been argued that individuals have a moral identity that is at one of the highest levels (the principal level) in the overall hierarchy of identities (Stets and Carter 2006). Stets and Carter (2006) argued that the moral identity operates like a "master" identity in that it influences the selection of other identities such as role and group identities. In this way, the moral self operates across various roles and within different groups. It guides moral conduct. When there is a discrepancy between the meanings of the moral identity and the meanings implied by individuals conduct, negative moral emotions emerge. Indeed, Stets and Carter found that when individuals are faced with moral dilemmas and do not respond in accordance with their moral identities, they report negative moral emotions. For example, when individuals' moral identities carry meanings of being caring and just, they report feeling shame and guilt when they do not return extra money that they receive or, alternatively, that they do not donate to a charity.

People tend to make moral evaluations of their various identities. Verification of self is an affirmation about what an individual perceives as good (and bad) about self, while a failure to verify self calls into question the moral evaluation of self. This moral dimension to self adds extra emotional fuel to interaction. It is one thing to sense that one has violated a moral code or behaved incompetently, and quite another to view self as not realizing the standards of morality contained in self-definitions or identity standards. Additionally, the higher in the hierarchy an identity is, the more likely it is to be evaluated in moral terms. Hence, its confirmation or disconfirmation will generate intense emotions.

Because the referent of moral emotions such as shame or guilt is the identities high in the hierarchy, these emotions can be particularly painful because self has much at stake. When there is a lack of verification of the moral self, verification can be achieved through apologies, role-taking, and behavioral modifications. Alternatively, if the pain is particularly acute, it may cause individuals to activate defense mechanisms, transmute the emotions into variants and combinations of anger, and make projections, displacements, and attributions onto others and social units.

Thus, the more a person's identity is high in his or her hierarchy and the more it is sanctioned negatively by others (or the person through introspection), the more intense will be the negative emotional arousal, and the more likely the person will activate defense mechanisms. Conversely, the less the negative sanctioning and the lower in the hierarchy the identity subject to disconfirmation is, the more likely a person will engage in corrective behaviors to verify self and identity.

It is possible for self to engage in moral misconduct and for self and others to not respond with negative emotions. The self may be experiencing multiple negative life events, (e.g., losing a job and going through a divorce), and under such stressful conditions, the person's moral misconduct may be tolerated. Self may be given "short-term credit" for past behavior that can be applied to "ride out" the current situation (McCall and Simmons 1978). Alternatively, self and others may engage in "selective perception" (i.e., they do not attend to the moral misconduct); they may engage in "selective interpretation," as in putting a "good spin" on the moral misconduct; or self may deny responsibility for his or her actions and others agree that self is not to be held responsible (McCall and Simmons 1978). Thus, not all moral misconduct leads to negative emotional arousal.

There are sociopaths, those who lack moral concern, who will not experience moral emotions in response to their own behavior. They also will not feel the harm when others express moral emotions in response to their misdeeds. They are not members of the moral community; in fact, they disregard the moral community as legitimate. Thus, Braithwaite's (1989) thesis that we should respond to criminal behavior by shaming offenders rather than imprisoning them in order to punish them, reduce recidivism, and build consciences only is possible for those who are not shameless, remorseless, and beyond conditioning by shame.

SOCIAL STRUCTURE AND MORAL EMOTIONS

Standing between culture and the individual is social structure. Some cultural codes such as values are highly general, but eventually they must be attached to encounters among individuals operating within the status-roles of social systems. Other cultural codes like norms and expectation states cut across diverse structures and become activated within a local situation. For example, the expectation of competence exists across various institutional domains and emerges in local situations such as the boardroom, the classroom, or the courtroom. Thus, individuals consider the morality of a situation as it is filtered down to them through the more inclusive structure in which they are interacting. Surprisingly, as the profession that presumably studies social structure, sociologists have not developed a consensus over how to conceptualize this centerpiece of the discipline.

The most traditional conceptualization of social structure is as a system of status positions, with individuals playing roles guided by the cultural codes attached to positions. In the study of emotions, the two most important components of status positions are their relative power and prestige (Houser and Lovaglia 2002; Kemper 1991; Stets and Burke 2005; Thamm 2004). Power and status can be resources that are differentially distributed in terms of moral criteria (competence, tradition, skill, and the like). Given this differential distribution, individuals will experience moral emotions to the degree that they evaluate the allocation of power and prestige as just and fair. Thus, moral emotions are often entailed in the status structure of encounters and groups as well as the larger social structures in which encounters and groups are embedded. Individuals can accept or resist this status structure, and their moral assessment is measured largely through the yardstick of justice and fairness.

Another conception of social structure is as a network, with the network consisting of nodes that are, to varying degrees, connected to each other. The links among nodes are generally conceptualized as a resource flow. Resources can be information, emotions, exchanges of rewards, or anything that individuals can share or exchange. When individuals stand at different places in a network, they develop expectations for exchanges of resources with other nodes in the network. Once this process operates to connect nodes in the network, it is likely to activate those biological systems generating expectations, reciprocity, and justice. These biologically based reactions to resource flows are, of course, also likely to be enshrined in cultural codes, thus making the arousal of moral emotions that much more predictable. As a general rule, the greater the level of density in the network, the more individuals know each others' respective resources, and, hence, the more likely is the receipt of resources to be monitored in terms of moral standards that codify expectation states for reciprocity and justice.

Still another concept of social structure is the substantive organization of the division of labor. For example, a productive division of labor coordinates individuals' activities and pools their contributions toward completion of a task or realization of goals. Such structures are more likely to develop a morality against free-riding in favor of norms and other evaluative symbols about the importance of individuals contributing their fair share (Coleman 1990; Hechter 1987; Lawler 2001). Productive organization is thus more likely to activate moral emotions than are alternative structures that do not pool and coordinate labor to a high degree. Status and prestige can intersect with dense networks and productive divisions of labor, adding new layers of morality to expectations for performance by those with varying degrees of power and prestige and to the rewards that actors should receive by virtue of their status and performance.

A final way to visualize social structure is as a target of defense mechanisms and attribution processes. When individuals experience negative emotions, particularly powerful ones like shame, they may repress these emotions and make external attributions to others, the local encounter, or more inclusive social structures. In an effort to protect self, individuals often see social structures as somehow violating expectations and justice norms. In general, there is a distal bias to negative emotions (Lawler 2001), and the more negative the emotions experienced by individuals, the more likely are they to repress the emotions and transmute them into negative emotions directed at social structures. These are moral emotions because they often come from repressed or bypassed shame or anger at perceived injustices meted out by others or social structures.

Before exploring the implications of the above for expanding the conceptualization of the moral emotions, we should review the various ways that social scientists have conceptualized emotions as moral. We divide this review into four parts: the self-critical moral emotions of shame and guilt (Tangney and Dearing 2002), the other-critical moral emotions of contempt, anger, and disgust (Rozin et al. 1999), the other-suffering responses of sympathy and empathy (Clark 1997; Hoffman 2000), and the other-praising moral emotions of gratitude and elevation (Haidt 2003). While self-critical moral emotions are the negative emotions directed at self for violating moral codes, other-critical moral emotions are the negative emotions directed at others for the violation of moral codes. Also, whereas other-suffering emotions are the negative feelings associated with witnessing another experience something bad, other-praising emotions are the positive feelings associated with witnessing another do something good.

Self-Critical Moral Emotions: Shame and Guilt

In reviewing shame and guilt, we first turn to the work of Lewis. As a psychotherapist, Lewis (1971) offered an important corrective to Freud's and other clinicians' overemphasis on guilt. In her review of transcripts of therapy sessions, she observed that shame appeared to be the more common emotion. Indeed, she argued that therapists often mislabeled shame as guilt. Both shame and guilt are self-referential in that they make individuals self-conscious, unless defense mechanisms are activated. Both shame and guilt arise when individuals or others in the situation perceive that there has been a transgression of cultural codes or a failure to live up to these codes. Despite these similarities, there are some very important differences between shame and guilt.

Lewis argued that shame is an emotion that focuses on a person's global self, making the individual feel small, worthless, powerless, and otherwise in disfavor with others. The individual, when experiencing shame, must observe self as both an insider and outsider, viewing self as unworthy from within as well as from the perspective of others. Shame leads individuals to be concerned with others' evaluation of self and motivates them to hide, escape, or strike back. Shame impairs self because it is so painful, increasing the probability that persons will activate defense mechanisms to protect self. As a result, shame often leads individuals to transmute their shame into anger and direct this anger at others, with such anger giving people a sense of efficacy and control (Lewis 1971; Retzinger 1987; Scheff 1987). The overall consequence is that, as defense mechanisms are activated, individuals become less attuned to others.

An interesting finding in the literature is that narcissism is inversely related to shame, but not guilt, and shame is positively associated with "splitting," whereby the narcissistic person swings from one pole where others are praised to the opposite pole where they are criticized and attacked (Gramzow and Tangney 1992). One interpretation of splitting is that narcissism—the concern with self and the constant focus on self—is a defense mechanism that enables individuals to avoid their accumulated shame. Like all shame-prone individuals, narcissists do not experience sympathy and empathy for others. Indeed, they are rather poor at role-taking.

In contrast to shame, which attacks the whole self, guilt is about a particular behavior that is perceived by a person to have violated moral codes. Rather than seeing the global self in negative terms, guilt leads individuals to perceive that they "did a bad thing" while generally leaving the level of evaluation of the whole self in place. As a result, guilt is less painful, leading people to experience emotions such as remorse and regret while motivating them to confess, apologize, and repair. Guilt increases the likelihood that individuals will role-take with others because guilt motivates them to adjust their behaviors in ways that facilitate cooperation with others (Leith and Baumeister 1998). As a result, guilt can lead to greater interpersonal attunement and, indeed, sympathy and empathy for others. In general, since guilt is not as harmful an emotion for the person because the entire self is not under siege, Tangney (1991) labeled guilt a "bad" feeling and shame as an "ugly" feeling.

Lewis' distinction between guilt and shame is supported by a variety of studies (Tangney and Dearing 2002). There are, however, several points that remain ambiguous in conceptualizations of shame and guilt, particularly shame. While guilt is an emotion that clearly arises when individuals perceive that they have violated moral codes, shame is less obviously connected to moral codes, at least highly evaluative ones. For example, shame often arises when individuals sense that they have behaved incompetently in a situation (Turner 2002). Although such behaviors may be seen as violating a moral code, this is not always the case. The person may gaze into the "looking glass" and simply perceive that he or she has not behaved competently. The shame is private rather than public, the negative evaluation is based on one's self-evaluation rather than social evaluation from others, and the shame may not attack the whole self.

Moreover, it is now well established in the sociological literature that self operates at many levels. Individuals have a transsituational self in that they carry a general view of themselves from situation to situation, but they also have a situational self that is activated in specific encounters and expressed in particular role identities (McCall and Simmons 1978; Stryker 2002). Shame may only attack a specific role identity in a situation, and although individuals seek consistency between their numerous identities in situations and their transsituational self, there is considerable cognitive slippage between the two (Turner 2002). Hence, shame may not always be devastating to the whole self as Lewis would argue, especially since her clinical sample is highly biased toward individuals whose biographies are filled with repressed and bypassed shame.

Conversely, guilt is not always confined to specific behaviors. In other words, specific behaviors do not have to be committed for one to feel guilty (Morris 1987). For example, individuals can feel guilty for wishing harm to a close other (guilt from a "state of mind"), for benefiting from something that cannot be defended as fair or deserved (fortuitous and unjust enrichment), or from thinking of the wrongful acts that have been enacted by others with whom one identifies (vicarious guilt).

Although there are "guilt-prone" individuals and the data appear to show that these individuals focus on specific behaviors rather than the whole self (Tangney and Dearing 2002), most of these data come from experimental settings in which the intensity of all emotions is rather low. These studies tend to underemphasize the extent to which persons with a long history of guilt begin to see their whole self in negative terms, as unworthy and as reprehensible.

Moreover, most studies add the caveat that any conclusions about guilt are only true for "shame-free guilt" (i.e., guilt that is not fused with shame). Guilt that is shame-free does not appear to generate dysfunctional and pathological symptoms in individuals, whereas shame is associated with depression, anxiety, eating disorders, low self-esteem, and subclinical pathologies. In guilt, when one feels bad for having done a bad thing, the negative feeling is restricted to the objectionable behavior and not generalized to the self as a "horrible person." If the generalization did occur, then shame has intruded into the process. Some have labeled this "maladaptive guilt" (Tangney and Dearing 2002). The fact that researchers need to differentiate between "adaptive" and "maladaptive" guilt underscores that often the two emotions occur simultaneously. People can be ashamed of themselves when they have done something "bad," and they can see themselves as unworthy because they have violated moral codes, with the result that many of the defensive behaviors associated with shame alone can also be activated when guilt is mixed with shame.

Guilt is seen as the moral emotion because it fosters responsible, normative, moral behavior, while shame promotes illicit, self-destructive behavior. The latter may be in response to the more negative and deeply painful feelings associated with shame when the whole self is attacked. The relationship among guilt, shame, and moral behavior is particularly compelling when longitudinal data are examined (Miller and Tangney 1994). Tangney (1994) identified children in the fifth grade as either guilt-prone or shame-prone, and then tracked them 8 years later (age 18 or 19). Shame-proneness in the fifth grade predicted later drug use, arrest, imprisonment, suicide attempts, and risky sexual behavior. On the other hand, guilt-prone youths were less likely to engage in these counternormative behaviors years later. Instead, in high school, they were more likely to apply to college, be involved in community service, have fewer sexual partners, and practice "safe sex."

Tangney and Dearing (2002) maintained that shame is a destructive emotion because it leads to the activation of defense mechanisms and the transmutation of shame into anger directed outward. Guilt, on the other hand, is an emotion that leads to role-taking, sympathy, empathy, and attunement. However, shame may serve an adaptive purpose; it may be an effective mechanism for social control in order to ensure conformity to normative expectations (Tomkins 1963). Indeed, when one is behaving counternormatively, shaming may be an internal control device that can substitute for external control. This conclusion is consistent with Braithwaite's (1989) thesis as well as with an earlier argument made by Shott (1979) as to how shame can encourage normative, solidarity-generating behavior. Braithwaite maintained that reintegrative shaming, in which a person's act is disapproved but the whole person does not come under attack, can aid in deterring criminality since the disapproval from significant others, coupled with the shame and repentance that follows, can build a conscience. In turn, a conscience is the key to internal control, lowered recidivism, and reintegration into the larger community.

From an evolutionary perspective, Tangney and Dearing (2002) argue that shame had a purpose during earlier stages of evolution, but with increasing complexity of society, there was a corresponding development in cognitive and emotional complexity, including the ability to role take, to differentiate self from behavior and not blur them, and to empathize with another's plight. More primitive concerns of reducing potentially lethal aggression, affirming one's rank in the social system, and conforming to social norms are replaced in modern society with taking responsibility for wrongful actions and engaging in reparative moves. Thus, while shame was the moral emotion of the past, guilt is the moral emotion of the present.

Tangney and Dearing's conclusion seems naive. In all societies in all times and places, both guilt *and* shame have operated to keep behavior in compliance with normative expectations; at the same time, these emotions serve to maintain commitments to groups and moral codes (Turner 2002). Turner (2000) argued that natural selection worked on the hominid neuroanatomy to combine all of the negative primary emotions to produce emotions like shame and guilt that make individuals self-conscious of their behavior and likely to act in ways that avoid experiencing the pain of shame. In the smaller hunting-and-gathering societies, where shame as an emotion first evolved in hominids and then humans, the experience of shame in the band would be of low intensity; high intensity could lead to repressing the shame, and repressed shame can spiral out of control into more negative emotions such as anger and rage. Once the low-intensity shame was experienced, it would operate as an internal control mechanism, keep individuals "in line," and, in turn, sustain commitments to others and produce solidarity. This line of argument is consistent with the ideas of other evolutionary researchers; for example, Gilbert (1997) contended that acknowledged shame provides a basis for corrective action and attunement.

It is acknowledging shame that is difficult, and as Turner (2002) emphasized, the intensity and frequency with which shame has been experienced determines the likelihood that repression will occur. If individuals experience mild shame, they are less likely to repress this emotion and, instead, use it as a basis for behaving more competently or morally. This conclusion is consistent with Scheff's (1990) thesis, which argues that if shame is acknowledged, then individuals can reattune their relations with others in ways that promote solidarity.

Other-Critical Moral Emotions: Contempt, Anger, and Disgust

While shame and guilt are reactions to one's moral worth within a moral community, contempt, anger, and disgust are reactions to the moral violations of others (Haidt 2003; Rozin et al. 1999). Anger is least likely to be seen as an "other-oriented" moral emotion because it is often a reaction to one's goals being blocked, and the revenge that is sought may end up hurting another, thereby creating problems in attunement. However, it is also true that anger emerges when another is perceived as committing an intentional and unjustifiable act that is directed either at self or others, causing a desire to restore justice (Averill 1982, 1993).

Moral disgust occurs when people interpret others' actions as revolting and inhuman because others have committed moral offenses (e.g., betraying one's family or friends, physically abusing another, perhaps even killing another in cold blood) (Rozin et al. 2000). Individuals act without dignity or treat others without dignity (Rozin et al. 1999). Offenders blur the boundary of humanity and animality by degrading themselves given how they treat others (Haidt 2003). The response to feelings of disgust is to withdraw or break off contact with the offending party compared to attacking the other when one is angry. Essentially, when one is disgusted with another, the offender is ostracized for his or her immoral behavior, and in so doing, the moral order is protected.

Contempt is seen as falling in the middle between anger and disgust; it is a "cool" emotion in comparison to the "heat" of anger or "visceral" feeling associated with disgust (Haidt 2003). Like anger and disgust, it is a negative evaluation of another, but it involves looking down on another and feeling morally superior. Because another does not measure up, less warmth and affection are extended to him or her, thereby weakening other moral emotions such as compassion.

Rozin and his associates (Rozin et al. 1999) maintained that contempt, anger, and disgust emerge across cultures when there is a violation of three moral codes: community, autonomy, and divinity (Shweder et al. 1997). Contempt is linked to the violation of the moral code of community. This moral code involves respecting the social hierarchy, including deference to those in authority, being dutiful and loyal to the group, and honoring the community. Rozin et al. argued that contempt, a negative feeling toward others and their actions, is often triggered when others disrespect hierarchical relations or threaten the preservation of community.

Anger is associated with the violation of the moral code of autonomy. The ethic of autonomy involves respect for individuals' rights, freedoms, and choices. According to Rozin and his colleagues (1999), anger typically emerges when another's actions are seen as infringing upon one's rights and liberties. Such actions are judged unjust and unfair, and they elicit this strong, negative emotional reaction.

Finally, disgust is linked to the moral code of divinity. This ethic emphasizes that which is pure and sacred. There is a consideration of the natural order of things and protection of the soul or world from degradation and spiritual ruin. Rozin et al. (1999) pointed out that because disgust is a reaction to pollution or degradation of the body or soul, it is most closely associated with what may be seen as sinful or defilement of the sacred.

Rozin and his collaborators (1999) found that students in the United States and Japan consistently paired the emotion word and facial expressions of contempt with violations of community, anger with violations of autonomy, and disgust with violations of divinity. Thus, contempt, anger, and disgust act as guardians of different portions of the moral order (Haidt 2003). Each emotion encourages others to change their relationship with the moral violators. However, because anger is the emotion most likely to repair the moral order (since, in essence, the offender is asked to mend his or her ways), it may be the most prototypical other-critical moral emotion, followed by disgust, and then contempt (Haidt 2003).

Other-Suffering: Empathy and Sympathy

Empathy and sympathy can be distinguished in the following way. Empathy involves the capacity to understand the affective state of the other (the cognitive component) or actually feel the emotions that the other feels (the affective component) through taking another's perspective and, in so doing, recognizing and discriminating among the other's affective states (Davis 1994). Sympathy does not so much involve experiencing the emotions of another as an effort to understand the difficulties faced by another and to emit supportive and caring responses. It is the capacity to understand the plight of another and to emit variations of sadness, coupled with support, for another's situation (Clark 1997; Eisenberg 1986). Empathy is not necessary for sympathy; indeed, one could feel sympathy for another but not have an empathic reaction to the other (Clark 1997; Eisenberg 1986). For example, one can have care and concern for another but not necessarily feel what the other is feeling. Additionally, one could feel empathy for another, but this empathy does not lead to feelings of sympathy perhaps because the other is judged as deserving of what has befallen him or her (Clark 1997).

Empathy and sympathy are, in essence, role-taking behaviors, to use Mead's (1934) term. The gestures of others are *read* to determine their affective state, and when this state is on the negative side of the emotional spectrum and the person is judged as undeserving of this negative state, an individual can feel sympathy for the person (Clark 1997). In the case of empathy, the observer understands the other's feelings or feels the emotions experienced by the other (Davis 1994). If such is the case, we can ask: Are empathy and sympathy actual emotions or are they interpersonal mechanisms for understanding or feeling the emotional state of another? In Schutz's (1967) terms, sympathy and empathy simply operate to increase intersubjectivity. There can be no doubt that empathy and sympathy are critical to the social order because the capacity for empathy and sympathy temporarily relieves those in plight of the full range of social responsibilities while generating supporting responses from others (Clark 1997). Also, there is a large literature documenting that empathy and sympathy facilitate close personal relations and altruism (Eisenberg and Miller 1987) while inhibiting aggression (Miller and Eisenberg 1988). Still, are these capacities for empathy and sympathy actual emotions or role-taking abilities? Is there an actual emotion that we could define as empathy or sympathy? As Haidt (2003) pointed out, empathy is not an emotion at all; it is only the tendency or ability to feel what another is feeling. He indicated that the same applies to sympathy; sympathy only reflects two people thinking or feeling the same thing. In most research on these capacities, other emotions such as worry, righteous indication, or anger are typically seen as the outcome of empathy. Compassion, sorrow, or sadness is often seen as the outcome of sympathy. Thus, we question the conclusion that empathy and sympathy are definitive emotions.

We think that what makes researchers see empathy and sympathy as moral emotions is that they generally have moral consequences for social relations. They allow those in plight temporary respite from normal social responsibilities, and they motivate others to offer supportive responses and to feel solidarity-generating emotions. Since the capacities for empathy and sympathy are so critical to maintaining social order, they are regulated by cultural rules, and Clark (1997) identified a list of rules for sympathy givers and receivers. However there is also a darker side to sympathy, as Clark (1990) earlier identified. Sympathy can be used as a tool in games of micropolitics and microeconomics to gain advantage, status, and power over others. For example, sympathy can take the form of a "put down," as in showing concern for another, while drawing attention to the other's negative qualities. This use of "sympathy" makes the other feel inferior. Alternatively, a subordinate can offer sympathy to a superordinate and increase intimacy, thus gaining an advantage.

In general, we question whether empathy and sympathy are emotions, per se, as opposed to role-taking techniques that lead to the arousal of actual emotions. Further, although empathy and sympathy can help sustain the moral order, they may also undermine the moral order, as when actors use sympathy to maintain power over others. A similar argument has been made about guilt. Although guilt can help maintain civility in society as individuals take responsibility for harmful acts and honor commitments, guilt may also be used in interpersonal relationships to get another to do something (Baumeister et al. 1994). For example, one may let another know that a particular action (or inaction) will be hurtful. In turn, the potential transgressor avoids the behavior so as to avoid the aversive state of guilt. Thus, sympathy and guilt may uphold the social order, but they may also be used as tools to undermine the social order.

Other-Praising Moral Emotions: Gratitude and Elevation

Smith (1976), in 1790, was one of the first to discuss gratitude as an important social emotion. He suggested that gratitude was crucial in maintaining society because it promoted goodwill. Indeed, in gratitude, one expresses a pleasant feeling toward a benefactor who has bestowed good fortune on self. To not recognize what another has done for self surely can create problems in attunement.

As Simmel (1950) argued, gratitude is a powerful means of social cohesion, connecting the giver with the receiver.

Recently, McCullough and his colleagues (2001) have outlined how gratitude is a moral emotion. They argued that gratitude has three moral functions: as a moral barometer, a moral motive, and a moral reinforcer. As a moral barometer, gratitude is a response to another's generosity. It is an "affective readout" that the social relationship between two individuals has changed, and one has benefited from the benevolent actions of the other. Gratitude is also a moral motive because it encourages grateful people to behave benevolently themselves. The benevolent action is typically directed at the benefactor; thus, gratitude can underlie reciprocal altruism (Trivers 1971). Finally, when gratitude is expressed, it motivates the benefactor to behave more pro-socially in the future. People who are thanked for their acts of kindness are more likely to help their beneficiaries again. This extends to third parties as well.

Related to the feeling of gratitude is elevation. This is a feeling of warmth and expansion associated with witnessing acts of charity, kindness, and self-sacrifice that manifest humanity's higher nature (Haidt 2003). There is a positive feeling of awe and amazement. As Haidt (2003) pointed out, elevation is the opposite of disgust. Whereas disgust emerges when people blur the lower boundary of humans and nonhumans, elevation occurs when people blur the upper boundary of humans and the divine, as when one witnesses "saintlike" acts. Although the response of disgust involves escaping from the offending party so as not to be "contaminated," the response in elevation is to seek contact—to touch and be in the person's presence. Elevation is in response to moral beauty; disgust is in reaction to moral depravity.

Gratitude and elevation are positive emotions that encourage pro-social behavior. Whereas gratitude motivates pro-social behavior that is local because the action is most likely to be directed at the benefactor, elevation encourages acts of helping, kindness, and charity that are general, motivating one to become a better person and follow the example of the moral exemplar. The pro-social behavior shown in response to gratitude might serve to repay a debt, and thus it is somewhat self-interested, whereas the response to elevation is disinterested (Haidt 2003). Haidt (2003) maintains that elevation is the most prototypical moral emotion of all.

TOWARD A SOCIOLOGY OF MORAL EMOTIONS

From a sociological perspective, emotions arise under predictable conditions while having predictable effects on behaviors, interactions, social structures, and cultural systems. Sociology thus takes a wide view of emotional dynamics (see Turner and Stets, 2005, for a review of the sociological literature), and in the case of the "moral emotions," the goal is to understand the causes and effects of these emotions. The problem is isolating moral emotions from many other emotional states and identifying what is unique about moral emotions.

What Makes an Emotion Moral?

As mentioned earlier, a moral emotion is one that is aroused in reference to cultural codes that contain evaluative content. Sometimes the evaluative content is intense, as is the case of values and ideologies; at other times, the evaluative content is less intense and may only involve the prescription to abide by norms (see Figure 23.1). From a sociological perspective, guilt is perhaps the prototypical moral emotion because it is an affective state generated when a person perceives that he or she has emitted behaviors that violate evaluative cultural codes. Shame is probably less moral because this is an emotion that comes when a person perceives that he or she has behaved incompetently (often in reference to expectations and norms) or when a person senses that others devalue his or her self (Turner 2002). However, there can be many other emotions that are equally moral.

When an individual violates a cultural code, others may have a variety of anger responses to the violation—annoyance, hostility, anger, or rage—and these emotions can be seen as moral emotions. Similarly, the individual who has violated the cultural code can experience a diversity of fear responses (anxiety, alarm, or panic) or a range of sad feelings (downcast, dismayed, sorrowful, or despondent), and these emotions can be considered as moral as shame, guilt, contempt, and disgust. They are, after all, emotions aroused in reference to moral codes. Thus, we need to examine the full range of human emotions and assess if they can become moral in the sense of being aroused by conformity to or deviance from moral codes. One way to get a rough sense of the potential for moral emotional arousal is to examine the range of variation in primary emotions and various complex emotions built from primary emotions to see which ones can, under what circumstances, become moral.

Variations and Elaborations of Emotions

VARIATIONS OF PRIMARY EMOTIONS. All researchers agree that happiness, fear, anger, and sadness are hard wired into human neuroanatomy (Turner and Stets 2005). These emotions can vary in intensity, thereby generating one source of variation in human emotions. Table 23.1 offers one effort to map the variations of these four primary emotions (Turner 2000). Those emotions that are boldfaced are, we believe, potentially moral because they are likely to be activated in situations where behaviors are assessed by the person and others with reference to moral codes. Interestingly, the satisfaction-happiness dimensions of primary emotions do not reveal a large number of emotions that are obviously moral. People are content and satisfied when self and others abide by moral codes, and they may emit friendly and amiable gestures as mild positive sanctions to encourage continued conformity to moral dictates. As we will see, more complex moral emotions emerge when we look at combinations of primary emotions, suggesting that the human brain was rewired to generate these combinations because they had fitness-enhancing value in increasing the cultural regulation of hominid and eventually human conduct.

When we move to the three negative primary emotions, it is immediately evident that there are more emotional valences that can potentially be moral. Thus, an individual who has violated a moral code can feel concern, misgivings, trepidation, anxiety, alarm, panic, and potentially high anxiety. Others responding to this individual can feel unnerved and reveal misgivings. More typically, however, others responding to transgressions of cultural codes by a person will reveal a variety of anger responses from annoyed, agitated, irritated, vexed, perturbed, rankled, and piqued on the low-intensity side to being displeased, belligerent, hostile, irate, and offended at intermediate levels of intensity, to loathing, disgust, hatred, furious, inflamed, incensed, and outraged on the high-intensity end. In essence, almost any variant of anger can become a moral emotion when others feel that a person has violated moral codes.

For the individual violating the codes, this person might reveal anger at self, manifesting itself as annoyance, agitation, displeasure, and loathing (with or at self). More typically, the individual will experience some variant of disappointment-sadness when violating moral codes such as feeling discouraged, downcast, and dispirited at the low-intensity end through dismayed, disheartened, and glum at a moderate intensity level to sorrow, anguished, and crestfallen at the high-intensity end. Others responding to transgressions by an individual, however, are less likely to experience these emotions revolving around sadness, unless they are sympathizing or empathizing with the other. In this case, they might be sorrowful, pained, heartsick, anguished,

TABLE 23.1. Moral Variants of Primary Emotions

	Low Intensity	Moderate Intensity	High Intensity
Satisfaction-happiness	Content	Cheerful	Joy
	Sanguine	**Buoyant**	Bliss
	Serenity	Friendly	Rapture
	Gratified	Amiable	**Jubilant**
		Enjoyment	Gaiety
			Elation
			Delight
			Thrilled
			Exhilarated
Aversion-fear	**Concern**	**Misgivings**	Terror
	Hesitant	**Trepidation**	Horror
	Reluctance	**Anxiety**	**High anxiety**
	Shyness	Scared	
		Alarmed	
		Unnerved	
		Panic	
Assertion-anger	**Annoyed**	**Displeased**	Dislike
	Agitated	Frustrated	**Loathing**
	Irritated	**Belligerent**	**Disgust**
	Vexed	Contentious	**Hate**
	Perturbed	**Hostility**	Despise
	Nettled	**Irate**	Detest
	Rankled	Animosity	Hatred
	Piqued	**Offended**	Seething
		Consternation	Wrath
			Furious
			Inflamed
			Incensed
			Outrage
Disappointment-sadness	**Discouraged**	**Dismayed**	**Sorrow**
	Downcast	**Disheartened**	Heartsick
	Dispirited	**Glum**	Despondent
		Resigned	**Anguished**
		Gloomy	**Crestfallen**
		Woeful	
		Pained	
		Dejected	

Note: Bold indicates an emotion that is potentially moral.

and dispirited about the plight of the person who is the object of sympathy or empathy. However, it is not sympathy or empathy that is the emotion. Rather, the capacities for sympathy and empathy lead individuals to feel variants of sadness for another.

FIRST-ORDER ELABORATIONS OF PRIMARY EMOTIONS. In ways that are only beginning to be understood, the human brain has the capacity to generate emotions that appear to be combinations of primary emotions. Recent imaging studies document some of the areas of the brain responsible for these elaborations of primary emotions (Chen and Singer 1992). Thus

TABLE 23.2. Moral First-Order Elaborations of Primary Emotions

Primary Emotions	→	First-Order Elaborations
	Satisfaction-happiness	
Satisfaction-happiness + *aversion-fear*	→	**Wonder**, hopeful, relief, gratitude, pride, reverence
Satisfaction-happiness + *assertion-anger*	→	**Vengeance, appeased, calmed, soothed**, relish, triumphant, bemused
Satisfaction-happiness + *disappointment-sadness*	→	Nostalgia, yearning, hope
	Aversion-fear	
Aversion-fear + *satisfaction-happiness*	→	**Awe, reverence, veneration**
Aversion-fear + *assertion-anger*	→	**Revulsed, repulsed, antagonism, dislike**, envy
Aversion-fear + *disappointment-sadness*	→	**Dread, wariness**
	Assertion-anger	
Assertion-anger + *satisfaction-happiness*	→	**Condescension**, snubbing, **mollified**, rudeness, **placated, righteousness**
Assertion-anger + *aversion-fear*	→	**Abhorrence**, jealousy, **suspiciousness**
Assertion-anger + *disappointment-sadness*	→	**Bitterness, depression, betrayed**
	Disappointment-sadness	
Disappointment-sadness + *satisfaction-happiness*	→	Acceptance, **moroseness**, solace, **melancholy**
Disappointment-sadness + *aversion-fear*	→	**Regret, forlornness, remorseful, misery**
Disappointment-sadness + *assertion-anger*	→	**Aggrieved, discontent, dissatisfied, unfulfilled**, boredom, **grief**, envy, **sullenness**

far, these areas are generally at points of intersection among those areas of the brain responsible for the emission of primary emotions.

Table 23.2 represents an effort to summarize these first-order emotions. For each emotion listed, there is a greater amount of one primary emotion over another. For example, emotions such as wonder and reverence are mostly happiness "mixed" in some (neurological) way with smaller amounts of fear. What is immediately evident is that first-order combinations dramatically expand the palate of potentially moral emotions (as is emphasized for emotions in bold type). Wonder and reverence can be activated in reference to moral codes within religious institutions. Vengeance, appeased, calmed, and soothed can all be reactions by persons to violations of moral codes or apologies for violations of moral codes.

Moving to the aversion-fear spectrum of first-order emotions, when fear is mixed with happiness, emotions such as awe, reverence, and veneration can generate commitments and conformity to moral codes—again, often religious. Fear mixed with anger leads to emotions like repulsion, antagonism, and dislike that can become negative sanctions against those who have violated moral codes. Fear mixed with sadness can become moral if a person dreads and is wary of situations where he or she might violate moral codes.

Turning to the assertion-anger spectrum of first-order emotions, greater amounts of anger mixed with happiness produces emotions like condescension, mollified, placated, and righteousness, which can serve as responses to violations of moral codes or apologies for violations of moral codes. Anger mixed with fear produces emotions like abhorrence and suspiciousness, which can become negative sanctions for moral transgressions. Anger mixed with sadness leads to emotions such as bitterness, depression, and betrayed, which can become sanctions or, in the case of depression, an emotion experienced by those who have violated moral codes and are subject to sanctioning by others.

Finally, turning to the disappointment-sadness spectrum of first-order emotions, sadness mixed with satisfaction produces emotions like moroseness and melancholy, which can serve as internal sanctions by an individual. Similarly, sadness combined with fear produces regret, forlornness, remorsefulness, and misery, which also can serve as internal sanctions for those who violate moral codes. Sadness alongside anger produces a range of emotions—aggrieved, discontent, dissatisfied, unfulfilled, grief, and sullenness—which a person or others can experience when moral codes are violated by another.

Thus, first-order emotions dramatically expand the range of moral emotions. It is not unreasonable to conclude that natural selection rewired the hominid and human brain to experience these emotions as a means to foster tighter-knit patterns of social organization (Turner 2000). With first-order emotions, there are both subtle and forceful ways to sanction individuals who violate moral codes. Additionally, there are many internal emotions for individuals to experience when transgressing moral codes, with these emotions operating as internal sanctions to bring individuals back into line. Thus, with first-order emotions, the capacity to sanction self and be sanctioned by others is significantly expanded, allowing for more nuanced and complex patterns of moral social relations.

SECOND-ORDER ELABORATIONS OF PRIMARY EMOTIONS.   As briefly discussed earlier, there are also second-order emotions that are created when three primary emotions (anger, fear, and sadness) are combined by the neurology of the human brain. Shame and guilt are two such emotions, and as noted earlier, they represent the work of natural selection to mitigate the power of negative emotions, which, by themselves, will not promote high degrees of social solidarity. By combining these three negative emotions into shame and guilt, potentially disruptive negative emotions can be channeled to more moral ends. When people feel shame and acknowledge this shame (as they generally do when shame valences are low, as is the case of embarrassment), they are motivated to take corrective action and, thereby, reaffirm cultural codes. Similarly, when individuals experience guilt, they are motivated to take corrective actions to affirm cultural codes. Thus, for humans to be moral, they must have the capacity to experience shame and guilt and to use this emotion to offer apologies and adjust behaviors so as to conform to norms, ideologies, and values. Unless individuals can experience shame and guilt, they will become sociopaths, and the moral order will break down.

The very fact that humans reveal second-order emotions suggests that expanding the repertoire of primary emotions through increased variation and first-order combinations was insufficient to ensure social solidarity and control. Natural selection had to do more, and it clearly wired the brain for shame, as twin studies document (Zahn-Waxler and Robinson 1995), and probably for guilt as well, although guilt may be activated primarily through socialization. An animal like humans that must use culture to organize itself requires emotions like shame and guilt to keep people in line, but as we have illustrated above, a very high proportion of the full palate of human emotions can become a basis for morality.

THE PSYCHODYNAMICS OF MORAL EMOTIONS

Negative emotional arousal is unpleasant. The data on shame, in particular, document the pain suffered by individuals because this emotion makes self feel small and unworthy. As long as shame can be of low intensity and can be acknowledged, it operates as a mechanism of self-control and leads to better attunement of responses among individuals (Lewis 1971; Retzinger 1987; Scheff

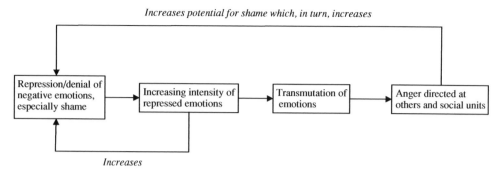

Increases potential for shame which, in turn, increases

Increases

FIGURE 23.2. Basic Model of Repression

1987, 1997). Other negative emotions such as guilt (Shott 1979) can work similarly as internal mechanisms of social control. Still other emotions like anger can be used in varied patterns of negative sanctioning. Yet, because negative emotions are painful, individuals often engage in defensive behaviors to protect self, at least for at time.

Defensive Strategies

There is a wide variety of defensive strategies and mechanisms that push negative emotions about self below the level of consciousness. Among the most common are defensive strategies that are used by individuals to deal with occasional negative sanctions from others about their conduct. These include selective perception of others' gestures, selective interpretation of these gestures, and invoking short-term credit from past successes to ride out a present episode of negative emotional arousal (McCall and Simmons 1978). Other defense mechanisms tend to be more chronic and begin with repression of the full impact of negative sanctions and the resulting feelings, particularly shame but also other negative emotions listed in Tables 23.1 and 23.2 as well.

Repression and Other Defense Mechanisms

There can also be varying levels and types of repression. For example, drawing from Lewis' analysis of shame, Scheff (1979) has argued that individuals can underdistance themselves from shame. In underdistancing, persons allow the shame to overwhelm their actions and speech as in averting gaze, blushing, covering of face, slowed speech, lowering of auditory level of speech, and gushing coded words such as "foolish," "stupid," or "silly"; the purpose is to not differentiate the nature of the shame and its source. Individuals can also overdistance themselves from shame by using rapid speech and gesturing before the shame can be experienced and acknowledged. Whatever the exact mechanisms, the shame and other negative feelings about self are repressed. Once repressed, the emotions build in intensity and require additional cognitive efforts at repression. Most important, the repressed emotions are often transmuted to other emotions, mostly revolving around anger and its variants and combinations (see Tables 23.1 and 23.2). The basic model of repression is delineated in Figure 23.2.

The interesting question becomes: Are repressed and transmuted emotions "moral emotions"? We think that they are if they are emotions such as repressed shame and, we could add,

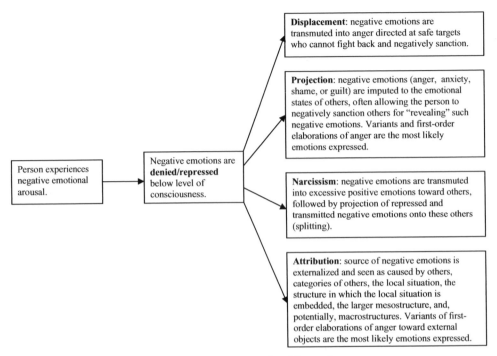

FIGURE 23.3. The Dynamics of Repression

repressed guilt (as well as the highlighted emotions in Tables 23.1 and 23.2) that originally emerged from a violation of shared values, beliefs, or norms. The specific mechanisms by which repression occurs often dictate the nature of the transmuted emotion. Figure 23.3 outlines some possibilities.

When repression leads to displacement of emotions, the repressed emotion is generally transmuted to variants of anger and directed at safe objects and persons who are typically not in a position to fight back. When repression revolves around projection, the emotion might not be transmuted but simply imputed to another, although transmutation often occurs. Thus, anxiety, shame, and guilt can be transmuted to anger and imputed as the emotional state of the other. Narcissism leads to an overconcern with self, which transmutes shame into cycles of positive and negative affect toward others who are seen to attend to, or fail to attend to, the needs of the narcissist. Also, attribution involves transmuting negative emotions about self into variants and combinations of anger, which can then be directed at six potential objects: (1) immediate others, (2) remote others or categories of others, (3) the local situation, (4) the structure in which the local situation is embedded, (5) the larger mesostructure (e.g., organization, community), and, potentially, (6) the macrostructures (institutions) of a society, another society, or system of societies.

Attribution as a Key Defense Mechanism

Attribution is generally considered to be a cognitive processes (Weiner 1986), which it certainly is, but it is also a defense mechanism that follows from repression of emotions about self (Turner 2002). When individuals make internal attributions and see self as the cause of their negative emotional arousal, they will experience variants and combinations of sadness and fear, often coupled with variants of anger toward self (with shame and guilt being combinations of all three negative emotions). Once repressed, negative emotions about self are generally transmuted and attributed to the actions or properties of others and social structures. Attribution is thus not only a cognitive process of assigning causality to events, it also operates as a defense mechanism. In fact, it may be the most important mechanism from a sociological perspective because attributions are often directed to social structures and the culture that they contain, thus affecting commitments to or alienation from micro-, meso-, and macrostructures that organize social life.

When shame, guilt, and other negative emotions about self are repressed, external attributions about the behaviors and properties of others and social units will often ensue. Because shame and guilt are composed of the three primary negative emotions, the attributions will be negative and will generally be transmuted into variants and combinations of anger, although other negative emotions are also possible. These are moral emotions to the extent that they arise from the repression and transmutation of negative emotions about self and the behaviors of self in relation to moral codes.

There is a distal bias for negative emotions, and, conversely, there is a proximal bias for positive emotions (Lawler 2001; Turner and Stets 2005). Individuals will generally make external attributions for negative emotional arousal and internal attributions directed at self for positive emotional experiences. If individuals experience positive emotions as a result of meeting moral expectations, they will also experience variants of happiness, and if there was some fear about meeting these expectations, they may also experience pride (a mix of happiness and fear). Moreover, if individuals experience positive emotions for their moral conduct, they will also generally express positive emotions to others in the local situation; they will become more committed to moral codes and to the structures in which they are entailed. Also, they will increasingly define self in terms of these codes. In contrast, if individuals experience negative emotional arousal as a consequence of being sanctioned by others for not meeting cultural codes or as a outcome of internal self-monitoring, their negative emotional arousal will often be repressed, transmuted, and imputed to others or social structures. It is the precise target of attribution that influences the exact emotions experienced by individuals making these attributions.

If immediate others in the situation are seen to cause negative emotional arousal, individuals will generally express variants and combinations of anger toward these others—annoyance, irritation, displeasure, dislike, and, in extreme cases, intense emotions like hatred and loathing. Moreover, if the anger is mixed with happiness, then very volatile emotions like righteous anger and vengeance emerge. If, however, others are powerful, a person might shift the target of attribution to others not present or to categories of others, such as members of a minority group or a social category like "management," that are generated by the hierarchical division of labor in many social structures. These are safer targets that generally remain unaware of the attribution and, hence, cannot negatively sanction a person. Again, the general emotion is anger at others and categories of others, and this anger is often codified into prejudicial beliefs that take on a moral character, especially when fueled by righteous anger. When the righteous anger is sufficiently intense, very intense emotions like hatred and vengeance may emerge.

If the attribution is to the social unit, then the immediacy of the unit influences the emotions aroused. If the anger is at the local situation in which the encounter producing negative emotions is embedded, then dissatisfaction, aggrievement, frustration, and annoyance are likely responses; if the repression is chronic, then a person is likely to experience a sense of alienation and negative emotions, such as being downcast, dismayed, resigned, gloomy, dejected, and disheartened, on the disappointment-sadness continuum. If the anger is at the structure within which the local situation is embedded, then the same emotions are likely to emerge.

When emotions move to meso- and macrostructures, the emotions become more like those directed at categories of others and reveal a distinctly moral tone. In fact, the more attributions are directed at mesounits and macrounits, the more likely they will be codified into prejudicial beliefs that are seen to justify righteous anger at, and alienation from, social structures and the culture that they embody. At times, the emotions become so intense that righteous anger leads to a desire for vengeance, as is the case of survivalists groups and others who "hate" the U.S. government or terrorists who seek revenge by acts of violence against meso- and macrostructures, including members of a whole society or even systems of societies. Righteous anger and vengeance are almost always moral emotions because they are codified into beliefs about what is "wrong" with a structural unit and about the necessity to act in ways to eliminate the "evil" forces in this unit.

For negative emotions to build to such intensity, the biographies of persons making the external attributions are generally filled with repeated episodes of shame and other negative emotions that are repressed or cannot be expressed except at distant targets whose members are dehumanized and placed into a social category about which prejudices are codified. Thus, what begins with iterated episodes of repressed shame and other negative emotions directed at self can, over time, fuel collective mobilizations that espouse a moral cause, which, in turn, makes it appropriate to have intense forms of anger and first-order combinations of anger like righteousness and vengeance in the name of this cause. Scheff and Retzinger (1991), for example, have analyzed the rise of Nazi Germany in these terms, viewing the hierarchical structure of prewar German society as shame-inducing; coupled with the continued humiliation demanded by the treaty ending World War I, Germans could be mobilized to initiate war couched in moral terms.

CONCLUSION: MORAL EMOTIONS AND THE MORAL ORDER

The macro-, meso-, and microstructures that organize social life all contain moral content. This is the moral order. The best way to see this moral content—this moral order—is for individuals to violate the values, ideologies, or norms, and then to observe people's emotional reactions to this violation. We have only to observe persons' expressed emotions when they hear of corporate leaders stealing from the pension fund of hard-working individuals, priests sexually abusing the young, or terrorists blowing up more human life. Such acts are evaluated as wrong and unacceptable, and the emotional reaction of anger or outrage signals to self and others that the moral order has been threatened. Humans are socialized into the moral order, and they act in ways to maintain it. Humans are moral animals (Smith 2003). Those who repeatedly violate the moral order, such as sociopaths, activate in others not only deep revulsion for the harm inflicted but also for the lack of remorse at having violated the order. Consequently, others find ways to isolate them in order to minimize their harm and preserve the moral order.

Humans may not do a good job of upholding the moral order when violations occur because they engage in defensive strategies such as repression. With repression, emotions are transmuted and displaced, projected, or attributed to the actions or properties of others or social structures. As a consequence, the moral order becomes complex and conflictual. When operating well, however, the moral order leads individuals to take responsibility for moral transgressions, to express the appropriate moral emotions such as regret or remorse, to recognize its harmful outcomes including role-taking and showing empathy or sympathy, and to engage in some action to repair things. Reparative action signals to others that personal and moral commitments are being honored. Essentially, the expression of moral emotions tells self and others much about what the self honors and values. However, repression and transmutation break the connections between self and the moral order, thereby making the emotional life of self and others difficult and often powerful. Yet, without moral emotions, the social order cannot be sustained, and so, the obstacles of repression and transmutation must be overcome to have viable societies.

REFERENCES

Averill, James R. 1982. *Anger and Aggression: An Essay on Emotion*. New York: Springer-Verlag.

———. 1993. "Illusions of Anger." Pp. 57–68 in *Aggression and Violence: Social Interactionist Perspectives*, edited by R. B. Felson and J. T. Tedeschi. Washington, DC: American Psychological Association.

Baumeister, Roy F., Arlene M. Stillwell, and Todd F. Heatherton. 1994. "Guilt: An Interpersonal Approach." *Psychological Bulletin* 115: 243–267.

Braithwaite, John. 1989. *Crime, Shame and Reintegration*. Cambridge: Cambridge University Press.

Chen, D. P., and R. N. Singer. 1992. "Self-Regulation and Cognitive Strategies in Sport Participation." *International Journal of Sport Psychology* 23: 277–300.

Clark, Candace. 1990. "Emotions and Micropolitics in Everyday Life: Some Patterns and Paradoxes of 'Place'." Pp. 305–333 in *Research Agendas in the Sociology of Emotions*, edited by T. D. Kemper. Albany: State University of New York Press.

———. 1997. *Misery and Company: Sympathy in Everyday Life*. Chicago: University of Chicago Press.

Coleman, James S. 1990. *Foundations of Social Theory*. Cambridge, MA: Belknap Press of Harvard University Press.

Davis, Mark H. 1994. *Empathy: A Social Psychological Approach*. Boulder, CO: Westview.

de Waal, Frans. 1996. *Good Natured: The Origins of Right and Wrong in Humans and Other Animals*. Cambridge, MA: Harvard University Press.

Eisenberg, Nancy. 1986. *Altruistic Cognition, Emotion, and Behavior*. Hillsdale, NJ: Erlbaum.

Eisenberg, Nancy, and Paul Miller. 1987. "Empathy, Sympathy, and Altruism: Empirical and Conceptual Links." Pp. 292–311 in *Empathy and Its Development*, edited by N. Eisenberg and J. Strayer. New York: Cambridge University Press.

Gilbert, Paul. 1997. "The Evolution of Social Attractiveness and its Role in Shame, Humiliation, Guilt and Therapy." *British Journal of Medical Psychology* 70: 113–147.

Gramzow, Richard, and June P. Tangney. 1992. "Proneness to Shame and the Narcissistic Personality." *Personality and Social Psychology Bulletin* 18: 369–376.

Haidt, Jonathan. 2003. "The Moral Emotions." Pp. 852–870 in *Handbook of Affective Sciences*, edited by R. J. Davidson, K. R. Scherer, and H. H. Goldsmith. New York: Oxford University Press.

Hechter, Michael. 1987. *Principles of Group Solidarity*. Berkeley: University of California Press.

Hoffman, Martin L. 2000. *Empathy and Moral Development: Implications for Caring and Justice*. New York: Cambridge University Press.

Houser, Jeffrey A., and Michael J. Lovaglia. 2002. "Status, Emotion, and the Development of Solidarity in Stratified Task Groups." Pp. 109–137 in *Advances in Group Processes*, Vol. 19, edited by S. R. Thye and E. J. Lawler. Greenwich, CT: JAI Press.

Jasso, Guillermina. 1980. "A New Theory of Distributive Justice." *American Sociological Review* 45: 3–32.

Kemper, Theodore D. 1991. "Predicting Emotions from Social Relations." *Social Psychology Quarterly* 54: 330–342.

Lawler, Edward J. 2001. "An Affect Theory of Social Exchange." *American Journal of Sociology* 107: 321–352.

Leith, Karen P., and Roy F. Baumeister. 1998. "Empathy, Shame, Guilt, and Narratives of Interpersonal Conflicts: Guilt-Prone People Are Better at Perspective Taking." *Journal of Personality* 66: 1–37.

Lewis, Helen. 1971. *Shame and Guilt in Neurosis*. New York: International Universities Press.

McCall, George J., and J. L. Simmons. 1978. *Identities and Interactions*. New York: Free Press.

McCullough, Michael E., Shelley D. Kilpatrick, Robert A. Emmons, and David B. Larson. 2001. "Is Gratitude a Moral Affect?" *Psychological Bulletin* 127: 249–266.

Mead, George H. 1934. *Mind, Self, and Society*. Chicago: University of Chicago Press.

Miller, Paul A., and Nancy Eisenberg. 1988. "The Relation of Empathy to Aggressive and Externalizing/Antisocial Behavior." *Psychological Bulletin* 103: 324–344.

Miller, Rowland S., and June Price Tangney. 1994. "Differentiating Embarrassment and Shame." *Journal of Social and Clinical Psychology* 13: 273–287.

Morris, Herbert. 1987. "Nonmoral Guilt." Pp. 220–240 in *Responsiblity, Character, and the Emotions*, edited by F. Schoeman. New York: Cambridge University Press.

Retzinger, Suzanne M. 1987. "Resentment and Laughter: Video Studies of the Shame-Rage Spiral." Pp. 151–181 in *The Role of Shame in Symptom Formation*, edited by H. B. Lewis. Hilldsdale, NJ: Erlbaum.

Rozin, Paul, Jonathan Haidt, and Clark R. McCauley. 2000. "Disgust." Pp. 637–653 in *Handbook of Emotions*, edited by M. Lewis and J. M. Haviland-Jones. New York: Guilford.

Rozin, Paul, Laura Lowery, Sumio Imada, and Jonathan Haidt. 1999. "The CAD Triad Hypothesis: A Mapping Between Three Moral Emotions (Contempt, Anger, Disgust) and Three Moral Codes (Community, Autonomy, Divinity)." *Journal of Personality and Social Psychology* 76: 574–586.

Scheff, Thomas J. 1979. *Catharsis in Healing, Ritual, and Drama*. Berkeley: University of California Press.
———. 1987. "The Shame-Rage Spiral: A Case Study of an Interminable Quarrel." Pp. 109–149 in *The Role of Shame in Symptom Formaqtion*, edited by H. B. Lewis. Hillsdale, NJ: Erlbaum.
———. 1990. "Socialization of Emotion: Pride and Shame as Causal Agents." Pp. 281–304 in *Research Agendas in the Sociology of Emotions*, edited by T. D. Kemper. Albany: State University of New York Press
———. 1997. *Emotions, the Social Bond, and Human Reality: Part/Whole Analysis*. Cambridge: Cambridge University Press.
Scheff, Thomas J., and Suzanne M. Retzinger. 1991. *Emotions and Violence: Shame and Rage in Destructive Conflicts*. Lexington, MA: Lexington Books/D. C. Heath.
Schutz, Alfred. [1932]1967. *The Phenomenology of the Social World*. Evanston, IL: Northwestern University Press.
Shott, Susan. 1979. "Emotion and Social Life: A Symbolic Interactionist Analysis." *American Journal of Sociology* 84: 1317–1334.
Shweder, Richard A., Nancy C. Much, Manamohan Mahapatra, and Lawrence Park. 1997. "The Big 'Three' of Morality (Autonomy, Conmmunity, and Divinity), and the Big 'Three' Explanations of Suffering." Pp. 119–169 in *Morality and Health*, edited by A. Brandt and P. Rozin. New York: Routledge.
Simmel, Georg. 1950. *The Sociology of Georg Simmel*. New York: Free Press.
Smith, Adam. [1790]1976. *The Theory of Moral Sentiments*. Oxford: Clarendon.
Smith, Christian. 2003. *Moral, Believing Animals: Human Personhood and Culture*. New York: Oxford University Press.
Stets, Jan E., and Peter J. Burke. 2005. "New Directions in Identity Control Theory." *Advances in Group Processes* 22: 43–64.
Stets, Jan E., and Michael J. Carter. 2006. "The Moral Identity: A Principle Level Identity." pp. 293–316 in *Purpose, Meaning, and Action: Control Systems Theories in Sociology*, edited by K. McClelland and T. J. Fararo. New York: Palgrave Macmillan.
Stryker, Sheldon. 2002. *Symbolic Interactionism: A Social Structural Version*. Caldwell, NJ: Blackburn.
Tangney, June Price. 1991. "Moral Affect: The Good, the Bad, and the Ugly." *Journal of Personality and Social Psychology* 61: 598–607.
———. 1994. "The Mixed Legacy of the Super-ego: Adaptive and Maladaptive Aspects of Shame and Guilt." Pp. 1–28 in *Empirical Perspectives on Object Relations Theory*, edited by J. M. Masling and R. F. Burnstein, Washington, DC: American Psychological Association.
Tangney, June Price, and Rhonda L. Dearing. 2002. *Shame and Guilt*. New York: Guilford.
Thamm, Robert. 2004. "Towards a Universal Power and Status Theory of Emotion." *Advances in Group Processes* 21: 189–222.
Tomkins, Silvan Solomon. 1963. *Affect Imagery Consciousness:* Vol. 2. *The Negative Affects*. New York: Springer.
Trivers, Robert L. 1971. "The Evolution of Reciprocal Altruism." *Quarterly Review of Biology* 46: 35–57.
Turner, Jonathan H. 2000. *On the Origins of Human Emotions: A Sociological Inquiry into the Evolution of Human Affect*. Stanford, CA: Stanford University Press.
———. 2002. *Face-to-Face: Towards a Sociological Theory of Interpersonal Behavior*. Stanford, CA: Stanford University Press.
Turner, Jonathan H., and Jan E. Stets. 2005. *The Sociology of Emotions*. New York: Cambridge University Press.
Weiner, Bernard. 1986. *An Attributional Theory of Motivation and Emotion*. New York: Springer-Verlag.
Williams, Robin Murphy. 1970. *American Society: A Sociological Interpretation*. New York: Knopf.
Zahn-Waxler, Carolyn, and JoAnn Robinson. 1995. "Empathy and Guilt: Early Origins of Feelings of Responsibility." Pp. 143–173 in *Self-Conscious Emotions: The Psychology of Shame, Guilt, Embarrassment, and Pride*, edited by K. W. Fischer and J. P. Tangney. New York: Guilford.

SECTION IV

EMOTIONS IN SOCIAL LIFE

CHAPTER 24

Emotions in the Workplace

Kathryn J. Lively

Over 20 years have passed since sociologists interested in emotion have turned their attention to the workplace. Often hierarchically ordered, the workplace setting offers a natural laboratory, of sorts, for exploring the roles that power and status (Kemper 1978) and cultural (Simon et al. 1992; Clark 1997) and organizational norms (Hochschild 1983; Pierce 1995; Sutton 1991) play in both the experience and expression of emotion.

The first truly sociological examination of emotion in the workplace was Hochschild's (1983) *The Managed Heart: The Commercialization of Feeling*. In a provocative study of the airlines industry (that ranged from the "toe" and the "heel"), Hochschild introduced the workplace as a worthy site to study emotion. Building largely upon her earlier theoretical work (Hochschild 1979) regarding the relationship between emotion and social structure, Hochschild introduced sociologists to the concept of *emotional labor* and raised sociological consciousness of how something that is often thought of as being inherently individual—emotion—is shaped, sometimes to individuals' detriment, by the very social structures and organizations in which they are embedded.

Arguably the most influential book regarding emotion, if not sociology more generally, Hochschild's groundbreaking study challenged not only the way we view emotion but also the way we think about work. Additionally, for good or ill, it has set the agenda for almost every other inquiry of workplace emotion (also see Smith-Lovin 2004). In this chapter, I will revisit Hochschild's *The Managed Heart* and review some of the specific lines of research that have developed as a response to some of her observations. I will also touch upon other related lines of research that have arisen as scholars attempt to more fully understand how emotion operates in the workplace. I will end by suggesting ways in which to enrich that understanding as well as to link the sociological study of emotion in the workplace with other developments within the sociology of emotion more broadly, as well as in social psychology.

Kathryn J. Lively • Department of Sociology, Dartmouth College, Hanover, NH 03755

THE MANAGED HEART

Drawing on numerous theoretical perspectives on emotion (Darwin 1955; Goffman 1959, 1961, 1967; Ekman 1971, 1973; Ekman and Friesen 1969; Ekman et al. 1972; James and Lange 1922; Schacter and Singer 1962), Hochschild (1983) posited that emotion, although culturally shaped, acts as a signal that tells an individual how he or she is faring in a particular social environment (also see Heise 1977; Thoits 1990). Instead of viewing emotion as something irrational or purely biological, Hochschild argued that emotions are subject to rules or norms, much in same way as other forms of behavior. Drawing on examples collected from college student writing, Hochschild illustrated that individuals are aware of which situations or occurrences called for which emotional responses (i.e., we should be happy on our wedding day or sad at a funeral).

Not only did individuals know what feelings they *should* experience, many purposefully managed their emotions so that their emotions would be appropriate to a given situation if they believed that what they were feeling was not owed a particular occurrence. Moreover, those who believed that they had not experienced the proper emotion but yet were unable or unwilling to change it into a more appropriate feeling oftentimes reassessed the meaning that the event had (e.g., I suppose I didn't love him all that much or I would be more upset than I am about his leaving).

Based on her own observations and Ekman's (1973; also see Ekman and Frieson 1969) discussion of display rules, Hochschild (1983) introduced the idea of feeling rules. Feeling rules, by definition, are cultural norms that govern both the display and the experience of emotion. Feeling rules tell us not only what emotions we should feel but also for how long and how intensely we should feel them (Thoits 1990; also see Francis 1997). Drawing on data collected from a variety of sources, Hochschild revealed that people actively manage their emotions by controlling their display (i.e., through *surface acting*) and manipulating their thoughts and memories (i.e., through *deep acting*) to make their feelings correspond to social norms.

When individuals manage their emotions in their private lives (i.e., trying to feel sad at a funeral or happy at a wedding), emotions are said to have use value. Hochschild referred to this social process as emotion work or emotion management. When individuals manage their emotions as part of a job, however, their emotions are turned into commodities; in other words, when emotion management is sold for a wage, emotion management is transformed into emotional labor. Emotional labor refers to one's ability to "induce or suppress feeling in order to sustain the outward countenance that produces the proper state of mind in others" (Hochschild 1983:7).[1]

Building upon arguments from labor scholars and Marxists alike, Hochschild (1983) shifted sociologists' attention to the emotional labor that workers engage in as part of their participation in the increasing U.S. service economy. In this new economy, which is built on the promises of smiling faces and authentic feelings, emotions, perhaps more so than even thought or action, are up for sale. Given emotion's unique relationship with identity (Burke and Harrod 2005; Heise 1977, 2002; Stets and Tsushima 2001; Stryker 2004), however, managing one's emotions *on* or *for* the job might have implications for the self that are not as apparent or relevant when considering other forms of labor. When workers sell their emotions for a wage, they run the risk not only of being alienated from the physical products of their labor but also the emotional ones; they might even be alienated from their very selves (also see Cahill 1989; Smith and Kleinman 1989).

Given sociologists' ongoing interest in the process of socialization, it is not surprising that Hochschild (1983) examined the systematic ways in which corporations socialize workers to engage in emotional labor (also see Leidner 1993; Van Maanen 1991). Focusing primarily on Delta Airlines, a corporation that employed a more Machiavellian approach than most, Hochschild showed that the company had selected individuals whom they perceived as being amenable to constraints being placed not only upon one's physical appearance (i.e., makeup, clothing, and weight) but also one's emotional experiences. In other words, with higher standards for customer service than other airlines at the time and ready access to a mostly nonunionized Southern workforce, Delta carefully hired and retained young, attractive, single women (and to a lesser degree men) who could successfully embody the corporate image that the airlines employed in order to reach and hold a particular segment of an increasingly competitive market.

Although emotional expression can largely be achieved through surface acting, Delta, like many other corporations and organizations, preferred that their employees actually manage their feelings (also see Leidner 1993; Van Maanen 1991), because it is understood that displays of "authentic" emotions are easier to maintain if the feelings are actually present (Hochschild 1983). As a result, Delta and other airlines created guidelines to assist flight attendants' use of deep acting in order to change their emotional experiences and, thus, their subsequent expressions. Specifically, they developed sophisticated strategies through which they trained the flight attendants to produce corporately mandated feeling states, which they believed would create, in turn, feelings of happiness, comfort, safety, and, perhaps most important of all, loyalty in their passengers.

One of Hochschild's (1983) concerns about jobs that routinely require emotional labor is that when individuals are put in the position of continually readjusting their emotional reactions to situations as part of their paid employment, they might put the signal function of their emotional system at risk—a consequence that has negative implications for the self. Specifically, Hochschild warned that individuals who were required to engage in emotional labor for extended periods were at the risk for one of three potential outcomes: a fusion of the self and the work role that might eventually result in the experience of burnout (Maslach 1976; Maslach and Pines 1977), an estrangement between the self and the work role that occurs at the expense of the self and lends itself to feelings of inauthenticity directed toward the self, or a fusion of the self that occurs at the expense of the work role that lends itself to feelings of inauthenticity or cynicism directed toward one's job. Although Hochschild warned about the negative consequences of all three outcomes, Wharton (1999) pointed out that later scholars seem to view the third alternative (e.g., cynicism toward one job) as a rather healthy response to the demands of emotional labor.

Although it might seem that the cost of emotional labor is purely individual, Hochschild (1983) argued that the social distribution of emotional labor is not equitable, thereby making emotional labor a social issue as well as an individual malady (Mills 1999). Despite the fact that emotional labor is necessary for the functioning of a service economy (and, indeed, society as a whole), jobs that Hochschild identified as requiring emotional labor are more commonly associated with service work, middle-class work, and women's work (see Hochschild's [1983] Appendix C for a complete list of so-called emotional labor jobs). To the degree that emotional labor is associated with poor psychosocial outcomes (e.g., feelings of burnout, alienation, or inauthenticity), middle-class women employed in the service industry stand at a greater risk of burnout and other forms of emotional dysfunction than other segments of the population.

Given the exploratory nature of Hochschild's (1983) study, several research agendas have arisen in response to the following questions: Who exactly engages in emotional labor in the workplace? How is emotional labor influenced by sociodemographic characteristics, such as occupational prestige, gender, and race? How does emotional socialization in the workplace or in preparation for a particular profession or occupation occur? What are the psychosocial and economic costs of engaging in emotional labor? In addition to those questions that stem directly from Hochschild's (1983) analysis of the airlines industry, others have also examined more tangential questions pertaining to emotion management, including, but not limited to, the likelihood of emotional expression and the role that others might play in managing emotions both on and for the job and to what degree the workplace is similar to or dissimilar from other important domains (i.e., the family).

Emotional Socialization

Given Hochschild's (1983) conclusions regarding the extent to which Delta socialized its employees to engage in emotional labor, it is not surprising that case studies of other corporations and professional schools were quick to follow. Perhaps the most elaborate of these was Leidner's (1993) examination of the recruitment, training, and monitoring practices that occur in other types of service industry occupations. Unlike Hochschild's single-minded focus on the airlines industry, Leidner compared two distinct interactive service occupations: fast-food handlers and insurance agents. Although these occupations are different in many ways (e.g., differing levels of training, prestige, client contact, autonomy), both are subject to more or less stringent training and monitoring regarding the way that their occupants should feel and express that feeling during interactions with clients. Specifically, food handlers, who received very little training, tended to be easily replaced and were subject to high levels of both routinization (e.g., greeting scripts, prompts for suggestive selling) and monitoring (e.g., surveillance equipment and line managers). The insurance agents, who were more highly trained and, therefore, not viewed as easily replaceable, were granted considerable latitude in their dealings with clients—dealings that typically took place in clients' homes or businesses, away from the prying eyes of supervisors or other forms of surveillance.

In place of the highly routinized scripts typically utilized by counter and drive-thru window help that specified opening greetings, suggestive selling transitions, and words of appreciation and invitation, insurance agents, similar to Hochschild's (1983) flight attendants, were granted sweeping guidelines that they could employ when necessary to gain the upper hand quickly and effectively at the beginning of each sales encounter (Leidner 1993). Many of the strategies crafted and supplied by the corporation assisted the insurance agents by enabling them to engage potential clients' positive feelings of care and responsibility for family members, as well as their negative emotions of fear and guilt.

In addition to the formal and, in some cases, regimented socialization that occurs on the clock in a variety of corporations (Hochschild 1983; Leidner 1993; VanMaanen 1991), others have also documented less tangible means of socialization that occur preemployment (Cahill 1989; Pierce 1995; Smith and Kleinman 1989). Turning their attention away from the workplace, per se, Smith and Kleinman (1989) and Cahill (1989) both illustrated the important role that professional schools play in emotional socialization (also see Pierce 1995). One of the things that set Smith and Kleinman (1989) and Cahill (1989) apart from other studies of the orchestrated efforts of corporations is the shared insight that educational institutions also facilitate informal methods of emotional socialization. In fact, it was often the case that the students themselves were active agents of their own socialization as they came to accept professional norms regarding emotion and to see themselves as members of their chosen profession (also see Lively 2001).

In particular, Smith and Kleinman's (1989) study of medical schools and Cahill's (1989) study of mortuary science students illustrated the processes through which students learn to manage their fear and disgust when handling the dead, as well as their embarrassment, repulsion, and, in some cases, attraction with dealing with live patients (Smith and Kleinman 1989). Although rarely mentioned by faculty or in textbooks, students nonetheless learned what emotions were appropriate and which ones were inappropriate by observing other students' and teachers' reactions to particular events and by participating in social interactions marked with jocular humor (see Coser 1964; Francis 1994). In addition to simply adhering to what Smith and Kleinman (1989) likened to a "hidden curriculum," Cahill (1989) also found that students' feelings of fear and disgust were blunted through the normalization of scenes (e.g., the repeated exposure to stainless-steel gurneys and corpses, plastic busts depicting the ravages of disease and traumatic head wounds, and open doorways between classrooms and embalming laboratories).[2]

Who Engages in Emotional Labor?

The initial studies of socialization that occurred in professional schools aside, most of the initial research on emotion in the workplace centered on the emotional labor performed by what sociologists have come to label as relatively low-status service workers or interactive service workers (McHammon and Griffin 2000). Interactive service workers are those individuals whose jobs are organized around face-to-face or voice-to-voice interactions (Macdonald and Sirriani 1996). Following Hochschild's initial analysis of the airlines industry and her guidance as to the types of jobs that were most likely to require emotional labor (see Appendix C in Hochschild [1983]), researchers have produced numerous studies of the emotional labor performed by occupants in a variety of interactive service occupations ranging from relatively lower-status occupations (e.g., amusement park greeter [Van Maanen and Kunda 1989], nail salon attendant [Kang 2003], food handler [Leidner 1993], emergency operators [Whalen and Zimmerman 1998], and waitress [Gatta 2002]) to their higher-status counterparts (e.g., bill collector [Sutton 1991], detective [Steinross and Kleinman 1989], insurance agent [Leidner 1993], paralegal [Lively 2002; Pierce 1999], nurse [Smith 1992], and attorney [Pierce 1995]).

As noted, early studies of workplace emotion focused on the emotional labor performed by interactive service workers (Leidner 1993). Although these studies tended to focus on relatively low-status workers who engaged in emotional labor in their interactions with clients or customers (Hochschild 1983; Leidner 1993; Rafaeli and Sutton 1990), later studies broadened the scope of what constitutes emotional labor jobs, as well as who constitutes a proper recipient of emotional labor. Both Pierce (1995) and Lively (2000) examined the emotional labor performed by paraprofessionals not strictly for the benefit of clients but also for the benefit of the professionals who employed them.

These two studies, which incorporated more fully than most the hierarchical nature of the settings investigated, revealed that, consistent with theoretical discussions of emotion and status (Hochschild 1979; Ridgeway and Johnson 1990) and experimental studies of small group interactions (Lovaglia and Houser 1996; Ridgeway and Johnson 1990; Ridgeway and Walker 1995), paralegals were typically expected to manage their own anger that arose from their interpersonal interactions with higher-status attorneys and the negative emotions of those same attorneys that might have arisen from either interactions with clients or other stressful events (also see Thoits 1984). Although not implicitly stated, these studies suggest that emotional labor might occur in any occupation in which the maintenance of a given status hierarchy is implicit within the "successful" enactment of an occupational role (also see Rollins 1985).

In addition to these studies of paraprofessionals who engage in emotional labor for the benefit of clients and for higher-status colleagues, Pierce (1995), Harlow (2003), and Bellas (1999) pushed the scope of who does emotional labor even further by studying the emotional labor of relatively high-status professionals (e.g., attorneys and college professors). In conjunction with her examination of the emotional labor performed by paralegals, Pierce (1995) also found that litigation attorneys engaged in significant amounts of emotional labor. However, unlike the paralegals, who were predominantly female and who were required to display caretaking emotions and stifle feelings of agitation (Erickson and Ritter 2001), the attorneys, who were predominantly male, were supposed to evoke agitated feelings.[3] Reminiscent of the earlier studies on emotional socialization (see above), Pierce (1995) reported that litigation attorneys were trained to view all interactions, including those with their paralegals, as interrogations and were taught how to *use* strong negative emotions such as anger and rage as a way to achieve influence over noncooperative clients and opposing counsel (see Clark's, 1990, 1997, theoretical discussions regarding the micropolitical uses of emotion). Although attorneys were typically rewarded for "destroying" witnesses or "tearing down" the opposing side's arguments in the courtroom, they were also taught to take advantage of role-taking emotions (Shott 1979), such as empathy, so as not to alienate jurors by inadvertently bullying a sympathetic witness (i.e., a child, a widow, or an invalid) as well as to engage in "strategic friendliness" in order to reach and retain clients (also see Hochschild 1983; Kang 2003).

Moving even further from what are typically viewed as emotional labor and service-oriented jobs, Bellas (1999) examined the emotional labor of college professors. Expanding upon the client-contact only model, Bellas argued that all four major aspects of an academic career—teaching, service, administration, and research—require emotional labor. Her analysis suggests, however, that the two aspects that openly require emotional labor and its concomitant interpersonal skills (e.g., teaching and service) are less valued, whereas the two evaluated more for their intellectual, technical, or leadership skills and less for the emotional ones are more highly rewarded. Although the emotional labor associated with research and administrative duties might be less time-consuming or obvious as that associated with teaching and service, these activities as sites of emotional labor should not be overlooked in future studies of academic life (Harlow 2003; also see Steinberg and Figart 1999).

The need to study a wide range of occupations in order to understand how emotional labor is utilized and the concomitant consequences has been verified further through the utilization of nationally representative data (Sloan 2003). Using combined data from the General Social Survey's Emotions Module (GSS emotions module; Davis and Smith 1996) and the Dictionary of Occupational Titles (DOT; England and Kilbourne 1988), Sloan (2003) illustrated that individuals in professional jobs were just as likely, if not more so, to perform emotional labor than individuals who were in so-called nonprofessional jobs (Becker 1970). Indeed, other studies using the GSS emotions module also revealed that relative status (e.g., the status difference between two or more actors) might be a better predictor of emotional expression than absolute status in hierarchical settings, of which the workplace is one (Lively and Powell 2006).

GENDER. As noted, Hochschild (1983) argued that women were more likely to engage in emotional labor than men. Her observations about gender differences arose from two sources: by comparing the experiences of male and female flight attendants and by comparing the emotional labor performed by flight attendants (who were disproportionately female) and bill collectors (who were disproportionately male). Even among flight attendants, Hochschild found that women were more likely to be subjected to the negative emotions of others as well as to be held to higher expectations regarding positive emotions, leading her to argue that women have weaker "status shields" than men, which place them at an interactional disadvantage. What this meant, empirically, was that female flight attendants were at a greater risk of being dumped upon by angry customers and that customers expected them to be more emotionally engaged, more caring, and friendlier than their male counterparts (also see Bellas 1999; Martin 1999; Pierce 1995). Hochschild suggested that women's reduced status shields are a function of normative expectations about women and emotion as well as broader structural considerations (e.g., women's lower status compared to that of men).[4]

Following Hochschild's (1983) perspective, other scholars examined gender differences within single occupations and, for the most part, replicated her findings (Martin 1999; Pierce 1995). Unfortunately, the bulk of these studies were centered on occupations that were either disproportionately male (e.g., police, detectives, or litigation attorneys) or those that were disproportionately female (e.g., paralegals, nurses, beauticians). Without exception, these studies confirmed that women were, indeed, held to both a quantitatively and qualitatively different standard of emotional labor than their counterparts. In other words, not only were women expected to engage in more emotional labor than men but also in different types (but see Steinberg and Figart 1999).

For example, whereas Pierce's female paralegals were expected to engage in caretaking or emotional cheerleading for the benefit of their attorneys, the male paralegals in her study were expected to remain emotionally neutral, but politically savvy, "yes men," a role that often garnered higher rewards than those experienced by their female counterparts (also see Heikes 1991; Kanter 1977; Williams 1992). Similarly, Martin's (1999) female police officers were often required to comfort and console witnesses, whereas their male counterparts were more likely required to bully or capture potential suspects (also see Steinross and Kleinman 1989; Sutton 1991). In both cases, the caretaking work that these female occupants provided was typically recognized as part of women's unpaid work and was, perhaps not surprising, among the most despised and devalued aspects of the job (also see Bellas 1999).

Despite what qualitative studies suggest regarding distinct and persisting gender differences in emotional labor in the workplace, the results have been somewhat less conclusive when turning to studies using survey data, whether of specific service organizations (Bulan et al. 1997; Erickson and Wharton 1997), communities (Erickson and Ritter 2001), or societies as a whole (Sloan 2004; Lively and Powell 2006). Although survey data tapping into the experience of emotion in the workplace reveal some subtle and nuanced differences in women's and men's experience, expression, and management of emotions, the findings suggest that the absolute effects of gender on emotion in the workplace or otherwise might, in fact, be overstated—a conclusion that mirrors Ridgeway and Smith-Lovin's (1999) comprehensive review of the literature on gender and face-to-face interaction in small groups.

Moreover, survey data of emotion, more broadly, also report few significant absolute differences between men and women (Lively and Powell 2006; Schieman 2000; Simon and Lively 2005; Simon and Nath 2004; Stets and Tsushima 2001). Looking less at absolute differences in occurrence and frequency, Lively and Heise (2004) revealed slight and subtle gender differences in both the structure of felt emotion as well as the shortest paths between emotion states (e.g., the shortest path between distress and tranquillity or between anger and joy). Further analyses (Lively 2004) suggest that the shortest path between positive and negative emotions differs in substantial ways for women in men. In particular, the shortest path between opposing emotions, for women, seems to be more complicated, to be less efficacious, and to utilize more stereotypically female emotions (Simon and Nath 2004). Although these models have not been tested in naturalistic settings, of which the workplace would be ideal (see below), these findings imply that the strategies that individuals might use in order to successfully manage their emotions on the job or for the job might, in fact, be qualitatively different, even if their outcomes (e.g., actual feeling and expression) are not.

RACE AND ETHNICITY. Unlike its closely studied counterpart, gender, the relationships between race and emotion and ethnicity and emotion within the workplace have been virtually ignored. Although some scholars have commented on the racialized nature of many of Hochschild's (1983) examples within *The Managed Heart*, there has been very little examination of how race or ethnicity affects workers' emotional experiences on the job (but see Gee and DeCastro 2001; Harlow 2003).

Drawing on Feagin's (1991) qualitative work regarding the experiences of middle-class blacks in public spaces and Hochschild's (1983) own examples of racial epithets tossed at flight attendants as dual starting points, Gee and DeCastro (2001) denoted the need to consider race as a complicating factor when considering emotional labor specifically, if not emotion and emotion management more generally, on the basis that racial and ethnic minorities might be required to engage in additional emotion management or emotional labor as a result of their devalued minority status. Despite the inherent logic in their argument—an argument that, in many ways, mirrors Hochschild's (1983) discussion of women's reduced status shields vis-à-vis men and Thoits's (1985) consideration of "normative double binds" (also see Ridgeway and Johnson 1990; Ridgeway and Walker 1995)—few have attempted to investigate this claim empirically.[5]

One noteworthy example, however, is Harlow's (2003) recent comparison of the experiences of black and white college professors employed in a predominantly white university. In her inquiry into the ways in which race affects emotion management in the classroom, Harlow found that the emotional experiences of black professors are different and more complex than those of their white counterparts.[6] Focusing specifically on professor-student interactions, Harlow reported that professors, regardless of race, routinely managed their own emotions in the classroom in an attempt to draw a desired response from their students (also see Bellas 1999). However, whereas all professors are often required to manage their emotions in response to behavioral or classroom management issues, Harlow's study found that black professors were more likely to have to further school their emotional reactions due to challenges to their competency, credentials, and ability to teach and assess student's work. In their attempt to protect themselves from the debilitating effects of day-to-day racism, Harlow argued, black professors are required to manage their emotions by "staying cognizant of macro-level racial barriers while diminishing the importance of those barriers on the micro-level" (p. 362).

Focusing on the experiences of Korean-immigrant nail salon owners, Kang (2003) also examined the influence of race and, in doing so, expanded upon traditional understandings of emotional labor, with the introduction of what she called, "bodily labor." Bodily labor designates a type of gendered work that involves the management of emotion in body-related service provision (also see Cahill 1989; Smith and Kleinman 1988) that is shaped not only by characteristics of the service workers (Hochschild 1983; Martin 1999; Pierce 1995) but also by the race, class, and expectations of the recipients. Specifically, she found that Korean-immigrant salon owners tend to provide high service bodily labor (e.g., physical pampering and emotional attentiveness) for middle- and upper-class white women. In contrast, they offered expressive bodily labor (e.g., artistry in technical skills and communication of respect and fairness) and routinized bodily labor (e.g., efficient, competent physical labor and courteous but minimal emotional labor) to working- and middle-class African American and Caribbean women and mostly lower-middle- and middle-class racially mixed female customers, respectively. Consistent with studies of gender inequality that have been linked to larger patterns of social stratification (Pierce 1995), Kang's findings illustrate how the gendered processes of bodily labor in nail salon work are "steeped with race and class meanings that reinforce broader structures of inequality and ideologies of difference among women" (p. 821).

Similar to investigations of gender that reveal qualitative, but not necessarily quantitative, differences in men's and women's emotional experiences (again, see Simon and Nath 2004), recent investigations of racial differences in emotional experience more generally also exhibit few significant variations. Using combined data from the GSS emotions module and the Chicago Crowding Study (Gove and Galle 1973), Mabry and Kiecolt (2005) found that African Americans generally neither feel nor express more anger than whites, when models control for age and gender, despite African American's lower average sense of control and higher levels of mistrust.

Unfortunately, scholars interested in pursuing racial and ethnic differences in the experience and expression of emotion in the workplace, or even more generally, are limited in their selection of representative data. Although obviously more recent than the Crowding Study, which is now over three decades old, the GSS emotions module was administered to a disappointingly small number of nonwhites. Moreover, the inadequate inclusion of groups other than black-white prevents much, if any, analysis.

Social Consequences of Emotional Labor

One of the most compelling questions that continues to plague researchers who study emotion in the workplace is whether individuals are, in fact, negatively affected by engaging in emotional labor (Hochschild 1983). As noted previously, Hochschild viewed feeling as a signal function that is related to identity, a view that led her to raise the dual specters of burnout (Maslach 1976; Maslach and Pines 1977) and alienation for those who were required to perform emotional labor for extended periods of time (also see Smith and Kleinman 1988).

Despite the intuitiveness of Hochschild's (1983) argument, qualitative studies of food handlers (Gatta 2002; Leidner 1993; Paules 1991) and insurance agents (Leidner 1993) have failed to corroborate her findings. Leidner's (1993) two-pronged study of fast-food workers and sales insurance agents, in particular, revealed fundamental contradictions to Hochschild's predictions regarding the psychosocial costs of emotional labor. Indeed, Leidner reported that both sets of workers actually benefited from emotional labor, albeit for different reasons. The fast-food workers, who, as noted, were typically low skilled, highly regulated, easily replaceable, and usually trapped behind counters or in drive-thru windows, enjoyed the anonymity afforded by the scripts that the corporation provided and the ease with which these routines allowed them to sidestep interactions with difficult or disgruntled customers (also see Rafaeli and Sutton 1990). The insurance agents, who, in contrast to their lower-skilled counterparts, were highly trained, granted a tremendous amount of job autonomy, and often tied to the company through lengthy associations with particular clients or customers, also reported favorably when asked about the emotional labor components of their jobs (Leidner 1993). The insurance agents, in particular, found that the training that they had received provided them with the tools necessary not only to manage their interactions with customers and potential clients but also to meet their professional goals (also see Lively 2001).[7]

Further, other qualitative studies also showcase the ways in which workers *resist* the demands of emotional labor rather than simply give in to their proposed consequences (Gatta 2002; Lively 2000; Pierce 1995). In fact, building upon Burawoy's (1979) ethnography of factory workers' resistance to the demands of management, Pierce (1995) introduced the notion of emotional resistance. Lively (2000) also illustrated how workers who have access to backstage regions (Goffman 1959) might in fact engage in reciprocal emotion management strategies that allow them to resist the costs of engaging in emotional labor.

In order to reconcile the inconsistencies brought about by the various ethnographic case studies, Wharton and her colleagues (Bulan et al. 1997; Erickson and Wharton 1997; Wharton 1993, 1999) undertook a systematic examination of the psychosocial costs of emotional labor using quantitative data collected from bank and hospital workers. Unlike ethnographic studies, where specific conditions or dimensions of meaning might be difficult to isolate or control, Wharton and her colleagues were able to tease apart not only the aspects of emotional labor that could potentially be damaging to workers but also to draw attention to the characteristics of both the jobs and the workers themselves that might have the potential to mediate or moderate the costs of emotional labor (Erickson and Wharton 1997; Wharton 1999; Wharton and Erickson 1995).

In the first of these studies, Wharton (1993) turned her attention to burnout—the predicted consequence of over identification or the fusion of the self to the work role (Hochschild 1983). Controlling for a variety of individual and job characteristics, Wharton (1993) reported that workers in jobs that required emotional labor were no more likely than other workers to experience job-related burnout (also see Wharton and Erickson 1995). In general, she found that burnout was better explained by more general job characteristics (e.g., autonomy and number of hours worked) than by emotional labor. Moreover, and perhaps even more surprising, she also found that workers who performed emotional labor were significantly more satisfied with their jobs than were workers who did not—a finding that suggests that there are, indeed, benefits associated with jobs that require emotional labor (Wharton 1993).

Shifting their focus to inauthenticity, the predicted result of an estrangement between the work role and the self, usually at the expense of the self (Hochschild 1983), Erickson and Wharton (1997) also examined the relationship between inauthentic feelings and emotional labor by comparing the experiences of workers who engaged in emotional labor and those who did not.[8] Unlike qualitative studies where, perhaps out of methodological necessity, researchers tend to treat emotional labor as a one-dimensional outcome (Hochschild 1983; Lively 2002), Erickson and Wharton (1997) measured emotional labor by tapping into three separate dimensions: contact with the public, the amount of time spent working with people on the job, and the degree to which "handling people well" is an important aspect of their job (also see Wharton 1999). Whereas other studies have focused almost exclusively on client contact (e.g., literally the presence or absence of clients; Hochschild 1983; Lively 2002; Sloan 2004), Erickson and Wharton found that "handling people well" was the only dimension of emotional labor positively related to feelings of inauthenticity (also see Wharton 1999).[9]

In another set of analyses, Wharton (1993) also examined whether different aspects of the work itself contribute to burnout and job satisfaction, once again by comparing the experiences of service workers who do and do not engage in emotional labor. Here, she found that high levels of job involvement were associated with lower levels of burnout among nonperformers of emotional labor, but that this was not the case with emotional laborers—a finding that supports Hochschild's (1983) original proposition that overidentifying might be problematic for individuals whose jobs require emotional labor (Wharton 1999). Another interesting difference was revealed when considering the factors that produce job satisfaction among performers and nonperformers of emotional labor. Wharton (1993) found that job *autonomy* affects job satisfaction more so for those who perform emotional labor than those who do not. However, job *involvement* seems to contribute more to the satisfaction levels of those who do not sell their emotions for a wage.

Finally, turning her attention to individual resources, Wharton (1993) also found evidence that suggests that performers and nonperformers of emotional labor differ in terms of the role that their interpersonal skills play in protecting them from or enhancing their susceptibility to burnout at work (also see Wharton 1999). Specifically, emotional laborers who score high on self-monitoring (e.g., the ability to monitor and react to the social environment) are better able to avoid burnout than workers who do not. Self-monitoring skills, however, contributed to burnout among those whose jobs do not require emotional labor.

Taken together, these studies offer support for some of Hochschild's (1983) broader claims while pointing to the need to be more systematic in the operationalization of concepts that are often vague or hard to measure in more naturalistic settings. Wharton and her colleagues' work furthers our understanding as to how complex and nuanced the effects of emotional labor can be and the ways in which these consequences might be mediated not only by the characteristics of the job but also by the psychological characteristics of the occupants themselves. Unfortunately, however, all of these studies were based on relatively small samples of particular organizations, raising important questions about the generalizability of their exact findings.

Using a much larger, community-based sample, but in the same tradition, Erickson and Ritter (2001) also utilized survey methods to tease apart the more potentially damaging dimensions of emotional labor and then tested whether there were differences for men and women. This work improves upon previous studies in important ways. First, Erickson and Ritter's analyses are not limited to data collected from workers in the service industry only, but, rather, from a random selection of workers more generally. This advance alone allows for a much needed assessment of the prevalence of particular emotions, as well as emotional labor and its resulting consequences in a variety of jobs. Second, instead of treating emotional labor as the management of emotions, broadly defined (Hochschild 1983; Lively 2000; Pierce 1995), Erickson and Ritter examined the management of three types of emotion: positive, negative, and agitated (also see Pugliesi and Shook 1997) and their distinctive effects. Third, because they were using a fairly representative sample Erickson and Ritter's results are not a function of skewed gender ratios (Kanter 1977), a problem too often associated with studies of interactive service work (see Hochschild 1983; Lively 2000; Martin 1999; Pierce 1995) given that most occupations remain stubbornly segregated by sex.

Drawing on a wide breadth of research on emotions and mental health, Erickson and Ritter (2001) posited that the management of agitation (i.e., anger, irritation, and frustration) is a form of emotional labor that is likely to be associated with increased feelings of burnout and inauthenticity. Taking into consideration research on gender and emotion and gender and mental health, they conjectured that this negative effect of agitation on well-being will be more pronounced for women than men, given that women are more likely to be subjected to the anger of others (Hochschild 1983; Thoits 1985), are placed in anger-eliciting interactions (Kemper 1978), and are expected to mask or manage those types of feeling (also Ridgeway and Johnson 1990).

Consistent with their expectations, Erickson and Ritter (2001) found that managing feelings of agitation (e.g., hiding feelings of anger) *is* significantly related to feelings of burnout and inauthenticity. Moreover, they found that the severity of one's feelings of inauthenticity corresponds with one's level of agitation. Contrary to their hypotheses regarding gender, however, the effects of managing agitation were not significantly different for women and men. Because women do, in fact, report higher levels of agitation than men, as well as other negative emotions (also see Simon and Nath 2004), Erickson and Ritter proposed that the meaning associated with hiding one's angry feelings might be different for women and men, a supposition that is, unfortunately, beyond the scope of their community-based survey data.

What Are the Economic Costs of Emotional Labor?

Perhaps somewhat surprisingly, given sociologists long-standing love affair with labor and capital, the *economic* costs of emotional labor have been less studied than the psychosocial costs, despite several qualitative studies that suggest that emotional labor—particularly the emotional labor performed by women—is, for the most part, undervalued and underpaid, if not unpaid. Much in the way that carework in the home is viewed as women's work and, therefore, devalued (Cancian 1987; Hochschild 1989), traditional forms of emotional labor (e.g., carework and other forms of on-the-job nurturing) are typically not recognized as skills that need to be compensated (Bellas

1999; Pierce 1995; Steinberg 1999; Steinberg and Figart 1999), especially when performed by women.

Perhaps the most comprehensive studies of the hidden costs of emotional labor comes not from those who would identify as scholars of emotion per se, but, rather, from scholars of inequality, labor, and stratification. The first of these studies was actually a comparable-worth investigation conducted for the state of New York. Here, Steinberg et al. (1985) found that several of 112 questions regarding job content, in fact, clustered around 2 factors associated with emotional labor (Hochschild 1983): "contact with difficult clients" and "communication with the public." When examining the effects of emotional labor on wages, the authors found that both factors were significantly related to the gender (female) composition of the job. However, only "communication with the public" produced a negative effect on earnings. This finding might be attributable to the fact that high-status service workers who deal primarily with clients (as opposed to customers) also engage in emotional labor (e.g., physicians, attorneys, investment bankers).

In a similar attempt, England, Kilbourne, and their colleagues also conducted a series of studies to test the effects of "nurturant social skills" on wages (England et al. 1994; Kilbourne et al. 1994). Like Steinberg et al., these scholars, too, found that nurturance is more likely to occur in historically female jobs than in historically male jobs. However, perhaps because of their operationalization of "nurturant skills" as involving interactions with both clients *and* customers, they also found that those occupations that require nurturance, be they historically male *or* female, are less compensated than occupations that do not. Although few have followed up on these studies, they, like Wharton's (1999) careful consideration of the psychosocial costs, point to the importance of teasing apart, using survey data, the observations documented in ethnographic studies. Having said that, however, it might be useful to turn to qualitative studies of domestic work to provide some insight on why "nurturant skills" are so devalued in an economy that remains based largely on service.

Not typically recognized as "emotional labor" or even "the workplace," ethnographic studies of Latina domestic workers reveal that employers are likely to pay less or to forgo other forms of monetary compensation (e.g., raises, overtime, or bonuses) once emotional ties are established, not only out of their desire to save money but to foster the belief that the domestic worker, particularly if she is a full-time caregiver, is caring for the employee's children out of love and not money (Hondagneu-Sotelo 2001). Although the nurturing work done at home—even if it is done by someone other than the "wife" or "mother"—is rarely recognized as work (Romero 1992, 1996, 1997), paid domestic labor might be a potential site through which to better understand, exactly, why emotions and care are not recognized as salable commodities.

The Role of Co-workers

Virtually absent in Hochschild's (1983) discussion of emotional labor, co-workers have nonetheless emerged as a topic of interest among those interested in how emotion operates in the workplace. Part of the reason why Hochschild's analyses purposefully excluded the role of co-workers in emotion management or emotional labor is that Delta instructed flight attendants not to turn to their flight partners when fearful, angry, or frustrated in part because most in-air interaction would be visible or audible to the customers themselves. Moreover, airline officials also believed that if flight attendants complained about a customer to a co-worker, it could potentially create an us-versus-them dichotomy that would interfere with the flight attendants' portrayal of the cabin as a living room (e.g., the proper setting for a party) and of the customers as guests.

Although co-workers can, in some cases, be more anger-producing or frustrating than clients or supervisors (Pugliesi and Shook 1997; also see Lively and Powell 2006), most view co-worker interaction as vital to emotional laborers' ability to manage their own emotions (Lively and Powell 2006; Sloan 2004) or engage in emotional labor for the benefit of others (Lively 2000). One source of data that holds insights as to the role that co-workers play in the emotional lives of workers is the GSS emotions module (1996). Examining a subset of questions that ask individuals to identify an anger-producing event within the last month, the target at whom the anger was directed, and a coping strategy they used in order to manage their negative feelings, scholars were able to determine how individuals report managing their emotions within a representative sample.

Focusing exclusively on those individuals who were angered at work, Sloan (2004) found that individuals were more likely to seek social support than they were to try to manage their emotions on their own (also see Lively and Powell 2006). Comparing the experiences of those who were angered by individuals in the workplace with those who were angered by family members, Lively and Powell (2006) also found that individuals who were angered with someone at work were significantly more likely to speak to someone other than the target of their anger compared to those individuals angered by someone at home. Although these two studies, in tandem, reveal the importance of considering the role that others play when managing emotion on the workplace, the data themselves mask important information as to the exact role that others play in managing emotions in the workplace. In order to grasp some of the details that are necessarily hidden when using quantitative data, it might be useful, once again, to consult qualitative studies of similar phenomena (see Lively 2000).

Another conceptual difficulty plaguing the emotions in the workplace genre is the distinction between emotion management that individuals do "voluntarily" for friends and co-workers and emotional labor that they are required to do for customers, clients, and status superiors. Is the voluntary emotion management that individuals perform to reach their professional goals, to maintain their sense of self, or simply because they want to perform emotional labor (Erickson 1997; Lively 2001)? Is the interpersonal emotion management that workers engage in strictly for the benefit of others (e.g., social support and coping assistance) (Francis 1997; Thoits 1985, 1995)? Conversely, is it ever the case that individuals voluntarily manage the emotions of higher-status others without necessarily feeling that it is part of their job? Finally, are there consequences to emotion management done voluntarily at work? If so, to what end?

Although most studies focus on emotion management (Smith and Kleinman 1989; Van Maanan and Kunda 1989) or emotional labor (Hochschild 1983; Kang 2003; Pierce 1995), a handful of studies show that individuals, perhaps not surprisingly, do both (Lively and Powell 2006; Sloan 2004; Lively 2000, 2001). Although it is clear from studies of emotional labor that there are rewards and punishments for emotional labor (be it increased sales and positive performance evaluations on the one hand and terminations on the other), there might also be informal rewards and punishments for those who either participate, or fail to participate in a less formally regimented emotional economy (Cahill 1989; Clark 1987, 1990; Lively 2000, 2001; Smith and Kleinman 1989).

Although individuals report that they benefit, both directly and indirectly, from engaging voluntarily in emotion management with others, Lively (2000) has suggested that workers' reciprocal emotion management comes at an individual cost, in that it can exact a heavy toll on one's own emotional and personal resources. Moreover, at a social level, workers' engagement in reciprocal emotion management becomes the safety valve that allows them to engage in emotional labor for the benefit of higher-status others. Finally, although reciprocal emotion management is viewed as strictly voluntary (yet is subject to the adherence of certain rules, much like sympathy [Clark 1997]), it does, ironically, lend itself to the reification of the existing status hierarchy and all of its emotional ramifications (Lively 2000; also see Pierce 1995). In fact, many of the paralegals in

Lively's (2000) study reported that they would not be able to manage consistently their emotions with regard to their interactions with clients and with attorneys if it were not for the emotion management assistance that they received from similar others.

Comparative Studies Between Work and Family

Despite the workplace being as good a place as any to study emotion, perhaps one of the reasons why researchers are so fascinated by the workplace is the natural comparison that it makes to one of the other most important life domains: the family. Unlike the workplace, family life has historically been characterized as emotionally authentic or as a refuge from the demands of the outside world (Stearns 1999; Stearns and Stearns 1986).

Hochschild's (1983) analysis of the airline industry underscores this difference, as one of the ways that corporations engineered emotional cultures was by convincing employees to treat customers as if they were family and the work space as a home. Pierce's (1995) study of law firms also highlighted differences between work and family to the degree that the disproportionately female paralegals were expected to engage in "mothering" behaviors (i.e., nurturing, cheering, or caring) for the benefit of their disproportionately male attorneys (also see Pierce 1999).

Although most researchers assume that there is a difference in the ways that emotions operate between work and family, there have been very few systematic studies that successfully compare the two. Instead, with the exception of a handful of studies (Hochschild 1997; Lively and Powell 2006; Wharton and Erickson 1995), we are left with examinations of work *or* family (but see Schieman 2000; Stets and Tsushima 2001). Justifications for a work-family dichotomy extend as far back as early discussions of professions (Becker 1970; Friedson 1970) and professionalism (Larson 1977; Ritzer 1971). Initial studies of the medical profession have historically stressed the importance of emotional neutrality as crucial to professional relationships, and more recent studies of professionalism have focused on the emotional component, almost to the exclusion of traditional markers of a professional career (Lively 2001; also see Pogrebin and Poole 1995).

Although most scholars assume that the workplace and the family hold emotionally distinct cultures, some have recently suggested a blurring of the emotional boundaries between work and family life. Hochschild (1997), for example, suggested that many workplaces have succeeded in creating an environment that is more emotionally welcoming and, consequently, rewarding for working parents, especially mothers. Similarly, Stearns (1999) has posited that norms regarding behavior, emotion, and self-control that once made the family a safe haven from the competitive ills of the workplace have been extended to public life, therefore obscuring important differences between the two spheres.

To date, there have been few studies that have systematically compared emotional experiences within the workplace and home. Moreover, because the majority of these studies have used the same dataset, all of the direct comparisons focus on one emotion: anger (see above).[10] Once again relying on the GSS emotions module, Schieman (2000), examining the relationship between education and anger, reported that education increased the likelihood of experiencing anger at work (compared to within the family)—a difference, however, that fell to nonsignificance when controlling for income and sense of control. Stets and Tsushima (2001), examining the experience of anger as it relates to particular types of identity, found that anger experienced as a result of one's worker identity is typically of longer duration than anger experienced as a result of one's family identity.

Focusing on the expression of anger, as opposed to its experience, Lively and Powell (2006) found that despite claims of the blurring boundaries between work and family, individuals are significantly more likely to express anger directly toward family members than they are to express anger directly toward people at work (e.g., customers, bosses, co-workers, subordinates). When examining the effects of status (both within and across the domains of work and family), however, Lively and Powell also found that individuals were less likely to express anger directly to individuals of higher status (e.g., customers or bosses) than they were to either equals (e.g., co-workers) or those of lower status (e.g., subordinates). Individuals angered by status equals were just as likely, if not slightly more so, to express their anger directly to co-workers than they were to those with lower status. Moreover, the patterns generated by considerations of status were not significantly different when considering work or family, which suggests that the difference between emotional expression at home and that at work might be more a matter of degree than substance.

CONCLUSION

The past two decades have spawned a tremendous amount of research regarding the role that emotion plays in the workplace. As noted, much of this early work was founded on overly descriptive studies of how emotions operate within particular occupations—first concentrated in relatively low-status service occupations and then extended to include professional schools and other higher-status professions. As part of their careful consideration of emotion norms and emotional cultures, these studies also documented the observable effects of personal characteristics on emotional experience, expression, and management—most notably those of gender and occupational prestige—suggesting that women and lower-status workers were required to engage in more caretaking behaviors and provide more care for men and individuals of higher status.

Because each workplace culture is different, as are the interdependent goals of workers, customers, and management (Leidner 1996; Lively 2002), it is not surprising that inconsistencies arose, the most controversial being the reported discrepancy surrounding the psychosocial costs of emotional labor (Hochschild 1983; Leidner 1993; Smith and Kleinman 1989). In order to reconcile empirical and, potentially, theoretical differences, scholars began collecting different types of data. Among these were survey data that, although not necessarily representative in scope, allowed for a greater specification of concepts and set up the tradition of multimethod investigation that has rapidly, and rightly so, become the norm in an area once dominated by qualitative methods (Erickson and Ritter 2001; Pugliesi and Shook 1997; Wharton 1999). This trend has escalated further with the release and utilization of the GSS (1996) module on emotion (Lively and Powell 2006; Schieman 2000; Sloan 2004; Stets and Tshushima 2001). The incorporation of both qualitative and quantitative methods to answer complementary questions has resulted not only in more generalizable conclusions but also in richer understandings of the problems at hand. This dual approach has also lent itself to a greater appreciation of statistically significant patterns that might require additional exploration using a more ethnographic or even experimental approach (see Lively and Powell 2006).

Although those studying emotion in the workplace have been receptive to the incorporation of new methodologies in order to answer their empirical questions, they typically have remained remarkably fixed in terms of their theoretical choices, a fact that might stem, in part, from the obdurate hold that Hochschild's (1983) legacy has retained over what seems to legitimately constitute the sociological inquiry of emotion in the workplace (but see Stets and Tsushima 2001). Historically, scholars of workplace emotion have limited their use of theory to what could rightfully be referred to as the cultural-normative perspective (Clark 1997; Heise and Calhan 1995; Hochschild 1975, 1983) and the structural perspective (Clark 1990, 1997; Collins 1990; Kemper 1978; Kemper and Collins 1990; Lovaglia and Houser 1996; for recent reviews see Lawler and Thye 2001, Smith-Lovin 1995; Stets 2003b). Often treated as mutually exclusive, a recent test of the relative effects of norms and status within hierarchically ordered domains illustrates that not only do culture and structure operate in tandem but that the relative effects are roughly the same (Lively and Powell 2006).

Despite scholars' overreliance on these two theoretical perspectives when addressing questions set in the workplace, social psychologists are beginning to theorize and specify the emotional implications of other, more middle-range theories. For example, in several recent theoretical and empirical pieces, affect control theory (Lively and Heise 2004; MacKinnon 1994; Smith-Lovin and Heise 1988), identity theory (Stryker 2004), identity control theory (Stets 2005; Stets and Tsushima 2001), exchange theory (Lawler and Thye 1999), and equity theory (Burke and Harrod 2005; Lively et al. 2004; Sprecher 1986, 1992; Stets 2003a) have been linked to the experience and expression of emotion. To date, however, the empirical tests of these theories have generally not been conducted in the workplace, despite the characteristics of the workplace that would make such an enterprise ideal (but see Stets and Tsushima 2001). Unlike laboratory settings, where groups of strangers are brought together for a short length of time to engage in tasks that might or might not be self-relevant or hold significant outcomes, tasks in the workplace are often highly self-relevant and tied to real outcomes (e.g., a wage or a promotion). Moreover, work-based tasks are routinely subject to both formal and informal evaluations that are embedded in real, if not significant, relationships that are clearly marked by both organizational norms and social status hierarchies.

Similar to the family (Steelman and Powell 1996), which has emerged as the critical site in which to test and enrich social psychological theory and to specify the scope conditions under which certain social psychological theories might offer the greatest explanations (Burke and Harrod 2005; Glass and Fujimoto 1994; Lennon and Rosenfield 1994; Lively et al. 2004 for recent empirical examples), the workplace holds the necessarily elements that would benefit both the testing and specification of theory as it pertains to the study of emotion. Moreover, because of the qualitative differences between the relationships within work and family, it is not at all clear that the emotional reactions associated with social psychological processes (say, perceptions of justice or inequity) would be the same in both settings; Stets and Tsushima's (2001) investigation of identity confirmation/disconfirmation suggests not.

In addition to simply providing a natural laboratory to test social psychological theory (and therefore play host to a series of questions outside of Hochschild's [1983] original considerations of emotion management and emotional labor), the empirical work being done in the workplace would benefit from a greater consideration of social psychological theory, particularly theories of identity (Burke 1991; Heise 1977; Lively and Heise 2004; Stets and Tsushima 2001; Stryker 2004). One assumption that is implicit in most studies of emotion management and emotional labor is that emotions are linked to the self. Although rarely acknowledged in workplace studies of emotion, this is also the underlying logic beneath most theories of identity, particularly control theories (Burke 1991; Heise 1977, 2002; Smith-Lovin and Heise 1988; Stets 2003a, 2005). In fact, when one reads descriptions of the emotion management strategies provided to workers (e.g., trying to see the irritating customer as a frightened child or a airplane as a living room), they read eerily like predictions straight from affect control theory (Heise 2002). Furthermore, Lively and Heise (2004), using multidimensional scaling and structural equation modeling, have illustrated that emotion management strategies (e.g., moving from anger to tranquillity) can actually be derived using postulates from affect control theory (also see Francis 1997).

Like all new subfields or inquiries of study, the study of emotion in the workplace is in an ongoing process of maturation. Hochschild (1983) provided the necessary building blocks to pique sociological interest in a relatively unknown or little considered arena and created one of the most prolific legacies within sociology today (Smith-Lovin 2004). Scholars have expanded their methodological practices in order to create a fertile dialogue between the empirical richness of ethnography and methodological specification associated with quantitative analyses, allowing them to create more complete understandings of emotion, the workplace, and the relationship between them.

Just as the inclusion of more diverse methods has resulted in a surge of research and knowledge, an infusion of theory, above and beyond the broad theoretical perspectives upon which Hochschild and others have based their work, might have a similar influence. Specifically, a greater use of middle-range and, therefore, more testable social psychological theories could provide scholars with a unique opportunity to enrich their ongoing efforts to understand emotion management and emotional labor. Perhaps even more important, for the future of the line of inquiry, the incorporation of more testable theories might open up new research agendas and, subsequently, make the study of workplace emotion more relevant for social psychology, as well as sociology as a whole.

NOTES

1. Although Hochschild's (1983) definitions of emotion management and emotional labor remain the most used, several scholars have introduced their own definitions that are more or less consistent with Hochschild's original statements. Rosenberg (1990:4), for example, used emotion management to refer to the "self-regulation of emotional exhibition for the purpose of producing intended effects on others' minds." Focusing more on emotional expression than the misuse of perception and memory that Hochschild was concerned with, Ashforth and Humphrey (1993:90) defined emotional labor as "the act of displaying the appropriate emotion." In an attempt to be more inclusive, while keeping the focus on service workers, Wharton (1999:160) defined emotional labor as "the effort involved in displaying organizationally sanctioned emotions be those whose jobs require interaction with clients or customers and for whom these interactions are an important component of the work."

2. Cahill (1989) also noted that students learned to manage their emotions via associations with other students outside of the classroom (i.e., the fact that mortuary students tend to live and socialize together) and through talk (i.e., the incorporation of occupational rhetoric and esoteric language, speaking of "cases," not "bodies").

3. Pierce (1995) argued that to the degree that paralegals and attorneys were successful in fulfilling their occupational roles and their emotional concomitants, they were also implicitly reproducing the larger gender hierarchy within society as a whole.

4. In particular, Hochschild (1983) argued that women were more suited to engage in emotional labor at work, because women are trained from childhood to be more in touch with their own and others' emotions than are men, and that as adults they learn to trade emotion (i.e., love and nurturing) for financial support from men.

5. Although not typically classed as studies within the sociology of emotion, other sources of information on the racialized nature of emotional labor and carework more generally come from an unlikely source (e.g., the growing literature on domestic workers), particularly foreign-born nannies employed not in traditional workplaces but, rather, in private homes throughout the United States (Ehrenreich and Hochschild 2002; Hondagneu-Sotelo 2001; Romero 1992, 1996, 1997; also see Rollins 1985).

6. Although Harlow (2003) referred to her topic exclusively as emotion management (and not, necessarily, labor), Bellas (1999) has argued that the emotion management that professors engage in during the course of teaching is done so as to elicit particular emotional responses from their students. This study, like others that focus on emotion management, but not labor per se (e.g., Lively 2000), might in fact obscure the relationship between emotion management that individuals engage in voluntarily and the emotional labor they do in order to achieve the goals of the organizations within which they are embedded.

7. Although both sets of workers in Leidner's (1993) study seem to benefit from engaging in emotional labor to the degree that their own goals match those of the corporations, she cautioned that when there is a *discrepancy* between goals, the workers' interests are the one's most likely sacrificed.

8. Erickson and Wharton (1997) captured inauthentic feelings with a two-item scale assessing how often respondents felt that they could not be themselves while at work or that they had to fake how they really felt at work.
9. In addition to Erickson and Wharton's (1997) careful analyses, Erickson and Ritter (2001), Morris and Feldman (1996), Steinberg and Figart (1999), and others all provided compelling theoretical arguments and empirical evidence for the need to consider multiple dimensions of emotional labor.

   Combining qualitative and quantitative analyses, Steinberg and Figart (1999) evaluated dimensions of emotional labor of three historically gender-specific jobs: nurses, police officers, and managers. Creating two indexes that measure a range of emotional skills and demands, they found that the emotional labor required of police officers and nurses is comparable despite the cultural ideology that portrays these jobs as requiring gender-specific skills, causing the authors to abandon their reliance on preconceived stereotypes of femininity when studying emotional labor, especially in service-sector jobs, and, instead, adopt an augmented conceptualization of emotional labor that takes into consideration what employees actually do in the course of performing their jobs.
10. Fewer, still, have examined the relationships between the emotional labor performed at work and the emotion management performed at home (but see Erickson and Wharton 1997).

REFERENCES

Ashforth, Blake E., and Ronald H. Humphrey. 1993. "Emotional Labor in Service Roles: The Influence of Identity." *Academy of Management* Review 18: 88–115.

Becker, Howard. 1970. "The Nature of a Profession." Pp. 87–103 in *Sociological Work: Method and Substance*, edited by H. Becker. Chicago: Aldine.

Bellas, Marcia L. 1999. "Emotional Labor in Academia: The Case of Professors." *Emotional Labor in the Service Economy. Annals of the American Academy of Political and Social Science* 561: 96–110.

Bulan, Heather Ferguson, Rebecca J. Erickson, and Amy Wharton. 1997. "Doing for Others on the Job: The Affective Requirements of Service Work, Gender, and Emotional Well-Being." *Social Problems* 44: 701–723.

Burawoy, Michael. 1979. *Manufacturing Consent: Changes in the Labor Process Under Monopoly Capitalism.* Chicago: University of Chicago Press.

Burke, Peter J. 1991. "Identity Processes and Social Stress." *American Sociological Review* 56: 836–849.

Burke, Peter J., and Michael M. Harrod. 2005. "Too Much of a Good Thing?" *Social Psychology Quarterly* 68: 359–374.

Cahill, Spencer. 1989. "Emotional Capital and Professional Socialization: The Case of Mortuary Science Students (and Me)." *Social Psychology Quarterly* 62: 101–116.

Cancian, Francesca. 1987. *Love in America: Gender and Self-Development.* Cambridge: Cambridge University Press.

Clark, Candace. 1987. "Sympathy Biography and Sympathy Margin." *American Journal of Sociology* 3: 290–321.

———. 1990. "Emotions and Micropolitics in Every Day Life: Some Patterns and Paradox of 'Place.'" Pp. 305–334 in *Research Agendas in the Sociology of Emotions*, edited by T. Kemper. Albany: State University of New York Press.

———. 1997. *Misery and Company: Sympathy in Every Day Life.* Chicago: University of Chicago Press.

Collins, Randall. 1990. "Stratification, Emotional Energy, and the Transient Emotions." Pp. 25–75 in *Research Agendas in the Sociology of Emotions*, edited by T. Kemper. Albany: State University of New York Press.

Coser, Rose Laub. 1964. "Some Social Functions of Laughter." *Human Relations* 12: 171–182.

Darwin, Charles. 1955. *The Expression of Emotions in Man and Animals.* New York: Philosophical Library.

Davis, James, and Tom Smith. 1996. *General Social Surveys, 1972–1996 Cumulative Codebook and Data File.* Chicago: National Opinion Research Center and University of Chicago.

Ehrenreich, Barbara, and Arlie Russell Hochschild. 2002. *Global Women: Nannies, Maids, and Sex Workers in the New Economy.* New York: Holt.

Ekman, Paul. 1971. "Universals and Cultural Differences in Facial Expressions and of Emotions." Pp. 207–283 in *Nebraska Symposium on Motivation*, edited by J. K. Cole. Lincoln: University of Nebraska Press.

———. 1973. *Darwin and Facial Expression.* New York: Academic.

Ekman, Paul, and Wallace Friesen. 1969. "Non-Verbal Leakage and Clues to Deception." Psychiatry 32: 88–106.

Ekman, Paul, W. V. Friesen, and P. Ellsworth. 1972. *Emotion in the Human Face: Guidelines for Research and an Integration of Findings.* New York: Pergamon.

England, Paula, Melissa S. Herbert, Barbara Stanek Kilbourne, Lori L. Reid, and Lori McCready Megdal. 1994. "The Gendered Valuation of Occupations and Skills: Earnings in 1980 Census Occupations." *Social Forces* 73: 65–99.

England, Paula, and Barbara Stanek Kilbourne. 1988. *Occupational Measures from the Dictionary of Occupational Titles for 1980 Census Detailed Occupations.* Ann Arbor, MI: Inter-University Consortium for Political and Social Research.

Erickson, Rebecca J. 1997. "Putting Emotions to Work (or, Coming to Terms with a Contradiction in Terms)." Pp 3–18 in *Social Perspectives on Emotion,* edited by R. J. Erickson and B. Cuthbertson-Johnson. Greenwich, CT: JAI Press.

Erickson, Rebecca J., and Christian Ritter. 2001. "Emotional Labor, Burnout, and Inauthenticity: Does Gender Matter?" *Social Psychology Quarterly* 64: 146–163.

Erickson, Rebecca J., and Amy Wharton. 1997. "Inauthenticity and Depression: Assessing the Consequences of Interactive Service Work." *Work and Occupations* 24: 188–213.

Feagin, Joe R. 1991. "The Continuing Significance of Race: Antiblack Discrimination in Public Places." *American Sociological Review* 56: 101–116.

Francis, Linda. 1994. "Laughter is the Best Mediation: Humor as Emotion Management in Interaction." *Symbolic Interaction* 17: 147–163.

———. 1997. "Ideology and Interpersonal Emotion Management: Redefining Identity in Support Groups." *Social Psychology Quarterly* 60: 153–171.

Friedson, Elliot. 1970. *Profession of Medicine: A Study of the Sociology of Applied Knowledge.* New York: Dodd, Mead.

Gatta, Mary. 2002. *Juggling Food and Feelings.* Lanham, MD: Lexington Books.

Gee, Gilbert C., and Butch DeCastro. 2001. "Race and Emotional Labor." Presented at the annual meeting of the American Public Health Association in Atlanta, GA.

Glass, Jennifer, and Tetsushi Fujimoto. 1994. "Housework, Paid Work, and Depression among Husbands and Wives." *Journal of Health and Social Behavior* 35: 179–191.

Goffman, Erving. 1959. *The Presentation of Self in Everyday Life.* New York: Doubleday Anchor.

———. 1961. *Encounters.* Indianapolis: Bobbs-Merrill.

———. 1967. *Interaction Ritual.* New York: Doubleday Anchor.

Gove, Walter R., and Omer R. Galle. 1973. *Chicago Crowding Study.*

Harlow, Roxanna. 2003. "'Race Doesn't Matter, But . . . ' The Effect of Race on Professors' Experiences of Emotion Management in the Undergraduate Classroom." *Social Psychology Quarterly* 66: 348–363.

Heikes, E. Joel. 1991. "When Men Are the Minority: The Case of Men in Nursing." *Sociological Quarterly* 32: 389–401.

Heise, David R. 1977. "Social Action as the Control of Affect." *Behavioral Sciences* 22: 163–177.

———. 2002. "Understanding Social Interaction with Affect Control Theory." Pp. 17–40 in *New Directions in Sociological Theory: Growth of Contemporary Theories*, edited by J. Berger and M. Zelditch, Jr. Boulder, CO: Rowman and Littlefield.

Heise, David R., and Cassandra Calhan. 1995. "Emotion Norms in Interpersonal Events." *Social Psychology Quarterly* 58: 223–240.

Hochschild, Arlie R. 1975. "The Sociology of Feeling and Emotion: Selected Possibilities." *Sociological Inquiry* 45: 280–307.

———. 1979. "Emotion Work, Feelings Rules, and Social Structure." *American Journal of Sociology* 85: 551–575.

———. 1983. *The Managed Heart: The Commercialization of Feeling.* Berkeley: University of California Press.

———. 1997. *The Time Bind: When Work Becomes Home and Home Becomes Work.* New York: Metropolitan Books.

Hochschild, Arlie R., with Anne Manchung. 1989. *The Second Shift: Working Parents and the Revolution at Home.* New York: Viking.

Hondagneu-Sotelo, Pierriete. 2001. *Domèstica: Immigrant Workers Cleaning and Caring in the Shadows of Affluence.* Berkeley: University of California Press.

James, William, and Carl G. Lange. 1922. *The Emotions.* Baltimore: Williams and Wilkins.

Kang, Miliann. 2003. "The Managed Hand: The Commercialization of Bodies and Emotions in Korean Immigrant-Owned Nail Salons." *Gender and Society* 17: 820–839.

Kanter, Rosabeth Moss. 1977. *Men and Women of the Corporation.* New York: Basic Books.

Kemper, Theodore. 1978. *A Social Interaction Theory of Emotions.* New York: Wiley.

Kemper, Theodore, and Randall Collins. 1990. "Dimensions of Microinteraction." *American Journal of Sociology* 96: 32–68.

Kilborne, Barbara Stanek, George Farkas, Kurt Baron, Dorthea Weir, and Paula England. 1994. "Returns to Skill, Compensating Differentials, and Gender Bias: Effects of Occupational Characteristics on the Wages of White Women and Men." *American Journal of Sociology* 100: 689–719.

Larson, Margaret S. 1977. *The Rise of Professionalism.* Berkeley: University of California Press.

Lawler, Edward J., and Shane R. Thye. 1999. "Bringing Emotions into Social Exchange Theory." *Annual Review of Sociology* 25: 217–244.

Leidner, Robin. 1993. *Fast Food, Fast Talk: Service Work and the Routinization of Everyday Life.* Berkeley: University of California Press.

———. 1996. "Rethinking Issues of Control." Pp. 29–49 in *Working in the Service Economy*, edited by C. MacDonald and C. Sirianni. Philadelphia: Temple University Press.

Lennon, Mary, and Sarah Rosenfield. 1994. "Relative Fairness and Division of Housework: The Importance of Options." *American Journal of Sociology* 100: 506–531.

Lively, Kathryn J. 2000. "Reciprocal Emotion Management: Working Together to Maintain Stratification in Private Law Firms." *Work and Occupations* 27: 32–63.

———. 2001. "Occupational Claims to Professionalism: The Case of Paralegals." *Symbolic Interaction* 24: 343–366.

———. 2002. "Upsetting the Balance and Evening the Field: The Effects of Client Contact on Emotional Labor." *Work and Occupations* 29: 198–225.

———. 2004. "Gender Indifference?: Reconsidering Gender and Emotion in the U.S." Presented at the annual meeting of the Southern Sociological Society, Atlanta, GA.

Lively, Kathryn J., and David R. Heise. 2004. "Sociological Realms of Emotional Experience." *American Journal of Sociology* 109: 1109–1136.

Lively, Kathryn J., and Brian Powell. 2006. "Emotional Expression at Work and at Home: Domain, Status, or Individual Characteristics?" *Social Psychology Quarterly* 69: 17–38.

Lively, Kathryn J., Lala Carr Steelman, and Brian Powell. 2004. "Equity, Emotion, and the Household Division of Labor." Presented at the annual meeting of the American Sociological Association, San Francisco.

Lovaglia, Michael J., and Jeffrey A. Houser. 1996. "Emotional Reactions to Status in Groups." *American Sociological Review* 61: 867–883.

Mabry, J. Beth, and K. Jill Kiecolt. 2005. "Anger in Black and White: Race, Alienation, and Anger." *Journal of Health and Social Behavior* 46: 85–101.

Macdonald, Cameron, and Carmen Sirriani. 1996. "The Service Society and the Changing Experience of Work." Pp. 1–26 in *Working in the Service Economy,* edited by C. Macdonald and C. Sirianni. Philadelphia: Temple University Press.

MacKinnon, Neil J. 1994. *Symbolic Interaction as Affect Control.* Albany: State University of New York Press.

Martin, Susan. 1999. "Police Work or Public Service? Gender and Emotional Labor." *Emotional Labor in the Service Economy. Annals of the American Academy of Political and Social Science* 561: 111–126.

Maslach, Christina. 1976. "Burned-Out." *Human Relations* 5: 16–22.

Maslach, Christina, and Ayala Pines. 1977. "The Burn-Out Syndrome in the Day Care Setting." *Child Care Quarterly* 6: 100–113.

McHammon, Holly J., and Larry J. Griffin. 2000. "Workers and Their Clients: An Editorial Introduction." *Work and Occupations* 27: 278–293.

Mills, C. Wright. 1959. *The Sociological Imagination.* New York: Oxford University Press.

Morris, J. Andrew, and Daniel C. Feldman. 1996. "The Dimensions, Antecedents, and Consequences of Emotional Labor." *Academy of Management Review* 21: 986–1010.

Paules, Greta Foff. 1991. *Dishing It Out: Power and Resistance among Waitresses in a New Jersey Restaurant.* Philadelphia: Temple University Press.

Pierce, Jennifer. 1995. *Gender Trials: Emotional Lives in Contemporary Law Firms.* Berkeley: University of California Press.

———. 1999. "Emotional Labor among Paralegals." *Annals of the American Academy of Political and Social Science* 56: 127–142.

Pogrebin, Mark R., and Eric D. Poole. 1995. "Emotion Management: A Study of Police Response to Tragic Events." Pp. 149–169 in *Social Perspectives on Emotion,* edited by D. D. Franks, M. G. Flaherty, and C. Ellis. Greenwich, CT: JAI Press.

Pugliesi, Karen, and Scott L. Shook. 1997. "Gender, Jobs, and Emotional Labor in a Complex Organization." Pp. 283–316 in *Social Perspectives on Emotion,* edited by R. J. Erickson and B. Cuthbertson-Johnson. Greenwich, CT: JAI Press.

Rafaeli, Anat, and Robert Sutton. 1990. "Busy Stores and Demanding Customers: How Do They Affect the Display of Positive Emotions?" *Academy of Management Journal* 33: 623–637.

Ridgeway, Cecilia, and Cathryn Johnson. 1990. "What Is the Relationship between Socioemotional Behavior and Status in Task Groups?" *American Journal of Sociology* 95: 1198–1212.

Ridgeway, Cecilia, and Lynn Smith-Lovin. 1999. "The Gender System and Interaction." *Annual Review of Sociology* 25: 191–216.

Ridgeway, Cecilia, and Henry Walker. 1995. "Status Structures." Pp. 281–310 in *Sociological Perspectives on Social Psychology,* edited by K. S. Cook, G. A. Fine, and J. S. House. Boston: Allyn and Bacon.

Ritzer, George. 1971. "Professionalism and the Individual." Pp. 59–74 in *The Professions and Their Prospects,* edited by E. Freidson, Beverly Hills, CA: Sage.

Rollins, Judith. 1985. *Between Women: Domestics and their Employers.* Philadelphia: Temple University Press.

Romero, Mary. 1992. *Maid in the U.S.A.* New York: Routledge.

———. 1996. "Life as a Maid's Daughter: An Exploration of the Everyday Boundaries of Race, Class, and Gender." Pp. 188–219 in *Feminisms in the Academy: Rethinking the Disciplines*, edited by A. J. Steward and D. Stanton. Ann Arbor: University of Michigan Press.

———. 1997. "Who Takes Care of the Maid's Children? Exploring the Costs of Domestic Service." Pp. 63–91 in *Feminisms and Families*, edited by H. L. Nelson. New York: Routledge.

Rosenberg, Morris. 1990. "Reflexivity and Emotion." *Social Psychology Quarterly* 53: 3–12.

Schacter, Stanley, and Jerome Singer. 1962. "Cognitive, Social and Psychological Determinants of Emotional State." *Psychological Review* 69: 379–399.

Schieman, Scott. 2000. "Education and the Activation, Course, and Management of Anger." *Journal of Health and Social Behavior* 41: 20–39.

Shott, Susan. 1979. "Emotion in Social Life: A Symbolic Interactionist Perspective." *American Journal of Sociology* 84: 1317–1334.

Simon, Robin, Donna Eder, and Cathy Evans. 1992. "The Development of Feeling Norms Underlying Romantic Love among Adolescent Females." *Social Psychology Quarterly* 55: 29–46.

Simon, Robin, and Kathryn J. Lively. 2005. "Gender Differences in Dimensions of Anger and Their Implications for Distressing Emotions." Presented at the annual meeting of the American Sociological Association, Philadelphia, PA.

Simon, Robin, and Leda Nath. 2004. "Gender and Emotion in the United States: Do Men and Women Differ in Self-Reports of Feelings and Expressive Behavior?" *American Journal of Sociology* 109: 1137–1176.

Sloan, Melissa. 2003. "Professional Emotion Management." Presented at the annual meeting of the American Sociological Association, Atlanta, GA.

———. 2004. "The Effects of Occupational Characteristics on the Experience of and Expression of Anger in the Workplace." *Work and Occupations* 31: 38–72.

Smith, Allen C., and Sherryl Kleinman. 1989. "Managing Emotions in Medical School: Students' Contacts with the Living and the Dead." *Social Psychology Quarterly* 52: 56–69.

Smith, Pam. 1992. *The Emotional Labour of Nursing: How Nurses Care.* New York: Palgrave, Macmillan.

Smith-Lovin, Lynn. 1995. "The Sociology of Affect and Emotion." Pp. 118–148 in *Sociological Perspectives on Social Psychology*, edited by Karen S. Cook, Gary A. Fine, and James S. House. Boston: Allyn and Bacon.

———. 2004. "They Got the Feeling, but They Missed the Marx: Twenty Years after *The Managed Heart*." Presented at the Annual Meeting of the American Sociological Association. San Francisco, CA.

Smith-Lovin, Lynn, and David Heise. 1988. *Analyzing Social Interaction: Advances in Affect Control Theory.* New York: Gordon and Breach.

Sprecher, Susan. 1986. "The Relation between Inequity and Emotions in Close Relationships." *Social Psychology Quarterly* 49: 309–321.

———. 1992. "How Men and Women Expect to Feel and Behave in Close Relationships." *Social Psychology Quarterly* 55: 57–69.

Stearns, Peter N. 1999. *Battleground of Desire: The Struggle for Self-Control in Modern America.* New York: New York University Press.

Stearns, Carol Z., & Peter N. Stearns. 1986. *Anger: The Struggle for Emotional Control in America's History.* Chicago: University of Chicago Press.

Steelman, Lala Carr, and Brian Powell. 1996. "The Family Devalued: The Treatment of the Family in Small Groups Literature." Pp. 213–238 in *Advances in Group Processes*, edited by B. Markovsky, M. Lovaglia, and R. Simon. Greenwich, CT: JAI.

Steinberg, Ronnie J. 1999. "Emotional Labor in Job Evaluation: Redesigning Compensation Practices." *Emotional Labor in the Service Economy. Annals of the American Academy of Political and Social Science* 561: 143–157.

Steinberg, Ronnie J., and Deborah M. Figart. 1999. "Emotional Demands at Work: A Job Content Analysis." *Emotional Labor in the Service Economy. Annals of the American Academy of Political and Social Science* 561: 177–191.

Steinberg, Ronnie J., Lois Haignere, Carol Possin, Donald Treiman, and Cynthia H. Chertos. 1985. *New York State Comparable Worth Study.* Albany, NY: Center for Women in Government.

Steinross, Barbara, and Sherryl Kleinman. 1989. "The Highs and Lows of Emotional Labor: Detectives' Encounters with Criminals and Victims." *Journal of Contemporary Ethnography* 17: 435–452.

Stets, Jan. 2003a. "Justice, Emotion, and Identity Theory." Pp. 104–122 in *Advances in Identity Theory*, edited by P. J. Burke, T. J. Owens, R. T. Serpe, and P. A. Thoits. New York: Plenum.

———. 2003b. "Emotions and Sentiment." Pp. 309–335 in *The Handbook of Social Psychology*, edited by J. DeLamater. New York: Kluwer Academic/Plenum.

———. 2005. "Examining Emotions in Identity Theory." *Social Psychology* 68: 39–56.

Stets, Jan, and Theresa M. Tsushima. 2001. "Negative Emotion and Coping Reponses within Identity Control." *Social Psychology Quarterly* 64: 283–295.

Stryker, Sheldon. 2004. "Integrating Emotion Into Identity Theory." *Advances in Group Processes* 21: 1–23.

Sutton, Robert. 1991. "Maintaining Norms about Expressed Emotion: The Case of Bill Collectors." *Administrative Science Quarterly* 36: 245–268.

Thoits, Peggy A. 1984. Coping, Social Support, and Psychological Outcomes: The Central Role of Emotion. Pp. 219–238 in *Review of Personality and Social Psychology*, edited by P. Shaver. Beverly Hills, CA: Sage.

———. 1985. "Self-Labeling Processes in Mental Illness: The Role of Emotional Deviance." *American Journal of Sociology* 91: 221–249.

———. 1986. "Social Support as Coping Assistance." *Journal of Consulting and Clinical Psychology* 54: 416–423.

———. 1990. "Emotional Deviance: Research Agendas. Pp. 180–206 in *Research Agendas in the Sociology of Emotions*, edited by T. Kemper. Albany: State University of New York Press.

———. 1995. "Managing the Emotions of Others." *Symbolic Interaction* 19: 85–109.

Van Maanen, John. 1991. "The Smile Factory: Work at Disney Land." Pp. 58–76 in *Reframing Organizational Culture*, edited by P. J. Frost. Newbury Park, CA: Sage.

Van Maanen, John, and Gideon Kunda. 1989. "Real Feelings: Emotional Expression and Organizational Culture." Pp. 43–104 in *Research in Organizational Behavior*, edited by L. L. Cummings and B. M. Shaw. Greenwich, CT: JAI Press.

Whalen, Jack, and Don H. Zimmerman. 1998. "Observations on the Display and Management of Emotion in Naturally Occurring Activities: The Case of 'Hysteria' in Calls to 9-1-1." *Social Psychology Quarterly* 61: 141–159.

Wharton, Amy S. 1993. "The Affective Consequences of Service Work." *Work and Occupations* 20: 205–232.

———. 1999. "The Psychosocial Consequences of Emotional Labor." *Annals of the American Academy of Political Science* 561: 158–176.

Wharton, Amy S., and Rebecca J. Erickson. 1995. "Consequences of Caring: Exploring the Links between Women's Job and Family Emotion Work." *Sociological Quarterly* 36: 301–324.

Williams, Christine. 1992. "The Glass Escalator: Hidden Advantages for Men in the 'Female' Professions." *Social Problems* 59: 253–267.

CHAPTER 25

Emotions and Health

Linda E. Francis

Although the study of emotions and health has been part of sociology internationally for over a decade, it is only beginning to garner interest as a sociological topic in the United States (James and Gabe 2003a). Direct connections between emotions and physical health have been the empirical province of health psychology, with very little recognition across disciplinary borders. In American sociology, the main tie between emotions and health has been the study of stress and mental health. Also, the broader implications of stress research for health have attracted more attention in public health than in American sociology.

The vast majority of sociological writings on emotions and health are published by British or Australian presses, although not all of the authors hail from those countries. These works reflect primarily two genres: social constructionist empirical work and theoretical essays. The former genre largely focuses on the role of emotions in medical encounters and extends our understanding of emotions as tools of interaction in social context. What work there is on this topic in the United States tends to be typical of this genre as well. The theoretical essays, on the other hand, are syntheses of a broad range of health- and emotions-related literature. They represent a small but growing movement for a new, multidimensional sociology of health and illness, with emotions as the cornerstone. This intriguing perspective opens the door to a sociology of emotions that is no longer peripheral, but central to the field of medical sociology. If it catches on, this movement will blur many divisions in the field and generate a new understanding of health as structural, social, interpersonal, psychological, and embodied.

In this chapter I will take this new movement as a starting point, highlighting its key ideas and contributors. The key point of the movement is to create an "embodied" sociology in which emotion is the connecting point between the biological and the social. As such, emotion is the touchstone for overcoming the rationalist dualism of Western thought, in which self and society are viewed as irreducibly separate and biology is unconnected to social structure.

LINDA E. FRANCIS • School of Social Welfare, SUNY at Stony Brook, Stony Brook, NY 11794

As the second task of this chapter, I will present an overview of the empirical work that has been done in each of several areas relevant to this movement. In this section I will review both work done in sociology and work done in areas outside the discipline but important to a complete understanding of the state of the field. In sociology, this work is represented by the social constructionist research on emotions and health care. Clinical essays in the health professions are also making growing use of this perspective. Another area, one that has been largely overlooked in sociology, is that of health psychology. Taking an almost exclusively experimental approach, this field has given little consideration to the social context emphasis of sociology. Nonetheless, it has made extremely useful strides in connecting emotion to physiology and thereby to health.

Third, I will summarize research that contributes to bridging the gaps identified along the way. The personality and social structure approach of stress research is the first field with insights upon which we can build. The stress literature excels in identifying and measuring the personal and psychological costs of social and interpersonal events. The second field considers the situated action approach of symbolic interactionism. This work adds the crucial dimension of the subjective experience of emotion, power, and conflict to the impersonal and rationalized model of stress.

Finally, I will conclude with some future directions for the development of the field of emotion and health. Drawing from the various literatures covered, I will outline some initial targets that are in particular need of exploration. In keeping with the tenor of the field, this chapter, and this volume more broadly, I will emphasize the rewards of disciplinary cross-fertilization for the growth of new ideas in the sociology of emotions.

THE SOCIOLOGY OF EMOTIONS AND HEALTH

Although the discourse of health and emotion is largely dominated by international writings, it was sparked by an American sociologist. More than 15 years ago, Freund (1990) defined the task of bringing emotions into the sociology of health and illness. Freund began by pointing out the mind-body dualism that exists in both the sociology of health and that of emotion. This dualism is reflected in the disease-versus-illness distinction, as well as rationalism/emotionality, nature/nurture, and constructionism/positivism. Drawing on Franks (1987), he argued that the sociology of emotions is the ideal field from which to begin the process of returning the "expressive body" to sociology, without reducing sociology to biology or ignoring biology altogether.

Freund used spatial metaphors from Goffman's work (1959, 1974) to show how emotion sits at the crux of a person's social, psychological, and physical existence. As we attempt to maintain our presentations of self, we manage our expressivity as well as other factors. As Freund pointed out, however, our environments are not always conducive to an expression of self that feels authentic or desirable. This can produce "dramaturgical stress," which results from

> responding to social situations in which there is a profound disjuncture between the ways in which one desires to present oneself and the social context which demands an "opposite" style of self-presentation and does not allow the actor to leave the field. (Freund 1998:276)

The similarity to the work of Hochschild (1983) here is not coincidental; Freund acknowledged that such stress is fundamentally the result of the need to engage in emotion work. He went on to argue that the long-term effects of dramaturgical stress can result in "emotional false consciousness," which leads to the individual colluding in the reproduction of his or her own stress. As Newton (1995) pointed out, this collusion is not recognized in most stress literature.

Freund also drew on Hochschild's (1983) concept of "status shields" as a proposed pathway by which social positions and social structure affect personal health. According to Hochschild, one's status is a key factor in determining how closely one has to conform to feeling rules in a given situation. Higher status produces stronger status shields, which protect a person from vulnerability to intrusion and social control by others. In other words, a high-status person (a boss, for instance) can disregard norms with impunity, whereas a line worker cannot. Thus, there is a reduced likelihood of a high-status person experiencing dramaturgical stress and an increased likelihood of its experience for a low-status person. Drawing on extensive research in social medicine (addressed in a later section of this review), he then drew on Kemper's (1978) theory of power and status to argue for differential effects of social standing on health.

Perhaps because of the publication of his seminal work in the British journal *Sociology of Health and Illness*, Freund's (1990) line of reasoning has been largely pursued on the other side of the Atlantic. Among the most prolific of the authors who have developed these ideas are Williams and Bendelow (2003), who expanded on the ideas of Freund to argue that the sociology of emotions could be the "missing link" in medical sociology. They traced the dualism of sociology and Western thought back to Cartesian rationalism: the notion of disembodied thought in *"cogito ergo sum."* They then tied that mind-body split to the existing disconnect between biological versus constructionist perspectives.

According to Williams, approaches to the sociology of emotions range from the conservative "organismic" to the radical "social constructionist" (2003:30). By his argument, both of these approaches are too extreme, each denying the validity of the other as a relevant facet of emotion. This is particularly clear in mental illness (Williams 2000). Here the division reflects either complete acceptance of the biomedical model, including the primacy of drug therapies and medical intervention, or the complete refutation of that model as a form of labeling (Scheff 1984) or social control (Szasz 1974). Neither model has been able to completely account for the incidence, prevalence, and experience of mental illness, and yet to deny either is to ignore reams of evidence (Thoits 2005). This is especially the case for depression, which, it is commonly agreed, is frequently sparked by life events or strains in the social environment (bereavement, unemployment, illness), in combination with existing psychological resources (lack of a sense of control and optimism), and which is treated through both pharmacological and interpersonal (psychotherapeutic) means. Despite the clear relevance of both nature and nurture in such a case, very little middle ground exists between the two perspectives, thus providing an ideal-type illustration of Cartesian dualism.

From this perspective, both the organic and constructionist views of the body are too divided, and a middle ground is needed. As Williams (2003) implied, however, it is only now that we have attained a point at which such a middle ground is within our reach. Until a sufficiently strong social constructionist view of illness and emotion developed, no true synthesis would be achievable: The primacy of the medical model would have ensured that the lived experience of embodiment would be subsumed as a secondary consideration to the objective medical body. Having reached a point at which the socially constructed world is accepted as being as "real" as the physiological one, we can now attempt to bridge the gap between two sturdy and self-supporting philosophies.

A truly embodied sociology of emotions, in the view of Williams, provides an opportunity to eliminate this dualism between the organic and the social, the rational and the emotional, the positivist and the constructionist. Drawing from Barbalet's (1998) model of "convergent" approaches to emotion, Williams (2000) argued that the line between emotion and reason is itself blurred—that cognition and emotion are inextricably linked. A *passion for objectivity* is neither merely a turn of phrase nor an oxymoron, but a portrayal of actual experience. Thus, to view mental illness as irrationality based in biological disorder is to ignore the fundamental social and emotional dimensions of the experience. In Williams' (2000) view, reconceptualizing "mental health" as "emotional health" is a step toward reducing the power of the medical imperialism that has so dominated the field, without reducing the experience to mere deviance.

Lyon (2003) elaborated a similar conception in her discussion of the overarching dominance of biomedical psychiatry in defining mental illness, particularly depression and related affective disorders. According to Lyon, we have seen the expansion of the biomedical definition to cover ever larger areas of life. Medicalization of an increasing range of forms of behavior is apparent diagnostic category creep: New disorders emerge because of the discovery of medications to change the associated behaviors.

Overmedicalization is a logical extension of the rationalization of Western thought, in which the individual self is seen as prior to and separate from society. As such, causes of emotional distress are seen as located in the biology of the individual, in, for example, the levels of the neurotransmitter serotonin. The proper response to rampant medicalization is to resituate the biological person in their social world:

> To represent the situatedness of understanding of human existence requires a concept which can give form to the relationship between the social structural milieu in which humans live, their subjective experience, and the flesh through which that existence is lived. (Lyon 2003:69)

She continued to say that it is the study of emotion that can provide this concept, bridging the gap without denying the uniqueness of either dimension of experience. Regarding affective disorders as multidimensional emotional concerns, rather than as unitarily biological, makes room for the conception of both the bodily and the social experience. Drawing on Mills (1959), she pointed out that acknowledging the social makes it possible to recognize as well that depression is not just an individual problem but also a social problem. Our "prozac society," then, becomes a concern to be "treated" at every level, from the biological to the structural.

Bendelow and Williams (1995, 1998) made a similar statement regarding the experience of pain. Specifically, they argued that the biomedical model currently has dominance over how pain is defined. However, as many others have argued (Melzack and Wall 2004; Nettleton 1992; Zbrowski 1969), to consider pain as only a sensation that can be objectively appraised and measured is reductionistic. Such a definition ignores the well-documented social and cultural variations in pain and pain expression and cannot account for the inadequacy of medical means to address pain in a consistent fashion.

Bendelow and Williams (1998a) argued for a strong emotional component to pain. Drawing on historical writings and their own research findings, they made a case that the line between physical and emotional pain is not nearly as distinct as is assumed in medical views. Rather, one can merge into the other, with emotional pain causing physical symptoms and vice versa. They stated that people need to find meaning for their pain, rather than merely treat it. Without a meaning to help them interpret their pain, individuals will begin to feel isolated, stigmatized, and discredited. Both physical and emotional pain can be increased by fear, powerlessness, anxiety, depression, and lack of control. Some pain, defined as "good pain" (Freund and McGuire 1995), such as the pain of athletic workouts or of childbirth in some societies, is more tolerable than that which indicates something is wrong. The emotional nature of pain underscores its social and cultural aspects and thus the connection between self and society.

Williams and Bendelow (2003) saw the most promising approach for blending the organic and constructionist approaches to emotion and health as interactionist. They argued that an interactionist approach sits "in the analytical space between organismic and constructionist accounts" (p. 34). As Denzin (1984) argued, emotions are inherently and intrinsically embodied experiences. According to Wentworth and Ryan (1994), an interactionist perspective allows for, quite literally, the *interaction* of biophysical, personal, and structural environments. Citing Wentworth and Yardley (1994), Williams and Bendelow argued that emotion is the medium through which we employ our biological ability of attaining intersubjectivity. We know, understand, and relate to the world and our position in it through emotion (Hochschild 1983). Our positions are affected by the macrostructural and ideological milieu via feeling rules and emotion management (Hochschild 1979, 1983). If we assume an active and embodied subject (Csordas 1994), we can also see the role of emotion in making our roles (Stryker 1980), our culture (Csordas 1994), and our institutions (Collins 1981; Lyon and Barbalet 1994).

Returning now to Freund (1990, 1998), we can see that the experience of disjuncture between self and social obligation can be felt first and foremost in the realm of emotion (i.e., through dramaturgical stress). One's position in the social world is felt as much as (or perhaps more than) cognitively perceived. Successes and failures, conflicts and companionships, ease and struggle are measured first by how they make us feel. By such logic, it should come as no surprise that one's structural situation and its correlate strains are reflected throughout one's embodied experience, up to and including health.

What is lacking in this argument, unfortunately, is the empirical sociological support for an otherwise compelling theory. Despite the argument for the elimination of philosophical dualism, most research continues to fall on one side of the divide or the other. In the following section, I outline the existing literature, in the sociology of emotions and health, using the above theoretical approach as a launching point.

THE DIVISION: BIOMEDICAL POSITIVISM AND SOCIAL CONSTRUCTIONISM IN RESEARCH ON EMOTIONS AND HEALTH

The organization of the following sets of research studies reflects the dualisms described by the preceding authors, most notably the social constructionist and the biomedical positivist. Included in the latter will also be material drawn not just from sociology but from health psychology as well. Following this review, I will highlight promising pieces of research that have already begun to narrow this divide. In conclusion, I will draw new directions for research in the field, taking the state of the theoretical and empirical literature as it stands now.

Social Construction: Emotions in Health Care

Since the sociology of emotions began as a recognized subfield in the 1970s (Kemper 1990), it has been dominated by the social constructionist perspective. This is not surprising, as a fundamental contribution of the field was the notion that emotions are social, manageable, and governed by normative expectations. Indeed, the field developed partially in reaction to the previously dominant view of emotions as primarily biological (Darwin 1969; James and Lange 1922) or even instinctual (Freud 1923).

Based in the constructionist tradition, the great majority of work on emotion and health has reflected the social role, usage, and effects of emotions in health-related situations. This body of work could be more accurately characterized as the sociology of emotions in health care, rather than health. There are two primary subdivisions in this field of work: that focused on personal emotion management in health care and that focused on emotions and emotional labor as social and political tools.

In the first division, we see a widespread emphasis on feeling rules and norms of the medical setting and the pervasive need to manage emotion. Drawing on Hochschild (1983), many studies report on the emotion management of health professionals when interacting with others in medical encounters. For instance, Smith and Kleinman (1989) illustrated the unacknowledged curriculum on emotion management in medical school. Through qualitative observations in a variety of academic medical settings, they showed the use of distancing, distraction, humor, and avoidance to manage "unprofessional" emotions. Although never explicitly discussed by faculty, medical students learn to maintain "affective neutrality" in the face of unwanted emotions when dealing with patients.

Thoits (1996) and Francis (1997, 1998) showed how support groups manage the emotions of group participants to achieve therapeutic ends. Thoits (1996) described a 1970 encounter group in which participants were encouraged to express (cathart) emotion. In her observations, she illustrated how screaming, yelling, crying, and other displays of strong emotion are encouraged. When participants are unwilling or unable to meet the dramatic expression norms of the group, other participants will gang up on the exception, attempting to induce the desired emotional display.

Francis (1997, 1998) studied more sedate groups focused on divorce and bereavement, but she found the same pressure to conform to the group's emotion norms. She found that each group was organized around a particular therapeutic ideology, and this ideology constrains the feeling rules for the group members. Specifically, each facilitator defines a different set of emotions as healthy and leading to recovery and others as unhealthy and producing pathology. These definitions lead to approval or disapproval of members' emotional expressions or coping behaviors, to the degree that they accord or not with the facilitator's therapeutic approach.

Francis et al. (1999) also illustrated health care providers' use of humor to manage the emotions of themselves, colleagues, and patients in medical encounters. Through qualitative interviews of health care providers in a large hospital, they showed that whether humor is helpful or harmful to the goals of a medical interaction depends on the adeptness of the humor user in assessing the dimensions of time, place, and person.

Meerabeau and Page (1998) illustrated the emotion work that nurses do in managing distance from dead and dying patients. According to these authors, the sanitized theory of cardiopulmonary resuscitation often bears little resemblance to the messiness of practice, and nurses sometimes find themselves required to apply procedures that feel inappropriate, ineffective, or even ludicrous. Echoing the themes of Smith and Kleinman (1989), Meerabeau and Page underscored the discomfort and "pollution" (Douglas 1975) of dealing with sick and damaged bodies and showed the demanding emotional labor of nurses in dealing with living and newly dead bodies.

In a similar vein, Van Dongen (2001) focused specifically on the messiness of the body, with nurses as mediators—in particular, how successful emotion work and body work when dealing with excrement and other unpleasant aspects of their elderly patients affects status in the wards of a mental hospital.

Three studies in particular emphasize the necessary role of emotion in physician-patient interaction. These studies take as a beginning a critique of the assumption that emotion has no place in a rational medical encounter. Baker et al. (2003) drew from transcripts of clinical visits to show the unequal expression of emotion of physicians and patients. They suggested that increased emotional expression on the physician's part could enhance care and patient confidence. Lupton (2003) contradicted the current consumerist movement in health care, which assumes a rational, self-reliant patient. She argued that emotion has a crucial place in the doctor-patient relationship. Without some degree of trust in their doctor's abilities and goodwill, seriously ill patients might find themselves experiencing even greater fear, uncertainty, and vulnerability than they already do. May et al. (2004) reported on how physicians negotiate meanings of patient illness and emotional responses to patients in everyday practice. The authors began with the historic shift toward an objectified model of the patient as an instance of a particular pathology rather than an experiencing subject. Using interviews with physicians, the authors argued that the degree of congruency between the physician's and the patient's models of explanation directly influences both the immediate and long-term emotional tenor of the clinical relationship.

Another theme in the emotion management in health care subdivision concerns the emotions of patients and families of patients in dealing with illness. Taylor (1995) argued that the dominance of victimization models in women's mental health overlook the agency of women when defining and recognizing women's emotional distress. She drew on Thoits (1986) self-labeling theory to describe the social construction of postpartum depression as a means that women use to respond to cultural norms about gender and motherhood.

Clarke (2005) described the unrecognized health care work, including emotion work, of fathers when a child has cancer. In addition to the stresses associated with the care and treatment of a gravely ill child, fathers had to cope with being stigmatized, excluded, and treated as a secondary parent even when they were the primary caregiver. Consedine and Magai (2002a, 2002b) compared four ethnic groups to understand the correlation among culture, emotional experience, emotional inhibition, and physical health. The results of their survey showed that ethnicity is associated with variations in emotional inhibition and negative affect and that these factors were, in turn, related to illness.

Finally, Wiley (1990) demonstrated a typology of emotion roles that clients assume in order to get along with staff in a holistic therapeutic community. In an environment where the "natural" expression of feelings by psychiatric clients is viewed as crucial therapy, Wiley described how clients adapt to the expectations for expression. When presented with cues for "appropriate" emotional display from the group therapist, clients must choose to accept, manipulate, or reject the situation as defined, with rewards and sanctions corresponding to their performances.

The second key subdivision in the field of emotions and health care reflects emotions as political tools in medical institutions. Unsurprisingly, most of these works focus on the profession of nursing as the field most torn between instrumental and emotional labor. In various forms, these authors pointed out that emotions can be a burden or a resource—or both—in dealing with competing demands. In some cases, the nurses must engage in emotional labor to meet the structural demands of employment, in much the same way as the flight attendants studied by Hochschild (1983). In others, the study focuses on how emotion work is used as a tool to generate more control and power among the less powerful actors in their work environment.

Bolton (2001) investigated how nurses adapt to conflicting expectations in an increasingly market-oriented health care environment. In her fieldwork at a large hospital, Bolton found that the nurses' language of "acting," "performances," and "masks" lends itself to a Goffmanesque inquiry. Viewing emotion work as part of a repertoire of self-presentations (Goffman 1959) clarifies nurses' ability to juggle the various emotional demands made of them.

O'Brien (1994) studied emotion work among nurses in the context of the growing emphasis on health promotion. Contrary to the health promotion ideals of community, social responsibility, and personal and collective control over health maintenance, the dominant medical practices are reoriented to health messages directed at individual health beliefs and behaviors. Nurses, O'Brien argued, are the primary implementers of this dominant program, and emotional labor is their primary tool for deployment. Thus, nurses develop their relationship with a patient with the intent of delivering messages targeted at the patient's personal health behaviors, and the original message of collective action and community-based health agendas is subverted.

Olesen and Bone (1998) took the perspective of stress on nurses by pointing out that the "speed up" of the health care system for cost containment has implications for emotion work and emotional labor, particularly among nurses. In this theoretical piece, the authors argud that structural and economic change entails alteration of emotion norms; as "patient" is shifted to "customer" in health care, the emotional tenor of the interaction changes as well. Rapid structural change requires correspondingly dramatic alteration in emotional response, and the change in emotion norms itself also incurs emotions in the nurses trying to adapt.

An exception to the focus on nursing is Treweek's (2003) study of care assistants in a residential home for the elderly in which she illustrates how emotional skills are a dynamic means of creating social order. She showed how an occupational group can develop their own norms for emotion work, rather than emotional labor done at the behest of management. With little outside support or formal power, the largely female staff was empowered to maintain order and control in the home through the use of emotion work.

The discussion of emotion in medical encounters has moved beyond health care research and has also infused clinical development. Articles have fairly recently begun to appear in practice journals for health care professionals that specifically address the issue of how to respond to emotion—one's own or others. Suchman et al. (1997) illustrated how physicians can improve their relationship with their patients by learning to recognize the opportunity to empathize with the patient. Robichaud (2003) argued that health care providers have a moral obligation to learn to pay attention to emotions of patients, families, and themselves in order to understand all factors influencing medical decision-making.

Thomas (2003) identified "mismanaged anger" as a significant problem in health care and provided strategies for dealing with the different kinds of angry encounter that a nurse is likely to face. She first described the kinds of setting in which a nurse is likely to either encounter anger or experience anger. She then suggested a hierarchy of effective problem-focused coping strategies, then emotion-focused coping strategies, and, finally, expression norms to maintain open communication.

Meier et al. (2001) presented a model to help doctors deal with their emotional reactions to critically ill patients. As these authors argued, working with such patients can produce a gamut of negative emotions, including frustration, grief, fear of contagion, and shame, all of which can interfere with effective practice. They argued that such emotions should not be viewed as unprofessional or abnormal. Rather they lay out a four-step process to recognize and manage the emotion effectively: naming the emotion, accepting its normalcy, reflecting on its potential consequences, and consulting a trusted colleague about it.

Even in the above attempts to recognize emotion, one finds the underlying message that emotions are dangerous—that they threaten the outcome of the medical interaction. For instance, Thomas (2003) saw anger as a problem with which nurses must deal. According to Meier et al. (2001), emotions might interfere with good practice. Robichaud (2003) implied that unrecognized emotions are a threat to good care because they might reflect incorrect values or beliefs or produce "unreasonable" decisions. Suchman et al. (1997) concluded that emotions are important because lack of empathy with patient emotions might increase the risk of lawsuits.

A shortcoming of most social constructionist studies of emotion in medical encounters is their tendency to ignore the existence of the body, as pointed out by Freund (1990, 1998) and Williams (2003). Bodies, for the most part, are objects that inspire emotions (disgust, desire, and so forth), but are not *part* of the emotion. Emotions, in turn, are disembodied experiences that can be cognitively appraised or expressed/not expressed for normative purposes. Their existence in this body of work is virtually entirely social or psychological, with little reference to how they might affect the health or well-being of the people involved.

Biomedical Positivism: Health Psychology and Emotion

At the most positivistic and biomedical end of the spectrum is the field of emotions in health psychology. Yet, despite what most sociologists would consider a peripheral position to our discipline, the psychology of emotion has a crucial contribution to make that we ignore at our epistemological peril. In particular, health psychology is undeniably set up to address issues of physiology to which sociologists have little recourse. This allows psychologists to investigate both direct and indirect connections between emotions and physical and/or mental health.

In the field of psychology, the focus of research has been on how emotion contributes to, or more commonly, how it detracts from health. Mayne (2001) has compiled a useful summary of the key arguments on the interrelation of emotions and health in psychological research. He posited two main relations: direct pathways to health, meaning the physiological activation effect of emotion, and indirect pathways, including behavioral and cognitive effects. The direct pathways refer largely to the physiological components of emotion, discussed at length by Franks in Chapter 2 of this volume. The relevant point here is that such physiological arousal can have an impact on the heart, lungs, immune, endocrine, circulatory, and other systems of the body. Excessive or persistent arousal has been shown to have damaging effects on these systems (Marmor and Mustard 1994). As Mayne pointed out, this understanding has been part of medicine since the early 1970s in the construct of the Type A personality. Colloquially, we can trace the origin back further, in, for instance, the nineteenth-century term of "apoplectic" anger leading to apoplexy (cardiac arrest).

In the study of physiology and emotion, a key body of work demonstrates that emotions and emotional expression do indeed have a direct impact on human physiology. Gross and his colleagues (Ochsner and Gross 2004; Oliver and Gross 2004) have demonstrated consequences of suppressing negative emotion. Suppressing refers to not expressing, or even smothering, a felt emotion. Gross (1998) found that suppressing emotion produces greater activation of the sympathetic nervous system, despite reduced reported emotion. Ochsner and Gross (2004) found that suppressing negative emotion produces the types of physiological stress that are associated over the long term with heart disease. In a related study, Oliver and Gross (2004) reviewed a large number of studies on emotional suppression versus reappraisal of the emotional stimulus (trying to think of it differently) and found that the later technique has better consequences for health.

Other authors have found similar results reflecting the adverse health effects of not expressing emotion, especially negative emotion. Cooke et al. (2003) studied repressive coping styles characterized by minimizing or denying stressful emotions. They found that using a repressive coping style has negative effects on lung function in asthma patients. Mehling and Krause (2005) have found clinical evidence that alexithymia (a form of dysfunctional expression of emotion) can be expressed as chronic pain. Martin et al. (1999) found that a person's style of anger expression predicted neuroticism, somatic complaints, and health behaviors.

Also of interest is that a number of health psychologists have found that certain forms of emotional expression can improve health outcomes. For instance, Spiegel (1995) has shown that group therapy among metastatic cancer patients has not only positive psychosocial effects but actually increases longevity. Frasure-Smith et al. (1995) found that depression, anxiety, anger, and emotional social support predict recovery from and relapse of myocardial infarction. Pennebaker and his associates (Greenberg et al. 1996; Pennebaker 2003; Smyth et al. 1999; Spera et al. 1994) found that writing about severe negative emotional experiences has dramatic physical health benefits, including significantly fewer physician visits for illness, reductions in symptoms among sufferers of asthma and rheumatoid arthritis, reduced depressive symptoms and faster reemployment, and decreased psychological symptoms among trauma victims.

The indirect pathways of emotion have generally been of greater immediate interest to sociologists, as they reflect interaction of the individual with the environment. Indirect pathways include both behavior and cognition, which, in turn, affect physiological activation. In terms of behavior, varieties of fear and distress, for instance, can motivate health behaviors such as seeking medical care, exercising, or adhering to prescribed diets or medication regimens. Such behaviors can help to alleviate fear of illness and also improve health. People also engage in behaviors to upregulate or downregulate emotions in other ways, such as thrill-seeking activities (e.g., skydiving) or substance use. Such activities can have indirect effects on health by putting the person at risk of injury or illness as a result of the behavior (Mayne 2001).

Cognition can influence health indirectly through either its impact on physiological activation or on behavior. Cognitions fall into three main categories: symptom perception, illness representation/beliefs, and behavioral response/coping. People must perceive a symptom in order to define themselves as sick, but, on average, most are highly inaccurate in this. When a symptom is perceived, beliefs about illness come into play. The symptom must be attributed to illness, the person must view himself or herself as vulnerable to that illness, and the illness must be seen as having undesirable consequences. Finally, the person must make the decision to seek help and adhere to treatment. Emotion is a key player in all three of these steps. Negative emotion has been shown to increase symptom perception, sense of vulnerability, and help seeking. However, it is also associated with poor treatment adherence and less optimal outcomes than positive emotion.

To a sociologist, the obvious drawback of the psychological literature is the eternal and nearly exclusive focus on the internal states of the individual. Nonetheless, by conceiving of emotion as a bridge connecting the physiological, the psychological, and the social, we can integrate bodily existence with the external environment.

BRIDGING THE GAP: STRESS AND INTERACTIONISM

Freund (1990, 1998) and Williams and Bendelow (2003) each identified a field of research that they saw as promising for creating an embodied sociology of emotions and health. For Freund, this field was stress research, and for Williams and Bendelow, it was the symbolic interactionist tradition. As Newton (2003) pointed out, neither of these fields is completely free of the mind-body dualism characteristic of the field more generally. Stress research either accepts the medical model of bodily realism as unproblematic—the objective body as opposed to the lived body—or retreats to a constructionist cognitive appraisal without reference to the embodied person. Interactionism tends to assume a bodily as well as a social experience of emotion, but, in general, it makes no connection of the lived body to the physiological implications of social living on that body—in short, to health. Nonetheless, each perspective has some key insights that point to ways to empirically investigate these crucial connections.

Emotions as Distress

As is well known, the term *stress* resulted from the research of endocrinologist Hans Selye (1956). Given that, it is not surprising that the stress literature leans toward the biomedical model of emotion. This is not to say that stress research accepts the purely organic James-Lange (1922) model of the visceral reaction as the actual emotion. Cognitive appraisals and perceptions of threat and support are key concepts in the field. However, by its nature, the field of stress research is focused on emotions that comprise mental health problems. Most stress research, therefore, defines emotion primarily in terms of anxiety or depression and measures it through instruments such as symptom scales.

Despite its medical origins, however, stress research has demonstrated that emotional distress is not merely a biological function but is a direct result of factors in an individual's social environment. An enormous body of literature exists demonstrating the social patterning of psychological and emotional well-being, so this chapter will reference only classic and new research.

Emotional distress is demonstrably *not* merely an individual characteristic, but a reflection of one's social position as well. Research has shown that distress is associated with social status and demographics, with lower-status groups suffering higher rates and intensities of negative emotion. This correlation of lower status to greater stress or poorer outcomes holds for socioeconomic status (Dohrenwend et al. 1992; Lorant et al. 2001; Ulbrich et al. 1989), gender (Gove and Shin 1989; Umberson et al. 1992), race (Breslau et al. 2005; Kessler and Neighbors 1986; Turner and Gil 2002), marital status (Pearlin et al. 1981; Turner et al. 1995), and education (McLeod and Kaiser 2004; Ross and Van Willigen 1997).

Distress is patterned not only by who experiences it but also by the category of stressor. Stress is not a uniform response to threat, but, rather, varies according to how the severity, duration, and configuration of stressors impact a person and his or her environment. The experience of stress can be sudden and dramatic, low level and long lasting, or a cumulative effect of multiple events and situations. Reflecting this, stressors have been categorized into four types: traumas, life events, role strains, and hassles (Thoits 1995). Traumas are rare and horrific events that are unexpected and long lasting in their effects: Disasters, rape, abuse, combat, and other events often associated with posttraumatic stress syndrome are considered traumas (Brewin et al. 2000; Rubonis and Bickman 1991). Life events are usually less overwhelming, but, like traumas, they tend to overshadow one's normal life during the time they are occurring. Life events can be either positive (e.g., marriage, childbirth, new job), or negative (e.g., divorce, death of a loved one, loss of job); however, only negative events are considered to increase the risk of health and mental health disorders (Avison and Turner 1988; Ensel and Lin 1991; Jackson and Finney 2002). Role strains are less time limited than either of the other two; that is, they are not events or situations, but ongoing struggles (Pearlin et al. 1981; Pearlin 1989). A parent juggling work and family conflicts experiences role strain, as does a caregiver for an ill or elderly relative or a worker with an abusive supervisor. Finally, hassles are the small but frustrating events of daily life that interfere with one's important obligations: parking tickets, leaky plumbing, traffic, annoying neighbors, and so forth (Serido et al. 2004).

Recent research indicates that these categories of stressors are also socially patterned; that is, some groups are more likely to be exposed to more stress than others. Turner and Turner (2005), for example, found that past cumulative adversity is the single greatest predictor of current experience of stress and of likelihood of exposure to future life events. McLeod and Owens (2004) tested a hypothesis of double jeopardy in mental health by various social statuses among children. They identified the interaction of race and socioeconomic class as the main significant predictor of adolescent outcomes, particularly for self-esteem and scholastic achievement. Pearlin et al. (2005) made a theoretical argument that health disparities can be tied to the persistence of stressors across the life course for low-status groups. They proposed that stressors related to status or status attainment that continue or occur repeatedly over life both put people at risk of additional adversity and take a long-term toll on health.

If types of stressor clarify the social and structural nature of distress, social supports and coping resources underscore the interpersonal and intrapersonal relevance. Social support reflects the availability of others in one's environment who can provide help in times of need. Coping resources are the strengths, both internal and external, on which a person can draw. Intricately connected, these two aspects are heavily invested with both cognitive and emotional meaning.

According to Thoits (1995), there are three types of social support: instrumental, socioemotional, and informational. Instrumental support is the provision of material help to a person in need. Financial support, transportation, shelter, babysitting, errand running, work coverage, and so forth are all examples of instrumental support. Socioemotional support is what one tends to think of as "the shoulder to cry on." Such support includes listening to, comforting, hugging, praying with, and even drinking with the distressed person. Informational support, the least studied kind, usually refers to the providing of useful information relevant to the person's need, such as sources of instrumental or socioemotional support (e.g., treatment, support groups). Social support has been shown to be an important factor in buffering stress (Lincoln 2003; Turner et al. 1998) and ameliorating depression (Lin et al. 1999). The loss of such support could in and of itself be a source of distress (Cornwell 2003).

A second key factor in the constellation of stress is how people cope with stressful life events. In the sociological stress literature, coping is divided into two categories: coping strategies and coping resources. The category of coping strategies can itself be divided into two categories: problem-focused and emotion-focused coping. Problem-focused coping, as its name suggests, is a category of strategy that attempts to find a solution to the problem that is causing the person distress. Examples would be searching want ads and attending job fairs upon becoming unemployed or addressing academic difficulties by hiring a tutor. Emotion-focused coping, on the other hand, is engaging in activities that relieve one's negative emotions. Confiding in a friend after discovering a partner's infidelity or watching TV to distract oneself from thinking about a loved one's illness would be examples of emotion-focused coping. Most severe stressors will require both emotion-focused and problem-focused coping.

Coping strategies are tied closely to social support. In Thoits' (1986) now classic work, she laid out the connections clearly by conceptualizing social support as coping assistance. She underlined the similarities between socioemotional support and emotion-focused coping, and instrumental support and problem-focused coping. Her conclusions emphasized the social nature of individual behavior, even so personal a behavior as responding to one's own sense of distress.

Finally, the category of coping resources is divided into two subcategories: psychological and environmental resources, each with its own components. Environmental resources can include many things, examples being the amount of each type of social support one has, one's financial resources, available time or leisure, availability of providers of services, and so forth (Moos 2002). Psychological resources include such things as self-esteem (one's self-evaluation as good or bad), self-efficacy (one's sense of control over events), and mastery (one's sense of power) (Folkman 1984, 1997; Rosenberg et al. 1995). Coping resources, then, refer to those sources of strength that one can tap at need.

The connection between stress and mental health has been well covered in the above literature. However, stress, social support, and coping have also been related to physical health. An interesting implication to draw from these pieces is the idea of coping strategies as health behaviors and vice versa. Peyrot et al. (1999) have linked psychosocial resources with glycemic control among diabetics. In their study, they found support for a biopsychosocial model of glycemic control, showing that stress and coping affect glucose levels through the intervening variable of regimen adherence. In addition, they found that biological factors have less of a direct impact on glycemic control than do psychosocial factors for Type I diabetics; and for both Type I and Type II, the effect of these factors is mediated by having stable psychosocial resources.

Alonzo and Reynolds (1998) argued that the outcome of cardiac arrest is heavily influenced by the emotional reaction of the patient to the attack. Excessive emotional arousal or denial are prime causes of delay in seeking treatment and are, therefore, indirect causes of death. Alonzo (2000) demonstrated that the cumulative stress of chronic illness can produce posttraumatic stress disorder. He argued for the additive effect of chronic illness, invasive therapies, change in illness trajectory, and external life events over the life course. Such traumatogenic experiences encourage maladaptive coping with illness symptoms, which, in turn, increases the risk of complications and death.

Reynolds et al. (2000) found that effective coping strategies predict better survival among breast cancer patients. In particular, expressing emotion as a coping strategy, combined with high levels of perceived emotional support, was predictive of survival. Women who reported low levels of both of these variables were significantly more likely to die of their cancer.

These studies have been criticized because they must rely on self-report measures of symptoms or fairly gross measures of illness (e.g., doctor visits). More important, however, they can be criticized for their penchant for locating the problem in the individual or the individual's networks. Maladaptive coping, poor social support, and even exposure to stressors are portrayed as personal problems, implying change to be made at the individual level.

As is evident from the above discussion, the research on stress spans the continuum from social structural position, to personal psychological characteristics, to health correlates. We can conclude from this work, for instance, that some demographic groups suffer more than other groups from stressors, have less complete social support networks, and experience more stress. For this reason, it is a powerful tool in closing the micro-macrosociology gap.

Distress is an emotion, and it is demonstrably tied to one's social environment. Thus, the stress literature could be an effective tool to chip away at the divide between biomedical and constructionist orientations. However, if its orientation toward distress is a medical problem subject to diagnosis (depression, anxiety, demoralization, dysthymia, somaticism, and so forth), it has largely overlooked the nature of emotion as a political, social, and interpersonal tool. In this field, then, emotion can be measured and correlated, but not "lived."

Emotions in Symbolic Interactionism

Unlike stress research, interactionism tends to emphasize the constructionist end of the continuum. Nonetheless, many interactionists have taken the step of considering the "lived experience" of the body in emotion and health. Denzin (1984) was one of the first to raise the question of the phenomenology of the lived and experienced body. Ellis and Bochner (1999) argued that medical social science needs to step out of merely biomedical observation and seek to understand the emotions and embodied experience of illness. Karp (1996) took the classically biomedical diagnosis of depression and explored it as a social, emotional, psychological, and embodied experience. Francis (2003) used health psychology findings and sociological theories of emotion and identity to develop a theory connecting health outcomes with emotional communication.

Ruane (2003) explicitly dealt with the mind-body dualism in her study of the techniques used by health care providers to promote "unbonding" among women giving up newborns for adoption. She demonstrated how the concept of maternal bonding is conceived of as having a firm biological (e.g., hormonal) basis, and yet the process of encouraging both bonding and unbonding is undeniably social. In her analysis, maternal-child attachment is clearly a fruitful example of the biopsychosocial continuum of emotion meriting further study.

Thoits (1985, 1986) was the first in sociology to make deliberate inroads on combining an interactionist approach to emotion with stress research. She pointed out the conceptual similarity of emotion-focused coping and emotion management, the main difference being simply that coping implies inherently negative emotions as the target. Her model of the cues of emotion management explicitly encompasses both biology and social influences. She identified four cues that people use to identify and manage their emotions: situational cues, expressive gestures, cultural labels, and physiological cues. Her work has provided fodder for a number of studies utilizing both emotions and stress concepts (Francis 1997, 1998; Lively 2002, Pugliesi and Shook 1997; Simon and Nath 2004, to name just a few). Thoits' research also serves as a pathway to connect the larger interactionist/constructionist concepts of emotional labor and ideology with distress and ultimately health.

More recently, Lively and Heise (2004) have established a clear correspondence between the approaches of managing and accounting for emotions. Specifically using theories of affect control (Heise 1979; Smith-Lovin 1990) and emotion management (Hochschild 1983), they compared expectations for each theory for contrast and congruency. In their findings, they demonstrated the "distance" between emotions in Euclidean space, showing how some emotions are "closer" to each other than others. It is easier, they concluded, to manage emotions (others' or one's own) into feelings that are closer than those that are further away. In other words, Lively and Heise have developed a means to operationalize the distance between ruling rules and feelings. Returning to Freund (1998), this is clearly a potential measure of degree of dramaturgical stress.

DISCUSSION

Public health research has drawn on the largely biomedically oriented health stress and health psychology literatures to develop a model of status gradients in health. Research has found that controlling for all known health risks, including physical environment, genetics, health-related behavior (exercise, smoking, drinking, diet, and so forth), and culture, and the lower that group's social status on any dimension (race, class, gender, and so forth), the worse that group's average morbidity and mortality (Hertzman et al. 1994; Marmor et al. 1994). In addition, the lower the social status, the more prolonged and unrelieved are the physical symptoms of stress in reaction to social demands (Wilkinson 1996; Shnurr and Green 2004). Studies in physiological psychology have related such long-term stress to immune function and allostatic load (how the body responds and adjusts to repeated stressors) (Dougall and Baum 2004; Friedman and McEwan 2004) as well as such concrete outcomes as heart disease (Marmor and Mustard 1994; Ford 2004). In theory, then, it is this negative stress that is the connection between the universal health gradient and status.

What this model ignores is the recognition that distress, the product of negative stress, is fundamentally an emotion. From the stance of a sociologist of emotion, what is lacking is the richness of constructionist and interactionist insights into conflict, power, and negotiated social order. Returning to Lyon's (2003) example of depression, we can clearly see the benefit of such insights.

Depression as an emotional state and a mental illness also follows social structural gradients. Those at the lower end of the social and economic ladder are much more at risk of depression than are those with greater social resources. Depression, in turn, has been linked to an increased risk of other illnesses as well, such as coronary heart disease (Todaro et al. 2003) and Alzheimer's disease (Zubenko et al. 2003). Rates of depression correlate with patterns of many other chronic or degenerative illnesses as well, including heart disease, diabetes, tuberculosis, schizophrenia, and high blood pressure, just to name a few. Thus, the clear social connections of depression to life conditions are increasingly now also being linked to physical health as well.

Yet, depression continues to be defined and treated as entirely an individual medical problem. This has created a society in which unhappiness—however valid—is medicalized into unhealthiness. Granted, the rise in rates of depression might be accounted for, in part, by the creep of this medical imperialism. It might, however, also reflect the rising discontent and anomie of much of our society in the face of enormous inequalities, prepackaged high-pressure goals, and socialized consumerism (Lyon 2003). As sociologists, we recognize the emotional tenor of our society as a potential commentary on the "unhealthiness" of our society (Bellah et al. 1985; Durkheim 1951;

Putnam 2000). The social order is not random, but aligned with the ideologies of those who benefit. Workers must adhere to the emotion norms of the workplace as part of their jobs. Occupations at risk of dramaturgical stress are an inherent component of a postindustrial economy (Freund 1998; Hochschild 1983, 1997). We understand alienation. Should we treat it with Prozac?

Viewing health and illness through the lens of emotion illustrates how we can resituate the biological body in the social world without denying either. Health, through this lens, becomes both individual trouble and a social problem (Karp 1996; Lyon 2003; Mills 1959). Drawing on Williams (2003), an embodied sociology of emotions and health does not intensify the tendency to locate social ills within the individual. Rather, it raises the question of where do the emotions come from and why. Medical problems are assumed to arise from within the body, but emotions are understood to emerge as a result of external events. Attention to the social as well as the biological etiology of negative, stressful emotion can move us from a unitary focus on the "treatment" of ill health to the political, cultural, social, and psychological context in which it occurs.

CONCLUSION

From this chapter I would like to draw three immediate directions for future research in the sociology of emotions and health. First, sociologists need to take up the theoretical gauntlets of Freund, Williams, Lyon, and others. We need empirical exploration of the validity and utility of their arguments for emotions as the point of closure for Cartesian dualism. In particular, as sociologists of emotion, we need to cease being afraid of the biological body. Although we have been effective in dealing with sexuality, gender, and violence as they relate to embodied life, we have tended to "throw out the baby with the bath water" in our view of traditionally medical territory.

Second, on a related note, we need increasing collaboration of emotions scholars with researchers in the sociology of health and mental health and illness. We currently have few people working across the two subfields of sociology, and we are in need of more connections to create discourse across models. As argued in this chapter, stress and interactionist approaches would be good places to begin. From interactionists, I foresee important contributions in fleshing out the nature of distress as an emotion and placing it in the context of power relations and social order. From stress researchers, we have need of empirical work connecting stress and psychological/emotional well-being to physical health outcomes, but with a focus on the constellation of stress as a social as well as an individual problem.

Third, we need to begin crossing disciplinary boundaries to reap the insights of other disciplines, including psychology, anthropology, and public health. Sociologists of emotion have excelled in infusing our topic across our own discipline, but we have little contact with most other fields, with the possible exception of communication. As we are no longer in need of tight boundaries to establish our identity, it is time to transcend ideological and methodological limitations and seek cross-fertilization with other modes of thought. The same argument, of course, holds for national boundaries as well, particularly given the sources of this chapter.

These directions by no means exhaust the possibilities; they merely scratch the surface. My hope is to see the development of the sociology of emotions and health as an opportunity to connect biology to political economy, with emotions as the first bridge. We have as a canvas the experienced body within the context of the negotiated, encultured, conflictual, unequal, and dynamic social world. In this, there is the potential for sociologists of emotions to build upon our central, rather than decentered, position in sociology, as well as more broadly in all the fields of health and illness.

REFERENCES

Alonzo, Angelo A. 2000. "The Experience of Chronic Illness and Post-traumatic Stress Disorder: the Effects of Cumulative Adversity." *Social Science and Medicine* 50: 1475–1484.

Alonzo, Angelo A., and Nancy R. Reynolds. 1998. "The Structure of Emotions during Acute Myocardial Infarction: A Model of Coping." *Social Science and Medicine* 46: 1099–1110.

Avison, William R., and R. Jay Turner. 1988. "Stressful Life Events and Depressive Symptoms: Disaggregating the Effects of Acute Stressors and Chronic Strains." *Journal of Health and Social Behavior* 29: 253–264.

Baker, Patricia S., William C. Yoels, and Jeffrey M. Clair. 2003. "Emotional Expression During Medical Encounters: Social Disease and the Medical Gaze." Pp. 173–200 in *Health and the Sociology of Emotions,* edited by V. James and J. Gabe. Oxford: Blackwell.

Barbalet, James. 1998. *Emotion, Social Theory, and Social Structure.* Cambridge: Cambridge University Press.

Bellah, Robert N., Richard Madsen, William M. Sullivan, Ann Swidler, and Steven M.Tipton. 1985. *Habits of the Heart.* Berkeley: University of California Press.

Bendelow, Gillian, and Simon J. Williams. 1995. "Transcending the Dualisms: Toward a Sociology of Pain." *Sociology of Health and Illness* 17: 139–165.

———. 1998. "Emotions, Pain and Gender." Pp. 253–267 in *Emotions in Social Life: Critical Themes and Contemporary Issues,* edited by G. Bendelow and S. Williams. London: Routledge.

Bolton, Sharon C. 2001. "Changing Faces: Nurses as Emotional Jugglers." *Sociology of Health and Illness* 23: 85–100.

Breslau, Joshua, Kenneth S. Kendler, Maxwell Su, Sergio Gaxiola-Aguilar, and Ronald C.Kessler. 2005. "Lifetime Risk and Persistence of Psychiatric Disorders across Ethnic Groups in the United States." *Psychological Medicine* 35: 317–327.

Brewin, Chris R., Bernice Andrews, and John D. Valentine. 2000. "Meta-analysis of Risk Factors for Posttraumatic Stress Disorder in Trauma-Exposed Adults." *Journal of Consulting and Clinical Psychology* 68: 748–766.

Clarke, Juanne N. 2005. "Fathers' Home Health Care Work When a Child has Cancer." *Men and Masculinities* 7: 385–404.

Collins, Randall. 1981. "On the Microfoundations of Macrosociology." *American Journal of Sociology* 86: 984–1014.

Consedine, Nathan S., and Carol Magai. 2002a. "The Uncharted Waters of Emotion: Ethnicity, Trait Emotion and Emotion Expression in Older Adults." *Journal of Cross-Cultural Gerontology* 17: 71–100.

———. 2002b. "Ethnic Variation in the Impact of Negative Affect and Emotion Inhibition on the Health of Older Adults." *Journals of Gerontology, Series B* 57: 396–408.

Cooke, Lucy, Lynn B. Myers, and Naz Derakshan. 2003. "Lung Function, Adherence and Denial in Asthma Patients Who Exhibit a Repressive Coping Style." *Psychology, Health and Medicine* 8: 35–44.

Cornwell, Benjamin. 2003. "The Dynamic Properties of Social Support: Decay, Growth, and Staticity, and Their Effects on Adolescent Depression." *Social Forces* 81: 955–978.

Csordas, Thomas J. 1994. "Words from the Holy People: A Case Study in Cultural Phenomenology." Pp. 269–290 in *Embodiment and Experience: The Existential Ground of Culture and Self,* edited by T. J. Csordas. Cambridge: Cambridge University Press.

Darwin, Charles. 1969. *The Expression of Emotion in Man and Animals.* New York: Greenwood.

Denzin, Norman K. 1984. *On Understanding Emotion.* San Francisco: Jossey-Bass.

Dougall, Angela Liegey, and Andrew Baum. 2004. "Psychoneuroimmunology and Trauma." Pp. 129–155 in *Trauma and Health: Physical Health Consequences of Exposure to Extreme Stress,* edited by P. Schnurr and B. Green. Washington, DC: American Psychological Association Press.

Douglas, Mary. 1975. *Implicit Meanings.* London: Routledge and Kegan Paul.

Dohrenwend, Bruce P., Itzhak Levav, Patrick E. Shrout, Sharon Schwartz, Guedalia Naveh, Bruce G. Link, Andrew E. Skodol, and Ann Stueve. 1992. "Socioeconomic Status and Psychiatric Disorders: The Causation-Selection Issue." *Science* 255: 946–952.

Durkheim, Emile. 1951. *Suicide; A Study in Sociology.* Translated by John A. Spaulding and George Simpson. Edited by G. Simpson. New York: Free Press.

Ellis, Carolyn, and Arthur P. Bochner. 1999. "Bringing Emotion and Personal Narrative into Medical Social Science." *Health* 3: 229–237.

Ensel, Walter M., and Nan Lin. 1991. "The Life Stress Paradigm and Psychological Distress." *Journal of Health and Social Behavior* 32: 321–341.

Folkman, Susan. 1984. "Personal Control and Stress and Coping Processes: A Theoretical Analysis." *Journal of Personality and Social Psychology* 46: 839–852.

———. 1997. "Positive Psychological States and Coping with Severe Stress." *Social Science and Medicine* 45: 1207–1221.

Ford, Daniel E. 2004. "Depression, Trauma and Cardiovascular Health." Pp. 73–98 in *Trauma and Health: Physical Health Consequences of Exposure to Extreme Stress*, edited by P. Schnurr and B. Green. Washington, DC: American Psychological Association Press.

Francis, Linda E. 1997. "Ideology and Interpersonal Emotion Management: Redefining Identity in Two Support Groups." *Social Psychology Quarterly* 60: 153–171.

———. 1998. "Emotion, Coping, and Therapeutic Ideologies." Pp. 71–101 in *Social Perspectives on Emotion*, Vol. 5 edited by B. Cuthbert-Johnson and R. Erikson. Greenwich, CT: JAI Press.

———. 2003. "Feeling Good, Feeling Well: Identity, Emotion and Health." Pp. 123–134 in *Advances in Identity Theory*, edited by P. J. Burke, T. J. Owens, R. T. Serpe and P. A. Thoits. New York: Kluwer Academic/Plenum.

Francis, Linda, Kathleen Monahan, and Candyce Berger. 1999. "A Laughing Matter? The Uses of Humor in Medical Interactions." *Motivation and Emotion* 23: 155–174.

Franks, David. D. 1987. "Notes on the Bodily Aspect of Emotion: A Controversial Issue in Symbolic Interaction." Pp. 219–233 in *Studies in Symbolic Interaction: Research Annual*, edited by N. K. Denzin. Greenwich, CT: JAI Press.

Frasure-Smith, Nancy, Francois Lesperance, and Mario Talajic. 1995. "The Impact of Negative Emotions on Prognosis Following Myocardial Infarction: Is It More than Depression?" *Health Psychology* 14: 388–398.

Friedman, Matthew J., and Bruce McEwan. 2004. "Posttraumatic Stress Disorder, Allostatic Load, and Medical Illness." Pp. 157–188 in *Trauma and Health: Physical Health Consequences of Exposure to Extreme Stress*, edited by P. Schnurr and B. Green. Washington, DC: American Psychological Association Press.

Freud, Sigmund. 1923. *The Ego and the Id.* London: Hogarth Press and the Institute for Psychoanalysis.

Freund, Peter E. S. 1990. "The Expressive Body: A Common Ground for the Sociology of Emotions and Health and Illness." *Sociology of Health and Illness* 12: 452–477.

———. 1998. "Social Performances and their Discontents: The Biopsychosocial Aspects of Dramaturgical Stress." Pp. 268–294 in *Emotions in Social Life: Critical Themes and Contemporary Issues*, edited by G. Bendelow and S. Williams. London: Routledge.

Freund, Peter E. S., and Meredith B. McGuire. 1995. *Health, Illness and the Social Body*. Englewood Cliffs, NJ: Prentice-Hall.

Goffman, Erving. 1959. *The Presentation of Self in Everyday Life*. Garden City, NY: Doubleday.

———. 1974. *Frame Analysis: An Essay on the Organization of Experience.* Cambridge, MA: Harvard University Press.

Gove, Walter R., and Hee-Choon Shin. 1989. "The Psychological Well-Being of Divorced and Widowed Men and Women: An Empirical Analysis." *Journal of Family Issues* 10: 122–144.

Greenberg, Melanie A., Camille B. Wortman, and Arthur A. Stone. 1996. "Emotional Expression and Physical Health: Revising Traumatic Memories or Fostering Self-Regulation?" *Journal of Personality and Social Psychology* 71: 588–602.

Gross, James J. 1998. "Antecedent- and Response-Focused Emotion Regulation: Divergent Consequences for Experience, Expression, and Physiology." *Journal of Personality and Social Psychology* 74: 224–237.

Heise, David R. 1979. *Understanding Events.* Cambridge: Cambridge University Press.

Hertzman, Clyde, John Frank, and Robert G. Evans. 1994. "Heterogeneities in Health Status and the Determinants of Population Health." Pp. 67–92 in *Why Are Some People Healthy and Others Not?*, edited by R. Evans, M. Barer, and T. Marmor. New York: Aldine De Gruyter.

Hochschild, Arlie R. 1979. "Emotion Work, Feeling Rules and Social Structure." *American Journal of Sociology* 85: 551–575.

———. 1983. *The Managed Heart.* Berkeley: University of California Press.

———. 1997. *The Time Bind: When Work Becomes Home and Home Becomes Work.* New York: Metropolitan Books.

Jackson, Pamela Braboy, and Montenique Finney. 2002. "Negative Life Events and Psychological Distress among Young Adults." *Social Psychology Quarterly* 65: 186–201.

James, Veronica, and Jonathan Gabe. 2003a. "Connecting Emotions and Health." Pp. 1–23 in *Health and the Sociology of Emotions*, edited by V. James and J. Gabe. Oxford: Blackwell.

———, eds. 2003b. *Health and the Sociology of Emotions.* Oxford: Blackwell.

James, William, and C. Lange. 1922. *The Emotions.* Baltimore: Wilkins and Wilkins.

Karp, David A. 1996. *Speaking of Sadness: Depression, Disconnection, and the Meanings of Illness.* New York: Oxford University Press.

Kemper, Theodore D. 1978. *A Social Interactional Theory of Emotions.* New York: Wiley.

———. 1990. "Themes and Variations in the Sociology of Emotions." Pp. 3–23 in *Research Agendas in the Sociology of Emotions*, edited by T. D. Kemper. Albany: State University of New York Press.

Kessler, Ronald C., and Harold W. Neighbors. 1986. "A New Perspective on the Relationships among Race, Social Class, and Psychological Distress." *Journal of Health and Social Behavior* 27: 107–115.

Lin, Nan, Xiaolan Ye, and Walter M. Ensel. 1999. "Social Support and Depressed Mood: A Structural Analysis." *Journal of Health and Social Behavior* 40: 344–359.

Lincoln, Karen D., Linda M. Chatters, and Robert Joseph Taylor. 2003. "Psychological Distress among Black and White Americans: Differential Effects of Social Support, Negative Interaction and Personal Control." *Journal of Health and Social Behavior* 44: 390–407.

Lively, Kathryn J. 2002. "Client Contact and Emotional Labor: Upsetting the Balance and Evening the Field." *Work and Occupations* 29: 198–225.

Lively, Kathryn J., and David R. Heise. 2004. "Sociological Realms of Emotional Experience." *American Journal of Sociology* 109: 1109–1136.

Lorant, Vincent, Isabelle Thomas, Denise Deliege, and Rene Tonglet. 2001. "Deprivation and Mortality: The Implications of Spatial Autocorrelation for Health Resources Allocation." *Social Science and Medicine* 53: 1711–1719.

Lupton, Deborah. 2003. "'Your Life in Their Hands': Trust in the Medical Encounter." Pp. 157–172 in *Health and the Sociology of Emotions*, edited by V. James and J. Gabe. Oxford: Blackwell.

Lyon, Margot L. 2003. "C. Wright Mills Meets Prozac." Pp. 55–76 in *Health and the Sociology of Emotions*, edited by V. James and J. Gabe. Oxford: Blackwell.

Lyon, Margot L., and James Barbalet. 1994. "Society's Body: Emotion and the 'Somatization' of Social Theory. Pp. 48–67 in *Embodiment and Experience: The Existential Ground of Culture and Self*, edited by T. J. Csordas. Cambridge: Cambridge University Press.

Marmor, Theodore R., Morris L. Barer, and Robert G. Evans. 1994. "The Determinants of a Populations Health: What Can Be Done to Improve a Democratic Nation's Health Status?" Pp. 217–231 in *Why Are Some People Healthy and Others Not?* edited by R. Evans, M. Barer, and T. Marmor. New York: Aldine De Gruyter.

Marmor, Theodore R., and J. Fraser Mustard. 1994. "Coronary Heart Disease from a Population Perspective." Pp. 189–215 in *Why Are Some People Healthy and Others Not?* edited by R. Evans, M. Barer, and T. Marmor. New York: Aldine De Gruyter.

Martin, Rene, Choi K. Wan, James P. David, Elizabeth L. Wegner, Bradley D. Olson, and David Watson. 1999. "Style of Anger Expression: Relation to Expressivity, Personality, and Health." *Personality and Social Psychology Bulletin* 25: 1196–1207.

May, Carl, Gayle Allison, Alison Chapple, Carolyn Chew-Graham, Clare Dixon, Linda Gask, Ruth Graham, Anne Rogers, and Martin Roland. 2004. "Framing the Doctor-Patient Relationship in Chronic Illness: A Comparative Study of General Practitioners' Accounts." *Sociology of Health and Illness* 26: 135–158.

Mayne, Tracy J. 2001. "Emotions and Health." Pp. 361–397 in *Emotions,* edited by T. J. Mayne and G. A. Bonnano. New York: Guilford.

McLeod, Jane D., and Karen Kaiser. 2004. "Childhood Emotional and Behavioral Problems and Educational Attainment." *American Sociological Review* 69: 636–658.

McLeod, Jane D., and Timothy J. Owens. 2004. "Psychological Well-Being in the Early Life Course: Variations by Socioeconomic Status, Gender, and Race/Ethnicity." *Social Psychology Quarterly* 67: 257–278.

Meerabeau, Liz, and Susie Page. 1998. "Getting the Job Done." Pp. 295–312 in *Emotions In Social Life: Critical Themes and Contemporary Issues*, edited by G. Bendelow and S. Williams. London: Routledge.

Mehling, Wolf E., and Niklas Krause. 2005. "Are Difficulties Perceiving and Expressing Emotions Associated with Low-Back Pain? The Relationship Between Lack of Emotional Awareness (Alexithymia) and 12-Month Prevalence of Low-Back Pain in 1180 Urban Public Transit Operators." *Journal of Psychosomatic Research* 58: 73–81.

Meier, Diane E., Anthony L. Back, and R. Sean Morrison. 2001. "The Inner Life of Physicians and Care of the Seriously Ill." *Journal of the American Medical Association* 286: 3007–3014.

Melzack, Ronald, and Patrick D. Wall. 2004. *The Challenge of Pain.* London: Penguin Global.

Mills, C. Wright. 1959. *The Sociological Imagination.* London: Oxford University Press.

Moos, Rudolf H. 2002. "The Mystery of Human Context and Coping: An Unraveling of Clues." *American Journal of Community Psychology* 30: 67–88.

Nettleton, Sarah. 1992. *Power, Pain and Dentistry.* Milton Keynes, UK: Open University Press.

Newton, Tim. 1995. *Managing Stress: Emotion and Power at Work.* London: Sage.

———. 2003. "Truly Embodied Sociology: Marrying the Social and the Biological." *The Sociological Review* 51: 20–42.

O'Brien, Martin. 1994. "The Managed Heart Revisited: Health and Social Control." *Sociological Review* 42: 393–413.

Ochsner, Kevin N., and James J. Gross. 2004. "Thinking Makes It So: A Social Cognitive Neuroscience Approach to Emotion Regulation." Pp. 229–255 in *Handbook of Self-Regulation: Research, Theory, and Applications*, edited by R. F. Baumeister and K. D. Vohs. New York: Guilford.

Olesen, Virginia, and Debora Bone. 1998. "Emotions in Rationalizing Organizations: Conceptual Notes from Professional Nursing in the USA." Pp. 313–329 in *Emotions in Social Life: Critical Themes and Contemporary Issues*, edited by G. Bendelow and S. Williams. London: Routledge.

Oliver, John P., and James J. Gross. 2004. "Healthy and Unhealthy Emotion Regulation: Personality Processes, Individual Differences, and Life Span Development." *Journal of Personality* 72: 1301–1333.

Pearlin, Leonard I. 1989. "The Sociological Study of Stress." *Journal of Health and Social Behavior* 30: 241–256.

Pearlin, Leonard I., Morton A. Lieberman, Elizabeth G. Menaghan, and Joseph T. Mullan. 1981. "The Stress Process." *Journal of Health and Social Behavior* 22: 337–356.

Pearlin, Leonard I., Scott Schieman, and Elena M. Fazio. 2005. "Stress, Health, and the Life Course: Some Conceptual Perspectives." *Journal of Health and Social Behavior* 46: 205–219.

Pennebaker, James W. 2003. "The Social, Linguistic and Health Consequences of Emotional Disclosure." Pp. 288–313 in *Social Psychological Foundations of Health and Illness*, edited by J. Suls, K. Wallston, and M. A. Malden. New York: Blackwell.

Peyrot, Mark, James F. McMurry, Jr., and Davida F. Kruger. 1999. "A Biopsychosocial Model of Glycemic Control in Diabetes: Stress, Coping and Regimen Adherence." *Journal of Health and Social Behavior* 40: 141–158.

Pugliesi, Karen, and Scott L Shook. 1997. "Gender, Jobs, and Emotional Labor in a Complex Organization." Pp. 283–316 in *Social Perspectives on Emotion*, edited by R. J. Erikson and B. Cuthbertson-Johnson. Greenwich, CT: JAI Press.

Putnam, Robert D. 2000. *Bowling Alone: The Collapse and Revival of American Community*. New York: Simon and Schuster.

Reynolds, Peggy, Susan Hurley, Myriam Torres, James Jackson, Peggy Boyd, Vivien W. Chen, and the Black/White Cancer Survival Study Group. 2000. "Use of Coping Strategies and Breast Cancer Survival: Results from the Black/White Cancer Survival Study." *American Journal of Epidemiology* 152: 940–948.

Robichaud, Allyson L. 2003. "Healing and Feeling: The Clinical Ontology of Emotion." *Bioethics* 17: 59–68.

Rosenberg, Morris, Carrie Carmi Schooler, and Florence Rosenberg. 1995. "Global Self-Esteem and Specific Self-Esteem: Different Concepts, Different Outcomes." *American Sociological Review* 60: 141–156.

Ross, Catherine E., and Marieke Van Willigen. 1997. "Education and the Subjective Quality of Life." *Journal of Health and Social Behavior* 38: 275–297.

Ruane, Sally. 2003. "Maternal-Baby Unbonding: Rituals for Undoing Nature." Pp. 133–156 in *Health and the Sociology of Emotions*, edited by V. James and J. Gabe. Oxford: Blackwell.

Rubonis, Anthony V., and Leonard Bickman. 1991. "Psychological Impairment in the Wake of Disaster: The Disaster-Psychopathology Relationship." *Psychological Bulletin* 109: 384–399.

Scheff, Thomas J. 1984. *Being Mentally Ill: A Sociological Theory*. New York: Aldine De Gruyter.

Schnurr, Paula P., and Bonnie L. Green, eds. 2004. *Trauma and Health: Physical Health Consequences of Exposure to Extreme Stress*. Washington, DC: American Psychological Association Press.

Simon, Robin W., and Leda E. Nath. 2004. "Gender and Emotion in the United States: Do Men and Women Differ in Self-Reports of Feelings and Expressive Behavior?" *American Journal of Sociology* 109: 1137–1176.

Selye, Hans. 1956. *The Stress of Life*. New York: McGraw-Hill.

Serido, Joyce, David M. Almeida, and Elaine Wethington. 2004. "Chronic Stressors and Daily Hassles: Unique and Interactive Relationships with Psychological Distress." *Journal of Health and Social Behavior* 45: 17–33.

Smith, Allen, and Sheryl Kleinman. 1989. "Managing Emotions in Medical School: Students' Contacts with the Living and the Dead." *Social Psychology Quarterly* 52: 56–69.

Smith-Lovin, Lynn. 1990. "Emotion as the Confirmation and Disconfirmation of Identity: An Affect Control Model." Pp. 238–270 in *Research Agendas in the Sociology of Emotions*, edited by T. D. Kemper. Albany: State University of New York Press.

Smyth, Joshua M., Arthur A. Stone, Adam Hurewitz, and Alan Kaell. 1999. "Effects of Writing about Stressful Experiences on Symptom Reduction in Patients with Asthma or Rheumatoid Arthritis." *Journal of the American Medical Association* 281: 1304–1309.

Spera, Stefanie P., Eric D. Buhrfeind, and James W. Pennebaker. 1994. "Expressive Writing and Coping with Job Loss." *Academy of Management Journal* 37: 722–733.

Spiegel, David. 1995. "How Do You Feel About Cancer Now?" *Public Health Reports* 110: 298–300.

Stryker, Sheldon. 1980. *Symbolic Interactionism: A Social Structural Version*. Menlo Park, CA: Benjamin/Cummings.

Suchman, Anthony L., Kathryn Markakis, Howard B. Beckman, and Richard Frankel. 1997. "A Model of Empathic Communication in the Medical Interview." *Journal of the American Medical Association* 277: 678–682.

Szasz, Thomas. 1974. *Ceremonial Chemistry: The Ritual Persecution of Drugs, Addicts, and Pushers*. Garden City, NY: Doubleday.

Taylor, Verta. 1995. "Self-Labeling and Women's Mental Health: Postpartum Illness and the Reconstruction of Motherhood." *Sociological Focus* 28: 23–47.

Thoits, Peggy A. 1985. "Self-Labeling Processes in Mental Illness: The Role of Emotional Deviance." *American Journal of Sociology* 91: 221–249.

————. 1986. "Social Support as Coping Assistance." *Journal of Consulting and Clinical Psychology* 54: 416–423.

————. 1995. "Stress, Coping, and Social Support Processes: Where Are We? What Next?" *Journal of Health and Social Behavior* 35: 53–79.

————. 1996. "Managing the Emotions of Others." *Symbolic Interaction* 19: 85–109.

————. 2005. "Differential Labeling of Mental Illness by Social Status: A New Look at an Old Problem." *Journal of Health and Social Behavior* 46: 102–119.

Thomas, Sandra P. 2003. "Anger: The Mismanaged Emotion." *Dermatology Nursing* 15: 51–57.

Todaro, John F., Biiung-Jiun Shen, Raymond Niaura, Avron Spiro, and Kenneth Ward. 2003. "The Effect of Negative Emotions on Frequency of Coronary Heart Disease." *American Journal of Cardiology* 92: 901–906.

Treweek, Geraldine Lee. 2003. "Emotion Work in Care Assistant Work." Pp. 115–132 in *Health and the Sociology of Emotions*, edited by V. James and J. Gabe. Oxford: Blackwell.

Turner, Heather A., Leonard I. Pearlin, and Joseph T. Mullan. 1998. "Sources and Determinants of Social Support for Caregivers of Persons with AIDS." *Journal of Health and Social Behavior* 39: 137–151.

Turner, Heather A., and R. Jay Turner. 2005. "Understanding Variations in Exposure to Social Stress." *Health* 9: 209–240.

Turner, R. Jay, and Andres G. Gil. 2002. "Psychiatric and Substance Use Disorders in South Florida—Racial/Ethnic and Gender Contrasts in a Young Adult Cohort." *Archives of General Psychiatry* 59: 43–50.

Turner, R. Jay, Blair Wheaton, and Donald A. Lloyd. 1995. "The Epidemiology of Social Stress." *American Sociological Review* 60: 104–125.

Ulbrich, Patricia M., George J. Warheit, and Rick S. Zimmerman. 1989. "Race, Socioeconomic Status, and Psychological Distress: An Examination of Differential Vulnerability." *Journal of Health and Social Behavior* 30: 131–146.

Umberson, Debra, Camille B. Wortman, and Ronald C. Kessler. 1992. "Widowhood and Depression: Explaining Long-Term Gender Differences in Vulnerability." *Journal of Health and Social Behavior* 33: 10–24.

Van Dongen, Els. 2001. "It Isn't Something to Yodel About, but It Exists! Faces, Nurses, Social Relations and Status within a Mental Hospital." *Aging and Mental Health* 5: 205–215.

Wentworth, William M., and John Ryan. 1994. "Introduction." Pp. 1–19 in *Social Perspectives on Emotions*, edited by W. Wentworth and J. Ryan. Greenwich, CT: JAI Press.

Wentworth, William M., and Darrell Yardley. 1994. "Deep Sociality: A Bioevolutionary Perspective on the Sociology of Emotions." Pp. 21–56 in *Social Perspectives on Emotions*, edited by W. Wentworth and J. Ryan. Greenwich, CT: JAI Press.

Wiley, Juniper. 1990. "The Dramatisation of Emotions in Practice and Theory: Emotion Work and Emotion Roles in a Therapeutic Community." *Sociology of Health and Illness* 12: 127–150.

Wilkinson, Richard G. 1996. *Unhealthy Societies: The Afflictions of Inequality*. New York: Routledge.

Williams, Simon J. 2000. "Reason, Emotion and Embodiment: Is 'Mental' Health a Contradiction in Terms?" *Sociology of Health and Illness* 22: 559–581.

———— 2003. "Marrying the Social and the Biological: A Rejoinder to Newton." *Sociological Review* 51: 550–561.

Williams, Simon J., and Gillian Bendelow. 2003. "Emotions, Health and Illness: The 'Missing Link' in Medical Sociology?" Pp. 25–54 in *Health and the Sociology of Emotions*, edited by V. James and J. Gabe. Oxford: Blackwell.

Zbrowski, Mark. 1969. "Cultural Components in Response to Pain." *Journal of Social Issues* 8: 16–30.

Zubenko, George S., Wendy N., Zubenko, Susan McPherson, Eleanor Spoor, Deborah B. Marin, Martin R. Farlow, Glenn E. Smith, Yonas E. Geda, Jeffrey L. Cummings, Ronald C. Petersen, and Trey Sunderland. 2003. "A Collaborative Study of the Emergence and Clinical Features of the Major Depressive Syndrome of Alzheimer's Disease." *American Journal of Psychiatry* 160: 857–866.

CHAPTER 26

Emotions and Social Movements

Jeff Goodwin
James M. Jasper

The study of emotions in politics and protest has emerged (or reemerged) in the past decade through a messy inductive process of recognizing the obvious: Emotions of many sorts permeate political action. In grappling with the inadequacies of existing theories of politics, researchers grabbed pieces of emotion theory opportunistically where they could find them. Few existing approaches in the sociology of emotion have been applied systematically, much less compared, in this field, but almost all have found their way into the mix to some degree. This inductive and relatively atheoretical approach may make social movements a useful venue for comparing theories of emotions developed in other settings.

We begin with a review of the place of emotions in the field of collective behavior and then social movements over the past 100 years, as they fell out of explanations in the 1970s, only to reemerge in the late 1990s (for more details, see Goodwin et al. 2000, from which we draw). We then look at recent research that has tried to specify the role of emotions in social movements and related forms of political action, categorizing this research crudely by the type of interactional setting in which the emotions are generated and displayed. Finally, we reach out to theoretical perspectives in the sociology of emotions, suggesting ways that research from movements could be extended to engage these theories more explicitly than it has in the past.

Aristotle launched the study of emotions and politics almost 2,400 years ago by examining the effects of orators on audiences—insights buried first by the rationalistic traditions of recent centuries and later by the structural predispositions of sociology. By pointing out the different interactive contexts of meaning and feeling (such as leaders and followers, recruiters and potential recruits, insiders and outsiders, pairs of opponents, and so on), we suggest Aristotle—and

Jeff Goodwin • Department of Sociology, New York University, New York, NY 10012
James M. Jasper • 346 West 15th Street, New York, NY 10011-5939

rhetoric—as a starting point for a rethinking of emotions that recognizes the strategic purposes that often lie behind them.

FEARING EMOTIONS: A BRIEF HISTORY

Crowds

Crowd-based theories dominated protest research until the 1960s, typically combining vague macrostructural strains with pejorative (often psychoanalytic) views of participants and their emotions. Emotions were considered the driving force of virtually all political action that occurred outside normal institutions. In nineteenth-century images of the mob, normal, reasoning individuals were thought to be transformed in the presence of a crowd, becoming angry, violent, impressionable, and generally unthinking. Crowds were assumed to create, through hypnotic processes such as contagion and suggestion, a kind of "primitive" group mind and group feelings, shared by all participants outside of their normal range of sensibilities, overwhelming their individual personalities and capacity for reason. Well into the twentieth century, crowds and their dynamics were conceived as the heart of protest movements, the core around which other forms of action were built. We see a stark contrast in this literature, as in so much Western thought, between emotions and rationality. In this vision, institutions were calmly reasonable, and crowds were emotional and irrational.

In the most influential expression of this pathologizing perspective, Le Bon (1960) described crowds as impulsive, irritable, suggestible, and credulous. They were guided primarily by unconscious motives and exhibited "very simple and very exaggerated" emotions: "A commencement of antipathy or disapprobation, which in the case of an isolated individual would not gain strength, becomes at once furious hatred in the case of an individual in a crowd" (p. 50). Given these traits, crowds are susceptible to the emotional appeals of demagogues. "Given to exaggeration in its feelings," wrote Le Bon, "a crowd is only impressed by excessive sentiments. An orator wishing to move a crowd must make an abusive use of violent affirmations. To exaggerate, to affirm, to resort to repetitions, and never to attempt to prove anything by reasoning are methods of argument well known to speakers at public meetings" (p. 51). Most social scientists of the early and mid-twentieth century, including Weber, Durkheim, Freud, and Smelser, accepted some version of Le Bon's viewpoint.

Fascism and communism prompted scholars to look for individuals peculiarly susceptible to mass movements. They were alienated (Kornhauser 1959), for example, or predisposed toward violence (Allport 1924). Others used Freudian psychology to show that participants were immature: narcissistic, latently homosexual, oral dependent, or anal retentive (Lasswell 1930, 1948). Lasswell was only the most explicit in elaborating a political "type" for whom politics was an effort to fulfill needs not met in private life. Hoffer (1951) similarly saw a desperate fanatic who needed to believe in *something*, no matter what. Because driven by inner needs, especially frustrations due to a lack of a stable identity or to "barren and insecure lives," Hoffer's "true believer" could never be satisfied, hoping to lose herself in a collective identity, a "mass movement," in which she believed with utter certainty. When one movement ended, she moved on to another.

In protest, Smelser (1968) speculated, ambivalence toward one's father in the oedipal crisis reemerges, split between two objects:

> On the one hand there is the unqualified love, worship, and submission to the leader of the movement, who articulates and symbolizes "the cause." On the other hand there is the unqualified suspicion, denigration, and desire to destroy the agent felt responsible for the moral decay of social life and standing in the way of reform, whether he be a vested interest or a political authority. (pp. 119–120)

External circumstances such as strain mostly provide an opportunity for the expression of internal emotional dynamics.

Pejorative views of participation were developed into a model of a "mass society" of "atomized" individuals, abandoned by intermediary organizations and left vulnerable to charismatic national leaders like Hitler, who could manipulate them through the mass media (Kornhauser 1959). Causal priority shifted from personality to social structure, but the vision was the same as Hoffer's. The "masses" swept aside traditional sources of authority in order to rule directly or through their leader in "extremist" style. The affective ties of community broke down, leaving many with an ill-defined sense of self. These theorists dismissed the affective ties of informal networks and the social control they provided on the grounds that they opened workers to the appeals of rabble-rousers. Only formal organizations protected against alienation.

Scholars in this period set out to explain a form of politics they already knew was dangerous, and thus everything associated with it was dangerous too, including strong emotions. Psychological dynamics such as "self-estrangement" or "alienation" were poorly specified. Misleadingly, Kornhauser (1959) applied them not to socially isolated individuals but to those whose primary groups (such as family and friends and co-workers) had no broader linkages. Those with the strongest local bonds would therefore have less allegiance to broader social institutions or the state (a view recently reversed by Robert Putnam and others).

Even Turner and Killian (1957), who were more sympathetic to protesters and explicitly rejected the distinction between rational individuals and irrational crowds (p. 17), often expressed hostile attitudes toward "mobs." As individuals "mill" about in crowds, according to Turner and Killian, their emotions are intensified and focused by their "circular reaction" to one another. Such individuals become suggestible and uninhibited in their actions. Crowds come to be "dominated by a uniform mood and uniform imagery" (p. 58) and, when frustrated, become angry and aggressive: "Crowd behavior consists, in essence, of deviations from the traditional norms of society" (p. 143). From this vantage point, Turner and Killian were unable to see that protesters often fully accept and even seek to defend traditional norms, including feeling rules.

In trying to deal with emotions or psychology, researchers in this period had little to use except a rather simplified form of Freudian psychoanalysis. Smelser (1968:92) called for an integration of social and psychological theory, on the grounds that protest "has a psychological dimension, since the deepest and most powerful human emotions—idealistic fervor, love, and violent rage, for example—are bared in episodes of collective behavior, and since persons differ psychologically in their propensity to become involved in such episodes." Jasper (2004b) has recently argued that psychoanalysis provided the main way for researchers to grapple with crucial issues of meaning and feeling before the cognitive revolution created numerous additional tools.

From a jaundiced psychoanalytic or crowd-based perspective, even the social movements of the 1960s did not always arouse sympathy, because they could be dismissed as the work of confused youngsters suffering from oedipal fantasies. As late as 1969, Klapp (1969:11–13) described the signs of "identity trouble" that led people to seek fulfillment in collective action: self-hatred, oversensitivity, a feeling of being blemished, excessive self-concern (including narcissism), alienation, a feeling that "nobody appreciates me," a desire to be someone else, a feeling of fraudulent self-presentation, Riesman's "other-directedness," and an identity crisis. In academic traditions like these, protest was either a mistake, a form of acting out, or a sign of immaturity.

Applying a more organizational and rhetorical view to the Chicago tradition, Gusfield (1963) managed to tame emotions in his study of the temperance movement. Feelings such as "hostility, hatred, and anger toward the enemy," said Gusfield (p. 110), "nurtured" the movement, and he analyzed the dynamics of moral indignation in detail. He linked these emotional responses to the declining status of parts of the middle class, taking a big step beyond most crowd theories. He anticipated later theories (even while limiting the importance of emotions) by seeing the issue of drinking as a "symbol" of underlying—and more economic, structural—shifts in society. He famously, and perhaps misleadingly, distinguished symbolic from instrumental action (and by implication, movements themselves), implicitly suggesting that strong emotions were a hallmark of the former but not the latter. The symbolic politics of status were not entirely irrational, but they were clearly not rational in the way that "normal" interest politics were.

The portrait of emotions in these traditions was flawed in many ways. In the crowd tradition, emotions come directly from crowds (or demagogues), having little to do with individuals' own lives and goals. They appear and disappear in response to one's immediate surroundings, with little lasting resonance. In the Freudian tradition, emotions were seen as emanations from individual personality conflicts rather than as responses to the social environment. Thus, only certain kinds of flawed people are susceptible to movement appeals. Their emotions are inevitably negative or troubled rather than positive and joyful; they reflect a psychological problem, albeit one that might go away with maturity. Participants do not *enjoy* protest; they are *compelled* to it by their inner needs and drives.

These traditions also faced methodological problems: The salient emotions are often vague and difficult to identify except through the very actions they are meant to explain. Can we recognize a propensity to violence except when it results in violence? Can we identify states of anomie or alienation before they lead to participation? In the absence of empirical investigation, what Le Bon and Hoffer thought they saw in crowds was more a projection of their own fears and anxieties than an accurate psychological portrait of protestors.

Little was recognized between the individual and the macrosocial: no social networks, organizations, shared cultural meanings, or processes of negotiation and interaction. Driven by mysterious forces outside their control, whether subconscious motivations or the pull of the crowd, protestors were not rational agents with purposes of their own. The more emotional an individual (or crowd) became, the less rational he or she (or they) became. The actual stuff of contentious politics—moral principles, stated goals, processes of mobilization, the pleasures of participation—was ignored.

Such views would not long survive the explosion of noninstitutional politics in the 1960s, but along with these early theories went some of the topics they had addressed, including the power of strong emotions to either mobilize or inhibit collective action. Even if they pathologized the emotions accompanying protest (indeed they emphasized emotions *in order to* pathologize protest generally), early theorists had at least paid attention to them. This would not be the case, alas, for the next generation of movement scholars.

Structuralism

By the early 1970s, many sociologists had been active in or were sympathetic to the movements they studied. Civil rights, antiwar, new left, and labor activists were clearly not atomized individuals, defeated in their personal aspirations, swept up by charismatic leaders. To the contrary, they were politically shrewd and instrumentally rational. In the new models, accordingly, activists campaign outside institutional politics because they are blocked from pursuing their interests through regular political channels, not because they are personally alienated. Rather than being studied alongside fads, crazes, and panics, social movements were now seen as "politics by other means."

To replace pathological explanations, sociologists turned to rational actor models and organizational theory, shifting from motivational "why" to strategic "how" questions. Given scarce resources and people's tendency to free ride on the efforts of others, how were activists sometimes able to mobilize people around long-standing grievances? The grievances themselves were rarely viewed as causally important or interesting. Grievances, and the emotions that accompanied them, were seen as "relatively constant and pervasive" (Jenkins and Perrow 1977:250). Their persistence could not explain why frustration only sometimes lead to collective action. To account for the emergence of social movements, "resource mobilization" and "political process" theorists turned primarily to the occasional largesse of elites. Lacking resources themselves, powerless groups need the attention, money, and political clout of powerful sponsors such as foundations, organized labor, and the government (Jenkins and Perrow 1977; McCarthy and Zald 1977).

In one of the most comprehensive statements of this new structuralism, Oberschall (1973) briefly listed a number of emotions in discussing the dynamics of conflict. He cited, for instance, impatience, trust, and the bitterness of protracted conflicts. Even more than social movements, conflict is hard to understand without recognizing the emotions involved. Oberschall mentioned emotions at key moments in his analysis without dissecting their dynamics.

In his influential model, Tilly (1978) depicted collective action as a function of interests, organization, the mobilization of resources, power, repression (or facilitation), and opportunities (or threats). Tilly presented these variables, including interests, as "structural," or independent of individuals' beliefs and feelings. He recognized, if implicitly, that emotions matter for what people want (i.e., their interests) and for their collective identities (a component of organization in his scheme) and that emotional reactions mediate between repression, opportunities, and threats, on the one hand, and actual collective action, on the other. Yet Tilly's rationalistic, organizational language and formulas discouraged any further attention to emotions.

The view of protestors as rational calculators was applied to ongoing movement dynamics as well as mobilization. In Kitschelt's (1986) view, for instance, antinuclear protestors of the 1970s deployed more radical tactics when blocked in normal political channels. They were rationally searching for effective strategies, with no emotional loyalties to their tactics. Similarly, Gamson (1975) treated strategic choice as a cognitive exercise. Emotions were absent from his discussion of factionalism, for example. Internal divisions arise because participants "will disagree on strategy and tactics. They will differ in the priorities they give to different subgoals and in their emphasis on the pursuit of short-range or long-range solutions. And they may compete for control of the organizational apparatus with power as an end in itself" (pp. 99–100). Nothing on the allegiances, jealousies, hatreds, demonizations, disappointments, hopes, and so on that not only accompany but help create—even define—schisms.

In structural accounts, emotions dropped out of view, along with many other things (Goodwin and Jasper 2004). Presenting activists as rational seemed to prevent their being emotional. Theorists depicted shrewd entrepreneurs, rational actors coolly calculating the costs and benefits of participation, and people mobilized by incentives rather than by passionate anger or righteous indignation. Much as they disliked everything else the crowd tradition had done, the new generation of theorists shared with the older ones one big assumption—*that emotions are irrational*. If the earlier theorists had portrayed protestors as emotional to demonstrate their irrationality, the new theorists demonstrated their rationality by denying their emotions.

Some structural theorists recognized a role for grievances, and McAdam's (1982) concept of "cognitive liberation" was intended to capture the subjective processes by which people suddenly come to believe that protest is possible and might succeed. However, he defined those processes as cognitive: "the altered responses of members to a particular challenger serve to transform evolving political conditions into a set of 'cognitive cues' signifying to insurgents that the political system is becoming increasingly vulnerable to challenge" (p. 49). Even though the term implied a radical change in perspective, cognitive liberation was portrayed as a relatively instrumental reading of available information about the likelihood of repression. "Liberation" implies heady emotions that "cognitive" then denies. All that potential protestors need, it seems, is a cognitive signal that they can succeed or at least will not be severely repressed (also Klandermans 1984). These are calculating automatons, not passionate human beings.

Research techniques account for part of the inattention to emotions, which are hard to identify from brief newspaper accounts of protest events. Historical research precludes participant observation, which is a good way to identify the emotions of protest. Nor can questionnaires always do the trick. The problem, however, was also conceptual. Metaphors of formal organizations and conflict over material interests encouraged an assumption of strategic purpose that did not seem to require attention to emotions. A view of collective actors as rational, political, and organized made sense as a counter to crowd theories. Activists are rarely crazy. But by defining rationality in contrast to and incompatible with emotion, resource mobilization and political process theorists missed powerful springs of collective action. (Ironically, emotions disappeared from the study of collective action just before the late 1970s, when the sociology of emotions emerged as a distinct subfield.)

The Cultural Turn

In the late 1980s, American scholars began to recognize cultural dimensions of social movements, partly inspired by European researchers who saw a range of so-called new social movements as efforts to transform dominant cultural codes and identities rather than as bids for political or economic power (Cohen 1985; Laraña et al. 1994). As the economy shifted from manufactured goods to the production of knowledge, Touraine (1977) argued, domination took the form of an increasing penetration of "technocratic power" into all spheres of life. New movements sought not economic gains or greater participation in the system, but spaces of autonomy in which to enact new lifestyles and relationships.

Melucci (1995) drew attention to participants' "emotional investment" in the new collective identities that are the chief product of mobilization, and he cautioned that "there is no cognition without feeling" (p. 45). Yet his view of collective identity as an "interactive and shared definition . . . concerned with the orientation for action and the field of opportunities and constraints in which the actions take place" (p. 44) emphasizes its cognitive components. Nevertheless, Melucci's recognition of emotions was a departure from structural analyses, and new social movement theorists' focus on culture, identity, and intersubjective processes encouraged attention to those processes even in "old" movements.

In the 1990s researchers criticized structuralists' indifference to cultural processes (Johnston and Klandermans 1995; Laraña et al. 1994; Morris and Mueller 1992). Culture had a distinctly cognitive cast in these writings, however, made up of "customs, beliefs, values, artifacts, symbols, and rituals" (Johnston and Klandermans 1995:3), "ideas and beliefs" (Mueller 1992:13), and "ideas, ideology, [and] identity" (McAdam 1994:36). Culture influences activists and potential activists by shaping their understandings, not their emotions.

A cognitive bent was also apparent in the scholarship on "framing"—the term originally used to describe the rhetorical processes by which a movement recruits members (Snow et al. 1986). Snow and Benford (1992:137) defined a frame as "an interpretive schemata that simplifies and condenses the 'world out there' by selectively punctuating and encoding objects, situations, events, experiences, and sequences of actions within one's present or past environment." Snow and Benford (1988) saw three types of framing as necessary for successful recruitment: *diagnostic*, in which a movement convinces potential converts that a problem needs to be addressed; *prognostic*, in which it convinces them of appropriate strategies, tactics, and targets; and *motivational*, in which it exhorts them to get involved in these activities. The many definitions and applications of frames and framing processes deal almost entirely with their cognitive components. "Motivational framing," which implicitly refers to emotions, is rarely discussed, although it is apparently what gets people actually to do something. Benford (1997:419) later admitted:

> Those operating within the framing/constructionist perspective have not fared much better than their structuralist predecessors in elaborating the role of emotions in collective action. Instead, we continue to write as though our movement actors (when we actually acknowledge humans in our texts) are Spock-like beings, devoid of passion and other human emotions.

As usual, Gamson (1992:32) saw what many others missed. He argued that "injustice frames," essential to protest, depend on "the righteous anger that puts fire in the belly and iron in the soul." In experiments that exposed ordinary people to transgressions by authority figures, Gamson and his collaborators (1982) found that hostility to authority preceded the development of an injustice frame. Suspicion, anger, and other emotions may arise even before blame is allocated through more cognitive processes. Gamson (1992:33) later elaborated on the sources of injustice frames, including "concreteness in the target, even when it is misplaced and directed away from the real causes of hardship." The need to elicit strong emotions, in other words, may lead organizers to distort their analyses. They may "exaggerate the role of human actors, failing to understand broader structural constraints, and misdirect their anger at easy and inappropriate targets" (p. 33). Le Bon redux.

Recent work on collective identity partly reflects a desire to capture the emotional motivations for protest, even though these are rarely discussed explicitly (Polletta and Jasper 2001). Identity is usually contrasted to "interest" in accounts of participation, suggesting a connection to movement aims that is closer to kinship than material interest. It is also used to describe a sense of solidarity among members of a social movement itself, again suggesting bonds of trust, loyalty, and affection. However, most discussions define collective identity as the drawing of a cognitive boundary rather than as a set of positive affects toward other group members on the grounds of that common membership. Perhaps the latter sounds too much like Hoffer or Klapper.

Methodological barriers to getting at emotions in social movements persist, since the rigorous questionnaires favored by social psychologists who study emotions are not always appropriate or feasible in studies of protest. The result is that emotions have remained unrecognized and untheorized, even as they have supplied much of the causal force behind some of the key mechanisms identified in recent years. This is as true of cultural concepts such as collective identity and frames as it is of structural concepts such as political opportunities and social networks (Jasper 1998).

REDISCOVERING EMOTIONS: RECENT RESEARCH

In the spirit of Aristotle, we distinguish several different interactional contexts in which emotions are generated and displayed. Some emotions arise outside of movements altogether, in individuals who are influenced by any number of others, including the media. These have been studied as the raw materials from which mobilization may be built. There are also internal dynamics in which participants engage each other, including the interactions between leaders and followers. In between these, participants engage potential recruits. This encounter may include specific efforts to build confidence, which is crucial to all strategic action (Jasper 2006b). It may include a great deal of moral work, labeling various players as good or bad. Then there are external interactions with other players, be they opponents, authorities, or bystanders. Finally, there are a number of trade-offs between internal and external dynamics, or ways in which internal processes affect external actions, in which emotions play an important part.

We also try, when possible, to apply a typology of emotions that we have used elsewhere (Goodwin et al. 2004; Jasper 2006a). One category consists of reflexes, such as anger or surprise, that are quick to appear and to subside and which have clear bodily programs associated with them (Ekman 1972). Another group are long-standing affects, especially love and hate but also others such as trust and respect. There are, in addition, a number of moral emotions of approval and disapproval, including shame and pride, or sometimes sympathies such as compassion. Our final category, moods, does not take a direct object the way most emotions do; moods color our action, especially giving us more or less confidence, and we usually carry them with us from one setting to the next.

Raw Materials

Some emotions form the raw materials for movement sympathy and recruitment. These may consist of cultural sensibilities such as compassion for different groups, or it may consist of individual personality dynamics—as well as an interaction between the two.

Broad sensibilities are raw materials for political mobilization. Shifts in emotions and their expression have created new vocabularies of motive, new subjects, and new targets of protest. Compassion for animals was the most important precondition for the emergence of animal protection movements (Jasper 1997). Barker-Benfield (1992) argues that "sensibility," the capacity to be swept up by excesses of pathos, pity, and sympathy, was promoted in the eighteenth century by British manufacturers purveying luxury entertainments and goods. It "disciplined" women's attachments "into tasteful domesticity," stimulating the demand for domestic objects (Barker-Benfield p. xxvi). But sympathy also drew women out of the house and into a public world of shopping and luxury entertainment. It encouraged middle-class women to speak publicly and collectively of their sufferings at the hands of men, nurturing a protofeminism. Stearns and Stearns (1986) noted that worker unrest as well as growing female employment in the twentieth century prompted managerial concerns about workers' emotions. Preventing anger became an important labor relations goal. Collective action can change institutionalized practices in part through its association with broad shifts in moral emotions.

Emotion norms also affect whether people think they can engage in politics and in which ways. Gender norms are the most studied example. Women's emotions (and those of other relatively powerless groups like racial and ethnic minorities, the physically disabled, and so on) are often characterized in ways that blunt their challenges to authorities or cultural norms. Women are particularly susceptible, Campbell (1994) argues, to having their opinions dismissed as bitterness or sentimentality. To say that someone is "bitter" is to say that her anger is without effective expression as well as to blame her for her own failure to be taken seriously. Bitterness, along with emotionality and sentimentality generally, "are used to interpret our expressions narrowly and critically as always either being on the edge of excess, or already excessive" (p. 55). Sentimentality is paradoxically encouraged in women but only in certain (private or domestic) spheres; it is thus used to control and limit the public occasions on which women may express emotions.

Scheff's (1994) approach has been to identify patterns of pride and shame that allow varying degrees of recruitment to collective action because of their rhetorical resonance. These two emotions are eminently social, having to do with our attachment to others—pride issuing from positive connections and shame issuing from disconnection. When shame is not acknowledged, according to Scheff, it can lead to aggression, at an individual, a group, or even at the national level. Also, when people feel ashamed of their anger, a "shame-rage" spiral can quickly spin out of control. Leaders mobilize through appeals to these emotions and especially promises to avenge shame.

Scheff (1994) has applied these ideas to nationalist movements and to nazism in particular, arguing that such movements "involve an intense and passionate quest for belonging" as "individuals and groups seek to increase their pride/shame balance (pp. 282, 286). For Scheff, "Hitler's appeal [to Germans] was that he promised that pride and community would replace shame and alienation"; "the promise of ending Germany's shame after the Treaty of Versailles and raising its pride formed the core of virtually all of his speeches and writings" (pp. 286–287).

Honneth (1995) has linked patterns of respect in a society to its politics and protest. When groups lack certain kinds of recognition from others—affective bonds, respect for their rational autonomy, and esteem—they develop a righteous anger that leads to mobilization. Eventually, they force others to grant them the recognition due to all humans. Honneth sees an important role in this process for negative emotional reactions such as anger and indignation. He also shows the tight bond between cognition, morality, and emotion.

Psychoanalytic approaches, which treat individual preoccupations and neuroses as raw materials for political organizers, have persisted, gaining new energy from narrative and other cognitive approaches that allow a less pejorative understanding of symbols and decision-making (Schafer 1976). For instance, psychoanalytic approaches have addressed the sources of cynicism and despair, moods that discourage political action (Hoggett 1992). Psychoanalytic theories, complementing Scheff, have also suggested a number of pathways by which shame operates in politics (Thompson forthcoming).

Occasionally, a movement will take a society's emotion norms as the target of its political work. Thus, self-help groups of women suffering from postpartum depression (Taylor 1996) explicitly aim at transforming the emotions associated with certain gender roles, as does the women's movement more generally (Hochschild 1975).

Confidence and Recruitment

Most often, movements use a culture's emotional expectations to recruit members. Blee's (1991) study of the 1920s Ku Klux Klan showed how the Klan joined a rhetoric of women's rights with a virulently racist agenda through inflammatory (and sexually titillating) portrayals of the sexual abuse of white Protestant women by blacks, Catholics, and Jews—themes still present, Blee has found, in the worldview and propaganda of contemporary racist activists (Blee 2002). Moral emotions, including indignation based on perceived threats, are the core of political rhetoric.

One way that activists must grapple with the emotions they bring to the movement is to try to transform deactivating emotions into activating ones. Shame cripples action, as do moods of resignation or depression. Anger, outrage, indignation, and pride, on the other hand, encourage action. Growing research has examined how action is sparked through emotional dynamics. A sense of agency is important for both recruiting new members and motivating existing ones.

Pride activates and shame deactivates, and their interplay has been analyzed. For instance, since the Stonewall riot pride has been the desired stance among lesbian and gay men. As Gould (2001, 2002) shows, however, pride can motivate very different forms of protest. Whereas expressions of pride accompanied militant and confrontational protest in the years after Stonewall, activists also invoked pride when calling for volunteerism, remembrance of the dead, and quiet lobbying in the early years of the AIDS crisis. According to Gould, lesbian and gay men's continuing ambivalence about their homosexuality—proud but also ashamed—discouraged expressions of anger in favor of demonstrating a quiet nobility in the face of a deadly epidemic. Five years into the epidemic, however, the movement's emotion rules changed again. Morally shocked and angered by the Supreme Court's *Bowers v. Hardwick* antisodomy decision, as well as by the government's inaction and state legislatures' willingness to consider quarantines, gay men and lesbians began to express indignation and outrage and to form militant groups like ACT UP. "Pride" once again demanded militant confrontation.

The transformation of shame into pride also operates at the other end of the political spectrum. Stein (2001a, 2001b) found signs of shame in interviews with Christian conservative activists, who accounted for their activity in terms of a selfless commitment to higher authorities—family, nation, and God—but also expressed feelings of rejection and passivity in describing themselves as victims of forces beyond their control. Through their activism, Stein argues, they try to construct a positive sense of themselves and their families as strong and independent, in contrast to weak, shameful others, in this case the gays and lesbians that they feared and detested.

Connecting movement emotions to broader theories of culture, Polletta (2002) argues that the stories activists tell one another are critical in mobilizing the emotions of confidence. In an analysis of students' contemporary accounts of the 1960s sit-ins, she shows how black student "apathy" was reinterpreted as the repression of political aspirations—they were "tired of waiting" for the rights denied them—and thus transformed into a motivation for action.

A sense of confidence and agency is not the same as a cold calculation of likely repression or success. Whereas structuralists and many culturalists viewed the latter as necessary for recruitment, it may be the emotions of the former that matter more.

Moral Work

Political activists do extensive rhetorical work to transform emotional raw materials into specific beliefs and suggestions for action. One way they inspire activity is through moral shocks, which occur when an unexpected event or piece of information raises such a sense of outrage in a person that he or she becomes inclined toward political action, whether or not the person has acquaintances in the movement (Jasper 1997, 1998; Jasper and Poulsen 1995). Whether the underlying image is a state of shock or an electric shock, it implies a visceral, bodily feeling, on a par with vertigo or nausea. The prospect of unexpected and sudden changes in one's surroundings can arouse feelings of dread and anger. The former can paralyze, but the latter can become the basis of mobilization. Activists work hard to create moral outrage and anger and to suggest targets against which these can be vented. Luker's (1984) research on antiabortion activists emphasizes how a Supreme Court decision—*Roe v. Wade*—morally angered and shocked certain women, mainly Catholic housewives, into lives of activism.

Nepstad and Smith (2001) have demonstrated how affective solidarities become the raw materials for moral shocks. When covert U.S. involvement in Central America became broadly known in the early 1980s, many members of American religious communities were especially likely to respond with activism because of their prior personal connections with Central Americans. Missionaries returning to the United States and Central America refugees given asylum by American congregations brought with them stories of atrocities suffered at the hands of U.S.-backed regimes. American churchgoers developed strong bonds with their foreign fellow Christians. Accordingly, when they heard about the CIA-sponsored mining of Nicaraguan harbors and the CIA counterinsurgency "murder manuals," they expressed their shock by turning to activism not on behalf of strangers but on behalf of people they felt they *knew*.

Young (2001) has studied another group of activists who mobilized on behalf of a group with whom they had even less contact. In the 1830s, American evangelical Protestants began to call for an immediate end to slavery with an urgency unthinkable only a few years earlier. What had changed, Young argues, was the cosmology and, even more important, the temperament of evangelical Christianity. Having long viewed slavery as a metaphor for Christians' own sinfulness, evangelicals now began to see slavery itself as sinful. Abolishing slavery was linked with personal redemption. Young shows how shifts in "emotion cultures" can create new motivations for, and targets of, protest. Again, activists must craft rhetoric to tap into moral sensibilities in the broader culture.

Whereas rational choice and even some structural traditions view morality as fairness calculations about the distribution of rewards, morality resides as much or more in emotions of approval and disapproval (Jasper 2006a). In all cases, words and images are crafted to arouse feelings and actions.

Internal Dynamics

Recent work has also examined the role of emotion in the internal dynamics of social movements proper. Gender is again prominent. In her study of a holistic health center, Kleinman (1996) found that men and women were rewarded differently for expressing the same emotions, with men praised for exhibiting caring emotions (or any emotions at all!) and women discouraged from being too emotional. Emotions, she found, were often used to attribute problems to personal failings rather than to structural inequities.

However, affective ties are the most studied way in which emotions affect the internal coherence of protest groups. In her study of women in the civil rights movement, for instance, Robnett (1997) pointed out that whereas national spokesmen like Martin Luther King, Jr., used emotional appeals to mobilize audiences, grassroots leaders, who were predominantly women, did a different kind of emotion work. Their day-to-day interaction with residents of Southern communities built the emotional loyalty necessary for persuading the latter to act in dangerous circumstances. In Lofland's (1996) book-length treatment of social movement organizations, emotions appear primarily as affective bonds that make social networks such important mechanisms for recruitment. Other sociologists have also revealed the affective bonds that forge solidarity and motivate participation, but without theorizing those processes explicitly (Epstein 1991; Lichterman 1996; McAdam 1988).

Rupp and Taylor's research on the "abeyance structures" that sustain movements during difficult times reveals the affective ties that permeate them (Rupp and Taylor 1987; Taylor 1989). The National Women's Party (NWP) provided the resurgent women's movement of the 1960s with activist networks, goals, tactics, and a collective identity. These contributions were made possible by the NWP's continuity over time, purposive commitment, exclusiveness, centralization, and culture. Emotions were important for all these dimensions. "Personal ties of love and friendship among members were an important cultural ideal," Taylor (1989:769) observed. A willingness to shape personal relationships around the cause was, in large measure, what made possible the intense commitment of members. Many activists were actually couples, and many had an intense personal devotion to the party's leader, Alice Paul.

Positive affective bonds toward fellow participants can weaken as well as strengthen individual commitments. Reinterpreting the insights of Freud (1959) and Slater (1963), Goodwin (1997) stresses the potentially disintegrative impact of affective ties, pointing to the Communist-led Huk rebellion in the Philippines as a case in point. Love and erotic attraction can lead individuals and dyads out of movement participation and into private life. In strategic terms, Jasper (2004a) refers to this as the common Band of Brothers Dilemma: Strong affective loyalties are a boon to a movement, but they may attach themselves to a subunit of the movement instead of the movement as a whole.

In addition, extremely tight bonds between some participants can alienate participants who do not share in them. In her history of radical feminism, Echols (1989) showed that the intense bonds of "sisterhood" promoted by the movement also ended up alienating some activists who felt stifled by those bonds. This suggests another way that emotions can motivate movement *dis*affiliation.

Researchers have remarked on the pleasures of protest without always analyzing what kinds of emotions accompany them. In some cases, these pleasures may be great enough to motivate participation without relying on a cognitive belief that success is likely or even possible. The deepest consist of dignity and pride. According to Bell (1992), many black civil rights protestors participated to gain dignity in their lives through struggle and moral expression, not necessarily because they expected to gain equal rights from that struggle. As he says of one participant, "her goal was defiance, and its harassing effect was likely more potent precisely because she did what she did without expecting to topple her oppressors" (p. xvi). This dignity is similar to Scheff's concept of pride.

Wood (2001, 2003) has similarly argued that Salvadoran peasants took pleasure and pride in their rebellion against long-dominant economic and political elites, regardless of their calculations about the likely success of their actions, which hardly seemed encouraging. Some *campesiños* engaged in collective action for its own sake: to assert agency was to reclaim their dignity; not to act was to be less than human. Protest itself was the main goal. Only later in the war, after the worst repression had passed, did some insurgents further their material interests through coordinated action.

In addition to pride, pleasures arise from the joys of collective activities, such as losing oneself in collective motion or song: Durkheim's classic "collective effervescence." Lofland (1982) described the "joys of crowds" in some detail—an important counter to older images of what inspired crowds. Eyerman and Jamison's (1998) research on the role of music in social movements emphasizes its cognitive functions, but they also note how music has helped to build collective identities and sustain solidarity and hope. Similar themes are sounded in Danaher and Roscigno's (2004) study of music in Southern textile communities. Berezin (2001) has shown how Italian fascists employed public rituals to induce strong feelings of national belonging—the neglected underside of political identities, according to Berezin—a cultural project that other movements have also pursued. Rituals are enjoyable in part because they reactivate affective bonds, in part because of the coordinated action.

Just as affective bonds can weaken as well as strengthen a movement, so the pleasures of participation have their negative counterpart in frustration and fatigue. In Hirschman's (1982:120) account, people "burn out" and retreat from the public to the private sphere because "participation in public life offers only this unsatisfactory too-much-or-too-little choice and is therefore bound to be disappointing in one way or another." Voting offers too little political involvement; social movements often demand too much. We become addicted to protest activities, commit huge amounts of time to them, and become exhausted; we have unrealistic expectations of social change and are easily disappointed. Hirschman's description of these dynamics depends (albeit mostly implicitly) on emotions such as excitement, disappointment, and frustration: "The turns from the private to the public life are marked by wildly exaggerated expectations, by total infatuation, and by sudden revulsions" (p. 102).

An important component of internal group dynamics involves the interactions between leaders and followers, a topic (like leadership more generally) that is currently out of fashion. Lalich (2004), examining Heaven's Gate and the Democratic Workers Party, has resuscitated

Hoffer's notion of a "true believer," giving it a more sociological twist by looking at the social mechanisms that sustain charismatic cults rather than blaming participation on defective personalities. Utter group loyalty depends on "singlemindedness, a way of thinking characterized by dogmatism and rigidity, and no identity outside the context of the group" (p. 255). Members feel both intense love and fear for their leaders, who in these particular cases were distant, disapproving, paranoid, and able to arouse guilt in members. The result is an overwhelming sense of duty to and unity with the group. Few groups manage, as these did, to absorb members so utterly, but successful groups need some of the same dynamics. So far, however, little research has examined the attraction of leaders or the "brainwashing" that groups can do, no doubt because of the shadow cast by Hoffer and similar thinkers.

External Engagements

Emotions are crucial to the interactions between social movements and others, just as they are to all social interactions. Participants may feel a certain way, usually negative, about opponents. They try to arouse sympathy and respect from bystanders. Interaction generates further emotions, including reflex emotions such as fear and moral emotions like shame and pride.

Gender reappears in the interactions between protest groups and outsiders as part of the goal or self-presentation of the movement. The animal protectionists studied by Groves (1997, 2001) were worried that their movement would appear too emotional because of its preponderance of women. Activists often used the term "emotional" to criticize colleagues they considered unprofessional, irrational, or (if they were women) feminine. Groves found that the career-oriented women who made up the bulk of the movement believed it was necessary to substantiate their feelings about animal cruelty with scientific arguments and the visible support of men.

Negative affects toward opponents (and sometimes outsiders generally) help mobilize people as surely as positive ones toward fellow group members. Jasper (1997, 2006b) analyzes the negative emotions produced by threats and blame, so important because they generate the strong emotions of Gamson's injustice frames. For example, when pro-choice and antiabortion newsletters "identify concrete and specific adversaries, characterize enemy action in an entirely negative light, attribute corrupt motives to the foe, and magnify the opponents' power" (Vanderford 1989:174), they enhance protestors' outrage and sense of threat. They transform emotions at the same time as understanding. Demonization fuels powerful emotions for social movements, such as hatred, fear, anger, suspicion, paranoia, and indignation.

The same myths that arouse positive feelings of national and ethnic belonging often inspire fierce hatred and resentment of other nations and ethnicities (Kaufman 2001; Petersen 2002). Hatred is far more than the absence of love; it is a passionate obsession with the other (Alford forthcoming). Still, although difficult, it is not impossible to forge intense positive bonds across national boundaries (Taylor and Rupp 2002), although perhaps only by defining an "in group" at the international level.

At the extreme, strategic engagement can be dangerous. Even in democratic societies, protestors often fear arrest, the loss of employment, bodily injury, harm to family members, and even death. Ongoing participation in "high-risk" movements typically requires the mitigation of participants' fears. Goodwin and Pfaff (2001) discovered several "encouragement mechanisms" whereby civil rights activists in the United States and the former East Germany managed to do just this. They showed that factors and processes that movement analysts have typically invoked for other explanatory purposes—including networks, mass gatherings, rituals, new collective identities, shaming, the possession of guns—also helped participants deal with their fears (sometimes as unanticipated consequences of these processes). Flam (1998) has similarly argued that overcoming or managing fear was important for East German and Polish dissidents.

Trade-Offs

Protestors may find that they need to display different emotional packages in different settings, while at the same time trying to avoid appearing duplicitous. Whittier (2001) shows that the activist survivors of child abuse encourage different emotions in conferences dominated by fellow survivors, on talk shows, and in courts of law. When among their own, survivors are urged to experience and express strong emotions—anger, grief, and shame, but also pride at overcoming their victimization. When pressing claims for crime victims' compensation, survivors must demonstrate grief, fear, and shame in order to legitimate their claims of injury, but not anger or pride. Justified as "strategy," the emotional injunctions that Whittier describes reveal activists' normative assumptions about gender, feeling, and rationality.

This is only one example of a very common trade-off: The emotional appeals and displays that will have the desired effect on one audience will have an undesirable effect on others. In the days of Aristotle and face-to-face communication, the orator had to think about his audience as a whole, largely ignoring individual differences. This is still a challenge, but one matched by differences among entire groups. Thanks to modern communications, words, gestures, and bodily expressed emotions can go to friends, foes, authorities, and bystanders all at once. Telling your group that your opponents are incorrigibly evil may strengthen your group, but it will not help you deal with those you have demonized once they find out.

THEORIZING EMOTIONS: ENGAGING BROADER THEORIES

Few of the scholars who rediscovered the emotions in social movements in the late 1990s were self-consciously working in any of the recognized traditions in the sociology of emotions. In our own cases, Goodwin (1997) drew on a Freud tamed by Slater (1997), and Jasper turned to a variety of cultural-constructionist approaches. Their cultural approach differed from Hochschild's in recognizing the ontological importance of emotions, not just their management and display. Although there was room for rituals and interactions, these were not emphasized as the sole or even main sources of influential emotions. Kemper's hierarchies were not emphasized because most of the "new social movements" did not seem driven by status or power issues, unlike the citizenship movements exemplary for political-process theories. Justice was central to the new research on movement emotions, but few links were made with existing sociologies of justice, largely because these are mostly limited to fairness. In this section we examine what links might be made to these literatures.

Culture

Movement research has touched on, without always explicitly engaging, several cultural and cognitive approaches to emotions. By defining culture as consisting of cognition, emotion, and morality, Jasper (1997) suggests both parallels and distinctions between cognitions and emotions. Among similarities, both of them have at the same time a public, shared component and an interior, personal component. We have expectations about cognitive meanings and about what emotions someone should experience in a given situation—expectations that can be disappointed (Thoits 1985, 1990). Methodologically, there are parallel challenges in linking the public expressions and the interior versions of the feelings and meanings. And both cognitions and emotions have a neurological/physiological component as well as an interpreted cultural component.

Yet our beliefs about the world are not quite the same as our feelings about the state of the world—at least analytically. In practice, the two prove hard to disentangle, so that most research on movements came to adopt a cognitive view of emotions as a form of belief about the world, but one with special relevance to our own flourishing or desires (well articulated by Nussbaum (2001)). Initially, there was also an adoption of a constructionist approach (from scholars such as Rom Harré) that proved unnecessary. Indeed, debates over biology and culture were never important in the field of movement emotions.

Symbolic interactionism (discussed in Chapter 7 of this volume) has been a central theoretical influence on the study of social movements, in a kind of Chicago-school shadow that survived alongside the structural-functional paradigm in the 1950s and 1960s. In this line, Lofland (1982) gave explicit attention to the emotions of collective action. He wrote about the joys of crowd interactions and the affective bonds that aid conversion to religious cults (Lofland and Stark 1965), adding affective variables without linking to explicit theories of emotions or showing how the feelings are related to cognitions. Although little research has followed up on Lofland's work, his research suggests the need to distinguish among interactive contexts. Lalich's (2004) work on sects, for instance, examines mechanisms of social control: what happens after the conversion.

Another form of symbolic interactionism, affect control theory, looks at culturally accepted definitions of identities and the emotions that result when our expectations of them are either met or not met (see Chapter 8 of this volume). Heise (1977, 1979, 1989), Smith-Lovin (1990), and others working in this tradition posited three main dimensions that define identities: evaluation (good or bad), potency (powerful or powerless), and activity (animated or passive), or EPA. When our transient impressions of an event or situation do not coincide with our fundamental expectations (a "deflection"), we experience emotions, usually negative ones (although we may experience positive emotions if our expectations are surpassed).

Affect control theory might help us understand common expectations and images of protestors in the general culture. The role of protestor, incorporated in several studies, gets a rating in North American culture of slightly good, slightly powerful, and very active—placing them in three-dimensional EPA space near identities such as fanatic, salesman, vigilante, jock, lobbyist, nymphomaniac, boy, and extrovert! This rating seems intuitively reasonable, especially if news coverage pits protestors in angry confrontations with police (verbs associated with imagined encounters between the two include "haggle with," "oppose," "hoot" or "holler" at, and "cajole"). At the same time, fictional media portrayals of protestors, as in sitcoms, often seem to paint them as rather powerless and ineffectual, in which case, protestors would end up near a number of childlike roles, which seems to be how they are often portrayed, especially by business interests and conservative politicians. There may be an ongoing cultural conflict over how to think and feel about protestors, which raises a range of issues that affect control theory has yet to address.

Because cultural impressions like these presumably affect outcomes, they seem a fertile research area. We could observe what steps protest groups take to generate impressions of power—for instance relying on men rather than women as spokespersons or using discourses of science rather than emotion (Groves 1997, 2001). In addition to self-presentation, we might also observe how protest groups aim to change popular characterizations of other strategic players: how they praise friends and demonize opponents. Struggles over the public images concerning particular players will always reflect underlying cultural images of general roles.

Associating a player with a common cultural role, although important rhetorical work, involves a number of dilemmas. Do you portray opponents as strong and threatening, to emphasize the urgency of stopping them, or as inept and ridiculous, to undermine their confidence and sense of agency? Similarly, do you present your own side as strong and heroic, able to contain evildoers, but possibly not in need of anyone else's support? Do you present yourselves as victims instead, gaining sympathy but undermining your sense of your own power, a recurrent dilemma for adult survivors of child abuse (Whittier 2001)? Politics is filled with efforts to define players as heroes, villains, and victims in EPA space.

One dimension of EPA is often overlooked, even though it is crucial to collective action: active versus passive. For a movement to succeed, as we saw, activists must devote enormous effort to giving participants a sense of their own agency. They need confidence in their own ability to act, something that requires the suppression of demobilizing emotions such as apathy and fear.

A final source of cultural theorizing about emotions—as we saw—came from feminism, largely suggested by Hochschild's (1975) analysis of how women's anger had to be legitimated and deployed in the face of widespread expectations for women to be passive. Taylor (1996) applied this view to the case of postpartum depression, highlighting the special difficulties women face in dealing with emotions "inappropriate" to the mother role, and Kleinman (1996) showed the different amounts of credit that men and women receive for expressing highly gendered emotions. This kind of research should provide a way to extend affect control theory to cover explicit challenges to cultural expectations, one possible (but understudied) reaction to continual "deflections." Gendered roles set up enormously strong expectations about actions and trigger strong emotions when they are not met.

Structure

One of the most fruitful approaches to emotions has linked them to individuals' positions in social hierarchies (see Chapter 14 of this volume). Kemper (1978; Kemper and Collins 1990) suggests that our emotions differ according to our relative power and status in hierarchies as well as in response to changes in these. When individuals have or gain power or status, they tend to feel positive emotions such as pride, security, and confidence. When they lack or lose them, they tend to feel fear, anxiety, and other negative emotions. Kemper distinguishes dozens of emotions according to people's positions in social structures.

Research might investigate whether the emotions that individuals feel in their work or personal lives carry over into their political lives. Those who feel powerless at work may seek power through collective action, as Kemper suggests. For status, he explicitly predicts that losses will lead to collective action if they are attributed to the actions of others (through anger and indignation) but not if they are blamed on oneself. A long tradition of research on right-wing, so-called status movements has found just these dynamics: Shame leads to demonization of those who are blamed for the loss of status (Aho 1990; Gusfield 1963; Lipset and Raab 1978; Rieder 1985). This tradition, currently out of favor, needs to specify better the mechanisms by which these feelings are referenced in rhetorical contexts.

More generally in the field of social movements, the structural emphasis on political constraints and financial resources that emerged in the 1970s, although it tended to ignore emotions altogether, was conceivably consistent with Kemper's theory. Protestors, typically visualized as insurgents, were seen as outsiders, in subordinate positions economically, legally, politically, and often personally. The U.S. civil rights movements, and southern blacks, were taken as the exemplar, although early modern labor movements in Europe also fit the pattern. Here we might expect hierarchical dynamics, with the emotions felt in everyday life (generated by structural positions) being the motivation to join collective action. But most social movements do not comfortably fit these exemplars, and despite Kemper's efforts (2001), structural approaches have not been widely adopted by students of social movements.

Another possible application would be to examine hierarchies *within* social movements. We must distinguish between a movement's internal dynamics and its attitudes toward the broader society it hopes to change. In the former, status and power differences may emerge more clearly. Relations between leaders and followers (currently an ignored research topic) may especially take the form of a social hierarchy. Authoritarian sects and cults, in particular, often have strong leaders to whom deference is given, as we saw with Lalich's (2004) account of Heaven's Gate and the (ironically named) Democratic Workers Party. In hierarchic groups like these, we should expect to see mechanisms that reinforce or rationalize hierarchies. For instance, the leaders of Heaven's Gate reinforced and exploited the age gap between them and their followers through nicknames and other language that infantilized the latter. Even those groups that, unlike Heaven's Gate, try to hide internal differences of power and status may still generate the emotions typical of them.

Nonetheless, today's protest groups, especially the so-called new social movements, rarely exhibit the kind of internal hierarchy that defines structure in Kemper's sense. Most are relatively egalitarian societies of equals, which try hard to minimize status differences among members, although informal hierarchies of status may nonetheless arise, capable of triggering the emotions that Kemper predicts.

Most protestors belong to groups that are explicitly critical of hierarchies, an observation compatible with Kemper's point about attributing blame for status decline. Ridgeway (1978, 1982; Ridgeway and Johnson 1990) has examined the cultural expectations people bring to interactions, expecting more competence from individuals of higher status (male, white, older, and so on) and becoming angry when lower-status individuals dominate instead. She has demonstrated these dynamics in the operations of small groups, a lead that might help us understand protest groups, especially gender dynamics (Kleinman 1996). Individuals of lower status, she suggests, may improve their ranking quietly and slowly without triggering negative emotions. With this exception, however, most structural factors will have more to do with constructions of outsiders than with the internal dynamics of ongoing movement groups. (Ridgeway's work has as much to do with cultural expectations about hierarchies as with hierarchies themselves.)

In another structural approach, Barbalet (1998) attempts to define macrosocial conditions for the spread of emotional raw materials useful in collective mobilization. When people lose the resources and capacities to maintain their social connections, they become resentful and vengeful against those they believe have denied them the status they deserve (resentment) or who have used their power against them (vengefulness). In rhetorical settings, organizers can appeal to these feelings whether or not they are held consciously.

In addition, Barbalet (1998) argues, confidence and fear can advance or hinder collective action. Jasper (2006b) also emphasizes confidence in his examination of strategic engagements in a variety of institutional arenas, and Goodwin and Pfaff (2001) have shown how important it is for protestors to manage fear. Barbalet points out that fear can inspire action as well as dampen it, tapping into recent work on the importance of threats as triggers of collective or strategic action (Jasper 1997, 2006b). Further, he notes that fear equally affects elites, frequently pushing them to innovate politically and organizationally. Students of protest might here learn something from international relations, which has often demonstrated how one nation's fears can lead it to strengthen its military, frightening its neighbors in turn and leading to hostile spirals (e.g., Buzan 1983).

In some ways, Barbalet (1998) has put the flesh of emotions on the spare bones of Smelser's (1962) idea of "social strain" (similar to many other early concepts). But it is not simply social change that causes strain; strategic actions by organized groups also place stress on others. Research on protest should be able to identify rhetorical references to and symbols of resentment and vengeance. Research on frames, for instance, should devote more attention to the emotional effects as well as the cognitive ones.

We saw that Scheff (1990, 1994, 1997), working in a similar vein, has documented the presence of shame in several collective mobilizations, although he has primarily examined nationalist wars rather than domestic and more local forms of mobilization. Like Barbalet (1998), he makes a plausible case that shame or pride can be widely distributed in a society and thus become an effective referent in pleas from political leaders. He adds more micromechanisms—for example the idea that leaders themselves can exhibit the emotions and thus embody the widespread feelings. Hitler, in one of Scheff's richest examples, displayed the signs of shame and called obsessively for revenge against his designated scapegoat: Europe's Jews.

Research on moral panics has explored many of the anxieties and fears suggested by Barbalet (1998) and Scheff (1990, 1994, 1997), especially among the elites who function as "moral entrepreneurs" in bringing attention to what they consider urgent social problems and in castigating "folk devils" responsible for them (Cohen 1972). The media, the police, politicians, and religious leaders are frequently prominent in defining a panic and organizing efforts to suppress it. Again, shame, anxiety, resentment, and other threatening feelings shape action primarily when leaders deploy or activate them rhetorically.

Although critics have decried the term "panic" as overly pejorative, it squarely suggests emotional processes. Its real weakness has been that the emotional mechanisms have not been specified. Perhaps Barbalet's (1998) descriptions of the emotions attendant on social change could remedy this problem. Moral panics are rooted in ongoing fears and anxieties about particular groups, especially those arriving from elsewhere, those at the bottom of economic hierarchies, and the young who have not yet been fully socialized. (These are the folk devils of many types of political mobilization, including revolutions.) There are clear social-structural sources for these feelings of threat.

Ritual

Drawing on Durkheim's concept of collective effervescence and Goffman's insights into interaction rituals (this is the subject of Chapter 6 in this volume), Collins (1975, 1981, 2004) has developed a theory of rituals and emotional energy, which he has applied to social movements (2001). Face-to-face social interactions can generate emotional energy that people crave, seeking out situations that generate more of it. In a way, Collins has specified new mechanisms for the old crowd image that dominated research through the 1960s. Rituals involve the physical copresence of individuals, who share awareness of one another, a focus of attention, and a mood. They synchronize their actions and develop symbolic and moral representations of their activity or group, thus helping to sustain it. Among other outcomes, righteous anger over infractions of the norms generated in the rituals may lead to collective action.

As we saw when discussing the pleasures of protest, existing research has remarked on a number of these mechanisms (e.g., Epstein 1991; Hirsch 1986, 1990), but it has tended to focus on the symbols that emerge as a kind of precipitate out of the interactions rather than the interactions themselves—no doubt because of easier methodological access. Group boundaries are reinforced, enemies demonized, insiders praised, and symbols promulgated. This research has gone in two directions somewhat different from Collins's. On the one hand, it is clear that some symbolic and presumably emotional resonance occurs in settings beyond the face-to-face, through more impersonal media (Jasper and Poulsen 1995). The vast literature on collective identities is filled with emotional solidarities not always connected to rituals—and not always acknowledged (Polletta and Jasper 2001). On the other hand, there are numerous emotions generated in personal interactions that fill in the rather vague notion of emotional energy: angry reactions, lustful responses, the joys of crowds, the fears of engagement. We need more research on the relationship between reflex emotions and the longer-lasting moods they help to generate. All organized groups face the Janus dilemma of reaching out versus reaching in (Jasper 2004a, 2006b), and the emotional dynamics for the two kinds of activity differ enormously (Summers-Effler 2004). Research needs to both extend and further specify the emotional energies that rituals especially generate.

Fairness and Morality

Exchange theories have examined experimental subjects' emotional reactions to transactions that they consider unfair (Cook and Hegtvedt 1983; Hegtvedt and Cook 1987). Researchers have posited that individuals carry both substantive and procedural norms of justice, which allow them to see either outcomes or the underlying procedures as unfair. Students of politics, trying to get at the indignation that motivates action, have made parallel distinctions (Jasper 1997; Spector and Kitsuse 1987). Plus, a growing army of behavioral economists have conducted similar experiments (for an overview, see Camerer 2001).

Disadvantaged people become indignant when they perceive outcomes or procedures as unfair, but most exchange theories distinguish only two possible attributions of this unfairness: Individuals can attribute the outcome to structural position or to their own characteristics. What is usually missing is a third attribution: to blame the outcomes on the actions of others. This is the righteous anger that so often leads to collective action (Gamson et al. 1982). The construction of blame, fusing emotion and cognition, is a central activity of movement groups. Here is a potentially rich engagement between research on emotions and on politics.

Another potential dialogue has to do with comparisons between procedural and substantive justice norms. According to Turner and Stets (2005), it is not altogether clear if one of these trumps the other when they are in conflict. But if we see norms as partly rhetorical strategies, we see instead a trade-off or dilemma over which one of them to refer to in a given situation. Jasper (2006b) has labeled this the Dilemma of Form and Content, observing that it is usually difficult to return to conflict over substance once a strategic player has switched to issues of procedure.

The limitation of most experiments in this tradition is that injustice is defined as an unfair distribution of payoffs, typically in the monetary terms that economists and exchange theorists favor for their mathematical properties. However, there are numerous moral principles and intuitions that can be violated, such as religious or political principles, professional norms, communicative norms, and community norms of empathy and compassion (Jasper 1997, chap. 6). Like procedural norms, these are hard to quantify. But the softer techniques of movement research may help extend the insights of fairness theories.

The moral dimension of protest is often recognized but rarely linked to the emotions that make up such a large part of it. We follow moral rules because we are afraid of the consequences of breaking them; or we follow them because it feels good to "do the right thing." Contrary to Kant's recommendations, we do not act morally out of an abstract calculation or principle but from a gut feeling. Shame and guilt perhaps begin to get at these moral emotions better than sociological theories of justice do. Moral emotions have to do with *approval and disapproval,* including approval and disapproval about ourselves. Pride and shame elude mere fairness theories, for the most part, even though they are central mechanisms reinforcing social norms (Scheff 1990, 1997; Elster 1999).

"Moral shock," we saw, is a term intended to get at the anger and outrage that can sometimes trigger political action in response to information or events that disrupt one's ontological security. It involves cognitive recognition that the world is not as it seems, with moral outrage and strong emotions about this gap. But these emotions have never been sorted out adequately. Fairness theories are only a start, and other sociological theories of emotion may help distinguish different sources of moral shocks.

Theories of justice might help us understand one of the puzzles of research into collective action: Sometimes repression dampens it and sometimes it stimulates it. Political-process and rational-choice theories have been unable to grapple effectively with situations in which higher costs to action lead to more of it. At best, they have suggested that short-run dampening may give way to longer-run stimulation (Andrews 2004), but the different effects can never be sorted out without attention to emotional dynamics. When repression is seen as grossly unjust, indignation is more likely to broaden protest, but it has to overcome fear to do so. Mediating factors probably include the attribution of blame; constructions of heroism, villainy, and victimhood; sheer hatred, fury, and revenge, alongside expectations about the costs and benefits of repression.

CONCLUSION

Sociological theories of emotions offer a number of leads to researchers on social movements, and we hope that such research can help advance these theories in turn. Different theories seem to be suited for different interactive contexts, and there are many such contexts in the recruitment, internal dynamics, and external engagements of social movements. The sociological study of political action desperately needs new microfoundations to counter those of rational choice theory, and the extensive tool kit of emotional mechanisms is a promising source for these (Jasper forthcoming).

Nonetheless, there seem to be several lacunae in which existing theories offer little if any guidance to the movement researcher. The first is how people negotiate different kinds of inter-personal and rhetorical settings, beginning with the contrast between dealing with insiders and outsiders. Just as different symbols and claims will resonate with each, so will different emotional appeals. Emotional appeals and displays that work with one audience may hurt with another, and it is difficult in today's world to segregate these audiences.

A similar gap in existing theories seems to be that most of them lump all emotions together, whereas the inductive research on social movements suggests differences. In particular, the abiding affective loyalties that go into collective identity and collective demonization must have sources and effects that differ from those of the reflex emotions such as anger and surprise. Moral emotions are also stable aspects of culture that differ from urges and reflexes. Moods too would seem to have different sources, although they are important in dampening or facilitating action.

Moral emotions are especially important in public rhetoric, suggesting another gap: Existing theories have little to say about mediated rhetorical settings and how they differ from direct one-on-one interactions. Systematic discussions of emotions began with Aristotle's observations on the emotional effects of rhetoric, an extremely sociological interest that has somehow been lost. Who arouses what emotions in whom? How and when? Specifying different emotional effects will help us understand politics, and political research can help us specify those effects.

REFERENCES

Aho, James A. 1990. *The Politics of Righteousness: Idaho Christian Patriotism.* Seattle: University of Washington Press.

Alford, C. Fred. Forthcoming. "Hate and Love and the Other." In *Emotional Dimensions of Politics*, edited by S. Clarke, P. Hoggett, and S. Thompson. London: Palgrave-Macmillan.

Allport, Floyd. 1924. *Social Psychology.* Boston: Houghton Mifflin.

Andrews, Kenneth T. 2004. *Freedom Is a Constant Struggle: The Mississippi Civil Rights Movement and its Legacy.* Chicago: University of Chicago Press.

Barbalet, J. M. 1998. *Emotion, Social Theory, and Social Structure: A Macrosociological Approach.* Cambridge: Cambridge University Press.

Barker-Benfield, G. J. 1992. *The Culture of Sensibility: Sex and Society in Eighteenth-Century Britain.* Chicago: University of Chicago Press.

Bell, Derrick. 1992. *Faces at the Bottom of the Well: The Permanence of Racism.* New York: Basic Books.

Benford, Robert D. 1997. "An Insider's Critique of the Social Movement Framing Perspective." *Sociological Inquiry* 67: 409–430.

Berezin, Mabel. 2001. "Emotions and Political Identity: Mobilizing Affection for the Polity." Pp. 83–98 in *Passionate Politics: Emotions and Social Movements*, edited by J. Goodwin, J. M. Jasper, and F. Polletta. Chicago: University of Chicago Press.

Blee, Kathleen M. 1991. *Women of the Klan: Racism and Gender in the 1920s.* Berkeley: University of California Press.

———. 2002. *Inside Organized Racism: Women in the Hate Movement.* Berkeley: University of California Press.

Buzan, Barry. 1983. *People, States, and Fear: The National Security Problem in International Relations.* Chapel Hill: University of North Carolina Press.

Camerer, Colin F. 2001. *Behavioral Game Theory: Experiments in Strategic Interaction.* Princeton, NJ: Russell Sage Foundation and Princeton University Press.

Campbell, Sue. 1994. "Being Dismissed: The Politics of Emotional Expression." *Hypatia* 9: 46–65.

Cohen, Jean L. 1985. "Strategy or Identity: New Theoretical Paradigms and Contemporary Social Movements." *Social Research* 52: 663–716.

Cohen, Stanley. 1972. *Folk Devils and Moral Panics: The Creation of the Mods and the Rockers.* New York: St. Martin's Press.

Collins, Randall. 1975. *Conflict Sociology: Toward an Explanatory Science.* New York: Academic Press.

———. 1981. "On the Micro-Foundations of Macro-Sociology." *American Journal of Sociology* 86: 984–1014.

———. 2001. "Social Movements and the Focus of Emotional Attention." Pp. 27–44 in *Passionate Politics: Emotions and Social Movements*, edited by J. Goodwin, J. M. Jasper, and F. Polletta. Chicago: University of Chicago Press.

———. 2004. *Interaction Ritual Chains.* Princeton, NJ: Princeton University Press.

Cook, Karen S., and Karen A. Hegtvedt. 1983. "Distributive Justice, Equity, and Equality." *Annual Review of Sociology* 9: 217–241.

Danaher, William F., and Vincent J. Roscigno. 2004. "Cultural Production, Media, and Meaning: Hillbilly Music and the Southern Textile Mills." *Poetics* 32: 51–71.

Echols, Alice. 1989. *Daring to be Bad: Radical Feminism in America, 1967 to 1975.* Minneapolis: University of Minnesota Press.

Ekman, Paul. 1972. *Emotions in the Human Face.* New York: Pergamon.

Elster, Jon. 1999. *Alchemies of the Mind: Rationality and the Emotions.* Cambridge: Cambridge University Press.

Epstein, Barbara. 1991. *Political Protest and Cultural Revolution: Nonviolent Direct Action in the 1970s and 1980s.* Berkeley: University of California Press.

Eyerman, Ron, and Andrew Jamison. 1998. *Music and Social Movements: Mobilizing Traditions in the Twentieth Century.* Cambridge: Cambridge University Press.

Flam, Helena. 1998. *Mosaic of Fear: Poland and East Germany Before 1989.* New York: Columbia University Press.

Freud, Sigmund. [1921]1959. *Group Psychology and the Analysis of the Ego.* New York: Norton.

Gamson, William A. 1975. *The Strategy of Social Protest.* Homewood, IL: Dorsey.

———. 1992. *Talking Politics.* Cambridge: Cambridge University Press.

Gamson, William, Bruce Fireman, and Steven Rytina. 1982. *Encounters with Unjust Authority.* Homewood, IL: Dorsey.

Goodwin, Jeff. 1997. "The Libidinal Constitution of a High-Risk Social Movement: Affectual Ties and Solidarity in the Huk Rebellion." *American Sociological Review* 62: 53–69.

Goodwin, Jeff, and James M. Jasper, eds. 2004. *Rethinking Social Movements: Structure, Meaning, and Emotion.* Lanham, MD: Rowman and Littlefield.

Goodwin, Jeff, James M. Jasper, and Francesca Polletta. 2000. "Return of the Repressed: The Fall and Rise of Emotions in Social Movement Theory." *Mobilization* 5: 65–82.

———. 2004. "Emotional Dimensions of Social Movements." Pp. 413–432 in *The Blackwell Companion to Social Movements*, edited by D. A. Snow, S. A. Soule, and H. Kriesi. Malden, MA: Blackwell.

Goodwin, Jeff, and Steven Pfaff. 2001. "Emotion Work in High-Risk Social Movements: Managing Fear in the U.S. and East German Civil Rights Movements." Pp. 282–302 in *Passionate Politics: Emotions and Social Movements*, edited by J. Goodwin, J. M. Jasper, and F. Polletta. Chicago: University of Chicago Press.

Gould, Deborah B. 2001. "Rock the Boat, Don't Rock the Boat, Baby: Ambivalence and the Emergence of Militant AIDS Activism." Pp. 135–157 in *Passionate Politics: Emotions and Social Movements*, edited by J. Goodwin, J. M. Jasper, and F. Polletta. Chicago: University of Chicago Press.

———. 2002. "Life During Wartime: Emotions and the Development of ACT UP." *Mobilization* 7: 177–200.

Groves, Julian McAllister. 1997. *Hearts and Minds: The Controversy over Laboratory Animals.* Philadelphia: Temple University Press.

———. 2001. "Animal Rights and the Politics of Emotion: Folk Constructs of Emotions in the Animal Rights Movement." Pp. 212–229 in *Passionate Politics: Emotions and Social Movements*, edited by J. Goodwin, J. M. Jasper, and F. Polletta. Chicago: University of Chicago Press.

Gusfield, Joseph R. 1963. *Symbolic Crusade: Status Politics and the American Temperance Movement.* Urbana: University of Illinois Press.

Hegtvedt, Karen A., and Karen S. Cook. 1987. "The Role of Justice in Conflict Situations." *Advances in Group Processes* 4: 109–136.

Heise, David R. 1977. "Social Action as the Control of Affect." *Behavioral Science* 22: 163–177.

———. 1979. *Understanding Events: Affect and the Construction of Social Action.* Cambridge: Cambridge University Press.

———. 1989. "Effects of Emotions Displays on Social Identification." *Social Psychology Quarterly* 52: 10–21.

Hirsch, Eric L. 1986. "The Creation of Political Solidarity in Social Movement Organizations." *Sociological Quarterly* 27: 373–387.

———. 1990. "Sacrifice for the Cause: Group Processes, Recruitment, and Commitment in a Student Social Movement." *American Sociological Review* 55: 243–254.

Hirschman, Albert O. 1982. *Shifting Involvements: Private Interest and Public Action.* Princeton, NJ: Princeton University Press.

Hochschild, Arlie Russell. 1975. "The Sociology of Feeling and Emotion: Selected Possibilities." Pp. 280–307 in *Another Voice*, edited by M. Millman and R. M. Kanter. Garden City, NY: Anchor.

Hoffer, Eric. 1951. *The True Believer.* New York: Harper and Row.

Hoggett, Paul. 1992. *Partisans in an Uncertain World: The Psychoanalysis of Engagement.* London: Free Association Books.

Honneth, Axel. 1995. *The Struggle for Recognition: The Moral Grammar of Social Struggles.* Cambridge: Polity Press.

Jasper, James M. 1997. *The Art of Moral Protest: Culture, Biography, and Creativity in Social Movements.* Chicago: University of Chicago Press.

———. 1998. "The Emotions of Protest: Affective and Reactive Emotions in and around Social Movements." *Sociological Forum* 13: 397–424.

———. 2004a. "A Strategic Approach to Collective Action: Looking for Agency in Social-Movement Choices." *Mobilization* 9: 1–16.

———. 2004b. "Intellectual Cycles of Social-Movement Research: From Psychoanalysis to Culture?" Pp. 234–253 in *Self, Social Structure, and Beliefs: Explorations in Sociology*, edited by J. C. Alexander, G. T. Marx, and C. L. Williams. Berkeley: University of California Press.

———. 2006a. "Emotion and Motivation." Pp. 157–171 in *Oxford Handbook of Contextual Political Studies*, edited by R. Goodin and C. Tilly. Oxford: Oxford University Press.

———. 2006b. *Getting Your Way: Strategic Dilemmas in Real Life.* Chicago: University of Chicago Press.

———. Forthcoming. "Emotions and the Microfoundations of Politics." In *Emotional Dimensions of Politics*, edited by S. Clarke, P. Hoggett, and S. Thompson. London: Palgrave-Macmillan.

Jasper, James M., and Jane D. Poulsen. 1995. "Recruiting Strangers and Friends: Moral Shocks and Social Networks in Animal Rights and Anti-Nuclear Protests." *Social Problems* 42: 493–512.

Jenkins, J. Craig, and Charles Perrow. 1977. "Insurgency of the Powerless: Farm Worker Movements (1946–1972)." *American Sociological Review* 42: 249–268.

Johnston, Hank, and Bert Klandermans, eds. 1995. *Social Movements and Culture*. Minneapolis: University of Minnesota Press.

Kaufman, Stuart J. 2001. *Modern Hatreds: The Symbolic Politics of Ethnic War*. Ithaca, NY: Cornell University Press.

Kemper, Theodore D. 1978. *A Social Interactional Theory of Emotions*. New York: Wiley.

———. 2001. "A Structural Approach to Social Movement Emotions." Pp. 58–73 in *Passionate Politics: Emotions and Social Movements*, edited by J. Goodwin, J. M. Jasper, and F. Polletta. Chicago: University of Chicago Press.

Kemper, Theodore D., and Randall Collins. 1990. "Dimensions of Microinteraction." *American Journal of Sociology* 96: 32–68.

Kitschelt, Herbert. 1986. "Political Opportunity Structures and Political Process: Anti-Nuclear Movements in Four Democracies." *British Journal of Political Science* 16: 57–85.

Klandermans, Bert. 1984. "Mobilization and Participation: Social-Psychological Expansions of Resource Mobilization Theory." *American Sociological Review* 49: 583–600.

Klapp, Orrin. 1969. *Collective Search for Identity*. New York: Holt, Rinehart, and Winston.

Kleinman, Sherryl. 1996. *Opposing Ambitions: Gender and Identity in an Alternative Organization*. Chicago: University of Chicago Press.

Kornhauser, William. 1959. *The Politics of Mass Society*. Glencoe, IL: Free Press of Glencoe.

Lalich, Janja. 2004. *Bounded Choice: True Believers and Charismatic Cults*. Berkeley: University of California Press.

Laraña, Enrique, Hank Johnston, and Joseph R. Gusfield, eds. 1994. *New Social Movements: From Ideology to Identity*. Philadelphia: Temple University Press.

Lasswell, Harold D. 1930. *Psychopathology and Politics*. Chicago: University of Chicago Press.

———. 1948. *Power and Personality*. New York: Norton.

Le Bon, Gustave. [1895]1960. *The Crowd*. New York: Viking.

Lichterman, Paul. 1996. *The Search for Community: Political Activists Reinventing Commitment*. Cambridge: Cambridge University Press.

Lipset, Seymour Martin, and Earl Raab. 1978. *The Politics of Unreason: Right-Wing Extremism in America, 1790–1977*, 2nd ed. Chicago: University of Chicago Press.

Lofland, John. 1982. "Crowd Joys." *Urban Life* 10: 355–381.

———. 1996. *Social Movement Organizations*. New York: Aldine.

Lofland, John, and Rodney Stark. 1965 "Becoming a World-Saver: A Theory of Conversion to a Deviant Perspective." *American Sociological Review* 30: 862–875.

Luker, Kristin. 1984. *Abortion and the Politics of Motherhood*. Berkeley: University of California Press.

McAdam, Doug. 1982. *Political Process and the Development of Black Insurgency, 1930–1970*. Chicago: University of Chicago Press.

———. 1988. *Freedom Summer*. New York: Oxford University Press.

———. 1994. "Culture and Social Movements." Pp. 36–57 in *New Social Movements*, edited by E. Laraña, H. Johnston, and J. R. Gusfield. Philadelphia: Temple University Press.

McCarthy, John D., and Mayer N. Zald. 1977. "Resource Mobilization and Social Movements: A Partial Theory." *American Journal of Sociology* 82: 1212–1241.

Melucci, Alberto. 1995. "The Process of Collective Identity." Pp. 41–63 in *Social Movements and Culture*, edited by H. Johnston and B. Klandermans. Minneapolis: University of Minnesota Press.

Morris, Aldon, and Carol McClurg Mueller, eds. 1992. *Frontiers in Social Movement Theory*. New Haven, CT: Yale University Press.

Mueller, Carol McClurg. 1992. "Building Social Movement Theory." Pp. 3–25 in *Frontiers in Social Movement Theory*, edited by A. Morris and C. M. Mueller. New Haven, CT: Yale University Press.

Nepstad, Sharon Erikson, and Christian Smith. 2001. "The Social Structure of Moral Outrage in Recruitment to the U.S. Central America Peace Movement." Pp. 158–174 in *Passionate Politics: Emotions and Social Movements*, edited by J. Goodwin, J. M. Jasper, and F. Polletta. Chicago: University of Chicago Press.

Nussbaum, Martha C. 2001. *Upheavals of Thought: The Intelligence of Emotions*. Cambridge: Cambridge University Press.

Oberschall, Anthony. 1973. *Social Conflict and Social Movements*. Englewood Cliffs, NJ: Prentice-Hall.

Petersen, Roger D. 2002. *Understanding Ethnic Violence: Fear, Hatred, and Resentment in Twentieth-Century Eastern Europe*. Cambridge: Cambridge University Press.

Polletta, Francesca. 2002. *Freedom Is an Endless Meeting: Democracy in American Social Movements*. Chicago: University of Chicago Press.

Polletta, Francesca, and James M. Jasper. 2001. "Collective Identity and Social Movements." *Annual Review of Sociology* 27: 283–305.

Ridgeway, Cecilia L. 1978. "Conformity, Group-Oriented Motivation, and Status Attainment in Small Groups." *Social Psychology Quarterly* 41: 175–188.

———. 1982. "Status in Groups: The Importance of Motivation." *American Sociological Review* 47: 76–88.

Ridgeway, Cecilia L., and Cathryn Johnson. 1990. "What Is the Relationship between Socioemotional Behavior and Status in Task Groups?" *American Journal of Sociology* 95: 1189–1212.

Rieder, Jonathan. 1985. *Canarsie: The Jews and Italians of Brooklyn against Liberalism.* Cambridge: Harvard University Press.

Robnett, Belinda. 1997. *How Long, How Long? African-American Women in the Struggle for Civil Rights.* New York: Oxford University Press.

Rupp, Leila J., and Verta Taylor. 1987. *Survival in the Doldrums: The American Women's Rights Movement, 1945 to the 1960s.* Oxford: Oxford University Press.

Schafer, Roy. 1976. *A New Language for Psychoanalysis.* New Haven, CT: Yale University Press.

Scheff, Thomas J. 1990. *Microsociology: Discourse, Emotion, and Social Structure.* Chicago: University of Chicago Press.

———. 1994. *Bloody Revenge.* Boulder, CO: Westview.

———. 1997. *Emotions, the Social Bond, and Human Reality: Part/Whole Analysis.* Cambridge: Cambridge University Press.

Slater, Philip. 1963. "On Social Regression." *American Sociological Review* 28: 339–364.

Smelser, Neil J. 1962. *Theory of Collective Behavior.* New York: Free Press.

———. 1968. "Social and Psychological Dimensions of Collective Behavior." Pp. 92–121 in *Essays in Sociological Explanation*, edited by N. J. Smelser. Englewood Cliffs, NJ: Prentice-Hall.

Smith-Lovin, Lynn. 1990. "Emotion as the Confirmation and Disconfirmation of Identity: An Affect Control Model." Pp. 238–270 in *Research Agendas in the Sociology of Emotions*, edited by T. D. Kemper. Albany: State University of New York Press.

Snow, David A., and Robert D. Benford. 1988. "Ideology, Frame Resonance, and Participant Mobilization." *International Social Movement Research* 1: 197–217.

———. 1992. "Master Frames and Cycles of Protest." Pp. 133–155 in *Frontiers in Social Movement Theory*, edited by A. D. Morris and C. M. Mueller. New Haven, CT: Yale University Press.

Snow, David A., E. Burke Rochford, Jr., Steven K. Worden, and Robert D. Benford. 1986. "Frame Alignment Processes, Micromobilization, and Movement Participation." *American Sociological Review* 51: 464–481.

Spector, Malcolm, and John I. Kitsuse. 1987. *Constructing Social Problems.* New York: Aldine de Gruyter.

Stearns, Carol Zisowitz, and Peter N. Stearns. 1986. *Anger: The Struggle for Emotional Control in America's History.* Chicago: University of Chicago Press.

Stein, Arlene. 2001a. "Revenge of the Shamed: The Christian Right's Emotional Culture War." Pp. 115–131 in *Passionate Politics: Emotions and Social Movements*, edited by J. Goodwin, J. M. Jasper, and F. Polletta. Chicago: University of Chicago Press.

———. 2001b. *The Stranger Next Door: The Story of a Small Community's Battle over Sex, Faith, and Civil Rights.* Boston: Beacon.

Summers-Effler, Erika. 2004. "Radical Saints and Reformer Heroes: Culture, Interaction, and Emotional Intensity in Altruistic Social Movement Organizations." Ph.D. dissertation, University of Pennsylvania.

Taylor, Verta. 1989. "Social Movement Continuity: The Women's Movement in Abeyance." *American Sociological Review* 54: 761–775.

———. 1996. *Rock-a-by Baby: Feminism, Self-Help, and Postpartum Depression.* New York: Routledge.

Taylor, Verta, and Leila J. Rupp. 2002. "Loving Internationalism: The Emotion Culture of Transnational Women's Organizations, 1888–1945." *Mobilization* 7: 125–144.

Thoits, Peggy A. 1985. "Self-Labeling Processes in Mental Illness: The Role of Emotional Deviance." *American Journal of Sociology* 91: 221–249.

———. 1990. "Emotional Deviance: Research Agendas." Pp. 180–203 in *Research Agendas in the Sociology of Emotions*, edited by T. D. Kemper. Albany: State University of New York Press.

Thompson, Simon. Forthcoming. "Shame and Resistance." In *Emotional Dimensions of Politics*, edited by S. Clarke, P. Hoggett, and S. Thompson. London: Palgrave-Macmillan.

Tilly, Charles. 1978. *From Mobilization to Revolution.* Reading, MA: Addison-Wesley.

Touraine, Alain. 1977. *The Self-Production of Society.* Chicago: University of Chicago Press.

Turner, Jonathan H., and Jan E. Stets. 2005. *The Sociology of Emotions.* Cambridge: Cambridge University Press.

Turner, Ralph, and Lewis M. Killian. 1957. *Collective Behavior.* Englewood Cliffs, NJ: Prentice-Hall.

Vanderford, Marsha L. 1989. "Vilification and Social Movements: A Case Study of Pro-Life and Pro-Choice Rhetoric." *Quarterly Journal of Speech* 75: 166–182.

Whittier, Nancy. 2001. "Emotional Strategies: The Collective Reconstruction and Display of Oppositional Emotions in the Movement against Child Sexual Abuse." Pp. 233–250 in *Passionate Politics: Emotions and Social Movements*, edited by J. Goodwin, J. M. Jasper, and F. Polletta. Chicago: University of Chicago Press.

Wood, Elisabeth Jean. 2001. "The Emotional Benefits of Insurgency in El Salvador." Pp. 267–281 in *Passionate Politics: Emotions and Social Movements*, edited by J. Goodwin, J. M. Jasper, and F. Polletta. Chicago: University of Chicago Press.

———. 2003. *Insurgent Collective Action and Civil War in El Salvador*. Cambridge: Cambridge University Press.

Young, Michael P. 2001. "A Revolution of the Soul: Transformative Experiences and Immediate Abolition." Pp. 99–114 in *Passionate Politics: Emotions and Social Movements*, edited by J. Goodwin, J. M. Jasper, and F. Polletta. Chicago: University of Chicago Press.

Index

Absolute value, of justice evaluation, 329
Accessibility principle, in self-verification theory, 217
Accountability, and sympathy, 469
Actors, relations between
  and justice evaluation, 330
  and love, 402
Admiration, differentiating from envy, 427
Adulation, by fans, as a version of love, 103
Adultery taboo, culturally determined definition of, 414
Affect
  control of, as a key feature of social life, 179–180
  defined, 181–182
  dimensions of, 20
  and hemisphere of the brain involved with emotion, 45
Affect control theory, 179–202
  classifying emotion in, 15, 18
  and emotion management strategies, 584
  evaluation, potency, and activity dimensions in, 28–29
  and expectations in social movements, 625
  generation of new situational definitions in, 264
  versus power-status theory, study of, 108–109
  research in, 173
Affection
  as an emotion toward exploited groups, 400
  valuing of, by women, 76
Affective concerns
  bonds in social movements, affiliative and disaffiliative
    effects of, 621–622
  commitment to identities, 206–207
  disorders as multidimensional emotional concerns, 594
  maximization and inequality, 29
  meanings, dimensions of, 182
  mood in a group, influence of high-status members on,
    364
  outcomes of empathic processes, 446, 453–454
Affect theory of social exchange, 304–305, 311–316
Age, and social distribution of anger, 505–506
Agency
  for assigning responsibility for social structural
    variations, 23
  attribution of, to the sacred self, 141
  capacity for, and alignment of feelings with social
    expectations, 156

defined, 97–98
Aggression
  and empathy, 457–458
  in response to devaluation, 242
  in response to ego threat, 239
Aggression-approval proposition, anger or pleasure
    produced by, 299
Agitation, managed feelings of, association with burnout
    and inauthenticity, 579
Agreement, in groups, emotions resulting from, 352
Alexithymia, expression of, as chronic pain, 599
Alienation, in chronic repression, 563
Allostatic load, relationship with long-term stress, 604
Altruism, emotion bonuses for, 383
Ambiguity, and self-report about gender and emotions,
    69
Ambivalence, in the conflict between the individual and
    society, 373
Amygdala
  fear and anger enabled by, 47
  and the limbic system, 50–51
Analytic dimensions, of emotions, 258–261
Anatomy, functional, of emotion in the brain, 42–45
Anger, 493–515
  from decrease in status, 121
  embarrassing, management of, 127
  as emotional capital for social movements, 195
  interaction with grief, 519
  interaction with shame, 280–281
  from lack of identity verification, 215–216
  mismanaged, in health care, 598
  as an other-critical emotion, 553–554
  relationship with power, status, and gender, 71, 73–74
  in response to insufficient status, 100
  righteous
    association with attribution, 563–564
    leading to social movements, 619, 629
  transmutation of repressed emotion to, 561–562
  with violation of the moral code of autonomy, 554
  at work, comparison with anger in the family, 581
  in the workplace and at home, comparative studies,
    582–583
Anger processes, social causes of, 495–503

Animate objects, loss of, and grief, 534–535
Annoyance, as a response to disagreement in a group, 352
Antecedents, to empathy, 444–445, 447–449
Anticipation, of responses to counter-stereotypical
emotion displays, 70–71
Anticipatory emotions, 97, 101
grief, 531
Anxiety, as an outcome of low self-esteem, 246
Appraisal, in classification of emotions, 16–17
Appraisal models, valence as a dimension in, 20
Approaches, to love, 396–397
"As if" loops, as the basis for learning, 143–144
Assertive influence, 357
Athletes, male, solidarity of, 168–169
Attachment, and grief, 520–521
Attachment theory, place of love in, 396
Attainment
extreme and dangerous, to enhance status, 94
formal, to enhance status, 93
Attention space, competition for, and shape of networks,
146–147
Attorneys, emotional socialization of, 573–574
Attraction, distinguishing love from, 393
Attributional judgments, and empathy, 446
Attribution-emotion-action model, effect on sympathy,
470
Attribution emotion family, 26–29
Attribution process, emotions related to identity
disruption, 211–212
Attributions
as defense mechanisms, 562–563
internal, for positive emotional experiences, 563
Attribution theory, 27
formalization of categories of, 30
global emotions, 302
outcomes of assigning responsibility for identity
disruption, 214–215
Authentic feminine self, and the female sexual script, 76
Autonomy, job, interaction with emotional labor to
produce job satisfaction, 578
Avoidance
of envy, 429–430
of self-devaluation, 242
Awareness, of envy, and economic productivity of
societies, 428–429
Axons, defined, 43

Bads, defined for justice analysis, 323–324
Balance of fortune principle, in sympathy worthiness
assessments, 471
Behavioral manipulations, for emotion management,
125
Behavior control, and power, 299
Beliefs
conflicts from competing sets of, 161–162
about gender and emotion, 64, 67
about status, consensual, 66

Beneficence, logic of, in socioemotional exchange, 476
Benefits, of emotional labor, 577–579
Bereavement
defined, 518
rules governing, 526
Biological capacity, for empathy, 444
Biological perspective, on love, 405
Biology, of morality, 546–548
Biomedical positivism
health psychology and emotion, 598–603
in research on emotions and health, 595–600
Blood pressure, diastolic, and responsibility for other
individuals, 237
Bluffing, to nullify power of the other, 96
Boasting, for status enhancement, 95
Bodily feelings, association with emotional experiences,
57–59
Bodily labor, example, 576
Bodily sensations, and cultural definitions, 115
Boundary defining process versus social bonding,
experimental comparison, 310–311
Brain
maintenance of, 42
structures of, top-down, 45–49
Brain stem, description and functions of, 48–49
Breast cancer, coping strategies in, and survival, 603
Building blocks, of the brain, 43–44
Burnout, in jobs requiring emotional labor, study, 578
Business policies, impact on grief and grief practices, 525

Capital
cultural
and emotional energy in interaction ritual chain
theory, 266
and sympathy margins, 477
human, education symbolized from the perspective of,
507
social
from bonding, 502–503
judgments of sympathy worthiness based on, 472
See also Emotional capital
Cardiac arrest, emotional reaction of the patient to, and
outcome, 602
Categoric units, key properties of, table, 289
Categories, of emotion, classifying, 18–19
Causation model, top-down and bottom-up, in
neuroscience, 41
Cell body of neurons, 43
Cerebral cortex
defined, 45
evolution of, 262
Cerebrum, defined, 46
Change
accompanying grief, 534
in emotional culture, documentation of, 122
in the justice evaluation, 330–331
social

and jealousy, 415
obstacles to, 172–173
Characteristic emotions, defined, 183
Chronic stressors
conflict between work and family roles, 501
and psychological functioning, 496–501
Cingulate cortex, description of, 46–47
Circumplex model, for describing emotion, 302
Classes of emotions, 21–22
Classes of self-referent constructs, 224–225
Classical conditioning, leading to empathic outcomes, 445
Classic construction of emotion categories, 18
Classification, of emotions, 11–37
Class resentment, macrosociological analysis of, 159
Coalition building, to augment power, 96
Coercion
in the exercise of power, scale of, 89–90
as transmission of a negative sanction for a positive
sanction, 300
Coercive emotions, to maintain social control, 74
Cognition
indirect effect on health, 600
interaction with emotion, 39
neuroscience approach to, 56–57
interdependence with emotion, 262–263
relationship with emotion, 55–59, 179–202
and structure of the self, Mead's view, 255
Cognitive appraisal, of differences expressed in group
task discussions, 352
Cognitive bias, of sociological approaches to the self,
256–258
Cognitive dimension, of jointness, in affect theory of
social exchange, 312
Cognitive dissonance theory, 228
Cognitive liberation, as belief in the power of protest,
615–616
Cognitive outcomes, of empathic processes, 452–453
Cognitive processes
advanced, leading to empathic outcomes, 445–446
in empathy, 469
simple, leading to empathic outcomes, 445
Cognitive psychology, emotions as defined in,
55–56
Cognitive reflexivity, 116
Cognitive representations, in empathy, 446
Cognitive strategies, for emotion management, 125
Cognitive theory, of emotion, 15
Cognitive work, on global emotions, 302
Collective action, variables in, 615
Collective consciousness, 136–137
Collective effervescence
defined, 135
focused, and rhythmic activity, 136
group-focused solidarity in, 138
individual-focused emotional energy in, 138
in social movements, 622
Collective identity, defined, 617

Collective memory, retaining the dead in, 528–529
College professors, emotional labor of, 574
comparison of blacks and whites, 576
Commercialization, of emotion management, 127–128
Commitment, defined as attachment to a social unit, in
relational cohesion theory, 305
Commodification of love, 400–401
Communication, through displays of emotion, 364, 370
Communities, of sympathy, 484–485
Companionate love, defined, 393
Comparative view
of envy, 428–429
of jealousy, 413–415
Comparison level (CL), as an internal standard, 299
Compassionate love, relationship with socially supportive
behavior, 396
Compassion fatigue, from demands for sympathy, 474
Complementarity, logic of, in socioemotional exchange,
476
Complicated grief, 531–532
after death of an individual from a previous attachment,
533
Concealment, to avoid envy, 429
Concepts
involved in sympathy, 469
transpersonal nature of, 141–146
Conceptualization, of anger, 494–495
Confidence
and collective action, 627
and recruitment to social movements, 619–620
Conflicts
from competing sets of beliefs, 161–162
as exchange of negative sanctions, 300
as intensely focused interaction, 138
lack of shared emotion in, 139–140
between valued and stigmatized identities, 165–166
Confluent love, and the democratization of intimacy,
398–399
Congruence
between identity standard meanings and
self-in-situation meanings, 3, 227
between self-perceptions and self-standards, 236
Connectedness, threads of, and grief, 118–119
Connections
of the justice evaluation function, 330
loss of, by survivors, 533
Conscience collective, defined, 137
Conscious domain, of mental life, changes in, 277
Consciousness
collective, 136–137
"feeling feelings" as the basis for, 298
of feelings versus emotions, 55
place in evolutionary development, 53
Consequent emotions, 101–103
defined, 97
Considerate social style, measuring, 459
Constitutive model, sentiments in, 359, 362–363

Construction, cultural
  of grief, 521–523
  of love, 399–400
Constructionism
  classification of emotions from the perspective of, 15
  grief from the perspective of, 522
Constructivism, emotions from the perspective of, 259
Contemporary classification, 14–15
Contempt, link to violation of the moral code of the
      community, 554
Content, of unconscious emotion, 51
Context
  cultural, expression of emotional responses, 270–271
  and emotional practices, 159–164
  of experienced emotion, in justice analysis, 333
  family, of anger, 498–501
  justice evaluation in, 329
  neighborhood, anger in, 501–503
  social, of anger provocation, 495–501
  for systems and learning, 151–152
  See also Settings; Social context
Context conditioning, roles of the hippocampus and
      amygdala in, 48
Contextual nature, of gender-emotion stereotypes, 68–71
Control
  over emotional labor, 129
    in law firms, study, 131
  over mate choice, 398
  sense of, and anger, 507–509
  over subordinates, reactions to failure of, 169
  See also Social control
Control identity, 204
Controllability, and responsibility, 23–24
Control principle, 186–187
Convergent evidence, validity contributed by, 40
Coping resources, for managing stressors, 601–602
Coping responses
  to negative emotions, 209
    anger, 216
  problem-focused strategies and emotion-focused, 602
Core elements, of the theory of emotions, 281–286
Core self, image-based, nonverbal self, 263
Core self-feelings, and roles of individuals in the social
      world, 266
Core symbolic interaction principle, 196–198
Corporate units, key properties of, table, 289
Corrective facework, ritual interaction in, 117
Cortical regions of the brain, interactions with subcortical
      regions, 57
Counter-role identity, defined, 204
Couple-level system, love as, 401–403
Courtroom trials, role of sympathy in, 481–484
Co-workers, role of, in satisfaction of emotional labor, 580
Criminal defendants, judgements about, empirical study,
      192–193
Cross-cultural comparison
  and the constructionist view of grief, 522–523

between German and U.S. undergraduates, affect
      control theory study, 195–196, 522
Crowds
  behavior of, as deviation from the traditional norms of
      society, 613
  theories of social movements based on, 612–614
Cults, charismatic, social mechanisms that sustain, 623
Cultural capital
  and emotional energy in interaction ritual chain theory,
      266
  and sympathy margins, 477
Cultural change, and the meanings of jealousy, 416
Cultural codes, activation of, 549
Cultural conditions, as constraints on the interaction
      order, 150
Cultural content of emotions, 116–118
Cultural labels, in the social construction of emotional
      response, 181
Cultural repertoire, and love, 400
Cultural rules, for returns on social and emotional gifts,
      475–476
Cultural schemas, of status and emotion, 353–355
Cultural theory, 114–134
Cultural variation, in emotional displays, 231
Culture
  versus content in classification of emotions, 16–17
  defined, in a unified theory of sociobehavioral
      processes, 342
  and emotion, 115
  Russian, envy in, 436–438
  Rwandan, genocide and envy in, 438–439
  and sexual scripts, 77–78
  and social movements, 616–617, 624–626
Culture-making institutions, 124

Dating relationships, gender-related difference in
      expectations about, 74–75
Decision making
  role of emotion in, 58–59
  as a selection pressure for increased emotionality, 371
Decompositions, of the justice evaluation function, 330
Deep acting, in order to follow feeling rules, 124
Deep sociality
  evolutionary basis for, 261, 369
  in human infants, 262
Defect, personal, jealousy as, 417
Defense mechanisms
  activation of, 290–292, 548–549
    by negative emotions, 560–564
  paradox of reflexivity generated by defensive strategies,
      144–145
  and targeting of emotions, table, 290
Defense system, attribution in, 291
Deference
  exchange of, for competent task efforts, 355–356,
      363–364
  power based on the ability to command, 140

Deficiency aversion, effect of sympathy and dyspathy on, 336–337
Deficit
   in power, 95–96
   in status, responses to, 93–95
Definitions, of affect control theory, 181–184. *See also* Dimensions
Deflection
   defined, for affect control theory, 187
   predicting emotional response to, empirical study, 192
Democratic Workers Party, deference to leaders in, 627
Demography of encounters, expectations over, 289
Dendrites, defined, 43
Denial
   to avoid envy, 430
   of envy, 425–427
Depression
   Cartesian dualism in treatments for, 593
   from decrease in status, 121
   effect of neighborhood problems, 501
   as emotional state and mental illness, 604
   postpartum, social construction of, 597, 626
   as a response to disagreement in a group, 352
   as a social problem, 594
   sympathy from family members in, 478–479
Diagnostic category creep, in emergence of new mental health disorders, 594
Diagnostic framing, in mass movements, 616–617
Diencephalon, structure and functions of, 48
Differences approach, for studying gender and emotion, 65
Differentiated emotions theory, 302
Dimensions
   analytic, of emotions, 258–261
   cognitive, of jointness, in affect theory of social exchange, 312
   cultural, of social movements, 616–617
   evaluation, potency, and activity, of affect control theory, 184, 625
   of evaluation, potency, and activity; active versus passive, 626
   expectation-sanction, 24
   formal category, 19
   integrative, of power, 305
   interpersonal
       of emotions, 258–259
   interpersonal-constructivist, of emotions and the self, 269–271
   interpersonal-positivist, of emotions and the self, 264–267
   intrapersonal-constructivist, of emotions and the self, 267–269
   intrapersonal-positivist, of emotions and the self, 261–263
   macro-, power and status as, 92–93
   structural, for classification of emotions, 12–13, 18
   in the study of emotions, figure, 260

   See also Evaluation, potency, and activity dimensions
Direct association, leading to empathic outcomes, 445
Directionality, as a dimension of emotion classification, 15, 24
Discovery, of envy, 424–425
Disenfranchised grief, 516, 530–531
Disengagement theory, and anger in the aged, 506
Disgust, moral
   link to the moral code of divinity, 554
   protecting the moral order with, 553–554
Displacement, Freud's definition of, 278
Display
   private and public, of grief, 522–523
   of sympathy, 469
Display rules
   cultural and gender standards for, 231
   culturally expected expressive displays as, 354
   gendered, for battered women, 167–168
   as norms, 118
   for social movement participants, 524
Distress, emotions as, 600–603
Distribution emotion family, 29
   formalization of categories of, 30
Distributive justice, in exchange theory, 3–4, 33
Divine, external, attachment to symbols of ritual, 137
Divine love, power and status in, 105
Division of labor, in human groups, 89
Doctors
   affective neutrality of, 161
   emotional detachment of, 130–131
   empathy of, for patients, 598
Doing emotion as doing gender, 63, 66–67
   for studying gender and emotion, 65
   view of men's emotional inexpressivity, 75–76
Domain relevance hypothesis, for identifying circumstances creating envy, 425
Domains
   institutional, norms emerging from, 546
   of mental life, 277
Dominance, defined, 357
Dominants, and emotions, 168–171
Double standard, sexual, 167
   as a consensual status belief, 76–77
Down time, need for, in groups, 150
D power, defined, 140
Dramaturgical stress
   from disjuncture between self and social obligation, 594–595
   measurement of, 604
   source of, 592
Dramaturgical theory
   as a foundation for symbolic interactionist study of emotion, 157
   model of the self in, 270–271
Dyspathy, in framing goods and bads for the self and other, table, 336

Ecology, of encounters, expectations over, 289
Economic costs, of emotional labor, 579–580
Economy of gratitude, in gender culture shifts, 160
Effervescence. *See* Collective effervescence
Ego, defenses developed by, 278
Elaborated cognitive networks, leading to empathic
    outcomes, 446
Elaborations, of primary emotions, 15
    first-order, 558–560
    second-order, 283, 560
Elemental emotions, in social interaction, 25
Elevation, as the opposite of disgust, 556
Embarrassment, threat of, and legitimacy of social norms,
    158
Embeddedness
    of encounters, 289
    of face-to-face interactions, 286
Embodied sociology, 591–592
Emergence versus reductionism, as a false dualism, 40–41
Emergent mentalism, defined, 41
Emergent systems, self and thinking as, 142–143
Emotional arousal, and identity nonverification,
    216–218
Emotional brain
    generalizations about, 41–42
    reasons for existence of, 39–41
Emotional capital
    of men, sources of, 169
    in a mortuary science program, study, 130
    for social movements, 195
Emotional connectedness, in dating relationships, gender
    difference in emphasis on, 75–76
Emotional consequences, of legitimacy, 356–358
Emotional contagion, mimicry as, 449–450
Emotional culture, variations in, 121–122
Emotional detachment
    of doctors, 130–131
    fostering inequality by encouraging, 163
Emotional deviance
    defined, 125–126
    emotional responses to, 232
Emotional display, dimensions of, 129–130
Emotional distress, effects of marital and parental roles
    on, 499
Emotional double bind, imposed by the culture of
    romance and presentation against stalkers, 167
Emotional effervescence, from social interaction, 266
Emotional empathy, 469
Emotional energy (EE)
    maximizing, 138–146
    negative, 292
    and social movements, 628–629
Emotional expression, defined, for intimate relationships,
    74
Emotional gifts, 474–481
Emotionality, association with the female/feminine, 63–64
Emotional practices, and contexts, 159–164

Emotional processes, in social exchange theory, 301–305
Emotional responses, qualitatively distinct, 240–241
Emotional socialization
    learning, 122–123
    research on, 123–124
    in the workplace, 572–573
Emotion-based self theory, 254–275
Emotion culture, 269–271
Emotion differentiation, levels of, 20–34
Emotion-focused copying, 602
Emotion management
    in an animal shelter, example, 161–162
    cues of, 603
    of health professionals, 596
    with surface and deep acting, 270–271
    in theoretical justice analysis, 334
    voluntary versus required, in the workplace, 581
Emotions
    basic, with deep neurological modules, 372
    coercive, role-taking and, 158
    the concept of, 297–298
    defined, 16, 183
        from an evolutionary point of view, 53
        for expectation states theory, 347
    defining, 115
    describing in affect control theory, 188–190
    and gender hierarchies, 2
    and grief, 523–525
    indirect pathways of, 599–600
    intense and uncontrollable, for maintenance of
        identities, 207
    interaction with cognition, 55–59
    as internal rewards and punishments, 299
    in justice processes, 332–334
    and the justice reflections, 334
    linking with the social, 158–159
    negative, source of in identity theory, 205
    neuroscience approach to, 56–57
    predicting, 107
    second-order, 547
    separation from feeling, 52–53
    in social movements, rediscovering, 617–624
    symbolic interactionism perspective on, 155–178
    in a unified theory of sociobehavioral processes, 342
Emotion work, 127–128, 156–157, 569–570
    of college professors, 574, 576
    control over, 129
        in law firms, study, 131
    of nurses, 596–597
    psychosocial costs of, 577–579
    psychosocial outcomes of, 571
    situations involving, 271
    of women, as furthering oppression, 171–173
    See also Gender, emotional work
Empathic accuracy paradigm, 452–453
Empathic concern (EC) scale, 448
    research about, 453–454

Empathy, 443–466
  defined, 443–444, 554
  as part of sympathy, 469
  of physicians for patients, 598
Empirical evidence, for relational cohesion theory,
    306–311
Empirical studies
  support from, for self-evaluation and emotional
    responses, 236, 241
  using affect control theory, 191–193
Empirical work, on emotion culture, 118–121
Employment, paid, emotional control in, 129
Emulation, differentiating from envy, 427–428
Encounter, elements of, 117
Encounter group, pressure to express dramatic expression
    norms in, 596
Engulfment, diminishing returns from ritual due to, 150
Enhancement imperative, 378–379
Entitled grief, 530–531
Entitlement, perceived, and expressions of anger, 73–74
Environmental resources, for coping, 602
Environment of evolutionary adaptedness (EEA), 372
Envy, 410–412
  defined, 412, 424
  distinguishing from other emotions, 424–439
  and jealousy, 421
E power, defined, 140
Equations
  for describing deflection, 187
  for describing social events, 185–186
  for predicting emotional response, 188–190
Equilibrium, in meanings assigned to an interaction, 180
Ethnicity
  and emotional work, 575–577
  and expression of grief, 536–537
  and relationship to illness, 597
Euphoria, of love, 391
Evaluation, potency, and activity (EPA) dimensions, of
    affect control theory, 28–29, 184
  and social movements, 625
Evolution
  as narrative, 40
  social, and emotions, 375–383
Evolutionary analysis, of the origins of human emotion, 4
Evolutionary biology, of emotions, 370–378
Evolutionary existentialism, 369–370
Evolutionary origins, of empathy, 447–448
Evolutionary perspective, on the unconscious, 53–54
Evolutionary psychology, and natural selection, 372
Evolutionary theory
  and emotions, 368–385
  love in, 397
  of the origins of localization of emotion processing,
    49–51
Exchange
  defined, generalized and reciprocal, 313–314
  generalized, defined, 313–314

  as mutual transmission of positive sanctions, 300
  productive
    defined, 313–314
    test of in relational cohesion research, 309–311
  of sympathy, principles in the socioemotional economy,
    476–481
  See also Social exchange
Exchange logics, reciprocity in, about sympathy, 480
Exchange networks, experimental manipulation of dyadic
    exchange embedded in, 308
Exchange payoffs
  failure to realize, and negative emotional energy, 292
  positive, need for, 287–288
Exchange relations
  frequency as the basis of, 305
  from repeated transmission of positive sanctions, 300
Exchange theory, 3–4
  and emotions, 32–33
  social, and emotions, 295–320
Exclusive connections, defined, 314
Exodus, and emotion rewards, 381–383
Expectations
  of death, and grief, 520
  as a dimension of interactions, 15
  dimensions of, 23–24
  and interactions, 283
  notation for, 25
  power and status in terms of, 28
  shared, in groups, 149
Expectation-sanction dimensions, 24
Expectation states theory, 23, 347–366
  application to gender, 65–66
  and gender-emotion beliefs, 63
Experience, deep, claims to, to enhance status, 94
Experienced justice evaluation function, 329
Exploitation, of subordinates who are satisfying with
    relationships with dominants, 172
Expressed justice evaluation function, 329
Expression rules, for expression of grief, 119
Expressive behaviors, solidarity maintained through, 348
Expressiveness
  extravagant, as nurturing at the expense of power and
    control, 70
  gestures of, 115
Expressiveness coefficient
  and emotion display, in theoretical justice analysis, 333
  transformation of the experienced to the expressed
    justice evaluation, 332–333
Expressiveness-impartiality, in theoretical justice
    analysis, 337
External engagements, of social movements, 623–624

Face
  claiming, defined, 138
  defined, 117, 141
  restoring, 117–118
Facial expressions, association with anger, 494

Facticity, as a transactional need, 288
Fairness
    in exchange theory, 3–4
        defined, 33
        and social movements, 629–630
    resulting from fear of being envied, 431
Families of emotions, comparative, 25–31
Family
    as the context of anger, 498–501
    emotions of, in dealing with illness, 597
Family control system, for learning emotional labor, 128
Fantasy (FS) scale, 448
Fate control, defined, 299
Fear
    and collective action, 627
    as emotional capital for social movements, 195
    of emotions, 612–617
    of envy, 429
    from intentional decrease in status, of a partner, 121
    study of relationship with consciousness, 53–54
    transition emotion class of, 22
Feeling
    and culture, 523
    currency of, 474
    role of the cingulate cortex in, 47
    separation from emotion, 52–53
Feeling rules, 118
    constraint on, by therapeutic ideologies, 596
    culturally expected emotional responses as, 354
    governing sympathy, data sources for research about, 173–174
    proper responses to, 156
    regarding death, 119
    in the social construction of emotional response, 181
    social emergents circumscribed by, 269–271
    for social movement participants, 524
    supporting gender ideologies about household labor, 120–121
    about sympathy, 468, 480
    about the timing and management of grief, 530
Feminization, of love, 399
Financial issues, in the family, anger provoked by, 499–500
Five-Factor model (FFM), for assessing personality, 92
Flexibility
    of the brain, 42
    in gender performance, 67
Focused interactions
    intensity of, 139
    as ritual, 135–136
Forces
    macro- and mesolevel, table, 285
    microlevel, table, 285
    social reality driven by, 283
Forgiveness, and empathy, 446, 454–455
Formal category dimensions, 19
Formal construction, of emotion categories, 17

Formalization
    of comparative emotions, 29–31
    of elemental emotions, 25
    of emotion syndromes, 33–34
    equations to describe impression formation, 185–186
    of subtle emotions, 31–32
Formal mapping, of emotion categories, 17
Formal structure, of affect control theory, 184–190
Frames
    emotional effect of, future research on, 628
    injustice, in protest, 617, 623
Framework
    integrative, for the sociology of emotions, self theory as, 224–229
    for justice analysis, 323
    organizational, for empathy, 444–447
    for studying gender and emotion, 65–68
Framing
    of grief
        of children, 535
        in metaphor, 529–532
    of mass movements, for recruitment, 616–617
Framing coefficient, in theoretical justice analysis, 333
Framing-impartiality, 335–336
Fraud, in claims to sympathy, 477–480
Freedom, as a power issue, 92
Function, social, of jealousy, 413
Functional magnetic resonance imaging (fMRI), data on areas of the brain involved in love, 391
Fundamental actors, in justice analysis, 323
Fundamental contexts, for justice analysis, 327
Fundamental distributions, in justice analysis, 326–327
Fundamental forces, in a unified theory of sociobehavioral processes, 341
Fundamental functions, for justice analysis, 324–325
Fundamental matrices, observer-by-rewardee, 325–326
Fundamental quantities of justice analysis, 324
Future
    explorations of emotion-based self theory, 271–272
    explorations of empathy, 460–462
    explorations of social exchange theory, 315
    questions for research about gender systems, 78
    of research on emotions and health, 604
    of scholarship on love, 401–405

Gay support groups
    identity work in, 164–165
    religious, study of, using affect control theory, 194–195
Gender
    and display of sympathy, 473
    and emotion, 63–82
    and emotional work, 166, 580
        in the workplace, 574–575
    and grief, 536–537
    hierarchies of
        and emotion, 2
        and emotional labor, 131

as an indicator of status, study of identity nonverification, 219–220

in interactions of protest groups with outsiders, 623–624

norms of, and social movements, 618

and rating of love, 396

and rewards for exhibiting emotions, 621–622

and social distribution of anger, 504–505

Gender ideology, and household division of labor, 120–121

Gender solidarity, male, evolutionary origin of, 379–380

Gender strategies, to manage disjuncture between ideology and feeling, 120–121

Genera, of subtle emotions, 31

General function, for justice evaluation, 327–328

Generalizations, of emotion theory, 286

Generalized exchange, defined, 313–314

Genetic selection, of the capacity to adapt to the group, 143

Gift giving, group cohesion as the proximate cause of, 311

Gifts, sympathy in the realm of, 473

Goal impediment, and anger, 501

Goods, defined for justice analysis, 323–324

Gossip, as an outward expression of envy, 412, 424

Grandiose self-image, and unstable self-esteem, negative emotions predicted by, 239

Gratitude, as a means of social cohesion, 555–556

Greed

the institutional demands of work as, 498

to manage envy, 435

Grief, 516–543

defined, 518

emotion culture content of, 118

meanings of, 518–520

Grief work

defined, 527–528

for management of grief, 530

Group cohesion, effects on, of positive emotion and uncertainty reduction, 310–311

Group-focused solidarity, as an emotion in collective effervescence, 138

Group Goal Facilitation factor, 88

Group identity, and relational cohesion, 309

Group inclusion, as a transactional need, 288

Groups

defined, in a unified theory of sociobehavioral processes, 342

homogeneous, performance expectations in, 350–351

Group Sociability factor, 88

as status, 91

Group therapy, health benefits of, 599

Guilt

behaviors causing a sense of, 552

compensatory action to reinstate an individual, 100

as an example of the moralizing role for emotions, 370

interaction with grief, 519

longitudinal study of, 552

maladaptive, 552

as a self-critical moral emotion, 550–553

as a tool to undermine the social order, 555

twin study assessing the genetic and environmental effects of, 547

Habituation, as an example of preconscious discounting, 377

Happiness

findings in studies of, 383

from increase in status, 121

in a unified theory of sociobehavioral processes, 342

Hard wiring

and moral emotion development, 546–548

for selected emotions, 372

Hassles, stress from, defined, 601

Health

and emotions, 591–610

emphasis on promotion of, versus dominant medical practices, 597

mental, reconceptualizing as emotional health, 593–594

pathways to

direct, physiological activation by emotion, 599–603

indirect, behavioral and cognitive effects, 599–603

physical, relationship with stress, social support, and coping, 602

See also Mental illness

Heaven's Gate (organization), deference to leaders in, 627

Helping, and empathy, 455–460

Hierarchies

of gender

and emotion, 2

and emotion work, 131

maintaining, 78

of identities, self as self-conceptions in terms of, 265

micro-

the roles of sympathy in, 474–475

and sympathy margins, 477

prominence, defined, 205

social

and emotions, 626

and status beliefs, 65–66

within social movements, 627

See also Salience hierarchy; Status hierarchy

Hippocampus, role in memory, 47–48

Historical context

of emotional experiences, 159–161

of grief, constructionist view, 522

Historical social transformations, and the expression of love, 398–399

History

access to material resources through, 149–150

of a system, and the dynamics of interaction between elements of, 152

Holistic therapeutic community, adaptation of clients to the expectations of, 597

Homogeneity, of categoric unit membership, and positive
    emotions, 290–292
Hopes, transition emotion class of, 22
Humility, to increase status, 94
Humor
    for decreasing resistance to influence, 73–74
    for defusing embarrassment, 127
    for enhancing status, 95
    for managing emotions in medical encounters, 596
Hypothalamus, functions of, 48

Id, defined, 277
Ideal love, 103
Identification, projective, and grief, 521
Identities, 27–29
    background, gender as, 66
    group-based, expressive strategies for emotion
        management in, 126
    maintaining in a social situation, 186–187
    power and status relations in, 32
    role
        defined, 203–204
        effect of nonverification of, 215
    role-based, strategies for emotion management in, 126
    of the self
        in different roles, 203
        hierarchy of, 548
Identity
    collective, defined, 617
    commitment to, in identity theory, 206–207
    disruption in the control system of, 210–211
    effect of emotions and beliefs on, 164
    frequency of interruption, and emotional arousal,
        218–219
    qualitative dimension of, due to depth of ties, 206–207
    standard for, 27
        changing, 242–243
    in a unified theory of sociobehavioral processes, 342
    verification of
        in the family, and anger over threats to, 500
        lack of and emotional arousal, 219–220
    See also Social identity
Identity control theory
    comparison with affect control theory, 196–198
    on interpersonal verification of salient identities, 258,
        265
Identity theory, 2–3
    and emotions, 203–223
    research about, 173
    salience and verification of identities in, 264
    sanctions and expectations in, 27
Identity work, as an emotional process, 164–166
Ideologies
    and levels of emotional codes, 545–546
    and sustained social inequalities, 168–173
Idiosyncratic meanings of roles, 205
    negotiation about in interactions, 204

Imagined social situations, emotions evoked by, empirical
    study, 192
Impartiality, in the justice process, 334–339
    empirical assessment of, 339–341
Impression, change in, 185–186
Impression management
    appearance of rationality as a technique for, 161
    working together to save face, 157
Inauthenticity, in jobs requiring emotional labor, study,
    578
Inclusive connections, defined, 314
Indirect expression, of envy, 426
Individual-focused emotional energy, in collective
    effervescence, 138
Individualism
    excessive, of American culture, 423–424
    and love, 399–400
Individual Prominence and Achievement factor, 88
    characteristics of, 91
Individuals
    characteristics of, in mass movements, 612
    differences among, in capacity for empathy, 444
        Questionnaire Measure of Emotional Empathy
            (QMEE), 448
Industrial societies, jealousy in, 414–415
Inequality
    and emotion rewards, 379–380
    link with love, 402
    perceived, and anger, 503
    rationalization of, and management of envy in society,
        433–434
    and self, in the culture of emotions, 166–168
    social, and ideology, 168–173
    understanding the reproduction of, 155
    in a unified theory of sociobehavioral processes, 342
Inequity, perceived, and anger provocation, 498
Informational support, 602
Information processing, complex emotionality as the key
    to, 370
Injustice frames, in protest, 617, 623
Instrumental support, defined, 601–602
Insula, feeling processed by, 47
Integrative framework, for the sociology of emotions, self
    theory as, 224–229
Intensity
    of emotions, and social or role identities, 236
    of grief, 519–520
    of love, and style of love, 394–395
    of negative emotions, 564
    of primary emotions, 372
    of response to negative emotions, 209–210
    of the triggered emotion, matching in justice analysis,
        333
Intentionality, of emotions, 56
Interactional emphasis, of identity theory, 205–206
    research from, 207–208
Interaction emotion family, 29

Interaction order, in ritual theory,
136
constraints on, 149–152
dynamics of, 137–140
Interaction ritual chain (IRC) theory
applications to empirical problems, 140
cultural capital and emotional energy in, 266
linking past, present and future, 139
thinking in, connection to network position, 142
Interaction ritual theory, 2, 135
and acquisition of emotional energy, 264
Interactions
dimensions of, from studies, 88
informal, ritual in, 137–138
Interaction theory
assumptions of, about directionality of interactions, 24
formalization of dimensions of, 30–31
interaction of biophysical, personal, and structural
environments in, 594–595
INTERACT software program, for use with affect control
theory, 190–191
Interchanges, of human emotions, 468
Interdependence, role of, in exchange theories, 300
Intergenerational shame-anger cycle, 281
Internal dynamics, of social movements, 621–622
Interpersonal accuracy, and empathy, 446, 452–453
Interpersonal Circle (IPC), for assessing personality, 92
Interpersonal-constructivist dimensions, of emotions and
the self, 269–271
Interpersonal control, and anger, 500–501
Interpersonal dimension, of emotions, 258–259
Interpersonal interaction, schematic content of the self
stemming from, 268
Interpersonal outcomes, empathic, 446–447, 455–460
Interpersonal-positivist dimensions, of emotions and the
self, 264–267
Interpersonal Reactivity Index (IRI), 448
Interpretive mechanism, of the left hemisphere of the
brain, 44–45
Intrapersonal-constructivist dimensions, of emotions and
the self, 267–269
Intrapersonal outcomes, of empathic processes, 446,
451–455
Intrapersonal-positivist dimensions of emotions and the
self, 261–263
Investment principle, in self-verification theory, 217

Jealousy, 412–424
association with passionate love, 394
defined, 208, 411
and envy, 410–442
confusion between, 426
differentiating, 427
Job authority, links with anger, 497
Jointness, of an exchange task, and the social unit as a
source of global emotion, 311–313
Jurors, factors affecting sympathy of, 483

Justice
expectation states for, in networks, 550
sense of, among monkeys, 547
as a status issue, 92
time series profile, 331
in a unified theory of sociobehavioral processes, 342
Justice analysis, 322–327
Justice evaluation, 324
Justice evaluation function (JEF), 325, 327–331
Justice processes, emotion in, 321–346
Just reward
defined, 324
sources of, and types of emotion, 333
true, means for estimating, 337–339
Just reward function (JRF), 324–325

Kingdoms of emotion, 21

Labeling
of emotion categories, 17
leading to empathic outcomes, 445
prototypical versus structural dimension, 12–13
Language
development of, from communication of emotion, 373
and development of the self, 255
effects of, on emotional expression, 122
emotional, evolution of, 262
emotional scripting with, 163–164
of the mind, versus emotion, 39
Language-mediated association, leading to empathic
outcomes, 445–446
Lateralization, of the brain, 44–45
Leaders, of social movements, interactions with followers,
622–623
Learned helplessness, in response to uncontrollable events
blocking goals, 219
Learning
capacity for, and solidarity, 143
of jealousy, 421–422
Legislation, effects on, of sympathy, 485
Legitimacy
dynamics of, 355–358
emotional consequences of, 356–358
of a status hierarchy, 355–356
Levels
of differentiation, 19–20
in the justice evaluation, 330–331
Libido, defined, 276–277
Life effects, stress from, defined, 601
Liking
defining, 106–107
versus love, 393
See also Love
Limbic system, debate about, 49–51
Literature
of grief, 517–518
of love, integration of, 404

Lived experience
  of the body, in emotion and health, 603
  of the self, 267–269
Looking glass self, 115, 180–181, 280
Loss
  of animate objects, 534–535
  categories of, 534
  of a couple's relationship, and the nature of love, 403
  of inanimate object, grief in, 535–536
  leading to grief, 516
  prevention of, and social movements, 524
Love, 389–409
  nonvolitional nature of, 105–106
  as a relationship, defined, 103
"Love is blind", neurological evidence for, 391
Love scale (Rubin), 394
Luck, concept of, and management of envy in society, 433

Macrodimensions, power and status as, 92–93
Macrojustice, estimates of principles of, 327
Macrosociology, on shaping of emotions by society and
        culture, 411
Macrostructural events, and population-level shame and
        anger, Germany before World War II, 281
Management
  of emotions, 124–126
  of envy in society, 431–434
  of jealousy, 417–418, 422–423
Manly emotion, defined, 70
Markers
  for maleness/masculinity and femaleness/femininity,
        66–67
  somatic, for storing symbols attached to bodily
        responses, 143
Marriage rules, and the expressions of jealousy
        appropriate to a culture, 413–414
Mastery of a task, in groups, effects of agreement or
        disagreement with an actor, 351–352
Mate choices, influence of social networks on,
        403
Material conditions
  as a constraint on involvement in ritual activity,
        149–150
  for women, consequences of emotional experiences of
        pleasure and romance, 172
Measurement
  of dramaturgical stress, 604
  of sympathy
    not too little, 479–480
    not too much, 478
Media, as culture-making institutions, 124
Medical model, of grief, 527–528
Memorials, and grief, 524–525
Memories
  collective, retaining the dead in, 528–529
  consolidating, by the amygdala, 47
  and feeling, studies of, 54–55

Mental health, reconceptualizing as emotional health,
        593–594
Mental illness
  biomedical model of, acceptance or refutation, 593
  grief by a family member over, 536–537
  sympathy for a family member in, 478–479
Mentalism, the appeal of, 51–52
Mentor love, power and status in, 105
Mesosociology, on the utility of emotions, 411
Methodological perspective, for interactionist studies of
        emotion, 173–174
Microdynamic processes, 288–289
Microfoundations, for social exchange theorizing, 296
Microhierarchical arrangements
  place, and sympathy margins, 477
  the roles of sympathy in, 474–475
Micropolitics
  of emotion, power and status in, 64
  and sympathy, 480–481
Microsociology, on learning of emotions, 411
Midlevel forces, in a unified theory of sociobehavioral
        processes, 341
Mimicry, motor, leading to empathic outcomes, 445,
        449–450
Mind, communal nature of, 43
Misconceptions, about jealousy, 421–423
Moderator model, and influence of salient sentiments in
        groups, 359, 363
Moderators
  of self-enhancing or self-protective patterns, 243–244
  between self-evaluation and emotional response,
        238–239
Modernity, and grief, 525, 529
Moods, defined, 183–184
Moral codes, levels of, 545
Moral emotions, 544–566
  characteristics of, 556–560
  and political rhetoric, 619–620
Moral identity, 204
Morality
  and emotion, 371
  nature of, 544–546
  of protest, 629–630
Moralizing role, for emotions, 370
Moral order, moral emotions and, 564
Moral panics, defined, 628
Moral work, in social movements, 620
Mother identity, salience of, and jealousy, 208
Motivational framing in mass movements, 616–617
Motivational outcomes, of empathic processes, 446
Motivational state
  change in, as an outcome of empathy-related processes,
        454–455
  love defined as, 391
Mourning, defined, 518
Multiple-reward-per-rewardee study, rating instructions,
        343

Multiple-reward-per-reward study of justice of earnings, 344
Multiple simultaneous justice evaluations, 330
Mutual verification, of identities, outcomes of, 213–214
Mythopoetic men, identity work of, 169–170

Narcissism
    defense mechanisms in, 562
    relationship with shame and guilt, 551
    as a response to negative self-feelings, 243
Natural selection, and synaptic alteration, 379
Nazism, accounting for, in pride and shame, 619
Need dispositions, defined, 226
Needs
    behavior that permits satisfaction of, 241–242
    defined, 234
    fundamental, 281–282
    and self-feelings, 234–235
Negative affects, mobilization by, 623
Negative emotions, directing at social structures, 550
Negative sentiments, influence on acceptance of
        influence, 362
Negative state relief (NSR) model, helping in, 455
Negotiated exchange, defined, 313–314
Negotiation
    to obtain mutually sustaining identities, 205
    of sympathy, participants and processes, 468
Neocortex
    change in the evolution of humans, 371
    defined, 45–46
Network processes, cohesion and form of exchange, 315
Networks
    elaborated cognitive, leading to empathic outcomes,
        446
    exchange
        branch and stem forms, 308–309
        experimental manipulation of dyadic exchange
            embedded in, 308
    organization of thinking in, 142
    pulsating connections in, 151
    religion as an extender for connections in, 379
    social, perspective on love, 403–404
    social structures as, 549–550
    types of connections in, 314
Neurological effects, of emotions, 298
Neuronal channels, between emotional centers and
        cognitive centers of the brain, 39
Neuroscience, of emotions, 38–62
Neurotransmitters, effects of, on dendrites, 43
Nonverbal behavior, gender differences in, mirroring
        power and status differences, 72
Normality, of emotion, 21
Normative appeals, about status, 93–94
Normative theory of emotions versus power-status theory,
        108–109
Norms
    of emotion, and social movements, 618

    for emotion work, development by an occupational
        group, 598
    of encounters in face-to-face interactions, 546
    institutional, indications of actions in, 546
    procedural, of justice, 629–630
Nostalgia retrieval, to enhance status, 95
Notations
    for describing emotions, 22–23
    for describing long-term power and status attributions,
        28–29
Nurturant social skills, effect of, on wages, 580

Observer
    characteristics of, that influence empathy, 444
    independence of mind of, in justice analysis, 323
Orders of emotions, 22–25
Organizational conditions, emotional norms fostering, 163
Organizational contexts, and emotions, 161–164
Organizational dynamics, linking emotions to the self, 266
Organizational theory, and social movements, 614–615
Other, responsibility of, 23–24
Other-critical moral emotions, 553–554
Other-praising moral emotions, 555–556
Other-suffering, 554–555
Outcomes
    affective, of empathic processes, 446, 453–454
    of assigning responsibility for identity disruption,
        214–215
    cognitive, of empathic processes, 452–453
    motivational, of empathic processes, 446
    primordial sociobehavioral, 341–343
    of social exchange, 297
    See also Interpersonal outcomes, empathic
Oxytocin, control of release of, by the hypothalamus, 48

Pain, social and cultural variations in, 594
Parallel emotion, in empathy, 446
Parent-infant love, power and status in, 105
Parents
    grief of, 535
    love of, power and status in, 105
Passionate love
    defined, 393
    scale for, 394
Paternalism
    emotions associated with, using coercively, 73–74
    and romantic love, 400
Pathological defense mechanisms, action of the
        experience of negative emotions, 246
Pathological emotional responses, 237
Peer group, for practicing emotion, 67
Perception
    differences in, associated with anger, 495
    emphasis on control of, in identity theory, 208–215
    of similarity, and liking, 359
Perception action mechanism (PAM), 450
Perceptual control, and identity theory, 215–220

Performance, in ritual theory, 140
Performance expectations, 350
   as a determinant of legitimacy in a group, 355–356
   effects of sentiments and emotions on, 362–363
Personal distress (PD)
   research about, 453–454
   scale for, 448
Personality, defined, in a unified theory of sociobehavioral
     processes, 342
Personal style, comprised of "as if" loops, 144
Person identities, defined, 204
Persons, defined, in a unified theory of sociobehavioral
     processes, 342
Perspective taking (PT)
   and aggression, 458
   and the capacity for empathy, 450–451
   scale for, in assessing the capacity for empathy, 448
   studying, future research directions, 460–461
Phyla of emotions, 21
Physical empathy, 469
Physical environments, noxious, in the workplace, 498
Physical health, relationship with stress, social support,
     and coping, 602
Physician-patient interaction, role of emotion in,
     596–597
Physiological basis of emotions, and the social
     psychological development of infants, 261–262
Physiology
   of the brain, 43
   and emotion, effects of emotional suppression, 599
Place attachment, and grief, 535–536
Pleasure/satisfaction
   effect on behavioral commitment, empirical evidence,
     306–308
   in protest, in social movements, 622
Polarity
   in emotion categories, 14–15
   in kingdoms of emotions, 20
Politics
   of envy management, 434–436
   micropolitics
     of emotion, power and status, 64
     and sympathy, 480–481
   role of emotions in understanding, 193–198
Positive sentiments, 361–362
Positivism, emotions from the perspective of, 259
Positron emission tomography (PET) scans, to follow
     activation of brain regions, 54–55
Postpartum depression, social construction of, 597, 626
Poststructuralism, views on grief, 518
Potential principle, in sympathy worthiness assessments,
     472
Potlatch, to reduce envy, 430
Power
   adequacy of, and safety or security, 98–99
   and anger, 507–509
   defined, 89–90, 121

as a dimension of emotion, 14, 27–28
displays of, and emotions, 70
evolution of, as the primary organizational principle for
     human groups, 374–375
excessive, leading to guilt, 98
in the family context, and anger, 500
and the feminization of love, 399
and gender
   differences in emotional behaviors, 71
   men's and women's beliefs about, 77, 160
indirect forms of attaining compliance with, 90
and jealousy, 420–421
of the other, and corresponding emotions, 99
relative, defined, 305
and status, moral emotions entailed in, 549
and status dynamics, 289
as a theme in analyses of gender, 64
total, defined, 305
types of, in ritual theory, 140
in a unified theory of sociobehavioral processes, 342
Power dependence theory
   network-embedded dyads in, 299–300
   relative and total power in, 305
Power-identity syndromes, formalization of, 33–34
Power-status theory, 96–107
   versus normative theory of emotions, study, 108–109
   predictions about anger in, 509
Practical uses of empathy, research on, 461–462
Preconscious arousal release rules, support for expanded
     social networks in, 376–384
Preconscious discounting, of emotional rewards,
     377–378
Preconscious domain of mental life, 277
Predictions
   of the effect of network connections, affect theory of
     social exchange, 315
   of emotions, 107
     from identity control theory, 216
     from power and status, 72–73
   of forms of exchange, affect theory of social exchange,
     313–314
   of theoretical justice analysis, examples, 332
Preferences, conscious and unconscious, influence on
     thought and behavior, 39
Prefrontal lobe, damage to, effect on decision making,
     58–59
Prejudices
   codification of, 564
   moderation of emotional responses to, 239
Prestige, and status dynamics, 289
Pride
   activation as a result of, 619–620
   and recruitment to collective action, 618–619
Primary circular reaction, leading to empathic outcomes,
     445
Primary emotions
   elaborations of, table, 284

from facial analysis, 370
lists of, 261
negative, 283
variations of, 557–558
Primordial sociobehavioral outcomes (PSO), 341–343
Problem, of examining and explaining order producing
  effects of emotions, 296–298
Problem-focused coping, 602
Problem solving, emotional energy and cultural capital
  used for, 145
Process
  anger, social causes of, 495–503
  dynamic, groups sustained by, 151
  emotional, in social exchange theory, 301–305
  of generation of empathy in the observer, 445–446
  justice, emotion in, 321–346
  microdynamic, 288–289
  network, 146–147
    cohesion and form of exchange, 315
  relational metaprocesses, 93–96
  self, 3
  of social exchange, role of emotions in, 297, 449–451
  sociobehavioral, unified theory of, 341–343
  versus structure, in self theory, 256
  See also Cognitive processes
Productive exchange
  defined, 313–314
  test of, in relational cohesion research, 309–311
Professional schools, role in emotional socialization,
  572–573
  medical schools, 596
Prognostic framing in mass movements, 616–617
Prohibitions, of envy, 432
Projection, repression in the form of, 562
Prominence hierarchy, defined, 205
Propaganda, to nullify power of the other, 96
Properties, of the justice evaluation function, 328
Protection, of relationships with jealousy, 413
Protest, in social movements, description of, 612–613
Protestant ethic, assumptions about grief in, 530
Protocols, for sympathy exchanges, 477
Proto-self, emotions of, 263, 267–268
Prototype approach, to love, 396
Prototypical labeling, 12–13
Psychoanalytic approaches, to political organization, 619
Psychoanalytic sociological theories, and emotions,
  276–294
Psychoanalytic theory, redirection of, 279–280
Psychodynamics, of moral emotions, 560–564
Psychoevolutionary approach, 13–14
Psychological approaches, to love, 393–397
Psychological resources, for coping, 602
Psychology, of jealousy, 422
  and sociology, 423–424
Psychometric approach, for describing emotion, 301–302
Psychophysiological responses, to identify stress, 237
Psychosocial costs of emotional labor, 577–579

Psychosocial outcomes of emotional labor, 571
Public health research, on social status of groups, and
  morbidity and mortality, 604

Quadrangle, jealousy as a, 413
Questions
  about love as an emotion, 389–393
  about workplace emotional management, 571–572

Race
  and beliefs about men's and women's behavior, 68
  and emotional work, 575–577
  interaction with socioeconomic class, to affect health
    through stress, 601
Rates of change, in a unified theory of sociobehavioral
  processes, 341
Rating task
  for empirical assessment of impartiality, 339
  for justice evaluation, 339
Rational actor models, of social movements, 614–615
Rational-choice theory
  connection with interaction ritual chains, 142
  as a microfoundation for social exchange theorizing,
    296, 303–304
Reactive emotions, and empathy, 446
Realist interactionist studies, qualitative methods in, 173
Reciprocal exchange, defined, 313–314
Reciprocal relationship, love as, 402
Reciprocity
  expectation states for, in networks, 550
  among higher primates, 547
  logic of, in socioemotional exchange, 476
  in sympathy exchanges, 480
  timing of, in sympathy exchanges, 480
  in voluntary emotion management, 581–582
Recognition, of jealousy and envy, 411–412
Reconceptualization, of grief, 529–532
Reconstruction principle, in affect control theory, 187
Recovery
  from grief, 528
  rituals of small groups for, 148
Recreational activity, skill in, as a means of gaining status,
  95
Recruitment, to social movements, 619–620
  grief as a motivator in, 524
Reductionism versus emergence, as a false dualism, 40–41
Reference groups, in the justice evaluation function, 330
Reflexivity
  defined, 115, 255–256
  and emotions, 115–116
Regard, conveying by offering sympathy, 474
Regulation, emotional, lack of after prefrontal lobe
  damage, 59
Reinforcement theory, 296
Relational cohesion theory, 304–311
Relational consequences, of social exchanges, 300
Relational metaprocesses, 93–96

Relationship Assessment Scale, for measuring power
        differences in love relationships, 420–421
Relationship problem, jealousy as, 420
Religion
    neurophysiological studies of arousal release in,
        378–379
    role of evolution in the emergence of, 376
Religious communities, activism of, about United States
        policies in Central America, 620
Reparative action, as a signal that commitments are being
        honored, 564
Representation, of emotional meaning, 56
Repression
    effect on behavioral pathology, 278
    as the master defense system, 286
    in response to intensity and frequency of shame, 553
    of shame, 560–564
    and targeting of emotions, table, 290
Research
    on the experience of grief, 534–537
    future, and self theory, 247–249
    and identity theory, 204–220
Research agenda
    for emotional labor, 128–130
    for emotional socialization, 123–124
    for emotion management, 126
    expanded measurements of affect control theory
        predictions, 198–199
    for identity theory, 220–221
    for power-status theory, 109–110
Research design
    for studying impartiality empirically, 339–340
    for studying impartiality in framing and expressiveness,
        337
Research evidence, relevant to the model of empathy,
        447–460
Respondent sample, for research about empirical
        assessment of impartiality, 340
Results, of empirical assessments of impartiality, 340–341
Retrospect, 247–249
Reward, actual, defined for justice analysis, 323–324
Rewardee, in justice analysis, 323
Rewardee sample, for empirical assessment of
        impartiality, 339
Rewards, means for generating individual, social units as,
        296
Rhythmic activity
    entrainment in interaction ritual, 138
    focused, collective effervescence generated from, 136
    history as a constraint on, 150
Rhythms, being out of sync with, and interaction failure,
        151
Righteous anger, leading to social movements, 619, 629
Rituals
    of collective sympathy, 484–485
    and emotional energy, application to social movements,
        628–629

mourning, integration into collective life through, 525
    for pointing out and correcting deviant acts, 117–118
    in preindustrial social life, 374
    role in creating the emotional and cultural foundations
        of society, 152
Ritual theory, 2, 135–154
Role captivity, and anger in a neighborhood context, 502
Role identities
    defined, 203–204
    effect of nonverification of, 215
Role performance, influence of emotions on, 207
Roles, structuring, and grief, 525–527
Role-set, workplace, interdependence in, 497
Role strains, stress from, defined, 601
Role strain theory, incompatible demands of work and
        family, and anger processes, 501
Role taking
    in empathy and sympathy, 554–555
    and guilt, 551
    leading to empathic outcomes, 446
Role-taking emotions
    coercive and controlling, 158
    self-conscious emotions as, 257–258
Romance, culture of, double standards in, 167
Romantic love
    effect of love for network members on, 404
    power and dependency in, 104

Sadness-depression, in response to insufficient power, 100
Salience, of self-evaluative standards as a moderating
        influence, 238
Salience hierarchy
    defined, 205
    roles of emotions in developing and maintaining, 265
    and self-values, 233
Salient identity
    effect of affect on, 207
    situations for enacting, 206–207
Sanctioning
    defined, 300
    dimensions of, 24
    emotional arousal determined by, 283
    notations for, 25
Sanctions, as a dimension of interactions, 15, 26
Satiation, diminishing returns from ritual due to, 150
Secondary emotional responding, example of,
        232
Self
    as agent, 23
    attributions of, from interactions, 138
    civil religion of, sympathy in, 472
    context for developing and maintaining,
        157
    deriving from ritual encounters, 137
    and emotions, 115–116
    gendered sense of, 63–64, 78
    gender performance for verifying the authenticity of,

67–68
and inequalities, in the culture of emotions, 166–168
layers of, Damasio's view, 263
as a level of social life, 142–143
loss of, and grief, 532–533
meaning of, in identity theory, 203
moral, 548–549
processes to, 143–144
as sacred symbol of interaction, 141
semiotic, 145
situational, 551–552
and thinking, 141–146
Self-attributions, negative, as a self-protective
    mechanism, 245–246
Self-cognition
    defined, 225
    and emotional experiences, 230–232
    stimulation of self-evaluations by, 232
Self-concept
    effect of emotional experiences on, 232
    specificity of content of, 227
    threats to, anger elicited by, 500
Self-conception, of emotional experiences, 230
Self-conceptualization, the self as a structured social
    process of, 256
Self-confirmation, effect of, on emotional energy,
    292
Self-conscious emotions, as role-taking emotions,
    257–258
Self-control, development of, 158
Self-critical moral emotions, 550–553
Self-defining memories, dimensions of, 236
Self-discrepancy theory, 228, 233
Self-efficacy, and anger, 500–501
Self-enhancing mechanisms, 244–245
    and self-feelings, 245–246
Self-enhancing responses, and emotions, 241–243
Self-esteem
    and jealousy, 418–420
    as a moderating influence on emotional effects of
        success or failure, 238–239
Self-evaluation
    and emotion, 235–240
    of emotional experiences/expression, 231
    self-feeling responses to, 232
    versus self-verification needs, 227–229
Self-evaluation theory, predictions about role identity
    nonverification, 229
Self-evaluative circumstances, 240–241
Self-evaluative responses, defined, 225–226
Self-expansion theory, love from the viewpoint of, 396
Self-feelings
    assessing identity in terms of, 257–258
    defined, 226
    and needs, 234–235
    self-conceptions tagged with, and ranking in the
        salience hierarchy of identities, 265

Self-identity meanings, emotions as signals about
    maintaining, 180
Self-locus, effect of, on emotional socialization, 123
Self-monitoring skills, interaction with emotional labor, in
    burnout, 578
Self-organizing systems, 151
Self-perceptions, matching with identity standard
    meanings, 209, 226
Self processes, 3
Self-protective mechanisms
    emotional responses as, 244–245
    and self-feelings, 245–246
Self-protective responses, 242–243
Self-protective/self-evaluative responses, defined, 226
Self-referent linkages, emphasis on, in self theory,
    227
Self-referent responses, emotions as, 229–230
Self-reports, about stereotypical gendered behavior, 69
Self-talk, for establishing a sense of self, 267–269
Self theory
    emotion-based, 254–275
    and emotions, 224–253
Self-values, 233
    approximating, 243
    and needs, 234
    revision of, in response to negative self-evaluation,
        242–243
    ultimate, 234
Self-verification theory, accessibility principle in, 217
Senses, as transducers, 42
Sensibility, social movements rising out of, 618–620
Sentiment
    defined, 182
        for expectation states theory, 347
    love as, 393
    modification of status hierarchies by, 361–362
    of sympathy, 469
Sentiment relations
    linking to status, 359
    mutual liking among individuals involved in, 360
Septum, structure of the brain, functions of, 48
Service economy, emotional labor in, 571
Service workers, interactive, emotional labor of,
    572–573
Settings
    for giving or receiving sympathy, 479
    for social encounters, 117
    See also Context
Sexual desire, in dating relationships, gender difference in
    emphasis on, 75–76
Sexual identity, Freud's view of, 277
Sexuality, and gender stereotypes, 74–78
Sexual scripts
    competing, for men and women, 77
    female, 76–77
    for intimacy, 64
    male, 75–76

Shame
  adaptive purpose of, 552–553
  deactivation as a result of, 619–620
  from decrease in status, 121
  defined, 551
    Lewis, 279–280
  distribution in a society, and social movements, 628
  as an example of the moralizing role for emotions, 370
  longitudinal study of, 552
  and recruitment to collective action, 618–619
  as a self-critical moral emotion, 550–553
  transforming into pride, 620
  twin study assessing the genetic and environmental
    effects in, 547
  from violating norms, 546
Shame-rage spiral, and recruitment to collective action,
    618–619
Shared expectations, in groups, 148–149
Shared poverty, and management of envy in society, 432
Sheltered workshop, conflicting conditions in, 162–163
Short-term credit, to the self experiencing negative life
    events, 549
Sibling rivalry, as jealousy, 417
Simple and mixed experienced emotions, in justice
    analysis, 333
Situation, empathy evoked by, 445, 448–449
Situational relevance, of self-values, 233
Small groups, 147–149
Smiling, frequency of, as an indication of power or status,
    72
Social behavior, and empathy, 458–460
Social bonding versus a boundary defining process,
    experimental comparison, 310–311
Social caging, 373–375
Social capital
  from bonding, 502–503
  judgements of sympathy worthiness based on, 472
  and sympathy margins, 477
Social change
  and jealousy, 415
  obstacles to, in attachment of subordinates to approval
    of dominants, 172–173
Social characteristics, of survivors, 536–537
Social class, and distribution of anger, 506–507
Social cognitive perspective, on anger, 494
Social consequences, of emotional labor, 577–579
Social constructionism
  emotions in health care, 595–598
  and grief, 521–523
  perspective on emotions in, 2, 267–268
    grief, 518
  in research on emotions and health, 595–604
Social content, and phyla of emotions, 21
Social context, 16–17
  analyzing in terms of activities, interaction, and
    sentiments, 298–299
  of social exchange, 297

stable meanings and situated meanings in, 181
Social control
  anger as a mechanism for, 508–509
  emotion as a mechanism for, 181
  through shame, 552–553
Social cues, influence on performance expectations,
    350
Social distribution, of anger, 503–507
Social emergents, emotions as, 269–271
Social environment, stress from factors in, 600–601
Social evolution
  and emotions, 375–383
  and power, 381–383
Social exchange, nature of, 300–301
Social exchange, affect theory of, 304–305, 311–316
Social exchange theory, and emotions, 295–320
Social hierarchies
  and emotions, 626
  sustaining with status beliefs, 65–66
Social identity
  defined, 204
  gender-differentiated, 231
  gender in formation and change in, 67
  response to nonverification of, 215
  status-marked aspects of the self constituting, 63
Social interactions, expectations about emotion outcomes
    of, and gender, 72–73
Socialization
  emotional, 122–123
  internalization of cultural codes as, 277
  learning self-evaluation in the process of, 232–233
  of men, and grief, 537
Social movements
  emotions in understanding, 193–198, 611–635
    the place of grief, 523–525
  motivation for, in negative emotions, 243
Social networks
  generation of, in anticipation of positive interactions,
    146–147
  perspective on love, 403–404
Social objects, and emotions, 303–304
Social order, and envy, 430–431
Social organization, arising from elaboration of emotions,
    373
Social relations
  outcomes in, and emotions, 96
  power and status dimensions of, 89
  precedence in, as a research topic, 109–110
Social sources, of the view of jealousy, 416–417
Social structural form
  classes of emotions, 21–22
  phyla of emotions, 21
Social structural perspective, 14
  on love, 397–398
Social structure
  for classification of emotion, 17
  effect on social exchanges, 300–301

of emotional labor, reproduction across generations,
130
grief in, 525–529
macro, love in, 397–398
and moral emotions, 549–556
Social support
as coping assistance, 602
for managing stressors, 601–602
Social-unit attributions, and the structure of exchange, 313
Social units
instability of, 296
as objects of value, 303–304
Social usefulness of jealousy, 421
Social worth principle, in sympathy worthiness
assessments, 472
Society
as defined in identity theory, 203
patterns of interaction creating, 157
Sociobehavioral processes, unified theory of, 341–343
Sociocultural context, circumscribing cultivation of
self-feelings, 271
Socioemotional economy, for addressing sympathy, 468,
475–476
Socioemotional support, defined, 601–602
Socioevolutionary approach, 13–14
Sociological approaches, to the self, 255–258
Sociological contributions, to concepts of grief, 531–532
Sociological perspectives, on love, 397–401
Sociological study, of envy, 436
Sociological theories
of pride and shame, 280–281
of the self, 255–256
Sociology of emotions
and health, 592–595
locating the emotion-based self in, 258–271
moral, 556–560
Sociopaths, failure of to experience moral emotions, 549
Sociophysiological integration, 110
Solidarity
affective, as the raw material for moral shocks, 620
through deep acting, Stockholm syndrome example,
139–140
of dominant groups, as process and product of
reinforcing privilege, 168
and feeling with the group, 364
separating from emotional energy, 139–140
with women objecting to generalizations, example,
193
Somatic marker hypothesis, 57–59
Sorrow, in grief, 519
Special burden principle, in sympathy worthiness
assessments, 471
Special responsibility principle, in sympathy worthiness
assessments, 472
Species, of emotion syndromes, 32–34
Specific emotions, forms of, 303–304
Specific function, justice evaluation function, 327–328

Split-brain research, 44–45
Stalkers, study of, 169
Status
adequacy of, 99
and affect, early studies, 348–349
and conformity to feeling rules, 593
defined, 121
as a dimension of emotion, 14, 27–28
emotional micropolitics of, 158
excessive, corresponding to shame/embarrassment, 99
and expression of anger, 508–509
and gender differences in expression of, 71
inferring from emotions displayed, 353
insufficient, anger and sadness-depression in response
to, 100
links with power and gender, 71
loss of, and participation in social movements, 626
and the nature of identity discrepancy, 212
other's
adequacy of, 100
insufficient, 101
power and prestige as components of, 549
relationship with power, 90–92
shaping of, by emotions and sentiments, 358–364
and solidarity, 354
in a unified theory of sociobehavioral processes, 342
Status characteristics, salience of, and performance
expectations, 350
Status competition, zero-sum element to, 380
Status differentiation, after the exodus, 381–383
Status dynamics, and distribution of prestige and power,
289
Status hierarchy, 4, 347
creation of, by sentiment, 360–361
maintenance of, in the workplace, 573
and predominance of positive behavior in a group, 353
Status-identity syndromes, formalization of, 33
Status processes, role of affect in, 351–353
Status shields, as a pathway for social position and
structure to affect health, 592–593
Stereotypes
defined, 68
emotion, 64
gender-emotion, 68
Story, love as, 395, 402
Strategic engagement, in social movements, dangers of,
623–624
Stress
and emotional deviance, 126
from incongruence between evaluations and self-image,
198
and interactionism, 600–604
Stress hormones, effect of, on the hippocampus, 48
Stressors, types of, 601
Structural dimensions
for classification of emotions, 12–13, 18
for social unit attributions, 312

Structural emotions (static), 21–22, 98–99
  defined, 97, 183
  social dimensions of, 34
Structural emphasis, of identity theory, research from, 207–208
Structural forms of exchange, 313–314
Structuralism, and social movements, 614–616
"Structuration" perspective, on love, 398–399
Structure, of social movements, 626–628
Studies
  of the airline industry, emotional management, 570–571
  of classification of love, 391–392
  of emotional management in the workplace, food handlers and insurance agents, 572
  of twins, assessing genetic and environmental effect in guilt and shame, 547
Styles, of love, 394–395
Subcortical regions of the brain, interactions with cortical regions, 57
Subcortical structures of the brain, functions of, 47–48
Subgroups, defined, in a unified theory of sociobehavioral processes, 342
Subordinates
  and emotion, 171–173
  reinforcing differences from, service work example, 170
Subordination hypothesis, predictions of, 72
Subtle emotions, formalization of, 31–32
Suffering, in grief, 520
Support groups
  emotion management in, for therapeutic ends, 596
  modifying negative identities in, empirical study of, 193
Survivors, social characteristics of, 536–537
Symbolic interactionism, 2–3, 155–178
  descriptions of the self in, 256
  emotions in, 603–604
  the roots of affect control theory in, 180–181
  and social movements, 625
Symbolic sharing, to avoid envy, 430
Symbols
  circulation through networks, 142
  in interaction, 138
  ritual, of groups, 135–136
Sympathy, 467–492
  defined, 469, 554
  as an exchange process, 119–120
  in framing goods and bads for the self and other, table, 336
  in justice situations, 335
  as a tool to gain advantage, 555
Sympathy brokers, 471
  in courtrooms, 482
  examples, 470–471
Sympathy margins
  implicit bookkeeping involving, 159

variables affecting, 476–477
Synapse, defined, 43
System dynamics, second-order, in ritual theory, 140
Systems logic, in ritual theory, 140

Taxation, to reduce envy, 430
Technology, effects on rewards and inequality, 382–383
Temperance movement, study of, 613–614
Thalamus, processing of sensory and motor information in, 48
Theoretical justice analysis, 331–332
Theorizing emotions, 624–630
Theory
  empirical tests of, in the workplace, 584
  tests of, power-status interactions, 107–109
Theory of emotions, expanding, 281–292
Thinking
  and selection pressure for increased emotionality, 371
  and the self, 141–146
  self-conscious nature of, 51–52
Threat, perceived, as a site of anger provocation, 502
Time
  as the basic constraint on interaction order, 149
  duration of
    for conditions entitling sympathy, 478
    for grief, 523
Timing
  for giving gifts, 474–475
  for giving or receiving sympathy, 479
  and the potential for positive interaction in groups, 151
Tipping, as a form of symbolic sharing, 430
Top-down brain structures, 45–49
Traits, defined, 183–184
Transactional needs
  anxiety over failure to meet, 283
  and self verification, 287–288
Transformation rules, in perspective taking, 451
Transient impressions, defined, 182
Transition emotions (dynamic class), 22
Transmutation, and targeting of emotions, table, 290
Trauma
  defined, in terms of effects, 601
  and grief, 524
Trial lawyers, feeling rules and emotional displays among, 166–167
Triangular theory of love, 395
Triggers, of experienced emotion, in theoretical justice analysis, 333
True sharing, to avoid envy, 430
Trust
  defined, 311
  role in sympathy claims, 477–480
  as a transactional need, 288

Types
of experienced emotion, in justice analysis, 333
of love, 402
table, 404

Uncertainty
reduction of
comparison with the emotional-affective process of
relational exchange theory, 309–310
effect on group cohesion, 310–311
shared, about interaction outcomes, 139
Unconscious, in evolutionary perspective, 53–54
Unconscious domain, of mental life, 277
Unconscious emotion, neuroscience and, 51–55
Unfaithful love, power and status in, 105
United States, contemporary, jealousy in, 415–416
Universality
of envy, 428
of power-status theory, 109–110
of romantic love, 391
Unrequited love, power and status in, 105
Utility, of anger, 507–509

Valences
emotional, attached to cognitions, 257–258
in emotion categories, 14–15, 20
in experienced emotion, matching in justice analysis,
333
and identities, 27
mixed, components of, 26
power represented in terms of, 28
of the self, 548

status represented in terms of, 28
Values, moral content of, 545
Vasopressin, control of release of, by the hypothalamus,
48
Verification, of an identity, outcomes of, 213, 548
Victimhood, to increase status, 94–95
Victims, in court trials, sympathy for, 482
Vocabularies, emotion, defined, 118
Volunteerism, and empathic concern, 457
Vulnerability principle, in sympathy worthiness
assessments, 471

Wealth addition, greed as, 435
Will of God, as a rationalization, and management of envy
in society, 433
Wish, innocent, differentiating from envy, 427
Work
cognitive, on global emotions, 302
conflict with family contexts, and anger, 501
as a context for anger provocation, 496–498
empirical, on emotion culture, 118–121
and family, comparative studies, 582–583
identity, as an emotional process, 164–166
moral, in social movements, 620
See also Emotion work
Work ethic, and management of envy in society, 434
Workplace
emotions in, 569–590
in role-set interdependence in, 497

Yurok Indians
jealousy as defined by, 413–414

23792577R00375

Made in the USA
San Bernardino, CA
30 January 2019